Demand for and supply of periodic financial reports

Statement of comprehensive income
Chapter 4: Revenue recognition

Balance sheet – assets
Chapter 5: Cash and receivables
Chapter 6: Inventories
Chapter 7: Financial assets
Chapter 8: Property, plant, and equipment
Chapter 9: Intangible assets, goodwill, mineral
          resources, and government assistance
Chapter 10: Applications of fair value to
            non-current assets

Balance sheet – liabilities
Chapter 11: Current liabilities and contingencies
Chapter 12: Non-current financial liabilities

Balance sheet – equity
Statement of equity
Chapter 13: Equities

Special topics
Chapter 14: Complex financial instruments
Chapter 15: Earnings per share
Chapter 16: Pensions and other employee
            future benefits
Chapter 17: Accounting for leases
Chapter 18: Accounting for income taxes
Chapter 19: Accounting changes

Cash flow statement
Chapter 20: Statement of cash flows

Volume II

INTERMEDIATE
ACCOUNTING

FOURTH
EDITION

INTERMEDIATE ACCOUNTING

FOURTH EDITION

KIN LO
University of British Columbia

GEORGE FISHER
Douglas College

WITH CONTRIBUTIONS BY

KIM TROTTIER
Simon Fraser University

DESMOND TSANG
McGill University

VOLUME 1

Pearson

Pearson Canada Inc., 26 Prince Andrew Place, North York, Ontario M3C 2H4.

978-0-13-482008-8

Library and Archives Canada Cataloguing in Publication
Lo, Kin, 1970-, author
   Intermediate accounting / Kin Lo, George Fisher. — Fourth edition.
Includes index.
Contents: v. 1. Chapters 1-10 — v. 2. Chapters 11-20.
ISBN 978-0-13-482008-8 (v. 1 : softcover).—ISBN 978-0-13-482007-1 (v. 2 : softcover)

   1. Accounting--Textbooks. I. Fisher, George, 1957-, author II. Title.

HF5636.L6 2019   657'.044   C2018-903284-7

Notice

About the Authors

Kin Lo, PhD, FCPA, FCA is the Senior Associate Dean—Students at the Sauder School of Business, University of British Columbia. He holds the CPA Professorship in Accounting established by the Chartered Professional Accountants of British Columbia (CPABC). After receiving a Bachelor of Commerce from the University of Calgary, he articled at PricewaterhouseCoopers and subsequently earned his doctorate from the Kellogg School of Management at Northwestern University in Chicago in 1999. His research has been published in the most important accounting journals, including *The Accounting Review, Journal of Accounting Research,* and *Journal of Accounting and Economics,* and he served as an Associate Editor at the *Journal of Accounting and Economics* from 2003 to 2011.

Since joining UBC in 1999, Professor Lo has taught extensively in intermediate-level financial accounting for undergraduates, as well as master and doctoral-level courses. He has coached numerous winning teams in regional, national, and global case competitions. His outstanding teaching has been recognized by the Killam Teaching Prize. Kin has also been a visiting professor at MIT Sloan School of Management and the University of California at Irvine's Merage School of Business.

Aside from research and teaching, Kin is also active in the professional accounting community, serving on provincial and national committees and contributing as a columnist to the Institute of Chartered Accountants of British Columbia's magazine *Beyond Numbers*. From 2008 to 2011, Professor Lo was a member of the Board of Evaluators for the Chartered Accountants' national Uniform Final Evaluation (UFE). He is a member of the Academic Advisory Council for the Accounting Standards Board of Canada. In recognition of his contributions to accounting education, he was awarded Fellowship by the CPABC in 2013. Kin is also an avid sailor.

George Fisher, MBA, CPA, CGA is the coordinator for the accounting option in the Bachelor of Business Administration degree program offered by Douglas College. He teaches financial reporting in the College's BBA and Post-Degree programs and facilitates financial reporting courses for the Chartered Professional Accountants' Western School of Business.

Mr. Fisher has been actively involved in the development of curriculum for CPA Canada since its inception. His publications for CPA Canada include *IF1, Intermediate Financial Reporting 1; IF2, Intermediate Financial Reporting 2;* and *AFR, Advanced Financial Reporting.* Mr. Fisher previously co-led the development of the finance elective for the CPA Professional Education Program.

Mr. Fisher was associated with the Certified General Accountants for more than 15 years in several roles, including authoring the final exams for CGA Canada's Financial Accounting 3 course (Financial Accounting: Liabilities & Equities). Other publications for CGA Canada include the domestic and international versions of *Financial Accounting: Assets (FA2), Financial Accounting: Consolidations and Advanced Issues (FA4),* and *Corporate Finance Fundamentals (FN1).*

Brief Contents

Contents

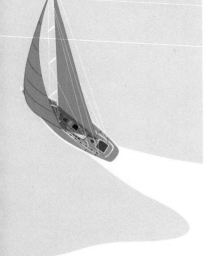

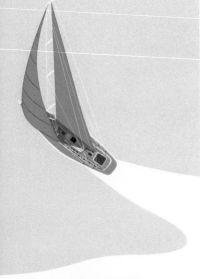

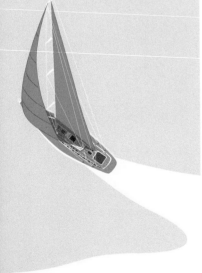

Preface

"There is too much material to learn!" is a complaint commonly heard among both students and instructors of intermediate-level financial accounting. The current environment in Canada involving multiple accounting standards certainly adds to the problem. However, this sentiment was prevalent even before the splintering of Canadian generally accepted accounting principles (GAAP) in 2011. So what is the source of the problem, and how do we best resolve it?

Regardless of one's perspective—as an instructor of intermediate accounting, as a student, or as a researcher reading and writing papers—often *the problem of too much content is an illusion.* Instead, the issue is really one of *flow*, not just of words, but of *ideas.* Why does a class, research paper, or presentation appear to cover too much, and why is it difficult to understand? Most often, it is because the ideas being presented did not flow—they were not coherent internally within the class, paper, or presentation, or not well connected with the recipients' prior knowledge and experiences.

Connecting new ideas to a person's existing knowledge and efficiently structuring those new ideas are not just reasonable notions. Modern neuroscience tells us that for ideas to be retained they need to be logically structured and presented in ways that connect with a person's prior knowledge and experiences.

OUR APPROACH

How can we better establish the flow of ideas in intermediate accounting? One way is to apply more accounting theory to help explain the "why" behind accounting standards and practices. Inherently, humans are inquisitive beings who want to know not just how things work, but also why things work a particular way. When students understand "why," they are better able to find connections between different ideas and internalize those ideas with the rest of their accumulated knowledge and experiences.

This approach contrasts with that found in other intermediate accounting textbooks, which present accounting topics in a fragmented way, not only between chapters but within chapters. For example, how is the conceptual framework for financial reporting connected with other ideas outside of accounting? How do the components such as qualitative characteristics relate to the elements of financial statements? Fragmented ideas are difficult to integrate into the brain, which forces students to rely on memorization tricks that work only for the short term. For example, a frequently used memory aid for the conceptual framework is a pyramid; this is a poor pedagogical tool because the concepts within the diagram are not logically connected and the pyramid shape itself has no basis in theory. In contrast, we anchor the conceptual framework on the fundamental notions of economic demand and supply.

Also different from other textbooks, we do not aim to be encyclopedic—who wants to read an encyclopedia? This textbook is designed as a learning tool for students at the intermediate level, rather than as a comprehensive reference source they might use many years in the future. Being comprehensive burdens students with details that are not meaningful to them. At the rate at which standards are changing, books become outdated rapidly, and students should learn to refer to official sources of accounting standards such as the *CPA Canada Handbook*.

ARE INTERMEDIATE ACCOUNTING STUDENTS READY FOR ACCOUNTING THEORY?

Most programs that offer an accounting theory course do so in the final year of their programs, with good reason—concepts in accounting theory are difficult. Thorough exploration of these concepts requires a solid grounding in accounting standards and practices and higher-level thinking skills. However, not exposing students to these concepts earlier is a mistake.

Other management (and non-management) disciplines are able to integrate theory with technical applications. For example, when finance students study investments and diversification, the capital asset pricing model is an integral component. Finance students also learn about firms' capital structure choices in the context of Modigliani and Miller's propositions, the pecking order theory, and so on. Students in operations management learn linear programming as an application of optimization theory. Relegating theory to the end of a program is an exception rather than the rule.

Accounting theory is too important to remain untouched until the end of an accounting program. This text exposes students to the fundamentals of accounting theory in the first chapter, which lays the foundation for a number of *threshold concepts* (see Meyer and Land, 2003[1]).

THRESHOLD CONCEPTS

While by no means perfect, this textbook aims to better establish the flow of ideas throughout the book by covering several threshold concepts in the first three chapters. Threshold concepts in this case are the portals that connect accounting standards and practices with students' prior knowledge and experiences. As Meyer and Land suggest, these threshold concepts will help to *transform* how students think about accounting, help students to *integrate* ideas within and between chapters, and *irreversibly improve* their understanding of accounting. Introducing these concepts is not without cost, because threshold concepts will often be troublesome due to their difficulty and the potential conflict between students' existing knowledge and these new concepts.

The previous two pages of this Preface identify the threshold concepts and the layout of the chapters in both volumes of this text. Crucially, the first chapter in Volume 1 begins with the threshold concepts of *uncertainty* and *information asymmetry*. The need to make decisions under uncertainty and the presence of information asymmetries results in *economic consequences of accounting choice*. Those consequences differ depending on whether the accounting information interacts with *efficient securities markets*. These concepts open up the notion of *supply and demand for accounting information*, which forms the basis of the conceptual frameworks for financial reporting (Chapter 2). Decision making under uncertainty leads to the issues surrounding the *timing of recognition* under accrual accounting (Chapter 3), which in turn lead to the concept of *articulation* between financial statements. Accounting choices having economic consequences leads to considerations of the *quality of earnings* and the potential for earnings management (Chapter 3).

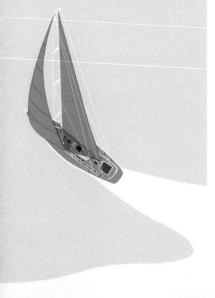

---

[1] Meyer, J.H.F., and R. Land. 2003. "Threshold Concepts and Troublesome Knowledge 1: Linkages to Ways of Thinking and Practicing." In *Improving Student Learning: Ten Years On*, C. Rust (Ed.), Oxford, UK: Oxford Centre for Staff and Learning Development.

These concepts then resurface at different points in the remaining 17 chapters. For example, the concept of information asymmetry is fundamental to understanding the reasons that companies issue complex financial instruments (Chapter 14). Another example is the important role of the moral hazard form of information asymmetry in explaining why accounting standards do not permit the recognition of gains and losses from equity transactions through net income. A third example is the influence of uncertainty and executives' risk aversion on the accounting standards for pension plans, which allow the gains and losses to flow through other comprehensive income rather than net income. A fourth example is the application of information asymmetry to the accounting for leases (Chapter 17).

As an aid for students, we have put threshold concepts icons in the margin to identify when these concepts appear in the various chapters. To further clarify these icons, we include the name of the specific concept next to the icon to ensure students understand which concepts are being referenced.

THRESHOLD
CONCEPT

ACCOUNTING STANDARDS AND PRACTICES

Along with the unique approach of introducing and integrating theory through the use of threshold concepts, this text also provides thorough coverage of accounting standards and practices typically expected of an intermediate accounting course. This edition reflects recently issued standards, including IFRS 15 on revenue recognition and IFRS 16 on leases.

Following an overview of the four financial statements in Chapter 3 in Volume 1, Chapter 4 explores revenue and expense recognition to highlight the connection financial reporting has to enterprises' value-creation activities. Chapters 5 to 10 in this book then examine, in detail, issues involving the asset side of the balance sheet.

The second volume begins with coverage of the right-hand side of the balance sheet in Chapters 11 to 13. Coverage in Chapters 14 to 18 then turns to special topics that cut across different parts of the balance sheet and income statement: complex financial instruments, earnings per share, pension costs, leases, and income taxes. Chapter 19 revisits the topic of accounting changes introduced in Chapter 3. Chapter 20 examines the statement of cash flows, which integrates the various topics covered in Chapters 4 through 19.

INTEGRATION OF IFRS

This is the first Canadian text written with International Financial Reporting Standards (IFRS) in mind throughout the development process, rather than as an afterthought. For example, we devote a separate chapter (Chapter 10) to exploring issues surrounding asset revaluation and impairment because these issues cut across different asset categories under IFRS. The complete integration of standards in the development process adds to the smooth flow of ideas in and between chapters. Another example is Chapter 10's coverage of agriculture activities, a topic covered by IFRS but not by past Canadian standards.

COVERAGE OF ASPE

While this text puts emphasis on IFRS, we do not neglect Accounting Standards for Private Enterprises (ASPE). Near the end of each chapter is a table that identifies differences between IFRS and ASPE. In contrast to other textbooks, we identify only substantive differences rather than every detail. In addition to the summary table, we carefully choose to discuss certain important differences in the main body of the chapters to create opportunities for understanding the subjective nature of accounting

A·S·P·E

standards, and the advantages and disadvantages of different standards. For example, Chapter 8 discusses the different treatments of interest capitalization under IFRS and ASPE. In the end-of-chapter Problems, we have placed icons in the margin to identify questions that apply ASPE instead of IFRS.

REFERENCE TO ACCOUNTING STANDARDS

Consistent with the threshold concepts described above, this textbook avoids treating accounting standards as written in stone and with only one interpretation. Ultimately, it is people who make accounting standards and it is important to analyze and evaluate the choices that standard setters make to understand the rationale behind the standards. Where appropriate, the chapters provide specific quotations from authoritative standards so that students begin to develop their ability to interpret the standards themselves rather than rely on the interpretations of a third party.

INTEGRATION OF LEARNING OBJECTIVES

To enhance the flow of material, each chapter fully integrates learning objectives from beginning to end. Each chapter enumerates four to six learning objectives that the chapter covers. The end of each chapter summarizes the main points relating to each of these learning objectives. We have also organized the Problems at the end of each chapter to match the order of these learning objectives as much as possible.

INTEGRATION OF CPA COMPETENCIES

To ensure students are building the knowledge and skills required for the CPA designation, we have integrated the competencies outlined in the CPA Competency Map and Knowledge Supplement. Each chapter now opens with a list of CPA Competencies, related Knowledge Items, and levels that are covered in that chapter; also, a master list of all the financial reporting Competencies and Knowledge Items is available at the end of this textbook. As well, all the Problems on MyLab Accounting for *Intermediate Accounting* 4e are mapped to the Competency, Knowledge Item, and level that is being assessed. These features will allow students and faculty interested in the CPA designation to become familiar with the Competency Map and the material covered in the book.

CHAPTER FEATURES

This text contains a number of features that augment the core text. We are mindful that too many "bells and whistles" only serve to distract students, so we have been selective and have included only features that reinforce student learning. The result is an uncluttered page layout in comparison to competing textbooks. We firmly believe that clean design supports clear thinking.

Opening Vignettes

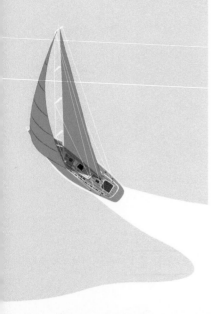

Each chapter opens with a short vignette of a real-world example that students will easily recognize and to which they will relate. These examples range from household names such as Bank of Montreal, Bombardier, and Telus, to car shopping and Christopher Columbus. As mentioned earlier, this connection to existing knowledge and experiences is crucial to learning new concepts. Each vignette serves to motivate interesting accounting questions that are later addressed in the chapter.

Charts and Diagrams

We have chosen to use graphics sparingly but deliberately. These graphics always serve to augment ideas in a logical way rather than to serve as memory "gimmicks" that lack meaning. For instance, it has been popular to use a triangle to organize the Conceptual Framework for financial reporting. We eschew the use of this triangle because that shape has no logical foundation or connection with the Conceptual Framework. Instead, we develop the Conceptual Framework from fundamental forces of supply and demand, so we provide a diagram that illustrates the interaction of those forces:

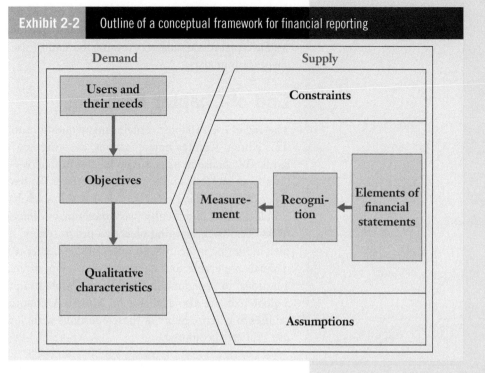

Exhibit 2-2   Outline of a conceptual framework for financial reporting

Feature Boxes

When warranted, we provide more in-depth discussions to reinforce the core message in the main body of the chapters. These discussions often take the form of alternative viewpoints or surprising research results that serve to broaden students' perspectives on the issues. Compass icons identify these feature boxes to denote the different perspectives on various issues.

STILL WAITING…

In 1670, an incorporation under the British royal charter created "The Governor and Company of Adventurers of England trading into Hudson's Bay." The charter gave the company exclusive rights to the fur trade in the watershed flowing into Hudson Bay. The company continues to operate today as The Hudson's Bay Company. It was publicly traded until January 2006, when it was purchased by private equity firm NRDC Equity Partners. In late 2012, the company became a public company again by issuing $365 million of shares on the Toronto Stock Exchange (ticker HBC). If investors had to wait until dissolution to find out what happened to their investments, they would have been waiting for three and a half centuries—and counting!

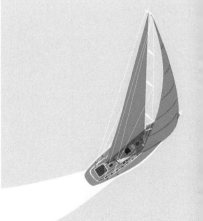

Checkpoint Questions

At important transitional points in each chapter, we pose "Checkpoint Questions" to engage students to reflect upon what they have just read, and to review, if necessary, before proceeding to the next portion of the chapter. These questions appear at the end of sections and there are five to ten such questions within each chapter. To encourage students to think about these questions before looking at the answers, we have placed the answers toward the end of each chapter, immediately after the chapter summary.

End-of-Chapter Problems

The end of each chapter contains many questions to help students to hone their skills. This edition features new questions, covering new chapter material and IFRS standards. We choose to use a single label—Problems—for all questions. This choice follows from our focus on learning objectives. We have organized the Problems in the order of the learning objectives, and within each learning objective according to the Problem's level of difficulty (easy, medium, or difficult). This approach allows students to work on each learning objective progressively, starting with easier questions and then mastering more difficult questions on the same learning objective. This approach is much preferable to having students jump around from "exercises" to "discussion questions" to "assignments," and so on. Problems in the textbook that are marked with a globe icon are also available on MyLab Accounting. Students have endless opportunities to practise many of these questions with new data and values every time they use MyLab Accounting.

> **MyLab Accounting**   Make the grade with **MyLab Accounting:** The problems marked with a 🌐 can be found on **MyLab Accounting.** You can practise them as often as you want, and most feature step-by-step guided instructions to help you find the right answer.

Cases

We have included Mini-Cases that are based on, or mimic, real business scenarios. The distinguishing feature of these cases is their focus on decision making. While they are technically no more challenging than Problems, cases bring in additional real-world subjective considerations that require students to apply professional judgment.

We have also included an appendix that provides case solving tips to students, as well as three comprehensive cases that cover topics across multiple chapters. MyLab Accounting for Volume 2 also contains two capstone cases that cover many of the topics in both volumes of the textbook. These cases simulate those on professional exams that require four to five hours of an entry-level professional accountant.

TECHNOLOGY RESOURCES

MyLab Accounting

MyLab delivers proven results in helping individual students succeed. It provides engaging experiences that personalize, stimulate, and measure learning for each student, including a personalized study plan.

MyLab Accounting for the fourth edition of *Intermediate Accounting* includes many valuable assessments and study tools to help students practise and understand key concepts from the text. Students can practise an expanded number of select end-of-chapter questions, review key terms with glossary flashcards, and review accounting fundamentals with the online, interactive Accounting Cycle Tutorial.

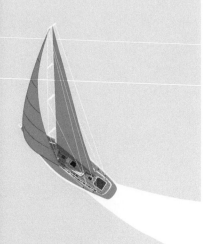

MyLab Accounting can be used by itself or linked to any learning management system. To learn more about how MyLab Accounting combines proven learning applications with powerful assessment, visit www.pearson.com/mylab.

Pearson eText

Pearson eText gives students access to their textbook anytime, anywhere. In addition to note taking, highlighting, and bookmarking, the Pearson eText offers interactive and sharing features. Instructors can share their comments or highlights, and students can add their own, creating a tight community of learners within the class.

Learning Solutions Managers

Pearson's Learning Solutions Managers work with faculty and campus course designers to ensure that Pearson technology products, assessment tools, and online course materials are tailored to meet your specific needs. This highly qualified team is dedicated to helping schools take full advantage of a wide range of educational resources, by assisting in the integration of a variety of instructional materials and media formats. Your local Pearson Canada sales representative can provide you with more details on this service program.

SUPPLEMENTS

These instructor supplements are available for download from a password-protected section of Pearson Canada's online catalogue (www.pearsoncanada.ca/highered). Navigate to your book's catalogue page to view a list of those supplements that are available. Speak to your local Pearson sales representative for details and access.

- **Instructor's Solutions Manual.** Created by Kin Lo and George Fisher, this resource provides complete, detailed, worked-out solutions for all the Problems in the textbook.
- **Instructor's Resource Manual.** The Instructor's Resource Manual features additional resources and recommendations to help you get the most out of this textbook for your course.
- **Computerized Test Bank.** Pearson's computerized test banks allow instructors to filter and select questions to create quizzes, tests, or homework. Instructors can revise questions or add their own, and may be able to choose print or online options. These questions are also available in Microsoft Word format.
- **PowerPoint® Presentations.** Approximately 30–40 PowerPoint® slides, organized by learning objective, accompany each chapter of the textbook.
- **Image Library.** The Image Library provides access to many of the images, figures, and tables in the textbook, organized by chapter for convenience. These images can easily be imported into Microsoft PowerPoint® to create new presentations or to add to existing ones.

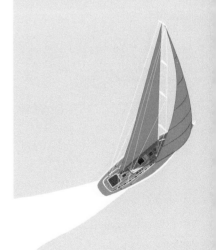

ACKNOWLEDGMENTS

During the development of this book, we obtained many helpful and invaluable suggestions and comments from colleagues across the country. We sincerely thank the following instructors who took the time and effort to provide thoughtful and meaningful reviews during the development of this fourth edition:

Ann-Marie Cederholm, Capilano University
Kathy Falk, University of Toronto Mississauga
Jing Lu, University of Guelph
Kelsie McKay, Georgian College
Jean Pai, University of Manitoba
Dal Pirot, MacEwan University
Zvi Singer, HEC Montreal
Barbara Wyntjes, University of British Columbia

Thanks also go to Desmond Tsang of McGill University and Zvi Singer of HEC Montreal for their hard work in creating many of the end-of-chapter Mini-Cases, and to Kim Trottier of Simon Fraser University and Trevor Hagyard of Concordia University for their creative and challenging Comprehensive Cases.

We would also like to acknowledge the assistance of the many members of the team at Pearson Canada who were involved throughout the writing and production process: Megan Farrell and Keara Emmett, Acquisitions Editors; Nicole Mellow, Program Manager; Anita Smale, Developmental Editor; Sarah Gallagher, Project Manager; Tania Andrabi, Production Editor; Laura Neves, Copy Editor; and Spencer Snell, Marketing Manager.

Kin Lo
George Fisher

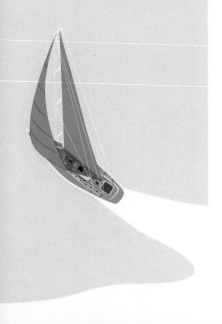

CHAPTER 1

Fundamentals of Financial Accounting Theory

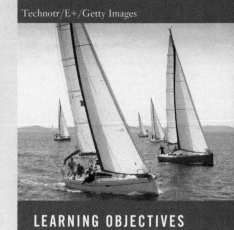

CPA competencies addressed in this chapter:

1.1.1   Evaluates financial reporting needs (Level B)
1.1.2   Evaluates the appropriateness of the basis of financial reporting (Level B)
1.1.3   Evaluates reporting processes to support reliable financial reporting (Level B)
1.2.1   Develops or evaluates appropriate accounting policies and procedures (Level B)

LEARNING OBJECTIVES

After studying this chapter, you should be able to:

L.O. 1-1.   Explain the sources of demand and supply of accounting information.

L.O. 1-2.   Apply concepts of information asymmetry, adverse selection, and moral hazard to a variety of accounting, management, and related situations.

L.O. 1-3.   Describe the qualitative characteristics of accounting information that help to alleviate adverse selection and moral hazard.

L.O. 1-4.   Evaluate whether and what type of earnings management is more likely in a particular circumstance.

L.O. 1-5.   Explain how accounting information interacts with securities markets.

A sailboat leaves port with its skipper and crew for a weekend cruise along the coast. During the trip, the sailors harness the wind, cope with waves, navigate around rocks and shallows, and avoid collisions with other vessels. However, *before departure,* they must familiarize themselves with how to operate all of the equipment onboard. *And even before that,* they must have a good understanding of the theory of sailing: the Bernoulli principle (lift from the airfoil effect that allows birds and planes to fly), drag, gravity, buoyancy, compass directions, theory of tides and tidal currents, ocean currents, and how all of these factors potentially affect the boat and its motion. These three stages, in chronological order, can be labelled as *theory*, *instrument*, and *application*.

Understanding accounting involves these same three stages. The actual practice of accounting is just the last step in the process—the *application* of accounting standards and the accounting framework to the situation at hand, in conjunction with the use of professional judgment. Before you can practise accounting, you need to thoroughly understand the *instrument* that you are using: the set of accounting standards and the framework that underlies those standards. But first of all, it is essential that you understand the *theory* behind why the accounting standards are the way they are so that you will be able to apply your judgment while using those standards to different circumstances that you face.

This chapter looks at the fundamental concepts in accounting theory, such as uncertainty, information asymmetry, and the demand and supply of information. This theory leads to Chapters 2 and 3, which discuss the conceptual framework and accrual accounting principles that underlie more specific accounting standards. The remainder of this book and Volume 2 (Chapters 11–20) cover the specific accounting standards and their application.

	Theory	Instrument		Application
Sailing	Lift, drag, gravity, buoyancy, compass directions, tides, and currents	General structure of sailboats	Components specific to the vessel	Sailing, navigating, avoiding collisions
Accounting	Uncertainty, information asymmetry, demand and supply	Conceptual framework, general principles	Specific accounting standards	Accounting for specific balances and transactions
Textbook structure	Chapter 1	Chapter 2 Chapter 3	Chapters 4 to 20	Introductory level accounting

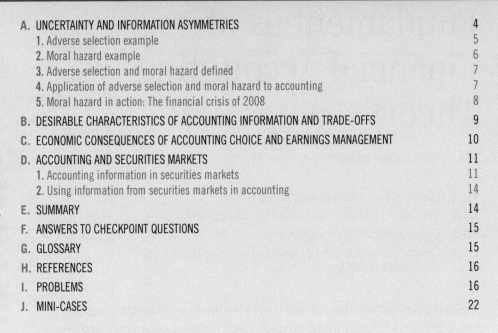

1 CONTENTS

L.O. 1-1. Explain the sources of demand and supply of accounting information.

generally accepted accounting principles (GAAP) Broad principles and conventions of general application as well as rules and procedures that determine accepted accounting practices.

Accounting is the production of information about an enterprise and the transmission of that information from those who have it to those who need it.

Despite what else you may know about accounting, the above sentence succinctly encapsulates what accounting is. Yes, the debits and credits, double-entry bookkeeping system, journal entries, and financial statements are all components of how we do accounting but, fundamentally, accounting is about communicating information. *Financial* reporting is the process by which enterprises provide information to external parties. *Managerial* accounting, on the other hand, involves reporting within the enterprise. We can even include *tax* accounting, which is the reporting of taxable amounts to government revenue authorities. What ties all the branches of accounting together is the idea that some people have information that others need. In managerial accounting, for example, a production manager needs to obtain relevant information on variable and fixed production costs, or top management requires information from division managers for budgeting purposes. Financial reporting involves the issuance of financial statements, forecasts, commentary, press releases, and even conference calls and webcasts to interested parties external to the enterprise.

In your introductory-level financial accounting course, you learned the basic approach and techniques for preparing accounting entries, compiling financial statements, and understanding financial reports using **generally accepted accounting principles (GAAP)**. Financial accounting at the intermediate level will not only raise your level of technical expertise in the "what" and "how" of accounting, but it will also help you to understand *why* we account for and report transactions in particular ways. That understanding will come from considering the range of possible methods of accounting and evaluating whether and how a particular method of accounting is consistent with the conceptual framework underlying GAAP, together with an appreciation for the underlying economic forces at work. This chapter on financial accounting theory exposes this important economic underpinning for accounting; Chapter 2 will delve into the conceptual framework.

The need for financial accounting theory is summed up in the common misunderstanding that the current financial reporting regime results from the proclamations issued by government or quasi-government regulatory agencies, such as the International Accounting Standards Board (IASB) located in London, England, or the Accounting Standards Board (AcSB) in Canada. Rather, financial reporting is an economic good and is therefore subject to the laws of supply and demand. Accounting standards reflect and respond to, although imperfectly, the demand for financial information and the ability of enterprises to supply that information. Financial accounting theory helps us to understand the complexities in the production and consumption (use) of accounting information. Viewed in this way, financial information can be, and is, a subject of rigorous economic analysis.

Consider the following scenario involving entrepreneur Susan Anthony, who is the sole proprietor of a thriving business buying and selling collectible coins and stamps. Susan has operated her business for over two decades and her business income has provided her with a comfortable lifestyle. At age 63, she is starting to look forward to retirement. In order to retire, she will have to sell her business.

This situation brings up a whole host of accounting-related questions. For example:

- Should Susan provide financial statements to outsiders such as potential buyers?
- What economic incentives are there for Susan to provide financial statements to potential buyers?
- What are the risks of providing this information to potential buyers?
- Should Susan have the financial statements for her business audited, even though she is not required to do so?
- For the preparation of her financial reports, should Susan follow International Financial Reporting Standards or Accounting Standards for Private Enterprises?
- What other information would be useful to potential buyers to maximize Susan's proceeds from selling her business?

Financial accounting theory can help business owners like Susan address questions like these, and can also provide insight into many other business issues:

- Why do some companies voluntarily disclose information and others do not?
- Why has a system of mandatory disclosures been put in place?
- What are the reasons behind the conceptual framework for financial reporting?
- How do capital (stock/bond) markets react to financial statement information?
- Why do capital markets react to financial statement information?
- How are financial statements used for contracting purposes (e.g., between shareholders and senior managers, between corporations and creditors)?
- Why are financial statements (instead of something else) used in contracting?
- How does the contracting role of accounting affect accounting practice?
- What are the considerations supporting the use of historical cost or current value reporting?

These are large, complex questions that require a separate book or course to address fully. This chapter serves as an introduction to the range of issues that affect the practice of accounting. Later chapters will apply some of these ideas in the context of specific accounting practices. To begin this journey, we start with the foundations of information economics.[1]

[1.] Information economics is an important and, relative to other areas of economics, recent development. The 2001 Nobel Prize in economics was awarded to three economists who laid the foundations for information economics in the 1970s: George Akerlof, Michael Spence, and Joseph Stiglitz.

L.O. 1-2. Apply concepts of information asymmetry, adverse selection, and moral hazard to a variety of accounting, management, and related situations.

information Evidence that can potentially affect an individual's decisions.

THRESHOLD CONCEPT
DECISION MAKING UNDER UNCERTAINTY

THRESHOLD CONCEPT
INFORMATION ASYMMETRY

information asymmetry A condition in which some people have more information than others.

A. UNCERTAINTY AND INFORMATION ASYMMETRIES

Accounting involves the communication of information, so let us clearly define what we mean by "information."

Information: Evidence that can potentially affect an individual's decisions.

It is important to notice that the evidence need only *potentially* affect decisions; it need not in fact alter any particular decision. For example, suppose Sally is planning a sailing trip. Before departure, she checks the weather forecast, which predicts that it will be sunny with winds of 10 to 15 knots from the northwest—great conditions, so Sally proceeds with her trip.[2] Did the weather forecast provide information to Sally? The fact that she did not change her mind is not important. What is crucial is that the forecast *could have* indicated gale force winds, in which case it would have been prudent for Sally to stay home. The forecast is informative to Sally, whether she ends up going on her sailing trip or not.

In thinking about this definition, it is important to note that some evidence can be information to one person but not to another. It all depends on the decision context. For example, the weather forecast could have no information value to Sally if she were only deciding between going to see a movie and playing indoor volleyball.

In the above examples, and indeed in most other contexts that we can think of, people make decisions under uncertainty. For the simple reason that decisions affect the future, even the very near future, outcomes will be uncertain to some extent. "The future is unpredictable," as is commonly said—or, more accurately, the future is not completely predictable. Only in hypothetical scenarios could uncertainty be entirely ruled out. For example, a managerial decision to sell a particular product involves uncertainties in demand, purchase costs, exchange rates, transportation costs, delivery times, product quality, and so on.

In financial reporting, the issue of uncertainty is particularly salient. Parties external to the reporting enterprise make decisions regarding whether they should lend to, invest in, sell product to, or work for an enterprise. The outcomes of these decisions depend on the firm's performance in the future (among other things), and past performance is a good source of information to help predict the future. *Thus, decision-making needs of external parties create the demand for financial reporting.*

Who supplies the information demanded by these external parties? Those who have more and better information, of course. Senior managers and members of a company's board of directors (i.e., insiders) most certainly have superior information about the company in comparison to the company's creditors, investors, suppliers, and employees (outsiders). *Thus, the supply and demand for financial reporting is due to the presence of* **information asymmetry**, whereby some people have more information than others.

The idea that some people have more or better information than other people is easy to comprehend. What is more important is to appreciate the pervasiveness of information asymmetry and the ramifications it has on what we do in (and outside of) financial reporting. To obtain a deeper understanding, we need to distinguish between two types of information asymmetry in the context of markets: adverse selection and moral hazard. As these are fairly abstract concepts, let's look at two examples to illustrate these ideas before formally defining these concepts.

 CHECKPOINT **CP1-1**

Describe how uncertainty and information asymmetry create the demand and supply of accounting information.

---

[2] A knot is a measurement of speed, meaning one nautical mile per hour. One nautical mile equals 1.852 km, or approximately 1.15 statute miles.

1. Adverse selection example

In this example, think about buying a car. As a student with meagre resources, you cannot afford a new car, so you consider buying a used one. What information problem do you face? Clearly, the seller has more information about the condition of the car than you do. Sure, you can see the exterior condition of the car, the amount of mileage from the odometer, and perhaps a few other details. However, if you are buying from an individual, that person knows how well the car runs, any problems including annoying squeaks, history of maintenance and collisions, and how hard the car has been driven in the past (e.g., running over speed bumps at 50 km/h). If you are buying from a car dealership, it still has a significant advantage over you even though the dealer's knowledge about the car's history is not as intimate as that of the previous owner. The dealership is in the business of buying and selling cars, so it employs experienced mechanics with the expertise to evaluate the quality of used cars much better than you can.

Suppose that as a potential buyer you believe a reasonable price range for a 10-year-old Honda Civic with 150,000 km is $2,000 to $4,000. You find a number of cars on the market that match these criteria, each identified by a letter in Exhibit 1-1. Based on what you know about these cars, they are nearly identical. All of the cars are advertised as selling for the best offer. How much should you pay? Would the midpoint of your range ($3,000) be a good start? As you would have an equal chance of over- and underpaying, this price would appear to be fair.

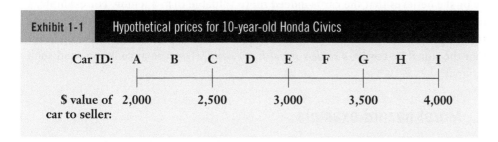

| Exhibit 1-1 | Hypothetical prices for 10-year-old Honda Civics |

Car ID:	A	B	C	D	E	F	G	H	I
$ value of car to seller:	2,000		2,500		3,000		3,500		4,000

This intuition is incorrect—the midpoint would *not* be a fair price. The problem is that the seller has better information than you do. Those sellers who know their cars to be higher than average quality (cars F, G, H, I) will not accept your offer of $3,000 (assuming they are not desperate to sell). Only those sellers who have below average quality cars (A, B, C, D, E) will like your offer. This means that you will always overpay if you offer $3,000. So you revise your strategy to reflect the new range of values to be between $2,000 and $3,000. Should you offer $2,500? If you did, you would still overpay, since owners of cars D and E will not accept this offer because they value their cars above $2,500. Repeat the process and you should see that the smart and rational strategy is to pay only the lowest price in the range: $2,000.

Given your price limit, a transaction will occur only if one or more sellers value their car at or below this value. In other words, you will be successful buying this car only if it is the worst possible car in the group that you are considering. This is why we call this *adverse* selection.

As it happens, there is one car owner who will accept an offer of $2,000 in this example. So what happens to the cars that the sellers feel are worth more than $2,000? The owners do not sell them because other potential buyers are just like you and are willing to pay only $2,000, less than the amount at which the owners are willing to sell. If the sellers think through this process beforehand, they do not put their cars on the market at all since it would be futile. As a result, the used cars that are available on the market tend to be the bad ones, or "lemons."[3]

[3.] George A. Akerlof, "The Market for 'Lemons': Quality Uncertainty and the Market Mechanism," *Quarterly Journal of Economics* 84, no. 3 (1970): 488–500.

Now, the actual used car market is somewhat better than that portrayed above. Motivated sellers, such as car dealerships, can use a number of different ways to help assure you of the quality of their cars so that you will be willing to pay a price higher than the price for lemons. In other words, sellers who truly believe that their cars are worth more than $2,000 will voluntarily provide information that demonstrates the quality of the car so that you will be willing to pay that price. However, only information that is verifiable is useful for this purpose. A claim such as, "It runs beautifully" is not verifiable; you cannot take the seller to court for misrepresentation should the car not meet such a vague claim about quality. In contrast, if the seller provides you with detailed documentation of the routine maintenance that has been carried out, the seller would be liable for fraud should that documentation be fake. As another example, a used car seller can provide an assessment of the car's quality from an independent mechanic.

In many instances, the seller cannot credibly communicate the quality of the vehicle to you because the factors that contribute to that quality are not readily observable or verifiable. To overcome this problem, the seller can resort to using a **costly signal**.

The need for costly signalling arises because unverifiable disclosures are **cheap talk** and cannot be believed. A claim by the car seller that his or her car is a bargain is an example of cheap talk, because anyone can make such a claim and they cannot be sued for making such a claim. Instead, the seller needs to use costly signalling if he or she believes that the car is indeed more valuable than a lemon. For example, a used car dealer can provide a guarantee against defects for a year; cars that are not truly high quality will result in significant future costs for the dealer. It is important that the signal be costly; *a costless signal is not credible* because anyone can send such a signal.

costly signalling (or just signalling) Communication of information that is otherwise unverifiable, by means of an action that is costly to the sender; contrast with **cheap talk**.

cheap talk Communication of unverifiable information, by means that are virtually costless; contrast with **costly signalling**.

2. Moral hazard example

Suppose you were successful in purchasing a car. Now you need to buy insurance. Whether you are legally required to have insurance or not, it is likely that your behaviour would differ from what it would be had you been *un*insured. With insurance, you will not be liable to pay damages if you unintentionally injure someone while driving, nor will you have to pay for repairs in a collision. (We will discuss insurance deductibles later.) Knowing this, you are likely to drive a bit faster and in a less careful, more reckless manner, since you do not bear the full consequences of accidents. We call this *moral hazard* because the provision of insurance encourages less care and effort, and therefore higher risk (i.e., it creates a hazard to our morals), but the higher risk is expected by both sides of the insurance contract.

The insurance company must anticipate the higher risk and increase insurance premiums accordingly. Thus, moral hazard is costly. In practice, this cost cannot be eliminated because the insurance company cannot monitor the insured to make certain that they drive carefully, and neither can the insured credibly commit to drive carefully. However, there are ways to mitigate the cost. For example, the insured can agree to pay for part of the damages incurred in the form of a deductible or percentage co-payment. When the insured bears some of the cost of damages, he or she is expected to take more care than when he or she is fully insured. Nevertheless, the insured is still expected to be less careful than when uninsured.

Thus, there is an inverse relationship between risk and the extent of moral hazard. When the insured has full insurance he or she faces low risk, and therefore provides little effort to prevent accidents; the moral hazard is accordingly high, and the cost of insurance must also be high. As we increase the risk faced by the insured, he or she will become more careful, which reduces the amount of moral hazard and the cost of insurance.

3. Adverse selection and moral hazard defined

Having discussed the background behind adverse selection and moral hazard by way of examples, we are now ready to consider these information asymmetries formally.

Adverse selection: A type of information asymmetry whereby one party to a contract has an information advantage over another party.

Moral hazard: A type of information asymmetry whereby one party to a contract cannot observe some actions relating to the fulfillment of the contractual terms by the other party.

adverse selection   A type of information asymmetry whereby one party to a contract has an information advantage over another party.

moral hazard   A type of information asymmetry whereby one party to a contract cannot observe some actions relating to the fulfillment of the contractual terms by the other party.

These definitions look similar but there is a crucial difference: moral hazard involves information about one party's actions that is not available to the other party. For this reason, moral hazard is succinctly summed up as *hidden actions*. Because actions are involved, moral hazard involves information about what happens in the *future*. In contrast, adverse selection concerns no actions other than whether the parties choose to reveal information that they possess. Consequently, adverse selection involves *hidden information* from the *past and present* (although such information could have ramifications for the future).

In the used car sale/purchase example, the information asymmetry involves the past history of how the car has been operated and its present condition. The buyer is not interested in what the seller does after the transaction, and the seller has no interest in how the buyer drives the car or what happens to it after it is sold. Thus, this is a case of adverse selection.

In the insurance example, the insurance provider is concerned about how much care the insured takes to prevent accidents in the future, but is unable to monitor the actions of the insured. Therefore, this is a case of moral hazard.[4]

THRESHOLD CONCEPT
INFORMATION ASYMMETRY

CHECKPOINT CP1-2

Identify two features that distinguish adverse selection from moral hazard.

4. Application of adverse selection and moral hazard to accounting

The astute reader will already see how the above discussion relates to accounting information. For example, buying and selling a used car is not all that different from buying and selling shares. Investors are at an information disadvantage relative to a firm's insiders (i.e., management and the board of directors). Consequently, a firm's management needs to provide credible evidence to investors so that its shares are not priced as "lemons." A claim by the CEO that the firm is underpriced is just cheap talk, since any CEO could make such a claim. Instead, useful evidence must be credible and verifiable. Such evidence can come in the form of financial statements that help summarize the financial condition and operations of the enterprise. To add credibility, the firm can hire independent auditors to attest to the financial statements' compliance with accounting standards, just as a car seller can obtain an independent assessment of the car's condition.

To overcome the adverse selection problem relating to a company's share price, the company can also use costly signalling, such as the payment of dividends. To be able to pay dividends on a regular basis, a firm needs to be profitable enough to generate sufficient cash flows in the future to fund those dividends. Thus, the commitment to pay dividends reveals management's beliefs about the firm's future prospects. For this reason, investors react quite strongly to announcements of new dividend

---

[4.] The provision of insurance often involves adverse selection as well, but the example given would need to be expanded to see that effect.

increases and decreases. Paying dividends is management's way of "putting money where its mouth is."

The issue of moral hazard is a little less straightforward. Who has the hidden actions? In relation to accounting, we are concerned with the actions of management. When there is a separation of ownership and management, we have an **agency problem** (also called a **principal–agent problem**): the owners (principals) are not able to monitor management personnel (the agents) to ensure that management makes decisions in the best interests of the owners. Because of the separation of ownership and management, managers neither obtain the full benefit of maximizing firm value nor do they bear the cost of not doing so. If executives are paid on a fixed salary basis, short of being fired they would be largely insured against bad performance, so they would not be motivated to strive for good performance. To mitigate this moral hazard problem, accounting reports can be used to provide information to owners about the firm's performance as an indirect indicator of management performance. Furthermore, incentive pay (bonuses) can be used to link compensation to performance measures such as net income or earnings per share. Another way to mitigate moral hazard is for management to take partial ownership of the company through stock purchase and stock option programs. These various tools ensure that managers share in the rewards of their efforts and will thus be motivated to create value for the company's owners.

A somewhat different moral hazard problem arises between the company and its creditors. Again, the company has the use of someone else's money. The lender faces the risk that the company will not repay the loan's principal and interest. To protect the lender's interest, loans will specify covenants that the company must satisfy during the term of the loan. For example, covenants may require that a firm maintain a current ratio higher than 2, a debt-to-assets ratio of less than 0.5, or an interest coverage ratio greater than 3.

agency problem   Arises from the inability of the principals to monitor the agents to ensure that the agents make decisions in the best interest of the principals.

principal–agent problem   See **agency problem**.

5. Moral hazard in action: The financial crisis of 2008

The financial crisis of 2008 is the most significant event affecting financial markets since the Great Depression in the 1930s and the market crash of 1929 that preceded it. The crisis resulted in, among other casualties, the bankruptcy of Lehman Brothers, the buyout of Merrill Lynch by Bank of America, and the bailout of American International Group (AIG) and Citigroup by the US government through equity stakes of 80% and 36%, respectively. *Each* of these four companies had between US$700 billion and US$2 trillion in assets. The colossal scale of these companies and the ramifications of their failure are immense.

It is now clear that moral hazard played a critical role in creating this crisis. Traditionally, commercial banking relies on earning a "spread" between interest rates paid on deposits from individuals and the interest rates received from money-lending activities, such as issuing mortgages.[5] Since banks bear the cost of borrowers defaulting on their loans, it is in the banks' interest to carefully assess the creditworthiness of borrowers. However, through financial innovation, it became possible to package thousands of mortgages together and sell them to other investors as *mortgage-backed securities*, or MBS. Furthermore, it was possible for investors to ensure that the MBS would be able to pay according to schedule by buying insurance through a financial instrument called a *credit default swap*, or CDS. For instance, Citigroup would package 10,000 mortgages with an average value of $200,000 into $2 billion worth of MBS. Investment banks like Merrill Lynch would buy these MBS; sometimes they would buy a CDS from AIG to insure against borrowers defaulting on their loans.

Both mortgage-backed securities and credit default swaps contributed to the spread of moral hazard. Since banks like Citigroup could offload the risk of default to

---

[5.] Commercial banking is the type of banking you experience day to day: making deposits and withdrawals, writing cheques, and borrowing funds. It is distinguished from investment banking, which involves activities in the capital markets such as underwriting share and bond offerings.

investors who buy the MBS, banks were no longer concerned about mortgage defaults. As a result, banks became more and more careless screening borrowers, lending to customers that were less and less creditworthy. Lending in the "subprime" mortgage market surged as a result. Banks even made "ninja loans" to people with <u>n</u>o <u>i</u>ncome, <u>n</u>o <u>j</u>ob, and no <u>a</u>ssets. Investors who purchased the MBS should have been concerned, because they would bear the cost of default. However, investors could insure against that risk by purchasing CDSs, thus offloading the risk to the insurance providers, such as AIG. Thus, the ability to offload risk allowed lenders and investors to be careless. The problems did not become apparent right away because defaults remained low as housing prices in the United States continued to increase through 2006. However, as house prices began dropping in 2007 and accelerated in 2008, mortgage default rates skyrocketed, exposing the low credit quality of the loans. Ultimately, it is moral hazard that caused banks to make such questionable loans in the first place.

B. DESIRABLE CHARACTERISTICS OF ACCOUNTING INFORMATION AND TRADE-OFFS

L.O. 1-3. Describe the qualitative characteristics of accounting information that help to alleviate adverse selection and moral hazard.

Depending on the type of information asymmetry that users face, they demand information with different characteristics. In the case of investors deciding whether to buy a company's shares and how much the price should be, the presence of adverse selection means that investors are wary of overpaying, which leads the company to provide as much credible information as possible so that the company obtains the highest price for its shares.[6] Thus, investors demand information that is relevant to investment decisions, such as information that helps them forecast future cash flows and assess the risks of those cash flows. Appendix B introduces some simple ways in which accounting information can be used for estimating the value of shares.

In the case of moral hazard, the demand for information is different. Investors need to ensure that management is properly using the company's assets, making the company profitable, growing sales, and so on. Lenders need to ensure that the company complies with the terms of loan agreements. However, since management is also the producer of information, investors and creditors need to be assured that the information provided is reliable. Since managers have the incentive to exaggerate so as to improve investors' and lenders' perception of their performance, investors and lenders demand information that is verifiable and not prone to manipulation by management.

Given the multiple user groups and conflicting demands placed on accounting information described above, trade-offs must necessarily be made. Not everyone can be satisfied with the same accounting information. For example, forward-looking information is useful for investment decisions, but predictions about future events are not verifiable and therefore not useful for evaluating management performance. On the other hand, an income measure based on the historical cost model is verifiable and less prone to management manipulation, but historical costs are not as useful as current values for estimating the value of the company and for pricing its shares.

Chapter 2 will further explore how accounting standards deal with the conflicting demands placed on accounting information.

 CHECKPOINT **CP1-3**

Explain how adverse selection and moral hazard lead to different demands on accounting information.

[6.] Even if the company is not currently issuing shares in an offering, firms generally want to maintain as high a share price as possible in the secondary market (i.e., shares traded on stock exchanges).

THRESHOLD CONCEPT
DECISION MAKING UNDER UNCERTAINTY

positive accounting theory   A theory for understanding managers' motivations, accounting choices, and reactions to accounting standards.

THRESHOLD CONCEPT
ECONOMIC CONSEQUENCES OF ACCOUNTING CHOICE

C. ECONOMIC CONSEQUENCES OF ACCOUNTING CHOICE AND EARNINGS MANAGEMENT

The end of the previous section alluded to the idea that management is prone to exaggerating financial reports. We explore this idea in more detail here.

Management is responsible for both operating the enterprise and preparing financial reports that help depict the company's performance. While financial reports are based on a set of accounting standards, these standards allow for considerable latitude in the choice of accounting policies and estimates. Why does this flexibility exist? There are at least two reasons. First, accounting standards are written in general terms so that they can be applied to a variety of businesses. The availability of choice in accounting policies reflects the simple idea that one size does not fit all. For example, the first-in, first-out (FIFO) method for inventory accounting provides information that is more useful than the weighted-average cost method for some firms; for other firms the opposite applies. Second, accrual accounting necessitates making estimates regarding the future—for example, how much of outstanding receivables will default, and how long will a piece of equipment be economically useful? Accounting standards cannot possibly specify what those estimates should be as they need to be made on a case-by-case basis.

Given that this latitude exists, we can expect managers to take advantage of it. If we understand the incentives that managers face, then we can anticipate the ways in which managers will use the flexibility at their disposal. In the same vein, we may be able to predict how they will respond to proposed or new accounting standards. For example, if there is a proposal to eliminate the first-in, first-out method of inventory accounting, which managers will lobby the accounting standard setters and what positions will they take? Understanding managers' motivations, accounting choices, and reactions to accounting standards is called **positive accounting theory**. ("Positive" is used in the sense of being descriptive rather than prescriptive—what do managers do and why do they do it?)

Managers' efforts to bias reported accounting information in one way or another are called *earnings management*. While the term refers to the income statement, it has been used more broadly to also apply to biases in the balance sheet or other financial information. As noted previously, managers have a tendency to exaggerate—that is, to manage earnings, assets, and equity upward and liabilities downward. They are motivated to do this for a number of reasons:

- To influence investors to make higher estimates of future earnings and cash flows, and therefore pay more for the firm's shares.
- To give the appearance of lower risk so that lenders provide more funds or charge a lower interest rate.
- To make it more likely that the firm will be able to meet its contractual obligations, such as debt covenants.
- To make it more likely that the firm will meet regulatory requirements, such as capital requirements for banks.
- To provide a stronger bargaining position in merger negotiations.
- To obtain higher compensation through profit-sharing agreements or profit-based bonuses.
- To obtain higher compensation through stock-based compensation if stock price responds to the upward bias in income.

While there are many reasons why managers would upwardly bias the financial statements, there are also some reasons or circumstances to do the opposite:

- To reduce the likelihood of additional taxes or regulations sometimes imposed on highly profitable companies, such as petroleum producers or Microsoft.
- To increase the likelihood of receiving government subsidies and trade protection.

- To take a "big bath" in a bad year by recording more expenses than usual so that future years are more likely to show higher and rising profitability, resulting in higher future compensation or share price.
- To improve the firm's bargaining position relative to employee unions.

Given the various motivations for earnings management, it is important to identify the factors that are most salient in a particular situation.

 CHECKPOINT **CP1-4**

Explain the connection between moral hazard, positive accounting theory, and earnings management.

D. ACCOUNTING AND SECURITIES MARKETS

In this section, we discuss how accounting interacts with securities markets. A *security market* is a general term used to refer to markets for securities (e.g., stocks and bonds), such as the Toronto Stock Exchange or the New York Stock Exchange. Securities markets take accounting information as inputs in the formation of prices, but they can also provide information for use in the accounting process. We look at these two different aspects below.

1. Accounting information in securities markets

The previous sections on uncertainty, information asymmetry, adverse selection, moral hazard, and positive accounting apply to all types of enterprises, whether or not they have securities traded in public markets. Firms with equity, debt, or other securities traded in public markets are called **public companies**, which is the focus of the following discussion.[7] To make this discussion more concrete, the following example uses Apple Inc., the maker of iPods, iPhones, iPads, and Macintosh computers. Exhibit 1-2 shows the closing prices and trading volume of the company's shares over a 12-month period ending December 31, 2016. At that time, Apple was the most valuable publicly traded company in the world measured by the market value of its shares (US$600 billion).

One idea that is quite important for publicly accountable enterprises like Apple is the theory of efficient markets. An **efficient securities market (semi-strong form)** is one in which the prices of securities traded in the market at all times properly reflect all information that is publicly known about those securities.[8] Efficient market theory has several important implications for accounting:

a. *Security prices react quickly to accounting information.* In markets where there are many buyers and sellers seeking to maximize profits, traders are constantly analyzing and acting on information they receive. Consequently, when accounting reports are publicly released, security prices adjust to that information rapidly. Voluminous academic research shows that accounting is an important source of information to securities markets and that prices do indeed react quickly to accounting information—in a matter of minutes for heavily traded securities, or within a day or two for securities that are traded more lightly. In the case of Apple, observe the significant price movements around the four earnings report dates identified in Exhibit 1-2. Furthermore, notice the higher-than-average trading volume on those days, indicating that investors were buying and selling shares based on the release of accounting information.

L.O. 1-5. Explain how accounting information interacts with securities markets.

THRESHOLD CONCEPT
EFFICIENT SECURITIES MARKETS

public companies   Firms with equity, debt, or other securities traded in public markets.

efficient securities market (semi-strong form)   A market in which the prices of securities traded in that market at all times properly reflect all information that is publicly known about those securities. A market that is strong form efficient has prices that reflect all information, whether publicly or privately known.

---

[7] Other types of enterprises are private enterprises without publicly traded securities, not-for-profit enterprises, and government entities.

[8] We do not consider weak form or strong form efficient markets, which are discussed in finance textbooks.

| Exhibit 1-2 | Daily closing price and trading volume for Apple Inc. (ticker: AAPL) |

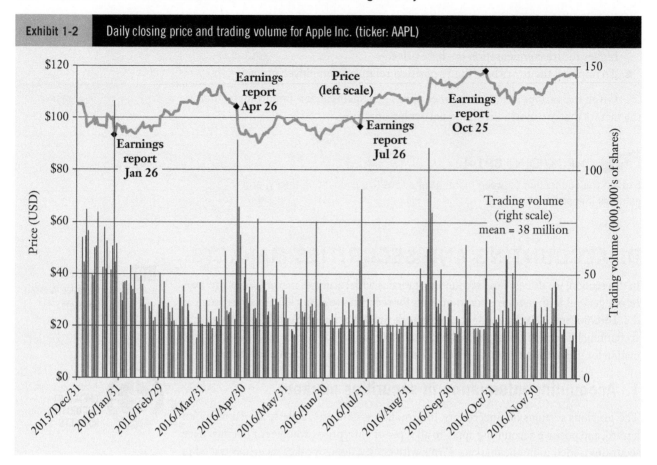

b. *Accounting information competes with other sources of information.* Because market participants demand all information that is relevant to the pricing of securities, they seek out and use many sources of information in addition to accounting reports. As a result, the demand for accounting reports depends on the ability of these reports to convey information useful for security pricing purposes, incremental to any other information available and in a timely fashion. The importance of timeliness is evident in the issuance of quarterly financial statements in addition to annual reports in many jurisdictions, as required by regulators or securities exchanges. For Apple, you will notice that its stock price changes throughout the year even though it issues earnings reports only four times a year. Those price changes suggest that other (non-accounting) information is influencing investors' decisions. For instance, trading volume spiked in the second week of September after the Apple "Keynote" announcement.

c. *It is important to distinguish new information from what has already been reflected in prices.* Users of financial statements (and other information) must recognize whether the information they are reviewing has already caused a change in security prices. For example, what may appear to be good news could already have been reflected in a higher share price, meaning that the stock no longer represents a good buying opportunity. In Apple's case, the company reported earnings on July 26, 2016, after the markets closed for the day. The report showed profits of $1.42 per share, exceeding expectations of $1.36 per share by 4.4%. In response to this good news, the price increased by $6 the following day. Had an investor learned of this news a week or even a day late, he or she would have been looking at old news, the effect of which had already been reflected in the share price on July 27.

d. *Using only publicly available information, it is difficult to earn abnormal profits.* A corollary to point (c) is that you must act fast to profit from new information—you must trade before the security price has fully adjusted for the new information to make an abnormal amount of profit (i.e., an amount more than the expected rate of return on the investment). Consider Apple's earnings report of July 26, 2016. The stock price adjusted rapidly to the earnings, which exceeded expectations. Because the earnings report was issued publicly, it would have been difficult to earn abnormal profits by trading on the information contained in the earnings announcements. Both buyers and sellers adjusted their valuations of the company's shares, so anyone wanting to buy the shares would have had to buy them at the higher price reflecting the high earnings.

e. *It is possible to earn abnormal profits using information that is **not** publicly available.* Academic research shows that securities markets are generally semi-strong form efficient, not strong form efficient; the latter requires security prices to reflect all information, public or private. Consequently, individuals who are privy to information that is not publicly available can buy or sell securities at significant profits. In the case of Apple, insiders who had early access to the earnings report of July 26, 2016, could have profited handsomely had they purchased the company's shares prior to July 26 and sold them a few days later.

THRESHOLD CONCEPT
INFORMATION ASYMMETRY

   To limit the extent to which insiders can exploit their information advantage, securities laws restrict the amount and timing of trades by company insiders and others who gain access to inside information. Without such regulation, the presence of information asymmetry (specifically adverse selection) would deter investors from trading in the securities markets because they would, on average, lose money trading against more knowledgeable insiders. The insiders' gains are the outsiders' losses.

f. *Accounting reports and standards can assume that users have a reasonable level of sophistication.* There are many participants in securities markets with a range of sophistication in terms of their knowledge of accounting, finance, and business in general. If publicly traded securities are efficiently priced, it is not necessary for accounting information and accounting standards to be understandable to all potential users. Rather, it is sufficient to ensure that a substantial portion of the market participants are able to process the information for prices to properly reflect that information. The less sophisticated users who have difficulty interpreting accounting (and other) information can rely on market prices. Of the 64 million shares of Apple that trade on an average day, a significant number of those trades would have relied on the market price rather than financial reports. This reliance on market prices also has implications in the legal arena, discussed next.

g. *Efficient market theory influences legal doctrine.* The central implications of efficient market theory have found their way into law, at least in the United States. The US Supreme Court, in the case of *Basic, Inc. v. Levinson* (1988),[9] articulated the concept of "fraud on the market," which states that "in an open and developed securities market, the price of a company's stock is determined by the available material information regarding the company and its business [i.e., an efficient market]... Misleading statements will therefore defraud purchasers of stock even if the purchasers do not directly rely on the misstatements. . . . The causal connection between the defendants' fraud and the plaintiffs' purchase of stock in such a case is no less significant than in a case of direct reliance on misrepresentations" (pp. 241–242). The gist of this ruling is that investors need not show direct reliance on information provided by companies for them to have a claim against companies and their management for misrepresentation; they merely need to have relied on the prevailing security price. Thus, management's provision of financial or other information needs to consider not only specifically identifiable users who will rely

---

[9.] *Basic, Inc. v. Levinson*, US Supreme Court Cases, Volume 485, 224–263 (1988).

on that information, but also the overall impact on the security prices and anyone who relies on those prices.

This discussion highlights the significant implications that efficient security markets have on the use of accounting information. Next, we turn things around and look at how securities markets provide information for accounting.

2. Using information from securities markets in accounting

In addition to obtaining financing from securities markets, firms often have investments traded in these markets. Many firms have investments in Treasury bills, corporate bonds, or shares in other corporations. If the markets for these securities are efficient, then the prices of the securities traded in these markets are reliable indicators of their fundamental values.

With an average daily trading volume of 38 million shares, Apple's stock is likely to be efficiently priced. If Company X holds some of Apple's shares as an investment, the value of that investment to Company X can be readily and reliably determined by multiplying the market price per share by the number of shares held. The ability to measure the value of investments in publicly traded securities, such as Apple's shares, has resulted in accounting standards measuring such investments at their market prices (see Chapter 7).

In contrast, many other components in financial statements, such as inventory or equipment, are measured using historical cost. The result is that financial statements report some items at their historical costs and other items at their market prices.

 CHECKPOINT **CP1-5**

Explain the accounting consequences of having efficient markets for securities.

E. SUMMARY

L.O. 1-1.   Explain the sources of demand and supply of accounting information.

- The demand for information arises from people's need to make decisions under uncertainty about the future. In many contexts, there are asymmetric distributions of information among people. Those who have more information are the potential suppliers of information to those who have less.

L.O. 1-2.   Apply concepts of information asymmetry, adverse selection, and moral hazard to a variety of accounting, management, and related situations.

- There are two types of information asymmetry. Adverse selection involves hidden information about the past and the present, while moral hazard involves hidden actions in the future.

L.O. 1-3.   Describe the qualitative characteristics of accounting information that help to alleviate adverse selection and moral hazard.

- The presence of adverse selection depresses outsiders' perception of the value of an enterprise, creating a demand for full disclosure of information that is relevant to the value of the enterprise. Moral hazard causes outsiders to be suspicious of information supplied by management regarding its actions, creating a demand for information that is reliable and verifiable.

L.O. 1-4. Evaluate whether and what type of earnings management is more likely in a particular circumstance.

- Insiders have many incentives to manage earnings: to influence share price, to lower the cost of financing, to meet contractual and regulatory requirements, to increase management compensation, to lower political costs, or to gain regulatory protection. Most often, the incentives lead to an upward bias in earnings and net assets, but sometimes the incentives lead to a downward bias.

L.O. 1-5. Explain how accounting information interacts with securities markets.

- Accounting is an important source of information for securities markets, and information from securities markets is also useful for accounting. The theory of efficient securities markets has important implications for the practice of accounting, particularly with regard to the timely provision of information, the need to protect outside investors from insider trading, and the level of sophistication expected of financial statement users.

F. ANSWERS TO CHECKPOINT QUESTIONS

CP1-1: People need to make decisions about the future, which is uncertain. Because information helps to reduce uncertainty and contribute to better decisions, such as investing and lending, this creates the demand for accounting information. Insiders in a company inherently have more and better information about the company; that information asymmetry allows them to supply others with information such as accounting reports.

CP1-2: The two features that distinguish adverse selection from moral hazard are whether they involve (1) hidden information or hidden action; and (2) the past and present or the future. Adverse selection results from one party having hidden information about the past and present, to which another party does not have the same access. Moral hazard results from one party's actions in the future being unobservable to another party.

CP1-3: The existence of adverse selection and moral hazard causes users to place different demands on accounting information. The reduction of adverse selection requires information be provided that is relevant to the decision. On the other hand, the reduction in moral hazard requires management to provide information that is reliable and not prone to manipulation.

CP1-4: The principal–agent relationship between owners and managers creates a moral hazard where the owners cannot directly observe the actions of management. The use of risk-sharing arrangements, such as income-based bonuses and stock option plans, creates incentives for management to manipulate earnings reports to their own benefit. Positive accounting theory helps us to understand when and why management would use their discretion to influence accounting outcomes.

CP1-5: Having efficient securities markets leads to several important consequences for accounting. First, security prices react quickly and unbiasedly to accounting information. Second, accounting information needs to be provided in a timely manner because it must compete with other sources of information. Third, it is difficult to earn abnormal profits using public information, but having inside information will allow for such profits. Fourth, accounting standards do not need to cater to every investor; instead, they only need to be understandable to a significant portion of investors. Fifth, the market prices of publicly traded securities, if efficiently priced, are reliable measures of value, so such values could be used in financial reports of enterprises that invest in these securities.

G. GLOSSARY

adverse selection: A type of information asymmetry whereby one party to a contract has an information advantage over another party.

agency problem: Arises from the inability of the principals to monitor the agents to ensure that the agents make decisions in the best interest of the principals.

cheap talk: Communication of unverifiable information by means that are virtually costless; contrast with **costly signalling**.

costly signalling (or just signalling): Communication of information that is otherwise unverifiable by means of an action that is costly to the sender; contrast with **cheap talk**.

efficient securities market (semi-strong form): A market in which the prices of securities traded in the market at all times properly reflect all information that is publicly known about those securities. A market that is strong form efficient has prices that reflect all information, whether publicly or privately known.

generally accepted accounting principles (GAAP): Broad principles and conventions of general application as well as rules and procedures that determine accepted accounting practices.

information: Evidence that can potentially affect an individual's decisions.

information asymmetry: A condition in which some people have more information than others.

moral hazard: A type of information asymmetry whereby one party to a contract cannot observe some actions relating to the fulfillment of the contractual terms by the other party.

positive accounting theory: A theory for understanding managers' motivations, accounting choices, and reactions to accounting standards.

principal–agent problem: See **agency problem**.

public companies: Firms with equity, debt, or other securities traded in public markets.

H. REFERENCES

Akerlof, George A. "The Market for 'Lemons': Quality Uncertainty and the Market Mechanism." *Quarterly Journal of Economics* 84 no. 3 (1970): 488–500.

Watts, Ross, and Jerold Zimmerman. *Positive Accounting Theory.* Englewood Cliffs, NJ: Prentice Hall, 1986.

MyLab Accounting   Make the grade with **MyLab Accounting:** The problems marked with a  can be found on **MyLab Accounting.** You can practise them as often as you want, and most feature step-by-step guided instructions to help you find the right answer.

I. PROBLEMS

P1-1.   Supply and demand for accounting information   **L.O.** 1-1) (Easy – 5 minutes)

Describe how uncertainty and information asymmetry are the sources of supply and demand for information.

P1-2.   Supply and demand for accounting information   **L.O.** 1-1) (Easy – 10 minutes)

In the context of an entrepreneur seeking an initial public offering (IPO) of shares in her company, discuss the concepts of uncertainty, information asymmetry, and the supply of and demand for information.

P1-3.   Supply and demand for accounting information   **L.O.** 1-1) (Easy – 10 minutes)

Discuss the concepts of uncertainty, information asymmetry, and the supply of and demand for information when a corporation applies for a bank loan.

P1-4.   Types of information asymmetries and their characteristics

   **L.O.** 1-2) (Easy – 5 minutes)

Using the following table, identify the characteristics of adverse selection and moral hazard and when they are most likely to apply. For example, for the first item, which of hidden action or hidden information is more closely associated with adverse selection? Which is more closely associated with moral hazard?

	Adverse selection	Moral hazard
Hidden action or information?		
Information about past, present, or future?		
Associated with the market for "lemons" or insurance deductibles?		
Mitigation of information asymmetry involves risk sharing or full disclosure?		
Most closely associated with investment decisions or compliance with contractual terms?		
Creates demand for provision of relevant or reliable information?		

P1-5.   Information asymmetries   (**L.O.** 1-2) (Easy – 5 minutes)

Based on your understanding of adverse selection, explain why it is not correct to assume that companies' management will generally withhold information from investors.

P1-6.   Information asymmetries   (**L.O.** 1-2) (Easy – 5 minutes)

Explain why signalling needs to be costly to be credible. When would a company need to engage in such signalling?

P1-7.   Information asymmetries   (**L.O.** 1-2) (Easy – 5 minutes)

Explain how the separation of ownership and management creates moral hazard, and how accounting information helps to alleviate this moral hazard.

P1-8.   Information asymmetries   (**L.O.** 1-2) (Medium – 10 minutes)

When a bank lends money to a company, moral hazard arises. Describe the detrimental effects of moral hazard in this context, and explain how accounting information can be valuable in alleviating this moral hazard.

P1-9.   Information asymmetries   (**L.O.** 1-2) (Medium – 10 minutes)

Agency problems arise from the inability of the principals to monitor the agents to ensure that the agents make decisions in the best interests of the principals. Briefly explain how this statement applies when shareholders hire a manager to run the business for them and list three approaches to mitigating the problem.

P1-10.   Types of information asymmetries   (**L.O.** 1-2) (Medium – 5 minutes)

Think about a person's age. Each person knows his or her own age, but this fact is generally not known to others with much precision, except for close friends and relatives (and they often forget, too). Looks can deceive, so people need to provide independent proof of age in the form of government-issued identification for various purposes, such as to purchase alcoholic products or to purchase life and health insurance. Let's focus on the latter.

An important aspect of life and health insurance is the age of the insured. Without documentation, each person clearly has an information advantage over others regarding his or her own age, so there is information asymmetry. Is this a case of adverse selection or moral hazard? Explain.

P1-11.   Types of information asymmetries   (**L.O.** 1-2) (Medium – 10 minutes)

Identify whether each of the following is most likely a case of adverse selection or moral hazard and briefly explain why.

a. A mortgage company intends to sell pools of loans (mortgages) to investors on a non-recourse basis. The mortgage company does not attempt to confirm the veracity of the mortgage applicant's declared income.

b. Your friend intends to declare bankruptcy at the end of the month. Between now and then he plans to charge the maximum amount possible on his credit cards.

c. You do not use the alarm system in your fully insured home because it is "too much trouble."

P1-12. Supply and demand for information and types of information asymmetries

(**L.O.** 1-1, **L.O.** 1-2) (Medium – 15 minutes)

Consider the following simple game between you and your good friends Julia and Scott. You are using a deck of playing cards that is in all respects normal except that there are no face cards (jack, queen, king), so there are 40 cards ranging from 1 to 10. Scott thoroughly shuffles the deck. There are two versions to this game, and you will play each one many times. The differences between the two versions of the game are highlighted in italics.

Version A: Scott pulls out a card, face down. None of you sees the card. You and Julia then have the opportunity to bid between $1 and $10. You can bid more than once, but each bid must be higher than the previous. The highest bidder pays the amount of the bid to Scott. Scott reveals the card, and he pays the winning bidder an amount equal to the value of the card. In this game, what is your optimal strategy? Why?

Version B: Scott pulls out a card *and looks at it*, then places it face down. Without having seen the card, you and Julia have the opportunity to bid between $1 and $10. You can bid more than once, but each bid must be higher than the previous. *During the bidding process, Scott is able to provide information about the card, as long as he does not lie.* The highest bidder pays the amount of the bid to Scott. Scott reveals the card, and he pays the winning bidder an amount equal to the value of the card. In this game, what is your optimal strategy? Why? What type of information asymmetry does this game illustrate?

P1-13. Application of financial accounting theory (**L.O.** 1-2, **L.O.** 1-3) (Medium – 15 minutes)

Imagine that you have just flown to another city and that you are taking a taxi from the airport to your hotel. As usual, you see a meter prominently displaying the cost of the fare. As the taxi continues toward your destination, the displayed fare ticks upward. On the car window, you notice the following information:

Flag (includes first 1/13th km)	$2.70
Per kilometre	$1.58
Per hour	$28.20

Required:

Applying concepts from accounting theory, discuss the rationale for the metered taxi fare system and evaluate its effectiveness.

P1-14. Application of financial accounting theory

(**L.O.** 1-2) (Difficult – 20 minutes)

On April 24, 2008, *The Economist* news magazine published an article entitled, "Gattaca! Gattaca!" in reference to a 1997 movie of that name, in which a genetically inferior man takes on the identity of a superior one to qualify for space travel. The article concerned the *Genetic Information Non-Discrimination Act*, or GINA, which became law in the United States later that year.

This law prevents the use of genetic test results in activities ranging from hiring to insurance. Companies are not able to selectively hire based on genetic profile, and insurers cannot limit insurance coverage or charge different rates based on genetic tests. The author fears this could lead to the collapse of private insurance. Genetic testing technology could provide information that would be helpful in assessing a person's risk profile, and this technology will become ever more precise. The author foresees one or both of the following outcomes: a market overrun with adverse selection or insurers choosing not to cover many medical conditions that are strongly influenced by genetics. The latter outcome would be ironic since the goal of the legislation is, according to its title, non-discrimination.

Required:

Focus on the medical insurance aspect and ignore the employment implications of the above. Explain how adverse selection problems could lead to the collapse of private medical insurance.

P1-15. Application of financial accounting theory (**L.O.** 1-2, **L.O.** 1-3) (Difficult – 20 minutes)

In February 2010, Vancouver hosted the XXI Olympic Winter Games. As part of the Games, the city commissioned the construction of an Olympic village, which housed the athletes during the Games. The construction project was completed by a private property developer. The plan was for the property developer to sell the housing as condominium units at market prices after the end of the Games. Also part of the plan was a requirement that the developer build more than 150 social-housing units that would be owned by the City of Vancouver and rented out.

On September 13, 2010, *The Globe and Mail* published an article by Frances Bula entitled, "City Demands of Non-profit Housing Operators Keeping Olympic Village Empty." Excerpts of this article follow.

> "The controversial city-owned rental units at Vancouver's Olympic village have been sitting empty since the [Winter Olympic] Games ended in March—and they'll continue that way for at least two more months."
>
> "The city's complex and unusual demands for future non-profit operators have produced so much confusion and concern that the already much-delayed bid process had to have its deadline extended last week to the end of September."
>
> "Non-profit organizations considering whether to bid to operate one or all of the city's three buildings say they've been taken aback by city demands that they turn over any surpluses they might generate."
>
> "[The City's representative justified this requirement by saying] it wouldn't be responsible of the city to give away the surplus to an operator."
>
> "Barbara Bacon, the long-time director at the Housing Foundation of B.C., also expressed concern. 'If you make money, you have to give it up to the city. If you lose money, you're on the hook for it.'"
>
> "She is also perplexed by an arrangement that provides no operating subsidies for the 151 social-housing units and requires operators to prepay millions of dollars for the 60-year leases on the building."
>
> "Added to that, many operators are wary about how much it's going to cost to maintain unfamiliar new heating and water systems in the development that incorporated many new green-building technologies. …"

Required:

Discuss the issues raised by the above excerpts by applying concepts from financial accounting theory.

 P1-16. Application of financial accounting theory (**L.O.** 1-2, **L.O.** 1-4) (Medium – 15 minutes)

In February 2003, the *Vancouver Sun* printed an editorial entitled, "Equity Contracts a Student Loan Solution." In this article, the paper identified the affordability of post-secondary education as an important issue. It argued that a potential solution is to use "human capital contracts," which are equity-like private financial instruments.

The editorial described these contracts thus: "Under a human capital contract, a student will receive funding and, in return, will have to hand over a predefined percentage of his or her income during a fixed period of time … like an equity investment. … the investor's rate of return will be a function of the earnings of the student, not a predetermined interest rate as in a student loan. As a result, students will face a much lower risk of going bankrupt [and] financial risks will be transferred to a private entity."[10]

Required:

Applying concepts from financial accounting theory, discuss the pros and cons of "human capital contracts."

 P1-17. Information asymmetries and accounting (**L.O.** 1-3, **L.O.** 1-4) (Medium – 15 minutes)

Positive accounting theory suggests that managers usually have incentives to report more income now than later—for instance, to increase their bonus compensation. This is expected given the substantial evidence from stimulus–response experiments dating back to the early

[10.] From "Equity Contracts a Student Loan Solution," February 2003. Copyright © 2003 by *The Vancouver Sun.*

20th century by Ivan Pavlov. However, management's tendency to exaggerate reduces the reliability of the financial statements. In light of this problem, consider the following proposals:

Companies shouldn't pay bonuses based on income. Instead, they should either (i) pay managers a fixed salary, or (ii) pay them using stock options. The accounting information given by management will then be more reliable for making investment decisions.

Required:

Evaluate the two proposed alternatives to paying income-based bonuses.

 P1-18. Moral hazard and accounting information (**L.O.** 1-3, **L.O.** 1-4) (Difficult – 15 minutes)

QAF Company is a clothing retailer with locations in major Canadian cities. Its shares are publicly traded. In 2021 and 2022, the company's financial performance was less than stellar, as shown in the table below:

	2021	2022	2023
Operating profit margin	4.0%	3.9%	5.5%
Return on assets (ROA)	5.0	4.8%	4.4
Year-end stock price	$23	$21	$16
Days of accounts receivable (A/R)	35	33	50

Operating profit margin is the ratio of after-tax operating profit divided by sales. ROA is equal to after-tax operating profit divided by average total assets. Days of A/R is the balance of A/R at year-end divided by credit sales and multiplied by 365 days.

In response to declining performance, the company's board of directors decided to initiate an incentive compensation plan starting in fiscal year 2023. The incentive plan provides for management bonuses based on the following formula:

$$Bonus = \$500,000 \times (Operating\ profit\ margin - 4\%)$$

Required:

Provide plausible reasons why the company is performing poorly despite the new incentive compensation plan.

 P1-19. Moral hazard and the accounting profession

(**L.O.** 1-1, **L.O.** 1-3) (Difficult – 20 minutes)

In the late 1990s and early 2000s, accounting firms came under scrutiny for providing non-auditing services to their clients. Statistics for the (then) "Big Five" accounting firms (Andersen, Deloitte & Touche, Ernst & Young, KPMG, and PricewaterhouseCoopers) indicate that about 45% of their revenues came from auditing, 25% from tax work, and the remainder from consulting and other services, which included information systems consulting and internal audits.

Some observers called for a ban on the provision of non-audit services by accounting firms. They argued that auditor independence was being compromised under the status quo.

As a partial response to this lobbying, in late 2000 the US Securities and Exchange Commission (SEC) adopted new rules requiring public companies to disclose the amount of fees paid to their auditors separately for audit and non-audit services.

In the wake of the collapse of Enron in 2001, there were renewed calls for the separation of audit and non-audit services. On February 6, 2002, Deloitte & Touche announced that it would separate its accounting and consulting divisions; a week earlier, PricewaterhouseCoopers made a similar announcement. Previously, the consulting arm of Arthur Andersen had become a separate consulting firm now known as Accenture.

Required:

Discuss the relevant issues raised by the above facts in relation to financial accounting theory.

 P1-20. Efficient securities markets   (**L.O.** 1-5) (Easy – 5 minutes)

Explain why accounting reports are useful to investors even if securities markets are efficient in the semi-strong form.

P1-21. Efficient securities markets    **1-5)** (Medium — 10 minutes)

It seems that everyone has a get-rich quick scheme, and some get rich by selling their ideas to others. Whether it's counting cards, flipping real estate, day trading, or otherwise playing the securities markets, in a bull market the forecasts are all blue skies and happy days.

Ms. Richquik promises that commodities provide a much better return than stocks, on the basis that there are only 20 commodities compared to thousands of stocks. She claims it is easier to succeed by focusing on commodities such as gold, silver, platinum, oil and gas, wheat, orange juice, and so on. Simply use her system and watch the returns roll in.

Required:

Evaluate this claim based on your knowledge of efficient securities markets and basic economics.

 P1-22. Accounting information in securities markets    **1-5)** (Medium — 10 minutes)

Maple Leaf Foods (MLF) is a Canadian manufacturer of meat and baked products that is listed on the Toronto Stock Exchange. On the morning of July 27, 2007, the company issued a press release with its second-quarter financial results:

> "Earnings per share from continuing operations before restructuring and other related costs, net of taxes, were $0.13, compared to $0.12 last year, while year-to-date earnings per share on a comparable basis were $0.25 compared to $0.20 last year."

On July 27 MLF's stock price opened at $16.20 and closed at $15.94, and dropped further to $14.89 over the next three days.

Because the products made by MLF are widely available on supermarket shelves, the company is well known to the public. In fact, the company is so well known that one of your friends studying liberal arts approaches you and makes the following comments:

> "I'm not a business expert, but I'm pretty confident in saying that investors have no idea what they're doing. Maple Leaf's financial statements say that the company is doing pretty well, and the company's share price tumbles!"

Another one of your friends who majors in finance comments:

> "Accounting information is useless to the stock market. Maple Leaf proves my point. The accounting numbers have no relation with share prices!"

Required:

How would you respond to your friends' comments?

P1-23. Accounting information in securities markets    **1-5)** (Difficult — 20 minutes)

In the past, accounting standards in Canada required intangible assets to be recorded at purchase cost if they were purchased from a market transaction. Costs incurred on internally generated intangibles could not be capitalized in most cases. Enterprises had to expense costs incurred to create a patented invention, to build up a brand or trademark, or to improve customer loyalty. In other words, many intangible assets were not recognized as assets on the balance sheet, or they were recognized at a nominal value of $1.

Since adopting IFRS beginning January 1, 2011, publicly accountable Canadian companies have the option of using the cost basis, as they have in the past, or the revaluation basis. The revaluation basis reports intangible assets at their estimated current value. While the revaluation option is available, companies can also choose to continue using the historical cost basis.

Required:

a. You are a believer of efficiency in securities markets. Everything else being equal, do you predict the stock price to be higher for a firm that revalues its intangible assets compared with the share price for a firm that uses the historical cost basis? Why?
b. Apply the concepts of information asymmetry, earnings management, relevance, and reliability in this context.

J. MINI-CASES

"When in doubt, blame the accountants," said Mathew Ingram in the title of his article that appeared in *The Globe and Mail* on January 31, 2002. The long-suffering accounting profession, mocked for boring personalities and overconsumption of trees to produce financial reports, was now being blamed for making a company's financial records more, rather than less, confusing.

The backdrop for the article was the spectacular collapse of Enron, a US energy company that had, at its peak, the seventh largest market capitalization in the country. (Interested readers can find more information on Wikipedia under "Enron scandal.") The bankruptcy was the largest in US history up to that time.

One key ingredient in Enron's rise and fall was the thousands of entities the company created to hold some of its assets and liabilities, but which did not appear on Enron's books. Many of these entities were controlled by Enron's executives and financed by Enron. Because these entities were not consolidated (i.e., were not included in Enron's books), Enron's financial statements did not sufficiently reflect the risks of these related entities. These risks became apparent when conditions in energy markets turned against the company. In Ingram's words, "It became a wobbling house of cards, until a stiff breeze from the market blew it apart."

Enron's failure triggered a "wave of concern" about the credibility of other companies' financial information. One might liken the phenomenon to cockroaches—when you see one, you know others are not far behind. Investors began to take a second look at companies like Tyco International, a conglomerate that had full or partial ownership in 170 different companies ranging from electronics to health care. The company paid for most of these acquisitions with its own shares, similar to Enron. Other large companies put under the microscope included AOL Time Warner and General Electric.

According to Ingram, one of the positive outcomes of Enron's collapse was that investors no longer believed in the idea of a company being "too big to fail." Investors were reminded of the need to carefully analyze any company, regardless of size. Ingram noted that many of Enron's questionable transactions were actually contained in its financial statements, albeit in footnote disclosures that were often difficult to decipher. This scenario suggests that if investors do not understand a company's operations, they should not buy its shares.

The problems at Enron didn't go completely unnoticed. Some analysts did raise concerns about how Enron was able to make the money it claimed it was making, and how these profits increased year after year. However, these few cautionary voices were overwhelmed by the numerous others who believed the company to be a "buy" or "strong buy," as the share price continued its upward trajectory.

In addition to Enron's management, much blame was placed on the company's auditors, Arthur Andersen. The audit firm also did a considerable amount of consulting work for Enron, which could have created a substantial conflict of interest. Did Andersen compromise its independence in its audit? Or did Enron's management deceive the auditor as well?

Ingram stated that, ultimately, investors need to take responsibility for their own investments rather than rely too heavily on the opinions of others such as analysts and auditors. There are good reasons for regulators to require companies to file various reports (financial statements, prospectuses, proxy statements)—investors need to spend the time to read these reports, even if they may be boring.

Required:
Discuss the issues raised above by applying financial accounting theory.

"What makes Jack Grubman the Michael Jordan of analysts?"[11] asks Geoffrey Smith, in his article "The Superstar Who Wears Two Hats." Jack Grubman was the lead stock analyst in the telecom sector for Salomon Smith Barney, a division of Citigroup (owners of Citibank). Like superstar athletes, Grubman had a superstar annual paycheque of $25 million in cash and shares.

Smith notes that "Grubman gets the big bucks because he's among Wall Street's hottest 'superanalysts,' high-ranked analysts who also bring in lots of investment-banking business. In the past two years, he has helped orchestrate some of telecom's biggest deals. His friendship with WorldCom Chairman Bernard C. Ebbers helped land Salomon the role of lead investment banker in the $35 billion WorldCom–MCI merger."[12] (WorldCom later entered and emerged from bankruptcy in 2003, and was purchased by Verizon in 2006.) Deals such as the WorldCom–MCI merger helped Salomon bring in $200 million in investment banking fees in the telecom sector, half of which is attributable to Grubman, according to Smith, based on his discussions with industry sources.

However, Smith notes that Jack Grubman's dual roles, both as analyst and investment banker, put him in an "awkward position." Companies provide investment bankers information not normally available to stock analysts. "Sources close to the WorldCom–MCI deal say Grubman sat in on closed-door meetings weeks before the merger was announced that are normally off limits to analysts," writes Smith. A Salomon spokes person said "the firm maintains strict ethical wall procedures to insulate [stock analyst] research from confidential information related to the firm's banking clients."[13]

Grubman's investment banking activities do not appear to have harmed his reputation as an analyst—and have perhaps enhanced it. *Institutional Investor* rated him the top analyst for "wireline services." "He's accessible, knowledgeable, and I don't think he is unduly influenced by investment banking," said Brian B. Hayward, manager of the Invesco Worldwide Communications Fund. "All the big-name analysts have investment-banking ties, and those of us on the other side have to keep that in the back of our minds."

Required:

Discuss the above article using financial accounting theory.

In 1996, *The Wall Street Journal* reported the following headline: "Exxon Completes Big Debt Restructuring, Raising 2nd-Quarter Profit $130 Million." The article described how the world's largest petroleum company used a technique called "in-substance defeasance" to bolster its sagging profits, which were under pressure from low oil prices that had been below $20 per barrel for a number of years.

"Defeasance" is the act of undoing something, and in this case refers to the cancellation of debts owed by Exxon. However, instead of an outright repurchase or redemption of the debt, the in-substance defeasance technique achieves results with similar economic substance (hence "in-substance") using a series of other transactions.

1. Exxon purchased a $312 million portfolio of bonds issued by the US federal government.
2. These government bonds were transferred to a trust and managed by a trustee. At the same time, Exxon transferred to the trust $515 million of its debt.
3. The trust used the cash flows received from the government bonds to cover the cash payments on Exxon's debt. (See Exhibit 1.)

Exxon structured this series of transactions such that the cash flow from the government bonds would balance out interest and principal payments on Exxon's debt. Since the trust was now making the payments on Exxon's debt, the company had in substance redeemed the debt; economically, Exxon did not need to make any further payments on the debt, although nominally and legally the company was still responsible

CASE 2
The superstar who wears two hats
(30 minutes)

CASE 3
In-substance defeasance of long-term debt
(90 minutes)

Note: This is a difficult case intended for guided classroom discussion.

[11.] Michael Jordan was considered the best basketball player in the NBA during the late 1990s.

[12.] From Geoffrey Smith, "The Superstar Who Wears Two Hats," October 5, 1998. Copyright © 1998 by Bloomberg L.P. Reprinted by permission from The YGS Group.

[13.] In the finance industry, the separation of analyst/research activities from investment banking/advisory services is known as a "Chinese wall."

Exhibit 1	Structure of Exxon's in-substance defeasance transactions

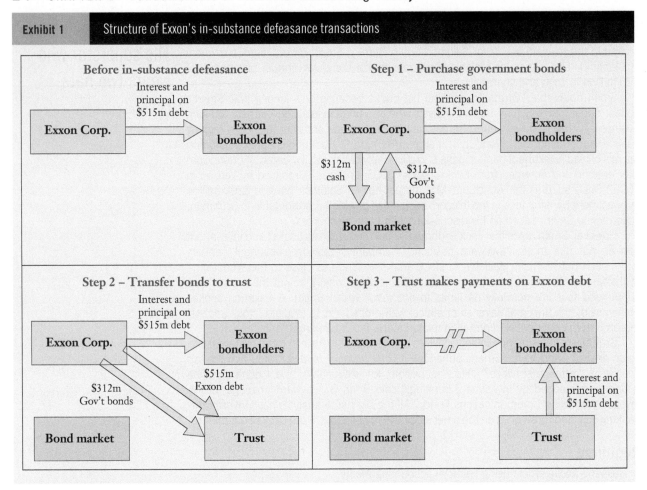

to the bondholders. From the bondholders' perspective, nothing had changed—they still held debt issued by Exxon and they would receive bond payments as scheduled.

As a result of the in-substance defeasance, Exxon removed $515 million of liabilities from its balance sheet. As it spent only $312 million to purchase the government bonds, the company recorded a gain of $203 million before tax and $130 million after tax in the second quarter of 1996.

In the previous quarter, Exxon earned $1.24 billion, or $1.43 a share, down about 23% from the year before. Revenue in this quarter was $27.11 billion, down about 10%.

The older Exxon bonds bear interest coupons of 5.8% to 6.7%, and they were issued close to par value. At the time of the in-substance defeasance, they were selling at a sharp discount from their face value due to much higher yields.

Exxon said the refunding would be financed out of cash balances, short-term borrowings, and medium-term debt, if necessary. In May 1995, Exxon said it planned to raise as much as $500 million by selling debt securities in 1996. The external financing would be the first Exxon debt sold in the United States in several years, and analysts viewed the announcement as another sign of financial pressure on the company.

In addition to the in-substance defeasance, Exxon had also used debt-for-equity swaps to bolster its earnings and balance sheet. In such swaps, a corporation exchanges shares of its stock for outstanding debt. In the six months preceding the in-substance defeasance Exxon had completed three such swaps, retiring a total of $147 million of debt.

The in-substance defeasance, together with the earlier debt-for-equity swaps, practically eliminated parent Exxon Corporation's long-term debt, which totalled $627 million on December 31, 2005. However, long-term debt of Exxon Pipeline Company and other Exxon subsidiaries totalled an additional $4.53 billion as of that date.

Required:

a. What motivated Exxon's "retirement" of the debt?

b. Why did the company opt to use the relatively complex in-substance defeasance rather than an outright repurchase or redemption?

c. Did the bond retirement make financial sense? How do you interpret the before-tax gain of $203 million?

d. Who won and who lost in this transaction?

e. Should the share price appreciate or depreciate because of this refinancing?

f. If you were the partner in charge of the audit of Exxon Corporation, what would be your position regarding the $203 million gain from the in-substance defeasance?

g. Exxon was not the only company to use in-substance defeasance; in fact, it was gaining in popularity in the mid-1990s. How would you expect accounting standard setters to react to this trend?

CASE 4
Bremner Health Insurance Company
(30 minutes)

Bremner Health Insurance Company (BHIC) is a publicly traded medical insurance company in the United States. At the time of establishment in 2019, the company decided to provide medical insurance to consumers without conducting a medical exam or asking for information about medical history. BHIC believed that everyone should have the right to medical insurance coverage, regardless of his or her medical health.

In its first two years of operation, the company generated earnings of $1.13 per share in 2019 and $1.25 per share in 2020 and was becoming very popular among consumers as the go-to place for medical insurance. Several financial analysts have been closely following the company and have forecast earnings of $1.45 per share for 2021, as they believe the company will present good news on its earnings announcement date. On February 9, 2022, its shares were trading on the market for $128.60 per share. The next day the company released its 2021 year-end earnings and announced earnings of $1.38 per share, well short of analysts' expectations of $1.45 per share. The company disclosed in the notes that it had incurred large medical coverage expenses during 2021 primarily because of many of its customers suffering from terminal illnesses. After the earnings announcement, BHIC's share price fell to $124.40 per share.

Required:

a. What type of information asymmetry is present in this case and how could BHIC decrease its effects?

b. Assuming a semi-strong form efficient market, why do you believe the share price fell on the day of the earnings announcement?

c. If BHIC had reported earnings of $1.46 per share as its earnings, what reaction would you expect from the market in the days following the announcement?

d. How important do you believe meeting forecast expectations is for publicly traded companies, and what kind of problems do you see arising as a result of attempting to meet these forecasts?

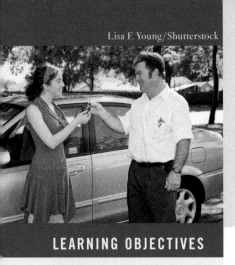

CHAPTER 2

Conceptual Frameworks for Financial Reporting

After studying this chapter, you should be able to:

L.O. 2-1. Explain the role of a conceptual framework for financial reporting and the reasons for having conceptual frameworks.

L.O. 2-2. Explain the rationale for each of the eight major components of these frameworks and synthesize these components into an integrated whole.

L.O. 2-3. Apply the conceptual frameworks in IFRS and ASPE to specific circumstances and evaluate the trade-offs among different concepts within the frameworks.

L.O. 2-4. Describe the standard-setting environment in Canada.

CPA competencies addressed in this chapter:

1.1.1 Evaluates financial reporting needs (Level B)
a. Framework of standard setting

1.1.1 Evaluates financial reporting needs (Level B)
b. Financial statement users and their broad needs, standard setting, and requirement for accountability

1.1.1 Evaluates financial reporting needs (Level B)
c. Objectives of financial reporting

1.1.2 Evaluates the appropriateness of the basis of financial reporting (Level B)
a. Fundamental accounting concepts and principles (qualitative characteristics of accounting information, basic elements)

1.1.2 Evaluates the appropriateness of the basis of financial reporting (Level B)
b. Methods of measurement

1.2.1 Develops or evaluates appropriate accounting policies and procedures – Ethical professional judgment (Level B)

Imagine that you are fresh from graduating from your accounting/business program, and you feel it might be time to reward yourself with a new car. You weigh the convenience, cost, practicality, fitness potential, and environmental impact of a car against the alternatives: a bicycle, walking, and a transit pass. Complicating your decision are the myriad car makes and models, types of bikes, shoe styles, and transit options available. On the other side of your potential purchase are the suppliers—car dealerships, bike shops, shoe stores, and the local transit authority—vying for your business. Each tries to anticipate your needs and the needs of thousands of other potential customers.

This scenario is, of course, not unique. It represents routine activities in markets: the interaction of demand and supply. It is repeated many times over every day in every corner of the world.

This interaction of demand and supply also applies to accounting. While complex and potentially intimidating, the Conceptual Framework for Financial Reporting in International Financial Reporting Standards (IFRS) can be viewed and better understood as a plan for the supply of accounting information to meet the demands of potential users.

The IFRS Conceptual Framework is just one possible plan. Accounting Standards for Private Enterprises (ASPE) has another, though similar, conceptual framework, and the US Financial Accounting Standards Board (FASB) has yet another. And like business plans, these frameworks change over time with changing conditions.

Chapter 1 discussed the sources of demand and supply of accounting information. Briefly, to review, people making decisions under uncertainty demand information to alleviate that uncertainty; an asymmetric distribution of information allows some individuals to supply information to others. This chapter looks at this idea more closely and explores how the accounting profession has formalized something akin to a business plan to anticipate the demand for information and to structure a reporting system to supply information that meets that demand.

THRESHOLD CONCEPT
DECISION MAKING UNDER UNCERTAINTY

THRESHOLD CONCEPT
INFORMATION ASYMMETRY

A. CONCEPTUAL FRAMEWORKS FOR FINANCIAL ACCOUNTING AS STRATEGIES TO MEET MARKET DEMANDS FOR INFORMATION

L.O. 2-1. Explain the role of a conceptual framework for financial reporting and the reasons for having conceptual frameworks.

This section examines the conceptual frameworks that provide the foundation for detailed accounting standards. Conceptual frameworks in general, not just in accounting, help to organize various concepts that are important. Conceptual frameworks involve *concepts*, which by their nature are abstract, so the relationship among concepts can be hard to understand. To make these ideas more concrete, we will first sketch out a business plan for an automobile manufacturer, then relate this to the conceptual framework for financial reporting. In the next section, we will look at the Conceptual Framework as laid out in International Financial Reporting Standards (IFRS), followed by a discussion of the different standard-setting bodies and the different frameworks and standards that are applicable.

1. Sketch of a business plan for a carmaker

Imagine that you are part of the management team of one of the automobile manufacturers. Your team is thinking about launching a new product. Clearly, it would be foolhardy to just go ahead and make the product and then hope for the best. Instead, you would go through a considerable amount of planning. What would be some of the important components of this planning process?

a. Assessing demand

One of the first things to consider is the structure of the market. Potential car buyers have a wide range of incomes, transportation needs, and tastes. One product is not likely to satisfy the entire market, so you need to be selective about choosing a *target market* and understanding the *needs* of this group of potential customers. Do these customers need a vehicle primarily for commuting, leisure, or hauling goods? Will they be using the automobile alone or with children? With an understanding of customers' needs, your team can then identify the overall *strategic goal or objective* of the new product as well as the *desirable product characteristics* to achieve that objective. The characteristics include fuel efficiency, speed and acceleration, reliability, storage space, seating room, and so on. These three steps so far can be summarized as an assessment of demand.

b. Supply planning

On the supply side, your management team needs to identify the *potential product components* that will help meet customer needs. Will the vehicle be a car, truck, or minivan? Will it have a gas or electric motor? Will it have a big or small engine? After this initial identification, the more specific *product design* can begin. Of course, you cannot just conjure up a car that uses 1 L per 100 km travelled and goes from 0 to 100 km/h in three seconds, carrying six passengers. Product design has to take into account the *technological and economic feasibility* of the designs.

Throughout this planning process, your team will have made numerous *simplifying assumptions* that support the analysis. For instance, it is not possible to identify consumer tastes perfectly, so you might use demographic data about age, gender, marital status, family size, income, education, and so on, as well as survey data to sort out these preferences and to discern trends. You cannot take into account every data point, so you simplify by using some summary statistics and assume that these statistics are representative of the whole population.

Exhibit 2-1	Outline of a business plan

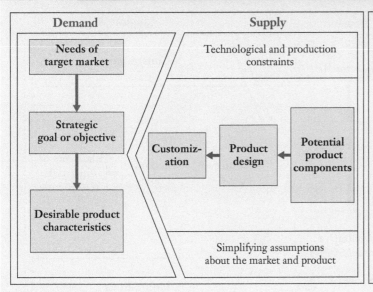

Demand

Needs of target market

Strategic goal or objective

Desirable product characteristics

Supply

Technological and production constraints

Customiz-ation

Product design

Potential product components

Simplifying assumptions about the market and product

- On the left are demand considerations, with the target market defining customer needs and desirable product characteristics.
- On the right side, supply points leftward to meet consumer demand.
- A carmaker would consider what product components would be desirable to meet consumer needs.
- Not every need can be satisfied, so only some components will be in the product design.
- Given an overall design, the product can be customized to suit different consumer tastes.
- Technological and production constraints limit what configurations of the product are feasible.
- Simplifying assumptions made through the design and customization process also affect how well the product meets customers' needs. These assumptions are at the bottom because they form the foundation of the analysis—poor assumptions are likely to result in unsuccessful products that do not meet customers' needs.

Exhibit 2-1 summarizes the business plan components discussed above and shows how they relate to each other.

Clearly, this is an extremely simplified way of looking at a business plan. It is neither as comprehensive nor as detailed as it needs to be for a real business plan. For example, it deliberately omits the important issue of the source of financing for the project, which has no corresponding component in the accounting conceptual frameworks. Nonetheless, this exercise helps to introduce the idea of conceptual frameworks for financial reporting, which can be illustrated by a diagram very similar to the one in Exhibit 2-1.

 CHECKPOINT **CP2-1**

Explain how a conceptual framework for financial reporting is similar to a business plan.

2. Outline of a conceptual framework for financial reporting

Similar to a business plan, Exhibit 2-2 shows the demand side on the left, which is determined by the set of intended users, their information needs, and the characteristics of the information they desire. The supply side on the right identifies the elements of financial statements (such as assets and liabilities). Whether these elements are reported on the financial statements (recognition) and at what value they should be reported (measurement) correspond to the product design stage of a business plan. Whether the supply of information fits users' demands partly depends on the constraints faced by accountants and the validity of the simplifying assumptions they make.

The above is an overview laying out the eight major components of a conceptual framework for financial reporting and how these components fit together. The following section explores these eight components in more detail in the context of IFRS.

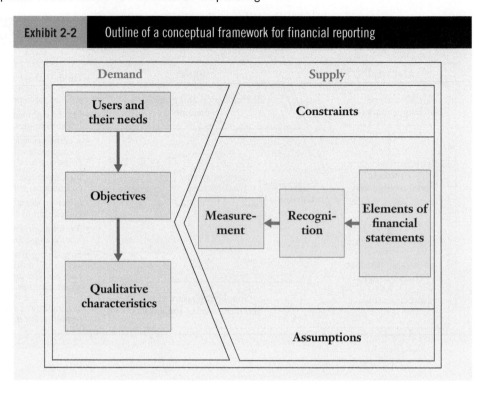

| Exhibit 2-2 | Outline of a conceptual framework for financial reporting |

B. COMPONENTS OF THE IFRS CONCEPTUAL FRAMEWORK

L.O. 2-2. Explain the rationale for each of the eight major components of these frameworks and synthesize these components into an integrated whole.

Having laid out the general structure of conceptual frameworks for financial reporting, we are now prepared to delve more deeply into the specific components. The following diagram fills in the details of the IFRS Conceptual Framework. Refer to Exhibit 2-3 frequently as you proceed through the discussion below to remind you of where you are in the framework.

This framework appears in the "Conceptual Framework for Financial Reporting" (denoted by "IFRS Conceptual Framework" in short), a separate document near the beginning of the printed hardcopy version of IFRS. However, note that the IFRS document does not have a diagrammatical depiction such as Exhibit 2-3; rather the diagram is an interpretation that is helpful for understanding the framework's components and their interrelationships.

1. Users and their needs

In paragraph OB2, the IFRS Conceptual Framework specifically identifies the set of users as "existing and potential investors, lenders, and other creditors." In other words, IFRS focuses on parties that have provided financial resources to the enterprise in the past and those who may decide to do so in the future. "Investors" includes parties who invest in the company's equity or debt.

The implication of defining the set of users specifically is that the reporting standards can better accommodate the needs of this group of potential users. However, this also means that the needs of other potential users are likely to be less well served. For example, customers and employees are also potential users of financial reports, but they are not included in the IFRS Conceptual Framework.

Paragraph OB5 in the IFRS Conceptual Framework notes that many investors and creditors are not in a position to demand a particular reporting entity to provide them with information beyond what is available in general purpose financial statements required by laws and regulations. General purpose financial statements are therefore a

Exhibit 2-3   The IFRS Framework

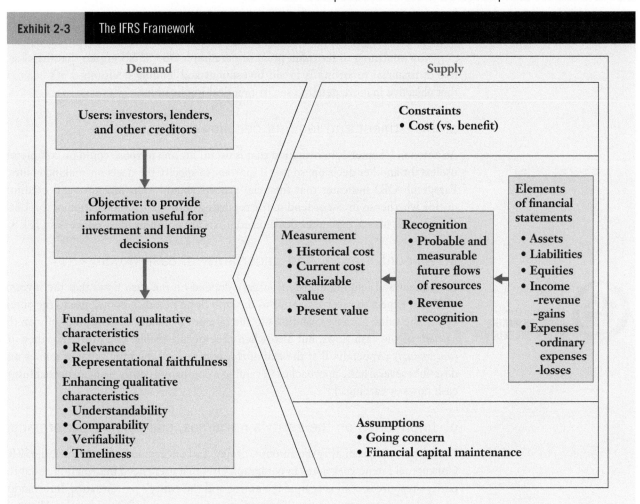

key tool for reducing information asymmetry for these users. Thus, these investors and creditors form the primary users of financial reports contemplated by IFRS.

The focus on a narrow set of users is a conscious choice, as is the choice of a target market. In the past (as recent as 2010), the Conceptual Framework in IFRS included a much broader set of users, including not just investors and lenders, but also employees, suppliers, customers, governments, and the public.

2. Objectives of financial reporting

After identifying the users (target market), we must think about their information needs. The needs of financial statement users define the objectives of financial reporting. The IFRS Conceptual Framework describes the objective of financial reporting as follows.

> ¶OB2   The objective of general purpose financial reporting is to provide finan-
> cial information about the reporting entity that is useful to existing and
> potential investors, lenders, and other creditors in making decisions about
> providing resources to the entity. Those decisions involve buying, selling,
> or holding equity and debt instruments, and providing or settling loans
> and other forms of credit.[1]

The first part of this short paragraph refers to *general purpose financial reporting,* which are the financial reports publicly available to outsiders. In other words, enterprises can choose to issue other financial reports that are not general purpose financial reports, and such reports would not need to follow the IFRS Conceptual Framework.

[1.] Copyright © 2012 IFRS Foundation.

For example, management can choose to compile reports for specific management decision-making purposes.

Now returning to the main point of paragraph OB2, IFRS argues that the objective of financial reporting is to aid investment and lending decisions. Let's examine that objective in more detail to see its practical implications.

a. Investment and lending decisions

As noted in Chapter 1, information that is useful for one purpose could be completely useless for another decision, so it is important to specify the decision-making context. Paragraph OB2 indicates that financial reports should help investors and creditors decide whether to invest or lend to the reporting entity. The specification of this decision context means that other decision contexts are not of primary concern in IFRS.

b. Amount, timing, and uncertainty of cash flows

THRESHOLD CONCEPT
DECISION MAKING
UNDER UNCERTAINTY

Investment and lending decisions largely depend on the cash flows that the investor or lender expect to receive relative to the cash flows that they contribute to the enterprise. The value of those cash flows to the investor or lender depends not only on the *amounts* of the cash flows, but also when they occur (*timing*) and how risky they are (*uncertainty*). (Appendix B at the end of this text reviews the time value of money and describes several basic approaches to valuing a company's equity using expected future cash flows or earnings.)

c. Information on the entity's resources, claims, and performance

For purposes of predicting the amount, timing, and uncertainty of cash flows, the IFRS Conceptual Framework notes in paragraph OB4 that users need information about the entity's resources, claims against the entity, and the entity's performance. Information on available resources is useful for predicting future cash inflows—we should expect abundant resources to generate high cash flows in the future. Likewise, information about claims against the entity help to predict future cash outflows—large claims entail large cash outflows in the future. Information on past performance is helpful for predicting future performance, which in turn affects future cash inflows and outflows.

While measuring past performance is done for the purpose of predicting future cash flows, this does not mean that past performance needs to be measured using cash flows. Past cash flows are *one* set of useful figures for predicting future cash flows, but other measures of performance are also useful. An example with which you are thoroughly familiar is academic performance: how you performed in a past course can be a predictor of your performance in future courses, but other factors can also be useful. In the financial context, IFRS suggests that accrual accounting produces useful performance measures.

accrual accounting A basis of accounting that records economic events when they happen rather than only when cash exchanges occur.

Accrual accounting includes economic events when they happen rather than only when cash exchanges occur. This basis of accounting is not constrained by the timing of cash flows: we record transactions and events even if the related cash flows occur in other periods. You are already familiar with the accrual basis of accounting from introductory accounting. For example, we record sales revenue today even if the customer pays for the goods 30 days later.

 **CHECKPOINT CP2-2**

According to the IFRS Conceptual Framework, who are the primary users of financial reports? To satisfy the needs of these users, what types of information should financial reports provide?

3. Qualitative characteristics

The discussion above has already covered two of the three components on the demand side of Exhibit 2-3: *users and their needs* and *objectives of financial reporting*. The third component contains the *qualitative characteristics*, which enumerate the desirable characteristics of financial reports that help to meet users' information needs. The IFRS Conceptual Framework enumerates six qualitative characteristics, categorized as either fundamental or enhancing characteristics.

The framework considers **fundamental qualitative characteristics** as those that must be present for information to be useful for decision making. There are two such characteristics: relevance and representational faithfulness. These characteristics are essential or "must haves." (See IFRS Conceptual Framework paragraph QC17.)

In comparison, **enhancing qualitative characteristics** are those that affect the information's degree of usefulness. There are four such characteristics: understandability, comparability, verifiability, and timeliness. These characteristics are desirable or "nice to have."

a. Fundamental qualitative characteristics

The IFRS Conceptual Framework argues that financial information must be both relevant and representationally faithful for it to be useful in decision making. **Relevance** is the ability to influence users' economic decisions. Information is relevant if it has *confirmatory value*, if it provides feedback about past events, or if it has *predictive value* for future outcomes. Note that the idea of relevance is very similar to the definition of information. A subtle distinction is that information is usually a yes/no classification, whereas relevance can be a matter of degree. A piece of data either is or is not informative to a person, but we can refer to how relevant that piece of information is to the decision maker in addition to saying that it is relevant or not.

In the context of relevance, the IFRS Framework also introduces the idea of **materiality**, whether omitting, misstating, or obscuring a particular piece of information about a reporting entity would influence the primary users' economic decisions. In other words, if an item has so little relevance that it would not change decisions, then it is considered immaterial.

Of course, whether a piece of information is material or not is a matter of professional judgment. That judgment should take into account who the users are and the decision contexts in which they will use the accounting information. For example, information about future growth as a result of a technological breakthrough is highly relevant and material to equity investors. However, creditors who do not share in the upside potential of the company will find the information less relevant and potentially immaterial. The identification of "primary users" in the definition of materiality indicates that materiality should be assessed in light of the decisions that investors, lenders, and other creditors are likely to make.

Materiality should also be assessed on the basis of a class of items or transactions, rather than on an item-by-item, transaction-by-transaction basis. For example, each smart phone is likely to be immaterial for its maker. However, the manufacturer cannot use the immateriality of each individual phone to justify omitting inventories from its balance sheet—all items of inventory as a whole are material to the readers of the financial statements.

The second fundamental qualitative characteristic is **representational faithfulness**—the extent to which financial information reflects the underlying transactions, resources, and claims of an enterprise. Financial statements provide a summary representation of some underlying phenomena, just as movies, paintings, or photographs are representations of real events and items. Some paintings are more abstract interpretations of reality while others are more direct representations. A more faithful representation allows the financial statement users to better

fundamental qualitative characteristics   The characteristics that must be present for information to be useful for decision making. Compare with **enhancing qualitative characteristics**.

enhancing qualitative characteristics   The characteristics that affect the information's degree of usefulness. Compare with **fundamental qualitative characteristics**.

relevance   The ability to influence users' economic decisions. Information that is able to provide feedback about past performance or helps make predictions is more relevant.

materiality   Whether omitting, misstating, or obscuring a particular piece of information about a reporting entity would influence the primary users' economic decisions.

representational faithfulness   The extent to which financial information reflects the underlying transactions, resources, and claims of an enterprise.

understand the underlying transactions, resources, and claims. Three attributes contribute to representational faithfulness: completeness, neutrality, and freedom from error.

completeness   The inclusion of all material items in the financial statements. One of three attributes of **representational faithfulness**.

Completeness: This attribute simply means that the financial statements should not omit any material items or transactions. In order for users to be able to make informed decisions, they need to see a comprehensive picture of the enterprise's operations, not just a piece of it. For example, in a parent–subsidiary group of companies, presenting the financial statements of the parent without including the operations of the subsidiary would be incomplete because the group acts as one economic unit. For this reason, we prepare consolidated financial statements that combine the operations of parents and subsidiaries. (See Chapter 7 for more discussion of consolidated financial statements.) Completeness also encompasses the time dimension: financial statements for a fiscal year need to include all of the transactions in that year. Chapter 3 discusses how we determine whether a transaction belongs in a particular fiscal period.

neutrality   The extent to which information is free from bias. One of three attributes of **representational faithfulness**.

Neutrality: There is a substantial amount of subjectivity, choice, and estimation involved in the preparation of financial statements, so generally it is inappropriate to refer to "true" amounts of income, assets, or liabilities. However, we can refer to amounts that are neutral, that is, free of bias. For example, suppose we polled 10 or 100 accountants who have no particular incentives to over- or underreport a company's financial position. While there is likely to be a range of outcomes, we can think of the average (mean or median) from this poll as representing what we should expect under neutrality. When actual financial statements systematically report above or below this hypothetical average, we can say that the financial statements lack neutrality.

freedom from error   The extent to which information is absent of errors or omissions. One of three attributes of **representational faithfulness**.

Freedom from error: While some aspects of accounting involve subjectivity, there are other aspects that involve objective quantities and descriptions. For example, errors in addition would undermine the representational faithfulness of the reported information. Similarly, classifying an amount that has yet to be received as "cash" would be an error. Financial reports that are free of errors enhance the usefulness of those reports.

understandability   The ease with which users are able to comprehend financial reports. One of four **enhancing qualitative characteristics**.

THRESHOLD CONCEPT
EFFICIENT SECURITIES MARKETS

comparability   Refers to the ability to compare one set of financial statements with another. The comparison may be with the financial statements of the same enterprise in a different year or with those of a different enterprise. One of four **enhancing qualitative characteristics**.

b. Enhancing qualitative characteristics

This category of qualitative characteristics contributes to the usefulness of financial reports. The IFRS Conceptual Framework suggests that they are desirable, but not essential. The four enhancing qualitative characteristics are understandability, comparability, verifiability, and timeliness.

The characteristic of **understandability** is fairly self-explanatory. Financial reports need to be understandable to the readers for them to be useful in decision making. As noted in Chapter 1, a certain degree of sophistication can be expected from financial statement users, particularly when the company is widely traded so that its security prices can be presumed to be efficient.

Comparability refers to the ability to compare one set of financial statements with another. The comparison may be with the financial statements of the same enterprise in a different year or with those of a different enterprise. Using consistent accounting policies from one period to the next improves comparability over time.

AN EVALUATION OF THE QUALITATIVE CHARACTERISTICS

The six qualitative characteristics identified above, stratified into two categories of fundamental and enhancing characteristics, are just one possible scheme for describing the characteristics of financial information that we would expect to be useful to readers of financial reports. Prior to September 2010, there was no stratification of the qualitative characteristics, and there were a total of four such characteristics (understandability, relevance, reliability, and comparability). The International Accounting Standards Board, the body that issues IFRS, believes that the current list and categorization of qualitative characteristics is an improvement over the past system; whether this is the case remains to be seen.

For example, if you thought about it carefully while you were reading the above section, you might have wondered whether it makes sense to classify relevance and representational faithfulness as "fundamental" characteristics that must be present for information to be useful. If we limited ourselves to dichotomous conclusions of whether a piece of information is relevant or not, or is faithfully represented or not, then these two characteristics could also be considered "fundamental." However, the usual meanings of relevance and representational faithfulness, as well as the meanings within the IFRS Conceptual Framework, are that they are matters of degree. Information can be more or less relevant and more or less faithfully represented. When characteristics are measured on a continuum, is it logical to say that those characteristics are fundamental or essential? When is a piece of information sufficiently relevant or represented with sufficient faithfulness? There is no clear answer to these questions; perhaps more clarity will develop over time as practitioners gain experience applying this version of the Conceptual Framework.

Verifiability is the degree to which different people would agree with the chosen representation in the financial reports. In other words, a representation or assertion in the financial report that can be objectively confirmed is more verifiable than one that cannot be. A cash balance can be verified with the banks that hold the deposits, whereas the value of research requires subjective assessments of future market potential, competitive actions, and so on, so, for example, "cash" is more verifiable than "intangible assets."

Timeliness refers to how soon the information is available to decision makers. The older the information, the less timely and less useful it is. Timeliness matters because accounting information competes with other sources of information, as discussed in Chapter 1.

 CHECKPOINT **CP2-3**

Identify the two fundamental qualitative characteristics and the four enhancing qualitative characteristics. How does IFRS distinguish characteristics that are fundamental from those that are enhancing?

verifiability The degree to which different people would agree with the chosen representation in the financial reports. One of four **enhancing qualitative characteristics**.

 THRESHOLD CONCEPT **EFFICIENT SECURITIES MARKETS**

timeliness How soon the information becomes available to decision makers. One of four **enhancing qualitative characteristics**.

4. Elements of financial statements

Having now covered the three demand components of the IFRS Framework, let's turn our attention to the supply side. Beginning with the far right side of Exhibit 2-3, we have the elements of financial statements. These elements define the items

asset A resource controlled by an entity as a result of past events and from which future economic benefits are expected to flow to the entity.

income Increases in economic benefits during an accounting period in the form of inflows or enhancements of assets or decreases of liabilities that result in increases in equity, other than those relating to contributions from equity participants. Income encompasses both **revenue** and **gains**.

revenue A type of income that arises in the course of ordinary activities.

gains A type of income other than revenue.

liability A present obligation of the entity arising from past events, the settlement of which is expected to result in an outflow from the entity of economic resources embodying economic benefits.

expenses Decreases in economic benefits during an accounting period in the form of outflows or depletions of assets or incurrence of liabilities that result in decreases in equity, other than those relating to distributions to equity participants. Expenses include **ordinary expenses** and **losses**.

losses A type of **expense** that is not an **ordinary expense**.

ordinary expense A type of **expense** that arises from the ordinary activities of the entity.

equity The residual interest in the assets of an entity after deducting all its liabilities.

Exhibit 2-4	Elements of financial statements
Elements relating to measuring financial position	**Elements relating to measuring performance**
An **asset** is a resource controlled by an entity as a result of past events and from which future economic benefits are expected to flow to the entity.	**Income** is increases in economic benefits during an accounting period in the form of inflows or enhancements of assets or decreases of liabilities that result in increases in equity, other than those relating to contributions from equity participants. Income encompasses both revenue and gains.
	Revenue arises in the course of ordinary activities.
	Gains represent other items that meet the definition of income and may or may not arise in the course of ordinary activities.
A **liability** is a present obligation of the entity arising from past events, the settlement of which is expected to result in an outflow from the entity of economic resources embodying economic benefits.	**Expenses** are decreases in economic benefits during an accounting period in the form of outflows or depletions of assets or incurrence of liabilities that result in decreases in equity, other than those relating to distributions to equity participants.
	The definition of expenses encompasses **losses** as well as those expenses that arise in the course of ordinary activities of the entity (**ordinary expenses**).
Equity is the residual interest in the assets of an entity after deducting all its liabilities.	

Source: IFRS Framework ¶4.4–4.35. Copyright © 2012 IFRS Foundation.

(or category of items) that appear in the financial statements. Corresponding to the information needs of users discussed previously, these elements can be separated into those relating to financial position and those relating to performance, as shown in Exhibit 2-4.

A quick read of these definitions reveals a strong focus on assets and liabilities, since *equity, income,* and *expenses* are defined in terms of assets and liabilities. Because these two elements are so important, it is worthwhile to examine them in more detail. Exhibit 2-5 separates each of these two definitions into three parts.

As you see, the definitions of assets and liabilities are mirror images of each other. Beginning from the bottom of Exhibit 2-5, an *asset* involves future inflows of economic benefits while a *liability* involves future outflows. These future flows must arise from past events, not anticipated transactions. Finally, control of a resource and an obligation are two sides of the same coin: the party who has control holds the decision rights, whereas a party who has an obligation lacks decision rights (i.e., he or she must fulfill the obligation). A *present* obligation is distinguished from a commitment to do something in the future, such as a contract to purchase a piece of equipment.

Exhibit 2-5	Definitions of asset and liability
An asset is …	**A liability is …**
a resource controlled by an entity	a present obligation of the entity
as a result of past events and	arising from past events,
from which future economic benefits are expected to flow to the entity.	the settlement of which is expected to result in an outflow from the entity of economic resources embodying economic benefits.

An important aspect that is implicit in the definitions of assets and liabilities is that they are two distinct concepts and we do not offset one against the other. Rather than just defining "net assets" or equity, we specify assets separately from liabilities. Showing that a company has $500 million in assets and $300 million in liabilities conveys more information than simply showing $200 million in net assets. In particular, the characteristics of the assets can differ dramatically from those of the liabilities. Only in limited circumstances in which an asset is closely linked to a specific liability would offsetting be appropriate. (Chapter 14 will look at this issue in more detail in the context of financial instruments.)

 CHECKPOINT **CP2-4**

Among the various elements of financial statements, explain how two of them, assets and liabilities, form the basis of the others.

5. Recognition

Financial statements contain both items that are **recognized** in the body of the balance sheet, income statement, statement of comprehensive income, statement of cash flows, or statement of capital, as well as items that are merely disclosed in the notes. Recognition criteria set down the guidelines for when to report something as a *line item* (e.g., sales revenue) on one of the main financial statements instead of in the notes, while measurement provides the basis for *quantifying* the items reported (e.g., how much revenue to report). Recognition criteria and measurement bases are choices made by standard setters among several alternatives. General accounting principles guide choices regarding more specific accounting pronouncements. For example, historical cost is only one among several alternative measurement bases (current cost is another). These choices should be made in light of the desirable qualitative characteristics demanded by users.

> **recognition** The process of presenting an item in the financial statements, as opposed to merely disclosing that item in the notes.

Generally, accounting elements are recognized in the financial statements if the future inflows or outflows of resources are *probable* and the amounts are *reasonably measurable*. For example, accounts receivable usually have a high probability of being collected, and the amount that can be collected is estimable, so accounts receivable are usually recorded as assets. On the other hand, the probability of success in research and development is low or unknown, and the future benefits from such investments are difficult to estimate with precision, so R&D expenditures are not usually recognized as assets. More specific recognition and measurement rules will be provided for specific items in future chapters. For instance, Chapter 4 will thoroughly examine *revenue recognition* (i.e., when revenue should be reported in the income statement).

6. Measurement

Measurement refers to the quantification of the amounts to be reported on the financial statements. The measurement basis most commonly used is **historical cost**, the amount of cash or cash equivalents paid or received in a transaction. Exchanges involving non-monetary items rather than cash will be discussed in Chapter 8.[2]

In addition to historical cost, other measurement bases used for different financial statement items include current cost, realizable/settlement value, and present value.

> **measurement** The basis for quantifying items reported in the financial statements.

> **historical cost** The actual cost of an asset at the time it was purchased; can also refer to amounts based on historical cost but adjusted by depreciation or impairment.

- *Current cost* is the amount of cash or cash equivalents that would be paid to purchase an asset or that would be paid to extinguish a liability currently.

---

[2] Briefly, a non-monetary item would be converted to a monetary amount using an estimate of its fair value at the time of the transaction. Fair value is the amount for which an asset could be sold, or a liability settled, between market participants.

- *Realizable value* is the amount of cash or cash equivalents that could be obtained from selling an asset. The corresponding basis for liabilities is *settlement value,* the amount that would be needed to settle the obligation. Both realizable value and settlement value are determined in the context of orderly, normal business transactions (e.g., not in a forced sale).
- *Present value* is the discounted value of future cash inflows or outflows expected in the normal course of business. Appendix B at the end of this text reviews present value concepts.

 CHECKPOINT **CP2-5**

Explain the differences between the definition of financial statement elements, their recognition, and their measurement.

7. Constraints

cost constraint A constraint stating that the cost of reporting financial information should not exceed the benefits that can be obtained from using that information.

Just as it does not make good business sense to build a product that costs more to produce than its sale price, the IFRS Framework acknowledges that the supply of accounting information must be cost-effective. The **cost constraint** simply says that the cost of reporting financial information should not exceed the benefits that can be obtained from using that information. The costs include not only the cost of data collection and financial report preparation, but also the cost of users reading and interpreting the information. Some of these costs are explicit and quantifiable, but others are more subjective. Likewise, the assessment of benefits from the use of the financial information is likely to be subjective.

8. Assumptions

In deriving detailed accounting rules, certain assumptions need to be made. These are not necessarily based on theory. *Assumptions* are simplified generalizations about the real world that are deemed to be appropriate for most circumstances (but not always). For example, a marketing plan makes generalizations about the target market based on summarized demographic data. The IFRS Conceptual Framework makes one important explicit assumption that the reporting entity will be a going concern. A second assumption that is appropriate for the Canadian environment is financial capital maintenance.

a. Going concern

going concern The assumption that the reporting entity will continue operating into the foreseeable future.

Financial statements are prepared assuming that the reporting entity is a **going concern**—that it will continue operating into the foreseeable future. For example, this means that we consider an asset's value in use in the entity rather than its liquidation value in a forced sale. The going concern assumption is also necessary for the various accruals we record, such as accounts receivable, which assume that the enterprise will collect those receivables in the future. Likewise, recording accounts payable assumes that the entity will pay those amounts in the future. Thus, the going concern assumption underlies the accrual basis of accounting.

b. Financial capital maintenance

Capital maintenance refers to the amount of resources required to ensure the economic sustainability of an entity—what is necessary for the entity to continue in operations for the foreseeable future at a level similar to how it has operated in the past. The assumption of capital maintenance importantly determines how we measure profit. Amounts that are earned beyond what is necessary for an entity to maintain its capital are profit. If the entity does not earn enough, such that its capital diminishes over time, then it has a loss.

THE ROLE OF THE IFRS FRAMEWORK IN RELATION TO SPECIFIC ACCOUNTING STANDARDS

Having now seen what the Conceptual Framework looks like, an important question that arises is how it interacts with more specific standards, such as those relating to the accounting for inventories or financial instruments. Should the general principles in the Conceptual Framework supersede specific standards in the same way that a constitution overrides specific statutes if the two should conflict?

The International Accounting Standards Committee (IASC, the predecessor of the IASB) specifically considered this issue and answered in two different ways.

First, the introduction to the IFRS Conceptual Framework indicates a lower authority for the framework:

> This Conceptual Framework is not an IFRS and hence does not define standards for any particular measurement or disclosure issue. Nothing in this Framework overrides any specific IFRS.
>
> The Board recognizes that in a limited number of cases there may be a conflict between the Conceptual Framework and an IFRS. In those cases where there is a conflict, the requirements of the IFRS prevail over those of the Framework. As, however, the Board will be guided by the Framework in the development of future Standards and in its review of existing Standards, the number of cases of conflict between the Framework and IFRSs will diminish through time.

Second, IAS 1 on *Presentation of Financial Statements* allows firms to depart from the specific standards in IFRS if following such standards would result in financial statements that did not meet the objectives in the framework. Specifically, paragraph 19 indicates

> In the extremely rare circumstances in which management concludes that compliance with a requirement in an IFRS would be so misleading that it would conflict with the objective of financial statements set out in the Framework, the entity shall depart from that requirement in the manner set out in paragraph 20 [by providing specific disclosures about the departure] …

Thus, there is no clear-cut dominance in authority of the IFRS Framework and specific IFRS.

IFRS contemplates two ways to define capital maintenance: physical and financial. Correspondingly, there are two ways to measure profit. Physical capital maintenance requires an entity to be capable of producing as much at the end of a period as at the beginning, measured in physical quantities (e.g., tonnes of coal, number of cars). **Financial capital maintenance** requires the entity to have as much resource in monetary terms at the end of a period as it did at the beginning of that period.

The two concepts of capital maintenance differ to the extent that there are changes in the prices of a firm's assets and liabilities. If there is high inflation, then each dollar of financial capital will buy less and less physical capital as time progresses, so merely maintaining financial capital means that physical capital is declining. When there is significant inflation, the financial capital maintenance concept reports profits that are too high (i.e., the reported profits include both a return on capital and a return of capital invested).

financial capital maintenance The assumption that an entity needs to have as much resource in monetary terms at the end of a period as it did at the beginning of that period to maintain its operating capacity. Amounts in excess of that required to maintain financial capital are profit.

For instance, if you had $100 and you were able to purchase a product and later resell it for $160, this produces a *profit of $60*, but this assumes that we use the financial capital maintenance concept. However, what if during that time, inflation was 100%? Did you really earn a profit? With prices doubling, you would actually need $200 just to be as well off as you were at the beginning. Measured in physical capital terms, you would have a *loss of $40* ($160 − $200). This is an extreme example used to demonstrate the difference between financial and physical capital maintenance. When prices are stable, as they are in Canada, measuring financial capital is reasonably valid. For this reason, Canadian enterprises generally use the financial capital maintenance assumption.

The Appendix to this chapter discusses and illustrates the concept of capital maintenance in more detail (see page 50).

9. Example for illustrating the application of the IFRS Framework

L.O. 2-3.   Apply the conceptual frameworks in IFRS and ASPE to specific circumstances and evaluate the trade-offs among different concepts within the frameworks.

Elmo Company operates a plant that processes limestone into quicklime and hydrated lime. The plant, where most of the equipment was installed several years ago, continually deposits a dusty substance over the surrounding countryside. Citing the unsanitary conditions on the neighbouring community, the pollution of the Elmo River, and the high incidence of lung disease among citizens of Elmotown, the provincial Pollution Control Agency has ordered the installation of air pollution equipment. The agency has also assessed a substantial penalty, which will be used to clean up Elmotown. After considering the costs involved (which could not have been reasonably estimated before the agency's action), Elmo decides to comply with the agency's order, the alternative being to cease operations at the end of the current fiscal year. The board of directors agrees that the air pollution equipment should be capitalized and depreciated over its useful life, but they disagree over the period(s) to which the penalty should be charged.

Required:

Consider three alternatives to account for the penalty: charge against current period income, charge against prior years' income, or capitalize the expenditure and amortize over future years. Using the framework for financial reporting, discuss the conceptual merits of each alternative.

Suggested solution:

Exhibit 2-6	Arguments for and against three alternatives to account for the pollution penalty	
Accounting alternative	**Arguments for alternative**	**Arguments against alternative**
Charge against current period income	■ Penalty has *no future benefits* because future cash flows have not changed with the payment; it is not an asset so it should be expensed. ■ Provides information to financial statement readers *relevant* to the monetary costs of Elmo's pollution. ■ Significantly reduces current year reported *performance*, which can result in reduced income-based compensation to management, giving them incentive to avoid pollution in the future.	■ Recognizing expense in the current period is *not representationally faithful* because the pollution that led to the penalty occurred in past periods. ■ The one-time impact on income would have an excessively negative impact on reported *performance* and the compensation of current managers, while the managers responsible for the past pollution may no longer be employed by Elmo. ■ The large expense recorded in the current period would reduce the *comparability* of the income statement with other periods.

(*Continued*)

Exhibit 2-6	Continued

Charge against prior years' income	■ Penalty *matches* revenue record in past years, when the pollution was generated. ■ Provides for more *comparable* (*consistent*) financial statements for year-to-year comparisons if the charges are recorded in the years the pollution was generated; future expenses will increase due to depreciation of new pollution control equipment. ■ Charging against prior years' income is consistent with recognizing liabilities in past years: the current penalty implies that the company had an *obligation* to abate pollution in those past years, and those past decisions to not do so result in future outflows in the form of penalties.	■ The current income statement does not show the penalty so it could be considered *incomplete* as users may not become aware of the significant penalty and degree of pollution created by Elmo's operations. ■ Management compensation is unlikely to be affected because past compensation is unlikely to be adjusted for retroactive changes to reported income (*performance*). ■ The penalty did not arise until the Pollution Control Agency issued its decision; no liabilities arose in past years for this penalty since the event *had not yet occurred*.
Capitalize expenditure and amortize over future years	■ The penalty is an asset: it *has future economic benefits* because the payment allows Elmo to remain in operation to generate future cash flows from operations (which are likely to be significant since the company decided to remain in Elmotown). The payment arose from *past events* and the company has *control* over whether it continues to operate in Elmotown.	■ The Pollution Control Agency assessed the penalty for past pollution, so there are *no future benefits* associated with this cost. ■ Any future benefits are unclear, so should not capitalize, to be conservative. ■ Future period of benefit is unclear, so there is no *reliable* basis for amortization and *matching*.

10. Financial information prepared on other bases

As noted previously, the Conceptual Framework according to IFRS is based on the primary users and, by necessity, cannot satisfy the needs of everyone. This is no different from a carmaker not being able to satisfy the needs of every possible car buyer. However, this does not mean that those other needs cannot be met. An enterprise can always present additional information that it thinks will be useful to readers.

For example, many companies report "pro forma" measures of income in addition to the net income amount required under IFRS. These pro forma measures remove certain items such as financing costs, depreciation, or the costs of restructuring the company. While these pro forma income numbers would be incomplete (detracting from one of the desirable attributes contributing to representational faithfulness), companies can choose to report these figures in addition to the net income figure prescribed by IFRS. They might choose to do this because they perceive the pro forma figure to be more relevant to some users. In the analogy of a car, these pro forma measures could be thought of as "after-market" modifications that the car owner makes after buying the vehicle to satisfy his or her particular tastes.

C. OTHER CONCEPTUAL FRAMEWORKS

The previous section discussed the Conceptual Framework as contained in IFRS. As mentioned earlier, the IFRS Framework is just one of many possible conceptual frameworks, just as there are many possible business plans.[3] Accounting Standards for Private Enterprises (ASPE) contains a conceptual framework that is different from, though similar to, the IFRS Framework. The conceptual framework in the United States was different from the IFRS Framework in the past, but the two frameworks have partly converged and will eventually become one since the United States and the

---

[3.] The frameworks change over time as well. The IFRS Conceptual Framework was partially revised in 2011.

Exhibit 2-7	Summary comparison of conceptual frameworks in IFRS and ASPE	
Demand Considerations	**IFRS**	**ASPE**
Users	Investors, lenders, and other creditors	Investors, creditors, and other users
Objectives	To provide information useful for investment and lending decisions	To provide information useful for making resource allocation decisions and/or assessing management stewardship
Qualitative characteristics		
Relevance	✓	✓
—Materiality	✓	See constraints
Representational faithfulness	✓	✓
—Completeness	✓	
—Neutrality	✓	✓
—Freedom from error	✓	✓
Understandability	✓	✓
Comparability	✓	✓
Verifiability	✓	✓
Timeliness	✓	✓
Classification into fundamental vs. enhancing characteristics	✓	
Trade-offs among characteristics	✓	✓
Elements of financial statements		
Assets	✓	✓
Liabilities	✓	✓
Equities	✓	✓
Revenue and gains	✓	✓
(Ordinary) expenses and losses	✓	✓
Comprehensive income	✓	
Recognition		
Probable and measurable future flows of resources	✓	✓
Revenue recognition	✓	✓
Matching	✓	✓
Measurement		
Historical cost	✓	✓
Current (replacement) cost	✓	✓
Realizable value	✓	✓
Present value	✓	✓
Constraints		
Cost (vs. benefit)	✓	✓
Materiality	See qualitative characteristics	✓
Assumptions		
Going concern	✓	✓
Financial capital maintenance	✓	✓
Length/detail of framework		
Number of pages	22	9
Number of paragraphs	136	52
Number of words (approx.)	11,000	3,800

IASB have been working together to develop a common conceptual framework. The table in Exhibit 2-7 summarizes where these differences occur between the IFRS and ASPE frameworks.

As Exhibit 2-7 shows, there is a considerable degree of similarity in the conceptual frameworks issued by the two standard-setting bodies. One seemingly trivial but notable difference shown at the bottom of the exhibit is the length of the frameworks. The IFRS Framework is two to three times the size of ASPE's. This situation is not unique to the conceptual frameworks. These statistics reflect the differences in standard-setting approaches in the different jurisdictions.

D. STANDARD SETTING: INTERNATIONALLY AND IN CANADA

L.O. 2-4.   Describe the standard-setting environment in Canada.

1. Standards internationally

IFRS are standards issued by the International Accounting Standards Board (IASB), a private body headquartered in London, England, with representation from a range of countries. Of the 14 seats on the board, four are allocated to Europe, four to the Americas, four to Asia-Oceania, one to Africa, and one at-large. In the current board (late 2017), one of the four members for the Americas represents Canada. IFRS has authority in a particular country if that country has legislation or regulation that requires the use of IFRS. The European Union required IFRS for publicly accountable enterprises beginning January 1, 2005. Currently, more than 100 countries around the world use IFRS.

2. Standards in Canada

In Canada, the Chartered Professional Accountants of Canada (CPA Canada) issues standards contained in the *CPA Canada Handbook*. Prior to January 1, 2011, a single set of accounting standards applied to all non-government entities, ranging from publicly traded companies to private enterprises to not-for-profit organizations. Beginning January 1, 2011, the accounting standards in the *Handbook* split into five parts. Part I contains IFRS; these standards are applicable to Canadian publicly accountable enterprises, which are defined as follows in the *Handbook* preface:

¶3(a)   a **publicly accountable enterprise** is an entity, other than a not-for-profit organization, that:

  i. has issued, or is in the process of issuing, debt or equity instruments that are, or will be, outstanding and traded in a public market . . . or
  ii. holds assets in a fiduciary capacity for a broad group of outsiders as one of its primary businesses.[4]

The second part of this definition includes entities such as banks and mutual funds that hold cash, shares, and other investments on behalf of others.

Part II of the *Handbook* contains Accounting Standards for Private Enterprises (ASPE). In these standards, a **private enterprise** means any for-profit entity that is not a publicly accountable enterprise.[5] Part III applies to not-for-profit enterprises (NFPOs) that are not government controlled beginning January 1, 2012. Part IV applies to pension plans. Part V contains legacy standards that were in effect prior to January 1, 2011. In addition to these five parts, governments and government-controlled entities

publicly accountable enterprise   An entity, other than a not-for-profit organization, that has issued debt or equity instruments that are outstanding and traded in a public market (or is in the process of issuing such instruments) or an entity that holds assets in a fiduciary capacity for a broad group of outsiders as one of its primary businesses.

private enterprise   In the ASPE standards, any for-profit entity that is not a publicly accountable enterprise.

[4.] Reprinted from Canadian Institute of Chartered Accountants Handbook–Accounting, 2015, with permission from Chartered Professional Accountants of Canada, Toronto, Canada. Any changes to the original material are the sole responsibility of the author (and/or publisher) and have not been reviewed or endorsed by the Chartered Professional Accountants of Canada.

[5.] In common English, "private enterprises" include both privately held enterprises and enterprises with publicly traded securities. For accounting standards, "private enterprises" refers to privately held businesses.

Exhibit 2-8 Standards applicable to different types of reporting entities

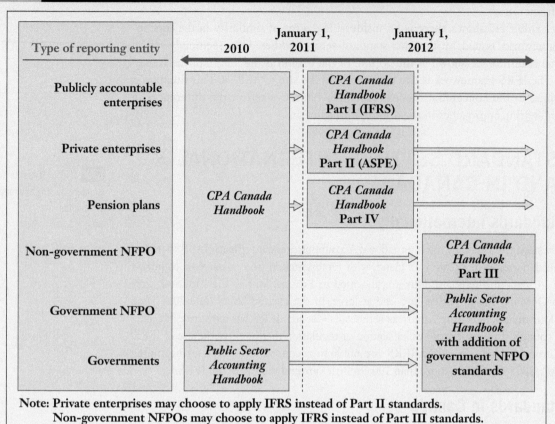

Note: Private enterprises may choose to apply IFRS instead of Part II standards.
Non-government NFPOs may choose to apply IFRS instead of Part III standards.

(e.g., Crown corporations) use a separate handbook that contains public sector accounting standards. Effective January 1, 2012, the public sector accounting standards were augmented to apply to government not-for-profit entities (e.g., public universities).

In this text we focus on Part I of the *CPA Canada Handbook* (i.e., IFRS), and point out significant differences where standards in Part II differ from Part I. For ease and clarity of reference in this textbook, we will use "IFRS" to refer to Part I of the *Handbook,* while citations to "ASPE" refer to Part II of the *Handbook*. For general purpose reference, the term "generally accepted accounting principles" (GAAP) refers to all standards in the *Handbook* (including IFRS), as well as principles and practices that are not in the *Handbook* but which are generally accepted by virtue of common practice.

Exhibit 2-8 summarizes the different standards that are applicable to various types of Canadian reporting entities over different time periods.

3. Organization and authority for setting accounting and auditing standards in Canada

In Canada, the *Canada Business Corporations Act* refers to accounting and auditing standards in the *Handbook* as the standards to be met for compliance with its regulations, thus effectively granting CPA Canada authority to set accounting and auditing standards.[6] The *Handbook* contains a relatively comprehensive set of standards, comprising:

---

6. *Canada Business Corporations Act,* Part XIV, Section 155; and *Canada Business Corporations Act,* Regulation 70. At the time of writing, the Act still refers to the CICA, the predecessor organization of CPA Canada, but the wording is expected to be amended.

- accounting standards for entities not in the public sector (including all for-profit enterprises whether publicly traded or privately held, and not-for-profit organizations);
- public sector accounting standards for governments and related entities such as government-owned universities and hospitals; and
- standards for auditing and other assurance engagements for both the public and private sectors.

Responsibility for non–public sector accounting standards rests with the Accounting Standards Board (AcSB), while the Public Sector Accounting Board (PSAB) issues standards for the public sector. While IFRS is contained within Part I of the *Handbook,* the AcSB has no authority to alter IFRS since these standards are set by the IASB in London. The Auditing and Assurance Standards Board (AASB) issues guidance for auditing and other assurance engagements.

Given the dual role of CPA Canada as an association of accountants and a standard-setting body, there is a potential for a real or perceived conflict of interest. In response, in 2000 the association established two independent governance bodies to oversee these three boards in order to increase the independence of the three standard-setting bodies. Each of these two oversight bodies has majority representation outside the accounting/auditing profession. The Accounting Standards Oversight Council (AcSOC) oversees the two accounting boards (AcSB and PSAB), while the Auditing and Assurance Standards Oversight Council (AASOC) oversees the AASB. See Exhibit 2-9 for a summary of the structure in Canada.

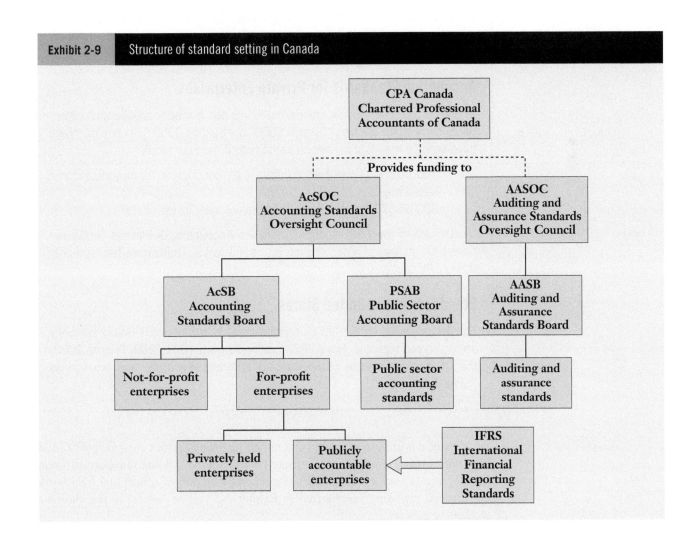

Exhibit 2-9   Structure of standard setting in Canada

UNDERSTANDING THE ORGANIZATION AND LABELLING OF ACCOUNTING STANDARDS

One seemingly trivial but important and practical issue is how the various accounting standards are organized and labelled (i.e., the filing system). For example, what are the meanings of references to "IFRS 2," "IAS 18," "ASPE Section 1000," or "SFAS 123"? What is the difference between an IFRS and an IAS? Do the numbers have any meaning?

International Financial Reporting Standards (IFRS)

Standards within IFRS are in chronological order by date of original issuance. For example, IFRS 1 precedes IFRS 2 chronologically. Subsequent revisions to the standards do not change the numbering. IFRS also includes standards with the label "IAS ##"; these are standards issued by the International Accounting Standards Committee (IASC), the predecessor to the current International Accounting Standards Board. The standards with IAS labels number from 1 to 41; those with the IFRS label begin from 1 and will continue to increase over time as more standards are issued. IAS- and IFRS-labelled standards have equal authority.

As noted earlier, the IFRS Conceptual Framework has lower authority than specific standards. In addition, IFRS includes interpretations of standards for specific circumstances. These are issued by the IFRS Interpretation Committee and its predecessor, the Standing Issues Committee; these interpretations carry the labels "IFRIC ##" and "SIC ##." Interpretations have less authority than IAS and IFRS.

Accounting Standards for Private Enterprises

In contrast to international standards, ASPE has a topical organization. Standards carry labels such as "Section 1000" or "Section 3065." Section numbers have specific meaning in relation to the rest of the *Handbook*.

> 1000–1800 General accounting (e.g., conceptual framework, income statement)
> 3000–3870 Specific items (e.g., inventories, investments)

Outside of the ASPE sections there are Accounting Guidelines (AcG) that have a chronological order, numbered from 1 to 19. These have less authority than ASPE sections.

Standards in the United States

Standards issued by the US Financial Accounting Standards Board currently are organized topically, like ASPE, numbered from 100 to 999. Prior to 2008, the US standards were chronologically ordered, like IFRS, and labelled as "SFAS ###."

Finally, it is important to note that not all reporting entities need to apply GAAP. In particular, if the owners agree, private enterprises may choose to report on a non-GAAP basis. In such circumstances, the general structure of conceptual frameworks for financial reporting summarized in Exhibit 2-2 will be helpful in the choice of accounting policies.

 CHECKPOINT **CP2-6**

Who sets accounting standards in Canada?

4. Globalization of standard setting

The convergence of accounting standards around the world is a topic that attracts heated debate. For many accountants, convergence is an attractive goal because it will provide increased comparability of financial statements of companies in different countries, reduce reporting costs for multinational companies, provide a common financial "language" for investors, and increase the mobility of accountants between countries. These benefits are intuitive and potentially large. However, others see significant costs that outweigh these benefits. For instance, the Financial Accounting Standards Committee of the American Accounting Association[7] issued a statement in April 2009 that opposed global convergence under IFRS.[8] The abstract of the article states: "[W]e propose that the need for a global [accounting standards] regulator is overstated. A global regulator is unlikely to help achieve the stated goals of comparability and consistency of financial reporting on a global basis. We favour allowing U.S. companies to choose use of U.S. GAAP or IFRS rather than mandating one global monopoly set of standards."

The two boxed articles on the following pages further explore this debate on global convergence in standard setting.

 GOING BANANAS: LESSONS FROM EVOLUTIONARY BIOLOGY

Bananas are yellow, right? Yes, if we are referring to the fruit eaten in most of the world: bananas of the "Cavendish" variety. As I learned from a fascinating radio program recently, the Cavendish is only one of over 1,000 varieties of the banana fruit that range broadly in terms of size, taste, and colour. Some varieties are red; some are quite round; many have hard seeds; and some are barely edible.

You may have read or heard about the fungal plague that is killing banana "trees" (technically, bananas are herbs) around the world, and that the species faces a real risk of extinction in the next decade. What you might not know is that this has happened before.

Some older readers might recall (with fondness) a different kind of banana that was available five decades ago. Before 1960, the "Gros Michel" was the predominant variety cultivated, as it was generally considered to be the best banana for its taste and its relative hardiness during shipping from producer to consumer. So what prompted the switch from the Gros Michel to the Cavendish?

(Continued)

[7.] The American Accounting Association is the principal association of accounting academics in the United States. The Financial Accounting Standards Committee has 11 leading academics from the United States and Canada.

[8.] Jamal, Karim, et al. "A Research Based Perspective on SEC's Proposed Rule on Roadmap for Potential Use of Financial Statements Prepared in Accordance with International Financial Reporting Standards (IFRS) by U.S. Issuers." Johnson School Research Paper Series No. #21-09 (2009). Available at SSRN: http://ssrn.com/abstract=1381292. Used with permission.

Banana growers had no choice but to change. The problem is that the Gros Michel was susceptible to a fungus commonly known as "Panama Disease." For a century, growers were engaged in a race against the disease: As they abandoned infected plantations and moved to new fields, the disease would follow. By 1960, banana companies had run out of new land and the Gros Michel had practically become extinct. Reluctantly, growers switched to the inferior-tasting Cavendish banana, as it was resistant to Panama Disease.

Which brings us to today: The history of the Gros Michel is now repeating itself as a new strain of Panama Disease spreads to Cavendish plantations around the world.

So why am I talking about bananas? Well, while it may seem unlikely, this banana saga has important lessons for the accounting profession. The main reason the banana fruit is such an important commodity is because it is uniform and consistent—a banana purchased here is the same as a banana bought in Brampton, Boston, or Brussels, regardless of whether it was grown in China, Colombia, or Costa Rica. However, this sameness and lack of diversity is what sealed the fate of the Gros Michel and what could seal the fate of the Cavendish as well. These banana plants propagate by growing new stems from the same roots (natural cloning, essentially). The fruits do not bear seeds of the next generation, and there is neither sexual reproduction nor genetic variation. Every Cavendish plant is as susceptible to Panama Disease as any other. Thus, banana cultivation is highly efficient but not robust to external changes.

Now take a leap with me and consider the global movement toward uniform accounting and auditing standards. Without doubt, uniformity will bring about increased efficiency, just as it did for bananas. But what are the long-term costs? How much risk are we creating if we rely only on a single set of standards and a single standard-setting body? Without alternative, competing standards, will standard setting become unresponsive to the changing business environment and eventually become irrelevant? How do we ensure accountability from global standard setters so that they keep the standards relevant and vital? Would the world be better off with multiple standard setters competing to have the best standards?

Stay tuned for next month's column in which I will continue to explore this important topic. Meanwhile, you may want to eat a few bananas while you can still get them.

Source: This article was written by Kin Lo, and the original version appeared in the September 2008 issue of *Beyond Numbers* magazine, published by the Institute of Chartered Accountants of BC. It has been altered and reprinted with the Institute's permission.

A PERSPECTIVE ON GLOBAL STANDARD SETTING

Last month, I used the history of banana cultivation as a cautionary tale to raise some important questions about the global movement toward uniformity for accounting and auditing standards. Now, I will provide some additional thoughts on global standard setting.

Consider the following examples of standards, all of which should be familiar to readers:

■ In North America, we drive on the right side of the road.

(Continued)

- I'm writing this column using the QWERTY keyboard standard that most of the English-speaking world uses.
- Microsoft Windows® is the *de facto* standard for personal computer operating systems.

What do we learn from these examples in terms of standard setting? What distinguishes one type of standard from another?

One general way to categorize the different settings is in terms of the costs and benefits to producers and consumers/users. The first example is considered a convention: as long as there is a rule, it matters little whether the rule says we must drive on the right or left (as they do in some parts of the world), but we would have chaos on the roads without the rule. In other words, there is no difference in cost whether the rule is one way or the other, but drivers gain enormous benefits from having a rule, any rule. Since nothing is gained by having a different standard, competition among standards serves no purpose.

The standard for keyboards is an example where standardization changes costs and benefits for producers and consumers. Users benefit from transferability of skills. Imagine the headache of having to cope with a new keyboard layout with every new computer, or going from computer to BlackBerry®, or from desktop to laptop. For producers, it costs the same whether the keyboard layout is QWERTY or Dvorak, but once the standard has been set, they can realize economies of scale. The cost of this standard is that some users who prefer to use alternate layouts bear extra cost of hardware or software. Another cost is the entrenchment of QWERTY as a standard, even though many argue it is less efficient than other alternatives.

The last example is also one where standardization's effect on producer and consumer welfare is not clear. Having a standard operating system provides a single platform for development of application software, lowering the cost of that development. However, similar to the QWERTY standard, there are many (myself included) who criticize the Windows® operating system as being inferior to others. One significant impediment against users switching is the network externality involved—people use Windows® because other people with whom they interact also use Windows®.

In these latter two examples, the keyboard and particular computer operating systems, there are considerable benefits from having competing standards. As a testament to the significance of those benefits, there are substantial numbers of users of the Dvorak keyboard and the Mac® operating system, despite the predominance of QWERTY and Windows®. In the case of operating systems, would we still be using MS-DOS® without competition from Apple (and others)?

Thus, when standards involve something more than conventions, we have to consider two opposing forces. Uniformity facilitates transferability/compatibility but stifles innovation, whereas competition encourages experimentation but makes it costly to deal with multiple standards.

So where do accounting standards fit in this scheme? Is it a case of setting conventions where competition is not needed, or the more complex scenario where the costs and benefits are less clear?

In fact, accounting is a mix of both. However, the portion of accounting that involves conventions is, while important, limited in scope. The debit-credit double-entry system is such a convention, and so is much of bookkeeping. In contrast, the accounting standards that are in the *CICA Handbook* (now the *CPA Canada Handbook*) or International Financial Reporting Standards involve everything but bookkeeping—they do not involve conventions and therefore the costs and benefits of each standard are not *a priori* clear.

(Continued)

The current movement in accounting standard setting is toward uniformity for publicly accountable enterprises. Implicit in this movement is the value judgment that transferability (i.e., comparability in accountants' words) is more important than innovation. For companies participating in capital markets that are ever more international, perhaps this is the correct trade-off. Nevertheless, having a monopoly always entails a risk of stagnation or of standards developing in a direction that does not reflect users' needs.

For private enterprises, the trade-off between transferability and innovation is very different. The benefits of transferability between countries are much reduced for such companies, which makes the case for global accounting standards for private enterprises much less compelling.

The Accounting Standards Board in Canada is proposing to have a set of private enterprise accounting standards based on the current *CICA Handbook*. I believe this is the correct direction, if for no other reason than to provide an independent alternative that helps to maintain a degree of competition and global innovation in accounting standards.

Source: This article was written by Kin Lo, and the original version appeared in the September 2008 issue of *Beyond Numbers* magazine, published by the Institute of Chartered Accountants of BC. It has been altered and reprinted with the Institute's permission.

E. STANDARDS IN TRANSITION

The International Accounting Standards Board (IASB) has an eight-phase project to revise the conceptual framework. The framework discussed in this chapter reflects the completion of two of these eight phases (objectives and qualitative characteristics) in 2010. The IASB had issued in the spring of 2015 an exposure draft (ED) that covers the elements of the financial statements, recognition, measurement, presentation and disclosure, income versus other comprehensive income, and the reporting entity. In addition, the ED revisited some of the conclusions already reached in 2010. Notably, the ED proposed increased prominence for the objective of assessing stewardship, and reintroduced the concept of prudence as a qualitative characteristic. At the time of writing, the IASB planned to issue a new conceptual framework near the end of the first quarter of 2018. For further information on this project, visit www.ifrs.org.

F. APPENDIX: ILLUSTRATION OF CAPITAL MAINTENANCE CONCEPTS

This appendix provides an example to illustrate the difference between physical and financial capital maintenance concepts.

Suppose Charles starts a new but simple business that uses a single piece of equipment, costing $1 million at the beginning of 2021, and it has a useful life of five years. He sets up a partnership called Charles and Friends and finances the equipment acquisition with $1 million from himself and his family and friends. His business plan projects $300,000 of income before equipment depreciation in the first year. As this is a very stable business, Charles anticipates that the $300,000 figure will continue in the foreseeable future, other than changes with the general price level. Charles and Friends, as a partnership, does not have income tax expense. Since the business is expected to be stable, Charles believes that the partnership should pay out to the owners as much profit as is available while maintaining the viability of the company indefinitely. How much can the partnership pay out over the next five years?

The answer to this question depends on the environment for price inflation faced by the company. We will consider two scenarios: one with zero inflation and one with 15% inflation per year.

ZERO INFLATION   Under a zero-inflation environment, the projected financial statements for Charles and Friends are quite straightforward, as shown in Exhibit 2-10.

Exhibit 2-10	Summary projected financial statements for Charles and Friends; no inflation					
(Amounts in $000's)	2021	2022	2023	2024	2025	Total
Income statement						
Income before depreciation	300	300	300	300	300	1,500
Depreciation expense	200	200	200	200	200	1,000
Net income	100	100	100	100	100	500
Statement of retained earnings						
Retained earnings —Jan. 1	–	100	200	300	400	
Net income	100	100	100	100	100	
Payout to owners	–	–	–	–	–	
Retained earnings —Dec. 31	100	200	300	400	500	
Balance sheet						
Cash (Note 1)	300	600	900	1,200	1,500	
Equipment net of acc. depr. (Note 2)	800	600	400	200	–	
Total assets	1,100	1,200	1,300	1,400	1,500	
Owners' equity	1,000	1,000	1,000	1,000	1,000	
Retained earnings	100	200	300	400	500	
Total liabilities and equity	1,100	1,200	1,300	1,400	1,500	
Note 1: For simplicity, assume cash balance does not earn interest income.						
Note 2: Straight-line depreciation over five-year useful life.						

Notice that the cash balance increases by $300,000 each year, an amount equal to the income before depreciation. (Recall that depreciation is a non-cash expense.) By the end of the fifth year, Charles and Friends has accumulated $1,500,000, more than enough to purchase equipment to replace the original that has reached the end of its useful life. If the price of the equipment changes in the same way as general inflation, then we would expect it to cost $1 million at the end of 2025. This means that Charles and Friends has an extra $500,000 that it could pay to its owners without affecting the viability of the business. The partnership could pay this amount in one lump sum or as five payments of $100,000 each year. In other words, *when there is zero inflation, the business can pay out to its owners an amount equal to its net income.*

INFLATION AT 15% PER YEAR   In this scenario, the projected financial statements for Charles and Friends are just slightly more complex (Exhibit 2-11).

Due to inflation, the income before depreciation increases each year. Since depreciation is a constant $200,000 each year, the net income also increases each year. More importantly, notice that the cash balance increases to $2,023,000 by the end of 2025, compared with $1,500,000 in the zero-inflation scenario. The retained earnings balance at that time would be $1,023,000. If Charles and Friends pays out all retained earnings as in the zero-inflation scenario (i.e., $1,023,000), then it will have $1,000,000 of cash. This amount would be enough to purchase the equipment necessary to replace

Exhibit 2-11	Summary projected financial statements for Charles and Friends; 15% inflation					
(Amounts in $000's)	2021	2022	2023	2024	2025	Total
Income statement						
Income before depreciation (Note 1)	300	345	397	456	525	2,023
Depreciation expense	200	200	200	200	200	1,000
Net income	100	145	197	256	325	1,023
Statement of retained earnings						
Retained earnings—Jan. 1	–	100	245	442	698	
Net income	100	145	197	256	325	
Payout to owners	–	–	–	–	–	
Retained earnings—Dec. 31	100	245	442	698	1,023	
Balance sheet						
Cash	300	645	1,042	1,498	2,023	
Equipment net of acc. depr.	800	600	400	200	–	
Total assets	1,100	1,245	1,442	1,698	2,023	
Owners' equity	1,000	1,000	1,000	1,000	1,000	
Retained earnings	100	245	442	698	1,023	
Total liabilities and equity	1,100	1,245	1,442	1,698	2,023	

Note 1: Assumed to increase at the same rate as inflation.

the piece that has reached the end of its useful life *only if the price of the equipment has not increased.* However, it is most likely that the equipment price has also increased along with general inflation. If so, then the equipment should cost $2.011 million ($1 million × 1.15^5). This means the partnership will have just a little more cash than the expected replacement cost of the equipment even without paying out any profits to owners. Indeed, the partnership will have a mere surplus of $12,000 in excess of what is needed to replace the equipment ($2.023–$2.011 million) after operating the business for five years. Thus, the income over the five years ($1.023 million) substantially overstates the economic profitability of the business.

The above two tables (Exhibit 2-10 and Exhibit 2-11) demonstrate what financial statements would look like under the assumption of *financial capital maintenance.* When there is no inflation, net income is an appropriate measure of profitability in that it reflects the amount that could be paid out without impairing the ability of the business to continue operations. However, when inflation is significant, net income overstates profitability such that payouts to owners based on net income will negatively affect the company's ability to continue operations.

When inflation is significant, the *physical capital maintenance* assumption produces financial statements that better reflect profitability by adjusting for changes in price levels. However, financial statements prepared using the physical capital maintenance concept are considerably more complex and not used in the North American context, which has been characterized by low to modest inflation in the past several decades.

G. SUMMARY

L.O. 2-1. Explain the role of a conceptual framework for financial reporting and the reasons for having conceptual frameworks.

- A conceptual framework can be viewed as a strategic business plan that identifies demands of users and how to supply a product that meets those demands. These frameworks provide overall plans to guide implementation: the evaluation of more specific accounting standards and the application of accounting standards to specific circumstances. As business plans, they differ in response to variations in the environments for which they are developed, and they change from time to time to respond to changes in market conditions.

L.O. 2-2. Explain the rationale for each of the eight major components of these frameworks and synthesize these components into an integrated whole.

- Analysis of the demand for accounting information requires specifying the users (target market), the objectives for the information gathered, and the desirable characteristics of information (desirable product characteristics).
- The supply side of a conceptual framework involves identifying the elements of financial statements (potential components), followed by criteria for recognition in the financial statements (product design) and measurement (customization to specific needs).
- Whether the supply of information is able to meet the users' demands also depends on constraints on financial reporting and the suitability of assumptions made in the planning process.

L.O. 2-3. Apply the conceptual frameworks in IFRS and ASPE to specific circumstances and evaluate the trade-offs among different concepts within the frameworks.

- Implementing a conceptual framework requires a thorough understanding of the specific reporting environment, which affects the relative desirability of the various qualitative characteristics and the trade-offs that should be made among those characteristics. The reporting environment also affects the reporting constraints (such as cost versus benefit) and the suitability of the assumptions (such as capital maintenance).

L.O. 2-4. Describe the standard-setting environment in Canada.

- Canada's standard-setting environment is a mixture of international and domestic standards. After 2010, publicly accountable enterprises must comply with IFRS, issued by the International Accounting Standards Board (IASB) in London, England. Private enterprises follow ASPE standards issued by the Accounting Standards Board of Canada (AcSB), but may choose to follow IFRS. Public sector entities follow guidance issued by the Public Sector Accounting Board of Canada (PSAB). The *CPA Canada Handbook* encompasses all these sets of standards.

H. ANSWERS TO CHECKPOINT QUESTIONS

CP2-1: A conceptual framework for financial reporting is similar to a business plan in that both need to consider the demands of the market and the ability of the suppliers to meet those demands.

CP2-2: IFRS identifies investors, lenders, and other creditors as the primary users of financial reports. To aid these users in their investing and lending decisions, financial reports should provide information that is useful for predicting the amounts, timing, and uncertainty of future cash flows. Information about the enterprise's resources, claims, and performance are also useful for these purposes.

CP2-3:   The fundamental qualitative characteristics are relevance and representational faithfulness, while the enhancing qualitative characteristics are understandability, comparability, verifiability, and timeliness. IFRS views fundamental characteristics as those that are essential and must be present for information to be useful. Enhancing characteristics are desirable and help to increase the usefulness of that information, but they are not essential.

CP2-4:   Assets and liabilities are the two elements of financial statements that form the foundation for the other elements. IFRS defines equity as assets net of liabilities. Income is the increase in equity while expenses are decreases in equity, which, as just noted, is defined by assets and liabilities.

CP2-5:   The financial statement elements are defined in general terms without regard to whether the items are shown in the body of the financial statements. Recognition means the inclusion of an item in the financial statements. Measurement is the method used to quantify the amounts for recognition in the financial statements.

CP2-6:   The overall responsibility for setting accounting standards in Canada rests with the Accounting Standards Board (AcSB). With the adoption of IFRS for publicly accountable enterprises beginning in January 2011, the AcSB has delegated standard setting for these entities to the International Accounting Standards Board located in London, England. The AcSB continues to set accounting standards for other (non-governmental) entities.

I. GLOSSARY

accrual accounting: A basis of accounting that records economic events when they happen rather than only when cash exchanges occur.

asset: A resource controlled by an entity as a result of past events and from which future economic benefits are expected to flow to the entity.

comparability: Refers to the ability to compare one set of financial statements with another. The comparison may be with the financial statements of the same enterprise in a different year or with those of a different enterprise. One of four **enhancing qualitative characteristics**.

completeness: The inclusion of all material items in the financial statements. One of three attributes of **representational faithfulness**.

cost constraint: A constraint stating that the cost of reporting financial information should not exceed the benefits that can be obtained from using that information.

enhancing qualitative characteristics: The characteristics that affect the information's degree of usefulness. Compare with **fundamental qualitative characteristics**.

equity: The residual interest in the assets of an entity after deducting all its liabilities.

expenses: Decreases in economic benefits during an accounting period in the form of outflows or depletions of assets or incurrence of liabilities that result in decreases in equity, other than those relating to distributions to equity participants. Expenses include **ordinary expenses** and **losses**.

financial capital maintenance: The assumption that an entity needs to have as much resource in monetary terms at the end of a period as it did at the beginning of that period to maintain its operating capacity. Amounts in excess of that required to maintain financial capital are profit.

freedom from error: The extent to which information is absent of errors or omissions. One of three attributes of **representational faithfulness**.

fundamental qualitative characteristics: The characteristics that must be present for information to be useful for decision making. Compare with **enhancing qualitative characteristics**.

gains: A type of income other than revenue.

going concern: The assumption that the reporting entity will continue operating into the foreseeable future.

historical cost: The amount of cash or cash equivalents paid or received in a transaction.

income: Increases in economic benefits during an accounting period in the form of inflows or enhancements of assets or decreases of liabilities that result in increases in equity, other than those relating to contributions from equity participants. Income encompasses both **revenue** and **gains**.

liability: A present obligation of the entity arising from past events, the settlement of which is expected to result in an outflow from the entity of economic resources embodying economic benefits.

losses: A type of **expense** that is not an **ordinary expense**.

materiality: Whether omitting, misstating, or obscuring a particular piece of information about a reporting entity would influence primary users' economic decisions.

measurement: The basis for quantifying items reported in the financial statements.

neutrality: The extent to which information is free from bias. One of three attributes of **representational faithfulness**.

ordinary expense: A type of **expense** that arises from the ordinary activities of the entity.

private enterprise: In the ASPE standards, any for-profit entity that is not a publicly accountable enterprise.

publicly accountable enterprise: An entity, other than a not-for-profit organization, that has issued debt or equity instruments that are outstanding and traded in a public market (or is in the process of issuing such instruments) or an entity that holds assets in a fiduciary capacity for a broad group of outsiders as one of its primary businesses.

recognition: The process of presenting an item in the financial statements, as opposed to merely disclosing that item in the notes.

representational faithfulness: The extent to which financial information reflects the underlying transactions, resources, and claims of an enterprise.

relevance: The ability to influence users' economic decisions. Information that is able to provide feedback about past performance or helps make predictions is more relevant.

revenue: A type of income that arises in the course of ordinary activities.

timeliness: How soon the information becomes available to decision makers. One of four **enhancing qualitative characteristics**.

understandability: The ease with which users are able to comprehend financial reports. One of four **enhancing qualitative characteristics**.

verifiability: The degree to which different people would agree with the chosen representation in the financial reports. One of four **enhancing qualitative characteristics**.

J. REFERENCES

Authoritative standards:

IFRS	ASPE Section
The Conceptual Framework for Financial Reporting	1000—Financial Statement Concepts
	1100—Generally Accepted Accounting Principles
IAS 1—Presentation of Financial Statements	1400—General Standards of Financial Statement Presentation

MyLab Accounting   Make the grade with **MyLab Accounting:** The problems marked with a ⊕ can be found on **MyLab Accounting**. You can practise them as often as you want, and most feature step-by-step guided instructions to help you find the right answer.

K. PROBLEMS

 **P2-1.**   Role of the conceptual framework for financial reporting

(**L.O.** 2-1) (Medium – 10 minutes)

IFRS, ASPE, and US GAAP each have a conceptual framework. Explain why a conceptual framework is necessary for a set of high quality accounting standards. Provide three reasons by considering the concepts in the framework, the standard setters, and the financial statement preparers.

P2-2.   Role of the conceptual framework for financial reporting

(**L.O.** 2-1) (Easy – 5 minutes)

Identify whether each statement in the following table is true or false.

	Statement	True	False
a.	Conceptual frameworks for financial reporting are purely conceptual and do not relate to the practice of accounting.		
b.	Conceptual frameworks for financial reporting are a list of concepts that are theoretically desirable.		
c.	Conceptual frameworks for financial reporting can be understood through the economic lens of supply and demand.		
d.	Conceptual frameworks for financial reporting describe the demands from financial statement users.		
e.	The IFRS Conceptual Framework is a mathematical representation of the double-entry bookkeeping system.		

P2-3.   Role of the conceptual framework for financial reporting and its components

(**L.O.** 2-1, **L.O.** 2-2) (Easy – 5 minutes)

For each of the following eight components of the framework for financial reporting, identify whether the component relates to (i) the *demand* for financial information from potential users, or (ii) the approach the accounting profession is taking to *supply* information to meet that demand.

	Concept	Demand	Supply
a.	User needs	✓	
b.	Measurement criteria		
c.	Assumptions for the preparation of financial statements		
d.	Objectives of financial reporting		
e.	Definitions of the elements of financial statements		
f.	Recognition criteria		
g.	Constraints		
h.	Desirable qualitative characteristics		

P2-4. Components of the framework for financial reporting   (**L.O.** 2-2) (Easy – 5 minutes)

For each concept in the following table, identify whether the concept is (i) a qualitative characteristic, (ii) an assumption, or (iii) a constraint in the IFRS Framework.

	Concept	Qualitative characteristic	Assumption	Constraint
a.	Understandability	✓		
b.	Going concern			
c.	Relevance			
d.	Benefits vs. costs			
e.	Verifiability			
f.	Representational faithfulness			
g.	Comparability			
h.	Financial capital maintenance			

 P2-5. Components of the framework for financial reporting   (**L.O.** 2-2) (Easy – 10 minutes)

For each concept in the following table, identify whether the concept relates to (i) representational faithfulness, (ii) recognition, or (iii) measurement.

	Concept	Representational faithfulness	Recognition	Measurement
a.	Current cost			✓
b.	Completeness			
c.	Historical cost			
d.	Revenue recognition			
e.	Probable and measurable future flows of resources			
f.	Neutrality			
g.	Present value			
h.	Realizable value			

P2-6. Components of the framework for financial reporting   (**L.O.** 2-2) (Easy – 10 minutes)

Identify whether each concept in the following table relates to (i) an element, (ii) an assumption, or (iii) a constraint in the IFRS framework.

	Concept	Element	Assumption	Constraint
a.	Expense			
b.	Capital maintenance			
c.	Cost			
d.	Liability			
e.	Going concern			
f.	Income			
g.	Equity			
h.	Asset			

P2-7.   Components of the framework for financial reporting   (**L.O.** 2-2) (Easy – 5 minutes)

Identify the three essential characteristics that define an asset, one of the key elements of financial statements.

 P2-8.   Components of the framework for financial reporting   (**L.O.** 2-2) (Easy – 5 minutes)

Identify the three essential characteristics that define a liability, one of the key elements of financial statements.

P2-9.   Components of the framework for financial reporting   (**L.O.** 2-2) (Easy – 10 minutes)

The IFRS Framework identifies five elements of financial statements: assets, liabilities, equities, income, and expenses. Briefly discuss how the latter three elements are related to assets and liabilities.

P2-10. Components of conceptual frameworks   (**L.O.** 2-2) (Medium – 15 minutes)[9]

Over the years, considerable debate has surrounded the use of the historical cost model and whether it should be replaced by a current cost model to better reflect the concept of physical capital maintenance. The fact that the IFRS Framework and the financial statements of Canadian companies continue to use the historical cost and financial capital maintenance concepts demonstrates that there are good reasons in favour of retaining this basis of financial statement presentation.

Required:

Discuss the reasons why the current cost accounting model has not received general acceptance as a basis for the preparation of financial statements in Canada.

 P2-11. Components of conceptual frameworks   (**L.O.** 2-2) (Medium – 15 minutes)

Companies often invest significant amounts of time and money in training their employees, whether the company engages in manufacturing, retail, or professional services. Accounting standards generally do not permit these costs to be recorded as assets (such as "investment in employees"), but instead require such costs to be expensed.

Required:

a. Discuss the rationale for this approach by considering the qualitative characteristics in the IFRS Conceptual Framework.
b. Discuss the rationale for this approach by considering the elements of financial statements and the recognition of those elements in the IFRS Conceptual Framework.

P2-12. Components of conceptual frameworks   (**L.O.** 2-2) (Medium – 15 minutes)[10]

Financial statements are now beyond the comprehension of the average person. Many of the accounting terms and methods of accounting used are simply too complex to understand just from reading the financial statements.

Additional explanations should be provided with, or in, the financial statements to help investors understand the financial statements.

[9.] Reprinted (or adapted) from Uniform Final Examination, 1981, with permission from Chartered Professional Accountants of Canada, Toronto, Canada. Any changes to the original material are the sole responsibility of the author (and/or publisher) and have not been reviewed or endorsed by the Chartered Professional Accountants of Canada.

[10.] Reprinted from Uniform Final Examination, 1991 with permission from Chartered Professional Accountants of Canada, Toronto, Canada. Any changes to the original material are the sole responsibility of the author (and/or publisher) and have not been reviewed or endorsed by the Chartered Professional Accountants of Canada.

Required:

Discuss the above opinions.

 P2-13. Components of conceptual frameworks   (**L.O.** 2-2) (Medium – 20 minutes)[11]

The president of a public corporation recently commented, "Our auditor states that our financial statements present a 'true and fair view' of our financial position and financial performance. I challenged him as to how he determined such fairness. He replied that fairness means that the financial statements are not misstated in amounts that would be considered material.

"I believe that there is some confusion with this materiality concept, since different users of our financial statements may have different ideas as to what is material. For example, bankers, institutional investors, small investors, and tax assessors all have different perceptions of materiality."

Required:

Discuss the issues raised by the president.

 **P2-14.** Application of the IFRS Framework   (**L.O.** 2-3) (Medium – 20 minutes)

Public Company Ltd. is a large, publicly held company with shares actively traded on the Toronto Stock Exchange and earnings before tax of $300 million per year. Public Company has spent $45 million in the current year to improve the basic literacy skills of its employees (i.e., reading, writing, and arithmetic) to allow for the introduction of high-tech, computerized, automated equipment. Without this training, efficient and effective implementation of the new production process is unlikely to occur. Management of Public Company proposes that the entire amount be capitalized and amortized over the next 15 years (the estimated average remaining working life of the trained workers).

The partner in charge of Public Company's external audit has approached you to prepare a memo for her on this matter. The memo should identify and discuss important theoretical and practical issues that might influence her, as the external auditor, as to whether she is prepared to accept Public Company's proposal as appropriate accounting for this $45 million expenditure. If she rejects the proposal, the alternative is to expense the training costs.

Required:

Identify important concepts, principles, and ideas that you should incorporate into your memo.

P2-15. Application of IFRS Framework   (**L.O.** 2-3) (Medium – 15 minutes)

In recent years there has been increasing concern about the inadequacies of historical cost financial statements. One particular area that has been the focus of attention is that of "intellectual capital"—the value of knowledge/know-how that firms' employees have. For example, much of the value of a software company may be attributable to the ability of its programmers and designers to come up with popular new products on a regular basis. Critics of historical cost accounting propose that companies' balance sheets should include the value of intellectual capital.

Required:

Discuss the conceptual issues surrounding the proposed capitalization of intellectual capital as an asset on the balance sheet.

 P2-16. Application of IFRS Framework and accounting theory (**L.O.** 2-3) (Easy – 15 minutes)

On February 4, 2002, the stock of Tyco International Ltd. (Tyco) plunged 10.4% as investors reacted to a report in *The Wall Street Journal* (*WSJ*) that questioned its disclosure practices. The

---

[11.] Reprinted from Uniform Final Examination, 1982 with permission from Chartered Professional Accountants of Canada, Toronto, Canada. Any changes to the original material are the sole responsibility of the author (and/ or publisher) and have not been reviewed or endorsed by the Chartered Professional Accountants of Canada.

WSJ reported that Tyco had not publicly announced US$8 billion of spending on 725 acquisitions in its past three fiscal years, broken down as follows:

Fiscal year	# of acquisitions	Amount ($billions)
1999	350	$4.2
2000	225	2.3
2001	150	1.5
Total	725	$8.0

Tyco's chief financial officer explained that the company clearly reports the net amount of cash it pays for all acquisitions, but does not disclose the details on its many smaller deals because they are immaterial.

Tyco is an international conglomerate whose recent years' earnings have been about $5 billion; it has a market value of equity of $60 billion.

Required:

Discuss the issues raised by the above fact pattern in relation to the IFRS Framework and financial accounting theory.

P2-17. Application of IFRS Framework
(**L.O.** 2-3) (Medium – 10 minutes)

In the revision to the IFRS Conceptual Framework, scheduled for issuance in 2018, the IASB considered whether to clarify that trade-offs need to be made between the qualitative characteristics.

Required:

Discuss (1) the trade-off between the two fundamental qualitative characteristics of relevance and representative faithfulness, and (2) why explicitly acknowledging this trade-off in the IFRS Framework is necessary.

P2-18. Application of IFRS Framework
(**L.O.** 2-3) (Medium – 15 minutes)

On February 9, 2002, an article in *The Economist* stated that the high-tech industry seems to be inventing new accounting documents and rules. Non-standard "pro forma" accounting is popular. Earnings are not calculated according to GAAP, but by creating unique formulas that exclude "special expenses." This tends to improve the bottom line. In January 2002, Amazon announced three different kinds of profit: $5 million net profit in the previous quarter, calculated under GAAP; $59 million "pro forma operating profit"; and $35 million "pro forma net profit." "Pro forma operating profit" excludes stock option expense, amortization of goodwill, and restructuring costs. "Pro forma net profit" excludes currency gains and losses and the "cumulative effect of changes in accounting principles."

Required:

Discuss the pros and cons of the types of disclosures described above.

P2-19. Applying the conceptual frameworks
(**L.O.** 2-3) (Medium – 20 minutes)

There are a variety of rankings for educational institutions and programs around the world. Among them are university rankings by Times Higher Education (www.timeshighereducation.co.uk) and Academic Ranking of World Universities (www.arwu.org). For business schools specifically, the popular business news magazine *BusinessWeek* compiles a ranking of master of business administration (MBA) programs every two years. Since the publication targets US readers, the rankings focus on MBA programs in the United States.

To compute its rankings, *BusinessWeek* uses information gathered primarily from surveys of MBA graduates and corporate recruiters. The survey of MBA graduates asks former students to score (on a 10-point scale) their own school's quality in terms of teaching, facilities, career services, and so on. The student survey elicits close to 10,000 responses each year. The survey sent to recruiters asks them to score MBA programs based on their experience with graduates from these programs. The recruiter survey has about 230 responses each year. Each of the two surveys contributes 45% to the final ranking. (The remaining 10% weight is for schools' contributions to "intellectual capital," which is not important for the purposes of this question.)

Required:

Discuss the usefulness of these rankings. More specifically, consider the reliability of the results from the two surveys (student and recruiter) that determine the rankings. Pay particular attention to the incentives of each group of survey respondents.

P2-20. Applying the conceptual frameworks and accounting theory
(L.O. 2-3**)** (Medium – 20 minutes)

The September 29, 2012, issue of *The Economist* contained an article called "Shape shifters" about the "Big Four" accounting firms. The article noted that these four accounting firms seem to grow bigger every single year. However, *where* that growth occurs is of concern to regulators and lawmakers. "[C]onsulting has been growing much faster than the audit business in recent years. In fiscal 2012, Deloitte increased its revenues from consulting by 13.5% and from financial advisory by 15%—compared with just 6.1% for audit and 3.9% for tax and legal services. Barry Salzberg, Deloitte's boss, says he expects consulting to continue to grow by double digits, whereas the audit market is mature." The number of employees in the consulting arm has been growing twice as fast as in the audit part of the firm. Continuing this trend would see the firm engaged in more consulting than auditing by 2017.

In the early 2000s, the accounting firm Arthur Andersen also experienced this fast growth in consulting, before it was shut down following the demise of one of its major clients, Enron, and revelations of severe accounting irregularities at that company.

Required:

Discuss the issues raised by the above article by applying concepts from the conceptual framework for financial reporting (this chapter) and financial accounting theory (Chapter 1).

P2-21. Applying the conceptual frameworks
(L.O. 2-3**)** (Difficult – 20 minutes)

On October 13, 2010, *The Globe and Mail* reported that Google is using the information from its search engine as economic indicators. Entitled "Google's Price Index to Measure Inflation of Online Sales," the article explains that Google is using its enormous database to start a "Google price index" in real time.

This price index would be constructed from tracking prices of purchases made over the Internet. Items frequently purchased online include "cameras, baby toys, and watches," notes the article. Because the data is electronically collected, the price index can be made available almost instantaneously. In contrast, official price index information from statistical agencies lags by several weeks. For example, Statistics Canada releases its consumer price index for October in the third week of November. Statistics Canada compiles its information by using data of 80 shoppers visiting various stores.

Google's chief economist, Hal Varian, notes that deflation is a clear trend in the United States based on Google's price index. In contrast, the official annual inflation rate in the United States in September was +1.14%.

Required:

Evaluate the merits of the Google price index by applying concepts from the IFRS Conceptual Framework.

P2-22. Applying the conceptual frameworks and accounting theory

(**L.O.** 2-3) (Difficult – 20 minutes)

The September 17, 2011, issue of *The Economist* contained a short article called "The R-word Index: Up Means Down."

At the time, the developed world was facing a combination of anemic growth, high unemployment, and underperforming stock markets. Contrary to official gross domestic product (GDP) statistics indicating moderate growth, the article argues that there will be further headwinds based on readings from *The Economist's* own "R-word index."

This R-word index counts mentions of the word "recession" in news articles over quarterly periods. *The Economist* argues that its index is more timely because it makes the index available just after the end of each quarter whereas official government statistics on economic growth take a month to compile. The magazine also boasts that the index has been able to predict previous recessions in 1990 and 2007 in the United States.

The article goes on to describe the recent trends in the index, which counts the use of the "R-word" in the *Financial Times* and *The Wall Street Journal* newspapers. From a peak of 4,300 in early 2009, the R-word index dropped almost continuously to about 1,000 by the first quarter of 2011. However, the index turned up again in the second half of 2011, reaching about 1,400 by September. The article concludes that, based on the R-word index, the recovery from the recession might be in jeopardy.

Required:

Evaluate the merits of the R-word index by applying concepts from the IFRS Conceptual Framework as well as from financial accounting theory from Chapter 1. Basic concepts from macroeconomics may also be useful in your response.

P2-23. Application of the IFRS Framework

(**L.O.** 2-3) (Difficult – 10 minutes)

The application of the IFRS Conceptual Framework in relation to specific standards in IFRS has several similarities compared with the application of constitutional law in relation to specific statute laws. Identify and discuss three similarities.

P2-24. Prudence in the IFRS Framework and evolution of accounting standards

(**L.O.** 2-3, **L.O.** 2-4) (Medium – 15 minutes)

Prior to 2010, the IFRS Conceptual Framework paragraph 37 indicated the following relating to the principle of conservatism or prudence:

> The preparers of financial statements . . . have to contend with the uncertainties that inevitably surround many events and circumstances, such as the collectability of doubtful receivables, the probable useful life of plant and equipment and the number of warranty claims that may occur. Such uncertainties are recognized by the disclosure of their nature and extent and by the exercise of prudence in the preparation of the financial statements. Prudence is the inclusion of a degree of caution in the exercise of the judgments needed in making the estimates required under conditions of uncertainty, such that assets or income are not overstated and liabilities or expenses are not understated. However, the exercise of prudence does not allow, for example, the creation of hidden reserves or excessive provisions, the deliberate understatement of assets or income, or the deliberate overstatement of liabilities or expenses, because the financial statements would not be neutral and, therefore, not have the quality of reliability.[12]

For the past few years, the International Accounting Standards Board (IASB) has been working on revising the IFRS Framework. In the first part of this revision, the IASB excluded the principle of prudence/conservatism from the framework.

Required:

Evaluate the merits of excluding prudence/conservatism from a revised IFRS Framework. Consider both arguments for keeping and for excluding prudence in the new framework.

[12.] Copyright © 2012 IFRS Foundation.

P2-25. Standard-setting and financial accounting theory (**L.O.** 2-4) (Medium – 10 minutes)

In January 2000, in an article in *The New York Times,* Andrew Pollack described the world's first treaty regulating trade of genetically modified products. The treaty, established between 130 nations, is focused on protecting the environment. To allow countries to monitor genetically modified products and to protect natural species from potential competition from new species, it establishes guidelines for labelling international shipments of food containing genetically altered ingredients. It does not, however, address such labelling of products in stores. Despite this agreement, the controversies that surround biotechnology are expected to continue. A significant portion of American-grown crops contain genetically modified grains or soybeans, and American farmers are losing millions of dollars of exports as increasing numbers of Europeans are rejecting food that is genetically modified.

Required:

Using some of the concepts from standard-setting and financial accounting theory, discuss the implications of there being no requirement to label products with genetically modified ingredients. [*Hint:* As a start, would you expect companies to label their products?]

 P2-26. Application of the IFRS Framework—online exercise (**L.O.** 2-3) (Easy – 10 minutes)

The *CPA Canada Handbook* is available to most post-secondary students through their educational institution's subscription. Visit http://edu.knotia.ca to complete this exercise. (You may need to complete this exercise on campus, or log in through your institution's VPN portal.)

Consider the following: recognition is the process of presenting an item in the financial statements, as opposed to merely disclosing it in the notes.

Required:

a. Go to the standards in Part I (IFRS) of the "Accounting" portion of the *Handbook*. View the "Conceptual Framework for Financial Reporting." Identify the paragraphs that discuss the recognition of the elements of financial statements.
b. Summarize the substance of the first three paragraphs.

 P2-27. Application of the IFRS Framework—online exercise (**L.O.** 2-3) (Easy – 10 minutes)

The *CPA Canada Handbook* is available to most post-secondary students through their educational institution's subscription. Visit http://edu.knotia.ca to complete this exercise. (You may need to complete this exercise on campus, or log in through your institution's VPN portal.)

Consider the following: measurement is the basis for quantifying items reported in the financial statements.

Required:

a. Go to the standards in Part I (IFRS) of the "Accounting" portion of the *Handbook*. View the "Conceptual Framework for Financial Reporting." Identify the paragraphs that discuss the measurement of the elements of financial statements.
b. Summarize the substance of these paragraphs.

 P2-28. Accounting standards in Canada—online exercise (**L.O.** 2-4) (Medium – 20 minutes)

The *CPA Canada Handbook* is available to most post-secondary students through their educational institution's subscription. Visit http://edu.knotia.ca to complete this exercise. (You may need to complete this exercise on campus, or log in through your institution's VPN portal.)

Required:

a. Click on the "CPA Canada Standards and Guidance Collection." Look at the table of contents that is presented. In addition to accounting standards, what other standards are included?
b. Go to the "Accounting" section of the *Handbook*. Read the "Preface to the *CPA Canada Handbook—Accounting*." What is the importance of the five definitions provided in this preface?

   c. Go to the standards in Part I (IFRS) of the "Accounting" portion of the *Handbook*. View the "Conceptual Framework for Financial Reporting." Identify the paragraphs that discuss (i) the objectives of financial statements, (ii) the fundamental qualitative characteristics, and (iii) the enhancing qualitative characteristics.

   d. Identify the standard (IFRS ## or IAS ##) that addresses each of the following topics:
  - presentation of financial statements
  - inventories
  - property, plant, and equipment
  - exploration for and evaluation of mineral resources
  - revenue

   e. While completing part (d), did you notice any logical structure in the IFRS or IAS numbers? In what order are these standards numbered? Are there any meaningful differences between IFRS and IAS standards?

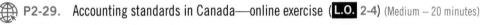

P2-29.   Accounting standards in Canada—online exercise (L.O. 2-4) (Medium – 20 minutes)

This exercise should be completed after P2-26.

   The *CPA Canada Handbook* is available to most post-secondary students through their institution's subscription. Visit http://edu.knotia.ca to complete this exercise. (You may need to complete this exercise on campus, or log in through your institution's VPN portal.)

Required:

   a. Go to the standards in Part II (ASPE) of the *CPA Canada Handbook*. View "Section 1000 – Financial Statement Concepts." Identify the paragraphs that discuss (i) the qualitative characteristics of financial statements and (ii) recognition criteria.

   b. Identify the section numbers that address each of the following topics:
  - generally accepted accounting principles
  - general standards of financial statement presentation
  - balance sheet
  - inventories
  - property, plant, and equipment
  - revenue

   c. While completing part (b), did you notice any logical structure in the ASPE section numbers? In what order are these standards numbered?

   d. Go to Section 1100 on generally accepted accounting principles. What does this section identify as primary sources of GAAP (applicable to entities using ASPE)? Why are primary sources distinguished from other sources of GAAP?

   e. Use the Search feature on the website. Enter "inventories" as a search term. What do you find?

P2-30.   Globalization of accounting standards (L.O. 2-4) (Medium – 15 minutes)

For more than a century, financial accounting has followed many paths throughout the world. Each country established its own standard-setting body to codify generally accepted accounting principles (GAAP) for entities operating in that country. These GAAP developed according to the country's characteristics, such as the following:
- legal regime (e.g., common law in Canada and United States versus code law in France);
- tax laws (i.e., whether taxable income is based on accounting income); and
- litigiousness (e.g., the United States is more litigious than most other countries).

   For example, US GAAP tends to be more detailed or "rules-based" because such detail helps lawyers to make a claim of misrepresentation or to defend against such a claim in court.

   Over the past decade, the world has steadily marched toward a uniform set of accounting standards across the globe. The biggest move occurred in 2005 when the European Union required publicly traded firms in member countries to use International Financial Reporting Standards (IFRS) issued by the International Accounting Standards Board (IASB) based in London, England. Canadian companies that are publicly accountable were also required to apply IFRS after January 1, 2011. The United States, with the biggest capital market in the world, is also considering following rules issued by the Financial Accounting Standards Board (FASB) to use IFRS.

Required:

Evaluate the merits (both for and against) of having one set of financial accounting standards across the world.

P2-31. The role of conceptual frameworks and standard setting

(**L.O.** 2-1, **L.O.** 2-4) (Difficult – 20 minutes)[13]

Consider the following three statements:

(i) Although the standards in the *CPA Canada Handbook* provide general guidance, the application of these standards is dependent upon particular circumstances.

(ii) In practice, accountants may encounter situations where authoritative standards do not exist or may not apply.

(iii) Since there is no substitute for the exercise of professional judgment in the determination of what constitutes fair presentation and good practice, it has been suggested that too much effort is being directed toward the development of standards.

Required:

Discuss the issues raised in the above statements.

[13.] Reprinted from Uniform Final Examination, 1982 with permission from Chartered Professional Accountants of Canada, Toronto, Canada. Any changes to the original material are the sole responsibility of the author (and/or publisher) and have not been reviewed or endorsed by the Chartered Professional Accountants of Canada.

L. MINI-CASES

CASE 1
West Pacific's mortgage-backed securities
(45 minutes)[14]

West Pacific (WP) is a financial institution incorporated in 2007 and traded on the Toronto Stock Exchange. Its performance has been exceptional since the original issue. Your firm of chartered accountants has been the auditor for WP since its inception. It is now December 2022.

Across Canada, WP has 200 offices that issue residential mortgages. All mortgages issued are insured by Canada Mortgage and Housing Corporation (CMHC). All CMHC-approved issuers must grant mortgages in accordance with policies that CMHC has developed to protect the quality of the mortgages. A qualified borrower can seek a mortgage for up to 95% of the value of the property, and WP will grant the funds since CMHC promises to pay principal and interest in the event of default. For this arrangement, the borrower pays a fee to CMHC.

WP initially records the mortgages as receivables. When WP has $50 million in mortgages with similar terms (e.g., 4½- to 5-year term, paying 9–9.5% interest), it pools the mortgages and sells the pool to investors. At this point, WP removes the mortgages from its books. The borrower continues to make payments to WP, which passes them on to the investors less a 0.6% fee, which WP retains. The investor's interest in this mortgage pool is called a mortgage-backed security (MBS).

Besides the CMHC guarantee on the individual mortgages, WP provides a guarantee of timely payment to the investor in the event of default. The MBS, therefore, entails almost no risk for the investor and is considered to be as safe as Government of Canada bonds. Since the mortgage-backed security yields about 0.5% more than government bonds, it has enjoyed tremendous success in the marketplace.

WP has no problem selling the security, but it may take several months to accumulate the pool of mortgages it wishes to sell. After a pool of mortgages has been raised, it can take an additional three months to sell the pool to investors because of the administration involved. During this period, WP is exposed to changes in interest rates.

WP's ratio of assets to equity must not exceed 25 times. WP provides a monthly financial statement to the federal financial institution regulator that monitors this ratio.

Since 2007, WP has been a leader in establishing the accounting rules in this evolving area. Its vice-president of finance is proud of the policies it has adopted. The Ontario Securities Commission (OSC) has started a program to review annual reports and is now questioning some of the company's accounting policies, even though there are no specific regulations covering these policies. Concerns raised by the Ontario Securities Commission are as follows:

1. The OSC questions whether mortgage receivables should be removed from the balance sheet when the company issues the MBSs.
2. The OSC disagrees with WP's policy of recognizing the present value of the 0.6% fee it earns on each mortgage as revenue when an MBS is sold.
3. Unsold mortgage receivables held at year-end remain on WP's books at cost and are not revalued because they will be sold in the short term. The OSC does not agree with this practice.

Required:

Provide arguments that support WP's position on the accounting policies being questioned and arguments that the OSC could present to support its position. Be specific in your arguments, using relevant ideas from the conceptual framework in IFRS.

[14.] Reprinted from Uniform Final Examination, 1993 with permission from Chartered Professional Accountants of Canada, Toronto, Canada. Any changes to the original material are the sole responsibility of the author (and/or publisher) and have not been reviewed or endorsed by the Chartered Professional Accountants of Canada.

WHAT IS THIS THAT ROARETH THUS?

Transport: The untold story of a failed attempt to introduce electric buses in London a century ago offers a cautionary technological tale

ON MONDAY, July 15, 1907, an unusual bus picked up its first passengers at London's Victoria Station before gliding smoothly off to Liverpool Street. It was the beginning of what was then the world's biggest trial of battery-powered buses. The London Electrobus Company had high hopes that this quiet and fume-free form of transport would replace the horse. At its peak, the firm had a fleet of 20 buses. But despite being popular with passengers, the service collapsed in 1909. The history books imply that the collapse was caused by technical drawbacks and a price war. It was not. The untold story is that the collapse was caused by systematic fraud that set back the cause of battery buses by a hundred years.

Indeed, the London electrobus trial remained the largest for the rest of the 20th century. Only recently has American interest in keeping city air clean encouraged trials on anything approaching the same scale. For the past 15 years Chattanooga has had a dozen battery buses. Today the world's biggest fleet, excluding minibuses, is in Santa Barbara, California. The city has 20 buses and is buying five more.

The replacement of horses by internal-combustion engines may now look to have been inevitable, but it certainly did not seem so at the time. At the beginning of 1906 there were only 230 motor buses in London. They were widely reviled for their evil smells and noise. At any one time a quarter of them were off the road for repairs. In 1907 *The Economist* predicted "the triumph of the horse." The future of public-transport technology was up for grabs.

The paradox at the heart of the electrobus story is that the electrobuses themselves were well engineered and well managed. All battery buses have a limited range because of the weight of their batteries. The electrobus needed 1.5 tonnes of lead-acid batteries to carry its 34 passengers. It could travel 60 km (38 miles) on one charge. So at lunchtime the buses went to a garage in Victoria and drove up a ramp. The batteries, slung under the electrobus, were lowered onto a trolley and replaced with fresh ones. It all took three minutes. "It just goes to show there's nothing new under the sun," says Mark Hairr, of the Advanced Transportation Technology Institute. "That's almost exactly what we do here in Chattanooga. And we knew nothing about this."

In April 1906 the London Electrobus Company floated on the stock market. It wanted £300,000 to put 300 buses on the streets of the capital. On the first day the flotation raised £120,000 and the share offer was on course to be fully subscribed. But the next day some awkward questions surfaced. The firm was buying rights to a patent for £20,000 (£7.5 million, or $15 million, in today's money) from the Baron de Martigny. But the patent was old and had nothing to do with battery buses. It was a scam. Investors asked for their money back, and the firm had to return £80,000. The investors would have been even less impressed had they known the true identity of the "Baron," who was a Canadian music-hall artist.

Martigny was only the front man. The mastermind behind this and a clutch of subsequent scams was Edward Lehwess, a German lawyer and serial con artist with a taste for fast cars and expensive champagne. After this initial fiasco, the London Electrobus Company struggled to raise money. But Lehwess had

(Continued)

set up a network of front companies to siphon off its funds. Chief among these was the Electric Vehicle Company of West Norwood, which built the buses.

The London Electrobus Company paid the Electric Vehicle Company over £31,000 in advance for 50 buses. Only 20 were ever delivered. The buses were hugely overpriced. Eventually the London Electrobus Company went into liquidation. Even then the scams continued. Lehwess bought eight buses for £800 from the liquidators and sold them to Brighton for £3,500—a mark-up of 340%—where they ran for another six years. At the time, the life of a motor bus was measured in months.

Whether the fraud was truly a tipping point for electric vehicles is, of course, impossible to say. But it is a commonplace of innovation—from railway gauges to semiconductors to software—that the "best" technology is not always the most successful. Once an industry standard has been established, it is hard to displace. If Lehwess and Martigny had not pulled their scam when they did, modern cities might be an awful lot cleaner.

Source: Republished with permission of The Economist Newspaper Ltd., from What is this that roareth thus? Transport: The untold story of a failed attempt to introduce electric buses in London a century ago offers a cautionary technological tale (Sep. 6, 2007). Permission conveyed through Copyright Clearance Center, Inc.

Required:

Consider the above article and thoughtfully discuss how various ideas from financial accounting theory and accounting standards played a role in the development of battery-powered electric buses.

CASE 3
More disclosure equals more pain?

(30 minutes)

Note: Each paragraph has been numbered sequentially for ease of reference.

1. Every so often, journalists writing business columns in newspapers and magazines provide interesting commentary on the state of accounting standards. For instance, Mathew Ingram, in the March 28, 2002, edition of *The Globe and Mail,* discussed the fallout from the dramatic rise and fall of Enron, which at the time was the largest bankruptcy in US history. Entitled "More Disclosure Could Mean More Pain," Ingram's article did not question the long-term benefits of more transparent disclosures but wondered whether there are unintended consequences from all the additional attention paid to financial statements in the short term.

2. For example, around the time of the article it was common practice for companies to disclose "pro forma" financial results that excluded various items (usually expenses) that companies considered to be one-time occurrences and did not reflect their ongoing business. Ingram argued that, post-Enron, investors and regulators were "pushing companies to declare their 'real' earnings."

3. Another practice that was accepted at the time was to not account for the cost of stock options given to employees. These stock options allow employees to buy shares in their company's stock at a fixed price, which could be substantially below the market price depending on the company's performance. The focus on financial reporting issues post-Enron has increased the pressure for companies to record the cost of awarding these stock options to employees. As Ingram writes, such stock options are often used by start-up tech companies. If they were recorded, the cost of such options could amount to billions of dollars industry-wide. Alan Greenspan, the US Federal Reserve chairman, argued that options replace cash compensation and should therefore be expensed.

4. The effect of expensing the cost of stock options could be substantial. The Federal Reserve estimates that the exclusion of stock option costs increases the annual growth rate in earnings by as much as 2.5%. Another study suggests that most companies it examined would have had their profits shaved by 20 to 30%. As an extreme case, it is estimated that Microsoft's $4.5 billion profit in 1998 would have turned to a loss of $17.8 billion had it purchased shares in the open market to pay the shares on the options owned by its employees.

5. While financial statements do include most of the data in the notes, news reports rarely report such information but rather focus on the headline numbers such as revenue and net income. If the information in the notes were suddenly included in the financial statements, the revised figures could be shocking to investors. The market reaction could be damaging when the economy is fragile and sensitive to bad news.

6. There were, of course, concerns more closely related to problems seen at Enron, which kept many debts off its balance sheet by using "special purpose entities," or SPEs. Many other companies also use these SPEs, and their reputations could be tarnished as well. For example, a company may have sold its office building and transferred the related debt to an SPE to isolate the debt and decrease the risk to the operating company. The company then leases the building back from the SPE. This kind of "synthetic lease" is legal, but frowned upon after the Enron bankruptcy, as Ingram writes.

7. While this information is disclosed in the fine print, suddenly incorporating significant debt into the financial statements could not only frighten investors but also cause a company's credit rating to be downgraded. The combination of lower profits and higher debt could put much downward pressure on shares, concludes Ingram.

Required:

Answer the following four questions by applying financial accounting theory and the IFRS Framework.

a. What are the pros and cons of the change in reporting described in paragraph 2?

b. Refer to paragraphs 3 and 4. Discuss whether the cost of employee stock options should be (i) not recorded, as rules permitted at the time; (ii) expensed when the options are granted; or (iii) capitalized as an asset.

c. Discuss the conceptual merits of consolidating or excluding SPEs in companies' financial statements (paragraphs 6 and 7).

d. Evaluate Ingram's sentiments regarding the consequences of more disclosure.

CASE 4
Wicon Waste
(30 minutes)[15]

Wicon Waste Facilities Inc. (WWF) is a large, diversified Canadian company with several subsidiaries operating mainly in the waste management and disposal industry. WWF was incorporated in 1980 and has grown to become one of the top four waste management firms in Canada. The business was started by the Wicon family, but currently no family members are actively involved in the management of the company. Family members, family trusts, and a limited number of friends own the common shares. In 2019, the Wicon family decided that they would begin the process of selling the company over the next two or three years. In preparation for the sale, the company has engaged your firm, Hoa and Partners, to audit the company's financial statements.

WWF has an August 31 year-end. It is now September 18, 2021, and your firm is partway through the audit of WWF for the year-ended August 31, 2021. The materiality for the engagement has been set at $6.5 million. You are reviewing the files that your junior auditors have prepared, and you note the following events:

1. On June 23, 2021, WWF received a wire transfer of 20 million Guinean francs (GNF) to its general Canadian dollar bank account in payment of an outstanding customer invoice. WWF's bank converted the funds to $10 million Canadian, incorrectly assuming that the transfer was in the currency of Papua New Guinea, the kina (PGK). On that day, 8,000 Guinean francs bought one Canadian dollar. WWF has not informed the bank of the error and has taken the difference into income.

2. During 2021, WWF lost a decision in the Federal Court of Appeal in a lawsuit brought by Waste Systems Integrated Limited for patent infringement. In an unusual award, the court ordered WWF to pay $18 million for shares of Waste Systems Integrated Limited, a private company, which had been in some financial difficulty. WWF has decided not to appeal the decision to the Supreme Court, and the company bought the shares in Waste Systems before year-end.

[15.] Reprinted from Uniform Final Examination, 1996 with permission from Chartered Professional Accountants of Canada, Toronto, Canada. Any changes to the original material are the sole responsibility of the author (and/or publisher) and have not been reviewed or endorsed by the Chartered Professional Accountants of Canada.

3. WWF issues debt for long-term financing purposes through three major investment dealers. In July 2021, Moody's, the credit-rating agency, put WWF's credit rating on alert for downgrade due to the potential negative effects of progressive toughening of environmental legislation applying to waste disposal sites.

4. WWF bids on various municipal waste pickup and disposal contracts. WWF buys waste disposal sites to dump the waste collected. WWF defers and amortizes the cost of the sites over the expected useful lives of the sites, stated in tonnes of capacity, years of remaining usage, or cubic metres of waste capacity. Amortization of the cost of these sites represents 41% of WWF's operating expenses. Of WWF's assets, 64% are waste disposal sites. Provisions for cleanup and site sealing costs are accrued on the same basis as the amortization of the sites.

5. WWF defers and amortizes over five years the costs of locating new waste disposal sites and negotiating agreements with municipalities.

6. Every year WWF updates the estimates of the remaining useful lives of waste disposal sites using the services of a consulting engineering firm. In the past, WWF used Folk & Co., Environmental Engineers, for these reviews. Folk & Co. did no other work for WWF. Starting in 2021, WWF used Cajanza Consulting Engineers for the reviews. Based on the new consultants' report, the useful lives of all waste disposal sites have been increased between 4 and 26% and the sealing/cleanup provision reduced by $13.6 million.

7. WWF's management is aware that to comply with the audit, the company's financial statements need to be prepared in accordance with GAAP. However, management is unclear which set of standards within GAAP the company should follow.

Required:

The partner has requested a memo that deals with the significant accounting issues for WWF.

CASE 5
Douglas Décor Company
(30 minutes)

Douglas Décor Company (DDC) is a private decoration company that has been in business for over 25 years in the Montreal area. Two brothers, Doug and Dez, established the company and have made it very profitable over the years. As they are approaching retirement, Doug and Dez have decided to sell the company. A potential buyer of the company, Perfect Decorations Inc. (PDI), has approached them about the purchase and has asked Doug and Dez for DDC's financial statements to evaluate firm performance over the years. PDI is a publicly accountable enterprise based in Calgary that is looking to expand into the Montreal market. The management at PDI believes the DDC acquisition presents a great opportunity for the company.

Dez has been responsible for the bookkeeping of the company. He had little accounting training in school, but believed it was enough to account for the company's transactions. DDC submitted the financial reports to PDI, and after close review PDI was very unhappy with the financial reports presented. They noticed the following problems:

- The transactions were recorded on a cash basis.
- There was no balance sheet, income statement, or cash flow statement; there was only a journal of transactions for the year and a summary of sales and expenses.

Since PDI could not reliably value DDC, they decided not to pursue the acquisition of the company.

Required:

a. What types of information did PDI require when reviewing the financial statements? Did DDC's financial reports fulfill those requirements?

b. Should DDC have produced more sophisticated financial statements over its 25 years of operations? Explain your reasoning.

c. Suppose Doug and Dez hired you to help them assemble the financial statements. Explain to them the qualitative characteristics that will help meet the users' information needs.

d. Suppose DDC had produced reliable financial statements under ASPE and PDI decided to purchase the company. Discuss the financial reporting effects PDI will have to deal with after the acquisition.

CHAPTER 3
Accrual Accounting

Morphart/Fotolia

CPA competencies addressed in this chapter:

1.1.1 Evaluates financial reporting needs (Level B)
b. Financial statement users and their broad needs, standard setting, and requirement for accountability

1.1.2 Evaluates the appropriateness of the basis of financial reporting (Level B)
c. Difference between accrual accounting compared to cash accounting

1.2.1 Develops or evaluates appropriate accounting policies and procedures—Ethical professional judgment (Level B)

1.2.2 Evaluates treatment for routine transactions (Level A)
o. Changes in accounting policies and estimates, and errors

1.2.2 Evaluates treatment for routine transactions (Level A)
r. Events after the reporting period

1.3.1 Prepares financial statements (Level A)
a. The accounting cycle

LEARNING OBJECTIVES

After studying this chapter, you should be able to:

L.O. 3-1. Explain the source of demand for periodic reporting and how accrual accounting satisfies that demand.

L.O. 3-2. Explain why accrual accounting is fundamentally inexact, why estimates are central to accrual accounting, and why there is no "true" income for typical situations; evaluate the "quality of earnings."

L.O. 3-3. Apply accrual accounting in relation to issues of timing: periodicity, cut-off, and subsequent events.

L.O. 3-4. Evaluate whether an accounting change is an error, a change in accounting policy, or a change in estimate, and apply the retrospective and prospective treatments appropriate to that type of accounting change.

L.O. 3-5. Integrate the structure and connections among the four financial statements and explain how this structure relates to accrual accounting.

In the late 16th century, the Dutch were at the forefront of trade with the rest of the known world, sailing as far as modern-day Indonesia to bring back spices that were in high demand in Europe. The large profits from this lucrative trade overcame the significant risks involved in traversing the oceans to the other side of the globe.

These voyages were also very expensive, requiring significant investment upfront to fund the construction and purchase of ships, as well as the hiring of crews for the long journeys, which lasted anywhere from several months up to more than a year. At the time, it was common for a company to be set up for each individual voyage, then dissolved when the ship returned to port (or sank) and the goods were sold. There was little in the way of financial accounting, other than to record the amount of funds initially invested and the amount at the end of the voyage for disbursement to the investors.

In 1602, the Dutch government sponsored the creation of the Dutch East India Company (Verenigde Oost-Indische Compagnie). The new company had monopoly powers to trade with Asia as far as the Dutch were concerned (although other European countries had their own ideas about the monopoly). For this company, accounting no longer centred on each voyage as was previously the case. Rather, the company reported its accounts periodically, which resulted in the development of accrual accounting.

Why did the Dutch companies before 1602 not report on a periodic basis, and why did the formation of the Dutch East India Company change that practice? What is accrual accounting and why is it a consequence of periodic reporting?

③ CONTENTS

In modern times, we take for granted that companies produce financial statements every year, or even more frequently. While much of this practice is due to regulation, the regulations themselves reflect the economic demands for periodic reporting. This chapter will first discuss the demand for and supply of periodic reporting. We will also see why periodic reporting naturally leads away from cash accounting toward accrual accounting (i.e., the way we currently present accounting reports; a formal definition of accrual accounting will follow). The chapter will then revisit the concept of uncertainty from Chapter 1 and how it impacts the preparation of accrual accounting reports through the use of estimates. This conceptual background will help explain the structure of the income statement (the main report measuring periodic performance)

and the idea of "quality of earnings," a concept that is used frequently in the press but often poorly understood.

After showing that periodic reports using accrual accounting are necessary to satisfy users' information needs, this chapter proceeds to explore several issues that surface as a consequence. First, what kinds of financial statements (balance sheet, income statement, etc.) are necessary under an accrual accounting regime? How do we define the reporting periods, and which events should be included in a particular period? Given the need to make accounting estimates and the need to change accounting policies from time to time, how do we deal with changes in these estimates and policies? How do we address errors in accounting reports that were previously issued?

While this range of issues may seem diverse, they all are addressed in this chapter because they all are connected by the idea of timing: when do events, transactions, and accounting occur relative to each other. In accrual accounting, as you will see, *timing is everything*.

A. DEMAND FOR PERIODIC REPORTING AND THE NEED FOR ACCRUAL ACCOUNTING

L.O. 3-1. Explain the source of demand for periodic reporting and how accrual accounting satisfies that demand.

Recall from Chapter 1 that accounting involves the production and transmission of information about an enterprise from those who have it to those who need it. In the context of financial reporting to external users, accounting can be very simple, as it was for businesses like the Dutch trading ships before 1602. Accountants needed only to record how much each investor contributed to the voyage; then, when the ship returned, the accountant tallied up how much the ship's goods fetched on the market and disbursed the funds to the investors according to their share of investment. In other words, the accounting was on a *cash basis*: track how much money comes into the enterprise at the beginning and how much goes back to each investor. This approach was efficient and practical because the cash cycles had all been completed.

TYPES OF CASH CYCLES

A **cash cycle** is a set of transactions that converts a cash inflow to a cash outflow or vice versa. We can categorize cash cycles into three types: financing, investing, and operating. A **financing cash cycle** is the receipt of funding from investors, using those funds to generate returns from investments and operations, and returning the funds to investors. An **investing cash cycle** begins with the use of funds to purchase property that has long-term future benefits for the enterprise (e.g., equipment), using that property to obtain economic benefits that ultimately result in cash inflows, and disposing of the property. An **operating cash cycle** involves the purchase of items such as inventory; production, sales, and delivery of goods or provision of services; and receipts from customers. The distinction between financing and the other two cycles is quite clear because of the *direction* of cash flows: financing involves inflows to the enterprise followed by outflows, while investment/operations involve outflows then inflows. The distinction between the investing and operating cash cycles is less clear as it requires subjective judgments about long versus short term: investing cycles tend to be longer than operating cash cycles.

Exhibit 3-1 summarizes each of these three cash cycles as well as their tendency to be nested: financing provides cash flows for investment and operations, investment provides benefits for operations, and operations generates cash flows to fund more investments and payments to investors.

cash cycle: A set of transactions that converts a cash inflow to a cash outflow, or vice versa. A **financing cash cycle** is the receipt of funding from investors, using those funds to generate returns from investments and operations, and returning the funds to investors. An **investing cash cycle** is the purchase of property that has long-term future benefits for the enterprise, using that property to obtain economic benefits that ultimately result in cash inflows, and disposing of the property. An **operating cash cycle** involves the purchase of items such as inventory; production, sales, and delivery of goods or provision of services; and receipts from customers.

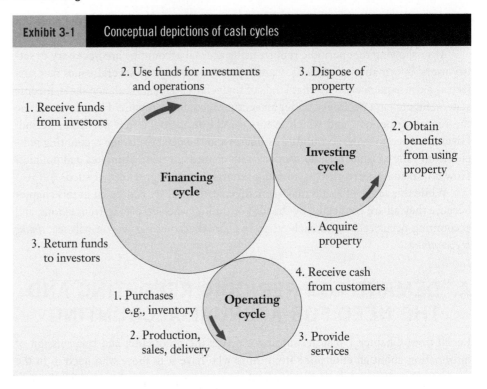

Exhibit 3-1   Conceptual depictions of cash cycles

2. Use funds for investments and operations

3. Dispose of property

1. Receive funds from investors

Financing cycle

Investing cycle

2. Obtain benefits from using property

1. Acquire property

3. Return funds to investors

4. Receive cash from customers

1. Purchases e.g., inventory

Operating cycle

2. Production, sales, delivery

3. Provide services

THRESHOLD CONCEPT
ACCOUNTING INFORMATION'S SUPPLY AND DEMAND

Why was there no reporting in between the departure and return of the ships? The reason is simple: there were no credible and timely ways to obtain information about a voyage until the ship returned to port. (Credibility is important here, as there could be unverifiable rumours from other ships that happened to cross paths with the ship of interest.) Without such information, no one was in any mood to buy or sell investments in the voyage once the ship had started its journey. It was only practical to wait until each ship returned to port. In other words, there was an *inability to supply* the information during the voyage, even if people demanded it. Given the limited duration of each company/voyage, investors were willing to wait for the ship's return.

The formation of corporations like the Dutch East India Company changed all that. These corporations, and other types of entities, had indefinite lives. They were intended to continue operating until the owners at a future date collectively decided to dissolve the entity. With the uncertain length of time until dissolution, which could be a very long time in the future, it is clearly not practical for investors to wait until the dissolution of the company to find out if they made any money!

The rise of entities with indefinite lives meant that investors in such entities needed to sell their investments at some point before the dissolution of the entity. These sellers and any potential buyers needed information to help them value the investment. Given a multitude of investors, it only made sense that enterprises report at pre-specified intervals rather than respond to information requests coming from each investor or potential investor. In the case of the Dutch East India Company, this interval was 10 years.[1] Today, the interval is typically a year or a quarter according to incorporation laws, securities regulations, and securities exchange rules.

[1.] The reports were required every 10 years. While this seems like a long time in current times, bear in mind that each voyage could last for more than a year. Given the nature of the Dutch East India Company's operations, 10 years is perhaps not such an unreasonable reporting period.

⚓ ## STILL WAITING...

In 1670, an incorporation under the British royal charter created "The Governor and Company of Adventurers of England trading into Hudson's Bay." The charter gave the company exclusive rights to the fur trade in the watershed flowing into Hudson Bay. The company continues to operate today as the Hudson's Bay Company. It was publicly traded until January 2006, when it was purchased by private equity firm NRDC Equity Partners. In late 2012, the company became a public company again by issuing $365 million of shares on the Toronto Stock Exchange (ticker HBC). If investors had to wait until dissolution to find out what happened to their investments, they would have been waiting for three and a half centuries—and counting!

Except for coincidental occasions, the end of a reporting period such as a year will not correspond with the completion of transactions. For instance, consider the hypothetical series of trading voyages for Tradewinds Company shown in Exhibit 3-2.

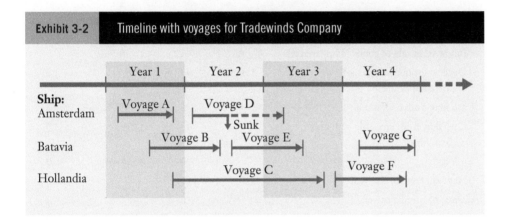

Exhibit 3-2	Timeline with voyages for Tradewinds Company

At the end of the first year, Voyage A had been completed. However, Voyages B and C also began in Year 1, but the ships had not returned by the end of the year. Should Tradewinds Company report only the results of Voyage A? What should Tradewinds report regarding the investments it made for Voyages B and C?

As you can gather from this example, reporting only information for completed voyages using cash basis accounting provides incomplete information to investors. (Recall the concept of completeness in the conceptual frameworks of Chapter 2.) Investors need to know that Tradewinds has invested in other voyages that are in progress at the end of the year—and, if the information is available, the status of those voyages. The accrual basis of accounting would try to capture the voyages in progress.

Formally, **accrual accounting** is a basis of accounting that reflects economic events when they happen rather than only when cash exchanges occur. For instance, for Year 1 accrual accounting would include information relating to the one completed voyage (A) as well as the two that are in progress at year-end (voyages B and C). Investors would find all of this information useful. Indeed, the financial report would be misleading were it to omit information about the two unfinished voyages. As you can see, accrual accounting arises naturally when enterprises report periodically.

THRESHOLD CONCEPT
CONCEPTUAL FRAMEWORK

accrual accounting A basis of accounting that records economic events when they happen rather than only when cash exchanges occur; contrast with **cash accounting**.

🔭 ## CHECKPOINT **CP3-1**

Explain the historical and logical reasons why we prepare periodic financial reports.

B. ACCRUAL VERSUS CASH ACCOUNTING

cash accounting A method of accounting that records only cash exchanges; contrast with **accrual accounting**.

We can use Exhibit 3-2 to illustrate the differences between accrual and **cash accounting** by applying some simple numbers to the voyages.[2]

- Investors provide $20 million in financing to start up the company.
- Each ship costs $5 million and on average can complete 10 voyages, unless it is sunk by storms, hazards, or pirates.
- Operating costs for each voyage are $1 million to pay for the crew's wages and to stock the ship with inventories and supplies. The company must pay these costs in advance because the goods and the crew may perish at sea.
- A successful voyage usually returns within a year (sometimes longer, depending on weather conditions) with goods that can be sold for $5 million.

The cash basis accounting report for Years 1 and 2 would look as shown in Exhibit 3-3 (Years 3 and 4 will be left as an exercise).

Exhibit 3-3	Cash basis financial report for Tradewinds Company			
	Year 1		Year 2	
	Voyages	$m	Voyages	$m
Operations				
Inflow from sale of goods ($5m/arrival)	A	5	B	5
Outflow for operating costs ($1m/departure)	A, B, C	(3)	D, E	(2)
Cash flow from operations		2		3
Cash flow from investing activities ($5m/ship)		(15)		0
Cash flow from financing activities		20		0
Net cash flow for the year		7		3
Cash at beginning of year		0		7
Cash at end of year		7		10

Note that the cash financial report is a statement of flows, with the balance of cash reported at the bottom. We can also produce a balance sheet, but it would be very short and redundant: it would show only cash of $7 million and $10 million for Years 1 and 2, respectively, and equity equal to those amounts. *The cash basis balance sheet has only cash and equity in equal amounts; there are no other items because all non-cash items are accruals.*

accrual An accounting entry that reflects events or transactions in a period different from its corresponding cash flow.

deferral An accounting entry that reflects events or transactions after the related cash flow.

Accruals are accounting entries that record events in a period different from the corresponding cash flows. Accruals encompass both instances where the accounting record reflects (i) events before cash flows and (ii) events after cash flows. Sometimes accountants will refer to the latter more specifically as **deferrals**. For example, recognizing sales revenue after the receipt of cash is a deferral of revenue.

To prepare the accrual basis financial report, we need to provide some additional guidance on Tradewinds Company's accrual policies:

- Record the cost of products shipped out and traded in exchange for products from Asia when the Asian products are sold at the home port. Similarly, record the cost of supplies and wages as well as depreciation when the ship returns home. This is a reasonable but arbitrary allocation rule that maintains the logical relationship between revenues and related costs (conventionally called "matching" of costs to revenues).

[2.] We use "dollars" and "$" for convenience. The actual Dutch currency since the 13th century had been the guilder, until the Netherlands adopted the euro.

- When the company receives information about the sinking of one of its ships, the company writes off the recorded value of that ship and expenses any inventories, prepaid wages, and prepaid supplies on the books.

Based on the previous information and these two accrual accounting policies, the accrual basis financial report would look like the one shown in Exhibit 3-4:

Exhibit 3-4	Accrual basis financial report for Tradewinds Company			
	Year 1		Year 2	
	Voyages	$m	Voyages	$m
Statement of income and retained earnings				
Revenue ($5m/arrival)	A	5.0	B	5.0
Operating expenses ($1m/arrival)	A	(1.0)	B	(1.0)
Depreciation ($0.5m/arrival)	A	(0.5)	B	(0.5)
Write-off of sunken ship		0.0	D	(4.5)*
Write-off of operating costs due to sunken ship ($1m/ship)		0.0	D	(1.0)
Net income (loss)		3.5		(2.0)
Retained earnings at beginning of year		0.0		3.5
Retained earnings at end of year		3.5		1.5
Balance sheet Cash (see Exhibit 3-3)		7.0		10.0
Prepaid expenses ($1m/voyage in progress)	B, C	2.0	C, E	2.0
Ships at cost ($5m/ship)		15.0		10.0
Less: accumulated depreciation	A	(0.5)	B	(0.5)
Total assets		23.5		21.5
Contributed capital		20.0		20.0
Retained earnings		3.5		1.5
Total equity		23.5		21.5
Cash flow statement (same as cash basis report—see Exhibit 3-3)				

*The *Amsterdam* sank in Voyage D. After depreciation of $0.5m for Voyage A, it had a book value of $4.5m, so this is the amount written off.

Let's compare and contrast the differences in the two sets of reports. What can we say about the complexity of the reports? It is evident that the cash basis report is much simpler. Tradewinds' cash balance increased from $7 million to $10 million, and we can see the sources of that change. In contrast, the accrual reports are more complex; there are many more items in the accrual accounting reports. Observe that all the items other than cash in the balance sheet result from accrual accounting.

Second, which set of reports provides more useful information about performance? The cash basis report shows operating cash flows of $2 million in Year 1, increasing to $3 million in Year 2. The accrual basis report shows $3.5 million income in Year 1, turning into a loss of $2 million in Year 2.

Exhibit 3-5	Summary of performance measures for Tradewinds Company		
Reporting basis	**Performance measure**	**Year 1**	**Year 2**
Cash basis	Operating cash flow	$2.0m	$3.0m
Accrual basis	Net income (loss)	3.5m	(2.0)m

These are quite dramatic differences and trends. To decide which one better reflects the underlying facts known to us (and to insiders, but not necessarily to people outside the company) we can summarize Tradewinds' activities as follows:

Exhibit 3-6	Summary of trading activities for Tradewinds Company	
Activity	Year 1	Year 2
Ships departed	3	2
Ships returned	1	1
Ships sunk	0	1

THRESHOLD CONCEPT
TIMING OF RECOGNITION

The company did not increase its trading activity in Year 2 and actually lost a ship during the year. Since the value of each voyage is constant year to year, it only makes sense that Year 2's performance should be lower than that in Year 1. From this example, we can say objectively and unambiguously that the accrual basis more closely reflects underlying events. The accrual basis of accounting provides more useful financial information to readers because it permits companies and their management to communicate their expectations of future outcomes.

To summarize these last two sections, we observe from history that a change from (i) single-purpose enterprises with limited life to (ii) enterprises that had indefinite lives created a demand for periodic reporting. In turn, periodic reports are more useful in terms of reflecting the economic conditions of the enterprise if they use an accrual basis rather than a cash basis. The illustration using Tradewinds Company demonstrates the differences in the resulting financial reports.

 CHECKPOINT **CP3-2**

Explain how accrual accounting better satisfies the demand for information in comparison to cash accounting.

L.O. 3-2. Explain why accrual accounting is fundamentally inexact, why estimates are central to accrual accounting, and why there is no "true" income for typical situations; evaluate the "quality of earnings."

THRESHOLD CONCEPT
DECISION MAKING UNDER UNCERTAINTY

C. UNCERTAINTY AND THE ESSENTIAL ROLE OF ESTIMATES IN ACCRUAL ACCOUNTING

Accrual accounting involves reporting amounts before the completion of some or all of the cash cycles. The inherent uncertainty of the future means that accrual accounting necessarily requires the use of estimates—no one, including the company's management, knows precisely the likelihood and amounts of future cash flows that will occur later in the cash cycles.

Refer to Tradewinds Company from the previous section, for example. The mere act of recording the three ships as assets uses estimates of the future cash flows expected to result from the use of the ships. Sometimes these estimates turn out to be incorrect—the vessel *Amsterdam* sank in Voyage D in Year 2, taking with it the inventories, supplies, and most likely the souls on board.

The need to use estimates means that all accrual accounting reports are imprecise—there is no single "true" accounting report for any set of circumstances. However, this does not mean that any arbitrary accrual accounting report is acceptable. Rather, there is a range of acceptable alternatives. For instance, Tradewinds Company could have used an alternate allocation policy for the ships' cost that recorded the depreciation expense when a ship departed instead of when it returned to port. On the other hand, not recording an expense for the supplies used would not be acceptable.

If we cannot describe financial statements as "true," or even more or less true, what *can* we say? Because of uncertainty and the need for estimates, the appropriate reference point should be "unbiased" financial statements. If we were to ask a sample of accountants (say, a hundred) without vested interests in the company concerned what they would do, we are likely to hear a range of answers. We can think of **unbiased accounting** as some average or consensus from this sample of disinterested accountants. Unbiased accounting is similar to the attribute of neutrality, which contributes to the qualitative characteristic of representational faithfulness in the IFRS Conceptual Framework discussed in Chapter 2.

THRESHOLD CONCEPT
CONCEPTUAL
FRAMEWORK

unbiased accounting   A conceptual accounting outcome that would result from taking an average or consensus from a sample of disinterested accountants.

true and fair   An overall evaluation of a set of financial statements as being a fair representation of the enterprise's economic conditions and performance.

Historically, IFRS has had a concept called the **true and fair** view, which states that accountants and auditors have a duty to evaluate the financial statements as a whole and determine whether those financial statements present a "true and fair" presentation of the company; if the financial statements are not true and fair, then the responsible accountant should amend them such that they are true and fair. This overall assessment can be used to override individual estimates, accounting choices, and even accounting standards if those estimates, choices, or standards produce financial statements that are not "true and fair."[3]

This is unfortunate wording, however. As we have seen in the above discussion, there can be no "true" financial statements under accrual accounting within the ordinary meaning of the word "true." Thus, we should not interpret "true and fair" literally; instead, we should take it to mean simply "fair." Appropriately, the new IFRS Conceptual Framework makes no mention of this concept. Furthermore, Canadian Auditing Standards note that to present financial statements that are "true and fair" and to "present fairly" have the same meaning.[4]

 CHECKPOINT **CP3-3**

Explain why accrual accounting numbers are fundamentally inexact.

D. QUALITY OF EARNINGS AND EARNINGS MANAGEMENT

A close relative of fair presentation is the idea of "quality of earnings." While many people have a general idea of what would constitute high-quality or low-quality earnings, there is often confusion over this concept. Some believe that earnings quality should be measured by comparing actual reported profits to what "true" earnings would be. On the other hand, many finance professionals such as stock analysts evaluate the quality of earnings by comparing income to cash flows.

While both of these ideas make some sense, they are both inadequate characterizations of earnings quality in different ways:

- Since a measure of true earnings does not exist, as discussed previously, we cannot evaluate earnings quality relative to true earnings. This applies both at the conceptual level and at a practical level.
- Using cash flow to evaluate the quality of earnings implies that cash flow is a better measure of performance. As the Tradewinds' example demonstrates, cash flow is usually an inferior measure of performance compared with accrual basis earnings.

[3.] Copyright © 2012 IFRS Foundation.

[4.] See IFRS Framework prior to 2011 paragraph 46, and Canadian Auditing Standard 700 paragraph 35.

quality of earnings How closely reported earnings correspond to earnings that would be reported in the absence of management bias.

THRESHOLD CONCEPT
QUALITY OF EARNINGS

Instead, the **quality of earnings** refers to how closely reported earnings correspond to earnings that would be reported in the absence of managerial bias. To understand this idea, let's take a simple example. Suppose Quantum Company has cash flows equal to $500, and reported earnings are $800. As defined earlier, accruals reflect events and transactions that occur in periods different from their corresponding cash flows. Thus, accruals represent the difference between reported earnings and cash flows, or $300 ($800 − $500).

We can think of separating this $300 of accruals into two components:

■ *unbiased accruals* that reflect economic conditions and accounting standards with the application of professional judgment and considering professional ethics
■ *excessive accruals* that result from contractual incentives for the firm or management as well as any unethical managerial opportunism to over- or under-accrue

Suppose that Quantum Company has unbiased accruals of $200, meaning that excessive accruals amount to $100 ($300 − $200). Ideally, if we were able to observe the amount of unbiased accruals, then we could determine the amount of unbiased earnings = cash flows + unbiased accruals = $500 + $200 = $700. However, the actual earnings that we observe are $800, which includes both unbiased and excessive accruals. The relationships among cash flows, accruals, and earnings are shown in Exhibit 3-7.

Exhibit 3-7	Relationship among cash flows, accruals, and earnings, including figures for Quantum Company

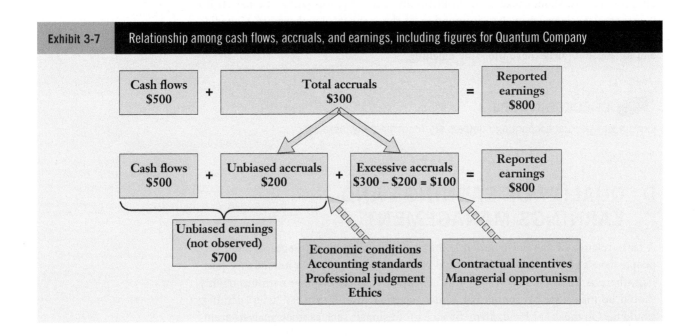

If it were possible, *we would evaluate the quality of earnings by identifying the excessive component of accruals.* Lower excessive accruals translate into higher-quality earnings. However, we can only observe total accruals. To distinguish the portion of total accruals that is excessive from the portion that is unbiased, users need to make conjectures about the incentives faced by management that would lead them to make more or less excessive accruals. Several of these motivations to manage earnings were discussed in Chapter 1 in relation to positive accounting theory and the economic consequences of different accounting choices.

THRESHOLD CONCEPT
ECONOMIC CONSEQUENCES OF ACCOUNTING CHOICE

The discussion in this section has focused on the quality of earnings, but the general ideas apply to the other financial statements as well. For instance, we can also think about the quality of the balance sheet: which assets and liabilities are potentially over- or understated relative to unbiased reporting, and by how much? Furthermore, excessive accruals on the income statement will have direct implications for the other financial statements because of the connections among them. For instance, recognition of more revenue on the income statement results in higher accounts receivable on the balance sheet. This and other connections among the financial statements will be explored further later in this chapter.

 CHECKPOINT **CP3-4**

Explain what is meant by "quality of earnings." How can financial statement readers evaluate the quality of earnings?

E. PERIODICITY, CUT-OFF, AND SUBSEQUENT EVENTS

L.O. 3-3. Apply accrual accounting in relation to issues of timing: periodicity, cut-off, and subsequent events.

Once in a while, those who are not familiar with accounting (and some who are) will say something to the effect of "It's only a matter of timing" in reference to the accounting of a transaction—and, in so doing, try to play down the importance of an accounting issue. However, as mentioned in the introduction, in accrual accounting *timing is everything*! Accrual accounting exists precisely because users desire to know what events and transactions occurred in a particular period of time. Therefore, it is essential to properly define the reporting period. Related to this issue, how do we deal with events and information that arise near the cut-off date at the end of the period and subsequent to that date?

**THRESHOLD CONCEPT
TIMING OF
RECOGNITION**

1. Periodicity

The typical reporting period for an enterprise is 12 months. Aside from regulatory and tax reporting requirements, this length of time makes sense in terms of the annual cycles of the seasons and the resultant ebb and flow of economic activity. However, an annual period does not need to match the calendar year of January 1 to December 31. Many businesses choose a year-end that coincides with a time of lower activity. For instance, Canadian retailers will tend to have year-ends at the end of January—after the holiday season when sales peak, inventory is at a low level, and any returns from customers have been processed. In addition, some enterprises will have reporting periods that are close to, but not exactly, 12 months. Again, retailers provide a good example: they have reporting periods of 52 weeks (364 days) and 53 weeks once every several years because doing so provides more comparable information year to year due to sales being significantly higher on some days of the week. In practice, about two-thirds of public enterprises have year-ends on December 31 or within a few days before or after.

2. Cut-off

Cut-off refers to the point in time at which one reporting period ends and the next begins. Defining this point is crucial to financial statements reported on a periodic basis. Because accrual accounting reflects some cash cycles that are not complete, it is necessary to formulate rules regarding which events will be reflected in the reporting period (i.e., prior to the cut-off date) and which others will not. As we proceed through later chapters, we will see this idea again and again. For example, Chapter 4 will discuss whether revenue should be recorded prior to the cut-off date or in a later period.

cut-off The point in time at which one reporting period ends and the next begins.

In addition to deciding which events should be reflected in the reporting period, we also need to consider the timing of information relating to these events. While accrual accounting estimates are inherently imprecise, we should use the best information available to maximize the precision as much as possible. This usually means

**THRESHOLD CONCEPT
DECISION MAKING
UNDER UNCERTAINTY**

using information that is as up-to-date as possible. However, we cannot wait for all uncertainty to disappear, as that would require all the cash cycles to be complete, which goes against the idea of periodic reporting.

For instance, suppose that a company has inventories of $2 million at year-end. During the preparation of the annual financial statements, the company's management learns that a quarter of the inventories have declined in value because of a technological change that has made the inventory obsolete. This information affects how much the company reports for inventories because these goods need to have future benefits for the company to satisfy the definition of an asset. The subsequent event indicates that the inventories do not have such future benefits, so the company needs to write down or write off the value of the affected inventory. The period between the cut-off date and the date when the company authorizes its financial statements for issuance is called the **subsequent-events period**. (IFRS uses "events after the reporting period" to refer to subsequent events; we opt for the more succinct terminology.)

A common point of confusion involves whether an event is merely a subsequent event and not part of the reporting period. A useful way to distinguish the difference is in terms of recognition and measurement. We *recognize* transactions and events occurring within the reporting period (i.e., up to the cut-off date), but the *measurement* of those transactions can use the best information available whether that information is from the reporting period or the subsequent-events period. The timeline in Exhibit 3-8 illustrates this difference.

subsequent-events period
The period between the cut-off date and the date when the company authorizes its financial statements for issuance.

| Exhibit 3-8 | Timeline showing subsequent-events period in relation to recognition and measurement |

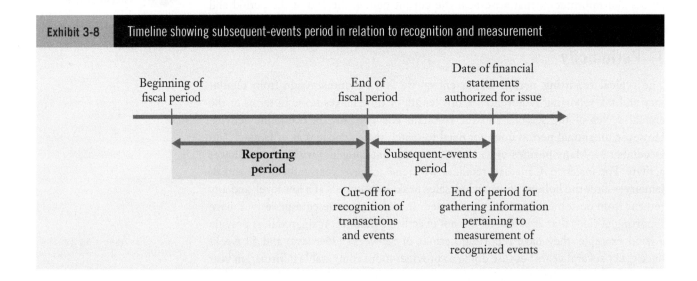

For the inventories just mentioned, the inventories are on hand at year-end, so they should be recognized on the balance sheet. If some of the inventories become obsolete prior to the cut-off date (i.e., the fiscal year-end), then the obsolescence should be recognized even if *the information about* the technological change becomes available later during the subsequent-events period. That information affects the measurement of the financial consequences of the technological change and the value of inventory at year-end.

On the other hand, if the *technological change itself* occurs during the subsequent-events period, then there would be no impact on the amounts recognized. If the effect is material, the company should disclose the information about the technological change in the notes to the financial statements.

Another common example to illustrate subsequent events relates to accounts receivable. Enterprises can and should use information in the subsequent period to estimate the amount to record in the allowance for doubtful accounts. Such information includes actual collections and defaults in the subsequent-events period for accounts outstanding at year-end.

In contrast, suppose an accident results in the destruction of a transport truck that had a carrying value of $400,000 on the year-end date of December 31. The accident occurred on January 15, two weeks after the cut-off date, so the reported value of the truck on December 31 would not include the effect of the accident. If the amount were material, the reporting entity would provide note disclosure regarding the effect of the accident.

 CHECKPOINT CP3-5

What key dates define the subsequent-events period? Explain how information obtained in the subsequent-events period should be used.

F. ACCOUNTING CHANGES: ERRORS, CHANGES IN ACCOUNTING POLICY, AND CHANGES IN ESTIMATES

As noted previously, accounting is inherently inexact because accruals depend on uncertain future outcomes. Therefore, we should expect changes in circumstances over time. To reflect changed circumstances, management may find it appropriate to change accounting estimates. At other times, a change in accounting policy is more appropriate since, ideally, a company chooses accounting policies that best reflect its economic circumstances. In addition, to err is human, so we need to know how to handle accounting errors. IFRS–IAS 8 and ASPE Section 1506 provide guidance on how to deal with these three types of accounting changes.

L.O. 3-4. Evaluate whether an accounting change is an error, a change in accounting policy, or a change in estimate, and apply the retrospective and prospective treatments appropriate to that type of accounting change.

THRESHOLD CONCEPT
DECISION MAKING UNDER UNCERTAINTY

1. Correction of errors

An error occurs when a company reports an incorrect amount *given the information available at the time*—hindsight must not be used. For instance, a forecast of useful life for equipment that turns out to be wrong is not an error as long as the forecast was made in good faith based on the available information. However, if management estimates the useful life to be five years but then applies a 10% straight-line depreciation rate, this would be an error. For a **correction of an error**, the appropriate treatment is **retrospective adjustment with restatement**. "With restatement" means that any financial statements from prior years presented for comparative purposes must be restated. The reason for retrospective correction of errors is to restore the previous financial statements to *what they should have been* given the information available at that prior date.

correction of an error An accounting change made necessary by the discovery of an incorrect amount, given information available at the time the amount was reported.

retrospective adjustment (also retroactive adjustment) Applying an accounting change to all periods affected in the past, present, and future. Retrospective adjustment **with restatement** shows any comparative figures on the same basis as the current period figures. Retrospective adjustment **without restatement** reflects the accounting change's impact on past periods in the current period.

2. Changes in accounting policy

A **change in accounting policy** is a change in, for example, inventory accounting from weighted average to first-in, first-out (FIFO). Such changes are at the discretion of management but should be made to reflect economic circumstances. (Recall that standards allow a range of accounting policies because there are a variety of economic circumstances.) The appropriate treatment for changes in accounting policy is retrospective adjustment with restatement.

Requiring retrospective adjustment with restatement increases comparability of financial statements (i.e., consistency over time). If a switch from weighted average to

change in accounting policy An accounting change made at the discretion of management.

FIFO increases income for the current year, for example, users need to have financial statements from the prior year to make a meaningful comparison. Retrospective adjustment with restatement also reduces the temptation to change accounting policies to manage earnings, because the effect of the change applies not just to the current year but also to all prior years. If the change were not retrospective, then the cumulative effect of the accounting policy change could significantly impact the current year's income. In fact, US GAAP treats changes in accounting policy retroactively *without* restatement. Comparative financial statements are not adjusted, and the income statement reports the retroactive effect through current-year income as "cumulative effect of accounting change" at the bottom of the income statement.

To illustrate the effect of the different methods, consider a change in depreciation policy that is treated as a change in accounting policy. (As will be seen in Chapter 8, a change in depreciation can also be considered a change in accounting estimate.) Assume that a company has a single piece of equipment, purchased at the beginning of 2020 for $1 million. The equipment has an estimated useful life of 10 years and zero residual value. The company initially decides to use a declining-balance method of depreciation at double the straight-line rate. The straight-line rate is 10%, so the depreciation in 2020 is 20% of $1 million, or $200,000. Also assume that the company earns income before depreciation of $500,000 in both 2020 and 2021. In 2021, the company chooses to change the depreciation policy from double-declining-balance to straight-line. (For simplicity, ignore income taxes.) This change in depreciation was not due to any change in circumstances or new information; the useful life remains 10 years and there is no change in usage of the equipment. Exhibit 3-9 shows the effect of this change in accounting policy under different reporting methods.

With the given assumption of stable operations (constant income before depreciation), we observe that the method of retrospective adjustment with restatement provides the most comparable financial information, particularly net income, which is

Exhibit 3-9	Illustration of potential methods to reflect a change in accounting policy						
($000's)	As originally reported	Retrospective with restatement (IFRS, CICA)*		Retrospective without restatement (US GAAP)†		Prospective treatment (not permitted for change in policy)‡	
	2020	2020	2021	2020	2021	2020	2021
Equipment—at cost	1,000	1,000	1,000	1,000	1,000	1,000	1,000
Accumulated depreciation	(200)	(100)	(200)	(200)	(200)	(200)	(289)
Equipment—net	800	900	800	800	800	800	711
Income before depreciation	500	500	500	500	500	500	500
Depreciation expense	(200)	(100)	(100)	(200)	(100)	(200)	(89)
Income before the following	300	400	400	300	400	300	411
Cumulative effect of accounting change	—	—	—	—	100	—	—
Net income	300	400	400	300	500	300	411

* Retrospective with restatement: Apply straight-line depreciation from the beginning of the equipment's life, so annual depreciation equals 10% of $1 million cost.

† Retrospective without restatement: Determine how much straight-line depreciation would be if it had been used from the beginning of the equipment life, and reflect the effect in the year of change (2021). The 2021 depreciation should be $100,000. Previously, $200,000 had been recorded for depreciation in 2020. Cumulative depreciation is $300,000, but straight-line depreciation over two years would require only $200,000. The excess $100,000 of depreciation is reversed by the item "cumulative effect of accounting change."

‡ Prospective treatment: Do not adjust prior year. Apply new depreciation policy beginning in 2021. The undepreciated cost at the beginning of 2021 is $800,000, depreciated over the remaining nine years results in straight-line depreciation of $800,000/ 9 = $88,889 per year.

$400,000 each year. The US approach of retrospective adjustment without restatement shows a pattern of increasing income from $300,000 to $500,000, although the separate reporting of the cumulative effect of accounting change of $100,000 makes evident the source of the increase. However, even backing out this $100,000 results in a pattern of increasing income: $300,000 in 2020 and $400,000 in 2021.

The last two columns show what would be reported under the prospective method, which is not permitted for changes in accounting policy. However, the prospective method is appropriate for changes in accounting estimates, which we discuss next.

3. Changes in accounting estimates

Accounting estimates are, for example, the percentage of bad debts or the number of years of useful life for a piece of equipment. These estimates should be based on the best information available at the time of financial statement preparation. However, as time progresses, new information could suggest that alternate estimates would be more accurate. Since such information was not predictable at the time of the prior estimates, the appropriate treatment is **prospective adjustment**: applying the change only to the current and future reporting periods without any changes to past financial statements. The two columns on the far right of Exhibit 3-9 show how this method would be applied if a change in depreciation method were considered a **change in estimate**. A change from the declining-balance method to the straight-line method can be justified as a change in estimate if the straight-line method more closely resembles the pattern of usage or value derived from the equipment.

prospective adjustment
Applying an accounting change only to the current and future reporting periods without any changes to past financial statements.

change in estimate   An accounting change made necessary by the arrival of new information.

4. Illustrative example for practice

You have been provided with the following information related to two recent financial years for Random Home Inc. (amounts in $millions):

Balance sheet data	2019	2020
Retained earnings—beginning of year	800	920
Accounts receivable—gross	850	900
Income statement		
Revenues	2,500	2,650
Cost of goods sold	1,600	1,650
Selling, general, and administrative expenses	300	320
Depreciation	100	100
Interest expense	260	240
Income before tax	240	340
Income tax expense	72	102
Net income	168	238

Required:

While preparing the 2020 financial statements, you realize that, in anticipation of uncollectible accounts, there needs to be a downward adjustment to end-of-year accounts receivable by 4% of the accounts receivable balance. Using the following table, indicate the impact on the financial statements if this change is due to one of the following reasons (ignore the effect of income tax):

a. An error correction because the company should have known that receivables were overvalued as early as 2019.
b. A change in accounting policy because the company had not previously provided for bad debts as they had been deemed immaterial.

c. A change in estimate due to new information showing a deterioration of economic conditions.

Type of accounting change	2019 Statement of comp. income	2019 Accounts receivable	2019 Retained earnings	2020 Statement of comp. income	2020 Accounts receivable	2020 Retained earnings
(a)						
(b)						
(c)						

Suggested solution:

($000's) Type of accounting change	2019 Statement of comp. income	2019 Accounts receivable	2019 Retained earnings	2020 Statement of comp. income	2020 Accounts receivable	2020 Retained earnings
(a) Error correction	−34	−34	−34	−2	−36	−36
(b) Change in policy	−34	−34	−34	−2	−36	−36
(c) Change in estimate	0	0	0	−36	−36	−36

The change in estimate in (c) is the simplest as it requires prospective adjustment. In the current reporting period, the company needs to record an allowance for doubtful accounts (a reduction in net accounts receivable) equal to 4% of the receivable balance of $900,000, which is $36,000. The adjusting journal entry would be:

2020	Dr. Bad debts expense	36,000	
	Cr. Allowance for doubtful accounts		36,000

When the income statement accounts are closed for the period, the bad debts expense also reduces retained earnings.

The error correction and change in accounting policy in (a) and (b) both require retrospective adjustment with restatement. To properly reflect this accounting change, the company needs to consider the effect on current as well as prior reporting periods. Had the company provided for bad debts in 2019, it would have recorded 4% of the receivable balance of $850,000, which is $34,000. After making this provision, the company would then record only an additional $2,000 for bad debts to bring the balance up to $36,000. Thus, the journal entries are:

2019	Dr. Retained earnings (bad debts expense)	34,000	
	Cr. Allowance for doubtful accounts		34,000
2020	Dr. Bad debts expense	2,000	
	Cr. Allowance for doubtful accounts		2,000

Notice that the 2019 entry debits retained earnings. While conceptually the $34,000 adjustment is for bad debts expense, which is denoted in parentheses, it is not correct to debit the "bad debts expense" account. All income statement accounts, such as bad debts expense, are temporary accounts representing the current fiscal year. To debit "bad debts expense" would record the expense in 2020. The "bad debts expense" account for 2019 had already been closed to retained earnings, so the adjustment goes directly to retained earnings.

For a review of temporary accounts, closing entries, and other aspects of the accounting cycle, see the Appendix at the end of this chapter.

 CHECKPOINT **CP3-6**

Which type(s) of accounting changes require retrospective adjustment? Which one(s) require prospective treatment?

5. Summary

We can summarize the three types of accounting changes and their treatments in IFRS and ASPE as shown in Exhibit 3-10:

Exhibit 3-10	Summary of types of accounting changes and corresponding treatments
Type of accounting change	**Treatment under IFRS and ASPE**
Correction of errors	Retrospective with restatement
Changes in accounting policy	Retrospective with restatement
Changes in estimates	Prospective

We can distinguish the type of accounting change by answering two questions, as illustrated in the decision tree shown in Exhibit 3-11. First, is the accounting change due to new information or just management choice? If it is just management choice, then it would be a change in accounting policy and treated retrospectively. If the change is due to new information, when was the information known or when should it have been known? If it was known or should have been known in a prior period, then we have an error that needs to be corrected retroactively. If the information could not have been known until the current period, then it is a change in estimate that is treated prospectively.

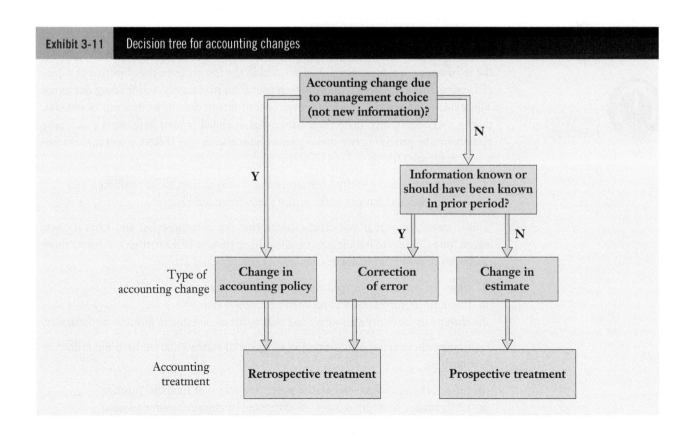

| Exhibit 3-11 | Decision tree for accounting changes |

This section has provided the basic tools necessary to deal with accounting changes. Future chapters will show many more applications of these tools. For example, Chapter 4, on revenue recognition, will show an important application of changes in estimates relating to the accounting for long-term contracts, and Chapter 6 will illustrate the effect of errors in inventory accounting.

G. THE STRUCTURE OF FINANCIAL REPORTS AND THEIR RELATIONSHIPS

L.O. 3-5. Integrate the structure and connections among the four financial statements and explain how this structure relates to accrual accounting.

Earlier in this chapter, we showed the key differences between cash and accrual accounting. Cash accounting is relatively straightforward, and likewise are the resulting financial statements, which involve a cash flow statement that shows the change in cash from the beginning to the end of the period. Accrual accounting, on the other hand, results in more extensive financial statements. The statement of comprehensive income arises as an alternative to the cash flow statement as a report on performance, while the balance sheet accumulates all of the accruals. In addition, accrual accounting developed when enterprises were no longer short-lived; these enterprises obtained multiple rounds of financing from owners and made periodic payments to them (dividends), creating a need for a report that distinguished such capital transactions with owners from other transactions with everyone else. In comparison, a Dutch trading company before 1602 would simply have had one financing prior to the beginning of the voyage and one set of payments upon dissolution of the company.

In this section, we look at the interrelationship of these four financial statements (cash flow statement, statement of comprehensive income, balance sheet, statement of changes in equity), how they relate to the IFRS Conceptual Framework from Chapter 2, and the requirements for their presentation according to IFRS. The following discussion will be quite general; we will look at many of the specific items in the financial statements in later chapters.

1. Overview of financial statement presentation and interrelationships

THRESHOLD CONCEPT
CONCEPTUAL FRAMEWORK

Financial statements are the end product of the accounting process, made to meet the information needs of users. As discussed in the last chapter, the objective of financial statements is to provide information useful for investment and lending decisions. These decisions depend on users' assessment of future cash flows in terms of amount, timing, and uncertainty. IFRS then asserts that financial reports help users make these assessments by providing two main types of information (see IFRS Conceptual Framework paragraph OB12):

1. information on the entity's resources and claims against those resources; and
2. information on changes in the entity's resources and claims.

Simply stated, resources and claims mean what the enterprise has and what it owes, where "owes" refers to both lenders and equity investors. IFRS further considers three categories of information about changes in resources and claims:

1. financial performance according to accrual accounting;
2. financial performance according to cash flows; and
3. changes in the entity's resources and claims that are not due to financial performance.

Translating these types of information to financial statements, we have the following relationships:

- resources and claims → balance sheet (statement of financial position)
- performance on accrual basis → statement of comprehensive income

- performance on cash basis → cash flow statement
- changes in resources and claims not due to performance → statement of changes in equity

The diagram in Exhibit 3-12 lays out these four key financial statements and the relationships among them. As well, the diagram shows the scope of IFRS, which covers all of the financial statements as well as note disclosures. IFRS does not cover commentary on financial performance in management's discussion and analysis (MD&A) and other types of reports, such as those on environmental performance, corporate social responsibility, value added, and so on.

Exhibit 3-12	Financial statements, relationships, and the scope of IFRS

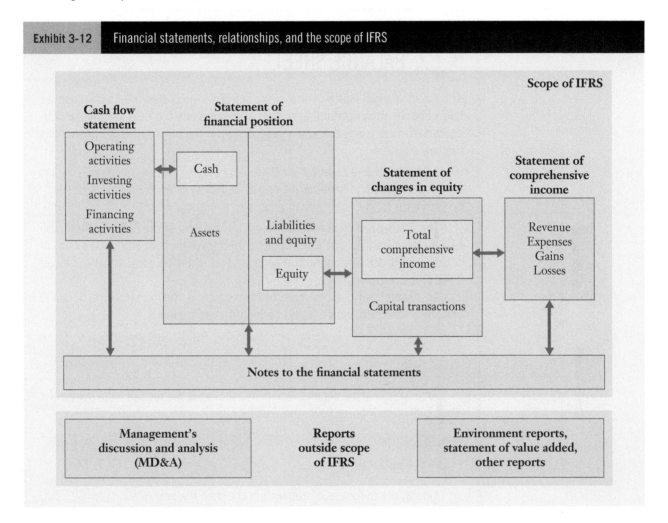

Central to the set of financial statements is the statement of financial position (traditionally called the balance sheet), as it records the *stock* or balances of assets, liabilities, and equity; that is, it shows the financial position at a point in time. The other three financial statements track the *flows* of items on the balance sheet. The cash flow statement shows the different activities that explain the change in cash balance over the year. The statement of equity explains changes to equity, differentiating comprehensive income or loss from other changes in equity. The statement of comprehensive income provides further details of items comprising comprehensive income. The notes to the financial statements provide additional disclosures that improve the understanding of the financial statements.

THRESHOLD CONCEPT
ARTICULATION

The relationships among the four financial statements shown above embed an important concept called **articulation**. In financial accounting, articulation does not have its common meaning relating to communication (e.g., "the articulate speaker delivered a convincing speech"). Rather, articulation refers to the *connection* of the financial statements with each other, similar to the usage in reference to human joints.

articulation   The connection of financial statements with each other.

The accounting system that we use is articulated: the amounts reported on the statement of comprehensive income connect with the balance sheet through the equity accounts. In other words, what happens on the statement of comprehensive income also impacts the balance sheet. In a different system in which the financial statements are not articulated, the measure of performance on the statement of comprehensive income can be independent from the amount of equity reported on the balance sheet. Such alternatives have been proposed from time to time because they can produce financial statements that better represent financial position and performance; however, these alternatives have not received wide acceptance.

 # DOUBLE-ENTRY ACCOUNTING AND THE BALANCE SHEET

The balance sheet is the centre of the set of financial statements because we use a double-entry accounting system. In this system, the balance sheet is self-contained. To see why this is the case, consider the three types of transactions that are possible:

a.   exchange of one asset for another;
b.   exchange of one financial claim (i.e., a liability or equity) for another; or
c.   increase (or decrease) of an asset and a financial claim.

The first type of transaction involves the left side of the balance sheet, the second involves the right side, and the third involves both sides. One can, of course, construct compound transactions that involve a combination of these three types of transactions.

An example of the first type of transaction is the purchase of $16,000 inventory with cash, which would be recorded as follows:

| Dr. Inventories | 16,000 | |
| Cr. Cash | | 16,000 |

An example of the second type of transaction is the receipt of an invoice for electricity costs incurred over the past month:

| Dr. Equity (Utility expense) | 2,000 | |
| Cr. Accounts payable | | 2,000 |

Finally, the third type of transaction could be the sale of goods for $25,000 on credit:

| Dr. Accounts receivable | 25,000 | |
| Cr. Equity (Revenue) | | 25,000 |

Notice from these examples that the second and third types of transactions can involve accounts you would normally think of as accounts on the income statement, which have been noted in parentheses in the journal entries. As you will recall from introductory accounting, utility expense, revenue, and other income statement accounts are temporary accounts; they exist as a more detailed representation of the changes that affect equity, and at the end of each period they are reset to zero with the net balance transferred to the retained earnings component of equity. Thus, only the balance sheet is a direct result of a double-entry system. All of the other financial statements result from additional information requirements we impose on the accounting system.

Another issue of practical importance is the degree of aggregation in the financial statements. A large company will have thousands of items in its general ledger, distinguished by the nature of the item (e.g., cash or inventory), the function of the item (manufacturing, administration), geographic location, division within the company, and so on. Clearly it is not useful for financial statements to contain so much detail, which tends to obscure rather than illuminate the overall picture. The concept of materiality comes into play here. IAS 1, Presentation of Financial Statements, indicates the following:

> ¶29 An entity shall present separately each material class of similar items. An entity shall present separately items of a dissimilar nature or function unless they are immaterial.[5]

This means items in the financial statements should be grouped together in a logical fashion. Cash and equipment are dissimilar, so they should not be grouped together as "cash and equipment," but cash in different currencies could be grouped together as "cash." Groupings that are immaterial should be enlarged to include other similar groupings. If the grouping of immaterial items results in a category without a suitably descriptive label, then the group would be called "other."

So far in this section we have looked at the overall presentation and relationships among the different financial statements. Let's now examine each component in more detail.

 CHECKPOINT **CP3-7**

What is articulation? How are financial statements articulated?

2. Balance sheet (statement of financial position)

The balance sheet, or statement of financial position, shows the financial position of an enterprise at a point in time. Financial position is the amount and composition of assets and the composition of the claims on those assets. In a double-entry accounting system, total assets equal total financial claims; that is, the two sides of the balance sheet balance, as you know from basic accounting.

Exhibit 3-13 provides a sample balance sheet for a hypothetical company called Illustrator Ltd. In examining this balance sheet and the other financial statements, focus on the overall structure and how the parts connect with each other; it is not important what transactions generated this set of financial statements. Also note that some of the features in this sample balance sheet will be discussed later in this section (e.g., comparative figures, discontinued operations).

There are potentially many different ways to organize the balance sheet to show the composition of assets and liabilities. IFRS generally requires a current/non-current presentation of assets and liabilities (which is the method used in Exhibit 3-13), unless ordering the items by liquidity provides more useful information. In particular, IAS 1 indicates the following:

> ¶60 An entity shall present current and non-current assets, and current and non-current liabilities, as separate classifications in its statement of financial position . . . except when a presentation based on liquidity provides information that is reliable and is more relevant. . . .
>
> ¶61 Whichever method of presentation is adopted, an entity shall disclose the amount expected to be recovered or settled after more than twelve months

Exhibit 3-13	Balance sheet (statement of financial position) for Illustrator Ltd.

Illustrator Ltd.
Balance Sheet
As at December 31

In $000's	2021	2020
Current assets		
Cash and cash equivalents	1,215	11,405
Trade and other receivables	15,820	13,600
Inventories	8,180	7,230
	25,215	32,235
Non-current assets		
Available-for-sale investments	3,620	3,200
Investments in associates	5,500	5,000
Grapevines	22,000	20,000
Property, plant, and equipment - net	34,000	30,500
Intangible assets	1	1
Deferred income tax	27	24
	65,148	58,725
Assets held for sale (discontinued operations)	—	2,630
Total assets	90,363	93,590
Current liabilities		
Trade and other payables	10,700	9,450
Provision for warranties	90	80
Taxes payable	280	250
Current portion of finance lease obligation	370	340
Current portion of long-term debt	10,000	8,000
	21,440	18,120
Non-current liabilities		
Finance lease obligation	2,480	2,850
Long-term debt	20,000	30,000
Deferred income tax	3,720	3,190
Employee pension benefits	1,470	1,350
	27,670	37,390
Liabilities of discontinued operations	—	1,440
Total liabilities	49,110	56,950
Equity		
Share capital (1,000,000 issued and outstanding)	15,000	13,000
Reserves	660	240
Retained earnings	25,593	23,400
Total equity	41,253	36,640
Total liabilities and equity	90,363	93,590

Annotations (margin):

Current/non-current presentation

Current/non-current presentation

Presentation of comparative figures for prior year

Minimum categories:
- cash and equivalents
- receivables
- investments (equity method)
- financial assets not above
- inventories
- biological assets
- property, plant, and equipment
- investment property
- intangible assets
- deferred tax assets

Separate item for discontinued operations

Partition of debt into current and long-term portions

Minimum categories:
- payables
- provisions
- financial liabilities not above
- taxes payable
- deferred taxes

Separate item for discontinued operations

Minimum categories:
- contributed capital
- retained earnings
- reserves
- non-controlling interest

for each asset and liability line item that combines amounts expected to be recovered or settled (a) no more than twelve months after the reporting period and (b) more than twelve months after the reporting period.[6]

In other words, enterprises should separate current (short-term) and non-current (long-term) items, or at least provide disclosures that allow users to make that

---

[6.] Copyright © 2012 IFRS Foundation.

determination. The definition of what constitutes current assets or liabilities will be discussed below.

With regard to the exception from the current/non-current presentation, IAS 1 specifically identifies financial institutions as an example for which a presentation by liquidity could be more useful. For instance, depositors' confidence in a bank's viability significantly depends on liquidity—its ability to pay depositors when they need funds. Furthermore, banks' cash cycles differ from other enterprises in that it is difficult to distinguish their operating and financing cycles (see Exhibit 3-1 and related discussion on cash cycles).

Other than the current/non-current (or liquidity) presentation, there is a substantial degree of flexibility in the organization of the balance sheet. For example, European companies have a tradition of showing equity before liabilities, non-current items before current items, and items in increasing order of liquidity (e.g., inventory before cash); the implementation guidance that accompanies IAS 1 illustrates this approach. However, North American companies have the opposite tradition. Both approaches are equally acceptable under IFRS.

Let's now examine the three major components of the balance sheet.

a. Assets

Assets and liabilities are fundamental elements in the IFRS Conceptual Framework, so it is worthwhile to reinforce some of the discussion from Chapter 2. Recall that for an amount to be recorded as an asset, it must meet the definition of an asset as well as the criteria for recognition and measurement. The Conceptual Framework defines an asset as that which gives rise to future inflows of economic benefits, arose from past transactions, and is under the control of the enterprise. For recognition on the balance sheet, the inflow of future economic benefits must be probable, and there must be a reasonable basis of measurement.

THRESHOLD CONCEPT
CONCEPTUAL FRAMEWORK

After meeting the criteria in the definition, recognition, and measurement of an asset, the fourth step is presentation. In addition to the general concept of materiality that affects the aggregation of assets, IAS 1 paragraph 54 specifically identifies the following asset groups as having a sufficiently different nature or function to warrant separate categories:[7]

1. cash and cash equivalents
2. trade and other receivables
3. investments accounted for using the equity method
4. financial assets other than those shown above in (1), (2), and (3)
5. inventories
6. biological assets (such as sheep, cattle, trees, grapevines)
7. property, plant, and equipment
8. investment property
9. intangible assets
10. receivables for current tax
11. deferred tax assets

These are the coarsest groupings under IFRS; finer partitions should be made according to the circumstances to achieve the objective of providing useful information. For example, "property, plant, and equipment" could be split into "land," "buildings," and "equipment," especially if each category uses a different measurement base, such as historical cost or current value.

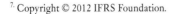

[7.] Copyright © 2012 IFRS Foundation.

Enterprises using the current/non-current classification of the balance sheet need to determine which of the above assets are current and which are not. IAS 1 provides the following guidance:

¶66   An entity shall classify an asset as current when:
(a) it expects to realize the asset, or intends to sell or consume it, in its normal operating cycle;
(b) it holds the asset primarily for the purpose of trading;
(c) it expects to realize the asset within twelve months after the reporting period; or
(d) the asset is cash or a cash equivalent (as defined in IAS 7) unless the asset is restricted from being exchanged or used to settle a liability for at least twelve months after the reporting period.
An entity shall classify all other assets as non-current.[8]

Criteria (a) and (c) together mean that an asset is current if it will be realized (sold or used) within a year or during the operating cycle, *whichever is longer*.

b. Liabilities

THRESHOLD CONCEPT
**CONCEPTUAL
FRAMEWORK**

Mirroring the definition of an asset, a liability is a present obligation arising from past transactions that entail future outflows of economic resources. Similar to an asset, if the future outflows are probable and reasonably measurable, the enterprise recognizes the liability on the balance sheet. Similar to assets, once the reporting entity has decided that an item should be reported as a liability, it needs to determine the presentation of the item—the degree of aggregation and where it should appear on the balance sheet.

IFRS requires at a minimum the following categories of liabilities (again, as long as they are material):

1. trade and other payables
2. provisions (e.g., warranty liability, pension benefits, restructuring costs)
3. financial liabilities other than the above
4. liability for taxes payable
5. liability for deferred taxes

If the reporting entity uses the current/non-current classification of the balance sheet, it would classify a liability as current using the following guidance in IAS 1:

¶69   An entity shall classify a liability as current when:
(a) it expects to settle the liability in its normal operating cycle;
(b) it holds the liability primarily for the purpose of trading;
(c) the liability is due to be settled within twelve months after the reporting date; or
(d) it does not have an unconditional right to defer settlement of the liability for at least twelve months after the reporting period....
An entity shall classify all other liabilities as non-current.[9]

Criteria (a) to (c) parallel those for current assets. Criterion (d) applies to, for example, revolving debt such as a line of credit—debt with a short nominal maturity that is rolled over from one period to another. At a particular date, the debt is non-current if the reporting entity has an agreement in place that gives it discretion to refinance the debt such that the debt need not be settled until more than a year after the balance sheet date.

---

c. Equity

In the double-entry system, equity is the residual amount after deducting total liabilities from total assets. Aside from its residual nature, equity can be classified into several distinct components that differ significantly in their nature:

1. contributed capital
2. retained earnings
3. reserves
4. non-controlling interest

Reserves can arise from a number of sources such as the revaluation of land, which will be discussed in Chapter 10. The last item relates to subsidiaries that the reporting entity does not own entirely; accounting for parents and subsidiaries is a complex topic covered in advanced financial accounting and will not be addressed further in this text except for a brief discussion in Chapter 7 on investments. While IAS 1 does not specifically require the first three items to be separated on the balance sheet, in practice companies will list them as separate line items because their natures significantly differ from each other. It should be apparent that profits retained are different from capital contributed by the owners.

3. Statement of changes in equity

One of the objectives of financial statements is to provide information on changes in financial position. The statement of changes in equity aims to achieve this objective by identifying the reasons for the change in total equity and its components from the beginning to the end of the period. Exhibit 3-14 shows an example of such a statement.

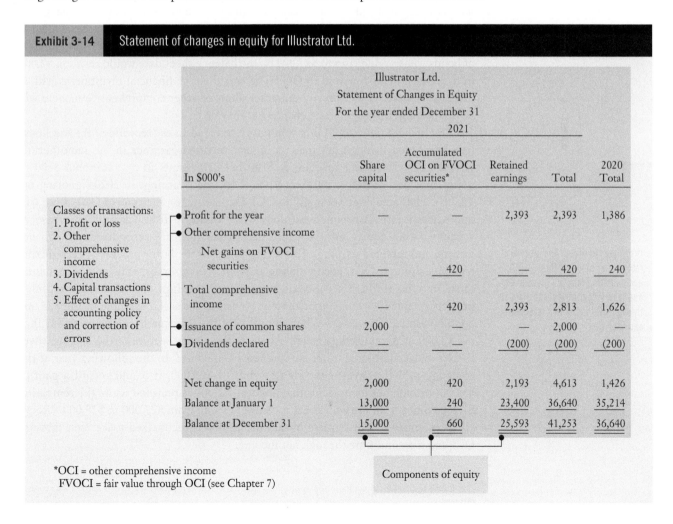

Exhibit 3-14   Statement of changes in equity for Illustrator Ltd.

Illustrator Ltd.
Statement of Changes in Equity
For the year ended December 31
2021

In $000's	Share capital	Accumulated OCI on FVOCI securities*	Retained earnings	Total	2020 Total
Profit for the year	—	—	2,393	2,393	1,386
Other comprehensive income					
Net gains on FVOCI securities	—	420	—	420	240
Total comprehensive income	—	420	2,393	2,813	1,626
Issuance of common shares	2,000	—	—	2,000	—
Dividends declared	—	—	(200)	(200)	(200)
Net change in equity	2,000	420	2,193	4,613	1,426
Balance at January 1	13,000	240	23,400	36,640	35,214
Balance at December 31	15,000	660	25,593	41,253	36,640

Classes of transactions:
1. Profit or loss
2. Other comprehensive income
3. Dividends
4. Capital transactions
5. Effect of changes in accounting policy and correction of errors

*OCI = other comprehensive income
FVOCI = fair value through OCI (see Chapter 7)

Components of equity

There are three components of equity, as shown in Exhibit 3-14 that we will consider:[10]

1. *Contributed capital*—the amount of funds provided by owners, net of any repayments to the owners or repurchases of ownership units (shares).
2. *Retained earnings*—the amount of cumulative profits (or losses) recognized through the statement of comprehensive income less dividends (and a few other adjustments discussed in Chapter 13).
3. *Reserves*—amounts accumulated from events or transactions increasing equity that are not transactions with owners and which have not flowed through profit or loss. An example of a reserve is "accumulated other comprehensive income," or AOCI.

There are potentially up to five classes of transactions that explain the change in these three components:

1. *Profit or loss*—income and expenses as recognized on the statement of comprehensive income, other than (2) below
2. *Other comprehensive income* (OCI)
3. *Dividends*
4. *Capital transactions*—transactions with owners such as share issuances or repurchases
5. *Effect of changes in accounting policy and correction of errors*

Item 2, other comprehensive income or OCI, requires a brief explanation, as it will be unfamiliar to some students. Other comprehensive income is a relatively recent development, being first included in IFRS in 2008. Currently, there are only a few items that qualify as OCI. In general, these items reflect changes in value that have not yet been "realized" via a transaction. An example of OCI arises from changes in the value of investments prior to the date of sale when the investments are classified as "fair value through other comprehensive income" (FVOCI). An investment in $25,000 of bonds whose value rises to $27,000 by the balance sheet date would result in $2,000 in unrealized gains reported in OCI. The treatment of financial investments will be explored in detail in Chapter 7, and other items of other comprehensive income will be discussed in the appropriate chapters as they arise.

One issue unique to OCI is commonly referred to as "recycling." As you know, items recorded through net income impact retained earnings in the same period. For example, recording revenue of $100 in 2020 results in an additional $100 of net income and therefore an extra $100 of retained earnings in 2020 (ignoring tax effects). The same does not apply to OCI. Depending on the type of OCI, some will immediately impact retained earnings while others will be "parked" in a reserve account within equity until a future date when they are recognized through net income and retained earnings. **Recycling** refers to the latter process of recognizing amounts through OCI, accumulating that OCI in reserves, and later recognizing those amounts through net income and retained earnings. OCI that is not recycled impacts retained earnings immediately. Consider again the example of the $25,000 bond investment just given. When the value of the investment increased to $27,000, the $2,000 of unrealized gains are shown in the equity section of the balance sheet as part of "accumulated other comprehensive income." In the following year, if the company sold the investment for proceeds of $28,000, it would record a gain of $3,000 through net income. Of that amount, $2,000 is recycled while the remaining $1,000 comes from the additional increase in value from $27,000 to $28,000. "Recycling" is somewhat descriptive in that the $2,000 is recognized twice: first through OCI and a second time through net income.

recycling (of OCI) The process of recognizing amounts through OCI, accumulating that OCI in reserves, and later recognizing those amounts through net income and retained earnings.

[10.] A fourth component of equity is non-controlling interest, which, as mentioned above, is beyond the scope of this text.

Exhibit 3-15 summarizes the typical relationship between the five classes of transactions and the three components of equity, along with the two presentation options.

Exhibit 3-15	Content and alternative presentations of the statement of changes in equity
Class of transaction	**Component of equity affected**
1. Profit or loss (also called net income)	Retained earnings
2. Other comprehensive income	Accumulated other comprehensive income (a component of reserves)
Total comprehensive income (1 + 2)	
3. Dividends*	Retained earnings
4. Capital transactions (e.g., share issuance or repurchase)	Contributed capital and sometimes retained earnings
5. Effect of changes in accounting policy and correction of errors	Contributed capital or retained earnings

*Dividends may be disclosed outside the statement of changes in equity.

It is important to note that there can be several types of contributed capital, such as when a company has more than one class of shares. Also, each type of OCI needs to be tracked as a separate component of reserves. Due to there being five different classes of transactions and multiple components of equity, it is usually most convenient to use a matrix-style presentation as illustrated in Exhibit 3-14.

 CHECKPOINT **CP3-8**

When is other comprehensive income recycled? What is the effect of recycling on net income?

4. Statement of comprehensive income

The statement of changes in equity specifically separates total comprehensive income from other changes in equity (items 1 and 2 in Exhibit 3-15). Comprehensive income for the period is a measure of the return on capital and therefore the statement of comprehensive income provides a measure of performance, which is one of the objectives of the financial statements in the IFRS Framework. Useful measures of performance should distinguish results due to operating activities from results due to financing activities because the effect of financial leverage significantly affects performance and risk. In addition, tax costs are only partially under the control of management, so such costs should be separately identified. Likewise, the reporting entity has limited influence over decisions at associated companies (i.e., companies that they do not control), so income or loss from such associates should be a separate item as well. As noted previously, specific items considered to be OCI need to be separated. For these reasons, IAS 1 requires reporting, at a minimum, items relating to each of these five components, plus two summary measures of performance: a subtotal for profit or loss and total comprehensive income.

THRESHOLD CONCEPT
CONCEPTUAL FRAMEWORK

Enterprises have the option to present the seven items in Exhibit 3-16 in one of two ways. The first way is to use a single statement of comprehensive income. The second is to break up the information into two parts: an income statement that includes items 1 to 5, and a statement of comprehensive income that includes items 5 to 7. The title "statement of comprehensive income" can thus be a little confusing since it can refer to the single statement comprising items 1 through 7 or the separate statement containing only items 5 to 7.

Exhibit 3-16	Minimal line items on the statement of comprehensive income per IAS 1 paragraph 82

1. Revenue
   Operating expenses
2. Finance costs
3. Share of profit or loss of associates
4. Tax expense
5. Profit or loss (net income)
6. Other comprehensive income
7. Total comprehensive income

One line item that is notably absent from the list in Exhibit 3-16 is "extraordinary items." Permitted under Canadian standards prior to 2011, IFRS specifically prohibits the classification of income or expenses as extraordinary. ASPE also follows this prohibition.

IAS 1 does not specifically require the item "operating expenses" as shown in Exhibit 3-16. However, the requirement to show profit or loss implies an amount for operating expenses. Furthermore, IAS 1 paragraph 99 recommends including on the income statement an analysis of expenses, although this information may be presented in the notes. The analysis of expenses should classify expenses according to their nature or function.

nature (of an expense)   The source of the expense (depreciation from equipment, costs of employee labour, cost of raw materials, or other means of production); contrast with **function**.

- **Nature** relates to the *source* of the expense (depreciation from equipment, labour costs from employees, cost of raw materials, or other means of production).
- **Function** refers to the *use* to which the expense has been put (cost of sales, distribution, administration, or other activities).

function (of an expense)   The use to which the expense has been put (e.g., cost of sales, distribution, administration, or other activities); contrast with **nature**.

Entities choosing the latter option must also provide information on the nature of expenses, disclosing, at a minimum, employee benefits expense, depreciation, and amortization. In other words, *information on the nature of expenses is mandatory*, but information about their function is optional.

Exhibit 3-17 shows an example of a statement of comprehensive income with expenses classified by function. The disclosure by the nature of expenses appears as separate disclosure at the bottom of the exhibit.

This exhibit also illustrates a multi-step financial statement, because Illustrator's statement of comprehensive income includes subtotals such as gross margin and operating profit. These subtotals are optional. Enterprises can choose to use a single-step statement that omits these subtotals; the only required totals are for net income and comprehensive income.

For many reporting entities, the profit for the entire enterprise may not be meaningful to an owner who has 500 shares out of a total of 50 million shares. To help owners gauge the performance of the enterprise, IFRS requires the disclosure of earnings per share (EPS), either on the face of the statement of comprehensive income or in the notes. Chapter 15 explores the details of EPS calculations and the different versions of this measure (basic EPS, diluted EPS). These EPS amounts are displayed in Exhibit 3-17.

5. Statement of cash flows

cash equivalents   Short-term, highly liquid investments that are readily convertible to known amounts of cash and which are subject to an insignificant risk of changes in value.

Similar to the statement of changes in equity, the statement of cash flows helps the reader understand the change in financial position of the enterprise in terms of the most liquid assets available: cash and cash equivalents. **Cash equivalents** are short-term, highly liquid investments that are readily convertible to known amounts of cash

Exhibit 3-17 Statement of comprehensive income for Illustrator Ltd.

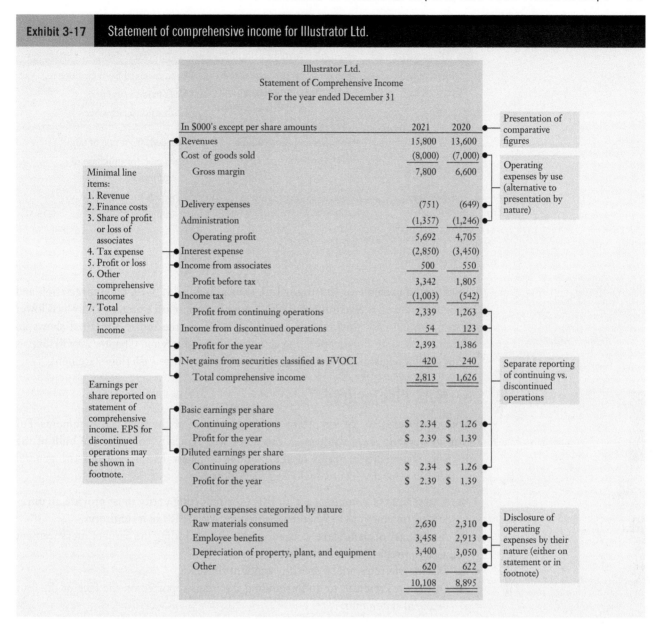

Illustrator Ltd.
Statement of Comprehensive Income
For the year ended December 31

Presentation of comparative figures

In $000's except per share amounts	2021	2020
Revenues	15,800	13,600
Cost of goods sold	(8,000)	(7,000)
Gross margin	7,800	6,600
Delivery expenses	(751)	(649)
Administration	(1,357)	(1,246)
Operating profit	5,692	4,705
Interest expense	(2,850)	(3,450)
Income from associates	500	550
Profit before tax	3,342	1,805
Income tax	(1,003)	(542)
Profit from continuing operations	2,339	1,263
Income from discontinued operations	54	123
Profit for the year	2,393	1,386
Net gains from securities classified as FVOCI	420	240
Total comprehensive income	2,813	1,626
Basic earnings per share		
Continuing operations	$ 2.34	$ 1.26
Profit for the year	$ 2.39	$ 1.39
Diluted earnings per share		
Continuing operations	$ 2.34	$ 1.26
Profit for the year	$ 2.39	$ 1.39
Operating expenses categorized by nature		
Raw materials consumed	2,630	2,310
Employee benefits	3,458	2,913
Depreciation of property, plant, and equipment	3,400	3,050
Other	620	622
	10,108	8,895

Minimal line items:
1. Revenue
2. Finance costs
3. Share of profit or loss of associates
4. Tax expense
5. Profit or loss
6. Other comprehensive income
7. Total comprehensive income

Earnings per share reported on statement of comprehensive income. EPS for discontinued operations may be shown in footnote.

Operating expenses by use (alternative to presentation by nature)

Separate reporting of continuing vs. discontinued operations

Disclosure of operating expenses by their nature (either on statement or in footnote)

and that are subject to an insignificant risk of changes in value. Different from equity, however, is the fact that equity has a number of distinct components (share capital, reserves, retained earnings), for which a matrix-style presentation is effective. Cash is a single category, so a linear format similar to the income statement suffices.

The cash flow statement has three sections corresponding to the three cash cycles discussed at the beginning of this chapter: operating, investing, and financing activities. The amounts in the three categories combined must fully explain the net change in cash from the beginning to the end of the year. Appendix A, at the end of this text (Volume 1) and Chapter 20, will discuss in detail what types of items go into which of the three categories of the cash flow statement. At this point, it suffices to make generalizations based on the nature of the three cash flow cycles, which are shown in Exhibit 3-18.

Exhibit 3-18 lists examples of cash flows in terms of the **direct method**, which shows the amounts attributable to each activity. Doing so satisfies the requirements in IAS 7, Statement of Cash Flows. For operating activities, IAS 7 allows an alternative presentation, called the **indirect method**. This method uses the profit or loss from the income statement as a starting point and then itemizes adjustments to arrive at operating cash

direct method (cash flow statement) A method of presenting the cash flow statement that shows the amounts attributable to each activity, such as sales to customers; contrast with **indirect method**.

indirect method (cash flow statement) A method of presenting the operating section of the cash flow statement that uses the profit or loss from the income statement as a starting point and then itemizes adjustments to arrive at the net amount of operating cash flows; contrast with **direct method**.

Exhibit 3-18	Categories of cash flows	
Cash flow from:	**General nature of cash flows**	**Examples**
Operating activities	Changes in current assets and liabilities resulting from day-to-day operations of the enterprise	Cash received from customers Cash paid to suppliers Cash paid to employees
Investing activities	Purchases and sales of non-current assets	Proceeds from sale of land Cash paid for purchase of equipment
Financing activities	Issuances and redemptions of the reporting entity's debt and equity	Proceeds from issuance of common shares Repayment of long-term debt

flows. In the example of Illustrator Ltd. shown in Exhibit 3-19, the depreciation and amortization total is $3.4 million. This amount is a non-cash expense, so profit is lower than operating cash flow by this amount. Therefore, the indirect method shows an addition of $3.4 million in operating activities. Appendix A and Chapter 20 will discuss other similar adjustments and the preparation of the entire cash flow statement.

6. Note disclosures

Note disclosures are an important and integral part of the financial statements. For even moderately sized companies, the notes will typically comprise the bulk of the financial statements in terms of the number of pages. IAS 1 provides the general requirements for disclosure, including the following:

- A statement of compliance with IFRS—a reporting entity must provide an unreserved statement as to whether it complies with IFRS in its entirety
- A summary of significant accounting policies, including the bases of measurement used in preparing the financial statements
- Disclosures required by specific standards in IFRS
- Disclosures relevant to understanding the items reported on the face of the four financial statements

IAS 1 also requires cross-referencing of items on the face of the financial statements and the related note disclosures. While this is an obvious and sensible requirement to help readers locate relevant information, it is not required in US standards.

7. Discontinued operations and other non-current assets held for sale

THRESHOLD CONCEPT
CONCEPTUAL FRAMEWORK

As discussed in Chapter 2, one of the important assumptions in accrual accounting in the IFRS Framework is that the reporting entity is a going concern—meaning that the entity will continue to operate, realizing the benefits of assets and discharging liabilities in the ordinary course of business. From time to time, companies will decide to discontinue some part of their operations. For example, a national retail chain could decide to sell its operations in the Atlantic provinces to focus more on other regions, or an integrated oil producer could decide to sell its downstream consumer products division to focus attention on the company's upstream extraction and refining activities. Once management has made the decision to dispose of these groups of assets and related liabilities, they no longer satisfy the assumption of going concern. Consequently, IFRS requires separate reporting for discontinued operations and other non-current assets held for sale. (We specify "non-current" to distinguish from current assets held

Exhibit 3-19   Cash flow statement for Illustrator Ltd.

Illustrator Ltd.
Cash Flow Statement
For the year ended December 31

In $000's	2021	2020	
			Presentation of comparative figures
Cash flows from operating activities			
Profit before tax from continuing operations	3,342	1,805	Separate reporting of discontinued operations
Profit before tax from discontinued operations	77	176	
Profit before tax	3,419	1,981	
Non-cash items			
Depreciation of property, plant, and equipment	3,400	3,050	
Income from associates	(500)	(550)	
Interest expense	2,850	3,450	Indirect method reconciles profit to operating cash flow
Increase in liability for employee pension benefits	120	140	
Working capital adjustments			
(Increase) decrease in trade and other receivables	(2,220)	(1,050)	
(Increase) decrease in inventories	(950)	(682)	
Increase (decrease) in trade and other payables	1,250	470	
Increase (decrease) in warranty provision	10	—	
Income tax paid	(469)	(244)	
Net cash from (used in) operating activities	6,910	6,565	
Cash flows from investing activities			
Proceeds from net assets held for sale	1,190	—	
Purchase of property, plant, and equipment	(6,900)	—	
Investment in grapevines	(2,000)	(1,500)	
Net cash from (used in) investing activities	(7,710)	(1,500)	
Cash flows from financing activities			
Payment of finance lease obligation	(340)	(320)	
Repayment of long-term debt	(8,000)	(6,000)	
Proceeds from issuance of common shares	2,000	—	Interest and dividends paid may be shown in operating activities instead
Interest paid	(2,850)	(3,450)	
Dividends paid	(200)	(200)	
Net cash from (used in) financing activities	(9,390)	(9,970)	
Net increase (decrease) in cash and cash equivalents	(10,190)	(4,905)	Net cash flow reconciles opening and closing cash balances
Cash and cash equivalents, January 1	11,405	16,310	
Cash and cash equivalents, December 31	1,215	11,405	

Three types of activities:
1. Operating
2. Investing
3. Financing

for sale, such as inventories.) We will look at this issue in more detail in Chapter 10. At this point, it suffices to understand that the financial statements should segregate discontinued operations using separate line items and disclosures. For example, "profit from discontinued operations" would be a separate line item on the income statement. The financial statements for Illustrator Ltd. (Exhibit 3-13, Exhibit 3-14, Exhibit 3-17, and Exhibit 3-19) show how we would present discontinued operations.

8. Comparative figures

As discussed in Chapter 2, comparability is an important qualitative characteristic that enhances the usefulness of financial information. To help users discern trends for a particular company, IAS 1 requires the presentation of comparative information for the relevant prior period. For comparisons to be meaningful, items need to be measured and reported on the same basis over time (i.e., consistently). For instance,

THRESHOLD CONCEPT
CONCEPTUAL FRAMEWORK

a change may involve something as simple as splitting what was one line item in the prior year into two items for the current year because each of the components has become material. When companies make such changes, they need to ensure that they also present comparative figures for past periods on the same basis.

9. Putting it all together: An illustrative example

In this section, we first had an overview of the financial statements as a whole, then we looked at each component separately. Now it is time to bring it all together again. Exhibit 3-20 illustrates the financial statements of Illustrator Ltd. in a condensed fashion, showing the articulation of the items and amounts in the four financial statements.

10. A practical illustration: Canadian Tire Corporation

So far in this section, we have used a constructed example to show the basic application of the general reporting requirements for financial statements. To see a real-life example, we now turn to the 2016 financial statements for Canadian Tire Corporation, which begin on page 56 of the company's Report to Shareholders. These financial statements have been reproduced in Appendix D at the end of this text. The following are some observations about these financial statements:

1. Note that the financial statements begin with a declaration of management's responsibility for the financial statements. While companies hire auditors to verify their books and records, it is not the responsibility of auditors to prepare the financial statements. Rather, financial statement preparation is management's responsibility. (The auditor's report issued by Deloitte LLP has been omitted from Appendix D due to copyright limitations.)

2. The second thing to note about these financial statements is the considerable length of the report. Aside from the first page containing the declaration of management's responsibilities, there are a total of 46 pages, of which only the first five are tabular financial statements and the remaining 41 pages are note disclosures. This length underscores the point made previously that disclosures can be very extensive.

3. The company has chosen the two-statement presentation of comprehensive income: an income statement and a separate statement of comprehensive income. The other three financial statements are the balance sheet (statement of financial position), the statement of cash flow, and the statement of changes in equity. All are denoted as "consolidated" because these financial statements present information not only for the legal entity of Canadian Tire Corporation, Limited, but also for all of the subsidiaries that are owned by the company.

4. Exhibit 3-21 shows condensed versions of the five financial statements shown on pages D3 to D7. This summary makes clear the articulation among the financial statements. Due to the complex corporate structure of Canadian Tire, which involves many parent–subsidiary relationships, there are several items relating to "non-controlling interests" about which you do not need to be concerned.

5. Now, look more carefully at each of the five financial statements. The first one is the income statement, displayed in Exhibit 3-22. Following IFRS requirements, Canadian Tire has separately presented line items for expenses by function (not by nature). Furthermore, this income statement separately shows line items for each of the following: interest expense, tax expense, and income from discontinued operations. The bottom of the income statement shows earnings per share.

6. Exhibit 3-23 shows the statement of comprehensive income. The statement is relatively short—as noted previously, there are only a few possible items of OCI. In the case of Canadian Tire, there are just four items of OCI.

Exhibit 3-20   Condensed financial statements for Illustrator Ltd. showing interrelationships

Cash Flow Statement
For the year ended December 31

In $000's	2021	2020
Net cash from operating activities	6,833	6,566
Net cash from investing activities	(7,633)	(1,500)
Net cash from financing activities	(9,390)	(9,970)
Net increase (decrease) in cash	(10,190)	(4,905)
Cash and cash equivalents, Jan. 1	11,405	16,310
Cash and cash equivalents, Dec. 31	1,215	11,405

Statement of Comprehensive Income
For the year ended December 31

In $000's	2021	2020
Revenues	15,800	13,600
Cost of goods sold	(8,000)	(7,000)
Delivery expenses	(751)	(649)
Administration	(1,357)	(1,246)
Interest expense	(2,850)	(3,450)
Income from associates	500	550
Income tax	(1,003)	(542)
Income from discontinued operations	54	123
Profit for the year	2,393	1,386
Other comprehensive income	420	240
Total comprehensive income	2,813	1,626

Balance Sheet
As at December 31

In $000's	2021	2020
Current assets		
Cash and cash equivalents	1,215	11,405
Trade and other receivables	15,820	13,600
Inventories	8,180	7,230
	25,215	32,235
Non-current assets	65,148	58,725
Assets held for sale	–	2,630
Total assets	90,363	93,590
Current liabilities	21,440	18,120
Non-current liabilities	27,670	37,390
Liabilities of disc. operations	–	1,440
Total liabilities	49,110	56,950
Equity		
Share capital	15,000	13,000
Reserves	660	240
Retained earnings	25,593	23,400
Total equity	41,253	36,640
Total liabilities and equity	90,363	93,590

Statement of Changes in Equity
For the year ended December 31
2021

In $000's	Share capital	Accum. OCI	Retained earnings	Total	2020 Total
Profit for the year	–		2,393	2,393	1,386
Other comprehensive income					
Net gains on FVOCI securities	–	420	–	420	240
Total comprehensive income	–	420	2,393	2,813	1,626
Issuance of com. shares	2,000	–	–	2,000	–
Dividends declared	–	–	(200)	(200)	(200)
Net change in equity	2,000	420	2,193	4,613	1,426
Balance at January 1	13,000	240	23,400	36,640	35,214
Balance at December 31	15,000	660	25,593	41,253	36,640

Notes to the financial statements
1. Statement of compliance:
   The financial statements of Illustrator Ltd. have been prepared in accordance with International Financial Reporting Standards (IFRS).
2. Significant accounting policies, estimates, assumptions, and judgments.
3. Specific disclosures cross-referenced to the four financial statements.

Exhibit 3-21   Condensed financial statements for Canadian Tire Corporation showing interrelationships

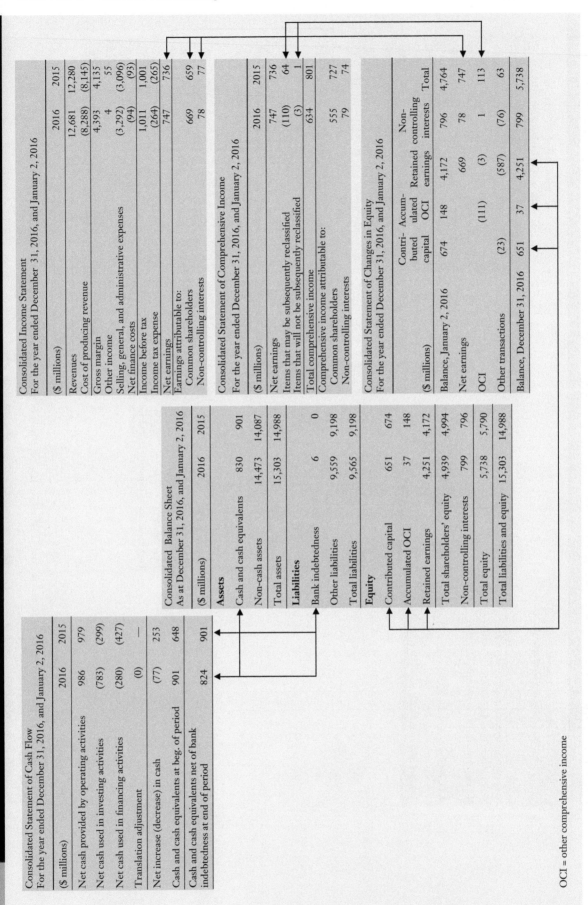

Consolidated Statement of Cash Flow
For the year ended December 31, 2016, and January 2, 2016

($ millions)	2016	2015
Net cash provided by operating activities	986	979
Net cash used in investing activities	(783)	(299)
Net cash used in financing activities	(280)	(427)
Translation adjustment	(0)	—
Net increase (decrease) in cash	(77)	253
Cash and cash equivalents at beg. of period	901	648
Cash and cash equivalents net of bank indebtedness at end of period	824	901

Consolidated Balance Sheet
As at December 31, 2016, and January 2, 2016

($ millions)	2016	2015
Assets		
Cash and cash equivalents	830	901
Non-cash assets	14,473	14,087
Total assets	15,303	14,988
Liabilities		
Bank indebtedness	6	0
Other liabilities	9,559	9,198
Total liabilities	9,565	9,198
Equity		
Contributed capital	651	674
Accumulated OCI	37	148
Retained earnings	4,251	4,172
Total shareholders' equity	4,939	4,994
Non-controlling interests	799	796
Total equity	5,738	5,790
Total liabilities and equity	15,303	14,988

Consolidated Income Statement
For the year ended December 31, 2016, and January 2, 2016

($ millions)	2016	2015
Revenues	12,681	12,280
Cost of producing revenue	(8,288)	(8,145)
Gross margin	4,393	4,135
Other income	4	55
Selling, general, and administrative expenses	(3,292)	(3,096)
Net finance costs	(94)	(93)
Income before tax	1,011	1,001
Income tax expense	(264)	(265)
Net earnings	747	736
Earnings attributable to:		
Common shareholders	669	659
Non-controlling interests	78	77

Consolidated Statement of Comprehensive Income
For the year ended December 31, 2016, and January 2, 2016

($ millions)	2016	2015
Net earnings	747	736
Items that may be subsequently reclassified	(110)	64
Items that will not be subsequently reclassified	(3)	1
Total comprehensive income	634	801
Comprehensive income attributable to:		
Common shareholders	555	727
Non-controlling interests	79	74

Consolidated Statement of Changes in Equity
For the year ended December 31, 2016, and January 2, 2016

($ millions)	Contributed capital	Accumulated OCI	Retained earnings	Non-controlling interests	Total
Balance, January 2, 2016	674	148	4,172	796	4,764
Net earnings			669	78	747
OCI		(111)	(3)	1	113
Other transactions	(23)		(587)	(76)	63
Balance, December 31, 2016	651	37	4,251	799	5,738

OCI = other comprehensive income

Source: From Canadian Tire Corporation 2016 Report to Shareholders. Copyright ©2016 by Canadian Tire Corporation, Limited. Reprinted by permission.

Exhibit 3-22   Income statement for Canadian Tire

Consolidated Statements of Income

For the years ended
(C$ in millions, except per share amounts)

	December 31, 2016	January 2, 2016	
Revenue (Note 27)	$ 12,681.0	$ 12,279.6	Expenses itemized by function of expenses. Required disclosure of expenses by nature provided in notes.
Cost of producing revenue (Note 28)	8,288.5	8,144.3	
Gross margin	4,392.5	4,135.3	
Other (income)	(4.3)	(54.9)	
Selling, general, and administrative expenses (Note 29)	3,291.9	3,096.1	
Net finance costs (Note 30)	93.9	92.8	
Income before income taxes	1,011.0	1,001.3	Interest expense separately identified.
Income taxes (Note 15)	263.5	265.4	
Net income	$ 747.5	$ 735.9	Tax expense separately identified.
Net income attributable to:			
Shareholders of Canadian Tire	$ 669.1	$ 659.4	
Non-controlling interests (Note 14)	78.4	76.5	
	$ 747.5	$ 735.9	
Basic EPS	$ 9.25	$ 8.66	
Diluted EPS	$ 9.22	$ 8.61	Earnings per share reported on income statement.
Weighted average number of Common and Class A Non-Voting Shares outstanding:			
Basic	72,360,303	76,151,321	
Diluted	72,555,732	76,581,602	

Source: From Canadian Tire Corporation 2016 Report to Shareholders. Copyright ©2016 by Canadian Tire Corporation, Limited. Reprinted by permission.

Exhibit 3-23   Statement of comprehensive income for Canadian Tire

Consolidated Statements of Comprehensive Income

For the years ended
(C$ in millions)

	December 31, 2016	January 2, 2016	
Net income	$ 747.5	$ 735.9	Begin with net income from the income statement.
Other comprehensive (loss) income, net of taxes			
Items that may be reclassified subsequently to net income:			
Cash flow hedges and available-for-sale financial assets:			
(Losses) gains	(40.5)	275.1	
Reclassification of gains to non-financial assets	(67.9)	(207.4)	
Reclassification of gains to income	(1.7)	(3.0)	Each source of other comprehensive income (OCI) identified.
Item that will not be reclassified subsequently to net income:			
Actuarial (losses) gains	(3.0)	0.8	
Other comprehensive (loss) income	(113.1)	65.5	
Other comprehensive (loss) income attributable to:			
Shareholders of Canadian Tire	$ (114.3)	$ 68.0	
Non-controlling interests	1.2	(2.5)	
	$ (113.1)	$ 65.5	
Comprehensive income	$ 634.4	$ 801.4	
Comprehensive income attributable to:			
Shareholders of Canadian Tire	$ 554.8	$ 727.4	
Non-controlling interests	79.6	74.0	
	$ 634.4	$ 801.4	

Source: From Canadian Tire Corporation 2016 Report to Shareholders. Copyright ©2016 by Canadian Tire Corporation, Limited. Reprinted by permission.

7. The statement of financial position (balance sheet) is in Exhibit 3-24. We can see that Canadian Tire is a large company, with total assets of over $15 billion. Consistent with IFRS requirements, the statement separates current from non-current assets, and likewise for liabilities. Equity is separated into four components, as required by IFRS. "Share capital" and "Contributed surplus" together comprise the component of contributed capital.

Exhibit 3-24	Balance sheet for Canadian Tire

Consolidated Balance Sheets

As at (C$ in millions)	December 31, 2016	January 2, 2016	
ASSETS			
Cash and cash equivalents (Note 7)	$ 829.7	$ 900.6	
Short-term investments	117.2	96.1	
Trade and other receivables (Note 8)	690.8	915.0	
Loans receivable (Note 9)	5,138.4	4,875.5	
Merchandise inventories	1,710.7	1,764.5	
Income taxes recoverable	42.5	42.2	
Prepaid expenses and deposits	103.8	96.1	
Assets classified as held for sale	4.6	2.3	
Total current assets	8,637.7	8,692.3	
Long-term receivables and other assets (Note 10)	763.7	731.2	
Long-term investments	175.2	153.4	Current assets separated from non-current assets.
Goodwill and intangible assets (Note 11)	1,280.3	1,246.8	
Investment property (Note 12)	266.4	137.8	
Property and equipment (Note 13)	4,097.2	3,978.2	
Deferred income taxes (Note 15)	82.3	48.1	
Total assets	$ 15,302.8	$ 14,987.8	
LIABILITIES			
Bank indebtedness (Note 7)	$ 5.9	$ —	
Deposits (Note 16)	950.7	880.7	
Trade and other payables (Note 17)	1,856.9	1,957.1	
Provisions (Note 18)	253.2	216.1	
Short-term borrowings (Note 20)	199.4	88.6	
Loans payable (Note 21)	700.3	655.5	
Income taxes payable	61.1	61.5	Current portion of debt separated from long-term portion
Current portion of long-term debt (Note 22)	653.4	24.3	
Total current liabilities	4,680.9	3,883.8	
Long-term provisions (Note 18)	45.9	45.7	
Long-term debt (Note 22)	2,667.1	2,971.4	Current liabilities separated from non-current liabilities.
Long-term deposits (Note 16)	1,230.8	1,372.2	
Deferred income taxes (Note 15)	104.2	111.1	
Other long-term liabilities (Note 23)	836.6	813.9	
Total liabilities	9,565.5	9,198.1	
EQUITY			
Share capital (Note 25)	648.1	671.2	
Contributed surplus	2.9	2.9	Equity separated into the four required categories (share capital and contributed surplus together equals contributed capital).
Accumulated other comprehensive income	36.7	148.1	
Retained earnings	4,250.9	4,172.0	
Equity attributable to shareholders of Canadian Tire	4,938.6	4,994.2	
Non-controlling interests (Note 14)	798.7	795.5	
Total equity	5,737.3	5,789.7	
Total liabilities and equity	$ 15,302.8	$ 14,987.8	

The related notes form an integral part of these consolidated financial statements.

Maureen J. Sabia
Maureen J. Sabia
Director

Diana L. Chant
Diana L. Chant
Director

Source: From Canadian Tire Corporation 2016 Report to Shareholders. Copyright ©2016 by Canadian Tire Corporation, Limited. Reprinted by permission.

8. Next, the cash flow statement in Exhibit 3-25 explains the change in the cash balance from $900.6 million at the beginning of 2016 to $823.8 million at the end of the year. The cash flows appear in three categories matching the three cash cycles: operating, investing, and financing. Canadian Tire chose the indirect method to present cash flows from operating activities; this method begins with net income and adjusts for deviations of accrual numbers from cash flows.

9. The fifth and final financial statement is the statement of changes in equity, shown in Exhibit 3-26. This financial statement is relatively complex compared to the other four. The presentation is in a matrix format, with a separate matrix for 2016

Exhibit 3-25	Statement of cash flow for Canadian Tire

Consolidated Statements of Cash Flows

For the years ended (C$ in millions)	December 31, 2016	January 2, 2016	
Cash (used for) generated from:			
Operating activities			
Net income	$ 747.5	$ 735.9	
Adjustments for:			
Depreciation on property and equipment and investment property (Note 28 and 29)	330.8	312.8	
Income tax expense	263.5	265.4	Indirect method
Net finance costs (Note 30)	93.9	92.8	reconciles net
Amortization of intangible assets (Note 29)	126.1	111.9	income to operating
Changes in fair value of derivative instruments	(15.8)	6.9	cash flow.
Gain on disposal of property and equipment, investment property, assets held for sale, intangible assets, and lease terminations	(14.9)	(43.9)	
Interest paid	(114.0)	(101.4)	Cash flows for
Interest received	6.5	8.4	interest and taxes
Income taxes paid	(262.8)	(284.0)	separately identified.
Other	5.6	14.6	
Total adjustments, except as noted below	1,166.4	1,119.4	
Change in operating working capital and other (Note 31)	126.1	(115.3)	
Change in loans receivable	(306.1)	(25.2)	
Cash generated from operating activities	986.4	978.9	
Investing activities			
Additions to property and equipment and investment property	(617.3)	(515.9)	
Additions to intangible assets	(163.5)	(94.7)	
Total additions	(780.8)	(610.6)	
Acquisition of short-term investments	(422.3)	(177.4)	
Proceeds from the maturity and disposition of short-term investments	441.4	426.6	
Acquisition of long-term investments	(61.4)	(35.0)	
Proceeds on disposition of property and equipment, investment property, and assets held for sale	32.8	101.5	
Other	7.5	(4.1)	
Cash (used for) investing activities	(782.8)	(299.0)	
Financing activities			
Dividends paid	(157.5)	(152.2)	
Distributions paid to non-controlling interests	(76.4)	(53.8)	
Total dividends and distributions paid	(233.9)	(206.0)	
Net issuance (repayment) of short-term borrowings	110.7	(111.2)	
Issuance of loans payable	288.3	270.1	
Repayment of loans payable	(243.5)	(219.0)	
Issuance of long-term debt (Note 22)	350.0	856.1	
Repayment of long-term debt and finance lease liabilities (Note 22)	(24.5)	(588.5)	
Payment of transaction costs related to long-term debt	(3.2)	(6.5)	
Repurchase of share capital (Note 25)	(449.4)	(434.6)	
Change in deposits	(74.9)	12.5	
Cash (used for) financing activities	(280.4)	(427.1)	
Cash (used) generated in the period	(76.8)	252.8	Net cash flow
Cash and cash equivalents, net of bank indebtedness, beginning of period	900.6	647.8	reconciles opening and closing cash
Cash and cash equivalents, net of bank indebtedness, end of period (Note 7)	$ 823.8	$ 900.6	balances.

Source: From Canadian Tire Corporation 2016 Report to Shareholders. Copyright ©2016 by Canadian Tire Corporation, Limited. Reprinted by permission.

Exhibit 3-26   Statement of changes in equity for Canadian Tire

Consolidated Statements of Changes in Equity

(C$ in millions)	Share capital	Contributed surplus	Total accumulated other comprehensive income	Retained earnings	Equity attributable to shareholders of Canadian Tire	Equity attributable to non-controlling interests	Total equity
Balance at January 2, 2016	$ 671.2	$ 2.9	$ 148.1	$ 4,172.0	$ 4,994.2	$ 795.5	$ 5,789.7
Net Income	—	—	—	669.1	669.1	78.4	747.5
Other comprehensive (loss) income	—	—	(111.4)	(2.9)	(114.3)	1.2	(113.1)
Total comprehensive (loss) income	—	—	(111.4)	666.2	554.8	79.6	634.4
Contributions and distributions to shareholders of Canadian Tire							
Issuance of Class A Non-Voting Shares (Note 25)	9.3	—	—	—	9.3	—	9.3
Repurchase of Class A Non-Voting Shares (Note 25)	(449.4)	—	—	—	(449.4)	—	(449.4)
Excess of purchase price over average cost (Note 25)	417.0	—	—	(417.0)	—	—	—
Dividends	—	—	—	(170.3)	(170.3)	—	(170.3)
Contributions and distributions to non-controlling interests							
Issuance of trust units to non-controlling interests, net of transaction costs	—	—	—	—	—	2.0	2.0
Distributions and dividends to non-controlling interests	—	—	—	—	—	(78.4)	(78.4)
Total contributions and distributions	(23.1)	—	—	(587.3)	(610.4)	(76.4)	(686.8)
Balance at December 31, 2016	$ 648.1	$ 2.9	$ 36.7	$4,250.9	$ 4,938.6	$ 798.7	$ 5,737.3
Balance at January 3, 2015	$ 695.5	$ 2.9	$ 82.0	$ 4,075.1	$ 4,855.5	$ 775.3	$ 5,630.8
Net income	—	—	—	659.4	659.4	—	659.4
Other comprehensive income (loss)	—	—	66.1	1.9	68.0	(2.5)	65.5
Total comprehensive income	—	—	66.1	661.3	727.4	74.0	801.4
Contributions and distributions to shareholders of Canadian Tire							
Issuance of Class A Non-Voting Shares (Note 25)	8.3	—	—	—	8.3	—	8.3
Repurchase of Class A Non-Voting Shares (Note 25)	(434.6)	—	—	—	(434.6)	—	(434.6)
Excess of purchase price over average cost (Note 25)	402.0	—	—	(402.0)	—	—	—
Dividends	—	—	—	(162.4)	(162.4)	—	(162.4)
Contributions and distributions to non-controlling interests							
Issuance of trust units to non-controlling interests, net of transaction costs	—	—	—	—	—	1.8	1.8
Distributions and dividends to non-controlling interests	—	—	—	—	—	(55.6)	(55.6)
Total contributions and distributions	(24.3)	—	—	(564.4)	(588.7)	(53.8)	(642.5)
Balance at January 2, 2016	$ 671.2	$ 2.9	$ 148.1	$ 4,172.0	$ 4,994.2	$ 795.5	$ 5,789.7

The four components of equity are contributed capital (share capital, + contributed surplus), AOCI (a reserve), retained earnings, and non-controlling interest. Other columns shown are sub-components.

Changes in equity identified by type of transaction:
1. Profit or loss
2. OCI
3. Dividends
4. Capital transactions
5. Effect of retrospective changes in accounting

There are two types of OCI: those that will be recycled ("may be classified subsequently to net income") and those that will not be recycled.

Comparative information for prior year.

Source: From Canadian Tire Corporation 2016 Report to Shareholders. Copyright ©2016 by Canadian Tire Corporation, Limited. Reprinted by permission.

and the comparative year 2015. The columns represent the four components of equity, with additional columns showing sub-components of these four. The rows contain the different types of transactions that caused the changes in the different components of equity.

10. Following the five financial statements are 41 pages of note disclosure. (Refer to pages D8 to D48 in Appendix D.) Note 3 is particularly long, taking up almost nine pages. However, this is important information, because Note 3 summarizes the significant accounting policies used in the preparation of the financial statements. Note 2 includes among other items "Judgments and estimates" management has made, underscoring the subjectivity inherent in the accounting process. The remainder of the notes provides additional details relating to certain items appearing in the five financial statements discussed above, ranging from the company's operations in different geographic areas to the computation of earnings per share. Cross-referencing of the line items in the five financial statements with the notes is useful to help readers understand the connections among the different pieces of information.

H. SUBSTANTIVE DIFFERENCES BETWEEN RELEVANT IFRS AND ASPE

Issue	IFRS	ASPE
Comprehensive income	An enterprise distinguishes items of other comprehensive income from items included in net income (profit or loss).	There is no concept of "other comprehensive income" in ASPE. Therefore, there is also no concept of comprehensive income.
Financial statement for performance measurement	An enterprise presents either: (i) a statement of comprehensive income; or (ii) an income statement plus a statement of comprehensive income that details the items of other comprehensive income.	An enterprise presents an income statement.
Statement of compliance	IAS 1 ¶16 requires an enterprise to make an "explicit and unreserved statement of compliance" with IFRS.	Section 1400 ¶16 requires an enterprise to state that it has prepared its financial statements in accordance with ASPE.

I. APPENDIX: REVIEW OF THE ACCOUNTING CYCLE

This appendix provides a brief review of the accounting cycle that you studied in introductory accounting. A more thorough review is available through an interactive online module in MyLab Accounting.

The accounting cycle involves the practical procedures that companies and individuals go through to record financial data and to transform those data into financial statements. It is a cycle because financial statements are prepared on a periodic basis, so the end of one accounting period/cycle is the beginning of the next period/cycle. Exhibit 3-27 summarizes the steps in this cycle and the documents associated with each step (note that "documents" is often in the form of an electronic database).

As Exhibit 3-27 shows, there are six steps in the accounting cycle, consisting of the following processes:

1. Journalizing
2. Posting
3. Adjustments

Exhibit 3-27	The accounting cycle

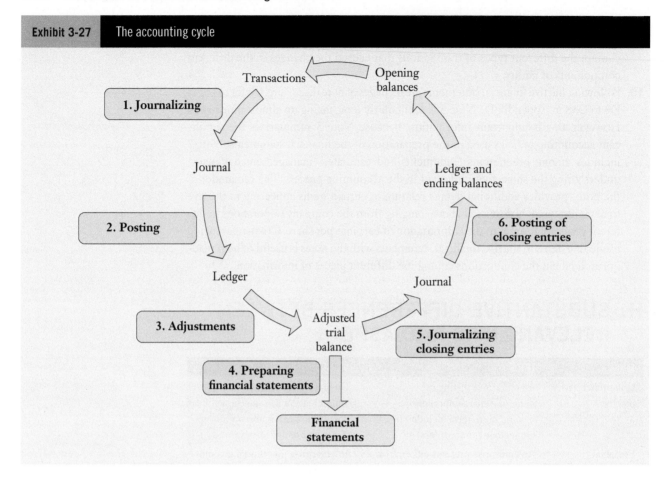

4. Preparing the financial statements
5. Journalizing closing entries
6. Posting of closing entries

The remainder of this appendix will discuss these six steps in more detail using the data inputs provided in Exhibit 3-28.

Exhibit 3-28	Data inputs for example to illustrate accounting cycle

i. Red and White Ltd. (RWL) provides wine consulting services. The company prepares financial statements on a monthly basis. At the beginning of June 2019, the company had the following account balances:

Cash	$2,800 Dr.	Taxes payable	$1,500 Cr.
Accounts receivable	4,600 Dr.	Common shares	100 Cr.
Equipment—cost	3,600 Dr.	Retained earnings	8,100 Cr.
Accumulated depreciation	1,300 Cr.		

ii. On June 15, the company paid the $1,500 taxes owing.

iii. On June 22, the company collected $3,500 on accounts receivable.

iv. On June 25, RWL billed a client for $5,000 plus $600 HST (harmonized sales tax) for services provided in the month of June. (Note: The $600 is collected on behalf of the government, so the amount becomes a tax payable.)

v. The equipment relates to computer hardware and software, which is being depreciated over 36 months on a straight-line basis.

1. Journalizing

This step involves recording all the transactions that RWL engages in. For the month of June, RWL had three transactions: the payment of taxes, collection of receivables, and billing a client for services rendered. These would be recorded in the journal as follows:

#1, June 15	Dr. Taxes payable	1,500	
	Cr. Cash		1,500
#2, June 22	Dr. Cash	3,500	
	Cr. Accounts receivable		3,500
#3, June 25	Dr. Accounts receivable	5,600	
	Cr. Sales revenue		5,000
	Cr. Taxes payable		600

The first two transactions are purely balance sheet transactions in which the journal entries involve only balance sheet accounts. On the balance sheet, assets have debit balances while liabilities and equities have credit balances (assuming they have positive balances). Assets = liabilities + equities, so debits = credits.

For entry #1, taxes payable is a liability account, so the debit to that account reduces the liability. This reduction in liability comes from a reduction in cash, which is an asset account, so we credit cash. Entry #2 records a receipt of cash for an amount owing from a customer, so we debit cash for the $3,500 received, and credit accounts receivable to reduce the amount owing from customers.

Entry #3 is a compound transaction that involves both the balance sheet and the income statement. Income statement accounts are in essence components of equity. Equity accounts have a credit balance, so increases in equity are credits while decreases in equity are debits. Earning revenue increases equity, so entry #3 credits revenue for $5,000. Including taxes, RWL is expecting to collect $5,600 from the customer, so we debit accounts receivable for that amount. The difference of $600 is payable to the government, which is recorded as a credit to taxes payable.

Note that the journal is a chronological record of transactions affecting a company's financial position. Next we look at posting, which involves the general ledger, which organizes information according to the general ledger account (such as cash, accounts receivable, etc.).

2. Posting

Posting is the process of transferring the amounts recorded in journal entries into the general ledger. The amounts entered in the general ledger (G/L), together with the opening balances, determine the ending balance of each account in the G/L. In June 2019, the G/L for Red and White Ltd. would be as follows:

Account	Date	Source	Debit	Credit
Cash	June 1	Opening balance	2,800	
	June 15	Entry #1		1,500
	June 22	Entry #2	3,500	
	June 30	Ending balance	4,800	
Accounts receivable	June 1	Opening balance	4,600	
	June 22	Entry #2		3,500
	June 25	Entry #3	5,600	
	June 30	Ending balance	6,700	
Equipment—cost	June 1	Opening balance	3,600	
		Ending balance	3,600	

Account	Date	Source	Debit	Credit
Accumulated depreciation	June 1	Opening balance		1,300
		Ending balance		1,300
Taxes payable	June 1	Opening balance		1,500
	June 15	Entry #1	1,500	
	June 25	Entry #3		600
	June 30	Ending balance		600
Common shares	June 1	Opening balance		100
		Ending balance		100
Retained earnings	June 1	Opening balance		8,100
		Ending balance		8,100
Sales revenue	June 1	Opening balance		0
	June 25	Entry #3		5,000
	June 30	Ending balance		5,000

Recall from introductory accounting that the income statement accounts show how much activity there is over an accounting period, so they start with a balance of zero at the beginning of each period. The sales revenue account begins the period with a zero balance; the ending balance of $5,000 represents how much revenue RWL recorded during the month.

The tabular presentation just shown is what would be used in practice. For pedagogical purposes, many textbooks (including this one) use T-accounts to show the same information. T-accounts show debits on the left side and credits on the right side of a T. The bottom of each T-account shows the balance in the account. The T-account representation of RWL's general ledger is as follows (with #1, #2, and #3 denoting the three transactions described above):

Cash		Accounts receivable		Equipment		Accum. depreciation	
(Bal) 2,800		(Bal) 4,600		3,600	Balance	Balance	1,300
	1,500 (#1)						
(#2) 3,500		3,500 (#2)					
		(#3) 5,600					
4,800		6,700		3,600			1,300

Taxes payable		Common shares		Retained earnings		Sales revenue	
Balance	1,500	Balance	100	Balance	8,100		
(#1) 1,500							
	600 (#3)						5,000 (#3)
	600		100		8,100		5,000

In manual records, as shown above, there are two separate steps for recording journal entries and posting them to the general ledger. In computerized systems, only one step will be required—after recording the journal entry, the posting step will be done automatically.

So far, we have looked at the process for recording and posting journal entries that reflect transactions with other entities (customers, suppliers, employees, government, etc.). Next, we look at entries that do not involve transactions.

3. Adjustments

In addition to transactions with other entities, enterprises also need to record non-transactional events that affect the company's financial position. Common examples of adjustments include depreciation expense, interest income or expense, and insurance expense. A common element in such adjustments is that they result from the passage of time (and hence there are no explicit transactions with outside parties).

For RWL, we need to record depreciation on its equipment. Straight-line depreciation of $3,600 over 36 months is $100/month. Therefore, we record the following journal entry:

#4, June 30	Dr. Depreciation expense	100	
	Cr. Accumulated depreciation		100

After posting this entry, the general ledger is as follows:

Cash		Accounts receivable		Equipment		Accum. depreciation	
(Bal) 2,800		(Bal) 4,600		3,600	Balance	Balance	1,300
	1,500 (#1)						
(#2) 3,500			3,500 (#2)				
		(#3) 5,600					
							100 (#4)
4,800		6,700		3,600			1,400

Taxes payable		Common shares		Retained earnings		Sales revenue	
Balance	1,500	Balance	100	Balance	8,100		
(#1) 1,500							
	600 (#3)						5,000 (#3)
	600		100		8,100		5,000

Depreciation expense	
(#4) 100	
100	

After all transactions and adjustments have been recorded, we would prepare a trial balance. A trial balance simply lists all of the G/L accounts with their corresponding balances. The total of all the debit balances must equal the total of all credit balances. The trial balance for RWL at the end of June is shown in Exhibit 3-29.

Exhibit 3-29	Trial balance for RWL at the end of June	
Account	**Debit**	**Credit**
Cash	4,800	
Accounts receivable	6,700	
Equipment	3,600	
Accumulated depreciation		1,400
Taxes payable		600
Common shares		100
Retained earnings		8,100
Sales revenue		5,000
Depreciation expense	100	
Total	15,200	15,200

4. Preparing the financial statements

At this point, the financial statements can be prepared based on the trial balance. A small private company would most likely follow ASPE, which requires a balance sheet, income statement, a statement of retained earnings, and a cash flow statement. For RWL, the financial statements are fairly straightforward, as shown in Exhibit 3-30, with the income statement and statement of retained earnings combined into one.

Exhibit 3-30	Financial statements for RWL for the month ending June 30, 2019

Red and White Ltd.
Balance Sheet
As at June 30, 2019

Cash	$ 4,800
Accounts receivable	6,700
Current assets	11,500
Equipment	3,600
Less: Accum. depreciation	(1,400)
Total assets	$13,700
Taxes payable	$ 600
Common shares	100
Retained earnings	13,000
Total equity	13,100
Total liabilities and equity	$13,700

Red and White Ltd.
Statement of Income and Retained Earnings
For the month ended
June 30, 2019

Sales revenue	$ 5,000
Depreciation expense	100
Net income	4,900
Retained earnings, June 1	8,100
Retained earnings, June 30	$13,000

Red and White Ltd.
Cash Flow Statement
For the month ended
June 30, 2019

Cash received from customers	$3,500
Cash paid for taxes	(1,500)
Cash flow from operations	2,000
Cash flow from investing	0
Cash flow from financing	0
Net cash flow	2,000
Cash, June 1	2,800
Cash, June 30	$4,800

5. Journalizing closing entries

After preparing the financial statements, the next step is to close the temporary accounts so that they have zero balances and are ready for the beginning of the next fiscal period. To close a temporary account, we determine the balance of that account and record an entry for the opposite amount; that is, if the temporary account has a debit balance, we record a credit in that account for the same amount; the other side of the closing entry goes to retained earnings.

To determine the balance in the temporary accounts, refer to the trial balance shown in Exhibit 3-29, which shows a credit balance of $5,000 for sales revenue and a debit balance of $100 for depreciation expense. For RWL, the closing entry is as follows:

#5, June 30	Dr. Sales Revenue	5,000	
	Cr. Depreciation expense		100
	Cr. Retained earnings		4,900

6. Posting of closing entries

The closing entry then needs to be posted to the general ledger. After posting, RWL's G/L would be as follows:

Cash		Accounts receivable		Equipment		Accum. depreciation	
(Bal) 2,800		(Bal) 4,600		3,600	Balance	Balance	1,300
	1,500 (#1)						
(#2) 3,500			3,500 (#2)				
		(#3) 5,600					
							100 (#4)
4,800		6,700		3,600		1,400	

Taxes payable		Common shares		Retained earnings		Sales revenue	
Balance	1,500	Balance	100	Balance	8,100		
(#1) 1,500							
	600 (#3)						5,000 (#3)
					4,900(#5)	(#5) 5,000	
600		100		13,000		0	

	Depreciation expense	
	(#4) 100	
		100 (#5)
	0	

After closing, the temporary accounts for the income statement have zero balances. Balances for permanent accounts (i.e., balance sheet accounts) carry forward as the opening balances for the next period (July 1, 2019).

7. Summary

The accounting cycle is the set of procedures that captures financial data and transforms that data into financial statements. This appendix used a simple example to review the accounting cycle that you learned in introductory accounting. Computerization reduces the need for some of the steps, but it is still important to understand the underlying procedures. For additional review, access the Accounting Cycle Tutorial on MyLab Accounting.

J. SUMMARY

L.O. 3-1. Explain the source of demand for periodic reporting and how accrual accounting satisfies that demand.

- Cash accounting sufficiently meets information demands when enterprises have finite and short lives because all cash cycles close when the entity dissolves.
- The demand for periodic reporting arises from the creation of enterprises with indefinite lives and the consequent need for information prior to the dissolution of the enterprise, so that investors, creditors, and others can ascertain the enterprise's financial position and performance.
- Accrual accounting better satisfies the demand for information because it provides additional information on cash cycles that are not yet complete at the reporting date.

L.O. 3-2. Explain why accrual accounting is fundamentally inexact, why estimates are central to accrual accounting, and why there is no "true" income for typical situations; evaluate the "quality of earnings."

- Since accrual accounting includes information about cash cycles that are not yet complete, management/accountants need to estimate the cycles' outcomes, which are inherently uncertain. There are better or worse estimates based on available information, but since the future is unknowable, none of the predictions about the future can be considered to be true; therefore, "true" income does not exist.
- While no true income exists for any particular circumstance, we can think of unbiased accounting—that is, the average or consensus among a sample of disinterested accountants or managers. Real people, however, have vested interests in the accounting numbers reported, so actual financial numbers reflect the biases that result from those incentives. Quality of earnings conceptually refers to how close the reported earnings are to the unbiased amount. Since we cannot observe unbiased earnings, quality of earnings is difficult to measure in practice.

L.O. 3-3. Apply accrual accounting in relation to issues of timing: periodicity, cut-off, and subsequent events.

- In accrual accounting, it is essential to properly define the reporting period. The cut-off date is the end of the period for the recognition of events. Subsequent events, while not recognized in the reporting period, may provide relevant information for the measurement of items recognized before the cut-off date.

L.O. 3-4. Evaluate whether an accounting change is an error, a change in accounting policy, or a change in estimate, and apply the retrospective and prospective treatments appropriate to that type of accounting change.

- Correction of errors and changes in accounting policies require retrospective adjustment of financial statements. Changes in estimates due to new information require prospective treatment.

L.O. 3-5. Integrate the structure and connections among the four financial statements and explain how this structure relates to accrual accounting.

- To meet the information needs of users, a complete set of financial statements consists of four statements plus note disclosures. The balance sheet (statement of financial position) shows an entity's financial position at a point in time. The statement of changes in equity and the cash flow statement show changes in financial position. The statement of comprehensive income reports financial performance for the period. Notes provide information about the accounting policies used, additional information relevant to items displayed on the four financial statements, and other pertinent disclosures to help users understand the reporting entity's financial position, performance, and changes in financial position.

■ The balance sheet is at the centre of the financial reports. The cash flow statement explains the changes in the cash account, while the statement of changes in equity explains changes in share capital, reserves, and retained earnings. The statement of comprehensive income further analyzes the components of profit/loss and other comprehensive income that contribute to the change in retained earnings.

K. ANSWERS TO CHECKPOINT QUESTIONS

CP3-1: The need for periodic financial reports arose from the creation of indefinite life enterprises. Investors in such enterprises could not, and did not want to, wait until the dissolution/ liquidation of these enterprises. These investors needed information to help them value the investment so that they would know what would be a fair price to buy or sell an enterprise or a portion thereof. Instead of drafting financial reports each and every time such information needs arose, it was more practical to publish financial reports at fixed intervals.

CP3-2: Accrual accounting better satisfies the demand for information than cash accounting does because accrual accounting information includes information on partially complete cash cycles that cash accounting information omits. As a result, the information is more timely, more complete, and more faithfully represents the transactions and events affecting the enterprise.

CP3-3: Accrual accounting numbers are fundamentally inexact because accruals involve incomplete cash cycles and therefore management needs to make forecasts of future outcomes to estimate the amounts for the accruals.

CP3-4: Quality of earnings refers to how closely reported accounting numbers resemble those that would be reported without managerial bias. Readers cannot directly observe the quality of earnings, but it is possible to make indirect assessments of this quality by evaluating the degree to which management is motivated to make excessive accruals to bias the financial information.

CP3-5: The subsequent-events period is the interval between the cut-off date (the end of the fiscal period) and the date when the company authorizes the financial statements for issuance. Information obtained in the subsequent-events period can be used to improve the *measurement* of transactions and events occurring prior to the cut-off date. However, information on transactions and events after the cut-off date cannot be *recognized*.

CP3-6: Both corrections of errors and changes in accounting policy require retrospective adjustment. In contrast, changes in estimates due to the arrival of new information or changed circumstances require prospective treatment.

CP3-7: Articulation refers to the connections among the financial statements. The cash flow statement connects with the cash balances shown in the balance sheet. Comprehensive income flows into retained earnings and reserves in the statement of changes in equity. The equity account balances in the statement of changes in equity connect with the equity portion of the balance sheet.

CP3-8: Recycling of other comprehensive income (OCI) results in the recognition of previously recorded OCI in net income (and therefore retained earnings as well). OCI that is *not* recycled does not pass through net income.

L. GLOSSARY

accrual: An accounting entry that reflects events or transactions in a period different from its corresponding cash flow.

accrual accounting: A method of accounting that records economic events when they happen rather than only when cash exchanges occur; contrast with **cash accounting**.

articulation: The connection of financial statements with each other.

cash accounting: A method of accounting that records only cash exchanges; contrast with **accrual accounting**.

cash cycle: A set of transactions that converts a cash inflow to a cash outflow, or vice versa. A **financing cash cycle** is the receipt of funding from investors, using those funds to generate returns from investments and operations, and returning the funds to investors. An **investing cash cycle** is the purchase of property that has long-term future benefits for the enterprise, using that property to obtain economic benefits that ultimately result in cash inflows, and disposing of the property. An **operating cash cycle** involves the purchase of items such as inventory; production, sales, and delivery of goods or provision of services; and receipts from customers.

cash equivalents: Short-term, highly liquid investments that are readily convertible to known amounts of cash and which are subject to an insignificant risk of changes in value.

change in accounting policy: An accounting change made at the discretion of management.

change in estimate: An accounting change made necessary by the arrival of new information.

correction of an error: An accounting change made necessary by the discovery of an incorrect amount given information available at the time the amount was reported.

cut-off: The point in time at which one reporting period ends and the next begins.

deferral: An accounting entry that reflects events or transactions after the related cash flow.

direct method (cash flow statement): A method of presenting the cash flow statement that shows the amounts attributable to each activity such as sales to customers; contrast with **indirect method**.

function (of an expense): The use to which the expense has been put (e.g., cost of sales, distribution, administration, or other activities); contrast with **nature**.

indirect method (cash flow statement): A method of presenting the operating section of the cash flow statement that uses the profit or loss from the income statement as a starting point and then itemizes adjustments to arrive at the net amount of operating cash flows; contrast with **direct method**.

nature (of an expense): The source of the expense (depreciation from equipment, costs of employee labour, cost of raw materials, or other means of production); contrast with **function**.

prospective adjustment: Applying an accounting change only to the current and future reporting periods without any changes to past financial statements.

quality of earnings: How closely reported earnings correspond to earnings that would be reported in the absence of management bias.

recycling (of OCI): The process of recognizing amounts through OCI, accumulating that OCI in reserves, and later recognizing those amount through net income and retained earnings.

retrospective adjustment (also retroactive adjustment): Applying an accounting change to all periods affected in the past, present, and future. Retrospective adjustment **with restatement** shows any comparative figures on the same basis as the current period figures. Retrospective adjustment **without restatement** reflects the accounting change's impact on past periods in the current period.

subsequent-events period: The period between the cut-off date and the date when the company authorizes its financial statements for issuance.

true and fair: An overall evaluation of a set of financial statements as being a fair representation of the enterprise's economic conditions and performance.

unbiased accounting: A conceptual accounting outcome that would result from taking an average or consensus from a sample of disinterested accountants.

M. FOR FURTHER READING

Lo, Kin. "Earnings Management and Earnings Quality." *Journal of Accounting and Economics* 45 (2008): 350–357.

N. REFERENCES

Authoritative standards:

IFRS	ASPE Section
The Conceptual Framework for Financial Reporting	1000—Financial Statement Concepts
IAS 1—Presentation of Financial Statements	1400—General Standards of Financial Statement Presentation
	1505—Disclosure of Accounting Policies
	1520—Income Statement
	1521—Balance Sheet
IAS 7—Statement of Cash Flows	1540—Cash Flow Statement
IAS 8—Accounting Policies, Changes in Accounting Estimates, and Errors	1506—Accounting Changes
IAS 10—Events After the Reporting Period	3820—Subsequent Events
IFRS 5—Non-current Assets Held for Sale and Discontinued Operations	3475—Disposal of Long-Lived Assets and Discontinued Operations

MyLab Accounting   Make the grade with **MyLab Accounting:** The problems marked with a can be found on **MyLab Accounting.** You can practise them as often as you want, and most feature step-by-step guided instructions to help you find the right answer.

O. PROBLEMS

P3-1.   The nature of accrual accounting   (**L.O.** 3-1) (Easy – 5 minutes)

For the factors listed below, indicate whether each significantly contributes to the practice of reporting financial statements **periodically** (annually or quarterly).

Factor	Significant contributor	Not a significant contributor
a. Improved technological capability (computers, Internet)		
b. A diffuse investor base comprising many people		
c. Increased pace of business transactions		
d. Invention of the printing press		
e. Establishment of regulators such as the Ontario Securities Commission		
f. Creation of indefinite-life entities like corporations		
g. Establishment of professional accounting organizations		

P3-2. **The nature of accrual accounting** **(L.O.** 3-1) (Easy – 10 minutes)

For the factors listed below, indicate whether each significantly contributes to the use of accrual accounting for financial reports (rather than using the cash basis).

Factor	Significant contributor	Not a significant contributor
a. Establishment of accounting standard setters such as the International Accounting Standards Board		
b. Invention of the double-entry system of bookkeeping		
c. Creation of indefinite-life entities like corporations		
d. Development of credit cards and other substitutes for cash		
e. Preparation of periodic financial reports		
f. Incomplete transactions at reporting dates		
g. The going concern assumption		
h. Accounting standards such as IFRS requiring accrual accounting		
i. Financial reports using accrual accounting being simpler to understand compared to those prepared using cash accounting		

P3-3. **The nature of accrual accounting** **(L.O.** 3-1) (Medium – 10 minutes)

Explain why companies prepare and present financial statements annually.

P3-4. **Demand for periodic reporting** **(L.O.** 3-1) (Easy – 5 minutes)

The IFRS Conceptual Framework paragraph OB2, states: "The objective of general purpose financial reporting is to provide financial information about the reporting entity that is useful to existing and potential investors, lenders and other creditors in making decisions about providing resources to the entity. Those decisions involve buying, selling or holding equity and debt instruments, and providing or settling loans and other forms of credit."

Required:

Explain how and why periodic reports such as annual or quarterly financial statements help to meet the objective stated in OB2.

P3-5. **The nature of accrual accounting** **(L.O.** 3-1) (Medium – 5 minutes)

The IFRS Conceptual Framework paragraph OB17, states: "Accrual accounting depicts the effects of transactions and other events and circumstances on a reporting entity's economic resources and claims in the periods in which those effects occur, even if the resulting cash receipts and payments occur in a different period. This is important because information about a reporting entity's economic resources and claims and changes in its economic resources and claims during a period provides a better basis for assessing the entity's past and future performance than information solely about cash receipts and payments during that period."[11]

Required:

Discuss why you would expect accrual accounting numbers to be better predictors of future cash flows in comparison to cash basis accounting.

[11.] Copyright © 2012 IFRS Foundation.

P3-6.   The nature of accrual accounting    3-1) (Medium – 10 minutes)

In finance, the calculation of net present value involves cash flows rather than accrual account-ing numbers. Indeed, one often takes accounting reports and adjusts for non-cash items such as depreciation to arrive at cash flows, which are then discounted. Some finance professionals proclaim that "cash is king" and believe accounting accruals should be ignored.

Required:

Do you agree with the above statements? Explain.

P3-7.   Role of the going concern assumption in accrual accounting

(**L.O.** 3-1) (Medium – 20 minutes)

The accrual basis of accounting implicitly assumes that the firm will continue to operate well into the future such that the incomplete transactions will be completed or concluded and the results will be known. This assumption is called the "going concern assumption." Because of this assumption we can use the historical cost basis of valuing most of the accounts on the balance sheet. The opposite of the going concern assumption is the notion that the firm is or will soon become bankrupt, and therefore will no longer continue to operate.

Required:

a. How does the going concern assumption relate to the valuation of property, plant, and equipment (PPE) on the balance sheet? Why is this assumption essential to the use of depreciation methods for PPE?
b. If the going concern assumption is no longer valid, how should assets be valued?
c. A company purchased a machine for $10,000,000 on January 1, 2021. The machine has a 10-year estimated useful life and an estimated residual value of $1,000,000. The company uses the straight-line depreciation method. During 2022 the company experiences signifi-cant and unexpected financial difficulty such that it goes into bankruptcy on December 31, 2022. At this time, the machine has a resale value in an auction of $5,500,000.
    i. How much is depreciation expense for 2021 and 2022?
    ii. Should depreciation expense for 2022 be the same as for 2021? Why?
    iii. What should be the value of the machine on the balance sheet on December 31, 2022?
    iv. What should be the adjustment to the carrying value of the machine in 2022?
d. A company has prepaid rent of $100,000 on December 31, 2022. If the company were a going concern, how should this amount be valued? If the company were *not* a going con-cern, how should it value the prepaid rent?
e. How should inventory be valued if a company goes into bankruptcy? Can the company use first-in, first-out or average cost?

 P3-8.   Accrual accounting and need for estimates   (**L.O.** 3-2) (Easy – 10 minutes)

For each of the following financial statement items, identify an estimate that is required in the measurement of that item on the financial statements.

Item
a. Accounts receivable
b. Inventories
c. Equipment
d. Warranty liability
e. Sales revenue
f. Revenue from long-term contract
g. Cost of goods sold

P3-9.   Uncertainty and estimates in accounting   (**L.O.** 3-2) (Easy – 10 minutes)

Explain why estimates are an essential part of financial reporting that cannot be avoided. Also explain how the need for estimates leads to the potential accounting numbers to be biased. In your answer, use accounts receivable as an example.

P3-10. Relation between accrual accounting and cash flows; quality of earnings

(**L.O.** 3-2) (Medium – 10 minutes)

Finance professionals often evaluate the quality of earnings by looking at the difference between earnings and cash flows. In particular, financial analysts often compute the difference between (i) net income from the income statement and (ii) cash flow from operations from the cash flow statement; the bigger the difference between the two, the lower the level of earnings quality is.

Required:

a. What is the meaning of "quality of earnings?"
b. Evaluate the practice of assessing earnings quality by comparing earnings and cash flows.

P3-11. The relation between accrual accounting and cash flows

(**L.O.** 3-2, **L.O.** 3-3) (Medium – 20 minutes)

Refer to the example of Tradewinds Company illustrated by the timeline in Exhibit 3-2 and the facts given at the beginning of Section B, "Accrual versus Cash Accounting." In addition, assume that the remaining ships are sold for $3.5 million each just before the end of Year 4 in preparation for the dissolution of the company.

Required:

a. Complete the financial statements for Years 3 and 4 using the tables below.
b. In the following tables, complete the column for "4-Year Total." Compare the 4-year totals for cash flow and income. Comment on the similarities and differences.

$ millions	Year 1	Year 2	Year 3	Year 4	4-Year Total
Cash flow statement					
Operations					
Inflow from sale of goods	5	5			
Outflow from operating costs	(3)	(2)			
Cash flow from operations	2	3			
Cash flow from investing activities	(15)	0			
Cash flow from financing activities	20	0			
Net cash flow for the year	7	3			
Cash at beginning of year	0	7			
Cash at end of year	7	10			

($ millions)	Year 1	Year 2	Year 3	Year 4	4-Year Total
Statement of income and retained earnings					
Revenue ($5m/arrival)	5.0	5.0			
Operating expenses ($1m/ arrival)	(1.0)	(1.0)			
Depreciation ($0.5m/ arrival)	(0.5)	(0.5)			
Write-off of sunken ship	0.0	(4.5)			
Write-off of prepaid expenses	0.0	(1.0)			
Net income (loss)	3.5	(2.0)			
Retained earnings at beginning of year	0.0	3.5			
Retained earnings at end of year	3.5	1.5			

($ millions)	Year 1	Year 2	Year 3	Year 4	4-Year Total
Balance sheet					
Cash	7.0	10.0			
Prepaid expenses	2.0	2.0			
Ships at cost	15.0	10.0			
Less: accumulated depreciation	(0.5)	(0.5)			
Total assets	23.5	21.5			
Contributed capital	20.0	20.0			
Retained earnings	3.5	1.5			
Total equity	23.5	21.5			

P3-12. No "true" net income

L.O. 3-2) (Medium – 30 minutes)

Computer Consulting Limited was started in early 2021 and continued to operate until early 2024, when it was wound up due to disputes between the two principal owners. When it started, the company considered two sets of accounting policies:

Accounting policy set 1:
a. Use straight-line depreciation method on the firm's only asset. The computer cost $1,000,000 and has an estimated useful life of four years.
b. Estimate warranty expense as 9% of sales.
c. Estimate bad debts expense as 5% of sales.

Accounting policy set 2:
a. Use 50% declining-balance method for depreciation.
b. Estimate warranty expense as 10% of sales.
c. The year-end allowance for doubtful accounts should be 40% of gross accounts receivable.

Actual events, cash flows, and transactions are as follows:

	2021	2022	2023	2024
Sales (all on account)	$3,000,000	$3,500,000	$4,000,000	$ 500,000
Warranties paid	250,000	275,000	410,000	180,000
Proceeds on disposal of computer	—	—	—	400,000
Accounts receivable collected during the year	2,600,000	2,800,000	3,800,000	1,200,000
Accounts receivable written off during the year	100,000	125,000	200,000	175,000
All other expenses (paid in cash in the year incurred)	2,100,000	2,500,000	2,700,000	350,000

Required:

a. Derive net income for 2021 to 2024 using the first set of accounting policies. For the year-end balance for 2024, assume accounts receivable, allowance for doubtful accounts, and the warranty accrual are $0, as the firm wound itself up during the year and all timing differences have been resolved.
b. Derive net income for 2021 to 2024 using the second set of accounting policies. For the year-end balance for 2024, assume accounts receivable, allowance for doubtful accounts, and the warranty accrual are $0, as the firm wound itself up during the year and all timing differences have been resolved.
c. Derive the annual net cash flows for 2021 to 2024.
d. What is the sum of the net income for the four years for the two sets of accounting policies? What is the sum of the net cash flows for the four years? What does this tell us about net income and accrual accounting?
e. Why were the net incomes different between the two sets of accounting policies?
f. What caused the net income in 2024 to be so high for the second set of accounting policies?

P3-13. Quality of earnings
L.O. 3-2) (Medium – 20 minutes)

Multi-Earnings Company had the following different patterns of net income based on different accounting policies and estimates/assumptions. These differing net incomes were the result of using different depreciation methods and assumptions about the useful life of assets, different methods of estimating bad debts expenses, different revenue recognition methods, different inventory valuation methods, and different methods of accruing liabilities such as vacation pay and warranties. In all cases, at the end of the fifth year the company had the same retained earnings, total assets and liabilities, and cash.

$ millions	2021	2022	2023	2024	2025	5-Year Total
Net Income A	30	30	30	30	30	150
Net Income B	22	25	29	34	40	150
Net Income C	39	35	30	25	21	150
Net Income D	35	27	30	34	24	150

Required:

a. Assuming that the company is publicly traded, which of these net income streams (A, B, C, or D) would likely result in the highest share price in early 2026? The lowest share price? Justify your conclusion.

b. Imagine you are the president of this company and the company is publicly listed/traded. Which representation of earnings would likely give you the largest aggregate bonus if your compensation were based on net income?

c. If you were the sole owner and chief executive officer of the company, which method of deriving net income would you prefer?

d. Does the selection of accounting policies change the actual achievements of the company? Does it change the future of the company? Does it change what people believe the past, present, or future of the company was, is, or will be? Discuss these differing perceptions and views of the company's financial condition.

P3-14. Evaluating accrual accounting and earnings quality
L.O. 3-2) (Medium – 20 minutes)

In the federal budget delivered on February 18, 2003, Finance Minister John Manley announced that the federal government will use full accrual accounting according to Canadian GAAP, as recommended by the auditor general. Other countries, such as the UK, Australia, and New Zealand, have also made similar changes.

In the past, the method of accounting was a "modified cash basis," which can be roughly summarized as follows:

- revenues = cash received in the fiscal year
- expenses = cash disbursed in the fiscal year
- surplus (or deficit) = revenues − expenses = cash received − cash disbursed

Under this old method of accounting, non-financial assets were not recognized on the balance sheet. For example, spending on the construction of roads or hospitals would be counted as expenses. (Financial assets and liabilities such as cash and bond obligations are recorded.)

Accounting critic Al Rosen, who has a reputation for being blunt, complained that this move by the government was "trading one pile of manure for another even larger, more stinky pile" (*Canadian Business*, May 13, 2003). He argued that GAAP-based rules are "looser," creating "thousands of new ways for the government to engineer the books."[12]

Required:

Discuss the pros and cons of the government adopting GAAP accrual accounting standards.

P3-15. Quality of earnings and other information
L.O. 3-2) (Medium – 20 minutes)

Section 8 of Canada's *Constitution Act, 1867*, required the federal government to conduct a census of its population every 10 years, starting in 1871. There are two versions of the census: a short form sent to every household, and a long form sent to a third of households. Responding to the

---

[12.] Courtesy of L.S. (Al) Rosen.

census was mandatory by law. However, for the 2011 census, the Conservative government of Stephen Harper made the long-form census voluntary.

On October 4, 2013, *The Globe and Mail* newspaper published an article by Professors Hulchanski, Murdie, Walks, and Bourne, entitled "Canada's voluntary census is worthless. Here's why."* Excerpts follow.

"Finally. There is good news about income inequality in Canada. Statistics Canada's recently released income data reveals that we are a much more equal society than we were a few years ago.

"It seems the income-inequality deniers may have been right all along. They just didn't have the 'correct' data from the most recent census [with which] to convince us.

"We have to thank Prime Minister Stephen Harper's voluntary National Household Survey (NHS), which replaced the mandatory long-form census, for this good news.

"The problem is that the voluntary survey has, as predicted, widely varying non-response rates. The response rates vary by location, socioeconomic status, ethno-cultural origin, family status, and so on. The non-response rate for Montreal was 20%, for Vancouver and Toronto about 25% … Peterborough, at 36%, was the highest for a metropolitan area.

"People with higher levels of education, higher-status jobs, higher (but not the highest) incomes and older people had higher response rates. Single parents and one-person households as well as renters had lower response rates. So did those living in the richest and poorest census tracts.

"These missing responses explain why the Prime Minister's NHS paints a rosy picture of a country with a growing middle-income group and fewer low-income areas. The fact is, fewer low-income people filled in the voluntary long form. …"[†]

Note: The mandatory long-form census was subsequently restored in 2016 after the defeat of the Conservative government in the 2015 election. Statistics Canada reported that the response rate for the long-form census increased to 98%, compared to 68% for the 2011 voluntary NHS.

Required:

Discuss the issues raised above that are analogous to earnings quality, earnings management, the Conceptual Framework for Financial Reporting, and financial accounting theory.

 P3-16. Subsequent events—online exercise   **L.O.** 3-3) (Easy – 10 minutes)

The *CPA Canada Handbook* is available to most post-secondary students through their educational institution's subscription. Visit http://edu.knotia.ca to complete this exercise. (You may need to complete this exercise on campus, or log in through your institution's VPN portal.)

Go to the standards in Part I (IFRS) of the "Accounting" portion of the *Handbook*. View IAS 10—Events after the Reporting Period (i.e., subsequent events).

Required:

a. Identify the paragraph that defines "events after the reporting period." Summarize the substance of this paragraph.
b. What action(s) must an entity take with respect to adjusting events after the reporting period?
c. What action(s) must an entity take with respect to non-adjusting events after the reporting period?

P3-17. Subsequent events   **L.O.** 3-3) (Medium – 10 minutes)

The date is February 26, 2021, and you are in the process of making adjusting entries for Bellevue Company for the year ended December 31, 2020. In your analysis of accounts receivable and bad debts, you come across the accounts for two customers that require additional attention:

■ Kingston Pen Ltd. owed Bellevue $55,000 as at December 31, 2020. You learned that Kingston Pen filed for bankruptcy on February 14, 2021, due to continuing financial difficulties.

■ Trenton Homes owed Bellevue $79,000 as at December 31, 2020. You learned that the owners decided to cease operations on February 22, 2021. An ice dam on the Trent River caused an uninsured flooding incident that damaged most of Trenton Homes's assets. Due to the vastly diminished assets of Trenton Homes, you expect to recover only $15,000 out of the $79,000 from the liquidation of the company's assets.

---

* The Globe and Mail newspaper published an article by Professors Hulchanski, Murdie, Walks, and Bourne, entitled "Canada's voluntary census is worthless. Here's why." Used with permission. https://www.theglobeandmail.com/opinion/canadas-voluntary-census-is-worthless-heres-why/article14674558/.

† The Globe and Mail newspaper published an article by Professors Hulchanski, Murdie, Walks, and Bourne, entitled "Canada's voluntary census is worthless. Here's why." Used with permission. https://www.theglobeandmail.com/opinion/canadas-voluntary-census-is-worthless-heres-why/article14674558/.

Required:

Identify and explain the appropriate treatment of the two accounts receivable in the books of Bellevue Company. Assume the amounts are material. Comment on any similarities or differences in treatment.

P3-18. Subsequent events   (**L.O.** 3-3) (Medium – 15 minutes)

You and your team of auditors are examining the financial statements of Capilano Water Company (CWC) for the fiscal year ended June 30, 2019. It is October 11, 2019. During the audit, you identified the following issues (assume all amounts are material):

a. CWC's draft financial statements show $100,000 of inventory of bottled water as of June 30, 2019. On August 17, 2019, it was discovered that the spring from which the company sources its water had been contaminated. Samples from the year-end inventory show that a quarter of it had been contaminated and is not suitable for sale.

b. On September 7, 2019, one of CWC's water delivery trucks was destroyed in an accident. This truck had a value of $80,000 on the books of CWC as of June 30, 2019.

c. In February 2019, CWC purchased 1,000 shares of Royal Bank Corporation (RBC) at $60 per share. These shares are widely traded on the Toronto Stock Exchange and share prices are available on a daily basis. The share price on June 30, 2019, was $55, and as of October 11, 2019, the share price has further declined to $48.

d. You noted that the closing cash balance on the bank statement dated September 30, 2019, was $3,000, much lower than the $67,000 shown on the draft financial statements that you are auditing.

Required:

Using the table below, identify the accounting treatment that would be most appropriate for each of the four issues described above, and explain why that is the appropriate treatment.

Item	Balance sheet amount after adjustment (if any), June 30, 2019	Explanation
a. Inventory—bottled water		
b. Equipment—truck		
c. Investment—RBC shares		
d. Cash		

P3-19. Subsequent events   (**L.O.** 3-3) (Medium – 15 minutes)

Below are several events that occur after the December 31, 2021, year-end but before the completion of the audit for Fundy Capital Inc. (Fundy). All amounts are considered to be material.

a. Fundy declares an $80,000 dividend on its ordinary (common) shares payable on January 31, 2022.

b. The Supreme Court of Canada finds Fundy liable for breach of contract and awards the plaintiff $153,698 in damages. Fundy had previously disclosed the lawsuit in its financial statements but had not recognized a provision.

c. Fundy issues $500,000 worth of ordinary (common) shares for cash.

d. Canada Revenue Agency notifies Fundy that they have disallowed a deduction on the company's 2020 tax return. The reassessment was for $58,496 plus interest and penalties of $6,105.

e. Fundy offers a bonus arrangement to its employees whereby the employees are collectively entitled to 10% of the company's pre-bonus, pre-tax earnings. Fundy provided for a $412,154 expense in 2021 based on its preliminary financial results prior to considering the above.

Required:

For each of the above events, determine whether the event:
a. requires an adjustment to the year-end financial statements,
b. requires note disclosure, or
c. requires neither adjustment to recognized amounts nor disclosure.
Justify your recommendation.

P3-20. Subsequent events   **L.O.** 3-3) (Medium – 15 minutes)

Below are several events that occur after your company's year-end but before the completion of the audit:

a. There is a fire at the company's only warehouse; the company has insufficient fire insurance to replace the warehouse and contents such that a material loss will result and operations will be curtailed for six months.

b. There is a significant fall in the market price of a major portion of inventory due to new technology making the existing items obsolete. The market price is lower than the current carrying value.

c. A new competitor enters the marketplace, which will result in serious price competition and, likely, reduced income next year.

d. New technology makes a major capital asset redundant or causes it to lose significant fair market and salvage value.

e. A major client unexpectedly goes bankrupt and it is determined that you will get 30% of the value of the accounts receivable as full and final settlement.

f. The company experiences a major labour strike. Workers are still on strike when the audit is finished. Does your answer change if this strike might force the company into bankruptcy?

Required:

For each of the above subsequent events, determine whether the event:

a. requires an adjustment to the year-end financial statements,

b. requires note disclosure, or

c. requires neither adjustment to recognized amounts nor disclosure.

Justify your recommendation.

P3-21. Accrual accounting and subsequent events   **L.O.** 3-3) (Medium – 20 minutes)

Xtra Foods is a meat processing company. The annual financial statements for the year ended July 31, 2020, were issued on September 25, 2020. Consider the following events (assume all amounts are material):

a. Xtra received a shipment of lambs (i.e., raw materials) on July 27, 2020. The company paid the related invoice of $325,000 on August 25, 2020.

b. The July 27 shipment was processed into finished goods over the following four days (July 28 to July 31). The company incurred processing costs of $550,000. (This amount appropriately includes labour and overhead costs.) This processed lamb was shipped to customers on August 3 for sales revenue totalling $1,230,000.

c. On September 15, Xtra staff discovered contamination of the products processed in the final four days of the fiscal year. Management did not include the effect of this discovery in the financial statements of July 31, 2020.

d. On October 1, 2020, the company issued a recall notice. The recall was for all lamb meat produced between July 28 and July 31. The recalled lamb no longer had commercial value. Management estimates the direct costs of the recall to be $1.5 million.

Required:

Analyze the above facts and, where appropriate, indicate the journal entries that should have been recorded for each transaction. Where journal entries are not adequate, describe the appropriate accounting treatment of the events. Be careful to specify the fiscal year in which each event should be recognized or disclosed. ("2020" means the fiscal year ended July 31, 2020.)

Fiscal year	Journal entries or explanation
a.	
b.	
c.	
d.	

P3-22. Accrual accounting and subsequent events   (**L.O.** 3-3) (Medium – 20 minutes)

Penticton Okanagan Vineyards (POV) is a grape grower and wine producer with a February 28 year-end. The annual financial statements for 2019 were issued on April 15, 2019. Consider the following events (assume all amounts are material):

a. During the fall of 2018, POV harvested 100 tonnes of grapes, extracted 50,000 litres of juice from these grapes, and began fermentation of the juice into wine. Labour costs for the harvest and production totalled $240,000, of which $15,000 remained unpaid as at February 28, 2019.

b. During the 2019 fiscal year, the company sold $950,000 of inventory with sales value totalling $1,850,000, of which $150,000 remained uncollected at the end of the year. Aging analysis indicates that $4,000 would be an appropriate amount in the allowance for doubtful accounts at year-end. Prior to recording the adjusting entry for bad debts, the allowance for doubtful accounts had a balance of $1,200.

c. On March 11, 2019, during routine testing, POV staff found that 10 barrels of wine having a work-in-process value of $50,000 had turned bad. The head winemaker concluded that the problem originated from defective yeast used in the fermentation process in the fall of 2018.

d. On May 1, 2019, vineyard staff noticed that a tract of vines did not grow after the spring thaw. The staff attributed the problem to cold winter conditions in January that damaged the roots of the vines. The dead vines had a value on the books of $80,000 as biological assets.

Required:

Analyze the above facts and, where appropriate, indicate the journal entries that should have been recorded. Where journal entries are not adequate, describe the appropriate accounting treatment of the events. Be careful to specify the fiscal year in which each event should be recognized or disclosed. ("2019" means the fiscal year ended February 28, 2019.)

	Fiscal year	Journal entries or explanation
a.		
b.		
c.		
d.		

P3-23. Accrual accounting and incomplete transactions

(**L.O.** 3-3) (Medium – 30 minutes)

Incomplete Transactions Company was started on January 1, 2021. During its first year of operations, the company had a choice of accounting policies. The chief financial officer identified the following as possible alternatives and provided the underlying assumptions/estimates for each:

	Accounting policy set A	Accounting policy set B
Inventory valuation	FIFO	Average cost
Bad debts	6% of sales	Allowance: 10% of closing gross accounts receivable
Warranties	4% of sales	Allowance: An analysis of sales and repairs

The following are the actual transactions for the first three years of operations:

	2021	2022	2023
Sales (all on accounts)	$11,000,000	$12,000,000	$12,800,000
Inventory purchases (paid immediately)	5,000,000	3,500,000	3,700,000
Ending inventory value, FIFO	2,000,000	2,300,000	2,500,000
Ending inventory value, average cost	1,800,000	2,000,000	2,500,000
Collections	9,000,000	10,500,000	13,270,000
Amounts actually written off	600,000	650,000	800,000
Warranties actually paid	300,000	460,000	502,000

	2021	2022	2023
Estimated warranties payable ending balance based on aging analysis of sales	150,000	180,000	170,000
Depreciation expense	1,000,000	1,000,000	1,000,000
All other operating expenses (paid immediately)	3,000,000	3,300,000	3,900,000

Required:

a. Derive net income for 2021, 2022, and 2023. Ignore income taxes.
b. What is the cumulative income for the three years for the two sets of accounting policies? What does this tell us about the closing balance sheet at the end of the third year?
c. What are the cumulative operating cash flows for the three years for either set of accounting policies? Why are these cumulative cash flows the same for the two sets of policies?
d. Carefully explain why the net incomes for each of the three years under review are not the same. What does this tell us about accruals and allocation methods?

 P3-24. Accounting changes  **3-4)** (Easy – 3 minutes)

For the following types of accounting changes, identify the appropriate treatment under IFRS.

Type of accounting change	Accounting treatment
a. Change in estimate	
b. Change in accounting policy	
c. Correction of an error	

 P3-25. Accounting changes **L.O. 3-4)** (Easy – 3 minutes)

For the following types of accounting changes, identify the relevant criteria for each accounting change by selecting "yes," "no," or "n/a" (not applicable).

Type of accounting change	Accounting change due to management choice?	Information known (or should have been known) in prior period?
a. Change in estimate	Yes No n/a	Yes No n/a
b. Change in accounting policy	Yes No n/a	Yes No n/a
c. Correction of an error	Yes No n/a	Yes No n/a

 P3-26. Accounting changes  **3-4)** (Medium – 15 minutes)

Evaluate each of the following independent situations to determine the type of accounting change (correction of error, change in accounting policy, or change in estimate) and the appropriate accounting treatment (retrospective or prospective).

Required:

a. A furniture maker decreases bad debts expenses from 3% to 2% of credit sales.
b. A manufacturer determines that credit losses are becoming material due to deteriorating economic conditions. As a result, it decides to set up an allowance for doubtful accounts at 5% of amounts over 90 days.
c. A parking service estimates bad debts to be 10% of the value of parking violations issued. In the current year, it changes to estimating the allowance for bad debts to be equal to 20% of accounts 30 to 90 days and 50% of accounts over 90 days.
d. A shipbuilder changes its revenue recognition policy from the point of receipt by the customer to when the ship leaves the factory shipyard. This change results from a change in shipping policy from F.O.B. destination to F.O.B. shipping point. (Recall from introductory accounting that F.O.B. means "free on board," and it refers to the point at which custody transfers from seller to buyer.)
e. An electronics retailer has never accrued for warranties or product guarantees. A new consumer protection law comes into effect, giving buyers of electronic products a guarantee against defects for 180 days after purchase and the ability to return defective products to the retailer.

f. A clothing company that has been operating for 20 years decides to obtain an external audit for the first time to meet the bank's demands. The audit firm recommends that management report inventories at the lower of cost and net realizable value, whereas the company has previously only tracked and reported inventory figures at cost.

P3-27. Accounting changes   **L.O.** 3-4) (Easy – 10 minutes)

Explain why a change in accounting policy requires the adjustment of both prior and future periods, whereas a change in estimate requires only adjustment of future periods.

P3-28. Accounting changes   **L.O.** 3-4) (Medium – 15 minutes)

Accrual accounting necessarily involves professional judgment, because accruals depend on decisions about uncertain future events. These judgments and decisions include the choices of accounting policies that management determines to be most appropriate for the circumstances.

Required:

Using the Conceptual Framework and other ideas, discuss whether a change in accounting policy should be treated prospectively or retrospectively.

P3-29. Accounting changes   **L.O.** 3-4) (Medium – 10 minutes)

For each of the following scenarios, determine the effects (if any) of the accounting change (correction of error, change in accounting policy, or change in estimate) on the relevant asset or liability, equity, and comprehensive income in the year of change and the prior year. Use the following table for your response.

		Year prior to change			Year of accounting change		
Type of accounting change	Treatment	Asset or liability	Equity	Income	Asset or liability	Equity	Income
a.							
b.							
c.							

a. Company A increases the allowance for doubtful accounts (ADA). Using the old estimate, ADA would have been $40,000. The new estimate is $45,000.
b. Company B omitted to record an invoice for an $8,000 sale made on credit at the end of the previous year and incorrectly recorded the sale in the current year. The related inventory sold has been accounted for.
c. Company C changes its revenue recognition to a more conservative policy. The result is a decrease in prior-year revenue by $3,000 and a decrease in current-year revenue by $4,000 relative to the amounts under the old policy.

P3-30. Accounting changes   **L.O.** 3-4) (Medium – 10 minutes)

During the audit of Keats Island Brewery for the fiscal year ended June 30, 2022, the auditors identified the following issues:
a. The company sells beer for $1 per bottle, plus $0.10 deposit on each bottle. The deposit collected is payable to the provincial recycling agency. During 2022, the company recorded $8,000 of deposits as revenue. The auditors believe this amount should have been recorded as a liability.
b. The company had been using the first-in, first-out cost flow assumption for its inventories. In fiscal 2022, management decided to switch to the weighted-average method. This change reduced inventory by $20,000 at June 30, 2021, and $35,000 at June 30, 2022.
c. The company has equipment costing $5,000,000 that it has been depreciating over 10 years on a straight-line basis. The depreciation for fiscal 2021 was $500,000 and accumulated depreciation on June 30, 2021, was $1,000,000. During 2022, management revises the estimate of useful life to 12 years, reducing the amount of depreciation to $400,000 per year.

Required:

For each of the three issues described above, using the following table, identify:
  a. the type of accounting change;
  b. the treatment required; and
  c. the effect of the accounting change on the financial statements of June 30, 2022.
    For (c), identify both the direction (increase or decrease) and the amount of the effect relative to the amount without the accounting change.

	Type of accounting change	Treatment	Effect of accounting change on the financial statements of June 30, 2022 (indicate both direction and amount)			
			Assets	Liabilities	Equity	Income
a.						
b.						
c.						

 P3-31. Accounting changes   (**L.O.** 3-4) (Difficult – 30 minutes)

Cross Company Limited, a private company, was started on January 1, 2021. For the first year, the chief accountant prepared the financial statements and a local accountant completed the necessary review of these statements. However, for the year ended December 31, 2022, an external auditor was appointed. The income statement for 2021 and the preliminary amounts for 2022 are as follows:

	2021	2022
Long-term contract income	$3,000,000	$4,000,000
Other income (loss)	(800,000)	(900,000)
Bad debts expense	(400,000)	(500,000)
Depreciation expense—machine	(500,000)	(500,000)
Depreciation expense—building	(300,000)	(270,000)
Warranty expense	(200,000)	(320,000)
Income before taxes	800,000	1,510,000
Income taxes (at 30%)	(240,000)	(453,000)
Net income	$ 560,000	$ 1,057,000

In the process of examining the accounting records the auditor noted the following issues:
  i. **Long-term contracts:** Cross Company used the completed contract method for revenue recognition in 2021. Management now believes that the percentage of completion method would be better. Income under the completed contract method for 2021 was $3,000,000 and for 2022 was $4,000,000. If the percentage of completion method had been used, the incomes would have been $4,200,000 (2021) and $3,700,000 (2022).
  ii. **Accounts receivable:** The accounts receivable on December 31, 2021, included a $100,000 account that was not provided for but subsequently was written off during 2022 as the customer went bankrupt after the issuance of the financial statements. Cross Company would like to adjust 2021 for this oversight as it sees this as an error.
  iii. **Machine depreciation:** Cross Company has one huge machine that cost $5,000,000 and was depreciated over an estimated useful life of 10 years. Upon reviewing the manufacturer's reports in 2022, management now firmly believes the machine will last a total of 15 years from the date of purchase. They would like to change last year's depreciation charge based on this analysis. Depreciation expense of $500,000 has been recorded for 2022.
  iv. **Building depreciation:** The company's building (cost $3,000,000; estimated salvage value $0; useful life 20 years) was depreciated last year using the 10% declining-balance method. The company and auditor now agree that the straight-line method would be more appropriate. A depreciation provision of $270,000 has been made for 2022.
  v. **Inventories:** The accountant last year failed to apply the lower of cost and net realizable value test to ending inventory. Upon review, the inventory balance for last year should have been reduced by $200,000. The closing inventory allowance for this year-end should be $300,000. No entry has been made for this matter.

vi. **Warranties:** Cross Company does not accrue for warranties; rather, it records the warranty expense when amounts are paid. Cross provides a one-year warranty for defective goods. Payments to satisfy warranty claims were $200,000 in 2021 and $320,000 in 2022. Out of the $320,000 paid in 2022, $150,000 related to 2021 sales. A reasonable estimate of warranties payable at the end of 2022 is $275,000.

Required:

a. As the audit senior on this engagement, what is your recommended treatment for each of these matters in terms of whether they are errors, changes in accounting policy, or changes in estimate? Explain your answers.

b. Assume that management of Cross Company agrees with your recommendations. Prepare the corrected statements of comprehensive income for 2021 and 2022.

 P3-32. Current and non-current assets  **L.O.** 3-5) (Easy – 5 minutes)

IFRS identifies a number of criteria to determine whether an asset can be classified as current. Satisfying *any one* of these criteria is sufficient. For the following list of criteria, identify whether each one is relevant for the classification of an asset as current instead of non-current.

Criteria	Relevant for classification as current? (Yes/No)
a. The asset is expected to be sold in the entity's normal operating cycle.	
b. The asset is traded in an active market.	
c. The asset is expected to be realized within 12 months after the balance sheet date.	
d. The asset is held primarily for the purpose of being traded.	
e. The asset is expected to be consumed in the entity's normal operating cycle.	
f. The asset is an item of inventory.	
g. The asset is cash or cash equivalent.	
h. The asset is a receivable from another company.	

 P3-33. Current and non-current liabilities **L.O.** 3-5) (Easy – 5 minutes)

IFRS identifies a number of criteria to determine whether a liability should be classified as current. A liability that satisfies *any one* of these criteria must be classified as current. For the following list of criteria, identify whether each one is relevant for the classification of a liability as current instead of non-current.

Criteria	Relevant for classification as current? (Yes/No)
a. The liability is expected to be settled in the entity's normal operating cycle.	
b. The liability requires settlement in cash.	
c. The liability is expected to be realized within 12 months after the balance sheet date.	
d. The liability is held primarily for the purpose of being traded.	
e. The entity does not have an unconditional right to defer settlement of the liability for at least 12 months after the balance sheet date.	
f. The liability is a line of credit owing to a financial institution.	
g. The liability is unavoidable.	

P3-34. Presentation of statement of comprehensive income

(**L.O.** 3-5) (Easy – 5 minutes)

IFRS requires certain line items to be presented in the statement of comprehensive income (rather than just disclosed in the notes). Identify whether the following items are required in the statement of comprehensive income.

Line item	Required? (Yes/No)
a. Revenue	
b. Profit or loss (net income)	
c. Cost of goods sold	
d. General and administrative expenses	
e. Comprehensive income	
f. Labour costs	
g. Income tax expense	
h. Other comprehensive income	
i. Finance costs (interest expense)	

 P3-35. Presentation of statement of comprehensive income

(**L.O.** 3-5) (Easy – 5 minutes)

Identify whether each of the following items of operating expense is described according to its *nature* or *function*.

Type of operating expense	Nature	Function
a. Cost of goods sold		
b. Delivery		
c. Wages and benefits		
d. Administration		
e. Building depreciation		
f. Utilities (electricity, heating, etc.)		
g. Marketing and advertising		
h. Sales commissions		
i. Raw materials consumed		
j. Insurance		

 P3-36. Preparation and presentation of financial statements with current/non-current classifications

(**L.O.** 3-5) (Easy – 20 minutes)

Below is an adjusted trial balance for Wan Industries Limited as at December 31, 2019.

Account (in alphabetical order)	Debit	Credit
Accounts payable		$142,000
Accounts receivable	$95,000	
Accumulated depreciation		50,000
Advertising expense	16,000	
Cash	334,000	
Common shares		200,000
Cost of goods sold	410,000	
Current portion of long-term loan payable		40,000
Depreciation expense	12,000	
Dividends	21,000	
Equipment	500,000	
Income tax expense	35,000	

Account (in alphabetical order)	Debit	Credit
Interest expense	41,000	
Interest payable		10,000
Inventory	51,000	
Long-term loan receivable	300,000	
Non-current portion of long-term loan payable		360,000
Prepaid rent	25,000	
Rent expense	75,000	
Retained earnings		385,000
Sales revenue		800,000
Stationery	5,000	
Stationery expense	14,000	
Unearned revenue		23,000
Wages expense	91,000	
Wages payable		15,000
Total	$2,025,000	$2,025,000

Required:

Prepare a balance sheet for Wan Industries Limited as at December 31, 2019 with items classified as current or non-current.

 P3-37. Articulation of financial statements   **(L.O. 3-5)** (Easy – 10 minutes)

Required:

Complete the missing numbers in the following table.

	Company A	Company B	Company C	Company D	Company E
Assets	?	$800	?	?	$4,000
Liabilities	?	425	1,100	1,800	?
Common stock	20	175	?	100	500
Retained earnings	130	?	275	?	700
Liabilities + Equity	$500	?	$1,500	$2,500	$4,000
Opening retained earnings	$100	$140	?	$500	$750
+ Net income (Loss)	70	?	160	?	?
− Dividends	?	(10)	(85)	(60)	(10)
Closing retained earnings	130	?	?	?	$700

P3-38. Accounting changes and articulation of financial statements
(L.O. 3-4, L.O. 3-5) (Medium – 20 minutes)

The following presents Echo Mike Sound Systems' *draft* financial statements for December 2021, with comparative figures for 2020. Amounts are in $000's.

Balance Sheet as at December 31					
	2021	2020		2021	2020
Cash	$ 280	$ 350	Accounts payable	$2,050	$1,900
Accounts receivable (gross)	3,500	3,000	Current portion of long-term debt	500	500
Less: allowance for doubtful accts	(70)	(60)	Current liabilities	2,550	2,400
Inventories	1,330	1,230	Long-term debt	1,500	2,000
Current assets	5,040	4,520	Total liabilities	4,050	4,400

Balance Sheet as at December 31					2021	2020
	2021	2020				
Land	800	800	Preferred shares		600	--
Plant and equipment (net)	2,500	2,890	Common shares		1,500	1,500
Goodwill	320	320	Retained earnings		2,510	2,630
Non-current assets	3,620	4,010	Total equity		4,610	4,130
Total assets	$8,660	$8,530	Total liabilities and equity		$8,660	$8,530

Cash flow statement for the year ended December 31	2021	2020		Income statement for the year ended December 31	2021	2020
Cash flow from operating activities	1,604	1,400	Revenue		$15,900	$14,200
Cash flow from investing activities	(100)	(700)	Operating expenses		(13,500)	(12,300)
Cash flow from financing activities	(1,674)	(550)	Interest expense		(180)	(200)
Net change in cash	(170)	150	Earnings before tax		2,220	1,700
Cash, January 1	450	300	Income taxes		(666)	(510)
Cash, December 31	280	450	Net income		$1,554	$1,190

During 2021 (2020), the company declared and paid $1,750,000 ($1,674,000) of dividends.

Required:

a. Before the above financial statements were finalized and issued, management found another sales invoice of $100,000 dated December 29, 2021. Describe how this information should be reflected in Echo Mike's financial statements. Ignore the effect of income taxes.
b. The company omitted to record a $350,000 account payable for goods purchased in the 2020 fiscal year. The inventory was correctly accounted for, and the payable was recorded and paid during the 2021 fiscal year. Identify the effect of this information on the financial statements for 2020 and 2021, and record any journal entries required.
c. Identify two articulation errors in the financial statements above.

P3-39. Accounting changes and articulation of financial statements
(**L.O.** 3-4, **L.O.** 3-5) (Medium – 20 minutes)

The following presents Oscar Equipment Company's *draft* financial statements for December 2022, with comparative figures for 2021. Amounts are in $000's.

Balance Sheet as at December 31					2022	2021
	2022	2021				
Cash	$ 280	$ 350	Accounts payable		$2,050	$1,900
Accounts receivable (gross)	3,500	3,000	Taxes payable		100	100
Less: allowance for doubtful accts	(70)	(60)	Long-term debt		1,600	2,070
Inventories	1,330	1,230	Wages payable		300	240
Current assets	5,040	4,520	Total liabilities		4,050	4,400
Land	800	800	Preferred shares		600	--
Plant and equipment (net)	2,500	2,890	Common shares		1,500	1,500
Goodwill	320	320	Retained earnings		2,510	2,630
Non-current assets	3,620	4,010	Total equity		4,610	4,130
Total assets	$8,660	$8,530	Total liabilities and equity		$8,660	$8,530

Cash flow statement for the year ended December 31		
	2022	2021
Cash flow from operating activities	1,604	1,400
Cash flow from investing activities	(100)	(700)
Cash flow from financing activities	(1,574)	(550)
Net change in cash	(70)	150
Cash, January 1	350	200
Cash, December 31	280	350

Income statement for the year ended December 31		
	2022	2021
Revenue	$6,220	$6,650
Operating expenses	(5,600)	(5,900)
Interest expense	(80)	(70)
Earnings before tax	540	680
Income taxes	(160)	(190)
Net income	$380	$490

During 2022 (2021), the company declared and paid $450,000 ($400,000) of dividends.

Required:

a. Before the above financial statements were finalized and issued, management decided to increase the allowance for doubtful accounts from 2% of gross receivables to 3% to reflect higher credit risk. Identify the effect of this change on the financial statements. Ignore the effect of income taxes. Indicate both the direction and magnitude of any effects.

	Assets	Liabilities	Equity	Income
2021				
2022				

b. The company discovered an error relating to land it had purchased in 2015. There were $50,000 of costs that should have been expensed but were incorrectly capitalized into the cost of land. Identify the effect of this change on the financial statements. Ignore the effect of income taxes. Indicate both the direction and magnitude of any effects.

	Assets	Liabilities	Equity	Income
2021				
2022				

c. Identify two substantive errors in the above financial statements.

P3-40. Components of the Conceptual Framework and the articulation of financial statements
(**L.O.** 3-5) (Medium – 20 minutes)[13]

A business earns income by converting assets and resources into other assets and resources. For example, through the efforts of its workforce and other resources, a business converts inventories of raw materials into receivables and cash. The value of the new assets generated may be termed "revenue," that of the assets and resources consumed may be termed "expense," and the increased value may be termed "income." Therefore, it can be argued that asset valuation, revenue recognition, and matching of expenses to revenues are interrelated. Some of these relationships are as follows:
a. The choice of asset valuation method affects revenue recognition.
b. The theory on which revenue generation is based affects the valuation of the related assets.
c. When the objectives of asset valuation and income recognition conflict, it becomes necessary to choose either the desired asset valuation method or the desired income recognition method.

Required:

Discuss each of the three relationships described above and provide examples where appropriate.

---

13. Reprinted from Uniform Final Examination, 1982, with permission from Chartered Professional Accountants of Canada, Toronto, Canada. Any changes to the original material are the sole responsibility of the author (and/ or publisher) and have not been reviewed or endorsed by the Chartered Professional Accountants of Canada.

P3-41. Preparation of articulated financial statements   (**L.O.** 3-5) (Easy – 15 minutes)

The following is a pre-closing trial balance for Axo Inc., a manufacturer of metal tubing, as at December 31, 2019:

	Debit	Credit
Accounts payable		$ 525,000
Accounts receivable	$ 1,360,000	
Accumulated depreciation		6,555,000
Cash	69,300	
Common shares		700,000
Depreciation	1,475,000	
Income from discontinued operations		25,000
Income tax expense	154,200	
Income tax on income from discontinued operations	7,500	
Interest expense	355,000	
Inventories	645,000	
Long-term debt		5,400,000
Plant and equipment	12,300,000	
Raw materials used	1,670,000	
Retained earnings		817,000
Salaries and wages	5,210,000	
Sales		9,224,000
Total	$23,246,000	$23,246,000

During the year, the company declared and paid dividends of $300,000, and issued shares for proceeds of $200,000.

Required:

Prepare, in good form, the following:
a. A multi-step income statement that includes relevant subtotals, with operating expenses listed by their nature, for the year ended December 31, 2019.
b. A statement of changes in equity for the year ended December 31, 2019.

 P3-42. Preparation of articulated financial statements

(**L.O.** 3-4, **L.O.** 3-5) (Medium – 15 minutes)[14]

The following is a partial list of the accounts for Boot Company for the year ended December 31, 2020, in alphabetical order:

	Dr. (Cr.)
Common shares	$(2,000,000)
Cost of goods sold	3,775,000
Depreciation expense	84,000
Dividends declared	150,000
Employee wages and benefits	957,000
Loss from discontinued operations before tax	107,000
Marketing and advertising expenses	642,000
Retained earnings, January 1, 2020	(443,000)
Sales	(4,661,000)
Utilities expense	315,000

[14.] Reprinted from CGA-Canada FA2 examination, December 2008, with permission from Chartered Professional Accountants of Canada, Toronto, Canada. Any changes to the original material are the sole responsibility of the author (and/or publisher) and have not been reviewed or endorsed by the Chartered Professional Accountants of Canada.

During the year, the company issued shares for proceeds of $400,000. In addition, the company had a change in depreciation policy that required a retroactive adjustment that increased the prior year's depreciation expense by $62,000. Boot pays income tax at the rate of 40%. Assume that all of the above items except for retained earnings are before tax.

Required:

Using the information above, prepare, in good form, the following:
a. A multi-step income statement that includes relevant subtotals, with operating expenses listed by their function, for the year ended December 31, 2020.
b. A statement of changes in equity for the year ended December 31, 2020.

 P3-43. **Preparation of articulated financial statements**   (**L.O.** 3-5) (Medium – 20 minutes)

The following is a pre-closing trial balance for Kalico Kats, as at December 31, 2021:

	Debit	Credit
Accounts payable		$ 1,235,000
Accounts receivable	$ 2,860,000	
Accumulated depreciation—equipment		1,740,000
Accumulated depreciation—plant		1,500,000
Cash	1,009,800	
Common shares		15,000,000
Depreciation—equipment	580,000	
Depreciation—plant	500,000	
Equipment	5,800,000	
Income tax expense	537,200	
Income tax on income from discontinued operations		200,000
Interest expense	165,000	
Inventories	645,000	
Land—cost	5,000,000	
Land—revaluation adjustment	3,000,000	
Long-term debt		3,500,000
Loss from discontinued operations	500,000	
Other comprehensive income—gain on land revaluation		3,000,000
Plant	10,000,000	
Raw materials used	4,670,000	
Retained earnings		1,834,000
Salaries and wages	7,210,000	
Sales		15,344,000
Utilities expense	876,000	
Total	$43,353,000	$43,353,000

During the year, the company declared and paid $500,000 of dividends and issued shares for proceeds of $5,000,000.

Required:

Prepare, in good form, the following:
a. A statement of comprehensive income that includes net income and comprehensive income in one schedule.
b. A statement of changes in equity.

P3-44. Preparation of articulated financial statements   (**L.O.** 3-5) (Easy – 15 minutes)

The following is a partial list of accounts and their balances for Davidson Company as at December 31, 2019:

	Debit	Credit
Accounts payable		$ 1,357,000
Accounts receivable	$ 3,035,000	
Accumulated depreciation—equipment		3,450,000
Accumulated depreciation—plant		2,500,000
Accumulated other comprehensive income—gain on available-for-sale investments		140,000
Cash	457,000	
Common shares		20,000,000
Depreciation—equipment	690,000	
Depreciation—plant	500,000	
Equipment	5,520,000	
Income tax expense	850,000	
Income tax payable		125,000
Intangible assets	1,750,000	
Inventories	820,000	
Land	12,000,000	
Long-term debt		30,000,000
Plant	50,000,000	
Preferred shares		10,000,000
Retained earnings, December 31, 2019		7,650,000
Available-for-sale investments—cost	1,500,000	
Available-for-sale investments—valuation adjustment	140,000	

Net income for the year was $838,000 and the company declared $400,000 in dividends during the year. There were items of other comprehensive income in the year. The investments are not expected to be sold in the next 12 months. The long-term debt is repayable over five years, with 20% of the balance due on June 30, 2020.

Required:

Prepare, in good form, the following:
a. A statement of changes in equity.
b. A balance sheet using the current/non-current presentation. When possible, group related items into one line to obtain the minimum number of line items to satisfy presentation requirements in IFRS.

 P3-45. Preparation of articulated financial statements

(**L.O.** 3-5) (Medium – 15 minutes)[15]

The following is a partial trial balance for Pluto, a public company, for the year ended December 31, 2020. Each item has its normal debit or credit balance, but the total does not equal to zero as it is a partial trial balance.

[15.] Adapted from CGA-Canada FA2 examination, December 2008. Used with permission.

Accounts receivable	$100,000
Sales	250,000
Prepaid expenses	45,000
Equipment, net (note 1)	60,000
Cost of goods sold	150,000
Accounts payable	65,000
Investments classified as fair value through other comprehensive income (FVOCI) (note 2)	90,000
Common shares	80,000
Unearned revenue	12,000
Retained earnings, January 1, 2020	50,000
Discount on bonds payable	8,000
Cash	22,000
Correction of error (note 3)	35,000
Bonds payable, due January 1, 2026	120,000
Loss on discontinued operations	25,000
Net income (note 4)	?

Notes:

1. The machinery is net of accumulated depreciation of $25,000.
2. The balance in the investments represents the original cost at the date of acquisition (January 1, 2020). As of December 31, 2020, none of these investments had been sold and market value was $120,000.
3. During 2019, a patent of Pluto's expired. The related writedown of $35,000 was subsequently recorded in March 2020.
4. Ignore income taxes for this question. Because only a partial trial balance is provided, net income cannot be directly calculated. It should be plugged in to make the financial statements balance.

Required:

Prepare a balance sheet as at December 31, 2020, and a statement of changes in equity for the year then ended, in good form and using appropriate terminology.

P3-46. Articulation of financial statements   (**L.O.** 3-5) (Medium – 10 minutes)

The following table presents summarized financial statements for Whiskey Golf Ltd., in $000's.

Balance Sheet, as at December 31					
	2021	2020		2021	2020
Cash	180	250	Accounts payable	740	1,400
Accounts receivable (net)	2,500	2,000	Current portion of long-term debt	300	300
Inventories	1,800	1,500	Current liabilities	1,040	1,700
Prepaid expenses	300	210	Long-term debt	900	1,200
Land	500	500	Preferred shares	800	800
Plant and equipment (net)	3,500	3,820	Common shares	2,000	2,000
Intangible assets	20	20	Retained earnings	4,860	3,400
Goodwill	800	800	Total equity	8,560	7,400
Total assets	9,600	9,100	Total liabilities and equity	9,600	9,100

Statement of Comprehensive Income For the year ended December 31		
	2021	2020
Revenue	7,500	7,000
Cost of goods sold	(4,900)	(4,800)
Interest expense	(400)	(400)
Earnings before tax	2,200	1,800
Income taxes	(660)	(540)
Income before discontinued operations	1,540	1,260
Loss on discontinued operations	(600)	0
Net income	940	1,260

Cash Flow Statement For the year ended December 31		
	2021	2020
Cash flow from operating activities	880	700
Cash flow from discontinued operations	(600)	0
Cash flow from investing activities	100	(400)
Cash flow from financing activities	(380)	(370)
Net change in cash	0	(70)

In addition, you also know that the company declared and paid $80,000 of dividends on preferred shares in each of the two years.

Required:

Identify five substantive errors in the above financial statements. There are no arithmetic errors. To save space, the above presentation is necessarily abbreviated, so do not consider omission of detailed line items to be errors. Assume that all required disclosures have been made in the notes to the financial statements. The company did not have any transactions involving other comprehensive income.

P3-47. Articulation of financial statements   (**L.O.** 3-5) (Difficult – 30 minutes)

A group of students are preparing for a presentation in their final-year business strategy course. The students have done all their analyses and are now finalizing their report. One of the students wisely suggests that a balance sheet and income statement should be included as part of their visual presentation and written report. As time is running out, one of the students prepares an income statement based on the competitive and market research completed and another student independently makes a comparative balance sheet based on what the financial plan suggests. The group feels proud they were able to complete this task so quickly and get their project in on time. However, during the presentation the instructor detects that the financial statements do not articulate and are unrealistic. Once this major error is uncovered the presentation quickly falls apart (and you can imagine how this story ends).

Required:

Identify three tests that the instructor might have done to determine whether the balance sheet and income statement fit together (articulate) or were developed independent of each other. Also suggest three tests of reasonableness the instructor might do to see whether the analysis is realistic.

P3-48. Preparation of articulated financial statements, error correction, and
subsequent events   (**L.O.** 3-3, **L.O.** 3-4, **L.O.** 3-5) (Difficult – 40 minutes)[16]

A friend of yours is the president of Maple Imports Ltd. The company sells and services cars
imported from Korea. Maple has just completed its first year of operations. The following balance sheet was prepared by the company bookkeeper:

Maple Imports Ltd.
Balance Sheet
As at December 31, 2021

Assets	
Cash in current account	$ 4,000
Accounts receivable (note 1)	90,000
Cars and car parts (note 2)	815,000
Accumulated depreciation on cars (note 3)	(87,500)
Equipment (note 4)	170,000
Land held for future development	228,000
	$1,219,500
Equities	
Accounts payable (note 5)	$ 419,000
Bank loan payable (note 6)	320,000
Common shares (40,000 shares authorized and issued)	400,000
Net income	80,500
	$1,219,500

Notes:

1. Accounts receivable is composed of the following:

Debit balances in customer accounts	$ 145,000
Credit balances in customer accounts	(55,000)
	$ 90,000

2. The cars and car parts account is composed of the following:

Car parts for service department (at cost)	$ 65,000
Cars intended for resale (at retail price)	645,000
Cars used by executives for business purposes	105,000
	$ 815,000

The purchase price of the cars intended for resale was $530,000. The cars for the executives
were purchased on June 30, 2021, at a cost of $105,000.
3. All cars that require depreciation are being depreciated on a straight-line basis with a
three-year estimated useful life and a residual value of 30% of original cost.
4. The equipment was purchased for $170,000 on January 2, 2021. The price paid was a bar-
gain because the regular price for this equipment was $218,000. The equipment should
last for seven years but will be worthless at that time. However, the company plans to
replace it at the end of five years and expects to be able to sell it for $25,000 at that time.
The company wants to use the declining-balance method for depreciation with a rate twice
the straight-line rate, but has not yet calculated or recorded the depreciation expense
for the equipment for the year.

[16.] Reprinted from CGA-Canada FA2 examination, December 2009 with permission from Chartered Professional
Accountants of Canada, Toronto, Canada. Any changes to the original material are the sole responsibility of the
author (and/or publisher) and have not been reviewed or endorsed by the Chartered Professional Accountants
of Canada.

5. Accounts payable is composed of the following balances:

Amounts owing to suppliers	$119,000
Loan received from the majority shareholder	300,000
	$419,000

The loan was received from the majority shareholder on October 1, 2021. The loan is repayable over four years with annual payments of $50,000 plus accrued interest at 6% per year. The first payment is due on October 1, 2022. No interest has been accrued on the loan.

6. The bank loan is due on demand and is secured by the cars held for resale.

Required:

a. After adjusting for any errors, prepare a balance sheet for Maple Imports as at December 31, 2021, using the current/non-current presentation. Ignore income taxes. (Do not calculate a revised net income; simply plug in a net income figure to balance the balance sheet.)

b. On February 2, 2022, a fire in Maple's warehouse destroys $30,000 worth of car parts. Unfortunately, Maple did not have insurance to cover this loss. The financial statements for 2021 were not finalized until the end of February 2022. Briefly explain how and why this fire loss should be recognized or disclosed in the 2021 financial statements.

P3-49. Analysis of articulated financial statements   (**L.O.** 3-5) (Medium – 10 minutes)

Refer to the financial statements of Canadian Tire Corporation, Limited, in Appendix D and answer the following questions:

a. Examine the Consolidated Balance Sheets presented for the two years. Why is one dated December 31, 2016, and the other January 2, 2016 (instead of December 31, 2015)?

b. The company has presented subtotals for "Total current assets" and "Total current liabilities." Are these subtotals required by IFRS or are they optional? Identify the relevant paragraphs from IAS 1 that support your answer. (Visit http://edu.knotia.ca to access the *CPA Canada Handbook*. You may need to complete this exercise on campus, or log in through your institution's VPN portal.)

P3-50. Analysis of articulated financial statements

(**L.O.** 3-4, **L.O.** 3-5) (Medium – 10 minutes)

Refer to the financial statements for Canadian Tire Corporation, Limited, in Appendix D and answer the following questions:

a. Where do you find operating expenses listed according to their nature (source)? Which is the company's largest operating expense by nature?

b. Where do you find operating expenses listed by their function (use)?

c. Why does the company present or disclose operating expenses both by their nature and by their function?

P. MINI-CASES

CASE 1
Effects of different accrual policies

(30 minutes)

Food Processing Company was started one year ago by three managers who had worked in the food processing industry for many years. They had combined their savings plus borrowed extensively from the bank such that the company was able to invest over $10 million to start the business. Their medium-term goal (next four years) is to get the business up and running successfully and then invite others to invest after the fourth year by taking the company public. One of the three managers is now the president, and the other two are vice-presidents of production and sales, respectively.

One important issue that the owners are struggling with as they prepare their first audited financial statements is setting policies for estimated bad debts and depreciation expense. Based on their years of experience in the food processing industry, they agree that the average bad debts as a percentage of credit sales has been 4%, but has varied from a low of 2.5% to a high of 5.5%. Similarly, for the type of equipment they are using in the manufacturing process, the average useful life has been eight years. Half of the firms in the industry use the double-declining-balance method and the other half use the straight-line method to estimate depreciation expense. The company is using very new technology and methods that give them an initial cost-saving advantage. The equipment makers suggest a 10-year useful life may be reasonable, but that the technological competitive advantage may be short lived as other firms adopt this technology.

Bad debts expense and depreciation expense are material and in aggregate will represent upward of 5% (bad debts) and 20% (depreciation) of all expenses for the current year if the most conservative methods of accounting are used. If neutral methods are used, the aggregate expense would be 17%, versus 12% if these expenses are estimated generously or liberally.

Required:

You are the vice-president of finance and chief financial officer. Write a memo to the executive committee (only the three owners sit on this committee) advising them on your recommendation as to which estimates or methods (neutral, conservative, or liberal) to use to derive bad debts and depreciation expenses.

CASE 2
Grosco's redeemable preferred shares

(45 minutes)

Note: This is a difficult case intended for guided classroom discussion. A good analysis/discussion of this case does not require technical knowledge specific to redeemable preferred shares.

Grosco Corporation (GC), a public company manufacturing farm equipment, was federally incorporated in 1926. Its common shares and bonds are widely held. The company's year-end is December 31.

The bond indentures contain the following covenants:

a. At the end of any quarter, if the debt-to-equity ratio exceeds 2.5:1, dividends may not be declared.

b. At the end of any quarter, if the debt-to-equity ratio exceeds 3:1, the bond principal becomes due and payable.

GC has experienced severe financial difficulties in the past four years and has sought refinancing in an effort to remain solvent. On May 1, 2021, GC issued a new class of preferred shares bearing a cumulative annual dividend of 12% (payable quarterly). The shares are retractable (the shareholders can redeem them for cash) on demand commencing one year from the date of issuance. As a result of the share issuance, the debt-to-equity ratio reported by management decreased from 2.7:1 to 2.2:1. By the end of 2021, the ratio had increased to 2.4:1 because of increased bank borrowings.

It is now April 2022. You are the accountant in charge of the audit of GC. The 2021 financial statements have been drafted and the audit is near completion. The 2022 first-quarter financial statements have just been compiled by the company and reveal a debt-to-equity ratio of 2.8:1.

Required:

Discuss the accounting issues implied in the above fact pattern. Pay particular attention to the timing of events while applying the IFRS Framework.

Note: You do not need to refer to any specific accounting pronouncements relating to retractable preferred shares.

Sleep King Manufacturing Company (SKMC) is a public manufacturing company specializing in the fabrication of mattresses. The company has been operating from its headquarters in Toronto since 1995. SKMC primarily sells to retailers, who in turn make final sales to customers. In 2020, the company reported net income of $100,000. The company has hired your firm, D & E Auditors, to conduct the year-end audit. As you are going through the financials, you come across a few accounting issues:

a. On December 28, 2020, a large client ordered a shipment worth $20,000 of mattresses. The terms of the sale were F.O.B. destination. The order was shipped on December 30, 2020, and the client received the mattresses on January 2, 2021. Management decided to report the revenue in the fiscal year of 2020 since the inventory left the building in 2020.

b. The company decided to change the useful life of the manufacturing machinery purchased 10 years ago from 15 years to 20 years. Management stated the machinery was still running well.

c. The company decided to reduce the allowance for doubtful accounts (ADA) from 8% of credit sales to 5% of credit sales. Management stated that it believes the new estimate more reliably represents its percentage of uncollectible amounts.

d. The company decided to change its accounting policy for inventory from the moving average-cost method to the FIFO method.

   In January 2020, SKMC decided to set the annual management bonus based on net income. The bonus is set to 5% of reported net income at the end of the year.

CASE 3

Sleep King Manufacturing Company

(30 minutes)

Required:

a. As the auditor of SKMC, which of the above issues would you be most concerned about and why?

b. Based on the information above, would you say that the quality of earnings of SKMC is high or low? Why?

c. What problems do you see arising from the extensive use of estimates in accrual accounting?

d. Between the balance sheet, income statement, and cash flow statement, which financial statement do you believe is least affected by estimates? Explain your reasoning.

CHAPTER 4
Revenue Recognition

LEARNING OBJECTIVES

After studying this chapter, you should be able to:

L.O. 4-1. Explain why there is a range of alternatives for revenue recognition that are conceptually valid and the rationale for accounting standards to prescribe a smaller set of alternatives.

L.O. 4-2. Apply the general revenue and expense recognition criteria to a variety of contexts.

L.O. 4-3. Apply the revenue and expense recognition criteria for long-term contracts, including the prospective treatment applicable to changes in estimates.

L.O. 4-4. Apply the accounting standards for long-term contracts when profitability is in doubt.

L.O. 4-5. Evaluate the risks of revenue misstatements and the appropriateness of revenue recognition policies in specific circumstances by applying professional judgment.

CPA competencies addressed in this chapter:

1.1.2 Evaluates the appropriateness of the basis of financial reporting (Level B)
   a. Fundamental accounting concepts and principles (qualitative characteristics of accounting information, basic elements)
   b. Methods of measurement
   c. Differences between accrual accounting compared to cash accounting

1.2.1 Develops or evaluates appropriate accounting policies and procedures – Ethical professional judgment (Level B)

1.2.2 Evaluates treatment for routine transactions (Level A)
   m. Revenue recognition/revenue from contracts with customers, and accounting for revenue and related expenses
   o. Changes in accounting policies and estimates, and errors

1.3.2 Prepares routine financial statement note disclosure (Level B)

1.4.2 Evaluates financial statements including note disclosures (Level B)
   c. Financial statements in accordance with applicable standards

BMW Group (Bayerische Motoren Werke or Bavarian Motor Works, www.bmwgroup.com, Frankfurt Stock Exchange ticker: BMW) is one of the world's leading luxury vehicle manufacturers. The company's portfolio includes well-recognized brands such as MINI, Rolls-Royce, and, of course, BMW.

You should already be familiar with the accounting for the revenue and cost of sales for tangible products such as cars: roughly speaking, revenue and costs are recorded "at the point of sale." However, BMW also sells some of its vehicles to car rental companies. In some cases, BMW has an obligation to take back the vehicles after a period of time. When should the company recognize revenues for such transactions? Is the appropriate time at the point of sale?

BMW often includes a package of services in conjunction with the sale of each vehicle. For example, if the sale of a BMW 323i sedan for $35,000 includes four years of maintenance services such as oil changes and tune-ups, should the company record the full $35,000 as revenue at the point of sale?

In addition to manufacturing and selling cars and motorcycles, BMW also provides financial services in the form of vehicle loans and leases. How should BMW recognize revenue from these financial services?

Recognition is the process of presenting an item in the financial statements, as opposed to merely disclosing that item in the notes. Many transactions and items that meet the definitions of financial statement elements (asset, liability, equity, revenue, ordinary expense, gain, loss; see Chapter 2) do not appear on the balance sheet or income statement. For example, some patents will meet the definition of an asset, but the value of patents usually is not recognized on the balance sheet. In this chapter, we focus on the recognition of revenues and expenses on the income statement.

recognition The process of presenting an item in the financial statements, as opposed to merely disclosing that item in the notes.

A. RANGE OF CONCEPTUAL ALTERNATIVES FOR REVENUE RECOGNITION

L.O. 4-1. Explain why there is a range of alternatives for revenue recognition that are conceptually valid and the rationale for accounting standards to prescribe a smaller set of alternatives.

THRESHOLD CONCEPT
EFFICIENT SECURITIES MARKETS

In theory, there is a wide range of possible points at which revenue could be recognized. The breadth of this range reflects a business's value creation process, as illustrated in Exhibit 4-1. (For simplicity, the diagram is linear even though the different stages can sometimes overlap.) In terms of value creation, the earliest point at which one can reasonably argue for revenue recognition is when the knowledge for a business, product, or process is developed—for example, a biotechnology company creates value for its owners when it discovers a new vaccine for a disease, or a mining company when it discovers a rich deposit of aluminum. For a publicly traded company, the value created will often be evident in the stock price of the enterprise if the discoveries are significant in relationship to the size of that enterprise. Conceptually, it is possible to argue for revenue recognition at this point because the company will be able to monetize these discoveries at some point in the future, either by commercializing the breakthroughs or selling the knowledge to another party.

Exhibit 4-1	A business's value creation process

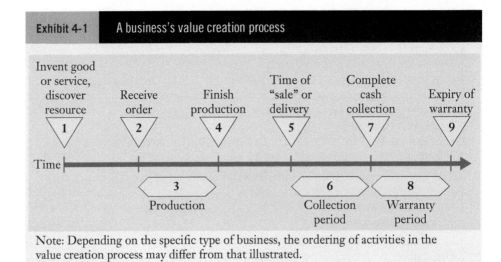

Note: Depending on the specific type of business, the ordering of activities in the value creation process may differ from that illustrated.

The value creation process continues with marketing efforts and the receipt of orders from customers. The production process, of course, also adds value. Depending on whether the product is a good or service, delivery occurs during production (for a service) or after production (for a good). If the business makes the sale on credit, then a portion of value added is in the form of financial services (i.e., lending to the buyer). Furthermore, many businesses provide a guarantee against product defects or provide warranties that their products will be in good operating condition for a certain length of time. These guarantees are also part of the value-added services provided by the business since they encourage more customers to buy from the enterprise. At the most conservative extreme, a business would delay revenue recognition to the point at which the warranty period has elapsed and it has received all payments from the customer. This is illustrated on the far right in Exhibit 4-1.

If the full range of alternatives discussed above and portrayed in Exhibit 4-1 were acceptable accounting policies, the potential disparities among the financial statements of different companies would be immense. This great scope of choice obviously impairs the comparability of financial statements among enterprises. More importantly, the methods that recognize revenue early in the value creation process entail substantially more uncertainties about the cash flows that the enterprise will ultimately realize and correspondingly lower degrees of verifiability and reliability.

THRESHOLD CONCEPT
CONCEPTUAL FRAMEWORK

As we discussed in Chapter 1, less reliable accounting numbers are less useful for contracting purposes, particularly for evaluating the performance of management. Less reliable performance measures allow for a greater degree of moral hazard: the easier it is for management to manipulate the reported performance, the more difficult it is to motivate desirable value creation activities. For example, if a biotechnology company were able to recognize revenue when it discovers a new vaccine, determining the amount of revenue would require estimates of the likelihood of the drug passing all regulatory approvals and, subsequent to that, future price and demand for the vaccine. In turn, future price and demand forecasts depend on the availability of similar or alternative treatments, the potential development of other new and superior vaccines in the future, whether government or private health insurance providers will cover the cost of the vaccine and the amount they would be willing to pay, and so on. As you can see, this would be a daunting forecasting exercise. Not only would the forecast results lack precision, they would be virtually impossible for an auditor to verify. Given the lack of verifiability, management will have significant latitude to bias the forecasts to its advantage, so this information has questionable value as a reflection of management performance.

In summary, early revenue recognition methods entail more uncertainty, requiring more estimates and judgments from management, resulting in financial statements that are less accurate gauges of managerial performance. Consequently, accounting standards specify revenue recognition criteria that allow only a subset of the revenue recognition policies depicted in Exhibit 4-1. The next section discusses these criteria.

THRESHOLD CONCEPT
INFORMATION ASYMMETRY

THRESHOLD CONCEPT
CONCEPTUAL FRAMEWORK

THRESHOLD CONCEPT
EARNINGS QUALITY

 CHECKPOINT **CP4-1**

Why do accounting standards for revenue recognition not reflect the value creation process?

B. AN OVERVIEW OF REVENUE RECOGNITION CRITERIA

The criteria for revenue recognition are contained in IFRS 15—Revenue from contracts with customers. Issued in 2014 jointly by the International Accounting Standards Board and the Financial Accounting Standards Board in the United States, it is a comprehensive standard that incorporates and unifies a vast number of previously existing disparate rules and regulations regarding revenue.

At the outset, it is important to note that the reference to "contract" in the standard includes all forms of contract, whether written or verbal, formal or implied by customary business practice. For instance, a common everyday sale of fruits and vegetables by a grocery retailer is included in the scope of this standard, as would be a complex contract to build a skyscraper. The standard covers any contract with a *customer*—a counterparty that has contracted to obtain goods or services from the reporting entity. That is, the contractual relationship has the potential to result in revenue for the reporting entity. On the other hand, there are some notable exclusions from IFRS 15:

L.O. 4-2.   Apply the general revenue and expense recognition criteria to a variety of contexts.

- lease contracts (covered by IFRS 16 and Chapter 17)
- insurance contracts (covered by IFRS 4, a specialized field not covered in this text)
- financial instruments (covered by IFRS 9 and Chapters 7, 11–14)
- non-monetary exchanges between entities in the same line of business to facilitate sales to customers or potential customers[1]

---

[1] IFRS 15 paragraph 5 provides the following example: "… a contract between two oil companies that agree to an exchange of oil to fulfill demand from their customers in different specified locations on a timely basis."

This standard specifies five steps for revenue recognition. These five steps encompass both recognition and measurement of revenue, and are as follows:

1. Identify the contract with the customer.
2. Identify the performance obligations.
3. Determine the transaction price.
4. Allocate the transaction price to performance obligations.
5. Recognize revenue in accordance with performance.

These steps will be explained in more detail below. At this point, it would be helpful to gain an overview of what they mean to see why we need these five steps. Basically, to recognize revenue in the final step, it is necessary to figure out first of all whether there is a contract that potentially results in revenue (Step 1). A contract has two sides/parties, so it should specify both (a) what the entity needs to do (Step 2) and (b) what it will receive as consideration from the customer (Step 3). By allocating the portion of the transaction price to the corresponding performance obligation (Step 4), we are then able to record revenue in amounts that correspond to completion of each performance obligation (Step 5). Exhibit 4-2 summarizes and illustrates this five-step process.

Exhibit 4-2	Schematic of five-step revenue recognition process

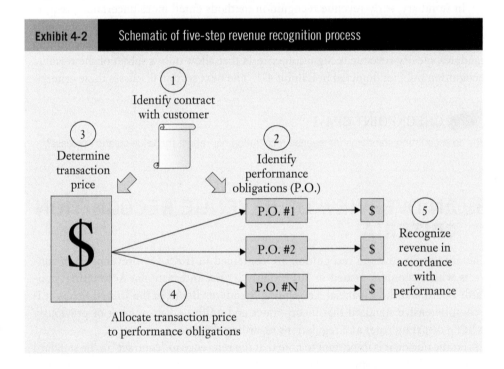

For many transactions that we experience on a daily basis, these steps are fairly straightforward to apply. For example, suppose a car dealership sells a car with a cost of $25,000 for $28,000 in cash. This sale does not involve any additional maintenance or warranty services. Exhibit 4-3 summarizes what the five steps entail for this simple transaction.

Exhibit 4-3	Simple example applying the five steps of revenue recognition to the sale of a car
Step	**Application**
1. Identify the contract	The written contract for the purchase and sale is readily identifiable.
2. Identify the performance obligation	The performance obligation is the delivery of the car by the dealership to the buyer.

(*Continued*)

Exhibit 4-3	Continued
3. Determine the transaction price	The contract specifies the price as $28,000 to be settled in cash.
4. Allocate the transaction price to performance obligations	There is a single performance obligation, which is the delivery of the car, so no allocation is required.

5. Recognize income in accordance with performance	Upon delivery of the car to the buyer, the car dealership can recognize revenue along with the associated expense with these journal entries:
	
	Dr. Cash 28,000
	  Cr. Sales revenue 28,000
	Dr. Cost of goods sold 25,000
	  Cr. Inventories 25,000

This simple example is representative of most transactions that we encounter on a daily basis, whether the transactions involve goods (as in this case) or services (such as a restaurant meal). However, there are also many transactions for which the application of these steps is less straightforward.

 CHECKPOINT **CP4-2**

Explain the need for the five-step revenue recognition process.

C. REVENUE RECOGNITION CRITERIA: A MORE DETAILED LOOK

Let us now look at these steps in more detail and uncover some of the complexities in each step. Exhibit 4-4 summarizes the key requirements in these steps as specified in IFRS 15.

1. Identify the contract

The first step in revenue recognition is by necessity the identification of the relevant contract. Simply, we need to know whether there is potential revenue for which we need to account. Requirements (a) to (c) are self-explanatory and do not require further elaboration here. Requirement (d) prevents revenue recognition in situations that have no commercial substance (i.e., shams), such as the exchange of coal between two mining companies. Requirement (e) prevents revenue recognition if there is a high enough probability of not obtaining the benefits from the transaction (usually in the form of cash); this requirement is consistent with the conceptual discussion in the previous section regarding the need to reduce the degree of uncertainty to an acceptable level before recognizing revenue.

2. Identify the performance obligation

Some contracts with customers involve more than one performance obligation. Those obligations can be a bundle of goods, or a combination of services, or some mixture of both. This step entails separating one performance obligation from another.

Separating performance obligations hinges on whether one good or service is *distinct* from another. Both of the following conditions need to be satisfied for a good or service to be distinct: (a) the customer can benefit from the good or service on its own or together with other readily available resources, and (b) the good or service is separately identifiable from other promises in the contract. The first condition is whether the good or service is *inherently* capable of being distinct while the second considers distinctiveness in the *context* of the contract. One can think of many examples that

Exhibit 4-4	Key requirements in the five steps of revenue recognition[2]
Step	**Key requirements in IFRS 15**
1. Identify the contract	¶9 An entity shall account for a contract with a customer that is within the scope of this Standard only when all of the following criteria are met: (a) the parties to the contract have approved the contract (in writing, orally, or in accordance with other customary business practices) and are committed to perform their respective obligations; (b) the entity can identify each party's rights regarding the goods or services to be transferred; (c) the entity can identify the payment terms for the goods and services to be transferred; (d) the contract has commercial substance (i.e., the risk, timing, or amount of the entity's future cash flows is expected to change as a result of the contract); and (e) it is probable that the entity will collect the consideration to which it will be entitled in exchange for the goods or services that will be transferred to the customer. . . .
2. Identify the performance obligation	¶22 At contract inception, an entity shall assess the goods or services promised in a contract with a customer and shall identify as a performance obligation each promise to transfer to the customer either: (a) a good or service (or a bundle of goods or services) that is distinct; or (b) a series of distinct goods or services that are substantially the same and that have the same pattern of transfer to the customer.
3. Determine the transaction price	¶47 An entity shall consider the terms of the contract and its customary business practices to determine the transaction price. The transaction price is the amount of consideration to which an entity expects to be entitled in exchange for transferring promised goods or services to a customer, excluding amounts collected on behalf of third parties (for example, some sales taxes). The consideration promised in a contract with a customer may include fixed amounts, variable amounts, or both.
4. Allocate the transaction price to performance obligations	¶73 The objective when allocating the transaction price is for an entity to allocate the transaction price to each performance obligation (or distinct good or service) in an amount that depicts the amount of consideration to which the entity expects to be entitled in exchange for transferring the promised goods or services to the customer. ¶74 To meet the allocation objective, an entity shall allocate the transaction price to each performance obligation identified in the contract on a relative stand-alone selling price basis. . . .
5. Recognize income in accordance with performance	¶31 An entity shall recognize revenue when (or as) the entity satisfies a performance obligation by transferring a promised good or service (i.e., an asset) to a customer. An asset is transferred when (or as) the customer obtains control of that asset.

satisfy inherent condition (a) but not the contextual condition (b). For instance, in a contract to construct a building involving the supply of bricks, piping, wiring, engineering, and construction labour, each of these components could satisfy condition (a), but not (b) because provision of all the individual components is for the purpose of fulfilling the overall promise of delivering a completed building. Similarly, the ingredients and labour in a restaurant meal could be separable in theory, but in context they should be combined.

Paragraph 22 (shown in Exhibit 4-4) also refers to "a series of distinct goods or services that are substantially the same." This clause refers to situations in which a contract specifies the repeated delivery of the same good or service over a period of time. For instance, a company may enter a contract to provide 5,000 tonnes of aluminum to a customer each month over a 24-month period. This has ramifications for the recognition of revenue in Step 5 below.

[2.] Copyright © 2015 IFRS Foundation.

3. Determine the transaction price

The transaction price in most situations is readily determined because most transactions involve fixed amounts of consideration. However, complications can arise from several sources as explained immediately below. Note, however, that the credit risk of the customer is not a factor to be considered in determining the transaction price.

a. Non-cash consideration

In transactions involving non-cash consideration, the seller needs to estimate the fair value of the non-cash consideration and combine it with the cash consideration to arrive at the transaction price. For example, a buyer of a new car trades in an old vehicle as partial consideration for the purchase, in addition to paying $20,000. If the dealership estimates the fair value of the old vehicle to be $7,500, then the transaction price would be $20,000 + $7,500 = $27,500.

In some cases, the fair value of the non-cash consideration cannot be reliably estimated. When this occurs, we can use the stand-alone selling price of the promised good or service to infer the value of the non-cash consideration. Continuing with the trade-in example, if the fair value of the old car is not reliably estimable, while the stand-alone selling price of the new car is $28,000, then the implied fair value of the old car traded in would be $28,000 − $20,000 cash = $8,000.

Note that non-monetary transactions involving assets not in an enterprise's main revenue generating activities (e.g., transfer of operating equipment) fall outside the scope of IFRS 15 as they are not contracts with customers. We address these other non-monetary transfers in Chapter 8.

b. Significant financing component

Enterprises need to reflect the time value of money when it is significant—that is, when the timing of payment differs substantially from the timing of delivery of the goods or services. In these circumstances, enterprises need to recognize revenue at the amount that would have been recorded had the customer paid in cash. For instance, if a company sells goods in exchange for payment of $121,000 in two years' time, then the transaction price would be less than $121,000, given a positive time value of money. How much less depends on the applicable interest rate. If the interest rate is 10%, then the transaction price would be $121,000 ÷ $1.10^2 = $100,000$.

Of course, many businesses extend trade credit to customers, especially those with business-to-business (rather than business-to-consumer) customer relationships. To account for the financing component of this trade credit would be very time consuming with little benefit—the transaction volume is often high while the time to collection is short. As a practical expedient, IFRS 15 allows enterprises to forgo the adjustment for financing if, at contract inception, the enterprise expects to collect the promised payment within one year of delivering the promised goods or services. This practical expedient applies to almost all trade credit arrangements.

c. Consideration payable to customer

In some instances, an enterprise promises to pay a cash consideration, for example, to provide incentive for the customer to continue purchasing from the enterprise. This incentive can be provided directly to the enterprise's customers, or indirectly to anyone in the supply chain down to the final consumer. For example, a detergent manufacturer issues coupons to consumers who purchase the company's products through grocery retailers, who in turn source their products from a wholesale distributor. In such situations, the detergent manufacturer needs to anticipate the amount of coupon redemptions, and deduct the estimated amount payable to consumers from the transaction price of the detergent sold to the distributor. This requirement prevents companies from recording sales revenue at artificially high prices upon sale, and only later recording the consequence of the promised consideration payable to customers.

For example, suppose Superclean Corp. sells 200,000 units of a new laundry detergent to Best Grocery Wholesale Ltd. at $3 per unit. This detergent has a manufacturing cost of $1.50 per unit, and the suggested retail price is $8. Suppose also that Superclean issues 400,000 store-shelf coupons for $2 each, redeemable at the cash register when a consumer purchases this new detergent. Superclean estimates that 30% of the coupons will be redeemed. Subsequently, retailers submit claims on the coupons collected, amounting to $250,000. As a result, Superclean would record the following journal entries:

Exhibit 4-5	Journal entries to recognize revenue, consideration payable to customers, and cost of sales for Superclean Corp.		
Upon delivery of 200,000 units to Best Grocery:			
Dr. Account receivable (200,000 units × $3/unit)		600,000	
Cr. Sales revenue			360,000
Cr. Consideration payable to customers (30% × 400,000 coupons × $2/coupon)			240,000
Dr. Cost of goods sold (200,000 units × $1.50/unit)		300,000	
Cr. Inventories			300,000
When claims on the coupons are received from retailers:			
Dr. Consideration payable to customers (from above)		240,000	
Dr. Sales revenue		10,000	
Cr. Accounts payable (given)			250,000

d. Variable consideration

Consideration is considered variable whenever there is some uncertainty over the amount of consideration involved. The coupon example just discussed can also be used as an example of variable consideration, because the final net amount received was dependent on the rate of coupon redemptions. In the example, the actual redemptions exceeded expected redemptions by $10,000.

A different example of variable consideration that is common is volume discounts, in which companies offer customers lower per-unit prices when a customer's purchases over a period of time exceed a certain threshold. For example, suppose Best Quality Bicycles (BQB) has a normal selling price of $100 per unit of its most popular model. The company offers retailers a 10% discount if a particular retailer purchases at least 500 units in a year. The discount applies to all units purchased in the year if the 500-unit threshold is met. Now consider Retailer X, whom BQB predicts with high probability will not meet the 500-unit threshold based on past experience. In the first half of the year, Retailer X purchases 200 units, and BQB charges the full $100 per unit, and records revenue of 200 units × $100/unit = $20,000. At this point, the purchase history is consistent with BQB's expectation that Retailer X will not exceed 500 units of purchases for the year. However, in the second half of the year, Retailer X makes an unexpectedly large purchase of 400 units, bringing the year's total to 600 units. As a result, BQB will record revenue of only $34,000 for the sale of 400 units, being $36,000 for the 400 units at $90/unit, less $2,000 of revenue reversal on the 200 units sold in the first half of the year (see Exhibit 4-6).

Exhibit 4-6	Calculation of transaction price on Best Quality Bicycles's sales to Retailer X		
	# units	Unit price	Total
Sale #1 (Jan. – Jun.)	200	$100	$20,000
Sale #2 (Jul. – Dec.)	400	90	36,000
Revenue reversal (200 units × $10/unit)			(2,000)
	600	$ 90	$54,000

This example brings up two additional issues relating to variable consideration. First, the estimate for the amount of variable consideration should use one of two methods, whichever is more suited to the circumstances. These methods use either (a) the expected value, which involves applying probabilities to possible outcomes and summing; or (b) the most likely amount. The latter is most appropriate when there are a small number of outcomes. In the case of Best Quality Bicycles, the customer either meets the threshold or does not meet the threshold, so only one of the two outcomes is possible. Therefore, it makes more sense to use the most likely amount of consideration ($100 or $90), rather than the expected value (some amount between $90 and $100).

The second issue is the variable consideration constraint. IFRS 15 states as follows:

> ¶56   An entity shall include in the transaction price some or all of the variable considerable estimated in accordance with paragraph 53 [referring to the expected value or most likely amount] only to the extent that it is highly probable that a significant reversal in the amount of cumulative revenue recognized will not occur when the uncertainty associated with the variable consideration is subsequently resolved.

This paragraph is somewhat difficult to read, but it essentially says that we should be prudent when we face uncertainty in the transaction price, because the paragraph refers to "highly probable" rather than just "probable" (the latter meaning "more likely than not"). In other words, we need to be quite sure that we will not have to reverse a significant amount of revenue in the future before recording that revenue. This variable consideration constraint is one-sided, so that revenue reversals should be rare but significant additional revenue could be realized regularly in the future when the uncertainty is resolved.

4. Allocate the transaction price to performance obligations

As noted in Exhibit 4-4, the allocation of the transaction price to performance obligations specified in the contract should be based on the relative stand-alone selling prices of the performance obligations.[3] The **stand-alone selling price** is the price at which an entity would sell a promised good or service separately to a customer. For instance, a contract has three performance obligations with a transaction price of $900. The stand-alone prices of performance obligations #1, #2, and #3 are $500, $300, and $200, respectively, totalling $1,000. The transaction price could be lower because the seller is providing a price concession to reward the customer for buying a bundle of the three products together, for example. In any case, the allocation of the $900 results in $450, $270, and $180 being allocated to the three performance obligations, as shown in Exhibit 4-7.

stand-alone selling price   The price at which an entity would sell a promised good or service separately to a customer.

[3.] Historically, the relative stand-alone selling prices method has also been called the relative fair value method, or the proportional method. The latter is appropriate because the allocation is based on each item's selling price in proportion to the total.

Exhibit 4-7	Example of transaction price allocation based on stand-alone selling prices			
	Stand-alone selling price	% of total selling price	Transaction × price	Amount allocated to each = performance obligation
Performance obligation #1	$ 500	50	$900	$ 450
Performance obligation #2	300	30	$900	270
Performance obligation #3	200	20	$900	180
	$1,000	100		$900

To the extent possible, enterprises should use *observable* stand-alone selling prices. However, this may not be possible in some situations, so estimates need to be made. IFRS 15 paragraph 79 identifies three alternatives but notes that other approaches may be suitable.

a. Adjusted market assessment approach—involves estimating what a customer would be willing to pay for the good or service or what competitors charge for a similar good or service.

b. Expected cost plus margin approach—involves estimating expected costs to provide the good or service and adding a profit margin typical for that good or service.

c. Residual approach—computes the stand-alone selling prices as the transaction price less the total of the observable stand-alone selling prices of other goods and services involved in the transaction. This approach is only acceptable if either (i) the good or service in question has a highly variable selling price, or (ii) the entity has not yet established a price for that good or service. Suppose in the example given in Exhibit 4-7, if the selling price for performance obligation #3 has not yet been established, then the residual approach would assign an estimated selling price of $100, being the transaction price of $900 less the stand-alone selling prices of the other performance obligations of $500 + $300.

5. Recognize revenue in accordance with performance

In the final step, an enterprise recognizes revenue according to the progress it makes toward complete performance of each obligation in the contract. Since the previous steps have allocated the transaction price to the various performance obligations, this final revenue recognition step is conducted for *each* performance obligation. Performance either occurs at a point in time or over a period of time. The sale of goods will typically result in performance at a point in time (i.e., delivery of the goods to the customer). More generally, IFRS 15 states that performance occurs when an enterprise transfers control of the promised good or service to the customer. In deciding whether control has been transferred at a point in time, management should consider whether the customer (IFRS 15 paragraph 38):

a. is obligated to pay for the asset;
b. has legal title to the asset;
c. has taken physical possession;
d. bears the significant risk and rewards of ownership; or
e. has accepted the asset.

This list of indicators is fairly comprehensive, although other factors may also be considered.

By default, IFRS presumes that revenue should be recognized at a point in time, unless the enterprise satisfies its performance obligation over time. The enterprise satisfies its performance obligation over time, and recognizes revenue accordingly if any one of three criteria are met, as per IFRS 15 paragraph 35:[4]

a. "the customer simultaneously receives and consumes the benefits" of the good or service;
b. "the entity's performance creates or enhances an asset that the customer controls"; or
c. "the entity's performance does not create an asset with an alternative use and the entity has an enforceable right to payment for the performance completed to date."

The commonality in the three criteria is that the enterprise transfers control of the good or service to the customer over time. In other words, the enterprise does not retain an asset because (a) the customer has consumed it; (b) the customer controls it; or (c) the seller has legally sold the asset in the sense that it will be compensated for it. These criteria are important in, for example, situations in which a company contracts to produce for a customer a series of identical goods or services over a period of time. In such situations, the company is able to recognize revenue over time by satisfying the criteria, rather than waiting until it transfers control of all of the promised units.

For accounting purposes, performance over a period of time only has consequences if the period of service extends over more than one reporting period. That is, there are many instances in which performance over a period of time has no accounting consequences (for example, a restaurant meal or haircut) because the period of performance is complete at the cut-off date for the reporting period. Later in this chapter, we will look in more detail at the procedures to recognize revenue on performance obligations that extend over a number of years (i.e., long-term contracts).

6. Examples of multiple performance obligations, allocation, and recognition: Franchise fees

A **franchise** arrangement is one in which one party (the franchisor) licenses its trademarks, business practices, and so on to another (the franchisee). For example, 80% of McDonald's restaurants are operated under franchise arrangements between McDonald's Corporation and thousands of independent franchisees.[5] In these arrangements, the franchisee typically pays the franchisor two types of fees: an initial fee for establishing the franchise and an ongoing fee. Accounting for the ongoing fee is usually straightforward: whether the fee is a fixed amount per period or a royalty related to revenues, the amount is revenue to the franchisor.

> **franchise** A commercial arrangement in which one party (the franchisor) licenses its trademarks, business practices, and so on to another (the franchisee).

On the other hand, accounting for the initial fees requires more judgment because it often involves multiple deliverables. Even though the franchisor has received payment, the issue is *whether the franchisor is entitled to recognize the entire initial fee as revenue* or whether it should defer a portion of the revenue to future periods. To what extent has the franchisor performed the services required to earn those fees? If the fee represents services to be provided during the term of the franchise agreement, over what period and in what amounts should the initial fee be amortized into income? There are no easy answers to these questions, and professional judgment must be applied on a case-by-case basis. For example, some portion of the initial franchise fee could represent compensation to the franchisor for a commitment to supply products to the franchisee at reduced margins. If the franchisor is the exclusive supplier of products such as hamburger patties, it may be very difficult to determine what the "normal" profit margin on the products should be.

[4.] Copyright © 2015 IFRS Foundation.

[5.] McDonald's Corporation website.

To illustrate the accounting for franchise revenue, suppose Delicio Restaurants signs a franchise agreement to allow a franchisee to operate in northwest Calgary for a 10-year period. The agreement requires the franchisee to pay Delicio $200,000 initially and a royalty of 2% of sales revenue thereafter. Sales at this franchise location for the first year are $2 million. The management of Delicio estimates that the value of services rendered to this franchisee—such as location and demographic analysis, initial staffing, and training—totalled $80,000. Management also believes that the remainder of the initial fee (i.e., $120,000) relates to services to be provided evenly over the 10-year period. To account for franchise revenue, Delicio would record the following entries shown in Exhibit 4-8.

Exhibit 4-8	Journal entries to record Delicio's franchise revenue from the northwest Calgary location		
To record receipt of initial franchise fee			
Dr. Cash		200,000	
Cr. Franchise revenue			80,000
Cr. Deferred revenue			120,000
To recognize annual revenue on initial franchise fee at end of one year			
Dr. Deferred revenue		12,000	
Cr. Franchise revenue ($120,000 ÷ 10 years)			12,000
To recognize annual revenue on sales royalty at end of one year			
Dr. Cash		40,000	
Cr. Franchise revenue (2% × $2,000,000)			40,000

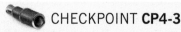 CHECKPOINT **CP4-3**

Why is it important to identify when a sale contains multiple performance obligations?

D. OTHER RELATED ISSUES

1. Expense recognition

IFRS does not provide much in the way of specific guidance for the recognition of expenses. Instead, the guidance is provided as part of the Conceptual Framework discussed in Chapter 2.[6] The definition of expenses in conjunction with general recognition criteria means that enterprises should recognize expenses when there is a decrease in an asset or an increase in a liability and the amount can be measured reliably. In addition, it makes logical sense to record an expense at the same time as the revenue to which the expense relates. Traditionally, this process has been called matching of expenses to revenue. For example, Exhibit 4-2 records the cost of goods sold at the same time as the related revenue.

Some costs do not have a direct link with revenues. For example, using up office equipment is part of the operations of an enterprise and allows it to generate revenues; however, one cannot (at least not easily) make a direct link with specific revenues. In

---

[6.] See paragraphs 4.49–4.53 of "The conceptual framework for financial reporting" in IFRS.

such instances, the recommended approach is a systematic and rational allocation of the costs. A common example of such an allocation is the depreciation of property, plant, and equipment. Another example is accruing interest expense in the period in which the borrowed funds are being used in operations.[7]

Some transactions give rise to expenses simply by virtue of not satisfying the condition for recognition as an asset. Recall from Chapter 2 that an asset's *definition* includes three characteristics (it must arise from past events, be controlled by the enterprise, and have future economic benefits), and *recognition* requires satisfying two additional criteria (the future benefits are probable and the asset's value can be measured reliably). For example, if an enterprise spends $5 million but cannot demonstrate future benefits attributable to that $5 million, then the amount cannot be recorded as an asset and it must be expensed instead. Thus, the default position is that expenditures are expenses unless they satisfy the definition and recognition criteria for assets.

2. Contract costs

In some situations, particularly for large contracts, enterprises incur significant costs to obtain a contract with a customer (e.g., costs to prepare bid documents to submit to a tendering process, legal fees for contract preparation, sales commissions). IFRS 15 recommends that such cost should be recognized as an asset *if it can identify the incremental costs*. It is important the costs be incrementally incurred to obtain the contract, rather than costs that would otherwise have been incurred. Some care is required in the interpretation of whether costs are incremental. Costs incurred to prepare bid documents mentioned above would be incurred whether the bidder is awarded the contract or not, so they are *not* considered incremental and therefore cannot be capitalized. On the other hand, the legal fees for contract preparation and sales commissions would be paid only when an enterprise obtains a contract with a customer, so these two costs can be capitalized.

Once capitalized, this asset would be amortized as an expense in a way consistent with the satisfaction of the performance obligations. As a practical expedient, IFRS 15 allows enterprises to expense contract costs if the period of amortization is one year or less.

3. Warranties

Many enterprises provide warranties on the goods and services that they provide. For accounting purposes, IFRS 15 distinguishes two types of warranties:

- assurance-type warranties that ensure that the customer receives the delivered product as specified in the contract; and
- service-type warranties that provide service beyond the assurance-type warranty.

An assurance-type warranty is a guarantee of quality—a guarantee that the product has the level of quality that is expected according to the contract. For manufactured products, this can be thought of as a guarantee against manufacturing defects. No manufacturing process is flawless, so this type of guarantee makes sense to eliminate the risk of the customer having to incur the cost in the event of being the unlikely one to be sold an item with an inherent defect. As this type of defect and the resulting warranty are inseparable from the production process, assurance-type warranties do not constitute a distinct performance obligation. Instead, the enterprise records a warranty liability for the estimated cost of fulfilling the terms of the warranty, in accordance with IAS 37—Provisions, contingent liabilities, and contingent assets (see Chapter 11).

[7.] For self-constructed assets, some interest costs may be capitalized instead of expensed. This issue will be addressed in Chapter 8 in relation to property, plant, and equipment.

On the other hand, a service-type warranty is a distinct performance obligation because it goes over and above simply guaranteeing that the product has no defects at the time of sale. An example is a warranty that allows a smart phone customer to obtain a replacement phone if the phone breaks for any reason (dropped, crushed under a car, etc.). Such breakage has no connection to the quality of the phone at the time of sale. This additional service is a performance obligation that is distinct from the delivery of the phone to the customer, and therefore should be accounted for accordingly.

Similarly, in the opening vignette of this chapter involving the sale of a BMW 323i sedan, the four years of maintenance services included in the $35,000 transaction price is a performance obligation distinct from the delivery of the car, so a portion of the $35,000 needs to be allocated to the service obligation and brought into income over the four-year period of service.

4. Onerous contracts

onerous contract   A contract in which the unavoidable cost of meeting the obligations under the contract exceeds the economic benefits expected to be received under it.

When enterprises enter into contracts with customers, it would be unusual for them to knowingly enter into a contract that would lead to negative expected net benefits. In some instances, they enter into such contracts for reasons beyond the particular contract itself, such as to establish a long-term relationship with an important client (known as a loss leader). In addition, over time, it is possible for circumstances to change and to result in expected net benefits that are negative, even though at the inception of the contract they were positive. Regardless of the reason, these situations result in an onerous contract. Formally, an **onerous contract** is one in which the unavoidable cost of meeting the obligations under the contract exceeds the economic benefits expected to be received under it (IAS 37 paragraph 68).

For accounting purposes, we need to identify onerous contracts because when an enterprise has such a contract, it needs to record the full effect of the expected loss in the period in which it identifies the contract as onerous. This treatment is different from non-onerous (i.e., profitable) contracts. Whereas we record only the portion of revenues and expenses according to the degree of completion of a profitable contract, we record all the expected losses on an onerous contract. The onerous contract might be only 20% completed, for instance, but 100% of the expected loss would be recognized in the period when the contract is identified as onerous. A detailed illustration of accounting for onerous contracts will follow in Section F.

E. SPECIFIC REVENUE RECOGNITION SITUATIONS

This and the next section discuss situations in which revenue is recognized at a time that is different from the point of sale to illustrate the importance of the different revenue recognition criteria, such as measurement uncertainty and the transfer of risks and rewards. This section provides relatively brief coverage of consignment sales, installment sales, and revenue recognition at point of production. The next section will address long-term construction contracts in considerable depth.

1. Consignment sales

consignment   An arrangement where one party (the consignor) provides goods to a second party to sell; however, the second party (the consignee) has the right to return all or a portion of the goods to the first party if the goods are not sold.

Recall from Section C that revenue recognition in Step 5 requires the transfer of control. Situations in which sales are made on consignment highlight the importance of this criterion. **Consignment** is an arrangement where one party (the consignor) provides goods to a second party to sell; however, the second party (the consignee) has the right to return all or a portion of the goods to the first party if the goods are not sold. As a result, the consignor retains control. In particular, the consignor retains legal title and bears the significant risks and rewards of ownership, while the consignee is not obligated to pay for the goods until they are sold. Therefore, the consignor does not record revenue when it delivers the product to the consignee; rather, it must defer the revenue to the date when the right of return expires. At that later date, control has been transferred and the amount of sales can be determined with a reasonable degree of accuracy.

A common example of consignment sales is the distribution of magazines. There are a number of business reasons for using consignment rather than the more typical supply chain, but the most important is related to the uncertainty in demand. By offering a consignment arrangement, the publisher removes the demand risk from the retailer, which increases the number of retailers willing to stock the product as well as the volume of inventory held by retailers, thereby increasing the total volume of product sales. For magazines sold at convenience stores, supermarkets, and bookstores, ensuring that consumers are able to browse the magazines is a critical factor in maintaining and increasing circulation, while the marginal cost of printing extra copies is low relative to the costs of developing the magazine content.

For example, suppose Prestige Publications on March 1 delivers 100,000 copies of one of its monthly magazines to its distributor, which in turn delivers the magazines to retailers. Retailers have the right to return unsold copies to the distributor, which also has the right to return them to the publisher. The retail price of each copy is $4.95, while the price charged to the distributor is $1.20. On April 15, the distributor returns 25,000 unsold copies to Prestige. Based on these facts, Prestige would recognize revenue on April 15 for 75,000 copies sold at $1.20 each, or $90,000. The inventory account would also be adjusted at this date to reflect the units sold and units that should be written down or written off.

2. Installment sales

Installment sales are arrangements whereby the vendor allows the buyer to make payments over an extended period of time even though the buyer receives the product at the beginning of the installment period. Often, legal title to the product does not transfer to the buyer until all the payments have been made. For example, a furniture retailer may allow consumers to pay for a sofa over 36 months. In such arrangements, there is a *higher degree of uncertainty over the amount that will ultimately be collected*, so it may be inappropriate to recognize all of the profits on the sale at the time of delivery to the buyer. In other words, the transaction does not satisfy criterion (e) in Step 1 of the revenue recognition process. Instead, it may be more appropriate to recognize profits in proportion to the amount of payment received. Whether collection is sufficiently uncertain to warrant the deferral of profit is a matter of professional judgment.

To illustrate the accounting for installment sales when uncertainty about collections is sufficiently high such that profits need to be deferred, consider the following example. Durable Furnishings makes installment sales of products with a retail price of $1,000,000 in the month of January. The cost of the products sold amounts to $800,000, so the average gross margin on these products is 20%. To record these transactions, Durable Furnishings would record the following for the initial sale:

installment sale An arrangement whereby the seller allows the buyer to make payments over an extended period of time while the buyer receives the product at the beginning of the installment period.

Exhibit 4-9	Journal entry for initial recognition of Durable Furnishings's installment sales	
Dr. Installment accounts receivable	1,000,000	
Cr. Inventory		800,000
Cr. Deferred gross profit [a liability account]		200,000

Thus, no revenue is recorded on the initial sale. Instead, we recognize the reduction in inventory ($800,000) and the deferred gross profit ($200,000), which appears as a liability on the balance sheet.

In February, Durable Furnishings receives $50,000 for these installment sales (after deducting amounts on account of interest).[8] To reflect these installment receipts and to recognize the revenue associated with those receipts, the company would record the following entries:

Exhibit 4-10	Journal entries to recognize installment receipts and revenue on Durable Furnishings's installment sales	
Dr. Cash	50,000	
Cr. Installment accounts receivable		50,000
Dr. Deferred gross profit ($50,000 × 20%)	10,000	
Dr. Cost of goods sold ($50,000 × 80%)	40,000	
Cr. Sales revenue		50,000

Thus, the second entry recognizes revenue of $50,000 and related cost of sales of $40,000, for a gross profit of $10,000 in the month of February. The liability for deferred gross profit declines by this same amount.

3. Bill-and-hold arrangements

Bill-and-hold arrangements involve the seller holding onto the goods at the request of the customer, even though the goods are in all other respects ready for delivery, the customer has inspected and accepted the goods, and the customer has already paid. The purchaser may not want immediate delivery because of, for example, limitations in storage space at its own premises, or it may need to have other goods or services rendered by other suppliers before it is able to take delivery of the goods in question. The seller has satisfied all the revenue recognition criteria for the sale of the promised goods, but is merely providing an incidental service of temporarily warehousing the goods. The seller can recognize revenue on the sale of goods even though the goods remain on the seller's premises.

 CHECKPOINT **CP4-4**

Why do we delay revenue recognition for consignment arrangements and installment sales past the delivery date?

L.O. 4-3.   Apply the revenue and expense recognition criteria for long-term contracts, including the prospective treatment applicable to changes in estimates.

percentage of completion method   An accounting method that recognizes revenues and expenses on a long-term contract in proportion to the degree of progress on the contracted project.

F. ACCOUNTING FOR LONG-TERM CONTRACTS

The key challenge in revenue recognition for performance obligations that extend over a long period of time is the amount to allocate to each reporting period (a fiscal year or a quarter for interim reporting). As discussed above, IFRS 15 indicates that revenue from performance obligations recognized over a period of time should be based on the progress toward completion, commonly called the **percentage of completion method**.

[8.] Accounting for the interest portion of the installment receivables is similar to that used for finance leases, which are discussed in Chapter 17. In fact, some of the characteristics of installment sales are very similar to finance leases.

A contract can be identified as being one of two types: fixed-price contracts or cost-plus contracts. Fixed-price contracts are ones in which the contractor agrees to a price before performance begins; the price of cost-plus contracts will depend on how much is spent on the project, plus a profit margin. Inherently, these two types of contracts have very different risk profiles for the contractor and the buyer. Who bears the risks and uncertainties associated with forecasting the cost of the project? Whichever party bears the risk has the incentive to control costs. Fixed-price contracts impose all the risk on the contractor, so it has the incentive to control costs. In contrast, cost-plus contracts leave the uncertainty in the hands of the buyer, so the contractor is not motivated to contain costs. This is a simple case of moral hazard, which was discussed in Chapter 1. Indeed, the contractor wants to maximize cost since the amount of profit on the cost-plus contracts increases with the total cost. Thus, buyers should be wary of cost-plus contracts and use them only when there is little uncertainty about the costs or when the buyer is able to supervise the project closely to contain the costs.

THRESHOLD CONCEPT
**INFORMATION
ASYMMETRY**

As an illustration of the pitfalls of cost-plus contracts, the City of Vancouver contracted with Millennium Group with a cost-plus contract to build 250 units of social housing on the site of the Olympic Village for the 2010 Winter Olympic Games. The original bid had a budget of $65 million. By February 2009, the estimated cost had increased to $110 million, an increase of 69%. While many factors played into the ballooning budget, the cost-plus contract was certainly one of the most important. By comparison, the other parts of the Olympic Village, also built by Millennium Group but not using a cost-plus contract, saw cost increases above budget in the neighbourhood of 10%.

1. Revenue recognition for cost-plus contracts

The accounting for cost-plus contracts is relatively straightforward. Suppose Adobe Building Company agrees to construct 360 condominium units for Century Homes, a real estate developer. Century Homes has staff with substantial experience to supervise the project, so it is willing to bear the risks inherent in a cost-plus contract. In return, Adobe agrees to a contract price of cost plus 5%, which is much lower than the 20% margin it charges on fixed-price contracts. The project covers three years, with the following cost estimates and actual costs:

Exhibit 4-11	Adobe Building Company: Example of a cost-plus contract			
(Amounts in $ millions)	2018	2019	2020	Total
Costs each year, estimated at beginning of contract	20.0	50.0	30.0	100.0
Actual costs incurred on the contract	24.0	64.0	22.0	110.0
Margin (5% of actual cost)	1.2	3.2	1.1	5.5
Revenue recognized each year	25.2	67.2	23.1	115.5

While accurate cost estimates are crucial to the management of long-term projects, these estimates do not play a role in the accounting for cost-plus contracts. The actual costs incurred by Adobe plus the 5% margin completely determine the amount of revenue to recognize in each year and in total.

2. Revenue recognition for fixed-price contracts: Application of changes in estimates

The accounting for fixed-price contracts would also be quite simple in a hypothetical and *unrealistic* scenario where there are no uncertainties about how much it will cost and how fast the project can be completed. For instance, suppose Century Homes awarded the contract for the 360 condominium units to Delta Engineering, which submitted a fixed-price proposal of $120 million.

If all the costs for the three years and the degree of completion can be estimated in advance *completely accurately*, then we could just use the percentage completed within each year to compute the amount of revenue to recognize. There would be no need to revise calculations to take into account new information as time goes on, because all the amounts are completely predictable. These amounts are shown in Exhibit 4-12.

Exhibit 4-12	Delta Engineering: Example of a fixed-price contract with no uncertainty		
(Amounts in $ millions)	2018	2019	Total
Contract price			120
Percentage completed during year*	30%	70%	100%
Revenue recognized each year†	36	84	120
Costs incurred and expensed each year‡	32	68	100
Gross profit on project recognized each year	4	16	20

*Estimated by the architectural engineer.
†Revenue = percentage completed during Year 3 × contract price.
‡The percentage of costs each year do not necessarily follow the physical rate of progress, because some parts of the project may be more labour intensive, use more materials, and so on.

In this unrealistic case without uncertainty, the amount of revenue recognized is just like the amount of depreciation using the units of production method that you learned in introductory accounting (which is also discussed in Chapter 8). For instance, 70% of the project was completed in 2019, so 70% of the revenue is recorded in that year. The costs recorded, however, are not based on these percentages; rather, the actual costs incurred in each year are expensed as cost of sales. Thus, *the percentage of completion method allocates revenue*, not expenses.

Turning to a more realistic scenario, suppose actual costs differ from the estimates made by Delta Engineering. Assume that we have the following data instead:

Exhibit 4-13	Delta Engineering: Example of a fixed-price contract *with* uncertainty, data only		
(Amounts in $millions)	2018	2019	Total
Contract price			120
% completed each year—in planning documents	30%	70%	100%
% completed each year—*actual estimate by engineer* at the end of each year	20%	80%	100%
Costs each year—in planning documents	32	68	100
Actual costs incurred on project each year	24	80	104
Additional cost to complete, estimated at the end of each year	72	0	—

For the first year, 2018, the amount of revenue that would have been recognized if the project developed as expected would be $36 million—30% of the contracted total of $120 million. However, actual experience differs from expectations, so how much revenue should be recognized instead? It does not make sense to use the 30% estimated in the planning documents, as that is outdated information. Instead, Delta should use the most recent information available. The engineer has estimated that the project is only 20% complete at the end of 2018. Based on this percentage complete, the revenue for 2018 should be 20% × $120 million = $24 million.

Given the existence of uncertainty, Delta needs to revise its estimates using the best available information at the end of each year. In other words, it needs to apply the guidance for changes in estimates and use the prospective treatment to incorporate this new information (see Chapter 3 and IAS 8). The past year(s) should not be revised, because the information was not available at that time. For the set of data shown in Exhibit 4-13, the amounts of revenues and expenses to recognize each year are shown in Exhibit 4-14.

THRESHOLD CONCEPT
TIMING OF RECOGNITION

Exhibit 4-14	Delta Engineering: Example of a fixed-price contract with uncertainty, data, and solution			
(Amounts in $ millions)	Labels and calculations	2018	2019	Total
Contract price	A			120
% completed each year, engineer's estimate	B	20%	80%	100%
Actual costs each year	C	24	80	104
Cumulative % completed to date	D = sum of B*	20%	100%	—
Cumulative revenue to date	E = A × D	24	120	—
Revenue recognized in prior years	F = prior E	0	24	—
Revenue for current year	G = E − F	24	96	120
Cost of sales for current year	H = C	24	80	104
Gross profit for current year	J = G − H	0	16	16

*Sum of current and prior year's % completed.

It is worth pointing out again that the percentage of completion method allocates revenue, not expenses. The amounts for cost of sales are the actual costs incurred on the project in each year. As a result, the gross profit on the contract can have a pattern that is very different from that of the percentage completed. In this example, the gross profit for 2018 is zero even though the project is 20% complete.

To summarize, the percentage of completion method uses the following formula shown in Exhibit 4-15 to determine the amount of revenue to recognize in each period.

Exhibit 4-15	Equation to compute percentage of completion revenue

Revenue = Percentage complete × Contract price − Revenue previously recognized

 CHECKPOINT **CP4-5**

How does the percentage of completion method relate to changes in estimates, discussed in Chapter 3?

3. Revenue recognition for fixed-price contracts: The cost-to-cost approach

In the examples just discussed, we assumed that the company has engineering estimates for the progress of the project. Another way to obtain an estimate of the percentage complete is to use the data available on the cost already incurred, plus estimates of how much additional cost needs to be incurred to finish the project. Thus, the formula for the percentage complete using the cost-to-cost approach is as follows:

Exhibit 4-16	Equation for cost-to-cost estimate of percentage complete

$$\text{Percentage complete} = \frac{\text{Cost incurred to date}}{\text{Estimated total cost}}$$

Using the information from Exhibit 4-13, the percentage of completion method under the cost-to-cost approach would result in the following figures:

Exhibit 4-17	Delta Engineering: Example of percentage of completion method using cost-to-cost approach			
(Amounts in $ millions)	Labels and calculations	2018	2019	Total
Contract price	A			120
Actual costs each year	C	24	80	104
Cumulative costs incurred to date	D = sum of C*	24	104	
Additional cost to complete, estimated at the end of each year	E	72	0	—
Total estimated cost of contract	F = D + E	96	104	
Cumulative % complete to date—cost-to-cost estimate	G = D ÷ F	25%	100%	—
Cumulative revenue to date	H = A × G	30	120	—
Revenue recognized in prior years	J = prior H	0	30	—
Revenue for current year	K = H − J	30	90	120
Cost of sales for current year	L = C	24	80	104
Gross profit for current year	M = K − L	6	10	16

*Sum of current and prior years' costs.

If you compare the revenue numbers in Exhibit 4-14 and Exhibit 4-17, you will see that the total is the same, $120 million, but the pattern over the three years differs significantly. Likewise, the gross profit using either method totals $16 million, but the amounts in each of the three years differ quite dramatically.

Returning to the formulas, we can substitute the equation in Exhibit 4-16 into the equation in Exhibit 4-15 to obtain the following formula:

Exhibit 4-18	Equation for revenue under percentage of completion method using the cost-to-cost approach

$$\text{Revenue} = \frac{\text{Cost incurred to date}}{\text{Estimated total cost}} \times \frac{\text{Contract}}{\text{revenue}} - \frac{\text{Revenue}}{\text{previously recognized}}$$

For example, applying this formula to Delta Engineering, we can obtain the revenue amount for 2019 as $[(104 \div 104) \times 120] - 30 = \$90$ million.

If we are interested in directly calculating the gross profit for each period, we can use the following formula:

Exhibit 4-19	Gross profit under percentage of completion method using the cost-to-cost approach

$$\text{Gross profit} = \frac{\text{Cost incurred to date}}{\text{Estimated total cost}} \times \frac{\text{Estimated}}{\text{gross profit}} - \frac{\text{Gross profit}}{\text{previously recognized}}$$

For Delta Engineering, we can calculate the gross profit amount for 2019 as $[(104 \div 104) \times (120 - 104)] - 6 = 16 - 6 = \$10$ million. Using this formula is more convenient if one is interested only in the amount of profit and not the breakdown between revenue and cost of sales.

So far, we have looked at how to compute the amounts of revenue and expenses to recognize for a long-term contract. We now turn our attention to recording these and other amounts relating to the contract in the accounts.

 CHECKPOINT CP4-6

What crucial assumption is needed for the cost-to-cost method to provide reasonable estimates of the percentage complete?

4. Accounting cycle for long-term contracts

The accounting entries for a long-term contractor can be broken down into five distinct phases: (i) incurring costs on the project, (ii) billing the client, (iii) receiving payments from the client, (iv) accruing revenue and any other adjustments for the accounting period, and (v) closing the accounts at the end of the contract. Exhibit 4-20 summarizes the journal entries for these five parts, along with the timing of when these entries would be made.

L.O. 4-4.   Apply the accounting standards for long-term contracts when profitability is in doubt.

Exhibit 4-20	Journal entries through the accounting cycle for a long-term contract	
Phase	**Timing**	**Journal entry**
1. Incurring cost on the project	As they occur	Dr. Construction in progress* Cr. Cash, A/P, etc.
2. Billing the client	When invoice is sent (usually scheduled in contract)	Dr. Accounts receivable Cr. Billings on construction in progress
3. Receiving payments from client	According to payment terms of invoice (usually specified in contract)	Dr. Cash Cr. Accounts receivable
4. Revenue and expense recognition	Once per period for each contract	Dr. Cost of sales Dr. Construction in progress Cr. Revenue
5. Completion of the project	Once per contract	Dr. Billings on construction in progress Cr. Construction in progress

*May also be called "work in progress" or "work in process."

Phase 1:   The contractor incurs costs for materials, labour, and overhead for the project. These costs are capitalized in "construction in progress," which is an inventory account.

Phase 2:   The long-term contract will usually specify when the contractor will be able to issue invoices. When the contractor does issue an invoice, an account receivable is recorded as usual. The credit goes to an account called "billings on construction in progress." This is a contra account associated with inventories (i.e., construction in progress). This journal entry should look different from what you may be used to. In other circumstances, the counterpart to the debit to accounts receivable is a credit to revenue. However, for long-term contracts, the amount of revenue needs to be computed, as we saw previously, and it is recorded in Phase 4.

Phase 3: The contractor records the cash received on invoices previously issued.

Phase 4: At the end of each year (or another reporting period), the contractor records the revenues and costs for the project. This is the point at which the effects of the contract flow through the income statement. The unusual aspect of this journal entry is that both revenue and cost of sales are in the same entry, with the difference going to increase construction in progress (or decrease, in the case of a loss). In other words, *the contractor adjusts the inventory value for the project's gross profit or loss for the year.* This is distinctly different from the standard revenue and cost of sales entries, which are two separate entries.

Phase 5: When the project is complete, the contractor removes the balances relating to the contract. Just before this closing entry, notice that the inventory account (construction in progress) has accumulated all the costs of the project (Phase 1 journal entries) and the gross profits or losses (Phase 4 entries). Thus, the balance in the account should equal the contract price. Likewise, the contra-inventory account (billings) is the accumulation of all the invoices sent to the client, so this account should also have a balance equal to the contract price. The closing entry removes these two offsetting amounts from the books.

In summary, the accounting in Phases 1 and 3 is the same as what would be done for short-term contracts. The unique aspects are in Phases 2 and 4. Phase 5 is a housekeeping entry so that offsetting amounts are not kept in the ledger indefinitely.

Let's now demonstrate how one would apply these entries using the information in Exhibit 4-17 for our Delta Engineering example. In addition, assume that the company issued invoices totalling $28 million and $92 million, and it received payments of $25 million and $95 million in 2018 and 2019, respectively.

Exhibit 4-21	Journal entries for Delta Engineering's long-term contract (amounts in $ millions)				
		2018		2019	
Phase	Journal entry	Dr.	Cr.	Dr.	Cr.
1. Incurring cost	Dr. CIP*	24		80	
	Cr. Cash		24		80
2. Billing the client	Dr. Accounts receivable	28		92	
	Cr. Billings on CIP		28		92
3. Receiving payments	Dr. Cash	25		95	
	Cr. Accounts receivable		25		95
4. Period-end accruals and adjustments	Dr. Cost of sales	24		80	
	Dr. CIP	6		10	
	Cr. Revenue		30		90
5. Completion of the project	Dr. Billings on CIP			120	
	Cr. CIP				120

*CIP = construction in progress

The balance sheet accounts for this project in the general ledger (other than cash), as represented by T-accounts, would have the following history:

Exhibit 4-22	T-accounts for Delta Engineering's long-term contract (amounts in $ millions)						
Year	**Accts Rec.**		**CIP (inventory)**			**Billings (contra-inventory)**	
2018	Issue invoice	28	Incur cost	24	Issue invoice		28
	Cash received	25	Gross profit adj.	6			
	Balance	3	Balance	30	Balance		28
2019	Issue invoice	92	Incur cost	80	Issue invoice		92
	Cash received	95	Gross profit adj.	10			
			Balance	120	Balance		120
			Completion		120	Completion	120
	Balance	0	Balance	0	Balance		0

Thus, at the end of the contract and after all payments have been received, all of the accounts related to the project have zero balances.

CHECKPOINT **CP4-7**

Identify the five sets of journal entries required for long-term contracts.

5. Onerous contracts

As discussed above, the contractor recognizes only a portion of revenue and profits in each year by following the percentage of completion method. However, if the contractor has information that indicates there will be a loss on the contract, then all of that loss must be recognized immediately.

In other words, when a long-term contract is expected to be profitable, the company recognizes the profits over the duration of the contract, but when the contract is expected to generate a loss, all of the loss is recognized at once. The idea behind this asymmetric treatment is to ensure that the financial statements do not overstate assets and income.

To illustrate, suppose Echo Construction has a three-year contract with a fixed price of $120 million. Exhibit 4-23 shows related cost figures over the life of the contract.

Exhibit 4-23	Echo Construction: Example of a long-term contract with an expected loss			
(Amounts in $ millions)	2018	2019	2020	Total
Actual costs each year	24	80	12	116
Additional cost to complete, estimated at the end of each year	72	26	0	

Due to the contract turning onerous in the second year, Echo Construction must report a loss of $16 million in 2019, as calculated in Exhibit 4-24.

Exhibit 4-24	Echo Construction: Example of percentage of completion method using cost-to-cost approach with expected loss				
(Amounts in $ millions)	Labels and calculations	2018	2019	2020	Total
Contract price	A				120
Actual costs each year	C	24	80	12	116
Cumulative cost incurred to date	D = sum of C*	24	104	116	
Additional cost to complete, estimated at the end of each year	E	72	26	0	—
Total estimated cost of contract	F = D + E	96	130	116	
Cumulative % complete to date—cost-to-cost estimate	G = D ÷ F	25%	80%	100%	—
Cumulative revenue to date	H = A × G	30	96	120	—
Revenue recognized in prior years	J = prior H	0	30	96	—
Revenue for current year	K = H − J	30	66	24	120
Cost of sales for current year	L = C	24	80	12	116
Gross profit (loss) before the below	M = K − L	6	(14)	12	4
Expected loss on portion not yet complete	N = P − M	0	(2)	2	0
Gross profit (loss) for current year	P (see Ex. 4-23)	6	(16)	14	4

*Sum of current and prior years' costs.

The "expected loss" of $2 million in 2019 represents 20% of the $10 million loss for the portion of the project that is yet to be completed at the end of 2019. The other $8 million loss has been accounted for via the standard percentage of completion method. Thus, the $16 million loss reported in 2019 includes the following components:

Exhibit 4-25	Echo Construction: Decomposition of loss recognized in 2019
Amounts in $ millions	
Loss on 80% portion of project already complete (80% × $10)	8
Reversal of profit previously recognized in 2018	6
Loss without applying onerous contract provisions	14
Expected loss on 20% portion of project not yet complete (20% × $10)	2
Total loss recognized in 2019	16

A quick way to determine this loss amount is to use a modified version of Exhibit 4-19 by replacing the percentage complete by 100%:

Exhibit 4-26	Equation for gross profit under the percentage of completion method using the cost-to-cost approach

$$\text{Gross profit (loss)} = 100\% \times \begin{matrix} \textit{Estimated} \\ \textit{gross profit (loss)} \end{matrix} - \begin{matrix} \textit{Gross profit (loss)} \\ \textit{previously recognized} \end{matrix}$$

For Echo Construction, the formula results in gross profit (loss) = (100% × −10) − 6 = −$16 million.

To complete this example, the following exhibit shows the journal entries (Phase 4) to recognize the revenue, cost of sales, and expected loss on the onerous contract.

Exhibit 4-27	Journal entries for Echo Construction's onerous contract (amounts in $ millions)								
	2018		2019		2020		Total		
Journal entry	Dr.	Cr.	Dr.	Cr.	Dr.	Cr.	Dr.	Cr.
Cost of sales	24		80		12		116	
CIP*	6			6	4		4	
Revenue		30		66		24		120
Provision for onerous contract			8		8		0	
Expected loss on onerous contract			2			2	0	
Provision for onerous contract				2	2		0	

*CIP = Construction in progress

6. Revenue recognition when outcome of a contract is uncertain: Cost recovery method

As discussed previously in this section, the percentage of completion method recognizes revenue, expenses, and profits in proportion to the degree of progress on the contracted project. However, in some instances there is sufficient uncertainty over the outcome of a contract that recognition of a portion of expected profits is unjustified. Specifically, if an enterprise is not able to reasonably measure the outcome of a performance obligation, then the cost recovery method should be used (IFRS 15 paragraph 45). The **cost recovery method** recognizes (i) contract costs incurred in the period as expenses, and (ii) an amount of revenue equal to the costs that are expected to be recoverable as part of the contract.[9] Thus, this method defers any profit on the contract to the completion date. In addition, any expected losses will continue to be recognized immediately.

cost recovery method
Recognizes contract costs incurred in the period as expenses and an amount of revenue equal to the costs that are expected to be recoverable as part of the contract.

 CHECKPOINT **CP4-8**

How do accounting standards for long-term contracts prevent the overstatement of income and assets?

7. Alternative in ASPE: Completed contract method

Under IFRS, the percentage of completion method is the prescribed method of accounting for long-term contracts, modified for circumstances in which the cost recovery method and early loss recognition apply. ASPE (paragraph 3400.16) allows an alternative, called the **completed contract method**. As the name suggests, this method defers revenue and expense recognition until the date when the contractor completes the project, instead of periodically over the life of the contract under the percentage of completion method. To prevent the overstatement of assets and income, any losses are still recognized in the period first anticipated. In short, profits are deferred but losses are not.

completed contract method   An accounting method that defers revenue and expense recognition until the date when the contractor completes the project.

While this alternative exists, ASPE limits its application. As Section 3400 notes,

¶18   The completed contract method would only be appropriate when performance consists of the execution of a single act or when the enterprise cannot reasonably estimate the extent of progress toward completion.[10]

[9.] Copyright © 2015 IFRS Foundation.

[10.] Reprinted from Accounting Standards for Private Enterprises application, Section 3400. The Canadian Institute of Chartered Accountants, with permission from Chartered Professional Accountants of Canada, Toronto, Canada. Any changes to the original material are the sole responsibility of the author (and/or publisher) and have not been reviewed or endorsed by the Chartered Professional Accountants of Canada.

Thus, even under ASPE, the percentage of completion method is the predominant method to follow for long-term contracts.

G. RISK OF EARNINGS OVERSTATEMENT IN LONG-TERM CONTRACTS

The nature of long-term contracts inherently makes this a high-risk area for accounting and auditing. The need to allocate revenue between two or more accounting periods, and the substantial amount of judgment required to make the estimates used in the calculations, provide significant pitfalls for intentional earnings management as well as unintentional judgment errors.

1. Intentional overstatement: Earnings management

L.O. 4-5. Evaluate the risks of revenue misstatements and the appropriateness of revenue recognition policies in specific circumstances by applying professional judgment.

From the above discussion, examples, and analysis, it should be clear that management makes a number of estimates that determine how much revenue and profit are recognized in a period. Consider the different results of using the engineer's estimate (Exhibit 4-14) versus the cost-to-cost approach (Exhibit 4-17) for the percentage complete. The key figures are repeated below for ease of comparison.

Exhibit 4-28	Delta Engineering: Comparison of results from using engineer's estimate vs. cost-to-cost approach for percentage complete		
(Amounts in $ millions)	2018	2019	Total
Cumulative % completed to date, **engineer's estimate**	20%	100%	—
Revenue for current year	24	96	120
Cost of sales for current year	24	80	104
Gross profit for current year	0	16	16
Cumulative % complete to date, **cost-to-cost estimate**	25%	100%	—
Revenue for current year	30	90	120
Cost of sales for current year	24	80	104
Gross profit for current year	6	10	16

THRESHOLD CONCEPT
QUALITY OF EARNINGS

While the total amount of gross profit is the same by the end of the contract ($16 million), the pattern of reported profits is dramatically different. The engineer's estimate results in all of the profit ($16 million) reported in the second year, and none in the first year. In contrast, the cost-to-cost approach shows $6 million profit in the first year. Both engineering estimates and the cost-to-cost approach are valid and acceptable for accounting purposes. Therefore, management has the ethical responsibility to choose the approach that best represents the underlying performance of the project. However, the latitude available also provides management an opportunity for earnings management.

Besides the ability to choose the approach for determining the percentage complete, management can open up additional earnings management opportunities by judiciously making estimates for the cost-to-cost approach. In particular, this approach uses estimates of future costs required to complete the project. Refer back to the formula in Exhibit 4-19, which is repeated here:

$$\text{Gross profit} = \frac{\text{Cost incurred to date}}{\text{Estimated total cost}} \times \begin{array}{c}\text{Estimated}\\\text{gross profit}\end{array} - \begin{array}{c}\text{Gross profit}\\\text{previously recognized}\end{array}$$

Underestimating future costs has two effects. First, it reduces the denominator in the percentage complete ratio, thereby increasing the percentage completed. Second, it increases the estimated gross profit. Thus, the two effects are in the same direction: underestimating costs increases the profit recognized in the current period (and lowers profit in future periods).

2. Unintentional overstatement: The winner's curse

As just discussed, estimated profits on long-term contracts can be biased if management has motives to manipulate earnings. In other instances, the overstatements are unintentional. Obviously, outright errors in the estimation process are a source of such unintentional overstatements. For example, a significant cost being omitted from the calculations, or an incorrect conversion from square feet to square metres, would be an error. For long-term contracts, however, a second source of unintentional overstatement is important.

Consider a typical bidding process for large contracts to build bridges, highways, schools, or hospitals. For each project, the business, organization, or government provides the project specifications and invites contractors to submit bids based on those specifications. Typically, the project is awarded to the lowest-priced bidder while taking into consideration some qualitative factors.

On the surface, such a bidding process (technically called a first-price sealed bid auction) is a good way for the party requesting the bids to get the lowest price, and in the process find the most efficient contractor. However, consider the following scenario. The Manitoba government requires a bridge to be built over the Saskatchewan River. Given the architect's design specifications, the architect believes that an unbiased estimate of the cost of this bridge is $720 million, plus a profit margin of $80 million for the contractor, for a total of $800 million. Five different contractors submit bids based on the best information available to each of them. Contractors A, B, C, D, and E, respectively, submit bids of $705 million, $737 million, $810 million, $855 million, and $893 million. If there are no convincing qualitative factors to choose one bid over another, then the $705 million bid wins. It is possible that Contractor A is better able to manage its crew, procure supplies more cheaply, and otherwise manage the project more efficiently than the other contractor. However, it is also possible that Contractor A has underestimated the amount of work required to build this bridge. For complex projects such as bridge building, there are myriad components to the projects and many sources of uncertainty, such as the factors affecting the construction of the caissons for the bridge foundations, the effect of rain, snow, and severe winter temperatures on the construction process, the price of steel over the duration of the construction, and so on.

THRESHOLDCONCEPT
DECISION MAKING
UNDER UNCERTAINTY

Given all these uncertainties, some contractors will overestimate while others will underestimate construction costs. Given the structure of the bidding process, the contract will tend to be awarded to the contractor who underestimates costs the most. In this example, it is possible that Contractor A has significantly underestimated costs in its submission of the winning bid of $705 million. In a real but somewhat sobering example, a foreign contractor bidding on a bridge project in Canada omitted to budget for provincial sales tax that is applied to construction materials used, simply because that contractor was not familiar with this basic but important feature of the Canadian tax environment.

The information problem facing the contractors is called a **winner's curse**: the winning bidder will tend to have underestimated the cost of the project the most, leading to a higher likelihood of a loss on the contract when actual costs are ultimately incurred.

It is important to note that the unintentional underestimation of costs and overstatement of expected profits is not due to errors. An error is a misstatement that is made when it should not have been, given the information available at the time. In contrast, the misstatement from the winner's curse occurs despite using all the information available correctly; the cost underestimate occurs because each contractor has different information arising from differences in experience with similar projects in the past and knowledge about the factors affecting the proposed project.

winner's curse   The higher likelihood of loss faced by winners of auctions when bidders each have different information.

H. PRESENTATION AND DISCLOSURE

1. General presentation and disclosure requirements

An entity separately reports the amount of revenue by type of activity—from the sale of goods, provision of services, royalties, interest, and dividends. The entity also separately reports the amounts of revenue in each of these five categories that arise from non-monetary exchanges. The notes to the financial statements need to describe the revenue recognition policies followed. In the case of services, the method of determining the stage of completion is also required to be reported.

Enterprises should also disclose in the notes a disaggregation of revenue recognized from contracts with customers using categories that help users understand the nature, amount, timing, and uncertainty of revenue and cash flows. There are many possible categorizations (e.g., whether the contracts are short term or long term, geographic source of revenue, type of customer, etc.), so professional judgment is required.

2. Presentation and disclosure for long-term contracts

Aside from the obvious implications for revenue on the income statement, long-term contract accounting also affects the balance sheet. Depending on the amount of costs and profits accumulated in construction in progress inventory compared with the amount billed to the client, there could be a net debit or credit, corresponding to a net asset or net liability, respectively. For example, refer to the T-accounts in Exhibit 4-22. At the end of 2018, Delta Engineering has $30 million in the construction in progress account and $28 million in the billings account, so the net debit amount of $2 million for this contract would be reported as an asset. If the company had a second contract with a net credit position of $5 million (i.e., the billings account exceeds the construction in progress account), the company would report a liability of $5 million separately from the $2 million asset for the first contract. The company *cannot* simply report a net liability of $3 million by offsetting the asset from one contract against the liability for another contract.

With regard to disclosures, the entity should report the following information:

- the amount of contract revenue recognized in the period;
- the method of revenue recognition (percentage of completion, cost recovery, etc.); and
- the method of estimating the percentage completed (the cost-to-cost approach, engineering estimates, etc.).

I. SUBSTANTIVE DIFFERENCES BETWEEN IFRS AND ASPE

Issue	IFRS Requirements	ASPE Requirements
General revenue recognition process	Use detailed five-step process applicable to both goods and services.	Apply general principles distinguished by goods vs. services.
Allocation of transaction price to performance obligations (Step 4)	Allocate based on relative stand-alone selling price.	No allocation method specified.
Performance obligations satisfied over a period of time (Step 5)	Use the percentage of completion method.	Use either the percentage of completion or the completed contract method.
Income and expenses for biological assets	Recognize income and expenses on changes in fair value of biological assets (see Chapter 10).	No specific guidance for agricultural activities.

J. SUMMARY

L.O. 4-1. Explain why there is a range of alternatives for revenue recognition that are conceptually valid and the rationale for accounting standards to prescribe a smaller set of alternatives.

- Value creation occurs during many different business processes: research, development, production, delivery, collection, and product guarantees are all potentially value-adding activities. Conceptually, revenue could be recognized to correspond to the value added by these activities.
- Accounting standards prescribe revenue recognition at later stages of the value creation process when the risks and uncertainties surrounding procurement, demand, price, credit, and indemnity risk are sufficiently low.

L.O. 4-2. Apply the general revenue and expense recognition criteria to a variety of contexts.

- Revenue recognition criteria involve a five-step process.
- After identifying the contract with a customer, identify the performance obligations and the transaction price. Then allocate the transaction price to the performance obligations. When or as performance occurs, recognize revenue.

L.O. 4-3. Apply the revenue and expense recognition criteria for long-term contracts, including the prospective treatment applicable to changes in estimates.

- IFRS prescribes the percentage of completion method to recognize revenue when performance occurs over time.
- The percentage of completion method recognizes revenue in proportion to the degree of progress on the contracted project.
- Enterprises may obtain estimates of the percentage complete from engineering estimates, the cost-to-cost approach, or other sources.
- Enterprises apply prospective treatment for changes in estimates for costs and percentage complete.
- The cost-to-cost approach expresses the fraction complete as the ratio of cost incurred divided by the estimated total cost.

L.O. 4-4. Apply the accounting standards for long-term contracts when profitability is in doubt.

- When the enterprise expects a loss on a contract, prudence requires that 100% of the loss be recognized immediately.
- The cost recovery method should be used when the enterprise cannot reasonably estimate the outcome of the contract.
- Enterprises eligible to use guidance in ASPE may use the completed contract method.

L.O. 4-5. Evaluate the risks of revenue misstatements and the appropriateness of revenue recognition policies in specific circumstances by applying professional judgment.

- Due to the wide variety of ways in which businesses operate, determining the appropriate revenue recognition policy requires the use of professional judgment that takes into account the information needs of users.
- As professional judgment may be misused by some financial statement preparers to further their own ends, auditors and financial statement readers should be aware of the degree to which revenue recognition policies are susceptible to management manipulation.
- The cost-to-cost approach for estimating the percentage completed in long-term contracts is particularly susceptible to understatements of future costs required to complete the project.

K. ANSWERS TO CHECKPOINT QUESTIONS

CP4-1: Accounting standards for revenue recognition do not reflect the value creation process because different stages of the value creation process have different degrees of uncertainty. Early stages of value creation are too uncertain for accurate estimates of the value created. In contrast, the final stages of the value creation process have a high degree of certainty and it is possible for management to make accurate estimates of the value created. Accounting standards have chosen a middle ground, late enough when the amount of probable future benefits can be estimated reliably, but not so late that the information becomes out-of-date.

CP4-2: The five-step revenue recognition process is needed due to the periodicity of accrual accounting. The process records an amount of revenue in a period depending on how much has been "earned" according to (i) progress on each performance obligation, and (ii) how valuable a performance obligation is when a transaction involves more than one performance obligation.

CP4-3: It is important to identify multiple performance obligations in a sale transaction because revenue needs to be allocated to the different components, and these components can have different timings for revenue recognition.

CP4-4: For consignment and installment sales, we delay revenue recognition because there remains too much risk and uncertainty regarding the amount of future benefits (i.e., cash flows) that will be received. Consignors retain the risks and rewards of ownership of the goods, while installment sales involve significant uncertainty regarding the amount of future payments that will be collected from customers.

CP4-5: The percentage of completion method uses current information to compute the amount of revenue to recognize. As time and construction progresses, the estimated stage of completion and total project costs will change. These changes reflect new information and therefore they are changes in estimate, requiring prospective treatment.

CP4-6: The cost-to-cost method relies on the assumption that costs are incurred in proportion to the progress made on the construction project. For instance, if an early stage in a project requires high cost for relatively little progress, then the cost-to-cost method will overstate the percentage completed.

CP4-7: The five entries are to record (i) costs incurred, (ii) billings to the customer, (iii) payments from the customer, (iv) revenue, and (v) completion of the project.

CP4-8: The accounting standards for long-term contracts require any anticipated loss to be recognized fully whenever management expects such a loss. Separately, if there is substantial uncertainty regarding the profitability of a contract, then the enterprise should use the cost recovery method, which defers any and all profit to the date of completion.

L. GLOSSARY

completed contract method: An accounting method that defers revenue and expense recognition until the date when the contractor completes the project.

consignment: An arrangement where one party (the consignor) provides goods to a second party to sell; however, the second party (the consignee) has the right to return all or a portion of the goods to the first party if the goods are not sold.

cost recovery method: Recognizes contract costs incurred in the period as expenses and an amount of revenue equal to the costs that are expected to be recoverable as part of the contract.

franchise: A commercial arrangement in which one party (the franchisor) licenses its trademarks, business practices, and so on to another (the franchisee).

installment sale: An arrangement whereby the seller allows the buyer to make payments over an extended period of time while the buyer receives the product at the beginning of the installment period.

onerous contract: A contract in which the unavoidable cost of meeting the obligations under the contract exceeds the economic benefits expected to be received under it.

percentage of completion method: An accounting method that recognizes revenues and expenses on a long-term contract in proportion to the degree of progress on the contracted project.

recognition: The process of presenting an item in the financial statements, as opposed to merely disclosing that item in the notes.

stand-alone selling price: The price at which an entity would sell a promised good or service separately to a customer.

winner's curse: The higher likelihood of loss faced by winners of auctions when bidders each have different information.

M. REFERENCES

Authoritative standards:

IFRS	ASPE Section
Framework for the Preparation and Presentation of Financial Statements	1000—Financial Statement Concepts
IFRS 15—Revenue from Contracts with Customers	3400—Revenue
IAS 37—Provisions, Contingent Liabilities, and Contingent Assets	3290—Contingencies
IAS 8— Accounting Policies, Changes in Accounting Estimates, and Errors	1506—Accounting Changes

---

MyLab Accounting Make the grade with **MyLab Accounting:** The problems marked with a 🌐 can be found on **MyLab Accounting.** You can practise them as often as you want, and most feature step-by-step guided instructions to help you find the right answer.

N. PROBLEMS

P4-1. Range of revenue recognition alternatives (**L.O.** 4-1) (Easy – 5 minutes)

Without restricting yourself to published accounting standards, explain how the potential range of revenue recognition policies corresponds to the idea of value added by an enterprise.

P4-2. Range of revenue recognition alternatives (**L.O.** 4-1) (Medium – 10 minutes)

One of your finance colleagues questions the usefulness of revenue recognition criteria that limit when revenue can be recorded. She cites evidence that stock prices respond reliably to news about corporate events such as the discovery of a mineral deposit; therefore, the company should record revenues to reflect that increase in value.

Required:

Respond to your colleague's criticism.

P4-3. **Range of revenue recognition alternatives**   (**L.O.** 4-1) (Medium – 10 minutes)

Throughout the years, there have been many instances in which companies have had to restate previously issued financial statements after investigations by security regulators. Usually, the restatements involve adjustments to reverse overstated assets or income. About half of these overstatements involve revenue recognition.

Required:

In light of this evidence, evaluate whether revenue recognition criteria should be changed to the cash basis.

P4-4. **Range of revenue recognition alternatives**   (**L.O.** 4-1) (Medium – 20 minutes)

The medication industry has at least two types of firms. The first type is biotechnology companies that focus their efforts on research and development (R&D) of new drugs. The second type is pharmaceutical companies that also engage in developing new drugs, but spend considerable efforts in the production, supply, and marketing of drugs.

Suppose pharmaceutical company ABC invests $500 million in R&D for the purpose of finding a vaccine for malaria. The company estimates the probability of success at 10% over a five-year period. If a vaccine is successfully developed, the estimated benefits in terms of future cash flows to the company will be in the range of $10 billion to $20 billion.

Pharmaceutical company XYZ also invests $500 million, but directs the funds to be invested in the equity of publicly traded biotechnology firms that are all in the search for a malaria vaccine. Suppose that XYZ invests $50 million in each of 10 such biotechnology firms. In return, XYZ receives approximately 10% of the common equity in each of these firms. XYZ accounts for these investments on a "mark-to-market" basis (meaning that changes in the biotechnology firms' stock prices are reflected in XYZ's assets and income).

Required:

a. How should ABC and XYZ account for each of their $500 million investments? Should they be capitalized as assets or expensed?
b. Suppose ABC successfully discovers a vaccine for malaria. How should it account for this discovery? If ABC were unsuccessful, how should the company account for this outcome?
c. Independent of (b), suppose one of the companies in which XYZ has an investment discovers a malaria vaccine, and the value of XYZ's investment increases to $2 billion. How should XYZ account for this outcome? Suppose the biotechnology company is unsuccessful and XYZ's investment becomes worthless. How should XYZ account for this outcome?
d. Using the following table, quantify the amount of revenue or income that would be recognized by ABC and XYZ in case of success or failure.

	ABC	XYZ
Vaccine success		
Vaccine failure		

e. Comment on the differences between ABC and XYZ that you observe from part (d).

 P4-5. **Revenue recognition policies**   (**L.O.** 4-1, **L.O.** 4-2) (Easy – 10 minutes)

The following disclosure is from Note 4 of the 2016 financial statements for BMW Group, the German automaker:

> Revenues from the sale of products are recognized when the risks and rewards of ownership of the goods are transferred to the dealer or customer, provided that the amount of revenue can be measured reliably, it is probable that the economic benefits associated with the transaction will flow to the entity and costs incurred or to be incurred in respect of the sale can be measured reliably. Revenues are stated net of settlement discount, bonuses, and rebates.
>
> If the sale of products includes a determinable amount for services ("multiple-component contracts"), the related revenues are deferred and recognized as income over the service period. Amounts are normally recognized as income by reference to the pattern of related expenditure.

Profits arising on the sale of vehicles, for which a Group company retains a repurchase commitment (buyback contracts), are not immediately recognized. The difference between the sales and buyback price is accounted for as deferred income and recognized in installments as revenue over the contract term.

Revenues relating to operating lease arrangements are recognized on a straight-line basis over the lease term. Interest income arising on finance leases and on retail customer/dealership financing is recognized using the effective interest method.

Required:

Identify the different types of activities for BMW Group and the method used to recognize the corresponding revenue.

P4-6.   Revenue recognition process   **(L.O.** 4-2) (Medium – 15 minutes)

List and briefly describe the purpose of each of the five steps involved in the revenue recognition process.

 P4-7.   Criteria for revenue and expense recognition   **(L.O.** 4-2) (Easy – 15 minutes)

For each of the following situations, identify the revenue or expense recognition method that you feel is most appropriate. The recognition methods are:

- at point of sale
- at time of delivery (if different from point of sale)
- when cash is received (if different from point of sale)
- at expiration of guarantee or warranty period
- when contract is signed
- over time
- when service/contract is complete
- according to degree of completion
- according to units of production

Situation	Method of recognition	Brief explanation
a. A vendor sells tomatoes at a farmers' market.		
b. A department store sells and delivers a washing machine with a three-year warranty against manufacturing defects.		
c. An electronics store sells a television set with a 14-day "lowest price" guarantee. (That is, if the customer finds a lower price on the same product offered by the company or a competitor, the company will refund the difference to the customer.)		
d. A bus manufacturer signs a contract to supply 280 buses over five years for the Toronto transit system.		
e. A university receives students' course registrations.		
f. An insurance company issues a one-year insurance policy on a car.		
g. A company deposits funds into a two-year term deposit that earns 4% per year.		
h. A company takes a five-year loan bearing interest at 8% per year.		
i. A company purchases computers for its accounting department.		
j. A company purchases manufacturing equipment that is expected to produce 50,000 widgets.		
k. A company incurs delivery costs on January 3 for a shipment of products sold five days earlier (before the year-end).		

P4-8.   Criteria for revenue recognition   (**L.O.** 4-2) (Medium – 15 minutes)

For each of the following circumstances, identify which revenue recognition criterion/criteria is/are NOT met at the point of sale, preventing the recognition of revenue at that time. (*Italics* identify the entity for which you are accounting.)

Circumstance	Revenue recognition criteria not met
a. An *apartment owner* receives a deposit of $1,200, equal to one month's rent.	
b. An *insurance company* receives annual premiums for fire insurance on June 25 for coverage beginning July 1.	
c. A city *transit authority* issues 200,000 monthly passes at $80 each for sale at various retailers. Retailers act as consignees for these passes.	
d. A city *transit authority* sells 50,000 monthly passes at $80 each to transit riders at its own retail offices/stores.	
e. A provincial *lottery corporation* delivers 10 million scratch-and-win cards to retailers. The cards retail for $2 and generate a commission of $0.20 per card for the retailer. The retailer can return unsold cards to the lottery corporation.	

P4-9.   Revenue recognition process—transaction price with consideration payable to a customer   (**L.O.** 4-2) (Medium – 20 minutes)

Mowers Unlimited Inc. (MUI) manufactures and distributes lawnmowers. To promote the sale of a new mower type, MUI offered a mail-in rebate to retail purchasers of $50 per mower. Pertinent details follow:

- During the promotional period MUI sold 10,000 mowers to distributors that included the mail-in rebate offer. The wholesale price was $350 per unit; the cost of goods sold was $180 per unit.
- MUI estimated that 60% of retail purchasers would take advantage of the rebate offer.
- The actual redemption rate was 55%.

Required:

a. Prepare a summary journal entry to record the sale of the lawnmowers to the distributors during the promotional period.
b. Prepare a summary journal entry to record the receipt and payment of the retail customers' rebate claims.

P4-10.   Revenue recognition process—variable consideration in transaction price   (**L.O.** 4-2) (Medium – 15 minutes)

Grocery Discounters (GD) is a wholesale distributor of grocery products to independent retail stores. To encourage loyalty from retailers, GD provides volume discounts on purchases, and the discount increases with the volume of purchase. The following is the schedule of discounts:

Total purchases in a calendar year (prior to discount)	Volume discount
Up to $999,999.99	0
$1,000,000 to $1,999,999.99	0.5%
$2,000,000 to $4,999,999.99	1.0%
$5,000,000 to $9,999,999.99	1.5%
$10,000,000 +	2.0%

Whichever level of discount is achieved by a retailer, the percentage discount is applied to all purchases for that calendar year.

Foothills Grocer is a long-time customer of GD. In recent years, Foothills Grocer has made purchases from GD annually totalling between $1 million and $2 million. It is currently October 31 and GD has sold $1.65 million of goods to Foothills Grocer so far in the year (prior to volume discount).

Required:

a. If the same rate of sales to Foothills Grocer is expected to continue in the remaining months of the year, how much revenue should FD record on a shipment of products in November priced at $30,000 (before volume discount)?
b. Given the discount schedule and the amount of purchases already made by Foothills Grocer in the first 10 months of the year, what do you think is the most likely outcome in terms of the volume discount level that Foothills Grocer will achieve for the year?

 P4-11. Revenue recognition criteria—multiple performance obligations

(**L.O.** 4-2) (Easy – 5 minutes)

A car manufacturer provides a service-type warranty for five years on sales of new vehicles. The following table provides information relating to two car models the company produces and sells:

Car model	Sale price	Estimated price of car	Estimated price of warranty
Nova	$15,000	$14,000	$1,500
Pinto	18,000	15,000	2,000

Required:

Using the relative stand-alone selling prices, compute the revenue that would be (i) recognized upon delivery of the vehicle and (ii) deferred and recognized over five years for each of the car models.

 P4-12. Revenue recognition criteria—multiple performance obligations

(**L.O.** 4-2) (Easy – 5 minutes)

Refer to the facts presented in the previous problem (P4-11).

Required:

Using the residual method, compute the revenue that would be (i) recognized upon delivery of the vehicle and (ii) deferred and recognized over five years for each of the car models. For the computations:

a. Assume that the selling price of the warranty has not been established.
b. Assume that the selling price of the car alone is highly variable.

 P4-13. Revenue recognition criteria—performance obligations

(**L.O.** 4-2) (Medium – 15 minutes)

Tenth Cup, a coffee retail chain, offers its customers a loyalty card whereby customers can receive their choice of drink free of charge after purchasing nine cups of coffee. Prices for small, medium, and large sizes are $1.50, $1.80, and $2, respectively. In one month, Tenth Cup sold the following quantities to customers who are on the loyalty program: small—100,000 cups; medium—250,000 cups; large—320,000 cups. (The company also made sales to other customers not on the loyalty program at the prices specified above.)

Required:

a. Assume that the relative stand-alone selling price method is appropriate, and that each customer always consumes the same size of coffee (whether purchased or obtained "free"). Record the journal entries for the sales to customers who are on the loyalty program.
b. Given the conditions of the loyalty offer, customers have a tendency to redeem for a large size even if they usually purchase a small or medium size. Assuming this is true for all

loyalty customers, use the residual value method to record the journal entries for the sales to customers who are on the loyalty program, assuming that all loyalty customers order a large size for their free 10th cup of coffee.

c. Taking into consideration your answer to part (b), explain why the residual value method described in part (b) would be more appropriate under the circumstances than the stand-alone selling price method. To answer this part, it may be helpful to compute the amounts of revenue that would be deferred if the alternative relative fair value method were used.

 P4-14. Revenue recognition criteria—multiple performance obligations

(**L.O.** 4-2) (Difficult – 20 minutes)

Oshawa Motors is a car dealership that has two types of operations: car sales and service. The two divisions operate independently and, in fact, the showroom for car sales is entirely separate from the service shop. (They are across the street from each other.) Despite the independence of the two divisions, the company provides incentives to its sales team to sell maintenance packages along with the sale of cars (new and used). Consider the following offer posted on one of the car windows:

	Price
Car	$45,000
Basic service package (2 years)	3,000
Increment for premium service package (4 years)	2,000
Total	50,000
Special offer for car + premium service	47,500
You save	**$ 2,500**

As is typical in car sales, the price negotiated between the salesperson and the customer varies in each transaction, even for identical vehicles, and there is a considerable amount of latitude given to the salesperson to adjust the price to "close the deal." In one such transaction for the above car including the premium service package, the final negotiated price was $45,900. (Ignore the time value of money in this problem.)

Required:

a. Assume that the three prices (for car, basic service package, increment for premium service package) reliably reflect the stand-alone selling price of these items. Compute the revenue that should be recorded on the date of delivery of the car and for each of the next four years.

b. Similar to part (a), assume that the component prices reliably reflect their fair values, except that the premium package (basic + increment for premium) should be considered together for a price of $5,000. Compute the revenue that should be recorded on the date of delivery of the car and for each of the next four years.

c. The service shop also offers the service packages to other car owners regardless of where they purchased their vehicles. The established price for the basic package is $1,500 and for the premium package is $3,300 (meaning the increment is $1,800 to upgrade from the basic to the premium package). Actual sale prices of the car itself are difficult to obtain due to various customizations that buyers demand, so it is only possible to determine a range of prices, from $42,000 to $46,000. Based on these assumed facts, determine the amount of revenue that should be recorded upon delivery of the car.

P4-15. Revenue recognition criteria—multiple performance obligations

(**L.O.** 4-2) (Medium – 10 minutes)

A cellular phone company offers two options to its customers who are interested in buying a JPhone.

Option A: The JPhone is provided for $600 to customers who do not sign a contract for service.

Option B: The JPhone is provided for $200 to customers who sign a two-year contract at $60 per month for cellular services.

The JPhone has an MSRP (manufacturer's suggested retail price) of $600 and is actually sold at this price by other retailers due to high demand for the product.

Required:

Determine the amount and timing of revenue the phone company should recognize for each option. You may ignore the time value of money for this question.

 P4-16. Revenue recognition criteria—multiple performance obligations

(L.O. 4-2) (Difficult – 20 minutes)

Smarty Phones is a company that provides cellular phone sales and services. The company offers different packages to suit different customers. For example, for one model of phone, the Raspberry 300, the company gives its customers the following options:

Option A: Raspberry 300 provided free with a three-year contract at $50 per month for cellular services.

Option B: Raspberry 300 purchased at $400 with a one-year contract at $50 per month for cellular services.

Option C: Raspberry 300 purchased for $600 with no contract.

Required:

a. Determine the amount and timing of the revenue that Smarty Phones should recognize if a customer chooses Option A. Repeat for Options B and C. You may ignore the time value of money for this question.

b. To ensure the validity of your approach in part (a), what else should you consider?

P4-17. Revenue recognition criteria—multiple performance obligations

(L.O. 4-2) (Difficult – 20 minutes)

The Royal Elbonian Yacht Club (REYC) is an association of members that offers a number of services: community and friendship among members, sailing courses for its members, meals in its restaurant, moorage for boats at the home port of Elbow City, and moorage at "outstation" facilities at ports outside of Elbow City. Access to the club facilities, including the club restaurant, is available to members only. To fund these services, the club charges a number of fees:

- A one-time initiation fee of $50,000; this fee is non-refundable and is valid for as long as the member continues to be a member in good standing.
- An annual membership fee of $10,000 due on January 1 each year, which is valid for the calendar year.
- Moorage on the home port is at market rates based on the size of the boat.
- Moorage at outstation facilities is included in the membership fee.
- Fees for skill improvement courses vary with each course.
- Fees for meals consumed in the club restaurant vary according to menu prices.

Along with the annual membership fee, members receive a $2,400 credit toward restaurant meals. Unused credits at the end of the year have no value. Because the club is operated on a break-even basis, the prices for restaurant meals are on average 25% below prices charged at comparable commercial restaurants.

REYC is a highly sought-after sailing club, so few members quit once accepted into membership, resulting in members remaining in the club for an average of 25 years.

Required:

Discuss how REYC should recognize revenue from its various sources.

P4-18. Revenue recognition process—multiple performance obligations and measuring extent of performance   **(L.O.** 4-2) (Difficult – 30 minutes)

Electronics Inc. (EI) manufactures and sells a computer tablet with two warranty packages available. The first package guarantees that the tablet will be free from manufacturing defects for two years. If the tablet fails during this time, EI will repair or replace it for no additional charge. The second package offers additional protection against loss, theft, and accidental damage. In the event of a mishap, EI will repair or replace the tablet for no additional charge. Other pertinent data follow:

- The sales price of the tablet with the assurance warranty is $500.
- The sales price of the tablet with the service warranty is $600. Note that this package also includes the assurance warranty.
- The service warranty can be purchased separately for $125.
- The cost of manufacturing each tablet is $300.
- The expected value of warranty claims under the assurance warranty is $25 per tablet.
- The expected value of warranty claims under the sales type warranty is $60, comprised of $35 pertaining to the service warranty and $25 relating to the assurance warranty.
- In 2018, EI sold 100 tablets with the assurance warranty and 150 tablets with the service warranty. No sales were made on credit terms.
- EI recognizes service warranty revenue over time based on the actual costs incurred (an input method).
- The cost of claims satisfied in 2018 under the assurance warranty for the 250 tablets sold totalled $2,000.
- The cost of claims satisfied in 2018 under the service warranty for the 150 tablets sold totalled $2,100.
- For both warranties, 50% of the cost was attributed to labour with the remainder being allocated to parts inventory.

Required:

a. Prepare a summary journal entry to record the sale of the tablets in 2018 with the assurance-type warranty.
b. Prepare a summary journal entry to record the sale of the tablets in 2018 with the sales-type warranty.
c. Prepare a summary journal entry to record the satisfaction of assurance-type warranty claims in 2018.
d. Prepare a summary journal entry to record the satisfaction of sales-type warranty claims in 2018.

P4-19. Revenue recognition criteria in specific situations—consignment sales

(**L.O.** 4-2) (Easy – 5 minutes)

A magazine publisher delivers 50,000 copies of its November magazine on October 26 to retailers. The retailers display the new magazines and remove the old (October) copies from the shelves by the end of October. Through an online system, the retailers report to the publisher the number of copies sold in a month by the third day of the following month. On November 3, the publisher learns that 42,000 copies of the October magazine had been sold. The unsold copies were finally returned to the publisher by December 31. The publisher charges $2 per copy of the magazine, which retails for $4.95.

Required:

How much revenue should the publisher record for the month of October for magazine sales?

 P4-20. Revenue recognition criteria in specific situations—consignment sales

(**L.O.** 4-2) (Medium – 15 minutes)

The publisher of *Business Weekly* received the following 52-week subscriptions during 2019. Each subscription is $99, which is a 52% discount off the newsstand price of $4 per issue. The company has a fiscal year that ends on the last Sunday of each calendar year. Each subscription becomes effective in the calendar month after the company receives the subscription.

Month	Subscriptions received	Month	Subscriptions received	Month	Subscriptions received
January	4,600	May	6,000	September	7,200
February	4,000	June	5,300	October	4,000
March	4,500	July	4,700	November	4,200
April	5,200	August	4,400	December	9,500
Total					63,600

Required:

Determine the amount of revenue from subscriptions *Business Weekly* should recognize in the year.

 P4-21. Revenue recognition criteria in specific situations—consignment sales

(**L.O.** 4-2) (Easy – 10 minutes)

Through non-subscription sales, *Business Weekly* (see P4-20) provides retailers with a 50% margin (or 100% markup) on its magazines. During 2019, the company distributed 1,950,000 copies to retailers, not all of which were sold. Retailers sent a total of 830,000 unsold copies back to the publisher, of which 35,000 copies were for the last two issues published in 2018. In January 2020, the company received 32,000 unsold copies for magazines published in the last weeks of December 2019.

Required:

Determine the amount of revenue from non-subscription sales *Business Weekly* should recognize in 2019.

P4-22. Revenue recognition criteria in specific situations—installment sales

(**L.O.** 4-2) (Easy – 5 minutes)

Why does revenue recognition on installment sales differ from that on more typical transactions involving the sale of goods?

P4-23. Revenue recognition criteria in specific situations—installment sales

(**L.O.** 4-2) (Easy – 5 minutes)

EasyOwn offers its customers an installment sales option whereby customers can pay monthly installments over 36 months. In July 2019, the company made $7.2 million of sales on installment. The average gross margin on such sales is 40%.

Required:

Using the installment sales method, record the journal entries that reflect EasyOwn's installment sales made in July 2019.

 P4-24. Revenue recognition criteria in specific situations—installment sales

(**L.O.** 4-2) (Easy – 10 minutes)

Mica Computers provides customers the option to purchase products with three installment payments made over 12 months (equal payments at the end of the 4th, 8th, and 12th months). In January 2019, Mica sold $30,000 of computers to one customer on this installment plan. The cost of these computers is $22,500.

Required:

Using the installment sales method, record the journal entries for Mica's installment sales made in January 2019 and the subsequent payments received. Assume all installment payments are received, and ignore the time value of money.

 P4-25. Revenue recognition criteria in specific situations—installment sales

(**L.O.** 4-2) (Easy – 10 minutes)

Oliver Furnishings frequently has sales involving "no down payment and no payments for three months." Three months after the purchase date, customers make four equal monthly payments (i.e., they make equal payments 3, 4, 5, and 6 months after purchase). Each payment is one-quarter of the purchase price.

The company has a December 31 year-end. During the current year, the company made the following sales on installment plans. Oliver makes a 40% gross margin on these sales.

Month	Sale price	Month	Sale price	Month	Sale price
January	$ 80,000	May	$ 90,000	September	$ 100,000
February	70,000	June	100,000	October	90,000
March	90,000	July	120,000	November	130,000
April	100,000	August	110,000	December	150,000
Total					$1,230,000

Required:

Using the installment sales method, record the journal entries for Oliver's installment sales made in the month of May and the subsequent payments received in August, September, October, and November. Assume all installment payments are received, and ignore the time value of money.

 P4-26. Revenue recognition criteria in specific situations—installment sales

(L.O. 4-2) (Medium – 15 minutes)

Refer to the facts given in the previous question (P4-25).

Required:

Using the installment sales method, determine the following amounts:

a. Balance of installment accounts receivable at December 31.
b. Amount of deferred gross profit as at December 31.
c. Sales revenue to recognize in the current year for installment sales made during the year. Assume all installment payments are received, and ignore the time value of money.

 P4-27. Computing revenue to recognize on long-term contracts

(L.O. 4-3) (Easy – 10 minutes)

Path Pavers began to resurface a 50-km running/cycling trail in March 2016 under a fixed-price contract of $25 million. The trail is to be completed by May 2020 at a total estimated cost of $18 million. In the five years of the contract, Path Pavers completes 8, 12, 12, 12, and 6 km of the trail, respectively. Actual costs are immaterially different from original estimates. Path Pavers is a publicly traded company listed on the Canadian Venture Exchange.

Required:

Determine the amount of revenue Path Pavers should recognize in each of the five years of the contract.

 P4-28. Computing profit to recognize on long-term contracts

(L.O. 4-3)[11] (Easy – 5 minutes)

Construction Co. started a contract in June 2017 to build a small foot bridge at a fixed price of $10 million. The bridge was to be completed by October 2019 at a total estimated cost of $8 million. Total cumulative costs incurred by the end of December 2017 and 2018 were $2 million and $5.5 million, respectively. Because of cost overruns in 2018, it is now expected that the project will cost $800,000 more than originally estimated. Final costs at the end of the project totalled $9 million. Construction Co. follows the guidance in IFRS.

[11.] Reprinted from Uniform Final Examination, 1997 with permission from Chartered Professional Accountants of Canada, Toronto, Canada. Any changes to the original material are the sole responsibility of the author (and/or publisher) and have not been reviewed or endorsed by the Chartered Professional Accountants of Canada.

Required:

Determine the amount of gross profit to be recognized for the year ended December 31, 2018.

 P4-29. Computing profit to recognize on long-term contracts

(**L.O.** 4-3) (Easy – 5 minutes)

Use the same facts for Construction Co. as in P4-28, but *also assume that the company is unable to estimate the total cost of the project prior to completion.*

Required:

Determine the amount of revenue, cost of sales, and gross profit Construction Co. would report in 2017, 2018, and 2019.

 P4-30. Understanding accounting policies for long-term contracts

(**L.O.** 4-3) (Easy – 10 minutes)

The following disclosure is from Note 2(G) of the 2016 financial statements for SNC-Lavalin (SNCL), an engineering firm headquartered in Montreal.

SNC-Lavalin 2016 Financial Statements Note 2(G)

REVENUES FROM E&C [Engineering and Construction]

Revenues from E&C are recognized based on the nature of the contract, which are mainly as follows:

- Revenues from cost-plus reimbursable contracts (usually providing for the reimbursement of costs related to time and material, plus an applicable margin) are recognized as costs are incurred, and include applicable margin earned as services are provided. Revenues from fixed-price contracts and unit-rate contracts are recognized on the stage of completion basis over the duration of the contract, which consists of recognizing revenue on a given contract proportionately with its stage of completion at any given time. Revenues from mixed contracts (providing for a mix of fixed-price and cost-plus reimbursable) are also recognized based on the stage of completion method. The stage of completion is determined by dividing the cumulative costs incurred as at the period end date by the sum of incurred costs and anticipated costs for completing a contract.
- The fixed-fee revenue portion from cost reimbursable with fixed-fee contracts for O&M [Operations and Maintenance] activity is recognized on a straight-line basis over the term of the contract, while the revenues from the cost-reimbursable portion are recognized as costs are incurred. Costs and anticipated revenues for completing a contract are recognized in the period in which the revisions are identified.

For contracts using the stage of completion method to recognize revenue, the cumulative effect of changes to anticipated costs and anticipated revenues for completing a contract are recognized in the period in which the revisions are identified. SNC-Lavalin has numerous contracts that are in various stages of completion. Estimates are required to determine the appropriate anticipated costs and revenues. Anticipated revenues on contracts may include future revenues from unapproved change orders, if such additional revenues can be reliably estimated and it is considered probable that they will be recovered. Also, anticipated revenues on contracts may include future revenues from claims, if negotiations have reached an advanced stage such that it is probable that the customer will accept the claim and the amount that it is probable will be accepted by the customer can be measured reliably. Revenues from performance incentives are recognized when specific indicators have been met and collection is reasonably assured.

In the event that the total anticipated costs exceed the total anticipated revenues on a contract, such loss is recognized in its entirety in the period it becomes known.

In all cases, the value of construction activities, material, and equipment purchased by SNC-Lavalin, when acting as purchasing agent for a client, is not recorded as revenue.

Required:

Identify the methods used by SNC-Lavalin to account for its construction contracts.

P4-31. Understanding accounting policies for long-term contracts

(L.O. 4-3, **L.O.** 4-4) (Easy – 10 minutes)

The following disclosure is from the 2016 Notes to the consolidated financial statements for EADS, the parent company of plane manufacturer Airbus.

Significant Accounting Policies

Revenue Recognition

Revenue is recognized to the extent that it is probable that the economic benefit arising from the ordinary activities of Airbus will flow to Airbus, that revenue can be measured reliably, and that the recognition criteria for each type of revenue-generating activity (sales of goods and services and construction contracts) have been met. Revenue is measured at the fair value of the consideration received or receivable.

Revenues from the sale of commercial aircraft are recognized when the aircraft is delivered, risks and rewards of ownership have been transferred to the customer, and revenues can be measured reliably except for launch customer contracts (see "Revenue from construction contracts"). Revenues from sales of aircraft (and related cost of sales) always include the engine component. Customers will generally benefit from a concession from the engine manufacturer, negotiated directly between the customer and the engine manufacturer. When reliable information exists, the engine prices considered in our revenues (and cost of sales) reflect the effect of the concessions.

Revenue from construction contracts

Construction contract accounting is applied for military programs, space projects, as well as for launch customer contracts in the civil aircraft business if customers have significantly influenced the structural design and technology of the aircraft type under the contract. As a result of certain airline customers' increasing involvement in the development and production process of the A350 XWB program, Airbus applies IAS 11 "Construction contracts" to a fixed number of launch customer contracts of the A350 XWB program. When the outcome can be estimated reliably, revenues and contract costs are recognized as revenue and expensed respectively by reference to the percentage of completion of the contract activity at the end of the reporting period ("PoC method"). Contract revenues include the purchase price agreed with the customer considering escalation formulas, contract amendments, and claims and penalties when assessed as probable. The PoC method used depends on the contract. The method is based either on inputs (*i.e.*, costs incurred for development contracts) or outputs (*i.e.*, contractually agreed technical milestones, delivered units).

Whenever the outcome of a construction contract cannot be estimated reliably – for example during the early stages of a contract or during the course of a contract's completion – all related contract costs that are incurred are immediately expensed and revenues are recognized only to the extent of those costs being recoverable (the "early stage," also called "zero profit margin" method of accounting).

Required:

Summarize the methods EADS uses to recognize revenue for construction contracts.

 P4-32. Computing revenue to recognize on long-term contracts and error correction

(L.O. 4-3) (Easy – 10 minutes)

Corus Corporation builds large cruise ships on a contract basis. The company uses the percentage of completion method of revenue recognition. The following information pertains to the construction contracts it had in place as of its year-end date of December 31, 2020.

($ million)	2019	2020
Cost incurred to date	108	320
Cost to complete contracts	612	480
Total price of contracts outstanding December 31, 2018	960	960
Revenue	144	?

Required:

a. Calculate the revenue to be recognized in 2020.

b. While examining the Corus financial statements, the auditors noted that there was an error in the estimate of costs to complete the contracts in 2019. The "cost to complete" should have been $792 million instead of $612 million. In light of this evidence, how much revenue should be recognized in 2020?

 P4-33. Accounting for long-term contracts   (**L.O.** 4-3) (Medium – 40 minutes)

Jones Contractors Inc. agreed to construct a building for $300,000. Construction commenced in 2018 and was completed in 2020. Data relating to the contract are summarized below:

	2018	2019	2020
Cost incurred during year	$ 80,000	$120,000	$ 50,000
Estimated costs to complete	158,000	39,000	—
Billings during year	65,000	130,000	105,000
Collections during year	60,000	128,000	112,000
Estimated profit on contract	?	?	?

Required:

a. For each of the three years, determine the following amounts relating to the above contract: revenue, expenses, gross profit, accounts receivable balance, and construction-in-process inventory balance.

b. Record the journal entries using T-accounts.

P4-34. Computing revenue and profit to recognize on long-term contracts with expected losses   (**L.O.** 4-3, **L.O.** 4-4) (Medium – 10 minutes)

Megacorp uses the cost-to-cost ratio to apply the percentage of completion method. It is currently early 2021. The following table provides information relating to one of its projects so far. The contract price is $45 million.

(Amounts in $ millions)	2019	2020	2021
Cost incurred to date	$ 12	$ 30	Not avail.
Additional costs to complete estimated at year-end	28	18	Not avail.
Total estimated cost	40	48	

Required:

Compute the amount of revenue and gross profit that Megacorp should recognize in each of 2019 and 2020.

 P4-35. Computing revenue and profit to recognize on long-term contracts with expected losses   (**L.O.** 4-3, **L.O.** 4-4) (Medium – 10 minutes)

Westel is a builder of large digital networks. In the midst of the high-tech euphoria, the company bid and won a $50,000,000 contract to build a network for the country of Elbonia. Details on the project over the past three years are as follows:

($000's)	Year 1	Year 2	Year 3
Cumulative costs incurred	12,000	30,000	55,000
Additional costs to complete estimated at year-end	48,000	20,000	0
Amounts invoiced to client in each year	8,000	19,000	23,000
Cash collected	7,000	18,000	25,000

Required:

Compute the amount of revenue, cost of goods sold (COGS), and gross profit (or loss) to be recognized in each of the three years. The company uses the percentage of completion method to account for long-term contracts. Record your answers in the following table.

($000's)	Year 1	Year 2	Year 3	Total
Revenue				50,000
− COGS	12,000			55,000
− Expected loss (recovery)		(8,000)		0
= Gross profit (loss)				(5,000)

 P4-36. Accounting for long-term contracts with price adjustments and expected losses

(**L.O.** 4-3, **L.O.** 4-4) (Medium – 10 minutes)

Cautious Construction Company has contracted to build an office building for Property Corporation. The construction started on January 1, 2018, and the project was completed on July 1, 2021. The contract price was $65 million. Due to uncertainties in the construction process, the two parties to the project agreed to a risk-sharing arrangement whereby Property Corporation covers 50% of all cost overruns in excess of the originally estimated cost of $60 million (e.g., if estimated total costs are $64 million, then Cautious Construction Company would receive an additional $2 million for the contract). The following data relate to the construction period:

($000's)	2018	2019	2020	2021
Costs incurred to date	15,000	30,000	50,000	63,000
Estimated cost to complete	47,000	42,000	11,000	0
Progress billings to date	25,000	45,000	55,000	unknown
Cash collected to date	20,000	42,000	51,000	62,000

Required:

Compute the estimated gross profit (loss) for 2018, 2019, 2020, and 2021, assuming that the percentage of completion method is used. [*Hint:* you need to compute revised contract prices each year due to the risk-sharing arrangement.]

P4-37. Accounting for long-term contracts with expected losses

(**L.O.** 4-3, **L.O.** 4-4) (Medium – 15 minutes)

On July 1, 2020, Hornby Construction Company Inc. contracted to build an office building for Ladysmith Corp. for a total contract price of $1,900,000. On July 1, Hornby estimated that it would take between two and three years to complete the building. In October 2022, the building was deemed substantially completed. Following are accumulated contract costs incurred, estimated costs to complete the contract, and accumulated billings to Ladysmith in 2020, 2021, and 2022.

	2020	2021	2022
Cost incurred to date	$ 150,000	$1,200,000	$2,100,000
Estimated costs to complete	1,350,000	800,000	0
Cumulative billings to Ladysmith	300,000	1,100,000	1,800,000

Required:

Using the percentage of completion method, compute the revenue and profit or loss to be recognized as a result of this contract for the years ended December 31, 2020, 2021, and 2022. The company used the cost-to-cost method to estimate the percentage complete. Use a schedule format similar to Exhibit 4-22 to show your calculations.

P4-38. Accounting for long-term contracts with expected losses

(**L.O.** 4-3, **L.O.** 4-4) (Medium – 15 minutes)

Refer to the information in the previous problem (P4-37). Complete the question assuming that Hornby Construction Company uses ASPE and applies the completed contract method.

A·S·P·E

 P4-39. Accounting for long-term contracts with expected losses

(**L.O.** 4-3, **L.O.** 4-4) (Medium – 10 minutes)

Assume the following facts for a construction contract that was completed over four years. The contract price is $5.5 million.

	2018	2019	2020	2021
Cost incurred to date	$ 1,000,000	$2,000,000	$3,000,000	$4,000,000
Estimated costs to complete	2,500,000	4,000,000	2,000,000	0

Required:

Using the percentage of completion method, compute the gross profit or loss to be recognized as a result of this contract for each of the four years. The company used the cost-to-cost method to estimate the percentage complete.

 P4-40. Accounting for long-term contracts with expected losses

(**L.O.** 4-3, **L.O.** 4-4) (Medium – 5 minutes)

Refer to the information in the previous problem (P4-39).

Required:

If this company were permitted to use guidance in ASPE, and the company chose to apply the completed contract method, what would be the gross profit or loss in each of the four years?

A·S·P·E

P4-41. Accounting for long-term contracts with expected losses

(**L.O.** 4-3, **L.O.** 4-4) (Difficult – 20 minutes)

Schott Construction is the contractor for a building project for an educational institution. The project was scheduled to be completed over three years from 2018 to 2020. The contracted price was $80 million. The following table provides information relating to this project:

(Amounts in $ millions)	2018	2019	2020
Project completion according to budget plan prior to project commencement	50%	80%	100%
Costs incurred to date	$42	$63	$81
Additional costs to complete, estimated at year-end	33	21	0
Billings on construction in progress to-date	38	58	81
Cash collected to-date	35	54	81

Required:

a. Compute the amount of gross profit to be recognized in each year.
b. Compute the amount of revenue to be recognized in 2019.
c. Prepare all the journal entries required in 2019.

 P4-42. Accounting for long-term contracts with expected losses

(**L.O.** 4-3, **L.O.** 4-4) (Difficult – 20 minutes)

Optimist Ltd. is constructing a residential high-rise in downtown Vancouver for a contract price of $12,000,000. Costs for this contract were initially estimated to be $9,000,000.

The company uses the percentage of completion method of revenue recognition, using the cost-to-cost method of estimating the percentage complete. The following information is available:

($000's)	Year 1	Year 2	Year 3
Costs incurred each year	3,500	6,500	2,000
Additional costs to complete estimated at year-end	6,500	3,000	0
Billings on construction in progress	5,000	4,000	3,000
Cash collected	4,700	4,200	3,100

Required:

a. Compute the amount of gross profit to be recognized in each year. Show computations in good form.
b. Compute the amount of revenue to be recognized in Year 2.
c. Prepare all the journal entries required in Year 2. [*Hint:* Four entries are required.]
d. Prepare the journal entry required in Year 3 to acknowledge completion and acceptance of the project.

P4-43. Accounting for long-term contracts with expected losses
(L.O. 4-3, L.O. 4-4) (Difficult – 20 minutes)

South Olympia Systems (SOS) has a long-term project to install a complex information system for a client. The project has a contract price of $40 million, and it was scheduled to be completed over four years from 2018 to 2021. SOS uses the percentage of completion method to account for long-term contracts using the cost-to-cost ratio. It is currently early 2021. The following table provides information relating to this project so far:

(amounts in $ millions)	2018	2019	2020	2021
Cost incurred in the year	4	20	10	Not avail.
Additional costs to complete, estimated at year-end	28	24	6	Not avail.
Billings on construction in progress to date	5	20	31	Not avail.
Cash collected to date	3	17	29	Not avail.

Required:

a. Compute the amount of revenue that SOS should recognize in each of 2018, 2019, and 2020.
b. The gross profit (loss) for the contract recognized in 2019 is a loss of $9 million. Compute the amount of gross profit for each of 2018 and 2020.
c. Prepare all the journal entries required in 2020, the third year of the contract.

P4-44. Accounting for long-term contracts with expected losses
(L.O. 4-3, L.O. 4-4) (Difficult – 25 minutes)

Condo King (CK) is building a luxury condominium for a contract price of $60,000,000. This is estimated to be a three-year project with an estimated cost of $48,000,000. CK uses the percentage of completion method of revenue recognition, using the cost-to-cost method of estimating the percentage complete. The following is the best available information at the end of each year:

($000's)	Year 1	Year 2	Year 3
Costs incurred each year	13,000	27,000	14,000
Estimated costs to complete	37,000	18,000	0
Billings on construction in progress	15,000	25,000	20,000
Cash collected	8,000	20,000	32,000

Required:

a. Compute the amount of gross profit to be recognized in Year 1, Year 2, and Year 3. Show computations in tabular form in a spreadsheet.
b. Prepare all the journal entries required in Year 2.
c. Prepare the journal entry required in Year 3 to close the accounts related to the project.
d. At the end of Year 2, if the estimated cost to complete is $22 million (instead of $18 million), how much gross profit would be recognized in Year 2?

 P4-45. Accounting for long-term contracts with expected losses

(**L.O.** 4-3, **L.O.** 4-4) (Difficult – 15 minutes)

In early 2018, Skyline Corp. won a contract to build a rapid transit line along the Broadway corridor. The contract was for $1.9 billion to be received over the construction period of six years, ending in November 2024. Skyline has a December 31 year-end and uses the percentage of completion method to account for long-term contracts.

Required:

a. Skyline's management expects the gross margin on the total project to be 20%, and that $228 million would be incurred on the project by December 31, 2018.
  i. How much gross profit (or loss) will Skyline record in the 2018 fiscal year if management's estimates are accurate?
  ii. Provide the journal entries to record revenue, cost of goods sold, and expected loss (if applicable) for fiscal 2018.
b. Assume that it is now early 2022 and you are preparing the adjusting entries for 2021. The accounting records indicate that, by the end of 2020, a total of $760 million in revenue and $684 million in cost of goods sold had been recorded. You also know that $380 million in costs were incurred on the project in 2021, and management's best estimates indicate another $912 million in costs will be required to complete the project.
  i. How much gross profit (or loss) should Skyline record in the 2021 fiscal year if management's estimates are accurate?
  ii. Provide the journal entries to record revenue, cost of goods sold, and expected loss (if applicable) for fiscal year 2021.

 P4-46. Accounting for long-term contracts with expected losses

(**L.O.** 4-3, **L.O.** 4-4, **L.O.** 4-5) (Difficult – 30 minutes)

Nautilus Resources is investing in a new heavy oil upgrader in northern Alberta. Nautilus has hired Rite Build Contractors to construct the facilities. The contract price is $3,600 million to be completed over four years. The following information pertains to this construction contract:

($ millions)	Year 1	Year 2	Year 3	Year 4
Cumulative costs incurred to date	480	1,250	2,660	3,750
Estimated additional costs to complete	2,520	1,875	1,140	0
Billings on construction in progress	500	900	1,000	1,200
Cash collected in the year	450	860	1,030	1,260

Required:

a. Compute the amount of revenue and expense to be recognized in the accounts of Rite Build Contractors in each of the four years. Show computations in tabular format in a spreadsheet.
b. Prepare all the journal entries required in Year 1.
c. Prepare the journal entry required in Year 4 to close the accounts related to the project.
d. If Rite Build were to underestimate the cost to complete to be $940 million instead of $1,140 million in Year 3, how much gross profit or loss would be recognized in each year? How much more or less gross profit or loss would be reported in that year? How much more or less gross profit would be reported in Year 4, and in total for all four years?

🌐 **P4-47.** Identifying errors in the accounting for long-term contracts

(**L.O.** 4-3, **L.O.** 4-4, **L.O.** 4-5) (Difficult – 15 minutes)

Fraternal Brothers provides consulting services on contract for a standard hourly rate of $100 per hour. The contracts allow the company to invoice the client evenly during the contract period. The company's average cost is $70/hour. At the end of December 31, 2019, its fiscal year-end, the company had the following projects still in progress:

Client	Project start date (y/m/d)	Contracted completion date	Budget hours in contract	Hours to date	% complete	Budgeted total revenue @ $100/hr	Revenue recorded	Billed to date	Accrued revenue*
Alpha	2019/2/5	2021/2/5	14,580	14,000	96.0	$1,458,000	$1,400,000	$ 656,100	$ 743,900
Beta	2019/2/28	2020/2/29	6,000	5,230	87.2	600,000	523,000	504,000	19,000
Chi	2019/4/9	2020/4/9	9,600	9,500	99.0	960,000	950,000	700,800	249,200
Delta	2019/5/19	2020/5/19	3,600	2,500	69.4	360,000	250,000	223,200	26,800
Epsilon	2019/6/28	2020/6/28	5,440	6,170	113.4	544,000	544,000	277,440	266,560
Phi	2019/8/7	2019/10/6	750	160	21.3	75,000	16,000		16,000
Gamma	2019/9/16	2020/9/16	4,400	1,960	44.5	440,000	196,000	127,600	68,400
Eta	2019/10/26	2019/11/25	350	150	42.9	35,000	15,000		15,000
			44,720	39,670	88.7	$4,472,000	$3,894,000	$2,489,140	$1,404,860

*Amounts reflected on the balance sheet in the item "Accounts receivable and accrued revenue."

Required:

Identify any errors or likely errors in Fraternal Brothers's revenue recognition for their contracts.

P4-48. Presentation, disclosure, and analysis

(**L.O.** 4-2, **L.O.** 4-3, **L.O.** 4-5) (Medium – 15 minutes)

Obtain the 2016 financial statements for Thomson Reuters Corporation either through the company's website or through SEDAR (www.sedar.com).

Required:

a. In addition to the general requirements for the recognition of revenue on the sale of goods and the provision of services, what other accounting policies does the company explain?
b. For sales arrangements involving multiple deliverables, what method of allocation does the company generally use?
c. For sales arrangements involving multiple deliverables, what are the two critical issues that the company identifies as requiring professional judgment? What process does the company use to resolve these issues?
d. For long-term service contracts, on what basis does the company estimate the percentage of completion?

P4-49. Presentation, disclosure, and analysis

(**L.O.** 4-2, **L.O.** 4-3, **L.O.** 4-5) (Medium – 15 minutes)

Refer to the financial report for Canadian Tire Corporation for the fiscal year ended December 31, 2016 in Appendix D.

Required:

a. Note 3 of the financial statements describes the company's accounting policies. Aside from a policy for "Sales and warranty returns," briefly describe the other six accounting policies relating to revenue.

b. In 2016, how much was recognized in revenue for each of the six categories described in (a)? How much was deferred as at December 31, 2016? Where is the largest source of growth in revenue?

P4-50.   Presentation, disclosure, and analysis
            (**L.O.** 4-2, **L.O.** 4-3, **L.O.** 4-5) (Medium – 10 minutes)

Obtain the annual report for Bombardier Inc. for the fiscal year ended December 31, 2016, either through the company's website or through SEDAR (www.sedar.com).

Required:

a. For revenue recognition on long-term contracts, how does the company estimate the percentage of completion? What does the company do when it anticipates a loss on a contract?

b. In relation to long-term contracts, how much work in process inventory did the company have at the end of 2016? How much was billings on construction in progress? How much was inventory before netting out the amount for billings on construction in progress?

O. MINI-CASES

CASE 1
Revenue recognition at telecom firms
(20 minutes)[12]

During the later 1990s, as the Internet blossomed around the world, Global Crossing thrived in the business of paving the Internet superhighway: laying cables to transport data criss-crossing the globe and charging a toll for the use of those cables. In 1999, the company's market capitalization reached $40 billion. In anticipation of the burgeoning demand, Global Crossing took on more than $7 billion of debt to lay 1.7 million miles of fibre-optic cable.

By 2001, the Internet boom had turned to bust. As this occurred, Global Crossing contracted with other telecom firms, such as Qwest Communications, to allow them to use the company's cables in future years. In the second quarter of 2001, Global Crossing sold some $600 million of fibre-optic capacity, amounting to almost 20% of revenues.

Separately, Qwest Communications also had its own set of cables. Due to the multi-modal nature of the Internet, the networks of Qwest and Global Crossing had significant overlap, while remaining distinct from each other. Like Global Crossing, Qwest also sold some of its fibre-optic capacity to other companies, including Global Crossing. Global Crossing recorded these purchases of fibre-optic capacity as capital investments and subsequently depreciated them over several years when the fibre could be used to generate revenues.

Required:
Evaluate the appropriateness of Global Crossing's accounting policies raised by the above facts.

CASE 2
Modern Electronics's product service plans
(25 minutes)

Modern Electronics Inc. (MEI) is a retailer that sells televisions, audio systems, computers, gaming consoles, related accessories, and appliances such as washing machines. Since its founding in 1995, MEI has grown to 28 locations across the country.

Many of the products stocked by MEI have warranties provided by the manufacturer, typically ranging from 90 days to one year. In addition to these manufacturer's warranties, MEI offers its customers, for a fee, "Guaranteed Advantage Plans" (GAPs). The box below provides a description of the Guaranteed Advantage Plan.

> ### Benefits of our Guaranteed Advantage Plan:
>
> Your Guaranteed Advantage Plan coverage goes beyond most manufacturers' warranties, ensuring that your product will perform to the standard you have come to expect from your manufacturer for the full period covered by the plan.
>
> We have customer service representatives available to assist you 24 hours a day.
>
> We'll do our best to fix your product. If we can't, we'll replace it. All free of charge while your product is covered by Guaranteed Advantage.
>
> If you decide to resell the product some time in the future, Guaranteed Advantage goes along, so you'll be able to get a better price.

[12.] Various facts for this case have been obtained from Harris Collingwood, David Sherman, and David Young, *Profits You Can Trust: Spotting and Surviving Accounting Landmines.* Upper Saddle River, NJ: FT Prentice Hall, 2003.

The fee and the coverage under the Guaranteed Advantage Plan differ according to the type of product and the option chosen by the customer. As a representative example, MEI offers the following coverage for a $1,500 television:

Length of guarantee	2 years	3 years	4 years
Price	$240	$270	$300

Competitors such as Best Buy and Future Shop also offer similar service plans.

The GAPs are highly profitable for MEI. On average, the cost of fulfilling the guarantee is well under a third of the fee charged to the customer. Because of this low cost, the company is considering a short-term promotion whereby customers would receive, for no additional charge, the shortest GAP available for the product purchased. The customer can obtain a longer GAP by paying the differential. In the above example, a customer who purchases the $1,500 television would receive the two-year plan for free, but could pay $60 to obtain the four-year coverage.

Required:

Assume that it is the first year that the company has offered the Guaranteed Advantage Plans. As the company's controller, prepare a memo to MEI's CFO explaining the accounting issues surrounding the GAP and how it affects the accounting for products sold. Assume that the company follows the guidance provided by IFRS.

CASE 3
Penguins in Paradise
(30 minutes)[13]

You have just met a new client, Darth Garbinsky, who has come to you for some accounting advice:

"The thing you have to understand is how these stage plays work. You start out with just an idea, but generally no cash. That's where promoters like me come in. We find ways of raising the money necessary to get the play written and the actors trained. If the play is a success, we hope to recover all those costs and a whole lot more, but cash flow is the problem. Since less than half of all plays make money, you cannot get very much money from banks.

"Take my current project, 'Penguins in Paradise.' You only need to look at the cash inflows (Exhibit I) to see how many sources I had to approach to get the cash. As you can see, most of the initial funding comes from the investors in the Penguins in Paradise Limited Partnership (PIP). They put up their money to buy a percentage of the future profits of the play.

"Some investors do not want to invest the amount required for a partnership unit. So, for them, we structure the deal a little differently. Instead of buying a unit in the partnership, they buy a right to a royalty—a percentage of future operating profits (i.e., gross revenue less true operating expenses). In this way, these investors get an interest in the play without being in the partnership. Since they do not have a vote at the partnership meetings, they are more concerned about their risks.

"Funding the play is not that easy. The money that the investors put up is not enough to fund all the start-up costs, so you have to be creative. Take reservation fees, for example. You know how tough it is to get good seats for a really hot play. Well, PIP sold the right to buy great seats to some dedicated theatre-goers this year for next year's performance. These amounts are non-refundable, and the great thing is that the buyers still have to pay full price for the tickets when they buy them.

"Consider the sale of movie rights. Lots of good plays get turned into movies. Once the stage play is a success, the movie rights are incredibly expensive. My idea was to sell the movie rights in advance. PIP got a lot less money, but at least we got it up front when we needed it.

"The other sources are much the same. We received the government grant by agreeing to have at least 50% Canadian content. We also negotiated a bank loan with an interest rate of 5% per year plus 1% of the gross revenue of the play, instead of the usual 20% interest a year. Even my fee for putting the deal together was taken as a percentage of operating profits, so just about everybody has a strong interest in the play's performance.

"Because of these various interests in PIP, I will require audited financial statements to determine how much is owing to each party."

[13.] Reprinted from Uniform Final Examination, 1991 with permission from Chartered Professional Accountants of Canada, Toronto, Canada. Any changes to the original material are the sole responsibility of the author (and/or publisher) and have not been reviewed or endorsed by the Chartered Professional Accountants of Canada.

Required:

Prepare a memo for your files summarizing the financial accounting issues raised in your conversation with Darth Garbinsky.

Exhibit I	Cash Flows for Penguins in Paradise

Penguins in Paradise
(A Limited Partnership)
Summary of Cash Flows
For the period ended December 31, 2020
($000's)

Cash inflows	
Investor contributions to limited partnership	$5,000
Sale of royalty rights	1,000
Bank loan	2,000
Sale of movie rights	500
Government grants	50
Reservation fees	20
	8,570
Cash outflows	
Salaries and fees	3,500
Costumes and sets	1,000
Miscellaneous costs	1,250
	5,750
Net cash flow	$2,820

CASE 4
Plex-Fame
Corporation
(30 minutes)[14]

You are engaged in the audit of Plex-Fame Corporation (PFC), a rapidly expanding, diversified publicly traded entertainment company with operations throughout Canada and the United States. PFC's operations include movie theatres, live theatre production, television production, and a 60% interest in Media Inc. (Media), a company that specializes in entertainment-related advertising and promotion.

It is June 22, 2021, the week before PFC's year-end. You meet with the chief financial officer of PFC to get an update on current developments and learn the following:

- PFC acquired real estate in prime locations where an existing theatre chain does not adequately serve the market. After acquiring a theatre site, the company engages a contractor to construct the theatre complex. During the year, the company received a $2 million payment from one such contractor who had built a 10-theatre complex for PFC in Montreal. This payment represents a penalty for not completing the theatre complex on time. Construction began in June 2020 and was to have been completed by December 2020. Instead, the complex was not completed until the end of May 2021.

- The company is staging a Canadian version of "Rue St. Jacques," which is to open in November 2021. The smash-hit musical has been running in Paris for three years and is still playing to sold-out audiences. PFC started receiving advance bookings in

14. Reprinted from Uniform Final Examination, 1997 with permission from Chartered Professional Accountants of Canada, Toronto, Canada. Any changes to the original material are the sole responsibility of the author (and/or publisher) and have not been reviewed or endorsed by the Chartered Professional Accountants of Canada.

November 2020, and the first 40 weeks of the show's run are completely sold out. Average ticket prices are $65; the show will play seven nights a week. The theatre used for production is relatively small, with about 1,200 seats. As at June 22, 2021, PFC had included in revenue $1.7 million of interest collected on the funds received from advance ticket sales. In addition to the substantial investment in advertising for this production ($4 million), the company will have invested $15 million in pre-production costs by November 2021 and will incur weekly production costs of $250,000 once the show opens.

■ PFC started selling movie theatres a couple of years ago. Each theatre's contribution to long-run operating cash flow is assessed, and if the value of the real estate is greater than the present value of future theatre operating profits, the theatre is sold. In the past, revenue from these sales has been relatively minor, but this year 25% of net income (i.e., $6 million) came from the sale of theatres. Since these sales are considered an ongoing part of the company's operations, proceeds from the sale of theatres are recorded as revenue in the income statement.

When you return to the office, you discuss these issues with the leader of the audit engagement. She asks you to prepare a report on the financial accounting issues you have identified as a result of your meeting with the chief financial officer.

Required:
Prepare the requested audit report.

Tom Mullins, a long-time client of your employer, Spinney and Smith, Chartered Accountants, approached one of the firm's partners concerning a new business opportunity. Tom is a well-established local real estate agent with an excellent reputation for integrity and client service. He is excited about a new development in the real estate field—the sale of "reverse mortgages."

Under such sales, senior citizens who own and live in homes with high market values, but who lack funds on which to live, enter into an agreement with a company whereby the senior citizens receive a cash settlement now in exchange for title to their home upon the death of the last survivor. The amount of the payment is based on the value of the home and actuarial assumptions about life spans.

The senior citizens continue to live in the house, rent free, for the rest of their lives. The only costs that they continue to bear after the transaction are the normal household expenses any homeowner bears, such as repairs, painting, cutting the lawn, insurance, and property taxes. Tom says that the price paid would be fair to both the senior citizens and the speculator: it would provide a reasonable return to the company without cheating the senior citizens.

Tom intends to incorporate a company (Happy Valley Homes Ltd.) to capitalize on this opportunity. Tom told the partner: "I can pay $200,000 for a reverse mortgage now, and the house should be worth $400,000 when sold. My average holding period should be about six years. That's a $200,000 gain, half of which would be taxable at, say, 40%. I would net $160,000."

Tom proposes to raise the necessary capital by way of an offering document to private investors. He wants Spinney and Smith to help put together a financial forecast and to attach "whatever opinion is appropriate. Use whatever accounting policies are best, as long as they are not too costly and complicated." Spinney and Smith will also be engaged as auditors, but for the moment Tom is primarily concerned with "getting the project off the ground." Accordingly, he is interested only in Happy Valley's immediate accounting and auditing concerns.

CASE 5
Happy Valley Homes
(75 minutes)[15]

[15.] Reprinted from Uniform Final Examination, 1988 with permission from Chartered Professional Accountants of Canada, Toronto, Canada. Any changes to the original material are the sole responsibility of the author (and/or publisher) and have not been reviewed or endorsed by the Chartered Professional Accountants of Canada.

In the interim, Tom intends to borrow funds from his bank to cover initial expenses for the first few houses.

After outlining his discussions with Tom, the partner has requested you to perform the initial research and to draft a preliminary report to the client on the issues raised.

Required:

a. Prepare the draft report requested by the partner.
b. Consider the business model and discuss the impact of information asymmetry (adverse selection and moral hazard) on the potential success or failure of the proposed venture.
c. Discuss the ethical issues involved in the proposed venture.

CASE 6
Revenue recognition
in governments

(24 minutes)

In late 2008, *The Globe and Mail* raised some concerns about the way provincial governments account for their revenues and implied that some of these practices are inappropriate. Entitled "B.C.'s $1.7-Billion Surplus Kept Under Wraps," the reporter, David Ebner, alleged that the government of British Columbia had been hiding a "secret surplus."[16]

At the time, the economies of British Columbia, Canada, and in fact most of the world were deteriorating rapidly following the financial crisis that began three months earlier. With shrinking tax revenues, the finance minister in BC updated the province's budget for the year ending March 31, 2009, to show a much reduced surplus of $450 million. Ebner alleged that this surplus could have been much higher had the government reported in a different way.

The issue that was the focus of Ebner's criticism is the way the BC government accounts for money the province receives from energy companies for rights for natural gas exploration, primarily in the northeast corner of the province. According to Ebner, Alberta and Saskatchewan record the full amount of such cash receipts as revenue. In contrast, British Columbia divides this revenue over eight years, which was the average duration for the exploration rights. Ebner calculates that, had BC recorded its revenues in the same way as its neighbouring provinces, it would have a surplus of $1.7 billion instead of $450 million, for a difference of $1.25 billion.

In 2008–2009, BC was paid $2.18 billion for natural gas rights, but the statement of revenues showed only $928 million. This latter figure includes a mere one-eighth of the $2.18 billion, and the remainder was carried over from a previous year. The gap between the amount accounted for and the cash received was $1.25 billion.

Ebner noted that the accounting method used in Saskatchewan contributed to a huge surplus in 2008–2009 of $2.3 billion, largely because of an additional and unexpected $1 billion received from selling exploration rights. (Saskatchewan has one-quarter the population of BC, so a surplus of $2.3 billion is enormous.)

Of key concern to Ebner was that, as a result of this accounting policy, money that existed could not be spent on programs or to make tax cuts that might help the province's floundering economy. On the other hand, Ebner acknowledges that the money was being spent on infrastructure, which has a capital budget that is separate from the operating budget, the latter of which is what produces government surpluses and deficits.

Each of the three provincial governments appear to believe that its interpretation of accounting rules is appropriate, so convergence is unlikely to happen anytime soon.

Required:

Discuss the issues raised by the above commentary by applying financial accounting theory, the Conceptual Framework for financial reporting, and accrual accounting concepts. In particular, evaluate the different revenue recognition policies used in the provinces mentioned, and critique the chosen perspective on the issues.

[16.] David Ebner, *The Globe and Mail*, December 2, 2008.

Patricia Leather Company (PLC) is a small private company located in Montreal. The company was established five years ago and has become increasingly popular with small local stores, which have been carrying its custom-made leather products. PLC sells its products to the stores, and the stores sell the merchandise to end-users. Due to its initial success, PLC decided to open its first retail store in 2021. In its first year of operations, the company did fairly well, reporting a net income of $80,000. Management was certain sales would increase in the next fiscal year and was considering three alternatives for growth:

- Alternative 1: Sales on Consignment
  Management believed it would be a good idea to start selling their products on consignment through retail stores. Instead of selling the products directly to the retail stores as they had been doing, they believed selling the merchandise on consignment would increase revenue.
- Alternative 2: Installment Sales
  Management was considering selling its products as installment sales in its retail boutique. They would allow clients to pay for their products in up to four separate payments. Since many of the leather products are pricey, they believed this would be a good idea to increase sales.
- Alternative 3: Franchise Revenue
  Management was also considering making PLC into a franchise. They have heard that franchisors collect initial fees and ongoing fees without really being involved in the franchisee stores. They believe this could also be a good idea to increase their sales.

PLC has hired you as an external consultant and has asked you to consider the three options above. They would like to go ahead with only one of the alternatives.

Required:

a. How should PLC account for revenue under each of the three alternatives?
b. What would be your main concerns with each of these alternatives?
c. Considering your answer in (b), which alternative would you advise the company to choose? Explain your reasoning.

CASE 7
Patricia Leather Company
(30 minutes)

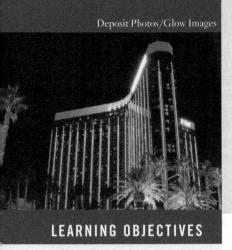

CHAPTER 5
Cash and Receivables

LEARNING OBJECTIVES

After studying this chapter, you should be able to:

L.O. 5-1. Apply the standards and procedures for recording, reconciling, and reporting cash and cash equivalents.

L.O. 5-2. Explain the need for internal controls for cash specifically and other assets more generally, and evaluate the adequacy of cash controls in different situations.

L.O. 5-3. Apply the standards and procedures for the initial recognition, subsequent measurement at the balance sheet date, and derecognition of trade receivables.

L.O. 5-4. Apply the standards to account for non-trade receivables.

CPA competencies addressed in this chapter:

1.1.2 Evaluates the appropriateness of the basis of financial reporting (Level B)
    c. Difference between accrual accounting compared to cash accounting

1.2.1 Develops or evaluates appropriate accounting policies and procedures – Ethical professional judgment (Level B)

1.2.2 Evaluates treatment for routine transactions (Level A)
    a. Cash and cash equivalents
    b. Receivables
    o. Changes in accounting policies and estimates, and errors

1.3.1 Prepares financial statements (Level A)
    a. Internal control and cash (bank reconciliation, control over cash receipts and disbursements)

1.4.1 Analyzes complex financial statement note disclosure (Level C)

MGM Resorts International (www.mgmresorts.com, New York Stock Exchange ticker: MGM) owns many casino/entertainment resorts—such as the Bellagio, the Luxor, and the Mirage in Las Vegas, as well as other locations around the globe. At the end of 2016, the company reported US$1,447 million in cash and cash equivalents on its balance sheet. A substantial portion of this balance is kept onsite rather than in bank accounts. As popularized in movies such as *Ocean's Eleven* (and *Ocean's Twelve* and *Ocean's Thirteen*), it is well known that casinos hold significant amounts of cash on their premises and that there are significant risks associated with the handling and storage of paper currency. For casinos and other more typical businesses, what are the internal controls necessary to reduce these risks to a sufficiently low level?

Furthermore, while the meaning of "cash" is quite clear, what constitutes "cash equivalents" and why are they classified together as one item on the balance sheet?

For December 31, 2016, MGM Mirage also reported $641 million and $543 million in gross and net accounts receivable, respectively. The difference between these two figures, the allowance for doubtful accounts, was $98 million, or 15% of the gross receivables. In addition, $92 million of this allowance relates primarily to casino accounts receivable, which amounted to $332 million out of the $641 million. Thus, the allowance for doubtful accounts represents 28% of casino receivables, compared with less than 1.1% for a typical company.[1] Why is it necessary for companies to establish an allowance for doubtful accounts—and why is it such a high figure for MGM Mirage?

[1.] Statistic based on 9,800 North American companies calculated from Compustat.

⑤ CONTENTS

Cash is unique among balance sheet assets. As discussed in Chapter 3, all of the non-cash assets (and liabilities) exist because of the accrual accounting system. Cash, in contrast, would be reported whether accounting is on a cash basis or an accrual basis. Given this difference, this chapter first addresses issues relating to cash accounting. Specifically, we first consider what "cash and cash equivalents" includes and excludes. We also look at bank reconciliations and internal controls, which for some readers will be a review of introductory accounting. The latter part of this chapter begins the study of non-cash assets with the coverage of receivables, both trade and non-trade. The coverage of other non-cash assets then continues in Chapters 6 through 10.

A. CASH AND CASH EQUIVALENTS

L.O. 5-1. Apply the standards and procedures for recording, reconciling, and reporting cash and cash equivalents.

In modern economies, the importance of cash is self-evident; it is, with few exceptions, the universally accepted medium of exchange. People and companies make purchases and pay debts with cash. Given the significance of cash, it is important to know what cash includes—and excludes—for accounting purposes.

1. Inclusions in cash and cash equivalents

cash   Cash on hand and demand deposits.

In common usage, "cash" refers to legal tender: bills and coins issued by the Bank of Canada (or a foreign government/central bank in the case of foreign currency). For security reasons, it is impractical to hold large quantities of currency or to transport millions of dollars of currency to pay for transactions. Thus, in addition to legal tender, **cash** in the context of accounting, includes demand deposits—accounts at banks or credit unions from which funds can be withdrawn on demand of the depositor without restriction, such as chequing accounts. Transactions completed by cheques, bank drafts, email transfers, wire transfers, and so on are all considered cash transactions.

While cash is useful for completing transactions, it is an idle asset. Cash on hand or in demand deposits earns no return (or a negligible amount at best). Consequently, firms find it beneficial to minimize the amount of cash and to hold funds in accounts that do earn a rate of return. To recognize the reality of this cash management activity, accounting standards allow firms to combine cash and cash equivalents. **Cash equivalents** refers to short-term, highly liquid investments that are *readily convertible* to known amounts of cash and that are subject to *insignificant risks of changes in value*. For example, a savings account, a term deposit with maturity of three months or less, an investment in a money market fund, or investments in three-month government Treasury bills would be cash equivalents because they can all be converted into cash on short notice and their market values change little over time.

cash equivalents   Short-term, highly liquid investments that are readily convertible to known amounts of cash and that are subject to insignificant risks of change in value.

2. Exclusions from cash and cash equivalents

As indicated above, the classification of items as cash and cash equivalents encompasses two criteria. The first is that the line item represents funds that can be readily accessed to settle debts. For this reason, any funds that are subject to restrictions that prevent their use for current purposes, or cash designated ("appropriated") for specific purposes, should be separately reported outside of current assets, with disclosure. For example, some loan agreements have "sinking fund" provisions that require the borrower to set aside money on a specified schedule. Cash that is appropriated for a sinking fund would be listed separately in non-current assets since such funds are not available for other uses.

The second criterion is that the amount must have little risk of changes in value. There are many financial investments that can be readily converted into cash, but they are subject to significant fluctuations in value. For instance, investments in shares traded on a public exchange can be sold easily and funds obtained in a matter of three days, but share prices can change dramatically on a daily basis. Consequently, these investments would not be considered cash equivalents.

The table in Exhibit 5-1 summarizes the treatment of commonly encountered items. Notice that both criteria—convertibility into cash and insignificant risk of change in value—need to be satisfied for the item to be included in cash and cash equivalents.

Exhibit 5-1	Determining whether commonly encountered items are cash and cash equivalents		
Item	Readily convertible into cash?	Risk of change in cash value?	Balance sheet classification
Domestic currency	Yes	None	Cash and cash equivalents
Chequing account	Yes	None	Cash and cash equivalents
Foreign currency	Yes	Mixed	Cash and cash equivalents if exchange rate is stable
Term deposit ≤ 3 months*	Yes	Low	Cash and cash equivalents
Term deposits > 3 months*	No	Low	Short-term investment[†]
Treasury bills ≤ 3 months*	Yes	Low	Cash and cash equivalents
Treasury bills, 3 to 12 months*	Yes	Moderate	Short-term investment[†]
Publicly traded bonds	Yes	Moderate	Short- or long-term investment[†]
Publicly traded shares	Yes	High	Short- or long-term investment[†]

*Refers to length of time after the balance sheet date.

[†]See Chapter 7 for details of classification for investments.

3. Cash held in foreign currencies

As noted in Exhibit 5-1, the treatment of foreign currency depends on the particular circumstances. For most currencies, there is an active market for exchanging one currency for another. There are a few currencies from smaller economies that are thinly traded, but we do not concern ourselves with such currencies for the purposes of this text. Some currencies are subject to capital controls imposed by governments to limit the volume of exchange transactions occurring in a short period of time (e.g., the Chinese yuan). However, these limits are usually high enough that they only affect very large transactions that are beyond the range of the typical enterprise. (This type of exchange control does affect financial institutions, which could have large flows of funds between currencies.) For the purposes of this text, we make the generalization that foreign currencies are readily convertible into Canadian currency, even though there could be a few exceptions.

While foreign currencies will usually satisfy the criterion of being readily convertible, it is less clear whether foreign currencies satisfy the second criterion of having a low risk of value changes. Consider the exchange rate between the Canadian and US dollars. Back in 2003, the average USD:CAD exchange rate was 0.72 (that is, it required US$0.72 to purchase one Canadian dollar, on average), and the rate fluctuated between 0.63 and 0.77, a range of 14 cents, or 19% relative to the average of 0.72. In comparison, in 2014, the exchange rate averaged 0.91, but fluctuated between 0.89 and 0.94, a range of 5 cents, or 5.5% of the average. Thus, in the more recent year, the amount of variability in the exchange rate was less than a third of that seen in 2003. Whether the exchange rate conditions in either or both of these years were stable enough to satisfy the criterion of having a sufficiently low risk of value changes is a matter of professional judgment.[2]

Some currencies have established a "peg" to another currency. For example, the Hong Kong dollar has been pegged, or fixed, to the US dollar at an exchange rate between HK$7.75 and HK$7.85 for each US dollar. Assuming that the government has sufficient resources to hold the peg, then Hong Kong dollars would be considered to have a low risk of value change relative to the US dollar. It is also readily convertible into US dollars, so cash in Hong Kong dollars would be equivalent to cash for an entity reporting in US dollars.

[2.] Exchange rate data obtained from Pacific Exchange Rate Service at http://fx.sauder.ubc.ca.

4. Negative balances

Cash management involves having a sufficient amount of cash to satisfy obligations as they become due, but not having too much cash sitting idle. To assist in maintaining a low level of idle cash, companies often have arrangements with banks that allow account balances to be negative (i.e., the account being in overdraft). Such balances should be reported as part of cash and cash equivalents (as a deduction) rather than listed as a liability. For example, a company with an overdraft of $3,000 in its chequing account, $20,000 in its savings account, and $50,000 in a term deposit maturing in 60 days would report cash and cash equivalents at $67,000. On the other hand, if the net balance of cash and cash equivalents is, say, −$35,000, then the enterprise should show a current liability for "bank overdraft" of $35,000.

5. Implications for the cash flow statement

The definition of cash and cash equivalents directly impacts the cash flow statement. Indeed, the definition of cash and cash equivalents in IFRS appears in IAS 7, Statement of Cash Flows. The definition is important because only exchanges of cash and cash equivalents for items that are not cash or cash equivalents result in cash flows. In other words, changing the composition of cash and cash equivalents (such as moving cash from a chequing account into a short-term deposit) does not constitute a cash flow; it is just a shift within cash and cash equivalents.

 CHECKPOINT **CP5-1**

Why do accounting standards allow cash equivalents to be classified together with cash?

B. BANK RECONCILIATIONS[3]

A bank reconciliation ties together the amount of cash according to a company's records and the amount of cash according to the bank that holds its funds. The reasons for preparing a bank reconciliation are threefold: (i) to understand why the two sets of records differ; (ii) to identify any bookkeeping errors by either entity; and (iii) to contribute to the internal control over cash. The issue of internal controls will be explored in more detail in the next section.

The reconciliation has two steps:

1. Begin with the bank balance and adjust for reconciling items to derive the corrected cash balance. These items are transactions that the bank has not yet recorded. These items do not require adjusting journal entries on the books of the reporting enterprise.
2. Begin with the company's balances and adjust for reconciling items to derive the corrected cash balance. The reconciling items in this step are transactions that affect cash but that have not yet been recorded by the reporting entity. The reconciling items from this step require the enterprise to make adjusting journal entries to bring the preliminary cash balance to the corrected cash balance.

Of course, the corrected cash balance from the two steps needs to agree; otherwise, further work is required to find additional reconciling items.

[3.] For some students, this section will be a review of material covered in introductory financial accounting.

To illustrate a bank reconciliation, consider the following facts relating to Cash Cow Corporation for its month ended May 31, 2020:

- The bank statement for the chequing account as at the close of business on May 31 shows a balance of $5,890, whereas Cash Cow's general ledger shows a balance of $66,010.

- The bank statement shows charges of $120 for administrative fees and overdraft interest for the month of May. Cash Cow became aware of this amount on June 10, when the company received the bank statement, so the amount was not reflected in the company's May 31 balance in the cash account.

- The company made deposits on May 30 and 31 (Saturday and Sunday) for $45,300 and $39,600, respectively. The bank did not record these deposits until its next business day, Monday, June 1.

- The following cheques issued by Cash Cow are still outstanding (not yet cashed by the recipient):

    #3345 for $7,500   #3351 for $4,200   #3352 for $12,400

- After review of the bank statement, Cash Cow noted that the bank made a transposition error: cheque #3347 written in the amount of $8,790 was processed for $7,890 instead.

- Cash Cow made an arithmetic error on the deposit slip used for its after-hours cash deposit of May 21: the amount was recorded on the books as $34,500 when it should have been $34,400. Cash receipts are for cash sales.

The above facts would result in the following bank reconciliation:

Exhibit 5-2	Bank reconciliation schedule for Cash Cow Corporation		
Cash Cow Corporation **Bank Reconciliation** **May 31, 2020**			
Step 1:			
Balance per bank statement			$ 5,890
+ Deposits in transit	May 30	$45,300	
	May 31	39,600	
			84,900
− Outstanding cheques	#3345	7,500	
	#3351	4,200	
	#3352	12,400	
			(24,100)
+/− Bank errors (cheque #3347 for $8,790 processed as $7,890)			(900)
Corrected cash balance			**$65,790**
Step 2:			
Balance per company's books			$ 66,010
+/− Book errors (over-recorded May 21 cash deposit)			(100)
− Bank charges not yet recorded on books			(120)
Corrected cash balance			**$65,790**

The overall idea in bank reconciliation is to identify all the items affecting cash that *should have been recorded but were not*. Deposits in transit should have increased the cash balance but were not included by the bank due to the deposits being made during the weekend when the bank was closed. Cheques already written but not yet cashed by the recipient have not yet been reflected in the bank balance, but they should be deducted from the cash balance. The bank should have reduced the account by $900 more for cheque #3347, so we make a downward adjustment relative to the bank's records.

On the company's side, Cash Cow over-recorded its May 21 cash deposit by $100, so the correct amount should be $100 less. Bank charges of $120 for the month had not yet been recorded on the books, but the amount also reduces cash. Following the completion of this bank reconciliation, Cash Cow would record the following journal entries to adjust its books for the reconciling items in Step 2:

Exhibit 5-3	Cash Cow's adjusting entries to correct for items noted in the bank reconciliation	
To correct over-recorded cash deposit and sales revenue		
Dr. Sales revenue	100	
Cr. Cash		100
To record unrecorded bank charges		
Dr. Administrative expense (bank charges)	120	
Cr. Cash		120

In general, accounting reconciliation is the process of making two related amounts compatible with each other. It is important to note that it is more than a recomputation of figures. A recomputation uses information from just one source, whereas a reconciliation uses information from two separate sources. The ability to prepare reconciliations is a core skill of accountants that will be required in later chapters, such as for pension accounting (Chapter 17) and the cash flow statement (Appendix A).

C. CASH MANAGEMENT, INTERNAL CONTROLS, AND FRAUD PREVENTION

L.O. 5-2. Explain the need for internal controls for cash specifically and other assets more generally, and evaluate the adequacy of cash controls in different situations.

The significant risks associated with cash are self-evident. This section discusses typical procedures used to help reduce those risks. As noted in the previous section, preparing bank reconciliations is an important internal control procedure; however, by itself, reconciling cash is not enough, as it is designed for detection after the fact. Preventive measures are equally if not more important.

1. Segregation of duties

Perhaps the most important control to reduce the risk of cash misappropriation is segregation of duties. Think about the following list of activities surrounding cash:

- Employees make sales to customers and record credit sales in accounts receivable.
- Customers pay using cash, cheques, or credit cards.
- Employees record payments against customers' accounts.
- Employees combine cash, cheques, and credit card receipts from different desks/counters and make deposits (or send them to the bank by security truck).
- The company makes purchases on credit.
- The company issues cheques for accounts payable.
- The bank issues a bank statement to the company.

Imagine what could happen if the same employee had responsibility for (i) recording sales, (ii) receiving payment from customers, and (iii) recording the receipt of payment from customers. If the sale is on credit, the employee could potentially modify the accounts receivable records to delete the initial sale and then take the funds personally. To reduce this risk, the company should do the following:

- Restrict the ability of sales staff to modify or delete accounts receivable. Credits or refunds (for defective items, for example) need to be recorded on a credit note.
- Assign employees with no access to receivable records the task of recording cash and cheques received.
- Assign different employees the task of depositing funds to the bank.
- Have accounts receivable staff (separate from the above) record payments against the specific accounts.

When a company segregates the duties in such a way, it prevents any single employee from mishandling cash or changing the accounts receivable record for personal gain. When duties are segregated, fraud requires collusion among two or more employees, which is much more difficult to execute.

On the payables side, it is important to limit who has access to the accounts payable master file that contains information on suppliers' names, addresses, and so on. Staff responsible for day-to-day processing of suppliers' invoices should not have this access; otherwise, they could obtain approval to pay a particular supplier, then redirect the cheque to a different payee and address, such as themselves or their relatives.

Finally, as mentioned in the previous section, a bank reconciliation should be done periodically, usually at the end of each month. The company should assign this responsibility to an employee who is not responsible for any of the other duties mentioned above.

In smaller enterprises, the opportunities available to segregate duties may be limited because of the small number of staff. Nevertheless, the enterprise should still try as much as possible. In the smallest enterprises, direct supervision by the owners can often substitute for other internal controls. We discuss the role of supervision next.

 CHECKPOINT **CP5-2**

Why is it important to segregate duties among different employees?

2. Monitoring by staff and customers

In some situations, it is not practically possible to segregate some duties. For example, in retail operations it is often too time consuming or costly to have one employee ring up a sale and a different employee receive the cash from the customer. When the transaction involves cash payment (not cheque or credit card), an unrecorded sale allows the employee to pocket the proceeds of the sale. Fraud prevention in such situations relies partially on monitoring by other staff and by customers. In fact, some retailers have policies along the lines of "your purchase is free if you don't get a receipt" to gain the cooperation of customers in ensuring that employees record all purchases through the cash register.

3. Implications for internal controls of other areas

The importance of internal controls and fraud prevention are of course not limited to cash. While common wisdom suggests that, among assets, cash has the greatest risk of being misappropriated, recent research suggests the opposite (see box inset). Thus, the discussion of internal controls for cash in this chapter serves as a sample of internal control considerations more generally. More detailed coverage of this topic is available in textbooks and courses on auditing.

ETHICS AND HONESTY IN RELATION TO CASH AND NON-CASH ITEMS

"Suppose your spouse calls you at work. Your daughter needs a red pencil for school next day. 'Could you bring one home?' How comfortable would you be taking a red pencil from work for your daughter? . . . Let me ask you another question. Suppose there are no red pencils at work, but you can buy one downstairs for a dime. And the petty cash box in your office has been left open, and no one is around. Would you take 10 cents from the petty cash box to buy the red pencil? Suppose you didn't have any change and needed the 10 cents. Would you feel comfortable taking it? Would that be OK?"

This situation is from Chapter 12 of *Predictably Irrational,* a book by behavioural economist Dan Ariely. If you are like most people, you would have likely found it to be relatively easy to take the pencil from the office, but not so for the 10 cents of petty cash. But what is the difference between the two? It is 10 cents of value either way! The implication is that people are more honest when dealing with cash compared with non-cash items.

Now, this thought experiment, as convincing as it may be, is not hard evidence. In his book, Ariely describes a real experiment that backs up the intuition of the mental exercise.* Ariely and his fellow researchers used three groups of 150 students each. Each student received 20 simple math problems to solve over five minutes, with the understanding that he/she would earn a reward of 50 cents per correct answer.

The first (control) group of students submitted their answers to a researcher who determined the students' scores and paid their reward. The second group self-marked the quiz, reported their scores to the researcher, and collected their reward. The third group also self-marked the quiz and reported their results to a researcher. However, instead of cash, the researcher paid these students a token for each correct answer, and the students then converted the tokens into cash (50 cents per token) at a table four metres away. The results are as follows (all differences in results among the groups are statistically significant):

	Group 1	Group 2	Group 3
Mean number of questions correct (max = 20)	3.5	6.2	9.4
Number of students scoring 20/20	0	0	24

Taken at face value, it would appear that students in Group 3 are systematically smarter than those in Group 2, who in turn are smarter than those in Group 1. However, recognizing the different conditions faced by the three groups, three important inferences arise from this experiment:

1.   Intuition suggests, if given the opportunity to cheat without a chance of being caught, people will lie to obtain personal benefit (compare Group 2 with Group 1).
2.   Even when their lies are never revealed, people tend to lie only a little— Group 2 on average inflated their scores by 2.7 answers compared with

(Continued)

*This was the third of six experiments. Republished with permission of American Marketing Association, from The Dishonesty of Honest People: A Theory of Self-Concept Maintenance, *Journal of Marketing Research* Vol. 45, Issue 6, 633–644, Nina Mazar, On Amir, Dan Ariely (2008) permission conveyed through Copyright Clearance Center, Inc.

Group 1, whereas they could have all reported 20 correct answers. Indeed, no one took the maximum opportunity to lie; none in Group 2 reported a score of 20/20.

3. Interestingly, directly involving cash makes people less willing to lie; said another way, dealing with non-cash items makes people more willing to lie. Students in Group 3 who were rewarded tokens exaggerated their performance by 5.9 questions on average compared to the control group, and 16% (24/150) of them saw no problem in reporting the maximum number of correct answers to claim the largest reward possible.

In terms of internal controls, the results of this study suggest that firms need to pay as much or more attention to the protection of non-cash assets than they devote to cash management.

D. OVERVIEW OF ACCOUNTING FOR NON-CASH ASSETS

As mentioned in the introduction, all of the non-cash assets are due to accrual accounting, which allows the recording of events and transactions separately from cash flows. For example, the expenditure of cash to buy inventories does not result in an immediate expense. Rather, the firm would record an asset for the inventories and recognize the expense at a later time when it sells the inventory. Thus, timing is everything in accrual accounting, as emphasized in Chapter 3.

The questions common to all non-cash assets are threefold:

1. Does a transaction give rise to an asset or an expense?
2. For a particular asset or class of assets, what is the appropriate value to be reported at the balance sheet date?
3. When should we remove an asset from the balance sheet?

We can ask similar questions in relation to liabilities and equities; Volume 2 of this text will address those issues.

1. Initial recognition and measurement: Asset or expense?

The first issue arises when an enterprise makes an **expenditure** in the form of a cash outflow, an incurrence of an account payable that results in a cash outflow in the future, or a similar credit entry. In accrual accounting, we permit the debit to be recorded as an asset, or **capitalized**, if it meets certain criteria; otherwise, we record it as an **expense**. As discussed in the Conceptual Framework in Chapter 2, capitalization of an asset requires that an expenditure satisfy the definition of an asset and meet the criteria for recognition and measurement. The definition of an asset requires it to have three characteristics. In brief, these are to:

■ have future economic benefits;
■ be under the entity's control; and
■ result from past transactions.

To recognize it on the balance sheet, the asset's future economic benefits must be reasonably measurable. If an expenditure does not satisfy the definition of an asset or the criteria for recognition, then by default we record the expenditure as an expense.

L.O. 5-3. Apply the standards and procedures for the initial recognition, subsequent measurement at the balance sheet date, and derecognition of trade receivables.

THRESHOLD CONCEPT
TIMING OF RECOGNITION

expenditure An outflow of cash or other resources; distinguish from **expense**.

capitalize Recording an **expenditure** as an asset on the balance sheet.

expense An amount reported on the income statement that reduces the amount of profit (or increases a loss) for the period.

2. Asset valuation on the balance sheet

Once an asset has been recorded, enterprises need to consider whether the asset is appropriately valued at each balance sheet date (e.g., quarter or year-end). To avoid presenting an asset with an overvalued amount, in general enterprises need to evaluate whether they need to adjust asset values downward to better reflect current values. In some cases, upward adjustments are also possible (see Chapter 10). Such valuation adjustments increase representational faithfulness.

3. Derecognition: Removal of an asset from the balance sheet

Once an asset has been recorded, we need to consider whether and when it needs to be removed from the balance sheet. For example, we remove inventory from the balance sheet when the inventory is sold, and we depreciate equipment costs over time.

The remainder of this chapter covers the specific asset of receivables. In particular, the three issues identified above will be discussed in more detail.

 CHECKPOINT **CP5-3**

What are the three accounting issues common to the different classes of assets?

E. TRADE RECEIVABLES: INITIAL CLASSIFICATION, RECOGNITION, AND MEASUREMENT

The most common receivables are those arising from ordinary sales transactions. We call these *trade receivables* or *accounts receivable.* The typical entry is to debit accounts receivable and credit sales revenue. So how does this match up with the general statements about assets in Section D? There is apparently no "expenditure" to speak of when the receivable is recorded.

The crucial point is to realize that a receivable can be viewed as cash flow that is temporarily forgone. For example, suppose ABC Company were to make a $100 credit sale. If the sale had not been on credit, the company *would have* received $100 in cash (or an amount very close to it). In essence, the company has advanced funds to its customer to make the purchase; this advance or loan is an expenditure. This expenditure meets the definition and recognition criteria for an asset because the company expects this expenditure to generate future benefits in the form of cash collection, the sales transaction has occurred, the company has control of the receivable, and the amount to be collected is reasonably measurable.

We can visualize the journal entry for the $100 credit sale as follows:

Exhibit 5-4	Standard and expanded representation of a journal entry for a sale made on credit		
Standard entry:			
Dr. Accounts receivable		100	
Cr. Sales revenue			100
Expanded entry to show advance to customer followed by cash sale:			
Dr. Accounts receivable		100	
Cr. Cash			100
Dr. Cash		100	
Cr. Sales revenue			100

Note that we show the expanded entry here merely to demonstrate the concept of an expenditure associated with an account receivable. The two offsetting cash entries are never recorded, no cash flows occur at this point, and there is no impact on the cash flow statement.

Conceptually, receivables are monetary assets because they are claims on specific future cash flows. Generally, monetary assets should be valued at their discounted present value. However, trade receivables are usually due in 90 days or less, and rarely extend over more than a year. In addition, the volume of transactions for trade receivables is usually high because they arise from the company's core operations. Consequently, the benefits to calculating the present value of these short-term receivables and any interest revenue are small, while the bookkeeping costs are high. Taking into consideration the cost constraint, we generally ignore the time value of money for trade receivables and record them at face value.

THRESHOLD CONCEPT
CONCEPTUAL FRAMEWORK

Cost–benefit considerations are also important when companies offer **cash discounts** to customers for immediate or timely payment.[4] Many companies record the accounts receivable at face value and later record any cash discounts taken as a reduction in revenue on the income statement. This is called the **gross method** of recording cash discounts. For instance, suppose the payment terms are 2/10 net 30, meaning that the seller will give a 2% discount if the customer makes payment within 10 days; otherwise, the full payment is due within 30 days. The 2% is called a cash discount—even though it is a credit sale with a 10-day grace period—simply because it is administratively impractical for customers to make immediate payment upon purchase/delivery, particularly if they have stringent cash control procedures, as discussed earlier in this chapter. After the 10 days, the customer loses the discount, so the 2% is essentially the interest for the customer to delay payment for 20 days.

cash discount A discount given for immediate or timely payment.

gross method (of accounting for cash discounts) Records the gross/face value of receivables and records any discounts taken as a reduction in revenue.

In this example, the interest amounts to a high rate, since it equals an annual rate of about $2\% \times 365 \text{ days} \div 20 \text{ days} = 36.5\%$.[5] Given this high rate, it would be irrational for most customers not to take advantage of the discount. Thus, by recording the full price as revenue and accounts receivable, the gross method assumes that customers will forfeit the discount. Relying on irrational behaviour on the part of others is not conceptually appealing.

The conceptually better alternative is the **net method**, which is to record the account receivable at the sale price less the cash discount. In this method, the company needs to make an adjustment for the interest earned if the customer fails to take advantage of the discount. This method is conceptually better because it assumes that customers will take the cash discount. It is also conceptually better because it more appropriately separates the portion of cash received that is on account of interest from the part that is due to the sale. That is, the net method is representationally more faithful.

net method (of accounting for cash discounts) Records receivables net of cash discounts and records any discounts forfeited as income.

Exhibit 5-5 illustrates these two methods using a sale of $1,000 made on May 1, 2020, with payment terms of 2/10 net 30.

THRESHOLD CONCEPT
CONCEPTUAL FRAMEWORK

Exhibit 5-5	Illustration of gross and net methods of accounting for cash discounts			
	Gross method (more common)		**Net method (conceptually better)**	
Sale made	Dr. Accounts receivable	1,000	Dr. Accounts receivable	980
May 1, 2020	Cr. Sales revenue	1,000	Cr. Sales revenue	980

(*Continued*)

---

[4] Cash discounts are sometimes called sales discounts. However, the latter terminology can be easily confused with discounted prices when companies have sales promotions.

[5] To be precise, the interest rate would be a little bit higher because it is $2 on every $98 borrowed. Thus, the calculation should be $2\% \times 365 \text{ days} \div 20 \text{ days} \div 0.98 = 37.2\%$.

Exhibit 5-5	Continued				
If payment received by May 10, 2020	Dr. Cash	980		Dr. Cash	980
	Dr. Cash discount	20			
	[income statement]				
	Cr. Accounts receivable		1,000	Cr. Accounts receivable	980
OR					
If payment received after May 10, 2020	Dr. Cash	1,000		Dr. Cash	1,000
				Cr. Interest or other revenue	20
	Cr. Accounts receivable		1,000	Cr. Accounts receivable	980

 CHECKPOINT **CP5-4**

What is the main difference between the gross and net methods of accounting for cash discounts?

F. SUBSEQUENT MEASUREMENT OF TRADE RECEIVABLES: ACCOUNTING FOR BAD DEBTS

While businesses hope that all their customers will pay their debts, the reality is that some will be unable to pay. Because there is almost always a risk of uncollectible accounts, the value of a receivable is less than its face value. Companies must therefore adjust the value of receivables at the balance sheet date to the amounts they expect ultimately to collect (the expected **net realizable value**). This adjustment reflects not only information on accounts *known* to be uncollectible (e.g., customers who have filed for bankruptcy), but also information about the portion of receivables that are *anticipated* to be uncollectible. Adjusting only for accounts known to be uncollectible is called the **direct write-off method**.

The reasons for adjusting accounts receivable for both known and anticipated amounts of uncollectible accounts are threefold; one relates to moral hazard, discussed in Chapter 1, and two are based on the IFRS Conceptual Framework of Chapter 2:

1. *Moral hazard:* Companies provide credit to customers not because they are altruistic, but because doing so facilitates and encourages sales. Dealing in cash is cumbersome, and requiring immediate payment for all purchases could turn away customers who would otherwise have made purchases on credit, particularly if competitors offer sales on credit. Thus, credit policy is an integral element of the sales package that a company offers its customers. Given this connection, it is necessary for management to estimate and record the cost of its credit policy. If it were not required to do so, then management would be motivated to have lax credit policies so as to increase sales, because the consequences in terms of bad debts would not be recorded until a future date.

2. *Timeliness:* Related to the last point, providing credit is part of the revenue-generating process, so the cost of providing credit in terms of bad debt losses should be recorded in the same period as when the company records the revenue.

3. *Neutrality and faithful representation:* The amount of accounts receivable reported on the balance sheet should not overstate (nor understate) the amount that will eventually be collected from customers, so management should use available information to make its best estimate of uncollectible accounts. Doing so ensures that the amount reported for accounts receivable is neutral and contributes to representational faithfulness.

net realizable value The value expected from the sale of an asset, net of any costs of disposal.

direct write-off method (for accounts receivable) A method that records the expense when an account receivable is deemed to be uncollectible.

THRESHOLD CONCEPT
INFORMATION
ASYMMETRY

THRESHOLD CONCEPT
CONCEPTUAL
FRAMEWORK

THRESHOLD CONCEPT
CONCEPTUAL
FRAMEWORK

The journal entry used to record the expense for bad debts and to adjust the value of accounts receivable to expected net realizable value (NRV) is as shown in Exhibit 5-6, using a hypothetical value of $100:

Exhibit 5-6	Journal entry to record bad debts expense and to adjust accounts receivable to NRV	
Dr. Bad debt expense	100	
Cr. Allowance for doubtful accounts		100

Notice that *we do not directly credit accounts receivable*, but instead use an allowance account. The **allowance for doubtful accounts (ADA)** is a **contra account**, which is a balance sheet account that has the opposite sign of the main balance sheet account to which it is connected (accounts receivable, in this case). The face value of accounts receivable, or **gross accounts receivable**, less the amount in the ADA contra account, equals the **net accounts receivable**.

There are three interrelated reasons for using a contra account in relation to accounts receivable:

1. It is necessary to keep track of how much the company is allowing for bad debts. If the credit entry in Exhibit 5-6 goes directly against accounts receivable, there would be no way of knowing how much lower NRV is compared to face value.
2. In practice, companies use a **sub-ledger** to record accounts receivable. The sub-ledger has details of each customer's name and amount owing (among other details). The total amount on the sub-ledger should match up with the amount in the general ledger account for receivables. If the above journal entry directly credited accounts receivable, it would reduce the amount in the general ledger without a corresponding decrease in the sub-ledger, and the two ledgers would no longer reconcile.
3. The allowance for doubtful accounts reflects an aggregate estimate of the amount that is *doubtful* rather than amounts for specific accounts that are uncollectible. At the time of setting up the allowance, it is not possible to write off any specific accounts from the receivables sub-ledger.

Exhibit 5-6 simply shows the form of the journal entry. Next, we need to determine the amount of the entry, which was arbitrarily shown as $100 for illustration purposes. There are two ways to estimate the amount for this journal entry: the percentage of sales method and the aging of accounts method.

1. Percentage of sales method (income statement approach)

This method uses the idea that some fraction of sales will be uncollectible, so to best match expenses with revenues, the *bad debts expense* should be some *percentage of credit sales*. We exclude cash sales since they do not have credit risk. Since this method focuses on the computation of the expense, it is known as the **income statement approach**. In more detail, the procedure is as follows:

1. Taking into consideration historical experience with bad debts, economic conditions, and so on, estimate the percentage factor to apply to the amount of net credit sales. This total determines what bad debts expense (BDE) should be for the period; call this amount x. If no BDE had been recorded previously, x is the amount to be used in the journal entry to record bad debts expense in Exhibit 5-6.
2. If some BDE had been previously recorded for the period, then the amount to be recorded would be the additional amount necessary to bring the total for the period up to the amount computed in (1). For example, if a company

allowance for doubtful accounts (ADA) A contra account relating to accounts receivable; the balance in the allowance for doubtful accounts is management's estimate of the amount that will not be collected from customers. Also called *allowance for bad debts* or *allowance for uncollectible accounts*.

contra account A balance sheet account that has the opposite sign of the main balance sheet account to which it is connected.

gross accounts receivable The face value of accounts receivable before deducting the allowance for doubtful accounts.

net accounts receivable The face value of accounts receivable minus the allowance for doubtful accounts.

sub-ledger A listing with details regarding individual accounts receivable including the name of the party who owes money to the firm, the amount they owe, and the dates on which the payments are due.

income statement approach An approach to accounting and standard setting that emphasizes the values of the income statement over the balance sheet.

determines that the BDE should be $x = \$54,000$ for the year, but had already recorded $40,000 for the first three-quarters of the year for interim reporting purposes, then the year-end adjustment would be the difference of $14,000 $(x - \$40,000 = \$54,000 - \$40,000)$.

3. The other side of the entry (usually a credit) adds to the balance in the allowance for doubtful accounts (ADA). In this method, ADA is the residual amount. In addition, note that ADA should always have a credit balance (or zero). A debit balance would result in the net realizable value of receivables exceeding face value, meaning that the enterprise expects to collect more than what it billed to customers, but of course no customer will pay more than what they need to.

2. Aging of accounts method (balance sheet approach)

The **aging of accounts** method focuses on the value of net accounts receivable on the balance sheet. The idea is that we are more concerned about the appropriate value shown as an asset for receivables, so this is known as the **balance sheet approach**. Thus, we begin by estimating the amount of the allowance account, which determines the net realizable value of receivables.

1. Categorize individual receivables based on how long each invoice has been outstanding (e.g., 0–30 days, 31–60 days, etc.).
2. For each age category, apply a percentage factor to estimate the amount uncollectible. This factor should be based on historical experience, economic conditions, and so on. The factor should also increase with the age of the receivables, since longer outstanding amounts indicate lower ability to pay by customers. Total the estimated ADA for all categories; call this total y.
3. Determine the existing balance in ADA. The amount to be recorded in the journal entry in Exhibit 5-6 equals y − existing balance. For example, if step (2) results in a required balance of $y = \$35,000$ in ADA, and the existing balance in ADA is $22,000, then we would credit ADA for $13,000 $(y - \$22,000 = \$35,000 - \$22,000)$.
4. The other side of the entry affects BDE. In this method, the expense is the residual figure. For example, at the end of the year Safeco analyzed its accounts receivable and produced the information in Exhibit 5-7 based on past experience with customers. Before making the year-end adjusting entry for bad debts, the balance in ADA had a credit balance of $510.

aging (of accounts receivable) A process of categorizing accounts receivable according to the length of time that has passed since the invoice date.

balance sheet approach An approach to accounting and standard setting that emphasizes the values of the balance sheet over the income statement.

Exhibit 5-7	Aging of accounts receivable for Safeco		
Days outstanding	Accounts receivable balance	Estimate of % uncollectible	Estimated amount uncollectible
0–30	$210,100	0.2%	$ 420
31–60	84,500	0.6	507
61–90	26,900	2.0	538
> 90	7,460	10.0	746
Total			$2,211

From this information, the adjusting journal entry that should be recorded is as follows:

Exhibit 5-8	Journal entry to record bad debts expense for Safeco
Dr. Bad debts expense	1,701
Cr. Allowance for doubtful accounts	1,701

The amount of $1,701 is the difference between the required balance in ADA from the aging schedule ($2,211 Cr.) and the pre-existing balance ($510 Cr.). This may be better understood in terms of a T-account for ADA:

Exhibit 5-9	T-account for Safeco's allowance for doubtful accounts
ADA	
510	Balance before adjustment
1,701	Amount to record in adjusting entry
2,211	Required balance from aging analysis

In practice, companies often use a combination of the two methods to estimate BDE and the ADA. The percentage of sales method is relatively easy to apply, so it is often used for interim reporting, such as for quarterly reports. The more detailed analysis of accounts using the aging method is then applied at year-end.

Both methods try to predict the amount of future defaults by customers using information available at the time of financial statement preparation. Even though these predictions are necessarily imperfect, we record them under the accrual accounting system because these represent the best estimates of future cash flows, which are useful to financial statement readers. If new information indicates that estimates need to be revised, such revisions would be reflected prospectively as changes in estimates, as discussed in Chapter 3. For example, if information suggests 3% of credit sales is an appropriate estimate for bad debts expense, but the company had been using 4% in previous years, the 3% rate would be used going forward without adjusting prior periods for the reduction.

THRESHOLD CONCEPT
**DECISION MAKING
UNDER UNCERTAINTY**

 CHECKPOINT **CP5-5**

Why is the percentage of sales method an income statement approach while the aging of accounts method is a balance sheet approach?

G. DERECOGNITION OF RECEIVABLES: COLLECTION, WRITE-OFFS, AND DISPOSALS

Receivables are removed from the accounts in one of three ways: as part of normal collections, through write-offs when they are determined to be uncollectible, and by selling the receivables. We will discuss each in more detail below. For simplicity, the illustrations use a hypothetical amount of $100 of accounts receivable.

1. Collection

For most businesses, the vast majority of receivables will be collected without too much trouble. The simple entry required is as follows:

Exhibit 5-10	Journal entry for cash collection	
Dr. Cash	100	
Cr. Accounts receivable (customer name)		100

In practice, the credit entry specifies the customer account in the receivables sub-ledger.

2. Write-offs

When management determines that a specific customer's account is uncollectible, the entry required is as follows:

Exhibit 5-11	Journal entry to write off an account	
Dr. Allowance for doubtful accounts	100	
Cr. Accounts receivable (customer name)		100

Again, the credit entry will go to the specific customer's sub-ledger account. Notice that this journal entry *does not involve an expense*—both the allowance and the receivable accounts are balance sheet accounts. Remember that the expense has already been recorded previously, when the percentage of sales or the aging method was used to estimate the bad debts expense and net realizable value of accounts receivable.

In some instances, an account that was previously written off as uncollectible becomes collectible again. The journal entry to record a recovery of an account written off involves first re-establishing the account receivable and then recording the cash collection. In most cases, the amount recovered will be less than the original amount outstanding. For example, if the recovery amount is 60% of the original $100 receivable, the journal entry would be as follows:

Exhibit 5-12	Journal entry to record the recovery of an account previously written off	
Dr. Accounts receivable (customer name)	60	
Cr. Allowance for doubtful accounts		60
Dr. Cash	60	
Cr. Accounts receivable (customer name)		60

Normally, an enterprise would record a recovery only when there is compelling evidence that it will be able to collect on the written-off account (e.g., actual cash receipt).

3. Transfer of receivables (factoring)

factor (for receivables)
A finance company that buys accounts receivable from other companies.

To improve cash flow and liquidity, a company may decide not to wait and collect on its receivables. Instead, the company can transfer the receivables to a **factor**, a financing company that specializes in buying receivables and then collecting the cash owed. Of course, the company with the receivables needs to pay for the benefits of earlier cash receipt and reduced processing/collection costs. Further, there is still risk that the receivables will not be collectible, so the factor will compensate for this risk by lowering the price it is willing to pay for the receivables. Thus, the amount of cash received from the factor will be significantly less than the face value of receivables.

The accounting treatment of such transfers depends crucially on whether there is a transfer of risk and rewards of ownership. Specifically, IFRS 9 paragraph 3.2.6 states the following with respect to the transfer of financial assets such as accounts receivable:

¶(a)   if the entity transfers substantially all the risks and rewards of ownership of the financial asset, the entity shall derecognize the financial asset and recognize separately as assets or liabilities any rights and obligations created or retained in the transfer.

¶(b)   if the entity retains substantially all the risks and rewards of ownership of the financial asset, the entity shall continue to recognize the financial asset.

¶(c)   if the entity neither transfers nor retains substantially all the risks and rewards of ownership of the financial asset, the entity shall determine whether it has retained control of the financial asset.[6]

These criteria are consistent with the definition of an asset in the Conceptual Framework from Chapter 2. That is, if the entity continues to expect future benefits from the receivables and is exposed to the risks inherent in owning those receivables, then those receivables continue to be recorded as assets. Otherwise, the entity derecognizes the receivable. Below, we consider in more detail two types of transfers in which the transfer of risks and rewards differs.

THRESHOLD CONCEPT
**CONCEPTUAL
FRAMEWORK**

a. Transfer without recourse

A transfer without recourse means that the factor (i.e., the buyer of the receivables) takes on the risk of uncollectible accounts and does not have recourse to go back to the company that transferred the receivable to seek funding for bad debts. Since the *risks and rewards of ownership have transferred*, we can consider this transaction to be a sale of receivables and remove this asset off the books. Suppose the company transfers $100 million of receivables without recourse for proceeds of $90 million. In this case, the entry would be as follows:

Exhibit 5-13	Journal entry for factoring accounts receivable without recourse ($ millions)	
Dr. Cash	90	
Dr. Interest expense	10	
Cr. Accounts receivable		100

Putting the $10 million in "interest expense" captures the character of this transaction because this is, in substance, a financial transaction in which the company obtains cash flow earlier than it otherwise would have had it held on to the receivables. Sometimes, the $10 million is less descriptively denoted as a "loss on sale of receivable."

b. Transfer with recourse

In this case, the factor can demand money back from the transferor if the customers do not pay. Since the transferor retains the risk of bad debts, the transfer does not constitute a sale. Consequently, the receivables cannot be removed from the balance sheet. Instead, a transfer with recourse would constitute a borrowing transaction: the transferor received cash from the factor in exchange for a loan.

In practice, the factor will demand a payment up front to cover possible non-collectibles (called a "holdback"). For example, if a company transfers $100 million of receivables to a factor in exchange for $98 million less a $3 million holdback, the entry on the transfer of receivables would be as follows:

Exhibit 5-14	Journal entry for factoring accounts receivable with recourse ($ millions)	
Dr. Cash	95	
Dr. Due from factor (for holdback amount)	3	
Cr. Short-term debt—asset-backed financing		98

[6.] Copyright © 2012 IFRS Foundation.

Later, when the factor completes the collection of the receivables and obtains $99 million (for example), meaning that it was not able to collect $1 million of receivables, it would pay the transferor $2 million. At this point, the receivables would be derecognized and the short-term debt would be extinguished. The journal entries would be as follows:

Exhibit 5-15	Journal entries for factoring receivables with recourse after completion of collection ($ millions)	
To recognize additional payments from the factor for the difference between the holdback amount and actual bad debts		
Dr. Cash	2	
Dr. Allowance for doubtful accounts (amount of actual bad debts)	1	
Cr. Due from factor		3
Dr. Short-term debt—asset-backed financing	98	
Dr. Interest expense	2	
Cr. Accounts receivable		100

In the above example, the difference in the amount of cash—$90 million when transferred without recourse versus $97 million ($95m + $2m) with recourse—is quite deliberate. The reason is that the amount of cash that the seller would expect to realize when factoring receivables with recourse should be higher than when it is done without recourse. When the transferor is willing to bear the risk of bad debts, it is a credible signal that the credit quality of the receivables is high. In contrast, when the seller offloads the risk of bad debts with a sale without recourse, the factor has to be wary that it is buying a set of accounts that has poor credit quality. In other words, there is adverse selection in a transfer of receivables, and it is potentially worthwhile for the seller to reduce the adverse selection problem by sending a credible signal through factoring with recourse. However, factoring with recourse is less favourable for financial reporting because the transaction creates a liability (short-term debt) in exchange for cash, which worsens measures of liquidity such as the current ratio or quick ratio. In comparison, factoring without recourse results in the derecognition of the accounts receivable in exchange for cash, so there is little effect on ratios. Thus, there is a trade-off between the amount of cash from the transaction and the financial reporting outcome at the date of transfer.

THRESHOLD CONCEPT
**INFORMATION
ASYMMETRY**

Exhibit 5-16	Summary of consequences for factoring transactions with and without recourse	
	Factor without recourse	**Factor with recourse**
Expected cash flow	Lower	Higher
Financial reporting	Treat as a sale of receivables	Treat as a borrowing transaction
Outcome	(↑cash, ↓receivables)	(↑cash, ↑liabilities)

There are other arrangements whereby the original company (not the factor) continues to collect on the accounts, but obtains funds from a financing company by pledging the accounts (using them as collateral). Since control of the receivables has not passed to the buyer, the receivables remain on the books of the original company. In other words, these are borrowing–lending transactions rather than sales of receivables.

Exhibit 5-17 provides an example from Fiat Chrysler, the Italian-American carmaker, of a transfer of receivables with recourse.

Exhibit 5-17	Example of factoring accounts receivable with recourse (Fiat Chrysler)

The Group transfers certain of its financial, trade and tax receivables, mainly through factoring transactions. Factoring transactions may be either with recourse or without recourse. Certain transfers include deferred payment clauses (for example, when the payment by the factor of a minor part of the purchase price is dependent on the total amount collected from the receivables), requiring first loss cover, whereby the transferor has priority participation in the losses, or requires a significant exposure to the variability of cash flows arising from the transferred receivables to be retained. These types of transactions do not meet the requirements of IAS 39*—*Financial Instruments: Recognition and Measurement*, for the derecognition of the assets since the risks and rewards connected with ownership of the financial asset are not transferred, and accordingly the Group continues to recognize these receivables within the Consolidated Statement of Financial Position and recognizes a financial liability of the same amount under Asset-backed financing. The gains and losses arising from the transfer of these receivables are recorded only when they are derecognized.

*Note: IAS 39 is the predecessor standard to IFRS 9.

Source: From *Fiat Chrysler Automobiles Annual Report* 2016. Copyright © 2016 by Fiat Chrysler Automobiles.

As noted in this disclosure, Fiat treats factoring transactions that have recourse ("first loss cover") as not meeting the requirements for the transfer of risks and rewards, and therefore as borrowing transactions.

4. Transfer of receivables (securitization)

Securitization simply means the process of transforming a financial asset (such as accounts receivable) into a security. For example, banks securitize packages of mortgage receivables from many different borrowers and then sell the resulting securities to investors. Similarly, large retailers with their own credit cards (e.g., Canadian Tire) often securitize their credit card receivables. Similar to factoring, the objective is to obtain cash from the receivables earlier than what would be obtained from collecting on the receivables.

> **securitization** The process of transforming a financial asset into a security.

Firms that securitize receivables often do so through special purpose entities (SPEs). While the technical definition is quite complex, for our purposes it suffices to say that a **special purpose entity** is one that, as the name suggests, is created for limited purposes; these purposes are specified in the legal documents that established the entity. To securitize receivables, a company creates an SPE so that the company can transfer the receivables to the SPE. The SPE then sells securities to investors, with the commitment to pay investors the cash flows collected from the receivables. Exhibit 5-18 summarizes the securitization transaction using an SPE. For example, Canadian Tire securitizes its credit card receivables through its SPE, Glacier Credit Card Trust.

> **special purpose entity (SPE)** An entity that is created for limited purposes; such purposes are specified in the legal documents that create the entity.

Just as for factoring transactions, the accounting treatment of receivables that are securitized depends on whether there is a transfer of risk and rewards. However, what

Exhibit 5-18	Summary of securitization transaction using a special purpose entity (SPE)

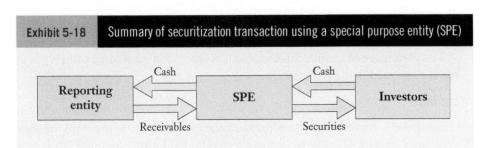

is different from factoring is the relationship between the reporting entity and the SPE—the reporting entity is usually the one that established the SPE in the first place. In some instances, the reporting entity will need to consolidate the SPE. The topic of consolidation is covered in advanced accounting, so we do not discuss this issue further.

 CHECKPOINT **CP5-6**

What is the general principle for deciding whether an enterprise should derecognize receivables when it transfers them to another entity?

H. COMPREHENSIVE ILLUSTRATION OF INITIAL RECOGNITION, SUBSEQUENT MEASUREMENT, AND DERECOGNITION OF ACCOUNTS RECEIVABLE

Exhibit 5-19 contains information pertaining to Tough Sell Corporation for the fiscal year ending December 31, 2019.

Exhibit 5-19	Information for Tough Sell Corporation

On January 1, 2019, the balance of accounts receivable was $1,550,000, and the balance of allowance for doubtful accounts (ADA) was $32,530.

a. For the first to fourth quarters of the year, the company sold goods on credit totalling $2,460,000, $2,320,000, $2,380,000, and $2,530,000, respectively.

b. For interim reporting, the company used the percentage of sales method to estimate bad debts, using a rate of 0.5%. This rate has been used for the last five years.

c. During the third quarter, Tough Sell introduced cash discounts to encourage prompt payment from customers. As a result, the company gave cash discounts totalling $27,000 and $39,000 in the third and fourth quarters, respectively. Tough Sell decided to use the gross method of recording cash discounts. During the year, the company collected $9,908,800 of receivables.

d. Tough Sell wrote off $37,200 of specific accounts that the company determined to be uncollectible.

e. On November 1, 2019, the company sold all of its accounts receivable on hand, totalling $500,000, without recourse, for proceeds of $450,000.

f. For the year-end, the company uses the aging method to determine the amount ADA, and the accounts receivable staff prepared the following aging schedule:

Days outstanding	Accounts receivable balance	Estimate of % uncollectible	Estimated amount uncollectible
0–30	$659,000	1%	$6,590
31–60	135,000	2	2,700
61–90	0	5	0
> 90	0	10	0
Total	$794,000		$9,290

The percentage of uncollectible accounts receivable in each aging category is the same as those used in the prior five years.

Required:

1. Using the T-accounts below, prepare summary journal entries to record the above transactions as well as the bad debts expense for the fourth quarter of 2019.

2. Evaluate the reasonability of the bad debts expense for the year and the balance in the ADA in light of the company's circumstances.

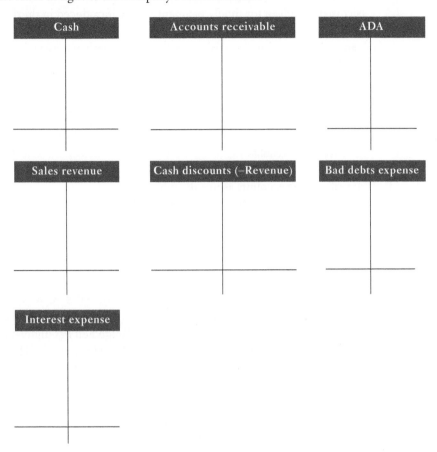

Suggested solution:

1. T-account journal entries:

Cash		Accounts receivable		ADA	
		1,550,000	Jan. 1, 2019	Jan. 1, 2019	32,530
		(a) 2,460,000			12,300 (b)
		(a) 2,320,000			11,600 (b)
		(a) 2,380,000			11,900 (b)
		(a) 2,530,000			
(c) 9,842,800			9,908,800 (c)		
			37,200 (d)	(d) 37,200	
(e) 450,000			500,000 (e)	(f) 21,840	
		794,000			9,290

Sales revenue		Cash discounts (–Revenue)		Bad debts expense	
	2,460,000 (a)			(b) 12,300	
	2,320,000 (a)			(b) 11,600	
	2,380,000 (a)	27,000 (c)		(b) 11,900	
	2,530,000 (a)	39,000 (c)			21,840 (f)
	9,690,000	66,000		13,960	

Interest expense	
(e) 50,000	

(a) Credit sales in the four quarters.

(b) BDE for the first three quarters at 0.5% of credit sales.

(c) Cash discounts given for timely payment. Policy introduced in third quarter of 2019. Due to the cash discounts, the amount of cash collected differs from the amount of accounts receivable credited. The summary journal entry for collections would be:

Dr. Cash	9,842,800	
Dr. Cash discounts (deduction from revenue)	27,000	
Dr. Cash discounts	39,000	
Cr. Accounts receivable		9,908,800

(d) Write off specific accounts as uncollectible.

(e) Factor without recourse $500,000 of receivable for proceeds of $450,000.

(f) The aging schedule indicates that the ADA account should have a credit balance of $9,290. The balance before the adjusting entry is $31,130 Cr. Therefore, the ADA account requires a debit adjustment of $31,130 − $9,290 = $21,840.

2. The BDE for the year, at $13,960, is only 0.14% of credit sales. As well, the year-end ADA balance of $9,290 is only a third of its balance at the beginning of the year of $32,530. On the surface, these facts suggest that Tough Sell has under-recorded BDE and overstated the net realizable value of accounts receivable. However, it is important to note that the company did two things that have a significant bearing on collections and bad debts. First, the company started a policy of cash discounts to encourage early payment. Second, the company sold a large portion of its receivables without recourse. As a result, the receivables balance has declined by about half, from $1,550,000 at the beginning of the year to $794,000 at the end of the year. In addition, all of these accounts are relatively current; they have been outstanding for 60 days or less because all the accounts as at November 1, 2019, had been sold. Given these additional considerations, and the fact that the company has not reduced its percentages for uncollectibles used in the aging schedule, the lower expense and ADA balance appear reasonable.

I. NON-TRADE RECEIVABLES

L.O. 5-4. Apply the standards to account for non-trade receivables.

promissory note   A written promise by one party to repay another party a specified amount at a specified date; sometimes colloquially called an "IOU."

THRESHOLD CONCEPT
CONCEPTUAL FRAMEWORK

Whereas trade receivables do not necessarily involve written contracts (the trade receivable contract may be verbal or constructive), non-trade receivables generally will have written contracts. For example, one company might supply funds to another company using a **promissory note** (a written contract that specifies the amount and date on which one party repays another). While trade receivables are frequent and generally outstanding for short periods of time, non-trade receivables are infrequent and can be outstanding for longer periods. The lower bookkeeping cost and the more significant time value of money suggest that non-trade receivables should be recorded using present value techniques.

For example, suppose Colwood Company provides services to Duncan Ltd. in exchange for a promissory note on January 1, 2017. The note requires Duncan to pay Colwood $100,000 in two years, on January 1, 2019. The market interest rate at the beginning of 2017 is 10%. Assuming that Colwood Company has a calendar year-end, it would record the note receivable as shown in Exhibit 5-20.

The example illustrates a basic application of the amortized cost method of accounting for receivables. With different combinations of cash flows and interest rates, the accounting can be substantially more complex. We leave the more detailed exploration of the amortized cost method for Chapter 7, which looks at financial assets including loans and receivables.

| Exhibit 5-20 | Accounting for Colwood Company's note receivable from Duncan Ltd. |

Initial recognition on January 1, 2017

Record the note receivable at the present value of $100,000 discounted for two years, which is $100,000 \div 1.10^2 = \$82,645$.

| Dr. Note receivable | 82,645 | |
| Cr. Service revenue | | 82,645 |

Subsequent measurement and income recognition on December 31, 2017

Record interest income and a corresponding increase in the value of the note receivable. The amount of interest equals the opening note receivable value multiplied by the interest rate, which amounts to $82,645 \times 10\% = \$8,264$.

| Dr. Note receivable | 8,264 | |
| Cr. Interest income | | 8,264 |

This entry brings the balance of the note receivable to $90,909.

Subsequent measurement and income recognition on December 31, 2018

Similar to the previous year, record interest and increase in the value of the note receivable. The amount of interest equals $90,909 \times 10\% = \$9,091$.

| Dr. Note receivable | 9,091 | |
| Cr. Interest income | | 9,091 |

This journal entry brings the balance of the note receivable to $100,000.

Derecognition on January 1, 2019

Assuming that Duncan pays the amount as promised, Colwood would record the following entry:

| Dr. Cash | 100,000 | |
| Cr. Note receivable | | 100,000 |

J. ACCOUNTING FOR RESTRUCTURED LOANS (FROM THE LENDER'S PERSPECTIVE)

The treatment of loans and notes receivable follows a general rule that we have discussed above: such non-trade receivables are recorded at present value. If there is evidence that the debtor will be unable to pay the originally agreed sums (e.g., an agreement for a restructured loan), then the loan/note needs to be marked down to reflect the present value of the new payment stream.

For example, a loan repayment of $100,000 was originally due to be received on June 30, 2018. As a result of financial difficulties faced by the borrower, the payment could not be made as scheduled, and the borrower and lender agreed to extend the due date of the loan by one year, to June 30, 2019. The amount to be repaid remained at $100,000. If the market interest rate for this type of loan is 5%, the loan restructuring would result in the following entry for the lender on June 30, 2018:

| Exhibit 5-21 | Journal entry for a restructured loan receivable |

Dr. Restructured loan receivable ($100,000 \div 1.05$)	95,238	
Dr. Loss on note restructuring	4,762	
Cr. Loan receivable		100,000

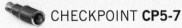 CHECKPOINT **CP5-7**

Why do enterprises record non-trade receivables differently from trade accounts receivables?

K. POTENTIAL EARNINGS MANAGEMENT USING RECEIVABLES

Investors, analysts, auditors, and other readers of financial statements need to be alert to the various ways in which a company can use accounts receivable to manage earnings, and how receivables can provide clues that earnings management is taking place. Because receivables relate to revenues, the largest single item on the income statement, the potential impact of manipulation is considerable.

1. Revenue recognition policy

A company seeking to temporarily boost earnings can do so by accelerating its revenue recognition policy (i.e., recognizing revenue at an earlier point in time relative to cash collection). Such actions will increase both sales revenue and accounts receivable, but the percentage change in receivables will tend to be higher because the increase in revenue will be in receivables—the amount of cash collected remains the same.

For example, if a consistent revenue recognition policy were followed, Company ABC would record $100 million in revenues, of which $15 million remains outstanding at the end of the year, representing 54.75 days of receivables ($15m ÷ $100m × 365 days). If the company accelerates revenue recognition so that it records $110 million in sales, then receivables would increase to $25 million and days of receivables will rise to 82.95 days ($25m ÷ $110m × 365 days). The days of receivables increase by 51.5% compared with the 10% increase in sales.

Readers therefore should be alert to increases in days of receivables that are out of proportion to any increases in sales, as such discrepancies could indicate an acceleration in revenue recognition policy that is possibly undisclosed. The discrepancy could also indicate a decline in credit quality of the customer base, or an active change in credit policy, which is discussed next.

2. Change in credit policy without change in allowance

A legitimate way to increase sales is to relax the company's credit policy. The company may sell to less creditworthy clients, or allow longer payment terms. However, if the company does not correspondingly increase its allowance for doubtful accounts and bad debts expense, then it will be able to increase current earnings. Future earnings will be lower when it is found that the allowance for bad debts was not sufficient for the lax credit policy.

3. Channel stuffing

Another way to temporarily increase revenues is through "channel stuffing." This practice involves filling the distribution channel by selling on favourable terms not usually offered by the company. For example, a manufacturer could offer its distributor an unlimited right of return so that the distributor would take more of the manufacturer's products than normal.

4. Change in the calculation of net realizable value

Calculation of the balance in the allowance for doubtful accounts and the net realizable value of receivables involves considerable judgment. This is the case whether we use the percentage of sales or aging of accounts methods. There may be good reasons to revise estimated percentages, perhaps based on experience, but management may have other motives to change the estimates. While auditors have access to these detailed calculations, investors typically cannot determine whether there has been any change in the estimates that go into the calculation of the net realizable value.

5. Sale of receivables

When receivables are sold without recourse, they are removed from the books entirely and no additional disclosure is required. This practice is particularly worrisome if a company does so to cover up the growth in receivables that would result from some of the other earnings management practices discussed above.

> ## CHANNEL STUFFING AT CHRYSLER
>
> In the midst of operational and financial difficulties, Chrysler LLC was reported to have been stuffing the distribution channels for the cars it manufactures, according to a January 2009 article in *The Wall Street Journal*. The article noted that automakers such as Chrysler recognize revenue when they ship vehicles from their plants to their dealers. In 2008, Chrysler vehicles sat on dealers' lots for about 140 days, compared with 82 days in 2007. The industry average was about 90 days in 2008. According to one dealer in Pennsylvania, Chrysler had been requesting dealers to order more stock despite full lots at the dealership, giving dealers financial incentives such as bonuses for ordering more. The pressure that Chrysler put on dealers was met with resistance by many who refused to take any more inventory.

L. PRACTICAL ILLUSTRATION: CANADIAN TIRE CORPORATION, LIMITED

Refer once again to the 2016 financial statements for Canadian Tire Corporation in Appendix D. The balance sheet shows $614.2 million for "Trade and other receivables" and $5,138.4 million for "Loans receivable." The former and smaller amount refers to receivables from dealers and franchisees, whereas the latter and larger amount refers to credit card balances and loans to dealers (see Note 9). Focusing on the larger category, Note 3—Significant accounting policies, management identifies the approach used to measure these loans.

Loans receivable

Loans receivable consist of credit card and line of credit loans, as well as loans to Associate Dealers ("Dealers"), who are independent third-party operators of Canadian Tire Retail Stores. Loans receivable are recognized when cash is advanced to the borrower. They are derecognized when the borrower repays its obligations, the loans are sold or written off or substantially all of the risks and rewards of ownership are transferred.

Losses for impaired loans are recognized when there is objective evidence that impairment of the loans has occurred. Impairment allowances are calculated on individual loans and on groups of loans assessed collectively. Impairment losses are recorded in cost of producing revenue in the consolidated statements of income. The carrying amount of impaired loans in the consolidated balance sheets is reduced through the use of impairment allowance accounts. Losses expected from future events are not recognized.

All individually significant loans receivable are assessed for specific impairment. All individually significant loans receivable found not to be specifically impaired are then collectively assessed for any impairment that has been incurred but not yet identified. Loans receivable that are not individually significant are collectively assessed for impairment by grouping together loans receivable with similar risk characteristics.

The Company uses a roll rate methodology to calculate allowances for credit card loans. This methodology employs statistical analysis of historical data, economic indicators, and experience of delinquency and default to estimate the amount of loans that will eventually be written off as a result of events occurring before the reporting date, with certain adjustments for other relevant circumstances influencing the recoverability of the loans receivable. Default rates, loss rates, and cash recoveries are regularly benchmarked against actual outcomes to ensure that they remain appropriate.

Dealer loans

Loans to Associate Dealers ("Dealers"), independent third-party operators of Canadian Tire Retail stores, are initially measured at fair value plus directly attributable transaction costs and are subsequently measured at their amortized cost using the effective interest method, less an allowance for impairment, if any.[7]

Note 9 of the financial statements then provides details regarding these balances, excerpted below:

Exhibit 5-22	Canadian Tire Corporation, Limited—Note 9: Loans receivable		
Continuity schedule of the Company's allowances for loans receivable			
(C$ millions)		**2016**	**2015**
Balance, beginning of year		$ 111.5	$ 113.2
Impairments for credit losses, net of [expected] recoveries		293.7	301.9
Recoveries		69.4	65.9
Write-offs		(367.7)	(369.5)
Balance, end of year		$ 106.9	$ 111.5
Aging of the loans receivable that are past due, but not impaired			
(C$ millions)		**2016**	**2015**
1–90 days past due		$ 308.6	$ 306.3
> 90 days past due		58.3	62.8
Total		$ 366.9	$ 369.1

Source: From Canadian Tire Corporation 2016 Report to Shareholders. Copyright ©2016 by Canadian Tire Corporation, Limited. Reprinted by permission.

In 2016, the Company recorded bad debt expense of $293.7 million, wrote off $367.7 million in loans receivable as uncollectible, and recovered $69.4 million on loans previously written off. The net additions or reversals are close to zero, so the company's estimates have proven reasonable in recent years. The balance of $106.9 million represents 2.0% of the $5,245.3 million gross loans receivable balance ($5,138.4 million + $106.9 million), which is a little less than twice as high as the 1.1% average mentioned at the beginning of this chapter.

[7.] Source: From Canadian Tire Corporation 2016 Report to Shareholders. Copyright ©2016 by Canadian Tire Corporation, Limited. Reprinted by permission.

M. SUMMARY

L.O. 5-1. Apply the standards and procedures for recording, reconciling, and reporting cash and cash equivalents.

- The category of cash and cash equivalents includes cash on hand, demand deposits, and other investments that are both highly liquid and have negligible risk of change in value.
- Bank reconciliations use records from the enterprise and its bank to determine the corrected cash balance that should be used for financial reporting purposes.

L.O. 5-2. Explain the need for internal controls for cash specifically and other assets more generally, and evaluate the adequacy of cash controls in different situations.

- Bank reconciliations and separation of duties are important internal controls to reduce the likelihood of cash misappropriation.
- Managerial and customer monitoring are alternative ways to reduce the risk of fraud.
- Internal controls for other assets are as important as for cash, because people have less aversion to misappropriating non-cash items.

L.O. 5-3. Apply the standards and procedures for the initial recognition, subsequent measurement at the balance sheet date, and derecognition of trade receivables.

- Trade receivables are usually recorded at face value due to the high cost of recordkeeping and the immateriality of the present value discount over short time periods.
- Enterprises can derecognize receivables for which they no longer retain the risks and rewards of ownership.
- Enterprises should report trade receivables at expected net realizable value to mitigate the moral hazard that would result from the mismatch in timing between the recording of bad debts expense and the recognition of revenue.
- Evaluation of receivables' value should take account of information available concerning the enterprise's revenue recognition policy, credit policy, sales return policy, whether the enterprise has factored a portion of their receivables, as well as whether management has particular incentives to bias earnings.

L.O. 5-4. Apply the standards to account for non-trade receivables.

- Non-trade receivables should generally be recorded at discounted present value because transactions giving rise to such receivables are usually less frequent and larger in amount than trade receivables, so the benefits exceed the costs of measuring the time value of money.
- When a lender restructures a loan receivable, it needs to revalue the loan using the new terms of the loan. Any resulting gain or loss flows through net income.

N. ANSWERS TO CHECKPOINT QUESTIONS

CP5-1: Cash equivalents can be classified together with cash because enterprises manage the amount of cash carefully. Since cash is an idle asset, enterprises often invest the funds in other assets that are nearly as liquid and nearly as safe as cash. Grouping cash and cash equivalents together is more relevant to financial statement users.

CP5-2: Segregation of duties is important as an internal control to reduce the chances of fraud. When two or more employees work on separate but related tasks, collusion among them is required to execute fraud without detection by others.

CP5-3: The three accounting issues common to the different classes of assets are (i) initial recognition and measurement, (ii) subsequent measurement, and (iii) derecognition.

CP5-4:   The main difference between the gross and net methods is whether the cash discount forfeited by customers is recorded as sales revenue (gross method) or as interest income (net method).

CP5-5:   The percentage of sales method is an income statement approach because it directly estimates the amount of bad debts expense, which is the effect of bad debts on income. The aging of accounts method is a balance sheet approach because it directly estimates the amount of the allowance for doubtful accounts, which is the effect of bad debts on the balance sheet.

CP5-6:   The principle dictating whether an enterprise should derecognize receivables when it transfers them to another entity is that the transferor can derecognize the receivables when it has transferred substantially all of the risks and rewards of ownership to another party.

CP5-7:   Enterprises should record non-trade receivables at their present value, but they can record trade accounts receivable at their nominal/face/undiscounted value. The difference reflects the cost constraint: trade receivables have a high volume of transactions and the length of time involved is relatively short, whereas the opposite is true for non-trade receivables.

O. GLOSSARY

aging (of accounts receivable): A process of categorizing accounts receivable according to the length of time that has passed since the invoice date.

allowance for doubtful accounts (ADA): A contra account relating to accounts receivable; the balance in the allowance for doubtful accounts is management's estimate of the amount that will not be collected from customers. Also called *allowance for bad debts* or *allowance for uncollectible accounts.*

balance sheet approach: An approach to accounting and standard setting that emphasizes the values of the balance sheet over the income statement.

capitalize: Recording an **expenditure** as an asset on the balance sheet.

cash: Cash on hand and demand deposits.

cash discount: A discount given for immediate or timely payment.

cash equivalents: Short-term, highly liquid investments that are readily convertible to known amounts of cash and which are subject to insignificant risks of change in value.

contra account: A balance sheet account that has the opposite sign of the main balance sheet account to which it is connected.

direct write-off method (for accounts receivable): A method that records the expense when an account receivable is deemed to be uncollectible.

expenditure: An outflow of cash or other resources; distinguish from **expense.**

expense: An amount reported on the income statement that reduces the amount of profit (or increases a loss) for the period.

factor (for receivables): A finance company that buys accounts receivable from other companies.

gross accounts receivable: The face value of accounts receivable before deducting the allowance for doubtful accounts.

gross method (of accounting for cash discounts): Records the gross/face value of receivables and records any discounts taken as a reduction in revenue.

income statement approach: An approach to accounting and standard setting that emphasizes the values of the income statement over the balance sheet.

net accounts receivable: The face value of accounts receivable minus the allowance for doubtful accounts.

net method (of accounting for cash discounts): Records receivables net of cash discounts and records any discounts forfeited as income.

net realizable value: The amount that can be obtained from the sale of an asset after deducting any costs that need to be incurred prior to the sale of the asset.

promissory note: A written promise by one party to repay another party a specified amount at a specified date; sometimes colloquially called an "IOU."

securitization: The process of transforming a financial asset into a security.

special purpose entity (SPE): An entity that is created for limited purposes; such purposes are specified in the legal documents that create the entity.

sub-ledger: A listing with details regarding individual accounts receivable including the name of the party who owes money to the firm, the amount they owe, and the dates on which the payments are due.

P. FOR FURTHER READING

Ariely, Daniel. *Predictably Irrational: The Hidden Forces That Shape Our Decisions.* New York, NY: HarperCollins, 2008.

Q. REFERENCES

Authoritative standards:

IFRS	ASPE Section
Framework for the Preparation and Presentation of Financial Statements ¶85	
IAS 7—Statement of Cash Flows ¶6	1540—Cash Flow Statement ¶6
IFRS 9—Financial Instruments	3856—Financial Instruments
	3856—Financial Instruments Appendix B: Transfers of Receivables

MyLab Accounting Make the grade with **MyLab Accounting:** The problems marked with a  can be found on **MyLab Accounting.** You can practise them as often as you want, and most feature step-by-step guided instructions to help you find the right answer.

R. PROBLEMS

 P5-1.   Cash and cash equivalents   (**L.O.** 5-1) (Easy – 3 minutes)

Identify the two criteria for classifying an investment as a cash equivalent.

P5-2.   Cash and cash equivalents   (**L.O.** 5-1) (Easy – 3 minutes)

Shares of large publicly traded companies can be readily sold and converted into cash. Explain why the value of such shares cannot be included in cash and cash equivalents.

 P5-3.   Cash and cash equivalents   (**L.O.** 5-1) (Easy – 3 minutes)

Guaranteed investment certificates (GICs) have a definite value upon maturity, and the principal amount is guaranteed by the Government of Canada (through the Canadian Deposit Insurance Corporation). Explain why a $50,000 GIC maturing two years after the balance sheet date cannot be included in cash and cash equivalents.

P5-4.   Cash and cash equivalents   (**L.O.** 5-1) (Easy – 5 minutes)

Identify whether each of the following items should be classified in cash and cash equivalents or some other category in the balance sheet. Assume that the reporting entity has operations in Canada.

a. Chequing account in Canadian dollars.
b. Investment in a mutual fund that invests in common shares.
c. Investment in long-term government bonds.
d. Term deposit maturing 120 days after the year-end.
e. Cash in a sinking fund account for a future redemption of bonds payable.

P5-5.   Cash and cash equivalents   (**L.O.** 5-1) (Medium – 10 minutes)

Identify whether each of the following items should be classified in cash and cash equivalents or some other category in the balance sheet. Assume that the reporting entity has operations in Canada.

a. Negative balance in a chequing account (i.e., an overdraft).
b. Investment in Treasury bills maturing 60 days after the year-end.
c. 100 ounces of gold, which is currently priced at $1,150/ounce.
d. Chequing account in US dollars.
e. Investment in US government Treasury bills maturing 60 days after the year-end.

P5-6.   Cash and cash equivalents   (**L.O.** 5-1) (Medium – 5 minutes)

A company spends $1,500 to purchase an airline ticket for a trip two months in the future. The company has the option to cancel the trip and obtain a full refund from the airline.

Required:

Discuss whether this refundable airline ticket is a cash equivalent.

P5-7.   Cash and cash equivalents   (**L.O.** 5-1) (Medium – 10 minutes)

Cryptocurrencies are digital currencies that use cryptography to ensure security of transactions and records. In the mid-2010s, cryptocurrencies such as Bitcoin, Ethereum, and Litecoin gained tremendous popularity, at least among a segment of the world's population. At the end of 2017, there were over 1,000 cryptocurrencies with total value equivalent to over US$600 billion. However, none are (as yet) affiliated with any national currencies or central banks.

Rising along with the popularity are also the values of cryptocurrencies. Expressed in terms of US dollars, Bitcoin's value increased more than 10-fold in 2017; Ethereum 100-fold; Litecoin 80-fold.

Required:

Suppose a company uses some idle cash to purchase cryptocurrencies. Should the company report such cryptocurrencies on the company's balance sheet as a part of cash and cash equivalents? Why or why not?

P5-8.   Cash reconciliation   (**L.O.** 5-1) (Easy – 5 minutes)

Jay Company's general ledger indicates a cash balance of $6,000 as at the end of October 2019, prior to completing a bank reconciliation. The bookkeeper has identified the following information:

■ Outstanding cheques $2,000.
■ Outstanding deposits $1,000.
■ Bank service charges $100 shown on the October 31 bank statement.

Required:

How much is the corrected cash balance of Jay Company as of October 31, 2019?

P5-9. Cash reconciliation   (**L.O.** 5-1) (Easy – 5 minutes)[8]

During May of the current year, AR Company wrote cheque #345 to a supplier as a payment on its account. The cheque was written for the correct amount of $15,200. The May bank statement listed the cheque at $51,200 and an ending account balance of ($48,300) in overdraft.

Required:

a. Prepare the portion of the May cash reconciliation that reconciles the bank balance to cash balance to be used in the financial statements.
b. Where on the balance sheet should the cash (or overdraft) balance be shown?

 P5-10. Cash reconciliation   (**L.O.** 5-1) (Easy – 5 minutes)[9]

Banana Company's bank balance on the bank statement for October 31 of the current year is $12,500. Banana's accountant is preparing a cash reconciliation and has determined that three cheques issued by Banana to its suppliers for a total of $8,500 have not yet cleared the bank. Also, a deposit for $1,500 made by Banana on October 31 does not appear on the bank statement. Bank service charges of $150 appear on the bank statement, but have not yet been recorded in the general ledger.

Required:

Prepare the cash reconciliation to determine the corrected cash balance that should be reflected in Banana's general ledger as at October 31.

P5-11. Cash reconciliation   (**L.O.** 5-1) (Medium – 10 minutes)

Barb Lee Inc. (BLI) is about to reconcile its bank statement for the month of May 2018. Pertinent information follows:

- Bank statement balance $11,003.74.
- General ledger balance $8,284.07.
- BLI mailed a deposit of $899.14 to the bank on May 28. The bank had not yet received it by month end.
- BLI issued cheques #124 for $2,041.25; #126 for $951.56; and #129 for $1,000 in May; however, these were not returned with the May 31 bank statement.
- BLI received notification that a cheque for $313 deposited to BLI's account was returned NSF. The bank levied a $32 returned cheque charge.
- The bank statement included a $29 service charge for the month.

Required:

a. Prepare the cash reconciliation for Barb Lee Inc. as at May 31, 2018.
b. Prepare adjusting journal entries to correct for items noted in the cash reconciliation.

P5-12. Cash reconciliation   (**L.O.** 5-1) (Medium – 10 minutes)

Chris Hacker Ltd. (CHL) is about to reconcile its bank statement for the month of September 2018. Pertinent information follows:

- Bank statement balance $6,627.87
- General ledger balance $5,685.45.
- The bank erroneously deducted another company's $800 cheque from CHL's bank account.

[8.] Reprinted from CGA-Canada FA2 examination, June 2009, with permission from Chartered Professional Accountants of Canada, Toronto, Canada. Any changes to the original material are the sole responsibility of the author (and/or publisher) and have not been reviewed or endorsed by the Chartered Professional Accountants of Canada.

[9.] Reprinted from CGA-Canada FA2 examination, December 2008, with permission from Chartered Professional Accountants of Canada, Toronto, Canada. Any changes to the original material are the sole responsibility of the author (and/or publisher) and have not been reviewed or endorsed by the Chartered Professional Accountants of Canada.

■ CHL issued cheques #222 for $456.23; #223 for $1,450; and #225 for $122.19 in September; however, these were still outstanding at month end.

■ CHL received notification that a cheque for $245 deposited to its account was returned NSF. The bank levied a $28 returned cheque charge.

■ The bank statement included a $14 service charge for the month.

Required:

a. Prepare the cash reconciliation for Chris Hacker Ltd. as at September 30, 2018.
b. Prepare adjusting journal entries to correct for items noted in the cash reconciliation.

 P5-13. Cash controls    **(L.O.** 5-2) (Easy – 5 minutes)[10]

Private Company (PC) is in its fourth year of retail operations. The owner/manager of PC previously employed a part-time bookkeeper to prepare and sign cheques, prepare the cash reconciliations, and prepare annual financial statements. PC has just hired you as the first full-time accountant to replace the bookkeeper.

Required:

a. Briefly explain the concept of "segregation of duties" to PC's owner/manager.
b. Identify the internal control issues relating to cash and provide your recommendations to improve PC's internal controls over cash.

P5-14. Cash controls    **(L.O.** 5-2) (Easy – 10 minutes)

The opening vignette in this chapter mentions the significant amount of cash held onsite at casinos. Relating to this cash, it is commonly asserted that video cameras are the most basic level of security. For example, www.gamblinginfo.com indicates the following:

> "Casinos generally hire a variety of security and surveillance officers to monitor both the interior and the exterior of the casino to be sure nothing is stolen. Numerous surveillance officers usually work the casino per shift. Monitoring is accomplished through surveillance cameras and other types of devices which are often hidden. Many gamers often refer to this as the eye in the sky; however, it has proven to be quite successful in detecting any type of theft. Surveillance officers also maintain constant communication with uniformed security officers spread throughout the casino as well as other employees such as floor supervisors to notify them of anything amiss or possible problems."[11]

Required:

This passage suggests that the "eye in the sky" is important and possibly the crucial security measure in a casino. Do you agree? Briefly explain why or why not. What would you consider to be basic security measures in a casino?

 P5-15. Cash controls    **(L.O.** 5-2) (Medium – 10 minutes)

You serve as a volunteer treasurer for your local hockey club. The club plans to hold a costume party on Halloween night to help raise funds for the team to travel to an out-of-town tournament. You anticipate about 200 guests at this event. Admission will cost $10 per person, which may be paid in advance or at the door. There will be beverages for sale. This venue has no cash register machine for recording sales.

Required:

Discuss the internal controls for cash you would recommend for this event.

[10.] Reprinted from CGA-Canada FA2 examination, March 2009, with permission from Chartered Professional Accountants of Canada, Toronto, Canada. Any changes to the original material are the sole responsibility of the author (and/or publisher) and have not been reviewed or endorsed by the Chartered Professional Accountants of Canada.

[11.] From Casino Management and Operations by Gamblinginfo.com. Copyright © by Endless Blue Inc. Reprinted by permission.

P5-16. Accounting for non-cash assets   (**L.O.** 5-3) (Easy – 5 minutes)

Explain the differences and relationships among expenditures, assets, and expenses.

 P5-17. Accounts receivable recognition and measurement—gross and net method
(**L.O.** 5-3) (Easy – 5 minutes)

Ajax Inc. has a policy of 1/10 net 30 for its accounts receivable. The company issues an invoice for $6,500.

Required:

How should Ajax record the invoice if it uses (a) the gross method or (b) the net method?

 P5-18. Accounts receivable recognition and measurement—gross and net method
(**L.O.** 5-3) (Medium – 10 minutes)

Beetles Geophysics issues an invoice to Yukon Goldmines for $300,000 on August 5, 2020. The invoice states the payment terms to be 2/10 net 45. Yukon pays the invoice on August 14, 2020.

Required:

How should Beetles record the invoice and its subsequent collection if it uses (a) the gross method or (b) the net method?

 **P5-19. Accounts receivable recognition and measurement—gross and net method**
(**L.O.** 5-3) (Medium – 10 minutes)

Continental Shelving Company made a sale to Excalibur Knives for $5,000 on December 10, 2020. Approaching year-end, Continental wanted to encourage prompt payment, so it provided generous discounts for those clients able to pay promptly. The invoices state the payment terms to be 3/10 net 45. Excalibur pays the invoice on January 20, 2021.

Required:

How should Continental record the invoice and its subsequent collection if the company uses (a) the gross method or (b) the net method?

P5-20. Accounts receivable recognition and measurement   (**L.O.** 5-3) (Easy – 10 minutes)

GAAP does not accept the direct write-off method as an appropriate method for accounting for bad debts.

Required:

Identify and discuss two different reasons why GAAP rejects the direct write-off method for accounting for bad debts.

 P5-21. Accounts receivable recognition and measurement   (**L.O.** 5-3) (Easy – 5 minutes)[12]

YM Company determines the allowance for doubtful accounts by aging its accounts receivable. At the end of 2020, the balance in the allowance account was $50,000. During 2021, YM wrote off $5,000 and collected a $3,000 receivable that had been previously written off as uncollectible. At the end of 2021, the aging schedule indicated that the balance of the allowance for doubtful accounts should be $64,000.

Required:

How much is the bad debts expense for 2021?

[12.] Reprinted from CGA-Canada FA2 examination, June 2009, with permission from Chartered Professional Accountants of Canada, Toronto, Canada. Any changes to the original material are the sole responsibility of the author (and/or publisher) and have not been reviewed or endorsed by the Chartered Professional Accountants of Canada.

P5-22. Accounts receivable recognition and measurement   (**L.O.** 5-3) (Easy – 5 minutes)

Grayson Co. (GC) uses the percentage of sales method for estimating bad debts for monthly reporting purposes. On January 1, 2020, the allowance for doubtful accounts balance was $5,000 Cr. GC had credit sales of $100,000 for the month of January, and, in the past, 1.5% of credit sales had not been collected. During the month, the company wrote off $3,000 of accounts receivable relating to bankrupt customers.

Required:

What should be the balance in the allowance for doubtful accounts on January 31?

 **P5-23.** Accounts receivable recognition and measurement   (**L.O.** 5-3) (Easy – 5 minutes)

McKenzie Ltd. provides for doubtful accounts based on 4% of credit sales. The following data are available for the current fiscal year:

Credit sales during the year	$3,250,000
Allowance for doubtful accounts January 1	26,000 Cr
Collection of accounts written off in prior years	5,000
Customer accounts written off as uncollectible during the year	39,850

Required:

How much should be the balance in the allowance for doubtful accounts on December 31?

 P5-24. Accounts receivable recognition and measurement

(**L.O.** 5-3) (Medium – 10 minutes)

At the end of the current fiscal year, Felicity Ltd.'s accounts show the following amounts:

Accounts receivable	$789,000
Allowance for doubtful accounts (prior to any adjusting or closing entries)	12,000 Dr.
Customer accounts written off as uncollectible during the year	?
Bad debts expense for the year (prior to any adjusting or closing entries)	62,000 Dr.

Felicity estimates the following percentages of accounts receivable will not be collectible:

	Days outstanding				
	0–30	31–75	76–120	> 120	Total
Amount	$345,000	$133,000	$175,000	$136,000	$789,000
% not collectible	2%	6%	12%	20%	—

Required:

What should be the amount of bad debts expense for the year?

P5-25. Accounts receivable recognition and measurement   (**L.O.** 5-3) (Medium – 10 minutes)

Stanger Corp.'s December 31, 2020, year-end *unadjusted* trial balance showed the following amounts:

Accounts receivable	$1,067,000
Allowance for doubtful accounts	14,521 Cr.
Customer accounts written off as uncollectible during 2020	16,379
Bad debts expense for 2020	20,000 Dr.

Stanger Corp. estimates the following percentages of accounts receivable will not be collectible:

	Days outstanding				
	0–30	31–60	61–90	> 90	Total
Amount	$722,000	$214,000	$89,000	$42,000	$1,067,000
% not collectible	1%	3%	6%	30%	—

Required:

a. Calculate the *total* bad debts expense for the year ended December 31, 2020.
b. Prepare the year-end adjusting journal entry to record bad debts expense.

 P5-26. Accounts receivable recognition and measurement

(**L.O.** 5-3) (Medium – 15 minutes)

Pessimist Inc. had credit sales totalling $4,900,000 and $5,100,000 for the years ended December 31, 2020 and 2021, respectively. Information on trade accounts receivable for the company is presented below:

	Days outstanding from invoice date			
	Current	30–60	61–90	Over 90
Balance in accounts receivable, December 31, 2020	$400,000	$150,000	$40,000	$10,000
Balance in accounts receivable, December 31, 2021	440,000	160,000	30,000	20,000
% of receivables estimated to be uncollectible	0.5%	1%	2%	5%

The balance of the allowance for doubtful accounts as of January 1, 2020, was $5,000. In addition, you learn that the company wrote off specific accounts of $6,500 in 2020, and the bad debts expense was $8,000 in 2021.

Required:

a. Determine the bad debts expense for 2020.
b. Determine the amount of receivables written off during 2021.
c. Prepare the journal entry to record the bad debts expense for 2020.

P5-27. Accounts receivable recognition and measurement (**L.O.** 5-3) (Medium – 10 minutes)

At the end of the 2018 fiscal year, Reversiflex Filing Company reported net accounts receivable of $755,000 and allowance for doubtful accounts of $15,000. At the following year-end, the corresponding figures were $649,000 and $13,000, respectively. During 2019, the company had credit sales of $3,210,000 and wrote off $19,000 of accounts that became uncollectible.

Required:

Determine the amount of cash collected from customers and the amount of bad debts expense for fiscal year 2019.

 P5-28. Accounts receivable recognition and measurement (**L.O.** 5-3) (Medium – 10 minutes)

Upsidedown Cake Company produces dessert products for sale in grocery stores, but it also has a retail location. At the end of 2020, the company had $349,000 in accounts receivable before netting out $6,000 of allowance for doubtful accounts. At the prior year-end, the corresponding amounts were $335,000 and $5,000, respectively. The company's sales in 2020 totalled $2,450,000, of which $2,200,000 was sold on credit. The company recorded bad debts expense of $9,000 in 2020.

Required:

Determine the amount of cash collected from customers for the year 2020 and the amount of receivables written off in the fiscal year.

 P5-29. Accounts receivable recognition and measurement (**L.O.** 5-3) (Medium – 10 minutes)

Verdant Vines specializes in cultivating rootstock for grape vines. The company sells to both vineyards and consumers. At the beginning of the year, the company had $120,000 in accounts receivable before netting out $17,000 of allowance for doubtful accounts. At the end of the year, the corresponding amounts were $125,000 and $16,000, respectively. The company's sales in the year totalled $7,670,000, of which $7,200,000 was sold on credit. During the year, the company estimated bad debts expense using the percentage of sales method, and at the end of the year recorded a further $5,000 of bad debts expense by applying the aging method. Write-offs amounted to $42,000.

Required:

Determine the amount of cash collected from customers for the current year and the percentage the company used to estimate bad debt expense.

 P5-30. Accounts receivable derecognition—transfer without recourse

(**L.O.** 5-3) (Easy – 5 minutes)

Kemano Motorcycles sold $800,000 of receivables to a factor to increase the company's liquidity. The company chose to factor these receivables without recourse. In exchange for these receivables, the factor paid Kemano $720,000 on the date of transfer. Ultimately, the factor collected $780,000 from these receivables.

Required:

Record the entry on Kemano's books relating to the sale of the $800,000 of accounts receivable.

 **P5-31.** Accounts receivable derecognition—transfer with recourse

(**L.O.** 5-3) (Medium – 10 minutes)

McBride Motors both sells and leases vehicles. Due to sales that have temporarily slowed with the economy, the company factored a significant portion of its lease receivables. The company factored with recourse receivables with a carrying amount of $15 million in exchange for $14.5 million less a holdback of $500,000 for potential uncollectible accounts. Due to poor economic conditions, the actual uncollectible accounts amounted to $900,000.

Required:

Record the entries on McBride's books relating to the $15 million of lease receivables.

 P5-32. Accounts receivable derecognition—transfer with recourse

(**L.O.** 5-3) (Medium – 10 minutes)

Ladysmith Furnishings extends generous payment terms to its customers. As a result, it has accumulated a substantial portfolio of accounts receivable. To improve cash flow, the company decided to sell $500,000 of these receivables to a factor. The company had previously checked the creditworthiness of its customers, so it is confident that few accounts will become uncollectible. Therefore, the company chose to factor these receivables with recourse. In exchange for these receivables, the factor paid Ladysmith 95 cents on each dollar of receivables on the date of transfer. The factor also held 2 cents on each dollar for potential uncollectible accounts. Ultimately, the factor collected $496,000 from these receivables.

Required:

Record the entries on Ladysmith's books relating to the $500,000 of accounts receivable.

P5-33. Accounts receivable derecognition—transfer with recourse

(**L.O.** 5-3) (Medium – 10 minutes)

Cassiar Aerodynamics specializes in the manufacture and sale of helicopters. Its customers include governments, hospitals and ambulance services, and corporations. Due to unfavourable payment terms negotiated on a large contract to supply the federal government, Cassiar is facing a cash shortage. To alleviate the pressure, the company decided to factor $45 million of its receivables with recourse. In exchange, the factor agreed to pay Cassiar 98% of the face value of the receivables less a 1% holdback on the date of transfer. After several months, the factor collected a total of $44.8 million from the debtors.

Required:

Record the entries on Cassiar's books relating to the $45 million of accounts receivable.

 P5-34. Accounts receivable derecognition—securitization   (**L.O.** 5-3) (Easy – 10 minutes)

Sparwood Credit Union is a small, regional financial institution with a loyal customer base. Like most financial institutions, Sparwood has a significant portfolio of home mortgages. Because of the nature of its operations, the risks relating to these mortgages are geographically concentrated. To reduce this risk, the credit union securitized $20 million of mortgages receivable for proceeds of $19.5 million. Under the securitization arrangement, investors in the mortgage-backed securities bear the cost of any defaults on the mortgages. Sparwood's only continuing involvement in the mortgages is the administration of the cash receipts and the transfer of that cash to the investors.

Required:

a. Should Sparwood record this securitization as a sale or as a borrowing transaction? Explain.
b. Record the entry in Sparwood's books relating to Sparwood's securitization of mortgage receivables.

 P5-35. Accounts receivable recognition and measurement   (**L.O.** 5-3) (Medium – 15 minutes)

The accounting records of 2Com Ltd. show the following for the current year:

Balance in accounts receivable, January 1	$ 90,000
Balance in accounts receivable, December 31	120,000
Balance in allowance for doubtful accounts, January 1	3,000
Bad debts expense before year-end adjustment, December 31	4,500 Dr.*
Accounts written off as uncollectible during the year	2,500 **

* The credit side of the journal entry (or entries) related to this amount went to allowance for doubtful accounts.
** Account write-offs went against the allowance for doubtful accounts.

Cash sales were $900,000, while credit sales were $650,000. Recently, 2Com's management has become concerned about various estimates used in its accounting system, including those relating to receivables and uncollectible accounts. The company is considering two alternatives.

For the purpose of comparing these two alternatives, the company has made the following estimates for each alternative:
- Alternative 1: Bad debts approximating 0.75% of credit sales.
- Alternative 2: Aging of the accounts receivable at the end of the period, where 80% would incur a 2% loss, while the remaining 20% would incur a 10% loss.

Required:

For each of the two alternatives listed above, calculate the bad debts expense for the year and the allowance for doubtful accounts balance at the end of the year.

P5-36. Accounts receivable recognition, measurement, and derecognition

(**L.O.** 5-3) (Medium – 15 minutes)

Pacific Communication Systems (PCS) uses the aging method for its accounts receivable. On January 1, 2020, the balance in the allowance for doubtful accounts was $2.25 million. For the year ended December 31, 2020, PCS made $945 million of credit sales and wrote off $12.5 million of accounts as uncollectible. For interim reporting purposes, the company recorded bad debts expense equal to 1% of credit sales during 2020. The aging analysis at the end of 2020 indicates the estimated uncollectible accounts total $2.5 million.

Required:

a. Record the year-end adjusting entry to record bad debts expense.
b. During 2020, PCS factored $50 million of its receivables with recourse. The factor paid PCS $47 million cash after deducting a holdback of $2 million for potential uncollectible accounts. Show the journal entry to record this transaction.
c. Six months later, the factor determined that $0.5 million are uncollectible and therefore paid PCS $1.5 million out of the $2 million holdback. In total, PCS received $48.5 million from this factoring transaction. Record the journal entries for this transaction.

 P5-37. Accounts receivable recognition, measurement, and derecognition

(**L.O.** 5-3) (Difficult – 20 minutes)

Quagmire Company is preparing its financial statement for the year ended. A summary of Quagmire's accounts receivable sub-ledger shows the following information:

	Days outstanding from invoice date			
	0–30 days	31–90 days	> 90 days	Total
Balance outstanding, December 31	$7,100,000	$1,800,000	$375,000	$9,275,000
Estimated default rate	0.5%	2%	10%	—
Accounts written off during the year				70,000
Collections on accounts written off				3,000
Allowance for uncollectibles, January 1				120,000

Required:

a. Determine the amount of bad debts expense required for the year.
b. Show the journal entry to record bad debts expense for the year.
c. Show the journal entry that was used to record write-offs for the year.
d. Independent of the information above, suppose Quagmire factored $2,000,000 of receivables without recourse. In exchange, it received $1,900,000. Show the journal entry to record this transfer of receivables.
e. In part (d), suppose Quagmire instead factored the $2,000,000 of receivables *with* recourse and received $1,930,000 cash. Both Quagmire and the factor anticipate that 2% of these receivables will prove to be uncollectible, so the factor has held this amount to cover any uncollectible accounts. Should the amount of uncollectibles prove to be more or less than 2%, the difference will be paid by/refunded to Quagmire. Show the journal entry to record this transfer of receivables.

 P5-38. Accounts receivable recognition, measurement, and derecognition

(**L.O.** 5-3) (Difficult – 15 minutes)

Wahlberg Design Partners (WDP) uses the aging method for its accounts receivable. On January 1, the balance in the allowance for doubtful accounts was $25,000. For the year, WDP made $2,560,000 of credit sales, wrote off $50,000 of accounts as uncollectible, and $850,000 remained outstanding at year-end. The following table is the aging schedule for these receivables:

	Days outstanding from invoice date			
	0–30 days	31–90 days	> 90 days	Total
Balance outstanding, December 31	$600,000	$170,000	$80,000	$850,000
Estimated default rate	1%	2%	5%	—

During the year, WDP factored $600,000 of its receivables with recourse. The company received $550,000, net of a holdback of $20,000 for potentially uncollectible accounts. Of the total amount factored, $585,000 was collected, and the factor made a final payment to WDP for $5,000.

Required:

a. Record the journal entries relating to the factoring transaction.
b. Determine the amount of bad debts expense for the year.
c. Show the journal entry to record bad debts expense for the year.
d. Show the journal entry that was used to record write-offs for the year.

 P5-39. Accounts receivable and accounting changes   5-3) (Medium – 10 minutes)

You are auditing the receivables section for one of your clients. The company provides you with its schedule of accounts receivable categorized by age and expected default rate, as follows:

| | Days outstanding from invoice date | | | |
	0–30 days	31–90	> 90 days	Total
Balance outstanding, December 31	$700,000	$180,000	$37,000	$917,000
Estimated default rate	0.5%	2%	10%	—

Based on the above information, the company's accounting clerk recorded $10,800 as bad debts expense. You collect additional relevant information as follows:

Allowance for doubtful accounts (ADA), January 1	$12,000
Accounts written off during the year	$7,000

Required:

Determine what adjustment, if any, is required to correct the company's accounts relating to receivables or bad debts. Provide the journal entry or entries accordingly.

 P5-40. Accounts receivable and accounting changes   5-3) (Difficult – 15 minutes)

At December 31, 2020, Kneeland Inc. had $150,000 of accounts receivable and $5,000 in the allowance for doubtful accounts.

In 2021, the company had $750,000 in credit sales and collected $776,500 on accounts. Kneeland also wrote off $3,500 for specific accounts determined to be uncollectible. The company uses the aging of accounts method to estimate bad debts, and management has estimated that the allowance for doubtful accounts for December 31, 2021, should be $4,000.

Required:

a. Provide the journal entry to record bad debts expense for 2021. (Ignore information contained in part (b) below.)
b. While auditing the books of Kneeland, you discover that the company's bookkeeper has erroneously recorded a transaction: for one customer who went bankrupt in 2021, Kneeland wrote off the receivable (of $1,500) with a debit directly to bad debts expense. Determine the error's effects (overstated/understated) on the balance sheet as at December 31, 2021, (accounts receivable, allowance for doubtful accounts) and the income statement for the year ended 2021.
c. In January 2022, the company factored all of its receivables ($120,000) without recourse for proceeds of $110,000. Provide the journal entry to record this transaction.

P5-41. Accounts receivable and accounting changes   **L.O.** 5-3) (Difficult – 15 minutes)

Aberdeen Co. started applying the percentage of sales method to account for bad debts in 2021. In 2020, the company's first fiscal year, the company had used the direct write-off method because the amount of bad debts was judged to be immaterial. The following information relates to the company's sales and receivables:

	2020	2021
Credit sales	$13,800,000	$26,400,000
Estimated bad debts as a percentage of credit sales	0.5%	0.5%
Accounts written off	$35,000	$160,000

Required:

a. Determine the correct balance in the allowance for doubtful accounts at the end of 2021. Remember to include the effect of the change in accounting policy on 2020 accounts.
b. Record the write-off entry for 2021 and the year-end adjusting journal entry for 2021 to adjust the ADA.

 P5-42. Non-trade receivables recognition and measurement

L.O. 5-4) (Easy – 5 minutes)[13]

On January 1, 2019, Carat Company agreed to sell a diamond to a customer at a special price of $5,000. Payment terms were $1,000 on January 1, 2019, and $1,000 each January 1 from 2020 to 2023. Carat normally charges 6% interest to its customers, but did not charge interest on this special sale.

Required:

How much revenue, and how much in accounts receivable, should Carat recognize on January 1, 2019?

P5-43. Trade and non-trade receivables recognition and measurement

L.O. 5-3, **L.O.** 5-4) (Medium – 10 minutes)

Evans Shielding Products (ESP) uses the aging method for its accounts receivable. On January 1, 2020, the balance in the allowance for doubtful accounts was $20,000. For the year ended December 31, 2020, ESP made $1,942,000 of credit sales, wrote off $75,000 of accounts as uncollectible, recovered $8,000 on an account previously written off, and had $430,000 outstanding at year-end.

On January 1, 2020, ESP received a promissory note from a customer in exchange for a large purchase of goods from ESP. The note pays interest at 7% annually, matures on December 31, 2022, and will pay ESP $150,000 upon maturity. The market yield for this type of note is 10%.

During 2020, ESP factored $200,000 of its receivables without recourse for net proceeds of $186,000.

The following table is the aging schedule for ESP's receivables:

	Days outstanding from invoice date			
	0–30 days	31–90 days	> 90 days	Total
Balance outstanding, December 31, 2020	$320,000	$80,000	$30,000	$430,000
Estimated default rate	1%	2%	4%	—

13. Reprinted from CGA-Canada FA2 examination, March 2009 with permission from Chartered Professional Accountants of Canada, Toronto, Canada. Any changes to the original material are the sole responsibility of the author (and/or publisher) and have not been reviewed or endorsed by the Chartered Professional Accountants of Canada.

Required:

a. Determine ESP's bad debts expense for 2020.
b. Record the journal entry or entries relating to the factoring transaction.
c. Record the sale made in exchange for the promissory note.
d. For 2020, how much interest income should ESP record for the promissory note?

P5-44. Trade and non-trade receivables recognition and measurement

(**L.O.** 5-3, **L.O.** 5-4) (Medium – 20 minutes)

Cascadia Products uses the aging method for its accounts receivable. On January 1, 2020, the balance in the allowance for doubtful accounts was $320,000. For the year ended December 31, 2020, Cascadia made $6,450,000 of credit sales, wrote off $250,000 of accounts as uncollectible, and recovered $12,000 that had been written off in the prior year. The aging analysis at the end of 2020 indicates the estimated uncollectible accounts total $350,000.

During the year, the company issued a note receivable.

Required:

a. Record the year-end adjusting entry to record bad debts expense.
b. During 2020, Cascadia factored $500,000 of its receivables without recourse. The factor paid Cascadia $440,000 cash. Show the journal entry to record this transaction.
c. Cascadia also factored $800,000 of its receivables with recourse. The factor paid Cascadia $750,000 cash after deducting a holdback of $30,000 for potential uncollectible accounts. Show the journal entry to record this transaction.
d. Cascadia loaned $300,000 to a customer to finance the purchase of goods from Cascadia on January 1, 2018. The customer was to pay Cascadia on December 31, 2020, the principal plus the market rate of interest at 12% compounded annually. No payments were due during the three-year period. At the end of 2020, Cascadia and the customer renegotiated the terms of the loan such that the total amount originally due would be due at the end of 2022. Show the journal entry to record the loan restructuring on Cascadia's books.

P5-45. Non-trade receivables recognition and measurement

(**L.O.** 5-4) (Medium – 15 minutes)

On January 1, 2018, Hicks Corp. sold inventory costing $32,000 and received $6,000 cash and a $40,000 promissory note. The five-year note was repayable at $8,734 per annum including interest at 3%. The market rate of interest for similar transactions was 7%. The first payment was due on January 1, 2019.

Hicks Corp. had a December 31 year-end and prepared its financial statements in accordance with IFRS. It did not prepare interim statements or make accruals during the year.

Required:

Prepare journal entries to record:
a. The sale of inventory.
b. Interest revenue earned in 2018.
c. Receipt of the loan payment on January 1, 2019.
d. Interest revenue earned in 2019.

P5-46. Accounting for restructured loans

(**L.O.** 5-4) (Medium – 10 minutes)

Alberni Port Authority has had a long-term relationship with a nearby lumber company, which ships a significant amount of lumber through the port. To help finance the lumber company's operations, Alberni advanced $5 million to the lumber company in return for a promissory note that specified payment of the $5 million plus interest at 10% annually, due at the end of two years. However, due to adverse conditions in the lumber industry, the lumber company was unable to meet its obligation and pay Alberni at the end of two years. In light of the importance of the relationship between Alberni and the lumber company,

Alberni extended the due date by three years (after the original two years), but increased the repayment amount to $7 million, inclusive of interest. The market interest rate for the loan remained at 10%.

Required:

Record the journal entries relating to the note receivable from the date of issuance to the restructuring date, inclusive.

 P5-47. Non-trade receivables and accounting changes  **(L.O.** 5-4) (Difficult – 15 minutes)

The financial statements of Bavarian Sausage Works (BSW) dated December 31, 2020, show $50,000 for "Note receivable." You learn that the company provided $50,000 cash to a customer (a new chain of hot dog stands) in exchange for a promissory note. The note was issued on January 1, 2019, bearing interest at 12% per year (which approximates the market interest rate), with principal and interest of $56,000 due on January 1, 2020. The hot dog chain has had numerous delays obtaining the required licences to operate on street corners. Consequently, on January 1, 2020, the chain and BSW renegotiated the promissory note so that the $56,000 in principal and interest would come due on January 1, 2022. Aside from the initial recording of the note receivable on January 1, 2019, BSW has not recorded any other journal entries relating to this note.

Required:

Provide the necessary journal entries to correct BSW's accounts in 2019 and 2020.

P5-48. Cash and receivables presentation, disclosure, and analysis

(L.O. 5-1, **L.O.** 5-3, **L.O.** 5-4) (Medium – 20 minutes)

Obtain the annual report for Encana Corporation for the fiscal year ended December 31, 2016, either through the company's website or through SEDAR (www.sedar.com).

Required:

a. How much cash did the company not include in "cash and cash equivalents" on the balance sheet at the end of 2016?
b. At the end of 2016, how much were the gross and net amounts of trade receivables?
c. Taking into consideration the answer to part (b), the nature of the company's business, and the discussion of credit risk in Note 24(c) of the financial statements, assess the reasonability of Encana's allowance for doubtful accounts.
d. At the end of 2016, how much did Encana have in non-trade, non-current receivables?

P5-49. Cash and receivables presentation, disclosure, and analysis

(L.O. 5-1, **L.O.** 5-3, **L.O.** 5-4) (Medium – 20 minutes)

Obtain the annual report for Air Canada for the fiscal year ended December 31, 2016, either through the company's website or through SEDAR (www.sedar.com).

Required:

a. How much did the company have in cash and cash equivalents at the end of 2016? Of the amount in cash and cash equivalents, how much is actually cash? [*Hint:* review Note 15 of the financial statements.]
b. How much restricted cash was not included in cash and cash equivalents but was instead listed in current assets? What comprised this restricted cash?
c. How much in net accounts receivable did the company have at the end of 2016? How much was the gross amount of accounts receivable? How do accounts receivable arise for Air Canada?

P5-50. Cash and receivables presentation, disclosure, and analysis

(**L.O.** 5-1, **L.O.** 5-3, **L.O.** 5-4) (Medium – 15 minutes)

Refer to the Report to Shareholders for Canadian Tire Corporation, Limited for the fiscal year ended December 31, 2016, in Appendix D.

Required:

a. How much did the company have in cash and cash equivalents at the end of 2016? What is peculiar about this amount in the context of IFRS requirements?

b. How much, if any, did the company record as the allowance for doubtful accounts, denoted as "allowance for credit losses," at the end of 2016 for all of its receivables (trade receivables, loan receivables, and other receivables)?

c. How much in loans receivable did the company have at the end of 2016? Of that amount, how much is expected to be collected by December 31, 2017? Does the portion that is current seem reasonable given the types of loans involved?

S. MINI-CASES

The opening vignette in this chapter provided an introduction to MGM Mirage, a casino/entertainment company. As noted there, the company has significant accounts receivable, and an extraordinarily high allowance for doubtful accounts.

Most patrons of casinos are required to use cash to purchase chips and tokens to participate in casino games. However, casinos also provide credit (or "markers") to some customers, particularly those who gamble large sums of money ("high rollers"). An MGM Mirage disclosure in its 10-K filing with the U.S. Securities and Exchange Commission (SEC) for 2008 noted the following:

CRITICAL ACCOUNTING POLICIES AND ESTIMATES

Marker play represents a significant portion of the table games volume at Bellagio, MGM Grand Las Vegas, Mandalay Bay, and the Mirage. Our other facilities do not emphasize marker play to the same extent, although we offer markers to customers at those casinos as well. We maintain strict controls over the issuance of markers and aggressively pursue collection from those customers who fail to pay their marker balances timely. These collection efforts are similar to those used by most large corporations when dealing with overdue customer accounts. . . . Markers are generally legally enforceable instruments in the United States. At December 31, 2008 and 2007, approximately 52% and 47%, respectively, of our casino accounts receivable was owed by customers from the United States. Markers are not legally enforceable instruments in some foreign countries, but in the United States, assets of foreign customers may be reached to satisfy judgments entered in the United States. At December 31, 2008 and 2007, approximately 34% and 38%, respectively, of our casino accounts receivable was owed by customers from the Far East.

We maintain an allowance, or reserve, for doubtful casino accounts at all of our operating casino resorts. . . . At resorts where marker play is significant, we apply standard reserve percentages to aged account balances under a specified dollar amount and specifically analyze the collectibility of each account with a balance over the specified dollar amount, based on the age of the account, the customer's financial condition, collection history, and any other known information. We also monitor regional and global economic conditions and forecasts to determine if reserve levels are adequate.

Source: From MGM Mirage (2008) U.S. Securities and Exchange Commission (SEC).

The final quarter of 2008 saw the beginning of a global financial crisis and a deep recession triggered by high debt loads and falling real estate prices.

The following table shows key statistics for MGM Mirage:

($ millions)	2008	2007	2006
Entity-wide			
Net revenue	$7,209	$7,692	$7,176
Net income	855	1,584	648
Accounts receivable (gross)	403	499	453
Bad debts expense	80	33	48
Write-offs net of recoveries	66	37	35

(*Continued*)

($ millions)	2008	2007	2006
Allowance for doubtful accounts receivable	100	86	90
Casino operations only			
Revenues—Tables	$1,079	$1,228	$1,251
Revenues—Slots	1,795	1,898	1,770
Revenues—Other	101	113	109
Total casino revenues	2,976	3,239	3,130
Casino accounts receivable (gross)	244	266	248
Allowance for doubtful casino accounts receivable	92	77	83
Median age of casino accounts receivable	36 days	28 days	46 days

Source: From MGM Mirage (2008) U.S. Securities and Exchange Commission (SEC).

Required:

a. Using the above qualitative and quantitative information, evaluate whether MGM Mirage has under-, over-, or adequately provided for bad debts.
b. Considering the high percentage of casino receivables that go uncollected, would you advise MGM Mirage to curtail the issuance of markers? Why or why not?
c. Discuss the ethical considerations in the issuance of markers and how they should factor into your answer to part (b).

CASE 2
West Pacific's mortgage receivables
(45 minutes)[14]

West Pacific (WP) is a financial institution incorporated in 2007 and traded on the Toronto Stock Exchange. Its performance has been exceptional since the original issue. Your firm of chartered accountants has been the auditor for WP since its inception. It is now December 2022.

Across Canada, WP has 200 offices that issue residential mortgages. All mortgages issued are insured by Canada Mortgage and Housing Corporation (CMHC). All CMHC-approved issuers must grant mortgages in accordance with policies that CMHC has developed to protect the quality of the mortgages. A qualified borrower can seek a mortgage for up to 95% of the value of the property, and WP will grant the funds since CMHC promises to pay principal and interest in the event of default. For this arrangement, the borrower pays a fee to CMHC.

WP initially records the mortgages as receivables. When WP has $50 million in mortgages with similar terms (e.g., 4½- to 5-year term, paying 9 to 9.5% interest), it pools the mortgages and sells the pool to investors. At this point, WP removes the mortgages from its books. The borrower continues to make payments to WP, which passes them on to the investors less a 0.6% fee, which WP retains. The investor's interest in this mortgage pool is called a mortgage-backed security (MBS).

Besides the CMHC guarantee on the individual mortgages, WP provides a guarantee of timely payment to the investor in the event of default. The MBS, therefore, entails almost no risk for the investor and is considered to be as safe as Government of Canada bonds. Since the mortgage-backed security yields about 0.5% more than government bonds, it has enjoyed tremendous success in the marketplace.

WP has no problem selling the security, but it may take several months to accumulate the pool of mortgages it wishes to sell. After a pool of mortgages has been raised, it can take an additional three months to sell the pool to investors because of the administration involved. During this period, WP is exposed to changes in interest rates.

WP's ratio of assets to equity must not exceed 25 times. WP provides a monthly financial statement to the federal financial institution regulator that monitors this ratio.

Since 2007, WP has been a leader in establishing the accounting rules in this evolving area. Its vice-president of finance is proud of the policies it has adopted. The Ontario Securities Commission (OSC) has started a program to review annual reports and is now questioning some of the company's accounting policies, even though there are

---

[14.] This case also appeared in Chapter 2 but is particularly relevant to this chapter as well. Reprinted from Uniform Final Examination, 1993 with permission from Chartered Professional Accountants of Canada, Toronto, Canada. Any changes to the original material are the sole responsibility of the author (and/or publisher) and have not been reviewed or endorsed by the Chartered Professional Accountants of Canada.

no specific regulations covering these policies. Concerns raised by the Ontario Securities Commission are as follows:

1. The OSC questions whether mortgage receivables should be removed from the balance sheet when the company issues the MBSs.

2. The OSC disagrees with WP's policy of recognizing the present value of the 0.6% fee it earns on each mortgage as revenue when an MBS is sold.

3. Unsold mortgage receivables held at year-end remain on WP's books at cost and are not revalued because they will be sold in the short term. The OSC does not agree with this practice.

Required:

Provide arguments that support WP's position on the accounting policies being questioned and arguments that the OSC could present to support its position. Be specific in your arguments (for example, "policy X is more relevant" is too general).

CASE 3
Kanata Motor Company

(30 minutes)

Kanata Motor Company (KMC) began producing automobiles in the 1950s. Taking advantage of the baby boom, the company designed and sold cars targeted toward families. Later, when urban dwellers migrated to the suburbs, the company recognized the needs of the suburban demographic (such as "soccer moms") who value practicality over style, economy over performance, and reliability over luxury. KMC is a full-service automobile company, manufacturing, distributing, and selling vehicles through its network of corporate-owned dealerships. The company also provides loans to customers who wish to finance their purchases. KMC has remained largely profitable over the decades in the face of stiff competition from domestic and foreign competitors, although there have been ups and downs with the economic cycle.

The global recession that began in mid-2008 hit the auto sector particularly hard. Sales of cars and light trucks plunged by 22% in the first quarter of 2009 relative to the same quarter in 2008, from 363,800 to 284,600 units. KMC was caught in this downdraft along with the rest of the industry. Indeed, the demographic that KMC targets was especially hard hit by job losses and belt tightening by businesses and consumers alike.

It is now mid-April 2009. KMC's chief executive officer, Tom Delorian, knows that he has to do something in light of these dire economic conditions. Privately, he knows that his company's sales have declined by 30% in the number of units and 40% in dollar value, as customers shifted toward buying cheaper vehicles. There has been mounting pressure from shareholders, who are becoming concerned about the profitability and future viability of the business. The company is due to report its results for the year ending June 30, 2009, some time in late July.

To help come up with a plan, Delorian called a meeting of his key staff:

- VP of marketing—Susan Marvel
- VP of dealership relations—Willy Nelson
- VP of credit services—Bruno Charles
- VP of finance—Kate Moffat

The following are some key excerpts from their meeting:

SUSAN: We should have a big promotion to get people into our stores. We have great products. All we need to do is bring them in and they will like what we have to offer so much that a sale will be a piece of cake.

WILLY: I wouldn't go that far—my salespeople work pretty hard. But I agree that getting people through the door is essential. As bad as the economy is, people are hesitant to spend. So why don't we give them an offer they can't refuse? Here's my credit protection proposal: if the customer loses his or her job and can't make the car payments, we'll take the car off their hands.

TOM: What do you think about this, Bruno?

BRUNO: Well, it sounds like a reasonable idea. It does take the risk off the customers, so they might be quite tempted to buy our cars. It shouldn't be a problem for our people to do the usual check-up on their credit history to approve the financing.

WILLY: I'm confident that we can kick up our sales by 50% with this plan. As you know, our salespeople have been starved of commissions lately. They'll love this new plan, since they get 5% of the sale price.

KATE: Wait a minute ... what happens if the customer does bring the car back in?

BRUNO: I guess our dealers will take the keys off their hands, and put the car back on the lot for resale.

KATE: What would happen to the car loan?

BRUNO: We would forgive the loan in exchange for the return of the car.

KATE: Any guess as to how often a customer might use this offer and return the car?

BRUNO: Well, this recession has been harder than any in recent memory, so we're in uncharted territory. Your guess is as good as mine.

TOM: Okay, I think we have an interesting idea here. I need to think it through in more detail over the next couple of days. Kate, can you draft a memo analyzing this proposal? I know you don't have a lot to work with in terms of numbers. All I'm looking for is a qualitative discussion of the issues and how they would end up impacting our bottom line.

Required:

Play the role of Kate and draft the memo requested by Tom.

Barkwood Winery (BW) is a small winery located in the Niagara region of Ontario. The winery used to be closed to the public as the wines were solely for distribution to wholesalers. Recently, its owner, Edmond Tang, built a tasting room on the premises such that the vineyard could be open to the public for wine tasting. Edmond was hoping the opening of the new tasting room would generate additional revenue for the company through tasting fees as well as retail sales at the tasting room.

Edmond believed it may take some time for customers to learn about the BW tasting room. Hence, in its first six months of operations, he expected the tasting room to be less busy so he hired only one full-time employee. The employee worked by himself from Monday to Friday and was responsible for everything from serving the wine to making sales and recording these sales transactions. The employee was also responsible for keeping track of the wines consumed and sold. On weekends, the full-time employee would have his days off and Edmond would run the tasting room himself with a part-time employee. However, there was no separation of duties between Edmond and the part-time employee, and both of them would be serving wine to customers, making sales, and recording sales transactions. Edmond and his full-time and part-time employees all shared the same cash register with a single cash drawer. Edmond would count the cash once a week on Sunday night and would make the bank deposit on Monday morning. The wines were stored in the 1,000-bottle wine cellar behind the tasting room, and Edmond did an inventory count at the end of each month and replenished the wine cellar to its full capacity for the next month.

Since the tasting fee was only $5 per person, customers would typically pay cash for the tasting fee, and they would pay by credit card only when they decided to make a wine purchase. The company would issue receipts and retain a copy of the receipts for wine purchase, but not for tasting. So far, most customers who visited the winery were more into tasting the wine than buying the wine.

CASE 4
Barkwood Winery
(20 minutes)

Required:

a. Based on the information provided above, discuss the internal control weaknesses (if any) of BW.

b. Discuss whether you think internal control mechanisms would be stronger on the weekend operation of the tasting room when compared to the weekday operation.

c. Do you think the employees would be more likely to misappropriate cash or inventory in this situation? Explain your position.

CHAPTER 6
Inventories

After studying this chapter, you should be able to:

L.O. 6-1. Describe the informational differences between perpetual and periodic systems of inventory control.

L.O. 6-2. Analyze costing information to determine the types and amounts of costs that can be included in the cost of inventories.

L.O. 6-3. Apply the different methods of allocating costs between inventory and cost of sales.

L.O. 6-4. Evaluate whether and by how much inventories should be written down.

L.O. 6-5. Synthesize the relationship between the income statement and balance sheet through analysis of inventory errors.

CPA competencies addressed in this chapter:

1.1.2 Evaluates the appropriateness of the basis of financial reporting (Level B)
b. Methods of measurement

1.1.3 Evaluates reporting processes to support reliable financial reporting (Level B)
a. Accounting information systems

1.2.1 Develops or evaluates appropriate accounting policies and procedures – Ethical professional judgment (Level B)

1.2.2 Evaluates treatment for routine transactions (Level A)
c. Inventories
o. Changes in accounting policies and estimates, and errors

1.3.2 Prepares routine financial statement note disclosure (Level B)

Valeant Pharmaceuticals International Inc. (www.valeant.com) is a Canadian company headquartered in Laval, Quebec. The company is listed on the Toronto and New York stock exchanges (ticker VRX in both locations). For the fiscal year ended December 31, 2016, the company reported on its income statement $9.54 billion in product sales and $2.57 billion in cost of goods sold. The balance sheet showed $1,061 million in inventories, which is net of an allowance for obsolescence. This total is comprised of the following components, as disclosed in the financial statement notes.

Inventories	(in millions of USD)[1]
Finished goods	$ 680
Raw materials	256
Work in process	125
	$1,061

How does a company like Valeant determine the values to report for inventories and cost of sales? What kinds of costs are included in raw materials, work in process, and finished goods? What is the "allowance for obsolescence"? How do inventory costs relate to cost of sales?

[1.] A significant number of Canadian companies use the US dollar as their reporting currency when they are listed on US exchanges or make most of their sales in US currency.

Source: From Valeant company's 2016 annual report. Copyright 2017 by Valeant Pharmaceuticals International.

CONTENTS

Inventories are assets held for sale. For companies that sell tangible goods, inventories are, of course, critical to the revenue-generating process. Estimates suggest that while the goods-producing sector of the Canadian economy (as in other developed countries) has declined to one-quarter of gross domestic product (and services making up the other three-quarters), tangible products continue to be important and they will always be so. People need food, clothing, shelter, transportation, and so on. Even the virtual world of cyberspace requires computers, software, and networks.

This chapter continues the coverage of inventories from introductory accounting and examines in more depth the three issues that are relevant to any asset:

- *Initial recognition and measurement*—Section B looks at which expenditures enterprises should capitalize. Should a cost go into inventories, or should it be an expense?

- *Derecognition*—Sections C and D look at how much of the costs recognized in inventories should be expensed through the income statement and how much should remain as inventories on the balance sheet.
- *Measurement*—Section E looks at the valuation of inventories that remain on hand on the balance sheet date. At what value should they be reported?

This chapter will also examine the effect of inventory errors and how we should account for them. This discussion, in Section F, illustrates the general rules for accounting errors discussed in Chapter 3 and highlights the sometimes difficult task of determining the effect of accounting errors due to the articulation of inventories (balance sheet) and cost of sales (income statement).

Before delving into these three issues, in Section A we will take a quick look at the practical issue of how enterprises obtain the information necessary to account for their inventories.

A. INFORMATION SYSTEMS FOR INVENTORY CONTROL

L.O. 6-1. Describe the informational differences between perpetual and periodic systems of inventory control.

In practice, there are two general methods for gathering information about inventory costs: perpetual and periodic. The method used will determine the nature and quality of information available to account for inventories and cost of sales.

1. Perpetual system

perpetual inventory system An inventory control system that directly keeps track of additions to and withdrawals from inventory.

A **perpetual inventory system** is one that directly keeps track of additions to and withdrawals from inventory. With such a system, an enterprise can determine the inventory quantity on hand and cost of goods sold (COGS) from the accounting records at any point in time. With advancing technology and decreasing data management costs, this method continues to increase in popularity because the system produces more information for management of inventory levels on a timely basis. Note that companies still need to conduct an inventory count even if they use the perpetual method because the perpetual records may not correctly represent actual inventory quantities.

2. Periodic system

periodic inventory system An inventory control system that relies on periodic inventory counts to infer the amounts withdrawn from inventory.

The **periodic inventory system**, in contrast, does not keep continual track of inventories and COGS. On the financial statement date, the enterprise conducts an inventory count to determine the ending inventory quantity and applies product costs to these quantities to determine the cost of ending inventory. Combined with the value of beginning inventory (i.e., ending inventory from the prior period) and the amount purchased in the period, the accountant then calculates COGS.

3. Comparison and illustration

To compare and illustrate the two inventory systems, assume the following facts for Vanderhoof Limited:

- Inventory at the beginning of the year: $200,000
- Inventory purchases: $700,000
- The year-end inventory count shows $300,000 in inventory

In addition to the above facts, *if Vanderhoof uses the perpetual system,* that system indicates $500,000 of goods sold during the year. The inventory T-accounts for the two systems would be as follows:

Exhibit 6-1	T-accounts for Vanderhoof's inventory under two inventory control systems ($000's)

Perpetual inventory system				Periodic inventory system			
Beg. bal.	200			Beg. bal.	200		
Purchases	700			Purchases	700		
		500	COGS*				
		100	COGS†			600	COGS†
End. bal.	300			End. bal.	300		

*Determined from perpetual records.

†Determined at year-end after inventory count. This is the "plug" figure that balances the inventory account.

Under both systems, the balance sheet shows $300,000 for inventory while the income statement shows $600,000 for COGS. Thus, the use of a perpetual or periodic system does not affect the amounts ultimately reported in the financial statements.

The difference between the two systems is that the perpetual system has the ability to identify both the expected and the actual amounts of COGS, whereas the periodic system can only identify the actual amount. If Vanderhoof uses the perpetual system, it would expect COGS of $500,000, while the amount determined after the inventory count is $600,000. As a result, the company is able to identify $100,000 in "shrinkage"—inventory losses from theft or breakage. This information allows Vanderhoof's management to decide whether it would be worthwhile to put in place additional inventory management practices, for example. In contrast, the periodic system is able to identify only a single sum of $600,000 for COGS, so it is not possible to determine how much is from actual goods sold versus the amount from shrinkage.

To complete this example, Exhibit 6-2 shows the journal entries for the purchase and sale of inventory in the two systems. (Journal entries for revenue recognition would also be recorded but are not shown below.)

Exhibit 6-2	Journal entries to account for Vanderhoof's inventory transactions ($000's)

	Perpetual system			Periodic system	
Purchase	Dr. Inventory	700		Dr. Purchases	700
	Cr. Cash, accounts payable		700	Cr. Cash, accounts payable	700
During year	Dr. Cost of goods sold	500		Not applicable	
	Cr. Inventory		500		
After inventory count	Dr. Cost of goods sold	100		Dr. Cost of goods sold	600
	Cr. Inventory		100	Dr. Inventory	100
				Cr. Purchases	700

The journal entries under the perpetual system are intuitive and require no further explanation. The periodic system, however, uses an account called "purchases," which is a temporary account that is closed at the end of each year. Purchases go into this account rather than directly into the inventory account so that the company can distinguish changes in inventory arising from purchases rather than adjustments to the inventory balance resulting from the inventory count (or other reasons such as writedowns—see Section E below).

In summary, in comparison to the periodic system, a perpetual inventory system provides more information that allows an enterprise to better manage its inventories. The two systems also result in different bookkeeping entries, although the final amounts reported in the financial statements are the same. Whether an enterprise uses a periodic or perpetual system also affects the implementation of different cost flow assumptions; we defer this discussion until Section D.

Having considered the bookkeeping, we now turn our attention to issues that require some professional judgment.

 CHECKPOINT **CP6-1**

Explain why a periodic inventory system is unable to identify the amount of inventory shrinkage separately from the cost of goods actually sold.

B. INITIAL RECOGNITION AND MEASUREMENT

L.O. 6-2. Analyze costing information to determine the types and amounts of costs that can be included in the cost of inventories.

Whenever an asset is to be recorded, the first question that naturally arises is which costs qualify to be included. IAS 2 lays out the general criterion as follows:

¶10.   The cost of inventories shall comprise all costs of purchase, costs of conversion, and other costs incurred in bringing the inventories to their present location and condition.[2]

As later chapters will show, most assets will use criteria similar to this one for inventories. Enterprises should include costs incurred to obtain the inventory (or other asset) and to bring it to the desired location. Purchased and manufactured goods are quite different from each other, so we separately discuss them below.

1. Purchased goods

For goods purchased for resale, inventory cost includes the purchase price, any taxes that are not recoverable from the government,[3] shipping and handling costs, and any other costs incurred up to the point where the product is at the desired location for sale. Subsequent costs, such as for retail space and sales staff, cannot be included in inventory.

Transportation times for goods, especially in a globalized economy, can be substantial. Therefore, it is important to determine whether goods in transit from a supplier or to a customer should be included in inventory. For this purpose, it is important to understand the shipping term **free on board** (**F.O.B.**), which indicates the point at which the buyer takes legal possession of the goods. F.O.B. origin (or shipping point) means that the buyer takes possession as soon as the goods leave the supplier's premises. In contrast, F.O.B. destination means that the buyer takes possession when the goods reach the buyer's premises.[4] At the year-end, an enterprise should include in inventories not only goods that are on its premises, but also inbound goods in transit that are F.O.B. origin and outbound goods in transit that are F.O.B. destination.

Most businesses that resell goods do so by first purchasing their products. As discussed in Chapter 4 in relation to revenue recognition, in some instances companies

free on board (F.O.B.)   The point at which the buyer takes legal possession of the goods.

[2.] Copyright © 2010 IFRS Foundation. All rights reserved. No permission granted to reproduce or distribute.

[3.] For taxable products, enterprises can recover the goods and services tax (GST) or harmonized sales tax (HST) that they pay as "input tax credits." Goods purchased for resale are usually also exempt from provincial sales taxes. Other taxes that are not recoverable would be included in inventory cost.

[4.] The uses of F.O.B. can be quite technical and differ internationally. For instance, F.O.B. can be somewhere in between origination and destination, such as at a port of entry into a country.

will work on a consignment basis, in which they sell products on behalf of the products' owners (and take a commission in the process). In such arrangements, the company that is put in trust to sell the goods (the consignee) is merely acting as an intermediary between the owner of the goods (the consignor) and the ultimate buyer. Therefore, the risks and rewards of ownership do not transfer from the consignor to the consignee, and the latter should not include consigned goods in its inventories.

2. Manufactured goods

For goods that an enterprise manufactures, inventory costing is somewhat more complicated. The production process, by definition, involves more than simply purchases of raw materials, which are accounted for as just described for purchased goods. Production involves the conversion of raw materials to finished goods using labour, machines, and other resources. All costs incurred in the acquisition of raw materials and in the conversion process are **product costs**. Product costs include materials, production labour including factory supervision, variable overhead such as electricity, and fixed overhead such as heating costs. In contrast, **period costs** are not closely related to production. Examples include marketing, administration, accounting, and finance. We expense period costs in the period incurred.

product costs   Costs that should be capitalized in inventory because they are incurred as part of the production process.

period costs   Costs that should not be capitalized in inventory because they are not closely related to the production process.

While it is straightforward to identify materials and labour costs—and even variable overhead costs—as product costs, the same is not true for fixed overhead. There are two views for determining whether an expenditure on *fixed* overhead (e.g., factory rent or depreciation) is a product or a period cost.

- *Variable costing*—considers fixed manufacturing overhead to be a period cost because such costs do not vary according to production level (by definition of fixed cost).
- *Absorption costing*—considers fixed overhead as a product cost because production cannot take place without these costs.

The table in Exhibit 6-3 summarizes the treatment of various types of costs under these two methods. Product costs are capitalized in inventory; period costs are expensed when incurred.

Exhibit 6-3	Product costs versus period costs under variable and absorption costing	
Type of cost	**Variable costing**	**Absorption costing**
Materials	Product	Product
Labour	Product	Product
Variable overhead	Product	Product
Fixed overhead	Period	Product
Selling, general, and administrative expenses	Period	Period

While managerial accounting and internal decision-making purposes favour the variable costing method, IFRS and ASPE require the use of absorption costing for external financial reporting (see IAS 2 paragraph 10 presented above). Absorption costing is consistent with the Conceptual Framework: enterprises incur fixed overhead costs to produce goods that generate revenue in the future, so such costs meet the definition of an asset. In addition, the later expensing of these costs through COGS when the products are sold matches costs to the revenues generated, which is more timely, not in the sense of being early, but in the sense of logical consistency— recognizing expenses in the same period as the related revenue makes logical sense. Recognizing COGS in this manner is likely to make predictions about the future more accurate. For example, if an enterprise recognizes revenue in one period but recognizes the related expenses in the following period, then the enterprise would

THRESHOLD CONCEPT
TIMING OF RECOGNITION

appear to be more profitable than is otherwise the case, and financial statement readers are likely to overpredict future cash flows.

CHECKPOINT CP6-2

Describe the general principle for the measurement of assets such as inventory upon initial recognition.

3. Manufactured goods with abnormal production levels

While consistent with the Conceptual Framework, the capitalization of fixed overhead creates issues when production levels significantly deviate from normal production levels. We look first at the case when production is above normal, then at the case when production is below normal.

a. Fixed overhead capitalization when production is above normal

Consider the following two scenarios for Winfield Weavers using absorption costing. In Scenario A, the company produces at a normal level, just enough units to meet sales demand of 200 units. In Scenario B, the company produces 100 more units than are sold. Variable costs are $40 per unit and sale price is $100 per unit. Fixed overhead totals $3,000 for the year.

Exhibit 6-4	Results of absorption costing for Winfield Weavers at two production levels	
	Scenario A: Normal production level	Scenario B: Abnormally high production level
Units of beginning inventory	0	0
Units produced	200	300
Units sold	200	200
Units in ending inventory	0	100
Fixed overhead	$ 3,000	$ 3,000
Units produced	÷ 200	÷ 300
Fixed overhead per unit	15	10
Variable cost per unit	40	40
Total cost per unit	$ 55	$ 50
Ending inventory (units in inventory × total cost/unit)	$ 0	$ 5,000
Revenue	$20,000	$20,000
Cost of goods sold	(11,000)	(10,000)
Gross margin	$ 9,000	$10,000
Gross margin %	45%	50%

From this example, it should be clear that an enterprise using absorption costing can lower COGS by increasing production volume. If a manager needed a little extra income to, say, meet an earnings target, then he or she could raise production at the end of the year so that ending inventories absorbed more fixed overhead.

While absorption costing is the treatment required for financial reporting, an auditor should be alert to such manipulations, as this behaviour could be indicative of other earnings management activities as well. An analyst or investor should be careful when interpreting gross margin figures and take into consideration the impact of possible

THRESHOLD CONCEPT
QUALITY OF EARNINGS

changes in inventory levels. In particular, it is important to distinguish increasing gross margins that are due to improved cost management from the portion due to changes in production levels. In this example, the gross margin increased significantly, from 45% to 50%.

b. Fixed overhead capitalization when production levels are below normal

As just discussed, increases in production volume will result in decreases in the fixed cost per unit. However, unusually low production volumes will result in unusually high fixed costs per unit being capitalized into inventory, and this outcome potentially overstates the value of inventory. Consequently, enterprises should allocate fixed overhead based on the normal production level expected over several periods.[5] If the actual production volume is significantly below normal, some fixed overhead would remain unallocated. Such unallocated overhead should be expensed, as indicated in IAS 2:

> ¶13   . . . The amount of fixed overhead allocated to each unit of production is not increased as a consequence of low production or idle plant. Unallocated overheads are recognized as an expense in the period in which they are incurred.[6]

The logic behind this recommendation should be clear from considering the extreme but reasonable case of a plant that is idle due to, for example, a strike. In this situation, there would be no units of production to absorb the fixed overhead incurred. The only reasonable way to account for the unallocated overhead is to expense it.

To illustrate this issue, consider Winfield Weavers, presented in Exhibit 6-4. As before, assume that normal production volume is 200 units. With fixed overhead at $3,000, the standard fixed overhead per unit is $15/unit ($3,000 ÷ 200 units). If actual production is only 120 units, then only $1,800 (120 units × $15/unit) of fixed overhead would be capitalized to inventories, so $1,200 ($3,000 − $1,800) remains unallocated. Winfield Weavers would need to expense this $1,200 of unallocated overhead.

 CHECKPOINT CP6-3

Why do we need to reduce the per-unit fixed overhead rate when the production level is above normal? For the opposite scenario, why do we not increase the per-unit fixed overhead rate when the production level is significantly below normal?

C. SUBSEQUENT MEASUREMENT AND DERECOGNITION: COST ALLOCATION BETWEEN THE BALANCE SHEET AND INCOME STATEMENT

Once an enterprise capitalizes costs into inventories, those costs eventually need to be removed. For a particular reporting period, an enterprise needs to determine how much of these costs should remain on the balance sheet versus be derecognized (i.e., expensed through the income statement).

There are a number of methods to determine these amounts. Due to the articulation of the financial statements (see Chapter 3), all of these methods are governed by

L.O. 6-3. Apply the different methods of allocating costs between inventory and cost of sales.

[5.] Managerial accounting refers to a system of using expected amounts in costing as a "standard costing system."

[6.] Copyright © 2012 IFRS Foundation.

the inventory cost flow equation, which states that all costs that go into the inventory costing system must either (i) be derecognized by being expensed or (ii) remain in ending inventory:

Exhibit 6-5	Inventory cost flow equation

Beginning inventory + Purchases = Cost of goods sold + Ending inventory

$$\underbrace{\text{Beginning inventory + Purchases}}_{\text{Cost of goods available for sale}}$$

In this equation and the following discussion, "purchases" should be interpreted broadly to include goods manufactured by the reporting enterprise. It should also be interpreted to be purchases net of any purchase discounts and returns. We simply use "purchases" for ease of exposition.

We discuss three methods of allocating costs between the income statement and balance sheet: specific identification, application of cost flow assumptions, and the retail inventory method.

1. Specific identification

specific identification A method of assigning costs to inventories and cost of sales based on actual costs of each item.

The most straightforward but also most costly method to implement is **specific identification**. This method is usually applied to high-value items. However, as technology to identify each unit of product becomes ever cheaper, this method is becoming more feasible for a wider range of products.

A significant drawback of this method is that it is prone to earnings management when an enterprise sells items that are indistinguishable from each other. For example, suppose a furniture store buys a number of identical chairs at different times, some at $100 per chair and others at $105 per chair. If the store wanted to report higher income, it would choose to expense the $100 units and show the $105 units in ending inventory. Recognizing this problem, IAS 2 specifies the following:

¶23.   The cost of inventories of items that are not ordinarily interchangeable . . . shall be assigned by using specific identification of their individual costs.

¶25.   The cost of inventories, other than those dealt with in paragraph 23, shall be assigned by using the first-in, first-out (FIFO) or weighted-average cost formula.[7]

Thus, the specific identification method should be used only for items that are distinguishable from each other using information such as serial numbers.

2. Cost flow assumptions

cost of goods available for sale (COGAS) The total of beginning inventories plus purchases (or goods manufactured).

Aside from specific identification, we have conceptually a bundle of costs comprising beginning inventory and purchases (or finished goods produced in the period for manufacturers), which is the left side of the cost flow equation shown in Exhibit 6-5. This bundle of costs is the **cost of goods available for sale (COGAS)**. We need to assign these costs to COGS and ending inventory because what was available for sale must be either "sold" or in inventory. ("Sold" includes shrinkage due to theft, damage, etc.) Now, because this bundle of costs is not split up and identified with specific units,

---

[7.] Copyright © 2012 IFRS Foundation.

we need to choose a systematic method for allocating between COGS and ending inventory. Based on tradition, this choice is called the *cost flow assumption*.

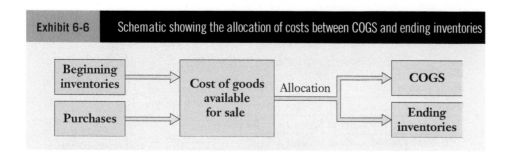

Exhibit 6-6	Schematic showing the allocation of costs between COGS and ending inventories

Several options are possible:

1. Remove the oldest costs first—first-in, first-out (FIFO)
2. Remove the newest costs first—last-in, first-out (LIFO)
3. Do something in between—weighted average

Note that these assumptions are about the *flow of costs*, rather than the flow of goods. This distinction is important. For a grocer, the flow of goods is (one hopes) first-in, first-out, especially for perishable items like milk. However, the store may use a different method for accounting purposes.

In the following discussion of these three methods, assume the following information for Westwold Water Company:

Exhibit 6-7	Information on Westwold Water Company's inventories		
Activity	# units	Cost/unit	Total cost
Beginning inventories	100	$1	$ 100
Purchase #1:	100	1	100
Purchase #2:	100	2	200
Purchase #3:	100	3	300
Purchase #4:	100	4	400
Goods available for sale	500		$1,100
Units sold	(300)	?	?
Ending inventory	200	?	?

An important figure to note is the COGAS of $1,100. This is the amount that must be allocated between COGS and ending inventory using a cost flow assumption. Also assume that the company uses the periodic method of inventory control.[8]

a. First-in, first-out (FIFO)

The **first-in, first-out (FIFO)** method expenses the oldest costs first. This also means that the most recent costs remain on the balance sheet, so that this method is equivalently called last-in-still-here (LISH). The following schematic

first-in, first-out (FIFO)   A cost flow assumption that uses the oldest costs in the computation of cost of sales.

---

8. We will discuss any differences between the results for the periodic and perpetual systems in Section D.

illustrates this method of allocation with corresponding numbers for Westwold Water Company:

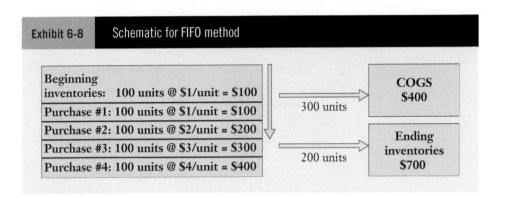

This means that COGS is determined by starting with beginning inventories (shown at the top), then going through purchases until we obtain the required number of units sold. Equivalently, one can determine the ending inventory by starting with the costs from the most recent purchases and working upward until the required number of units in inventory is obtained. For Westwold's $1,100 COGAS, FIFO allocates $400 to COGS and $700 to ending inventory.

b. Last-in, first-out (LIFO)

last-in, first-out (LIFO) A cost flow assumption that uses the most recent costs in the computation of cost of sales.

The **last-in, first-out** (**LIFO**) method expenses the most recent costs first. This also means that the oldest costs remain in inventory. Exhibit 6-9 shows the results of LIFO applied to Westwold Water Company:

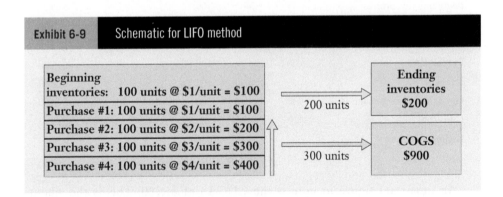

For Westwold's COGAS of $1,100, LIFO allocates $900 to COGS and $200 to ending inventory. When costs are rising, as is the case for Westwold, LIFO shows higher COGS and lower income compared with FIFO.

Currently, *IFRS and ASPE prohibit the use of LIFO*. However, the LIFO method is permitted and used by many companies in the United States. The method was also permitted under *CICA Handbook* rules until the end of 2007.

weighted-average cost A cost flow assumption that uses the weighted-average cost in the computation of cost of sales; weighted average is computed using cost of goods available for sale divided by the number of units available for sale.

c. Weighted-average cost

A third method uses the **weighted-average cost** (WAC) per unit for both COGS and ending inventory. We obtain the WAC per unit in the usual way for obtaining any weighted average, as follows:

Exhibit 6-10	Weighted-average cost formula

$$\text{WAC per unit} = \frac{\text{Beginning inventory} + \text{Purchases}}{\text{Units available for sale}} = \frac{\text{Cost of goods available for sale}}{\text{Units available for sale}}$$

For Westwold, the WAC per unit is computed as follows:

Exhibit 6-11	Weighted-average cost calculation for Westwold Water Company

$$\text{WAC per unit} = \frac{\text{Cost of goods available for sale}}{\text{Units available for sale}} = \frac{\$1,100}{500 \text{ units}} = \frac{\$2.20}{\text{Unit}}$$

As a result, the WAC method allocates $660 to the 300 units sold ($300 \times \$2.20 = \$660$), and $440 to the 200 units remaining in inventory ($200 \times \$2.20 = \$440$). The total of COGS and ending inventory again equals the amount for COGAS ($\$660 + \$440 = \$1,100$).

The table in Exhibit 6-12 shows the amounts Westwold Water Company would report under the three different cost flow assumptions.

Exhibit 6-12	Result of using different cost flow assumptions for Westwold Water Company		
	FIFO	**Weighted average**	**LIFO**
Cost of goods available for sale	$1,100	$1,100	$1,100
Cost of goods sold	400	660	900
Ending inventory	$ 700	$ 440	$ 200

From this example, we can see that FIFO results in the lowest COGS and therefore the highest income. In contrast, LIFO results in the lowest income. This pattern results from the fact that the unit cost increased over time from $1 to $4 per unit. Weighted average produces results that are intermediate between FIFO and LIFO.

d. Comparison of cost flow assumptions

The example of Westwold Water Company demonstrates that amounts reported on financial statements for inventory and COGS depend on the cost flow assumption employed. To evaluate the quality of the information that results, we should consider information conveyed both by the balance sheet and the income statement. In addition, the resilience of the method to earnings management is also important because this affects the representational faithfulness of the reported information. Exhibit 6-13 summarizes these three considerations, as well as the jurisdictions/purposes for which the cost flow assumption may be used.

The balance sheet is most relevant for valuation if the amount reported for an asset approximates current value. Since FIFO leaves the cost of the most recent purchases in ending inventory, it provides high-quality information about the value of inventory. In contrast, LIFO values for ending inventory are low quality because they consist of the oldest costs, potentially years or decades old, which have little resemblance to current value.

The income statement is most relevant for evaluating performance if the basis for recognizing expenses matches the basis for revenue recognition. Sales revenue will generally reflect market conditions in the reporting period, so inventory costs that also come from the reporting period are the most relevant. The FIFO method includes

THRESHOLD CONCEPT
CONCEPTUAL FRAMEWORK

THRESHOLD CONCEPT
CONCEPTUAL FRAMEWORK

Exhibit 6-13	Comparison of cost flow assumptions		
	FIFO	**Weighted average**	**LIFO**
Quality of balance sheet for valuation	High	Medium	Very low
Quality of income statement expense (matching)	Low	Medium	High
Ease of income manipulation	Difficult	Difficult	Easy
Permitted for Canadian financial reporting?	Yes	Yes	No
Permitted for Canadian tax reporting?	Yes	Yes	No
Permitted for US financial reporting?	Yes	Yes	Yes
Permitted for US tax reporting?	Yes	Yes	Yes

costs from beginning inventory in the calculation of COGS, so some of these costs are outdated. In contrast, LIFO COGS consists of costs from the most recent purchases. Therefore, LIFO provides better matching of COGS with revenue.

There is, however, an important caveat: the conclusion that the LIFO method provides the most relevant information in the income statement depends on there being no decrease in inventory level. If the quantity sold exceeds purchases, then the LIFO method will withdraw costs from older inventory layers (purchases from prior years), which are outdated. This occurrence is called "LIFO dipping."

THRESHOLD CONCEPT
QUALITY OF EARNINGS

The fact that the LIFO method will use old cost layers when inventory levels decrease creates an opportunity for management to manipulate earnings. This can be accomplished by lowering purchases (or production in the case of a manufacturer) near year-end such that purchases fall below quantities sold for the year. This type of earnings management is not possible with FIFO or weighted average.

As noted earlier, IFRS and ASPE both prohibit the use of the LIFO method. In addition, Canadian companies cannot use LIFO for income tax reporting. In contrast, the United States allows LIFO for financial reporting and income taxes. This application of LIFO in the United States will be discussed further in the Appendix to this chapter.

3. Retail inventory method

retail inventory method A method of estimating the cost of ending inventory by applying an average sales margin to the retail price of products.

As the name suggests, the **retail inventory method** is a popular method for retailers. Many retail stores have a wide variety of products each at low value (e.g., supermarkets, department stores). Because the retail price is marked on the product or on product displays, it is relatively easy to identify the products' selling prices, and more laborious to obtain their costs. The retail inventory method relies on an average profit margin to estimate the cost of each product by discounting the retail price by that average profit margin. Multiplying these costs by quantities obtained from an inventory count produces the amount for ending inventory. Management can then determine cost of sales using the inventory cost flow equation (Exhibit 6-5).

For example, suppose an enterprise has an average markup of 25%. An average product with a cost of $80 would retail for $100 ($80 × 1.25). The average margin would be 20% ($20 profit on $100 of revenue) and the COGS percentage would be 80%. We then take this average margin and apply it to specific products. If a particular product has a retail price of $40, then under the retail inventory method that product would be assigned a cost of $32 ($40 × 80%).

Clearly, the validity of the retail inventory method depends on the accuracy of the average profit margin. If an enterprise has significantly different margins on different categories of products (e.g., clothing versus kitchen appliances), then these different categories would need to be separately tabulated and a different margin applied to each. Furthermore, discounts from normal selling prices would affect the profit margin, so discounted products need to be segregated from regular, non-discounted products.

RETAIL PRICING TERMINOLOGY

As you are probably aware from experience, retailers adjust their prices quite frequently by having sales events in response to competitive pressures. A number of terms are used for the different price changes, and they are best understood by seeing them in a diagram with a specific example. Suppose a product costing $100 has a normal selling price of $150 based on the standard markup of 50% above cost. After setting this regular price, the retailer adjusted the price to $160, $130, $80, and $110.

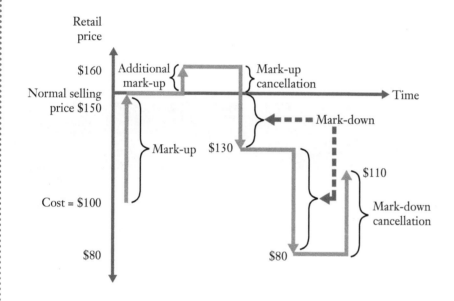

A key reference point is the normal selling price. This point separates upward price adjustments into regular markup and additional markup. For downward price adjustments, this point separates markup cancellations from markdowns. In this example, we have:

— a markup of $50 (from $100 cost up to $150);
— an additional markup of $10 (from $150 to $160);
— a price reduction of $30 (from $160 to $130), of which $10 is a markup cancellation and $20 is a markdown;
— a markdown of $50 (from $130 to $80); and
— a markdown cancellation of $30 for the increase from $80 to $110.

While these terms are important in the retail sector, for accounting purposes the essential amount is the estimated gross margin on the products on the financial statement reporting date, regardless of what combination of markups and markdowns is involved.

For example, suppose specialty clothing retailer Keats Kotton has two product lines: standard and deluxe. Each product line has between 40 and 50 specific products. The company normally marks up its products by 100% on standard products and 150% on deluxe products. In the week prior to the year-end, Keats discounted the prices on 10 of the products in the standard line by offering

40% off the regular price. Summary information on the company's inventory is as follows:

Exhibit 6-14	Inventory information for Keats Kotton
Product category	**Amount**
Ending inventory (at retail price)	
Deluxe products	$ 24,500
Standard products—undiscounted	15,800
Standard products—discounted	5,700
Beginning inventory (at cost, from prior year financial statements)	27,600
Purchases (at cost, from purchase records)	524,300

To apply the retail inventory method, first estimate the margins on each product line:

Exhibit 6-15	Computing Keats Kotton's margins for each product line				
Product category	**Markup (% on cost)**	**Markdown (% of normal price)**	**Retail price per dollar of cost**	**Cost as % of retail price†**	**Profit margin as % of retail price**
Deluxe	150%	—	$2.50	40.00%	60.00%
Standard—undiscounted	100	—	2.00	50.00	50.00
Standard—discounted	100	40%	1.20*	83.33	16.67

*A product costing $1 would be marked up 100% to $2, then discounted by 40% down to $1.20.

†Average cost % = $1 / Price × 100%

After obtaining these estimated costs and margins, we can apply the retail inventory method to estimate the ending inventory cost for Keats Kotton:

Exhibit 6-16	Estimating Keats Kotton's ending inventories using the retail inventory method		
Product category	**Cost as % of retail price**	**Retail value of ending inventory**	**Estimated cost (cost % × retail value)**
Deluxe	40.00%	$24,500	$ 9,800
Standard—undiscounted	50.00	15,800	7,900
Standard—discounted	83.33	5,700	4,750
Total ending inventory			$22,450

The ending inventory is thus $22,450. COGS can then be computed using the inventory cost flow equation (Exhibit 6-5):

Exhibit 6-17	Computation of Keats Kotton's cost of goods sold
Beginning inventory (from prior year financial statements)	$ 27,600
+ Purchases (from purchase records)	524,300
− Ending inventory (estimated using retail inventory method)	(22,450)
Cost of goods sold	$529,450

Related to the retail inventory method is the gross margin method. The retail inventory method just discussed (i) estimates ending inventory cost using retail prices and an average gross margin, then (ii) computes an estimate of COGS using the inventory cost flow equation. The **gross margin method** reverses this process by (i) estimating COGS by applying an average gross margin to the amount of sales recorded for the period, then (ii) computing an estimated ending inventory balance by using the inventory cost flow equation. This method is sometimes used for interim reporting when it is not cost-effective to conduct inventory counts in interim periods. However, this method relies entirely on the estimated gross margin—there is no direct information on actual COGS or ending inventories, so this method is not normally accepted for annual financial statements whereas the retail inventory method is accepted (IAS 2 paragraphs 21–22).

> **gross margin method** A method for estimating cost of goods sold by applying an average gross margin to the amount of sales recorded in a period.

 CHECKPOINT **CP6-4**

Explain why standards permit several different methods for determining inventory cost flows (specific identification, FIFO, weighted-average cost, retail inventory method).

D. SUBSEQUENT MEASUREMENT: INTERACTION OF COST FLOW ASSUMPTIONS AND INFORMATION SYSTEMS FOR INVENTORY CONTROL

The last section discussed the different assumptions that an enterprise can make regarding the flow of inventory costs (FIFO or weighted-average for Canadian firms). The implementation of these cost flow assumptions can potentially differ depending on whether the enterprise uses a periodic or perpetual system for inventory control, as discussed in Section A. As the following will demonstrate, whether a periodic or perpetual system is used *does not* affect the amount under the FIFO method, but *does* affect the amounts resulting from the weighted-average method. Due to that difference, the perpetual weighted-average cost method is also called the *moving-average method* to distinguish it from the periodic weighted-average method.

To illustrate the potential differences, consider Vallican Polypropylene (polypropylene is a chemical used in plastics):

- Beginning inventory is 30,000 tonnes at $1,000/tonne, which is $30,000,000 in total.
- The polypropylene production process is continuous except for interruptions for equipment maintenance and servicing once at the end of each month. Production for the first three months of the year is as follows:

Month	Quantity (tonnes)	Cost per tonne	Total cost
January	10,000	$1,100	$11,000,000
February	8,000	1,250	10,000,000
March	11,000	1,300	14,300,000
Total			$35,300,000

- On February 20, Vallican shipped 12,000 tonnes of product to a customer.
- On March 11, Vallican shipped 20,000 tonnes to another customer.

For the quarterly financial statements at the end of March, Vallican would compute the following inventory and COGS figures under the periodic or perpetual systems if it used the weighted-average cost flow assumption:

Exhibit 6-18	Vallican's inventory using the weighted-average cost method under periodic or perpetual systems			
Periodic weighted-average method	**Quantity (tonnes)**	**Total cost**		**Weighted-average cost per tonne**
Beginning inventory	30,000	$ 30,000,000		$1,000.00
Production, Jan.–Mar.	+29,000	+35,300,000		
Available for sale	59,000	65,300,000	→	1,106.78
Shipments out, Jan.–Mar.	−32,000	−35,416,949	←	1,106.78
Balance, March 31	27,000	$29,883,051	→	1,106.78
Perpetual moving-average method	**Quantity (tonnes)**	**Total cost**		**Moving-average cost per tonne**
Beginning inventory	30,000	$ 30,000,000		$1,000.00
January production	+10,000	+11,000,000		
Balance, January 31	40,000	41,000,000	→	1,025.00
February 20 shipment out	−12,000	−12,300,000	←	1,025.00
February production	+ 8,000	+10,000,000		
Balance, February 28	36,000	38,700,000	→	1,075.00
March 11 shipment out	−20,000	−21,500,000	←	1,075.00
March production	+11,000	+14,300,000		
Balance, March 31	27,000	$31,500,000	→	1,166.67
COGS for first quarter:				
February 20 shipment		$ 12,300,000		
March 11 shipment		21,500,000		
Total for first quarter		$33,800,000		

Note: The arrows (→, ←) indicate the direction of the calculation.

As you can see from Exhibit 6-18, the results can differ materially depending on whether Vallican uses the periodic or the perpetual system. The periodic method results in COGS of $35.4 million and an inventory balance of $29.9 million. In comparison, the perpetual method results in a lower COGS of $33.8 million and a correspondingly higher inventory balance of $31.5 million. However, note that this pattern cannot be generalized—the amounts can be either higher or lower, depending on whether costs are increasing or decreasing.

Moving on to the FIFO method, Exhibit 6-19 shows the results using the periodic and perpetual systems. This example demonstrates the point noted above: the result using the FIFO method is the same whether the periodic or perpetual system is used. Both systems produce inventory balances of $33.1 million and COGS of $32.2 million.

Exhibit 6-19	Vallican's inventory using the FIFO method under periodic or perpetual systems		
Periodic FIFO method	**Quantity (tonnes)**	**Cost per tonne**	**Total cost**
Beginning inventory	30,000	$1,000	$30,000,000
Production, January	10,000	1,100	11,000,000
Production, February	8,000	1,250	10,000,000
Production, March	11,000	1,300	14,300,000

(*Continued*)

| Exhibit 6-19 | Continued | | |

Periodic FIFO method	Quantity (tonnes)	Cost per tonne	Total cost
Cost of goods available for sale	59,000		65,300,000
Shipments out*	−30,000	1,000	−30,000,000
Shipments out†	− 2,000	1,100	− 2,200,000
Inventory balance, March 31	27,000		$33,100,000

Perpetual FIFO method	Quantity (tonnes)	Cost per tonne	Total cost
Beginning inventory	30,000	$1,000	$30,000,000
Production, January	10,000	1,100	11,000,000
Shipment out, Feb. 20*	−12,000	1,000	−12,000,000
Production, February	8,000	1,250	10,000,000
Shipment out, Mar. 11*	−18,000	1,000	−18,000,000
Shipment out, Mar. 11†	− 2,000	1,100	− 2,200,000
Production, March	11,000	1,300	14,300,000
Inventory balance, March 31	27,000		$33,100,000

*Cost taken from beginning inventory as per FIFO method.
†Cost taken from January production as per FIFO method.

CHECKPOINT **CP6-5**

Why is the FIFO cost flow assumption not affected by whether an enterprise uses a periodic or perpetual inventory system? Why is the weighted-average cost method affected?

E. SUBSEQUENT MEASUREMENT: AVOIDING OVERVALUATION OF INVENTORIES

Representational faithfulness requires assets not to be overvalued on the balance sheet. This principle of course applies to inventories, so accounting standards require inventories to be reported at the lower of cost and market (LOCM). That is, if the prevailing market price of inventory declines below cost, then that lower value should be used, and a loss is recorded. However, if the market price exceeds cost, no upward adjustment is made. The journal entry for an inventory writedown of $100 would be as follows:

L.O. 6-4. Evaluate whether and by how much inventories should be written down.

THRESHOLD CONCEPT
CONCEPTUAL FRAMEWORK

Dr. Loss from decline in inventory value (COGS)	100	
Cr. Inventory		100

In practice, companies report this loss from an inventory writedown as part of COGS.

1. Meaning of "market"

Conceptually, the term *market* in "lower of cost and market" has several potential interpretations.

- *Input market view:* market value is the **replacement cost** of inventory—how much it would cost to repurchase or re-manufacture the inventory.
- *Output market view:* market value is the **net realizable value**—how much can be obtained from sale in the ordinary course of business, net of any selling costs.

Currently, IFRS and ASPE emphasize the latter view (net realizable value). In particular, raw materials used in a production process are evaluated for writedown *only if* the finished

replacement cost The amount required to be expended to replace an item (of inventory).

net realizable value The value expected from the sale of an asset, net of any costs of disposal.

product requires a writedown. If the end product is expected to sell for more than cost, then the inputs would not be written down, even if the cost of inputs has decreased.

In instances when the finished product needs to be written down, the enterprise should also evaluate the raw materials (and work in process) for impairment. In such instances, the enterprise can use the replacement costs of raw materials for purposes of the LOCM evaluation because replacement costs are usually more readily and reliably available for raw materials. The alternative is to determine the net realizable value of raw materials, which requires estimating all of the costs and quantities necessary to convert the raw materials to the end product, as well as the net realizable value of the end product.

For example, suppose Yahk Petroleum is a refinery that buys crude oil and produces gasoline. The company has crude in inventory that has a purchase cost of $150 per barrel. To refine this crude into a barrel of gasoline, Yahk incurs $100 of processing costs. At year-end, the prices of crude and gasoline fell to $50 and $200, respectively. Based on these facts, Yahk Petroleum would do the following:

- The ending inventory of gasoline has a cost of $250 per barrel ($150 + $100), whereas the net realizable value is only $200, so each barrel of gasoline needs to be marked down by $50.
- Since the finished goods required an LOCM adjustment, the raw materials also need to be assessed for a potential writedown. The carrying value of crude oil is $150, but the replacement cost is only $50 per barrel, so Yahk will need to write down each barrel of crude held in inventory by $100.

If the market value of inventory recovers in a subsequent period, an enterprise can reverse some or all of the writedown in the prior period(s) and record a gain. However, this reversal is rare because it can apply only to the same inventory on hand both at the time of the writedown and the reversal. For most enterprises, the turnover in inventory is such that items will not be on hand long enough for reversal to occur.

2. Unit of evaluation

In order to evaluate inventories for impairment, it is necessary to define the size of the unit or group for that evaluation. For instance, if there are two products in inventory, can the LOCM evaluation be conducted for both products together such that higher valuations of one product offset lower valuation of the other? Likewise, can raw materials, work in process, and finished goods be evaluated together? IFRS resolves this issue as follows in IAS 2:

> ¶29.   Inventories are usually written down to net realizable value item by item. In some circumstances, however, it may be appropriate to group similar or related items. This may be the case with items of inventory relating to the same product line that have similar purposes or end uses, are produced and marketed in the same geographic area, and cannot be practicably evaluated separately from other items in that product line. It is not appropriate to write inventories down on the basis of a classification of inventory, for example, finished goods, or all the inventories in a particular operating segment.[9]

Thus, inventories should be evaluated for writedowns at the most detailed level possible. For instance, a bicycle manufacturer that has five products would evaluate each product separately. On the other hand, all of the parts (i.e., raw materials) that go into assembling a particular bicycle would be considered together.

CHECKPOINT CP6-6

In applying lower of cost and market, which interpretation of "market" do IFRS and ASPE emphasize? When is replacement cost relevant?

[9.] Copyright © 2012 IFRS Foundation.

F. ACCOUNTING FOR INVENTORY ERRORS

The inventory account is one where the effects of mistakes are sometimes not clearly evident, at least not initially. It is worth noting that the inventory account is involved twice in the calculation of COGS in a periodic inventory system (i.e., the beginning balance and the ending balance; see the inventory cost flow equation, Exhibit 6-5). This means one inventory error will usually affect two periods. Furthermore, misstatements of transactions involving inventories are often accompanied by errors in related accounts such as purchases and accounts payable.

INVENTORY ERROR EXAMPLE 1 (INVENTORY INCLUDED, PURCHASES OMITTED): Suppose Zeballos Inc. omits to process an invoice for $5,000 for a purchase made near the year-end of December 31, 2018, while the inventory involved was properly included in the inventory count.

To see the effects, we repeat the inventory cost flow equation here for ease of reference:

$$\text{Beginning inventory} + \text{Purchases} = \text{Cost of sales} + \text{Ending inventory}$$

We know that ending inventory is correctly stated, and we should assume that beginning inventory is also correctly stated (unless there is information to indicate otherwise). Therefore, a $5,000 omission to purchases results in a $5,000 understatement in cost of sales. We can see this by rewriting the inventory cost flow equation as follows:

$$\text{Cost of sales} = \text{Beginning inventory} + \text{Purchases} - \text{Ending inventory}$$

Now, while the purchases were omitted in one fiscal period, they are likely to be included in the following period because the vendor will ensure that Zeballos is aware of the invoice. Therefore, the omission in 2018 will result in an overstatement in purchases in 2019 by the same amount.

To further illustrate the effects of inventory errors, consider three additional examples involving Zeballos Inc. For purposes of illustration, each error is independent of the others.

INVENTORY ERROR EXAMPLE 2 (INVENTORY OMITTED, PURCHASES INCLUDED): Zeballos omits to include $5,000 of inbound inventories that were shipped F.O.B. shipping point; on December 31, 2018, the goods were in transit. However, the company recorded the invoice in the accounts payable and purchases for December 31, 2018.

The direct effect of omitting the inbound inventories is to understate ending inventories. The indirect but equally important effect is on cost of sales. The inventory cost flow equation shows that an understatement of ending inventories by $5,000 increases COGS by that amount.

INVENTORY ERROR EXAMPLE 3 (INVENTORY OMITTED, PURCHASES OMITTED): Zeballos omits to include $5,000 of inbound inventories. The company also does not include the related invoice for these inventories until the following fiscal year.

Example 1 omitted purchases, while example 2 omitted goods from the inventory count. This example has both omissions. The direct effects on inventory and accounts payable should be clear. The indirect effects are twofold, as can be seen by applying the inventory cost flow equation: the understated ending inventory overstates COGS by $5,000, while the understated purchases understate COGS by $5,000. The net effect on COGS is zero. This should make sense in terms of the balance sheet equation as well. Assets (inventories) and liabilities (accounts payable) are both understated by the same amount while the retained earnings balance is correct because income is correctly stated.

L.O. 6-5. Synthesize the relationship between the income statement and balance sheet through analysis of inventory errors.

THRESHOLD CONCEPT
ARTICULATION

INVENTORY ERROR EXAMPLE 4 (INCORRECT COSTING): Zeballos omits to include $5,000 of shipping costs on goods it purchased. Instead, the amount was charged to "miscellaneous expenses." By the year-end, 80% of the affected goods have been sold.

The incorrect accounting for an inventory cost as an expense overstates the expense by $5,000. At the same time, this error understates purchases by $5,000. Since by year-end only 20% of the goods remains on hand, ending inventories are understated by 20% × $5,000 = $1,000. Applying the inventory cost flow equation, the $5,000 of understated purchases and the $1,000 understated ending inventory balance result in a net $4,000 understatement in COGS.

In addition to the effects noted above, the errors will have follow-through effects in the following year. Exhibit 6-20 summarizes the effects of the four errors over the two years.

As the table shows, the balance sheet amounts are all correct by the end of the two years. The errors affect the balance sheet amounts in the year of the error, as well as the allocation of income between the two years, but the cumulative effect after two years is zero.

Exhibit 6-20	Summary of effect of inventory errors on inventories and cost of goods sold (COGS)			
	Example 1	Example 2	Example 3	Example 4
Goods included in inventory count	Included	Omitted	Omitted	Included
Purchase recorded during year	Omitted	Included	Omitted	Included
Freight costs included in inventories	Included	Included	Included	Omitted
2018				
Beginning inventories	$ 0	$ 0	$ 0	$ 0
+ Purchases	−5,000	0	−5,000	−5,000
− Ending inventories	0	−5,000	−5,000	−1,000
= Cost of goods sold	−5,000	+5,000	0	−4,000
Miscellaneous expenses				+5,000
Net income	+ $ 5,000	− $ 5,000	$ 0	− $ 1,000
Assets (ending inventories)	$ 0	− $ 5,000	− $ 5,000	− $ 1,000
Liabilities (accounts payable)	−5,000	0	−5,000	0
Equity (retained earnings)	+5,000	−5,000	0	−1,000
2019				
Beginning inventory	0	−5,000	−5,000	−1,000
+ Purchases	+5,000	0	+5,000	0
− Ending inventory	0	0	0	0
= Cost of goods sold	+5,000	−5,000	0	−1,000
Miscellaneous expenses				0
Net income	− $ 5,000	+ $ 5,000	$ 0	− $ 1,000
Assets (ending inventories)	0	0	0	0
Liabilities (accounts payable)	0	0	0	0
Equity (retained earnings)	0	0	0	0

Note: In this table "−" is understated; "+" is overstated; 0 is correctly stated.

 CHECKPOINT **CP6-7**

Which equation is often useful in the analysis of inventory errors? Why?

G. PRESENTATION AND DISCLOSURE

As noted in Chapter 3, the balance sheet must present inventories as a line item separate from other assets. However, there is no corresponding requirement for cost of sales on the income statement, only "operating expenses," which includes cost of sales as an implied requirement in IAS 1.[10] Instead, cost of sales is just a required disclosure (not necessarily presented on the income statement), although most enterprises do choose to report it in the income statement.

If an enterprise has recorded material writedowns of inventory, it should disclose the amount of writedowns and any writedown reversals in the period as well as the amount of inventories that have been written down. If the enterprise has pledged inventories as collateral for loans or other liabilities, it needs to disclose that fact.

As for most other financial statement items, the note disclosures should include the enterprise's accounting policies for inventories. Going back to the vignette at the beginning of this chapter, Valeant's financial statement notes disclose the following accounting policy for inventories:

> Inventories comprise raw materials, work in process, and finished goods, which are valued at the lower of cost or market, on a first-in, first-out basis. Cost for work in process and finished goods inventories includes materials, direct labor, and an allocation of overheads. Market for raw materials is replacement cost, and for work in process and finished goods is net realizable value.
>
> The Company evaluates the carrying value of inventories on a regular basis, taking into account such factors as historical and anticipated future sales compared with quantities on hand, the price the Company expects to obtain for products in their respective markets compared with historical cost and the remaining shelf life of goods on hand.[11]

H. A PRACTICAL ILLUSTRATION: CANADIAN TIRE CORPORATION, LIMITED

Canadian Tire's 2016 financial statements in Appendix D reported $1,711 million in merchandise inventories. Note 3 of these financial statements on page 69 indicates that all inventories are finished goods, and measured at the lower of cost and net realizable value (NRV). NRV is the estimated selling price in the normal course of business less estimated selling expenses. To determine cost, the company uses the weighted-average cost method, where costs include "costs incurred in bringing the merchandise inventories to their present location and condition." In some instances, suppliers pay Canadian Tire certain subsidies, which are in essence negative costs. The company's policy is, "Cash consideration received from vendors is recognized as a reduction to the cost of related inventory, unless the cash consideration received is either a reimbursement of incremental costs incurred by the Company or a payment for assets or services delivered to the vendor." Hence, there is some amount of judgment required in determining which subsidies reduce inventory cost and which reduce expenses.

[10.] As discussed in Chapter 3, the requirement to report operating expenses as a line item is implied rather than explicit because IAS 1 requires line items for revenue, finance costs, share of profit or loss of associates, tax expense, and profit or loss. The remaining amount that can be inferred is operating expenses.

[11.] From Valeant Pharmaceuticals International, Inc. 2016 Annual Report, Copyright © 2017 Valeant.

I. POTENTIAL EARNINGS MANAGEMENT USING INVENTORIES

The discussion in this chapter points to several ways in which management could manipulate earnings using inventories. These actions could involve the use of accounting estimates or real operating decisions.

1. Overproduction

For manufacturing companies, producing more goods than the optimal amount for good inventory management can give a boost to income. As discussed in Section B, production volume that is over the normal level results in lower per-unit costs because there are more units to absorb the fixed costs. The lower per-unit cost then reduces the amount of COGS that flows through income, increasing net income. For users and auditors, it is important to be alert to a buildup of inventory at year-end, which could indicate excessive production for the purpose of earnings management.

2. Including non-production costs in inventory

When an enterprise incurs an expenditure, it either expenses that cost or capitalizes it as an asset such as inventory. Including a cost that would otherwise be expensed would keep that cost from flowing through the income statement temporarily until the inventory itself is sold. For example, including in inventory cost the wages of management staff who are not involved in production would inflate the cost of inventory and reduce wage expense. Auditors need to scrutinize whether costs are production related. Users will have a difficult task of discerning this type of earnings management, but a potential sign is a decrease in the gross margin percentage because including too much cost in inventories would increase COGS.

3. Not identifying impaired or discounted items

Inventories need to be assessed for impairment using the lower of cost and net realizable value of the inventories. Clearly, not recording a writedown on impaired inventory (e.g., obsolete items, damaged items, demo units not for sale) will increase income. For retailers, the application of the retail inventory method relies on an accurate separation of discounted products from those that have normal markups. If management reverses markdowns just prior to year-end, then those items would appear to be regularly priced products and counted as such; the retail inventory method would then impute a higher value to that product. Financial statement readers will be unable to discern this type of earnings management, but auditors should verify that recent sale prices support the value of the items in inventory.

J. SUMMARY

L.O. 6-1. Describe the informational differences between perpetual and periodic systems of inventory control.

- A perpetual inventory system maintains information about purchases and cost of sales (i.e., information about flows) on an ongoing basis, whereas the periodic system calculates these amounts when the enterprise completes an inventory count. Consequently, the perpetual system is more informative and allows for better inventory management.

L.O. 6-2. Analyze costing information to determine the types and amounts of costs that can be included in the cost of inventories.

- For financial reporting purposes, enterprises should include all costs necessary to purchase or to produce the inventory. Manufactured inventories should include product costs but exclude period costs. Product costs include materials, labour, and variable overhead as well as fixed overhead.
- An enterprise should allocate fixed production overhead using actual units produced unless production volume is abnormally low, in which case it should use the normal production level and expense any unallocated overhead.

L.O. 6-3. Apply the different methods of allocating costs between inventory and cost of sales.

- IFRS and ASPE permit specific identification, first-in, first-out (FIFO), and weighted-average cost flow assumptions. Due to the use of historical cost and the articulation of balance sheet and income statement numbers, more current inventory values result in less current cost of sales, and vice versa.
- The retail inventory method estimates ending inventory cost by using retail prices adjusted by the sales margin. Retailers use this method due to the relative ease of determining selling prices of each item.

L.O. 6-4. Evaluate whether and by how much inventories should be written down.

- Enterprises should write down inventories when their net realizable value falls below their cost.
- Enterprises should evaluate whether they should write down raw materials and work in process only if finished products' net realizable value falls below cost.

L.O. 6-5. Synthesize the relationship between the income statement and balance sheet through analysis of inventory errors.

- Inventories and cost of sales are related amounts such that errors in one account also result in errors in the other.

K. ANSWERS TO CHECKPOINT QUESTIONS

CP6-1: The periodic inventory system relies on the beginning and ending inventory balances along with the amount of purchases to determine the total for cost of goods sold (COGS). This amount for COGS cannot be further broken down into components for shrinkage and for goods actually sold because at least one of them needs to be tracked to determine the other, and the periodic system does not produce that information.

CP6-2: The general principle for the measurement of assets upon initial recognition is to include all costs necessary to bring the asset to the location and condition for its sale or use. For inventories, this means all costs necessary to purchase, manufacture, or transport the goods to their point of sale.

CP6-3: When production is above normal, the fixed overhead per unit must be reduced because total overhead remains constant. However, to fully allocate fixed overhead when production falls significantly below normal, the fixed overhead per unit would need to increase above the standard rate, which would lead to anomalously high inventory values. To prevent this undesirable outcome, accounting standards do not allow the per-unit fixed overhead rate to increase when production volume is low. The fixed overhead that is not allocated to the units produced must be expensed.

CP6-4: Accounting standards permit a variety of methods for determining inventory cost flows because of practical limitations, the cost constraint, and quality of information. In some instances, it is feasible to specifically identify the cost of individual items of inventory, but in many other instances it is not feasible, at least not at a reasonable cost. The FIFO, weighted-average cost, and retail inventory methods are different ways to approximate the cost flows (as well as the ending inventory value) by making simplifying assumptions. The retail inventory method is most practical in retail settings with many items of inventory. The standards permit a choice between FIFO and weighted-average cost because each produces information that is more representationally faithful for either inventory or COGS, but not for both.

CP6-5: FIFO assumes that the first costs from beginning inventories and earliest purchases flow out to COGS first. The ordering of cost layers transferred to COGS is the same whether a periodic or perpetual system is used. In contrast, the weighted-average cost is computed once per period under the periodic system, but recomputed each time the enterprise makes a purchase of inventory under the perpetual system.

CP6-6: IFRS and ASPE emphasize net realizable value (output market view) for the lower of cost and market rule. However, replacement cost is still relevant for raw materials because this value is much more easily and more reliably determined in comparison to net realizable value. Note that raw materials would only need to be evaluated for impairment when the finished product is impaired.

CP6-7: In the analysis of inventory errors, it is often useful to use the inventory cost flow equation, which is beginning inventory + purchases = cost of sales + ending inventory. This equation is useful because of the articulation between the balance sheet and income statement— errors in inventory balances can lead to errors in COGS, and vice versa.

L. GLOSSARY

cost of goods available for sale (COGAS): The total of beginning inventories plus purchases (or goods manufactured).

first-in, first-out (FIFO): A cost flow assumption that uses the oldest costs in the computation of cost of sales.

free on board (F.O.B.): The point at which the buyer takes legal possession of the goods.

gross margin method: A method for estimating cost of goods sold by applying an average gross margin to the amount of sales recorded in a period.

last-in, first-out (LIFO): A cost flow assumption that uses the most recent costs in the computation of cost of sales.

LIFO liquidation: The effect on income due to an enterprise using old LIFO cost layers when quantities sold exceed quantities purchased in the year.

LIFO reserve: The difference between the LIFO inventory cost and current replacement cost.

net realizable value: The amount that can be obtained from the sale (of inventory) less selling costs.

period costs: Costs that should not be capitalized in inventory because they are not closely related to the production process.

periodic inventory system: An inventory control system that relies on periodic inventory counts to infer the amounts withdrawn from inventory.

perpetual inventory system: An inventory control system that directly keeps track of additions to and withdrawals from inventory.

product costs: Costs that should be capitalized in inventory because they are incurred as part of the production process.

replacement cost: The amount required to be expended to replace an item (of inventory).

retail inventory method: A method of estimating the cost of ending inventory by applying an average sales margin to the retail price of products.

specific identification: A method of assigning costs to inventories and cost of sales based on actual costs of each item.

weighted-average cost: A cost flow assumption that uses the weighted-average cost in the computation of cost of sales; weighted average is computed using cost of goods available for sale divided by the number of units available for sale.

M. REFERENCES

Authoritative standards:

IFRS	ASPE Section
IAS 2—Inventories	3031—Inventories

N. APPENDIX: USAGE OF LAST-IN, FIRST-OUT (LIFO) IN THE UNITED STATES

In Canada, LIFO is not accepted for tax purposes. To use LIFO for financial reporting purposes, a company would have to maintain two sets of records for inventories. Consequently, few companies in Canada used the LIFO cost flow assumption even when it was permitted prior to 2008. In contrast, over 50% of large US companies use this method for at least some of their inventories, and 30% use LIFO for more than 50% of their inventories. The high use of LIFO in the United States reflects a different tax environment: US companies are permitted to use LIFO for tax reporting if they also use LIFO for financial reporting—this is called the "LIFO conformity rule." Because of the prevalence of LIFO in the United States, it is likely that you will come across this method in the future. Thus, it is worthwhile to spend a little time considering some issues specific to the use of LIFO in the United States.[12]

1. Balance sheet effect and the LIFO reserve

Each year, LIFO retains the oldest costs in the inventory account. Starting from the beginning of the life of an enterprise, the oldest cost layer develops from the purchases in the first year that remain unsold at year-end. Subsequent cost layers are added on each year when quantities purchased exceed quantities sold. This occurs year after year, so that the costs in inventory can be many years and even decades old. For most companies, inventory prices have been rising, so old inventory costs could have very low costs per unit under LIFO. For example, many oil companies that use LIFO have oil inventories valued at less than $10 per barrel, whereas the prevailing prices are several times that amount.

If a US company uses LIFO, it is required to disclose in the financial statement notes the amount of its **LIFO reserve**, the difference between the LIFO inventory cost and current replacement cost.

LIFO reserve The difference between the LIFO inventory cost and current replacement cost.

2. Income effect and LIFO liquidation

As long as the inventory quantity sold does not exceed purchases, and prices are rising, the LIFO reserve will grow. However, in any year that the quantity sold exceeds the quantity purchased, then one or more old (low) cost layers will be expensed. This "dipping" into low cost

---

[12.] The LIFO conformity rule is contained in IRS Regulation, Subchapter A, Part 1, Section 1.472-2 paragraph (e).

LIFO liquidation The effect on income due to an enterprise using old LIFO cost layers when quantities sold exceed quantities purchased in the year.

layers results in apparently high margins in the year of dipping because the sale price is unaffected by the accounting procedure. Fortunately for financial statement users, the effect on income of such dipping, or **LIFO liquidation**, is required to be disclosed in the notes so that a financial statement user can recalculate income without such dipping. Technically, the LIFO liquidation amount equals the difference between the LIFO cost and current replacement cost. Thus, one can reverse the effects of LIFO dipping by adding back the amount of LIFO liquidation to COGS.

3. Distortion of turnover ratio

We usually calculate the inventory turnover ratio as COGS divided by average inventory. While this ratio uses dollar amounts, an important thing to note about inventory turnover is that, ultimately, the ratio should reflect the physical turnover of inventory. When inventory consists of two or more products, measuring physical turnover is impossible as it involves (sometimes literally) adding together apples and oranges. The dollar value of inventory is how we convert different products to the same units. However, for this conversion to be meaningful, the prices used in the numerator and denominator of the ratio need to be consistent.

Under LIFO, the inventory turnover ratio is not valid because LIFO distorts at least one and possibly both parts of the ratio.

- First, the denominator is always based on the oldest (lowest) costs under LIFO. This means that it is usually understated relative to COGS, which is based on the most recent (higher) costs. Thus, the denominator effect is to overstate the turnover ratio.
- Second, the numerator may be understated if there is any LIFO dipping, which understates the ratio.

Therefore, two adjustments need to be made to obtain a better measure of turnover when a company uses LIFO. These adjustments put both the numerator and denominator on the same basis, at approximately replacement cost.

Exhibit 6-21	Formula for inventory turnover ratio correcting for LIFO distortions

$$\text{Inventory turnover} = \frac{\text{LIFO COGS} + \text{LIFO liquidation}}{\text{Average LIFO inventory} + \text{Average LIFO reserve}}$$

For example, Exxon Mobil Corporation provides the following information in its financial report for the year ended December 31, 2014:

Exhibit 6-22	Information on Exxon Mobil's inventories		
Amounts in $ millions		2014	2013
Income statement:			
Cost of sales		266,831	284,681
Balance sheet:			
Inventories of crude oil, products, and merchandise		12,384	12,117
Note disclosures:			
Inventories are carried at the lower of LIFO and current market value			
LIFO liquidation		187	282
LIFO reserve		10,600	21,200

Based on this information, we can compute the inventory turnover ratio with and without the correction for LIFO.

Exhibit 6-23	Inventory turnover ratios for Exxon Mobil

$$\text{Uncorrected inventory turnover} = \frac{\text{LIFO COGS}}{\text{Average LIFO inventory}} = \frac{\$266{,}831}{(12{,}384 + 12{,}117)\ /\ 2} = 21.8$$

$$\text{Corrected inventory turnover} = \frac{\text{LIFO COGS} + \text{LIFO liquidation}}{\text{Average LIFO inventory} + \text{Average LIFO reserve}}$$

$$= \frac{\$266{,}831 + 187}{(12{,}384 + 10{,}600 + 12{,}117 + 21{,}200)\ /\ 2} = 9.5$$

Using the figures as reported in the income statement and balance sheet, the turnover ratio is 21.8 times a year. After correcting for the LIFO distortion, primarily the artificially low inventory value under LIFO, the turnover ratio drops more than half—to only 9.5 times per year. As this example illustrates, the distortion in the turnover ratio under LIFO can be quite substantial.

MyLab Accounting   Make the grade with **MyLab Accounting:** The problems marked with a  can be found on **MyLab Accounting.** You can practise them as often as you want, and most feature step-by-step guided instructions to help you find the right answer.

O. PROBLEMS

 P6-1.   Perpetual and periodic inventory systems   (**L.O.** 6-1) (Easy – 5 minutes)

Identify whether the following are benefits of using a perpetual inventory system (in comparison to a periodic system).

Potential benefit	True/False
A perpetual system is less costly than a periodic system.	
A perpetual system produces information that is more useful for inventory management.	
A perpetual system helps to estimate expected amounts of inventory at year-end.	
A perpetual system allows a company to avoid conducting costly inventory counts.	
A perpetual system is required by IFRS and ASPE.	
A perpetual system helps determine the amount of shrinkage.	

 P6-2.   Perpetual and periodic inventory systems   (**L.O.** 6-1) (Medium – 15 minutes)

For each of the following businesses, provide your recommendation for the type of inventory system (perpetual or periodic). In making this recommendation, consider three criteria: (i) the feasibility of tracking inventory continuously under the perpetual system, (ii) the benefits of such tracking, and (iii) the costs of using the perpetual system.

a. A supermarket that has 10,000 products and inventory turnover of 50 times per year
b. An ice cream store that makes its only products onsite and sells by the scoop
c. A car dealership
d. An electronics store

P6-3.   Perpetual and periodic inventory systems   (**L.O.** 6-1) (Medium – 10 minutes)

For each of the following types of businesses, would you recommend a perpetual or periodic inventory system? Briefly discuss the reasons for your recommendation.

a. A department store such as The Bay or Nordstrom
b. A furniture manufacturer
c. A restaurant
d. A post office

P6-4.   Inventory costing—initial recognition   (**L.O.** 6-2) (Easy – 10 minutes)

For each of the following items, identify whether the item is a product cost or a period cost for a clothing retailer.

Item	Product	Period
a. Invoice cost of purchased inventory		
b. Non-refundable tariffs on imported inventory		
c. Cost of shelves and racks at retail store		
d. Cost of shipping from distributor to warehouse		
e. Transportation from warehouse to retail store		
f. Cost to courier products to VIP customers		
g. Rent for warehouse		
h. Rent for retail store		
i. Wages of staff at retail store		
j. Salary of purchasing manager		

P6-5.   Inventory costing—initial recognition   (**L.O.** 6-2) (Easy – 10 minutes)

Identify whether the following costs for a manufacturer should be included in inventories or expensed in the period.

Item	Include in inventories	Expensed
a. Raw materials		
b. Salary for production line supervisor		
c. Salary for sales manager		
d. Pension benefits for assembly line workers		
e. Electricity used in production plant		
f. Production accountant (who tracks costs and variances)		
g. Cost of shipping to company's warehouse prior to sale		
h. Heating cost for production plant during operating hours		
i. Heating cost for production plant during off-hours		
j. Depreciation on production plant		

P6-6.   Inventory costing—initial recognition   (**L.O.** 6-2) (Medium – 10 minutes)

One of Zoe Inc.'s suppliers was going out of business. Zoe agreed to purchase the supplier's remaining inventory stored in the spa manufacturer's warehouse for $1.7 million cash plus 10% HST (harmonized sales tax). Zoe also paid a shipping company $30,000 to deliver the inventory to its (Zoe's) warehouse. The inventory consisted of three categories of items:

Inventory item	Number	Estimated retail selling price
2 person spa	200	$5,000
4 person spa	140	6,000
6 person spa	90	7,500

Zoe used the relative fair value method to allocate costs to the three categories of inventory.

Required:

a. Prepare journal entries to record the purchase of the inventory and payment of related costs.
b. Calculate the amount to be allocated to each of the three types of inventory.

P6-7.   Inventory costing—initial recognition   (**L.O.** 6-2) (Medium – 15 minutes)

Formula Fabricating Inc. (FFI) is a publicly reportable enterprise. At the beginning of the year, FFI did not have in inventory any completed units or work in progress. However, it did have $20,000 in raw materials inventory. Extracts from the company's general ledger as at the December 31 year-end follow:

General ledger account	Amount
Administration expense	$42,000
Depreciation – office building	16,000
Depreciation – manufacturing facility	22,000
Depreciation – equipment	14,000
Direct labour	60,000
Executive salaries	120,000
Plant supplies	13,000
Property taxes (30% for office building, 70% for manufacturing facility)	8,000
Production manager's salary	75,000
Raw material inventory, December 31	30,000
Raw material purchases	140,000
Utilities expense (15% for office building, 85% for manufacturing facility)	40,000

At December 31, there was no work in process, but 15% of the units manufactured remained in ending finished goods inventory.

Required:

a. What was the cost of goods sold for the year?
b. What was the value of the finished goods inventory on December 31?

P6-8.   Inventory costing—initial recognition   (**L.O.** 6-2) (Medium – 20 minutes)

Inventive Controls Ltd. was incorporated and started business early in January 2019 to manufacture electronic control devices to monitor traffic. Inventive purchased a small manufacturing plant and office building in a new industrial park and was in operation immediately. General ledger account balances at December 31, 2019, are as follows:

General ledger account	Amount
Sales commissions	$ 75,000
Supervisory salaries, production manager	65,000
Executive salaries	100,000
Raw material purchases	123,500
Miscellaneous plant supplies	12,400
Amortization, office building	8,000
Amortization, plant, equipment	10,000
Property taxes (1/5 for office building, 4/5 for plant building)	5,000
Sales	527,000
Direct labour	62,000
Raw material inventory, December 31	14,600
Utilities expense (1/10 related to the office)	20,000
General administration expenses	38,800

At December 31, 2019, there was no work in process, but 20% of the units manufactured remained in ending finished goods inventory. Inventive uses the straight-line method to calculate amortization.

Required:

a. Compute the value of cost of goods sold and ending finished goods inventory under IFRS.
b. Prepare an income statement for Inventive for the year ended December 31, 2019.

 P6-9. Inventory costing—initial recognition and fixed cost allocation

(**L.O.** 6-2) (Easy – 5 minutes)

For the explanations listed below, identify whether they are reasons under IFRS and ASPE to include fixed manufacturing overhead in inventory costs.

Potential reason for requirement to capitalize under IFRS and ASPE:	Yes/No
The fixed overhead is relatively constant, which contributes to stable values of earnings and inventories.	
Fixed overhead contributes to the production of goods that have future benefits.	
Capitalizing fixed overhead into inventories helps to match costs to revenues.	
Capitalizing fixed overhead into inventories helps to smooth earnings.	
Fixed overhead costs are reliable and verifiable.	
Capitalizing fixed overhead is consistent with the going concern assumption.	
Fixed overhead costs are measurable and are usually material.	

 P6-10. Inventory costing—initial recognition and fixed cost allocation

(**L.O.** 6-2) (Easy – 3 minutes)

A company has fixed production overhead costs totalling $10,000. The normal production level is 1,000 units per year, yielding a standard fixed overhead rate of $10 per unit. If the actual production level is 1,250 units, how much would be the amount of fixed overhead per unit and the amount of total fixed overhead included in inventory? Select the letter for the best answer.

Fixed overhead per unit	Fixed overhead included in inventory
a. $ 8	$ 8,000
b. 8	10,000
c. 10	10,000
d. 10	12,500

P6-11. Inventory costing—initial recognition and fixed cost allocation

(**L.O.** 6-2) (Easy – 3 minutes)

A company has fixed production overhead costs totalling $20,000. The normal production level is 1,000 units per year, yielding a standard fixed overhead rate of $20 per unit. If the actual production level is 500 units, how much would be the amount of fixed overhead per unit and the amount of total fixed overhead included in inventory? Select the letter for the best answer.

Fixed overhead per unit	Fixed overhead included in inventory
a. $20	$10,000
b. 20	20,000
c. 40	10,000
d. 40	20,000

 P6-12. Inventory costing—initial recognition and fixed cost allocation

(**L.O.** 6-2) (Easy – 5 minutes)

A company has a normal production level of 100,000 units per year, and production that is more than ±5% from this level is considered abnormal. Fixed overhead costs are $500,000.

Required:

For the following production levels, determine the amount of fixed overhead that should be capitalized in inventories and the amount that should be directly expensed. ("Directly expensed" does not include amounts recognized when the units are sold.)

Production level	Amount capitalized into inventories	Amount directly expensed
120,000 units		
110,000 units		
100,000 units		
98,000 units		
90,000 units		
80,000 units		
0 units		

 P6-13. Inventory costing—initial recognition and fixed cost allocation

(**L.O.** 6-2) (Easy – 5 minutes)

A company has a normal production level of 40,000 units per year, and production that is more than ±10% from this level is considered abnormal. Fixed overhead costs are $4,000,000.

Required:

For the following production levels, determine the fixed overhead allocation rate per unit of production:

Production level	Fixed overhead allocation rate
50,000 units	
46,000 units	
42,000 units	
40,000 units	
39,000 units	
30,000 units	
0 units	

P6-14. Inventory costing—initial recognition and fixed cost allocation

(**L.O.** 6-2) (Medium – 10 minutes)

Boomerang Devices Inc. manufactures sport hunting equipment. The company's operations had the following results for the year just ended. Actual production volume approximated normal levels. F = favourable variance, meaning actual costs were below standard; U = unfavourable variance, meaning actual costs exceeded standard. Assume all variances are material.

Item	Amount
Raw materials, at standard cost	$ 210,000
Production wages, at standard cost	670,000
Variable production overhead, at standard cost	180,000
Fixed production overhead, at standard cost	350,000
Total production cost, at standard cost	$1,410,000
Raw materials variance	$ 15,000 U
Labour variance	20,000 F
Variable overhead variance	3,000 F
Fixed overhead variance	50,000 U
Net variances	$ 42,000 U

Required:

a. Determine the amount that Boomerang should include in the cost of inventories produced in the year.
b. If actual production volume were to be higher than normal, what would be the effect on the cost of inventories on a per-unit basis? What if actual production volume were lower than normal?

 P6-15. Inventory costing—initial recognition and fixed cost allocation

(**L.O.** 6-2) (Medium – 15 minutes)

Durable Concrete mixers and trucks concrete to construction sites. The company uses a standard costing system for the batches of concrete produced. The company has a fleet of 10 mixing trucks, each of which goes on three runs per day, 250 days per year under normal circumstances. The standard costs are as follows:

Standard costs per batch based on 750 batches per year	Amount
Raw materials—gravel, sand, cement, chemicals	$ 1,500
Wages	500
Variable overhead—mixing truck depreciation, diesel, etc.	200
Fixed overhead—depreciation on raw materials silos	300
Total production cost per batch	$ 2,500
Opening inventory cost—all raw materials	$1,200,000
Ending inventory cost—all raw materials	$ 900,000

During the year, the company received an unusually large order for a big construction project. As a result, Durable Concrete had to extend its operating hours and days, temporarily increasing output to 900 batches for the year. The company uses the first-in, first-out cost flow assumption. Actual variable costs approximated standard costs per batch. Depreciation rates established at the beginning of the year remain valid for the year.

Required:

Determine the amount of cost of goods sold for the year.

P6-16. Inventory costing—initial recognition and fixed cost allocation

(**L.O.** 6-2) (Medium – 15 minutes)

Grand Yachts manufactures sailboats. Due to recessionary conditions that have significantly depressed sales, the company had to cut back production to levels significantly below the normal level of 500 units a year. In the current year, the company's production resulted in the following amounts:

Item	Amount
Number of boats	
Opening inventory	40
Production	320
Sales	(280)
Ending inventory	80
Standard costs per unit based on 500 units per year	
Raw materials	$ 18,000/unit
Production wages	37,000/unit
Variable production overhead	15,000/unit
Fixed production overhead	20,000/unit
Total production cost	$ 90,000/unit
Opening inventory cost	$ 3,600,000
Sales	$ 42,000,000

Actual amounts of variable and fixed costs were not materially different from standard costs.

Required:

Determine the amount of cost that should be included in inventories and the gross profit for the year. Grand Yachts uses the first-in, first-out cost flow assumption.

 P6-17. Inventory costing—initial recognition and fixed cost allocation

(**L.O.** 6-2) (Medium – 15 minutes)

Variety Appliances produces two lines of refrigerators. Typically, the company sells (and makes) an equal number of each product line. Both product lines are manufactured in the same facility using the same equipment and staff; the plant changes from making one product line to the other as the production plan requires. Both product lines take about the same amount of time to produce. The main difference is in the quality of materials used in the products.

Recently, consumers shifted toward the higher-end products in home furnishings, which resulted in the following operating results for Variety Appliances:

	Economy line	Deluxe line
Number of units		
Normal volume of production	20,000	20,000
Actual volume of production	16,000	24,000
Opening inventory	4,000	4,000
Closing inventory	5,000	3,000
Actual production costs		
Raw materials ($100 or $200 per unit)	$1,600,000	$4,800,000
Production wages ($150 per unit)	2,400,000	3,600,000
Variable production overhead ($50 per unit)	800,000	1,200,000
Total variable production costs ($300 or $400 per unit)	4,800,000	9,600,000
Fixed production overhead	?	?
Opening inventory ($425 or $525 per unit)	$1,700,000	$2,100,000

Fixed production costs, comprising factory depreciation and production manager salary, totalled $5 million. Variety Appliances uses the first-in, first-out cost flow assumption.

Required:

a. Consider the two product lines separately. Determine the cost of goods sold for each line and for Variety Appliances as a whole.
b. Consider the two product lines as a single manufacturing process. Determine the cost of goods sold for Variety Appliances as a whole.
c. Discuss the difference between (a) and (b). Which approach is better?

 P6-18. Absorption costing and cost flow assumptions

(**L.O.** 6-2, **L.O.** 6-3) (Difficult – 20 minutes)

Greenfor is a large producer of lumber and paper products. The company has a periodic inventory system and uses the weighted-average cost flow assumption. You gathered the following information regarding the company's lumber operations. [*Note:* mbf = million board feet, which is a quantity of production or inventory.]

■ The variable manufacturing cost of production is $90,000/mbf.
■ Fixed production costs including depreciation are $120 million.
■ Inventory at the beginning of 2020 was $216 million, with physical quantity of 1,540 mbf.
■ Inventory quantity at December 31, 2020, was 1,950 mbf.
■ In 2019, the company sold 2,270 mbf.
■ In 2020, the company sold 2,820 mbf.

Required:

a. Using absorption costing, calculate the cost per mbf for lumber produced in 2020.
b. Using absorption costing, calculate the cost of goods sold for 2020 and the ending inventory at December 31, 2020.
c. Calculate the inventory turnover ratio using the above information.
d. Describe the purpose of the turnover ratio. What does the ratio mean?
e. Using the available information, provide an alternate calculation of the inventory turnover ratio that is conceptually superior to that used in part (c).
f. If the variable costing method had been used (for the current and all prior years), how much would be the cost of goods sold for 2020?

 P6-19. Cost flow assumptions and inventory valuation   (**L.O.** 6-3) (Easy – 5 minutes)

Consider the following inventory information:

	# Units	Cost per unit	Total cost
Beginning inventory, January 1	2,000	$12.50	$ 25,000
Purchase, March	3,000	12.00	36,000
Purchase, July	2,000	13.50	27,000
Purchase, October	4,000	11.00	44,000
Goods available for sale	11,000		$132,000

The company uses a periodic inventory system. The year-end inventory count indicated 2,500 units in inventory.

Required:

Using the first-in, first-out (FIFO) method, compute the amount of cost of goods sold for the year and the cost of inventory on December 31.

 P6-20. Cost flow assumptions and inventory valuation   (**L.O.** 6-3) (Easy – 5 minutes)

Consider the following inventory information from P6-19:

	# Units	Cost per unit	Total cost
Beginning inventory, January 1	2,000	$12.50	$ 25,000
Purchase, March	3,000	12.00	36,000
Purchase, July	2,000	13.50	27,000
Purchase, October	4,000	11.00	44,000
Goods available for sale	11,000		$132,000

The company uses a periodic inventory system. The year-end inventory count indicated 2,500 units in inventory.

Required:

a. Compute the weighted-average cost (WAC) per unit for the period.
b. Using the periodic WAC method, compute the cost of goods sold and the ending inventory for the year.

 P6-21. **Cost flow assumptions and inventory valuation**   **(L.O.** 6-3) (Easy – 10 minutes)

Consider the following inventory information:

	# Units	Cost per unit
Beginning inventory, January 1	300	$200
Purchase, January 7	200	210
Purchase, January 22	400	205
Units sold in January	(700)	?
Ending inventory, January 31	200	?

Required:

Using the first-in, first-out (FIFO) method, compute the amount of cost of goods sold in January and the cost of inventory on January 31.

 P6-22. **Cost flow assumptions and inventory valuation**   **(L.O.** 6-3) (Easy – 10 minutes)

Consider the following inventory information:

	# Units	Cost per unit
Beginning inventory, January 1	3,000	$5.00
Purchase, January 4	5,000	5.10
Purchase, January 25	6,000	5.15
Sales, month of January	(12,000)	?
Purchase, February 14	8,000	5.00
Sales, month of February	(7,000)	?
Purchase, March 7	4,000	4.95
Purchase, March 21	5,000	5.10
Sales, month of March	(11,000)	?

Required:

Using the first-in, first-out (FIFO) method, compute the amount of cost of goods sold for the quarter ending March 31 and the cost of inventory on March 31.

 P6-23. **Cost flow assumptions and inventory valuation**   **(L.O.** 6-3) (Medium – 15 minutes)

Refer to the information in problem P6-22. Assume that the company uses a periodic inventory system and counts inventory at the end of each month.

Required:

Using the weighted-average cost method, compute the amount of cost of goods sold for the quarter ending March 31 and the cost of inventory on March 31.

 P6-24. Cost flow assumptions and inventory valuation   (**L.O.** 6-3) (Medium – 15 minutes)

Refer to the information in problem P6-22. Assume that the company uses a periodic inventory system and counts inventory at the end of each month.

Required:

Using the LIFO cost method that is commonly used in the United States, compute the amount of cost of goods sold for the quarter ending March 31 and the cost of inventory on March 31.

P6-25. Cost flow assumptions and inventory valuation   (**L.O.** 6-3) (Medium – 10 minutes)

Blixi Bikes manufactures commuter bicycles in the United States. The following information pertains to the company's inventories for 2020:

	# Units	Total cost
Beginning inventory	400	$ 80,000
Production during year	2,400	508,000
Ending inventory	320	67,200
Variable costs (raw materials, labour, variable overhead)		408,000
Fixed manufacturing overhead		100,000

The company had no work in process at the end of both 2019 and 2020. Blixi uses a periodic inventory system.

Required:

Using the above information, identify the cost flow assumption used by Blixi Bikes (i.e., FIFO, LIFO, or weighted-average cost).

 P6-26. Cost flow assumptions and inventory valuation   (**L.O.** 6-3) (Medium – 10 minutes)[13]

Ferro Ltd. began operations on January 1, 2020. Merchandise purchases and four alternative methods of valuing inventory for the first two years of operations are summarized below:

	2020	2021
Purchases	$600,000	$700,000
Ending inventory		
Specific identification	212,000	192,000
First-in, first-out (FIFO)	220,000	188,000
Average-cost	216,000	190,000
Lower of cost and market	196,000	176,000

Required:

a. Which of the four methods listed above does not apply matching? Briefly explain.
b. Determine the cost flow assumption or inventory valuation method that would report the highest net income for 2020.
c. Assuming that FIFO had been used for both years, how much would be the cost of goods sold for 2021?

[13.] Adapted from CGA-Canada FA2 examination, June 2009.

P6-27. Perpetual and periodic inventory systems and cost flow assumptions

(**L.O.** 6-1, **L.O.** 6-3) (Medium – 5 minutes)

Holden Inc. sells one major product. Purchase prices have been rising steadily for this product for several years. Which of the following inventory costing methods would tend to provide the lowest year-end inventory value? Explain your answer.

a. First-in, first-out, perpetual system
b. Weighted-average cost, periodic system
c. Specific identification
d. Last-in, first-out, periodic system

 P6-28. Perpetual and periodic inventory systems and cost flow assumptions

(**L.O.** 6-1, **L.O.** 6-3) (Medium – 15 minutes)[14]

Eagle has been selling cellular phones for the past five years. Its best-selling model is the E-PHONE, and costs have been falling quickly recently (although selling prices to Eagle's customers are stable). The following information pertains to inventory of the E-PHONE for August of the current year:

	Units	Unit cost
Opening inventory	3,600	$40
Purchase #1	2,400	$36
Sale #1	(1,500)	
Purchase #2	3,000	$28
Sale #2	(3,500)	
Total	4,000	

Required:

a. If Eagle uses the periodic FIFO inventory system, what would be the cost of ending inventory for August?
b. If Eagle uses the weighted-average method for costing its periodic inventory, what would be the cost of goods sold for August?
c. If Eagle uses the weighted-average method under a perpetual inventory system, what would be the cost of ending inventory for August?

 P6-29. Perpetual and periodic inventory systems and cost flow assumptions

(**L.O.** 6-1, **L.O.** 6-3) (Medium – 15 minutes)[15]

The inventory records of RST indicate the following regarding its best-selling product in the month of January:

	Units	Unit cost
Opening inventory	3,000	$8.00
Purchase #1	2,000	7.65
Sale #1	(1,500)	
Purchase #2	4,000	7.50
Sale #2	(2,500)	
Total	5,000	

Required:

Calculate the dollar amount of ending inventory and cost of goods sold under each of the following cost flow assumptions:

a. Weighted-average cost, periodic inventory
b. FIFO, perpetual inventory
c. Weighted-average cost, perpetual inventory

[14.] Adapted from CGA-Canada FA2 examination, March 2009.

[15.] Adapted from CGA-Canada FA2 examination, December 2008.

P6-30. Perpetual and periodic inventory systems and cost flow assumptions

(**L.O.** 6-1, **L.O.** 6-3) (Medium – 25 minutes)

GFF's inventory records included the following information regarding one of its product lines for the month of August:

	Units	Unit cost
Opening inventory	10,000	$16.00
Purchase #1	5,000	17.50
Sale #1	(500)	
Purchase #2	4,000	17.25
Sale #2	(11,000)	
Purchase #3	6,000	16.75
Sale #3	(13,000)	
Total	500	

Required:

Calculate the dollar amount of ending inventory and cost of goods sold under each of the following cost flow assumptions:
a. First-in, first-out, periodic inventory
b. Weighted-average cost, periodic inventory
c. Weighted-average cost, perpetual inventory

P6-31. Perpetual and periodic inventory systems and cost flow assumptions

(**L.O.** 6-1, **L.O.** 6-3) (Medium – 15 minutes)

Refer to the facts in problem P6-30. Assume that GFF uses a perpetual inventory system and the weighted-average cost flow assumption to account for its inventory. All purchases were made on account; all sales were for cash. GFF's supplier offered terms of 2/10 net 30. GFF recorded purchases at the gross amount. Additional information follows:

	Purchase discount taken
Purchase #1	Yes
Purchase #2	No
Purchase #3	No
	Sales price per unit
Sale #1	$24.00
Sale #2	26.00
Sale #3	25.50

Required:

a. Prepare journal entries to record:
   i. The purchases of the inventory
   ii. The sales of the inventory
   iii. Payment of the accounts payables
b. Assume that GFF's opening and closing balances of its accounts receivable and payable for the year were $0. If the company uses the direct method to prepare its statement of cash flows, how much would be reported as a cash inflow from the sale of inventory? As a cash outflow from the purchase of inventory?

 **P6-32.** Inventory cost allocation—retail inventory method   (**L.O.** 6-3) (Easy – 5 minutes)

A retailer has a standard markup of 100% on invoiced cost. At the year-end, 200 out of 5,000 products had been discounted by 30% of retail price.

Required:

Compute the estimated costs as percentages of retail price separately for regular and discounted products.

P6-33. Inventory cost allocation—gross margin method   (**L.O.** 6-3) (Easy – 5 minutes)

A retailer has a standard markup of 50% on cost. For the month of June, the company recorded sales of $330,000 and purchases of $200,000. Inventory at the beginning of June was estimated to be $160,000.

Required:

Using the gross margin method, estimate the cost of goods sold for the month of June and the cost of inventory at the end of June.

 P6-34. Inventory cost allocation—retail inventory method   (**L.O.** 6-3) (Easy – 10 minutes)

Trail Outfitters is a retailer of outdoor clothing and equipment. The company has a standard markup of 100% on invoiced cost. Inventory at the beginning of the fiscal year was $1,790,000. During the year, the company purchased $13,700,000 of goods and recorded sales of $25,780,000. The year-end inventory count showed $3,380,000 of inventory measured at actual retail prices. Included in this total of $3,380,000 was $520,000 of goods that had been discounted by 35% relative to regular prices.

Required:

Using the retail inventory method, estimate the cost of inventory at year-end and the amount of cost of goods sold.

P6-35. Inventory valuation   (**L.O.** 6-4) (Easy – 5 minutes)

For each of the following scenarios, determine if raw materials (RM) would be written down below cost. Briefly explain.

	RM cost	RM replacement cost	WIP cost	WIP NRV	FG cost	FG NRV
a.	$100	$ 80	$200	$250	$500	$600
b.	100	120	200	150	500	400
c.	100	80	200	250	500	400
d.	100	80	200	150	500	600

Abbreviations: RM = raw materials; WIP = work in process; FG = finished goods;
NRV = net realizable value

 P6-36. Inventory valuation    (**L.O.** 6-4) (Easy – 5 minutes)

A specialized retailer has a selection of five products. The following is information relating to these products:

Product	# Units	Cost per unit	Selling price
A	200	$ 40	$ 80
B	100	150	120
C	300	60	100
D	200	100	100
E	300	65	70

The company estimates selling costs to be 10% of selling price, primarily for sales commissions.

Required:

Determine the amount of inventory writedown, if any.

P6-37. Inventory valuation

(**L.O.** 6-4) (Easy – 10 minutes)

A manufacturer produces four products, each using a different raw material. The following table provides cost and market value information on these inventories.

Inventory item	Cost per unit	Replacement cost	Net realizable value
Finished good A	$100	—	$200
Raw material A	50	$50	—
Finished good B	100	—	220
Raw material B	50	45	—
Finished good C	100	—	80
Raw material C	50	50	—
Finished good D	100	—	80
Raw material D	50	45	—

Required:

For each of the above inventory items, determine whether a writedown is required.

 P6-38. Inventory valuation

(**L.O.** 6-4) (Medium – 10 minutes)

A particular production process requires two types of raw materials to produce the end product. Each unit of finished product requires three units of raw material A and two units of raw material B and processing costs of $40. The following provides information on inventories at year-end:

Inventory item	# Units	Cost per unit	Replacement cost	Net realizable value
Finished goods	300	$200	n/a	$180
Raw material A	200	20	$25	n/a
Raw material B	100	50	45	n/a

Required:

a. Evaluate these inventories to determine the amount of writedown, if any.
b. Would your answer change if the replacement cost of raw material A were $21/unit?

 **P6-39.** Inventory valuation

(**L.O.** 6-4) (Medium – 10 minutes)

A manufacturer produces two products: Alphas and Betas. Information on these products along with their raw material inputs and costs incurred to convert the raw materials into finished products are below:

Inventory item	# Units	Cost per unit	Replacement cost	Net realizable value
Alphas				
Raw material A	50	$ 30	$20	—
Raw material B	100	10	11	—
Raw material C	80	50	40	—
Conversion cost	—	300	—	—
Finished goods	20	450	—	$425
Betas				
Raw material D	600	5	4	—
Raw material E	1,000	10	11	—
Conversion costs	—	120	—	—
Finished goods	16	520	—	600

Required:

Evaluate these inventories to determine the amount of writedown, if any.

P6-40. Inventory cost allocation and inventory errors

(**L.O.** 6-3, **L.O.** 6-5) (Medium – 20 minutes)

Comfy Feet manufactures slippers. In 2020, the company hired a new bookkeeper who did not have appropriate training. The bookkeeper charged to "production expense" all of the following costs for manufacturing 70,000 pairs of slippers:

Raw materials	$ 30,000
Factory labour	100,000
Variable manufacturing overhead	8,000
Fixed manufacturing overhead	12,000
Factory depreciation	25,000
Finished goods storage	4,000
Interest for carrying finished goods	3,000
Total	$182,000

The company had zero work in process at the end of both 2019 and 2020. Finished goods amounted to 5,000 pairs of slippers at $2.40/pair at the end of 2019. There were 6,000 pairs of slippers in finished goods inventory at the end of 2020.

Required:

a. Provide the adjusting journal entry or entries to correct the bookkeeper's errors and properly record the above expenditures recorded in the "production expense" account.
b. Assume the company uses a periodic inventory system and the FIFO cost flow assumption for finished goods. Compute the cost of goods sold and the ending value of finished goods inventory for 2020.
c. Now assume the company uses the weighted-average cost flow assumption. Compute the cost of goods sold and the ending value of finished goods.

 P6-41. Inventory valuation and inventory errors

(**L.O.** 6-4, **L.O.** 6-5) (Medium – 10 minutes)

In early 2021, Darwin's Pet Shop discovered that some of its inventory of dogs were not what the supplier purported them to be. More than 300 puppies that were supposed to be purebred (and therefore expensive) were in fact sired by parents with unknown history. As at the fiscal year ended December 31, 2020, 210 of these puppies had been sold while 90 remained in inventory. Purebred puppies cost $150 each and they would retail for $400. Non-purebreds have a replacement cost of $40 each, and the estimated sale price is $100 each. Darwin is pursuing the supplier to obtain a refund for the cost difference. However, whether there will be compensation is uncertain.

Required:

a. Record the journal entry for the writedown of puppy inventory on December 31, 2020. Note any assumptions necessary.
b. Suppose the error (non-purebreds treated as purebreds) had not been discovered. Indicate the effect of this error on the following accounts (i.e., were they over- or understated, and by how much?):
   i. Inventory, December 31, 2020
   ii. Cost of goods sold, year 2020
   iii. Cost of goods sold, year 2021

 P6-42. Inventory errors   (**L.O.** 6-5) (Medium – 10 minutes)[16]

For each of the following independent scenarios, indicate the effect of the error (if any) on:
   i. 2020 net income
   ii. 2021 net income
   iii. 2021 closing retained earnings

[16.] Adapted from CGA-Canada FA2 examination, March 2009 and June 2009.

The company uses the periodic system of inventory and its fiscal year-end is December 31. Ignore income tax effects.

a. Your analysis of inventory indicates that inventory at the end of 2020 was overstated by $15,000 due to an inventory count error. Inventory at the end of 2021 was correctly stated.

b. Invoices in the amount of $24,000 for inventory received in December 2020 were not entered on the books in 2020. They were recorded as purchases in January 2021, when they were paid. The goods were counted in the 2020 inventory count and included in ending inventory on the 2020 financial statements.

c. Goods received on consignment amounting to $37,000 were included in the physical count of goods at the end of 2021 and included in ending inventory on the financial statements.

P6-43. Inventory errors   (**L.O.** 6-5) (Medium – 10 minutes)

For each of the three scenarios in P6-42, provide the journal entry that should be recorded in 2021 to correct the error.

P6-44. Inventory errors   (**L.O.** 6-3, **L.O.** 6-5) (Difficult – 10 minutes)

Below is information relating to Knoclew Inc., a subsidiary of a US publicly traded manufacturer of murder mystery games. The company uses the last-in, first-out (LIFO) cost flow assumption. Additional information on inventory during Year 1 includes the following:

Beginning-of-year finished goods inventory	20,000 units
Units finished during Year 1	200,000 units
End-of-year finished goods inventory	15,000 units
Beginning-of-year work in process (in equivalent units*)	10,000 units
Ending work in process (in equivalent units*)	10,000 units

*For example, 10 units that are each 40% complete are equal to 4 equivalent units.

a. One of Knoclew's products became obsolete and worthless during Year 1, but the inventory writedown did not occur until Year 2. The cost of this inventory was $25,000.

b. In the Year 1 closing inventory count, employees improperly included 1,000 units of finished goods that had already been sold to customers. These units had a cost of $8,000 under LIFO.

c. An invoice for $15,000 of materials received and used in production arrived after the year-end. Neither the purchase nor the accounts payable was recorded. However, the amount of raw materials in ending inventory was correct based on the inventory count.

d. In Year 1, Knoclew incurred the following expenditures:

Factory labour	$1,000,000
Materials used in manufacturing	800,000
Variable overhead	300,000
Subtotal	2,100,000
Transportation cost of raw materials	200,000
Factory depreciation	700,000
Salary of production vice-president	100,000
Salary of marketing vice-president	120,000
Advertising cost for new game	200,000
	$3,420,000

Knoclew's accountants debited only $2,100,000 into the inventory (work in process) account. The remainder was expensed as period costs.

Required:

For each of the above independent scenarios (a) through (d), indicate in the following table the effect of the accounting errors on the books of Knoclew Inc. Specifically, identify the amount and direction of over- or understatement of inventory and income for Year 1 and Year 2. If an account requires no adjustment, indicate that the account is "correct."

	Year 1			Year 2	
Scenario	Inventory	Income		Inventory	Income
a.					
b.					
c.					
d.					

P6-45. Inventory costing, cost flow assumptions, and inventory errors

(L.O. 6-2, **L.O.** 6-3, **L.O.** 6-5) (Difficult – 15 minutes)

Orca Crafts manufactures high quality kayaks and canoes. Although the company makes boats of different styles, the production process for each is similar, as are the costs of production. The following information pertains to the company's inventories for 2020:

	# units	Total cost
Beginning inventory	50	$100,000
Production during year	200	440,000
Ending inventory	90	?
Variable costs (raw materials, labour, variable overhead)		240,000
Fixed manufacturing overhead		200,000

The company had no work in process at the end of both 2019 and 2020. Orca uses a periodic inventory system.

Required:

a. Using the weighted-average cost method, compute the ending value of finished goods inventory and cost of goods sold (COGS).

b. For this part, assume the company uses the first-in, first-out (FIFO) method. During the preparation of the 2020 financial statements, the accountant discovered an error in the beginning inventory balance. Five units that had already been sold in 2019 had been included in beginning inventory balance. Ignoring any income tax effects, determine the effect of the error on the following balances:

	Direction (overstated or understated)	Amount ($)
2019 Cost of goods sold		
2019 Ending retained earnings		
2020 Cost of goods sold		
2020 Ending retained earnings		

c. For planning purposes, the company president has asked you for information about the inventory costs in 2021 at various levels of production. The normal level of production is 200 units ±10%. Complete the following table based on production data from 2020.

Production volume	Total variable costs	Fixed costs	Per unit cost of production for financial reporting purposes
250 units		$200,000	
200 units		200,000	
100 units		200,000	

P6-46. Inventory errors **(L.O. 6-2, L.O. 6-3, L.O. 6-5)** (Difficult – 20 minutes)

Monster Bikes manufactures off-road bicycles. In 2021, the company's accountant recorded the following costs into the inventory account:

Variable costs (raw materials, labour, variable overhead)	$10,680,000
Fixed manufacturing overhead	2,000,000
Salary of factory manager	100,000
Salary of company president	300,000
Advertising and promotion	500,000
Total	$13,580,000

The company had no work in process at the end of both 2020 and 2021. Finished goods at the end of 2020 amounted to 6,000 bikes at $250/bike. Production was 50,000 bikes, and 4,000 bikes remained in the inventory at December 31, 2021. The company uses a periodic inventory system and the FIFO cost flow assumption.

Required:

a. Of the $13,580,000, how much should have been capitalized into inventories?
b. Compute the ending value of inventory and the cost of goods sold for 2021.
c. If the error in inventory costing had not been corrected as per part (a), by how much would inventory be overstated at the end of 2021?
d. Record the journal entry to correct the error in inventory costing.
e. If the company uses the weighted-average cost method, how much would be the ending value of inventory and cost of goods sold for 2021?

P6-47. Change in inventory accounting policy **(L.O. 6-5)** (Difficult – 40 minutes)

Oculus is a proprietorship that produces a specialized type of round window. It is after the fiscal year-end for 2021 and the owner has drafted the financial statements for the business for presentation to the bank and for tax purposes. The following provides a summary of those financial statements, along with comparative information for the prior year:

Balances as at December 31	2021	2020
Cash	$ 8,900	$ 7,600
Accounts receivable	42,600	40,900
Inventories: raw materials	7,900	5,500
Inventories: work in process	5,100	6,200
Inventories: finished goods	48,400	29,400
Other assets	320,000	310,000
Total assets	$432,900	$399,600
Total liabilities	$113,800	$137,900
Contributed capital	5,000	5,000
Retained earnings	314,100	256,700
Total liabilities and equity	$432,900	$399,600

For the year ended December 31	2021	2020
Sales	$561,000	$529,000
Cost of goods sold	321,200	305,000
Gross margin	239,800	224,000
Operating expenses	182,600	178,300
Net income	$ 57,200	$ 45,700

Raw materials consist of glass and aluminum. Due to their nature, these inventories cannot be specifically identified. Consequently, Oculus has used the first-in, first-out (FIFO) method for all of its inventories. Oculus uses a periodic inventory system, and the above financial information has been prepared using FIFO.

Input prices had been reasonably stable prior to 2020. However, as a result of rapidly rising prices for raw material inputs, the owner of Oculus feels that the FIFO method is overstating income. He wonders whether and by how much his financial results would change if he were to use the weighted-average cost method for inventories. To help address this issue, he has assembled additional information on the inventories for Oculus (raw material quantities are expressed in units equivalent to one standard finished window):

	2021		2020	
	Quantity	$	Quantity	$
Glass: beginning inventory	75	$ 3,400	80	$ 2,500
Glass: purchases	1,235	74,700	1,297	53,500
Glass: used in production	(1,250)	(73,200)	(1,302)	(52,600)
Glass: ending inventory	60	$ 4,900	75	$ 3,400
Aluminum: beginning inventory	75	$ 2,100	80	$ 1,600
Aluminum: purchases	1,235	50,700	1,297	33,500
Aluminum: used in production	(1,250)	(49,800)	(1,302)	(33,000)
Aluminum: ending inventory	60	$ 3,000	75	$ 2,100
WIP: beginning inventory	25	$ 6,200	23	$ 4,600
WIP: materials, labour, overhead used	1,250	339,100	1,302	311,800
WIP: cost of goods completed	(1,260)	(340,200)	(1,300)	(310,200)
WIP: ending inventory	15	$ 5,100	25	$ 6,200
Finished goods: beginning inventory	120	$ 29,400	121	$ 24,200
Finished goods: production	1,260	340,200	1,300	310,200
Finished goods: cost of goods sold	(1,230)	(321,200)	(1,301)	(305,000)
Finished goods: ending inventory	150	$ 48,400	120	$ 29,400

Required:

Prepare the revised balance sheets and income statements for Oculus under the weighted-average cost method. [*Hint:* Pay attention to how costs flow between raw materials to WIP to finished goods.]

P6-48. Inventory presentation, disclosure, and analysis
(**L.O.** 6-2, **L.O.** 6-3, **L.O.** 6-4, **L.O.** 6-5) (Medium – 15 minutes)

Obtain the 2011 annual report for Canadian Tire Corporation, Limited from the company's website or from SEDAR (www.sedar.com).

Required:

a. Which types of inventories does the company have (raw materials, work in process, finished goods)?
b. What does the company include in inventory cost?
c. Which cost flow assumption does the company use?
d. How does the company define net realizable value for purposes of determining whether inventory is impaired?
e. How many days of merchandise inventory does the company have as at December 31, 2011? How many days was it in 2010? What is the most identifiable explanation for the significant change in this ratio from 2010 to 2011? Qualitatively, without doing any calculations, how would you adjust the numbers going into the ratio to make the comparison more meaningful?

P6-49. Inventory presentation, disclosure, and analysis

(**L.O.** 6-2, **L.O.** 6-3, **L.O.** 6-4, **L.O.** 6-5) (Medium – 15 minutes)

Obtain the 2016 annual report for Bombardier Inc. from the company's website or from SEDAR (www.sedar.com).

Required:

a. How much in inventories did the company have at the end of 2016? What three components comprise this amount?
b. How does the company determine the amount for work in progress on long-term contracts?
c. For finished products, how does the company determine the cost of finished goods on aircraft inventories?

P6-50. Inventory presentation, disclosure, and analysis

(**L.O.** 6-2, **L.O.** 6-3, **L.O.** 6-4, **L.O.** 6-5) (Medium – 15 minutes)

Obtain the 2016 financial statements for Teck Resources Limited from the company's website or from SEDAR (www.sedar.com).

Required:

a. How much in inventory did the company have at the end of 2016? What four components comprised this amount?
b. The company separately reported the current and long-term portions of its inventory. What did the long-term inventory consist of? What was the rationale for segregation? Where was the long-term portion reported on the balance sheet?
c. What does the company include in inventory cost?
d. Which cost flow assumption does the company use?

P. MINI-CASES

John Lotter established Rocky Dilemma (RDL) on January 5, 2020. The accounts on December 31, 2020, the company's year-end, had balances as follows:

CASE 1
Rocky Dilemma
(30 minutes)

Account			Balance
Current assets, excluding inventory			$ 10,000
Non-current assets			107,000
Current liabilities			32,600
Long-term bank loan			50,000
Owner's investment (excludes retained earnings)			40,000
Purchases			
January 9:	3,500 units @ $11/unit	$ 38,500	
March 30:	12,300 units @ $13/unit	159,900	
December 10:	3,200 units @ $16/unit	51,200	249,600
Sales			284,000
Expenses, other than cost of goods sold			40,000

The inventory count at December 31, 2020, showed 4,000 units on hand. Of this amount, 3,500 units are from the January 9 purchase and 500 are from the March 30 purchase. RDL uses a periodic system for inventories.

Lotter is now preparing financial statements for the year. He is aware that inventory may be costed using the FIFO, weighted-average, or specific identification method. He is unsure of which one to use and requests your assistance. In discussions with Lotter, you learn the following:

i.   Suppliers to RDL provide goods at regular prices as long as the current ratio is at least 2 to 1. If this ratio is lower, the suppliers increase the price charged by 10% to compensate for what they consider to be a substantial credit risk.

ii. Based on the terms of a long-term bank loan, the bank can put RDL into a state of bankruptcy if the total debt to total assets ratio exceeds 50%.

iii. Lotter has an agreement with the company's general manager that, for each percent above a 25% rate of return on ending total assets (based on pre-bonus income), she will be given an additional $1,000 bonus in the following year. As this is a proprietorship, the business does not pay income taxes.

Required:

a. Compute the cost of goods sold and ending inventory under each of the three cost flow assumptions.

b. What is the recommendation you would give to John Lotter? Explain.

Eastern Pacific Lumber (EPL) is a private forestry company located on Vancouver Island in British Columbia. The company uses a bonus plan to reward its management staff according to their areas of responsibility. For example, the chief operating officer receives a bonus of 1% of net income, the sales manager receives 0.1% of revenues, and the production manager receives $20,000 for each dollar that per-unit production costs fall below $280/mbf.[17] The CEO owns 40% of the company and receives no explicit bonuses; rather, the board of directors sets his pay after considering many different performance factors.

CASE 2
Eastern Pacific
Lumber
(45 minutes)

[17.] One mbf is a thousand board feet, which equals one thousand square feet of lumber one inch thick.

You are an internal auditor at EPL. As an internal auditor, you report directly to the board of directors. While conducting your review of the preliminary financial statements for 2021, you collected the following information:

	Preliminary 2021 (000's)	Audited 2020 (000's)
Cash	$ 5,365	$ 3,830
Accounts receivable	20,357	18,754
Inventories	72,970	47,050
Other	4,322	2,883
Total current assets	$103,014	$ 72,517
Revenue	$247,592	$222,659
Cost of goods sold	176,642	164,203
Gross profit	$ 70,950	$ 58,456

Accounting policies:

Inventories are carried at the lower of cost, derived using the FIFO method, and net realizable value. Cost of goods sold includes export tariffs amounting to $17.7 million in 2021 (2020 – $28.5 million); these amounts were paid on exports to the United States.

Operating information:

Sales volume increased from 500,000 mbf in 2020 to 600,000 mbf in 2021. Average sales price declined from $445/mbf in 2020 to $413/mbf in 2021.

Fixed costs of production have been approximately $34 million per year.

Inventory at the beginning of 2020 was $46,053,000.

In conversations with the controller, she tells you that she felt 2021 had been a successful year despite the significant decline in lumber prices. She attributed the success to the ability of the factory to control costs, which resulted in cost of goods sold per unit declining by 2.4%. The production manager was in agreement with this assessment and pointed out that production costs decreased by $10/mbf from $272 to $262/mbf.

Required:

Analyze the information you have collected and evaluate EPL's performance in 2021. As the internal auditor, do you have any concerns? If so, what would you recommend to the board of directors to address these concerns in the future?

CASE 3
Mountain Mines Lubrication
(60 minutes)[18]

Mountain Mines Lubrication Ltd. (MML) supplies lubricant to mining operations in northern British Columbia and the Northwest Territories. MML commenced operations four years ago and is based in Prince George, British Columbia. MML has two lubricant products: Slip Coat and Maximum Guard. MML's lubricants are used in large, expensive mining machines and are crucial to the operation of the machines. Without good lubrication, the machines will overheat and break down.

The mining industry has not performed well in recent years, but over the last summer the economy has picked up and, according to MML's owner, Max Mulholland, the BC mines are running at peak capacity. Customer service is key to the business. Max says that MML has been able to survive the hard times because it is more flexible and its products cost less than those of its competitors.

[18.] Reprinted from Uniform Final Examination, 1999 with permission from Chartered Professional Accountants of Canada, Toronto, Canada. Any changes to the original material are the sole responsibility of the author (and/or publisher) and have not been reviewed or endorsed by the Chartered Professional Accountants of Canada.

MML is a new client of your firm. You, a CA, have been assigned to conduct the review engagement. You have met with Max and with Nina Verhan, the bookkeeper. Your notes are in Exhibits I and II. You have been working at the client's office for two days. The partner would like a memo analyzing the issues you have identified in the review.

Required:

Prepare the memo to the partner.

Exhibit I	Excerpts from your discussion with Max Mulholland

"I do everything I can to keep costs down. Minimizing costs is vital in our business. Take shipping costs. Some of my clients are in pretty remote areas, and it costs a lot to ship lubricant up there. So I send enough lubricant up there in one shipment to last them for a year. They put the stuff in their machines as they need it, and report to me how much they've used. When my sales rep makes the annual delivery, he confirms the information they have provided. That way they are happy because they don't have to wait for lubricant to be delivered, and I keep my costs and my prices low.

"Of course, there are always problems. On August 30, the supervisor at Scorched Earth called to warn me they were really low on lubricant. That was a bit of a surprise to me, because we shipped a lot up there in the spring, but I know they've been working hard in August and those older machines really go through the stuff.

"Flexibility is another strong point. You know things have been bad in the mining industry, but they have picked up this year, which means that our business has picked up as well. Some mines were experiencing cash flow problems and, even though lubricant is not their biggest expense, every little bit helps. So instead of charging them for product as they put it into their machines, I've arranged to have meters installed to read the number of hours a machine is in use and they are charged based on hours of usage. It takes about four weeks before a machine needs to have its lubricant tanks refilled, if it is running at peak capacity."

Exhibit II	Excerpts from your discussion with Nina Verhan, bookkeeper

"Max is excited about this year. A lot of orders have come in since the mines started picking up. We were concerned about cash flows, but Max thinks they are going to be okay. Big Scar Mine, a new diamond mine in the Northwest Territories, has started operations, and we are its supplier.

"Max told you about our new charging plan, based on hourly usage. When the mine workers pour lubricant into the tank on one of their machines, they let me know by fax. I send them a "no charge" invoice, and at the same time I charge the cost of lubricant to cost of sales. Max thinks that it is a good reminder of the special deal we are giving them. Then, each week, they fax in their meter readings, and I charge them based on the hours of operation of the machine and I record the revenue at that time. We just started doing it this way this year, for three of our four customers. Here is our inventory list for all our mines (see Exhibit III).

"I've also prepared draft financial statements for you. Here are some excerpts (see Exhibit IV), and the gross margins by product (Exhibit V).

"Our three BC mine customers have really picked up over the summer. For July, August, and September they have been running at full capacity. The Scorched Earth Mine is the only one in BC not owned by Broken Wing Properties, and it has really been financially squeezed lately. Scorched Earth was pretty eager to switch to our new hourly usage billing, because its cash flow was tight.

"Based on our average selling prices and costs, you will see that our percentage gross margins have increased over last year, and our volume of sales has also increased nicely. I would say we have had a pretty good year.

"The Big Scar Mine has a large amount of our inventory onsite. That mine is owned and operated by North Canadian Developments Ltd., a subsidiary of Broken Wing Properties.

"We have received all the meter readings from our hourly usage customers up to August 31. I noticed that the Scorched Earth Mine meter reading is low, so I will ask our sales rep to recheck the meter when he makes another delivery this week. I have billed Scorched Earth for August on the hours that the mine has provided."

Exhibit III	Current inventory list, as at August 31, 2020		
		Slip Coat	Maximum Guard
Average sale price per kg			
2020		$16.00	$22.50
2019		15.00	21.00
Average cost per kg			
2020		$13.50	$18.25
2019		13.00	17.25
Prince George warehouse		3,000 kg	1,000 kg
Scorched Earth Mine (BC)			
Onsite (Note 2)		0 kg	20 kg
Mining machine capacity		50 kg	50 kg
Date of last top-up		August 25	August 25
Moon Crater Mine (BC)			
Onsite (Note 2)		300 kg	300 kg
Mining machine capacity		50 kg	50 kg
Date of last top-up		August 13	August 13
Dead Fish Mine (BC)			
Onsite (Note 2)		800 kg	900 kg
Mining machine capacity		20 kg	20 kg
Date of last top-up		n/a	n/a
Big Scar Mine (NWT)			
Onsite (Note 2)		3,500 kg	5,000 kg
Mining machine capacity		200 kg	300 kg
Date of last top-up		August 28	August 28

Notes:

1. Scorched Earth Mine, Moon Crater Mine, and Big Scar Mine are billed by hourly machine usage. Dead Fish Mine is billed for product when it is poured into the tanks.

2. Onsite does not include lubricant contained in the machines.

Exhibit IV	Excerpts from draft financial statements		
Income statement, for the years ended August 31		**2020**	**2019**
Sales		$336,250	$276,390
Cost of sales		286,291	232,090
Gross margin		49,959	44,300
Other expenses		37,309	36,150
Income before taxes		12,650	8,150
Income tax expense		3,500	2,490
Net income		9,150	5,660
Retained earnings—opening		37,750	32,090
Retained earnings—closing		$ 46,900	$ 37,750

(*Continued*)

Exhibit IV	Continued		
Balance sheet, as at August 31		**2020**	**2019**
Cash		$ —	$ 8,790
Accounts receivable		67,540	57,423
Inventory		234,365	156,837
Property, plant, and equipment		146,600	113,600
		$448,505	$336,650
Bank overdraft		$ 37,929	$ —
Accounts payable		143,476	63,700
Current portion, long-term debt		60,000	20,000
Long-term debt		115,000	175,000
Common shares		45,200	40,200
Retained earnings		46,900	37,750
		$448,505	$336,650

Exhibit V	Gross margin by product			
		Slip Coat	**Maximum Guard**	**Total**
2020	Sales	$136,000	$200,250	$336,250
	Cost of sales	117,933	168,358	286,291
	Gross margin	$ 18,067	$ 31,892	$ 49,959
	Number of kg sold	8,500	8,900	17,400
2019	Sales	$111,750	$164,640	$276,390
	Cost of sales	96,850	135,240	232,090
	Gross margin	$ 14,900	$ 29,400	$ 44,300
	Number of kg sold	7,450	7,840	15,290

James Television Inc. (JTI) is a privately owned television wholesaler located in Yellowknife that specializes in selling high-end Japanese televisions to retailers. It has been in business for 10 years and has been recording increasing profits for the last five years. Its inventory information for the quarter ending March 31, 2019, was as follows:

Beginning Inventory, January 1, 2019: 10 units @ $400/unit
January 20, 2019: Purchased 20 units @ $500/unit
February 12, 2019: Sold 10 units @ $700/unit
March 1, 2019: Purchased 30 units @ $550/unit
March 28, 2019: Sold 25 units @ $700/unit
Ending Inventory, March 31, 2019: 25 units @ $550/unit

JTI accounts for its inventory using the perpetual system and it uses FIFO as its costing method. The company recorded revenues of $24,500 and COGS of $16,750, resulting in a gross profit of $7,750 for the quarter ending March 31, 2019. However, the cost of the product has been rising because of currency appreciation of the yen.

JTI is considering introducing lower-cost televisions as another line of its products. In the past year, the company consulted with an external company, Global Manufacturing Inc., for the possibility of importing lower-cost Chinese televisions. Global Manufacturing Inc. specializes in the manufacturing of televisions in China, and it operates as an order-to-manufacture company. Customers of Global Manufacturing Inc. can order products to their specifications and product price is determined based on the specifications of the product and the production volume. In a sense, the customers of Global Manufacturing

CASE 4
James Television Inc.

(30 minutes)

Inc. are themselves the manufacturers of the products. Based on JTI's specifications and order size, Global Manufacturing Inc. submitted the following financial information to JTI:

Costs for the manufacturing of 20 units:
- Raw Materials: $100/unit
- Labour: $10/hour, 15 hours/unit
- Variable Overhead: $50/unit
- Fixed Overhead: $2,000/month

JTI is currently considering whether to continue buying all its televisions from the Japanese manufacturers or to make part of its purchases from Global Manufacturing Inc. If the company imports the 20 units from Global Manufacturing Inc., it is expected that the company would reduce the order of the high-end Japanese televisions by 10–15 units. The company is expecting to continue to sell the Japanese televisions at $700 per unit and the new televisions from Global Manufacturing Inc. would be introduced at $500 per unit.

Required:

a. Suppose JTI chooses to purchase 20 televisions from Global Manufacturing Inc. Would you advise the company to use the variable costing or the absorption costing method to account for inventory expenses?
b. Suppose JTI chooses to continue purchasing all its televisions from the Japanese manufacturers. Is JTI using the optimal inventory system (i.e., perpetual system) and costing method (i.e., FIFO) to account for its inventory?
c. Suppose you are the manager at JTI. Would you recommend the company continue buying all its televisions from the Japanese manufacturers, or should the company diversify into the new product line? Use both financial and non-financial information to support your argument.

CHAPTER 7
Financial Assets

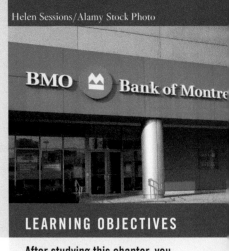

CPA competencies addressed in this chapter:

1.1.2 Evaluates the appropriateness of the basis of financial reporting (Level B)
b. Methods of measurement

1.2.1 Develops or evaluates appropriate accounting policies and procedures—Ethical professional judgment (Level B)

1.2.2 Evaluates treatment for routine transactions (Level A)
k. Financial instruments
l. Investments in associates/significant influence*

1.2.3 Evaluates treatment of non-routine transactions (Level B)
h. Consolidated financial statements subsequent to acquisition date*
i. Joint ventures: proportionate consolidation or equity method*

1.3.2 Prepares routine financial statement note disclosure (Level B)

The Bank of Montreal, also known as BMO Financial Group (www.bmo.com, Toronto Stock Exchange ticker: BMO), is one of the six national chartered banks in Canada with a history dating back two centuries to 1817. Among the company's $710 billion in assets reported on its balance sheet of October 31, 2017, are the following financial assets (in billions of dollars):

Measurement basis	Amount
Fair value, with changes flowing through profit or loss	$128.0
Fair value, with changes flowing through OCI	54.1
Amortized cost	372.6
Consolidation (11 companies)†	—
Total	$554.7

†The amount for subsidiaries is not presented in this table because there is no single amount on the financial statements that would represent the investment in subsidiaries.

The items in this table raise a number of interesting questions. What is the meaning of the different measurement bases? What types of assets are in each category? Why is there such a variety of reporting methods?

LEARNING OBJECTIVES

After studying this chapter, you should be able to:

L.O. 7-1. Explain what financial assets are, how they differ from other types of assets, and why there is a variety of measurement standards for different categories of financial assets.

L.O. 7-2. Evaluate the nature of a financial asset to classify it into one of seven categories: subsidiaries, joint operations, joint ventures, associates, fair value through profit or loss, fair value through OCI, and amortized cost.

L.O. 7-3. Identify the measurement approach appropriate to the seven categories of financial assets and explain the general nature of the various measurement approaches.

L.O. 7-4. Analyze historical cost and fair value information to determine the appropriate balance sheet measurement and income recognition subsequent to purchase for three categories of financial assets: fair value through profit or loss, fair value through OCI, and amortized cost.

L.O. 7-5. Apply present value techniques to account for investments in debt instruments.

---

*These items are discussed at Level C in this chapter, as they are covered in greater detail in advanced textbooks and courses.

A. INTRODUCTION

financial asset An asset arising from contractual agreements on future cash flows.

L.O. 7-1. Explain what financial assets are, how they differ from other types of assets, and why there is a variety of measurement standards for different categories of financial assets.

What are financial assets and how do they differ from other kinds of assets? In accounting, finance, and to a large extent in general usage, **financial assets** are those based on contractual agreements relating to future cash flows. Common examples of financial assets are investments in stocks and bonds; these investments entitle the holder to future dividends and interest, even if those future payments could be uncertain. An investment in equipment is not a financial asset—while the equipment could help generate future cash flows, there is no contract that identifies the potential cash flowing to the owner of the equipment. Items such as equipment, land, buildings, and inventory are typically called "real assets."[1]

Because financial assets are based on contracts, another way to think about the difference between financial and real assets is to consider whether there is a "counterparty." An investment in shares has a counterparty who issued those shares and who is expected to pay dividends in the future. An investment in bonds has a counterparty who is obligated to repay interest and principal on the bonds. A financial asset appears on the left-hand side of the balance sheet of the investor;

[1.] "Real assets" should not be confused with "real property," which is a term originating from common law referring to land and buildings (i.e., real estate).

a similar item should be on the right-hand side of the balance sheet of the counterparty as a liability or equity. Thinking about it this way, it is clear that a piece of equipment is not a financial asset—there is no counterparty opposite the equipment owner, and the equipment does not appear on the right-hand side of anyone's balance sheet.

From the above, we can see that one entity's financial asset and the counterparty's liability or equity are two sides of the same coin. That "coin" is a **financial instrument**, which is formally defined as follows in IAS 32 paragraph 11:

> ¶11   A financial instrument is any contract that gives rise to a financial asset of one entity and a financial liability or equity instrument of another entity.[2]

financial instrument   Any contract that gives rise to (i) a financial asset for one entity and (ii) a financial liability or equity instrument for another entity.

This chapter will focus on the asset side of financial instruments; Chapters 11 through 14 discuss financial liabilities, equity, and more complex financial instruments.

The most important accounting issue for financial assets is the measurement basis for reporting their values on the balance sheet date. There is no single measurement basis that is suitable for all financial assets because the trade-off between relevance and other qualitative characteristics of those measurements depends on management's intent with respect to those investments. For instance, an enterprise investing in the common shares of another company can own anywhere from a small fraction up to 100% of the latter company. When the investment is relatively small, the market price (if available) is a relevant and verifiable measure of how much the company would be able to obtain from selling those shares. In the case where one company (the "parent") owns a majority of the shares of another (the "subsidiary"), the market price is not particularly relevant because in such instances the parent does not intend to sell its holdings. In addition, the majority ownership implies a special economic relationship between the two companies—a relationship that would significantly change if the parent company were to sell its shares in the subsidiary. The parent also has inside information about the subsidiary not available to potential buyers. For all these reasons, the subsidiary's share price (again, if available), which is based on publicly available information, is not necessarily a reliable indicator of value of the subsidiary to the parent.

THRESHOLD CONCEPT
CONCEPTUAL FRAMEWORK

THRESHOLD CONCEPT
INFORMATION ASYMMETRY

The need for different measurement bases, however, does not imply that all measurement bases are possible for every kind of investment. Instead, accounting standards specify the criteria for different classifications of financial assets and the corresponding accounting treatment that is judged to be appropriate for that category. These standards have experienced significant changes over the last two decades, with this chapter reflecting the comprehensive overhaul in IFRS 9 issued in 2014 and effective beginning January 1, 2017.

The next section lays out a comprehensive system for classifying financial assets and provides an overview of the accounting method appropriate to each category. Sections C, D, and E will then look at the accounting for specific types of financial assets in more detail.

CHECKPOINT **CP7-1**

Why are accounts receivable financial assets and inventories are not?

---

2. Copyright © 2012 IFRS Foundation.

B. OVERVIEW OF FINANCIAL ASSET CLASSIFICATION

equity instrument A contract that gives the holder the residual interest in an entity after deducting all of its liabilities; an example is a common share.

derivative A financial instrument with all three of the following characteristics: (i) its value changes according to a specified variable, such as an interest rate or stock price; (ii) it requires no initial net investment or a small investment relative to non-derivative contracts with similar exposure to the specified variable; and (iii) it is settled at a future date.

debt instrument Any financial instrument that is not an equity instrument or a derivative.

In general, people tend to think about financial instruments in terms of whether they have the nature of equity, a derivative, or debt. These three general groupings reflect the economic characteristics of the instruments themselves. An **equity instrument** is a contract that gives the holder the residual interest in an entity after deducting all of its liabilities; an example is a common share (see IFRS—IAS 32). A **derivative** is a financial instrument with all three of the following characteristics: (i) its value changes according to a specified variable, such as an interest rate, stock price, and so on; (ii) it requires no initial net investment or a small investment relative to non-derivative contracts with similar exposure to the specified variable; and (iii) it is settled at a future date. An example of a derivative is a stock option, which entitles the holder of the option to buy (or sell) a certain number of shares at a particular price over a specified period of time. A **debt instrument**, while not specifically defined in IFRS, includes any financial instrument that is not an equity instrument or a derivative. A bond is a common example of a debt instrument.

While this three-way grouping is useful for describing the nature of the financial instruments, they are not sufficiently specific to reflect the reasons why enterprises invest in them, and those reasons are important factors in determining the appropriate accounting method. As a result, accounting standards separate financial assets into seven mutually exclusive categories:[3]

1. subsidiaries
2. investments in joint operations
3. investments in joint ventures
4. investments in associated companies
5. measured at fair value through profit or loss (FVPL)
6. measured at fair value through other comprehensive income (FVOCI)
7. measured at amortized cost

These categories will be explained more fully below. At this point, it is useful to obtain an overview of how these seven categories arise, how they relate to the three-way grouping (equity, derivative, debt), and which accounting methods are appropriate for each. Exhibit 7-1 illustrates these relationships.

As this diagram shows, depending on the reason for the investment, an equity investment can be classified into one of five categories: a subsidiary, a joint operation, a joint venture, an associate or FVPL. In contrast, derivatives are always classified as FVPL. Investments in debt instruments can be classified as FVPL, FVOCI, or amortized cost.

We now look at each of the seven categories of financial assets individually in the following two sections. Section C will look at the top four categories in Exhibit 7-1, which are known as strategic equity investments and usually held for the long term. Section D will look at the remaining categories, which are non-strategic in nature.

 CHECKPOINT **CP7-2**

Why is it not sufficient to simply identify investments as equity, debt, or a derivative for accounting purposes?

[3.] Technically, cash is another category of financial assets. The accounting for cash is straightforward and previously addressed in Chapter 5, so it is not repeated here.

| Exhibit 7-1 | Accounting classification of financial assets and the corresponding accounting treatment |

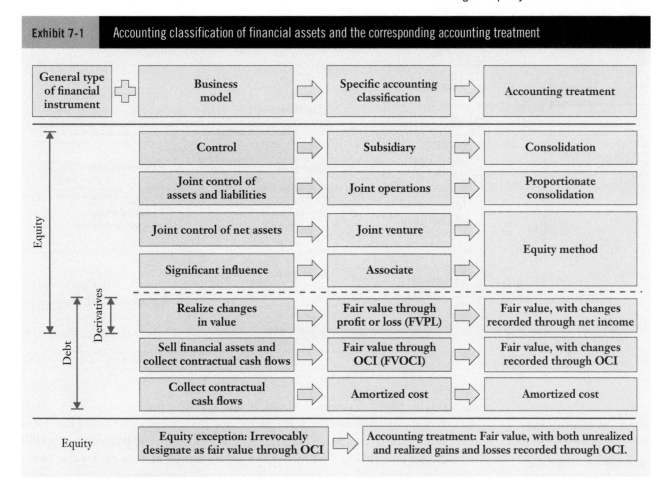

C. STRATEGIC EQUITY INVESTMENTS[4]

This section examines equity investments in other enterprises that are under the control, joint control, or significant influence of the investor enterprise. As these three labels suggest, enterprises hold these investments for strategic reasons—to access resources, extend their market reach, increase operational efficiency, and so on by directing or influencing the management decisions in the investee company. Furthermore, joint control can be exerted in two ways, resulting in four categories of strategic equity investments: subsidiaries, joint operations, joint ventures, or associates. The distinctions among these four categories depend on how much influence the investor is able to exert over the investee. In most circumstances, the determining factor will be the amount of voting power held by the investor. Exhibit 7-2 provides an overview of the four categories of equity investments.

This section does not look at all aspects of these types of investments, as the accounting issues are relatively complex and covered in textbooks at the advanced level. Instead, *we will solely focus on the classification* of financial assets into the four categories of subsidiaries, joint operations, joint ventures, and associates. Examples will serve to illustrate the overall consequence of these classifications without going into detail of the accounting procedures.

1. Subsidiaries

When one enterprise invests in the equity of another, that investment could be so substantial that it gives the investor control of the latter enterprise. **Control** in this

L.O. 7-3. Identify the measurement approach appropriate to the seven categories of financial assets and explain the general nature of the various measurement approaches.

control   The power to govern the financial and operating policies of an entity.

[4.] References to investments in equity also apply to ownership of organizations other than a corporation, such as a partnership. For ease of language, we will generally refer to investments in corporations.

| Exhibit 7-2 | Equity investment classification and accounting according to degree of influence |

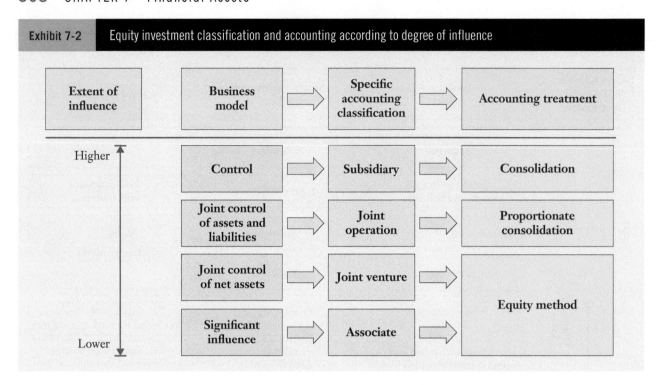

parent   An entity that controls another entity (the **subsidiary**).

subsidiary   An entity that is controlled by another entity (known as the **parent**).

THRESHOLD CONCEPT
CONCEPTUAL FRAMEWORK

context is the power to govern the financial and operating policies of an entity. When such control exists, the investor is the **parent** and the company that issued the shares is the **subsidiary**. Typically, we can presume that an investor company has control if it holds greater than 50% of the voting power of the investee, because such voting power allows the appointment of the board of directors, which sets the strategic direction of the investee. The presumption of control when an enterprise has more than 50% of the voting power can be rebutted with specific evidence to the contrary.

It is important to emphasize that it is the percentage of voting power that is important rather than the amount of investment. Some companies have more than one class of shares where the voting power is disproportionate to the amount of investment. For example, most preferred shares do not have voting rights. Another example is where one class of common shares has one vote per share and another class has a hundred votes per share (called super-voting shares).

ACCOUNTING TREATMENT—CONSOLIDATION   When the extent of investment gives one company control of another, it is reasonable to treat both companies as one economic unit, since the management of the parent company can direct the subsidiary's affairs as well as the parent's. For this reason, we prepare consolidated financial statements that show the two legal entities as one economic unit. This presentation is a more complete presentation of the economic resources and claims of the enterprise, contributing to representational faithfulness. In essence, we add together the financial statements of the two companies, but with a number of adjustments. Consolidation is a relatively complex topic that is covered in advanced financial accounting.

EXAMPLE   Princeton Powerboats holds all of the common shares of Sidney Sails, which has net assets of $100 million. Exhibit 7-3 shows condensed balance sheets for the two companies separately, and the consolidated balance sheet that combines the two entities.

As shown in this example, consolidated financial statements combine the amounts from the separate financial statements of the parent and subsidiary. The elimination column removes double counting that would result from simply adding the two columns of numbers together: Princeton's $100 million investment in

| Exhibit 7-3 | Separate and consolidated balance sheets and income statements for Princeton Powerboats and Sidney Sails |

$ millions	Sidney Sails (assumed)	+	Princeton Powerboats (assumed)	+	Elimination	=	Consolidated Princeton + Sidney
Balance sheets							
Investment in Sidney	—		100		−100		—
Other assets	300		600		—		900
Total assets	300		700		−100		900
Liabilities	200		400		—		600
Common shares	60		200		−60		200
Retained earnings	40		100		−40		100
Total liabilities and equity	300		700		−100		900
Income statements							
Income from Sidney Sails	—		14		−14		—
Revenue	50		150				200
Expenses	−36		−100				−136
Net income	14		64		−14		64

Sidney represents the net assets of Sidney ($300m in assets − $200m in liabilities = $100m net assets = $100m equity).

2. Joint operations

As defined in IFRS 11, joint operations and joint ventures are two types of joint arrangements. A **joint arrangement** is a contractual arrangement whereby two or more parties undertake an economic activity that is subject to joint control by those parties. **Joint control** is a contractually agreed upon sharing of control over an economic activity; joint control exists only when the strategic decisions relating to the activity require the unanimous consent of the parties sharing control. Joint arrangements usually have a limited life and a defined set of objectives or activities. For example, companies in the oil and gas industry often enter joint arrangements for the purpose of exploration and production at a particular geographic location. A joint arrangement is distinct from a typical partnership because partnerships do not generally require unanimous consent of the partners. A partnership that has a partnership agreement that does require unanimous consent would be a joint arrangement for accounting purposes.

For accounting purposes, IFRS further classifies joint arrangements as joint operations or joint ventures, depending on the nature of the investor's economic interests in the arrangement. A joint arrangement is a **joint operation** if the investor has rights to the assets and obligations for the liabilities of the arrangement. For example, a joint operation could involve a contractual arrangement that uses an unlimited liability partnership in which the partners share control of the assets and are exposed to the liabilities of the partnership. In contrast, a joint arrangement is a **joint venture** if the investor has rights to the *net* assets of the arrangement. For example, a joint venture could involve the sharing of control over a corporate entity that has limited liability.

joint arrangement A contractual arrangement whereby two or more parties undertake an economic activity that is subject to **joint control** by those parties.

joint control A contractually agreed upon sharing of control over an economic activity; joint control exists only when the strategic decisions relating to the activity require the unanimous consent of the parties sharing control.

joint operation A joint arrangement in which the investor has rights to the assets and obligations for the liabilities of the arrangement.

joint venture A joint arrangement in which the investor has rights to the net assets of the arrangement.

ACCOUNTING TREATMENT—PROPORTIONATE CONSOLIDATION Because joint operations have the characteristic of joint control, and the control relates to the specific assets and liabilities of the investee, some form of consolidation makes sense, just as control of a subsidiary requires consolidation as discussed above. However, full consolidation is inappropriate because more than one party shares control. Consequently, the appropriate accounting method is proportionate consolidation, which takes the investor's proportionate share of the joint operation's assets, liabilities, and income and adds it to the investor's accounts. For example, if Parson Petroleum is a 40% partner in a joint operation, then it includes 40% of the joint operation in its consolidated financial statements.

EXAMPLE   Suppose Princeton Powerboats has a 40% interest in Joy of Boating (JOB), a partnership. According to a contractual agreement, Princeton shares joint control of JOB with two other companies that together hold the remaining 60% ownership in JOB, and each party to the joint arrangement shares rights to JOB's assets and responsibilities for JOB's liabilities. Net assets of JOB total $250 million, so Princeton's 40% share equals $100 million. The separate and proportionately consolidated financial statements for Princeton and JOB are as shown in Exhibit 7-4.

Exhibit 7-4	Separate and proportionately consolidated balance sheets and income statements for Princeton Powerboats and Joy of Boating (JOB)						
$ millions	100% of JOB (assumed)	40% of JOB	+	Princeton (assumed)	+ Elimination	=	Proportionally consolidated Princeton + 40% of JOB
Balance sheets							
Investment in JOB	—	—		100	−100		—
Other assets	750	300		600	—		900
Total assets	750	300		700	−100		900
Liabilities	500	200		400	—		600
Common shares	150	60		200	−60		200
Retained earnings	100	40		100	−40		100
Total liab. and equity	750	300		700	−100		900
Income statements							
Income from JOB	—	—		14	−14		—
Revenue	125	50		150			200
Expenses	−90	−36		−100	—		−136
Net income	35	14		64	−14		64

The numbers in this example have been chosen to make Exhibit 7-3 and Exhibit 7-4 easy to compare. In both cases, Princeton's investment is $100 million. This $100 million represents all of the net assets of the subsidiary (Sidney Sails), while it represents 40% of the net assets of a larger joint operation (JOB) with total net assets of $250 million (40% × $250m = $100m). Comparing the two exhibits, you will note that there are essentially no differences between the results of full consolidation and proportionate consolidation when the amount of investment is the same.

3. Joint ventures

As just discussed, a joint venture is one type of joint arrangement in which the rights and responsibilities of the parties to the arrangement are limited to the net assets of the investee. That is, the joint ventures do not have direct control over the assets nor direct exposure to the liabilities of the venture.

ACCOUNTING TREATMENT—EQUITY METHOD   To reflect the exposure to the net assets of the venture, the appropriate accounting treatment is the equity method. The **equity method** can be thought of as a condensed consolidation that shows the

equity method   A method of accounting whereby the balance sheet value of the investment equals the purchase cost adjusted by the investor's share of the investee's post-acquisition changes in net assets, and the income recognized equals the investor's share of the investee's net income.

financial position and results of operations of the investee on a net basis on the balance sheet and income statement in one line (each). The balance sheet shows the value of the investment equal to the purchase cost adjusted by the investor's share of the investee's post-acquisition changes in net assets. The income statement shows the investor's share of the investee's net income. An example of the equity method will follow the discussion of associates, which also uses the equity method.

4. Associates

In some instances, an enterprise's investment in another is not sufficient to give it control, but nevertheless it is able to affect the strategic direction of the latter company. In these situations, we say that the investor has **significant influence**, the power to participate in the financial and operating policy decisions of the investee (but not to the extent of control or joint control). When the investor company has significant influence, we call the investee an **associate** of the investor; sometimes, entities also use the term "affiliate." We presume that significant influence exists if the investor holds between 20% and 50% (inclusive) of the voting power of the investee, and no significant influence otherwise. Similar to the determination of whether control exists, if the percentage voting power results in the presumption of significant influence, that presumption can be refuted with specific evidence to the contrary.

> significant influence   The power to participate in the financial and operating policy decisions of the investee (but not to the extent of **control** or **joint control**).
>
> associate   An entity over which the investor has **significant influence** and that is neither a **subsidiary** nor an interest in a **joint venture**.

While it is clear that the upper limit of 50% makes sense in that any higher investment would confer control, why can we presume that there is significant influence for investments with 20%, 25%, or 45% voting power? Why do we presume that there is no significant influence below 20%?

There are two distinct reasons for this presumption. The first is that an investor often does not require more than 50% of votes to be in a position to appoint/elect members onto the investee's board of directors, particularly for publicly traded firms with diffused ownership. Representation on the board of directors gives the investor influence, but not control, over the strategic direction of the investee.

The second reason is more subtle but perhaps more important. It is that the extent of the investment itself provides strong positive evidence, not just a presumption, that the investor does have significant influence. Why? It is because significant influence is the most likely reason for a level of ownership that is as high as 50%. Portfolio theory in finance concludes that investors can achieve better risk–return trade-offs by diversifying investments. Thus, if the only reason for an investment is to obtain the highest return at the lowest risk, an enterprise can do better by having a portfolio of many investments rather than one large, concentrated holding in one company. The fact that an enterprise does have a high level of investment in another indicates that it is willing to bear the additional risk of the concentrated investment in return for the ability to influence the direction of the investee. In other words, finance theory suggests that it is not rational for an enterprise to hold a large position in the equity of another company if it did not want, and is not able to exercise, significant influence.

The ability to exert significant influence is valuable to the investor because it helps reduce the two types of information asymmetry discussed in Chapter 1. Having representation on the board of directors and generally being able to participate in the governance of the investee alleviates the moral hazard inherent in the agency relationship between ownership and management. At the same time, an investor company with significant influence faces less adverse selection because it is able to obtain better (i.e., inside) information on the investee in comparison to other investors who do not have such influence.

THRESHOLD CONCEPT
INFORMATION ASYMMETRY

If you reflect on these points about why significant influence confers advantages over portfolio investments—advantages that compensate for the additional risk of concentrated holdings—you should see that the same arguments apply to situations of full control or joint control discussed above. For this reason, the accounting treatment for investments with significant influence has some of the features of consolidation. However, significant influence is not control, so the investor and investee cannot be considered one economic unit. Thus, we do not combine the financial statements of the two entities. The accounting method that produces results similar to consolidation but without actually consolidating the financial statements is called the equity method.

ACCOUNTING TREATMENT—EQUITY METHOD As noted above, the equity method can be thought of as a condensed consolidation that shows the investor's share of the net assets and net income of the investee. The following example uses an investment in an associate to illustrate the equity method. The effects are similar for a joint venture accounted for under the equity method.

EXAMPLE Princeton Powerboats has a third investment, a 20% interest in Asymmetric Spinnaker Company (ASC). Princeton has determined that it can and does exert significant influence over ASC.

As shown in Exhibit 7-5, ASC has total assets of $1,500m and liabilities of $1,000m, so net assets equal $500m. Princeton owns 20% of ASC, so it shows $100 million (20% × $500m = $100m) as "Investment in ASC" on the balance sheet. On its income statement, Princeton shows $14 million as "Income from ASC" for its 20% share of ASC's net income of $70 million.

Exhibit 7-5	Balance sheets and income statements for Princeton Powerboats and Asymmetric Spinnaker Company (ASC)		
$ millions	**100% of ASC**	**20% of ASC**	**Princeton under equity method**
Balance sheets			
Investment in ASC	—	—	100
Other assets	1,500	300	600
Total assets	1,500	300	700
Liabilities	1,000	200	400
Common shares	300	60	200
Retained earnings	200	40	100
Total liab. and equity	1,500	300	700
Income statements			
Income from ASC	—	—	14
Revenue	250	50	150
Expenses	−180	−36	−100
Net income	70	14	64

To compare and contrast consolidation, proportionate consolidation, and the equity method, let's review the financial statements of Princeton in the three examples given above. Note that Princeton has an equal dollar amount of investment in each of the three companies ($100 million) so that the only difference is the accounting method.

As Exhibit 7-6 shows, the net asset positions for the three scenarios are identical ($300 million), as are the amounts of net income ($64 million). However, the equity method differs from consolidation and proportionate consolidation in the components of net assets and net income. Whereas the two consolidation methods include the individual line items (assets, liabilities, revenues, expenses) of the subsidiary, the equity method nets out liabilities against assets and expenses against revenue. Thus, the three methods are equivalent on a net basis, but they differ in terms of the individual line items.

Another important point to note is that for all four types of strategic investments, the value of the investment goes up and down with the income earned or losses incurred

Exhibit 7-6	Comparison of consolidated, proportionately consolidated, and equity method balance sheets and income statements for Princeton Powerboats

$ millions	Consolidated Princeton + Sidney	Proportionally consolidated Princeton + 40% of JOB	Princeton + 20% of ASC using the equity method
Balance sheets			
Investment in ASC	—	—	100
Other assets	900	900	600
Total assets	900 } 300	900 } 300	700 } 300
Liabilities	600	600	400
Common shares	200	200	200
Retained earnings	100	100	100
Total liabilities and equity	900	900	700
Income statements			
Income from ASC	—	—	14
Revenue	200	200	150
Expenses	−136	−136	−100
Net income	64	64	64

by the investee and any capital contributed to or withdrawn from the investee. In other words, for accounting purposes, the value of the investment does not have a direct connection to the market price of the shares in the investee (or other equity instrument). In contrast, the market price is much more important for non-strategic investments, which we discuss next.

As mentioned at the beginning of this section, the coverage here is to provide you with the ability to classify an investment according to the degree of influence that an investor company has over another, to identify the appropriate accounting method for each classification, and to generally understand the effect of the three methods. Consolidation, proportionate consolidation, and the equity method can be much more complex; we leave thorough coverage of these complexities to advanced financial accounting texts.

 CHECKPOINT **CP7-3**

What are the four categories of strategic investments and how do we account for them under IFRS?

D. NON-STRATEGIC INVESTMENTS

The four categories of financial assets discussed in the last section relate solely to equity investments, and only those equity instruments that have voting rights, which allows the investor to exert varying degrees of influence on the investee. We now turn our attention to three categories of financial assets that are not limited to equity investments. These three categories are those diagrammed on the bottom half of Exhibit 7-1, which is reproduced in Exhibit 7-7 for ease of reference. Note that the very bottom row shows an exception for equity; it is not associated with a particular business model, so it does not fit the overall classification framework. We will address this exception after the three categories determined by business models.

L.O. 7-4. Analyze historical cost and fair value information to determine the appropriate balance sheet measurement and income recognition subsequent to purchase for three categories of financial assets: fair value through profit or loss, fair value through OCI, and amortized cost.

Exhibit 7-7	Accounting classification and accounting treatment of non-strategic financial assets

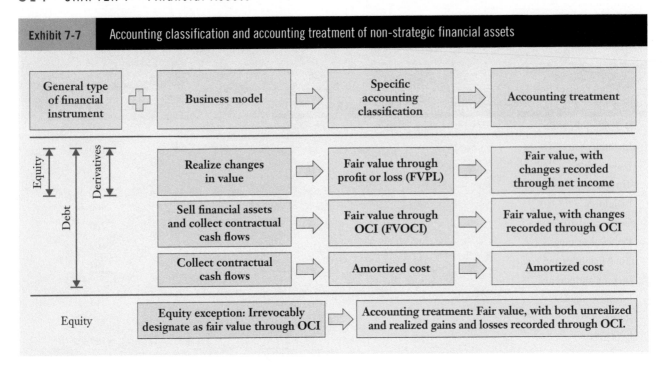

1. Fair value through profit or loss (FVPL)

Aside from the strategic reasons for investing in the equity of other companies discussed in the previous section, firms also buy equity with the intent (i.e., business model) of benefiting from changes in the value. In other words, these are portfolio investments that management intends to trade with the expectation of profit. Reflecting this business model, IFRS requires such investments to be categorized as FVPL so that changes in investment values are recognized in net income (as opposed to OCI).

In addition, the nature of derivatives is that they involve a higher level of risk for a particular amount of investment in comparison to non-derivative investments (i.e., debt and equity), so they are considered to be speculative investments. Consequently, accounting standards classify derivatives as FVPL so that net income includes the effects of these investments.[5]

Other than derivatives and equity held to earn profits, FVPL is also the default category for any financial assets not classified into one of the other categories. Importantly, the FVPL category includes investments in debt instruments not classified into one of the next two categories (FVOCI or amortized cost). Many companies do have short-term investments in bonds to earn a return; these funds would otherwise be held as cash.

THRESHOLD CONCEPT
CONCEPTUAL
FRAMEWORK

Fair value is the relevant measure of value because financial statement readers find it useful to know for how much these investments could be sold, since they are likely to be sold in the near future. Fair value is also assumed to be verifiable because there is likely to be an active market for these securities; if there were no active market, then companies would not buy these investments with a business model of profiting from trading.

Changes in fair value are also called unrealized gains and losses, where "unrealized" refers to the fact that the investments have not yet been sold. The unrealized gains or losses of FVPL investments should flow through net income (profit or loss) because the intention to trade for a profit implies that the trading activity is part of the enterprise's regular operating activities.

[5.] Technically, FVPL includes all derivatives *other than those used for hedging.* Hedging is a topic beyond the scope of this chapter. Chapter 14 will discuss hedges.

For example, suppose Holberg Enterprises had the following transactions relating to its equity portfolio (and had no other portfolio equity investments):

Exhibit 7-8	Holberg Enterprises's equity investments				
Date	Transaction	Company	# Shares	Amount per share	Total
2020					
Sept. 20	Bought	Royal Bank	400	$60.00	$24,000
Nov. 15	Bought	TELUS	500	40.00	20,000
Nov. 24	Dividends	Royal Bank	400	0.50	200
Dec. 31	Year-end closing price	Royal Bank	400	63.00	25,200
Dec. 31	Year-end closing price	TELUS	500	39.00	19,500
2021					
Jan. 10	Sold	Royal Bank	400	62.50	25,000

If Holberg classifies these investments as FVPL, the company would record the following journal entries:

Exhibit 7-9	Journal entries to record Holberg's investments if classified as FVPL		
Sept. 20	Dr. FVPL investments—Royal Bank	24,000	
	Cr. Cash		24,000
Nov. 15	Dr. FVPL investments—TELUS	20,000	
	Cr. Cash		20,000
Nov. 24	Dr. Cash	200	
	Cr. Dividend income		200
Dec. 31	Dr. FVPL investments—Royal Bank	1,200	
	Cr. Gain (loss) on FVPL investments ($25,200 − $24,000)		1,200
Dec. 31	Dr. Gain (loss) on FVPL investments ($19,500 − $20,000)	500	
	Cr. FVPL investments—TELUS		500
Jan. 10	Dr. Cash	25,000	
	Dr. Gain (loss) on FVPL investments ($25,000 − $25,200)	200	
	Cr. FVPL investments—Royal Bank		25,200

Notice that the year-end journal entries to adjust the investments to fair value result in gains or losses, which are unrealized and flow through income. The write-up of the Royal Bank shares to $63/share at the year-end later results in a loss of $0.50/share, or $200 in total, when the shares are sold for $62.50. Through the entire holding period of these shares, Holberg recorded $1,200 − 200 = $1,000 of gains and $200 of dividend income.

Regarding the year-end journal entries for the re-measurement of the investments to fair value, the above shows the simplest way to represent the adjustment to the balance sheet (i.e., the debit to FVPL investments). In practice, enterprises will use a valuation account, such as "Valuation adjustments on FVPL investments." This practice is similar to the use of a contra account for allowance for doubtful accounts. Doing so allows the records to reflect fair value adjustments while preserving cost information, which is required to compute gains or losses for tax purposes when the enterprise later sells the investments. However, it is important to note that the valuation account can be positive or negative, whereas the allowance for doubtful accounts must always reduce the value of receivables (i.e., it must have a credit or zero balance).

2. Fair value through other comprehensive income (FVOCI)

The FVOCI category includes debt securities included in a business model with which the entity intends (i) to profit from changes in value and (ii) to collect cash flows to which the entity is entitled. Note that neither equity investments nor derivatives can be classified as FVOCI.

FVOCI means that the balance sheet reports these investments at fair value, while changes in value flow through OCI in the statement of comprehensive income (not through net income). Therefore, FVPL and FVOCI have the same reporting outcomes on the balance sheet, but they differ in the statement of comprehensive income. The effect of fair value changes flows through net income under FVPL, but through OCI under FVOCI. When an entity sells investments measured at FVOCI, the total gain or loss flows through income.

Since equity investments cannot be classified as FVOCI, Holberg's investments in the shares of Royal Bank and TELUS cannot be used to illustrate the accounting for this category. Instead, we will defer briefly until subsection 6 for a complete example illustrating the accounting for FVOCI.

Note that the difference in treatment between FVPL and FVOCI applies only to *unrealized* gains and losses. For both categories, *realized* gains and losses from actual disposals of the financial assets flow through net income, not OCI. In other words, OCI is recycled into net income.

 CHECKPOINT **CP7-4**

What is the key difference between the accounting treatments for FVPL and FVOCI investments?

3. Amortized cost

Amortized cost is a category of financial investments that have fixed or determinable payments representing principal and interest, and the entity intends to collect these contractual cash flows. This category applies only to debt investments. Implementation of the amortized cost method requires discounted cash flow analysis, which we discuss in Section E.

4. Exception for equity investments with an irrevocable election

IFRS 9 provides for an exception to the treatment of *equity* investments that would otherwise be classified as FVPL. This exception allows an entity to elect to present changes in the fair value of an investment through OCI. This election must satisfy three conditions: it must be made when the entity initially acquires the investment; the investment must be in equity; and the election is irrevocable, meaning that the investment cannot be reclassified later into another category.

The results of designating a particular equity investment in this manner are not exactly the same as discussed above for the FVOCI category. While the entity holds the investment, any dividends received would be recorded in net income, while changes in fair value flow through OCI, just like for the FVOCI category. However, upon sale/derecognition, any gain or loss does *not* flow through net income, but continues to go into OCI. At this time, the accumulated other comprehensive income (AOCI) for this investment would then directly transfer over to retained earnings. In other words, *there is no recycling of OCI into net income* when an entity chooses to make this election for an equity investment. Because of this difference, we do not use the FVOCI acronym to identify investments with this irrevocable election.

In the example given for Holberg Enterprises in Exhibit 7-8, had the company made the irrevocable election, at the time of purchase, to measure the investments in the shares of Royal Bank and TELUS at fair value with changes flowing through OCI, it would record the transactions as follows:

Exhibit 7-10	Journal entries to record Holberg's investments if elected to record through OCI		
2020			
Sept. 20	Dr. Equity investments with OCI election—Royal Bank	24,000	
	Cr. Cash		24,000
Nov. 15	Dr. Equity investments with OCI election—TELUS	20,000	
	Cr. Cash		20,000
Nov. 24	Dr. Cash	200	
	Cr. Dividend income		200
Dec. 31	Dr. Equity investments with OCI election—Royal Bank	1,200	
	Cr. OCI—Gain (loss) on equity investments with OCI election—Royal Bank ($25,200 − $24,000)		1,200
Dec. 31	Dr. OCI—Gain (loss) on equity investments with OCI election—TELUS ($19,500 − $20,000)	500	
	Cr. Equity investments with OCI election—TELUS		500
2021			
Jan. 10	Dr. Cash	25,000	
	Dr. OCI—Gain (loss) on equity investments with OCI election—Royal Bank ($25,000 − $25,200)	200	
	Cr. Equity investments with OCI election—Royal Bank		25,200

Notice that (i) the year-end unrealized gains or losses as well as (ii) the realized gain on the sale of Royal Bank shares both go through OCI. The difference between the above and the FVPL journal entries in Exhibit 7-9 (other than account names) is that all of the gains and losses pass through OCI. For the investment in Royal Bank that was sold in 2021, the accumulated other comprehensive income (AOCI) is $1,000 ($1,200 gain for the fair value adjustment in 2020 less $200 loss on sale in 2021; or equivalently, proceeds of $25,000 less cost of $24,000), so at the end of 2021, a closing entry will transfer $1,000 from AOCI to retained earnings.

One might question why IFRS 9 precludes the recycling of OCI generated by investments with this election, in contrast to the treatment of FVOCI investments, which do result in recycling. The reason has to do with earnings management. If the standards specified recycling of OCI, then management can pick the opportune time to sell financial assets with this election in order to transfer unrealized gains (or losses) out of AOCI and into profit (or loss) to boost (or reduce) net income. Without recycling, all of the accumulated gains and losses bypass the income statement and transfer directly into retained earnings, precluding the earnings management.

This rationale then raised another question: why does the FVOCI category specify that OCI needs to be recycled into income when the investments are sold? Wouldn't that create the earnings management opportunities we just identified? It does. Indeed, an earlier version of IFRS 9 in 2012 did anticipate this problem and did not have the FVOCI category at all. The category was later added in 2014 after considerable feedback and lobbying, particularly from financial institutions with large holdings of

THRESHOLD CONCEPT
EARNINGS QUALITY

debt investments that would otherwise have been classified as either FVPL or amortized cost. Many commenters stated that they used a business model for their debt investments that was neither solely to trade for profit, nor solely to collect contractual cash flows, but was rather a combination of the two. The IASB agreed and added the FVOCI category to accommodate the hybrid business model.

5. Reclassifications from one category to another

THRESHOLD CONCEPT
EARNINGS QUALITY

The classification of financial assets into the different categories discussed above depends on business models selected by management rather than the characteristics inherent in the investments themselves. Consequently, changes in management intention can result in a change in classification. However, if there are no constraints on the ability of management to reclassify, then there could be significant opportunities for companies to manage earnings. For example, consider what would happen if a company were to reclassify an investment with unrealized gains from FVOCI to FVPL. Similarly, what if a company reclassifies an investment with unrealized losses from FVPL to FVOCI? These reclassifications would allow management to increase earnings by recognizing unrealized gains and deferring losses. To prevent this opportunistic activity from occurring, IFRS 9 provides specific guidance for these situations.

Note that derivatives can only be classified as FVPL (again, with the exception of derivatives used in hedging). Likewise, investments in equity can only be classified as FVPL, with the exception of those for which the entity has made an irrevocable election to measure at fair value through OCI. In all these cases, no reclassifications are possible. Thus, what remain are investments in debt.

As illustrated in Exhibit 7-1 and again in Exhibit 7-7, debt investments can be classified as FVPL, FVOCI, or amortized cost. Reclassifications out of and into these three categories produce six possible permutations, which are all addressed in IFRS 9, in paragraphs 5.6.2 to 5.6.7. Exhibit 7-11 summarizes these six reclassification scenarios. Note that in all cases, the reclassification is treated prospectively, such that there are no restatements of prior results.

We can make some generalizations from this table. First, with the exception of Case 4, when a reclassification occurs, the financial asset is re-measured to fair value.

Exhibit 7-11		Reclassifications of debt investments			
Case	From	To	IFRS 9 para.	Balance sheet value on reclassification	Changes in value up to reclassification date
1.	FVPL	FVOCI	5.6.6	Fair value	(Fair value – carrying value) recognized in income
2.	FVPL	Amortized cost	5.6.3	Fair value	(Fair value – carrying value) recognized in income
3.	FVOCI	FVPL	5.6.7	Fair value	OCI up to reclassification date recognized in income
4.	FVOCI	Amortized cost	5.6.5	Amortized cost computed using information from original purchase	OCI up to reclassification date offset against fair value
5.	Amortized cost	FVPL	5.6.2	Fair value	(Fair value – carrying value) recognized in income
6.	Amortized cost	FVOCI	5.6.4	Fair value	(Fair value – carrying value) recognized in OCI

FVPL = fair value through profit or loss

FVOCI = fair value through other comprehensive income

Second, with the exception of Cases 4 and 6, changes in value up to the reclassification date flow through income. These two observations suggest that the treatment of reclassifications is as if there were a sale and then a repurchase of the same financial asset on the same date.

As for the exceptions of Cases 4 and 6, they involve reclassifications between FVOCI and amortized cost, in either direction. The end result of the exceptions is that the balance sheet outcome after reclassification is as if the investment had always been in the category into which the entity has reclassified it, and a one-time adjustment is made to OCI. In Case 4, where an entity reclassifies from FVOCI to amortized cost, it is as if the investment had always been carried at amortized cost. In Case 6, where an entity reclassifies from amortized cost to FVOCI, it is as if the investment had always been carried at FVOCI.

For example, suppose a debt investment purchased for $100 had increased in fair value to $120 at the reclassification date, but the amortized cost remained at $100. In Case 4, FVOCI accounting up to the reclassification date would require the investment to be valued at $120, and $20 would have been recorded in OCI. Upon reclassification, the investment is written back down to $100 by debiting OCI by $20 and crediting the investment by $20. Result: the investment is carried at the amortized cost of $100 and OCI is zero.

In Case 6, using the same facts, amortized cost accounting up to the date of reclassification would show the carrying amount at $100. Upon reclassification, the investment would be written up to the fair value of $120, with the increment of $20 recognized in OCI of the current period.

These two exceptions (Cases 4 and 6) would seem to present opportunities for management to improve the appearance of their financial position by reclassifying investments with losses out of FVOCI and into amortized cost, while reclassifying investments with gains out of amortized cost and into FVOCI. These opportunities are limited by paragraph 4.4.1, which states, "When, and only when, an entity changes its business model for managing financial assets it shall reclassify all affected financial assets...." In other words, management is not allowed to "cherry pick" particular assets with gains or losses for reclassification; instead, it must consider the overall business model for a portfolio of financial assets being managed, and reclassify the entire portfolio if the business model changes.

 CHECKPOINT **CP7-5**

Why is it important for accounting standards to specify rules concerning the reclassification of financial assets?

6. Example: A debt investment to illustrate the differences among FVPL, FVOCI, and amortized cost

On January 1, 2021, Terrace Co. pays $100,000 to purchase 100 Government of Canada bonds that have a maturity date of December 31, 2025 (five years later). Each bond has a face value of $1,000 and a coupon interest rate of 6%, payable annually. That is, the bonds will pay Terrace Co. interest of $6,000 (6% × 100 bonds × $1,000/bond) each year on December 31, and the face value of $100,000 (100 bonds × $1,000/bond) on December 31, 2025. Since the purchase price and the face value are both $1,000 per bond, Terrace purchased the bonds at par.

On Terrace Co.'s fiscal year-end of December 31, 2021, the bonds had a quoted price of $1,022 per bond. How should Terrace Co. report this investment on its

December 31, 2021 balance sheet? How should the company report any changes in fair value? How much income or comprehensive income would be reported (ignoring income taxes)?

Intend to trade:	If Terrace Co. holds the bonds in a business model that sells bonds for a profit, it would classify this investment as FVPL. It would report the bonds on its balance sheet at fair value of $102,200 (100 bonds × $1,022/bond). On its income statement, Terrace Co. would report an unrealized gain of $2,200 ($102,200 − $100,000). The interest income is $6,000, so the net effect is $6,000 + $2,200 = $8,200 reported in income.
Intend to hold or trade:	If Terrace Co. holds the bonds in a business model that both holds the investments to collect contractual cash flows and sells them for profit, it would classify the bonds as FVOCI. It would report the bonds on its balance sheet at fair value of $102,200, the same as for the held-for-trading category. However, it would not report an unrealized gain of $2,200 on the income statement. Rather, Terrace Co. would report the unrealized gain in other comprehensive income. The $6,000 interest income would be reported in the income statement.
Intend to hold:	If Terrace Co. intends to hold the bonds until December 31, 2025, so as to collect all the cash flows from the bond, then it would classify them as held to maturity. In this case, its balance sheet would report the amortized cost of the bonds at $100,000. The income statement would report interest income of $6,000.

Exhibit 7-12 summarizes the accounting treatment for these bonds using the three methods:

Exhibit 7-12	Accounting treatment of Terrace Co.'s bond investments		
Financial asset category	**Fair value through profit or loss**	**Fair value through OCI**	**Amortized cost**
Dec. 31, 2021 Balance sheet	$102,200	$102,200	$100,000
Interest income	$ 6,000	$ 6,000	$ 6,000
Unrealized gain on income statement	2,200	0	0
Total recognized income	8,200	6,000	6,000
Unrealized gain in OCI	0	2,200	0
Total comprehensive income	$ 8,200	$ 8,200	$ 6,000

Notice that the balance sheet amounts for FVPL and FVOCI are the same because they both reflect fair value of $102,200. However, the amounts of income are different—whereas FVPL recognizes the fair value change of $2,200 through income (profit or loss), FVOCI shows this amount as other comprehensive income.

The journal entries that would be recorded for the three classifications are shown in Exhibit 7-13.

To close this example, suppose Terrace sells 20 of the 100 bonds (20%) on June 30, 2022 for $1,050 per bond, giving total proceeds of $21,000. Of this amount, $600 represents accrued interest (20% × $100,000 × 6%/year × 0.5 year). The proceeds excluding accrued interest are thus $20,400 ($21,000 − $600), and the realized gain relative to purchase cost is $400 ($20,400 − $20,000). The journal entries in Exhibit 7-14 would be recorded under the three different classifications:

| Exhibit 7-13 | Journal entries to account for Terrace's bond investments | | | | | |

Financial asset category	FVPL		FVOCI		Amortized cost	
	Dr.	**Cr.**	**Dr.**	**Cr.**	**Dr.**	**Cr.**
Jan. 1, 2021 Purchase						
Dr. FVPL investments	100,000		—		—	
Dr. FVOCI investments		—	100,000		—	
Dr. Amortized cost investments		—		—	100,000	
Cr. Cash		100,000		100,000		100,000
Dec. 31, 2021						
Recognition of interest income						
Dr. Cash or interest receivable	6,000		6,000		6,000	
Cr. Interest income		6,000		6,000		6,000
Dec. 31, 2021 Re-measurement						
Dr. FVPL investments	2,200		—		—	
Cr. Gain on FVPL investments		2,200		—		—
Dr. FVOCI investments		—	2,200		—	
Cr. OCI on FVOCI investments		—		2,200		—

| Exhibit 7-14 | Journal entries to account for the sale of 20% of Terrace Co.'s bond investments |

If classified as FVPL		
Dr. Cash	21,000	
Dr. Loss on sale of FVPL investments*	40	
Cr. FVPL investments (20 × $1,022)		20,440
Cr. Interest income		600

If classified as FVOCI		
Dr. Cash	21,000	
Dr. OCI on FVOCI investments (20 × $22)	440	
Cr. FVOCI investments (20 × $1,022)		20,440
Cr. Interest income		600
Cr. Gain on sale of FVOCI investments[†]		400

If classified as amortized cost		
Dr. Cash	21,000	
Cr. Amortized cost investments (20 × $1,000)		20,000
Cr. Interest income		600
Cr. Gain on sale of Amortized cost investments[‡]		400

*Gain (loss) = Proceeds net of interest − Carrying value = $20,400 − $20,440

[†]Gain = Proceeds net of interest − Cost = $20,400 − $20,000

[‡]Gain = Proceeds net of interest − Cost = $20,400 − $20,000

Several points are worth noting about the above journal entries.

1. Regardless of the investments' categorization, the amount removed/credited from the balance sheet is proportionate to the amount recorded on the balance sheet account.
2. The entry to record the proceeds from sale needs to distinguish the interest component, if any. (For equity investments, any dividend income would be similarly separated.)

3. For FVPL investments, the gain or loss recognized through the income statement is the difference between (i) the proceeds net of interest income and (ii) the fair value on the balance sheet. In this case, the proceeds net of interest are $20,400, while the balance sheet fair value is $20,440, resulting in a loss of $40.

4. For FVOCI and amortized cost investments, the gain or loss equals the difference between (i) the proceeds net of interest income and (ii) the amortized cost of the investment. Thus the gain is equal to $20,400 − $20,000 = $400.

5. For FVOCI investments, OCI related to the investment needs to be reversed out of equity. In this case, $440 of OCI is debited out of equity.

The example of Terrace Co.'s investment is the simplest of examples, as the company purchased the bonds at par. In such cases, there is no amortization and the amortized cost method is just the cost method. In instances where a bond is purchased at a non-par amount, there will be amortization. Furthermore, this amortization is necessary not just for the amortized cost method, but also for FVOCI investments. We look at this issue in more detail now in Section E.

E. AMORTIZATION OF DEBT INVESTMENTS

L.O. 7-5. Apply present value techniques to account for investments in debt instruments.

effective interest method Calculates the amortized cost of a financial asset at each reporting date as the present value of the asset's cash flows discounted at the **effective interest rate** or **yield.**

effective interest rate (or yield) The discount rate that results in a present value equal to the purchase price of a financial asset. In finance, this is called the internal rate of return (IRR).

As you learned in introductory accounting, enterprises can use a number of different methods to amortize (or depreciate) non-financial items such as property, plant, and equipment. In contrast, IFRS permits only one method to amortize debt instruments: the **effective interest method**. This method calculates the amortized cost of a financial asset at each reporting date as the present value of the asset's cash flows discounted at the **effective interest rate** or **yield**. The yield is the discount rate that produces a present value equal to the purchase price of the financial asset. The yield is also called the internal rate of return (IRR) in finance. (For a review of present value techniques, refer to Appendix B at the end of this book. For instructions on how to use a financial calculator to solve time value of money problems, refer to the box titled Using Financial Calculators.)

1. The effective interest method

To understand this method, consider the underlying substance of an investment in a debt instrument such as a bond. Suppose a bond has a $1,000 face value and a coupon interest rate of 6% per year. This bond promises to pay $60 (6% × $1,000) each year, plus $1,000 when the bond matures. (At this point, we do not yet need to be explicit about when this bond matures.)

- If the investors in the market for these bonds demand a higher yield, say 7%, then the bond price must be lower than $1,000 for investors to be willing to buy this bond, because the coupon rate of 6% is too low compared to the market yield. When the bond price is lower than the face value, we call it a *discount bond*.
- If investors demand a yield exactly equal to the coupon rate of 6%, then the bond price will exactly equal the $1,000 face value or par value. We call this a *par bond*.
- If investors demand a yield lower than 6%, say 5%, then the bond price must rise above $1,000 because the coupon rate exceeds the rate demanded by investors;

Exhibit 7-15	Summary of general bond pricing		
Coupon rate	**Market yield**	**Bond price**	**Bond type**
6%	5%	> $1,000	Premium bond
6%	6%	= $1,000	Par bond
6%	7%	< $1,000	Discount bond

the price increases to a point such that the bond's price equals the present value at the 5% market rate. When the bond price is higher than face value, the bond is a *premium bond.*

Thus, depending on the prevailing yield at the time of investment, the purchase price can be higher or lower than the face value, while the value at maturity remains $1,000. The effective interest method produces the sequence of values between the purchase price and the maturity value. This sequence of values is the present value of the bond's cash flows at a particular date discounted at the effective interest rate, which is the yield of the bond. While the exact figures depend on each circumstance, the patterns in general should look like the following in Exhibit 7-16:

Exhibit 7-16	Stylized patterns of bond values between purchase and maturity dates

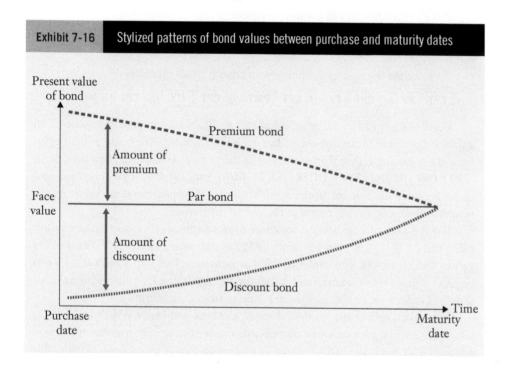

While somewhat difficult to discern, the lines for premium and discount bonds are curved rather than linear. The slopes are flatter farther away from maturity and become steeper toward the maturity date.

So far, the discussion of the effective interest method has been qualitative to outline the general ideas. To apply the method quantitatively, we need to identify one additional fact in addition to the three pieces of information already identified: the maturity. Thus, we need four pieces of information in total:

- the maturity date (or length of time to maturity)
- the maturity value or face value
- the coupon payments (or rate) and frequency
- the market yield or effective interest rate

With these four pieces of information, we can compute the price of the bond.

For illustration purposes, we assume a short time to maturity of two years to keep the computations simple. We assume the facts in Exhibit 7-17 for three bonds purchased by Ucluelet Umbrellas at the beginning of Year 1.

Realistically, an investor will know the purchase price from the amount paid rather than having to value the bond. Using the price of the bond, the investor then computes the effective interest rate using a financial calculator or a spreadsheet.

Using Financial Calculators

It is very important that you understand how to use a financial calculator, as you will need one to solve many of the problems related to time value of money (TVM) in this textbook. The financial calculator keystrokes illustrated in this text are for the Texas Instruments BA II Plus, given its widespread use. Most other financial calculators employ a similar methodology; however, the required keystrokes may differ slightly across brands and models of calculators. Refer to your owner's manual for specifics.

The abbreviations that follow are used throughout the text in TVM illustrations:

- PV — present value
- FV — amount due at the end of N periods (i.e., the future value)
- PMT — amount of the annuity payment
- I/Y — interest rate per period
- N — number of periods

To solve for (compute) the unknown variable, press these keys:

`CPT` `PV` or `CPT` `FV` or `CPT` `PMT` or `CPT` `I/Y` or `CPT` `N`

BGN—You need to set your calculator to BGN to compute the value of an annuity due. An annuity due is one in which the payments are made at the beginning of the period, rather than at the end of the period. To do this, press these keys: `2ND` `PMT` [BGN] `2ND` `ENTER` [SET] `CE/C`. Your calculator's display will now include a small BGN in the upper right-hand corner. Repeat the same keystrokes to return to the mode for payments at the end of the period.

For the sake of consistency, we enter present values (PVs) as negative values using the (`+`|`−`) key, and payments (PMTs) and future values (FVs) as positive values. (Alternatively, you can enter PVs as positive values and PMTs and FVs as negative values. What is important is that the signage of the PVs differs from that of the PMTs and FVs, to distinguish cash inflows from cash outflows.)

When you follow the methodology in the text and input PMTs and FVs as positive values, the calculator's output will display a negative number when you solve for PVs, such as −1.074.257426. The negative sign is ignored when using this information to prepare journal entries.

CAUTION: The Texas Instruments BA II Plus allows you to specify the number of interest-compounding periods per year. Before you start, it is important to check the factory default setting by pressing `2ND` `I/Y` [PY] and verify that it shows 1. If the compounding frequency (number of payments per period) is set at 1, do not change it as the examples in this text assume P/Y = 1 and use the number of periods to maturity. If the compounding period is other than P/Y = 1, reset the compounding period to 1 by following the instructions in your owner's manual on how to make this change.

There are a couple of reasons why we set the compounding period at 1 irrespective of the number of payments in a year:

1. Conceptually, many people find it easier to think in terms of an interest rate per period and the number of periods to maturity.

2. It is consistent with the format for entering the data into an Excel spreadsheet.

Note that the `CE/C` key does not clear the data in your TVM registry keys (`N` `I/Y` `PV` `PMT` `FV`). The required keystrokes to clear this information are `2ND` `FV` [CLR TVM].

Exhibit 7-17	Sample bond valuation on date of purchase		
	Bond A Premium bond	**Bond B** Par bond	**Bond C** Discount bond
Facts			
Face value (P)	$ 1,000	$ 1,000	$ 1,000
Time to maturity (t)	2 years	2 years	2 years
Coupon payments (C)	$ 60 (6%) per year	$ 60 (6%) per year	$ 60 (6%) per year
Effective interest rate (r)	5%	6%	7%
Total present value	$1,018.59^A	$1,000.00^B	$ 981.92^C

[A]1,000 **FV** 60 **PMT** 2 **N** 5 **I/Y** **CPT** **PV** → PV = −1,018.59 (rounded)
[B]1,000 **FV** 60 **PMT** 2 **N** 6 **I/Y** **CPT** **PV** → PV = −1,000.00
[C]1,000 **FV** 60 **PMT** 2 **N** 7 **I/Y** **CPT** **PV** → PV = −981.92 (rounded)

Given the above facts and calculations, we can now prepare bond amortization schedules. The par bond needs no amortization, so we only need schedules for premium and discount bonds.

As the amortization schedules in Exhibit 7-18 show, the amortized cost of the premium bond begins at $1,018.59, decreases to $1,009.52 by the end of Year 1, and ends at $1,000 at the end of Year 2, which is the maturity date. In contrast, the discount bond's amortized cost begins at $981.92 and increases to $990.65 and finally ends at $1,000.

Exhibit 7-18	Amortization schedules for premium and discount bonds purchased by Ucluelet Umbrellas							
	Premium bond (Bond A)				**Discount bond (Bond C)**			
	Beginning of year amortized cost	+ Interest @ 5% yield*	− Coupon payment	= End of year amortized cost	Beginning of year amortized cost	+ Interest @ 7% yield*	− Coupon payment	= End of year amortized cost
Year 1	$1,018.59	$50.93	$60.00	$1,009.52	$981.92	$68.73	$60.00	$ 990.65
Year 2	1,009.52	50.48	60.00	1,000.00	990.65	69.35	60.00	1,000.00

*Interest = Beginning of year amortized cost × Effective interest rate; for example, $1,018.59 × 5% = $50.93.

2. Using amortized cost in the accounting for financial assets

Bond amortization schedules like Exhibit 7-18, as you would expect, are useful for the amortized cost method. However, it may surprise you that these schedules are also necessary for debt investments classified as FVOCI.

a. Debt instruments held at amortized cost

Once an enterprise has prepared the amortization schedule for an amortized cost investment, the accounting is relatively straightforward. Using the information from Exhibit 7-18, Ucluelet Umbrellas would record the following journal entries in Exhibit 7-19:

Exhibit 7-19	Journal entries for Ucluelet's bonds if held at amortized cost (AC)				
	Premium bond (Bond A)			**Discount bond (Bond C)**	
Purchase	Dr. AC invest. (Bond A)	1,018.59		Dr. AC invest. (Bond C)	981.92	
	Cr. Cash		1,018.59*	Cr. Cash		981.92*
End of Year 1	Dr. Cash	60.00		Dr. Cash	60.00	
	Cr. AC invest. (Bond A)		9.07[†]	Dr. AC invest. (Bond C)	8.73[†]	
	Cr. Interest revenue		50.93[‡]	Cr. Interest revenue		68.73[‡]
End of Year 2	Dr. Cash	60.00		Dr. Cash	60.00	
	Cr. AC invest. (Bond A)		9.52[†]	Dr. AC invest. (Bond C)	9.35[†]	
	Cr. Interest revenue		50.48[‡]	Cr. Interest revenue		69.35[‡]
Maturity	Dr. Cash	1,000.00		Dr. Cash	1,000.00	
	Cr. AC invest. (Bond A)		1,000.00	Cr. AC invest. (Bond C)		1,000.00

*See Exhibit 7-18 for these figures.

[†]The adjustment to the investment account (i.e., the amortization) is the difference between the cash coupon payment and the interest income at the effective interest rate.

[‡]The amount of interest revenue equals the beginning balance in the investment account, measured at amortized cost, multiplied by the effective interest rate. These amounts were previously calculated in Exhibit 7-18.

As shown in the journal entries at the end of Years 1 and 2, Ucluelet adjusts the investment account balance each year when the purchase price differs from the par/face/maturity value. The adjustments are the reason this method is called "amortized cost." The adjustment is downward in the case of the premium bond (Bond A) and upward in the case of the discount bond (Bond C). In both cases, the adjustment brings the investment balance, the amortized cost, toward the par value of $1,000. In addition, the amount of the amortization increases over time (e.g., Bond A amortization: Year 1 = $9.07, Year 2 = $9.52), just as illustrated in the increasing steepness of the lines graphed in Exhibit 7-16.

b. Debt instruments held at FVOCI

If an enterprise has *debt instruments* classified as FVOCI, it needs to keep track of the investments' amortized cost, and overlay the fair value through the OCI method. There are two distinct reasons for changes in the value of debt investments. The first is the predictable change in value according to the amortization schedule. The second is the unpredictable change in value due to changes in demand for the debt instrument, which could result from change in market interest rates, changes in credit risk for the instrument, and so on.

To see this interaction, we will use Ucluelet's investment in Bond A, which is a premium bond. Repeating the facts for ease of reference, Ucluelet purchased the $1,000 bond for $1,018.59, with two years to maturity, $60 per year annual coupon payments, and yield of 5%. To illustrate the fair value method, we now also assume that the price of the bond decreases to $987 at the end of Year 1. At the end of Year 2, the fair value increases back up to $1,000 (as would be expected on the maturity date).

Based on these facts, Ucluelet would prepare the following schedule to track the carrying value of the investment and to determine the amounts of unrealized gain or loss due to fair value changes:

Exhibit 7-20	Continuity schedule for Ucluelet's premium bond (Bond A) if carried at fair value					
	Beginning of year carrying value	+ Interest*	− Coupon payment	= Carrying value before fair value adjustment	Fair value at end of year	Unrealized gain (loss) = Fair value − Carrying value
Year 1	$1,018.59	$50.93	$60.00	$1,009.52	$ 987.00	($22.52)
Year 2	987.00	50.48	60.00	977.48	1,000.00	22.52

*The amount of interest was calculated in Exhibit 7-18; it is equal to the amortized cost × effective interest rate (5% in this case).

Notice that this schedule needs to refer to the amortization schedule previously prepared and shown in Exhibit 7-18. This is necessary because the amount of interest income depends on the amortized cost, which is not the carrying value; the carrying value on the balance sheet is fair value when the investment is classified as FVOCI.

Using this continuity schedule, Ucluelet would record the following journal entries in Exhibit 7-21:

Exhibit 7-21	Journal entries for Ucluelet's premium bond (Bond A) if classified as FVOCI			
	Bond A classified as FVOCI		Bond A classified as amortized cost (AC) (from Exhibit 7-19, shown here for comparison)	
Purchase	Dr. FVOCI invest. (Bond A)	1,018.59	Dr. AC invest. (Bond A)	1,018.59
	Cr. Cash	1,018.59	Cr. Cash	1,018.59
End of year 1	Dr. Cash	60.00	Dr. Cash	60.00
	Cr. FVOCI invest. (Bond A)	9.07	Cr. AC invest. (Bond A)	9.07
	Cr. Interest revenue	50.93	Cr. Interest revenue	50.93
	Dr. OCI—Unrealized gain (loss) on FVOCI investment	22.52		
	Cr. FVOCI investment (Bond A)	22.52		
End of year 2	Dr. Cash	60.00	Dr. Cash	60.00
	Cr. FVOCI invest. (Bond A)	9.52	Cr. AC invest. (Bond A)	9.52
	Cr. Interest revenue	50.48	Cr. Interest revenue	50.48
	Dr. FVOCI invest. (Bond A)	22.52		
	Cr. OCI—Unrealized gain (loss) on FVOCI investment	22.52		
Maturity	Dr. Cash	1,000.00	Dr. Cash	1,000.00
	Cr. FVOCI invest. (Bond A)	1,000.00	Cr. AC invest. (Bond A)	1,000.00

The important point to note is that, even though Ucluelet carries the bond investment at fair value on the balance sheet, the interest income and the associated amortization rely on the bond amortization schedule. Furthermore, the computation of unrealized gain or loss partly depends on the amortization; the gain or loss equals fair value less the carrying value after amortization. Thus, when an enterprise invests in a debt investment, it needs to use an amortization schedule if it classifies the investment as amortized cost or FVOCI.

An astute reader may question why we require amortized cost calculations for debt investments classified as amortized cost or FVOCI, but not for those classified as FVPL. The reason is actually quite straightforward. Changes in fair value for FVPL investments are recorded through the income statement, as is interest income. Little information is lost by reporting a combined investment income figure, and reporting a single investment income number is consistent with the rationale for the category. In contrast, fair value changes for FVOCI investments go to other comprehensive income and do not impact the income statement until those gains or losses are realized upon disposal of the investments, so it is necessary to distinguish interest income from fair value changes.

 CHECKPOINT **CP7-6**

An amortization schedule is necessary to apply the amortized cost method. Why is it also necessary to prepare an amortization schedule for debt investments classified as FVOCI?

F. IMPAIRMENT OF INVESTMENTS IN DEBT

In principle, the value of an investment is determined by both the expected cash flows and the discount rate that reflects the time value of money. Since a debt instrument specifies the sequence of contractual cash flows, fluctuations in fair value derive primarily from changes in the discount rate. As you know, the discount rate reflects both the risk-free rate and a premium for the risk of the particular security. Key among the factors contributing to the overall risk of debt investments is the credit risk of the borrower. Consequently, IFRS 9 requires companies with investment in debt to evaluate whether the credit risk of those investments has deteriorated, and if so, to record impairment losses on such investments.

How one goes about determining the impairment for credit losses is complex. Even when fair values are observable via market prices, those prices reflect changes in credit quality, but they also reflect other factors. From the previous discussion, we know of two such factors: (i) the mechanical increase or decrease toward maturity value for debt purchased at a discount or premium, respectively; and (ii) changes in the market interest rate. The difficulty is in distinguishing changes in value due to these two factors apart from that due to credit risk, which is beyond the scope of this text.

The requirement to evaluate debt investments for impairment due to credit risk applies for debt held at amortized cost or FVOCI. While debt held at FVOCI is already reported at fair value on the balance sheet, the impairment requirement is necessary because any impairment in value due to credit deterioration needs to be reported in income rather than in OCI. For debt investments classified as FVPL, fair value changes all flow through income, so it is not necessary to conduct the impairment evaluation.

Note that accounts receivable do not fall under the scope of these impairment requirements, since the allowance for doubtful accounts already includes expected credit losses when estimated in the normal fashion (as discussed in Chapter 5).

G. SUBSTANTIVE DIFFERENCES BETWEEN RELEVANT IFRS AND ASPE

Issue	IFRS	ASPE
Strategic investments—joint arrangements	IFRS distinguishes joint operations from joint ventures and requires proportionate consolidation for the first and the equity method for the second.	ASPE distinguishes "jointly controlled operations," "jointly controlled assets," and "jointly controlled enterprises." The first two categories use proportionate consolidation, while the third uses the equity or cost method.
Non-strategic investments—classification	IFRS 9 classifies financial assets according to the business model used to manage the assets.	ASPE does not refer to trading intentions. Instead, investments are categorized by their nature: equity, debt, and derivatives.
Non-strategic investments—FVOCI	FVOCI investments should be carried at fair value, with unrealized gains or losses going through other comprehensive income.	There is no concept of "other comprehensive income" in ASPE, so there is no treatment similar to FVOCI in IFRS.
Non-strategic investments—measurement of equity investments	Portfolio equity investments should be reported at fair value and unrealized gains or losses flow through net income.	Enterprises should measure equity investments that are quoted in an active market at fair value, with gains and losses going through income. Equity not quoted in an active market should remain at cost, subject to any impairment.
Non-strategic investments—measurement of debt	Investments in debt may be classified as FVPL, FVOCI, or amortized cost. Implementation of the amortized cost method uses the effective interest method.	Investments in debt should use the amortized cost method. ASPE does not state the amortization method required (i.e., either the effective interest or straight-line method may be used). Enterprises may irrevocably elect to measure a debt investment at fair value instead of amortized cost.
Non-strategic investments	—	An entity may elect to measure any financial asset at fair value despite the above.

H. SUMMARY

L.O. 7-1. Explain what financial assets are, how they differ from other types of assets, and why there is a variety of measurement standards for different categories of financial assets.

- Financial assets are contractual agreements that entitle the holder to future cash flows. Being contractual, financial assets have counterparties who have promised to pay these future cash flows, although these cash flows can be uncertain in both amount and timing (e.g., dividends).
- Accounting standards provide different measurement standards according to the goals or intents that enterprises have for these investments.

L.O. 7-2. Evaluate the nature of a financial asset to classify it into one of seven categories: subsidiaries, joint operations, joint ventures, associates, FVPL, FVOCI, and amortized cost.

- When an enterprise has control or significant influence over another enterprise, it classifies that investment as a subsidiary or associate, respectively. When an enterprise has joint control over the assets and joint obligation for the liabilities of another, it classifies the arrangement as a joint operation, whereas if it has joint control of the net assets, it classifies the arrangement as a joint venture. These four categories are strategic investments in which the enterprise has substantial and concentrated holdings in the equity of other enterprises.
- FVPL financial assets are those that the enterprise intends to sell in the short term for a profit. Any type of financial asset (debt, equity, derivative) can be classified as FVPL.
- FVOCI financial assets are debt instruments held in a business model that aims to profit from both trading and collection of contractual cash flows.
- Amortized cost financial assets are debt instruments that an enterprise intends to hold in order to collect contractual cash flows.

L.O. 7-3. Identify the measurement approach appropriate to the seven categories of financial assets and explain the general nature of the various measurement approaches.

- Enterprises should use consolidation and proportionate consolidation to account for subsidiaries and joint operations, respectively. Enterprises should use the equity method for joint ventures and associates. These three methods share substantial similarities in that they reflect the economic ties among the entities.
- Enterprises should use fair values to report FVPL and FVOCI financial assets.

L.O. 7-4. Analyze historical cost and fair value information to determine the appropriate balance sheet measurement and income recognition subsequent to purchase for three categories of financial assets: FVPL, FVOCI, and amortized cost.

- Unrealized gains or losses arising from changes in fair value flow through the income statement for FVPL financial assets, but through other comprehensive income for assets classified as FVOCI.
- Investments in debt instruments classified as FVOCI or amortized cost require the application of the effective interest method to determine amortized cost for the balance sheet and the amount of interest income to recognize on the income statement.

L.O. 7-5. Apply present value techniques to account for investments in debt instruments.

- Debt investments have five essential parameters: par/face/maturity value, maturity date, coupon rate and frequency, yield or effective interest rate, and purchase price. Any four of these parameters can be used to compute the fifth.
- A bond amortization schedule is useful for calculating the amount of interest and amortized cost through the duration of the investment.

I. ANSWERS TO CHECKPOINT QUESTIONS

CP7-1:   Accounts receivable are financial assets because they represent contractual arrangements for future cash flows between the customers and the company that holds the receivables. Inventories are not financial assets even though they are expected to generate future cash flows because there are no contracts that define the payer of those cash flows.

CP7-2:   Equity, debt, and derivative identify the nature of the financial instruments. These categorizations are not sufficient for classifying investments because they do not capture the reasons for the investment (e.g., whether to hold or to trade).

CP7-3:   The four categories of strategic investments and their accounting methods under IFRS are as follows: subsidiary—consolidation; joint operation—proportionate consolidation; joint venture—equity method; associate—equity method.

CP7-4:   The key difference between FVPL and FVOCI investments is the treatment of unrealized gains and losses. Such unrealized gains and losses flow through net income for FVPL investments, but flow through OCI for FVOCI investments.

CP7-5:   Rules concerning the reclassification of financial assets are important because, in the absence of such rules, enterprises may engage in earnings management by selectively reclassifying certain investments to increase or decrease income or assets.

CP7-6:   An amortization schedule is necessary for debt investments classified as FVOCI because we need to distinguish two sources of change in value: the predictable change caused by the amortization of premium or discount, and the unpredictable changes due to changes in market interest rates, credit risk, and so on.

J. GLOSSARY

associate: An entity over which the investor has **significant influence** and that is neither a **subsidiary** nor an interest in a **joint venture**.

control: The power to govern the financial and operating policies of an entity.

debt instrument: Any financial instrument that is not an equity instrument or a derivative.

derivative: A financial instrument with all three of the following characteristics: (i) its value changes according to a specified variable, such as an interest rate or stock price; (ii) it requires no initial net investment or a small investment relative to non-derivative contracts with similar exposure to the specified variable; and (iii) it is settled at a future date.

effective interest method: Calculates the amortized cost of a financial asset at each reporting date as the present value of the asset's cash flows discounted at the **effective interest rate** or **yield**.

effective interest rate (or **yield**): The discount rate that results in a present value equal to the purchase price of a financial asset. In finance, this is called the internal rate of return (IRR).

equity instrument: A contract, such as a common share, that gives the holder the residual interest in an entity after deducting all of its liabilities.

equity method: A method of accounting whereby the balance sheet value of the investment equals cost adjusted by the investor's share of the investee's post-acquisition changes in net assets, and the income recognized equals the investor's share of the investee's net income.

financial asset: An asset arising from contractual agreements on future cash flows.

financial instrument: Any contract that gives rise to (i) a financial asset for one entity and (ii) a financial liability or equity instrument for another entity.

joint arrangement: A contractual arrangement whereby two or more parties undertake an economic activity that is subject to **joint control** by those parties.

joint control: A contractually agreed upon sharing of control over an economic activity; joint control exists only when the strategic decisions relating to the activity require the unanimous consent of the parties sharing control.

joint operation: A joint arrangement in which the investor has rights to the assets and obligations for the liabilities of the arrangement.

joint venture: A joint arrangement in which the investor has rights to the net assets of the arrangement.

parent: An entity that controls another entity (the **subsidiary**).

significant influence: The power to participate in the financial and operating policy decisions of the investee (but not to the extent of **control** or **joint control**).

subsidiary: An entity that is controlled by another entity (known as the **parent**).

yield: See **effective interest rate**.

K. REFERENCES
Authoritative standards:

IFRS	ASPE section
IFRS 10—Consolidated financial statements	1601—Consolidated financial statements
IAS 28—Investment in associates and joint ventures	3051—Investments
IFRS 9—Financial instruments	3856—Financial instruments
IFRS 11—Joint arrangements	3056—Interests in joint arrangements

MyLab Accounting   Make the grade with **MyLab Accounting:** The problems marked with a 🌐 can be found on **MyLab Accounting.** You can practise them as often as you want, and most feature step-by-step guided instructions to help you find the right answer.

L. PROBLEMS

 P7-1.   The nature of financial assets   (**L.O.** 7-1) (Easy – 3 minutes)

Identify whether each of the following items is a financial asset:
a. Cash
b. Account receivable
c. Investment in property, plant, and equipment
d. Investment in a derivative
e. Investment in bonds

 P7-2.   The nature of financial assets   (**L.O.** 7-1) (Easy – 3 minutes)

Identify whether each of the following items is a financial asset:
a. Prepaid expense
b. Inventory
c. Investment in shares of another entity
d. Investment in a joint venture
e. Bond issued by the reporting entity

P7-3.   The nature of financial assets   (**L.O.** 7-1) (Medium – 5 minutes)

Briefly answer the following questions:
a. Describe the single most important characteristic of a financial asset that distinguishes it from a real asset.
b. Keeping in mind your answer to (a), does cash have this characteristic of a financial asset? Why is cash a financial asset?

P7-4. The nature of financial assets   (**L.O.** 7-1) (Medium – 10 minutes)

Company X contributes $17 million while Company Y contributes management expertise toward the creation of a joint venture called Zed. Zed purchases a building and incurs a mortgage to finance the purchase. The joint venture renovates the building with the help of contractors, who are paid 15 days after they render their services. After completion of renovations, Zed operates the building as a hotel. It also sells some of the rooms to individual investors. As a part of the purchase of each room, an investor has rights to 60% of the revenue from the hotel room purchased, while Zed retains 40% to cover operating costs.

Required:

Identify all the financial assets involved in the above situation.

 P7-5. The nature of financial assets   (**L.O.** 7-1) (Medium – 10 minutes)

Alpha purchases a hotel with 100 similar rooms. To help finance this purchase, Alpha sells these rooms to individual investors for $200,000 each. An investor that owns *a single room* receives 55% of 1/100th of the revenue of the hotel (i.e., 0.55%), while the hotel retains the other 0.45%. An investor who wishes to liquidate his or her investment may sell the room back to Alpha for the original $200,000, but cannot otherwise sell the room to other parties.

Required:

Identify all the financial assets involved in the above situation.

 P7-6. Classifying financial assets   (**L.O.** 7-2) (Easy – 10 minutes)

For each of the following financial asset classifications shown in the left column, identify the combinations of (i) the type of financial instrument in the middle column that can be put into that classification and (ii) the business model that would lead to that classification.

Example: FVPL = (Equity, debt, or derivatives) + To realize changes in value

Accounting classification	= Type of financial instrument	+ Business model
FVPL	Equity	Control
FVOCI	Debt	Joint control of net assets
Amortized cost	Derivatives	Significant influence
Associate		To realize changes in value
Joint venture		To collect contractual cash flows
Joint operations		Joint control of assets and joint obligation for liabilities
Subsidiary		To sell financial assets and collect contractual cash flows

P7-7. Classifying financial assets   (**L.O.** 7-2) (Medium – 10 minutes)

Consider the following six investments:

a. Atlantic Company buys 5,000 common shares of a publicly traded company that has 200 million shares outstanding.

b. Beetleweed buys $20,000 in bonds maturing in five years.

c. A bank lends $400,000 to a person to purchase a home.

d. An exporter enters into a currency swap (a derivative contract) to secure the Canadian dollar price of a sale.

e. Elite Cars buys 800,000 shares in Selective Autos.

f. Fanciful Gifts buys 3,000 preferred shares in another company. These shares have no voting rights.

Required:

Under IFRS 9, financial assets can be put into one of seven categories: subsidiaries, joint operations, joint ventures, associates, FVPL, FVOCI, and amortized cost. For each of the above investments, identify the possible categories into which it can be placed. More than one category is possible for some items.

 P7-8.   Classifying financial assets (**L.O.** 7-2) (Medium – 10 minutes) A·S·P·E

Consider the six investments listed in the problem P7-7.

Required:

Under ASPE, financial assets can be put into one of six categories: subsidiaries, joint ventures, associates, portfolio equity investment, debt investment, and derivatives. For each of the above investments, identify the possible categories into which it can be placed. More than one category is possible for some items.

 P7-9.   Classifying financial assets (**L.O.** 7-2) (Medium – 10 minutes)

Consider the following eight investments.
a. Investment in 500 shares of Bank of Montreal: Management believes the shares are currently underpriced.
b. Investment in bonds maturing in two years: Management made the purchase to park idle cash until after two years, when it will make a major capital expenditure.
c. Investment in 800,000 shares of Calisto Corp., a public company with 2 million shares outstanding.
d. Purchase of 800 shares of Dupree Donuts, a private company with 1,000 shares outstanding.
e. Purchase of 1,000 shares of Epic Adventures, a public company with 10 million shares outstanding.
f. Investment in 60% of the outstanding shares of Fruitloops Fountains: An agreement with the company's founder specifies that he retains the right to make all operating decisions for Fruitloops.
g. St. George Company buys 15% of the outstanding shares of Gigantic Gargoyles: After the purchase, St. George appoints its chief executive officer to the board of directors of Gigantic Gargoyles.
h. Investment in bonds maturing in 30 years.

Required:

Using IFRS 9, classify each of the above items into one of the seven categories of financial assets relevant for financial reporting purposes. Select the category that *best* suits the situation given.

 P7-10. Classifying financial assets (**L.O.** 7-2) (Medium – 10 minutes) A·S·P·E

Consider the eight investments listed in problem P7-9.

Required:

Using ASPE, classify each of the above items into one of the six categories of financial assets relevant for financial reporting purposes. Select the category that *best* suits the situation given.

 P7-11. Classifying financial assets (**L.O.** 7-2) (Medium – 10 minutes)

Foxtrot Ltd. made the following investments during its current fiscal year:
a. The company places $30,000 in a six-month term deposit with its bank.
b. The company purchases from its broker a call option on 1,000 shares of RBC Financial Group, a publicly traded company, for $3,500, in anticipation of an increase in the share price of RBC.
c. Foxtrot buys 25% of the outstanding shares of Quickstep Company. The purchase was made in anticipation of a bid by Tango Inc. to purchase all of the shares of Quickstep within the next nine months.
d. The company buys $15,000 of shares in Encana, a publicly traded corporation with a market capitalization of more than $20 billion.

Required:

Identify how Foxtrot should categorize the above financial assets under IFRS 9. Briefly explain the reason for the classification.

A·S·P·E   🌐   **P7-12. Classifying financial assets**   **L.O.** 7-2) (Medium – 10 minutes)

Refer to the information in the problem P7-11.

Required:

Using ASPE, identify how Foxtrot should categorize the above financial assets. Briefly explain the reason for the classification.

P7-13. Classifying financial assets   **L.O.** 7-2) (Medium – 10 minutes)

Investments in equity that are considered strategic in nature are generally accounted for differently from portfolio investments in equity. The former uses consolidation, proportionate consolidation, or the equity method, while the latter uses the fair value through profit or loss (FVPL) method.

Required:

Explain conceptually why this difference in accounting for strategic versus portfolio investments is justified. [*Hint:* consider how information asymmetry differs between them.]

P7-14. Initial recognition of financial assets   **L.O.** 7-3) (Medium – 15 minutes)

On January 1, 2018, Investor's Club Inc. (ICI) made a number of non-strategic investments detailed below:
   a. The company acquired 100,000 ordinary shares in Norman Inc. for $5 cash per share plus a $10,000 transaction fee. ICI's management did not make any specific election with respect to the classification of this investment.
   b. ICI purchased 5,000, $25, 3.0% cumulative preferred shares in Bleay Inc. for $130,000 including transaction costs of $5,000. ICI irrevocably elected to present changes in fair value through OCI.
   c. ICI paid $2,393,859 plus a $50,000 transaction fee for $2.5 million of 3.5% semi-annual bonds issued by Zoe Corp. that mature in five years. The effective rate of interest earned is 2.0% PER PERIOD. The objective of the company's business model for this type of asset is to hold the investment for the purpose of collecting the contractual cash flows.

Required:

Record the journal entries necessary to reflect the foregoing transactions. Briefly justify your chosen treatment.

P7-15. Subsequent measurement of financial assets   **L.O.** 7-4) (Medium – 15 minutes)

Refer to the facts set out in P7-14 above and consider the following additional information:
   a. On July 1, 2018, ICI received a $43,750 interest payment on the Zoe Corp. bonds. The next interest payment is due on January 1, 2019.
   b. On September 30, 2018, ICI received a $3,750 dividend on the Bleay Inc. cumulative preferred shares.
   c. On December 31, 2018, ICI received a $2,000 dividend on the Norman Inc. ordinary shares.
   d. The market value of the Norman Inc. ordinary shares as at December 31, 2018, was $4.90 per share.
   e. The market value of the Bleay Inc.'s cumulative preferred shares as at December 31, 2018, was $26.25 per share.
   f. The market value of the investment in the Zoe Corp. bonds as at December 31, 2018, was $2,500,000.

ICI has a December 31 year-end. It does not prepare interim financial statements.

Required:

Prepare the necessary journal entries to record income earned on these assets in 2018 and the requisite fair value adjustments at December 31, 2018.

P7-16. Subsequent measurement of financial assets   (**L.O.** 7-3) (Easy – 10 minutes)

After the initial purchase, financial assets can be reported using one of six measurement bases under IFRS:

consolidation	fair value with changes through income
proportionate consolidation	fair value with changes through OCI
equity method	amortized cost

Required:

For each of the following financial assets, identify the appropriate measurement basis according to IFRS.

	Measurement basis
a. Shares without an irrevocable election	
b. Bonds classified as FVOCI	
c. Bonds held to collect contractual cash flows	
d. Investment in an associate	
e. A derivative on foreign currency	
f. A subsidiary	
g. Bonds held to collect contractual cash flows and sold for profit	
h. Investment in a joint venture	

P7-17. Subsequent measurement of financial assets   (**L.O.** 7-3) (Medium – 15 minutes)

Accounting standards provide for a variety of different measurement bases for different types of financial assets. IFRS has six measurement bases:

consolidation	fair value with changes through income
proportionate consolidation	fair value with changes through OCI
equity method	amortized cost

Required:

a. Explain why reporting entities should, on the one hand, use consolidation, proportionate consolidation, and the equity method for investments in subsidiaries, joint operations, joint ventures, and associates, but on the other hand use the fair value methods for equity investments that are held for trading profits.
b. Explain, for investments in debt securities, why the amortized cost method is more appropriate for investments held in a business model that collects contractual cash flows, but why one of the fair value methods is more appropriate for other business models.

 P7-18. Subsequent measurement of financial assets   (**L.O.** 7-3) (Easy – 5 minutes)[6]

On January 1, 2019, Arch Ltd. purchased 30% of the common shares of AP Inc. for $1,700,000. In 2019, AP reported net income of $880,000 and paid dividends of $600,000.

Required:

a. Which of the following conditions must be met for Arch to use the equity method to report its investment in AP?
    i. Arch owns at least 20% of the voting shares of AP.
    ii. Arch has control over AP.
    iii. Arch has a significant interest in AP.
    iv. Arch is able to exercise significant influence over AP.
b. How much income would be reported by Arch in 2019 for its investment in AP under the equity method?

[6.] Reprinted from CGA-Canada FA2 examination, June 2009, with permission from Chartered Professional Accountants of Canada, Toronto, Canada. Any changes to the original material are the sole responsibility of the author (and/or publisher) and have not been reviewed or endorsed by the Chartered Professional Accountants of Canada.

P7-19. Subsequent measurement of financial assets   (**L.O.** 7-3) (Easy – 5 minutes)

Kay Company holds a financial asset that is classified as an associate; Kay owns 40% of the associate. At the beginning of the year, the investment had a carrying value of $25,500,000. During the year, the associate reported net income of $3,000,000, and declared and paid dividends of $1,000,000. At the end of the year, the market value of Kay's investment in the associate was $32,000,000.

Required:

a. For the year, how much income should Kay report for its investment in the associate?
b. At what value should Kay report its investment in the associate at the end of the year?

P7-20. The equity method   (**L.O.** 7-3) (Medium – 10 minutes)

On January 1, 2020, Sunshine Ltd. acquired 30% of the outstanding ordinary shares of Moonbeam Inc. for $270,000 and now has significant influence over the investee. The fair value of Moonbeam's net identifiable assets at acquisition date was $900,000. Pertinent information follows:

Moonbeam Inc.	Year ended Dec. 31, 2020	Year ended Dec. 31, 2021
Net income	$300,000	($ 80,000)
Dividends declared and paid	50,000	30,000
Market value of investment	370,000	320,000

Required:

a. Prepare Sunshine Ltd.'s journal entries related to its investment in Moonbeam Inc. for the years ending December 31, 2020, and December 31, 2021, including the journal entry to record the acquisition.
b. Determine the balance in the investment account as at December 31, 2021.

 P7-21. Subsequent measurement of financial assets   (**L.O.** 7-4) (Easy – 5 minutes)

On January 25, 2020, Douglas Ltd. purchased 1,000 common shares of BMO (Bank of Montreal) for $65 each. During the remainder of 2020, Douglas received $2.80/share in dividends and BMO's earnings per share were $5.30. The closing price of the shares on the fiscal year-end date of December 31, 2020, was $69.

Required:

Assume that Douglas classified the investment as FVPL.
a. At what value should the company report the BMO shares on its December 31, 2020, balance sheet?
b. How much income should the company report in relation to these shares?
c. How much OCI should Douglas report in relation to these shares?

 P7-22. Subsequent measurement of financial assets   (**L.O.** 7-4) (Easy – 5 minutes)

Refer to the facts presented in problem P7-21.

Required:

Assume that Douglas made the irrevocable election to measure the investment at fair value through OCI.
a. At what value should Douglas report the BMO shares on its December 31, 2020, balance sheet?
b. How much income should Douglas report in relation to these shares?
c. How much OCI should Douglas report in relation to these shares?

P7-23. Subsequent measurement of financial assets   **L.O.** 7-4) (Easy – 5 minutes)

On January 1, 2019, Ganges Marine Supplies purchased a Government of Canada bond at par for $5,000. The bond has an interest rate of 4% and matures in three years. By December 31, 2019, market interest rates had increased such that the fair value of the bond decreased to $4,900. The fair value of the bond decreased further to $4,700 on December 31, 2020 (two years after purchase).

Required:

Assume that Ganges classified the investment as amortized cost.
  a. At what value should Ganges report the bonds on its December 31, 2019, balance sheet?
  b. How much income or loss should Ganges report in relation to this bond?
  c. How much OCI should Ganges report in relation to this bond?

 P7-24. Subsequent measurement of financial assets   **L.O.** 7-4) (Easy – 10 minutes)

Refer to the facts in problem P7-23.

Required:

Assume that Ganges classified the investment as FVOCI.
  a. At what value should Ganges report the bonds on its December 31, 2019, balance sheet?
  b. How much income or loss should Ganges report in 2019 in relation to this bond?
  c. How much OCI should Ganges report for 2019 in relation to this bond?
  d. How much OCI should Ganges report for 2020 in relation to this bond?
  e. How much is accumulated OCI on the balance sheet at December 31, 2020?

 P7-25. Subsequent measurement of financial assets
L.O. 7-3, **L.O.** 7-4) (Medium – 15 minutes)[7]

On January 1, 2020, LL Company acquired 20,000 shares, representing 20% of the outstanding shares of TT Limited at a price of $15 per share. On July 31, 2020, TT declared and paid a dividend of $1 per share. TT's net income for 2020 was $250,000. On December 31, 2020, the shares of TT were trading on the Toronto Stock Exchange at $18 per share.

Required:

LL is not sure how to report its investment in TT shares. Using the following format, indicate the amounts that would appear on the balance sheet and the statement of comprehensive income for 2020 if the investment (a) has been irrevocably elected to be measured at fair value through OCI, (b) is classified as FVPL, or (c) is an associate.

	Fair value through OCI election	FVPL	Associate
Balance sheet			
Investment in TT shares			
Statement of comprehensive income			
Dividend income			
Other income (specify types)			
—			
—			
Subtotal (= effect on net income)			
Other comprehensive income			
Total (= effect on comprehensive income)	$80,000	$80,000	$50,000

[7.] Reprinted from CGA-Canada FA2 examination, June 2009, with permission from Chartered Professional Accountants of Canada, Toronto, Canada. Any changes to the original material are the sole responsibility of the author (and/or publisher) and have not been reviewed or endorsed by the Chartered Professional Accountants of Canada.

P7-26. Subsequent measurement of financial assets   **(L.O.** 7-3) (Medium – 5 minutes)

Refer to the facts provided in the problem P7-25. Provide the journal entries assuming that LL classifies TT as an associate.

 P7-27. Subsequent measurement of financial assets

(L.O. 7-3, **L.O.** 7-4) (Medium – 10 minutes)

Reversiflex Inc. purchased three equity investments during the current fiscal year ended December 31.

	Investment A	Investment B	Investment C
Balance sheet value, Dec. 31	$120,000	$63,000	$80,000
Dividends received	1,500	2,000	4,000
Dividend income	—	2,000	4,000
Total income (loss) recognized on the investment	7,000	2,000	(1,000)
Balance sheet reserve for cumulative OCI on unrealized gains (losses)	—	3,000 Cr.	—

Required:

a. Based on the available information, how did Reversiflex classify each financial asset?
b. Determine the cost of each of the three investments. If it is not possible to do so with the available information, indicate what additional information would be needed.

 P7-28. Subsequent measurement of financial assets

(L.O. 7-3, **L.O.** 7-4) (Medium – 10 minutes)

True Worth Hardware operates a chain of hardware stores. Recent operations have been stable and profitable, resulting in a significant amount of cash inflows. During the past fiscal year ended December 31, the company made a number of investments, described below.

a. True Worth bought 20,000 shares of MasterTrade, a supplier of equipment for construction and renovation. With in-depth knowledge of the hardware retailing business, True Worth's management believes that MasterTrade's shares are undervalued and that the company could make a quick profit selling the shares within the next 12 months. True Worth purchased the shares at a price of $42 each, and received $0.50 per share of dividends during the year. The shares traded at $46 at the fiscal year-end.
b. The company purchased 6,000 units of a mutual fund that cost $22 each. The mutual fund invests primarily in shares. At the end of the year, the units had a quoted market value of $21.
c. At the beginning of the year, True Worth bought 25% of the common shares in Unique Tools, one of its smaller suppliers, for $3 million. These shares had a fair value of $3.2 million at the end of the year. During the year, Unique Tools had profits of $800,000 and paid dividends of $160,000.

Required:

Determine how True Worth should report the above investments in its financial statements at its fiscal year end. Include effects both on the balance sheet and the statement of comprehensive income.

A·S·P·E   **P7-29.** Subsequent measurement of financial assets

(L.O. 7-3, **L.O.** 7-4) (Medium – 10 minutes)

Refer to the facts presented in problem P7-28.

Required:

Determine how True Worth should report the above investments in its financial statements if the company applies ASPE. Include effects both on the balance sheet and the income statement.

P7-30. Subsequent measurement of financial assets

(L.O. 7-3, L.O. 7-4) (Medium – 15 minutes)

Refer to the facts in problem P7-28. Record the journal entries appropriate for True Worth's three investments beginning with the initial purchase.

 P7-31. Subsequent measurement of non-strategic financial assets

(L.O. 7-4) (Medium – 10 minutes)[8]

Birch Corp. is a real estate developer with headquarters in Burlington, Ontario. As a result of recent increases in land prices, Birch has accumulated a substantial amount of excess cash. It is looking to invest in a building supply company, but has not yet found a suitable company. To earn a reasonable return and to minimize risk, Birch invests its excess cash in common shares of large, stable corporations. The following describes the events surrounding one of Birch's investments:

a. On January 1, 2019, Birch paid $1,000,000 to purchase 100,000 common shares of Poplar Inc.
b. On December 27, 2019, Poplar declared and paid a dividend of $0.50 per common share.
c. On December 31, 2019, the market value of the common shares was $1,030,000.
d. On June 30, 2020, Birch sold the common shares for $1,045,000.

Required:

Using the following table, indicate the amounts to be reported on the balance sheet, through profit or loss, and through other comprehensive income for 2019 and 2020 under two scenarios:

a. Birch makes the irrevocable election to measure at fair value through OCI.
b. Birch does not make the irrevocable election to measure at fair value through OCI.

	With election		Without election	
	2019	2020	2019	2020
Balance sheet				
Amount through profit or loss				
Other comprehensive income				

 P7-32. Subsequent measurement of non-strategic financial assets

(L.O. 7-4) (Medium – 10 minutes)

Laurel Ltd. has a December 31 fiscal year-end. During 2017, the company purchased 15,000 shares of Pinegreen Company for $4.40 per share ($66,000 total), and sold these shares in 2020 for $5.60 per share. Pinegreen declared and paid dividends of $0.10, $0.20, and $0.30 per share at the end of 2017, 2018, and 2019, respectively. Pinegreen's shares closed at $4.80, $4.20, and $5.20 at the end of 2017, 2018, and 2019, respectively.

Required:

Assume that Laurel classifies this investment in Pinegreen as FVPL. Determine the amounts to be reported on Laurel's balance sheet and statement of comprehensive income with respect to the company's investment in Pinegreen Company for the four years from 2017 to 2020.

P7-33. Subsequent measurement of non-strategic financial assets

(L.O. 7-4) (Medium – 10 minutes)

Refer to the facts presented in problem P7-32.

[8.] Reprinted from CGA-Canada FA2 examination, June 2009, with permission from Chartered Professional Accountants of Canada, Toronto, Canada. Any changes to the original material are the sole responsibility of the author (and/or publisher) and have not been reviewed or endorsed by the Chartered Professional Accountants of Canada.

Required:

Assume that Laurel irrevocably elects to record changes in the fair value of Pinegreen in OCI. Determine the amounts to be reported on Laurel's balance sheet and statement of comprehensive income with respect to the company's investment in Pinegreen Company for the four years from 2017 to 2020.

P7-34. Subsequent measurement of non-strategic financial assets
(**L.O.** 7-4) (Medium – 10 minutes)

Britannia Water Company (BWC) purchased 1,000 shares of Scotiabank on March 11, 2021, when the share price was $58 per share. At the close of December 31, 2021, the price of Scotiabank shares had declined to $50. On November 2, 2022, when BWC sold the shares, the price had recovered to $55. During 2022, BWC received dividends of $2.14/share.

Required:

a. Suppose BWC had classified the investment in Scotiabank as fair value through profit or loss (FVPL). Record all journal entries in 2022 relating to this investment.
b. Suppose BWC made the irrevocable election to measure changes in fair value through OCI. Record all journal entries in 2022 relating to this investment.

 P7-35. Subsequent measurement of non-strategic financial assets
(**L.O.** 7-4) (Medium – 15 minutes)

During 2019, Heather Ltd. purchased 6,000 shares of Oaktree Corp. for $31 per share ($186,000 total). Heather held these shares until September 2021, when it sold them for $36 per share. During these three years, Oaktree paid dividends of $1 per share on July 31. On Heather's fiscal year-end (December 31), shares of Oaktree closed at $34, $29, and $38 in 2019, 2020, and 2021, respectively.

Required:

Assume that the company designated half of the Oaktree shares as FVPL and the other half irrevocably elected to record fair value changes through OCI. Determine the amounts to be reported on Heather's balance sheet and statement of comprehensive income with respect to the company's investment in Oaktree Corp. What do you observe about the total amount of retained earnings for the three years combined?

 P7-36. Subsequent measurement of non-strategic financial assets
(**L.O.** 7-4) (Medium – 20 minutes)[9]

Lion had the following transactions relating to its investments during the current fiscal year. Lion uses the effective interest method of amortization of premiums or discounts when applicable.

a. On July 1, Lion acquired a $200,000, 6%, eight-year government bond with interest paid semi-annually on January 1 and July 1. Because the market rate of interest was 4% on that date, Lion paid $227,156 for the bond. The bonds were classified as amortized cost by Lion and had a fair value of $210,000 plus accrued interest on December 31.
b. On July 1, Lion acquired 6,000 shares of Zebra at a price of $25 per share. On December 31, dividends of $1.50 per share were declared with an expected date of payment 15 days later. On December 31, the fair value of the Zebra shares had increased to $28 per share. The shares are classified as fair value through profit or loss by Lion.
c. On July 1, Lion acquired 30,000 shares (30%) of the outstanding shares of Giraffe at a price of $11 per share, giving it significant influence over Giraffe. Giraffe had net income of $400,000 for the six months ended December 31, and declared and paid dividends of $220,000 to its shareholders on December 31. On December 31, Giraffe's shares had a fair value of $13 per share.

9. Reprinted from CGA-Canada FA2 examination, March 2009, with permission from Chartered Professional Accountants of Canada, Toronto, Canada. Any changes to the original material are the sole responsibility of the author (and/or publisher) and have not been reviewed or endorsed by the Chartered Professional Accountants of Canada.

Required:

Provide all required journal entries relating to these investments on July 1, and December 31, including any required journal entries relating to the change in fair value for the year (if no journal entry is required relating to the change in fair value, state so).

 P7-37. Applying present value techniques to debt instruments

(**L.O.** 7-5) (Easy – 5 minutes)

A bond has a maturity value of $100,000 payable in 10 years. These bonds have a 5% coupon rate payable annually, and the market yield was 6% when the bonds were purchased.

Required:

a. Is this a discount bond or a premium bond?
b. Compute the amount required to purchase this bond at the beginning of the 10-year period.

 P7-38. Applying present value techniques to debt instruments

(**L.O.** 7-5) (Easy – 5 minutes)

A bond has a maturity value of $10,000 payable in 10 years. These bonds have a 7% per year coupon rate payable semi-annually, and the market yield was 6% per year when the bonds were purchased.

Required:

a. Is this a discount bond or a premium bond?
b. Compute the amount required to purchase this bond at the beginning of the 10-year period.

 P7-39. Subsequent measurement of investments in debt instruments

(**L.O.** 7-5) (Easy – 10 minutes)

Armstrong Corp. purchased a bond with a maturity value of $10,000 payable in five years. These bonds have a 6% coupon rate payable annually. Armstrong paid $10,890 for these bonds, giving a yield of 4%.

Required:

Prepare an amortization schedule that shows the amortized cost of this bond at the end of each of the five years and the amount of interest income for each of those five years.

 P7-40. Subsequent measurement of investments in debt instruments

(**L.O.** 7-5) (Easy – 10 minutes) $\boxed{\text{A·S·P·E}}$

Refer to the facts in problem P7-39.

Required:

Using the straight-line alternative permitted under ASPE, prepare an amortization schedule that shows the amortized cost of this bond at the end of each of the five years and the amount of interest income for each of those five years.

 P7-41. Subsequent measurement of investments in debt instruments

(**L.O.** 7-5) (Easy – 10 minutes)

On January 1, 2016, Bamfield Company purchased bonds with a maturity value of $10,000 for $9,147. These bonds have a 4% per year coupon rate payable semi-annually on June 30 and December 31. The bond matures on December 31, 2020. On January 1, 2016, the market yield for bonds of equivalent risk and maturity was 6% per year.

Required:

Prepare an amortization schedule that shows the amortized cost of this bond at the end of each of the five years and the amount of interest income for each of those five years.

A·S·P·E 🌐 **P7-42.** Subsequent measurement of investments in debt instruments

(**L.O.** 7-5) (Easy – 10 minutes)

Refer to the facts in problem P7-41.

Required:

Using the straight-line alternative permitted under ASPE, prepare an amortization schedule that shows the amortized cost of this bond at the end of each of the five years and the amount of interest income for each of those five years.

P7-43. Subsequent measurement of investments in debt instruments

(**L.O.** 7-5) (Easy – 5 minutes)

Under IFRS, which of the following are possible patterns of amortization for an investment in debt carried at amortized cost? The investment was made at the beginning of Year 1 and matures at the end of Year 3.

	Year 1	Year 2	Year 3
a.	$31.89	$28.47	$25.42
b.	$28.47	$31.89	$35.71
c.	$31.89	$31.89	$31.89
d.	$0	$0	$0

🌐 **P7-44.** Subsequent measurement of investments in debt instruments

(**L.O.** 7-5) (Medium – 5 minutes)

Under IFRS, which of the following are possible patterns of amortized cost balances for a financial asset carried at amortized cost? The investment matures at the end of Year 4.

	End of Year 1	End of Year 2	End of Year 3	End of Year 4
a.	$ 889.00	$ 946.11	$ 974.58	$1,000.00
b.	$ 889.00	$ 924.56	$ 961.54	$1,000.00
c.	$1,111.00	$1,144.19	$1,038.46	$1,000.00
d.	$1,111.00	$1,075.44	$1,038.46	$1,000.00

P7-45. Determining the effective interest rate

(**L.O.** 7-3, **L.O.** 7-4, **L.O.** 7-5) (Medium – 15 minutes)

On January 1, 2018, Dudas Inc. paid $917,783 plus a $5,000 transaction fee to acquire $1,000,000 in bonds that mature in 10 years. The bonds pay interest annually at 4% per annum on December 31. Dudas Inc. classifies its investment as a financial asset at amortized cost, which is in keeping with the objective of its business model and the contractual cash flow characteristics of the investment.

Dudas Inc. has a December 31 year-end. It does not accrue interest income during the year.

Required:

a. Determine the effective interest rate that Dudas is earning on its investment. Use a financial calculator or spreadsheet.
b. Prepare the journal entry to record the acquisition of the investment.
c. Prepare the journal entry to record the receipt of interest on December 31, 2018.
d. Prepare the journal entry to record the receipt of interest on December 31, 2019.

P7-46. Subsequent measurement of investments in debt instruments
(**L.O.** 7-4, **L.O.** 7-5) (Medium – 15 minutes)

Brix Wines (BW) has a December 31 fiscal year-end. The company purchased BCE Inc. corporate bonds with face value of $100,000. These bonds were purchased on January 1, 2021, at a cost of $93,225. The bonds pay annual interest at 5%, and mature on January 1, 2025. The yield on the date of purchase was 7%. These bonds had a market value of $96,000 and $97,000 at the end of 2021 and 2022, respectively.

Required:

a. Suppose BW had carried the BCE bond investment at amortized cost. Determine the amount of income that BW should recognize in each of 2021 and 2022 for this investment.
b. Suppose BW had classified the BCE bond investment as fair value through other comprehensive income (FVOCI). Determine the amount of other comprehensive income (OCI) that BW should recognize in each of 2021 and 2022 for this investment.
c. Following part (b), suppose BW sells the BCE bond investment on January 1, 2023, for $97,000. Record the journal entry for the sale.

P7-47. Subsequent measurement of investments in debt instruments
(**L.O.** 7-4, **L.O.** 7-5) (Medium – 15 minutes)

Green Teaz (GT) has a December 31 fiscal year-end. The company purchased Hydro One bonds with face value of $10,000. These bonds were purchased on January 1, 2020, at a cost of $10,267. The bonds pay annual interest at 7% and mature on January 1, 2023. The yield on the date of purchase was 6%. These bonds had a market value of $10,200 and $10,100 at the end of 2020 and 2021, respectively. GT classified this investment as fair value through other comprehensive income (FVOCI).

Required:

a. Prepare the amortization schedule for GT's investment in Hydro One bonds.
b. Record the journal entries for GT's investment in Hydro One bonds for the years 2020 and 2021.
c. Suppose GT sells the Hydro One bonds for proceeds of $10,030 on June 30, 2022. Record the journal entry for the sale and the accrued interest income prior to sale.

 ### P7-48. Subsequent measurement of investments in debt instruments
(**L.O.** 7-4, **L.O.** 7-5) (Medium – 20 minutes)

The Argyle Company acquired a $10 million face value bond that has an 8% coupon rate (pays interest annually on December 31) on January 1, 2017. The bond matures on December 31, 2022. On January 1, 2017, the market yield for bonds of equivalent risk and maturity was 6%.

Required:

a. How much did Argyle pay for this bond on January 1, 2017?
b. On December 31, 2017, the market yield for bonds of equivalent risk and maturity is 7%. What would be the market value of this bond on December 31, immediately after the coupon payment on that date?
c. On December 31, 2018, the market yield for bonds of equivalent risk and maturity is 8%. What would be the market value of this bond on December 31, immediately after the coupon payment on that date?
d. Assume one of three scenarios: the bond is to be (i) amortized cost, (ii) FVOCI, or (iii) FVPL:
   ■ How much would the balance sheet value of this bond be on December 31, 2017, and December 31, 2018?
   ■ How much income would be reported in 2017 and 2018 for this bond?
   ■ How much would OCI and accumulated OCI be for fiscal years 2017 and 2018?

P7-49. Subsequent measurement of investments in debt instruments

(L.O. 7-4, L.O. 7-5) (Difficult – 20 minutes)

Adobe Financial specializes in providing financing for commercial real estate purchases. The company's main source of income is the interest charged on these loans. At the end of 2018, the company had approximately $700 million of mortgages outstanding. To facilitate financial reporting, the company groups these mortgages according to the time to maturity (up to one year, one to three years, and three to five years). The following table provides further information on these mortgages as at the year-end of December 31, 2018:

	Up to one year	1–3 years	3–5 years
Average maturity	6 months	2 years	4 years
Scheduled semi-annual payments	$4m	$5m	$20m
Average yield on loans at inception	6%/a	6%/a	8%/a
Principal amount outstanding as at Dec. 31, 2018	$100m	$200m	$400m
Estimated market value, Dec. 31, 2018	$101m	$203m	$420m

Adobe's standard policy for all mortgages is semi-annual payments of interest, which is compounded semi-annually, plus payment of principal upon maturity.

Required:

a. How should Adobe account for these mortgage receivables?
b. At what value should Adobe report its mortgage receivables at the end of 2018?
c. Considering only the mortgage receivables outstanding at the end of 2018, project the value of mortgage receivables that should be reported at the end of 2019 and 2020. For purposes of this projection, you can use the average maturity and ignore the fact that there is a range of maturities that form this average.

P7-50. Subsequent measurement of investments in debt instruments

(L.O. 7-4, L.O. 7-5) (Difficult – 30 minutes)

Gander Corp. is a small public company with a December 31 fiscal year-end. At the end of 2016, the company had $3 million of excess cash. The board of directors decided that the company should hold the funds until the right business opportunity appeared, rather than pay out the funds to its shareholders and then have to issue shares to obtain the financing later. The board directed management to invest the funds in a diversified portfolio of debt instruments. As a result, on January 1, 2017, management purchased $1 million of short-term government bonds, $1 million of medium-term government bonds, and $1 million of high-quality corporate bonds. (The amounts are face values, not investment cost.) The following table provides additional information about these investments:

	Short-term government bonds	Medium-term government bonds	Corporate bonds
Face value	$1,000,000	$1,000,000	$1,000,000
Coupon rate	3%	5%	6%
Yield	3%	4%	8%
Maturity	Jan. 1, 2019	Jan. 1, 2022	Jan. 1, 2022
Interest frequency	Annual	Annual	Annual
Accounting classification	Amortized cost	FVOCI	FVOCI
Investment cost	?	?	?
Market value, Dec. 31, 2017	$ 985,000	$1,040,000	$950,000
Market value, Dec. 31, 2018	$1,000,000	$1,028,000	$970,000
Market value, Dec. 31, 2019	—	$1,020,000	$1,050,000
Market value, Dec. 31, 2020	—	$1,010,000	$1,010,000
Market value, Dec. 31, 2021	—	$1,000,000	$1,000,000

Required:

a. Determine the investment cost of the three investments on January 1, 2017.

b. Prepare amortization schedules for the medium-term government bonds and the corporate bonds. Use a computer spreadsheet to help you do your calculations.

c. For each of the three investments, determine the following amounts for each fiscal year:
   - balance sheet asset
   - income
   - other comprehensive income
   - accumulated other comprehensive income component of equity

d. Had Gander classified the medium-term government bonds and the corporate bonds as amortized cost financial assets, how much would have been the total amount of income over the five years for each of the type of bonds?

e. Had Gander classified the medium-term government bonds and the corporate bonds as FVPL financial assets, how much would have been the total amount of income over the five years for each of the type of bonds? What would be different under this scenario?

M. MINI-CASES

CASE 1
Good Fortune Co.

(30 minutes)

Good Fortune Co. is a small public company that operates a chain of furniture stores throughout Canada. The company was founded by Kate Homewood, who still owns 25% of the outstanding shares and who remains the CEO. The company has been successful through its three decades of operations largely due to Kate's ability to accurately gauge customers' taste for home furnishings. With successful operations, significant additional funding from its initial public offering, and little reliance on debt financing, Good Fortune has been able to expand to 15 locations across the country despite the ups and downs of the business cycle.

Prior to the latest recession, the company had plans to open three more stores in Halifax, St. John's, and Regina. The expansion would have been funded by internal cash flows from existing operations. However, top management decided to shelve the expansion plans in light of the deep recession and to reconsider these expansion plans when the economy improves again.

With expansion plans on hold, Kate has been wondering what to do with the $30 million of cash that had been set aside for the three new locations. While adept at marketing and operations, Kate has no particular financial training. She has asked you, the chief financial officer, to draft a short report outlining the options she and the board of directors should consider. She mentioned that she would like to know what types of investments would be suitable, what the effects might be on the financial statements, and how investors might react.

Required:

As the CFO of Good Fortune, prepare the report requested by CEO Kate Homewood.

CASE 2
Tightrope Limited

(45 minutes)

Tightrope Limited (TRL) is a large public company with diversified operations in five different industries. Over the past decade, the company has generated significant cash flows from its operations. However, the company has paid out only a small portion of this cash flow to shareholders. Management and the board of directors believe in retaining significant financial assets so that the company has funds available to make strategic investments and so that it can survive through tough economic times. For the years ended 2016, 2017, and 2018, the company reported before-tax profits of $400, $450, and $380 million, respectively.

At the fiscal year-end of December 31, 2018, the company had the following investments:

Investment (in $millions)	Cost	Market value
Cash and cash equivalents	$ 50	$ 50
Affiliates under significant influence (cost approximates carrying amount)	450	750
Equity investments carried at fair value through profit or loss	200	300
Debt investments carried at fair value through other comprehensive income	350	300
Amortized cost debt instruments, purchased at par with average yield of 6%; five years remaining to maturity	800	500
Total	$1,850	$1,900

TRL also has non-financial assets with carrying value of $2 billion on the balance sheet.

As of the end of 2018, the company had bonds outstanding in the amount of $1.5 billion with an interest rate of 8%. Of this amount, $300 million will need to be repaid on March 30,

2019. Other liabilities (accounts payable, etc.) total $400 million; these liabilities do not bear interest. This long-term bond includes the following two covenants:

i.   TRL must maintain a debt-to-asset ratio under 50%, calculated at the end of each fiscal quarter. (For this ratio, the numerator includes all liabilities reported on the balance sheet, while the denominator equals total assets.)

ii. TRL must maintain an interest coverage ratio of 3:1, calculated at the end of each fiscal year. (For this ratio, the numerator is income before interest and taxes, while the denominator is interest expense.)

Should TRL violate either covenant, bondholders have the right to require the immediate repayment of the debt.

Required:

a. It is early March 2019, and you are TRL's chief financial officer. Discuss alternatives and provide a recommendation to the CEO on how you would fund the debt repayment on March 30, 2019.

b. Evaluate TRL's current investment and financing policy and propose changes that would improve the company's financial position.

Luca Merchandising Inc. (LMI) is a privately held import and export company located in Montreal considering going public in the next fiscal year. The company decided to purchase shares in two companies, Terra Nova Inc. (TNI) and McBeal Ltd. (ML). Information related to these investments is as follows.

Terra Nova Inc.:

- Acquired 100,000 shares of the company, accounting for 22% of total shares outstanding.
- Paid $20/share in 2018.
- Shares traded at $25/share at the end of 2018 and $28/share at the end of 2019.
- LMI does not have a seat on the board of directors.
- LMI and TNI do not engage in any trade activities.
- LMI accounts for its investment in TNI using the equity method.

McBeal Ltd.:

- Acquired 50,000 shares of the company, accounting for 10% of total shares outstanding.
- Paid $50/share in 2017.
- Shares traded at $43/share at the end of 2018 and $40/share at the end of 2019.
- LMI accounts for its investment using FVPL.

Balance sheet amounts at December 31, 2019:

- Investment in TNI $1,900,000.
- Investment in ML $2,000,000.

CASE 3
Luca Merchandising Inc.

(20 minutes)

Required:

a. Suppose LMI hired you as an advisor. Discuss the accounting method(s) you would recommend for the investment in TNI.

b. Discuss the alternative accounting methods available for the investment in ML. Which one of the methods would provide the best financial picture for LMI and why?

c. Now suppose that both TNI and ML are small-cap stocks that are not frequently traded in the market. What are the reporting issues related to these securities and how should firms account for these types of investments?

CHAPTER 8

Property, Plant, and Equipment

LEARNING OBJECTIVES

After studying this chapter, you should be able to:

L.O. 8-1. Evaluate whether a cost should be included in property, plant, and equipment, and how much should be classified in each category of asset or expense.

L.O. 8-2. Apply different depreciation methods, including the effect of changes in estimates on depreciation calculations.

L.O. 8-3. Apply the standards for derecognition of property, plant, and equipment and understand the meaning of gains and losses arising from derecognition.

L.O. 8-4. Analyze transactions with non-monetary consideration and apply the accounting standards for non-monetary transactions.

CPA competencies addressed in this chapter:

1.1.2 Evaluates the appropriateness of the basis of financial reporting (Level B)
  b. Methods of measurement
  c. Difference between accrual accounting compared to cash accounting

1.2.1 Develops or evaluates appropriate accounting policies and procedures – Ethical professional judgment (Level B)

1.2.2 Evaluates treatment for routine transactions (Level A)
  d. Property, plant, and equipment
  f. Depreciation, amortization, impairment, and disposition/derecognition
  o. Changes in accounting policies and estimates, and errors

1.2.3 Evaluates treatment for non-routine transactions (Level B)
  a. Uncommon capital assets (exchange of assets, decommissioning costs)

1.3.2 Prepares routine financial statement note disclosure (Level B)

1.4.1 Analyzes complex financial statement note disclosure (Level C)

1.4.5 Analyzes and predicts the impact of strategic and operational decisions on financial results (Level C)
  b. Impact of financial results on the whole organization

TELUS (www.telus.com, Toronto Stock Exchange ticker: T) is a major telecommunications company with shares traded on the Toronto Stock Exchange. At the end of 2016, the company reported $27.7 billion of total assets, of which $10.5 billion, or 38%, were in property, plant, and equipment (PPE). The statement of comprehensive income reported $1.56 billion in depreciation expense on revenues of $12.8 billion.

Clearly, these are important items in TELUS's financial statements. On what basis is the PPE presented? What does the $10.5 billion represent? Is it the current value of TELUS phone lines, cellular phone towers, and so on? How does TELUS determine the amount of depreciation?

In its note disclosures, TELUS explains that the company includes materials, direct labour, applicable overhead, as well as the cost of funds used to finance the construction of PPE that the company self-constructs. What costs can and cannot be included in PPE?

Finally, TELUS also discloses that the PPE account includes costs required in the future to dismantle plant and equipment and to restore the site to its previous condition. Why are these obligations for future costs included in PPE, and how should these costs be accounted for?

Chapter 5 introduced the idea that the reporting of assets under accrual accounting fundamentally involves an allocation problem: whether to record an expenditure as an *expense today* or as an asset that potentially results in *expenses in the future*. This allocation problem is particularly important for assets with long useful lives, such as property, plant, and equipment (PPE), as well as intangible assets. Recording an expenditure as inventory, for example, defers the expense recognition by perhaps one year at most, to the date when the inventory is sold. In contrast, recording costs in PPE results in expense deferral for many years, and indefinitely in the case of land. The long-lived nature of these assets makes the allocation problem particularly important.

THRESHOLD CONCEPT
TIMING OF RECOGNITION

In IFRS, PPE are *tangible* items lasting more than one year and *held for use* in production, for administrative purposes, or for rental to others.[1] The accounting for intangible assets will take place in Chapter 9. Chapter 10 will look at the accounting for non-current assets held for sale (rather than held for use).

In relation to PPE, this chapter explores the following three issues:

■ Initial recognition and measurement—what and how much an enterprise should recognize initially as an asset, and how to classify the amount.

■ Subsequent measurement—how much the enterprise should report on the balance sheet at the reporting date.

■ Derecognition—when and how the enterprise should remove the asset from the balance sheet.

[1.] Copyright © 2012 IFRS Foundation.

This chapter discusses these three issues using the historical cost basis of accounting, which is acceptable under both IFRS and ASPE. However, IFRS also permits the fair value basis; Chapter 10 addresses this alternative. Revaluing PPE to fair value affects the accounting for the second and third issues listed above (i.e., subsequent measurement and derecognition). In addition, Chapter 10 will deal with the **impairment** of PPE—when there are significant declines in the value of these assets.

In some instances, companies will buy or sell assets such as PPE for non-monetary consideration in exchange. This chapter also discusses the standards for how we should account for such non-monetary exchanges. Earlier in this text, Chapter 4 touched on this issue in the context of revenue recognition in barter transactions.

> **impairment** The process of writing down the value of an asset to recognize declines in its **fair market value**.

A. INITIAL RECOGNITION AND MEASUREMENT

The initial recognition of PPE must consider two distinct questions: what costs should an enterprise recognize as an asset, and to which asset account should the cost be recorded? In other words, we must consider the source of the costs and their destinations.

1. What should an enterprise capitalize?

Similar to other assets, enterprises should recognize an expenditure as PPE if it satisfies the definition of an asset and meets the criteria for recognition. In other words, costs meeting these criteria can be capitalized; otherwise, they should be expensed. To **capitalize** a cost is to record it on the balance sheet as an asset. Specifically, IAS 16 indicates the following:

> **L.O. 8-1.** Evaluate whether a cost should be included in property, plant, and equipment, and how much should be classified in each category of asset or expense.

THRESHOLD CONCEPT
CONCEPTUAL FRAMEWORK

> **capitalize** To record a cost on the balance sheet as an asset.

¶7   The cost of an item of property, plant, and equipment shall be recognized as an asset if, and only if:

(a) it is probable that future economic benefits associated with the item will flow to the entity; and

(b) the cost of the item can be measured reliably.[2]

Future economic benefits should be assessed broadly. Some PPE help to generate cash flows directly: furniture in a restaurant is directly related to the ability to serve customers. Other PPE generate cash flows indirectly: manufacturing equipment produces inventories, which are then sold in the future. Also, it is sometimes difficult to attribute specific benefits to a particular item of PPE other than if it is needed for the enterprise's operations: a piece of pollution-abatement equipment may have no direct benefits to the enterprise, but the equipment may be installed for necessary operating permits to be obtained. Alternatively, the enterprise may have chosen to voluntarily exceed environmental standards by installing such equipment.

Enterprises can capitalize all costs required to acquire or to construct the asset and to prepare it for its intended use. This is similar to the criteria for inventory costing. In Exhibit 8-1 are some examples of typical costs to include in various categories of PPE.

Exhibit 8-1 is just an illustration rather than an exhaustive list of costs that should be included in each category. It is important to reiterate that the overall criterion is that all costs necessary to prepare the particular asset for its intended use can be capitalized as part of the cost of the asset. While the idea can be succinctly stated, there are a number of areas where substantial professional judgment is required: self-construction costs; borrowing costs on self-constructed assets; period of capitalization; repairs or replacements; and costs of dismantlement, removal, and site restoration.

---

[2] Copyright © 2012 IFRS Foundation.

Exhibit 8-1	Common costs to include in land, building, and equipment accounts	
Land	**Building**	**Equipment**
Land purchase cost	Building purchase cost	Equipment purchase cost
Title search	Construction permits	Sales taxes
Legal fees	Architectural design	Transportation and delivery
Property transfer tax	Engineering survey of site	Installation
Demolition of old structures	Construction costs	Testing
Soil decontamination costs	Interest during construction	Equipment-specific training

 CHECKPOINT **CP8-1**

What are the criteria for determining what amounts should be capitalized as PPE?

a. Self-construction costs

When companies build their own PPE there are potential difficulties deciding whether an activity is part of the construction and to which asset it belongs. For example, suppose a group of investors started a company called Invermere Inc. to purchase an old industrial site with the intention of developing the property into 30 new rental apartment towers. In the process, the company incurred the following costs:

Exhibit 8-2	Costs potentially related to property development by Invermere Inc.
Transaction	**Amount**
a. Land purchase	$ 300 million
b. Building materials, labour, overhead	1,500 million
c. Property development application, including architectural design	30 million
d. Site decontamination	150 million
e. Green space, community centre, and other public amenities required by city to approve development application	200 million
f. Management salaries	$ 2 million per year
g. Rental office staff	1 million per year
h. Insurance	1 million per year
i. Average borrowing costs during construction period of 10 years	60 million per year

Some of these cost items are fairly straightforward: land should include $300 million for the land purchase, while buildings should include the $1,500 million cost of building materials, labour, and overhead. (Of course, the company should also identify the specific tower for the building cost.) Similarly, the $30 million cost of the development application and architectural design should be included in buildings.

One might consider including the $150 million site decontamination cost into the building cost as well, but instead it should be included as part of land costs. Management's intention for the land is to develop it into residential buildings, and decontamination is necessary to put the land into a developable state.

What is the appropriate treatment of the other costs? The $200 million for public amenities is required by the city for Invermere to obtain approval to build on the site, so perhaps this should be part of the land cost. However, the public amenities also benefit

> ### ⚓ HOW MUCH WOULD IT HAVE COST?
>
> When considering whether an amount is part of the cost of an item of PPE, it is often useful to ask the question, "How much would the enterprise have to pay if it had to purchase the item in the state that it wants?" For Invermere, if it were to purchase the land with the condition that the seller decontaminate the land such that the land is ready for building construction, the seller would price the land to include the cost of decontamination (i.e., $150 million more than the land price without decontamination).

the company by increasing the attractiveness of the developed neighbourhood and thus increasing the rental rates. Indeed, the company may even have provided similar amenities without the city requiring it to do so. Ultimately, the decision requires professional judgment, taking into consideration the details of circumstances that cannot be fully described in this example.

Professional judgment is also required to determine how much of management salaries can be included in the building costs. The company's operations are to develop this property and to rent out the units upon completion. Thus, a large portion of management's time and effort would be spent on construction project management, and such costs should be included in buildings. On the other hand, the activities of rental office staff are not part of construction, so their salaries should be expensed. Insurance costs relate partially to construction and partially to non-construction activities (e.g., directors' and officers' liability insurance), so further analysis should be performed to determine what portion of the insurance premiums relate to construction. Finally, some borrowing costs can be capitalized as part of building costs; we look at this issue in more detail next.

b. Borrowing costs on self-constructed assets

IFRS recommends capitalization of construction-related borrowing costs and expensing of any other borrowing costs. IAS 23 states the following:

> ¶8 An entity shall capitalize borrowing costs that are directly attributable to the acquisition, construction, or production of a qualifying asset as part of the cost of that asset. An entity shall recognize other borrowing costs as an expense in the period in which it incurs them.[3]

The interpretation of "directly attributable" in this paragraph requires some clarification. Borrowing costs incurred on debt issued specifically for the purpose of funding the construction of PPE clearly meets the criterion of being directly attributable. However, even in cases when the enterprise borrows generally, it can attribute a portion of general borrowing costs to the construction of PPE. The logic is that, had the construction not occurred, the enterprise could have avoided incurring the borrowing costs—it could have used the funds to repay debt incurred for other purposes. Specifically, IAS 23 provides the following interpretation of "directly attributable":

> ¶10 The borrowing costs that are directly attributable to the acquisition, construction, or production of a qualifying asset are those borrowing costs that would have been avoided if the expenditure on the qualifying asset had not been made.

[3.] Copyright © 2012 IFRS Foundation.

Based on this guidance, the $60 million incurred by Invermere during the construction period for the purpose of construction should be capitalized as part of the building cost, regardless of whether the borrowing was purpose-specific or general.

Conceptually, there are some problems with this IFRS rule specifying the capitalization of directly attributable interest. Economically, there is a cost of financing regardless of whether the source is debt or equity. Consider the following four scenarios for Invermere:

Exhibit 8-3	Four scenarios for Invermere's construction project	
	Method of financing	
	Financed with additional borrowing	Financed with builder's internal funds
Self-construction	**1a:** Invermere constructs buildings for $1,500 million; costs are evenly incurred over 10 years, with costs financed by a loan with an average balance of $750 million at an interest rate of 8%.	**1b:** Invermere constructs buildings for $1,500 million; costs are evenly incurred over 10 years, with costs financed by internal funds (available cash). The company has no significant debt financing.
Using a construction company	**2a:** Invermere hires construction company Alpha for a contract price of $2,200 million. The construction company borrows, on average, $750 million to finance the construction at 8% interest.	**2b:** Invermere hires construction company Beta for a contract price of $2,200 million. The construction company pays for construction costs with internal funds.

Method of construction applies to the left side (Self-construction / Using a construction company).

Scenario 1a satisfies the requirements of IFRS: the borrowing costs are directly attributable to the project, so the $750 million $\times$ 8% $\times$ 10 years = $600 million of interest should be capitalized into the cost of the building. In contrast, Scenario 1b does not qualify since there is no debt directly attributable to the construction.

Now consider the second pair of scenarios. Both involve Invermere hiring another company for the construction project. In Scenario 2a, we can readily compute the financing cost as $600 million, the same amount Invermere would have incurred in Scenario 1a. The contract price must cover not only construction materials, labour, and overhead, but also Alpha's financing costs. Therefore, the contract price must be more than $1,500 million (the amount without financing costs). As a result, the contract price is $2,200 million after taking into consideration debt financing costs of $600 million and a modest profit margin of $100 million. In Scenario 2b, the financing costs are not apparent because construction company Beta is able to use internal funds rather than debt to finance the project. Nevertheless, there is an economic cost of funds, so Beta also builds that cost into its contract price of $2,200 million. Thus, in either Scenario 2a or 2b, it would cost Invermere $2,200 to have the buildings constructed, and that would be the amount capitalized in the building account on the balance sheet—independent of the construction company's financing source. If this is the case, then the difference in treatment that IFRS imposes upon Scenarios 1a and 1b is rather arbitrary.

When an enterprise borrows specifically for construction, the interest rate is evident from the loan agreement. However, when the enterprise allocates general borrowing for a construction project, then the interest rate (or "capitalization rate") needs to be computed. IAS 23 paragraph 14 specifies that the interest rate "shall be the weighted average of the borrowing costs applicable to the borrowings of the entity that are outstanding during the period, other than borrowing made specifically for the purpose of obtaining a qualifying asset." It is possible for this calculation to result in an amount of interest that exceeds the actual total borrowing cost in the period; in such cases, the amount of interest capitalized would be capped at the amount of interest actually incurred. Exhibit 8-4 illustrates the application of these interest capitalization rules for one year of interest capitalization using three hypothetical companies. For each situation, assume that the enterprise has a weighted-average borrowing rate of 7% on its existing debt (i.e., general borrowing) and assume that the enterprise incurs $100 million in construction costs that require funding.

- Company A: All construction costs financed by general borrowing. Total interest cost for the enterprise for the year is $15,450,000.
- Company B: 80% of construction costs financed by a construction loan at an interest rate of 9%, and remainder financed by general borrowing. Total interest cost for the enterprise for the year is $15,450,000.
- Company C: Construction costs financed by general borrowing and internal funds. Total debt outstanding during the year was $40,000,000 and total interest cost incurred for the year was $2,600,000.

Exhibit 8-4	Examples of interest capitalization computations		
	Company A	**Company B**	**Company C**
Construction-specific borrowing	$ 0	$80,000,000	$ 0
Capitalization rate	× n/a	× 9%	× n/a
Interest on construction loan	$ 0	$ 7,200,000	$ 0
General borrowing used for construction	$100,000,000	$20,000,000	$40,000,000
Capitalization rate	× 7%	× 7%	× 7%
Interest on general borrowing for construction	$ 7,000,000	$ 1,400,000	$ 2,800,000
Total interest on construction-specific and general borrowing for construction	7,000,000	8,600,000	2,800,000
Total interest incurred by enterprise (given)	15,450,000	15,450,000	2,600,000
Lesser of above = Total interest for the year directly attributable to construction eligible for capitalization	$ 7,000,000	$ 8,600,000	$ 2,600,000

For Company A, the computation is straightforward since all of the borrowing was not construction-specific. Company B's borrowing was partly from construction-specific borrowing and general borrowing, so both components need to be accounted for. Company C financed by general borrowing and internal funds (i.e., equity), so the interest directly attributable to construction is based on only the debt portion ($40 million), not the equity portion ($60 million). Furthermore, since the actual interest incurred in the year for all borrowing by the enterprise was only $2.6 million, that amount becomes the cap for the amount of interest capitalization.

While IFRS provides specific guidance on the capitalization of borrowing costs, ASPE only requires enterprises to disclose their accounting policy for interest capitalization and the amount of interest capitalized (see ASPE Section 3850); neither is there a requirement to capitalize, nor is there a prohibition against capitalization. Exhibit 8-5 summarizes the accounting treatment of interest on self-constructed assets.

Exhibit 8-5	Summary of accounting standards applicable to interest capitalization	
Standard	**Cost of debt directly attributable to construction**	**Cost of internal funds**
ASPE	Can capitalize or expense	Can capitalize or expense
IFRS	Capitalize	Expense

This variation in standards illustrates the significant differences in position that can be taken by different standard-setting bodies. The requirements and prohibitions against interest capitalization in IFRS reflect a higher priority for comparability among reporting entities. The greater flexibility allowed by ASPE reflects a greater trust that enterprises will choose the policy that best reflects their circumstances and that disclosure of interest capitalization policies will sufficiently inform users.

THRESHOLD CONCEPT
CONCEPTUAL FRAMEWORK

 CHECKPOINT **CP8-2**

What amounts of financing cost can be capitalized into the cost of a constructed asset?

c. Period of capitalization

When does an enterprise stop capitalizing costs into PPE? In general, capitalization ends when the item is ready for its intended use. Whether the asset is in fact put into use is not important. For example, suppose Jaffray Company starts to construct a warehouse on April 1, 2018, and finishes on September 30, 2019; warehousing operations begin on November 15, and the construction loan is repaid on December 1. In this situation, Jaffray would capitalize construction costs, including any borrowing costs, for the 18-month period from April 1, 2018, to September 30, 2019.

d. Replacements versus repairs

The criteria for asset recognition are also important in transactions other than the initial purchase. Frequently, companies will incur expenditures related to existing assets, such as upgrading a building or servicing a vehicle. Similar to the treatment of the initial asset purchase, the issue is whether the additional subsequent expenditures have future benefit. If they do, then they should be capitalized to the cost of the asset; otherwise they should be expensed.

IFRS provides additional specific guidance in IAS 16 paragraphs 12 and 13. Enterprises should expense expenditures that would normally be considered repairs and maintenance, whereas replacements of significant asset components should be capitalized as replacements. This is another area that requires considerable professional judgment. For example, an oil change for a car would be considered part of ongoing maintenance, while putting in a new engine would be a replacement. Generally, repairs and maintenance costs are those that are insignificant relative to the value of the PPE or those that are incurred on a recurring basis.

If an expenditure qualifies as a replacement, it is then necessary to consider the treatment of any remaining costs previously included in the asset that pertain to the replacement. For example, suppose Kimberley Corporation spends $3 million to replace the roof on one of its buildings, Building 22, with a "green" roof that will reduce rainwater runoff and air conditioning costs by 30%. The old roof had not been classified as a separate asset, but instead was included as part of the $12 million purchase cost of the building. At the time of the roof replacement, Building 22 had a carrying value on the balance sheet (i.e., purchase cost less accumulated depreciation) of $8 million. Kimberley estimates that the roof comprises about 20% of the building's value.

This roof expenditure would likely qualify as a replacement as it is a significant cost relative to the value of the building and the cost is not a recurring cost. When Kimberley capitalizes the $3 million for the new roof, it will also need to remove the costs of the old roof. Since the company estimates that 20% of the building's cost relates to the roof, it should remove $1.6 million (20% of $8 million carrying value) from the balance sheet. Exhibit 8-6 shows the journal entries Kimberley should record if it treats the roof work as a replacement.

Exhibit 8-6	Journal entries for Kimberley's roof work on Building 22 treated as replacement	
Dr. Accumulated depreciation—Building 22	800,000	
Dr. Loss on roof replacement for Building 22	1,600,000	
Cr. Building cost—Building 22		2,400,000
Dr. Building cost—Building 22	3,000,000	
Cr. Cash		3,000,000

The net impact on the income statement is –$1.6 million (before tax). For the balance sheet, these entries would result in the building cost increasing by $0.6 million, accumulated depreciation decreasing by $0.8 million, and carrying value increasing by $1.4 million. The schedule in Exhibit 8-7 shows the derivation of these balance sheet amounts. In summary, the $3 million of expenditures is allocated between $1.6 million in expense and $1.4 million in increase in PPE.

Exhibit 8-7	Continuity schedule for Kimberley's Building 22 with roof work treated as replacement		
	Cost	Accumulated depreciation	Carrying value
Balance before roof replacement	$12,000,000	$4,000,000	$8,000,000
Deduct portion relating to old roof (20%)	(2,400,000)	(800,000)	(1,600,000)
Add cost of new roof	3,000,000	0	3,000,000
Balance after roof replacement	$12,600,000	$3,200,000	$9,400,000

For comparison, had Kimberley treated the roof replacement as a repair, it would have expensed the $3 million cost, reducing pre-tax income by the same amount. There would be no effect on the balance sheet accounts for PPE.

The replacement/repair dichotomy revises a betterment/maintenance classification used previously in IFRS before 2005, and still used in ASPE (see Section 3061 paragraphs .14 and .15). In this latter approach, an enterprise classifies subsequent expenditures on an asset as betterment if the expenditures enhance the quality or quantity of the asset's output (i.e., future benefits) and capitalizes such costs into the asset base; otherwise, it expenses the cost as maintenance expense.

 CHECKPOINT **CP8-3**

How do we distinguish replacements from repairs and maintenance of PPE?

e. Costs of dismantlement, removal, and site restoration

Acquisitions of PPE often entail obligations to incur future costs of dismantling and removing the item, and restoring the installation site to a predefined condition. For instance, government regulations often require companies engaged in heavy industry to restore the industrial site, at the end of the industrial activity, to conditions similar to the state before the commencement of the activities. Incurring these future costs is necessary to obtain regulatory approval to operate, so such costs should be included as part of the initial cost of the related PPE, and depreciated along with it. A common example is a gasoline station.

To understand the accounting required, suppose Liverpool Linens purchases a piece of land for the purpose of building a laundry facility for commercial customers such as restaurants. Because the cleaning process involves significant quantities of cleaning solvents and potential seepage into the ground, the municipality requires the company to restore the site at the end of the 20-year period for which the company is permitted to operate at the particular location. The company estimates that it will need to incur $500,000 to decontaminate the soil at the end of 20 years of operations. The present value of this $500,000 site restoration cost, assuming a discount rate of 8%, is $107,274. To recognize this site restoration cost, the company would record the following entries upon initial acquisition and subsequently (assuming straight-line depreciation):

Exhibit 8-8	Journal entries for Liverpool Linens's site restoration cost		
Acquisition:	Dr. Building site restoration cost	107,274	
	Cr. Obligation for future site restoration cost		107,274
Each year:	Dr. Depreciation expense ($107,274 ÷ 20 years)	5,364	
	Cr. Accumulated depreciation—building		5,364
Year 1:	Dr. Interest expense ($107,274 × 8%)	8,582	
	Cr. Obligation for future site restoration cost		8,582
Year 2:	Dr. Interest expense [($107,274 + 8,582) × 8%]	9,268	
	Cr. Obligation for future site restoration cost		9,268

By the end of 20 years, the accumulated depreciation will total $107,274 ($5,364/ year × 20 years), which is the present value of the $500,000 at the beginning of the 20 years. The amount of interest expense will increase each year, along with the balance of the obligation. By the end of 20 years, the account "Obligation for future site restoration costs" will be $500,000. Exhibit 8-9 shows the amount relating to the site restoration costs.

Exhibit 8-9	Schedule of expenses and balance sheet amounts related to Liverpool Linens's site restoration			
Year	Depreciation expense	Accumulated depreciation at end of year	Interest on obligation for site restoration at 8%*	Obligation for future site restoration at end of year**
0		$ 0		$107,274
1	$ 5,364	5,364	$ 8,582	115,856
2	5,364	10,727	9,268	125,124
3	5,364	16,091	10,010	135,134
4	5,364	21,455	10,811	145,945
5	5,364	26,819	11,676	157,621
6	5,364	32,182	12,610	170,231
7	5,364	37,546	13,618	183,849
8	5,364	42,910	14,708	198,557
9	5,364	48,273	15,885	214,442
10	5,364	53,637	17,155	231,597
11	5,364	59,001	18,528	250,124
12	5,364	64,364	20,010	270,134
13	5,364	69,728	21,611	291,745
14	5,364	75,092	23,340	315,085
15	5,364	80,456	25,207	340,292
16	5,364	85,819	27,223	367,515
17	5,364	91,183	29,401	396,916
18	5,364	96,547	31,753	428,669
19	5,364	101,910	34,294	462,963
20	5,364	107,274	37,036	500,000
Total	$107,274		$392,726	

*Interest = Prior year balance of obligation × 8%.

**Obligation = Prior year obligation + Current year interest.

Notice that the total expense (depreciation + interest) over the 20 years adds up to $107,274 + $392,726 = $500,000, the estimated cost of site restoration.

 CHECKPOINT **CP8-4**

What are the two expenses that result from future site restoration costs? How do we determine the amounts of these two expenses?

2. How should enterprises categorize costs capitalized into property, plant, and equipment?

a. Unit of measurement and componentization

THRESHOLD CONCEPT
CONCEPTUAL FRAMEWORK

To capitalize costs in PPE, it is necessary to define the unit of measurement—when are two or more items separate assets, and when are they merely components of a single asset? Should a car be considered as a single unit, or should it be componentized into engine, frame, wheels, and so on? How about a manufacturing plant and the equipment inside it? There are no clear-cut answers for all situations, and IFRS allows firms latitude to apply professional judgment according to the circumstances (IAS 16 paragraph 9). Reflecting the cost constraint, enterprises need only componentize significant parts of an item of PPE. Furthermore, the issue is only important to the extent that finer, more detailed classifications can accommodate more specific estimates of useful lives and depreciation patterns. Therefore, parts of an item with similar useful lives and usage patterns can be classified as a single asset because there are no additional information benefits from separating such components. Specifically, IAS 16 states the following:

¶43 Each part of an item of property, plant, and equipment with a cost that is significant in relation to the total cost of the item shall be depreciated separately.

¶45 A significant part of an item of property, plant, and equipment may have a useful life and a depreciation method that are the same as the useful life and the depreciation method of another significant part of that same item. Such parts may be grouped in determining the depreciation charge.[4]

Section B below discusses the specifics of the depreciation process. To the extent that capitalizing costs into different types of assets affects future depreciation, a useful way to categorize expenditures is according to their expected useful life and pattern of depreciation. For example, how does one treat the costs of putting down a sidewalk around a building? Is it part of the building cost, or part of the land cost? Since a sidewalk does have a finite life, it cannot be considered part of the land cost. If the sidewalk's usefulness matches that of the building, then the two can be combined together. On the other hand, if the sidewalk is expected to last longer or for less time than the building, then it would be put in a separate category such as "land improvements."

b. Bundled purchases

Enterprises often purchase groups of assets as a bundle in a single transaction. For example, a purchase of a warehouse will typically include both the land and building,

---

and possibly some inventory management equipment such as forklifts. If the purchase and sale agreement does not contain a list of values for each item of land, building, and equipment purchased, then the total purchase price will need to be allocated to the specific asset using estimates of each asset's fair value on the date of acquisition.[5] Further, as discussed above, a bundled purchase may result from an enterprise separating a single purchase into different components (e.g., such as separating a car into engine, frame, wheels, etc.).

For example, suppose Nelson Commercial Properties purchases a shopping centre for $200 million. The company estimated the fair values on the date of acquisition as follows:

- Land—$80 million
- Land improvements (sidewalks, parking lot, landscaping)—$10 million
- Building—$110 million

THRESHOLD CONCEPT
QUALITY OF EARNINGS

There is, however, considerable judgment required in making the estimates of fair value. How reliable is the $80 million value estimate for the land Nelson purchased? If management has incentives to increase reported income and assets, then there could be pressure to bias upward the estimated fair value of land and bias downward the land improvements and building. Why? It is because land is not depreciable while the other assets are. For instance, if management increased the fair value estimate for land by $10 million, and decreased the value of the building by the same amount, the total would still be $200 million, but there would be $10 million less to be depreciated in the future. If the useful life of the building is 20 years, straight-line depreciation would be reduced by $500,000 per year.

A second issue in bundled purchases is that it is possible that the total estimated fair value of the individual items together adds up to an amount more or less than the total purchase price. When this occurs, we allocate the purchase price in proportion to each item's fair value. For example, suppose Nelson Commercial Properties purchased the shopping centre for $192 million (instead of $200 million as illustrated above). The value of land, land improvements, and buildings totals $200 million, which exceeds the purchase price. Proportional allocation of the purchase price would result in the following values recorded in each of the three categories of PPE:

Exhibit 8-10	Calculation of costs to allocate to each category of PPE for Nelson Commercial Properties				
PPE category	**Percentage of total fair value**	×	**Total price**		**Cost allocated**
Land	$80m / $200m = 40%	×	$192m	=	$ 76.8m
Land improvements	$10m / $200m = 5%	×	$192m	=	9.6m
Building	$110m / $200m = 55%	×	$192m	=	105.6m
Total					$192.0m

 CHECKPOINT **CP8-5**

Why is it important to componentize items of PPE and to allocate the cost of bundled purchases to different items of PPE?

[5.] Buyers and sellers will usually agree on an itemized list of values; the seller also requires such values for tax reporting to determine tax gains and losses. There would not be an agreed-upon list of values if the assets were purchased through an acquisition of a corporation. The technical aspects of such transactions are beyond the scope of this text.

B. SUBSEQUENT MEASUREMENT

1. Basis of measurement: Historical cost versus current value

L.O. 8-2. Apply different depreciation methods, including the effect of changes in estimates on depreciation calculations.

After the purchase date, IFRS permits two methods of measuring the value of PPE: historical cost (adjusted for depreciation) or fair value. In comparison, ASPE allows only the former method. This chapter will apply the method using historical cost and leave the fair value method for Chapter 10.

Before looking at the details of depreciation under the historical cost method, we should take a moment to consider the potential alternative ways to measure the value of PPE on the balance sheet—historical cost or current value, the latter of which can be measured by three measurement bases: replacement cost, value in use, and net realizable value.

historical cost   The actual cost of an asset at the time it was purchased; can also refer to amounts based on historical cost but adjusted by depreciation or impairment.

current value   The value of an asset in an input market or output market on the date of measurement.

replacement cost (entry value)   The cost required to replace the productive capacity of an asset. For a used asset, the amount reflects the age and past usage of the asset, not a new asset.

value in use   The discounted value of cash flows expected from using an asset for its intended purpose.

net realizable value (exit value)   The value expected from the sale of an asset, net of any costs of disposal.

- **Historical cost**—this measurement basis uses the initial cost of purchase or construction (recorded according to the discussion in the previous section) and calculates depreciation over the useful life of the asset.
- **Current value**—the entry value, value in use, or exit value of the asset at the date of measurement, such as each year-end.

    — **Replacement cost (entry value)**—the value of an asset in terms of the dollar amount required to replace the asset's productive capacity.
    — **Value in use**—measures the value of PPE according to how much cash flow the enterprise expects from the output of the PPE.
    — **Net realizable value (exit value)**—the amount that can be obtained from the sale of the asset net of any costs of disposal.

The three different measures of current value are the same only in perfect markets—when there are no market imperfections such as transaction costs or information asymmetry. For example, a large company with significant buying power and a strong bargaining position relative to suppliers will be able to make purchases at prices below other buyers who do not have similar buying power. Also, on average, companies make positive net present value investments in operating assets—otherwise, there would be no reason to be in business. Thus, the value in use of PPE generally exceeds its entry and exit value. Value in use will also tend to exceed exit value because of adverse selection: as discussed in Chapter 1, buyers have less information about an item that is available for sale compared with the seller and they must discount the price accordingly. For PPE, the degree of this adverse selection could be quite severe. Folk wisdom suggests that the value of a new car drops by 30% the moment it is driven off the car dealer's lot; while probably an exaggeration, there is truth behind the sentiment—when the new car owner wishes to resell the car, skeptical buyers will ask, "Why is he or she selling and what is wrong with the car?"

THRESHOLD CONCEPT
INFORMATION ASYMMETRY

fair value   The price that would be received to sell an asset (or paid to transfer a liability) in an orderly transaction between market participants at the measurement date.

Fair value for PPE is the price that would be received to sell an asset (or paid to transfer a liability) in an orderly transaction between market participants at the measurement date (IFRS 13). This definition is similar to current value; the difference is that fair value identifies a priority ordering of the three measures of current value. The preference is to use exit values: what is the market value of the asset if sold? In terms of PPE such as land and buildings, exit values are usually obtained via appraisals by professional valuators who take into account market values of similar transactions (IAS 16 paragraph 32). However, many types of PPE are specialized in function, location, or in other ways such that market values cannot be reliably estimated. In such cases, these enterprises can estimate fair value by the value in use or replacement cost (entry value).

Companies can revalue PPE to fair value under certain circumstances. In particular, IAS 16 provides the following guidance if a company chooses to revalue its PPE:

¶31   After recognition as an asset, an item of property, plant, and equipment whose fair value can be measured reliably shall be carried at a revalued amount, being its fair value at the date of the revaluation less any subsequent accumulated depreciation and subsequent accumulated impairment losses. Revaluations shall be made with sufficient regularity to ensure that the carrying amount does not differ materially from that which would be determined using fair value at the end of the reporting period.[6]

Note that revaluation is not compulsory—a company may choose the cost model or the revaluation model. Furthermore, the fair value for the class of assets needs to be "measured reliably" for revaluation to be applied. Thus, this choice as permitted by IFRS aims to achieve higher relevance of reported numbers by providing more up-to-date information, as long as a sufficient degree of reliability can be obtained. Once an enterprise has chosen the revaluation model for an asset, it must continue to revalue that asset regularly to ensure that the reported value on the balance sheet is current.

Revaluation can result in asset values rising or falling. Revaluation has implications for depreciation, both subsequent to revaluation as well as in the year of revaluation. These issues will be discussed in detail in Chapter 10.

THRESHOLD CONCEPT
CONCEPTUAL FRAMEWORK

2. Impairment

To ensure neutrality and representational faithfulness, enterprises need to consider whether the accounts overstate the value of PPE relative to fair value. The need to record impairment applies whether an enterprise uses historical cost or fair value bases. As with revaluation, application of impairment to PPE is relatively complex and we defer addressing this issue until Chapter 10.

THRESHOLD CONCEPT
CONCEPTUAL FRAMEWORK

3. Depreciation under the historical cost basis

Depreciation is a systematic (yet arbitrary) process of **cost allocation** that apportions the cost of PPE over its economic useful life. Depreciation matches costs to the periods over which benefits are obtained. Despite the non-accounting use of "depreciation" to refer to the decline in value of assets, *the objective of accounting depreciation is not asset valuation,* so the depreciated value of an asset need not correspond to its current value. In particular, some PPE's current value may increase, but such assets would still need to be depreciated.

cost allocation   The process of apportioning the cost of an asset over its **useful life**.

In accounting, **depreciation** is synonymous with "depletion" and "amortization." Traditionally, accountants have used depreciation to refer to tangible human-made assets, depletion to refer to tangible natural resources such as minerals, and amortization to refer to intangible assets.

Most readers should be familiar with the basics of depreciation from introductory accounting. To review, the journal entry to record depreciation is as follows:

depreciation   The systematic allocation of an asset's depreciable amount over its estimated useful life. Depreciation usually refers to tangible human-made assets, depletion refers to tangible natural resources, and amortization refers to intangible assets. ASPE uses amortization as a generic term that covers all three types of assets.

Exhibit 8-11	Depreciation journal entry	
Dr. Depreciation expense		xx
Cr. Accumulated depreciation [PPE category]		xx

The process to determine the amount of depreciation expense for this journal entry involves three judgments: the total amount to depreciate, the period of depreciation, and the pattern of depreciation.

[6.] Copyright © 2012 IFRS Foundation.

a. Total amount to depreciate: The depreciable amount

depreciable amount The total amount to be expensed through depreciation: initial cost less residual value.

The **depreciable amount** is the total amount to be expensed through depreciation. This amount equals the initial cost less residual value. **Residual value** is the amount that the enterprise expects to be currently obtainable from the disposal of the asset (less disposal costs) if the asset has the age and condition expected at the end of its useful life. This combination of timing appears unusual. The residual value of an asset with a five-year useful life refers to the *present day* value of the asset if the asset were *five years old*. The reason for this combination of timing is to avoid having firms forecast the value of an asset and market conditions far into the future, which is difficult and unreliable. Instead, firms only need to estimate the value of the used asset under current market conditions. As a practical matter, enterprises will often ignore the residual value for many assets unless the residual value is substantial and readily estimable.

residual value The estimated amount that an entity would currently obtain from disposal of the asset, after deducting the estimated costs of disposal, if the asset were already of the age and in the condition expected at the end of its useful life.

For example, suppose a company purchased a truck for $60,000 in 2019. The company plans to use the truck for five years, at which point it would be sold. In 2019, the company sold a similar used truck that was five years old for $10,000. Based on these facts, the company could use $10,000 as the estimated residual value for the new truck. The company would not try to predict the value of the truck in 2024.

b. Period of depreciation

useful life The period of time over which an asset is expected to be available for use by an entity, or the number of production units an enterprise expects to obtain from the use of an asset.

The period of depreciation is the estimated useful life of the asset. **Useful life** is the period of time over which an asset is expected to be available for use by an entity, or the number of production units an enterprise expects to obtain from the use of an asset. "Useful" here is specific to the enterprise and the state of technology. An asset may still be operational, but if there were more efficient ways to perform the same functions then the asset would no longer be useful. For example, old computers may still function but are obsolete and impractical to use due to technological advances. Recognizing depreciation expense over the periods in which the enterprise obtains benefits conforms to the matching principle.

It is also important to note that depreciation should be recorded in a period as long as the PPE is *available for use* rather than actually in use. For example, a production machine may sit idle due to slow sales and the buildup of an excess amount of finished goods; depreciation should still be computed. As another example, for a newly constructed building, depreciation begins when it is available to be occupied, even if the company chooses to move into the building at a later date.

c. Pattern of depreciation

straight-line method A method of depreciation in which the (remaining) depreciable amount is evenly allocated over the asset's (remaining) estimated useful life.

To match expenses to revenue, the chosen pattern of depreciation should best reflect the expected pattern of consumption of the asset's future economic benefits (see IAS 16 paragraphs 60 and 62). For example, if an asset produces more benefits in its early years of use than in later years, then the enterprise should choose a depreciation method that results in higher depreciation in the early years. Three common patterns of depreciation in use:

declining-balance method A method of depreciation in which a period's depreciation equals the asset's net carrying amount multiplied by a fixed percentage.

- **Straight-line method**—allocates the depreciable amount evenly over the years of estimated useful life.
- **Declining-balance method**—determines depreciation as a fixed percentage of the asset's carrying value.
- **Units-of-production method**—allocates the depreciable amount in proportion to the fraction of production capacity used.[7]

units-of-production method A method of depreciation in which the (remaining) depreciable amount is allocated in proportion to the productive capacity used.

[7.] Another method that is less common is sum-of-the-years'-digits. For an asset with a three-year useful life, the sum of the years' digits is $1 + 2 + 3 = 6$. In time order, the depreciation would be $3/6$, $2/6$, and $1/6$ of the depreciable amount. Thus, this is a declining pattern of depreciation that fully allocates the depreciable amount over the estimated useful life.

Why have these methods developed if the goal is to record depreciation according to the amount of benefits consumed in each period? Why not let management decide, at the end of each year, how much depreciation to record? The reason is that these methods are systematic in the sense that management must determine the future stream of depreciation when the company acquires the asset by setting the three depreciation parameters (depreciable cost, useful life, depreciation pattern). *Having management commit to a depreciation schedule that covers the asset's useful life reduces earnings management opportunities because it prevents management from recording an amount of depreciation according to its judgment and motives each period.*

Traditionally, the straight-line and declining-balance methods have been the most commonly used depreciation methods because of their simplicity. In particular, the straight-line method is simplest for a single asset, but becomes more complex than the declining-balance method when an enterprise has several assets in the same depreciation group but acquired in different years. For example, suppose a company buys three machines, one at the beginning of each of Years 1 through 3, at a cost of $10,000 each, zero residual value, and a five-year expected useful life. All three machines remain in operation until the end of Year 7. Using the straight-line method, it is easy to determine the depreciation to be $2,000/year per machine. The table in Exhibit 8-12 shows the depreciation for Years 1 through 7.

THRESHOLD CONCEPT
QUALITY OF EARNINGS

Exhibit 8-12	Illustration of straight-line method with multiple assets			
		Machine A	Machine B	Machine C	Total
Year acquired		Year 1	Year 2	Year 3	
Cost		$10,000	$10,000	$10,000	$30,000
Depreciation	Year 1	2,000			2,000
	Year 2	2,000	2,000		4,000
	Year 3	2,000	2,000	2,000	6,000
	Year 4	2,000	2,000	2,000	6,000
	Year 5	2,000	2,000	2,000	6,000
	Year 6	—	2,000	2,000	4,000
	Year 7	—	—	2,000	2,000

To obtain the correct amount of straight-line depreciation for all three machines in total on the far right column, it is necessary to maintain accurate records on an *item-by-item basis* of (i) the original cost and (ii) the date of acquisition or the accumulated depreciation of each machine. For instance, in Year 6, the total depreciation is not the total cost ($30,000) divided by five years, which would be $6,000. Rather, it is $2,000 each for Machines B and C, for a total of $4,000, because Machine A has already been fully depreciated. In contrast, the declining-balance method only requires the aggregate carrying amount to obtain the amount of depreciation. This is one of the reasons that depreciation for tax purposes generally follows the declining-balance method.

d. Other considerations

As a practical matter, enterprises also need to have a policy regarding partial-year depreciation for assets acquired or disposed of during the year. Some enterprises will be precise and record depreciation according to the month it acquires or disposes of the PPE. Others will simply record a full year of depreciation in the year of acquisition and none in the year of disposal. Yet others take a compromise approach and use a half year in the year of acquisition and the year of disposal.

Finally, take note that when an enterprise uses PPE to produce other assets, the depreciation charges flow into those other assets rather than through the income statement as an expense. For example, the depreciation on a piece of manufacturing equipment would be included as part of the production cost of inventories and recorded as an asset. The depreciation affects the income statement as part of cost of sales when the enterprise sells the inventory.

e. Illustration

Once an enterprise establishes the above three parameters (depreciable amount, useful life, and depreciation pattern), the depreciation calculation can be done readily. Readers proficient with introductory accounting should have no difficulty with the following calculations.

Suppose Mackenzie Company purchases a piece of production equipment for $120,000 to replace an identical machine that has reached the end of its useful life. This equipment has an estimated useful life of five years. In terms of units of production, the company expects the useful life to be 1,000 units. At the end of its useful life, Mackenzie intends to sell the machine to a lower-quality manufacturer overseas, as it is doing with the old machine. The company has been able to obtain $20,000 for the old equipment after deducting shipping costs to the buyer. At the end of each year, Mackenzie determines the actual number of units produced to be, in chronological order, 150, 200, 250, 250, and 50 units, for a total of 900 units. For purposes of illustration, Mackenzie uses a 40% rate for the declining-balance method of depreciation.

The table and figures in Exhibits 8-13 and 8-14 show the amount of depreciation (in $000's) that Mackenzie would record in each year, as well as the carrying amount of the equipment on the balance sheet, using the three methods of depreciation.

Exhibit 8-13	Depreciation schedules for Mackenzie Company's production equipment ($000's)					
	Depreciation			Carrying amount (cost − accumulated depreciation)		
Year	Straight line over 5 years*	Declining balance†	Units of production‡	Straight line over 5 years	Declining balance	Units of production
0	—	—	—	120.0	120.0	120.0
1	20.0	48.0	15.0	100.0	72.0	105.0
2	20.0	28.8	20.0	80.0	43.2	85.0
3	20.0	17.3	25.0	60.0	25.9	60.0
4	20.0	5.9	25.0	40.0	20.0	35.0
5	20.0	0.0	5.0	20.0	20.0	30.0
Total	100.0	100.0	90.0			

*(Cost − Residual value) ÷ Useful life = (120 − 20) ÷ 5 years = 20/year.
†Carrying amount × Declining-balance rate = 120 × 40% = 48 in Year 1; (120 − 48) × 40% = 28.8 in Year 2; and so on. Years 4 and 5 do not correspond to this calculation method; see discussion below.
‡Depreciation per unit = (Cost − Residual value) ÷ Potential units = (120 − 20) ÷ 1,000 = 0.10/unit; Year 1 depreciation = 0.10/unit × 150 units = 15; Year 2 depreciation = 0.10/unit × 200 units = 20; and so on.

Notice that the total depreciation under the units-of-production method totals only $90,000, so that $30,000 remains as the carrying value at the end of five years. This can occur because the useful life of 1,000 units is only an estimate made when Mackenzie acquires the machine, while the actual production turned out to be

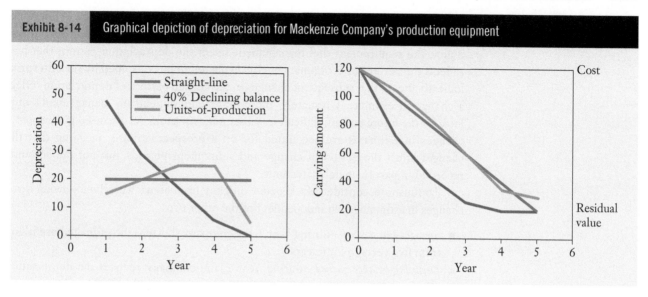

| Exhibit 8-14 | Graphical depiction of depreciation for Mackenzie Company's production equipment |

900 units over the five years. In contrast, the straight-line and declining-balance methods fully allocate the depreciable amount of $100,000 over the five years, leaving only the residual value of $20,000 in the carrying amount. Thus, the units-of-production method may better match depreciation with the benefits consumed in an ideal world where the future can be predicted precisely; in practice, the presence of uncertainty makes this advantage less clear.

In Exhibit 8-13, also note that the depreciation amounts for the declining-balance method in Years 4 and 5 do not follow the general declining-balance approach. In Year 4, 40% of the carrying amount of $25,900 equals $10,400. However, recording this amount of depreciation would bring the carrying amount below the residual value of $20,000, meaning that accumulated depreciation exceeds the depreciable amount. This result occurs because the declining-balance method does not factor in the residual value (in contrast to the straight-line method). To avoid this outcome, Mackenzie should record only $5,900 for depreciation, after which the carrying amount would equal $20,000. In Year 5, the company would record zero depreciation since the asset has been fully depreciated.[8] Of course, the zero depreciation in Year 5 suggests that the 40% rate for the declining-balance depreciation schedule is too high if the machine indeed has a five-year useful life, so perhaps a lower rate would be more appropriate.

 CHECKPOINT **CP8-6**

What are the three parameters that determine the amount of depreciation?

f. Impact of changes in estimates on depreciation

The three parameters (depreciable cost, useful life, depreciation pattern) used in the calculation of depreciation are only management's best estimates of the future. Any of the three can be revised when better information becomes available. For example, management may increase its estimate of the residual value, decrease the estimate of useful life, or determine that the declining-balance method better matches costs with revenues than the straight-line method does. Such changes could all be

---

[8] There are alternative ways to avoid overdepreciating an asset under the declining-balance method, but the one described here is probably the simplest. Accounting standards do not specifically address such situations.

considered *changes in estimate* rather than changes in accounting policy. While there is a valid argument that a change in depreciation pattern is a change in accounting policy, the requirement that management select the depreciation pattern that best reflects the pattern of economic benefits expected to be consumed by the enterprise logically means that subsequent changes in the chosen pattern of depreciation reflect a change in estimate. Ultimately, these judgments depend on management's outlook for the future and are difficult to substantiate or refute. As discussed in Chapter 3, changes in estimates are accounted for on a prospective basis, meaning that the changes affect the period of change and subsequent periods, but not the amounts recorded in past financial statements.

To illustrate, consider Mackenzie Company from above with the following three changes in estimate (each independent of the other two):

- *Straight-line method*—during Year 3, the company shortens the estimated useful life from five years to four years.
- *Declining-balance method*—during Year 2, the company reduces the depreciation rate from 40% to 30% to better reflect the five-year useful life.
- *Units-of-production method*—during Year 4, the company realizes that it had initially overestimated the number of units the machine can produce, so it revises the total units that it expects to produce from the machine from 1,000 to 920 units.

How much depreciation should Mackenzie record in each year? Exhibit 8-15 shows these amounts, with the figures in bold reflecting the three separate changes in estimates just described.

Exhibit 8-15	Depreciation schedules for Mackenzie Company with changes in estimate ($000's)					
	Depreciation			Carrying amount (cost − accumulated depreciation)		
Year	Straight line*	Declining balance†	Units of production‡	Straight line	Declining balance	Units of production
0	—	—	—	120.0	120.0	120.00
1	20.0	48.0	15.00	100.0	72.0	105.00
2	20.0	**21.6**	20.00	80.0	**50.4**	85.00
3	**30.0**	15.1	25.00	50.0	35.3	60.00
4	**30.0**	10.6	**31.25**	20.0	24.7	28.75
5	0.0	4.7	**6.25**	20.0	20.0	22.50
Total	100.0	100.0	**97.50**			

Bolded figures reflect changes in estimate.

*Year 3 depreciation = $(80 - 20) \div 2$ years = 30/year; same for Year 4.

†Year 2 depreciation = $72 \times 30\% = 21.6$; Year 3 = $50.4 \times 30\% = 15.1$; Year 4 = $35.3 \times 30\% = 10.6$; Year 5 = lesser of $(24.7 \times 30\%)$ or (remaining depreciable cost) = lesser of 7.4 or 4.7 = 4.7.

‡Depreciation per unit in Years 4 and 5 = $(60 - 20) \div 320 = 0.125$/unit; Year 4 depreciation = 0.125/unit $\times 250$ units = 31.25; Year 5 depreciation = 0.125/unit $\times 50$ units = 6.25.

The general idea behind the calculations used in Exhibit 8-15 is that each depreciation calculation takes into account the most current information, but does not apply that information to prior periods. That is, we apply the prospective method. To formalize these calculations, we can express the calculations using the formulas shown in Exhibit 8-16. In these formulas, any references to "remaining" refers to amounts before the current-period depreciation. These formulas will be useful not only for instances when there are changes in estimate, but also when estimates do not change. The table also shows how these formulas apply to Mackenzie both before and after the changes in estimate.

Exhibit 8-16	Depreciation formulas, including effects of changes in estimate and application to Mackenzie Company		
	Straight line	**Declining balance**	**Units of production**
Depreciation formula	$Depr = \dfrac{\text{Remaining depreciable cost}}{\text{Remaining useful life}}$	Depr $= $ Carrying amount $\times$ DB rate	Define UP rate $= \dfrac{\text{Remaining depreciable cost}}{\text{Est. remaining capacity}}$

Straight line — Application to Mackenzie Company

Year 1 = 100 / 5 = 20
Year 2 = 80 / 4 = 20
Change in estimate from 5 to 4 years' useful life.
Year 3 = 60 / 2 = 30
Year 4 = 30 / 1 = 30

Declining balance — Application to Mackenzie Company

Year 1 = 120 × 40% = 48
Change in estimate from 40% to 30%.
Year 2 = 72 × 30% = 21.6
Year 3 = 50.4 × 30% = 15.1
Year 4 = 35.3 × 30% = 10.6
Year 5 = 24.7 × 30% = 7.4

Units of production — Application to Mackenzie Company

then

Depr = Production × UP rate

Yr	UP rate	Depr.
1	100 / 1,000 = 0.10	150 × 0.10 = 15
2	85 / 850 = 0.10	200 × 0.10 = 20
3	65 / 650 = 0.10	250 × 0.10 = 25

Change in estimate of capacity from 1,000 units to 920 units.

4	40 / 320 = 0.125	250 × 0.125 = 31.25
5	8.75 / 70 = 0.125	50 × 0.125 = 6.25

CHECKPOINT **CP8-7**

How should enterprises reflect changes in one or more of the three depreciation parameters?

C. DERECOGNITION

Enterprises must derecognize a piece of PPE when it is sold or disposed of by other means (recycled or trashed). The depreciated historical cost of PPE that results from the accounting discussed above does not attempt to value these assets, so the carrying amount will generally differ from the proceeds of disposal, often by substantial margins. That difference will be recognized through net income. Refer to the Mackenzie Company example shown in Exhibit 8-13 in the previous section (without the change in estimates). Suppose the company sells this equipment, with a cost of $120,000, in Year 3 for $70,000. Assume that the company had been using the straight-line method, and the company does not record depreciation in the year of disposal. Mackenzie would record the following journal entry to reflect this sale:

L.O. 8-3 Apply the standards for derecognition of property, plant, and equipment and understand the meaning of gains and losses arising from derecognition.

Exhibit 8-17	Entry to record Mackenzie's disposal of equipment after two years of straight-line depreciation	
Dr. Cash	70,000	
Dr. Accumulated depreciation (2 years × $20,000/year)	40,000	
Dr. Loss on disposal of equipment	10,000	
Cr. Equipment		120,000

In other words, after two years of depreciation, the machine had a carrying value of $80,000 ($120,000 cost less $40,000 of accumulated depreciation). The $70,000 proceeds from disposal are less than the carrying value of $80,000, so Mackenzie recognizes a loss of $10,000.

Now consider what would happen if Mackenzie had been following the 40% declining-balance method. The journal entry would then be:

Exhibit 8-18	Entry to record Mackenzie's disposal of equipment after two years of declining-balance depreciation	
Dr. Cash	70,000	
Dr. Accumulated depreciation ($48,000 + $28,800)	76,800	
Cr. Gain on disposal of equipment		26,800
Cr. Equipment		120,000

In this case, the carrying value is $43,200 ($120,000 − $76,800). The $70,000 proceeds of disposal exceed this carrying value, resulting in a gain of $26,800.

Thus, depending on the depreciation policy, Mackenzie would realize a loss in one scenario and a gain in the other. The interpretation of these gains and losses is that they are "catch-ups" for the deviation of the PPE's carrying amount from the resale (market) value. In this example, the straight-line method results in relatively low amounts of depreciation (and high carrying value), while the declining-balance method results in the opposite. Combining the depreciation expense and the gain or loss on disposal results in the same total impact on income. As noted in Chapter 3, accrual accounting allocates income and expense to different periods of time. Through the entire investment cycle (purchase, use, and sale of PPE), the total income or expense reconciles with the amount of cash flow, as shown in Exhibit 8-19.

THRESHOLD CONCEPT TIMING OF RECOGNITION

Exhibit 8-19	Computation of total income impact of Mackenzie's PPE including depreciation and gain or loss on derecognition	
	Straight line	**Declining balance**
Depreciation		
Year 1	$ (20,000)	$ (48,000)
Year 2	(20,000)	(28,800)
Total depreciation	(40,000)	(76,800)
Gain (or loss) on disposal	(10,000)	26,800
Total income impact	$ (50,000)	$ (50,000)
Cash outflow for purchase	$(120,000)	$(120,000)
Cash inflow from disposal	70,000	70,000
Net cash flow	$ (50,000)	$ (50,000)

 CHECKPOINT **CP8-8**

What does a gain on the disposal of PPE represent? What about a loss?

DOES DEPRECIATION POLICY MATTER?

Back when I learned about depreciation in introductory accounting, my professors told me that depreciation policy choices are systematic and rational and, at the same time, arbitrary and subjective. Following the latter line of thinking, I later learned that financial statement users do not really care

(Continued)

much about depreciation policies as long as such policies are fully disclosed, since users can undo and redo depreciation policies as they like. Moreover, finance professionals typically ignore depreciation—by using measures such as "EBITDA" (earnings before interest, taxes, depreciation, and amortization) for example. So, is there really any reason to put effort into choosing a depreciation policy?

Well, yes, if you consider reinvestment decisions, according to Dr. Scott Jackson of the University of South Carolina. In a paper published in *The Accounting Review* (March 2008), Jackson analyzes how depreciation policies affect choices of fixed asset renewals. Enlisting approximately 200 MBA students to act as production managers in a controlled experiment, Jackson asked the students to make an important cost-saving decision involving one of two alternatives:

Option 1: Selling existing equipment and investing in new equipment via a lease; or

Option 2: Improving training and maintenance to make better use of the existing equipment.

The periodic cash flows (lease payments, training, and maintenance costs) were the same in both cases, as were the expected amount of cost savings and the probability of success. However, Option 1 generated an additional $43,000 from the disposal of the old equipment, so Option 1 was the preferable choice.

The important variable in this experiment was the depreciation policy on the old equipment. Some subjects were told that the company used accelerated (declining-balance) depreciation, which gave the old equipment a book value of $26,000. Other subjects were told that the company used the straight-line method, resulting in a book value of $60,000. Thus, if the students/production managers chose Option 1, accelerated depreciation resulted in a $17,000 accounting gain, while the straight-line method resulted in a $17,000 accounting loss.

The results are quite striking. Accelerated depreciation resulted in a significantly higher percentage of optimal decisions. A majority (65%) of the group subjected to accelerated depreciation preferred Option 1. In contrast, 65% of the group subjected to straight-line depreciation preferred Option 2.

Given the experimental setup, the only reasonable explanation for the difference in these results is that the students exposed to straight-line depreciation sought to avoid incurring a loss on the asset disposal, which would have occurred if they had chosen 1 over 2.

It is interesting to note that the subjects were told their compensation (as production managers) would not be impacted by any gains or losses from asset disposal. Thus, the students' loss aversion cannot be attributed to any direct economic implications for the production managers. Even though it is not rational to choose Option 2—thereby forgoing the $43,000 in incremental cash flow from sale of the old equipment under Option 1—the accounting loss of $17,000 was enough to make a significant percentage of subjects choose the sub-optimal alternative.

In summary, this study shows that using a less conservative depreciation policy is likely to discourage capital asset replacement, even if that asset replacement would add value. Companies whose competitiveness depends on having efficient capital assets should take note.

This article was written by Kin Lo and originally appeared in the May 2008 issue of *Beyond Numbers* magazine, published by the Institute of Chartered Accountants of BC. It is reprinted with the Institute's permission.

D. NON-MONETARY TRANSACTIONS

L.O. 8-4. Analyze transactions with non-monetary consideration and apply the accounting standards for non-monetary transactions.

monetary items Assets and liabilities that have fixed or determinable cash flows.

Monetary items are assets and liabilities that have fixed or determinable cash flows, such as cash, accounts receivable, and bonds. While the vast majority of transactions in our economy are carried out using money or monetary items, some transactions will primarily involve non-monetary exchanges. For example, a company may trade a delivery truck for a used car, or issue shares in exchange for a manufacturing plant or patents. How do we account for such non-monetary transactions? IAS 16 paragraphs 24–26 (and similarly ASPE Section 3831) provide guidance on these transactions.

1. Classification of non-monetary exchanges

Depending on the nature of the transaction, a non-monetary exchange fits into one of two cases. For simplicity, the discussion below involves a single asset exchanged for another, although actual transactions can involve multiple assets on each side of the exchange.

a. General case

In general, enterprises should record a non-monetary transaction using fair values of the asset given or received, whichever is more reliably measured. If both assets are measured with equal reliability, it is preferable to use the fair value of the *asset given up*. The idea behind using fair values is to reflect the substance of the transaction(s). In essence, there are two separate transactions:

- a sale at fair value, and
- a purchase using the proceeds of the sale.

As with other asset disposals, fair value will typically differ from book value, resulting in a gain or loss.

b. Exceptions

IFRS provides for two exceptions to the use of fair values in non-monetary exchanges. In these circumstances, enterprises should use the carrying amount of the asset given up to record the exchange, resulting in no gain or loss in the transaction. The two exceptions are:

1. there is no commercial substance to the transaction; or
2. the fair values of the assets exchanged are not reliably measurable.

The latter exception should be clear—an enterprise should not use fair values if they cannot be estimated reliably. Regarding the former exception, a transaction has *commercial substance* if (i) the assets exchanged are significantly different in terms of the risk, timing, or amount ("configuration") of cash flow; or (ii) the value of the entity's operations significantly changes as a result of the transaction.[9] In other words, we can evaluate commercial substance either by looking at the *objects* (the assets being exchanged), or by looking at the *subject* (the enterprise engaged in the exchange).

For example, the act of two airlines exchanging a Boeing aircraft for an Airbus plane of a similar age and capacity could be considered an exchange with no commercial

---

[9.] IFRS uses the technical wording, "the entity-specific value of the portion of the entity's operations affected by the transaction." This cumbersome wording is necessary for the purpose of evaluating the significance of a change in value. An exchange may not have a significant impact on an enterprise as a whole, but may have a significant impact on one part of its operations.

substance if the aircraft are ultimately used for the same routes. In contrast, if the two airlines were to exchange an Airbus super-jumbo plane for three smaller Boeing 737s, then the transaction would have commercial substance since the flight routes and schedules served by the planes must be different, so the configuration of cash flow must also differ. In many cases, commercial substance will be clearly evident, such as when an enterprise issues shares in exchange for PPE.

The commercial substance test makes sense as it helps to reduce the ability to manage earnings through artificial transactions. If the standards were to allow the use of fair values in exchanges without commercial substance, then enterprises could engage in exchanges of similar assets with other enterprises to generate artificial revenues and gains (or losses).

THRESHOLD CONCEPT
QUALITY OF EARNINGS

2. Recognition of non-monetary exchanges

To illustrate the accounting for both types of non-monetary exchanges, consider the following example. Nanaimo Boating is in the business of chartering (renting) boats to customers who want to explore the coast of Vancouver Island. In the current year, the company engaged in two non-monetary exchanges. Exhibit 8-20 shows the details of these exchanges and the corresponding accounting for them.

Exhibit 8-20	Nanaimo Boating's non-monetary exchanges
Transaction	**Analysis**
In the first exchange, Nanaimo gave up a Dufour 36 sailboat in exchange for a Beneteau 37 sailboat to have fewer makes and models of boats. Both sailboats are of almost identical size (36 and 37 feet). After the exchange, Nanaimo intends to rent out the Beneteau 37 for the same rate as the Dufour was rented out, at $500/day. On Nanaimo's books, the Dufour 36 had a cost of $200,000 and accumulated depreciation of $70,000, while similar boats have been advertised for $155,000.	This exchange would likely be considered an exchange without commercial substance due to the similar cash flow–generating ability of the two sailboats. Consequently, the transactions would be recorded as an exception to the general case, using the carrying amount of the asset given up (the Dufour 36): Dr. Beneteau 37 130,000 Dr. Accum. depreciation—Dufour 36 70,000 Cr. Dufour 36—cost 200,000

In the second exchange, Nanaimo traded a Dufour 36 for a Bayliner 32 (a motorboat). Sailboats and power boats have distinct clienteles, seasons, and sensitivity to fuel prices. On Nanaimo's books, this Dufour 36 also had a cost of $200,000 and accumulated depreciation of $70,000. Nanaimo believes that the Dufour 36 is worth $150,000, but there have been no recent sales of this make and model of boat. Two months before the exchange, there was a sale of a similar Bayliner 32 in Powell River for $140,000.	This exchange has commercial substance since the configuration of cash flows for the Dufour 36 and Bayliner 32 are significantly different. In this case, we use fair value to record the exchange. In particular, we use the fair value of the Bayliner because it is more reliably measured as it is based on an actual transaction.
	
	Dr. Bayliner 32 140,000
	Dr. Accum. depreciation—Dufour 36 70,000
	    Cr. Dufour 36—cost 200,000
	    Cr. Gain 10,000

Some exchanges will involve both monetary and non-monetary consideration. Such transactions would still need to apply the above standards: use fair values for the non-monetary items if the exchange has commercial substance and if fair values can be reliably measured. Otherwise, use the carrying amounts in the books. For example, in Nanaimo's second exchange above, suppose Nanaimo also received $15,000 in the transaction while all other facts remain the same. As a result, Nanaimo received assets with a total fair value of $155,000 ($140,000 fair value of Bayliner plus $15,000 cash). Since the carrying amount of the asset given up is $130,000, the gain amounts to $25,000. In this case, the company would modify the journal entry as follows:

Exhibit 8-21	Entry showing the effect of cash consideration on Nanaimo's non-monetary exchange with commercial substance	
Dr. Cash	15,000	
Dr. Bayliner 32	140,000	
Dr. Accumulated depreciation—Dufour 36	70,000	
Cr. Dufour 36—cost		200,000
Cr. Gain		25,000

 CHECKPOINT **CP8-9**

Non-monetary exchanges should generally be recorded at fair value. When should enterprises use the carrying amount of the asset given up?

E. POTENTIAL EARNINGS MANAGEMENT USING PROPERTY, PLANT, AND EQUIPMENT

THRESHOLD CONCEPT
QUALITY OF EARNINGS

The long-lived nature of PPE assets means that earnings management involving these assets can have long-lasting implications. As noted at the beginning of this chapter, capitalizing costs into PPE defers the expense recognition over the life of the asset. In the case of land, the deferral is indefinite, until the enterprise disposes of the land. Therefore, the rewards and incentives for using PPE to manage earnings are high. Combined with the subjective nature of some of the estimates required, the risk of earnings management could be significant. Financial statement readers and auditors should thus be alert to potential earnings management in this area. The following section discusses some areas of concern.

1. Including operating expenses in PPE

The issue here is similar to that discussed for inventories. The general principle is that enterprises should capitalize only costs directly attributable to the purchase or construction of the asset, be it inventory, PPE, or another asset. The problem lies in the determination of whether a particular activity is directly connected to the purchase or construction of the asset, which can be subjective. For example, the cost of personnel who have been partially assigned to supervise a construction project could be inappropriately fully allocated to the project to reduce wage expense (or not allocated to the project at all to increase wage expense). This type of earnings management is difficult for financial statement readers to detect, but auditors should seek evidence that costs capitalized into PPE are indeed directly attributable to its acquisition or construction.

2. Interest capitalization

Enterprises can capitalize interest as long as they can directly attribute the interest cost to the construction of PPE. As discussed earlier in the chapter, what is considered to be directly attributable depends on whether the borrowing was specifically for the purpose of constructing the PPE. An enterprise that wants to lower expenses and boost income would just need to arrange for an additional loan to finance the PPE, while a different enterprise that wants to lower income would choose not to borrow or engage in general borrowing that is not specifically identified as being for the purpose of PPE construction. For instance, a construction loan for $100 million at 8% for one year would result in $8 million capitalized into PPE. In comparison, $100 million raised from general corporate borrowing when the debt-to-assets ratio is 10% would result in only $0.8 million of interest capitalized.

3. Depreciation parameters

There is a significant amount of judgment used in the estimates and choices of the three depreciation parameters (depreciable amount, useful life, pattern of depreciation). The depreciable amount depends on the estimate of residual value at the end of the asset's useful life, which is difficult to forecast. The estimated useful life is a forecast of the future, which is inherently uncertain, so this estimate can be easily biased. Finally, the choice of the depreciation method determines how much expense will be recognized in which accounting period. In addition, an enterprise can justify a change to the pattern of depreciation as a change in estimate (rather than as a change in accounting policy) and reflect the change prospectively without disclosure of the change.

4. Opportunistic disposals of PPE

Accounting depreciation is merely a method of cost allocation and not a method of asset valuation. As a result, the carrying amount of PPE can significantly diverge from their fair values over time. When this occurs, enterprises can selectively sell assets to realize accounting gains (or losses in some cases). They may even repurchase the same or similar assets subsequently if those assets are essential to operations. The result of such transactions is not only higher income, but higher asset values as well.

F. PRESENTATION AND DISCLOSURE OF PROPERTY, PLANT, AND EQUIPMENT

The category of property, plant, and equipment potentially includes a wide variety of assets. Consequently, disclosure requirements dictate that enterprises provide disclosures for each significant class of PPE. To meet disclosure requirements, firms generally present a table that shows the cost, accumulated depreciation, and carrying amount for each asset class, as well as the prior period comparative figure for the carrying amount. In addition to these balance sheet amounts, enterprises also need to disclose the amount of depreciation, including both amounts directly expensed or capitalized into other assets such as inventories.

Additional quantitative disclosure includes reconciliations between beginning and ending carrying amounts showing the amount of additions to each class of PPE, and the amount of PPE reclassified out of PPE as assets held for sale. If the enterprise has self-constructed assets, it needs to disclose such amounts so users can identify them separately from acquired assets.

Enterprises also need to provide information on their accounting policies for PPE: the measurement base (historical cost or revalued amounts), the depreciation methods, and the useful lives or depreciation rates as appropriate to the depreciation method. Any changes in estimates used for depreciation (residual value, useful life, depreciation pattern) would need to be disclosed. Likewise, changes in estimates for dismantling and site restoration costs must be provided. If an enterprise has PPE that is restricted, for example, when it is pledged as collateral for a loan, it needs to disclose that fact.

There are additional disclosures when an enterprise uses the revaluation basis for PPE and when there are impairments to these assets. Chapter 10 will discuss these additional requirements.

Exhibit 8-22 provides an example of PPE disclosures from TELUS's 2016 annual report. The exhibit shows the costs and accumulated depreciation separately for major classes of assets. TELUS has also detailed its asset retirement obligations, separated between current and long-term portions. The disclosures also include a description of the accounting policies for PPE as well as the depreciation policies.

Exhibit 8-22	PPE disclosures from TELUS 2016 annual report

Note 17: Property, plant, and equipment ($ millions)

(millions)	Network assets	Buildings and leasehold improvements	Other	Land	Assets under construction	Total
At cost						
As at January 1, 2015	$26,415	$2,801	$1,163	$55	$ 504	$30,938
Additions[a]	732	24	93	–	1,252	2,101
Disposition, retirements, and other	(1,098)	(106)	(209)	–	–	(1,413)
Assets under construction put into service	1,142	128	73	–	(1,343)	–
As at December 31, 2015	27,191	2,847	1,120	55	413	31,626
Additions[a]	762	45	39	–	1,472	2,318
Additions arising from business acquisitions	–	1	1	–	–	2
Dispositions, retirements, and other	(739)	(78)	(223)	–	–	(1,040)
Assets under construction put into service	1,070	139	84	–	(1,293)	–
As at December 31, 2016	**$28,284**	**$2,954**	**$1,021**	**$55**	**$ 592**	**$32,906**
Accumulated depreciation						
As at January 1, 2015	$19,202	$1,808	$ 805	$ –	$ –	$21,815
Depreciation	1,268	95	112	–	–	1,475
Dispositions, retirements, and other	(1,119)	(93)	(188)	–	–	(1,400)
As at December 31, 2015	19,351	1,810	729	–	–	21,890
Depreciation	1,357	99	108	–	–	1,564
Dispositions, retirements, and other	(758)	(73)	(181)	–	–	(1,012)
As at December 31, 2016	**$19,950**	**$1,836**	**$ 656**	**$ –**	**$ –**	**$22,442**
Net book value						
As at December 31, 2015	$ 7,840	$1,037	$ 391	$55	$ 413	$ 9,736
As at December 31, 2016	**$ 8,334**	**$1,118**	**$ 365**	**$55**	**$ 592**	**$10,464**

(a) For the year ended December 31, 2016, additions include $(40) (2015 – $65) in respect of asset retirement obligations.

Note 8 Financing costs	2016	2015
Interest expense – capitalized long-term debt interest[b]	$52	$45
Interest accretion on provisions[c]	12	12

(b) Long-term debt interest at a composite rate of 3.31% was capitalized to intangible assets with indefinite lives.

(c) Interest on asset retirement obligations.

(Continued)

Exhibit 8-22	Continued

Note 1(q) Property, plant, and equipment

General: Property, plant, and equipment ... are recorded at historical cost, which for self-constructed property, plant, and equipment includes materials, direct labour, and applicable overhead costs. ... Where property, plant, and equipment construction projects are of a sufficient size and duration, an amount is capitalized for the cost of funds used to finance construction, as set out in Note 8. The rate for calculating the capitalized financing costs is based on our weighted-average cost of borrowing experienced during the reporting period.

When we sell property, plant, and/or equipment, the net book value is netted against the sale proceeds and the difference, as set out in Note 6, is included in ... Other operating income.

Asset retirement obligations: Provisions for liabilities, as set out in Note 25, are recognized for statutory, contractual, or legal obligations, normally when incurred, associated with the retirement of property, plant, and equipment (primarily certain items of outside plant and wireless site equipment) when those obligations result from the acquisition, construction, development, and/or normal operation of the assets. ... The obligations are measured initially at fair value, determined using present value methodology, and the resulting costs are capitalized into the carrying amount of the related asset. In subsequent periods, the liability is adjusted for the accretion of discount, for any changes in the market-based discount rate, and for any changes in the amount or timing of the underlying future cash flows. The capitalized asset retirement cost is depreciated on the same basis as the related asset and the discount accretion, as set out in Note 8, is included ... as a component of Financing cost.

Note 1(i) Depreciation ...

Assets are depreciated on a straight-line basis over their estimated useful lives as determined by a continuing program of asset life studies ...

Estimated useful lives for the majority of our property, plant, and equipment subject to depreciation are as follows:

Network assets	Estimated useful lives[d]
Outside plant	17 to 40 years
Inside plant	4 to 17 years
Wireless site equipment	5 to 10 years
Balance of depreciable property, plant, and equipment	3 to 40 years

(d) The composite depreciation rate for the year ended December 31, 2016, was 5.0% (2015 – 4.8%). The rate is calculated by dividing depreciation expense by an average gross book value of depreciable assets for the reporting period.

Source: From Telus Corporation, Consolidated Financial Statements, December 31, 2016. Copyright © 2017 by Telus Corporation. Reprinted by permission.

G. SUBSTANTIVE DIFFERENCES BETWEEN IFRS AND ASPE

Issue	IFRS	ASPE
Interest capitalization	Capitalize only borrowing costs directly attributable to the acquisition or construction of PPE.	Enterprise can choose to capitalize or expense interest incurred for the acquisition or construction of PPE. Disclose amount capitalized.
Costs incurred on existing items of PPE	Distinguish replacements versus repairs. Capitalize cost of replacements and derecognize carrying amount of item replaced. Expense repair costs.	Distinguish betterments versus maintenance. Capitalize cost of betterments. Expense maintenance costs.
Measurement bases	PPE measured using cost model or revaluation model.	PPE carried at cost adjusted for depreciation.
Depreciable amount and depreciation period	Cost less residual value over useful life.	Greater of (i) cost less residual value over useful life and (ii) cost less salvage over asset life.

H. SUMMARY

L.O. 8-1. Evaluate whether a cost should be included in property, plant, and equipment, and how much should be classified in each category of asset or expense.

- Enterprises should capitalize as PPE those expenditures on tangible, long-lived assets that give rise to future benefits for the reporting entity and for which the costs are reasonably measurable. Enterprises should capitalize all costs incurred for the acquisition or construction of PPE, including materials, labour, overhead, borrowing costs, and future costs for demolition and site restoration. Capitalization ends when the asset is ready for its intended use. Enterprises should capitalize replacements of PPE components but expense repairs.
- Enterprises need to distinguish among different components and types of PPE according to their useful lives and patterns of benefits consumed. Bundled purchases of PPE potentially require subjective allocations of costs to different items of PPE.

L.O. 8-2. Apply different depreciation methods, including the effect of changes in estimates on depreciation calculations.

- Enterprises should choose the depreciation method that best reflects the pattern of benefits consumed; however, IFRS does not specify the methods that should be used. Common methods include straight-line, declining-balance, and units-of-production.
- In addition to the depreciation method, enterprises need to estimate two other parameters: the depreciable amount (the difference between cost and residual value) and useful life (or depreciation rate, in the case of the declining-balance method).

L.O. 8-3. Apply the standards for derecognition of property, plant, and equipment and understand the meaning of gains and losses arising from derecognition.

- When an item of PPE is sold, dismantled, or otherwise disposed of, the enterprise should remove the item from the accounts along with the corresponding accumulated depreciation, and recognize any gain or loss through income.

L.O. 8-4. Analyze transactions with non-monetary consideration and apply the accounting standards for non-monetary transactions.

- Enterprises should generally account for exchanges involving non-monetary assets using the fair values of those assets, except when the exchange does not have commercial substance or when fair values are not reliably measurable. It is preferable to use the fair value of the asset given up in the exchange if both assets' fair values are reliably measured. In the exception case, the reporting entity should use the carrying value on its books.

I. ANSWERS TO CHECKPOINT QUESTIONS

CP8-1: To evaluate whether an expenditure should be capitalized as PPE, an enterprise should consider (i) whether the expenditure satisfies the definition of an asset and (ii) whether the expenditure satisfies the recognition criteria. To satisfy the former, an asset must have arisen from past transactions, be under the control of the enterprise, and have future benefits. To satisfy the latter, the future benefits must flow to the enterprise with sufficiently high probability and the cost of the PPE must be measured reliably.

CP8-2: The financing costs that can be capitalized into constructed assets are borrowing costs that are directly attributable to the construction. Such directly attributed borrowing costs can be derived from debt incurred specifically for the purpose of construction or general debt financing. The amount capitalized is capped at the total interest incurred in the period.

CP8-3: Repairs and maintenance of PPE are costs that are insignificant relative to the value of the PPE or that recur regularly. In contrast, replacements are significant costs and are usually irregular in occurrence.

CP8-4: The two expenses for future site restoration are depreciation and interest. The present value of the future site restoration cost is allocated over the useful life of the site to determine depreciation. The interest expense equals the present value of the site restoration liability multiplied by the discount rate, and the liability increases by the amount of interest for the period.

CP8-5: Componentization and allocation of bundled purchase costs are important to the extent that different items and parts of items have different useful lives or usage patterns that lead to different amounts of depreciation. In other words, there is little informational benefit to separating items and parts that have the same or similar useful lives and usage patterns.

CP8-6: The three parameters that determine the amount of depreciation are the depreciable amount, the asset's useful life, and the depreciation pattern.

CP8-7: Enterprises should reflect changes in the depreciation parameters on a prospective basis because these are normally considered to be changes in estimate. The change affects current and future depreciation amounts, but not depreciation recorded in past periods.

CP8-8: A gain on the disposal of PPE results from the sale of an asset whose carrying value is low relative to the resale value, so the gain represents the amount by which depreciation exceeded the amount that would have been needed to adjust the carrying amount to market value. A loss on the disposal of PPE is the opposite: it represents the amount by which depreciation was below the amount required to reduce the carrying amount to market value.

CP8-9: In non-monetary transactions, enterprises should use the carrying amount of the asset given up if either (i) the transaction does not have commercial substance or (ii) the fair values of the assets exchanged are not reliably measurable.

J. GLOSSARY

capitalize: To record a cost on the balance sheet as an asset.

cost allocation: The process of apportioning the cost of an asset over its **useful life.**

current value: The value of an asset in an input market or output market on the date of measurement.

declining-balance method: A method of depreciation in which a period's depreciation equals the asset's net carrying amount multiplied by a fixed percentage.

depreciable amount: The total amount to be expensed through depreciation; initial cost less residual value.

depreciation: The systematic allocation of an asset's depreciable amount over its estimated useful life. Depreciation usually refers to tangible human-made assets, depletion refers to tangible natural resources, and amortization refers to intangible assets. ASPE uses amortization as a generic term that covers all three types of assets.

fair value: The price that would be received to sell an asset (or paid to transfer a liability) in an orderly transaction between market participants at the measurement date.

historical cost: The actual cost of an asset at the time it was purchased; can also refer to amounts based on historical cost but adjusted by depreciation or impairment.

impairment: The process of writing down the value of an asset to recognize declines in its **fair value.**

monetary items: Assets and liabilities that have fixed or determinable cash flows.

net realizable value (exit value): The value expected from the sale of an asset, net of any costs of disposal.

replacement cost (entry value): The cost required to replace the productive capacity of an asset. For a used asset, the amount reflects the age and past usage of the asset, not a new asset.

residual value: The estimated amount that an entity would currently obtain from disposal of the asset, after deducting the estimated costs of disposal, if the asset were already of the age and in the condition expected at the end of its useful life.

straight-line method: A method of depreciation in which the (remaining) depreciable amount is evenly allocated over the asset's (remaining) estimated useful life.

units-of-production method: A method of depreciation in which the (remaining) depreciable amount is allocated in proportion to the productive capacity used.

useful life: The period of time over which an asset is expected to be available for use by an entity, or the number of production units an enterprise expects to obtain from the use of an asset.

value in use: The discounted value of cash flows expected from using an asset for its intended purpose.

K. REFERENCES

Authoritative standards:

IFRS	ASPE Section
IAS 16—Property, Plant and Equipment	3061—Property, Plant, and Equipment
	3110—Asset Retirement Obligations
	3831—Non-monetary Transactions
IAS 23—Borrowing Costs	3850—Interest Capitalized—Disclosure Considerations

MyLab Accounting   Make the grade with **MyLab Accounting:** The problems marked with a ⊕ can be found on **MyLab Accounting.** You can practise them as often as you want, and most feature step-by-step guided instructions to help you find the right answer.

L. PROBLEMS

 P8-1.   PPE capitalization   (**L.O.** 8-1) (Easy – 15 minutes)

Steve Manufacturing Limited (SML) purchased a large lathe. The invoice cost of the lathe was $5,500,000 but SML was able to reduce the price to $5,300,000. The seller provided terms whereby if the entire amount was paid within 30 days a further discount of 1% was available. SML paid on the 25th day. The machine was transported a long distance, costing SML $75,000. Insurance while in transit was $15,000. To encourage SML to purchase another machine, the manufacturer gave the company a $50,000 discount voucher on its next purchase of a similar machine. Workers were paid $60,000 to install the machine. Start-up and testing costs were $35,000. Unfortunately, during the installation, one of the workers accidently damaged the machine and it cost $40,000 to repair the damage. Sales tax paid was $500,000. A sales tax rebate of $45,000 was received relating to this transaction. During installation, part of the plant had to be shut down; lost profit from the shutdown was $100,000.

Required:

For each expenditure, identify whether it should be included in the cost of the lathe or expensed. Briefly justify each of your responses.

P8-2.   PPE capitalization   (**L.O.** 8-1) (Medium – 20 minutes)

Mike's Lemonade Stand (MLS) purchased a parcel of land for $10,000,000 on March 31. The site was available at a reasonable price. The company has a strategic plan to build a large warehouse in the area some time in the next five years. The real estate agent representing MLS was paid $50,000. Title search and legal fees were $40,000.

MLS paid a fee to have the site rezoned for use as a warehouse rather than for residential use: $100,000. The company paid the seller $30,000 for the unexpired portion of property tax on the site. This property tax expires on June 30. Property tax for the last half of the year was $70,000. A number of abandoned homes on the site were demolished for $90,000. In the process of demolition, MLS received $15,000 for items salvaged from the homes.

As the site will remain vacant for a few years, MLS spent $200,000 landscaping it and putting in a sports field. MLS did this as part of a deal with the local residents so they would support the rezoning application. MLS spent $10,000 on food and entertainment to host a groundbreaking ceremony for the park opening. Senior managers and the president visited the party and were paid $5,000 in salaries while there. The company further spent $35,000 to advertise their good corporate citizenship using the example of the park and ceremony. During the remaining part of the year $20,000 was spent to maintain the field. MLS erected fences for $55,000 around part of the site to prevent children from harming themselves.

MLS spent $25,000 on consulting fees to determine where the most appropriate site for the warehouse should be. Numerous sites were identified, including the one purchased.

Required:

Identify whether or not and to which account MLS should capitalize each of the above expenditures. Briefly justify each of your responses.

[*Hint:* Some of these costs may be capitalized as site development costs.]

P8-3.   PPE capitalization   (**L.O.** 8-1) (Difficult – 20 minutes)

Lower Seymour Manufacturing (LSM) is building a factory. It has signed a contract and paid a third-party construction company $25,000,000 to build the factory. LSM also paid for design changes and cost overruns totalling $1,000,000. In advance of signing the contract, LSM paid legal fees of $50,000 to oversee the process of collecting bids to construct the premises. A feasibility study costing $100,000 helped determine the design and facility needs. The president suggested that she spent about one-quarter of the past year thinking about and discussing matters related to the factory. Her annual salary is $500,000.

During the planning stage of the factory, the company paid $200,000 for design drawings and plans for a factory that was abandoned in favour of this project. Originally on the site was a building they had planned to renovate. When they bought the site they capitalized the cost of this building. The unamortized cost of the building is $750,000. It cost $95,000 to demolish this building.

During the construction period, one of the construction workers was injured. LSM was held partly liable for the injury and had to pay $300,000, as this was not covered by the company's insurance policy.

Interest costs paid that were directly attributable to this project while under construction amounted to $350,000. As senior management were distracted from their normal activities, it is conservatively estimated that at least $400,000 in profits were lost.

LSM spent $40,000 advertising the opening of the factory. During construction, local citizens unexpectedly challenged the project. The company spent $125,000 in legal fees resolving these matters. Property taxes of $110,000 were paid on the land while under construction. After the project was completed, but before occupancy, a further $35,000 in taxes was paid.

To get final permission to build the factory, LSM had to give the city 10% of the land it had bought for the factory to be converted into a park and green space. The cost of the entire parcel of land was $10,000,000. At the time the land was given up, the entire parcel had a value of at least $15,000,000.

Required:

Determine the cost of the PPE. Briefly justify the treatment of each cost component.

 ### P8-4.   PPE capitalization   (**L.O.** 8-1) (Difficult – 25 minutes)

Joliet Co. Ltd. was incorporated on January 2, 2021, but was unable to begin manufacturing immediately. The new factory facilities became available for use on July 1, 2021.

During the start-up period, the company provisionally used a "Land and factory building" account to record the following transactions, in chronological order:

Jan. 31	Purchase of land and building	$220,000
Feb. 19	Cost of removing existing building	9,000
Mar. 15	Proceeds on sale of scrap material from demolition	(3,000)
Mar. 15	Partial payment on new construction	50,000
Mar. 15	Legal fees paid (see note i below)	3,500
Apr. 1	Second payment on new construction	50,000
Jun. 3	Insurance premium (see note ii)	2,700
Jun. 20	Special tax assessment (see note iii)	5,500
Jun. 30	General expenses (see note iv)	24,400
Jul. 3	Final payment on new construction	70,000
Dec. 31	Asset write-up (see note v)	23,500
	Subtotal	455,600
Dec. 31	Less depreciation for 2021 (see note vi)	(18,224)
	Account balance	$437,376

Notes:

i. Legal fees of $3,500 covered the following:

Cost of incorporating the company	$ 700
Examination of title covering purchase of land	1,300
Legal work in connection with construction contract	1,500

ii. Insurance covered the building for a one-year term beginning April 1, 2021.
iii. The special tax assessment covered repaving the street in front of the building.
iv. General expenses covered the following for the period from January 2, 2021, to June 30, 2021:

President's salary	$20,000
Plant superintendent covering supervision of new building	4,400

v. The board of directors increased the value of the building by $23,500, believing that such an increase was justified to reflect the current market at the time the building was completed; however, there was no external validation of this higher value. Retained earnings were credited for this amount.

vi. Engineers estimate the useful life of the building to be 40 years. The company believes that the declining-balance method at a 5% rate is appropriate. The company's policy for new PPE is to depreciate the assets according to the time available for use in the fiscal year, rounded to the closest month.

Required:

Prepare entries to reflect correct land, factory building, and accumulated depreciation accounts at December 31, 2021.

 P8-5.   Cost of self-constructed assets  (**L.O.** 8-1) (Medium – 15 minutes)

Crayon Company Limited (CCL) is experiencing a temporary slowdown in demand due to an economic recession. The company is operating at 80% capacity and is struggling with what to do with its surplus workers. CCL expects demand to return to normal capacity in nine months. Most of its workers are highly skilled and hard to replace. The company could do one or more of three things with these extra workers:

i. Lay off the 30 surplus workers, requiring severance pay and other termination costs of $400,000.

ii. Continue to pay the idle workers and be assured of having them available in nine months when they will be needed. Salary, benefits, and other direct costs would total at least $700,000.

iii. Engage these workers in building new machinery. Besides the costs of these workers, additional materials costing $1,000,000 would be required. Based on how the company allocated overhead, $75,000 in fixed overhead costs could be assigned to these new machines if the labourers were working on this project.

Senior management has decided against laying off the workers as it would seriously harm labour relations, and replacing the workers later would be difficult, time consuming, and require significant training and hiring costs.

Required:

a. According to economics, finance, and net present value analysis, what would be the relevant costs associated with this project (i.e., using the workers to build new machinery)?
b. According to financial accounting, what would be the cost of these machines?
c. If the company chooses to build the machines instead of laying off the workers, will this decision affect net income in the current period? If so, by how much will income change?

 P8-6. PPE capitalization—interest cost **(L.O.** 8-1) (Medium – 15 minutes)

Capital Company built two similar buildings. Each building took one year to build and required $45,000,000 in construction costs. Capital had limited internal financial resources, so it could fund only Building A internally and financed Building B by borrowing the $45,000,000 evenly over the year (i.e., zero at the beginning of the year and increasing to $45,000,000 by the end of the year). The interest rate on the loan is 6%. Both projects were finished on December 31, 2018, and were ready for occupancy immediately. The buildings are estimated to have a useful life of 20 years with no residual value. Capital uses the straight-line method for depreciation.

Required:

a. How much interest cost should be capitalized on Building B under IFRS?
b. What will be the annual depreciation expense for each of the two buildings?
c. ASPE allows interest capitalization while IFRS requires the capitalization of borrowing costs directly attributable to the construction of assets. Ignoring the complexities of how to determine how much interest to capitalize, which treatment of interest costs is conceptually more correct? Explain your conclusion.
d. Why can interest costs not continue to be capitalized after the self-construction period is completed?

 P8-7. PPE capitalization—interest cost **(L.O.** 8-1) (Medium – 10 minutes) A·S·P·E

Dolan Enterprises constructed a new warehouse for its distribution facility. The construction period began on May 1, 2019, and continued until October 31, 2020. Dolan began operating the warehouse on January 1, 2021. Material and labour costs totalled $5 million. Payments for these costs were made as follows:

Date	Payment
May 31, 2019	$ 900,000
July 31, 2019	700,000
September 30, 2019	700,000
November 30, 2019	700,000
June 30, 2020	800,000
August 31, 2020	800,000
October 31, 2020	400,000
Total	$5,000,000

Dolan used internal funds to finance these payments. The company had long-term debt of $35 million to $40 million with an interest rate of 8% throughout the construction period.

Required:

a. How much interest cost should be capitalized on the building under IFRS?
b. What is the range of financing cost that can be capitalized under ASPE?

 P8-8. PPE capitalization—interest cost (**L.O.** 8-1) (Medium – 15 minutes)

Eeyore Toys made significant renovations to one of its retail stores. Total costs of the renovation were $800,000 completed over six months ending October 31, 2019. The company financed the renovation costs with a short-term bank loan with a 6% interest rate. The company received the $500,000 proceeds from this loan on May 1, 2019, and repaid it in full on February 28, 2020. The remaining $300,000 of construction costs were financed from existing debt, which had an average interest rate of 9%. Payments made for construction costs were as follows:

Date	Payment
May 31, 2019	$100,000
June 30, 2019	100,000
July 31, 2019	100,000
August 31, 2019	200,000
September 30, 2019	200,000
October 31, 2019	100,000
Total	$800,000

In the period when funds from the short-term loan had not been fully used (between May 1 and August 31, 2019), the company earned $6,000 of investment income.

Required:

How much interest cost should be capitalized on the building under IFRS?

 P8-9. PPE capitalization—replacements and repairs (**L.O.** 8-1) (Medium – 20 minutes)

Below are several situations related to replacements and repairs. For each case, prepare the necessary journal entry to record the transaction. Please provide a short justification for your chosen treatment.

Case A: Every three years a major component (Part #45) in a machine must be replaced. By doing this regular but expensive repair the machine can be used for 15 years. If Part #45 were not replaced, the machine could be used only for a maximum of six years. When the machine was originally purchased for $9,000,000 it was set up as one asset and depreciated over its estimated useful life of 15 years. Recently the repair was completed at a cost of $750,000 for Part #45. The earlier Part #45 cost $650,000 when it was installed three years ago. Neither the old nor the new Part #45 has residual value.

Case B: Same as Case A except Part #45 is recognized as a separate PPE asset and depreciated over three years.

Case C: An important piece of equipment requires major maintenance. Management has decided to upgrade the machine in the process by installing a new component that will extend the useful life of the machine from three remaining years to five more years. The regular part could have been purchased for $100,000 but the more durable part cost $175,000. The replaced part was not set up as a separate asset when the machine was purchased.

Case D: A large piece of earth-moving equipment was upgraded at a cost of $400,000 so that it can self-unload. After the upgrade was completed, management estimated that this feature would save the company $50,000 a year for the next six years.

Case E: A truck has a new engine installed for $140,000 that will increase gas mileage by 25% and reduce pollution. The truck and engine were not set up as separate assets. Management confidently estimates that the cost of the engine is one-third of the overall cost of the truck. The truck's original cost was $300,000 and it is 40% depreciated.

Case F: A car rental company has a fleet of 40,000 cars. Every three months all the cars are given scheduled oil changes, tire rotation, and replacement of small components. The cost per car is $150, which is $40 in parts and $110 for the wages of in-house mechanics. This is $6,000,000 in total. For half of the cars, a satellite radio receiver was installed at a cost of $75 each (total $1,500,000). The gadget allows the car to receive satellite radio. The company will provide this service free and promote it heavily to increase sales. This advertising campaign will cost $2,500,000. After the original free use of the satellite feature, the company will charge later users a fee for the use of satellite radio.

P8-10.   PPE capitalization—betterments and repairs   (**L.O.** 8-1) (Medium – 20 minutes)   **A·S·P·E**

Refer to the situations in problem P8-9. Using ASPE, prepare the necessary journal entries to record the transaction for each case. Please provide a short justification for your chosen treatment.

P8-11.   PPE capitalization—replacements and repairs   (**L.O.** 8-1) (Medium – 15 minutes)

Canadian Express provides overnight delivery of small parcels to locations throughout Canada. As a small public company, Canadian Express follows IFRS.

Required:

Record the journal entries necessary to reflect the following transactions. Briefly justify your chosen treatment if you feel it is necessary.

a. The company has the engines in its delivery trucks tuned up once every two years. The cost of the servicing in the year was $1 million. In addition, the tires are replaced three times per year, costing $3 million in the year.

b. During the year, the company paid $3.5 million to have the trucks in the fleet rust-proofed. As a result, management expects the trucks to last three extra years. Because each truck was out of service for about a week for rust-proofing, the company estimates that it lost $12 million of revenue.

c. The company spent $5 million during the year to develop a new parcel-tracking system to improve its efficiency and customer service quality. The new system was operational by September of the current year.

d. The company built a new transfer and sorting depot in Winnipeg to increase efficiency by reducing the number of flight routes necessary. The facilities became operational on December 1, just in time for the peak in parcel traffic during the holiday season. The company spent $5 million to purchase the land and incurred the following costs related to construction: materials, $15 million; labour, $20 million; managerial project supervision, $1.2 million; construction insurance, $400,000; interest incurred on construction loan from May 1 to December 31, $1.6 million.

P8-12.   PPE capitalization—betterments and repairs   (**L.O.** 8-1) (Medium – 15 minutes)   **A·S·P·E**

Refer to the situations in problem P8-11. Using ASPE, record the journal entries necessary to reflect the transactions. Briefly justify your chosen treatment if you feel it is necessary.

P8-13.   PPE capitalization—dismantlement, removal, and site restoration costs
(**L.O.** 8-1) (Easy – 10 minutes)

Abacus Energy drilled a natural gas well in northern Alberta and began producing from the well immediately. The company's geological engineers estimate that the well will be productive for 10 years. Environmental regulations require the company to restore the well site to its original state at the end of the well's useful life. Management estimates that it will cost $2 million to restore the site.

Required:

a. Compute the present value of the future site restoration costs at the beginning of the 10-year production life of the well. The appropriate discount rate is 8%.

b. Compute the annual depreciation expense related to the site restoration costs using the straight-line method.

c. Compute the amount of interest expense to be accrued on the obligation for site restoration for the first two years of the well's production life.

 P8-14. PPE capitalization—dismantlement, removal, and site restoration costs

(**L.O.** 8-1) (Medium – 20 minutes)

Acorn Mines began developing an open pit copper and zinc mine in northern Ontario in April of 2019. As part of the regulatory approvals to develop and to extract minerals from the site, the company committed to restore the mine site. Given the nature of open pit mining, it is not possible to fully restore the site to its original state. Nevertheless, the commitment requires the company to replant the area such that it will be suitable for wildlife and recreation (hiking, paddling, etc.). An independent environmental consultant hired by the mining regulator has estimated that the future site restoration costs will amount to $52 million at the end of the production life of the mine. Management estimates that the mine will begin production in the spring of 2021 and continue for 30 years. Acorn has a March 31 year-end and an incremental borrowing rate of 10%.

Required:

a. Compute the present value of the future site restoration costs as of the spring of 2019.

b. Compute the amount of depreciation expense related to the site restoration costs for the years ending 2020, 2021, and 2022 using the straight-line method.

c. Prepare a schedule showing the interest that will accrue on the site restoration liability each fiscal year from April 2019 to the end of the expected life of the mine.

d. Record the journal entries relating to the future site restoration costs for 2020, 2021, and 2022.

 P8-15. PPE capitalization—dismantlement, removal, and site restoration costs

(**L.O.** 8-1) (Difficult – 40 minutes)

Black Mountain Ski Resort has been granted a 20-year permit to develop and operate a skiing operation in a national park. After 20 years the site must be returned to its original condition. The roads may remain, as they can be used for fire prevention purposes. In the spring and summer before the ski hill opened, the following transactions and events occurred:

  i. Installed three ski lifts for a total cost of $150,000,000. It is estimated that the scrap metal from the lifts could be sold for $4,000,000 at the end of the 20 years.

 ii. Built a ski chalet for $70,000,000

iii. Removed trees and cleared the area for ski runs at a cost of $40,000,000

 iv. Received $10,000,000 for the trees that were removed for the ski runs

  v. Put in roads for a cost of $50,000,000

 vi. Paved an area at the base of the mountain for a parking lot at a cost of $10,000,000

vii. Estimated that it would cost $20,000,000 to dismantle the ski lifts in 20 years. The chalet could be removed for a cost of $15,000,000. Re-foresting the site would cost $5,000,000. Removing the parking lot will cost $3,000,000.

Required:

a. Prepare journal entries to record transactions (i) to (vi).

b. Prepare a journal entry to record transaction (vii). Assume all these costs will be set up in a single account called "site restoration cost." Assume a 6% discount rate.

c. Record all year-end journal entries for the above items for the first year of operations. The company used the straight-line method to record depreciation for all assets.

d. Prepare only those journal entries for the second and third year of operations, which would be different from those completed in (c).

e. Prepare the balance sheet presentation of all the accounts involved in this question for the end of the third year of operations.

f. Assume at the end of the project the actual total cost of restoring the site is $43,000,000, as originally estimated. Prepare the journal entry to record the payment of these costs.

g. What would be the total expenses associated with the site restoration in the first and second years of operations? In the last (20th) year?

P8-16. PPE capitalization—bundled purchases of assets   **L.O.** 8-1) (Easy –10 minutes)

Steiger Company paid $50,000,000 for a warehouse and related assets from a company that was in bankruptcy. The warehouse includes land, building, moving equipment, and a heating/ventilation/air conditioning (HVAC) system. An independent appraiser valued these items individually as follows:

PPE category	Appraised value
Land	$28,000,000
Building	21,000,000
Moving equipment	4,000,000
HVAC system	3,000,000
Total	$56,000,000

Required:

Allocate the purchase price among the assets acquired.

 P8-17. PPE capitalization—bundled purchases of assets

L.O. 8-1) (Medium – 10 minutes)

Staples Company bought an office building for $15,000,000 so it could consolidate its entire senior management staff in one location. An independent appraiser valued the items acquired individually as follows:

PPE category	Appraised value
Land	$ 5,600,000
Building	6,500,000
Computer network system	1,100,000
Elevator system	2,400,000
Landscaping and site improvements	900,000
Total	$16,500,000

Prior to completing the purchase, Staples's management decided that it will remove the existing computer network system and replace it with fibre-optic cables and related technologies.

Required:

Allocate the purchase price among the assets acquired.

P8-18. PPE capitalization—bundled purchases of assets   **L.O.** 8-1) (Medium – 10 minutes)

Clipper Company bought three used machines located in Toronto for $10,000,000. The arrangement with the seller is to move all the equipment to Clipper's factory in Edmonton. It is understood that some of the equipment will be sold as scrap or disassembled and used as spare parts. A careful inventory of all the equipment is shown below. Clipper plans to maximize the value of each item by using it in its most beneficial manner.

Machine	Value if installed and operated	Value as spare parts	Value as scrap
A	$3,000,000	$ 900,000	$ 500,000
B	4,500,000	5,000,000	2,000,000
C	2,000,000	1,600,000	2,500,000
Total	$9,500,000	$7,500,000	$5,000,000

Required:

Allocate the purchase price among the assets acquired.

P8-19. PPE capitalization—bundled purchases of assets (**L.O.** 8-1) (Medium – 15 minutes)

Van Deerman Inc. acquired various assets from a business in financial distress. Details of the assets acquired and related outlays follow:

Asset category	Estimated fair market value
Production equipment	$4,000,000
Motor vehicles	2,000,000
Computers	500,000
Furniture	1,000,000
Total	$7,500,000

Related expenditures	Amount
Cost of purchasing the bundle of assets excluding taxes	$7,000,000
Refundable taxes	290,000
Non-refundable taxes	220,000
Legal fees	50,000
Freight	20,000

Required:

Allocate the qualifying expenditures among the assets acquired.

 P8-20. Summarizing accounting concepts for PPE

(**L.O.** 8-1, **L.O.** 8-2) (Medium – 20 minutes)

There are numerous rules and standards behind PPE, with each providing guidance on specific topics and issues.

Required:

If you were to reduce all these rules and standards to a limited number of key concepts, what would those key concepts/principles be?

P8-21. Depreciation—conceptual discussion and analysis

(**L.O.** 8-2) (Medium – 20 minutes)

Perhaps of all the expense accruals that financial accounting requires, the most misunderstood and criticized is the provision for depreciation expense on income statements. From 2000 to 2008 in much of the world there was significant appreciation in the value of PPE. Managers and financial analysts ridiculed financial statements and financial accounting for ignoring the increase in value of PPE by continuing to record depreciation expense and reducing the value of PPE on balance sheets.

Required:

Identify and discuss three reasons why depreciation expense is recorded, even during times of PPE price increases.

P8-22. Depreciation—conceptual discussion and analysis

(**L.O.** 8-2) (Medium – 15 minutes)

This chapter states that "depreciation is a systematic (yet arbitrary) process of cost allocation that apportions the cost of PPE over its economic useful life. Depreciation matches costs to the periods over which benefits are obtained." It continues by noting that, for practical purposes, firms tend to use either the straight-line or declining-balance methods.

Required:

Three methods are introduced in the chapter: straight-line, declining-balance, and units-of-production. Assume that for the declining-balance method the rate is 2 divided by useful life (which is also called the "double-declining-balance" method). There are three classes of PPE assets: buildings, factory equipment, and computers. Which of these methods would conceptually be most suitable for each group of assets? Justify your conclusion.

 P8-23. Depreciation—straight-line method (**L.O.** 8-2) (Easy – 3 minutes)[10]

At December 31, 2020, the following data were available for a building owned by NU Company:

Building cost	$800,000
Accumulated depreciation—building	600,000
Estimated residual value at end of useful life	50,000
Estimated remaining useful life	10 years

A small room was built on the back of the building at a cost of $50,000. The room was completed on June 30, 2021, and was used as office space commencing July 2, 2021. The company uses the straight-line depreciation method and accounts for partial years using the number of months the asset is available for use.

Required:

How much is the impact of this expenditure on income before taxes for 2021?

 P8-24. Depreciation—straight-line method (**L.O.** 8-2) (Easy – 10 minutes)

Listed below are the long-lived assets of a company. The company uses the straight-line method to determine depreciation expense. Assume in all cases that the asset's first and last years are full years, and that all assumptions and estimates used to derive depreciation remain unchanged throughout the assets' useful lives.

Item	Cost	Estimated useful life	Estimated residual value
Lathe	$ 4,000,000	7 years	$ 200,000
Building	25,000,000	20 years	500,000
Earth-moving truck	700,000	6 years	70,000
Electric turbine	7,000,000	10 years	800,000
Stamping machine	10,000,000	9 years	3,000,000

Required:

For each asset, calculate the depreciation expense for the first, third, fifth, and last year of the assets' useful lives.

 P8-25. Depreciation—declining-balance method (**L.O.** 8-2) (Easy – 3 minutes)[11]

On April 1, 2021, STV Company acquired $30,000 of furniture. The furniture is expected to last 10 years with no residual value. STV uses the double-declining-balance method and fractional-year depreciation based on the number of months.

Required:

What would be the depreciation expense for the year ended December 31, 2021?

P8-26. Depreciation—declining-balance method (**L.O.** 8-2) (Easy – 15 minutes)

The table below itemizes several assets. The company uses the double-declining-balance method to determine depreciation expense, which means that the rate used will be 2 divided by useful life. For example, if estimated useful life is eight years, the declining balance rate would

[10.] Reprinted from CGA-Canada FA2 examination, June 2009, with permission from Chartered Professional Accountants of Canada, Toronto, Canada. Any changes to the original material are the sole responsibility of the author (and/or publisher) and have not been reviewed or endorsed by the Chartered Professional Accountants of Canada.

[11.] Reprinted from CGA-Canada FA2 examination, March 2009, with permission from Chartered Professional Accountants of Canada, Toronto, Canada. Any changes to the original material are the sole responsibility of the author (and/or publisher) and have not been reviewed or endorsed by the Chartered Professional Accountants of Canada.

be 2 ÷ 8, or 25%. Assume in all cases that the asset's first and last years are full years, and that all assumptions and estimates used to derive depreciation remain unchanged throughout the assets' useful lives.

Item	Cost	Estimated useful life	Estimated residual value
Lathe	$ 4,000,000	7 years	$ 200,000
Building	25,000,000	20 years	500,000
Earth-moving truck	700,000	6 years	70,000
Electric turbine	7,000,000	10 years	800,000
Stamping machine	10,000,000	9 years	3,000,000

Required:

a. Calculate depreciation expense for the first, third, fifth, and last years using the double-declining-balance method.
b. Assume in all cases the assets are sold at the end of their estimated useful lives at their estimated residual value. Prepare the journal entry to record their disposal.

 P8-27. Depreciation—units-of-production method   **L.O.** 8-2) (Easy – 5 minutes)[12]

At the beginning of the year, RU Company purchased a machine that cost $200,000. It has an estimated four-year life and a residual value of $20,000. The machine is expected to be used for a total of 6,000 hours over the four years. During the year, it was used for 1,720 hours.

Required:

How much is the depreciation for the year under the units-of-production method?

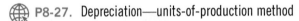 **P8-28.** Depreciation—units-of-production method   (**L.O.** 8-2) (Medium – 15 minutes)

The following table itemizes several assets. Assume in all cases that the asset's first and last years are full years and all assumptions and estimates used to derive depreciation remain unchanged throughout the assets' useful lives.

	Machine A	Machine B	Machine C
Cost	$9,000,000	$1,400,000	$2,400,000
Estimated residual value	600,000	90,000	300,000
Estimated total units of production over useful life	6,000,000 units	500,000 units	1,400,000 units
Actual production—Year 1	750,000 units	25,000 units	100,000 units
Actual production—Year 3	600,000 units	60,000 units	100,000 units
Actual production—Year 5	900,000 units	35,000 units	100,000 units
Actual production—Final year	350,000 units	62,000 units	100,000 units

Required:

For each asset, calculate the depreciation expense for the first, third, fifth, and last years of useful life using the units-of-production method.

 P8-29. Depreciation—various methods   (**L.O.** 8-2) (Medium – 15 minutes)

In January 2019, JN Norman Inc. (JNN) purchased and installed production equipment. It was first available for use on March 1, 2019. JNN has a December 31 year-end and accounts for

[12.] Reprinted from CGA-Canada FA2 examination, June 2009, with permission from Chartered Professional Accountants of Canada, Toronto, Canada. Any changes to the original material are the sole responsibility of the author (and/or publisher) and have not been reviewed or endorsed by the Chartered Professional Accountants of Canada.

partial years using the number of months that the asset is available for use. The following data were available for the machine:

Cost excluding the amounts below	$100,000
Delivery	1,000
Installation	6,000
Testing	3,000
Refundable sales taxes	5,000
Estimated residual value at end of useful life	4,000
Estimated useful life	8 years
Estimated total units of production over useful life	40,000 units
Actual production 2019	4,000 units
Actual production 2020	7,000 units

Required:

a. Calculate depreciation expense for 2019 and 2020 using the straight-line method.
b. Calculate depreciation expense for 2019 and 2020 using the double-declining-balance method $(2 \div 8 = 25\%)$.
c. Calculate depreciation expense for 2019 and 2020 using the units-of-production method.

 P8-30. Depreciation—partial years    **8-2)** (Easy – 25 minutes)

Below are three cases related to the depreciation of plant and equipment. In all cases the company has a December 31 year-end. The company records partial depreciation in the year of acquisition or disposal based on the number of months the asset is available for use in the year.

Case A: On March 31, 2011, a machine costing $5,000,000 was acquired. The company estimates that the asset will have a useful life of five years and a residual value of $500,000. On April 1, 2016, the asset is sold for $625,000. The company uses the straight-line method to determine depreciation expense. Prepare the entry to record depreciation expense for 2011, 2012, and all entries required for 2016 as they relate to this asset.

Case B: Same as Case A, except the company uses the declining-balance method at a rate of 40%.

Case C: Acquired land and building on June 1, 2011, for $16,000,000. An expert in real estate appraisal estimates that the land is worth 55% of the total purchase price. The building is estimated to have a useful life of 25 years and a residual value of $600,000. On September 1, 2021, the company moved and sold the property for $21,000,000. The buyer and seller agreed that 75% of the proceeds should be allocated to land. The company depreciates buildings using the straight-line method. Prepare the entry to record the purchase on June 1, 2011, depreciation expense for 2011 and 2012, and all entries required to record the disposal of the property on September 1, 2021.

Required:

For each case, prepare the journal entries requested.

 P8-31. Depreciation—changes in estimates and methods

 **8-2)** (Medium – 5 minutes)

Golden Bakery acquires a delivery truck for $60,000 and anticipates using it for eight years, at which time it will have logged 500,000 kilometres. Currently, market conditions suggest that a used truck with 500,000 kilometres on the odometer sells for $4,000. The company anticipates using the truck for about the same amount each year and therefore believes that the straight-line method is appropriate.

After using and depreciating the truck for three years, management believes that the truck will now be useful for a total of 10 years, after which the residual value will be $2,000.

Required:

Compute the amount of depreciation in the third and fourth years.

P8-32. Depreciation—changes in estimates and methods

(L.O. 8-2) (Medium – 10 minutes)

Fresh Juice Company installed a new juice press for $1,000,000. The company expects to use the press for 10 years, after which it can be sold for proceeds of $200,000. Management believes that the double-declining-balance method of depreciation is appropriate.

After six years the company reassessed the depreciation method and determined that a 10% declining-balance rate would be more appropriate. The residual value estimate remained unchanged.

Required:

Compute the amount of depreciation for the juice press for all 10 years.

 P8-33. Depreciation—changes in estimates and methods

(L.O. 8-2) (Medium – 10 minutes)

Below are two cases related to the depreciation of plant and equipment. In both cases the company has a December 31 year-end.

Case A: A machine was acquired on January 1, 2017, for $4,000,000. At that time it was estimated the machine would last eight years and have a residual value of $500,000. The company uses the straight-line method to record depreciation. Due to reduced levels of activity during 2019, management revised the estimate of useful life to 10 more years (the machine was to be operational until December 31, 2028, 12 years in total) and its residual value would be $300,000.

Case B: Same as Case A, except the company uses the declining-balance method. The rate used will be 2 ÷ 8 years, or 25%, for the first two years and then 2 ÷ 12 years, or 16.67%, thereafter.

Required:

For each case, prepare the journal entries for depreciation for 2017 and 2019.

 P8-34. Depreciation—changes in estimates and methods

(L.O. 8-2) (Medium – 10 minutes)

Below are two cases related to the depreciation of a building. In both cases the company has a December 31 year-end.

Case A: A building costing $6,000,000 was purchased on January 1, 2011. Based on management's best estimates, the useful life of the building was estimated to be 40 years with no residual value at that time. During 2017 it was discovered that the local government had plans to build a highway where the building stands. This project would require significant engineering and regulatory approval, so the site would be expropriated by January 1, 2023. The government agreed to pay $1,000,000 compensation for the building. The company uses the straight-line method to determine depreciation expense.

Case B: Same as Case A, except the company uses the declining-balance method. The rate will be 2 ÷ 40 years, or 5%, until 2017 and 2 ÷ 12, or 16.67%, thereafter.

Required:

For each case, prepare the journal entries to record depreciation for 2011 and 2017.

P8-35. Depreciation—changes in estimates and methods

(L.O. 8-2) (Medium – 5 minutes)

A large lathe was bought on January 1, 2013, for $7,000,000. It was expected to last for 12 years and have a residual value of $70,000. The company's policy for depreciating equipment is the straight-line method. During 2018 the remaining useful life of the lathe was revised to be four more years (for nine years in total). Management also felt that all equipment should now be depreciated using the declining-balance method at a 25% rate to better reflect the benefits obtained from the equipment.

Required:

Prepare the journal entries for depreciation for 2013 and 2018.

P8-36. PPE capitalization, site restoration costs, depreciation, and changes in estimates
(**L.O.** 8-1, **L.O.** 8-2) (Medium – 20 minutes)

A provincially-owned utility company is constructing a large hydroelectric dam. This dam is expected to operate for 100 years. During the construction period of 10 years, the company incurs the following costs:

Compensation to Indigenous Peoples who have land claims in the affected area	$ 300,000,000
Compensation to relocate non-Indigenous residents	200,000,000
Site preparation (e.g., clearing trees from land)	100,000,000
Materials for dam (e.g., concrete, steel)	2,000,000,000
Construction labour on dam	1,700,000,000
Power transmission lines	200,000,000
Power generation equipment	500,000,000
Total	$5,000,000,000

The useful lives of the transmission lines and power generation equipment are expected to be well under 100 years.

To fund the costs of the dam, the company issues $5 billion of bonds at the beginning of the construction period. These bonds bear interest at 6% paid annually, were issued at par, and mature in 30 years. The company reports using IFRS.

Required:

a. Determine the amounts that the company should capitalize into the following categories: land, facilities (dam).
b. The company believes that the straight-line method is appropriate for the dam and transmission lines to match revenues. The facilities are expected to last for the full 100 years and the transmission lines for 40 years. The power generation equipment should be depreciated on a declining-balance basis at a rate of 10% because their efficiency declines over time. Compute the amount of depreciation on the assets relating to this dam for the tenth year of operations. Assume that a full year of depreciation had been recorded in the first year of operations.
c. After 10 years of operations, the company revises the estimated useful life of the transmission lines from 40 to 30 years in total. How much would be the depreciation on the transmission lines in year 11?
d. During the environmental review process, regulators determined that the utility will need to restore the dam site to its original condition at the end of the dam's useful life. The estimated cost will be $2,000,000,000. Prepare the journal entry to record these site restoration costs. The discount rate is 6%.
e. For the first year of operations, record any entries related to the site restoration costs.

P8-37. PPE capitalization, depreciation, and derecognition
(**L.O.** 8-1, **L.O.** 8-2, **L.O.** 8-3) (Medium – 15 minutes)[13]

Pear Company (PC) had been renting its office building for several years. On January 1, 2016, it decided to have a new office building constructed. On that date, it acquired land with an abandoned warehouse on it for $100,000. Other costs included the following:

---

[13]·Reprinted from CGA-Canada FA2 examination, March 2009, with permission from Chartered Professional Accountants of Canada, Toronto, Canada. Any changes to the original material are the sole responsibility of the author (and/or publisher) and have not been reviewed or endorsed by the Chartered Professional Accountants of Canada.

Demolition of warehouse	$ 20,000
Legal fees for purchase of land	2,400
Construction costs of new building	400,000
Proceeds from salvage of warehouse materials	4,000
Installation of wiring and plumbing fixtures	16,000
Title guarantee insurance for fiscal year 2016	2,000
Architectural fees	24,000

Required:

a. Indicate what balance PC should record in the following accounts for the acquisition: (i) land account, (ii) building account.
b. Assume that the building was completed on December 31, 2016, and was occupied on that date. It has an estimated useful life of 40 years, with a residual value of $50,000. Calculate depreciation for 2017 using (i) the straight-line method and (ii) the double-declining-balance method.
c. Assume that management decided to use straight-line depreciation for the building. By 2020 PC had grown considerably and needed to relocate to a larger space; it sold the land and building to Sparrow Company on July 1, 2020, for $680,000. Assume depreciation expense has already been recorded for the first six months of the year (January 1 to June 30, 2020). Prepare all journal entries required relating to the land and building accounts on July 1, 2020.

P8-38. Derecognition

 **(L.O.** 8-3) (Easy – 5 minutes)

Taya Ltd. purchased equipment in February 2016 for $200,000. At the time of purchase it was estimated that the equipment would have a useful life of four years with no residual value. In September 2018, the equipment was destroyed in a flood. In February 2019, Taya Ltd. received an insurance settlement of $101,500. The company depreciates all equipment on a straight-line basis. Its policy is to record a full month of depreciation in all months that assets are available for use.

Required:

Prepare the journal entry to record the derecognition of the asset.

P8-39. Derecognition

 **(L.O.** 8-3) (Medium – 10 minutes)

Josh Inc. paid $2,400,000 cash for equipment on May 8, 2015, and immediately brought it into use. At the time of purchase it was estimated that the equipment would produce 4,000,000 casings over its useful life of five years and have a residual value of $600,000.

On August 1, 2019, the equipment was sold for $925,000. Josh Inc. depreciates its equipment using the straight-line method. Its policy is to record a full month of depreciation expense when assets are first available for use and no depreciation expense in the month of disposal.

Required:

a. Prepare the journal entry to record the derecognition of the asset on August 1, 2019.
b. Assume that rather than using the straight-line method the company uses the units-of-production method to derive depreciation expense. Further assume that 2,900,000 casings were produced during the time that the machine was owned. Prepare the journal entry to record the derecognition of the asset on August 1, 2019.

 P8-40. Derecognition

 **(L.O.** 8-3) (Medium – 15 minutes)

A machine was purchased during 2013 for $3,000,000. At the time of purchase it was estimated that the machine would have a useful life of nine years (ignoring year of purchase) and a residual value of $700,000. During 2019 the machine was sold for $1,700,000. The company does not record depreciation expense in the year of acquisition or disposal. The company uses the straight-line method to derive depreciation expense.

Required:

a. Prepare the journal entry to record the derecognition of the asset in 2019.
b. Assume that rather than using the straight-line method the company uses the declining-balance method to derive depreciation expense. The rate will be 2 ÷ 9. Prepare the journal entry to record the derecognition of the asset in 2019.
c. What is the aggregate income statement effect of using the straight-line and declining-balance method from 2013 to 2019? What is the net cash outflow associated with the purchase and subsequent sale of this machine? Is it coincidence or logical that the two income amounts and the net cash flows are the same (subject to rounding)?

P8-41. Derecognition    (**L.O.** 8-3) (Medium – 15 minutes)

Zoe Corporation bought a large piece of equipment for $9,000,000 during 2016. When the company purchased the equipment, it estimated a useful life of five years, ignoring the year of acquisition, and a residual value of $800,000. During 2019 the equipment was sold for $5,000,000. The company does not record depreciation expense in the year of acquisition or disposal.

Required:

a. Calculate the depreciation expense for 2016, 2017, and 2018, and compute any gain or loss on disposal for 2019 assuming the company used the straight-line method to determine depreciation expense.
b. Calculate the depreciation expense for 2016, 2017, and 2018 and any gain or loss on disposal for 2019 assuming the company used the declining-balance method to determine depreciation expense. The depreciation rate will be 2 ÷ 5, or 40%. What is the cumulative effect of the depreciation expense and any gain or loss for the four years under review?
c. What caused the gain on disposal for the declining method in 2019 or the loss on disposal for the straight-line method in 2019? Does a gain on disposal suggest good or excellent management and a loss on disposal indicate poor management? Explain your conclusion.
d. What can gains or losses on disposal tell us about prior years' reported net incomes?

P8-42. Derecognition—conceptual discussion and analysis
(**L.O.** 8-3) (Medium – 15 minutes)

Many companies do not record depreciation expense in the year of an asset's disposal.

Required:

Discuss three reasons for not recording depreciation expense in the year an asset is sold.

P8-43. PPE capitalization, depreciation, and non-monetary exchanges
(**L.O.** 8-1, **L.O.** 8-2, **L.O.** 8-4) (Medium – 15 minutes)[14]

Elm Limited had the following transactions and events during the year ended December 31, 2018:

a. In December 2018, Ami, the owner of Elm, paid for a parcel of land along with a warehouse on behalf of Elm, the registered owner of the property, for a total cost of $700,000. Ami also paid a real estate commission of $35,000 and legal fees of $5,000 in connection with this purchase, plus $25,000 for the demolition of the warehouse. Elm will reimburse Ami for these costs in January 2019 and will begin construction of an office building on this land. Prior to the purchase, the land and warehouse were appraised at $500,000 and $200,000, respectively.

[14.] Adapted from CGA-Canada FA2 examination, June 2009.

b. On December 31, 2018, Elm and Mahogany Corp. exchanged equipment. The exchange met the test for commercial substance for accounting purposes. Details of the carrying value and fair value of the equipment on the date of the exchange were as follows:

	Elm's equipment	Mahogany's equipment
Cost	$500,000	$820,000
Accumulated depreciation	200,000	505,000
Fair value	350,000	Not determinable

c. On October 1, 2018, Elm purchased some land by signing a four-year non-interest-bearing note payable for $400,000. Elm pays interest at the rate of 8% on other loans and was pleased to get a non-interest-bearing note payable on this deal.

Required:

Prepare the journal entries for Elm to record the above transactions and events, as well as any related year-end adjusting entries. Ignore income taxes.

P8-44. Non-monetary exchanges   (**L.O.** 8-3, **L.O.** 8-4) (Medium – 15 minutes)

The "backbone" of the Internet is made up of large fibre-optic cables that link major cities, countries, and continents. Due to the importance of these links, a number of different companies have overlapping networks that connect these different locations. Global Xing and Quest Communications are two such companies. The following provides information on transactions between these two companies.

Transaction 1: On January 5, 2020, Global Xing sold to Quest a part of its network connecting North and South America. In exchange, Quest sold to Global Xing cables connecting Europe and Asia. Global Xing paid $20 million as part of this transaction.

Transaction 2: On January 9, 2020, Global Xing sold to Quest some cables connecting the cities of Toronto and Montreal. These cables were laid along the shores of Lake Ontario and the St. Lawrence River. In exchange, Global Xing received from Quest cables connecting the same two cities, but running through a more inland route farther to the northwest. The rationale for the exchange was to facilitate servicing and maintenance of the cables. [*Note:* Fibre-optic cables require little maintenance in general.] In this transaction, Global Xing received $1 million.

The following table provides additional information on the assets exchanged in the transactions described above (in $ millions).

Information known to Global Xing	North–South America cables	Europe–Asia cables	Shoreline cables	Inland cables
Gross carrying amount	$300	n/a	$23	n/a
Accumulated depreciation	(90)	n/a	(8)	n/a
Net carrying amount	$210	n/a	$15	n/a
Fair value*	$390	$425	$21	$20

* The fair values of assets given up and received are measured with equal reliability.

Required:

a. Record Transaction 1 on the books of Global Xing.
b. Record Transaction 2 on the books of Global Xing if it is considered to have commercial substance.
c. Record Transaction 2 on the books of Global Xing if it is considered to lack commercial substance.

P8-45. Non-monetary exchanges   (**L.O.** 8-3, **L.O.** 8-4) (Medium – 15 minutes)

Lela Corp. purchased land and buildings in 2015 for $4,000,000. $1.4 million of the purchase price was allocated to land, the balance to buildings. At the time of purchase it was estimated that the building would have a useful life of 30 years but no residual value.

In 2024, Lela Corp. exchanged the land and buildings for an undeveloped land parcel and $100,000 cash. The fair market value of the assets given up was estimated to be $6.2 million; the fair value of the land received was $6.1 million.

Lela Corp. depreciates its buildings using the straight-line method. Its policy is to record a full year of depreciation expense in the year of acquisition and no depreciation expense in the year of disposal.

Required:

a. Prepare the journal entry to record the derecognition of the asset in 2024, assuming that the transaction has commercial substance.
b. Prepare the journal entry to record the derecognition of the asset in 2024, assuming that the transaction lacks commercial substance.

P8-46. Non-monetary exchanges   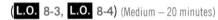 (**L.O.** 8-3, **L.O.** 8-4) (Medium – 20 minutes)

Quitzau Fishing Corp. (QFC) received a parcel of undeveloped land from another company in exchange for $45,000 cash and a second-hand forklift used in production. The fair values of the forklift and land have both been reliably measured. Pertinent details of the exchange follow:

Historical cost of the forklift	$50,000
Accumulated depreciation of the forklift	12,000
Fair market value of the forklift	42,000
Fair market value of the land	88,000
Cash paid	45,000

Required:

a. Does this transaction appear to have commercial substance? Why or why not?
b. Prepare the journal entry to record the exchange of assets assuming that the transaction has commercial substance.
c. Prepare the journal entry to record the exchange of assets assuming that the transaction lacks commercial substance.

P8-47. Non-monetary exchanges    (**L.O.** 8-4) (Medium – 20 minutes)

Douglas Company manufactures specialized golf clubs in Toronto. Anthony Corporation manufactures sports equipment, including golf clubs, but in Calgary. Anthony has a machine that it exchanges with Douglas Company on January 1, 2018. Below are details of the exchanged assets:

Historical cost of old asset on Douglas's accounting records	$6,000,000
Accumulated depreciation of old asset on Douglas's accounting records	2,100,000
Fair market value of old asset of Douglas "sold" to Anthony	4,250,000
Historical cost of old asset on Anthony's accounting records	7,200,000
Accumulated depreciation of old asset on Anthony's accounting records	3,000,000
Fair market value of old asset of Anthony "sold" to Douglas	4,000,000
Cash paid by Anthony to Douglas	250,000

Required:

a. Assume this exchange has no commercial substance. Prepare the journal entries to record this exchange for Douglas Company.
b. Assume this exchange does have commercial substance. Prepare the journal entries to record this exchange for Douglas Company.
c. Assume this exchange has no commercial substance. Prepare the journal entries to record this exchange for Anthony Company.

d. Assume this exchange does have commercial substance. Prepare the journal entries to record this exchange for Anthony Company.
e. Examine the journal entry of Anthony Company with no commercial substance (part c). Does any part of the entry look suspect?
f. Where did the "Gain on disposal" for the Douglas exchange go when the transaction was considered to have no commercial substance?

 P8-48. Non-monetary exchanges   **(L.O.** 8-4) (Medium – 15 minutes)

Trison Corporation traded a piece of equipment with another company in exchange for another piece of equipment. Details of the exchange are as follows:

Historical cost of old asset	$195,000
Accumulated depreciation of old asset	35,000
Fair market value of old asset	170,000
Fair market value of new asset	185,000
Cash paid	15,000

Required:

a. Record the transaction for Trison, assuming the exchange has no commercial substance.
b. Record the transaction for Trison, assuming the exchange has commercial substance.
c. Explain the rationale for the accounting treatment for exchanges without commercial substance.

P8-49. Non-monetary exchanges   **(L.O.** 8-4) (Medium – 15 minutes)

Pacific National Railway (PNR), a transportation company, has substantial investments in property, plant, and equipment. In the current year, the company exchanged some of these assets with other companies. [*Note:* Any depreciation expense prior to these transactions has already been properly recorded.] These transactions are as follows:

Transaction 1: PNR traded railway tracks running from Vancouver–Calgary–Winnipeg to its competitor, Transcanada Railway, in exchange for the Vancouver–Edmonton–Winnipeg route. PNR received $10 million from Transcanada because the southern route was shorter. Aside from this $10 million differential, there are no other significant differences in the amount, risk, and timing of future benefits from these two sets of tracks. The tracks, originally laid down in the late 19th century, had a cost of $100 million, accumulated depreciation of $70 million, and fair value of $200 million. The Vancouver–Edmonton tracks were recorded on Transcanada's books at a cost of $120 million and accumulated depreciation of $90 million.

Transaction 2: PNR is trying to expand its business in transportation beyond rail, so the company traded some railcars in return for several trucks. On PNR's books, the railcars had a cost of $5 million, accumulated depreciation of $3 million, and fair value of $4 million. The trucks had fair value of $3.8 million and were recorded on the seller's books at a cost of $4.5 million and accumulated depreciation of $1 million. No cash was involved in this exchange.

Transaction 3: PNR transported some luxury automobiles from the port in Vancouver to Winnipeg "for free." The company does not usually transport cars on this route, so a fair value was not determinable. However, there were negligible incremental costs because doing this involved simply attaching a few extra railcars to an existing train bound for Winnipeg. For doing this, PNR received two luxury cars, which the company awarded to executives as perquisites (perks). These cars had a retail value totalling $300,000.

Required:

Record the journal entries for the above transactions on PNR's books. State your reason(s) for the chosen accounting method.

P8-50. PPE capitalization, depreciation, and non-monetary exchanges

(**L.O.** 8-1, **L.O.** 8-2, **L.O.** 8-4) (Difficult – 20 minutes)[15]

Pebble Pasta Corporation (PPC) recently decided to add a new line of sauces to its product mix. To do so, it had to acquire new equipment for a new assembly line. The following costs were incurred in early 2017 relating to the assembly line:

Jan. 1, 2017	Mixing machine	$ 20,000
	Packaging machine	30,000
	Freight for machine delivery	8,000
Feb. 1, 2017	500-square-metre addition to factory	100,000
Mar. 1, 2017	Cost of testing and training on new assembly line	16,000

The mixing machine and the packaging machine are both about the same size, weight, and complexity.

On March 31, 2017, testing ended and the new assembly line went into full production; shipments to customers began immediately. The company intends to produce sauces for the next 20 years, at which time the assembly line is expected to be completely obsolete with no salvage value.

On January 1, 2019, PPC realized that its mixing machine was too small due to its very successful entry into the sauce business. The company exchanged its mixing machine for a newer, higher-capacity machine that had a fair value of $25,000. The original manufacturer accepted the old machine plus $1,000 for the exchange. PPC incurred $3,000 to ship the old and new machines to their respective destinations. No additional testing or training was needed for the new machine because of its similarity to the old machine; otherwise, it would have cost $8,000 to test and train on the new machine.

Required:

a. Calculate the amounts to be included in PPC's property, plant, and equipment. Use separate asset categories where appropriate.
b. PPC uses straight-line depreciation. Calculate the amount of depreciation expense for the year ended December 31, 2017, relating to the mixing machine, and prepare the related journal entry.
c. Prepare the journal entry (entries) for the exchange of the mixing machines on January 1, 2019. State any assumptions required.
d. What would be the journal entry (entries) for the exchange of mixing machines if your assumptions in part (c) were not valid?

P8-51. PPE presentation, disclosure, and analysis

(**L.O.** 8-1, **L.O.** 8-2, **L.O.** 8-3, **L.O.** 8-4) (Medium – 20 minutes)

Obtain the 2016 financial statements for Thomson Reuters Corporation either from the company's website or from SEDAR (www.sedar.com).

Required:

a. What are the major categories of PPE that the company owns?
b. On what basis does the company report its PPE (cost or revaluation)? What method of depreciation does the company use? What are the estimated useful lives for the different categories of PPE?
c. Using depreciation information, estimate the average age of assets at the end of 2016 as a percentage of estimated useful life. Do this for each of the three categories of PPE.
d. Using depreciation information, estimate the average useful life of computer hardware used by the company in 2016. Why might this estimate be inaccurate in this situation?

---

[15]·Adapted from CGA-Canada FA2 examination, December 2008.

P8-52. PPE presentation, disclosure, and analysis

(**L.O.** 8-1, **L.O.** 8-2, **L.O.** 8-3, **L.O.** 8-4) (Medium – 30 minutes)

Refer to the 2016 financial statements for Canadian Tire Corporation in Appendix D.

Required:

a. Which measurement basis does the company use for its PPE (cost or revaluation)? Where in the annual report does the company disclose this choice? What reason does the company provide for this choice?

b. How much does the company report for "Property and equipment" (net of accumulated depreciation) at the end of 2016?

c. Why does the company not report any depreciation on the income statement?

d. Where in the financial statements is the information on depreciation expense?

e. What method of depreciation does the company use? What are the company's depreciation rates on (i) buildings and (ii) fixtures and equipment?

f. Are the actual depreciation amounts in 2016 consistent with the rates in (e)?

g. How much interest did the company capitalize for property under construction in 2016? What interest rate did the company use for this purpose?

M. MINI-CASES

Pan Asia Airlines was founded in 1980. Headquartered in Hong Kong, the publicly traded company has routes throughout Asia and to major airports throughout Europe and North America. While Pan Asia charges a premium of 10 to 20% over its competitors, customers have not been deterred from using the airline. Since it began operations, Pan Asia has been consistently recognized for its quality of service.

A key reason for this reputation for high quality is the company's relatively young fleet of aircraft, with an average age of five years and no plane older than eight years. To maintain a young fleet, Pan Asia sells and replaces its planes regularly. The frequent replacement ensures that the planes are equipped with the latest technology and operate efficiently. Other full-service airlines typically have aircraft fleets with an average age of 10 years, while discount airlines have even older fleets, with an average age of 15 years. These older ages are partly due to the airlines using the same aircraft for more years, and partly a result of them buying used aircraft sold by other airlines and leasing companies. A well-maintained aircraft can last for 20 to 25 years, or even more in some cases.

The company has a decentralized management structure. Each of five regional managers has primary responsibility for all investment and operating decisions for his or her region (Asia north of Hong Kong, Asia south of Hong Kong, West Asia/Middle East, Europe, and North America). The company evaluates each region as a profit centre. The decentralized structure allows each region to respond quickly to changes in its market.

Financially, the company has been consistently profitable in recent years. Stock analysts have projected a target price that is 20% higher than the current price of $32.50 per share, based on their projections of earnings before interest, taxes, depreciation, and amortization (EBITDA). Because of its solid financial performance, Pan Asia has also earned a high credit rating, allowing it to borrow at a rate of 6%. Debt currently comprises about 40% of assets, while liquid assets (cash, short-term investments) amount to about 10% of assets, which total approximately $2 billion (Canadian dollars).

It is now February 2021. A new chief executive officer (CEO), William Chan, has been appointed following the retirement of the founding CEO. Chan has a background in mechanical engineering and served as Pan Asia's chief operating officer for the past 15 years.

While Chan has a thorough understanding of the company's central operations, he is less familiar with other aspects of the company. Consequently, he has spent the past three months reviewing the company's marketing program, human resources, information systems, treasury, as well as accounting. During this review, Chan has identified a few issues that he would like you, the chief financial officer, to explain to him.

1. The CEO noted that Pan Asia uses the declining-balance method of depreciation. He also noted that many (though not all) competitors use the straight-line method. He wonders whether Pan Asia should consider conforming to the majority in the industry.
2. In recent conversations with stock analysts, Chan noted that they often ask about the company's EBITDA and what his outlook is for that figure. He is wondering about the merits of using this figure in comparison to the bottom line net income that is reported in the financial statements.
3. One of the two aircraft manufacturers that Pan Asia uses has recently started a promotion that offers a significant discount to airlines that make advance payments on their aircraft orders. The discount amounts to 15% of the price that Pan Asia would otherwise have to pay. To obtain the discount, Pan Asia would need to pay in full when it orders a plane, rather than when the manufacturer delivers it. Typically, the amount of time between order and delivery is two years. Chan is unsure whether he should encourage the regional managers to take up this offer. He is also wondering what the effects might be for the financial statements.

CASE 1
Capitalization of PPE and depreciation policies
(30 minutes)

Required:

Draft a memo to the CEO that addresses the issues he raised.

CASE 2
Intrawest's interest capitalization policy

(30 minutes)

On January 20, 2000, the *Financial Post* published an article by Philip Mathias entitled, "Intrawest Points to Accounting Report for Fall in Stock Price." Intrawest owns and operates Whistler Blackcomb in British Columbia, Mont Tremblant in Quebec, and a number of other resorts around the world. In addition to ski resort operations, a significant part of the company's operations involves developing real estate in and around the resorts. At the time of the article, the company was publicly traded and followed the guidance in the *CICA Handbook*, since IFRS did not come into effect until 2011.

The article indicated that Intrawest attributed a decline in stock price to criticisms of the firm's accounting by forensic accountant L.S. Rosen. The company's stock price had been as high as $25 in late December 1999, but had fallen to about $21 by the date of the news article (see Exhibit I). While there had been rumours about such a critical report for several weeks, the reporter was unable to obtain a copy. According to the reporter, when he questioned Mr. Rosen about the criticism, Rosen "declined to confirm or deny reports he publicly criticized Intrawest's financial reports."

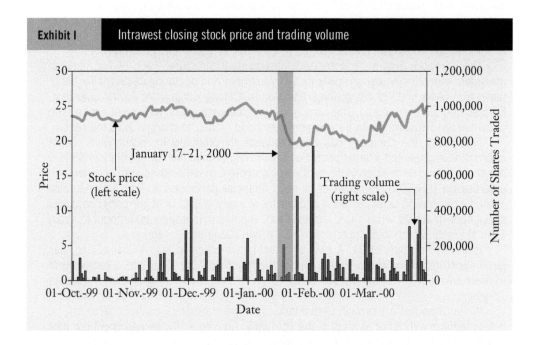

| Exhibit I | Intrawest closing stock price and trading volume |

At the heart of the criticisms was the company's policy for capitalizing costs on its real estate projects. In response to the allegations, Intrawest's executive vice-president, Daniel Jarvis, said, "Our statements are absolutely rock solid ... They present a fair and accurate picture of where the company is and ... are very conservative."

Specifically, the criticism focused on the company's policy to capitalize "interest on general and specific debt and administrative expenses" on its resort developments. The criticisms allege that Intrawest's earnings would be lower had it followed more conservative accounting policies.

The company justified its accounting policy on the basis that it financed some of its resort construction with the company's equity while others were financed with loans. Mr. Jarvis said that "there is always a cost of funding" regardless of where it comes from. The article noted that Mr. Jarvis said Intrawest's practice is required by GAAP.

In the year ended June 30, 1999, the company reported profits of $51.5 million, up from $41 million in 1998.

Required:

Discuss the above article using concepts from financial accounting theory (Chapter 1) and financial reporting framework (Chapter 2), and the standards for PPE accounting (this chapter).

CASE 3
Bedrock Quarries
(60 minutes)[16]

Bedrock Quarries Ltd. (Bedrock), wholly owned by Betty Rubble, has operated a sand and gravel pit since 1992. During that time, its revenues have increased moderately. On March 15, 2015, after almost two years of negotiation, a purchase and sale agreement between Flintstone Sand and Gravel Ltd. (Flintstone) and Betty Rubble was completed whereby Ms. Rubble sold Bedrock to Flintstone. Mr. Flintstone, sole shareholder of Flintstone, was optimistic about the synergistic benefits that would accrue to the combined operations.

Mr. Harrison, the senior partner of Harrison, Longo, and Chan (HLC), Chartered Accountants, and a cousin of Ms. Rubble, has recently been informed that a complaint was made to the Provincial Institute of Chartered Accountants (PICA) regarding his involvement with Bedrock. In February 2016, Mr. Flintstone submitted a complaint to the PICA alleging that HLC, and Mr. Harrison in particular, were associated with financial statements of Bedrock that were false and materially misleading. Apparently, Mr. Flintstone has retained counsel and is preparing to commence legal action against HLC for negligence in its work on the Bedrock engagements.

For each of the fiscal years ended January 31, 2012, and January 31, 2013, HLC prepared audited reports, and for the fiscal years ended January 31, 2014, and January 31, 2015, HLC prepared review engagement reports on the financial statements of Bedrock. Mr. Harrison is adamant that Bedrock's financial statements were prepared in accordance with International Financial Reporting Standards.

The PICA does not have the staff available at the moment and has asked Chapman & Partner (CP), Chartered Accountants, to investigate Mr. Flintstone's complaint. You are employed by CP. Jim Chapman, partner in charge of CP's litigation department, has asked you to prepare a memo discussing all relevant matters regarding the engagement. He will use it as a basis for discussion in a meeting he has scheduled for next week, on May 12, 2016, with staff from the PICA.

In order to prepare your memo, you have been provided with extracts from Bedrock's financial statements for the years 2013 to 2015 (see Exhibit I).

You have reviewed the working paper files of HLC and have held discussions with Mr. Flintstone. All significant issues arising from your investigation, including your discussions, are outlined in Exhibits II and III. Key points from the purchase and sale agreement are summarized in Exhibit IV.

Required:
Prepare the memo.

Exhibit I	Extracts from financial statements for Bedrock Quarries Ltd. (in $000's)		
Balance sheet as at January 31	2015 (unaudited)	2014 (unaudited)	2013 (audited)
Assets			
Cash and cash equivalents	$ 23,397	$ 21,215	$ 29,219
Accounts receivable	38,903	28,869	22,927
Inventory	18,155	17,011	29,019
Land at cost	3,637	3,637	3,637
Plant and equipment at cost	93,987	93,987	93,987
Accumulated depreciation and depletion	(56,091)	(51,714)	(47,195)
Investment in and advances to associated company	9,394	9,165	4,716
	$131,382	$122,170	$136,310

(*Continued*)

[16.] Reprinted from Uniform Final Examination, 1996 with permission from Chartered Professional Accountants of Canada, Toronto, Canada. Any changes to the original material are the sole responsibility of the author (and/or publisher) and have not been reviewed or endorsed by the Chartered Professional Accountants of Canada.

Exhibit I	Continued		
Balance sheet as at January 31	2015 (unaudited)	2014 (unaudited)	2013 (audited)
Liabilities and shareholder's equity			
Bank indebtedness	$ 628	$ 503	$ 21,120
Accounts payable	22,695	24,179	20,325
Long-term debt	43,076	39,114	47,161
Deferred taxes	6,296	5,454	396
Common shares	1,000	1,000	1,000
Retained earnings	57,687	51,920	46,308
	$131,382	$ 122,170	$ 136,310
Income statement for the years ended January 31	2015 (unaudited)	2014 (unaudited)	2013 (audited)
Revenue	$78,697	$ 74,750	$ 62,215
Operating expenses			
Cost of sales	54,534	50,988	59,223
Sales and general costs	4,490	3,819	5,051
Development	1,760	2,019	1,693
Depreciation and depletion	4,377	4,519	4,776
	65,161	61,345	70,743
Operating profit (loss)	13,536	13,405	(8,528)
Interest expense, net	1,227	1,119	1,315
Exploration expense	1,149	1,212	976
Research expense	463	404	391
	2,839	2,735	2,682
Income (loss) before income taxes	10,697	10,670	(11,210)
Income taxes	4,930	5,058	—
Net income (loss)	$ 5,767	$ 5,612	$(11,210)

Exhibit II	Notes from review of HLC working papers for the fiscal years 2012 to 2015

Based on your review of HLC's working papers, you have learned the following:
1. Materiality for the engagements was set at 1% of revenue for each year.
2. No review of subsequent events was conducted for any fiscal year.
3. A letter of representation was obtained from management in each fiscal year stating that no contingencies or commitments existed, that no unusual transactions had occurred, and that the financial statements were complete. Also, specific items mentioned include the following:
   - Related-party transactions did exist.
   - Inventory was counted, costed, and valued fairly.
4. In each year, one HLC staff member attended the year-end inventory count to observe the procedures employed by Bedrock staff for the physical count and valuation of inventory. Every year, accounts receivable were reviewed for mathematical accuracy.
5. Harrison's fees for each year were based on 1% of sales or $200,000, whichever was less, and the fees could not exceed a quotation from any accounting firm of similar size and expertise.
6. Accounts receivable include amounts owed to Bedrock by Rubble Sales and Haulage Ltd., a company owned by Ms. Rubble.
7. The bank loan is secured by an assignment of accounts receivable and land and equipment.

The accounting policies of Bedrock include the following:
1. Inventory is valued at net realizable value.
2. Revenue is recognized when products are ready for delivery.
3. Depreciation and depletion are calculated on a 10-year straight-line basis.

Exhibit III	Notes from discussions with Mr. Flintstone

From discussions with Mr. Flintstone, you have learned the following:

1. Mr. Flintstone initially heard of Bedrock's financial results and financial position from a friend of Mr. Harrison who had periodically discussed Bedrock's operations with Mr. Harrison.
2. Mr. Flintstone relied upon the Bedrock financial statements for the years 2012 to 2014 before entering into the purchase and sale agreement.
3. Mr. Flintstone claims that during a meeting on August 15, 2014, HLC assured him that the financial statements of Bedrock were free of any material errors for each of the fiscal years 2012 to 2014.
4. Mr. Flintstone reviewed the draft 2015 financial statements prior to closing the deal.
5. Mr. Flintstone had no knowledge of the nature and extent of HLC's procedures for 2015.
6. Mr. Flintstone considers himself very knowledgeable about the industry.

Exhibit IV	Summary of key points concerning the purchase and sale agreement

1. The purchase price of Bedrock's shares is $100 million plus three times net income for the fiscal years 2015 and 2016.
2. HLC will remain Bedrock's accountants for fiscal 2016, after which the auditors of Flintstone Sand and Gravel will assume the engagement.
3. Ms. Rubble provided a general representation and warranty in the purchase and sale agreement that all financial statements of Bedrock are true and correct.
4. Flintstone Sand and Gravel is entitled to have access to all of Bedrock's corporate records in the course of its due diligence procedures.

Dunstan Electric Inc. is a private company specializing in the sale of high-end home appliances and consumer electronics with over 40 stores across Canada. Dunstan Electric is known for its guaranteed delivery within 24 hours. The company has been owned and operated by the Dunstan family for over 30 years.

Tyler & Perry (T&P), Chartered Accountants, has audited Dunstan Electric for over 20 years. You are the audit senior on the engagement. It is now December 11, 2019, and Jack Dunstan, founder and chief executive officer (CEO), called you to say that one of the company's largest stores was completely destroyed in a fire on December 7. With less than a month until the year-end, this fire has happened at a bad time.

Dunstan Electric is insured for damage caused by fire. Inventory and capital assets that were destroyed in the fire are insured at their replacement cost, assuming that the replacement is of the same make and model as the asset destroyed or, if it is no longer available, the closest substitute. The insurance policy states that the insured will receive the fair value of the building that was destroyed whether or not it is rebuilt. There is no business interruption insurance policy.

The statement of claim is currently being prepared. Once the insurers receive the claim, it will be validated, approved, and then paid within 60 days of approval. The accounting staff started working on the claim but have not yet completed it.

Anne Cooper, the engagement partner, has just met with Mr. Dunstan to obtain more information about the incident and the losses sustained (Exhibit I). You also obtain the November 2019 financial statements to help you plan for this year's audit engagement (Exhibit II). Anne would like you to prepare a memo outlining the financial accounting considerations and any other issues resulting from the fire.

CASE 4
Dunstan Electric
(40 minutes)[17]

Required:

Prepare the memo to Anne Cooper.

[17.] Reprinted from Uniform Final Examination, 2004 with permission from Chartered Professional Accountants of Canada, Toronto, Canada. Any changes to the original material are the sole responsibility of the author (and/or publisher) and have not been reviewed or endorsed by the Chartered Professional Accountants of Canada.

Exhibit I	Information from Dunstan Electric

According to the records at head office, the book values of the destroyed capital assets are as follows:

	Building	Fixtures, computer hardware, and software
Cost	$722,000	$495,000
Net book value	545,000	221,000

Preliminary estimates include the following:

Building

Since the building was completely destroyed in the fire, a new one must now be built. As required by the insurance company, estimates from two contractors have already been received.

	Contractor A	Contractor B
Labour	$ 652,000	$ 523,000
Materials	963,000	942,000
	$1,615,000	$1,465,000

Jack Dunstan has never dealt with Contractor A, but the contractor has assured Jack that the building can be rebuilt similar to the newer, more modern Dunstan Electric stores. Contractor B was used for the construction of the last six Dunstan Electric stores. It is estimated to take six to eight months to rebuild the burnt store.

Jack and the insurers are currently negotiating which contractor to select. Jack has decided not to record any insurance proceeds until the negotiations are complete, and instead has booked a loss of $545,000 on the building for the year ended December 31, 2019.

Sales

No goods were sold or received after the fire. The salespeople estimated the week's worth of sales before the fire took place, since the weekly update to the main server was lost. Ninety percent of Dunstan's sales are on cash or credit card basis. For the cash and credit card sales, bank deposits are made on a daily basis by the stores. A printout of the web-based bank statement is made at head office to confirm the deposit information. The remaining 10% of sales are financed in-house. The financing application is approved at the time of the purchase by the store and the information is transferred to head office as part of the weekly update.

Inventory

The destruction of the IT systems also created havoc in determining year-end inventory for the destroyed store. Since it is the holiday season, inventory levels of electronic goods are kept at higher levels than normal. To expedite the receipt of proceeds from the insurers, Jack went ahead and estimated the ending inventory by obtaining the inventory levels as at the date of the fire for the other three similar-sized Dunstan Electric stores:

(in $ millions)	Store #26	Store #8	Store #37	Store #23 (destroyed)
Inventory—Dec. 7, 2019 (estimated)	1.6	1.3	1.9	Unavailable
Inventory—Nov. 30, 2019	1.5	1.2	1.8	1.6
Year-to-date revenues—Dec. 7, 2019 (estimated)	16.4	12.9	17.4	Unavailable
Year-to-date revenues—Nov. 30, 2019	15.3	12.0	15.8	15.5

Jack recorded insurance proceeds receivable of $1.9 million since he believes that Store #37 best approximates the destroyed store's activities. Jack noted, however, that some broken and older electronics items were being set aside at each of the stores in preparation for the year-end inventory count. He has no idea of the value of these items in the burnt store and has not attempted to back out an amount from the other stores' figures.

(Continued)

Exhibit I	Continued

Other fire-related costs

The loss of the store has meant additional costs will be incurred:

Salaries still to be paid while employees are not able to work: $110,000

Estimated site-demolition and clean-up cost: $500,000

Municipal bylaws require a demolition of the building within 30 days. These costs will be expensed for accounting purposes.

Other

Dunstan Electric just refinanced its operating line of credit with its bank in November. As a result of this agreement, the bank now requires the audited financial statements for 2019 to be finalized no later than February 5, 2020.

Jack was reviewing the draft financial statements and noticed the gross margin went up 6%. Jack believes that the increase is directly related to sales of electronic goods. Other staff believe otherwise. They do not have much management information on hand to help them analyze the reason for the increase.

Exhibit II	Draft income statement for Dunstan Electric

For the periods ended November 30
(in $000's)

	2019 (11 months)	2018 (11 months)
Sales	$352,653	$262,935
Cost of goods sold		
Opening inventory	45,644	49,885
Purchases	229,587	179,225
Closing inventory	(44,254)	(44,569)
	230,977	184,541
Gross profit	121,676	78,394
Operating expenses		
Salaries and commissions	23,568	16,555
Bonuses	5,522	2,215
Advertising	10,555	8,855
Freight and transportation	3,556	1,950
Amortization	7,587	5,963
Professional fees	2,559	1,754
Office	2,998	1,335
Utilities	4,659	3,445
Miscellaneous	4,445	1,442
	65,449	43,514
Income from operations	56,227	34,880
Other income and expenses	2,558	1,778
Income before taxes	53,669	33,102
Income taxes	21,468	13,240
Net income	$ 32,201	$ 19,862

CASE 5
MINID Property Corp

(30 minutes)

MINID Property Corp. (MINID) is a publicly held real estate company in Canada, specializing in retail real estate property. The company took advantage of the economic downturn and purchased several investment properties in the United States over the fiscal year of 2013. The following were the details of the purchase transactions (all in CAD).

The first property is a strip mall located in Silicon Valley, California. The property was appraised at $3 million, with $2 million attributed to land and $1 million to building. The company was informed of high competition for the property and thus decided to pay a premium to win the real estate bid. The purchase price was thus $3.5 million. Management booked 2/3 of the purchase price to land and 1/3 to building. At the end of the year, the company booked an impairment of $500,000 to its land account.

The second property that the company purchased was a small power centre located in Napa Valley, California. The property was appraised at $5.5 million, but management bargained with the owners for a purchase price of $5 million. Management believed the $0.5 million qualified as negative goodwill and that they were supposed to book this amount as profit. However, management did not want the amount to show up on the income statement; therefore, they recorded $5.5 million as the acquisition cost of the property and $0.5 million as a contra-asset account—"negative goodwill"—directly below goodwill in the intangible asset section of the balance sheet.

The third property the company purchased was a small retail store located in downtown San Francisco. Jon Shen, MINID's CEO, was the original owner of the store and he had paid $300,000 for the property 10 years ago. The property was appraised at $600,000 in 2013. The board of directors decided to buy this property from Jon Shen at a price of $750,000. The premium paid was intended to compensate Jon Shen for all the good things he had done for the company over the years. Management booked the property at $300,000, and $450,000 as compensation expense for the company.

Required:

a. Suppose you are hired by an accounting firm to audit the financial statements of MINID for the fiscal year 2013. Discuss the appropriateness of the accounting treatments with regard to the acquisition of the above-mentioned properties.

b. Publicly traded companies are usually under pressure to maximize income and to increase shareholder wealth. Why do you think MINID is motivated to decrease its earnings for reasons other than tax?

CHAPTER 9
Intangible Assets, Goodwill, Mineral Resources, and Government Grants

David Wei/Alamy Stock Photo

CPA competencies addressed in this chapter:

1.1.2 Evaluates the appropriateness of the basis of financial reporting (Level B)
   b. Methods of measurement

1.2.1 Develops or evaluates appropriate accounting policies and procedures – Ethical professional judgment (Level B)

1.2.2 Evaluates treatment for routine transactions (Level A)
   e. Goodwill and intangible assets
   f. Depreciation, amortization, impairment, and disposition/derecognition
   o. Changes in accounting policies and estimates, and errors

1.2.3 Evaluates treatment for non-routine transactions (Level B)
   a. Uncommon capital assets (natural resources, government grants)

1.3.2 Prepares routine financial statement note disclosure (Level B)

1.4.1 Analyzes complex financial statement note disclosure (Level C)

Bombardier Inc. (www.bombardier.com, Toronto Stock Exchange ticker: BBD.B) is a manufacturer of aerospace and ground transportation equipment with some 70,000 employees worldwide, headquartered in Montreal. For its fiscal year ended December 31, 2016, the company reported intangible assets and goodwill totalling US$7.14 billion, a larger amount than the $1.95 billion in property, plant, and equipment. What do intangible assets represent? Do companies recognize the value of brands? When does an enterprise record goodwill? Clearly, these are important questions for companies like Bombardier.

BP plc, also known as British Petroleum (www.bp.com, London Stock Exchange ticker: BP), is one of the largest energy companies in the world. To account for its oil and gas exploration activities, the company uses the "successful efforts" method. In Canada, Accounting Standards for Private Enterprises (ASPE) also allows the "full cost" method. What are the differences between these two methods of accounting for oil and gas exploration activities? What are the reasons for having these two different methods?

The previous chapter on property, plant, and equipment (PPE) dealt with tangible long-lived assets. This chapter will consider potential assets that are intangible—those items without physical substance. Of the three general stages of accounting for assets—initial recognition and measurement, subsequent measurement, and derecognition—the first stage has the most issues unique to intangibles, while the latter two stages are to a large extent similar to the accounting for PPE. Therefore, this chapter will devote most of the discussion to the initial recognition and measurement of intangible assets. The latter part of this chapter will examine the accounting issues relating to assets used in mineral exploration. We devote separate treatment to this industry not because it is specialized or secondary to other parts of the Canadian economy, but because it has unique accounting issues. Indeed, in some provinces/territories, exploration, development, and extraction of mineral resources comprise the largest sector of the economy. Finally, this chapter discusses the accounting for government grants.

A. INTANGIBLE ASSETS—INITIAL RECOGNITION AND MEASUREMENT

Recognition and measurement of intangible assets involve two steps. The first considers whether an item is an intangible asset (definition), while the second deals with the amounts that should be capitalized or expensed in the accounts (recognition and measurement).

L.O. 9-1. Evaluate whether a cost qualifies for capitalization as an intangible asset or goodwill.

1. What qualifies as an intangible asset?

As defined in IFRS–IAS 38 (as well as in ASPE), an **intangible asset** is an identifiable, non-monetary asset without physical substance. Such assets include patents, trademarks, copyrights, customer lists, software, movies, and so on. The definition of an intangible asset embodies three conditions: its lack of physical substance, non-monetary nature, and identifiability.

intangible asset An identifiable, non-monetary asset without physical substance.

COMMON ITEMS THAT ARE POTENTIALLY INTANGIBLE ASSETS

From everyday experiences, you are probably aware of quite a number of items that could be considered potential intangible assets. Here is a partial list.

Patents are exclusive rights given for the invention or discovery of a product or process. Patents must be obtained through an application process with the Canadian Patent Office (which is a part of the Canadian Intellectual Property Office; CIPO) or its equivalent in other countries. The Patent Office determines whether the proposed product or process is significantly original and distinct from existing products or processes. Canadian patents expire after 20 years, which is the minimum length of time specified by the World Trade Organization's Agreement on Trade-Related Aspects of Intellectual Property Rights (TRIPs); 20 years is the length of time specified in the patent laws of most countries.

Enterprises can also register *industrial designs,* which involve an original shape or visual pattern that appeals to the eye. Industrial design can involve very simple products that would not be patentable—the important feature is the outward appearance of the product. For example, a uniquely shaped chair could be registered as an industrial design. Registration protects an industrial design for 10 years.

Copyright is the right to copy or duplicate. Copyright applies to original works of art in any form (visual, audio, etc.) and literature (books, articles, and other writing including computer programs). Copyright arises automatically with the creation of the work of art or literature, but an official copyright may be obtained by applying to the CIPO. Canadian law protects copyrights during the life of the author and for 50 years thereafter.

Trademarks are distinctive signs used by a person or enterprise to identify its products or services. A trademark can be a word, a design, or a combination of words and designs. Trademarks can develop through use under common law, in which case they are unregistered trademarks. Trademarks can also be registered with the CIPO. Registered trademarks are denoted by ® or ™. Trademarks registered in Canada are valid for 15 years but renewable afterward, so they have potentially indefinite lives.

For more information on these and other intellectual property, visit the CIPO website (www.cipo.ic.gc.ca).

a. Lack of physical substance

In many cases, intangible assets will have tangible components, but the tangible portion is incidental to the value of the item. For example, a patent certificate is only a representation of the underlying patent. The storage medium or computer that holds a software program is usually separable from the program itself. In contrast, if the software were an integral part of a machine such that it was required for the machine's operations (such as a computer's operating system), then the software would be considered part of PPE.

b. Non-monetary nature

Some assets that lack physical substance are financial in nature and are not considered intangible assets in accounting. For example, accounts receivable and bond investments lack physical substance, but they are claims on cash flows, so they are financial rather than intangible assets. We previously examined the accounting for financial assets in Chapters 5 and 7.

c. Identifiability

This condition refers to whether one can distinguish and separate an item from other items. More specifically, IAS 38 provides the following guidance:

> ¶12   An asset is identifiable if it either:
> (a) is separable, i.e., is capable of being separated or divided from the entity and sold, transferred, licensed, rented or exchanged, either individually or together with a related contract, asset or liability regardless of whether the entity intends to do so; or
> (b) arises from contractual or other legal rights, regardless of whether those rights are transferable or separable from the entity or from other rights and obligations.[1]

Thus, an enterprise can meet the identifiability criterion by demonstrating either that the potential intangible asset is separable or that the enterprise has the legal rights to that asset. For example, a patent that is purchased meets both criteria: it can be sold to another party, and the patent confers legal rights to the owner.

The identifiability criterion distinguishes intangible assets from goodwill. Accounting **goodwill** represents the difference between the purchase cost of a business and the **fair value** of identifiable assets net of liabilities. Since it is a residual amount left over after values have been allocated to all other balance sheet items (including intangible assets), goodwill is not specifically identifiable. Thus, it is not classified as an intangible asset; goodwill is a separate type of asset altogether.

A related but distinct concept is *economic goodwill*, which can be created by branding, excellent customer service, acting in a socially responsible manner, and so on. Companies such as Apple, Nike, and Coca-Cola have strong and recognizable brands that contribute to the economic goodwill of these iconic companies. However, *accounting goodwill* arises only from the purchase of a business (an entire company or some portion of it, such as a division). Companies that have never made acquisitions of other businesses will have no accounting goodwill. (Accounting for business mergers and acquisitions is a topic usually reserved for advanced financial accounting texts and courses; this chapter will simply provide an introduction to the accounting for goodwill.)

Also embedded in the definition of an intangible asset are, of course, the criteria for an asset: it must arise from past transactions, have future benefits, and be under the control of the enterprise. With respect to the third criterion, control over the future benefits of intangible assets usually stems from legal or contractual rights.

goodwill   The difference between the purchase cost of a business and the fair value of identifiable assets, net of liabilities.

fair value   The price that would be received to sell an asset or paid to transfer a liability in an orderly transaction between market participants at the measurement date.

[1.] Copyright © 2012 IFRS Foundation.

CHECKPOINT CP9-1

What are the three characteristics of an intangible asset? From what other assets does each characteristic distinguish an intangible asset?

2. What amounts should an enterprise capitalize as intangible assets?

To be recognized in the financial statements, an item must meet the definition of an intangible asset, as described above, as well as the recognition and measurement criteria, which require that future benefits be probable and that the cost be measurable. More specifically, IAS 38 indicates the following:

¶21 An intangible asset shall be recognized if, and only if:
  (a) it is probable that the expected future economic benefits that are attributable to the asset will flow to the entity; and
  (b) the cost of the asset can be measured reliably.

¶22 An entity shall assess the probability of expected future economic benefits using reasonable and supportable assumptions that represent management's best estimate of the set of economic conditions that will exist over the useful life of the asset.[2]

Ultimately, whether and how an enterprise satisfies these criteria depends on the way it obtains the intangible asset—whether it acquires or internally develops the intangible asset. Whereas acquired intangibles readily satisfy the recognition and measurement criteria, internally developed intangibles must meet more stringent criteria, as discussed below. The difference is due to the subjectivity involved in measuring the benefits of internally developed intangibles, and the greater possibility of management bias in developing the estimates of those benefits. (Refer to Chapter 1 for a review of the motives for earnings management.)

THRESHOLD CONCEPT
**CONCEPTUAL
FRAMEWORK**

a. Acquired intangibles

In general, enterprises should record acquired intangibles at fair value on the acquisition date if they have been acquired from an arm's-length party (i.e., a party that acts independently of the enterprise in question, which excludes related companies, major shareholders, etc.). The acquisition may be through a separate purchase of the intangible, through a purchase of a business, or from a government grant. If the transaction involves non-monetary assets, then the rules relating to non-monetary exchanges discussed in Chapter 8 apply as well.

IFRS presumes that (i) intangibles acquired from arm's-length parties meet the criterion of having probable future benefits, and (ii) such benefits can be measured reliably. In particular, IAS 38 indicates the following:

¶25 Normally, the price an entity pays to acquire separately an intangible asset will reflect expectations about the probability that the expected future economic benefits embodied in the asset will flow to the entity.... Therefore, the probability recognition criterion in paragraph 21(a) is always considered to be satisfied for separately acquired intangible assets.

¶33 [relating to intangibles purchased in a business combination] The fair value of an intangible asset will reflect expectations about the probability that the expected future economic benefits embodied in the asset will flow to

---

[2.] Copyright © 2012 IFRS Foundation.

the entity.... Therefore, the probability recognition criterion in paragraph 21(a) is always considered to be satisfied for intangible assets acquired in a business combination.[3]

This presumption makes sense to the extent that management enters into the purchase willingly and rationally. Thus, purchased intangibles—whether bought separately or as part of a bundle of assets—can and must be recognized as an asset under IFRS.

Recognizing an acquisition of an intangible through a separate transaction is straightforward, as fair value equals the purchase cost. For example, Bombardier Inc. acquired $516 million of intangible assets for aerospace program tooling in 2016.[4] The company recorded these transactions as follows:

Exhibit 9-1	Journal entry for Bombardier's acquisition of intangible assets in 2016	
Dr. Intangible assets – Aerospace program tooling	516m	
Cr. Cash (or other consideration)		516m

In contrast to purchases of individual intangible assets, acquisitions of intangible assets through the purchase of another company are more complex due to the need to estimate the fair value of each intangible, since the purchase price is for a bundle of assets. To make such estimates, an enterprise should take account of any market prices for the same or similar intangibles, if available; otherwise, it should apply one or more appropriate valuation models. The nature of intangibles is such that market prices are rare, so assigning fair values to intangibles acquired in a bundled purchase requires a great deal of professional judgment.

Enterprises sometimes acquire intangibles from governments at fair value, such as wireless broadcasting rights obtained through an auction. At other times, enterprises will receive the intangible for free or nominal value, such as a grant of logging rights. In the latter case, the enterprise can record the intangible at the nominal price it paid or at fair value.

b. Internally developed intangibles

IAS 38 identifies two distinct stages for internally developed intangibles: a research phase and a development phase. Research encompasses activities that are not targeted toward a specific commercial product or process, and therefore it is not possible to satisfy the recognition criterion relating to the probability of future economic benefits. IAS 38 distinguishes research from development as follows:

research   Original and planned investigation undertaken with the prospect of gaining new scientific or technical knowledge and understanding. Contrast with **development**.

development   The application of research findings or other knowledge to a plan or design for the production of new or substantially improved materials, devices, products, processes, systems, or services before the start of commercial production or use.

¶8   **Research** is original and planned investigation undertaken with the prospect of gaining new scientific or technical knowledge and understanding. **Development** is the application of research findings or other knowledge to a plan or design for the production of new or substantially improved materials, devices, products, processes, systems, or services before the start of commercial production or use.[5]

The costs incurred in the research phase must be expensed because the activities do not relate to an identifiable product or process. Development activities are further advanced than research in terms of commercially viable products or processes, so it is possible to satisfy the criterion of probable future benefits. However, not all costs incurred in the development phase qualify for capitalization. IAS 38 provides a list of

---

[3.] Copyright © 2012 IFRS Foundation.

[4.] Figures in US currency.

[5.] Copyright © 2012 IFRS Foundation.

six criteria for the capitalization of development costs, *all* of which must be satisfied for capitalization to occur [emphasis added]:

¶57   An intangible asset arising from development (or from the development phase of an internal project) shall be recognized if, and only if, an entity can demonstrate all of the following:

(a) the technical *feasibility* of completing the intangible asset so that it will be available for use or sale.

(b) its *intention* to complete the intangible asset and use or sell it.

(c) its *ability* to use or sell the intangible asset.

(d) how the intangible asset will generate probable future economic benefits. Among other things, the entity can demonstrate the existence of a *market* for the output of the intangible asset or the intangible asset itself or, if it is to be used internally, the *usefulness* of the intangible asset.

(e) the availability of *adequate* technical, financial and other *resources* to complete the development and to use or sell the intangible asset.

(f) its ability to *measure reliably* the expenditure attributable to the intangible asset during its development.[6]

Basically, most of these criteria (a to e) focus on whether future benefits are probable. The final criterion relates to identifiability: what are the boundaries of the project and which costs are or are not part of the project eligible for capitalization? Exhibits 9-2 and 9-3 provide two examples to illustrate the accounting for research and development (R&D) costs:

Exhibit 9-2	R&D example 1

Scenario:

A pharmaceutical company is developing a drug to reduce the effects of Parkinson's disease, a condition of the central nervous system that impairs motor skills. After several years of research, the company has identified a compound that helps to restore the balance of the neurotransmitters. The company has begun drug trials to test the efficacy of the drug and to determine if there are significant side effects.

Analysis:

It remains uncertain as to whether the drug is effective and safe. Therefore, the company has not yet demonstrated that it has the ability to use or sell the intangible asset, so criterion (c) fails.

Conclusion:

As the project fails at least one of the six criteria of IAS 38 ¶57, the project has not yet reached the stage at which development costs could be capitalized.

Exhibit 9-3	R&D example 2

Scenario:

A company engages in a project to reengineer its information system. Dedicating 25 staff to the project, the company intends to streamline the flow of information and documents within the organization, which will reduce duplication and increase the efficiency of employees. The project is sufficiently staffed with qualified personnel who have the requisite training and experience to complete the project. The project team has already produced a report describing the existing information system, the changes that will be made, a project timeline, a budget for the project, and an analysis of the costs and benefits of changing the information system.

Analysis:

Criteria (IAS 38 ¶57)	Evaluation
Technical feasibility	The project plan outlines the feasibility and timeline of the project.
Management intention	Management has the intention to change the information system.

(Continued)

Exhibit 9-3	Continued

Criteria (IAS 38 ¶57)	Evaluation
Ability to use or sell	There is little doubt that the company will be able to use the new information system.
Marketability or usefulness	The company has performed a cost–benefit analysis to demonstrate the economic benefits of the project.
Resource adequacy	The project has a dedicated group of qualified staff.
Measurement reliability	The project is well defined and uses specific personnel, and there is a project budget that outlines the specific costs, so the costs of the project are likely to be measured with sufficient reliability.

Conclusion:

The circumstances suggest that the company would be able to demonstrate that the project meets all six criteria. Therefore, the costs of the project from this point forward would be eligible for capitalization.

The six requirements for the capitalization of development costs are quite stringent, and a development project needs to meet all of the criteria for capitalization to occur. This means that there are many costs in the development phase that cannot be capitalized. Furthermore, once a cost has been expensed it cannot be later reclassified as an asset when the project reaches a point when it is able to satisfy the capitalization criteria.

Note that the terms "research phase" and "development phase" apply to all types of internally generated intangible assets, not just R&D activities (see IAS 38 paragraph 52). For example, one does not usually associate brands and customer lists with R&D; however, we can still apply the above rules. Since branding and building customer lists do not relate to an identifiable product or process they do not qualify as development activities, so an enterprise cannot capitalize such costs.

Similar to the recognition of self-constructed PPE, the costs included for an internally generated intangible asset are those costs directly related to creating the intangible and making it ready for its intended use or sale. For example, in the development of a new production process, capitalization of development costs ceases when the production process is ready to produce commercial products for sale. Costs incurred prior to that point, such as test production runs, would be capitalized.

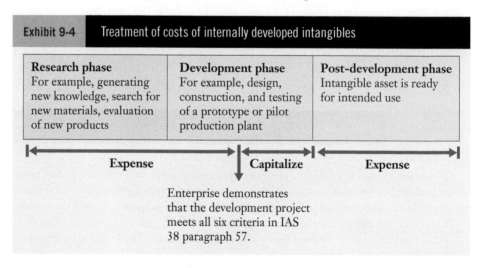

Exhibit 9-4	Treatment of costs of internally developed intangibles

To illustrate the treatment of R&D costs, Canadian Tire Corporation disclosed that it spent $153.8 million on internally developed software in 2016 and recorded the amount as finite-life intangible assets (see Note 11 in Appendix D). In Note 3, the company explains, "Intangible assets with finite useful lives … are amortized on a straight-line basis … generally for a period of two to ten years." We discuss amortization of intangible assets next.

CHECKPOINT CP9-2

What is the key reason that accounting standards treat acquired intangibles differently from internally developed intangibles?

B. INTANGIBLE ASSETS—SUBSEQUENT MEASUREMENT

Just as for PPE, the measurement of intangible assets can follow the historical cost model or the revaluation model. This chapter focuses on the **historical cost** approach, while Chapter 10 will address revaluation. Chapter 10 will also deal with **impairments** of intangible assets.

The treatment of an intangible asset subsequent to initial capitalization depends on whether it has a finite or an indefinite life. An indefinite **useful life** does not mean an infinite amount of time; rather, it means that the enterprise expects the particular intangible asset to continue providing economic benefits for the foreseeable future at a level similar to that expected when the enterprise capitalized the asset.

1. Intangible assets with indefinite useful lives

For intangible assets with indefinite lives, there is no reasonable basis for specifying the period over which to allocate the cost of such an asset. Instead, the enterprise should evaluate the assets for impairment each year (see Chapter 10). For example, a registered trademark in Canada can be renewed indefinitely in 15-year increments. As long as the trademark holder intends to renew the trademark, this intangible asset would have an indefinite life.

2. Intangible assets with finite useful lives

Similar to tangible assets with finite useful lives, an enterprise allocates/amortizes a finite-life intangible asset over its useful life because the enterprise expects to consume the benefits of the asset over that period of time. However, the nature of intangible assets is that they typically relate to knowledge or intellectual property, so the assessment of their useful lives is more complex than for PPE. As discussed earlier in this chapter, intellectual property with a finite legal life includes patents (20 years), copyrights (life of author plus 50 years), and industrial designs (10 years). An intangible asset with legal rights specified by laws, regulations, or contracts has a useful life that is at most equal to its legal life, but it could be much shorter. For example, a patent provides legal protection for a medication for 20 years, but if other technological developments are expected to result in competing, superior products after 10 years, then the useful life of the patent is only 10 years. On the other hand, if the medication is such a breakthrough that the enterprise expects no competing product to arise even after 30 years, then the useful life is the 20-year legal life of the patent. Likewise, copyright protects computer programs/software programs for decades, but the economic life of a program is likely to be only a few years given the rapid pace of software development. Thus, the useful life is the lesser of the legal life and the economic life.

The assessment of useful life should take into account all factors relevant to the ability of the asset to generate economic benefits. In addition to legal protection, the enterprise should consider factors affecting the intangible asset itself such as the speed of technical innovation and obsolescence, the market for the product(s) related to the intangible asset, the useful life of any other asset on which the intangible asset depends, competitive pressure, trends, and the stability of the industry.

L.O. 9-2. Evaluate whether a recognized intangible asset has an indefinite life or a finite life, and in the latter case, determine the appropriate useful life for amortization.

historical cost   The actual cost of an asset at the time it was purchased; can also refer to amounts based on historical cost but adjusted by depreciation, amortization, or impairment.

impairment   The process of writing down the value of an asset to recognize declines in its fair value.

useful life   The period of time over which an asset is expected to be available for use by an entity, or the number of production units an enterprise expects to obtain from the use of an asset.

Among the three parameters of amortization (useful life, amortizable amount/ residual value, and pattern of amortization), useful life is the one that involves the most judgment. IFRS presumes that the residual value of an intangible asset is zero and that the straight-line method reflects the pattern of economic benefits consumed, unless there is specific evidence to the contrary. In practice, nearly all firms amortize intangible assets using the straight-line method with no residual value.[7]

For example, Canadian Tire Corporation disclosed in Note 3 of its 2016 financial statements (Appendix D) the following amortization policies for intangible assets (other than computer software, which was previously described above).

Exhibit 9-5	Canadian Tire's amortization policies for intangible assets
Intangible assets	

Intangible assets with finite useful lives are measured at cost and are amortized on a straight-line basis over their estimated useful lives, generally for a period of two to ten years. The estimated useful lives and amortization methods are reviewed annually with the effect of any changes in estimates being accounted for on a prospective basis.

Intangible assets with indefinite useful lives are measured at cost, less any accumulated impairment, and are not amortized.

CHECKPOINT CP9-3

What is the key question to ask before proceeding with the amortization of an intangible asset?

C. INTANGIBLE ASSETS—DERECOGNITION

Derecognition of an intangible asset is the same as for an item of PPE. The difference between the proceeds and the carrying amount is a gain or loss that flows through profit or loss. The enterprise removes both the cost and accumulated amortization from the accounts.

D. GOODWILL

As discussed in Section A, although goodwill is intangible, it is an asset separate from "intangible assets." Accounting goodwill represents the difference between the purchase cost of a business and the fair value of identifiable assets net of liabilities. Conceptually, this difference represents how much the buyer is willing to pay for the business as a whole, over and above the value of the individual assets alone. Goodwill can sometimes comprise the majority of the value of a purchase. For example, Canadian Tire Corporation disclosed that in 2013, it paid $58 million to acquire Pro Hockey Life Sporting Goods Inc. Of that amount, only $10.4 million was in identifiable assets and liabilities, while $47.6 million was goodwill. Similar to intangible assets with an indefinite life, enterprises do not need to amortize goodwill; rather, they should evaluate it for impairment.

[7.] The specific evidence required to rebut the presumption of zero residual value includes a contractual commitment by an arm's-length buyer or an active market for the intangible asset that allows for reliable determination of a residual value.

For example, suppose Powell Company purchases Sooke Ltd. for $60 million.[8] After analyzing Sooke's balance sheet, Powell has estimated the following amounts for fair values in each category of asset and liability:

Exhibit 9-6	Calculation of goodwill for Powell Company's purchase of Sooke Ltd.	
($000's)	Carrying value	Fair value
Cash	5,000	5,000
Accounts receivable	20,000	19,500
Inventories	15,000	14,000
Property, plant, and equipment	50,000	45,000
Intangible assets (patents)	1	9,500
Total assets	90,001	93,000
Total liabilities	(50,000)	(50,000)
Net assets	40,001	43,000
Purchase price		60,000
Goodwill (Purchase price – Fair value of net assets)		17,000

Fair values on the date of acquisition will generally differ from the carrying amounts on the balance sheet. In the example of Sooke Ltd.:

- accounts receivable have fair value lower than recorded due to uncollectible accounts and the fact that the accounts receivable balance does not reflect the time value of money;
- inventories have lower value due to obsolescence;
- PPE have fair values below the carrying amount due to accounting depreciation being less than the decline in their fair values; and
- intangible assets have fair value far exceeding the nominal value of patents because Sooke's past R&D activities have not satisfied the criteria for capitalization.

On a fair value basis, assets total $93 million while liabilities total $50 million, for net assets of $43 million. Since Powell Company paid $60 million to purchase Sooke Ltd., the premium of $17 million is the amount of goodwill. Thus, goodwill is not an individually identifiable asset; rather, it is simply the portion of the purchase price not specifically accounted for by the identifiable assets and liabilities.

 CHECKPOINT **CP9-4**

Why is goodwill not an intangible asset for accounting purposes?

E. PRESENTATION AND DISCLOSURE

Due to the diverse range of intangible assets, disclosures should group together assets with a similar nature and use. These "classes" of intangible assets include, for example, patents, copyrights, computer software, licences, industrial designs, and so on. In addition, as discussed above, the accounting for intangible assets depends on whether the enterprise acquires them or develops them internally. Consequently, an enterprise should separately identify internally developed intangibles from acquired intangibles.

[8.] The purchase could be completed by a purchase of shares or the assets and liabilities of Sooke Ltd. For purposes of this example and this text, the differences in the methods of acquisition are not important.

For each class of intangible asset, the enterprise should identify whether the useful lives are indefinite or finite. In the case of indefinite lives, the enterprise should disclose the reasons for its determination of indefinite lives. In cases of finite useful lives, the disclosure should include information on amortization policy (useful life or amortization rate, and amortization pattern), the carrying amount and accumulated amortization (i.e., relating to the balance sheet), and the amount of amortization included in one or more line items of the statement of comprehensive income. An enterprise should disclose the amount of R&D costs expensed through profit or loss.

Finally, the enterprise should reconcile the beginning and ending balances of each class of intangible assets. The reconciliation should include increases due to acquisition or internal development, amortizations if any, and other changes.

With respect to goodwill, the disclosures requirements are simpler because goodwill is always considered to have an indefinite life. Thus, there is no amortization and no amortization-related disclosure. The enterprise should provide a reconciliation of beginning and ending balances similar to the requirement for intangible assets. As will be discussed in the next chapter, any impairments or revaluations to either goodwill or intangible assets also need to be disclosed.

The following exhibit shows excerpts from Bombardier's 2016 annual report as an example of disclosures for intangible assets and goodwill. The disclosures include the capitalization and amortization policies. Notice the separation of goodwill from intangible assets, and the major classes of intangibles.

Exhibit 9-7	Disclosures of intangibles from Bombardier's 2016 annual report

Note 2: Summary of significant accounting policies

Intangible assets

Internally generated intangible assets include development costs (mostly aircraft prototype design and testing costs) and internally developed or modified application software. These costs are capitalized when certain criteria for deferral such as proven technical feasibility are met. The costs of internally generated intangible assets include the cost of materials, direct labour, manufacturing overheads and borrowing costs and exclude costs which were not necessary to create the asset, such as identified inefficiencies.

Acquired intangible assets include the cost of development activities carried out by vendors for which the Corporation controls the underlying output of the usage of the technology, as well as the cost related to externally acquired licences, patents and trademarks.

Intangible assets are recorded at cost less accumulated amortization and impairment losses and include goodwill, aerospace program tooling, as well as other intangible assets such as licences, patents and trademarks. Other intangible assets are included in other assets.

Amortization of aerospace program tooling begins at the date of completion of the first aircraft of the program. Amortization of other intangibles begins when the asset is ready for its intended use. Amortization expense is recognized as follows:

	Method	Estimated Useful Life
Aerospace program tooling	Unit of production	Expected number of aircraft to be produced (1)
Licences, patents, and trademarks	Straight-line	3 to 20 years
Other intangible assets	Straight-line	3 to 5 years

(1) As at December 31, 2016, the remaining number of units to fully amortize the aerospace program tooling, except for aerospace program tooling under development, is expected to be produced over the next 14 years.

The amortization methods and estimated useful lives are reviewed on a regular basis, at least annually, and changes are accounted for prospectively. The amortization expense is recorded in cost of sales, SG&A or R&D expenses based on the function of the underlying assets.

The Corporation does not have indefinite-life intangible assets, other than goodwill. Goodwill represents the excess of the purchase price over the fair value of the identifiable net assets acquired in a business acquisition. After initial recognition, goodwill is measured at cost less any accumulated impairment losses.

(Continued)

Exhibit 9-7 Continued

Note 21: Intangible assets

Intangible assets were as follows:

| | Aerospace program tooling | | | | | |
	Acquired	Internally generated	Total	Goodwill	Other	Total
Cost						
Balance as at December 31, 2015	$ 1,864	$ 11,320	$ 13,184	$1,978	$ 683	$ 15,845
Additions	516	829	1,345	—	35	1,380
Disposals	—	—	—	—	(4)	(4)
Effect of foreign currency exchange rate changes	—	—	—	(123)	(15)	(138)
Balance as at December 31, 2016	$ 2,380	$ 12,149	$ 14,529	$1,855	$ 699	$ 17,083
Accumulated amortization and impairment						
Balance as at December 31, 2015	$ (1,449)	$ (7,760)	$ (9,209)	$ —	$ (569)	$ (9,778)
Amortization	(3)	(143)	(146)	—	(32)	(178)
Disposals	—	—	—	—	2	2
Effect of foreign currency exchange rate changes	—	—	—	—	12	12
Balance as at December 31, 2016	$ (1,452)	$ (7,903)	$ (9,355)	$ —	$ (587)	$ (9,942)
Net carrying value	$ 928	$ 4,246	$ 5,174	$1,855	$ 112	$ 7,141

[Comparative figures for fiscal year ended December 31, 2015, have been omitted for brevity.]

Aerospace program tooling

The net carrying value of aerospace program tooling comprises $2,586 million for Commercial Aircraft, $2,631 million for Business Aircraft, $8 million for Aerostructure and Engineering Services and $(51) million for Corporate and Elimination, respectively, as at December 31, 2016 ($1,914 million, $2,041 million, $20 million, and nil, respectively, as at December 31, 2015, and $4,347 million, $2,470 million, $9 million, and nil, respectively, as at January 1, 2015).

Goodwill

Goodwill is related primarily to the DaimlerChrysler Rail Systems GmbH (Adtranz) acquisition in May 2001. Goodwill is monitored by management at the Transportation operating segment level. During the fourth quarter of fiscal year 2016, the Corporation completed an impairment test. The Corporation did not identify any impairment.

Source: From Financial Report, 2016 Bombardier. Copyright © 2017 by Bombardier. Reprinted by permission.

F. MINERAL RESOURCES

L.O. 9-3. Apply the specialized standards for the initial recognition of assets relating to mineral resource exploration and evaluation.

IFRS 6 addresses accounting issues specific to costs incurred in the **exploration for and evaluation of mineral resources**, which includes activities involved in the search for mineral resources—minerals, oil, natural gas, and similar non-regenerative resources—after the entity has obtained legal rights to explore in a specific area, as well as the determination of the technical feasibility and commercial viability of extracting the mineral resource. For brevity, this chapter refers to these activities simply as "mineral exploration." Mineral exploration is one of three key phases in mining activities; the other two are development and extraction.

exploration for and evaluation of mineral resources Activities involved in the search for mineral resources, including minerals, oil, natural gas, and similar non-regenerative resources, after the entity has obtained legal rights to explore in a specific area, as well as the determination of the technical feasibility and commercial viability of extracting the mineral resource.

1. Three phases in mineral activities: Exploration, development, and extraction

Conceptually, mineral exploration has similarities with the research phase of R&D. The activities are aimed at gathering knowledge about the geology and the potential for mineral resources embedded underground. During mineral exploration, there are significant uncertainties regarding not only the existence of significant concentrations of mineral resources, but also whether the resources are commercially extractable using available technologies. Whereas IAS 38 requires enterprises to expense costs incurred during the research phase, IFRS 6 allows enterprises a choice in selecting the capitalization policy for mineral exploration costs. In other words, enterprises can choose to expense all exploration costs, which would result in the same outcome as applying IAS 38, or to capitalize exploration costs.

When (and if) an enterprise establishes that a project is technically feasible and commercially viable, the project enters the second phase—development. At this point, the guidance in IAS 38 for intangible assets applies to the development phase. If the enterprise establishes that the mineral site is not worthy of further exploration or development, costs up to that point would be written off to reflect the impairment of the asset. (See Chapter 10 for a more detailed examination of impairment.) This is called the **successful efforts method** because only costs accumulated on exploration efforts that are ultimately successful at discovering valuable minerals remain capitalized as assets by the end of the exploration phase.

When the mineral site is ready for mineral extraction, the project enters the extraction phase. In this phase, standard rules regarding the recognition of expenses would apply to match the recognition of revenue. The diagram in Exhibit 9-8 summarizes the three phases of mineral exploration, development, and production along with the relevant standards in IFRS.

successful efforts method (relating to mineral exploration)   A method of accounting that capitalizes costs of mineral exploration and evaluation only if the outcome is successful (i.e., production is technically feasible and commercially viable); contrast with the **full cost method**.

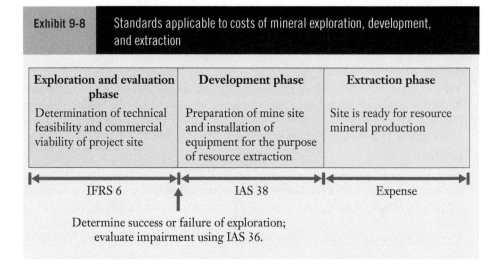

Exhibit 9-8   Standards applicable to costs of mineral exploration, development, and extraction

Exploration and evaluation phase	Development phase	Extraction phase
Determination of technical feasibility and commercial viability of project site	Preparation of mine site and installation of equipment for the purpose of resource extraction	Site is ready for resource mineral production
IFRS 6	IAS 38	Expense

Determine success or failure of exploration; evaluate impairment using IAS 36.

THRESHOLD CONCEPT
CONCEPTUAL FRAMEWORK

Why does IFRS allow a choice to capitalize the costs of mineral exploration? If mineral exploration is similar to research, why should the accounting standards allow capitalization in the case of mineral exploration but not scientific research? The reason is the difference in the degree of uncertainty. The markets for the mineral resources are well established, whereas a market for ideas is not. Deep and liquid commodity markets for gold, copper, uranium, oil, and gas ensure that mineral resources can be sold at some price, but there is no guarantee that a particular research finding can be sold at any price. For this same reason, when a mineral site enters the development phase, it would normally satisfy the six criteria for the capitalization of development costs in IAS 38 paragraph 57.

2. Full cost alternative under ASPE

full cost method (relating to mineral exploration)   A method of accounting that capitalizes costs of mineral exploration and evaluation costs without regard to outcome; contrast with the **successful efforts method**.

The **full cost method** allows enterprises to capitalize all mineral exploration costs without regard to the success or failure of specific projects. ASPE allows private enterprises to use either the full cost method or the successful efforts method, and this choice was also available to publicly accountable enterprises in Canada prior to the adoption of IFRS on January 1, 2011.

The two methods rely on different interpretations of the criterion in the definition of an asset that relates to probable future benefits. The successful efforts method takes the reasonable view that there are no future benefits flowing from costs incurred on a mineral site that will never enter production, and such costs should be expensed; costs incurred on successful sites do have future benefits, so they qualify as assets. On the other hand, the full cost method considers specific mineral exploration activities to be part of the larger process of discovering productive sites and generating future revenues. That is, exploration is risky by its very nature, so some sites will be successful while others will not, but costs from all sites are part of the same exploration process. From this perspective, costs generally incurred for mineral exploration activities have expected future benefits even though, after the fact, some sites will turn out to be unproductive.

The following exhibit provides examples to illustrate both methods of accounting for oil and gas exploration expenditures.

Exhibit 9-9	Examples of successful efforts and full cost methods in practice

Example of successful efforts method: 2016 annual report of BP plc, a large energy company headquartered in the UK, with US$260 billion in assets.

Oil and natural gas exploration, appraisal, and development expenditure

Oil and natural gas exploration, appraisal, and development expenditure is accounted for using the principles of the *successful efforts* method of accounting.

Licence and property acquisition costs

Exploration licence and leasehold property acquisition costs are capitalized within intangible assets and are reviewed at each reporting date to confirm that there is no indication that the carrying amount exceeds the recoverable amount. This review includes confirming that exploration drilling is still under way or planned or that it has been determined, or work is under way to determine, that the discovery is economically viable based on a range of technical and commercial considerations and sufficient progress is being made on establishing development plans and timing. If no future activity is planned, the remaining balance of the licence and property acquisition costs is written off. Lower value licences are pooled and amortized on a straight-line basis over the estimated period of exploration. Upon recognition of proved reserves and internal approval for development, the relevant expenditure is transferred to property, plant, and equipment.

Exploration and appraisal expenditure

Geological and geophysical exploration costs are recognized as an expense as incurred. Costs directly associated with an exploration well are initially capitalized as an intangible asset until the drilling of the well is complete and the results have been evaluated. These costs include employee remuneration, materials and fuel used, rig costs, and payments made to contractors. If potentially commercial quantities of hydrocarbons are not found, the exploration well is written off. If hydrocarbons are found and, subject to further appraisal activity, are likely to be capable of commercial development, the costs continue to be carried as an asset. If it is determined that development will not occur, then the costs are expensed.

Costs directly associated with appraisal activity, undertaken to determine the size, characteristics, and commercial potential of a reservoir following the initial discovery of hydrocarbons, including the costs of appraisal wells where hydrocarbons were not found, are initially capitalized as an intangible asset. When proved reserves of oil and natural gas are determined and development is approved by management, the relevant expenditure is transferred to property, plant, and equipment.

Development expenditure

Expenditure on the construction, installation, or completion of infrastructure facilities such as platforms, pipelines, and the drilling of development wells, including service and unsuccessful development or delineation wells, is capitalized within property, plant, and equipment and is depreciated from the commencement of production as described below in the accounting policy for property, plant, and equipment.

Example of full cost method: 2016 annual report of Encana Corporation, one of the largest Canadian oil and gas companies headquartered in Calgary. This report was prepared under US GAAP, which allows the full cost method.

Property, plant, and equipment

EnCana uses the full cost method of accounting for its acquisition, exploration, and development activities. Accordingly, all costs directly associated with the acquisition of, the exploration for, and the development of natural gas and liquids reserves, including costs of undeveloped leaseholds, dry holes, and related equipment, are capitalized on a country-by-country cost centre basis. Capitalized costs exclude costs relating to production, general overhead, or similar activities. Capitalized costs accumulated within each cost centre are depleted using the unit-of-production method based on proved reserves....

 **CHECKPOINT CP9-5**

Why does IFRS permit the capitalization of exploration costs but not research costs?

3. Other aspects of accounting for mineral exploration costs

Subsequent to the initial recording of mineral exploration costs, enterprises can apply either the cost model (discussed in the previous chapter for tangibles and this chapter for intangibles) or the revaluation model (discussed in the next chapter). Similar to other long-lived assets, enterprises need to evaluate the capitalized costs for impairment. Depletion of mineral exploration costs normally uses the units-of-production method.

4. Example to illustrate the accounting for mineral resources

Suppose Peace River Exploration Co. (PREC) incurred the following costs in its search for oil and natural gas in northern Alberta and British Columbia during 2019:

Well	Costs incurred in exploration and evaluation	Status at year-end December 31, 2019
A	$400,000	Producing
B	600,000	Abandoned
C	300,000	Abandoned
D	500,000	In development
E	200,000	Exploration and evaluation still ongoing

In addition to costs in the exploration phase, PREC incurred an additional $800,000 on PPE to develop Well A and $500,000 to develop Well D. During the year, Well A produced 20,000 barrels of crude out of an estimated reserve of 500,000 barrels (i.e., production equals 4% of reserves).

Based on the above information, the following entries would summarize PREC's accounting for the costs of exploration, development, and extraction under the successful efforts and full cost methods:

Exhibit 9-10	Accounting for the cost of PREC's mineral resource activities ($000's)			
Successful efforts method			**Full cost method**	
Record exploration costs				
Dr. Exploration expenses—Well B	600			
Dr. Exploration expenses—Well C	300			
Dr. Intangible assets—Well A	400			
Dr. Intangible assets—Well D	500			
Dr. Intangible assets—Well E	200		Dr. Intangible assets—exploration	2,000	
Cr. Cash		2,000	Cr. Cash		2,000
Record development costs				
Dr. PPE—Well A	800		Dr. PPE—Well A	800	
Dr. PPE—Well D	500		Dr. PPE—Well D	500	
Cr. Cash		1,300	Cr. Cash		1,300
Record depletion and depreciation				
Dr. Depletion expense	16		Dr. Depletion expense	80	
Cr. Accum. depletion—Well A			Cr. Accum. depletion		
($400,000 × 4%)		16	($2,000,000 × 4%)		80
Dr. Depreciation expense	32		Dr. Depreciation expense	32	
Cr. Accum. depreciation—Well			Cr. Accum. depreciation—		
A ($800,000 × 4%)		32	Well A ($800,000 × 4%)		32

Notice that the successful efforts method shown on the left side identifies exploration costs specifically by well/location. PREC would expense costs for wells that are unsuccessful (B, C). The company can carry forward as intangible assets those costs incurred on successful wells (A, D). Costs for wells still in the exploration phase remain as assets pending further evaluation (E). In contrast, the full cost method capitalizes all exploration-phase costs, and it is not particularly important whether the costs are specifically identified with a particular location.

In the development phase, the accounting treatment is similar under both methods. In the extraction phase, both methods would need to record depletion that reflects the 4% of reserves extracted. However, the full cost method has a larger amount previously capitalized ($2 million under full cost versus $400,000 under successful efforts), so the amount of depletion is correspondingly higher. The amount of depreciation is the same, as both methods capitalize the same amounts to PPE.

G. GOVERNMENT GRANTS

L.O. 9-4. Apply the standards for accounting for government grants.

For many different reasons, governments at all levels provide assistance to enterprises for engaging in certain activities. The federal government may provide investment tax credits for the purchase or construction of equipment and facilities to provide economic stimulus during a recession. A provincial government may provide rebates for the installation of equipment that reduces the output of greenhouse gases. A municipal government may provide property tax concessions to encourage the construction of low-cost housing.

If an enterprise receives the benefit of such grants, how should it account for the grant? To be concrete, suppose the federal government provides a four-year forgivable loan of $20 million to Ocean Falls Company to acquire a production facility in Canada. The government will forgive $5 million for each year that the company employs at least 500 people in Canada. The facility costs $100 million and has a useful life of 20 years. For this type of government assistance:

- How should Ocean Falls record the grant—in equity or income?
- When should Ocean Falls recognize the grant—when it first receives the loan, during the four-year period of the loan, or at the end when the loan is fully forgiven?
- Should the company present the effect of the grant on a gross or net basis?

This section addresses these three questions according to IAS 20. In addition, the end of this section looks at the treatment of government grants in cases where they become repayable due to the inability of the enterprise to meet the conditions of the grant.

1. How should enterprises recognize government grants—as equity capital or income?

Government grants ultimately confer benefits on enterprises' owners. Conceptually, the question is how equity should be increased: should the grant enter equity capital directly or indirectly through income and retained earnings? The direct (capital) approach argues that government grants are not part of the earning process and are therefore not revenue or reductions in expense. The indirect (income) approach argues that grants are indeed earned because enterprises need to satisfy certain conditions to receive the grants, so they are appropriately part of income.

IFRS requires enterprises to use the income approach. Specifically, IAS 20 states the following:

> ¶12   Government grants shall be recognized in profit or loss on a systematic basis over the periods in which the entity recognizes as expenses the related costs for which the grants are intended to compensate.[9]

In addition to requiring the income approach, this paragraph also indicates the importance of matching the income recognition to the incurrence of related costs.

Note that accrual accounting generally matches expenses to revenue, but not the reverse. Matching in both directions would result in a logical circularity. In other words, if we were to match expenses to revenues and also match revenues to expenses, then recognizing any amount would be as good as any other amount—there would be no external anchor to support one treatment over any other. Government grants provide an exception where we match income to cost/expenses. No circularity results because the government grant is secondary to the operating revenue of the enterprise: we apply the revenue recognition criteria, match expenses to those revenues, then match the government grant income to the related expenses.

Applying this matching process is fairly straightforward for items related to current period costs such as wages. In some cases, an enterprise receives a grant for performance in past periods; it would recognize the income effect of the grant in the period received. When an enterprise receives grants for investing in assets such as PPE, the related cost is the cost of the PPE, and enterprises should recognize the income effect of the grant over the useful life of the PPE in the same way that it depreciates the PPE.

In the case of Ocean Falls, the forgivable loan is for the purpose of acquiring production facilities, so it should recognize the benefit of the loan over the life of the PPE rather than all at the beginning when it receives the funds.

2. When should enterprises recognize government grants?

The nature of government grants is that they will generally specify conditions that enterprises must satisfy to be eligible for the grant. Consequently, enterprises should record these grants only when they are reasonably assured that they have complied with the conditions of the grants and that the grants will be received.

For Ocean Falls Company, if it intends to maintain at least 500 employees in Canada for the full four-year period, it can recognize the full $20 million as a grant when it first receives the funds. The alternative is to record a liability for the loan for $20 million, and then reduce the amount of the loan by $5 million for each year that the company meets the criteria for forgiveness. Assuming management feels reasonably assured of meeting the minimum employment levels, the company would record the following entry at the beginning of the four years:

Exhibit 9-11	Journal entry to record Ocean Falls' receipt of a government grant relating to PPE

Dr. Cash	$20,000,000	
Cr. Deferred income (a liability) or PPE*		$20,000,000

* Either of these two accounts may be used depending on the presentation method chosen. See discussion below.

In the example of Ocean Falls Company, the forgivable loan would result in $1 million of income each year for 20 years.[10]

---

[10] An astute reader may reasonably question whether the government grant relates to employee costs rather than to PPE. The loan is for the purpose of acquiring production facilities, but the conditions of forgiveness require minimum employee levels. If the loan were treated as being related to employee costs, then the income could be recognized over the four-year period covered by the forgiveness provision, resulting in $5 million of income each year. The treatment presented in this example uses the fact that the government advanced the full $20 million at the beginning of the four years, which suggests that the amount relates to the initial acquisition of facilities rather than the payment of ongoing costs of employees.

Exhibit 9-12	Journal entry to record income on PPE-related government grant received

Dr. Deferred income	$1,000,000
Cr. Other income (government grant)	$1,000,000
Or	
No separate entry required if the grant was initially recorded as a credit against PPE.	

Which of these two journal entries would be recorded depends on whether Ocean Falls chooses the gross or net method, which we discuss next.

3. How should enterprises present government grants?

There are two ways to present government grants. The gross method shows the effect of government grants as separate line items on the balance sheet and statement of comprehensive income, while the net method offsets the government grant against the related financial statement items. Exhibit 9-13 shows the different accounts used in each of these methods. Depending on the nature of the grant, whether it relates to the performance of certain activities over time ("related to income") or to the acquisition of assets ("related to assets"), the accounts affected differ.

Exhibit 9-13	Journal entries for gross and net methods of accounting for government grants	
	Gross method	**Net method**
Grants related to income		

—recognition in period matching related costs	Dr. Cash
	    Cr. Other income (government grant)
		Dr. Cash
		    Cr. Related expense

Grants related to assets		

—initial recognition	Dr. Cash
	    Cr. Deferred income
		Dr. Cash
		    Cr. PPE or other relevant asset

—subsequent periods	Dr. Deferred income Cr. Other income (government grant)	No specific entries; income recognized through reduced depreciation

Refer again to the example of Ocean Falls Company. The journal entries for the forgivable loan and the related production facilities are as follows (assume straight-line depreciation of the facilities over the 20-year useful life):

Exhibit 9-14	Comparison of journal entries for gross and net method of accounting for government grants				
	Gross method		**Net method**		

Initial recognition	Dr. PPE
	    Cr. Cash
		100m
		
			100m
				Dr. PPE
				    Cr. Cash
					100m
					
						100m

	Dr. Cash
	    Cr. Deferred income
		20m
		
			20m
				Dr. Cash
				    Cr. PPE
					20m
					
						20m

Subsequent periods	Dr. Deferred income Cr. Other income (government grant)	1m 	 1m	No specific entries for government grant; income recognized through reduced depreciation	

	Dr. Depreciation expense
	    Cr. Accumulated depreciation
		5m
		
			5m
				Dr. Depreciation expense
				    Cr. Accumulated depreciation
					4m
					
						4m

Thus, the effect on the statement of comprehensive income is $4 million in both cases. The difference is that the gross method shows $5 million depreciation expense separately from the $1 million income from the government grant, whereas the net method shows the net amount of $4 million in depreciation expense. Similarly, the balance sheet for the gross method shows a larger amount of assets and a partially off-setting liability, while the net method shows the net amount as an asset:

Exhibit 9-15	Comparison of balance sheet impact of gross and net method of presenting government grants for Ocean Falls Company

$ millions Dr. (Cr.)	Gross method					Net method		
End of year	PPE	Accumulated depreciation*	Net PPE	Deferred income (liability)†	Net PPE less deferred income	PPE	Accumulated depreciation‡	Net PPE
0	100		100	(20)	80	80	0	80
1	100	(5)	95	(19)	76	80	(4)	76
2	100	(10)	90	(18)	72	80	(8)	72
3	100	(15)	85	(17)	68	80	(12)	68
⋮								
18	100	(90)	10	(2)	8	80	(72)	8
19	100	(95)	5	(1)	4	80	(76)	4
20	100	(100)	0	(0)	0	80	(80)	0

*Straight-line depreciation of $100 million cost over 20 years equals $5 million per year.

†Straight-line amortization of $20 million government grant over 20 years equals $1 million per year.

‡Straight-line depreciation of $80 million over 20 years equals $4 million per year.

A reasonable question to ask at this point is, why does IFRS allow two different ways to present the same transaction? Neither presentation is more favoured than the other because there are good conceptual arguments for both presentations, as summarized in Exhibit 9-16:

Exhibit 9-16	Arguments for gross and net methods of presenting government grants	
Issue	**Gross method**	**Net method**
Financial statement items generally should not be offset against other items unless they are integrally related (IAS 1 ¶32).	A government grant is distinct from the incurrence of cost by an enterprise.	The enterprise acquires the asset or incurs the expense with full consideration of the cost reduction provided by government grants.
What is the cost of the acquired asset or expense incurred?	The actual purchase price or construction cost is the cost of the asset or expense.	In competitive markets, the costs of items include the effect of government grants, such that items with high subsidies have higher prices that partially or fully negate the effect of the subsidy. Thus, the cost of the item must include the government grant.[11]

While IFRS allows both approaches, enterprises will tend to favour the net approach because it results in lower liabilities and lower (i.e., better) leverage ratios. For instance, if Ocean Falls had no assets or liabilities other than the production facility and forgivable loan, then the gross method would result in a debt-to-assets ratio of $19 \div 95 = 20\%$ at the end of Year 1, while the net method would result in a ratio of zero.

 CHECKPOINT **CP9-6**

How should enterprises report government grants?

[11.] The effect of government subsidies increasing the prices of the subsidized items is technically called an "implicit tax." This topic is covered in some advanced courses on taxation.

4. Repayment of government grants

In some cases, enterprises will be unable to meet the stipulations of government grants, and consequently must repay the grant. Such situations would be accounted for as changes in estimate, with the usual prospective treatment *except* that the company also needs to recognize in expense the cumulative effect of the additional depreciation (net method) or corresponding income (gross method) that would have been recorded in the absence of the grant. This is an unusual application of the prospective method, and there is no clear rationale for why IAS 20 makes this exception for government grants (see IAS 20 paragraph 32). ASPE does not make this exception; instead, the normal prospective treatment applies, so that the change does not involve a cumulative adjustment for past depreciation (see ASPE Section 3800 paragraph 28).

For example, what if Ocean Falls' employment level falls below the minimum of 500 in the third and fourth years of the forgivable loan? Applying IFRS, the company would do the following:

- Step 1: Reclassify the $10 million portion of the loan that is repayable (gross method) or increase the cost of PPE by that amount (net method).
- Step 2: Record an expense for an amount equal to the additional expenses that it would have recorded in Years 1 and 2 had the grant been valued at $10 million instead of $20 million.
- Step 3: Change the amount of amortization/depreciation starting in Year 3. Exhibit 9-17 shows the effect of these changes.

If the company followed guidance in ASPE, it would complete only Steps 1 and 3 just described and omit Step 2.

| Exhibit 9-17 | Effect of Ocean Falls' forgivable loan becoming repayable during the third year |

$ millions Dr. (Cr.)	Gross method						Net method			
	Statement of comprehensive income			Balance sheet			Stmt of comprehensive income	Balance sheet		
End of Year	Depreciation expense	Other expense (income)	PPE	Accumulated depreciation	Deferred income	Net PPE less deferred income	Depreciation expense	PPE	Accumulated depreciation	Net PPE
0			100	0	20.0	80.0		80	0.0	80.0
1	5	(1.0)	100	(5)	(19.0)	76.0	4.0	80	(4.0)	76.0
2	5	(1.0)	100	(10)	(18.0)	72.0	4.0	80	(8.0)	72.0
Reclassify grant					10.0*			10		
Cumulative effect	1.0**		——	——	(1.0)		1.0**	——	(1.0)	
Subtotal			100	(10)	(9.0)	81.0		90	(9.0)	81.0
3	5	(0.5)†	100	(15)	(8.5)	76.5	4.5‡	90‡	(13.5)	76.5
4	5	(0.5)	100	(20)	(8.0)	72.0	4.5	90	(18.0)	72.0
⋮										

(*Continued*)

Exhibit 9-17	Continued									
18	5	(0.5)	100	(90)	**(1.0)**	**9.0**	4.5	90	**(81.0)**	**9.0**
19	5	(0.5)	100	(95)	**(0.5)**	**4.5**	4.5	90	**(85.5)**	**4.5**
20	5	(0.5)	100	(100)	**0.0**	**0.0**	4.5	90	**(90.0)**	**0.0**

Bold amounts reflect figures affected by the change in circumstances/change in estimates.

*Of the original $20 million forgivable loan recorded as deferred income, $10 million should be reclassified to government loan.

**Cumulative adjustment for past depreciation or corresponding income due to the need to repay forgivable loan: of the original $20 million loan, $10 million will be repayable, so $10m ÷ 20 years = $0.5m per year. For years 1 and 2, the cumulative adjustment is $0.5m × 2 = $1.0m negative income or additional expense.

†The company qualified for two years of forgiveness at $5 million per year for a total of $10 million. This amount amortized over 20 years is $0.5 million per year.

‡PPE cost of $100 million offset by $10 million of loans forgiven equals $90 million. This amount depreciated over 20 years is $4.5 million per year.

The journal entries corresponding to these three steps for the repayment of the government grant for Year 3 would be as shown in Exhibit 9-18.

Exhibit 9-18	Journal entries for Ocean Falls's forgivable loan becoming repayable				
Year 3	**Gross method**	**$ millions**	**Net method**	**$ millions**	

1. Reclassify $10m from grant to loan	Dr. Deferred income
	    Cr. Government loan
		10	10	Dr. PPE
				    Cr. Government loan
					10	10

2. Retroactively adjust for past depreciation	Dr. Other expense
	    Cr. Deferred income
		1	1	Dr. Depreciation expense
				    Cr. Accum. depreciation
					1	1

3. Current year depreciation	Dr. Depreciation expense
	Dr. Deferred income
	    Cr. Other income
	    Cr. Accum. depreciation
		5.0
		0.5
		
			0.5
			5.0
				Dr. Depreciation expense
				    Cr. Accum. depreciation
					4.5	4.5

THRESHOLD CONCEPT
QUALITY OF EARNINGS

H. POTENTIAL EARNINGS MANAGEMENT

The accounting for intangible assets, mineral resources, and government grants involves significant use of professional judgment, and the consequences are long lasting. As a result, there are significant incentives and opportunities for earnings management. The following discussion provides a sampling of the issues in these areas.

1. Capitalization of development costs

The criteria that need to be satisfied for the capitalization of development costs are quite strict, as discussed earlier in this chapter. However, that strictness is aimed at preventing overcapitalization. Undercapitalization is relatively easy because an enterprise only has to demonstrate that it does not satisfy any one of six criteria for capitalization. Clearly, this allows for understatement of earnings and assets. In addition, capitalization in one year after several years of no capitalization, even when the company could have capitalized but chose not to, could create an appearance of improved performance.

2. Estimated useful lives of intangible assets

As discussed in the last chapter, the useful life estimates for PPE can be biased. This is even more of an issue for intangible assets, because of the unique nature of many intangible assets. The length of time provided by legal protection is one guide, but the economic lives of intangible assets are inherently uncertain. How does one estimate the speed of advancement in knowledge and technology? This issue is not as important for internally developed intangibles, because of the strict criteria for capitalization, but is very important for acquired intangibles.

3. Determination of exploration success or failure

The successful efforts method of accounting for mineral exploration costs temporarily capitalizes such costs until the enterprise determines success or failure. Success results in continued capitalization with a transfer of the costs from exploration to development. Failure results in the costs being expensed. While it is clear what the accounting should be after the determination of success or failure, *when* that point is reached is not always clear. If an enterprise delays concluding that an exploration site is a failure, that delay could defer the recognition of the exploration expense from one fiscal year to the next.

I. SUBSTANTIVE DIFFERENCES BETWEEN IFRS AND ASPE

Issue	IFRS	ASPE
Mineral exploration costs	Only permits the successful efforts method. Costs of unsuccessful exploration are expensed via the impairment test.	Permits either successful efforts or full cost methods. The latter allows the capitalization of all costs in the extraction phase.
Repayment of government grants	Changes in circumstances resulting in the repayment of government grants should be accounted for as a change in estimate, but with a cumulative adjustment for additional past depreciation.	Changes in circumstances resulting in the repayment of government assistance should be treated prospectively.

J. SUMMARY

L.O. 9-1. Evaluate whether a cost qualifies for capitalization as an intangible asset or goodwill.

- Enterprises should capitalize the cost of acquired intangible assets and goodwill resulting from the purchase of another enterprise.
- Costs of internally developed intangibles should be expensed unless they are development costs that satisfy six criteria requiring the enterprise to demonstrate the existence of future benefits, the ability and intention of the enterprise to exploit the expected benefits, and reliable cost measurement.

L.O. 9-2. Evaluate whether a recognized intangible asset has an indefinite life or a finite life, and in the latter case, determine the appropriate useful life for amortization.

- An intangible asset has an indefinite life if the enterprise expects that the asset will maintain its level of benefits for the foreseeable future. Such assets are not amortized.
- Enterprises should amortize intangible assets with finite lives over their estimated useful lives. Generally, enterprises should assume nil residual values and use the straight-line method for amortization, unless they can provide reliable evidence to the contrary.

L.O. 9-3. Apply the specialized standards for the initial recognition of assets relating to mineral resource exploration and evaluation.

- Enterprises engaged in mineral exploration that apply IFRS must use the successful efforts method of accounting for costs associated with the exploration and evaluation of mineral resources. ASPE allows a choice between the successful efforts or full cost methods.
- The successful efforts method capitalizes only costs of mineral exploration and evaluation on projects where the enterprise has discovered mineral resources for which extraction is technically feasible and commercially viable.
- The full cost method capitalizes all costs of mineral exploration and evaluation regardless of the success or failure of the project.
- Development costs associated with mineral resources are generally capitalized.

L.O. 9-4. Apply the standards for accounting for government grants.

- Enterprises reasonably assured of receiving government grants should recognize the grant's fair value through profit or loss over the periods matching the related costs. Enterprises may present such grants using the gross or net method.

K. ANSWERS TO CHECKPOINT QUESTIONS

CP9-1: The three characteristics of an intangible asset are its lack of physical substance, non-monetary nature, and identifiability. Lack of physical substance separates intangible assets from tangible assets such as inventories. Non-monetary nature separates intangible assets from financial assets. Identifiability separates intangible assets from goodwill.

CP9-2: The key reason for the difference in treatment is the degree of subjectivity in measuring the future benefits of intangibles. For acquired intangibles, we can presume that the purchase price is a valid reflection of management's expectations of future benefits, so the purchase cost can be capitalized. In contrast, the costs incurred in developing intangibles internally do not closely correspond to expected future benefits, so strict criteria are required to limit the degree of management discretion in the capitalization of research and development costs.

CP9-3: Before proceeding with the amortization of intangible assets, it is necessary to ask whether the asset has a finite or indefinite life. We do not amortize intangible assets with indefinite lives.

CP9-4: Goodwill, specifically accounting goodwill, is not an intangible asset because it is not separately identifiable, which is one of three characteristics of an intangible asset. Instead, accounting goodwill is the excess of the purchase price of a business over the fair value of the identifiable assets.

CP9-5: IFRS permits the capitalization of exploration costs but not research costs because of the different amounts of uncertainty. While both activities aim to discover new knowledge, there is much less uncertainty about the value of knowledge regarding the existence of commercially viable quantities of minerals. There are well-developed markets for various mineral commodities, but no developed markets for research ideas.

CP9-6: Enterprises should record a government grant (i) using the income approach, (ii) when they are reasonably assured of satisfying the conditions of the grant, and (iii) using either the gross or net method.

L. GLOSSARY

development: The application of research findings or other knowledge to a plan or design for the production of new or substantially improved materials, devices, products, processes, systems, or services before the start of commercial production or use.

exploration for and evaluation of mineral resources: Activities involved in the search for mineral resources, including minerals, oil, natural gas, and similar non-regenerative resources, after the entity has obtained legal rights to explore in a specific area, as well as the determination of the technical feasibility and commercial viability of extracting the mineral resource.

fair value: The price that would be received to sell an asset or paid to transfer a liability in an orderly transaction between market participants at the measurement date.

full cost method (relating to mineral exploration): A method of accounting that capitalizes costs of mineral exploration and evaluation costs without regard to outcome; contrast with **successful efforts method.**

goodwill: The difference between the purchase cost of a business and the fair value of identifiable assets, net of liabilities.

historical cost: The actual cost of an asset at the time it was purchased; can also refer to amounts based on historical cost but adjusted by depreciation, amortization, or impairment.

impairment: The process of writing down the value of an asset to recognize declines in its fair value.

intangible asset: An identifiable, non-monetary asset without physical substance.

research: Original and planned investigation undertaken with the prospect of gaining new scientific or technical knowledge and understanding. Contrast with **development.**

successful efforts method (relating to mineral exploration): A method of accounting that capitalizes costs of mineral exploration and evaluation only if the outcome is successful (i.e., production is technically feasible and commercially viable); contrast with **full cost method.**

useful life: The period of time over which an asset is expected to be available for use by an entity, or the number of production units an enterprise expects to obtain from the use of an asset.

M. REFERENCES

Authoritative standards:

IFRS	ASPE
IAS 38—Intangible Assets	Section 3064—Goodwill and Intangible Assets
IFRS 3—Business Combinations	Section 1582—Business Combinations
IFRS 6—Exploration for and Evaluation of Mineral Resources	AcG 16—Oil and Gas Accounting—Full Cost
IAS 20—Accounting for Government Grants and Disclosure of Government Assistance	Section 3800—Government Assistance

*AcG = Accounting Guideline

MyLab Accounting   Make the grade with **MyLab Accounting:** The problems marked with a ⊕ can be found on **MyLab Accounting.** You can practise them as often as you want, and most feature step-by-step guided instructions to help you find the right answer.

N. PROBLEMS

 P9-1. Definition of intangible assets   **(L.O. 9-1)** (Easy – 5 minutes)

Identify whether the following items are intangible assets according to the definition under IFRS:

Item	Intangible asset (Yes / No)
a. Cash	
b. Costs of research and development	
c. Computer software applications	
d. A currency derivative	
e. Purchased goodwill	
f. Internally developed goodwill	
g. Trademark	

 P9-2. Definition of intangible assets   **(L.O. 9-1)** (Easy – 5 minutes)

IFRS defines intangible assets as lacking physical substance, being non-monetary in nature, and being identifiable. For the following items, identify the reason or reasons why the item is not considered an intangible asset.

Item	Has physical substance	Monetary	Not separately identifiable
a. Accounts receivable			
b. Investment in shares			
c. Cost of upgrading a computer system			
d. Purchased goodwill			
e. Development cost at a mineral site			

 P9-3. Capitalization of intangible assets   **(L.O. 9-1)** (Easy – 5 minutes)

Consider the following transactions for a new small business:
   a. Paid $500 as incorporation fees and to file articles of incorporation.
   b. Purchased accounting software for $200 and paid an accountant $800 to set up the accounting system.
   c. Spent $400 on dinner with the local mayor to develop goodwill.

Required:

For each transaction above, decide whether an intangible asset should be recorded for accounting purposes, and if so, at what value.

P9-4. Capitalization of intangible assets   **(L.O. 9-1)** (Easy – 10 minutes)

Below are several events or transactions:
   a. Paid the government $3,000,000 for the right to broadcast on a certain frequency for five years.
   b. Paid legal fees of $6,000,000 to successfully defend the company's exclusive right to a drug patent it had developed and registered. The drug is highly profitable, earning over $50,000,000 annually.
   c. Paid legal fees of $7,000,000 to defend the exclusive right to a drug patent the company had developed and registered. The court ruled the company did have the right but it was *not* exclusive. The drug is highly profitable, earning over $50,000,000 annually.

d. Paid $5,000,000 to an outside training firm to educate staff on the implementation and operation of a new decision support system.

e. Purchased a fleet of 100 taxis along with their taxi licences for $2,500,000 to operate in Winnipeg. The fair value of the cars is reasonably and reliably estimated to be $1,500,000.

Required:

For each case above, decide whether an intangible asset arose from the event and how it might be valued. Justify your recommendation.

P9-5.   Conceptual discussion—asset capitalization   (**L.O.** 9-1) (Easy – 15 minutes)

There is a range of items on the balance sheet that lack tangibility, including the following:
a. Short- or long-term accounts receivable
b. Prepaid expenses for rent or insurance
c. Deferred development expenses from R&D activities
d. Internally developed patents/copyrights, acquired patents/copyrights
e. Franchise rights held by a franchisee (e.g., an operator of a McDonald's restaurant)
f. Goodwill

Required:

Explain why each of these items can be recognized as an asset on the balance sheet.

P9-6.   Capitalization of intangible assets   (**L.O.** 9-1) (Medium – 10 minutes)

Consider the following items:
a. Lottery Company has a mailing list of people who have an established tendency to buy lottery tickets through the mail. It sold an exclusive copy of this mailing list for $500,000 to a charity. The charity can use the list for four years only. Lottery Company would like to set up a $500,000 asset for its copy of the list.
b. The charity noted above would like to set up the mailing list as an asset for $500,000. It plans to hold lotteries annually in the future.
c. A hockey team signed a three-year contract for a sensational new hockey player. The contract includes a $9,000,000 signing bonus.
d. A company acquired another firm that is developing several promising technologies. In putting the bid together on how much to pay for this company, a value of $10,000,000 was assigned to these in-process technologies.

Required:

For each case above, decide whether an intangible asset arose from the event and how it might be valued. Justify your recommendation.

 P9-7.   Capitalization of intangible assets   (**L.O.** 9-1) (Medium – 10 minutes)

Consider the following items:
a. A company has advanced $15,000,000 to an advertising agency to develop a branding strategy and advertisements for a new product it plans to launch next year.
b. A firm paid a $4,000,000 fine for infringement of environmental regulations in the past. If this fine had not been paid, the company would have been forced to shut down permanently.
c. A team is providing additional training to one of its most outstanding professional hockey players. This athlete is learning a new strategy for scoring. An outside consultant has been hired and additional ice time purchased. The overall cost of this training program is $500,000. The player has three years remaining on his exclusive contract with the team. Careful analysis by experts shows convincingly that this training will increase the team's likelihood of being successful during the season and playoffs. Currently there are thousands of unsold tickets, but over the season they will be sold if the team improves its standings in the league. Incremental revenue is cautiously estimated to be $1,000,000 per season from improved attendance.
d. Same as (c) above except currently all the seats for every game are sold out, and there are no plans to increase ticket prices.

Required:

For each item above, decide whether an intangible asset arose from the event and how it might be valued. Justify your recommendation.

P9-8.   Capitalization of intangible assets   (**L.O.** 9-1) (Medium – 20 minutes)

Public Company Ltd. is a large, publicly held company whose shares are actively traded on the Toronto Stock Exchange and that has earnings before tax of $300 million per year. The company has spent $15 million in the current year to improve the basic literacy skills of its employees (i.e., reading, writing, and arithmetic) to allow for the introduction of high-tech, computerized, automated equipment. Without this training, efficient and effective implementation of the new production process is unlikely to occur. Management of Public Company proposes that the entire amount be capitalized and amortized over the next 15 years (the estimated average remaining working life of the trained workers).

Required:

In answering this question, ignore specific accounting standards and refer to basic accounting principles and concepts to justify your positions.

a. Provide three arguments in support of expensing the $15 million in the year incurred.
b. Provide three arguments in support of capitalizing the $15 million.
c. Assuming these costs were capitalized, do you agree with the 15-year amortization period? Explain your conclusion.

 P9-9.   Acquired intangibles and bundled purchases

(**L.O.** 9-1, **L.O.** 9-2) (Medium – 20 minutes)

A professional sports team and its related items (including a stadium) were bought by an exceedingly wealthy investor and sports fan. The negotiated price was $175,000,000. Details of what was purchased and the agreed fair values are as follows:

Item	Fair value (in $ millions)
Stadium	45
Land	25
Cable television broadcasting contract	15
Player contracts	20
Spectators' leases on luxury viewing boxes	5
Product licensing agreements	14
Season ticket subscriber list	9
Contracts and commitments for use of stadium	10
The "team," imputed or residual value	32
Total	175

The team has been less than successful in its league and has been recording losses of $5,000,000 to $10,000,000 per year on its audited financial statements for the past five years. It was these losses that prompted the last owner to sell the team and related assets.

Required:

a. Of the $175 million purchase price, how much of it relates to tangible assets? What percentage of the purchase price relates to tangible assets?
b. Describe the nature of the future economic benefits associated with each of the intangible assets acquired. As an example, for the cable television broadcasting contract this would be the present value of the future payments expected from contracts for the broadcast of games on cable channels plus potential renewal contracts thereafter.
c. There are seven identified intangible assets noted on the list. Group these assets into three classes: those that are (i) easily measurable and identifiable; (ii) reasonably measurable and identifiable; and (iii) very difficult to measure and identify. For each group, what common quality or feature of these items distinguished their classification?
d. While all the items can be assigned a value, would you capitalize all these amounts? Explain your conclusion.

P9-10. Research and development costs (L.O. 9-1) (Easy – 10 minutes)

a. Why does IFRS make a precise distinction between research costs and development costs?
b. What unique features have led to the differing treatment between research and development costs? Why are these distinctions so fundamental to the treatment of these two classes of expenditures?

P9-11. Capitalization of development costs (L.O. 9-1) (Medium–20 minutes)

Six criteria must be satisfied for an expenditure to qualify as a development cost and be eligible for capitalization.

Required:

Identify each of the six criteria and explain why each one is essential for the classification of an expenditure to qualify as a development cost and therefore be eligible for capitalization. Continue by explaining why the absence of the identified criteria undermines the classification of the expenditure as an asset.

P9-12. Applying development cost capitalization criteria to tangible assets (L.O. 9-1) (Easy – 10 minutes)

IAS 38 paragraph 57 identifies six criteria for the capitalization of some development costs.

Required:

a. Are these criteria useful in deciding whether to capitalize an expenditure on a tangible asset, or are they relevant only for intangible assets? Explain your conclusion.
b. Assume a firm spends $20 million on a new machine that is subsequently used in production. Show how all six of these criteria would likely be met such that the machine would rightfully be treated as an asset with an assigned value of $20 million.

P9-13. Applying development cost capitalization criteria (L.O. 9-1) (Easy – 10 minutes)

The following are several independent transactions.
a. A telecommunications company sponsors $10 million of university research into whether quantum entanglement can be used as a method of instantaneous communication.
b. An automobile manufacturer spends $30 million on a project to improve the lithium-ion batteries used in its electric and hybrid vehicles. The project results in a 10% improvement in the capacity of each battery.
c. A social media company spends $5 million on a project examining the usage habits of its customer base in order to optimize the company's offering. This project is similar to a series of previous projects because the company is continuously engaged in improving its service.

Required:

Determine whether the expenditures should be capitalized as development costs or expensed.

P9-14. Applying development cost capitalization criteria (L.O. 9-1) (Medium – 15 minutes)

Listed below are several transactions that occurred during the year. All amounts in each case were capitalized to an account called "R&D costs." At the end of the year the company wants this account closed out and these amounts either expensed or capitalized to an asset account called "Development costs."
a. During the year, $3,000,000 was paid to staff to investigate whether a drug combination was effective in reducing a specific type of cancer in mice. Evidence showed it materially reduced the effects of this cancer on the mice.
b. During the year, $10,000,000 was paid to staff to investigate whether a drug combination was effective in reducing a specific type of cancer for terminally ill cancer patients. The trials were successful in a limited number of cases, but the results were mixed.

c. During the year, $30,000,000 was paid to staff to investigate whether a drug combination was effective in reducing a specific type of cancer. The drug was very successful in most cases. Market research shows a huge market for this drug. The board of directors has committed further resources to complete the development of this project and to market the drug.

d. During the year, $35,000,000 was paid to staff to investigate whether a drug combination was effective in reducing a specific type of cancer. The drug combination was very successful in most cases. Market research shows a huge market for this drug combination. The company is small and does not have adequate funds to complete the balance of the drug testing. The company is looking for a large pharmaceutical firm to take it over and complete the process.

Required:

Prepare the journal entry for each case. Where necessary or useful, explain your proposed treatment.

 P9-15. Applying development cost capitalization criteria  (**L.O.** 9-1) (Difficult – 15 minutes)

Listed below are several transactions that occurred during the year. All amounts in each case were capitalized to an account called "R&D costs." At the end of the year the company wants this account closed out and these amounts either expensed or capitalized to an asset account called "Development costs."

a. During the year, $45,000,000 was paid to staff in the research division of a pharmaceutical firm. Supplies used totalled $5,000,000. Rent on the research building totalled $2,000,000. Utilities totalled $1,000,000. Head office allocated $4,000,000 in general overhead to the research division. The total spent on research was therefore $57,000,000. The company is completing five different projects investigating whether five different drug combinations effectively reduce cancer in patients. One of the five drugs was very successful in most cases. Market research shows there is a huge market for this drug. The board of directors has committed resources to complete the project and market the drug; 15% of the total research staff are working on the successful drug combination.

b. During the year, $45,000,000 was paid to staff to investigate whether a drug combination was effective in reducing a specific type of cancer. The drug was very successful in most cases. Management is committed to continuing this project and has secured financial and technical resources to see if the drug will prove to be commercially viable.

c. Last year, $55,000,000 in costs were capitalized as all the development cost criteria were satisfied for a specific drug combination. During the current year a further $15,000,000 was spent that can be directly attributed to this drug's development. Near the end of the year a competitor surprisingly started selling a similar drug. The first-mover advantage of the competing drug seriously challenges the market usefulness and success of the drug this company is researching. Management and the board of directors are nonetheless financially and strategically committed to launching their drug in 18 months.

Required:

Prepare the journal entry for each case. Where necessary or useful, explain your proposed treatment.

P9-16. Finite and indefinite life intangibles (**L.O.** 9-2) (Easy – 5 minutes)

Identify whether the following items have finite or indefinite lives.

	Item	Finite life	Indefinite life
a.	Copyright		
b.	Trademark		
c.	Brand purchased from another company		
d.	Design for an office chair (industrial design)		
e.	Accounting goodwill		

P9-17. Amortization of intangibles　　　　　(**L.O.** 9-2) (Easy – 10 minutes)

Below are several intangible assets.
  a. A firm purchased a famous luxury good's brand name for $50,000,000. The firm has the exclusive right to use this name forever.
  b. Over the years, by consistently promoting its products' excellent features and high quality, a firm developed a reputation that is extremely high and sought-after in the luxury goods market. This year, the firm spent $40,000,000 advertising its brand in top-tier fashion magazines and at the top fashion shows around the world.
  c. A firm paid $5,000,000 for the right to use a song from a world-famous band as part of a product's promotion strategy. It has the exclusive right to use the song forever. The firm plans to run the advertising campaign for two years. The product's life cycle is conservatively estimated to be four years.
  d. A firm bought a patent for a drug for $60,000,000. The patent is good for 10 more years. The drug will likely command a large market share for six years and then other, newer drugs may make the drug redundant.

Required:

For each case suggest whether the item should be amortized. If amortization is recommended, what is the useful life that it should be amortized over? Provide justification for your recommendation.

 P9-18. Amortization of intangibles　　　　　(**L.O.** 9-2) (Medium – 10 minutes)

  a. Complete the table below to indicate whether the intangibles listed are amortizable assets as they have a finite life; are not amortizable as they have an indefinite life; or may be either depending on the nature of the agreement.
  b. Provide a brief explanation of the determining factors to be considered when deciding whether intangibles that are potentially either should be amortized or not.

	Finite life – amortize	Indefinite life – do not amortize	Potentially either
Goodwill			
Brand name			
Copyright			
Customer list			
Franchise			
Industrial design			
Licensing arrangement			
Patent			
Supply agreement			
Trademark			

 **P9-19.** Amortization of intangibles　　　　　(**L.O.** 9-2) (Medium – 15 minutes)

Below are several intangible assets.
  a. A firm paid $135,000,000 to acquire the eternal rights to distribute and collect any such royalties and other fees from the movie that won the Academy Award for best picture last year.
  b. A firm paid a very famous retired politician $1,000,000 for the publishing and distribution rights to her forthcoming autobiography. Several other politicians have written such books and most have been financially successful for the publisher.
  c. A firm bought the right to all future royalties from a famous rock band's entire music library for $8,000,000. The firm did a careful net present value analysis based on a 20-year time horizon, and a 20% cost of capital, to come up with the purchase price.
  d. A company paid $15,000,000 for the three-year exclusive privilege to have a famous sporting figure endorse and use its sports equipment. This contract entitles the company to renew the contract for a further four-year exclusive endorsement arrangement for a fixed fee of $10,000,000, due midway through the last year of the current contract.

Required:

For each case, suggest whether the item should be amortized. If amortization is recommended, what is the useful life that it should be amortized over? Provide justification for your recommendation.

 P9-20. Capitalization and amortization of intangibles

(**L.O.** 9-1, **L.O.** 9-2) (Medium – 10 minutes)

Axo Mirth Company paid $24 million to purchase a drug patent on April 1, 2019. At the date of purchase, the patent remained valid for another 12 years. In 2021, the company spent $4 million to successfully defend the patent, with the case closed on September 30, 2021. The company has a December 31 year-end.

Required:

Taking account of partial years, compute the amount of patent amortization for 2019, 2020, 2021, and 2022.

P9-21. Derecognition of intangibles

(**L.O.** 9-2) (Medium – 15 minutes)

Dudas Inc. sold a division of its business. Pertinent details follow:

Assets sold	Cost	Net book value	Fair value
Inventory	$ 100,000	$ 100,000	$ 110,000
Equipment	2,000,000	1,400,000	1,300,000
Patent	40,000	20,000	3,000,000
Trademark	10,000	10,000	55,000

Consideration received	
Cash	$2,000,000
Note receivable	$6,000,000 interest-free note payable in annual installments of $1,000,000. Market rate of interest 6.0% per annum.

Required:

Prepare the journal entry to record the sale of the assets assuming that Dudas Inc. uses the net method to record intangibles. Segregate the gain or loss on the sale into its component parts, for example, arising from the sale of the patent.

P9-22. Derecognition of intangibles

(**L.O.** 9-2) (Medium – 15 minutes)

Sandhawalia Inc. (SI) sold a division of its business in 2020 for $2,700,000 cash and a $1,800,000, 4% note repayable in annual installments of $495,882. The interest rate charged approximated the market rate of interest for similar transactions. Other pertinent details follow:

Tangible assets sold	Cost	Net book value	Fair value
Land	$1,000,000	$1,000,000	$2,100,000
Building and equipment	1,200,000	750,000	1,000,000

When SI acquired the division in 2013, $310,000 of the purchase price was allocated to goodwill. In 2014, the value of the cash generating unit was found to be impaired and $85,000 of goodwill was written off.

SI was granted a copyright in 2015 for original material produced by the company. The immaterial costs of obtaining the copyright were expensed at the time. In 2017, SI spent $240,000 to successfully defend the copyright. At the time of the defence, the remaining expected useful life of the copyright was 12 years. SI records a full year of depreciation expense in the year of origination but none in the year of disposal. The estimated fair value of the copyright at the time of the sale was $850,000.

Required:

Prepare the journal entry to record the sale of the assets assuming that Sandhawalia Inc. uses the net method to record intangibles. Segregate the gain or loss on the sale into its component parts, for example, arising from the sale of the land.

P9-23. Computing accounting goodwill   (**L.O.** 9-2) (Easy – 10 minutes)

Determine the amount of accounting goodwill or other amounts by completing the table below.

($000's)	Carrying value	Fair value
Cash	4,000	4,000
Accounts receivable	35,000	32,000
Inventories	45,000	41,000
Prepaid expenses	3,000	(c)
PPE, net	(a)	132,000
Intangible assets	1	25,000
Total assets	187,001	234,000
Total liabilities	(b)	115,000
Net assets	67,001	(d)
Purchase price		119,000
Accounting goodwill		(e)

 P9-24. Computing accounting goodwill   (**L.O.** 9-2) (Easy – 10 minutes)

Determine the amount of accounting goodwill or other amounts by completing the table below.

($000's)	Carrying value	Fair value
Cash	7,000	7,000
Accounts receivable	43,000	40,000
Inventories	(a)	31,000
Prepaid expenses	2,000	1,000
PPE, net	90,000	(c)
Intangible assets	0	21,000
Total assets	(b)	(d)
Total liabilities	92,000	105,000
Net assets	75,000	97,000
Purchase price		121,000
Accounting goodwill		(e)

P9-25. Computing accounting goodwill   (**L.O.** 9-2) (Easy – 10 minutes)

Determine the amount of accounting goodwill or other amounts by completing the table below.

($000's)	Carrying value	Fair value
Cash	(a)	9,000
Accounts receivable	55,000	47,000
Inventories	63,000	61,000
Prepaid expenses	0	0
PPE, net	167,000	112,000
Intangible assets	1	35,000
Total assets	294,001	(c)
Total liabilities	191,000	175,000
Net assets	(b)	(d)
Purchase price		(e)
Accounting goodwill		$ 6,000

P9-26. Economic goodwill   (**L.O.** 9-2) (Medium – 10 minutes)

Accounting goodwill is measured and identified as the difference between the amount paid for a firm and the net fair value of the assets and liabilities acquired. This accounting goodwill is an attempt to quantify economic goodwill.

Required:

    a. What is economic profit as it would be defined in finance or economics? Use a numerical example to illustrate the difference.

    b. Why is accounting net income not the same as an economist's determination of earnings, as measured from a shareholder's perspective?

 P9-27. Economic goodwill   (**L.O.** 9-2) (Medium – 20 minutes)

A company has accounting net income of $50 million and shareholders' equity of $350 million. Assume that carrying values for all assets and liabilities equal their fair value. Finally, assume the firm's risk-adjusted required rate of return for equity is 10%. What is the amount of economic profit earned in the year? If the company became more risky, would economic profit increase, decrease, or stay the same if accounting net income remained at $50 million? Explain your conclusion.

P9-28. Economic goodwill   (**L.O.** 9-2) (Medium – 10 minutes)

Consider the amount of economic goodwill implied in the following simplified example. Owners invested $6 million to start a firm with no debt financing. The firm purchased PPE for $5 million. It invested $1 million in net working capital. The owners hired management and workers and incurred other costs to operate the business. With total certainty and confidence, it is estimated that net income will be $900,000/year forever. Depreciation and amortization charges will be sufficient to replace depreciable assets as required. The risk-adjusted required rate of return for the owners is 13%.

Required:

Calculate the amount of economic goodwill implied by the above facts. What does this amount of economic goodwill mean? If this amount were negative, what would this mean?

 P9-29. Mineral exploration costs—IFRS 6 versus IAS 38   (**L.O.** 9-3) (Medium – 20 minutes)

Accounting standards provide flexibility in the treatment of mineral exploration costs. These costs can be expensed or capitalized at the discretion of the company (IFRS 6). Mineral exploration costs have similarities with research costs (IAS 38) but are afforded the privilege of being capitalized.

Required:

Identify and discuss four reasons for allowing mineral exploration costs to be capitalized despite the fact that they are similar to research expenditures (which must be expensed).

P9-30. Accounting for mineral resources   (**L.O.** 9-3) (Easy – 5 minutes)

Identify whether each of the following statements regarding the successful efforts method is true or false. Briefly explain.

Item	T/F	Explanation
a. Costs of mineral production are expensed.		
b. Costs incurred in the development phase are capitalized until production begins.		
c. Costs incurred in exploration are expensed as incurred.		
d. Costs incurred in exploration are capitalized until the feasibility of the mineral site has been determined.		

P9-31. Accounting for mineral resources **(L.O. 9-3)** (Easy – 10 minutes)

Kitimat Co. mines and produces aluminum. During 2018, the company explored two new sites and evaluated them for aluminum ore potential. By the year ended December 31, 2018, the sites remained in the evaluation stage. During 2019, evaluation of site Andromeda was completed and the site was deemed to have sufficient quantities of ore; consequently, development of the site began. However, site Bode was determined to have ore concentrations too low to be commercially viable. The following is the cost of exploration and evaluation incurred on the two sites:

	2018	2019
Andromeda	$2,380,000	$1,470,000
Bode	950,000	1,950,000
Total	$3,330,000	$3,420,000

Required:

Record the journal entries in 2018 and 2019 relating to the exploration and evaluation costs using the successful efforts method. Assume that Kitimat has a policy of capitalizing the costs of exploration and evaluation.

 P9-32. Accounting for mineral resources **(L.O. 9-3)** (Easy – 5 minutes) A·S·P·E

Consider the facts presented in problem P9-31.

Required:

Record the journal entries in 2018 and 2019 relating to the exploration and evaluation costs using the full cost method.

 P9-33. Accounting for mineral resources **(L.O. 9-3)** (Easy – 5 minutes)

Lillooet Company capitalized exploration and evaluation costs of $754,000. A further $1,348,000 was spent on tangible property, plant, and equipment to develop an oil well. Reserves at the beginning of the year were 240,000 barrels. During the year, the company produced 15,000 barrels of oil.

Required:

Compute the amounts for depletion and depreciation.

P9-34. Accounting for mineral resources **(L.O. 9-3)** (Easy – 5 minutes)

Cuprum Inc. specializes in copper mining and production. In 2019, the company spent $5,125,000 exploring a new site at Brass Mountain. In 2020, the site was determined to be viable and an additional $3,500,000 was spent on developing the site. The estimated extractable reserves were 5,000 tonnes. In 2021, the company began extraction from the site and produced 400 tonnes of copper.

Required:

Prepare the journal entries for Cuprum Inc. using IFRS. Assume that the company has a policy of capitalizing the costs of exploration and evaluation.

P9-35. Accounting for mineral resources **(L.O. 9-3)** (Medium – 5 minutes)

Petropower Corporation engages in the exploration, development, and production of oil and natural gas. In 2019, the company spent $8,500,000 exploring a new site in northern Alberta. The site was determined to be viable and an additional $4,000,000 was spent on developing the site. At the end of 2019, proven reserves were estimated to be 500,000 barrels-of-oil-equivalent (BOE). In 2020, the company began extraction from the site and produced 60,000 BOE. Estimated proven reserves at the end of 2020 were 540,000 BOE.

Required:

Prepare the journal entries for Petropower using IFRS. Assume that the company has a policy of capitalizing the costs of exploration and evaluation.

P9-36. Accounting for mineral resources   **(L.O.** 9-3) (Medium –15 minutes)

Graystone Resources explores, develops, and produces aluminum. The company has a December 31 year-end and follows IFRS. During 2018, the company engaged in the following activities.

- Alpha Hills: Produced and sold 30,000 tonnes of aluminum, leaving reserves of 170,000 tonnes at the end of 2018. The average selling price per tonne was $1,150 while operating costs were $15 million at Alpha Hills. Intangible exploration costs that remained unamortized at the end of 2017 amounted to $30 million, while undepreciated tangible development costs totalled $20 million.
- Beta Valley: Graystone spent the entire year and $8 million developing this mine site. However, it was not yet ready for production by the end of 2018.
- Chi Canyon: Graystone began exploring this area for aluminum deposits in April 2018. By December 31, the company had spent $5 million on geological tests and core samples. However, whether Chi Canyon will have sufficient concentrations of aluminum to be productive remains uncertain at year-end.
- Delta Ridge: Graystone also explored this area in July 2018. By November, the company had spent $2 million on geological tests and core samples. Due to results that did not look promising, the company ceased further exploration in the area.
- Research and development project: Graystone was also actively engaged in developing a new way to determine the existence of aluminum deposits in a particular location. In 2018, the company spent $12 million on this project. However, the company has not yet been able to demonstrate that its approach is any more effective than existing technologies.

Required:

Record the journal entries relating to the transactions. Assume that Graystone follows IFRS and has a policy of capitalizing the costs of exploration and evaluation. Ensure that the names of accounts clearly identify whether it is an asset or an expense.

A·S·P·E   **P9-37.** Accounting for mineral resources   **(L.O.** 9-3) (Medium – 15 minutes)

Consider the facts presented in problem P9-36.

Required:

Record the journal entries relating to the transactions assuming that Graystone Resources applies ASPE and chooses to use the full cost method.

 P9-38. Accounting for mineral resources   **(L.O.** 9-3) (Medium –20 minutes)

The following is the complete mineral exploration, development, and extraction history of Nikko Minerals Inc. Early in 2019, owners invested $50 million to start the company. No further financing was required. The company started explorations in 2019. However, all exploration efforts between 2019 and 2021 were unsuccessful. It was not until early in 2022 that Nikko found its one and only viable mineral deposit, which it immediately began to develop. It took two years to complete the development of the site and all the minerals were extracted in three years, starting in 2024.

Activity	Year	Amount
Exploration costs incurred and paid	2019	$5,000,000
Exploration costs incurred and paid	2020	$7,000,000
Exploration costs incurred and paid	2021	$8,000,000
Development costs incurred and paid	2022	$10,000,000
Development costs incurred and paid	2023	$11,000,000
Estimated units of mineral resource	2023	6,000,000 units
Revenues and cash collected from sale of ore @ $13/unit	2024	$26,000,000
Units of ore extracted	2024	2,000,000 units
Extraction costs incurred and paid	2024	$4,000,000
Revenues and cash collected from sale of ore @ $16/unit	2025	$40,000,000

(Continued)

Activity	Year	Amount
Units of ore extracted	2025	2,500,000 units
Extraction costs incurred and paid	2025	$5,000,000
Revenues and cash collected from sale of ore @ $8/unit	2026	$12,000,000
Units of ore extracted	2026	1,500,000 units
Extraction costs incurred and paid	2026	$3,000,000

Required:

Assume Nikko used the successful efforts method to account for exploration costs and complete the following table. Balance sheet amounts should be presented as at the year-end of December 31. Note also that when the ore is extracted, capitalized exploration and development (E&D) costs are amortized using a units-of-production depletion rate, which is the accumulated deferred costs divided by the estimated units of ore discovered (6,000,000 units).

($000's)	2019	2020	2021	2022	2023	2024	2025	2026
Cash								
Capitalized E&D costs								
Total assets								
Share capital								
Retained earnings (deficit)								
Total owners' equity								
Revenue								
Exploration costs								
Extraction costs								
Amortization of capitalized E&D costs								
Net income (loss)								

 P9-39. Accounting for mineral resources   (**L.O.** 9-3) (Medium – 20 minutes)

Refer to the facts in problem P9-38.

Required:

Assume Nikko uses the full cost method to account for exploration costs and complete the following table. Balance sheet amounts should be presented as at the year-end of December 31. Note also that when the ore is extracted, capitalized exploration and development (E&D) costs are amortized using a units-of-production depletion rate, which is the accumulated deferred costs divided by the estimated units of ore discovered (6,000,000 units).

($000's)	2019	2020	2021	2022	2023	2024	2025	2026
Cash								
Capitalized E&D costs								
Total assets								
Share capital								
Retained earnings (deficit)								
Total owners' equity								
Revenue								
Exploration costs								
Extraction costs								
Amortization of capitalized E&D costs								
Net income (loss)								

P9-40. Government grants  (Easy – 5 minutes)

Edelweiss Music Production received a government grant to subsidize the production of music with Canadian content (meaning using Canadian writers, singers, instrumentalists, etc., in the recordings). Based on activity in the current year, the company is eligible to receive $150,000 to offset labour costs, and $80,000 to offset equipment purchases.

Required:

Record the journal entries for the government grants using the gross method.

P9-41. Government grants (L.O. 9-4) (Easy – 5 minutes)

Refer to the facts in problem P9-40.

Required:

Record the journal entries for the government grants using the net method.

 **P9-42.** Government grants (L.O. 9-4) (Easy – 10 minutes)

Clear Energy is a builder of wind turbines that are used in electricity generation. To encourage the installation of wind turbines and the development of wind power technology, the provincial government has several programs in place that support the industry. In the current year, Clear Energy incurred the following costs that were potentially eligible for government subsidies:

　　i. The company spent $5 million on research and development (R&D); these costs are eligible for a 15% tax credit. The $5 million had been previously expensed.
　　ii. For each megawatt of wind power generating capacity installed, the government provides a subsidy of $200,000 to the utility. During the current year, Clear Energy installed 20 megawatts for its customers (utility companies).
　　iii. Clear Energy is eligible for a full tax rebate on sales tax normally levied on materials used in the construction of its turbine factory. This sales tax amounted to 7% of the materials cost of $20 million.

Required:

　a. Record the journal entries for the above transactions using the gross method for government grants.
　b. Record the journal entries for the above transactions using the net method for government grants.

P9-43. Government grants (L.O. 9-4) (Medium – 20 minutes)

Glanfield PEM Corp. (GPEM) designs and manufactures proton exchange membrane (PEM) fuel cell technology. Various levels of government have programs in place to encourage the development of solutions for a clean energy future. In 2018, GPEM took advantage of these incentives and constructed a new $4 million research facility. GPEM received the government subsidies listed below:

　　i. A $20,000 rebate of 2018's property taxes. GPEM had previously paid the full amount of the $80,000 assessment.
　　ii. A $200,000, interest-free, forgivable loan to assist with the construction of the research facility. The loan was repayable at $40,000 per annum with the first payment due January 1, 2020; however, installments were forgivable provided that the company was actively engaged in PEM research for the immediately preceding year.
　　iii. GPEM was eligible for a partial rebate of sales tax paid on materials used in the construction of the research facility. The rebate was for 4% of the materials cost of $3 million.

The estimated useful life and residual value of the research facility were 20 years and $400,000 respectively. GPEM prepared its financial statements in accordance with IFRS, and depreciated its long-term assets on a straight-line basis. Adjusting entries were only prepared at year-end.

Required:

Gross method

a. Prepare journal entries to record the receipt of the three government grants.
b. Prepare the journal entry(ies) arising from the above transactions for GPEM's December 31, 2020, year-end.

Net method

c. Prepare journal entries to record the receipt of the three government grants.
d. Prepare the journal entry(ies) arising from the above transactions for GPEM's December 31, 2020, year-end.

 P9-44. Government grants    **L.O.** 9-4) (Medium – 20 minutes)

Zachary Limited is planning to enlarge its factory in an economically challenged area of Canada. The federal, provincial, and municipal governments are all keen to assist the firm in making this investment successful and hopefully generate permanent and significant economic and social benefits for the region. Collaboratively, the three levels of government and the company have made the following commitments:

  i. The company will build a factory that will cost $100,000,000.
  ii. The city will donate the land for the factory, which has a fair market value of $5,000,000. Upon completing construction, the legal title of the land will be transferred to the company.
  iii. For the next five years, the city will reduce the property and municipal taxes the company has to pay on the new factory by 25%. It is estimated that these taxes would be $1,600,000 per year before the discount.
  iv. The federal government will provide a forgivable loan of $15,000,000 to assist in the financing of the factory. The loan will be forgiven over five years if the company employs at least 300 workers per year in the new factory.
  v. For the next five years, the provincial government will provide a training subsidy of $4,000,000/year to the company for the employment and skill development of local residents.
  vi The federal government will immediately give the company a $2,000,000 grant for having had a factory in the region for the past 10 years.
  vii. The federal government will give the company $10,000,000 in five years if it maintains an average workforce of 700 workers employed at the new factory. During the first year, an average of 313 workers were employed as the factory was in the start-up stage.

Required:

a. Prepare journal entries to record each of the seven items described above for the first year. Assume all estimates and expectations for the first year are correct and the factory is built and operational in the first year. Zachary Limited uses the net method to record grants. No depreciation will be accrued in the first year.
b. What will be the annual depreciation expense for the factory starting in year 2? Zachary Limited uses the net method to record grants. The factory is expected to have a useful life of 30 years (excluding the first year in the start-up phase) and no material residual value. The company uses the straight-line method for depreciation.
c. By how much was net income increased because of government assistance in the first year? For the second year, assume all continuing conditions to be eligible for the grants are met. How much was net income increased by in the second year? Ignore income taxes.

 P9-45. Government grants   **L.O.** 9-4) (Difficult – 50 minutes)

Due to concerns with climate change resulting from rising levels of carbon dioxide and other greenhouse gases, many companies and organizations have been seeking alternative energy sources (i.e., other than from burning hydrocarbons). To encourage the development of green technology in the manufacturing sector, the Ontario government introduced significant incentives for companies to engage in research, development, and production of equipment that produces power from alternative sources. The subsidies amount to 40% of research and development costs and 20% of production costs for the alternative power generators. Qualifying production costs include materials, labour, as well as capital costs required for facilities and equipment that are dedicated to the manufacture of the new alternative power generators. Production costs that do not meet this criterion do not qualify for the subsidy. Furthermore, a recipient of subsidies on capital costs can only retain the portion that is proportional to the length of time the plant or equipment is used for qualifying production; the remainder must be repaid to the government.

New Solar Inc. is a company that specializes in the production of equipment that captures solar energy. In response to the government incentives, the company spent $20 million on research in 2011 and a further $30 million in 2012 on developing a new solar technology. Out of the $30 million, the company had determined that $12 million satisfy the six criteria for the capitalization of development costs. In 2013, the company built a plant to produce the new solar power generators at a cost of $100 million and installed production equipment at a cost of $60 million. Production of the new power generators began in early 2014. The company expected the plant to be operational for 20 years and the manufacturing equipment to last 10 years, after which they would be replaced. The company expects the technology it has developed to remain competitive for 20 years. (All dollar amounts just presented do not include the effect of any government subsidies.)

Initially, demand for the new generators was modest, but picked up by 2016. However, by 2018, demand began to drop off drastically due to competition from other technologies. The government subsidy program was so successful that a number of different solar, wind, tidal, and other green power generation technologies had been developed and were economical. By early 2020, New Solar determined that it could no longer produce its solar power generators profitably and converted the plant to manufacture other products. As a result, it wrote off the balance of the development costs.

New Solar has a December 31 fiscal year-end, uses the straight-line method to depreciate/amortize its plant, equipment, and intangible assets, with a full year of depreciation/amortization recognized in the year of acquisition. The company uses the net method to record government subsidies.

Required:

a. Prepare three schedules, one each for plant, equipment, and intangible assets, showing the year-end cost, accumulated depreciation/amortization, and net carrying value covering the period from 2011 to 2020.

b. Record the journal entries for the transactions and events in 2011, 2012, 2013, 2014, and 2020.

A·S·P·E   **P9-46.** Government grants   (**L.O.** 9-4) (Difficult – 40 minutes)

Refer to the facts in problem P9-45.

Required:

Assume that New Solar is a private entity and applies ASPE. Prepare the schedules and journal entries as required in problem P9-45.

P9-47. Presentation, disclosure, and analysis   (**L.O.** 9-1, **L.O.** 9-2) (Medium – 15 minutes)

Refer to the 2016 financial statements for Canadian Tire Corporation in Appendix D.

Required:

a. What amount of intangible assets and goodwill did the company report on its December 31, 2016 balance sheet? What was the composition of this amount? Break it into the component parts as identified by the company and provide totals for finite life intangibles, indefinite life intangibles other than goodwill, and goodwill. What percentage of total assets did intangible assets and goodwill represent?

b. Using Canadian Tire's financial statements, and assuming nil residual values, estimate the average remaining useful life of the company's software and other finite intangibles at the end of 2016.

P9-48. Presentation, disclosure, and analysis (**L.O.** 9-1, **L.O.** 9-2) (Medium – 15 minutes)

Obtain the 2016 financial statements for Thomson Reuters Corporation from the company's website or from SEDAR (www.sedar.com).

Required:

a. How much in intangible assets did the company have at the end of 2016? How much in goodwill did the company have? What percentage of total assets did intangible assets and goodwill represent?
b. Using the balance sheet and income statement, and assuming negligible residual values, estimate the average remaining useful life of the company's computer software at the end of 2016. Estimate this figure also for "other identifiable intangible assets" other than computer software. Also do this for goodwill.
c. What do "other identifiable intangible assets" reported on the balance sheet represent?
d. Using the information in Note 16, estimate the average remaining useful lives of the four categories of "other identifiable intangible assets" at the end of 2016. What explains the difference between these estimates and that obtained for "other identifiable intangible assets" in part (b)?

P9-49. Presentation, disclosure, and analysis (**L.O.** 9-1, **L.O.** 9-2) (Medium – 15 minutes)

Obtain the 2016 annual report for TELUS Corporation either from the company's website or from SEDAR (www.sedar.com).

Required:

a. How much labour cost did the company capitalize into internally developed intangible assets?
b. How long is the average remaining useful life for software intangible assets at the end of 2016? Does this figure look reasonable?
c. What is the primary source of the company's intangible assets with indefinite lives? How does the company justify the use of indefinite lives (rather than finite useful lives)?

P9-50. Presentation, disclosure, and analysis (**L.O.** 9-3) (Medium – 10 minutes)

Obtain the 2016 financial statements for Canadian Natural Resources Ltd. either from the company's website or from SEDAR (www.sedar.com).

Required:

a. In 2016, how much in mineral exploration and evaluation costs did the company incur?
b. As a result of mineral exploration and evaluation projects that were deemed to be successful in 2016, how much was transferred from the asset account for mineral exploration and evaluation costs to property, plant, and equipment?

O. MINI-CASES

CASE 1
Capitalization of intangible assets
(40 minutes)

How we account for intangible assets is a controversial issue. There are many who adamantly support the treatment of expenditures on non-monetary intangibles as assets. Others strongly oppose this approach and think such expenditures should be expensed and not capitalized on the balance sheet.

Required:

a. Identify and discuss the reasons why many individuals oppose the capitalization of expenditures related to non-monetary intangibles.
b. Identify and discuss the reasons why many individuals support the capitalization of expenditures related to non-monetary intangibles.
c. If you were the chief financial officer of a large public company with a long history of strong ethical management, would you be inclined to support or oppose capitalizing expenditures on potential intangible assets? Explain your conclusion.
d. If you were the chief financial officer of a small, recently listed high-tech public company, would you be inclined to support or oppose capitalizing potential intangible asset expenditures? Explain your conclusion.
e. If you were an external auditor, how would you prefer management treat potential intangible asset expenditures? Explain your conclusion.

CASE 2
Creative Architects and Engineers
(30 minutes)

Since 1980, Creative Architects and Engineers (CAE) has been providing high-quality design services to property developers, city governments, and others in need of large-scale designs for office buildings, condominiums, art galleries, concert halls, bridges, train stations, and so on. The company has been successful largely due to the ability of its staff to generate designs that are functional yet attractive, and cost-effective while environmentally sustainable. The company has five office locations with a total staff of about 500 and is publicly listed.

Top management has always been attuned to the need to foster and maintain the creativity and expertise of its staff, as that is the key to the company's success. To stay at the forefront of human resource management practices, the company has recently introduced a number of enhancements:

- The company has undergone a complete review of its workplace to assess the ergonomics of its office furniture and fixtures. As a result of this review, the company spent $2 million to replace existing equipment that has a carrying value of $800,000. The company rents the office space using long-term leases, with typical lease terms of 10 years.
- Following the practices of other creative companies such as Google and Electronic Arts, the company opened up an area in each office location for relaxation/entertainment. This space includes sound isolation rooms, television sets, computer game consoles, wireless headsets, and tables for pool, foosball, and air hockey. The modification to the offices cost $1.5 million. Management believes these facilities contribute to the creative process of its staff.
- The company also implemented a health and wellness program. This program provides a reimbursement of up to $2,000 per employee toward membership fees at fitness centres and purchase of recreational equipment and clothing. Management estimates that this program benefits the company $1,500 per employee in terms of the reduction in the number of sick days alone, not counting the additional benefits of higher productivity.
- CAE encourages its staff to engage in professional development and continuing education by providing tuition reimbursements of up to $10,000 per year. Employees must remain employed at the company for two subsequent years; otherwise, the employee must repay the funds to CAE.

Required:

a. Discuss the accounting issues related to the above enhancements to CAE's human resource practices.

b. Compare the accounting treatments that you find appropriate for the four programs. Evaluate the accounting standards that led to those similarities and differences.

Autotech Corp. (Autotech) is a federally incorporated public company formed in 2009 to manufacture and sell specialty auto products including paint protection and rust proofing. By 2013, Autotech's board of directors felt that the company's products had fully matured and that it needed to diversify. Autotech aggressively sought out new "concepts," and in November 2013 it acquired the formula and patent of a synthetic motor lubricant (Synlube) and 25% of the outstanding voting shares of JDP Ltd. (JDP) for $400,000 cash. The formula was developed by JDP, a company then owned 100% by Jack Douglas. Although some members of the board of directors felt and continue to feel some concern about Mr. Douglas's continuing ownership of JDP, Mr. Douglas became the president of Autotech in February 2014.

Synlube is unlike conventional motor oils. Its innovative molecular structure accounts for what management believes is its superior performance. Although it is more expensive to produce and therefore has a higher selling price than its conventional competitors, management believes that its use will reduce maintenance costs and extend the life of the equipment in which it is used.

Autotech's main competitor is a very successful multinational conglomerate that has excellent customer recognition of its products and a large distribution network. To create a market niche for Synlube, management is targeting commercial businesses in western Canada that service vehicle fleets and industrial equipment.

Autotech's existing facilities were not adequate to produce Synlube in commercial quantities. Management believed that there was a growing market for this product in western Canada, and in June 2015 Autotech commenced construction of a new blending plant in Alberta. After lengthy negotiation, it received a $900,000 grant from the provincial government. The terms of the grant require Autotech to maintain certain employment levels in the province over the next three years or the grant must be repaid. The new facilities became operational on December 1, 2015.

In addition to the grant monies received, Autotech has financed its recent expansion with a term bank loan. Management is considering a share issue later in 2016 to solve the company's cash flow problems. Autotech's March 31, 2016, draft balance sheet is provided in Exhibit I.

Although they had been with the company since its inception, Autotech's auditors have just resigned. It is now April 22, 2016. You, a CA, and a partner in your firm met with Jack Douglas to discuss the services your firm can provide to Autotech for the year ended March 31, 2016. During your meeting, you collected the information contained in Exhibit II.

As you return to the office, the partner tells you that he is interested in having Autotech as an audit client. Before making a decision, however, he wants a memo from you covering in detail the accounting and audit issues that you see arising from this potential engagement.

Required:

Prepare the memo to the partner.

CASE 3
Autotech
(60 minutes)[12]

[12.] Reprinted from Uniform Final Examination, 1996 with permission from Chartered Professional Accountants of Canada, Toronto, Canada. Any changes to the original material are the sole responsibility of the author (and/or publisher) and have not been reviewed or endorsed by the Chartered Professional Accountants of Canada.

Exhibit I	Autotech Corp. draft balance sheet		
As at March 31 (in $000's)		**2016 (Unaudited)**	**2015 (Audited)**
Current assets			
Accounts receivable		213	195
Inventories		1,650	615
Prepaid expenses		45	30
		1,908	840
Non-current assets			
Property and equipment		2,120	716
Investment in JDP Ltd.		1	1
Deferred development costs		1,979	686
Patent		835	835
Total assets		6,843	3,078
Current liabilities			
Bank indebtedness		1,225	462
Accounts payable		607	476
Current portion of long-term debt		400	98
Advances from shareholders		253	—
		2,485	1,036
Non-current liabilities			
Long-term debt		3,114	650
Total liabilities		5,599	1,686
Share capital		2,766	2,766
Deficit		(1,522)	(1,374)
Total shareholders' equity		1,244	1,392
Total liabilities and shareholders' equity		6,843	3,078

Exhibit II	Information collected by CA

1. The "Capital assets—new plant" account in the general ledger has increased by $1.435 million during the year. An analysis of this increase is as follows:

Land	$ 200,000
Building, net of grant of $900,000	416,000
Advertising (promotion of Synlube product)	125,500
Relocation costs (moving plant management)	216,300
Equipment	319,200
Legal fees (Synlube patent-infringement lawsuit)	67,400
Labour costs (amounts paid to employees during training period)	90,600
	$1,435,000

As no significant orders of Synlube have been received to date, no amortization has been charged this year.

(*Continued*)

Exhibit II	**Continued**

2. Autotech has commenced a lawsuit against its major competitor for patent infringement and industrial espionage. Management has evidence that it believes will result in a successful action and wishes to record the estimated gain on settlement of $4 million. Although no court date has been set, legal correspondence shows that the competitor intends "to fight this action to the highest court in the land."

3. Deferred development costs represent material, labour, and subcontract costs incurred during 2014 and 2015 to evaluate the Synlube product and prepare it for market. Almost 80% of the subcontract costs were paid to JDP. Autotech has not taken any amortization to date but thinks that a period of 20 years would be appropriate.

4. Jack Douglas contacted your firm after Autotech's former auditors resigned. The previous auditors informed Mr. Douglas that they disagreed with Autotech's valuation of deferred development costs and believed that the balance should be reduced to a nominal amount of $1.

5. Royalties of $0.25 per litre of Synlube produced are to be paid annually to JDP.

6. Inventory consists of raw materials, semi-processed liquids, and finished goods. Approximately 60% of the value of inventory relates to Synlube production at the new plant. The fourth-quarter inventory count resulted in a significant book-to-physical adjustment. Management thinks that the standard costs used may have caused the problem.

7. The $3.514 million term bank loan is secured by a floating charge over all corporate assets.

8. Autotech has incurred substantial losses during the past three fiscal years.

CASE 4
Air Technologies
(90 minutes)[13]

You have recently been hired by International Products Inc.'s (IPI) internal audit department and are sitting in your office planning for your upcoming meeting with the head of internal audit. It is January 20, 2014. You just returned from a week visiting Air Technologies Ltd. (Air), IPI's newest subsidiary. Air has been part of the IPI group of companies since late in 2012 and up to now had never been visited by internal auditors. As is standard practice at IPI, the internal audit department visits the subsidiary companies once a year to check on the functioning of the accounting systems and internal controls, and to make sure that policies and procedures are being adhered to. This was your first assignment and you thought it was a tough one because you have to prepare a report not only addressing the internal audit findings, but also discussing the financial reporting issues you found related to IFRS.

As you sit down to write your report, you once again review the material gathered in your investigation. Exhibit I is a brief history of Air; Exhibit II contains notes from your meeting with Louis Shayne, Air's president; Exhibit III is a summary of the development costs incurred during 2013; Exhibit IV provides Air's financial statements for the year ended December 31, 2013; and Exhibit V contains other information you gathered.

[13] Reprinted from Uniform Final Examination, 2003 with permission from Chartered Professional Accountants of Canada, Toronto, Canada. Any changes to the original material are the sole responsibility of the author (and/or publisher) and have not been reviewed or endorsed by the Chartered Professional Accountants of Canada.

| Exhibit I | Brief history of Air Technologies Ltd. (Air) |

Louis Shayne is an amateur inventor. He developed a new technology for air cleaning that is especially useful for spaces that do not have central forced air heating and cooling. The technology is more effective at removing airborne pollutants than any existing technology. Air was formed in 2009. Louis's goal for the company was to develop and market a new method for residential and commercial air cleaning. In 2011, Louis built and tested commercial prototypes for the new technology, which performed very well under difficult conditions. Because of the increase in asthma in children and the perceived decrease in air quality in many parts of Canada, Louis knew his technology would be very successful.

While Louis was convinced that the product would be successful, he did not have the resources to take the project any further. He was unsuccessful in obtaining financing from banks or venture capitalists and could not find anyone interested in purchasing an equity stake in Air. Louis was about to give up when, in November 2011, he had a chance meeting with the chief executive officer of IPI, Fred Irving, at a local meeting of the asthma association. Mr. Irving is the father of two children who have severe asthma and Louis was demonstrating his product. Mr. Irving took an immediate interest. Louis loaned Mr. Irving his prototypes; Mr. Irving was very pleased that they helped improve his children's symptoms. Based on his personal experiences with the prototypes, Mr. Irving saw that the product had significant market potential and agreed to get involved in developing and marketing it.

In late 2012, Louis sold all the outstanding shares in Air to IPI for $250,000. IPI agreed to finance the remaining research and development necessary to complete the product and bring it to market. The sale agreement required that Louis remain as president of Air until December 31, 2013, to complete development of the product and launch it. Mr. Irving believed that Louis's knowledge was vital for the product's success. Louis's agreement with IPI stipulates that he receive a salary of $50,000 per year. In addition, he is to receive a bonus of $1 million if (i) the product is successfully brought to market, (ii) at least 10,000 units of the product are sold at a minimum average price of $65 per unit by December 31, 2013, and (iii) Air generates a profit for the year ended December 31, 2013.

| Exhibit II | Notes from meeting with Louis Shayne |

Louis explained that, from the time IPI acquired Air until the end of 2012, his efforts were directed toward refining the product. During that time, $300,000 was spent on improvements to the product and the full amount was expensed. Air reported a loss for tax purposes of $424,000.

In early 2013, everything came together. All the glitches with the product were solved, and testing results were consistent and met the specifications. Sure that the product would be successful, Louis then turned all of his attention to selling the product.

In January and February 2013, marketing studies and production feasibility studies were carried out. In late April, Louis made a presentation to Fred Irving and received commitment of the funds required to get production underway. The manufacturing process is quite straightforward and relatively inexpensive, requiring only about $800,000 for manufacturing and assembly equipment. Despite a number of initial problems, the first full production run occurred in July. The first 900 units produced did not meet specifications and could not be shipped. The first shipment of units to customers was in August. Louis explained that the 900 units with specification problems are currently in inventory and he expects that, when time permits, they will be repaired and sold.

Louis said that he agreed to stay on with Air for an additional three months (until March 31, 2014) by which time a new president for Air should be hired. He said that Fred Irving did all he could to convince him to stay on longer but Louis explained that he is an inventor at heart, not a manager, and that, with the right president, Air would continue its success.

(Continued)

Exhibit II	Continued

Louis was very satisfied with initial demand for the product. He had arranged contracts with a number of national and local distributors, and early feedback from the distributors was favourable. However, Louis thought that the initial orders made by the distributors were unrealistically low and that they would quickly run out of inventory, which would cost Air significant sales because customers might buy a competitor's product.

Louis thinks that market penetration is key and he is not prepared to miss any sales. As a result, he often shipped significantly more units to distributors than ordered. While Louis assured any distributors that objected that they would see that the extra units were merited, he allowed them to delay payment until six months after delivery. At that time, they have to pay in full or return any unsold units shipped in excess of the initial amount ordered. Louis's first priority is getting the product out the door. Once orders are sent to the shipping department, Louis wants the goods shipped within a day or two. Louis keeps production operating at full capacity to ensure there is enough inventory in place to meet the anticipated demand.

Louis acknowledged that paperwork was a bit sloppy. Because of the strong demand for Air's product, Louis had little time to pay attention to administrative tasks, devoting his time instead to selling, and to making sure production was kept on schedule and orders were shipped on time. He pointed out that IPI had kept Air on a fairly tight budget and, as a result, he was understaffed in the office.

Louis expects the paperwork to flow better once everyone gets used to the computer system and its glitches are fixed. The computer system was mandated by IPI and was installed by a small company recommended by IPI. The system was installed in May 2013. Louis complained that the computer company simply showed up one day, installed the system without any discussion of what was wanted or needed, and then left. It was never heard from again, except to render the bill.

Exhibit III	Summary of development costs during 2013
Costs incurred from January to March 2013	
Marketing surveys	$ 65,000
Consultant's report on air quality issues	80,000
Search costs for production facility	70,000
Feasibility study for production facility	92,000
Costs incurred from April to July 2013	
Cost of setting up production facility	37,000
Training of production staff	48,000
Costs incurred from August to December 2013	
Production cost overruns during first three months of production	97,000
Selling, marketing, and promotion costs	118,000
Total development costs incurred	$607,000

Exhibit IV	Extracts from internal financial statements of Air Technologies Ltd.

Balance sheet as at December 31	2013
Current assets	
Cash	$ 75,000
Accounts receivable	475,000
Inventories	303,620
Prepaid expenses	35,000
	888,620
Property, plant, and equipment	767,650
Development costs	607,000
Total assets	$2,263,270
Current liabilities	
Accounts payable	$ 302,000
Loan from parent company	2,500,000
	2,802,000
Share capital	278,670
Deficit	(817,400)
Total shareholders' equity (deficiency)	(538,730)
Total liabilities and shareholders' equity	$2,263,270

Income statement For the year ended December 31	2013
Revenue (Note 1)	$ 770,352
Cost of goods sold	295,352
Gross margin	475,000
Amortization of equipment (Note 2)	32,000
Selling, general, and administrative costs	201,000
Income before income taxes	242,000
Income taxes	75,400
Net income	$ 166,600

Note 1: Air recognizes revenue when merchandise is shipped to customers. This method is consistent with IPI's standard accounting policy for other manufactured products.

Note 2: Amortization of the equipment began in August 2013 and is calculated on a straight-line basis over 10 years.

Exhibit V	Other findings

Air shipped the first units to customers in August 2013. Total units shipped during 2013 were 11,672. No other products are produced by Air.

    During 2013, Air shipped 500 units as demonstration models to potential customers, and to a variety of lung and asthma associations. The units were treated as sales with a selling price of $0.

    Discussion with the accounts receivable clerk found considerable dissatisfaction with Air's computer accounting system. When the clerk tried to reconcile the receivables list to the general ledger, she found that the listing sometimes had the same invoice number assigned to more than one shipment. The clerk said that she knows "for a fact" that different numbers were assigned but the computer seems to have its own ideas.

(Continued)

| Exhibit V | Continued |

She also complained about difficulties with the monthly bank reconciliation, explaining that the accounting system keeps reporting as outstanding cheques that have cleared the bank. "No matter how hard I try, I can't figure out how to get those cheques off the computer-generated list. Now when I do the bank reconciliation, I ignore the outstanding cheque list generated by the system because I have no confidence in it. Instead, I rely on a manual record that I keep."

The accounts payable clerk complained that many of the outstanding payables balances are not true payables but that they cannot be removed from the system. He explained that Air uses a purchase order system. He thinks that the problem might be that the receiver enters the receipt of the back-ordered items as a new-order receipt instead of going back to the original order. When the accounts payable clerk tried to fix the problem using the "over/under shipment" menu item, access was denied. So he has had to leave the old balances on the aged accounts payable report. The accounts payable clerk is frustrated because he is sure that there is an easier way to handle the shipments but cannot figure it out.

Other members of Air's staff complained that they were not consulted in the development of the computer system and that they did not receive any training. It seemed they were supposed to figure it out for themselves. Some people complained that the system does not produce the information they need to do their jobs properly, generating useless reports instead. Some of these people have figured out how to circumvent the system to obtain the information they need.

From discussions with the shipper, there appear to be significant problems in the shipping department. The shipper seems overworked and extremely dissatisfied with the way shipping is managed. The shipper has been involved in shipping for 15 years and has never seen a mess like Air's. It is virtually impossible for him to keep up with the orders that have to be shipped. "I'd say I'm two to three weeks behind getting orders out." The shipper said that he could use more help in the department, but he could probably get the job done if Louis did not get involved in what gets sent out. "It seems he's down here every day telling me to add a few more units to this order and to that order. The shipping documents are almost useless. I'd say that most orders go out of here with a different number of units than what is recorded on the shipping documents I receive from sales. In fact, they're so useless I don't even bother filing them anymore. I just toss them into that box in the corner."

A review of the accounting system showed that the billing process is initiated as soon as an order is confirmed and sent to the shipping department. Trade receivables and sales are recorded at that time.

Inventory records are perpetual. The inventory is reduced when goods are shipped. The shipper maintains a log of units shipped and the log is used to update the inventory records each day.

Air operates in a rented facility. The production department occupies about 45% of the building, storage 25%, and offices and administration the rest. The full amount of rent is treated as a product cost and included in inventory. IPI's accounting policies state that only the rental cost associated with production should be inventoried. Air also includes the cost of office staff, managers, and production supervisors in the cost of inventory.

CASE 5
Clare Cherry Cola
(30 minutes)

Clare Cherry Cola (CCC) is a privately held soda company specializing in the manufacturing and distribution of soda across Canada. CCC is a fairly new entrant to the market, incorporated in 2008, but it has been doing well in the last few years, expanding to new markets across Canada and showing strong growth in current markets.

For the current fiscal year of 2019, the company decided to hire a Big Four accounting firm to review its financial statements. While doing preliminary audit work, the auditors were looking for more information concerning several intangible accounts and were informed of the following:

Note 1: Brand name is an intangible asset on the balance sheet for $300,000. The cost was related to legal and other trademark fees of the brand name and logo. The company claimed an indefinite useful life on the asset and therefore no amortization has been recorded so far.

Note 2: In 2019, the company decided to create a sophisticated client list with detailed information reported on each client. The company capitalized the client list as an intangible asset because there were future benefits associated with the asset. The list was valued at $50,000 and no amortization has been recorded so far.

Note 3: The company was also heavily involved in the research and development of new soda flavours. In 2019, the company capitalized $150,000 in research costs and $200,000 in product development costs.

Note 4: At the end of 2019, the company was granted a patent on the new soda flavour "strawberry-kiwi" that it had developed. The patent was valued at $50,000 and was amortized over 10 years, the legal life of the patent.

Note 5: The company also had internally generated goodwill valued at $100,000 on the balance sheet. The amount of goodwill was determined based on the company's excellent customer service, social responsibility, and increasing market share.

Required:

a. Suppose you are the auditor for CCC. Comment on CCC's accounting policies for the following intangible assets:

    i. Brand name

    ii. Client list

    iii. Research and development costs

    iv. Patent

    v. Goodwill

b. Discuss the earnings management potential with regard to intangible assets.

c. Do you believe that companies should capitalize intangible assets? Explain your position.

CHAPTER 10

Applications of Fair Value to Non-Current Assets

CPA competencies addressed in this chapter:

1.1.2 Evaluates the appropriateness of the basis of financial reporting (Level B)
b. Methods of measurement

1.2.1 Develops or evaluates appropriate accounting policies and procedures – Ethical professional judgment (Level B)

1.2.2 Evaluates treatment for routine transactions (Level A)
d. Property, plant, and equipment
f. Depreciation, amortization, impairment, and disposition/ derecognition

1.2.3 Evaluates treatment for non-routine transactions (Level B)
a. Uncommon capital assets (investment properties, biological assets)
c. Assets held for sale and discontinued operations

1.3.2 Prepares routine financial statement note disclosure (Level B)

1.4.1 Analyzes complex financial statement note disclosure (Level C)

5.4.1 Determines the value of a tangible asset (Level C)

5.4.2 Applies appropriate methods to estimate the value of a business (Level C)

5.4.3 Estimates the value of an intangible asset (Level C)

LEARNING OBJECTIVES

After studying this chapter, you should be able to:

L.O. 10-1. Apply the revaluation model of accounting for non-current assets.

L.O. 10-2. Evaluate whether a non-current asset should be tested for impairment, whether the asset is impaired, and the extent of impairment.

L.O. 10-3. Account for the impairment of different types of non-current assets.

L.O. 10-4. Apply the specialized standards for the recognition and measurement of assets relating to investment properties and agricultural activities.

L.O. 10-5. Apply the accounting standards relating to non-current assets held for sale and discontinued operations.

LVMH Moët Hennessy–Louis Vuitton (www.lvmh.com, Paris Stock Exchange ticker: MC) is a global collection of some 60 luxury brands with sales of €29 billion. Among the company's brands are Moët & Chandon, maker of Dom Pérignon, possibly the world's most recognized Champagne; Christian Dior perfume; TAG Heuer watches; De Beers diamonds; and, of course, fashion label Louis Vuitton.

In the company's 2016 financial statements, LVMH reported €1,077 million in "revaluation reserves" on its balance sheet for vineyard land, an increase of €113 million from the prior year. The company also reported that its gross goodwill value of €12,083 million had impairment of €1,682 million, leaving net goodwill of €10,401 million.

What is a revaluation reserve? What causes the balance to increase or decrease in a year? What is impairment and when do companies record impairment? How does a revaluation to decrease an asset's value differ from an impairment? How do companies determine the amount of revaluation or impairment?

Separately, LVMH disclosed that it reports its €855 million of investment property at cost. What is "investment property" for accounting purposes, and what alternatives are there to report these assets?

The production of Champagne and other wine products of course requires the cultivation of vines. Plants and livestock involved in agriculture are significant biological assets that change in value over their lifespans, unlike most other types of assets. How do companies like LVMH account for such biological assets?

THRESHOLD CONCEPT
CONCEPTUAL FRAMEWORK

The previous two chapters focusing on non-current assets discussed accounting using the historical cost basis. Another alternative is the revaluation method using fair values. While historical figures are reliable, they potentially provide irrelevant information if the prices of assets have changed significantly due to changing market conditions, technological change, inflation, or myriad other factors. For this reason, IFRS permits the alternate fair value basis for many non-current assets: fair values better reflect current conditions and therefore provide information that is more relevant to users. However, ASPE does not permit revaluations. For private enterprises, fair values have limited usefulness because the user base is limited to the private owners and their bankers. Furthermore, the historical cost method is simpler for the preparer and more readily understood by the reader.

At the same time, the qualitative characteristic of faithful representation from the IFRS Conceptual Framework and the conservatism concept in ASPE suggests that balance sheet figures should not overstate the value of assets. Consequently, firms need to assess non-current assets for impairment to determine if their carrying values need to be written down due to declines in the assets' worth. This impairment assessment may be necessary even if an enterprise follows the revaluation model, because the values used for impairment assessments can significantly differ from those used for revaluation. Thus, impairment needs to be assessed whether an enterprise follows the cost model or the revaluation model.

This chapter first discusses the revaluation alternative to the cost model, followed by impairment. In addition, fair values are important in the accounting for several specific categories of non-current assets, including investment property, agricultural assets, and non-current assets that an enterprise expects to sell in the near future; the third to fifth sections of this chapter address these topics.

A. REVALUATION MODEL OF MEASURING CARRYING VALUES SUBSEQUENT TO INITIAL ACQUISITION

As an alternative to the historical cost model, enterprises can choose to apply the revaluation model to measure the carrying values of non-current assets such as property, plant, and equipment (PPE) and intangible assets. The **revaluation model** restates the carrying value of an asset to its **fair value** on the date of revaluation. For example, IAS 16 provides the following guidance for PPE:

> ¶29   An entity shall choose either the cost model in paragraph 30 or the revaluation model in paragraph 31 as its accounting policy and shall apply that policy to an entire class of property, plant, and equipment.
>
> ¶30   After recognition as an asset, an item or property, plant, and equipment shall be carried at cost less any accumulated depreciation and any accumulated impairment losses.
>
> ¶31   After recognition as an asset, an item or property, plant, and equipment whose fair value can be measured reliably shall be carried at a revalued amount, being its fair value at the date of the revaluation less any subsequent accumulated depreciation and subsequent accumulated impairment losses. Revaluation shall be made with sufficient regularity to ensure that the carrying amount does not differ materially from that which would be determined using fair value at the end of the reporting period.[1]

L.O. 10-1.   Apply the revaluation model of accounting for non-current assets.

revaluation model   Restates the carrying value of an asset to the asset's fair value on the date of revaluation.

fair value   The price that would be received to sell an asset or paid to transfer a liability in an orderly transaction between market participants at the measurement date.

As indicated in the standards, revaluation is not compulsory. A company may choose the cost model or the revaluation model. The goal of IFRS allowing a choice is to achieve higher relevance of financial statements by allowing the use of the revaluation model when there is a sufficient degree of reliability in fair value estimates. However, if an enterprise cannot reliably measure fair value, then it must follow the cost model (as discussed in Chapters 8 and 9).

In particular, most intangible assets will not satisfy the requirement of having reliably measured fair values. IAS 38 notes that, "It is uncommon for an active market . . . to exist for an intangible asset, although this may happen. For example, in some jurisdictions, an active market may exist for freely transferable taxi licences, fishing licences, or production quotas. However, an active market cannot exist for brands, newspaper mastheads, music and film publishing rights, patents or trademarks, because each such asset is unique."[2] Without an active market, the fair value of an intangible asset cannot be reliably determined. Thus, the ability of an enterprise to use the revaluation model in place of the cost model depends on whether the particular assets have reliably measured fair values.

If an enterprise uses the revaluation model for an asset, it need not revalue the asset each and every year. The frequency of revaluation depends on how likely fair values materially deviate from carrying values, which is usually dependent on the type of asset being considered. Faster and larger changes in fair value require more frequent revaluations.

THRESHOLD CONCEPT
CONCEPTUAL FRAMEWORK

[1.] Copyright © 2012 IFRS Foundation.

[2.] IAS 38 paragraph 78.

Enterprises using the revaluation model need to apply it consistently across assets that are in the same "class." A class is a group of assets of similar nature, such as land, buildings, machinery, motor vehicles, office equipment, licences, and pollution permits. This requirement reduces the possibility of earnings management through selectively revaluing some assets in a class but not others (sometimes referred to as "cherry picking").

After establishing the fair value of an asset, how does an enterprise reflect that fair value in the accounts? We can divide the accounting into three issues. First, how do we adjust the asset value? This issue is not immediately clear for those assets subject to depreciation (or amortization) because we also have to deal with accumulated depreciation. Second, under double-entry accounting, these increases and decreases in asset values also affect owners' equity—should the impact on equity flow through profit/loss, or through other comprehensive income? Third, revaluation alters the depreciation base for future periods. The following discusses these three issues in turn.

1. Adjusting asset values for revaluation

For assets not subject to depreciation or amortization (land, intangible assets with indefinite lives), adjusting their carrying values is quite straightforward. For example, suppose Quesnel Company has a parcel of land that it carries at $80,000 prior to the revaluation adjustment. A professional appraisal determines the land's fair value to be $100,000. The revaluation entry would increase the carrying value of land by the increment of $20,000, as follows:

Dr. Land	20,000	
Cr. [Profit/loss account or other comprehensive income]		20,000

As noted above, the next subsection addresses the second half of the journal entry.

For an asset subject to depreciation or amortization, the *net* effect of a revaluation is the same as just illustrated. Instead of land, had Quesnel's revalued asset been a piece of equipment with net carrying value (i.e., gross carrying value less accumulated depreciation) of $80,000 and fair value of $100,000, it would also adjust the net carrying amount upward by $20,000. The question involves how we should split the adjustment between the gross carrying amount and the accumulated depreciation on the equipment. There are two ways to do this: the proportional method or the elimination method.

a. Proportional method

proportional method (of accounting for revaluation)   A method that adjusts the gross carrying value and accumulated depreciation (or amortization) by the same percentage such that the net carrying amount equals fair value after revaluation. Contrast with **elimination method**.

As the name suggests, the **proportional method** restates both an asset's gross carrying value and its accumulated depreciation on the date of revaluation proportionally, meaning that both amounts increase by the same percentage. Continuing with the example of Quesnel Company, suppose the equipment with net carrying amount of $80,000 has gross carrying value of $120,000 and accumulated depreciation of $40,000. As above, the company estimates that the fair value of the equipment has increased to $100,000.

Fair value exceeds the net carrying amount by 25% ([$100,000 ÷ $80,000] − 1), so the proportional method increases both the gross carrying amount and accumulated depreciation by 25%. As a result, Quesnel would increase the gross carrying value of equipment by 25%, from $120,000 to $150,000. Likewise, accumulated depreciation increases by 25%, from $40,000 to $50,000. The net carrying amount is thus $150,000 − $50,000 = $100,000, which is the fair value. Exhibit 10-1 summarizes these changes.

Exhibit 10-1	Amounts before and after revaluation for Quesnel Company using the proportional method			
Before revaluation		**After revaluation**		**Change**
Equipment	$120,000	Equipment	$ 150,000	+25%
Accum. depreciation	40,000	Accum. depreciation	50,000	+25%
Net carrying amount	**$ 80,000**	Net carrying amount	**$100,000**	+25%

b. Elimination method

The **elimination method** resets the balance of accumulated depreciation to zero on the date of revaluation, which means that the gross carrying amount equals the net carrying amount. Revaluation of the net carrying amount then simply involves adjusting the gross carrying amount. For Quesnel's equipment, the increase of $20,000 in net carrying amount from $80,000 to $100,000 results in the following figures:

elimination method (of accounting for revaluation)   A method that removes the balance in accumulated depreciation and restates the gross carrying amount to fair value. Contrast with **proportional method**.

Exhibit 10-2	Amounts before and after revaluation for Quesnel Company using the elimination method			
Before revaluation		**After revaluation**		**Change**
Equipment	$120,000	Equipment	$ 100,000	
Accum. depreciation	40,000	Accum. depreciation	0	
Net carrying amount	**$ 80,000**	Net carrying amount	**$100,000**	+25%

c. Comparison of the proportional and elimination methods

As noted above, both methods result in the same net carrying value after revaluation—$100,000 fair value of the asset—so the net amount of the adjustment is the same. However, there are significant differences in the journal entries, as shown in Exhibit 10-3, and the resulting balance sheet accounts as previously shown in Exhibit 10-1 and Exhibit 10-2.

Exhibit 10-3	Journal entries to adjust Quesnel Company's equipment to fair value		
Proportional method		**Elimination method**	
Dr. Equipment	$30,000	Cr. Equipment	$20,000
Cr. Accumulated depreciation	10,000	Dr. Accumulated depreciation	40,000
Cr. [Profit/loss or other comprehensive income]	20,000	Cr. [Profit/loss or other comprehensive income]	20,000

The result of the proportional method maintains the character of the original purchase since the ratio of accumulated depreciation to cost remains unchanged before and after the revaluation. The elimination method produces numbers that would result from a purchase at the revaluation date since there would be no accumulated depreciation.

Neither method is ideal. The proportional method restates gross carrying amounts and accumulated depreciation as if current prices prevailed at the time of the initial purchase, but such prices are purely hypothetical. On the other hand, the elimination method presents figures as if the asset had been newly purchased and reduces the ability of financial statement readers to approximate the age of assets. Which of the two methods an enterprise adopts is a matter of professional judgment.

2. Accounting for the effect of revaluation on equity

The above discussion addresses only one half of the accounting for revaluation; the offsetting side of the journal entry also needs to be considered. In the above example, what should Quesnel Company do with the $20,000 that must be credited?

Unfortunately, the answer is not simple. It depends on whether the revaluation is upward or downward, and what past revaluations have been *for the same asset.* IAS 16 indicates the following:

¶39   If an asset's carrying amount is increased as a result of a revaluation, the increase shall be recognized in other comprehensive income and accumulated in equity under the heading of revaluation surplus. However, the increase shall be recognized in profit or loss to the extent that it reverses a revaluation decrease of the same asset previously recognized in profit or loss.

¶40   If an asset's carrying amount is decreased as a result of a revaluation, the decrease shall be recognized in profit or loss. However, the decrease shall be recognized in other comprehensive income to the extent of any credit balance existing in the revaluation surplus in respect of that asset. The decrease recognized in other comprehensive income reduces the amount accumulated in equity under the heading of revaluation surplus.[3]

These two paragraphs are difficult to understand because they contain a number of conditional "if–then" statements. However, the conditions can be simplified considerably by picturing them in a graph, as shown in Exhibit 10-4.

Exhibit 10-4	Graphical depiction of treatment of revaluation adjustments

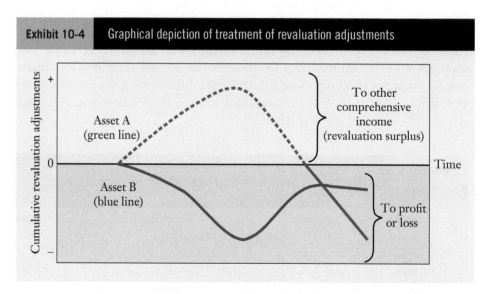

As shown in the graph, the treatment of a revaluation adjustment is asymmetric depending on the *cumulative* adjustment for the specific asset.

- Cumulative revaluation increases, illustrated by the dotted line, go through other comprehensive income (OCI) to the revaluation surplus component of equity.

- Cumulative revaluation decreases, illustrated by the solid lines, go through net income (profit or loss). We can describe the latter case as assets that are "under water": the cumulative revaluation adjustments are less than zero.

In a particular year, a revaluation adjustment can result in a portion going through profit or loss and a portion going to the revaluation surplus account if the adjustment involves a transition from below zero to above zero, or vice versa.

Take the example from above of Quesnel Company's equipment, with a $20,000 revaluation increase in the current year. Assume the company has chosen the proportional method to account for the accumulated depreciation. Now also suppose that the equipment has cumulative revaluation adjustments of the following amounts prior to the current revaluation: (i) $30,000; (ii) −$30,000; (iii) −$15,000. How should Quesnel account for the current-year revaluation increase of $20,000? Exhibit 10-5 shows the appropriate journal entries for each scenario.

Exhibit 10-5	Journal entries to adjust Quesnel Company's equipment to fair value			
Scenario	**Balance of cumulative revaluation adjustment**		**Journal entries (proportional method)**	
(i)	Opening	30,000	Dr. Equipment	30,000	
	Current adjustment	+20,000	Cr. Accumulated depreciation		10,000
	Closing	50,000	**Cr. OCI—revaluation surplus**		20,000
(ii)	Opening	−30,000	Dr. Equipment	30,000	
	Current adjustment	+20,000	Cr. Accumulated depreciation		10,000
	Closing	−10,000	**Cr. Gain on revaluation of equipment**		20,000
(iii)	Opening	−15,000	Dr. Equipment	30,000	
	Current adjustment	+20,000	Cr. Accumulated depreciation		10,000
	Closing	5,000	**Cr. Gain on revaluation of equipment**		15,000
			Cr. OCI—revaluation surplus		5,000

*OCI = other comprehensive income

Notice that in Scenario (iii), Quesnel would record only $15,000 of gain because the amount eliminates the balance of the cumulative revaluation loss. The remaining $5,000 of the $20,000 revaluation adjustment goes toward the revaluation surplus account in equity via OCI.

3. Adjusting depreciation in periods subsequent to revaluation

After an enterprise revalues a depreciable/amortizable asset, it also needs to revise depreciation calculations for subsequent periods. Since a revaluation is a change in asset values due to new information, it is a change in estimate, accounted for using the prospective method. For example, suppose Quesnel's equipment described above has a six-year useful life from the date of purchase, has zero residual value, and the revaluation occurs at the end of the second year/beginning of the third year. Recall that prior to revaluation the gross carrying value was $120,000 and accumulated depreciation was $40,000. Thus, depreciation prior to revaluation was $120,000 ÷ 6 years = $20,000/year. The revaluation increased the net carrying amount by $20,000, from $80,000 to $100,000. Depreciation after revaluation would be $100,000 ÷ 4 years = $25,000/year. Exhibit 10-6 details the depreciation for each of the six years of the equipment's useful life.

Exhibit 10-6	Depreciation schedule for Quesnel Company's equipment reflecting changes due to revaluation						
Year	Gross carrying amount	Accumulated depreciation before current year depreciation	Net carrying amount	Residual value	Remaining depreciable amount	Useful life remaining	Straight-line depreciation†
1	120,000	0	120,000	0	120,000	6 years	20,000
2	120,000	20,000	100,000	0	100,000	5 years	20,000
3	120,000	40,000	80,000				
RA*	+30,000‡	+10,000‡	+20,000				
3	150,000	50,000	100,000	0	100,000	4 years	25,000
4	150,000	75,000	75,000	0	75,000	3 years	25,000
5	150,000	100,000	50,000	0	50,000	2 years	25,000
6	150,000	125,000	25,000	0	25,000	1 year	25,000

*RA = revaluation adjustment occurred at the end of Year 2, so changes in depreciation begin in Year 3.
†Depreciation = Remaining depreciable amount ÷ Remaining useful life
‡Assume that Quesnel uses the proportional method for the revaluation adjustment.

Of course, if there are additional revaluations in later years, the depreciation schedule would be revised for each revaluation to reflect those changes on a prospective basis.

CHECKPOINT **CP10-1**

Identify and describe the two methods that can be used to reflect revaluation adjustments for depreciable assets.

CHECKPOINT **CP10-2**

When do revaluation adjustments for PPE flow through net income? When do they flow through OCI?

B. IMPAIRMENT

L.O. 10-2. Evaluate whether a non-current asset should be tested for impairment, whether the asset is impaired, and the extent of impairment.

Whereas revaluations of non-current assets just discussed are optional, impairments are not. In general terms, representational faithfulness requires reported asset values to not overstate the amount that can be obtained by the sale or use of the asset. If an enterprise determines that an asset's carrying value cannot be recovered by sale or use (i.e., the asset is impaired), the enterprise must write down its value. In Chapter 6, this principle resulted in the "lower of cost and net realizable value" rule for inventories. This section focuses on the impairment of non-current assets based on the standards in IAS 36. ASPE has different guidance, which we will examine later in this section.

Impairment accounting involves three distinct stages:

1. Preliminary steps to determine what should be tested for impairment
2. Testing for impairment
3. Recognition of any impairment in the financial statements

Exhibit 10-7 illustrates these three stages and summarizes the accounting activities in each. The following discussion will walk through this diagram systematically.

Exhibit 10-7   Flowchart depiction of steps in testing and accounting for asset impairment

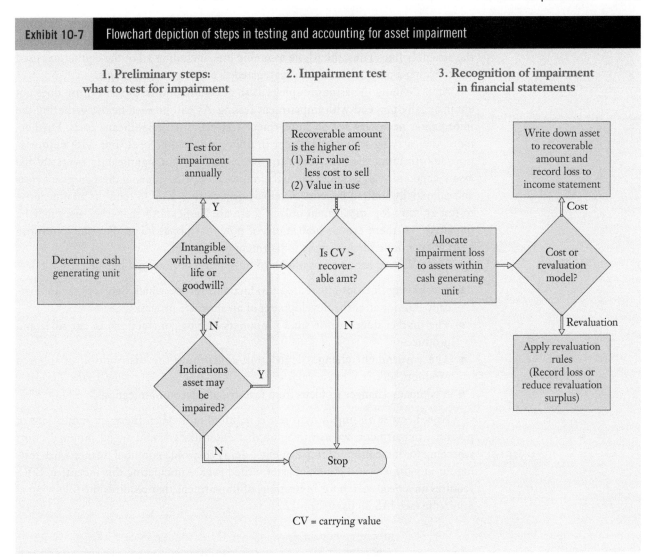

1. Preliminary steps: what to test for impairment

2. Impairment test

3. Recognition of impairment in financial statements

CV = carrying value

1. Preliminary steps: What to test for impairment

In order to think about whether something is impaired, it is first necessary to define what that "something" is. Where is the boundary between one asset and another, and when is it necessary to group different assets together for purposes of impairment testing? Is a wholesaler's delivery truck an appropriate unit for the evaluation of impairment? What about a subway car in a typical transit system?

While both the truck and the subway car are well-defined items separable from other items in a physical sense, what is important for purposes of impairment testing is whether the item generates *cash flows* independent from others. Depending on the details of the circumstances, the truck likely does generate independent cash flows. In contrast, the subway car is unlikely to produce independent cash flows because it operates in conjunction with subway tracks and other ancillary equipment, and it is part of a larger transit system in which riders can transfer from one subway line to another and to buses. In other words, it is not possible to isolate the cash inflows of a single subway car. In order to carry out impairment tests, enterprises need to separate or group assets such that they form **cash generating units**: the smallest identifiable group of assets that generates cash inflows that are largely independent of those from other assets.

cash generating units The smallest identifiable group of assets that generates cash inflows that are largely independent of those from other assets.

Another common example is an assembly line that comprises many different machines. Each machine cannot produce goods independent of the other machines in the assembly line. Thus, the whole assembly line, including all of the equipment used in producing a product, would be aggregated as a cash generating unit.

After defining the asset groupings/cash generating units, the enterprise does not automatically proceed with impairment testing. As will be seen below, gathering the information necessary for an impairment test can entail significant costs. Furthermore, the carrying values of assets with finite lives decline over time with depreciation/amortization, such that the carrying values will not significantly overstate the assets' economic values under normal circumstances. Recognizing the significant costs and potentially limited benefits of impairment testing, IAS 36 requires an enterprise to test an asset for impairment only if there are "indications that [the] asset may be impaired."[4] If there are no indications of potential impairment, then the enterprise need not continue further in the impairment procedures.

The following are some examples of indications of potential impairment:

- A company licenses a patented production process, which becomes technologically inferior after the development of an alternate process.
- The market demand for steel plummets due to contractions in car sales and production.
- The government changes legislation concerning the distribution of tobacco products.
- A company changes its focus from forestry to telecommunications.[5]

Now, because an impairment test is required only when there are indications of potential impairment, we can imagine that enterprises would spend minimal effort searching for indications of impairment—doing so avoids potential further work testing for impairment and potential asset writedowns. Anticipating this incentive, IFRS requires an *annual* search for indications of impairment that requires the following at minimum (see IAS 36 paragraph 12):

Exhibit 10-8	Minimum sources of information to find indications of impairment
Internal sources of information	**External sources of information**
■ Evidence of obsolescence or physical damage	■ Market value of the asset has declined more than would be expected due to normal aging
■ Changes in, or plans to change, the use of the asset	■ Adverse changes to the technological, legal, product market, or general economic environments
■ Evidence from internal reporting that shows performance below expectations	■ Increases in interest rates that would adversely affect the discounted value of cash inflows from using the asset
	■ The market value of the enterprise as a whole is less than the carrying value of net assets

For example, a company manufacturing parts for the auto sector in Ontario in 2008 would have needed to evaluate its equipment for impairment because of the collapse of the North American auto sector that year.

[4.] IAS 36 paragraph 9.

[5.] This example may seem far-fetched, but it actually happened in the case of Nokia, the Finnish communications company.

There is an exception to this rule (i.e., to test for impairment only if there are indications of impairment) for intangible assets with indefinite lives and goodwill, because there is no gradual diminishment of the carrying value over time due to amortization. It is therefore necessary to regularly check for overvaluation of these assets on the balance sheet. IAS 36 requires enterprises to test these assets for impairment every year.

2. Impairment test

As just discussed, an enterprise performs an impairment test for an asset:

- annually if it is goodwill or an intangible asset with an indefinite life; or
- when there are indications that the asset may be impaired.

The impairment test itself compares an asset's carrying value with a quantity called the "recoverable amount." If the carrying value exceeds the recoverable amount, then the asset is impaired and the enterprise writes down the asset to the recoverable amount. Otherwise, the asset is not impaired and no accounting adjustments are required.

Depending on the type of asset and the enterprise's accounting policy, the carrying amount may be based on the cost model or the revaluation model, adjusted by any accumulated depreciation/amortization.

The **recoverable amount** of an asset is the *higher* of two values: its fair value less cost to sell and its value in use. Conceptually, allowing the use of the higher of the two values as the recoverable amount makes economic sense. An enterprise can either sell the asset or continue to use it in its operations, so it should rationally choose the option that generates the most net benefits.

> recoverable amount   The higher of an asset's **fair value less cost to sell** and its **value in use**.

To complete the impairment test, it is not always necessary to estimate both alternatives of the recoverable amount. If a company first determines Asset X's fair value less cost to sell to be higher than its carrying value, it need not estimate the value in use. Likewise, if the company first determines Asset Y's value in use to be higher than its carrying value, it need not estimate its fair value less cost to sell. As long as one of these two amounts equals or exceeds the carrying value of the asset, the company concludes that the asset is not impaired and no further impairment procedures are required.

The following discussion goes into more detail regarding how one estimates the two alternative values of the recoverable amount.

a. Fair value less cost to sell

The reference to "fair value" in the recoverable amount has the same meaning as in previous chapters. Thus, **fair value less cost to sell** is the price that would be received to sell an asset or paid to transfer a liability in an orderly transaction between market participants at the measurement date, less the costs of disposal.

> fair value less cost to sell   The price that would be received to sell an asset or paid to transfer a liability in an orderly transaction between market participants at the measurement date, less the **costs of disposal**.

There are potentially different sources of evidence of fair value for a particular asset. In order of preference, these information sources include (see IAS 36 paragraphs 25–27):

1. The price of the particular asset in a binding sale agreement
2. The market price of the particular asset in an active market
3. Actual transactions involving similar assets within the same industry

The ordering is logical in that more precise and relevant sources of fair value are preferred over those that are less precise or less relevant. In all cases, the evidence must be based on arm's-length transactions, not transactions between related parties. Exhibit 10-9 provides examples of these three types of information sources for fair value:

Exhibit 10-9	Examples of fair value evidence
Source of evidence for fair value	**Example**
1. Actual price of the particular asset	Before the financial statements are issued, the enterprise signs a contract to sell one of its buildings to an unrelated party for $30 million.
2. Market price of the particular asset	A company holds carbon credits that allow it to release 200,000 tonnes of carbon dioxide. The company is able to sell these credits on a commodity exchange, and quoted prices on the exchange were $15/tonne at year-end.
3. Actual prices of similar assets	An enterprise receives a property assessment that was made for purposes of property tax collection. According to the government agency responsible for these property assessments, the estimated value of a particular property is based on actual transaction prices of neighbouring properties (and other factors such as the amount of interior space, lot size, etc.).

costs of disposal The incremental costs directly attributable to the disposal of an asset, excluding finance costs and income tax expense.

Fair value less cost to sell also involves estimates of the **costs of disposal**, which has its common everyday meaning. To be precise, IAS 36 defines it as "the incremental costs directly attributable to the disposal of an asset, excluding finance costs and income tax expense." Examples of disposal costs include removal and transportation costs if paid by the seller, and costs of cleaning and refurbishment.

b. Value in use

value in use The present value of the future cash flows expected to be derived from an asset.

An asset's **value in use** is the present value of the future cash flows expected to be derived from that asset. The need to forecast future cash flows for purposes of estimating value in use is the principal reason why it is necessary to identify the cash generating unit: in order to conduct discounted cash flow analysis, one must first define the unit that produces those cash flows.

The standard discounted cash flow techniques used in finance apply; Appendix B summarizes these techniques. However, IAS 36 provides additional detailed guidance on some of the more subtle aspects of applying the discounted cash flow model. These additional details are beyond the scope of this text; the interested reader should refer to IAS 36 paragraphs 30–57.

c. Example testing for impairment

Red Rocket Racers is a (hypothetical) builder of performance bicycles with retail prices in the range of $3,000 to $10,000. For several years, the company's sales have been increasing as people have become more health conscious and increasingly willing to spend money on products related to health and recreation. However, due to the recession that began in 2008 and the consumer belt-tightening that ensued, Red Rocket's monthly sales plummeted by 45% by September 30, 2009, its fiscal year-end, compared to the same month the year before. As of March 2009, the company had curtailed production and laid off one-half of its production staff.

The company does not own, but rents, its manufacturing and office facilities. However, Red Rocket does own several pieces of equipment for the manufacture of bicycle components. While the types of bicycles built by Red Rocket are often made-to-order and produced in low volume compared with lower-cost models made by other bike manufacturers, the equipment used in the industry is fairly standard and independent of the quality of the output (e.g., a machine for shaping the bike frame). In preparation for the 2009 year-end, staff compiled the following information related to the company's manufacturing equipment:

Exhibit 10-10	Information relating to the manufacturing equipment of Red Rocket Racers

1. The accounting records show the following amounts for each piece of equipment as at September 30, 2009, after recording depreciation for the year. All three machines were purchased four years ago and have been depreciated straight-line over 10 years.

	Machine A	Machine B	Machine C
Gross carrying amount	$360,000	$720,000	$120,000
Accumulated depreciation	(144,000)	(288,000)	(48,000)
Net carrying amount	$216,000	$432,000	$ 72,000

2. Due to the downturn in the economy, a number of used machines were sold at auction with the bankruptcy of several other high-end bicycle manufacturers. Recent auction results for equipment similar to the three machines in use by Red Rocket were as follows:

Machine A		Machine B		Machine C	
Age	Price	Age	Price	Age	Price
2 years	$200,000	4 years	$400,000	6 years	$40,000
6 years	100,000	6 years	250,000	8 years	20,000
8 years	50,000				

3. While sales of high-end bicycles dropped substantially, overall industry sales declined only modestly as value-conscious consumers downshifted to lower-priced models, resulting in increased sales for lower-end products. As a result, management has determined that there is still demand for the company's machines should it decide to sell them. After evaluating market conditions, management estimates that an orderly sale of Machines A, B, and C would fetch $170,000, $450,000, and $50,000, respectively.

4. Costs to move and transport the machines are negligible and all three machines have negligible residual values.

5. Management has compiled the following cash flows and forecasts associated with the use of the machinery for the remaining six years of the machines' useful lives. As all three machines are used in the same production process, there is only one forecast for all the machines combined. As shown in the table, market conditions are expected to continue to be weak, with a modest recovery in volume and margins starting in 2011.

Year ended or ending Sept. 30	2008	2009	2010	2011–2015
Number of bikes produced	1,200	800	800	1,000
Average contribution margin per bike	$ 600	$ 200	$ 250	$ 300
Total contribution margin	720,000	160,000	200,000	300,000
Other costs of sales and distribution	200,000	100,000	110,000	140,000
Net incremental cash flow	$520,000	$ 60,000	$ 90,000	$160,000

6. Management estimates that 12% is the appropriate cost of capital for discounting cash flows for the machinery.

ANALYSIS:

- *Cash generating unit(s):* The three machines comprise a single cash generating unit because cash inflows result from the concurrent use of all three machines, so the analysis of impairment should consider all the machines together.
- *Need for impairment test:* The machines are tangible assets, so an impairment test is required if there are indications that they may be impaired. The recessionary economic conditions and the severe drop in sales are clear indications that an impairment test is necessary.
- *Carrying amount:* The three machines together have a total carrying amount of $720,000 ($216,000 + $432,000 + $72,000).
- *Fair value less cost to sell:* The prices at auction do not constitute fair values of similar machines because they are liquidation prices resulting from bankruptcy; prices from forced sales are not fair values. The only other evidence of fair value are the estimates provided by management, which show a total of $670,000 ($170,000 + $450,000 + $50,000).
- *Value in use:* Using the forecasted cash flows provided by management, the present value of cash flows over the remaining six-year useful life of the machines is $595,000 (rounded to the nearest thousand).

	2010	2011	2012	2013	2014	2015
Net incremental cash flow	90,000	160,000	160,000	160,000	160,000	160,000
PV factor at 12%	0.8929	0.7972	0.7118	0.6355	0.5674	0.5066
Present value as at Sept. 30, 2009	80,357	127,551	113,885	101,683	90,788	81,061
Total present value	$595,325					

- *Recoverable amount:* The higher of fair value less cost to sell ($670,000) and value in use ($595,000) is $670,000.
- *Result of impairment test:* The carrying value of $720,000 exceeds the recoverable amount of $670,000. The equipment must be written down by the difference of $50,000.

Notice that while the impairment test reflects negative changes in market conditions, it is not intended to capture the worst-case scenario. That is, it does not require the use of the lower of the two estimates of the recoverable amount (i.e., $595,000). The reason, as noted previously, is that Red Rocket's management can always choose the better of the two alternatives. In this case, the company would be better off selling the machines in an orderly fashion rather than continuing to operate them.

Once an enterprise determines that an asset or cash generating unit is impaired, as is the case for Red Rocket, it then needs to recognize the impairment writedown in the financial records. We discuss these procedures next.

3. Recognition of impairment

L.O. 10-3. Account for the impairment of different types of non-current assets.

If the impairment test involves a single asset, then that asset, of course, bears all of the impairment loss as determined above. However, if the impairment test involves a cash generating unit with more than one asset, the enterprise needs to first allocate the impairment loss to the different assets. We discuss this allocation process before describing the journal entries used to recognize impairment losses.

a. Allocation of impairment loss to assets within a cash generating unit

Intuitively, a reasonable way to allocate impairment losses is to do so in proportion to some measure of value. Chapter 8 discussed the allocation of price for a bundled purchase using the fair values of the component assets. In the case of an impairment loss of a cash generating unit, the fair values of individual assets are not always available—since, by definition, the assets within the cash generating unit are dependent on each other. Consequently, IAS 36 recommends allocating impairment loss *in proportion to the net carrying amounts* of the assets in the cash generating unit.

There are two exceptions to this general allocation rule for impairment losses. First, if the cash generating unit includes goodwill, the impairment loss would first go toward reducing that goodwill prior to the allocation based on net carrying amounts. This exception reflects the idea that if a cash generating unit is impaired, the impairment more likely occurred in the goodwill rather than in the identifiable assets (tangible or intangible).

The second exception involves assets within the cash generating unit that can be identified to be unimpaired. By definition, assets within a cash generating unit do not have *both* fair values less costs to sell and values in use that are individually quantifiable for each asset; if they did, they would not need to be grouped in the same cash generating unit. However, it is possible that *one* of the two values can be identified for individual assets. If such information can be identified for assets within the cash generating unit, and the asset's net recoverable amount exceeds the carrying amount, then no loss should be allocated to that asset. If this exception applies, the loss that would have been recorded against the unimpaired asset would be allocated to the other assets.

We can use the example of Red Rocket Racers described in the last section to illustrate this allocation process. For ease of reference, we repeat some of the facts relevant to the allocation (CGU = cash generating unit).

Exhibit 10-11	Summary of information relevant to allocation of Red Rocket's impairment loss			
	Machine A	Machine B	Machine C	CGU Total
Net carrying amount	$216,000	$432,000	$72,000	$720,000
Fair value less cost to sell	170,000	450,000	50,000	670,000
Value in use				595,000
Recoverable amount				670,000
Impairment loss for CGU				50,000

Applying the general allocation rule, the impairment losses for each asset in proportion to its net carrying value are as indicated in Exhibit 10-12.

Exhibit 10-12	Allocation of impairment loss for Red Rocket in proportion to carrying amounts of machines			
	Machine A	Machine B	Machine C	CGU Total
Net carrying amount	$216,000	$432,000	$72,000	$720,000
Net carrying amount as % of total	30%	60%	10%	100%
Total loss to be allocated	$ 50,000	$ 50,000	$50,000	$ 50,000
Loss allocated to each asset*	15,000	30,000	5,000	50,000
Net carrying amount after impairment	$201,000	$402,000	$67,000	$670,000

*Loss allocated = Net carrying amount as % of total × Total impairment loss for CGU.

This allocation results in Machine B's carrying amount ($432,000) being lower than its recoverable amount, which is the fair value less cost to sell ($450,000). Indeed, the carrying amount before impairment ($432,000) was already below the fair value less cost to sell, so no impairment is attributable to Machine B. As a result, the $30,000 that would have been allocated to Machine B needs to be reallocated to the other machines, as shown in Exhibit 10-13.

Exhibit 10-13	Loss allocation for Red Rocket taking into account that Machine B is unimpaired			
	Machine A	Machine B	Machine C	CGU Total
Initial allocation				
Net carrying amount	$216,000	$432,000	$72,000	$720,000
Net carrying amount as % of total	30%	60%	10%	100%
Total loss to be allocated	$ 50,000	$ 50,000	$50,000	$ 50,000
Loss initially allocated to each asset	$ 15,000	nil*	$ 5,000	$ 20,000
Reallocation of loss that would have been allocated to Machine B in initial allocation				
Net carrying amount	$216,000	n/a	$72,000	$288,000
Net carrying amount as % of total	75%	n/a	25%	100%
Total loss to be allocated	$ 30,000	n/a	$30,000	$ 30,000
Loss reallocated	$ 22,500	n/a	$ 7,500	$ 30,000
Summary				
Net carrying amount before impairment	$216,000	$432,000	$72,000	$720,000
Loss initially allocated and reallocated	(37,500)	0	(12,500)	(50,000)
Net carrying amount after impairment	$178,500	$432,000	$59,500	$670,000

*Amount is nil because the net carrying amount should not be written down below the asset's recoverable amount of $450,000.

As you can see, while the general rule for impairment loss allocation is fairly intuitive, its application becomes more complex because of the exceptions allowed.[6]

b. Entries to record impairment loss

Subsequent to determining the amount of impairment loss for an asset—after allocation within a cash generating unit if necessary—we are now prepared to record that loss in the accounts. The procedures differ, depending on whether an enterprise follows the cost model or the revaluation model. Under both methods, both the asset side and the equity side of the balance sheet must decrease. The difference lies in which equity component is affected.

COST MODEL   Under the cost model, the writedown is recorded as a loss in the income statement, thus affecting retained earnings. For Red Rocket Racers, the journal entries would be as follows:

Exhibit 10-14	Journal entries to record impairment losses if Red Rocket Racers uses the cost model	
Dr. Impairment loss—Machine A	37,500	
Cr. Accumulated depreciation—Machine A		37,500
Dr. Impairment loss—Machine C	12,500	
Cr. Accumulated depreciation—Machine C		12,500

REVALUATION MODEL   If an enterprise carries an asset under the revaluation model, the treatment of the impairment loss is the same as for a revaluation decrease. More specifically, the impairment loss goes through profit or loss (and thus retained earnings)

[6.] A third exception to the general allocation rule is mentioned in IAS 36: an asset's net carrying amount should not become negative as a result of impairment. An allocated loss cannot exceed an asset's carrying amount under proportional allocation; however, the exception preventing the allocation of a loss to unimpaired assets creates the possibility of an allocated loss exceeding an asset's carrying amount.

unless the asset has a revaluation surplus. If the asset has a revaluation surplus, the loss would flow through OCI until the surplus is exhausted. The consistency with revaluation accounting makes sense because, conceptually, impairment is the downward half of revaluation, which is potentially upward or downward.

For the sake of illustration, suppose Red Rocket Racers' Machine A has a revaluation surplus of $20,000, while Machine C does not. Assuming all other facts as presented previously, the journal entries would be as follows (with differences from Exhibit 10-14 in bold):

Exhibit 10-15	Journal entries to record impairment losses if Red Rocket Racers uses the revaluation model		
Dr. OCI—revaluation surplus—Machine A		**20,000**	
Dr. Impairment loss—Machine A		**17,500**	
Cr. Accumulated depreciation—Machine A			37,500
Dr. Impairment loss—Machine C		12,500	
Cr. Accumulated depreciation—Machine C			12,500

For Machine A, the $37,500 impairment first goes to eliminate the $20,000 of revaluation surplus, and the remainder is an impairment loss that flows through net income.

c. Adjustments to depreciation/amortization

As just illustrated, impairment reduces the carrying amounts for assets. For assets subject to depreciation/amortization, this reduction also lowers the remaining depreciable amount. This is a change in circumstance that requires prospective adjustments of future depreciation/amortization charges. Such prospective changes were illustrated in Chapter 8.

d. Reversals of impairment

If an enterprise writes down an asset for impairment, what should it do if the asset increases in value in subsequent years? IFRS allows increases to assets' carrying amounts to reverse prior impairments. The increase is limited to an amount such that the reversal will not result in a net carrying amount that exceeds what would have been obtained had no impairment been recorded. Note this is different from saying that the reversal is limited to the amount of loss recorded, because the amount of depreciation/amortization had also changed in the time between the impairment and the reversal.

Consider Red Rocket Racers' Machine C. The asset has a cost of $120,000, zero residual value, and a useful life of 10 years. Straight-line depreciation before impairment was $12,000 per year. The impairment at the end of the fourth year changes the depreciation to $9,917 per year, as shown in these calculations:

Exhibit 10-16	Computation of Red Rocket Racers' depreciation on Machine C after impairment	
Cost		$120,000
Accumulated depreciation at end of Year 4 (Sept. 30, 2009)	$48,000	
Addition to accumulated depreciation due to impairment	12,500	
Accumulated depreciation at beginning of Year 5 (Oct. 1, 2009)		(60,500)
Net carrying amount (= remaining depreciable amount)		59,500
Remaining useful life at beginning of Year 5		6 years
Annual depreciation		$ 9,917

Exhibit 10-17 shows the depreciation schedules for Machine C with and without the impairment, and the maximum impairment reversal possible in Years 5 through 10 of the machine's useful life (2010 to 2015).

Exhibit 10-17		Depreciation schedule for Red Rocket Racers' Machine C reflecting impairment of 2009							
			Without impairment				With impairment at end of Year 4		
Yr	Year ended Sept. 30	Gross carrying amount	Depreciation for the year	Accumulated depreciation at end of year	Net carrying amount at end of year	Depreciation for the year	Accumulated depreciation at end of year	Net carrying amount at end of year	Maximum impairment reversal
1	2006	$120,000	$12,000	$ 12,000	**$108,000**	$12,000	$ 12,000	**$108,000**	n/a
2	2007	120,000	12,000	24,000	**96,000**	12,000	24,000	**96,000**	n/a
3	2008	120,000	12,000	36,000	**84,000**	12,000	36,000	**84,000**	n/a
4	2009	120,000	12,000	48,000	**72,000**	12,000	60,500*	**59,500***	n/a
5	2010	120,000	12,000	60,000	**60,000**	9,917	70,417	**49,583**	$10,417
6	2011	120,000	12,000	72,000	**48,000**	9,916	80,333	**39,667**	8,333
7	2012	120,000	12,000	84,000	**36,000**	9,917	90,250	**29,750**	6,250
8	2013	120,000	12,000	96,000	**24,000**	9,917	100,167	**19,833**	4,167
9	2014	120,000	12,000	108,000	**12,000**	9,916	110,083	**9,917**	2,083
10	2015	120,000	12,000	120,000	**0**	9,917	120,000	**0**	0

*See Exhibit 10-13 for calculation of the impairment loss.

Exhibit 10-18 graphically illustrates the maximum impairment reversal as the area between two lines representing the carrying amounts with and without impairment. The path of the actual carrying amount with impairment and any future reversals (solid line) can never exceed the dashed line—the carrying value that would have been reported in the absence of the impairment.

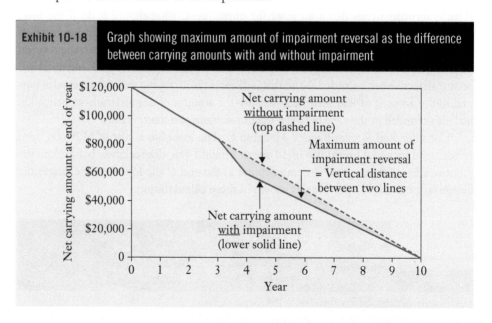

| Exhibit 10-18 | Graph showing maximum amount of impairment reversal as the difference between carrying amounts with and without impairment |

4. Differences between impairment and revaluation

As noted earlier, conceptually, impairment involves the downward half of asset revaluations. Does that imply that an enterprise that follows the revaluation model (rather than the cost model) for a class of assets automatically complies with the impairment standards? For instance, if revaluation results in a downward adjustment, would that adjustment take the place of the impairment loss?

Unfortunately, it is not that simple. Satisfying the revaluation rules does not imply compliance with the impairment standards, because even though impairment and revaluation overlap conceptually, the implementation details differ. Among the more important differences are the following:

	Revaluation	Impairment
Unit of measure	▪ By asset	▪ By cash generating unit
Frequency of evaluation	▪ At regular intervals according to the speed of price changes ▪ Not necessarily annual	▪ Annual if asset is intangible with an indefinite life ▪ Annual search for indications that the asset may be impaired
Value measurement	▪ Fair values ▪ Does not consider disposal costs	▪ Fair values less cost to sell or value in use, whichever is higher

Thus, enterprises that follow the revaluation model still generally need to assess their assets for impairment. When the differences are insignificant for the particular enterprise and assets, then revalued assets need not be assessed for impairment.

5. Impairment standards in ASPE

There are four significant differences between IFRS and ASPE with respect to impairments. First, ASPE also uses indications of impairment as a preliminary step to determine whether to quantitatively test for impairment, but it does not require an annual search for such indications. Second, ASPE defines the recoverable amount for an asset with a finite life as the *undiscounted* cash flows from the use of the asset. An asset is impaired if the carrying amount exceeds this recoverable amount. However, the amount of the impairment loss is based on the difference between the carrying amount and fair value, which ultimately reflects *discounted* cash flows. Third, ASPE does not permit reversals of impairments. Finally, since ASPE does not permit the revaluation model, impairment losses always flow through profit or loss and never through OCI.

6. Economic roles of impairments

IFRS and ASPE require enterprises to write down impaired assets to their recoverable amount. Doing so is consistent with the concepts of representational faithfulness (IFRS) and conservatism (ASPE) in the conceptual frameworks. At the same time, we should consider whether and what roles impairments play in a larger economic sense.

a. Communicating information to users

The first obvious role of the impairments is to convey to users information relevant to assessing the value of an enterprise's assets and the enterprise as a whole. Recording impairments alerts readers that the reporting enterprise's asset values have declined and that economic conditions facing the enterprise have changed adversely. However, this explanation does not fully explain why there should be only downward impairments but not upward adjustments (relative to historical cost).[7] In other words, the objective of conveying information relevant to asset valuation is best served by measuring assets using the revaluation model, which involves both downward and upward adjustments.

THRESHOLD CONCEPT
**DECISION MAKING
UNDER UNCERTAINTY**

[7.] As explained earlier in the chapter, upward adjustments in the form of impairment reversals are permitted.

b. Supporting efficient contracting and reducing earnings management

THRESHOLD CONCEPT
QUALITY OF EARNINGS

Debt contracts frequently make reference to the value of assets, and non-current assets in particular. Assets serve as collateral in debt contracts or in debt covenants based on financial ratios (such as debt to assets). Creditors bear the downside risk of asset value declines and business failure but do not share in the upside success. Thus, the creditors who rely on financial statements prefer the one-sided impairment standard.

The use of financial statement income in executive compensation contracts is another reason for the prudence/conservatism of impairments. Executives have incentives to present financial figures in a favourable manner, so permitting gains for upward adjustments to asset values would increase the opportunities for earnings management. For this reason, even the upward adjustments in the revaluation model flow through OCI rather than through profit or loss.

c. Facilitating rational decision making

THRESHOLD CONCEPT
ECONOMIC CONSEQUENCES OF ACCOUNTING CHOICE

Decision makers have a well-documented aversion to losses, whether such losses are real (in an economic sense) or apparent (as reported in financial statements). Chapter 8 discussed the influence of depreciation policy in managerial decision making regarding disposals and replacement of aging assets (see the article "Does depreciation policy matter?" in Chapter 8). If depreciation is relatively low such that the net carrying amount for an asset is high, disposal of that asset is more likely to result in a loss, or to increase the loss, in comparison to a more conservative depreciation policy. Likewise, if accounting standards did not require enterprises to write down assets when they are impaired, the overstated asset values would make management reluctant to dispose of the assets because doing so would result in an accounting loss. On the other hand, if the enterprise is required to write down an asset's carrying amount to its fair value, then there should be no significant loss upon disposal of the asset. As a result, it is more likely that management will make the disposal decision rationally based on incremental cash flows rather than accounting outcomes.

For example, suppose Salmo Company has an old machine with carrying value (without recording impairment) of $200,000, fair value of $160,000, and negligible disposal costs. The company could replace the machine with a more technologically advanced one, which would generate positive expected net present value of $20,000. Should Salmo replace the machine? Would Salmo's management actually choose to do it?

The answers depend on whether Salmo is required to record impairment and management's view of accounting losses. Without writing down the machine, choosing to replace the machine would generate proceeds of $160,000 from the sale of the old machine, its fair value less cost to sell. Since the machine has a carrying amount of $200,000, the replacement decision triggers an accounting loss of $40,000. This amount exceeds the $20,000 net present value expected from replacing the machine, so management may decide to forgo the investment to avoid the loss.

However, in such capital budgeting decisions, accounting losses are not relevant. The $20,000 positive net present value is already a summary measure that takes into account all the cash flows relevant to the decision, so Salmo should proceed with the replacement.

If Salmo first writes down the old machine for impairment, such that the carrying amount becomes $160,000, then the replacement decision would not trigger any significant accounting losses. Thus, the impairment process helps to reduce the influence of irrelevant accounting losses on management decision making.

 CHECKPOINT **CP10-3**

How frequently should PPE, intangible assets, and goodwill be tested for impairment?

CHECKPOINT **CP10-4**

In an impairment test, what are the two values that go into the determination of the recoverable amount?

C. INVESTMENT PROPERTY

IFRS provides accounting standards specific to investment property in IAS 40. Why is there a special standard for this type of property? The label "investment property" itself provides a clue. It suggests assets held for the purpose of earning a profit directly, similar to investments in financial assets. In the same way that financial investments can produce interest or dividend income as well as price increases, investment property can produce rental income and capital appreciation.

Investment property is distinct from PPE because we expect the former to generate profits directly (through rental income or capital appreciation) and the latter to generate profits indirectly (through production of goods or services). Investment property is distinct from inventories because inventories earn profits when they are sold, not when they are held.

> **L.O.** 10-4. Apply the specialized standards for the recognition and measurement of assets relating to investment properties and agricultural activities.

1. Definition of investment property and scope of IAS 40

Investment property is land or buildings held to earn rental income or for capital appreciation. This definition excludes property held for use in the supply of goods or services or for administrative purposes, which would be considered **owner-occupied property**, a category of PPE. It also excludes property that is held for sale in the ordinary course of business, which would be inventory. As discussed in Chapters 8 and 6, IAS 16 and IAS 2 are, respectively, the accounting standards for PPE and inventories.

The key issue in accounting for investment property is the value at which enterprises report investment property on the balance sheet date (i.e., subsequent measurement). Related issues involve the transfer of assets into and out of the classification of investment property.

> **investment property**   Land or buildings held to earn rental income or for capital appreciation.
>
> **owner-occupied property**   Land or buildings for use in the production or supply of goods or services or for administrative purposes.

2. Subsequent measurement

Similar to PPE, the initial recognition of investment property is at cost, which includes transaction costs incurred in the acquisition (legal fees, etc.). However, subsequent to initial acquisition, the measurement of investment property can differ from that for PPE.

Subsequent to initial recognition, IAS 40 provides enterprises with a choice of the cost model or the fair value model to measure the value of investment property. This choice applies to all of the enterprise's investment property, not to selective properties. This all-or-none designation helps to discourage earnings and balance sheet management through selective designation of appreciated property.[8] However, if an enterprise chooses the cost model, it must then also disclose fair values in the notes to the financial statements.

The fair value model is similar to but distinct from the revaluation model discussed earlier in this chapter. First, the **fair value model** reports investment property at fair value on the balance sheet date, with changes in value recognized in profit or loss. Thus, gains and losses always flow through income under the fair value

THRESHOLD CONCEPT
QUALITY OF EARNINGS

> **fair value model**   A measurement model that reports assets at fair value on the balance sheet date, with changes in value recognized in profit or loss.

[8.] There are two exceptions to this all-or-none designation, but they are outside the scope of this chapter. Refer to IAS 40 paragraphs 32A and 34.

model, not through OCI. (Recall from earlier in this chapter that revaluation gains and losses flow through either OCI or income, depending on whether the cumulative revaluation adjustment is positive or negative.)

Second, there is no need to record depreciation on investment property reported under the fair value model. This makes sense to the extent that the fair value estimate already takes into consideration any decline in the quality or useful life of the asset, and the changes in value flow through profit or loss, so no separate depreciation expense is needed. For revaluations of PPE under IAS 16, depreciation is still required.

Third, IAS 40 also indicates that fair values should reflect actual market conditions at the balance sheet date (IAS 40 paragraph 38). This requirement suggests that enterprises should obtain fair value estimates annually for investment property, in contrast to PPE, which may be revalued less frequently if fair values are changing gradually.

Exhibit 10-19 summarizes the cost and fair value models for investment property under IAS 40 and compares them to the corresponding standards for PPE in IAS 16.

Exhibit 10-19	Comparison of IAS 40 and IAS 16		
Choice of model for subsequent measurement	**Accounting issue**	**IAS 40 Investment Property**	**IAS 16 PPE**
Cost model	Measurement on balance sheet	At cost less depreciation	At cost less depreciation
	Disclosure of fair value	Required	Not required
	Depreciation	Required	Required
Fair value model	Measurement on balance sheet	At fair value	At fair value
(Revaluation model for IAS 16)	Frequency of measurement	Annual	Annual or less frequently
	Unrealized gains and losses	Record through profit or loss	Record through OCI or profit or loss depending on cumulative revaluation adjustments
	Depreciation	None	Required

As this exhibit shows, there are a number of important differences, particularly when fair value is involved.

EXAMPLE To demonstrate the effect of these reporting requirements, consider the following scenario. Arbutus Homes operates communal housing for senior citizens, including the provision of food, cleaning, and some paramedical services. At the beginning of 2019, the company acquired an apartment building on Laurel Street for $20 million ($8 million for land and $12 million for the building). At the time of purchase, Arbutus Homes estimates that the building would be useful for a further 20 years. Appraisals at the end of 2019, 2020, and 2021 estimated the value of the building to be, respectively, $11.78 million, $10.98 million, and $13 million, and for the land, $9 million, $9.5 million, and $10 million.

Without further details regarding management's intent, the land and building, either individually or together, could be treated as PPE under IAS 16 or investment property under IAS 40. Suppose that management intended for both the land and building to be held for use in the provision of housing for seniors.

Exhibit 10-20 shows the results over the first three years after purchase, using either the cost or revaluation model for PPE:

Exhibit 10-20	Reporting outcomes for Arbutus Homes' Laurel Street property treated as PPE (IAS 16)			
		2019	2020	2021
Cost model	Building—cost	$12,000,000	$12,000,000	$12,000,000
	Building—accum. depr.	(600,000)	(1,200,000)	(1,800,000)
	Building—net	11,400,000	10,800,000	10,200,000
	Land	8,000,000	8,000,000	8,000,000
	Total land and building	$19,400,000	$18,800,000	$18,200,000
	Depreciation expense	$ 600,000	$ 600,000	$ 600,000
Revaluation model (elimination method)	Building—gross	$11,780,000	$10,980,000	$13,000,000
	Building—accum. depr.	0	0	0
	Building—net	11,780,000	10,980,000	13,000,000
	Land	9,000,000	9,500,000	10,000,000
	Total land and building	$20,780,000	$20,480,000	$23,000,000
	Depreciation expense*	$ 600,000	$ 620,000	$ 610,000
	Revaluation reserve—bldg.	$ 380,000	$ 200,000	$ 2,830,000
	Revaluation reserve—land	1,000,000	1,500,000	2,000,000
	Total revaluation reserve	1,380,000	1,700,000	4,830,000
	Cumulative increase (decrease) in retained earnings	(600,000)	(1,220,000)	(1,830,000)
	Net effect on equity	$ 780,000	$ 480,000	$ 3,000,000

*Depreciation = Beginning of year depreciable amount ÷ Remaining useful life
2019: $12,000,000 ÷ 20 years = $600,000/year
2020: $11,780,000 ÷ 19 years = $620,000/year
2021: $10,980,000 ÷ 18 years = $610,000/year

For comparison, suppose that management intends to hold the property for capital appreciation rather than for use. That is, the company could sell the property if given the right price, and the company could still continue to provide seniors housing by renting the space from the buyer. Holding for capital appreciation would result in the Laurel Street property being considered investment property for accounting purposes. Exhibit 10-21 shows the results over the first three years after purchase, using either the cost model or fair value model for investment property.

Exhibit 10-21	Reporting outcomes for Arbutus Homes' Laurel Street property treated as investment property (IAS 40)			
		2019	2020	2021
Cost model	Same as for cost model under IAS 16 plus disclosure of fair values in footnotes.			
Fair value model	Building—net	$11,780,000	$10,980,000	$13,000,000
	Land	9,000,000	9,500,000	10,000,000
	Total land and building	20,780,000	20,480,000	23,000,000
	Opening carrying value	20,000,000	20,780,000	20,480,000
	Gain or loss on fair value change	$ 780,000	$ (300,000)	$ 2,520,000
	Cumulative increase (decrease) in retained earnings = Net effect on equity	$ 780,000	$ 480,000	$ 3,000,000

Notice that the revaluation model and the fair value model have the same net effect on equity (see bottom rows of the preceding exhibits). The difference is that the equity effect in the revaluation model for PPE is composed of a revaluation surplus offset by retained earnings reduction (due to depreciation), whereas the fair value model for investment property passes all of the fair value changes through retained earnings (via profit or loss).

3. Transfers into and out of investment property

THRESHOLD CONCEPT
QUALITY OF EARNINGS

The definition of investment property distinguishes these assets from PPE and inventories. That differentiation also suggests that, when there is a change in use, investment property should be reclassified as PPE or inventories and vice versa. Given the different measurement bases available for the three classifications, IFRS prescribes several rules to prevent earnings management through transfers into or out of investment property. For example, in the absence of such standards, management could take PPE measured at cost, but which has appreciated in value, and reclassify it as investment property carried at fair value so as to recognize the increase in value in income.

a. Change in use requirement

To reduce opportunities for earnings management, IAS 40 paragraph 57 requires a change in use for a transfer into or out of investment property. A change in use is, for example, a change from holding the property to earn rental income or capital appreciation to occupying the property, or vice versa.

b. Transfers when the enterprise uses the cost model for investment property

This is the most straightforward scenario, which encompasses both transfers into and out of investment property. The appropriate accounting is to continue to use the pre-transfer cost and carrying amount after the transfer; the cost and carrying amount under the old classification becomes the cost and carrying amount under the new classification. Any accumulated depreciation would be carried over (i.e., the accumulated depreciation is not reset to zero as would be the case with a purchase from an outside party). Note that the pre-transfer carrying amount need not be based on historical cost. For example, for transfers into investment property, pre-transfer PPE could be measured using the cost model or the revaluation model; pre-transfer inventory is at the lower of cost and net realizable value. Likewise, for transfers out of investment property, the use of the cost model pre-transfer does not restrict the measurement post-transfer.

c. Transfers when the enterprise uses the fair value model for investment property

When the enterprise uses the fair value model, the accounting for the transfer depends on the direction of transfer.

- Transfers *out of investment property* to PPE or inventories: Apply the fair value model at the date of transfer (i.e., record the change in value through profit or loss). The fair value on the date of transfer becomes the cost of the PPE or inventories.
- Transfers from inventories *into investment property*: Revalue inventory to fair value on the date of transfer and record the change in value through profit or loss.
- Transfers from PPE *into investment property*: Apply IAS 16 up to the date of transfer (i.e., record depreciation up to the date of transfer and any impairment), then revalue the asset according to the revaluation model of IAS 16. Revaluation is required independent of whether the company had been using the cost model or the revaluation model for that property. The revalued amount becomes the cost initially recognized in investment property.

Thus, these rules result in the transfers being recorded at fair value on the date of transfer in all cases. The pre-transfer accounting is where it becomes unintuitive. The first two transfers are as if the property had been sold on the date of transfer, since the gains or losses flow through income.

For the third transfer (from PPE into investment property), the accounting for the change in value depends on the circumstance. Applying IAS 16 up to the date of transfer requires understanding whether the cumulative revaluation adjustment for the asset, including the adjustment up to the date of transfer, is above or under water, as discussed in Section A. As long as the cumulative revaluation adjustment is positive, the changes in value go through OCI; otherwise, the adjustment goes through net income.

If an item of PPE has a cumulative revaluation surplus on the date of transfer, that surplus remains in equity until the enterprise disposes of the property. At that time, the revaluation surplus is transferred to retained earnings without passing through profit or loss (i.e., not recycled through income).

To illustrate these rules on transferring into and out of investment property, consider again the facts for Arbutus Homes' Laurel Street property. First suppose that the company initially classified the property as an investment property and applied the fair value model. At the beginning of 2021, the company no longer intends to hold the property for capital appreciation and instead the property would be part of the company's operating assets. With the change in use, the company reclassified the Laurel Street property as PPE. To reflect this transfer, Arbutus Homes would record the following entries:

Exhibit 10-22	Journal entries to record the transfer of Arbutus Homes' Laurel Street property out of investment property carried at fair value to PPE	
Dr. PPE—Laurel Street building	10,980,000	
Cr. Investment property—Laurel Street building		10,980,000
Dr. PPE—Laurel Street land	9,500,000	
Cr. Investment property—Laurel Street land		9,500,000

Thus, transfers out of investment property are reasonably straightforward.

To illustrate an inward transfer, suppose that Arbutus Homes had initially classified the Laurel Street property as PPE, and then changed the classification to investment property at the beginning of 2021. Further, assume that the company sells the property later in 2021 for $22 million, with $12 million allocated to the building and $10 million allocated to land. The following journal entries reflect this transfer if the PPE was carried at cost, and the subsequent sale:

Exhibit 10-23	Journal entries to record the transfer of Arbutus Homes' Laurel Street property from PPE carried at cost into investment property	
First, revalue the land and building to fair value at date of transfer:		
Dr. PPE—Laurel Street building	180,000	
Cr. Revaluation reserve—Laurel Street building (OCI)		180,000
Dr. PPE—Laurel Street land	1,500,000	
Cr. Revaluation reserve—Laurel Street land (OCI)		1,500,000
Second, record transfer:		
Dr. Investment property—Laurel Street building	10,980,000	
Dr. Accumulated depreciation—Laurel Street building	1,200,000	
Cr. PPE—Laurel Street building		12,180,000
Dr. Investment property—Laurel Street land	9,500,000	
Cr. PPE—Laurel Street land		9,500,000

(Continued)

Exhibit 10-23	Continued

Record the sale of property for $22 million in 2021:

Dr. Cash	22,000,000	
Cr. Investment property—Laurel Street building		10,980,000
Cr. Investment property—Laurel Street land		9,500,000
Cr. Gain on sale of investment property		1,520,000
Dr. Revaluation reserve—Laurel Street building (AOCI)	180,000	
Dr. Revaluation reserve—Laurel Street land (AOCI)	1,500,000	
Cr. Retained earnings		1,680,000

Observe in particular the final entry—the revaluation reserves for the property, which were established upon the transfer from PPE to investment property, must be transferred directly to retained earnings without passing through income.

For the sake of completeness, let us also consider what the journal entries would look like had Arbutus Homes transferred the PPE into investment property, and had the PPE been carried using the revaluation model.

Exhibit 10-24	Journal entries to record the transfer of Arbutus Homes' Laurel Street property from PPE carried on revalued basis into investment property

First, revalue the land and building to fair value at date of transfer:

(No entries required because transfer occurred at the beginning of the year and the assets had already been revalued at the prior year-end.)

Second, record transfer:

Dr. Investment property—Laurel Street building	10,980,000	
Cr. PPE—Laurel Street building		10,980,000
Dr. Investment property—Laurel Street land	9,500,000	
Cr. PPE—Laurel Street land		9,500,000

Record the sale of property for $22 million in 2021:

Dr. Cash	22,000,000	
Cr. Investment property—Laurel Street building		10,980,000
Cr. Investment property—Laurel Street land		9,500,000
Cr. Gain on sale of investment property		1,520,000
Dr. Revaluation reserve—Laurel Street building (AOCI)	200,000	
Dr. Revaluation reserve—Laurel Street land (AOCI)	1,500,000	
Cr. Retained earnings		1,700,000

In the final entry, notice that the revaluation reserve on the building transferred to retained earnings is $200,000, compared with $180,000 in Exhibit 10-23, where the PPE was carried at cost prior to transfer. The difference of $20,000 is due to the higher depreciation expense under the revaluation model, which in turn reduced retained earnings. The additional $20,000 transferred into retained earnings upon the sale of the property compensates for that additional depreciation expense taken while the property was classified as PPE.

 CHECKPOINT **CP10-5**

Identify three ways in which the fair value model for investment property differs from the revaluation model for PPE.

 CHECKPOINT **CP10-6**

How should enterprises record a change in use from property held for use to property held to earn income or capital appreciation?

D. AGRICULTURE

Agriculture receives special attention in IFRS through a separate standard (IAS 41) because of two unique features of the sector: the nature of agricultural activities and the lack of usefulness of historical cost figures.

- Agriculture, more than any other commercial activity, involves regular cycles of change (growth, degeneration/decay, and reproduction), managing those changes (by providing nutrients, water, etc.), and measuring changes in quantity and quality due to growth, degeneration, and reproduction.
- Due to the nature of agricultural activities just discussed, the historical cost of a biological item will bear little resemblance to the realizable value of that item. For example, the cost of seedlings will be a small fraction of the value of an apple tree. As a result, IAS 41 generally requires the use of fair values to measure biological items.

Due to the significantly different accounting for agriculture, it is important to first understand what is or is not an agricultural activity. We will then look at the accounting for these activities.

1. Definition of agricultural activity and scope of IAS 41

The scope of IAS 41 covers agricultural activity and the assets relating to those activities. The standard defines **agricultural activity** as the management by an entity of the biological transformation of biological assets for sale or for conversion into agricultural produce or into additional biological assets. Two parts of this definition require emphasis:

> **agricultural activity** The management by an entity of the biological transformation of biological assets for sale or for conversion into agricultural produce or into additional biological assets.

- The requirement for active management includes fish farming and tree plantations, but excludes, for example, fishing from the open ocean or logging from unmanaged forests.
- Agricultural activity extends only to the point of harvest but not beyond. Subsequent processing of agricultural produce would be covered by other accounting standards such as IAS 2 on inventories and IAS 18 on revenue recognition.

Exhibit 10-25 illustrates the scope of IAS 41 in relation to the stage of activity, whether agricultural or subsequent processing, along with the types of assets associated with the stage.

As shown in the diagram, two types of assets are associated with agricultural activity: a **biological asset** is a living animal or plant, whereas **agricultural produce** is the harvested product of biological assets.

> **biological asset** A living animal or plant.
>
> **agricultural produce** The harvested product of biological assets.

2. Accounting for biological assets and agricultural produce

As alluded to above, the accounting for agricultural activities uses fair values more than non-agricultural sectors do. Whereas the general recognition criteria for other

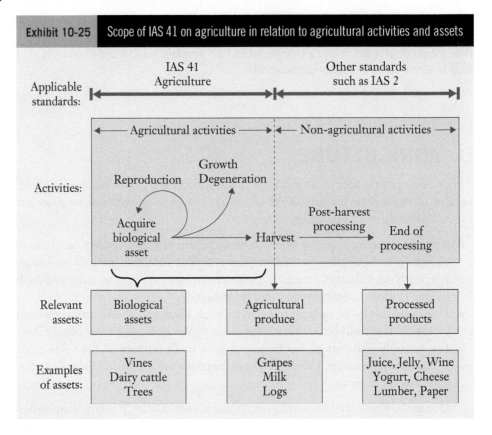

Exhibit 10-25 Scope of IAS 41 on agriculture in relation to agricultural activities and assets

types of assets involve a reliable measurement of *cost*, IAS 41 paragraph 10 instead refers to *fair value* in addition to cost:

> ¶10   An entity shall recognize a biological asset or agricultural produce when, and only when:
>   a. the entity controls the asset as a result of past events;
>   b. it is probable that future economic benefits associated with the asset will flow to the entity; and
>   c. the fair value or cost of the asset can be measured reliably.[9]

Contrast condition (c) with the corresponding measurement criterion for the recognition of PPE in Chapter 8 and intangible assets in Chapter 9: "The cost of the asset can be measured reliably." (e.g., IAS 16 paragraph 7(b))

a. Agricultural produce

When an enterprise harvests agricultural produce, it estimates the fair value of that produce on the date of harvest as well as the costs that the enterprise would incur if the produce were to be sold. The fair value net of the point-of-sale costs is the amount at which the enterprise records the agricultural produce.

b. Biological assets

For biological assets, IAS 41 also requires enterprises to use fair values less point-of-sale costs in both the initial recognition upon acquisition and subsequent measurement on each balance sheet date. An enterprise can make an exception and use cost (less any depreciation) instead of fair value *only if* the enterprise demonstrates that it cannot measure fair value reliably. In other words, for biological assets there is a presumption that

---

fair value can be measured reliably, and an enterprise must provide evidence to rebut that presumption. This *exception to applying fair value must be made upon initial recognition* of the biological asset—IAS 41 rules out the possibility of an enterprise determining that it can reliably measure fair value initially but being unable to do so later. However, the opposite is possible: an enterprise can initially determine that fair value is not reliably measurable but later conclude that it can be measured reliably.

There are aspects to the determination of fair values that are particular to biological assets and agricultural produce. Such detail is beyond the scope of this text. The interested reader should refer to paragraphs 15 to 25 of IAS 41, which describe these considerations thoroughly.

Take a moment to consider the fair value requirement. Contrast a dairy cow and a fruit-bearing tree. Which of these two biological assets is more likely to have reliable fair values and which one less?

For an asset to have a fair value, it needs to be capable of being sold. A dairy cow can be transported from seller to buyer quite readily. In contrast, one cannot uproot a mature fruit-bearing tree without extensively damaging its roots. This is not to say that the tree has a fair value of zero, because the tree has value where it has been planted, but its value is literally attached to the land. In other words, we would only be able to reliably determine a fair value for the fruit trees if the farm or land were to be sold, but not before then. This example illustrates the difficulty of measuring the fair value of **bearer plants**: biological assets that are used only to grow agricultural produce over several periods.

bearer plants Biological assets that are used only to grow agricultural produce over several periods.

Due to the inability of farmers to obtain reliable fair values of bearer plants, the IASB in 2014 issued an amendment to IAS 41 to exclude bearer plants from the fair value requirement. In other words, the IASB amended the standard to reflect actual practice and removed the presumption that bearer plants have reliable fair values. As a result of this amendment, enterprises should account for bearer plants in the same fashion as PPE. The amendment became effective January 1, 2014.

c. Gains and losses from fair value measurement

The initial recognition and subsequent measurement of agricultural produce and biological assets at fair values can give rise to gains or losses. For example, newborn chicks, lambs, or calves will likely result in gains, while a banana plantation afflicted with Panama disease (a fungus) would likely result in a loss. An enterprise would record such gains and losses through profit or loss (not comprehensive income) because they result from normal operating activities of the agricultural enterprise.

Exhibit 10-26	Example of accounting for agriculture in practice

Andrew Peller Limited is a Canadian-based winery that is publicly traded on the Canadian Securities Exchange (ticker: ADW-A). The following are excerpts from the company's annual report for the fiscal year ended March 31, 2017, to illustrate the accounting for agriculture using IFRS. Figures are in thousands of dollars.

Statement of financial position	2017	2016
Current assets		
Biological assets	1,400	1,196
Statement of comprehensive income		
Sale of goods	427	778
Cost of goods sold	(1,682)	(1,172)
Fair value adjustment on biological assets	(816)	(178)
Note 2: Summary of significant accounting policies		

(Continued)

Exhibit 10-26   Continued

Basis of measurement

The consolidated financial statements have been prepared under the historical cost convention, except for derivatives, which are measured at fair value, and biological assets, which are measured at fair value less costs to sell.

Cost of goods sold

Cost of goods sold includes the cost of finished goods inventories sold during the year, inventory writedowns, and revaluations of agricultural produce to fair value less costs to sell at the point of harvest.

Inventories

Inventories are valued at the lower of cost and net realizable value. Cost is determined on an average cost basis. The Company utilizes a weighted average cost calculation to determine the value of ending inventory (bulk wine and finished goods). Average cost is determined separately for import wine and domestic wine and is calculated by varietal and vintage year.

Grapes produced from vineyards controlled by the Company that are part of inventories are measured at their fair value less costs to sell at the point of harvest.

The Company includes borrowing costs in the cost of certain wine inventories that require a substantial period of time to become ready for sale.

Biological assets

The Company measures biological assets, consisting of grapes grown on vineyards controlled by the Company, at cost, which approximates fair value as there has been minimal biological transformation since the initial cost incurred. The initial costs incurred are comprised of direct expenditures required to enable the biological transformation of agricultural produce.

At the point of harvest, the fair value of biological assets is determined by reference to local market prices for grapes of a similar quality and the same varietal. At this point, agricultural produce is measured at fair value less costs to sell, which becomes the basis for the cost of inventories after harvest.

Gains or losses arising from a change in fair value less costs to sell are included in the consolidated statements of earnings in the period in which they arise.

Note 6. Biological assets

Biological assets consist of grapes prior to harvest that are controlled by the Company. The Company owns and leases land in Ontario and British Columbia to grow grapes in order to secure a supply of quality grapes for the making of wine.

During the year ended March 31, 2017, the Company harvested grapes valued at $6,238 (2016 – $6,479).

The changes in the carrying amount of biological assets are as follows:

	2017	2016
Carrying amount – Beginning of year	$ 1,196	$ 1,129
Net increase in fair value less costs to sell due to biological transformation	6,442	6,546
Transferred to inventory on harvest	(6,238)	(6,479)
Net gain	204	67
Biological assets	$ 1,400	$ 1,196

Note that Andrew Peller has an unusual classification of its vines and grapes. The above disclosures indicate that only unharvested grapes are included in biological assets. Additional disclosure in Note 5 relating to property, plant, and equipment includes $31.5 million in "vines, vineyard land, and infrastructure" as at March 31, 2017, and this amount represents cost less accumulated amortization. The examples included in IAS 41 include grapevines as biological assets, picked grapes as agricultural produce, and wine as products resulting from processing.

 CHECKPOINT CP10-7

How does IAS 41 differentiate between biological assets and agricultural produce?

 CHECKPOINT CP10-8

Which measurement basis does IAS 41 suggest is generally most appropriate for biological assets?

E. NON-CURRENT ASSETS HELD FOR SALE AND DISCONTINUED OPERATIONS

By definition, non-current assets are intended to be held for more than one year. However, on occasion enterprises will sell such assets rather than continue to use them in their operations. When an enterprise has decided to sell a non-current asset but has not yet sold it by the reporting date, that asset is considered to be "held for sale." Technically, IFRS 5 requires the following:

> ¶6   An entity shall classify a non-current asset (or disposal group) as held for sale if its carrying amount will be recovered principally through a sale transaction rather than through continuing use.[10]

L.O. 10-5.   Apply the accounting standards relating to non-current assets held for sale and discontinued operations.

In this standard, a **disposal group** refers to a group of assets and liabilities to be disposed of together in a single transaction. For example, a disposal group could be a subsidiary that a company intends to sell; this subsidiary would usually contain both assets and liabilities, and they could be either current or non-current. For simplicity, this section will refer to non-current assets as also referring to disposal groups.

disposal group   A group of assets and liabilities to be disposed of together in a single transaction.

The assets that IFRS 5 paragraph 6 intends to cover are those non-current assets which are both *available* for immediate sale and *expected to sell* within a year of their classification as held for sale. In some instances, non-current assets may be available for sale but market conditions are such that management cannot expect to sell the assets until more than a year in the future. In that case, the asset would continue to be classified as a regular non-current asset (i.e., held for use).

Similar to financial investments that are classified as held for sale, fair value becomes relevant to the measurement of non-current assets held for sale. When an enterprise classifies a non-current asset as held for sale, it should measure the asset's value at the lower of its carrying amount and fair value less cost to sell. Since the enterprise no longer intends to use the non-current asset in operations for any significant period of time (less than a year), the asset's value in use is not the most relevant measure.

THRESHOLD CONCEPT
CONCEPTUAL FRAMEWORK

Stated differently, an enterprise must complete an impairment test for any non-current assets classified as held for sale, using the measure of recoverable amount that is relevant under the circumstances (i.e., fair value less cost to sell, not the value in use). If the non-current assets held for sale are impaired, the accounting for the impairment follows the approach discussed earlier in Section B: the impairment loss flows through net income or OCI depending on whether the enterprise uses the cost or revaluation model and whether there is a revaluation surplus balance in equity.

Another interesting (and somewhat controversial) aspect of non-current assets held for sale is that depreciation or amortization ceases when the enterprise classifies these assets as held for sale. On the one hand, the enterprise expects to use the non-current asset for less than a year, so the amount of depreciation/amortization should not be large. Furthermore, any decline in value because of continued use of the asset would be reflected in lower proceeds on the sale, which would result in a lower gain or a larger loss when the sale transaction is completed. On the other hand, not recording depreciation/amortization is inconsistent with the decline in productive capacity from using the asset.

[10.] Copyright © 2012 IFRS Foundation.

component of an entity
A portion of an entity that comprises operations and cash flows that can be clearly distinguished, operationally and for financial reporting purposes, from the rest of the entity.

THRESHOLD CONCEPT
DECISION MAKING UNDER UNCERTAINTY

discontinued operations
A component of an entity that either has been disposed of or is classified as held for sale and (i) represents a separate major line of business or geographical area of operation, (ii) is part of a single coordinated plan to dispose of a separate major line of business or geographical area of operation, or (iii) is a subsidiary acquired exclusively with a view to resale.

Asset disposals are sometimes large enough to involve a **component of an entity**, which comprises operations and cash flows that can be clearly distinguished, operationally and for financial reporting purposes, from the rest of the entity. In other words, a component of an entity is at least one cash generating unit or a combination of cash generating units. A subsidiary or product division would usually be considered a component of an entity. When a component of an entity has been sold or held for sale as at the financial statement date, its operations are called **discontinued operations**. Formally, discontinued operations consist of a component of an entity that either has been disposed of or is classified as held for sale and (i) represents a separate major line of business or geographical area of operation, (ii) is part of a single coordinated plan to dispose of a separate major line of business or geographical area of operation, or (iii) is a subsidiary acquired exclusively with a view to resale.

Discontinued operations likely represent a significant portion of an enterprise's total operations. To aid readers of financial statements to evaluate performance and predict future operations, IFRS requires separate presentation of the results of discontinued operations on the face of the financial statements and in disclosure in the notes. Specifically, enterprises with discontinued operations should do the following:

1. Present a single amount in the statement of comprehensive income, on an after-tax basis, being the total of:
   - net profit or loss attributable to the discontinued operations, and
   - gain or loss on disposal (if sold by year-end) or from impairment of assets used in the discontinued operations (if not sold by year-end).
2. Disaggregate the single amount from (1), either on the statement of comprehensive income or in the notes, into the following six components:
   - revenue
   - expenses
   - pre-tax profit
   - income tax expense
   - gain or loss on disposal or from impairment of assets used in the discontinued operations
   - income tax expense on the gain or loss
3. Disclose the operating, investing, and financing cash flows of the discontinued operations either on the cash flow statement or in the notes.

As you can see, the additional presentation and disclosures for discontinued operations are quite extensive. The overall idea is to present a summary of the results of those operations that the enterprise will not carry on in the future so that financial statement users can adjust forecasts accordingly. Consistent with this idea, if an enterprise buys a new subsidiary with the intention of selling that subsidiary, then the results of the discontinued operations would never have been included in continuing operations. In such cases, IFRS 5 allows the omission of the detailed disclosures in (2) and (3); the single amount for after-tax income in (1) is sufficient.

This simplified reporting method can be seen in the 2010 annual report of Rio Tinto PLC, an Anglo-Australian mining company. In 2007, Rio Tinto purchased the Canadian company Alcan Inc., an aluminum producer. Notice the separate line item "Asset held for sale" on the balance sheet as well as the additional lines on the income statement for discontinued operations and EPS on discontinued operations. The note disclosure provides additional information on these discontinued operations.

Exhibit 10-27	Rio Tinto's reporting of discontinued operations

Excerpt from balance sheet

As at December 31 (millions USD)	2010	2009
Current assets		
Inventories	4,756	4,889
Trade and other receivables	5,582	4,447
Loans to equity accounted units	110	168
Tax recoverable	542	501
Other financial assets	521	694
Cash and cash equivalents	9,948	4,233
	21,459	14,932
Assets of disposal groups held for sale	1,706	4,782

Excerpt from income statement

For the years ended December 31 (millions USD)	2010	2009
Profit before taxation	20,577	7,860
Taxation	(5,296)	(2,076)
Profit from continuing operations	15,281	5,784
Discontinued operations—Loss after-tax from discontinued operations	(97)	(449)
Profit for the year	15,184	5,335
Earnings per share (USD)		
Basic earnings/(loss) per share		
Profit from continuing operations	7.35	3.02
Loss from discontinued operations	(0.05)	(0.26)
Profit for the year	7.30	2.76
Diluted earnings/(loss) per share		
Profit from continuing operations	7.31	3.00
Loss from discontinued operations	(0.05)	(0.25)
Profit for the year	7.26	2.75

Note 19: Assets held for sale

At 31 December 2010, assets and liabilities held for sale comprise Alcan's Engineered Products group (AEP), excluding the Cable Division following the receipt on 5 August 2010, of a binding offer from funds affiliated with Apollo Global Management, LLC. ("Apollo") and the Fonds Stratégique d'Investissement (FSI) to buy a 61 per cent stake in AEP, excluding the Cable Division. The divestment was completed on 4 January 2011. The terms of the transaction are confidential. Refer to note 48 – Events after the statement of financial position date.

Source: From Rio Tinto, 2010 Annual report. Copyright 2010 by Rio Tinto Ltd.

 CHECKPOINT **CP10-9**

In which way is the accounting for non-current assets held for sale similar to the accounting for impairment?

F. A PRACTICAL ILLUSTRATION: CANADIAN TIRE CORPORATION

The following excerpts from the 2016 financial statements of Canadian Tire Corporation serve to illustrate the result of applying some of the accounting standards discussed in this chapter.

Issue	Reference in financial statements	Excerpts [Discussion in brackets]
Revaluations of non-current assets	Page 63: Note 2: Basis of preparation: Basis of presentation	[The company disclosed that it uses "the historical cost basis" except for several instruments, implying that it does not use the revaluation model for non-current assets.]
Impairment	Page 71: Note 3: Significant accounting policies: Impairment of assets	The carrying amounts of property and equipment, investment property and intangible assets with finite useful lives are reviewed at the end of each reporting period to determine whether there are any indicators of impairment. Indicators of impairment may include a significant decline in asset market value, material adverse changes in the external operating environment which affect the manner in which the asset is used or is expected to be used, obsolescence, or physical damage of the asset. If any such indicators exist, then the recoverable amount of the asset is estimated. Goodwill and intangible assets with indefinite useful lives and intangible assets not yet available for use are not amortized but are tested for impairment at least annually or whenever there is an indicator that the asset may be impaired.
	Page 71: Note 3: Significant accounting policies: Cash generating units	When it is not possible to estimate the recoverable amount of an individual asset, the Company estimates the recoverable amount of the CGU to which the asset belongs. The CGUs correspond to the smallest identifiable group of assets whose continuing use generates cash inflows that are largely independent of the cash inflows from other assets or groups of assets.

Goodwill acquired in a business combination is allocated to each of the CGUs (or groups of CGUs) expected to benefit from the synergies of the combination. Intangible assets with indefinite useful lives are allocated to the CGU to which they relate. |
| | Page 71: Note 3: Significant accounting policies: Determining the recoverable amount | An impairment loss is recognized when the carrying amount of an asset, or of the CGU to which it belongs, exceeds the recoverable amount. The recoverable amount of an asset or CGU is defined as the higher of its fair value less costs to sell ("FVLCS") and VIU [value in use].

In assessing VIU, the estimated future cash flows are discounted to their present value. Cash flows are discounted using a pre-tax discount rate that includes a risk premium specific to each line of business. The Company estimates cash flows before taxes based on the most recent actual results or budgets. Cash flows are then extrapolated over a period of up to five years, taking into account a terminal value calculated by discounting the final year in perpetuity. The growth rate applied to the terminal values is based on the Bank of Canada's target growth rate or a growth rate specific to the individual item being tested based on management's estimate. |
Investment property	Page 70: Note 3: Significant accounting policies: Investment property	Investment property is property held to earn rental income or for appreciation of capital or both. The Company has determined that properties it provides to its Dealers, franchisees and agents are not investment property as these relate to the Company's operating activities. This was determined based on certain criteria such as whether the Company provides significant ancillary services to the lessees of the property. The Company includes property that it leases to third parties (other than Dealers, franchisees or agents) in investment property. Investment property is measured in the same manner as property and equipment.
Agricultural activities	—	[Not applicable to company.]
Non-current assets held for sale	Page 71: Note 3: Significant accounting policies: Assets classified as held for sale	Non-current assets and disposal groups are classified as assets held for sale when their carrying amount is to be recovered principally through a sale transaction rather than through continuing use. This condition is regarded as met only when the sale is highly probable and the asset (or disposal group) is available for immediate sale in its present condition. Management must be committed to the sale, and it should be expected to qualify for recognition as a completed sale within one year from the date of classification. Assets (and disposal groups) classified as held for sale are measured at the lower of the carrying amount or FVLCS and are not depreciated.

G. SUBSTANTIVE DIFFERENCES BETWEEN IFRS AND ASPE

Issue	IFRS	ASPE
Cost or revaluation model	Enterprises can choose to apply the cost model or revaluation model to each class of PPE or intangible assets.	Enterprises must use the cost model.
When to test for impairment	Annually test intangibles with indefinite lives and goodwill. Test other assets (PPE, intangibles with finite lives) when there are indications the asset may be impaired.	For any long-lived asset (PPE, intangibles, goodwill), test when there are indications the asset may be impaired.
When to search for indications of impairment	Annually search for indications of impairment.	ASPE does not refer to an active search for indications of impairment.
Recoverable amount in impairment test	The recoverable amount is the higher of (i) fair value less cost to sell and (ii) value in use.	The recoverable amount is the sum of undiscounted cash flows expected from the use of the asset.
Amount of impairment loss	Impairment = Carrying amount − Recoverable amount	Impairment = Carrying amount − Fair value
Reversal of impairment	Impairments may be reversed if the recoverable amount subsequently rises.	Impairment losses cannot be reversed.
Impairment of items carried using revaluation model	Impairment first reduces any revaluation surplus on the item, and the remainder flows through net income.	Not applicable since the revaluation model is not permitted. Thus, all impairment losses flow through net income.
Investment property	Enterprises with investment property may choose either the cost or fair value model; this choice applies to all of its investment property. If the cost model is chosen, fair values must be disclosed.	No specific guidance relating to investment property since ASPE does not permit the fair value model. Refer to general guidance in property, plant, and equipment.
Agriculture	IAS 41 specifically addresses issues relating to agricultural activities; emphasis on fair value measurements of biological assets and agricultural produce.	No specific guidance relating to agriculture. Refer to general guidance in inventories, property, plant, and equipment, etc., which are based primarily on historical cost.

H. SUMMARY

L.O. 10-1. Apply the revaluation model of accounting for non-current assets.

- IFRS allows enterprises to choose the revaluation model instead of the cost model to account for many non-current assets if those assets have fair values that are sufficiently reliable.
- For assets that are depreciable, enterprises have the option of accounting for the effect of the revaluation on accumulated depreciation using either the proportional or elimination methods. Subsequent depreciation changes prospectively.
- The effect of revaluation affects equity asymmetrically depending on whether cumulative revaluation adjustments are positive or negative for a particular asset. Positive cumulative adjustments go to the revaluation surplus component of equity, while negative cumulative adjustments go through profit or loss.

L.O. 10-2.   Evaluate whether a non-current asset should be tested for impairment, whether that asset is impaired, and the extent of impairment.

- An enterprise should annually search for indications that its assets may be impaired.
- An enterprise should annually test for impairment of goodwill and intangible assets with indefinite lives.
- For purposes of impairment procedures, an enterprise should group assets with interdependent cash flows into cash generating units.
- An asset (or cash generating unit) is impaired if its carrying amount exceeds its recoverable amount.
- The recoverable amount is the higher of fair value less cost to sell and value in use.
- The amount of impairment equals the amount by which the carrying amount exceeds the recoverable amount.

L.O. 10-3.   Account for the impairment of different types of non-current assets.

- An enterprise should allocate the impairment loss of a cash generating unit among the assets comprising that unit in proportion to each asset's carrying value. An exception to proportional allocation occurs when such allocation would result in an asset's carrying amount falling below its recoverable amount.
- An enterprise records an impairment loss by writing down the carrying amount of the asset and recording a loss through the income statement and retained earnings, except when the enterprise has a revaluation surplus, in which case the loss flows through other comprehensive income to reduce that surplus.

L.O. 10-4.   Apply the specialized standards for the recognition and measurement of assets relating to investment properties and agricultural activities.

- Investment property for accounting purposes under IFRS includes property held for the purpose of earning rental income or for capital appreciation.
- Enterprises can choose to measure investment property at cost or at fair value at the balance sheet date.
- The fair value method requires fair value estimates at the end of the reporting period.
- Investment property carried at fair value is not depreciated.
- IFRS provides specific rules to account for transfers into and out of investment property to reflect changes in use. These rules are aimed at mitigating opportunities for earnings management.
- Agricultural activities include acquisition, growth, reproduction, and production, including harvest. Subsequent processing is not part of agriculture for the purposes of IFRS.
- Enterprises should measure agricultural produce at fair value less point-of-sale costs.
- Enterprises should measure biological assets at fair value less point-of-sale costs, except in cases where they are unable to reliably measure fair value; in such cases, enterprises should measure biological assets at cost less accumulated depreciation. Once a biological asset is carried at fair value, it should continue to be carried on that basis.

L.O. 10-5.   Apply the accounting standards relating to non-current assets held for sale and discontinued operations.

- Enterprises should classify non-current assets as held for sale if those assets are available for sale and expected to be sold within one year from the classification date.
- Non-current assets held for sale should be tested for impairment, with the recoverable amount defined as fair value less cost to sell.
- Enterprises that have disposed of or plan to dispose of assets significant enough to be considered a component of the entity should provide separate presentation and disclosure of the results of the discontinued operations.

I. ANSWERS TO CHECKPOINT QUESTIONS

CP10-1: The two methods to reflect revaluation adjustments for depreciable assets are the elimination and proportional methods. The elimination method resets the accumulated depreciation balance to zero and sets the gross carrying amount equal to the revalued amount. The proportional method adjusts the gross carrying amount and accumulated depreciation by the same percentage, such that the net carrying amount of the depreciable asset equals the revalued amount.

CP10-2: Revaluation adjustments flow through net income when the revalued asset is "under water" (cumulative revaluations are below zero). The adjustments flow through OCI when the revalued asset is "above water" (cumulative revaluations are above zero).

CP10-3: The frequency of impairment testing depends on the type of asset and whether it has a finite or indefinite life. Intangible assets with indefinite lives and goodwill (which also has an indefinite life) should be tested for impairment annually. Other assets should be tested when there are indications of impairment.

CP10-4: The two values that go into the recoverable amount are (i) fair value less cost to sell and (ii) value in use.

CP10-5: Three differences between the fair value and revaluation models include the following: (i) the fair value model requires fair value estimates each year, but the frequency can be lower for the revaluation model; (ii) under the fair value model, fair value adjustments flow through net income, whereas, under the revaluation model, they flow through OCI or net income depending on whether the cumulative revaluations are above or below zero, respectively; and (iii) the fair value model does not require depreciation to also be recorded, as is necessary under the revaluation model.

CP10-6: A change in use from property held for use to property held to earn income or capital appreciation results in a transfer from PPE to investment property. To record the transfer, the enterprise accounts for the asset under IAS 16 up to the date of transfer and then revalues the asset according to IAS 16. The revalued amount becomes the new cost for the investment property, which is then accounted for under IAS 40.

CP10-7: Biological assets and agricultural produce differ because the former are alive (pre-harvest) whereas the latter has been harvested.

CP10-8: IAS 41 recommends the use of fair value less point-of-sale costs for biological assets. In exceptional cases, when fair value cannot be reliably measured, the cost method may be used.

CP10-9: Non-current assets held for sale are recorded at the lower of their carrying value and their fair value less cost to sell. This is just like applying the impairment test without considering the value in use since management plans to sell the assets.

J. GLOSSARY

agricultural activity: The management by an entity of the biological transformation of biological assets for sale or for conversion into agricultural produce or into additional biological assets.

agricultural produce: The harvested product of biological assets.

bearer plants: Biological assets that are used only to grow agricultural produce over several periods.

biological asset: A living animal or plant.

cash generating units: The smallest identifiable group of assets that generates cash inflows that are largely independent of those from other assets.

component of an entity: A portion of an entity that comprises operations and cash flows that can be clearly distinguished, operationally and for financial reporting purposes, from the rest of the entity.

costs of disposal: The incremental costs directly attributable to the disposal of an asset, excluding finance costs and income tax expense.

discontinued operations: A **component of an entity** that either has been disposed of or is classified as held for sale and (i) represents a separate major line of business or geographical area of operation, (ii) is part of a single coordinated plan to dispose of a separate major line of business or geographical area of operation, or (iii) is a subsidiary acquired exclusively with a view to resale.

disposal group: A group of assets and liabilities to be disposed of together in a single transaction.

elimination method (of accounting for revaluation): A method that removes the balance in accumulated depreciation and restates the gross carrying amount to fair value. Contrast with **proportional method.**

fair value: The price that would be received to sell an asset or paid to transfer a liability in an orderly transaction between market participants at the measurement date.

fair value less cost to sell: The price that would be received to sell an asset or paid to transfer a liability in an orderly transaction between market participants at the measurement date, less the **costs of disposal.**

fair value model: A measurement model that reports assets at fair value on the balance sheet date, with changes in value recognized in profit or loss

investment property: Land or buildings held to earn rental income or for capital appreciation.

owner-occupied property: Land or buildings for use in the production or supply of goods or services or for administrative purposes.

proportional method (of accounting for revaluation): A method that adjusts the gross carrying value and accumulated depreciation (or amortization) by the same percentage such that the net carrying amount equals fair value after revaluation. Contrast with **elimination method.**

recoverable amount: The higher of an asset's **fair value less cost to sell** and its **value in use.**

revaluation model: Restates the carrying value of an asset to the asset's fair value on the date of revaluation.

value in use: The present value of the future cash flows expected to be derived from an asset.

K. REFERENCES

Authoritative standards:

IFRS	ASPE Section
IAS 16—Property, Plant, and Equipment	3061—Property, Plant, and Equipment
IAS 36—Impairment of Assets	3063—Impairment of Long-lived Assets
IAS 38—Intangible Assets	3064—Goodwill and Intangible Assets
IAS 40—Investment Property	
IAS 41—Agriculture	
IFRS 5—Non-current Assets Held for Sale and Discontinued Operations	3475—Disposal of Long-lived Assets and Discontinued Operations

MyLab Accounting   Make the grade with **MyLab Accounting:** The problems marked with a 🌐 can be found on **MyLab Accounting.** You can practise them as often as you want, and most feature step-by-step guided instructions to help you find the right answer.

L. PROBLEMS

 P10-1. Accounting for revaluations on land   **(L.O.** 10-1**)** (Easy – 3 minutes)

Company One purchased land for $1,000,000 during the year. Fair value at the end of the year was $1,250,000.

Required:

Prepare the journal entry to record the revaluation adjustment.

 P10-2. Accounting for revaluations on land   **(L.O.** 10-1**)** (Easy – 3 minutes)

Company Two has land that was purchased for $1,000,000 in a prior year. Fair value was $500,000 at the beginning of the year and $400,000 at the end of the year.

Required:

Prepare the journal entry to record the revaluation adjustment.

 P10-3. Accounting for revaluations on land   **(L.O.** 10-1**)** (Easy – 5 minutes)

Company Three has land that was purchased for $1,000,000 in a prior year. Fair value was $600,000 at the beginning of the year and $1,100,000 at the end of the year.

Required:

Prepare the journal entry to record the revaluation adjustment.

 P10-4. Accounting for revaluations on land   **(L.O.** 10-1**)** (Easy – 5 minutes)

Company Four has land that was purchased for $1,000,000 in a prior year. Fair value was $1,250,000 at the beginning of the year and $800,000 at the end of the year.

Required:

Prepare the journal entry to record the revaluation adjustment.

 P10-5. Accounting for revaluations on land   **(L.O.** 10-1**)** (Easy – 20 minutes)

Simple Value Limited (SVL) was incorporated on January 1, 2019, when the sole shareholder invested $1,000,000. This was the only financing the firm needed. SVL had a single project that it developed over four years. Below are details of the four years of operations. SVL used $900,000 of the funds to purchase land. At the end of 2022 the land was sold for its fair value.

($000's)	2019	2020	2021	2022
Revenue (all cash)	$2,500	$3,000	$2,000	$1,500
Expenses (all cash)	2,300	2,600	1,700	1,400
Fair value of land at end of the year	900	1,000	1,200	1,100

Required:

Complete the following tables. The first table assumes that SVL uses the historical cost basis of measurement. The second table assumes that SVL uses the revaluation model of measurement. What do you observe about the total income for the four years? What do you observe about the balance sheet at the end of 2022?

Historical cost basis ($000's)	2019	2020	2021	2022	4-year total
Revenue	$ 2,500	$ 3,000	$ 2,000	$ 1,500	$ 9,000
Expenses	(2,300)	(2,600)	(1,700)	(1,400)	(8,000)
Gain on disposal of land					
Net income (= comprehensive income)					
Opening retained earnings	0				
Closing retained earnings					
Cash	$ 300	$ 700	$ 1,000	$ 2,200	
Land	900				
Total assets	$ 1,200				
Share capital	$ 1,000				
Retained earnings					
Total shareholder's equity					

Revaluation model ($000's)	2019	2020	2021	2022	4-year total
Revenue	$ 2,500	$ 3,000	$ 2,000	$ 1,500	$ 9,000
Expenses	(2,300)	(2,600)	(1,700)	(1,400)	(8,000)
Gain on disposal of land					
Net income					
OCI for revaluation gain (loss)					
Comprehensive income					
Cash	$ 300	$ 700	$ 1,000	$ 2,200	
Land	900				
Total assets	$ 1,200				
Share capital	$ 1,000				
Accumulated revaluation surplus					
Retained earnings					
Total shareholder's equity					

*OCI = other comprehensive income

P10-6. **Accounting for revaluations on land with reversals**

(**L.O.** 10-1) (Medium – 20 minutes)

Variable Value Limited (VVL) was incorporated on January 1, 2019, when the sole shareholder invested $1,000,000. This was the only financing the firm needed. VVL had a single project that it developed over four years. Below are details of the four years of operations. VVL used $900,000 of the funds to purchase land. At the end of 2022 the land was sold for its fair value.

($000's)	2019	2020	2021	2022
Revenue (all cash)	$2,500	$3,000	$2,000	$1,500
Expenses (all cash)	2,300	2,600	1,700	1,400
Fair value of land at end of the year	1,150	800	1,050	1,100

Required:

Complete the following tables. The first table assumes that VVL uses the historical cost basis of measurement. The second table assumes that VVL uses the revaluation model of measurement. OCI refers to other comprehensive income.

Historical cost basis ($000's)	2019	2020	2021	2022	4-year total
Revenue	$ 2,500	$ 3,000	$ 2,000	$ 1,500	$ 9,000
Expenses	(2,300)	(2,600)	(1,700)	(1,400)	(8,000)
Gain on disposal of land					
Net income (= comprehensive income)					
Opening retained earnings	0				
Closing retained earnings					
Cash	$ 300	$ 700	$ 1,000	$ 2,200	
Land	900				
Total assets	$ 1,200				
Share capital	1,000				
Retained earnings					
Total shareholder's equity					

Revaluation model ($000's)	2019	2020	2021	2022	4-year total
Revenue	$ 2,500	$ 3,000	$ 2,000	$ 1,500	$ 9,000
Expenses	(2,300)	(2,600)	(1,700)	(1,400)	(8,000)
Revaluation gain (loss)					
Gain on disposal of land					
Net income					
OCI for revaluation gain (loss)*					
Comprehensive income					
Cash	$ 300	$ 700	$ 1,000	$ 2,200	
Land	1,150				
Total assets	$ 1,450				
Share capital	1,000				
Accumulated revaluation surplus					
Retained earnings					
Total shareholder's equity					

*OCI = other comprehensive income

 P10-7. Revaluation adjustments on depreciable assets  **(L.O. 10-1)** (Medium – 10 minutes)

Alpha Company has a piece of equipment with original cost of $1,000,000. The equipment's carrying value at the beginning of the year (net of any accumulated depreciation) was $700,000. Alpha recorded $100,000 for depreciation during the year. The equipment's fair value at the end of the year was $900,000. This is the first year that the company has revalued this equipment.

Required:

a. Record the journal entry for the revaluation adjustment assuming that Alpha uses the elimination method.
b. Record the journal entry for the revaluation adjustment assuming that Alpha uses the proportional method.

 P10-8. Revaluation adjustments on depreciable assets  **(L.O. 10-1)** (Medium – 10 minutes)

Bravo Company has a piece of equipment with original cost of $1,000,000. The equipment's carrying value at the beginning of the year (net of any accumulated depreciation) was $700,000. Bravo recorded $100,000 for depreciation during the year. The equipment's fair value at the end of the year was $480,000. This is the first year that the company has revalued this equipment.

Required:

a. Record the journal entry for the revaluation adjustment assuming that Bravo uses the elimination method.
b. Record the journal entry for the revaluation adjustment assuming that Bravo uses the proportional method.

 P10-9. Effect of revaluation adjustments on depreciation   **10-1)** (Easy – 5 minutes)

Charlie Company purchased a building for $5 million. The building has a 20-year useful life and zero residual value. The company uses the straight-line method to depreciate buildings. After using and depreciating the building for 12 years, the company obtained an appraisal, which put the value of the building at $4 million; the company revalued the building to that amount.

Required:

Compute the annual amount of depreciation expense for the first 12 years and for the last 8 years of the building's useful life.

 P10-10. Effect of revaluation adjustments on depreciation

 **10-1)** (Easy – 10 minutes)

Delta Company purchased a piece of equipment for $400,000. The equipment has an eight-year useful life and zero residual value. The company uses the double-declining-balance method for depreciating equipment. After using and depreciating the equipment for two years, the company obtained an appraisal that put the value of the equipment at $320,000, and the company revalued the equipment to that amount. Despite the revaluation, Delta's management believed the existing depreciation policy and rate to be reasonable.

Required:

Compute the amount of depreciation expense for each of the first two years and for each of the two years after the revaluation.

 P10-11. Effect of revaluation adjustments on depreciation

(L.O. 10-1) (Medium – 20 minutes)

Echo Company purchased a machine some years ago. At the end of the current year, the company revalued the machine to its fair value. The machine has the following characteristics as at the end of the current year:

Original cost	$1,000,000
Residual value	$ 200,000
Estimated useful life (from acquisition date)	10 years
Years of use up to end of current year	4 years
Estimated useful life remaining (after current year-end)	6 years
Fair value at end of current year	$ 800,000
Depreciation method	Straight-line

Required:

a. Calculate the depreciation expense for the years prior to the revaluation.
b. Calculate the depreciation expense for the years following the revaluation.
c. Record the journal entry for the revaluation adjustment using the elimination method.
d. Assuming no other changes in estimates or revaluations, show the following three amounts at the end of each of the 10 years of the equipment's life: gross carrying value, accumulated depreciation, net carrying value. Do this for the historical cost method as well as for the revaluation method.

P10-12. Effect of revaluation adjustments on depreciation

(**L.O.** 10-1) (Medium – 20 minutes)

Foxtrot Company purchased a machine some years ago. At the end of the current year, the company revalued the machine to its fair value. The machine has the following characteristics as at the end of the current year:

Original cost	$2,000,000
Residual value	$ 500,000
Estimated useful life (from acquisition date)	6 years
Years of use up to end of current year	2 years
Estimated useful life remaining (after current year-end)	4 years
Fair value at end of current year	$1,650,000
Depreciation method	Straight-line

Required:

a. Calculate the depreciation expense for the years prior to the revaluation.
b. Calculate the depreciation expense for the years following the revaluation.
c. Record the journal entry for the revaluation adjustment using the proportional method.
d. Assuming no other changes in estimates or revaluations, show the following three amounts at the end of each of the six years of the equipment's life: gross carrying value, accumulated depreciation, net carrying value. Do this for the historical cost method as well as for the revaluation method.

 P10-13. Evaluating whether impairment testing is required

(**L.O.** 10-2) (Easy – 5 minutes)

Explain why it is necessary to identify cash generating units (CGUs) for purposes of impairment tests.

 P10-14. Evaluating whether impairment testing is required

(**L.O.** 10-2) (Easy – 5 minutes)

Identify whether each of the following statements is true or false under IFRS.

Statement	True/False
a. Enterprises should test all tangible assets for impairment annually.	
b. Enterprises should test all intangible assets for impairment annually.	
c. Enterprises should test goodwill for impairment annually.	
d. For all tangible assets, enterprises should annually search for indications of impairment.	
e. For all intangible assets, enterprises should annually search for indications of impairment.	
f. Enterprises should annually search for indications that goodwill is impaired.	

 P10-15. Evaluating whether impairment testing is required   (**L.O.** 10-2) (Easy – 5 minutes)

Explain why intangible assets with indefinite lives must be annually tested for impairment while intangible assets with finite lives need not always undergo this test.

P10-16. Evaluating whether impairment testing is required

(**L.O.** 10-2) (Medium – 10 minutes)

Golf Pro Inc. is approaching its year-end and the company is considering whether it needs to test the following non-current assets on its balance sheet for impairment. The company has been reasonably profitable and has had stable operations.

   a. Golf club moulding machine.

   b. Golf ball logo stamper; packaging equipment. (Golf Pro buys balls in bulk and adds the company's logo before distributing to wholesalers.)

   c. Patent for the company's own make of golf clubs, due to expire in 12 years.

   d. The Golf Pro brand name, which the company bought from the prior owner.

   e. Goodwill from the acquisition of a golf cart distributor.

Required:

Determine whether each of the above assets should be evaluated for impairment and justify your conclusion. Note that this task does not require you to actually carry out the impairment test, but just to indicate whether such a test is necessary.

 P10-17. Evaluating whether impairment testing is required   (**L.O.** 10-2) (Medium – 10 minutes)

Hotel Consolidators purchases blocks of hotel rooms at a discount and resells them on the Internet. In 2003, the company developed a proprietary system to help attract Internet users to its website, and the company capitalized $25 million for the development cost. This system cost includes all the software and hardware, as well as the design effort that went into the system. The company depends almost entirely on this system for its revenues.

     It is now 2009. Worldwide travel has declined significantly due to the deep recession that began in 2008.

Required:

Evaluate whether Hotel Consolidators needs to test the proprietary Internet system for impairment.

 P10-18. Evaluating whether there is impairment   (**L.O.** 10-2) (Easy – 3 minutes)

A company owns an office building that it rents out to other businesses. Due to a downturn in the economy, rental rates have dropped while vacancy rates have increased. Because of these circumstances, the company evaluated the building for impairment. The building has a cost of $50 million, accumulated depreciation of $15 million, and a value in use of $28 million. In addition, the company has recently received an offer to purchase the building for $32 million. Legal and other costs necessary to complete a sale of this type would amount to $100,000.

Required:

Determine the amount of impairment.

 P10-19. Evaluating whether there is impairment   (**L.O.** 10-2) (Medium – 10 minutes)

Due to increased competition from low-cost foreign manufacturers, Juliet's Toy Company is experiencing significant declines in sales. The company produces its toys from an assembly line. The equipment in this assembly line has not been previously revalued or impaired. For the year ending December 31, 2020, the company controller gathered the following information:

Original cost	$4,000,000
Accumulated depreciation	1,200,000
Fair value	1,700,000
Costs to sell	100,000
Incremental cash flow 2021	500,000
Incremental cash flow 2022	400,000
Incremental cash flow 2023	700,000
Incremental cash flow 2024	800,000
Incremental cash flow 2025 and later	0
Risk-adjusted cost of capital	12%

Required:

Determine whether the assembly line is impaired, and if so, the amount of the impairment.

P10-20. Evaluating whether there is impairment    **(L.O.** 10-2) (Medium – 5 minutes)   A·S·P·E

Complete problem P10-19 using ASPE.

 P10-21. Evaluating whether there is impairment    **(L.O.** 10-2) (Medium – 10 minutes)

Kilo Pascal is a maker of instruments for measuring weight, temperature, pressure, and so on. Due to the increasing use of digital instruments, one of the company's production lines based on analog technology is potentially impaired. Management has produced the following information relating to this production line:

Original cost	$7,000,000
Accumulated depreciation	4,300,000
Fair value	3,200,000
Costs to sell	145,000
Incremental cash flow 2021	800,000
Incremental cash flow 2022	900,000
Incremental cash flow 2023	900,000
Incremental cash flow 2024	1,000,000
Incremental cash flow 2025 and later	0
Risk-adjusted cost of capital	10%

Required:

Determine whether the production line is impaired, and if so, the amount of the impairment.

 P10-22. Evaluating whether there is impairment    **(L.O.** 10-2) (Medium – 5 minutes)   A·S·P·E

Complete problem P10-21 using ASPE.

 **P10-23.** Evaluating whether there is impairment   **(L.O.** 10-2) (Medium – 10 minutes)

Lima Bean Company produces two distinct product lines: dried beans and canned beans. Due to changing consumer tastes, the company is evaluating these two CGUs for impairment for the year ending December 31, 2020. Relevant information is as follows:

	Dried	Canned
Original cost	$9,000,000	$12,000,000
Accumulated depreciation	3,700,000	4,500,000
Fair value	6,100,000	7,300,000
Costs to sell	180,000	310,000
Incremental cash flow 2021	1,100,000	2,200,000
Incremental cash flow 2022	1,400,000	3,000,000
Incremental cash flow 2023	1,700,000	3,500,000
Incremental cash flow 2024	2,000,000	0
Incremental cash flow 2025 and later	0	0
Risk-adjusted cost of capital	12%	12%

Required:

Determine whether either product line is impaired and, if so, the amount of the impairment.

 P10-24. Evaluating whether there is impairment   **(L.O.** 10-2) (Medium – 5 minutes)   A·S·P·E

Complete problem P10-23 using ASPE.

P10-25. Allocation of impairment loss among assets   **(L.O.** 10-3) (Easy – 10 minutes)

Mike's Bikes produces specialized bicycle frames. The production process uses two machines, which together form a cash generating unit. The following information is relevant to the evaluation of impairment for these machines:

	Bending machine	Welding machine	Total cash generating unit
Net carrying value	$300,000	$200,000	$500,000
Fair value less costs to sell	180,000	See required	See required
Value in use			400,000

Required:

a. Assume that the welding machine has a fair value less cost to sell of $160,000. Determine the amount of impairment that should be recorded for the cash generating unit and for each of the two machines.
b. Assume that the welding machine has a fair value less cost to sell of $220,000. Determine the amount of impairment that should be recorded for the cash generating unit and for each of the two machines.

P10-26. Recording impairments under revaluation model

(L.O. 10-3) (Medium – 15 minutes)

Uplifting Co. is a manufacturer of escalators and elevators. The following provides information on two types of PPE as at the end of fiscal year 2020:

	Assembly-line equipment	Factory building
Cost	$8,000,000	$20,000,000
Estimated residual value	nil	2,000,000
Estimated useful life on purchase date	10 years	40 years
Remaining useful life at the end of fiscal 2020	6 years	25 years
Depreciation policy	Straight-line	Straight-line
Accumulated depreciation at end of 2020	$3,200,000	$6,750,000

Required:

a. Using the above information, compute the depreciation that would be recorded on each of the two assets for 2021. Do not use the information below.
b. At the beginning of fiscal year 2021, Uplifting conducted appraisals of these assets. The appraisals indicate that the factory building is worth $18 million while the equipment is worth $4,320,000. Although the company has conducted regular appraisals in the past, these are the first appraisals to show significant deviations of fair value from carrying value. In other words, there have been no revaluation surpluses or losses on these assets prior to 2021. For the revaluation on the equipment, the company has chosen to use the proportional method. For the building, the company will use the elimination method. Record the journal entries to revalue these two assets at the beginning of 2021.
c. Using the amounts after revaluation, compute the depreciation that would be recorded on each of the two assets for 2021.
d. At the beginning of fiscal year 2022, Uplifting conducted another appraisal, which showed a value of $16 million for the building and $3,800,000 for the equipment. For consistency of accounting policies, the company must use the same revaluation policies as in 2021 (see part b above). Record the journal entries to revalue these two assets at the beginning of 2022.

P10-27. Recording impairments   **(L.O.** 10-3) (Medium – 10 minutes)

November Raincoats uses three different machines to manufacture raincoats. Due to climate change and changes in consumer preferences, demand for raincoats has declined in recent years. The following information is relevant to the evaluation of impairment:

	Machine A	Machine B	Machine C	Total
Net carrying amount	$1,000,000	$1,500,000	$2,000,000	$4,500,000
Fair value less costs to sell	1,000,000	1,200,000	1,800,000	4,000,000
Value in use	n/a	n/a	n/a	3,800,000

Required:

Determine the amount of impairment that should be recorded for the cash generating unit and for each of the three machines.

 P10-28. Recording impairments   **(L.O.** 10-3) (Medium – 20 minutes)

The following information relates to Oscar Trophy Company (CGU = cash generating unit):

	Machine A	Machine B	Machine C	CGU total
Net carrying value	$900,000	$1,300,000	$1,700,000	$3,900,000
Fair value less cost to sell	600,000	1,400,000	1,300,000	3,300,000
Value in use	n/a	n/a	n/a	3,400,000
Net carrying value for CGU				
Less: recoverable amount for CGU				
Impairment loss for CGU				
Net carrying value for loss allocation				
Percentage of total carrying amount				
× Total impairment loss				
Impairment loss allocated				
Carrying value before impairment				
Less: impairment loss				
Carrying value after impairment				

Required:

a. Complete the above table to determine the amount of impairment.
b. Prepare the journal entries to record the impairment of Oscar's assets assuming that there have been no prior revaluations of these assets.
c. Record the journal entries for impairment assuming that Oscar had a prior revaluation. The revaluation surplus for Machine A is $50,000, and for Machine B is $100,000.

 P10-29. Recording impairments with reversals   **(L.O.** 10-3) (Medium – 15 minutes)

Papa Bear Co. has land and a building with a 20-year estimated useful life (from the date of acquisition). The company uses the straight-line depreciation method with a full year of depreciation in the year of acquisition. The land and building were purchased in 2011 together for $25 million, with $15 million allocated to land and $10 million allocated to the building. The company has a December 31 year-end.

At the beginning of 2014, Papa Bear evaluated its assets for impairment, and concluded the recoverable amount to be $12 million for the land and $6.8 million for the building. The company then wrote down both assets to these amounts.

At the beginning of 2021, the company again assessed the value of its assets and concluded the recoverable amounts to be $16 million for the land and $6 million for the building.

Required:

a. Determine the amount of depreciation for 2011 to 2013.
b. Determine the amount of impairment loss for 2014.
c. Determine the amount of depreciation for 2014 to 2020.
d. Determine the amount of impairment loss for 2021.
e. Determine the amount of depreciation for 2021 to 2030.

 P10-30. Recording impairments—reversals   (**L.O.** 10-3) (Difficult – 20 minutes)

Quebec Pulp and Paper (QPP) has plant and equipment that have been evaluated for impairment periodically in response to changing conditions in the industry. The plant and equipment together form a cash generating unit. They were purchased in 2011 for $150 million (plant) and $84 million (equipment). As of the acquisition date, the plant had an estimated useful life of 25 years; the equipment, 12 years. QPP uses the straight-line depreciation method and recorded a full year of depreciation in the year of acquisition. The company has a December 31 year-end.

At the beginning of 2016, QPP wrote down the plant and equipment for impairment due to the decline in prices of newsprint and other paper products. The recoverable amount of the plant was estimated to be $110 million; the equipment, $42 million.

Prices of paper products later recovered. At the beginning of 2019, the company re-evaluated the impairment of its plant and equipment. The new recoverable amounts were $105 million for the plant and $25 million for the equipment.

Required:

a. Determine the amount of depreciation for 2011 to 2015.
b. Determine the amount of impairment loss for 2016.
c. Determine the amount of depreciation for 2016 to 2018.
d. Determine the amount of impairment loss for 2019.
e. Determine the amount of depreciation for 2019.

P10-31. Impairment of assets   (**L.O.** 10-2, 10-3) (Difficult – 30 minutes)

Super Computers Inc. (SCI) is a publicly accountable enterprise that manufactures computer microchips. It is conducting various impairment tests in concert with the preparation of its financial statements for the year ended December 31, 2016. Management is concerned that due to the recent introduction of more mechanized production equipment, it is possible that the value of one of SCI's machines is impaired. SCI uses the cost model to account for the machine and is depreciating it on a straight-line basis over four years.

Other relevant information follows:

Original cost	$2,400,000
Accumulated depreciation	600,000
Estimated residual value	0
Fair value – December 31, 2016	1,400,000
Costs to sell	50,000
Incremental cash flow 2017	550,000
Incremental cash flow 2018	550,000
Incremental cash flow 2019	550,000
Incremental cash flow 2020 and later	0
Risk-adjusted cost of capital	9%

Required:

a. Determine whether the asset is impaired, and, if so, prepare the journal entry.
b. Management determined that the fair value less costs to sell off the machine as at December 31, 2017, was $975,000. Prepare the required journal entry, if any.

A·S·P·E   **P10-32. Impairment of assets**   (**L.O.** 10-2, 10-3) (Medium – 15 minutes)

Refer to problem P10-31. Assume that Super Computers Inc. is a private company that elects to report its financial results in accordance with ASPE. Provide the required information above.

P10-33. Investment property—identification   **(L.O.** 10-4) (Easy – 5 minutes)

Identify whether IAS 40 applies to the following items. In other words, are they investment properties? While there is some amount of judgment depending on the circumstances, consider the most plausible scenario.

a. A residential apartment building owned by an apartment rental company.
b. A building owned and used by a hotel operator as a hotel.
c. A building owned by Company A and rented to Company B, which operates a hotel in the building.
d. Land on which a company's production facilities are situated.
e. An empty parcel of land adjacent to a company's production facilities.

P10-34. Contrasting the revaluation provisions of IAS 16 and IAS 40

(L.O. 10-1, 10-4) (Easy – 10 minutes)

IAS 16, Property, Plant, and Equipment, and IAS 40, Investment Property, both include provisions permitting certain non-current assets to be subsequently measured at fair value. Use the chart that follows to summarize the primary differences in these two standards as they pertain to fair value measurement.

Accounting issue	IAS 16, Property, Plant, and Equipment	IAS 40, Investment Property
Measurement on balance sheet		
Frequency of measurement		
Unrealized gains and losses		
Depreciation		

 P10-35. Investment property—measurement   **(L.O.** 10-4) (Medium – 15 minutes)

Hinton Property Management Company (HPMC) owns several properties that it rents to major hotel chains such as The Westin and Holiday Inn. HPMC does not operate the hotels but instead simply provides the physical structures and maintains essential services for the building (heating, cooling, electricity, water, etc.). The hotel companies provide the management and staff needed to provide accommodations, meals, and business services.

In 2018, HPMC paid $50 million for a property in Halifax—$30 million for the building and $20 million for the land. The company then rented the property to a hotel chain. At the time of purchase, HPMC estimated that the building would have a remaining useful life of 25 years and residual value of $5 million. The company has a straight-line depreciation policy on buildings, with a full year of depreciation in the year of acquisition. For PPE, the company uses the revaluation model using the elimination method. The company has a December 31 year-end.

At the end of 2018, a professional appraisal indicates a value of $31.4 million for the building and $17.5 million for the land due to increasing construction costs for new buildings. At the end of 2019, the appraisal values changed to $32 million for the building and $19.5 million for the land.

Required:

a. Record the year-end adjusting entries relating to HPMC's property for 2018 and 2019.
b. Record the year-end adjusting entries for 2018 and 2019 relating to HPMC's property if the company, in addition to owning the property, also operates it as a hotel.

 P10-36. Investment property—measurement   **(L.O.** 10-4) (Medium– 5 minutes)   **A·S·P·E**

Refer to the information in problem P10-35. Answer the requirements assuming that HPMC follows ASPE.

P10-37. Investment property—measurement   **(L.O.** 10-4) (Medium – 15 minutes)

On July 1, 2019, Danielle Investments Corp. (DIC) purchased land and buildings and agreed to rent the facility to a non-affiliated company on a month-by-month basis. Pertinent details follow:

■ DIC paid $6 million for the investment property plus $200,000 in related legal fees and $100,000 to a rental agency company for negotiating the rental agreement.

- The purchase price was allocated 80% to the building and 20% to the land.
- The estimated useful life of the building is 30 years at which time the salvage value is expected to be $0.
- DIC uses the straight-line method to depreciate all depreciable assets.
- An appraisal valued the investment property at $6.4 million as at DIC's December 31, 2019, year-end—$5.1 million building and $1.3 million land.

Required:

a. Prepare the journal entry to record the purchase of the property.
b. Prepare the year-end adjusting entries for 2019 assuming that DIC elects to use the cost model to account for its investment properties.
c. Prepare the year-end adjusting entries for 2019 assuming that DIC elects to use the fair value model to account for its investment properties.

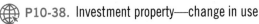 **P10-38.** Investment property—change in use   (**L.O.** 10-4) (Medium– 15 minutes)

Pronto Real Estate purchased a small warehouse in Winnipeg some years ago for $720,000. (The accompanying land was also purchased, but that information is not necessary for purposes of this question.) The company rented out the warehouse to different companies and expected increases in the property value over time as well. At the beginning of 2013, having held the property for 10 years, the company decided to use the warehouse to store excess office equipment from its head office. At the beginning of 2015, Pronto concluded that it did not require the warehouse for storage purposes and began renting out the property again. The fair value estimate at this date was $480,000.

For the December 31, 2012, year-end, the fair value of the warehouse was $500,000. At that time, the warehouse had a remaining useful life of 20 years, which is consistent with the estimated useful life at the time of acquisition. The company uses the straight-line method to depreciate buildings, recording a full year of depreciation in the year of acquisition and none in the year of disposal. The company uses the cost model to account for PPE.

In 2019, the company sold the building for proceeds of $450,000, which was also its appraised value at the end of 2018.

Required:

Record the journal entries to reflect the changes in use and the sale of the building, assuming that the company uses the cost model for investment property.

 **P10-39.** Investment property—change in use   (**L.O.** 10-4) (Medium– 15 minutes)

Refer to the information presented in problem P10-38.

Required:

Record the journal entries to reflect the changes in use and the sale of the property, assuming that the company uses the fair value model for investment property. For revaluations of PPE, use the elimination method.

 P10-40. Agriculture—classification   (**L.O.** 10-4) (Easy – 5 minutes)

Identify whether IAS 41 applies to the following items (i.e., are they used in or do they directly result from agricultural activities?).

Item	Related activity involves active management (Yes/No)	Item relates to activity up to and including point of harvest (Yes/No)	IAS 41 applies (Yes/No)
i. Strawberries			
ii. Strawberry jam			
iii. Trees in a virgin forest			
iv. Christmas trees on a tree farm			
v. Peach trees			

P10-41. Agriculture—classification (**L.O.** 10-4) (Easy – 5 minutes)

Consider the list of items in problem P10-40.

Required:

Classify each item as a biological asset, agricultural produce, or neither.

P10-42. Agriculture—classification (**L.O.** 10-4) (Easy – 5 minutes)

Identify whether IAS 41 applies to the following items (i.e., are they used in or do they directly result from agricultural activities?).

Item	Related activity involves active management (Yes / No)	Item relates to activity up to and including point of harvest (Yes / No)	IAS 41 applies (Yes / No)
i. Tuna in the ocean			
ii. Farmed salmon			
iii. Wheat			
iv. Potted tropical plants in a nursery			
v. Cattle used in breeding			

P10-43. Agriculture—classification (**L.O.** 10-4) (Easy – 10 minutes)

Consider the list of items in problem P10-42.

Required:

Classify each item as a biological asset, agricultural produce, or neither.

P10-44. Agriculture—measurement (**L.O.** 10-4) (Medium – 10 minutes)

Pommery Limited is a large producer of apples, with apple orchards in a number of different locations in southern Ontario and British Columbia. The company had the following transactions on one of its new orchards:

- Beginning of Year 1: Purchased and planted 40,000 young apple trees that will mature (i.e., begin bearing fruit) in 10 years, at a cost of $3,000,000.
- Years 1 to 10: Spent $50,000 on water, $100,000 on fertilizer, and $300,000 on labour cultivating the orchard each year for 10 years.
- Years 11 and on: At maturity, each apple tree produces about 100 kilograms of apples on average. Apple trees are productive for about 40 years. Harvested apples can be sold immediately or put into cold storage for up to six months without significant deterioration in quality. In addition to water, fertilizer, and labour costs as previously incurred, harvesting also requires an additional cost of $500,000 per year.

Other information about the orchard: The market price for apples is about $0.50/kg at the farm gate (wholesale and retail prices are considerably higher). Once apple trees have been planted, they are not movable without significant damage to their root system, so there is no market price for planted apple trees.

Required:

Record the journal entries for Years 1, 2, and 11 relating to the above information, assuming Pommery uses the cost method for the apple trees because they are bearer plants.

P10-45. Agriculture—measurement (**L.O.** 10-4) (Medium – 10 minutes)

Highland Packers (HP) is a breeder of llamas. Llamas are camel-like animals that are naturally found in the Andes Mountains in South America. They have been domesticated for some time for use as pack animals to carry heavy loads. Their fur can also be used, similar to sheep's wool.

Llamas grow to maturity and become fertile around 30–36 months of age. They continue to be reproductive for the next 15 years. On average, each female gives birth to one cria (a baby llama) each year.

Due to their hardiness in mountainous areas, HP is breeding llamas to rent and to sell as hiking companions to carry the hikers' equipment. The company has a December 31 year-end and it follows IFRS for its accounting.

HP entered the llama business in early 2020. Shortly after incorporation, the company paid $400,000 to purchase 10 pairs of three-year-old llamas from a Chilean ranch. HP allocated 75% of the cost to the llamas and 25% for the specialized knowledge obtained from the Chilean ranch for breeding and raising llamas. HP's owners believe that the knowledge has value over 10 years, the period of time necessary to make their ranch fully operational by breeding the llamas to a sufficiently large number. At the end of 2023, the company's balance sheet reported $520,000 for the llamas, composed of the following:

Llama age (rounded to whole years)	Quantity	Fair value per llama	Total
7 years	20	$11,000	$220,000
3 years	10	15,000	150,000
2 years	10	10,000	100,000
1 year	10	5,000	50,000
Total	50		$520,000

The fair values in this table are based on HP's estimates. These estimates indicate that the value of a newly mature (three-year-old) llama remains stable at $15,000 each. Prior to that point, a cria increases in value evenly over the three years. After reaching maturity, the llamas decline in value evenly over 15 years.

During 2024, the company did not have any sales, as all of the llamas were being raised for reproductive purposes. The company incurred the following costs during the year:

- Feed and labour: $90,000
- Depreciation on building (barn): $30,000

At the end of 2024, the company's llama population had increased to 65, as follows:

Llama age	Quantity	Notes
8 years	20	From initial purchase
4 years	10	Offspring from initial 20 llamas
3 years	10	Offspring from initial 20 llamas
2 years	10	Offspring from initial 20 llamas
1 year	15	Offspring from initial 20 llamas and 10 mature offspring
Total	65	

Required:

a. HP's management believes the estimates of fair value made in 2023 continue to be valid at the end of 2024. Estimate the fair value of HP's biological assets at the end of 2024.
b. Record the journal entries relating to HP's biological and intangible assets for 2024. Assume that the company follows IFRS.

 P10-46. Non-current assets held for sale and discontinued operations

(**L.O.** 10-5) (Medium – 10 minutes)

Romeo Partners is scaling back operations; the partnership has the following assets on its books that it is considering for sale:

a. The partnership has $120,000 in trade accounts receivable that it could sell to a factoring company in return for $105,000. Romeo has done this in the past and sees no impediments to doing so again.
b. Romeo has a parcel of land that is currently vacant. The land is located in an area of the city that was undeveloped and Romeo had purchased it a number of years ago in anticipation

of growth in the city's population and the development of that section of the city. Actual population growth has been below expectations and has in fact been declining in the past two years. It is not clear whether a willing buyer can be found under these conditions.

c. Romeo's operations are housed in an office and a separate storage facility. Romeo owns the land on which these facilities reside. The partnership is able to vacate the storage facility on short notice and there is an active market for similar storage. As for the office, Romeo still plans to continue its operations, so it does not foresee vacating the office space in the immediate future.

Required:

Determine whether Romeo should present the assets described above as non-current assets held for sale.

P10-47. Non-current assets held for sale and discontinued operations

(**L.O.** 10-5) (Medium – 10 minutes)

a. Explain why non-current assets held for sale should be presented separately from other non-current assets.
b. Explain why non-current assets held for sale should be recorded at the lower of their (i) carrying value or (ii) fair value less cost to sell.
c. Explain why non-current assets held for sale should be valued using fair value less cost to sell rather than the value in use.

 P10-48. Non-current assets held for sale and discontinued operations

(**L.O.** 10-5) (Medium – 10 minutes)

Sierra Mountain Gear Ltd. had retail operations throughout most of Canada. In 2019, the company decided to sell all of its stores in the western provinces to a competitor; however, the sale was not completed by the end of the year. While compiling the financial statements for the year ended December 31, 2019, the company's new controller prepared the following information relating to these discontinued operations. He believes that this information satisfies the requirements of IFRS:

($000's)	2019	2018
Income statement (excerpt)		
Earnings before interest and taxes	$22,800	$24,630
Interest expense	(3,960)	(4,550)
Income from discontinued operations (Note 13)	7,860	8,540
Income before taxes	26,700	28,620
Income tax expense	(8,010)	(8,586)
Net income	$18,690	$20,034
Note 13—discontinued operations		
Pre-tax profit	$ 7,860	$ 8,540
Income tax expense	(2,358)	(2,562)
After-tax profit	$ 5,502	$ 5,978

Required:

Identify three deficiencies in the presentation or disclosure relating to the discontinued operations.

P10-49. Non-current assets held for sale and discontinued operations

(**L.O.** 10-5) (Medium – 15 minutes)

Meagan Brandon Inc. (MBI) reports its financial results in accordance with IFRS. Selected financial information for the year ended December 31, 2019, follows:

- MBI's income for the year from continuing operations totalled $1.1 million.
- MBI's effective tax rate is 20%.

- MBI disposed of a subsidiary during the year that met the criteria of a discontinued operation and was classified accordingly. The subsidiary's pre-tax loss was $200,000. The pre-tax gain on disposal was $100,000.

Required:

a. Prepare a statement of profit or loss for the year starting with income from continuing operations. Ignore the requirement to report earnings per share.
b. List the component parts of the disaggregated information that enterprises with discontinued operations must present in either the statement of comprehensive income or the notes to the financial statements.

P10-50. Non-current assets held for sale and discontinued operations

(**L.O.** 10-5) (Medium – 15 minutes)

On August 31, 2019, Angela Corp. (AC) classified a surplus machine as held for sale. The equipment is available for immediate sale and is expected to sell within one year. Pertinent information follows:

- AC reports its financial results in accordance with IFRS. Its year-end is December 31.
- The surplus machine has historically been accounted for using the cost model.
- The net book value of the equipment at August 31, 2019, was $360,000 ($600,000 cost minus $240,000 accumulated depreciation). The equipment has been depreciated at $10,000 per month, which was last taken on August 31, 2019.
- The estimated costs of disposal are $15,000.
- Estimates of value follow:

	August 31, 2019	December 31, 2019
Fair value	$370,000	$350,000
Value in use	380,000	365,000

- AC sold the equipment on January 15, 2020, for $368,000 cash less disposal costs of $19,000.

Required:

Prepare the necessary journal entries to reflect the forgoing events.

M. MINI-CASES

Capilano Forest Company Ltd. (CFCL) has been owned and managed by an experienced forester, Don Strom, for 20 years. The company has performed well in the past few years, but the industry is cyclical. In the interior of British Columbia, CFCL manufactures lumber of all grades from raw logs. A small lumberyard and sales office is located in Vancouver.

Your firm has been reappointed auditor for CFCL. You, the senior on this engagement, have been going over some issues with the recently hired controller of the company, Everett Green. CFCL had been searching for a controller for several months. Green agreed to accept the position with the condition that his compensation include a bonus based on net income. Strom finally agreed to this form of remuneration, despite initial resistance.

A large Japanese lumber importer has recently expressed an interest in purchasing CFCL. Therefore, Green proposes to make changes to CFCL's accounting policies, which he believes will maximize the value of the company.

During the year, CFCL was granted, by the Ministry of Forests, the right to log a large area of standing timber on Crown land. Although CFCL does not own the land, it does have the right to log all the timber on it, not to exceed an allowable annual limit. This right was granted to the company at no initial cost. However, a fee is paid to the Ministry based on the number of logs removed from the forest. Shortly after CFCL received this right, the Ministry announced that all holders of logging rights over Crown land are responsible for reforesting the lands at their own expense; the ruling applies to all rights granted in the past five years. After eight months of logging, CFCL has still not carried out any reforestation. The controller is proposing that CFCL record receipt of this right at fair market value. In addition, he would like to include in the financial statements the fair market value of rights received from the Ministry two years ago. These rights do not currently appear on the company's balance sheet.

CFCL recently purchased the right to log the standing timber on a mine site. As part of the purchase contract, CFCL agreed that it would cease logging in five years, when mining would commence. Although CFCL would probably be unable to log all the timber in this period, the five-year rights were considered to be worth considerably more than the purchase price. Since logging operations began, however, it has become apparent that many of the trees are infested with insects, and are therefore worthless. Green does not think that this presents a valuation problem for financial reporting: "These rotten trees are part of the cost of the good ones, and will be expensed as the good trees are sold. The purchase price will be allocated to all the good trees on the mine site."

With respect to the costing of trees on land that CFCL owns, Green contends that these trees really have no cost: "We paid for the land that produces the trees. The trees themselves do not have any cost. If anything, replanting and pesticide expenses are the only costs we have. The situation is similar to owning land on which we have a building and machinery producing widgets. When we sell the widgets, we don't expense the land, do we?"

Last year the company acquired a large tract of land and timber along the Pacific coast for $2.9 million. This year, 20% of this tract along the shoreline was sold to a resort developer. CFCL has assigned a cost of $25,000 to this parcel. At the date of original purchase, CFCL considered this parcel to be worthless from a logging standpoint. The rest of this land is abundant in timber. CFCL paid a premium for the land, with its rich soil and moist, coastal climate ideal for tree growth. Lately, however, the company has been having problems logging the area. Environmentalists have vowed that no one will be allowed to destroy its natural beauty. Roadways have been blocked on several occasions by these protesters. In addition, they have campaigned aggressively against the company and its products. In response, CFCL has spent large amounts on public relations, advertising, and legal costs to obtain injunctions. These amounts, as well as the estimated costs of idle time related to the protests, will be capitalized as goodwill.

[11.] Reprinted from Uniform Final Examination, 1990 with permission from Chartered Professional Accountants of Canada, Toronto, Canada. Any changes to the original material are the sole responsibility of the author (and/or publisher) and have not been reviewed or endorsed by the Chartered Professional Accountants of Canada.

CASE 1
Capilano Forest Products
(80 minutes)[11]

Green intends to include in goodwill costs relating to forest fires, which are rampant in areas surrounding CFCL's land. Although none of CFCL's timber has been damaged by the blaze, the company did pay for resources to help control the disaster. As the controller explained, "It was in our best interests to help combat the fires because they were headed toward our timber." The fires are continuing, and CFCL has promised an additional $300,000 in aid.

CFCL has gained a reputation amongst Japanese companies as a good source of clear pine. CFCL can sell the Japanese as much pine as it can cut. Orders currently outstanding will take the company at least six months to fill. Under the terms of the contracts, the purchase price, denominated in yen, may be increased or decreased by a maximum of 5%, depending on the grade as determined by inspection at a Japanese harbour. The company would like to record the revenue on these contracts as soon as the lumber is cut.

The company sells wood chips as a byproduct of its sawmill operations. It entered into a three-year contract with a large pulp mill, Remul Ltd., under which Remul can purchase all the chips produced by CFCL. CFCL would have plenty of willing customers, given the current market demand, for any chips that Remul did not take. CFCL transports the chips by truck and rail car. The truck drivers have been on strike for the past two weeks. Green does not see this strike lasting much longer, and he would, therefore, like to recognize the revenue on the chips as they are produced.

The partner on this engagement has asked you to prepare a memo discussing the accounting alternatives of the issues raised with the controller.

Required:

Prepare the requested memo.

CASE 2
WW Development Inc.
(2 hours)[12]

WW Development Inc. (WW), a real estate developer, was incorporated in Canada in 1981 by two brothers, Peter and David Wang. In the 1980s and 1990s, WW was quite successful. In early 2008, Peter and David's children took over the operations of WW and began acquiring properties to be held as revenue-producing properties rather than for development.

In recent years, WW's profitability has suffered. Some of WW's creditors have expressed concern about WW's financial situation and are anxiously awaiting the results of the June 30, 2019, fiscal year-end. WW has some loans coming due in 2020. One creditor decided not to wait for the financial statements to be released and informed WW that it would not be renewing its loan.

Samuel & Samuel, Chartered Accountants/Chartered Professional Accountants, have been the auditors of WW since 1983 and have a good relationship with the Wang family. It is now September 5, 2019, and the fieldwork for the audit has been completed. The partner-in-charge of the WW engagement, Rylan Baseden, has completed his review of the working paper file. Samuel & Samuel recently established a quality control department to ensure that the firm meets professional standards for its work. Rylan has submitted the WW file to the quality control department for review, to take advantage of its expertise.

You, a new manager with Samuel & Samuel's quality control department, are to review the WW working paper file for the year ended June 30, 2019, and prepare a memo on the results of your review for the partner-in-charge of quality control. WW's relationship with its lenders is a major concern, and WW has undertaken to inform the lenders immediately of any issues identified by the auditors. The partner needs the memo for a meeting with Rylan that is to take place in three days.

You met with Rylan to familiarize yourself with WW's operations and gathered the information contained in Exhibit I. Rylan also gave you the WW financial statements, prepared in accordance with IFRS, and the WW working paper file. Extracts from the financial statements and the working paper file are provided in Exhibits II, III, and IV.

Required:

Prepare the memo.

[12.] Reprinted from Uniform Final Examination, 2000 with permission from Chartered Professional Accountants of Canada, Toronto, Canada. Any changes to the original material are the sole responsibility of the author (and/or publisher) and have not been reviewed or endorsed by the Chartered Professional Accountants of Canada.

Exhibit I	Excerpts from your conversation with the engagement partner

1. "I have been doing the audit of WW for the last 10 years. I'm glad to say I count the Wang brothers amongst my closest friends. They are not only great businessmen, they are excellent golfers!"

2. "WW has not been doing very well in the last few years, but the Wangs assure me that the real estate market is turning around. The children have prepared forecasted earnings for the next five years that are very promising. I have not seen these forecasted earnings myself, but I believe them when they say that WW will do better in the future."

3. "Audit risk was assessed as low this year, as in previous years, because of my in-depth knowledge of the industry and the client. We have never had any reason to doubt management integrity. Nothing of significance has occurred in the current fiscal year to warrant changing our risk assessment."

4. "Three years ago, WW acquired a piece of land on the outskirts of town at a bargain price. Before being acquired by WW, the land had been for sale for many years without anyone showing any interest in it. WW wants to develop the land into a large residential complex for young professionals. If WW is successful in obtaining the necessary financing for the project, it anticipates making a profit of approximately $16 million. The children have tried for the last 1½ years to obtain the financing, without any luck. The banks say the land has no resale value. Peter and David are so confident about the project that they are prepared to provide personal guarantees to the bank if required."

5. "The Rosdell shopping centre lost its anchor tenant in January 2019. The Wang children are not concerned because they can easily find a replacement."

6. "I almost forgot to tell you that the Glass Tower joint venture financial statements have not been audited. Another accountant issued a review engagement report on them. I told the staff that this was sufficient since we are accounting for the Glass Tower joint venture using the equity method."

7. "We also realized after we left the client's office that we had to issue an audit opinion on statements of operating expenses for the various revenue-producing properties. Thank goodness we had already done the work on those expenses for the regular audited financial statements of WW. We were able to rely on that work."

Exhibit II	Extracts from WW's financial statements of June 30, 2019—statement of operations

WW Development Inc.
Statement of Operations
For the years ended June 30 (in thousands of dollars)

	2019	2018
Revenue		
Rental operations	$23,306	$24,155
Other	631	218
	23,937	24,373
Expenses		
Rental operations	9,946	10,031
General and administration	739	960
Amortization of debt cancellation fee	123	0
	10,808	10,991
Income before the undernoted items	13,129	13,382
Interest and amortization		
Interest on debt	12,407	12,481
Depreciation	6,324	6,721
	18,731	19,202
Equity pick-up in net earnings of joint venture	589	0
Income (loss) before income taxes	(5,013)	(5,820)
Income taxes	117	109
Loss for the period	$(5,130)	$ (5,929)

Exhibit III	Extracts from WW's financial statements of June 30, 2019—supplementary information

WW Development Inc.
Supplementary Information Revenue-producing properties
For the year ended June 30, 2019 ($000's)

	Rental revenue	Rental operation expenses	Amortization	Interest
Rosdell Shopping Centre	$ 2,518	$1,908	$ 546	$ 1,803
Yellow Tower	3,996	1,635	932	1,298
WW Building	4,873	2,041	2,812	4,685
Bencroft Building	3,396	1,936	649	920
Silver Tower	4,194	1,298	690	1,026
Belanger Building	4,329	1,128	695	1,962
	$23,306	$9,946	$6,324	$11,694

Exhibit IV	Extracts from WW's working paper file

1. Revenue-producing properties

	Property	Tenant improvements	Total	Municipal valuation
Rosdell Shopping Centre	$ 7,352,000	$ 3,428,000	$ 10,780,000	$ 13,034,000
Yellow Tower	12,543,000	2,437,000	14,980,000	15,206,000
WW Building	37,841,000	6,113,000	43,954,000	48,920,000
Bencroft Building	8,422,000	1,557,000	9,979,000	9,543,000
Silver Tower	9,279,000	2,168,000	11,447,000	13,215,000
Belanger Building	9,355,000	1,665,000	11,020,000	14,122,000
	$84,792,000	$17,368,000	$102,160,000	$114,040,000

WW accounts for its investment properties using the cost model. The municipal valuations are based on market values that are reassessed every five years. WW's properties were last reassessed in 2015.

2. All properties have positive cash flows from operations except for the Rosdell Shopping Centre and the WW Building. Management says the Rosdell Shopping Centre will have a positive cash flow once the anchor tenant is replaced. As for the WW Building, management believes that even though the cash flows have been negative on this property for the last two years, the situation will soon turn around. Conclusion: no writedown necessary.

3. Land held for development includes various small properties as well as the land on which WW plans to develop its residential project. This piece of land has a carrying value of $1,287,000. The net realizable value of this land is not an issue because the project will generate a substantial profit once the financing is obtained.

4. Mortgages receivable

Mortgage A

Mortgage receivable on June 30, 2018	$1,988,000
Accrued interest	159,000
Mortgage receivable on June 30, 2019	$2,147,000

(*Continued*)

Exhibit IV   Continued

The mortgage is secured by a revenue-producing property with a fair market value of approximately $1,559,000. The property is located in a town where a car manufacturing plant is the town's sole industry. The plant closed down during the year and may not reopen.

No payments have been received on the mortgage since April 2018. The confirmation we sent came back from the borrower indicating the terms of the mortgage were changed by WW because the borrower was unable to make the previous debt repayments. The confirmation showed that the monthly payment was reduced by half. Starting in January 2020, the borrower will make monthly principal repayments of $16,567. The mortgage will continue to bear interest at 8%, the rate of the original mortgage.

Mortgage B

One of WW's revenue-producing properties was sold in 2017 to a developer, and a mortgage was taken back against the property. The property was sold because it was residential and the Wang children found the residential market to be too much work. No payments have been made by the developer since 2018, but the Wangs assured me that they spoke to the developer and were told that "he intends to resume making monthly payments as soon as possible." The balance of the mortgage is $3,288,000.

5. During the year, WW invested in a 40% interest in Glass Tower, a joint venture. The joint venture owns a revenue-producing property with a carrying value of $3.4 million and a mortgage of $3 million. Management accounted for this investment using the equity method. We agree with the treatment adopted by WW since the 60% venturer is operating the property and, even though the joint venture agreement gives one vote to each venturer, WW is not involved in the day-to-day operations.

6. WW must meet an interest coverage ratio of 0.50 or the bank can call its loan. The bank has agreed to such a low ratio because of its close relationship with the Wang family. Based on the financial statements of June 30, 2019, WW is in compliance with the covenant, having an interest coverage ratio of 0.60. The interest coverage ratio is calculated using income before interest and income taxes. For 2019, the calculation is:

$$\frac{(\$5,130,00) + \$117,00 + \$12,407,000}{\$12,407,000} = 0.60$$

7. Rental revenue analysis:

The decrease in rental revenue was mostly due to:

- the Rosdell anchor tenant leaving in January 1, 2019: $348,000
- an additional 13% vacancy in the Rosdell Shopping Centre since January 2019: $103,000
- vacancies throughout the year in the WW Building: $258,000

8. In April 2019, some of the tenants of the Rosdell Shopping Centre made a legal representation to WW. The tenants asserted that if the anchor tenant was not replaced within six months, their leases would cease to be in force on the basis of breach of contract. They claim that they rented space in Rosdell mainly because of the presence of that particular anchor tenant.

9. The anchor tenant in the Rosdell Shopping Centre had to pay a cancellation fee of $450,000 to cancel its lease. This amount was included in income for the year.

10. The rental agency hired in May 2019 to find an anchor tenant for Rosdell says it will be lucky to find an anchor-type tenant in the next eight to ten months.

11. During the year, WW refinanced one of its revenue-producing property loans. WW paid a penalty of $1,230,000 to get out of the existing mortgage. Management said that it was worth it because the old $15,263,000 mortgage bore interest at 10.5% and matured in 2025. The new mortgage is for a period of 10 years at 9.5%. The annual principal repayments were reduced from $750,000 to $575,000.

CASE 3
Ryland Storage Park

(40 minutes)

Ryland Storage Park (RSP) is a publicly held real estate investment trust (REIT) in Canada specializing in storage properties. In general, an REIT is a passive investment company focused on buying and holding quality real estate properties for the long term to generate rental income.

Before the adoption of IFRS, RSP had been classifying its real estate properties as property, plant, and equipment. Under IAS 40 of IFRS, a new category of "investment property" was introduced. The executives at RSP are debating whether it is more appropriate to reclassify the company's real estate properties as investment properties rather than as property, plant, and equipment. They are also wondering what the immediate impact will be on the financial statements should they switch their assets to the investment properties category.

Required:

a. Suppose you are one of the executives of RSP. Discuss whether the real estate properties would more appropriately be classified as property, plant, and equipment or as investment properties.

b. Assume the real estate market has been burgeoning over the last few years and RSP has been experiencing huge gains on its real estate portfolio. Discuss the immediate financial statement impact of classifying the real estate properties as investment properties instead of property, plant, and equipment.

c. Both IAS 16 and IAS 40 give companies the option of measuring non-current assets' carrying values using the historical cost basis and an alternative basis. Do you think firms would be more likely to adopt the alternative basis under IAS 16 or under IAS 40? Explain your position.

d. IAS 40 adopts the fair value model as the alternative basis of valuing non-current assets. What do you think are the benefits and shortcomings of the fair value model? Do you think allowing the choice would create more opportunities for financial statement manipulation? Explain your position.

APPENDIX A
Statement of Cash Flows

CPA competencies addressed in this appendix:

1.1.2 Evaluates the appropriateness on the basis of financial reporting (Level B)
c. Differences between accrual accounting compared to cash accounting

1.2.1 Develops or evaluates appropriate accounting policies and procedures (Level B)

1.2.2 Evaluates treatment for routine transactions (Level A)
a. Cash and cash equivalents and numerous others

1.2.3 Evaluates treatment for non-routine transactions (Level B)
Exchange of assets

1.3.1 Prepares financial statements (Level A)

1.3.2 Prepares routine financial statement note disclosure (Level B)

1.4.1 Analyzes complex financial statement note disclosure (Level C)

Learning Objectives

After studying this chapter, you should be able to:

L.O. A-1.   Describe the purpose of the statement of cash flows and the information it conveys.

L.O. A-2.   Define cash and cash equivalents.

L.O. A-3.   Differentiate among cash flows from operating activities, investing activities, and financing activities.

L.O. A-4.   Describe the difference between the direct and indirect methods of calculating cash flows from operating activities.

L.O. A-5.   Prepare a statement of cash flows using both the direct and indirect methods.

Canadian Tire Corporation (CTC), which bills itself as "one of Canada's most trusted companies," is a well-established Canadian retail chain.

For the year ended December 31, 2016, CTC reported comprehensive income of $634.4 million. Despite this reported profit, CTC's statement of cash flows disclosed a net decrease in cash of $76.8 million for the year. How are these seemingly inconsistent results possible?

The statement of cash flows indicates that the net decrease of $76.8 million was due to cash inflows of $986.4 million from operating activities, offset by a $782.8 million outflow from investing activities and a $280.4 million outflow from financing activities. Moreover, CTC presented operating cash flows using the indirect method, in contrast to the direct method used for investing and financing cash flows. Why does the company categorize cash flows as arising from operating, investing, or financing activities? What is the difference between the direct and indirect methods of reporting cash flows from operating activities? Why does CTC produce a statement of cash flows? What information does this statement provide?

CONTENTS

A. INTRODUCTION

L.O. A-1. Describe the purpose of the statement of cash flows and the information it conveys.

Net income is an important metric as it measures the financial performance of the company. Equally important is the firm's ability to generate cash—because it is ultimately cash, not income, that pays employees, suppliers, creditors, investors, and governments. Income statements are prepared on an accrual basis, and consequently net income seldom equals the change in cash during the period.

In the opening vignette, CTC's cash decreased by $76.8 million in 2016 despite the reported profit of $634.4 million. While CTC's affairs are complex, its financial statements do give some insight into sources of the substantive gap between the decrease in cash and comprehensive income. For example, CTC reported net cash outflows for investing and financing activities of $782.8 million and $280.4 million, respectively. These amounts represent outflows of cash that are not included in comprehensive income.

Investors, creditors, and managers are interested in how entities generate and use cash. Responding to this demand, IAS 1—Presentation of Financial Statements requires all companies to present both an income statement and a statement of cash flows (SCF). The SCF speaks to the capacity of a business to generate cash and the business's need for cash resources. Managing cash flow to ensure that the company has sufficient monies to pay bills when due is an essential function. Larger companies have a treasury department dedicated to managing cash resources.

To provide information useful to decision makers, IAS 1 requires companies to report cash inflows and outflows using standardized categories: operations, investments, and financing. Second, the SCF provides information on why the change in cash for a period differs from its reported income. Moreover, comparative SCFs provide a historical record of both the firm's ability to generate cash and its ongoing need for funds. The SCF thus provides useful information that is not available in other financial statements (i.e., the balance sheet, income statement, and so on).

The SCF is useful for evaluating a company's liquidity—its ability to generate sufficient cash to meet its obligations when due. Users can also glean valuable information about the timing and uncertainty of cash flows by analyzing past relationships between items like sales and cash flow from operations. Using these facts facilitates more accurate forecasts of future cash flows than relying solely on the income statement. Lastly, the SCF can also be used to ascertain the firm's quality of earnings. As discussed in Chapter 3, the quality of earnings refers to how closely reported earnings correspond to earnings that would be reported in the absence of managerial bias. One way to evaluate earnings quality is to compare the company's net income with cash from operating activities, because cash flows are less subject to managerial bias compared with accrual income. If the reported net income is consistently close to or less than cash from operating activities, the company's net income or earnings are said to be of a "high quality." If net income is consistently more than cash from operating activities, further investigation is needed to ascertain why the reported net income is not matched by an increase in cash.

THRESHOLD CONCEPT
QUALITY OF EARNINGS

For all of the reasons above, the SCF is a useful and important component of an enterprise's financial report. The next section discusses *what* should appear on the SCF. Section C will then describe the procedures for *how* one goes about compiling the figures that appear in the SCF.

 CHECKPOINT **CPA-1**

List three reasons why the statement of cash flows is a useful component of an enterprise's financial statements.

B. PRESENTATION OF THE STATEMENT OF CASH FLOWS

The general standards for the presentation of the SCF appear in IAS 1—Presentation of Financial Statements, with more specific standards provided by IAS 7—Statement of Cash Flows. To properly specify the reporting requirements for the SCF, it is necessary to identify what is a "cash flow." To do so, we need to review what are considered to be cash and cash equivalents (see also Chapter 5).

1. Cash and cash equivalents defined

In IAS 7, "cash and cash equivalents" is an important concept. The standard defines the two components separately as follows:

¶6   ... *Cash* comprises cash on hand and demand deposits.
     . . . **Cash equivalents** are short-term, highly liquid investments that are readily convertible to known amounts of cash and which are subject to an insignificant risk of changes in value.[1]

The reference to "demand deposits" means funds in accounts with financial institutions that can be withdrawn without notice or penalty; for example, a chequing account.

L.O. A-2.   Define cash and cash equivalents.

cash equivalents   Short-term, highly liquid investments that are readily convertible to known amounts of cash and which are subject to an insignificant risk of changes in value.

---

[1] Copyright © 2012 IFRS Foundation.

To qualify as a cash equivalent, an item must meet both requirements of *convertibility* and *insignificant risk*. Many items meet one but not both criteria. For example, an investment in widely traded stock is readily convertible to cash because it can be sold on a stock exchange, but its price is subject to significant risk of change. A non-redeemable term deposit is not subject to significant risk of change in value, but cannot be readily converted to cash if the maturity date is far in the future. Neither the stock investment nor the term deposit would be considered cash equivalents. In contrast, Treasury bills (which are government bonds with maturity under a year) that mature within 90 days of acquisition could be considered a cash equivalent because they can be readily sold in a public market and their value does not fluctuate significantly. Likewise, a term deposit with a short enough maturity also meets the criteria of convertibility and insignificant risk; IAS 7 paragraph 7 suggests that three months or less would be a short enough duration.

Note that investments in securities that satisfy the criteria of a cash equivalent are not always reported as such. In this respect, if an investment in a qualifying security is held for the purpose of meeting short-term cash commitments, then it is reported as a cash equivalent. If, though, the qualifying investment is held for other reasons, then the cash flows resulting from the purchase and sale of the investment are classified as follows:

- an operating activity, if the investment is held for trading purposes; or
- an investing activity, if the investment is held for purposes other than trading.

Cash is an idle asset that does not earn income. Consequently, most enterprises try to keep cash holdings close to zero, so it is common for bank balances to be in overdraft (i.e., to be negative). When a bank's overdraft facility is an integral part of an enterprise's cash management system, and if the balance often fluctuates between a positive balance and an overdraft, the overdraft is included in the balance of cash and cash equivalents.

The reason for considering the details of "cash" and "cash equivalents" above is that the two are considered together in the definition of cash flows. IAS 7 indicates the following:

> ¶9   Cash flows exclude movements between items that constitute cash or cash equivalents because these components are part of the cash management of an entity rather than part of its operating, investing and financing activities. Cash management includes the investment of excess cash in cash equivalents.[2]

Thus, for purposes of the SCF, we do not look at cash versus cash equivalents as two separate items but rather as a single unit of "cash and cash equivalents." For brevity, the remainder of this chapter will simply use "cash" to mean "cash and cash equivalents."

 **CHECKPOINT CPA-2**

Briefly describe cash equivalents.

2. Classifying cash flows

L.O. A-3.   Differentiate among cash flows from operating activities, investing activities, and financing activities.

As discussed in Chapter 3, there are three distinct cash cycles. The shortest cash cycle relates to operations, followed by investments, with the financial cycle being the longest. Consistent with these cash cycles, IAS 7 classifies cash flows into three categories: operating activities, investing activities, and financing activities.

---

[2] Copyright © 2012 IFRS Foundation.

a. Operating activities

Cash flows from operating activities arise from the day-to-day running of the business. Technically, IAS 7 defines operating activities as follows:

> ¶6 **Operating activities** are the principal revenue-producing activities of the entity and other activities that are not investing or financing activities.[3]

operating activities The principal revenue-producing activities of the entity and other activities that are not investing or financing activities.

Cash flows from operating activities give considerable insight into a firm's ability to generate sufficient cash to maintain its business operations, repay loans, and make new investments without having to arrange external financing. Exhibit A-1 lists some of the most common operating activities.

b. Investing activities

IAS 7 defines investing activities as follows:

> ¶6 **Investing activities** are the acquisition and disposal of long-term assets and other investments not included in cash equivalents.[4]

investing activities The acquisition and disposal of long-term assets and other investments not included in cash equivalents.

Cash flows related to investing summarizes the net expenditure on assets meant to generate future income. There are two distinct components of investing activities: (i) the acquisition and disposition of fixed assets; and (ii) the purchase and resale of financial assets. The first type of investing encompasses companies purchasing and selling property, plant, and equipment (PPE) to establish and maintain the infrastructure necessary to run their businesses. The second includes companies buying and selling debt and equity securities.

While most dealings in debt and equity securities are reported in the investing activity section, there are two exceptions to this:

- For reasons previously discussed, the purchase and resale of investments classified as cash equivalents are not reported as cash flows.
- Transactions involving the purchase and sale of investments at FVPL held for trading purposes are reported as operating activities, as they are similar to inventory held specifically for resale. The ASPE requirements in this respect are virtually identical to those of IFRS.

c. Financing activities

Companies raise money by issuing debt and by selling equity, using the proceeds to acquire fixed assets or for operating purposes. Financing activities record the cash flows associated with the issuance and retirement of debt and equity. Technically, IAS 7 defines financing activities as follows:

> ¶6 **Financing activities** are activities that result in changes in the size and composition of the contributed equity and borrowings of the entity.[5]

financing activities Activities that result in changes in the size and composition of the contributed equity and borrowings of the entity.

For purposes of the SCF, financing activities do not include financing resulting from ordinary operations. For example, supplier financing through accounts payable is an operating rather than a financing activity.

---

[3] Copyright © 2012 IFRS Foundation.

[4] Copyright © 2012 IFRS Foundation.

[5] Copyright © 2012 IFRS Foundation.

Exhibit A-1   Common examples of cash flows by type of activity

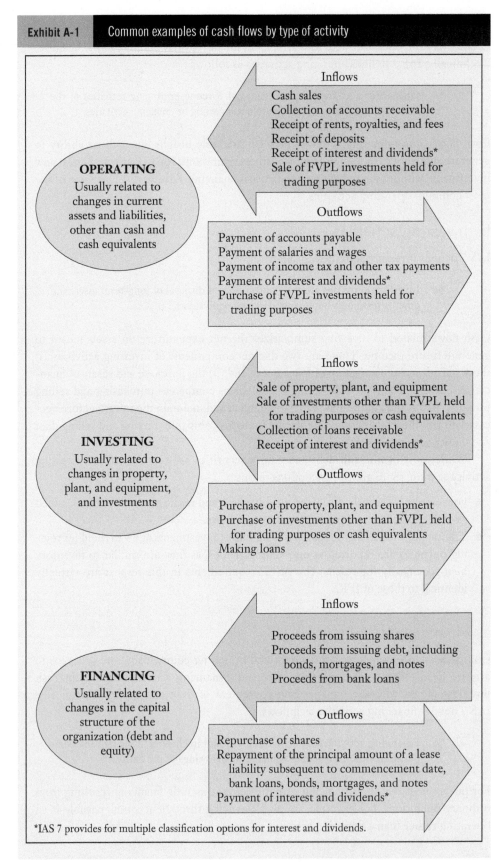

OPERATING
Usually related to changes in current assets and liabilities, other than cash and cash equivalents

Inflows
Cash sales
Collection of accounts receivable
Receipt of rents, royalties, and fees
Receipt of deposits
Receipt of interest and dividends*
Sale of FVPL investments held for trading purposes

Outflows
Payment of accounts payable
Payment of salaries and wages
Payment of income tax and other tax payments
Payment of interest and dividends*
Purchase of FVPL investments held for trading purposes

INVESTING
Usually related to changes in property, plant, and equipment, and investments

Inflows
Sale of property, plant, and equipment
Sale of investments other than FVPL held for trading purposes or cash equivalents
Collection of loans receivable
Receipt of interest and dividends*

Outflows
Purchase of property, plant, and equipment
Purchase of investments other than FVPL held for trading purposes or cash equivalents
Making loans

FINANCING
Usually related to changes in the capital structure of the organization (debt and equity)

Inflows
Proceeds from issuing shares
Proceeds from issuing debt, including bonds, mortgages, and notes
Proceeds from bank loans

Outflows
Repurchase of shares
Repayment of the principal amount of a lease liability subsequent to commencement date, bank loans, bonds, mortgages, and notes
Payment of interest and dividends*

*IAS 7 provides for multiple classification options for interest and dividends.

To illustrate these three classes of cash flows, consider an electronics retail store. Some of the operating activities include cash received from customers, payments for inventories, wages of the sales staff, and taxes to the government. Investing activities include purchasing cash registers and computer systems, buying a long-term bond issued by another entity, and selling a delivery vehicle. Financing activities include issuing bonds, repurchasing preferred shares, and reducing the principal on an outstanding lease liability.

d. Cash flows with classification options

For most transactions, the classification of a cash flow is unambiguous. However, there are two situations where the standards allow a choice of classification (IAS 7 paragraphs 31–34).

- *Interest and dividends received:* An enterprise may classify the receipt of interest and dividends as either an operating or an investing activity. The ambiguity here arises because it is not clear-cut whether this type of income is part of an enterprise's normal operations or part of its investments.
- *Interest and dividends paid:* An enterprise may choose to report the payment of interest and dividends as either an operating or a financing activity. The ambiguity occurs because, even though interest and dividend payments both arise from financing activities (issuance of debt and equity), interest is recorded through income, while dividends are not.

Note that a separate policy may be adopted for each type of cash flow. For example, a company may classify interest received as an operating activity and dividends received as an investing activity. Regardless of the choice for this accounting policy, the enterprise must apply it consistently to all similar transactions.

Accounting Standards for Private Enterprises (ASPE) does not provide options. Rather, the receipt of interest and dividends and the payment of interest are operating activities; the payment of dividends is a financing activity. This mandated treatment is illustrated in Section B, subsection 4.

Exhibit A-1 categorizes common cash inflows and outflows.

e. Non-cash transactions

When a company borrows money from the bank and then uses the funds to purchase a vehicle, the loan is recorded as a cash inflow from financing activities, and the automobile purchase as a cash outflow from investing activities. However, if the company leases this vehicle from the automobile dealer, the transaction is not recorded on the statement of cash flows as this is a non-cash transaction. **Non-cash transactions** are activities that do not involve cash. Investing and financing activities that involve non-cash transactions are not recorded on the SCF because the SCF reports only the cash effect of a company's activities. Common non-cash transactions include the following:

non-cash transactions Activities that do not involve cash.

- exchanging assets such as parcels of land with another company
- converting bonds or preferred shares into common shares
- stock dividends
- leasing a right-of-use asset

Certain transactions are only partially settled in cash; for example, a company acquires a building for $1,000,000 by paying $200,000 in cash and signing an $800,000 note payable. The SCF records only the $200,000 cash paid as an outflow in the investing activities section. Similarly, lease payments made on or before the commencement date are reported as a cash outflow in the investing activities section.

While the effect of non-cash transactions does not appear as line items in the SCF, enterprises must disclose significant non-cash transactions in the notes to the financial statements.

CHECKPOINT **CPA-3**

Briefly describe how the classification of cash flows arising from the purchase and sale of investments at FVPL is determined.

 CHECKPOINT **CPA-4**

List the three categories of cash flows reported on the statement of cash flows.

 CHECKPOINT **CPA-5**

Briefly describe the options available under IFRS with respect to classifying the receipt and payment of interest and dividends.

 CHECKPOINT **CPA-6**

Briefly describe non-cash transactions and how they are reported on the statement of cash flows.

3. Format of the statement of cash flows

a. Illustrative example

L.O. A-4. Describe the difference between the direct and indirect methods of calculating cash flows from operating activities.

Exhibit A-2 reproduces the 2016 statement of cash flows for CTC. Preliminary comments about the structure and format of the statement are provided as a prelude to a full discussion of these points later in the chapter:

- The cash flows are grouped by type of activity: operating, investing, and financing.
- Cash inflows and outflows are not netted against each other. Rather, they are presented separately; for example, CTC reports "issuance of loans payable" and "repayment of loans payable."
- The amount of dividends paid is presented as a line item in the SCF. CTC elected to present these amounts as a financing activity.
- The amount of interest paid and received is presented as a line item in the statement. CTC elected to present these amounts as an operating activity.
- The amount of income taxes paid is presented as a line item in the statement. CTC reported these as operating cash flow, which was consistent with their nature.
- The opening and closing cash and cash equivalents balances at the bottom of the SCF match those presented on the accompanying balance sheet net of bank indebtedness. While not reproduced here, these amounts are reconciled in note 7 to the financial statements. As previously discussed, including short-term bank indebtedness as part of cash and cash equivalents is consistent with paragraph 8 of IAS 7.
- CTC used the indirect method to present its cash flows from operating activities. The company could have also used the direct method. We discuss these two methods next.

Exhibit A-2	Canadian Tire's 2016 statement of cash flows

Canadian Tire Corporation, Limited

Consolidated Statements of Cash Flows

For the years ended (C$ in millions)	December 31, 2016	January 2, 2016
Cash (used for) generated from: Operating activities		
Net income	$ 747.5	$ 735.9
Adjustments for:		
Depreciation of property and equipment and investment property (Notes 28 and 29)	330.8	312.8
Income tax expense	263.5	265.4
Net finance costs (Note 30)	93.9	92.8
Amortization of intangible assets (Note 29)	126.1	111.9
Changes in fair value of derivative instruments	(15.8)	6.9
(Gain) on disposal of property and equipment, investment property, assets held for sale, intangible assets, and lease terminations	(14.9)	(43.9)
Interest paid	(114.0)	(101.4)
Interest received	6.5	8.4
Income taxes paid	(262.8)	(284.0)
Other	5.6	14.6
Total adjustments, except as noted below	1,166.4	1,119.4
Change in operating working capital and other (Note 31)	126.1	(115.3)
Change in loans receivable	(306.1)	(25.2)
Cash generated from operating activities	986.4	978.9
Investing activities		
Additions to property and equipment and investment property	(617.3)	(515.9)
Additions to intangible assets		
Total additions	(163.5)	(94.7)
	(780.8)	(610.6)
Acquisition of short-term investments	(422.3)	(177.4)
Proceeds from the maturity and disposition of short-term investments	441.4	426.6
Acquisition of long-term investments	(61.4)	(35.0)
Proceeds on disposition of property and equipment, investment property, and assets held for sale	32.8	101.5
Other	7.5	(4.1)
Cash (used for) investing activities	(782.8)	(299.0)
Financing activities		
Dividends paid	(157.5)	(152.2)
Distributions paid to non-controlling interests	(76.4)	(53.8)
Total dividends and distributions paid	(233.9)	(206.0)
Net issuance (repayment) of short-term borrowings	110.7	(111.2)
Issuance of loans payable	288.3	270.1
Repayment of loans payable	(243.5)	(219.0)
Issuance of long-term debt (Note 22)	350.0	856.1
Repayment of long-term debt and finance lease liabilities (Note 22)	(24.5)	588.5
Payment of transaction costs related to long-term debt	(3.2)	(6.5)

(Continued)

Exhibit A-2	Continued		
Canadian Tire Corporation, Limited			
Consolidated Statements of Cash Flows			
Repurchase of share capital (Note 25)		(449.4)	(434.6)
Change in deposits		(74.9)	12.5
Cash (used for) financing activities		(280.4)	(427.1)
Cash (used) generated in the period		(76.8)	252.8
Cash and cash equivalents, net of bank indebtedness, beginning of period		900.6	647.8
Cash and cash equivalents, net of bank indebtedness, end of period (Note 7)		$ 823.6	$ 900.6

The related notes form an integral part of these consolidated financial statements.

Source: From Canadian Tire Corporation 2016 Report to Shareholders. Copyright ©2016 by Canadian Tire Corporation, Limited. Reprinted by permission.

b. Direct and indirect methods of reporting cash flows from operating activities

Cash flows from operations can be reported using either the direct or indirect method. IAS 7 states the following:

¶18   An entity shall report cash flows from operating activities using either:

(a) the **direct method**, whereby major classes of gross cash receipts and gross cash payments are disclosed; or

(b) the **indirect method**, whereby profit or loss is adjusted for the effects of transactions of a non-cash nature, any deferrals or accruals of past or future operating cash receipts or payments, and items of income or expense associated with investing or financing cash flows.[6]

direct method   A method of presenting the statement of cash flows by showing major classes of gross cash receipts and gross cash payments.

indirect method   A method of presenting the statement of cash flows by adjusting profit or loss for the effects of transactions of a non-cash nature, any deferrals or accruals of past or future operating cash receipts or payments, and items of income or expense associated with investing or financing cash flows.

Although the net amount of operating cash flows remains the same, the direct and indirect methods involve different line items within cash flows from operating activities. Moreover, the choice of the direct or indirect method does not affect the reporting of cash flows from investing and financing activities as cash flows from investing and financing are presented using the direct method.

The International Accounting Standards Board (IASB) and the Accounting Standards Board in Canada (AcSB) have long favoured the direct method of reporting because, they argue, this method provides more useful information than the indirect method. Indeed, the first sentence of IAS 7 paragraph 19 reads "Entities are encouraged to report cash flows from operating activities using the direct method."[7] Notwithstanding this support, the vast majority of companies choose to use the indirect method of presentation. While hard statistics are not readily available, it is estimated that less than 1% of entities use the direct method of presentation in Canada. To reflect common practice, we focus on the indirect method in this chapter.

As IAS 7 provides only general guidance on the format of the statement of cash flows, users will observe that entities do present their results in different ways. The two exhibits that follow illustrate the general form of presentation. (Ignore the "Reference" column for now; these references will be used later in the chapter.)

---

[6] Copyright © 2012 IFRS Foundation.

[7] Copyright © 2012 IFRS Foundation.

Some observations about these two exhibits:

- Notice that net cash from operating activities of $590 is the same under both the direct and indirect methods.
- The format employed of separately disclosing related items together (e.g., income tax expense and income taxes paid) facilitates meeting disclosure requirements discussed elsewhere in this chapter.
- As set out above, paragraph 18 of IAS provides that the starting point for the indirect method is profit or loss. Profit or loss as defined in paragraph 7 of IAS 1 specifically excludes other comprehensive income. Notwithstanding that the illustrative example in Appendix A to IAS 7 uses profit before taxation as a starting point, we begin with net income as this is analogous to profit or loss and is consistent with past practice in Canada. As set out in Exhibit A-2, the first line of CTC's SCF is net income.

The above discussion reveals some flexibility in the presentation of the SCF. For the sake of consistency, unless specifically stated otherwise, the remainder of this chapter assumes that the company has adopted the following conventions:

- Net income is the starting point for determining cash flow from operating activities using the indirect method.
- Interest paid, interest received, dividends paid, and dividends received are all classified as operating activities.

Exhibit A-3	Sample operating section of a statement of cash flows using the indirect method

Illustrative Company (Partial) Statement of Cash Flows
Year Ended December 31, 2021

Cash flow from operating activities		Reference
Net income	$ 3,050	(i)
Adjustments for:		
Depreciation	450	(ii)
Gain on sale	(50)	
Investment income	(400)	
Interest expense	400	(iii)
Income tax expense	300	
Subtotal	3,750	
Increase in trade and other receivables	(500)	
Decrease in inventories	1,050	(iv)
Decrease in trade payables	(1,740)	
Cash generated from operating activities	2,560	
Dividends received*	200	
Interest received*	200	
Dividends paid†	(1,200)	(v)
Interest paid†	(270)	
Income taxes paid	(900)	
Net cash from operating activities	$ 590	(vi)

*Can also be shown as cash flows from investment.

†Can also be shown as cash outflows for financing.

Exhibit A-4	Sample operating section of a statement of cash flows using the direct method

Illustrative Company (Partial) Statement of Cash Flows
Year Ended December 31, 2021

Cash flow from operating activities	
Cash receipts from customers	$ 30,360
Cash paid to suppliers and employees	(27,800)
Cash generated from operating activities	2,560
Dividends received*	200
Interest received*	200
Dividends paid†	(1,200)
Interest paid†	(270)
Income taxes paid	(900)
Net cash from operating activities	$ 590

*Can also be shown as cash flows from investment.

†Can also be shown as cash outflows for financing.

4. Format of the statement of cash flows under ASPE

Section 1540 of Part II of the *CPA Canada Handbook*—Accounting governs the preparation of the statement of cash flows under ASPE. While Section 1540 is substantively the same as IAS 7, small differences do exist. These include the following:

- ASPE refers to this statement as a cash flow statement, rather than the statement of cash flows.
- Under ASPE, the receipt of interest and dividends and the payment of interest are normally classified as operating activities and the payment of dividends is reported as a financing activity. Unlike IFRS, ASPE does not permit choice in this respect.
- ASPE only requires that the amount of interest and dividends paid and charged directly to retained earnings be separately presented as financing activities. Unlike IFRS, it does not require separate disclosure of the amount of interest and dividends received and paid. Disclosure of this information is not prohibited, however, and many private companies choose to provide some or all of this information.
- Under ASPE the amount of income taxes paid need not be disclosed.

Exhibits A-5a and A-5b present two versions of ASPE cash flow statements using the same set of facts. (The underlying facts will be given in Section C.) The two versions differ as to whether there is separate disclosure of the amounts of interest and dividends received/paid and the amount of income taxes paid.

Contrasting this statement to that presented under IFRS in Exhibit A-10, you should note the following:

- The statement is referred to as a cash flow statement (i).
- The payment of interest is reported as an operating activity (ii). Under ASPE this is normally mandatory. Separate disclosure of this amount is not required, however.
- Separate disclosure of income taxes paid is not required under ASPE (iii).
- The payment of dividends is reported as a financing activity (iv). Under ASPE this is mandatory.
- While the net increase in cash ($48,000) is the same under ASPE and IFRS, the categorization of cash flows may differ. The determining factor is the entity's choice of accounting policy under IFRS with respect to reporting cash received and paid for interest and dividends. In this example, under ASPE the amount reported as net cash from operating activities is $46,000 more than that under IFRS; net cash from financing activities $46,000 less.

Exhibit A-5a	Result of applying procedures for cash flow statement, Example 1 (ASPE and IFRS compliant)		

Kimzoo Fireworks Ltd. Cash Flow Statement
Year Ended December 31, 2021

Cash flows from operating activities			Reference
Net income	$ 67,000		(i)
Adjustments for:			
Depreciation and amortization	32,000		
Interest expense	5,000		
Income tax expense	33,000		
Subtotal	137,000		
Increase in trade and other receivables	(14,000)		
Decrease in inventory	10,000		
Decrease in prepaid expenses	3,000		
Increase in trade payables	1,000		
Cash generated from operating activities	137,000		
Interest paid	(5,000)		(ii)
Income taxes paid	(33,000)		(iii)
Net cash from operating activities		$ 99,000	
Cash flows from investing activities			
Purchase of plant assets	(70,000)		
Net cash used in investing activities		(70,000)	
Cash flows from financing activities			
Dividends paid	(46,000)		(iv)
Retirement of mortgage payable	(150,000)		
Sale of preferred shares	215,000		
Net cash from financing activities		19,000	
Net increase in cash		48,000	
Cash and cash equivalents, January 1, 2021		51,000	
Cash and cash equivalents, December 31, 2021		$ 99,000	

Note that the amounts reported as cash flows arising from operating, investing, and financing activities in Exhibit A-5b are identical to those reported in Exhibit A-5a. The two statements differ only in the amount of information provided to the reader. Both statements are acceptable under ASPE as the governing standards primarily address the categorization of cash flows and establish the minimum amount of information that must be provided.

Having discussed what should be presented in the statement of cash flows, we now turn to how one goes about preparing this financial statement. Whereas the standards specify the required presentation, little guidance is provided with respect to the preparation and formatting of the statement of cash flows.

 CHECKPOINT **CPA-7**

Briefly describe the primary difference between IFRS and ASPE with respect to the presentation of the statement of cash flows.

Exhibit A-5b	Result of applying procedures for cash flow statement, Example 1 (ASPE)

Kimzoo Fireworks Ltd. Cash Flow Statement
Year Ended December 31, 2021

Cash flows from operating activities		
Net income	$ 67,000	
Adjustments for:		
Depreciation and amortization	32,000	
Increase in trade and other receivables	(14,000)	
Decrease in inventory	10,000	
Decrease in prepaid expenses	3,000	
Increase in trade payables	1,000	
Net cash from operating activities		$ 99,000
Cash flows from investing activities		
Purchase of plant assets	(70,000)	
Net cash used in investing activities		(70,000)
Cash flows from financing activities		
Dividends paid	(46,000)	
Retirement of mortgage payable	(150,000)	
Sale of preferred shares	215,000	
Net cash from financing activities		19,000
Net increase in cash		48,000
Cash and cash equivalents, January 1, 2021		51,000
Cash and cash equivalents, December 31, 2021		$ 99,000

C. PREPARING THE STATEMENT OF CASH FLOWS

L.O. A-5. Prepare a statement of cash flows using both the direct and indirect methods.

The SCF explains the change in cash and cash equivalents during the year, categorizing the cash flows by activity: operating, investing, or financing. The general format of the SCF is shown in Exhibit A-6.

Exhibit A-6	General format of the statement of cash flows

Company Name Statement of Cash Flows Period Ended

Cash flow from operating activities	
Details of the adjustments to profit or loss by category (indirect method)	
Details of cash inflows and outflows by category (direct method)	
Net cash from (used in) operating activities	$ xx
Cash flow from investing activities	
Details of cash inflows and outflows by category	
Net cash from (used in) investing activities	xx
Cash flow from financing activities	
Details of cash inflows and outflows by category	
Net cash from (used in) financing activities	xx
Net increase (decrease) in cash and cash equivalents	xx
Cash and cash equivalents at beginning of period	xx
Cash and cash equivalents at end of period	$ xx

Observe how the net increase (decrease) in cash and cash equivalents explains the difference between the opening and ending balance of cash and cash equivalents.

1. Sources of information

The balance sheet and income statement are prepared directly from the adjusted trial balance, as they each present select components of the general ledger. In contrast, preparing the SCF requires additional information outside of the trial balance, which only contains information about the ending cash balance but not changes in that balance. The required information comes from three primary sources:

- *Comparative balance sheets:* The change in cash for the year can be explained by the net change of all the non-cash accounts on the balance sheet.
- *The income statement for the period:* The income statement is a necessary starting point to determine cash from operating activities under the indirect method. It also provides information about the change in retained earnings.
- *Select transaction data:* The income statement and comparative balance sheets provide aggregated information that is insufficient for identifying some cash flows. For example, the purchase of furniture for $50,000 and the sale of land originally costing $20,000 would result in a net change of $30,000 in PPE on the balance sheet. The $30,000 net figure is inadequate for SCF purposes because the standards require that cash flows used for the purchase of assets be presented separately from cash arising from the sale of assets. Moreover, the cost of assets sold does not directly correlate to the proceeds from their sale.

2. The process—Indirect method

a. When are adjustments required?

When preparing the SCF, we consider the net change in each balance sheet account during the year. Nevertheless, it is instructive to contemplate individual transactions to gain greater insight into the underlying mechanics of preparing the SCF. There are four types of straightforward transactions to be considered, depending on whether each half of the transaction involves income/expenses or cash inflows/outflows:

As shown in Exhibit A-7, whenever the amount reflected in the income statement differs from the amount of cash flow for a transaction, there needs to be an adjustment

Exhibit A-7	Types of transactions according to impact on income/expense and cash inflows/outflows			
One-half of transaction involves income or expenses	Yes	No	Yes	No
One-half of transaction involves cash inflows or outflows	No	Yes	Yes	No
Label for convenience	**Transaction type 1**	**Transaction type 2**	**Transaction type 3**	**Transaction type 4**
Example transaction	Sale to a customer on credit	Purchase of equipment using cash	Cash sale	Purchase of equipment using note payable
Example journal entry	Dr. Accounts receivable Cr. Sales revenue	Dr. Equipment Cr. Cash	Dr. Cash Cr. Sales revenue	Dr. Equipment Cr. Notes payable
Adjustment required in indirect method	Yes	Yes	No	No
Reason	Income or expense recorded but not received/paid in cash	Cash received or paid but not reflected in income or expenses	Cash flow equals income or expense	No cash involved

in the SCF using the indirect method (transaction types 1 and 2). When the effect is the same on the income statement and on cash flows, then an adjustment would not be required (transaction types 3 and 4).

b. The indirect method described

The indirect method of compiling the SCF involves converting the company's accrual-based income statement to a cash-based statement. Net income, rather than comprehensive income, is the starting point as items that are included in other comprehensive income do not affect cash flows. The opening balance of cash plus (or minus) cash generated from (used in) operating, investing, and financing activities results in the closing balance, which should match the amount on the balance sheet. The process of preparing the SCF is as follows:[8]

Step 1: Determine the change in cash that needs to be explained. This is a simple matter of comparing this year's closing cash and cash equivalents balance to the prior year's balance.

Step 2: The numerical references below (i to vi) correspond to the noted areas of Exhibit A-3. Adjust net income as necessary to determine net cash from operating activities:

  i.   The starting point is the company's recorded profit or loss.

  ii. Adjust net income for all non-cash items including depreciation and gains and losses on the sale of assets or the settlement of debt.

  iii. Add back interest and income tax expense and subtract investment income from interest and dividends.

  iv. Adjust for the unexplained changes in working capital accounts representing operating activities, for example, trade receivables, inventory, trade payables, and prepaid expenses, amongst others. (Note that changes in interest and dividends receivable, interest and dividends payable, and income taxes payable accounts are adjusted for in (iii) and (v).)

  v.   Add dividends and interest received and subtract dividends, interest, and income taxes paid. Separately itemizing these cash flows meets the disclosure requirements set out in paragraphs 31 and 35 of IAS 7.

  vi. The total of items (i) to (v) equals net cash from operating activities for the year.

Step 3: Account for the changes in remaining balance sheet accounts. The reconciling items are recorded in the financing or investing activities section of the SCF according to their nature.

Step 4: Calculate subtotals for operating, investing, and financing activities and ensure the net change in cash and cash equivalents thus determined is equal to the actual change for the period computed from Step 1.

c. The indirect method illustrated—Example 1

The process of preparing a relatively straightforward SCF using the steps outlined above is set out in the three exhibits that follow. Exhibits A-8a and A-8b show the information necessary for compiling the SCF for Kimzoo Fireworks for the year 2021, Exhibits A-9a to A-9d illustrate the process to prepare the SCF, and Exhibit A-10 presents the results.

---

[8] The procedure discussed relates to the example of the indirect method SCF set out in Exhibit A-10. The process will vary slightly for companies that present their SCF differently.

Exhibit A-8a	Information necessary for the indirect method: Income statement, Example 1

Kimzoo Fireworks Ltd. Income Statement
Year Ended December 31, 2021

Sales	$660,000
Cost of sales	363,000
Gross profit	297,000
Operating expenses	160,000
Interest expense	5,000
Amortization and depreciation expense	32,000
Income before income taxes	100,000
Income tax expense	33,000
Net income	$ 67,000

Exhibit A-8b	Balance sheet and supplemental information, Example 1

Balance Sheets with Change in Balances Computed
As at December 31

	2021	2020	Change
Assets			
Cash and cash equivalents	$ 99,000	$ 51,000	$ 48,000
Accounts receivable	53,000	39,000	14,000
Inventory	50,000	60,000	(10,000)
Prepaid expenses	6,000	9,000	(3,000)
Property, plant, and equipment at cost	420,000	350,000	70,000
Accumulated depreciation	(150,000)	(125,000)	(25,000)
Patents	51,000	58,000	(7,000)
Total assets	$529,000	$442,000	
Liabilities			
Dividends payable	$ 2,000	$ 2,000	$ 0
Trade payables	69,000	68,000	1,000
Mortgage payable	0	150,000	(150,000)
Total liabilities	71,000	220,000	
Shareholders' Equity			
Preferred shares	215,000	0	215,000
Common shares	200,000	200,000	0
Retained earnings	43,000	22,000	21,000
Total shareholders' equity	458,000	222,000	
Total liabilities and shareholders' equity	$529,000	$442,000	

Supplemental information: The company's policy is to report interest and dividends paid as cash outflows from operating activities.

The first step is to determine the change in cash that needs to be reconciled. The process is illustrated in Exhibits A-9a to A-9d.

Exhibit A-9a	Applying the process for preparing a statement of cash flows using the indirect method, Step 1, Example 1

Step 1: Determine the change in cash that needs to be explained.

From the comparative balance sheet, the company's closing cash and cash equivalents balance was $99,000, an increase of $48,000 over the opening balance of $51,000.

Having determined the change in cash that needs to be explained, we adjust net income as necessary to determine net cash from operations. This process is illustrated in Step 2.

Exhibit A-9b	Process for the indirect method, Step 2, Example 1

Step 2: Adjust net income as necessary to determine net cash from operating activities.

i. Start with the company's net income.

The income statement shows net income of $67,000.

ii. Adjust for all non-cash items.

Depreciation and amortization expense reported on the income statement totalled $32,000. This amount is added to net income as the expense did not involve a cash outflow.

iii. Add back interest and income tax expense and subtract investment income.

The income statement reports interest expense of $5,000 and income tax expense of $33,000.

iv. Adjust for the unexplained changes in working capital accounts representing operating activities.

The working capital accounts included on the balance sheet requiring adjustment are accounts receivable, inventory, prepaid expenses, and trade payables.

Accounts receivable *increased* $14,000 during the year as the cash collected was *less* than the revenue recognized. While the $14,000 increase was the aggregate change for the year, to help visualize the required adjustment it is sometimes instructive to think of events that could have caused the noted difference in terms of an originating journal entry.

Dr. Accounts receivable	14,000	
Cr. Sales revenue		14,000

Revenue and income *exceeds* the amount of cash collected by $14,000 so, starting with net income, we need to deduct this $14,000 difference.

Once you understand this, you can apply a more straightforward method to determine the amount and direction of adjustment: think of what the cash balance must do in response to a change in a non-cash account on the balance sheet. If a non-cash asset increases, holding all else constant, the cash account must decline to keep the balance sheet in balance. Likewise, an increase in a liability results in an increase in cash. The increase in accounts receivable requires a –$14,000 adjustment in the SCF.

Inventory *decreased* $10,000 during the year. A decrease in a non-cash asset is accompanied by an increase in cash, so this requires a +$10,000 adjustment in the SCF.

Prepaid expenses *decreased* $3,000 during the year. A decrease in a non-cash asset is accompanied by an increase in cash, so this requires a +$3,000 adjustment in the SCF.

Trade payables *increased* $1,000 during the year. An increase in a liability is accompanied by an increase in cash, so this requires a +$1,000 adjustment in the SCF.

v. Add dividends and interest received and subtract dividends, interest, and income taxes paid.

Interest paid = interest expense − change in interest payable. Interest payable for both years was $0, so interest paid equals interest expense, which was $5,000 as shown in the income statement.

Income taxes paid = income tax expense − change in income taxes payable. Income taxes payable for both years was $0, so income taxes paid equals income tax expense, which was $33,000 as shown on the income statement.

Dividends paid = dividends declared − change in dividends payable. The balance in the dividends payable account remains unchanged, so dividends payable equals dividends declared. However, the amount of dividends declared is not directly apparent from the balance sheet and income statement. In the absence of capital transactions that directly affect retained earnings (see Chapters 13 and 14), changes in retained earnings are due to net income and dividends declared.

Retained earnings, beginning of year (from balance sheet)	$22,000
Plus: net income (from income statement)	67,000
Less: dividends declared (solve)	(46,000)
Retained earnings, end of year (from balance sheet)	$43,000

In practice, the amount of dividends declared can be determined from the general ledger. We show this analysis here to demonstrate the relationship between income, dividends, and retained earnings.

In all three of the above formulas, "change" is a positive number for increases and a negative number for decreases.

(Continued)

Exhibit A-9b	Continued

vi. The total of items (i) to (v) equals net cash from operating activities.

$67,000 + $32,000 + $5,000 + $33,000 − $14,000 + $10,000 + $3,000 + $1,000 − $5,000 − $33,000 − $46,000 = $53,000.

From a practical perspective, this step is fulfilled by completing the cash flows from operating activities section of the SCF.

As outlined in Step 3, we then account for the changes in the remaining balance sheet accounts.

Exhibit A-9c	Process for the indirect method, Step 3, Example 1

Step 3: Account for the changes in remaining balance sheet accounts. The reconciling items are recorded in the financing or investing activities section according to their nature.

The remaining account balances requiring adjustment are property, plant, and equipment (PPE) at cost, mortgage payable, and preferred shares. From the comparative balance sheet, the respective changes are a $70,000 increase, a $150,000 decrease, and a $215,000 increase. Note that the change in accumulated depreciation and patents was dealt with when depreciation and amortization was added back in the operating activities section. Similarly, the change in retained earnings was explained by net income and dividends declared, both of which were allowed for in cash flow from operating activities. Unless provided with specific information to the contrary, assume that these transactions are all cash based.

■ The company paid $70,000 to acquire the PPE, so record a $70,000 cash outflow in the investing activities section.

■ To reflect the $150,000 paid to extinguish the mortgage obligation, record a $150,000 cash outflow in the financing activities section.

■ The sale of preferred shares raised $215,000, so record a $215,000 cash inflow in the financing activities section.

We now complete the process as detailed in Step 4.

Exhibit A-9d	Process for the indirect method, Step 4, Example 1

Step 4: Calculate subtotals for operating, investing, and financing activities and ensure the net change in cash and cash equivalents thus determined is equal to the actual change for the period computed from Step 1.

The completed SCF follows. Note how the $48,000 increase in cash corresponds to the amount from Step 1.

Exhibit A-10	Result of applying procedures for statement of cash flows, Example 1 (IFRS)

Kimzoo Fireworks Ltd. Statement of Cash Flows
Year Ended December 31, 2021

Cash flows from operating activities	
Net income	$ 67,000
Adjustments for:	
Depreciation and amortization	32,000
Interest expense	5,000
Income tax expense	33,000
Subtotal	137,000
Increase in trade and other receivables	(14,000)
Decrease in inventory	10,000

(*Continued*)

Exhibit A-10	Continued	
Kimzoo Fireworks Ltd. Statement of Cash Flows **Year Ended December 31, 2021**		
Decrease in prepaid expenses	3,000	
Increase in trade payables	1,000	
Cash generated from operating activities	137,000	
Dividends paid	(46,000)	
Interest paid	(5,000)	
Income taxes paid	(33,000)	
Net cash from operating activities		$53,000
Cash flows from investing activities		
Purchase of plant assets	(70,000)	
Net cash used in investing activities		(70,000)
Cash flows from financing activities		
Retirement of mortgage payable	(150,000)	
Sale of preferred shares	215,000	
Net cash from financing activities		65,000
Net increase in cash		48,000
Cash and cash equivalents, January 1, 2021		51,000
Cash and cash equivalents, December 31, 2021		$ 99,000

d. The indirect method illustrated—Example 2

To help you master the process for preparing a statement of cash flows, we use the same steps to work through a more complex example, Fred's Fajitas Ltd. (FFL).

Exhibit A-11a	Information necessary for the indirect method: Income statement, Example 2
Fred's Fajitas Ltd. Income Statement **Year Ended December 31, 2021**	
Sales	$1,000,000
Cost of sales	400,000
Gross profit	600,000
General and administrative expenses	175,000
Interest expense	10,000
Depreciation expense	110,000
Operating income	305,000
Recycled loss on FVOCI* investments	2,000
Loss on sale of land	50,000
Income before income taxes	253,000
Income tax expense	107,000
Net income	$ 146,000
*FVOCI = at fair value through other comprehensive income	

Exhibit A-11b	Balance sheet and supplemental information, Example 2

Balance Sheets with Change in Balances Computed
As at December 31

Assets	2021	2020	Change
Cash and cash equivalents	$ 17,000	$ 43,000	$ (26,000)
Accounts receivable	104,000	90,000	14,000
Inventory	80,000	65,000	15,000
Prepaid expenses	48,000	45,000	3,000
Current assets	249,000	243,000	
Land	551,000	310,000	241,000
Buildings at cost	860,000	810,000	50,000
Accumulated depreciation	(250,000)	(220,000)	(30,000)
Investments (FVOCI*)	84,000	90,000	(6,000)
Total assets	$1,494,000	$1,233,000	
Liabilities			
Trade payables	$ 52,000	$ 65,000	(13,000)
Dividends payable	7,000	12,000	(5,000)
Income tax payable	9,000	4,000	5,000
Notes payable	129,000	116,000	13,000
Current liabilities	197,000	197,000	
Bank loan	620,000	410,000	210,000
Total liabilities	817,000	607,000	
Shareholders' Equity			
Preferred shares	0	100,000	(100,000)
Common shares	265,000	210,000	55,000
Retained earnings	412,000	316,000	96,000
Total shareholders' equity	677,000	626,000	
Total liabilities and shareholders' equity	$1,494,000	$1,233,000	

*FVOCI = at fair value through other comprehensive income

Supplemental information:

- FFL's policy is to report interest and dividends paid as cash outflows from operating activities.
- During the year, FFL bought and sold land. The historical cost of the land sold was $250,000.
- FFL sold a building originally costing $250,000 for proceeds equal to its carrying value.
- The cost of the investment at FVOCI sold during the year was $6,000. This was also its carrying cost immediately prior to sale.

Recall that the first step is to determine the change in cash that needs to be reconciled as demonstrated in Step 1.

Exhibit A-12a	Applying the process for preparing a statement of cash flows using the indirect method, Step 1, Example 2

Step 1: Determine the change in cash that needs to be explained.

From the comparative balance sheet, the company's closing cash balance was $17,000, a decrease of $26,000 from the opening balance of $43,000.

The second step requires that we determine the net cash from operating activities. While this example is more involved than example 1, the process remains the same.

| Exhibit A-12b | Process for the indirect method, Step 2, Example 2 |

Step 2: Adjust net income as necessary to determine net cash from operating activities.

i.   Record the company's net income.

The income statement reported net income for the year of $146,000.

ii. Adjust for all non-cash items.

Depreciation expense reported on the income statement was $110,000. This amount is added back on the SCF because the expense did not involve a cash outflow.

The income statement recorded a loss *on the sale of investments* of $2,000 and *a loss on the sale of land* of $50,000.

These losses are the difference between the sales price of the assets and their respective carrying values. It may be instructive to consider one of the underlying transactions to help visualize the required adjustments.

Dr. Cash	200,000	
Dr. Loss on sale of land	50,000	
Cr. Land		250,000

The $200,000 cash received is a cash inflow from investing activities. Since this $200,000 fully reflects the cash flow from this transaction, we need to add back $50,000 to cash flow from operating activities for the loss included in income.

iii. Add back interest and income tax expense and subtract investment income.

The income statement reports interest expense of $10,000 and income tax expense of $107,000.

iv. Adjust for the unexplained changes in working capital accounts representing operating activities.

The working capital accounts included on the balance sheet requiring adjustment are accounts receivable, inventory, prepaid expenses, trade payables, and notes payable.

Accounts receivable increased $14,000 during the year. Cash collected was less than the revenue recognized on the income statement, so this is a cash outflow from operating activities.

Inventory increased $15,000 during the year. The cash outflow was more than the related expense (cost of goods sold), so this is a cash outflow from operating activities.

Prepaid expenses increased $3,000. The cash outflow was more than the related expense, so this is a cash outflow from operating activities.

Trade payables decreased $13,000. The cash outflow was more than the related expense, so this is a cash outflow from operating activities.

v.   Add dividends and interest received and subtract dividends, interest, and income taxes paid.

Interest paid = Interest expense − Change in interest payable. Interest payable for both years was $0, so interest paid equals interest expense of $10,000.

Income taxes paid = Income tax expense − Change in income taxes payable. The balance of the income taxes payable account increased $5,000. Therefore, income taxes paid equals $107,000 − $5,000 = $102,000.

Dividends paid = Dividends declared − Change in dividends payable. First, the amount of dividends declared can be determined from the change in retained earnings and net income.

Retained earnings, beginning of year (from balance sheet)	$316,000
Plus: net income (from income statement)	146,000
Less: dividends declared (solve)	(50,000)
Retained earnings, end of year (from balance sheet)	$412,000

Second, the balance of the dividends payable account decreased $5,000 during the year. Dividends paid were thus $50,000 − (−$5,000) = $55,000.

vi. The total of items (i) to (v) equals net cash from operating activities for the year.

Cash flow from operating activities totalled $213,000 as set out on the SCF in Exhibit A-13.

Step 3 requires that we account for the changes in the remaining balance sheet accounts. Again, while this illustration is more complex than the preceding example, the process to prepare a statement of cash flows using the indirect method remains unchanged.

Exhibit A-12c	Process for the indirect method, Step 3, Example 2

Step 3: Account for the changes in remaining balance sheet accounts. The reconciling items are recorded in the financing or investing activities section according to their nature.

The remaining account balances requiring adjustment are land, building at cost, accumulated depreciation, investments, bank loan, preferred shares, and common shares. Note that the change in accumulated depreciation was only partially explained when depreciation was added back in the operating activities section. The change in retained earnings was fully explained by net income and dividends declared, both of which were allowed for in cash flow from operating activities.

We first deal with transactions that do not require supplemental calculations.

Notes payable increased $13,000 during the year and is recorded as a cash inflow from financing.

The *increased bank loan* is recorded as a cash inflow of $210,000 in the financing section.

The *retirement of preferred shares* is recorded as a cash outflow of $100,000 in the financing section.

The *issuance of common shares* is recorded as a cash inflow of $55,000 in the financing section.

Sale of investments at FVOCI: From the income statement, we know that the net realized loss of $2,000 on the sale of investments at FVOCI was recycled through net income. From the supplemental information, we know that the cost of the investment was $6,000 as was the carrying cost of the investment immediately prior to sale. Therefore, the sales proceeds were $4,000, which is recorded as a cash inflow from investing activities.

Journal entry immediately prior to sale of investment

Dr. OCI unrealized loss on investment at FVOCI 2,000

Cr. Investments (FVOCI) 2,000

Journal entry at time of sale of investment

Dr. Cash 4,000

Cr. Investments (FVOCI) 4,000

Journal entry to recycle the realized loss at period-end*

Dr. Loss on sale of investment at FVOCI[†] 2,000

Cr. OCI 2,000

*OCI will be closed to AOCI as part of the closing entry process.
[†]Reported in net income.

Land: There were two transactions involving land. The historical cost of the land sold is known ($250,000 from the supplemental information section) as is the loss on sale ($50,000 from the income statement). Therefore, as already established in point ii in Exhibit A-12b, the sales proceeds were $200,000. This amount is recorded as a cash inflow from investing.

A T-account can be used to solve for the cost of the land purchased. The $491,000 purchase price (from the T-account) is recorded as a cash outflow from investing.

	Land		
Jan. 1 balance	310,000		
		250,000	Cost of land sold
Cost of land purchased	**491,000**		
Dec. 31 balance	551,000		

Buildings: There were two transactions involving buildings, a sale and a purchase. For the building sold, the historical cost is known ($250,000 from the supplemental information section), but the related accumulated depreciation must be found by analyzing the T-account for accumulated depreciation. The T-account below shows that the building sold had accumulated depreciation of $80,000, so the carrying value of the building sold was $250,000 − $80,000 = $170,000. This is also the amount of the sale proceeds since there was no gain or loss on the sale. This amount is recorded as a cash inflow from investing.

(*Continued*)

Exhibit A-12c   Continued

For the building purchased in the year, analysis of the T-account for buildings shows that the purchase price was $300,000. This amount is recorded as a cash outflow from investing.

Building				Accumulated depreciation	
Jan. 1 balance 810,000				220,000	Jan. 1 balance
Cost of building purchased 300,000				110,000	Depr. expense
	250,000	Cost of building sold	Accumulated depreciation of building sold 80,000		
Dec. 31 balance 860,000				250,000	Dec. 31 balance

The process is then completed in Step 4.

Exhibit A-12d   Process for the indirect method, Step 4, Example 2

Step 4: Calculate subtotals for operating, investing, and financing activities and ensure the net change in cash and cash equivalents thus determined is equal to the actual change for the period computed from Step 1.

The completed SCF is shown in Exhibit A-13. Note how the $26,000 decrease in cash from Step 1 has been explained.

Exhibit A-13   Result of applying procedures for statement of cash flow, Example 2

Fred's Fajitas Ltd. Statement of Cash Flows
Year Ended December 31, 2021

Cash flows from operating activities	
Net income	$ 146,000
Adjustments for:	
Loss on sale of investment	2,000
Loss on sale of land	50,000
Depreciation and amortization	110,000
Interest expense	10,000
Income tax expense	107,000
Subtotal	425,000
Increase in accounts receivable	(14,000)
Increase in inventory	(15,000)
Increase in prepaid expenses	(3,000)
Decrease in trade payables	(13,000)

Exhibit A-13	Continued		

Fred's Fajitas Ltd. Statement of Cash Flows
Year Ended December 31, 2021

Cash generated from operating activities	380,000		
Dividends paid	(55,000)		
Interest paid	(10,000)		
Income taxes paid	(102,000)		
Net cash from operating activities		$ 213,000	
Cash flows from investing activities			
Purchase of land	(491,000)		
Sale of land	200,000		
Purchase of building	(300,000)		
Sale of building	170,000		
Sale of FVOCI* investment	4,000		
Net cash used in investing activities		(417,000)	
Cash flows from financing activities			
Issuance of notes payable	13,000		
Proceeds of bank loan	210,000		
Retirement of preferred shares	(100,000)		
Issuance of ordinary shares	55,000		
Net cash from financing activities		178,000	
Net increase in cash		(26,000)	
Cash and cash equivalents, January 1, 2021		43,000	
Cash and cash equivalents, December 31, 2021		$ 17,000	

*FVOCI = at fair value through other comprehensive income

CHECKPOINT **CPA-8**

Itemize the four-step process to prepare a statement of cash flows using the indirect method.

3. The process—Direct method

The indirect method just described and illustrated refers only to cash flows from operating activities. Cash flows from investing and financing activities are always presented using the direct method. We now apply the direct method also to operating activities. Moreover, the method of determining dividends and interest received and dividends, interest, and income taxes paid is the same for both methods. Therefore, discussion is confined to how to ascertain cash receipts from customers and cash paid to suppliers and employees.

a. The direct method described

The direct method differs from the indirect method as it does not directly consider net income; rather, it focuses on cash received from sales and cash ppaid to suppliers and employees to generate those sales.

The general format for presenting cash flows from operating activities, as first presented in Exhibit A-4, is partially reproduced below.

Exhibit A-14	Sample of operating section of statement of cash flows

Illustrative Company Statement of Cash Flows (Partial)
Year Ended December 31, 2021

Cash flow from operating activities		
Cash receipts from customers	$ 30,360	Described below
Cash paid to suppliers and employees	(27,800)	Described below
Cash generated from operating activities	2,560	
Dividends received	200	These amounts are determined in the same manner whether the direct or indirect method is used.
Interest received	200	
Dividends paid	(1,200)	
Interest paid	(270)	
Income taxes paid	(900)	
Net cash from operating activities	$ 590	

This example shows only two lines other than those involving dividends, interest, and taxes. This presentation is the minimum required since inflows should not be netted against outflows. Enterprises can choose to provide more details by using additional lines. For example, "cash paid to suppliers and employees" could be divided into "cash paid to suppliers," "cash paid to employees," and "other operating expenses." There is no concrete guidance as to what level of detail should be provided, so professional judgment is required. In the discussion and illustrations below, we will use this two-line presentation.

CASH RECEIPTS FROM CUSTOMERS The starting point for determining cash receipts from customers is sales. This accrual-based number is transformed to a cash-based figure by adjusting for the net change in accounts receivable (AR) during the period. If AR increased during the year, sales exceeded cash collections; if AR decreased during the year, sales were less than cash collections. Thus,

Cash receipts from customers = Sales − Change in accounts receivable

In this formula, "change" can be an increase or decrease, with increases being positive amounts and decreases being negative ones.

It may be instructive to consider the underlying summary journal entry of a simple example and compare it with the formula solution.

Exhibit A-15	Illustration for computing cash receipts from customers

Facts:
- Zil Baguettes Ltd.'s sales for the year totalled $1,000,000.
- Zil's receivables increased $10,000 during the year.

Summary journal entry		
Dr. Cash	990,000	
Dr. Accounts receivable	10,000	
Cr. Sales		1,000,000

Direct computation

Cash receipts from customers = Sales − Change in accounts receivable

= $1,000,000 − $10,000 = $990,000

CASH PAID TO SUPPLIERS AND EMPLOYEES Cash paid to suppliers and employees is the sum of the cash paid for inventory and cash paid for operating expenses.

Cash paid for inventory is determined in two steps: (i) establishing the cost of inventory purchased; and (ii) ascertaining the cash paid for the purchases. We first compute cost of inventory purchased (or produced) using the formula:

$$\text{Purchases} = \text{Cost of goods sold} + \text{Change in inventory}$$

Second, cash paid for purchases is:

$$\text{Cash paid for inventory} = \text{Purchases} - \text{Change in accounts payable}$$

We can then combine these into one calculation (COGS denotes cost of goods sold):

$$\text{Cash paid for inventory} = \text{COGS} + \text{Change in inventory} - \text{Change in accounts payable}$$

Cash paid for operating expenses is determined in much the same manner as just illustrated for inventories; that is, adjust the accrual-based income statement number to determine the cash outflow for the year:

$$\text{Cash paid for operating expenses} = \text{Operating expenses} + \text{Change in prepaid expenses}$$

In all of the above formulas, "change" is a positive number for increases and a negative number for decreases. The foregoing points are summarized in Exhibit A-16.

Exhibit A-16	Determining direct cash flows from operating activities

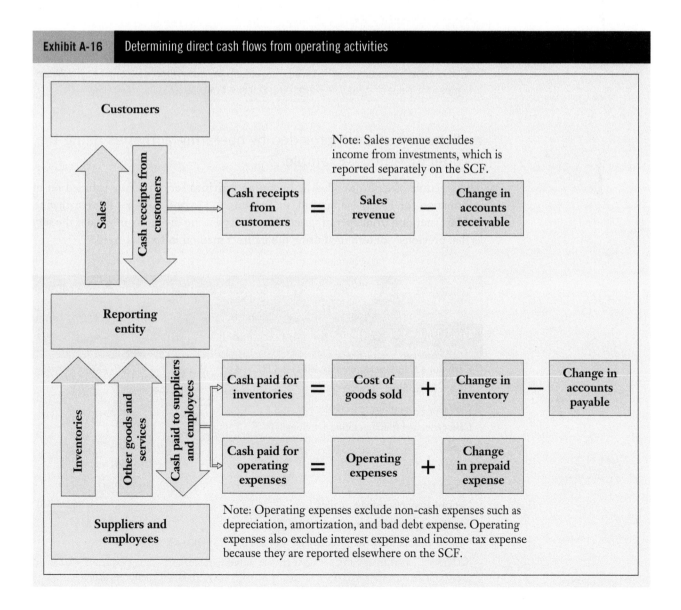

b. Schedule of cash provided by operating activities using the direct method—Example 1

The schedule of cash provided by operating activities set out below is based on the information for Kimzoo Fireworks in Exhibits A-8a and A-8b. Observe that the $53,000 net cash from operating activities derived using the direct method is the same as that previously determined using the indirect method in Exhibit A-10.

Exhibit A-17	Schedule of cash provided by operating activities using direct method, Example 1
Kimzoo Fireworks Ltd. Schedule of Cash Provided by Operating Activities Year Ended December 31, 2021	
Cash flows from operating activities	
Cash receipts from customers*	$ 646,000
Cash paid to suppliers and employees†	(509,000)
Cash generated from operating activities	137,000
Dividends paid	(46,000)
Interest paid	(5,000)
Income taxes paid	(33,000)
Net cash from operating activities	$53,000
Supporting computations	
*Sales − Change in accounts receivable = $660,000 − $14,000 = $646,000	
†COGS + Change in inventory − Change in accounts payable + Operating expenses + Change in prepaid expenses = $363,000 − $10,000 − $1,000 + $160,000 − $3,000 = $509,000	

c. Schedule of cash provided by operating activities using the direct method—Example 2

The schedule of cash provided by operating activities set out below is based on the information for Fred's Fajitas Ltd. in Exhibits A-11a and A-11b. Observe that the $213,000 net cash from operating activities derived using the direct method is the same as that previously determined using the indirect method in Exhibit A-13.

Exhibit A-18	Schedule of cash provided by operating activities using the direct method, Example 2
Fred's Fajitas Ltd. Schedule of Cash Provided by Operating Activities Year Ended December 31, 2021	
Cash flows from operating activities	
Cash receipts from customers*	$ 986,000
Cash paid to suppliers and employees†	(606,000)
Cash generated from operating activities	380,000
Dividends paid	(55,000)
Interest paid	(10,000)
Income taxes paid	(102,000)
Net cash from operating activities	$213,000
Supporting computations:	
*Sales − Change in accounts receivable = $1,000,000 − $14,000 = $986,000	
†COGS + Change in inventory − Change in accounts payable + Operating expenses + Change in prepaid expenses = $400,000 + $15,000 + $13,000 + $175,000 + $3,000 = $606,000	

 CHECKPOINT **CPA-9**

Describe the process of determining cash receipts from customers and cash paid to suppliers and employees.

4. Effects of specific items on the statement of cash flows

The process for preparing the SCF as described above provides general guidance on how to deal with common situations. The list that follows provides additional direction on select items not already addressed.

a. Accounts receivable—Allowance for bad debts

Companies often report receivables at the gross amount less an allowance. To obtain the amount of operating cash flow, the indirect method simply adjusts for the change in the net receivables. For the direct method of presentation, the calculation is a bit more involved. Cash receipts from sales is adjusted for the change in the gross amount of the receivables less the amount of receivables written off during the period. Thus,

$$\text{Cash receipts from customers} = \text{Sales} - \text{Change in gross accounts receivables}$$
$$- \text{Write offs}$$

Alternatively, cash from sales may be calculated as

$$\text{Cash receipts from customers} = \text{Sales} - \text{Change in net receivables}$$
$$- \text{Bad debt expense}$$

b. Complex financial instruments

As discussed in Chapter 14, complex financial instruments frequently include components of both debt and equity. As the cash received for the issuance of both debt and equity are classified as cash inflows from financing, reporting complex financial instruments on the SCF does not present any special challenges.

- *At time of issuance:* The consideration received for the issuance of the complex financial instrument is allocated to the constituent parts as per the guidance in Chapter 14. The elements are then normally reported separately as cash inflows in the financing activities section.
- *While the instruments are outstanding:* Cash inflows and outflows relative to the component parts are reported in the normal manner. In the event that a cash inflow or outflow contains multiple elements, they are each classified according to their nature. Paragraph 12 of IAS 7 indicates "*A single transaction may include cash flows that are classified differently . . .*"
- *At time of conversion:* The conversion is reported as a non-cash transaction. For example, a convertible bond is received in exchange for ordinary shares. If cash is involved, the cash received is reported as a cash inflow in the appropriate category, normally financing. For example, when warrants and cash are received in exchange for ordinary shares, the cash received is reported as a cash inflow from financing.
- *At time of derecognition:* The cash consideration paid is categorized according to its nature, normally financing.

c. Discontinued operations

Cash flows from discontinued operations are shown separately in the operating, investing, and financing sections of the SCF according to their nature. Alternatively, as per paragraph 33(c) of IFRS 5, Non-current Assets Held for Sale and Discontinued Operations, this information may be disclosed in the notes to the financial statements.

d. Discounts and premiums on bonds and other financial instruments

IAS 7 does not address the classification of the amortization of discounts and premiums on investments in debt instruments or financial liabilities. Recall that interest received may be classified as a cash inflow from operating or investing, while interest paid may be categorized as a cash outflow from operating or financing. The lack of specific guidance in this area does not present any particular difficulties, however, as the amortization of discounts and premiums does not involve cash flows, the SCF is adjusted as follows:

- For the direct method of presentation—report the amount of interest received or paid in the designated category.
- For the indirect method of presentation—subtract interest revenue and/or add back interest expense from/to net income in the operating activities section. Then report the amount of interest received and/or paid in the chosen category.

IFRS differs from ASPE. When the indirect method is used, ASPE requires that the amortization of discounts on both financial assets and liabilities be reported in the operating activities section. ASPE also requires that the amortization of premiums on financial assets and liabilities be included in the investing and financing activities sections respectively.

Exhibit A-19 and Exhibit A-20 illustrate the process of reporting the amortization of a bond premium and discount under IFRS. As previously established, the reporting entity can elect to classify cash outflows for interest payments as either an operating activity or a financing activity; we have presented both options for illustrative purposes. This is a simplified example that isolates the required treatment of the amortization of the premium and discount.

Exhibit A-19a	Amortization of bonds issued at a premium

Facts:

- Georgina's Stables Inc.'s (GSI) net income for the year ended December 31, 2018, was $100,000.
- GSI interest expense for the year was $10,000; interest paid was $12,000. The $2,000 difference is due to the amortization of a premium on a bond payable.
- Opening cash was $25,000; closing cash $123,000.
- There were no other items that needed to be reported on GSI's statement of cash flows.

Exhibit A-19b	Interest payments classified as an operating activity; indirect method

Georgina's Stables Inc. Statement of Cash Flows
Year Ended December 31, 2018

Cash flows from operating activities		
Net income	$100,000	
Interest expense	10,000	
Interest paid	(12,000)	
Net cash from operating activities		$ 98,000
Cash flows from investing activities		0
Cash flows from financing activities		0
Net increase (decrease) in cash		98,000
Cash, January 1, 2018		25,000
Cash, December 31, 2018		$123,000

Exhibit A-19c	Interest payments classified as a financing activity

Georgina's Stables Inc. Statement of Cash Flows
Year Ended December 31, 2018

Cash flows from operating activities		
Net income	$100,000	
Interest expense	10,000	
Net cash from operating activities		$ 110,000
Cash flows from investing activities		0
Cash flows from financing activities		
Interest paid	(12,000)	
Net cash from financing activities		(12,000)
Net increase (decrease) in cash		98,000
Cash, January 1, 2018		25,000
Cash, December 31, 2018		$ 123,000

Exhibit A-20a	Amortization of bonds issued at a discount

Facts:

- Georgina's Stables Inc.'s (GSI) net income for the year ended December 31, 2018, was $100,000.
- GSI interest expense for the year was $12,000; interest paid was $10,000. The $2,000 difference is due to the amortization of a discount on a bond payable.
- Opening cash was $25,000; closing cash $127,000.
- There were no other items that needed to be reported on GSI's statement of cash flows.

Exhibit A-20b	Interest payments classified as an operating activity; indirect method

Georgina's Stables Inc. Statement of Cash Flows
Year Ended December 31, 2018

Cash flows from operating activities		
Net income	$100,000	
Interest expense	12,000	
Interest paid	(10,000)	
Net cash from operating activities		$102,000
Cash flows from investing activities		0
Cash flows from financing activities		0
Net increase (decrease) in cash		102,000
Cash, January 1, 2018		25,000
Cash, December 31, 2018		$127,000

Exhibit A-20c	Interest payments classified as a financing activity

Georgina's Stables Inc. Statement of Cash Flows
Year Ended December 31, 2018

Cash flows from operating activities		
Net income	$100,000	
Interest expense	12,000	
Net cash from operating activities		$112,000
Cash flows from investing activities		0
Cash flows from financing activities		

(*Continued*)

Exhibit A-20c	Continued		
Georgina's Stables Inc. Statement of Cash Flows
Year Ended December 31, 2018			
Interest paid		(10,000)	
Net cash from financing activities			(10,000)
Net increase (decrease) in cash			102,000
Cash, January 1, 2018			25,000
Cash, December 31, 2018			$127,000

e. At fair value through profit or loss investments—Unrealized and realized gains and losses

The unrealized profit or loss on an investment at FVPL is reported in the income statement. When the indirect method of presentation is used, the unrealized profit or loss must be reversed in the cash flows from operating activities section of the SCF. No adjustment is required when the direct method of presentation is used.

The realized profit or loss on the sale of an investment at FVPL is a non-cash item and is treated in the same manner as gains and losses arising on the sale of other assets. When the indirect method of presentation is used, the realized profit or loss must be reversed in the cash flows from operating activities section of the SCF. No adjustment is required when the direct method of presentation is used.

The sales proceeds of an investment at FVPL held for trading purposes is reported as a cash inflow from operating activities under both the direct and indirect methods of presentation. The sales proceeds of an investment at FVPL held for other than trading purposes is reported as a cash inflow from investing activities under both the direct and indirect methods of presentation.

f. At fair value through other comprehensive income investments—Unrealized and realized gains and losses

The unrealized profit or loss on an investment at FVOCI is reported in other comprehensive income rather than in net income. As such, an adjustment is not necessary under either the direct or indirect methods of presentation. The unrealized gain or loss for the period needs to be factored in when reconciling that change in the value of investments at FVOCI reported on the comparative balance sheet, however.

As illustrated in Chapter 7, immediately prior to derecognizing (selling) an investment at FVOCI, the carrying value of the asset may be updated to the current market value with the as-yet-unrealized gains or losses reported in other comprehensive income. These unrealized gains and losses are treated in the same manner as those just described.

When an investment at FVOCI is derecognized, accumulated holding gains or losses on the investment are recycled (transferred) to profit or loss and are reported in net income.[9] This recycled income is a non-cash item and is treated in the same manner as gains and losses arising on the sale of other assets. When the indirect method

---

[9] As discussed in Chapter 7, the accumulated holding gains and losses on an investment in an equity security for which the investee elected to report the holding gains and losses in OCI are not recycled when the investment is derecognized. As such, the previously unrealized gain or loss is not reported in net income and, accordingly, an adjustment is not required when preparing the statement of cash flows.

of presentation is used, the realized profit or loss must be reversed in the cash flows from operating activities section of the SCF. No adjustment is required when the direct method of presentation is used.

The sales proceeds of an investment at FVOCI are reported as a cash inflow from investing activities under both the direct and indirect methods of presentation.

g. Income taxes—Classification

IAS 7 paragraph 35 requires that "taxes on income . . . shall be classified as cash flows from operating activities unless they can be specifically identified with financing and investing activities." In this text, all cash flows arising from income taxes are classified as operating activities.

h. Income taxes—Current and deferred

There are two components of income tax on both the balance sheet and the income statement—current and deferred. We compute cash paid for income taxes using the formula:

$$\text{Income taxes paid} = \text{Income tax expense} - \text{Change in income taxes payable}$$

This equation still holds provided you recognize that income tax expense includes both current and deferred tax expense and that taxes payable encompasses the current and deferred portions.

i. Investments in associates

Investments in associates are typically accounted for using the equity method. The SCF is concerned only with the cash received or advanced, rather than investment income. The required adjustment for the indirect method of presentation entails deducting income from investments in the operating section and recording dividends received in either the operating or investing section.

Exhibits A-21a and A-21b give a simplified example that isolates the illustration of the process of reporting cash flows arising from investments in associates using the indirect method of presentation of cash flows from operating activities.

Exhibit A-21a	Cash flows from investment in associates

Facts:

- Jaxxen's Hot Cars (JHC) Ltd.'s net income (including investment income) for the year ended December 31, 2018, was $100,000.
- JHC accounts for its investment in its associate, Belle's Racing Inc. (BRI), using the equity method. In 2018, JHC reported earning $20,000 from its investment in BRI.
- In 2018, BRI declared and paid $5,000 in dividends to JHC.
- JHC elects to report dividends received as an operating activity.
- Opening cash was $25,000; closing cash $110,000.
- There were no other items that had to be reported on JHC's statement of cash flows.

The $20,000 investment income is deducted from the SCF because the income did not involve a cash inflow. Similarly, the $5,000 dividend received is reported on the SCF as the cash received is not included in income. Note that JHC could also elect to report the dividend received as an investment activity.

Exhibit A-21b	Dividends received classified as an operating activity; indirect method

Jaxxen's Hot Cars Ltd. Statement of Cash Flows
Year Ended December 31, 2018

Cash flows from operating activities		
Net income	$100,000	
Investment income (investments in associates)	(20,000)	
Dividends received	5,000	
Net cash from operating activities		$ 85,000
Cash flows from investing activities		0
Cash flows from financing activities		0
Net increase (decrease) in cash		85,000
Cash, January 1, 2018		25,000
Cash, December 31, 2018		$110,000

j. Other comprehensive income

Other comprehensive income (OCI) is not reported on the SCF, as OCI does not affect cash since it records only unrealized gains and losses on select items.

k. Stock splits and dividends

Stock splits and dividends are non-cash transactions. They are not recorded on the SCF.

l. Treasury shares

Cash flows from the purchase and sale of treasury shares are reported as a financing activity.

5. Putting it all together—Comprehensive examples

This section has described the process for preparing the SCF using both the direct and indirect methods. You now have an opportunity to work through two comprehensive examples to confirm your knowledge of the topic. Many aspects of these examples are more involved than the previous two examples provided above. To solve, you will need to supplement the material in this chapter with your general knowledge of accounting. When complete, compare your answers to the solutions that follow.

a. Comprehensive example #1

Zippo Hosiery Inc.'s income statement, comparative balance sheet, and supplemental information follow:

Exhibit A-22a	Zippo Hosiery Inc.'s income statement

Zippo Hosiery Inc.
Income Statement
For the year ended December 31, 2021

Sales	$1,432,000
Cost of sales	756,000
Gross profit	676,000
Other expenses	256,600

(Continued)

Exhibit A-22a   Continued

Zippo Hosiery Inc.
Income Statement
For the year ended December 31, 2021

Interest expense	75,000
Depreciation expense	334,400
Income before income taxes	10,000
Income tax expense	4,000
Net income before discontinued operations	6,000
Discontinued operations, net of taxes ($100,000)	283,100
Net income	$ 289,100

Exhibit A-22b   Zippo Hosiery Inc.'s balance sheet

Zippo Hosiery Inc.
Comparative Balance Sheet
As at December 31

	2021	2020	Change
Assets			
Cash and cash equivalents	$ 172,000	$ 210,000	$ (38,000)
Accounts receivable	150,000	170,000	(20,000)
Inventory	575,000	498,000	77,000
Investments—FVPL held for trading purposes	140,000	190,000	(50,000)
Current assets	1,037,000	1,068,000	
Property, plant, and equipment at cost	1,984,000	1,396,000	588,000
Accumulated depreciation	(650,400)	(487,000)	(163,400)
Patents	690,000	552,000	138,000
Total assets	$3,060,600	$2,529,000	
Liabilities			
Trade payables	$ 93,000	$ 86,000	$ 7,000
Current liabilities	93,000	86,000	
Bank loan	0	100,000	(100,000)
Bonds payable	659,500	674,000	(14,500)
Total liabilities	752,500	860,000	
Shareholders' Equity			
Ordinary shares	1,150,000	700,000	450,000
Retained earnings	1,158,100	969,000	189,100
Total shareholders' equity	2,308,100	1,669,000	
Total liabilities and shareholders' equity	$3,060,600	$2,529,000	

Exhibit A-22c   Zippo Hosiery Inc.'s supplemental information

- The decrease in bonds payable is due entirely to the amortization of the related premium.
- Zippo's policy is to report interest and dividends paid as a cash outflow from operating activities.

(Continued)

Exhibit A-22c   Continued

- $10,000 of FVPL investments were purchased during the year; none was sold.
- Property, plant, and equipment costing $570,000 was sold for $422,000.
- 100,000 ordinary shares were issued to acquire $450,000 of property, plant, and equipment.
- The $212,000 cost of successfully suing a competitor for patent infringement was capitalized during the year.
- "Other Expenses" includes gains and losses on asset sales, holding losses, and patent amortization.
- Cash was received or paid for all revenues and expenses other than those relating to inventories, sales, depreciation, and amortization.
- Income from discontinued operations represents the operating profits of a plant that is in the process of being decommissioned. The recorded profit was received in cash.

Required:

1. Prepare Zippo Hosiery Inc.'s statement of cash flows for the year ended December 31, 2021, using the indirect method, including disclosure of non-cash activities.

2. Prepare a schedule of Zippo's cash provided by operating activities for the year ended December 31, 2021, using the direct method.

Solution to comprehensive example #1

For the year ended December 31, 2021, Zippo Hosiery Inc.'s cash inflows from operating activities totalled $560,000. Zippo's investing and financing activities for the year resulted in cash outflows of $498,000 and $100,000, respectively. These amounts were determined using the procedures illustrated in the chapter. Note that both the direct and indirect methods established that the aggregate cash inflows from operating activities were $560,000. Note that the references column is for expository purposes only. It would not normally be included in a formal statement of cash flows.

Exhibit A-23a   Solution to comprehensive example #1

Zippo Hosiery Inc. Statement of Cash Flows
For the year ended December 31, 2021

Cash flows from operating activities		References
Net income from continuing operations	$ 6,000	
Net income from discontinued operations	283,100	1
Adjustments for:		
Holding loss on FVPL investment	60,000	5
Gain on sale of property, plant, and equipment	(23,000)	3, 8
Depreciation and amortization expense	408,400	2, 7
Interest expense	75,000	
Income tax expense—continuing operations	100,000	
Income tax expense—discontinued operations	4,000	
Subtotal	913,500	
Purchase of FVPL investment held for trading purposes	(10,000)	
Decrease in accounts receivable	20,000	
Increase in inventory	(77,000)	
Increase in trade payables	7,000	
Cash generated from operating activities	853,500	

(Continued)

Exhibit A-23a Continued

Zippo Hosiery Inc. Statement of Cash Flows
For the year ended December 31, 2021

Cash flows from operating activities			References
Dividends paid	(100,000)		6
Interest paid	(89,500)		4
Income taxes paid—continuing operations	(100,000)		
Income taxes paid—discontinued operations	(4,000)		1
Net cash from operating activities		$ 560,000	
Cash flows from investing activities			
Purchase of property, plant, and equipment	(708,000)		8
Sale of property, plant, and equipment	422,000		
Patent	(212,000)		
Net cash used in investing activities		(498,000)	
Cash flows from financing activities			
Retire bank loan	(100,000)		
Net cash from financing activities		(100,000)	
Net increase (decrease) in cash		(38,000)	
Cash, January 1, 2021		210,000	
Cash, December 31, 2021		$ 172,000	

Exhibit A-23b Required disclosure—Notes to financial statement

Note: During the year, the company issued $450,000 of ordinary shares in exchange for property, plant, and equipment having a fair market value of $450,000.

Exhibit A-23c Supporting comments calculations as per the references in SCF

1. Income and income taxes pertaining to discontinued operations must be separately disclosed.

2. $334,400 depreciation (PPE) + $74,000 amortization (patent) = $408,400.
   Depreciation is reported on the income statement, while amortization is determined using a T-account (see #7 below).

3. Gain on sale = Sales proceeds − Net book value = $422,000 − ($570,000 − $171,000) = $23,000.
   The accumulated depreciation on the PPE sold is determined using a T-account (see #8 below).

4. Interest paid = Interest expense + Amortization of the bond premium = $75,000 + $14,500 = $89,500.
   Amortization of the bond premium is the change in the bonds payable balance from the comparative balance sheet.

5.

	Investment (FVPL—held for trading purposes)		
Jan. 1 balance	190,000		
Cost of investments purchased	10,000		
		60,000	Unrealized holding loss
Dec. 31 balance	140,000		

6.

	Retained earnings		
		969,000	Jan. 1 balance
		289,100	Net income
Dividends declared	100,000		
		1,158,100	Dec. 31 balance

(*Continued*)

Exhibit A-23c	Continued

7.

	Patent		
Jan. 1 balance	552,000		
Legal defence costs	212,000		
		74,000	Patent amortization
Dec. 31 balance	690,000		

8.

	PPE					Accumulated depreciation	
Jan. 1 balance	1,396,000					487,000	Jan. 1 balance
Cost of PPE purchased for shares	450,000					334,400	Depr. expense
		570,000	Cost of PPE sold	Accumulated depreciation of PPE sold	171,000		
PPE purchased for cash	708,000						
Dec. 31 balance	1,984,000					650,400	Dec. 31 balance

Exhibit A-23d	Cash flow from operations: Direct method

Zippo Hosiery Inc. Schedule of Cash Provided by Operating Activities
For the year ended December 31, 2021

Cash flows from operating activities	
Cash receipts from customers (1)	$1,452,000
Cash receipts from discontinued operations (2)	383,100
Cash paid to suppliers and employees (3)	(971,600)
Cash paid to acquire FVPL investment held for trading purposes	(10,000)
Cash generated from operating activities	853,500
Dividends paid	(100,000)
Interest paid	(89,500)
Income taxes paid—continuing operations	(4,000)
Income taxes paid—discontinued operations	(100,000)
Net cash from operating activities	$560,000

Supporting computations

1. $1,432,000 (sales) + $20,000 (decrease in accounts receivable) = $1,452,000

2. $283,100 (income net of tax from discontinued operations) + $100,000 (income tax paid—discontinued operations) = $383,100

3. $756,000 (COGS) + $256,600 (other expenses) + $77,000 (increase in inventory) – $7,000 (increase in trade payables) – $74,000 (amortization included in other expenses) – $60,000 (holding loss included in other expenses) + $23,000 (gain on sale included in other expenses) = $971,600

b. Comprehensive example #2

Gretta's Cat Products (GCP) Inc.'s statement of comprehensive income, statement of financial position, and supplemental information follow:

Exhibit A-24a	GCP's statement of comprehensive income

Gretta's Cat Products Inc.
Statement of Comprehensive Income
For the year ended December 31, 2021

Sales	$5,000,000
Cost of sales	3,500,000
Gross profit	1,500,000
Bad debt expense	(50,000)
Depreciation and amortization expense	(75,000)
Gain on sale of investments at FVPL	15,000
Holding gain on investments at FVPL	5,000
Interest expense	(60,000)
Loss on sale of property, plant, and equipment	(25,000)
Recycled loss on disposal of assets at FVOCI	(30,000)
Other expenses	(1,000,000)
Income before income from associates and income taxes	280,000
Income from associates	95,000
Income before income taxes	375,000
Current income tax expense	(125,000)
Deferred income tax expense	(80,000)
Net income	$ 170,000
Other comprehensive income, net of taxes	
Items that may subsequently be reclassified to net income:	
Holding loss on investment at FVOCI	$ (20,000)
Reclassification of holding losses to income	30,000
Other comprehensive income, net of taxes	$ 10,000
Comprehensive income	$ 180,000

Exhibit A-24b	GCP's statement of financial position

Gretta's Cat Products Inc.
Comparative Statement of Financial Position
As at December 31

	2021	2020	Change
Assets			
Cash	$ 758,000	$ 612,000	146,000
Investments for purpose of meeting short-term cash commitments	136,000	124,000	12,000
Investments at FVPL held for trading purposes	154,000	221,000	(67,000)
Accounts receivable (net)	492,000	474,000	18,000
Inventory	822,000	839,000	(17,000)
Prepaid expenses	28,000	26,000	2,000
Investments at FVPL held for other than trading purposes	83,000	85,000	(2,000)
Investments at FVOCI	91,000	84,000	7,000

(Continued)

Exhibit A-24b   Continued

Gretta's Cat Products Inc.
Comparative Statement of Financial Position
As at December 31

	2021	2020	Change
Investments in associates	412,000	365,000	47,000
Property, plant, and equipment (net)	1,064,000	1,226,000	(162,000)
ROU asset (net)	65,000	0	65,000
Intangible assets (net)	26,000	29,000	(3,000)
Total assets	$4,131,000	$4,085,000	
Liabilities			
Accounts payable and accruals	$ 372,000	$ 383,000	(11,000)
Interest payable	14,000	11,000	3,000
Income taxes payable	6,000	22,000	(16,000)
Dividends payable	121,000	129,000	(8,000)
Bank loan payable	640,000	1,250,000	(610,000)
Lease payable	57,000	0	57,000
Bonds payable	783,000	291,000	492,000
Deferred income taxes	126,000	114,000	12,000
Total debt	2,119,000	2,200,000	
Shareholders' equity			
Preferred shares	225,000	200,000	25,000
Common shares	950,000	1,000,000	(50,000)
Contributed surplus—conversion option	75,000	0	75,000
Retained earnings	712,000	645,000	67,000
Accumulated other comprehensive income	50,000	40,000	10,000
Total shareholders' equity	2,012,000	1,885,000	
Total debt and shareholders' equity	$4,131,000	$4,085,000	

Exhibit A-24c   GCP's supplemental information

- GCP's policy is to report interest and dividends received and paid as operating activities.
- GCP sold investments at FVPL held for trading purposes during the year.
- GCP did not buy or sell any investments held for other than trading purposes during the year.
- GCP purchased investments at FVOCI during the year.
- GCP sold an investment at FVOCI for $62,000 cash.
- GCP's shareholdings in its associate did not change during the year.
- GCP acquired an ROU asset valued at $70,000 during the year which was financed 100% by the lessor. Lease payments were made subsequent to the commencement date of the lease.
- GCP paid $5,000 in legal fees to successfully defend its patent (intangible asset) during the year.
- GCP borrowed an additional $220,000 from the bank during the year.
- GCP's interest expense included amortization of an $8,000 premium on its bonds payable.
- GCP issued $50,000 of preferred shares during the year in exchange for equipment with a fair value of $50,000.
- GCP distributed a common stock dividend during the year valued at $82,000.
- GCP issued a convertible bond during the year.

Solution to comprehensive example #2

For the year ended December 31, 2021, GCP's cash inflows from operating activities totalled $270,000. GCP's investing activities for the year resulted in cash inflows of $93,000, while its financing activities resulted in cash outflows of $205,000. These amounts were determined using the procedures illustrated in the chapter. Note that both the direct and indirect methods established that the aggregate cash inflows from operating activities were $270,000. The references column is for expository purposes only. It would not normally be included in a formal statement of cash flows.

Exhibit A-25a	Solution to comprehensive example #2		
Gretta's Cat Products Inc. Statement of Cash Flows **For the year ended December 31, 2021**			
Cash flows from operating activities	**References**		
Net income	1	$170,000	
Adjustments for:			
Gain on sale of investments at FVPL	2	(15,000)	
Holding gain on investments at FVPL	2	(5,000)	
Loss on sale of property, plant, and equipment	2	25,000	
Recycled loss on disposal of assets at FVOCI	2	30,000	
Income from associates	3	(95,000)	
Depreciation and amortization expense		75,000	
Interest expense		60,000	
Current income tax expense		125,000	
Deferred income tax expense		80,000	
Subtotal		450,000	
Sale of FVPL investment held for trading purposes	4	89,000	
Increase in accounts receivable		(18,000)	
Decrease in inventory		17,000	
Increase in prepaid expenses		(2,000)	
Decrease in accounts payable and accruals		(11,000)	
Cash generated from operating activities		525,000	
Dividends received	3	48,000	
Dividends paid	5	(29,000)	
Interest paid	6	(65,000)	
Income taxes paid	7	(209,000)	
Net cash from operating activities			$270,000
Cash flows from investing activities			
Purchase of investment at FVOCI	8	(89,000)	
Sale of investment at FVOCI		62,000	
Sale of property, plant, and equipment	9	125,000	
Capitalization of legal fees on intangible assets		(5,000)	
Net cash used in investing activities			93,000
Cash flows from financing activities			
Borrow by way of bank loan		220,000	
Payment on bank loan	10	(830,000)	
Payment on lease liability	11	(13,000)	
Sale of bonds	12	575,000	
Repurchase of preferred shares	13	(25,000)	
Repurchase of common shares	14	(132,000)	

(*Continued*)

Exhibit A-25a	Continued	

Gretta's Cat Products Inc. Statement of Cash Flows
For the year ended December 31, 2021

Net cash from financing activities		(205,000)
Net increase in cash		158,000
Cash and cash equivalents, January 1, 2021	15	736,000
Cash and cash equivalents, December 31, 2021	16	$ 894,000

Exhibit A-25b	Required disclosure—Notes to financial statement

Notes:

■ During the year, the company issued $50,000 of preferred shares in exchange for equipment having a fair market value of $50,000.

■ During the year, the company acquired a right-of-use asset valued at $70,000, financed by a lease liability of the same amount.

■ During the year, the company declared and distributed an $82,000 stock dividend on its common shares.

■ The cash and cash equivalents of $894,000 as at December 31, 2021, were comprised of $758,000 in demand deposits with a local bank and a short-term money market investment valued at $136,000 that is held to meet short-term cash commitments.

Exhibit A-25c	Supporting comments calculations as per the references in SCF

1. Net income, rather than comprehensive income, is the starting point for determining cash flows from operations (indirect method).

2. Gains and losses on investments are not cash flows and must be adjusted in the cash flows from operating activities section (indirect method).

3. Income from associates are not cash flows and must be adjusted in the cash flows from operating activities section (indirect method). Dividends received are cash flows and must be reported as a cash inflow from either operating or investing activities in accordance with the company's policy in this respect. See T-account in #20 below for determination of the amount of dividends received.

4. The sale of an investment at FVPL held for trading purposes is reported as a cash inflow in the cash flows from operating activities section. See T-account in #17 below and supporting commentary for determination of the sales proceeds.

5. Dividends paid = Cash dividends declared + Decrease in dividends payable account = $21,000 + $8,000 = $29,000. See T-account in #30 below for determination of the amount of dividends declared.

6. Interest paid = Interest expense − Increase in interest payable account + Amortization of bond premium = $60,000 − $3,000 + $8,000 = $65,000.

7. Income taxes paid = Current income tax expense + Deferred income tax expense + Decrease in income taxes payable − Increase in deferred taxes payable = $125,000 + $80,000 + $16,000 − $12,000 = $209,000.

8. The purchase of an investment at FVOCI is reported as a cash outflow in the cash flows from investing activities section. See T-account in #19 below for determination of the purchase price.

9. The sale of PPE is reported as a cash inflow in the cash flows from investing activities section. See T-account in #21 below and supporting commentary for determination of the sales proceeds.

10. The repayment of bank loans is reported as a cash outflow in the cash flows from financing activities section. See T-account in #24 below for determination of the amount repaid.

11. The repayment of the lease liability is reported as a cash outflow in the cash flows from financing activities section. See T-account in #25 below for determination of the amount repaid.

12. The sale of bonds is reported as a cash inflow in the cash flows from financing activities section. See T-account in #26 below and supporting commentary for determination of the sales proceeds.

(*Continued*)

13. The repurchase of preferred shares is reported as a cash outflow in the cash flows from financing activities section. See T-account in #27 below for determination of the purchase price.

14. The repurchase of common shares is reported as a cash outflow in the cash flows from financing activities section. See T-account in #28 below for determination of the purchase price.

15. Opening cash and cash equivalents = Cash + Investments held for meeting short-term obligations = $612,000 + $124,000 = $736,000.

16. Closing cash and cash equivalents = Cash + Investments held for meeting short-term obligations = $758,000 + $136,000 = $894,000.

17.

Investments at FVPL (trading)

Jan. 1 balance	221,000		
Unrealized holding gain*	7,000		
		74,000	Book value of FVPL (trading) sold**
Dec. 31 balance	154,000		

*$5,000 reported realized gain = $x - $2,000$ unrealized holding loss on FVPL (non-trading); $x = $7,000$

$74,000 book value + $15,000 gain on sale = **$89,000 sales proceeds

18.

Investments at FVPL (non-trading)

Jan. 1 balance	85,000		
		2,000	**Unrealized holding loss**
Dec. 31 balance	83,000		

19.

Investments at FVOCI

Jan. 1 balance	84,000		
		62,000	Sale of FVOCI
		20,000	Unrealized holding loss
Purchase of FVOCI	**89,000**		
Dec. 31 balance	91,000		

20.

Investments in associates

Jan. 1 balance	365,000		
Investment income	95,000		
		48,000	**Dividends received**
Dec. 31 balance	412,000		

21.

Property, plant, and equipment (net)

Jan. 1 balance	1,226,000		
Preferred shares issued	50,000		
		62,000	Depreciation*
		150,000	**Depreciated cost of PPE sold during year**
Dec. 31 balance	1,064,000		

*$75,000 depreciation and amortization expense − $5,000 depreciation of ROU asset − $8,000 amortization of intangible asset = $62,000

$150,000 depreciated cost − $25,000 loss on sale = **$125,000 sales proceeds

(Continued)

Exhibit A-25c   Continued

22.

	ROU asset (net)		
Jan. 1 balance	0		
Leased	70,000		
		5,000	**Depreciation**
Dec. 31 balance	65,000		

23.

	Intangible assets (net)		
Jan. 1 balance	29,000		
Legal fees	5,000		
		8,000	**Depreciation**
Dec. 31 balance	26,000		

24.

	Bank loan payable		
		1,250,000	Jan. 1 balance
		220,000	New borrowings
Repaid during year	**830,000**		
		640,000	Dec. 31 balance

25.

	Lease liability		
		0	Jan. 1 balance
		70,000	New borrowings
Repaid during year	**13,000**		
		57,000	Dec. 31 balance

26.

	Bonds payable		
		291,000	Jan. 1 balance
Amortization of premium	8,000		
		500,000	**New borrowings***
		783,000	Dec. 31 balance

*$500,000 bonds + $75,000 contributed surplus = **$575,000** sales proceeds

27.

	Preferred shares		
		200,000	Jan. 1 balance
		50,000	Issued for equipment
Redeemed during year	**25,000**		
		225,000	Dec. 31 balance

28.

	Common shares		
		1,000,000	Jan. 1 balance
		82,000	Stock dividend
Redeemed during year	**132,000**		
		950,000	Dec. 31 balance

29.

	Contributed surplus		
		0	Jan. 1 balance
		75,000	**Part of bond sales proceeds**
		75,000	Dec. 31 balance

(Continued)

Exhibit A-25c	Continued

30.

		Retained earnings	
		645,000	Jan. 1 balance
Net income		170,000	
Stock dividend distributed	82,000		
Cash dividend declared	**21,000**		
		712,000	Dec. 31 balance

31.

	AOCI	
	40,000	Jan. 1 balance
	10,000	**OCI 2021**
	50,000	Dec. 31 balance

Exhibit A-25d	Cash flow from operations: Direct method

**Gretta's Cat Products Inc. Schedule of Cash Provided by Operating Activities
For the year ended December 31, 2021**

Cash flows from operating activities	
Cash receipts from customers (1)	$4,932,000
Cash paid to suppliers and employees (2)	(4,496,000)
Cash received from sale of FVPL investment held for trading purposes	89,000
Cash generated from operating activities	525,000
Dividends received	48,000
Dividends paid	(29,000)
Interest paid	(65,000)
Income taxes paid	(209,000)
Net cash from operating activities	**$270,000**

Supporting computations

1. $5,000,000 (sales) – $18,000 (increase in accounts receivable) – $50,000 (bad debt expense) = $4,932,000

2. $3,500,000 (COGS) + $1,000,000 (other expenses) – $17,000 (decrease in inventory) + $11,000 (decrease in trade payables) + $2,000 (increase in prepaid expenses) = $4,496,000

D. PRESENTATION AND DISCLOSURE

The previous sections of this chapter have described the presentation and disclosure requirements regarding the SCF. These requirements are primarily contained in IAS 1 and IAS 7. The following table provides a summary of the principal requirements:

Exhibit A-26	Summary of presentation and disclosure requirements relating to the statement of cash flows

Presentation

- The change in cash and cash equivalents must be explained.
- Cash flows must be classified as arising from operating, investing, or financing activities.

(*Continued*)

Exhibit A-26	Continued

Presentation

- Cash flows from operating activities may be reported using either the direct or indirect method.
- Major classes of cash inflows and outflows for both investing and financing activities must be separately reported.
- Cash flows from interest paid and received, dividends paid and received, and income taxes paid must be individually disclosed. This information may be included directly on the statement of cash flows or discussed in the supporting notes to the financial statements.

Disclosure

- The components of cash and cash equivalents must be disclosed.
- The policy adopted to determine the composition of cash and cash equivalents must be disclosed.
- Non-cash investing and financing transactions are not reported on the statement of cash flows, but must be disclosed elsewhere in the financial statements.
- Sufficient information must be provided to enable users to evaluate changes in liabilities arising from financing activities, including both cash and non-cash transactions.

E. SUBSTANTIVE DIFFERENCES BETWEEN IFRS AND ASPE

ISSUE	IFRS	ASPE
Cash equivalents	Qualifying investments held to meet the entity's short-term cash commitments are reported as a cash equivalent.	Qualifying investments may be reported as (i) a cash equivalent or (ii) a trading asset or investment. The entity establishes a policy concerning which of these assets will be reported as cash equivalents.
Interest and dividends received	Enterprises may classify cash inflows arising from the receipt of interest and dividends as either an operating or an investing activity.	Cash inflows arising from the receipt of interest and dividends must be classified as an operating activity.
Interest paid	Enterprises may classify cash outflows arising from the payment of interest as either an operating or a financing activity.	Cash outflows arising from the payment of interest is normally classified as an operating activity.
Dividends paid	Enterprises may classify cash outflows arising from the payment of dividends as either an operating or a financing activity.	Cash outflows arising from the payment of dividends must be classified as a financing activity.
Interest and dividends received and paid	IFRS requires separate disclosure of the amount of interest and dividends both received and paid.	ASPE requires that interest and dividends paid and charged directly to retained earnings be separately presented as cash outflows from financing.
Income taxes paid	IFRS requires disclosure of the amount of income taxes paid.	ASPE does not require disclosure of the amount of income taxes paid.
Amortization of discounts on financial assets and financial liabilities	IFRS is silent on this matter.	ASPE requires that the amortization be accounted for as an adjustment to net income in the operating section (indirect method).
Amortization of premiums on financial assets	IFRS is silent on this matter.	ASPE requires that the amortization of the premium be reported as a cash inflow from investing.
Amortizапion of premiums on financial liabilities	IFRS is silent on this matter.	ASPE requires that the amortization of the premium be reported as a cash outflow from financing.

F. SUMMARY

L.O. A-1. Describe the purpose of the statement of cash flows and the information it conveys.

- The statement of cash flows helps users determine the entity's ability to make payments when due and to pay dividends.
- It also helps users assess the company's quality of earnings.

L.O. A-2. Define cash and cash equivalents.

- Cash is cash on hand and demand deposits.
- Cash equivalents are short-term, highly liquid investments that are easily convertible to a known amount of cash and which are subject to an insignificant risk of changes in value.

L.O. A-3. Differentiate among cash flows from operating activities, investing activities, and financing activities.

- Operating cash flows arise from the day-to-day running of the business.
- Cash flows from investing result from the acquisition and disposal of non-current assets and other investments.
- Cash flows from financing activities stem from issuing and retiring debt and equity.

L.O. A-4. Describe the difference between the direct and indirect methods of calculating cash flows from operating activities.

- Net income is the starting point for the indirect method of presenting cash flows from operating activities. Profit and loss is adjusted for non-cash transactions, deferrals and accruals, and income or expense items related to investing and financing activities.
- The direct method of presenting cash flows from operating activities discloses the gross amount of cash receipts and cash payments by category.

L.O. A-5. Prepare a statement of cash flows using both the direct and indirect methods.

- The statement of cash flows is prepared in accordance with the methodology outlined in this chapter.

G. ANSWERS TO CHECKPOINT QUESTIONS

CPA-1: Three reasons why the statement of cash flows is a useful component of an enterprise's financial statements include (i) it is useful for evaluating a company's liquidity, (ii) it provides information about the timing and uncertainty of cash flows, and (iii) it can be used to ascertain the firm's quality of earnings.

CPA-2: Cash equivalents are short-term, highly liquid investments that are readily convertible to a known amount of cash and which are subject to an insignificant risk of changes in value.

CPA-3: Cash flows arising from the purchase and sale of investments at FVPL are classified as operating activities if the investments are held for trading purposes, and as investing activities if held for other than trading purposes.

CPA-4: The three categories of cash flows reported on the statement of cash flows are those arising from operating activities, investing activities, and financing activities.

CPA-5: IFRS permits an enterprise to classify interest and dividends received as an operating or investing activity and interest and dividends paid as an operating or financing activity.

CPA-6: A non-cash transaction is one that does not involve cash. Non-cash financing and investing activities are not reported on the statement of cash flows. If significant, however, they are disclosed in the notes to the financial statements.

CPA-7: The primary differences between the two sets of standards governing the preparation of the statement of cash flows are as follows:

- ASPE refers to a cash flow statement; IFRS a statement of cash flows.
- ASPE does not normally provide options with respect to the classification of interest and dividends received and paid.
- ASPE does not require separate disclosure of the amount of interest and dividends paid and received. Rather, ASPE only requires separate disclosure of the amount of interest and dividends charged directly to retained earnings.
- ASPE does not require disclosure of the amount of income taxes paid.

CPA-8: The four-step process to prepare a statement of cash flows using the indirect method is as follows:

1. Determine the change in cash that needs to be explained.
2. Adjust net income as necessary to determine net cash from operating activities.
3. Account for the changes in remaining balance sheet accounts. The reconciling items are recorded in the financing or investing activities section according to their nature.
4. Calculate subtotals for operating, investing, and financing activities and ensure the net change in cash and cash equivalents thus determined is equal to the actual change for the period computed in the first step.

CPA-9: The process of determining cash receipts from customers is to start with sales and then deduct the net increase in accounts receivable (or add the net decrease) to determine the cash received. Cash paid to suppliers and employees is the sum of cash paid for inventory and cash paid for operating expenses. The cash paid for inventory is cost of goods sold plus the increase in inventory (or minus the decrease) minus the increase in accounts payable (or plus the decrease); the cash paid for operating expenses is operating expenses plus the increase in prepaid expenses (or minus the decrease in prepaid expenses).

H. GLOSSARY

cash equivalents: Short-term, highly liquid investments that are readily convertible to known amounts of cash and which are subject to an insignificant risk of changes in value.

direct method: A method of presenting the statement of cash flows by showing major classes of gross cash receipts and gross cash payments.

financing activities: Activities that result in changes in the size and composition of the contributed equity and borrowings of the entity.

indirect method: A method of presenting the statement of cash flows by adjusting profit or loss for the effects of transactions of a non-cash nature, any deferrals or accruals of past or future operating cash receipts or payments, and items of income or expense associated with investing or financing cash flows.

investing activities: The acquisition and disposal of long-term assets and other investments not included in cash equivalents.

non-cash transactions: Activities that do not involve cash.

operating activities: The principal revenue-producing activities of the entity and other activities that are not investing or financing activities.

I. REFERENCES

Authoritative standards:

IFRS	ASPE Section
IAS 1—Presentation of Financial Statements	1400—General Standards of Financial Statement Presentation
IAS 7—Statement of Cash Flows	1540—Cash Flow Statement
IFRS 5—Non-current Assets Held for Sale and Discontinued Operations	3475—Disposal of Long-lived Assets and Discontinued Operations
IAS 8—Accounting Policies, Changes in Accounting Estimates and Errors	1506—Accounting Changes

J. PROBLEMS

 PA-1.   Purpose of the statement of cash flows   (**L.O.** A-1) (Easy – 5 minutes)

Describe in a general way the purpose of the statement of cash flows and the information that it conveys.

 PA-2.   Usefulness of the statement of cash flows   (**L.O.** A-1) (Easy – 5 minutes)

The statement of cash flows provides information relative to the entity's cash inflows and outflows for the period. List three ways that stakeholders may use this information.

 PA-3.   Cash and cash equivalents   (**L.O.** A-2) (Easy – 10 minutes)

a. Describe cash equivalents.
b. Briefly discuss the factors that determine how investments that meet the criteria of cash equivalents are reported on the statement of cash flows.
c. What guidance does IFRS provide with respect to reporting bank overdrafts on the statement of cash flows?

 PA-4.   Classifying cash flows   (**L.O.** A-3) (Medium – 10 minutes)

a. Describe operating activities, investing activities, and financing activities and provide three examples of each.
b. Describe in a general way what information each category of cash flows provides.
c. Describe the options available with respect to classifying the receipt and payment of interest and dividends under IFRS. Contrast this with the options available, if any, under ASPE.

A·S·P·E

PA-5.   Classifying cash flows—indirect method   (**L.O.** A-3) (Medium – 15 minutes)

A list of items that may affect an IFRS-based statement of cash flows prepared using the *indirect* method follows. Assume that the transactions are for cash unless stated otherwise. For each item, indicate by using the associated letter whether it is:

A—a cash receipt reported as an operating activity or an amount added to net income in the cash flows from operating activities section
B—a cash outflow reported as an operating activity or an amount deducted from net income in the cash flows from operating activities section
C—a cash receipt in the cash flows from investments section
D—a cash outflow in the cash flows from investments section
E—a cash receipt in the cash flows from financing section
F—a cash outflow in the cash flows from financing section
G—not reported on the statement of cash flows
H—an item for which there is more than one alternative for reporting

Item	Transaction	Categorization on the statement of cash flows
1.	Receipt of dividends	
2.	Increase in accounts receivable	
3.	Decrease in deferred income taxes payable	
4.	Sale of an at fair value through profit or loss investment held for trading purposes	
5.	Issuing (selling) shares	
6.	Depreciation expense	
7.	Loss on the sale of a financial asset at amortized cost investment	
8.	Payment of interest	
9.	Goodwill impairment loss	
10.	Purchase of an at fair value through other comprehensive income investment	
11.	Decrease in accounts payable	
12.	Conversion of bonds to ordinary shares	
13.	Borrowing money from the bank	
14.	Sale of a computer at book value	
15.	Retirement of bonds	

PA-6.   Classifying cash flows—direct method   (**L.O.** A-3) (Easy – 10 minutes)

A list of items that may affect an IFRS-based statement of cash flows prepared using the *direct* method follows. Assume that the transactions are for cash unless stated otherwise. For each item indicate by using the associated letter whether it is:

A—a cash receipt in the cash flows from operations section
B—a cash outflow in the cash flows from operations section
C—a cash receipt in the cash flows from investments section
D—a cash outflow in the cash flows from investments section
E—a cash receipt in the cash flows from financing section
F—a cash outflow in the cash flows from financing section
G—not reported on the statement of cash flows
H—an item for which there is more than one alternative for reporting
I—none of the above

Item	Transaction	Categorization on the statement of cash flows
1.	Sale of land at a loss	
2.	Gain on the sale of equipment	
3.	Repurchasing own shares	
4.	Receipt of interest	
5.	Purchase of an investment that meets the criteria of a cash equivalent held to meet short-term cash commitments	
6.	Depreciation expense	
7.	Leased right-of-use equipment	
8.	Payment of dividends	
9.	Other comprehensive income	
10.	Impairment loss on a patent	

PA-7.   Analysis of changes in account balances—effects of specific transactions
(**L.O.** A-3) (Medium – 10 minutes)

Select financial information for Aaron and Jamie Ltd. appears below:

Aaron and Jamie Ltd. Select Financial Information As at December 31		
	2019	**2018**
Plant assets	$ 800,000	$ 500,000
Accumulated depreciation	(140,000)	(180,000)
Dividends payable	35,000	52,000
Retained earnings	1,058,000	1,029,000
		2019
Net income		$ 400,000
Depreciation—plant assets		74,000

- The company issued 20,000 ordinary shares to a supplier in exchange for plant assets having a fair value of $200,000.
- The company sold equipment (plant assets) with a net book value of $125,000 for $90,000 cash.
- The company declared and issued an ordinary stock dividend valued at $30,000.

Required:

a. Determine the amount of cash inflows from investing that should be reported on the statement of cash flows.
b. Determine the amount of cash outflows from investing that should be reported on the statement of cash flows.
c. Determine the amount of cash dividends declared and paid during the year.

PA-8.   Classifying cash flows—Other comprehensive income and non-cash transactions
(**L.O.** A-3, **L.O.** A-4) (Medium – 5 minutes)

a. Describe how other comprehensive income is reported on the statement of cash flows prepared using the direct method of presenting cash flows from operating activities.
b. Describe how other comprehensive income is reported on the statement of cash flows prepared using the indirect method of presenting cash flows from operating activities.
c. Describe how the statement of cash flows reports non-cash investing and financing transactions.
d. Provide three examples of non-cash investing or financing transactions.

PA-9.   Identifying and determining cash flows from operating activities—indirect method
(**L.O.** A-3, **L.O.** A-5) (Medium – 10 minutes)

Hobnob Corp.'s policy is to report all cash flows arising from interest and dividends in the operating activities section. Hobnob's activities for the year ended December 31, 2018, included the following:

- Net income after taxes for 2018 totalled $125,000.
- Declared and issued a stock dividend valued at $50,000.
- Accounts receivable decreased $32,000 in 2018.
- Sold an at fair value through profit or loss investment that was held for trading purposes for $12,000. The book value was $10,000.
- Interest revenue for the period was $12,000. The interest receivable account decreased $3,000.
- Declared a $20,000 dividend payable. The dividends payable account decreased $12,000 in 2018.
- Sold an at fair value through other comprehensive income investment for $8,000. The cost of the investment and its book value immediately prior to sale was $9,000.

■ Hobnob recorded a $10,000 goodwill impairment loss during the year.
■ Depreciation expense for the year was $8,000.

Required:

a. Prepare the cash flows from operating activities section of the statement of cash flows using the indirect method.
b. Identify how the activities listed above that are not operating activities would be reported in the statement of cash flows.

A·S·P·E **PA-10.** Identifying and determining cash flows from operating activities—indirect method
(**L.O.** A-3, **L.O.** A-5) (Medium – 10 minutes)

Refer to the information presented in PA-9. Assume that Hobnob Corp. is a private corporation that elects to report its financial results in accordance with ASPE.

Required:

a. Prepare the cash flows from operating activities section of the cash flow statement using the indirect method.
b. Identify how the activities listed above that are not operating activities would be reported in the cash flow statement.

Note: At fair value through profit or loss (FVPL) and at fair value through other comprehensive income (FVOCI) are IFRS terminology that is not used in Part II of the *CPA Canada Handbook— Accounting* (ASPE). For the purpose of this question, assume that the FVPL item is an equity instrument acquired for trading purposes and the FVOCI item is an equity instrument that was not acquired for trading purposes.

 PA-11. Cash flows from operating activities—direct method
(**L.O.** A-3, **L.O.** A-5) (Medium – 10 minutes)

Jill K. Ltd.'s policy is to report all cash flows arising from interest and dividends in the operating section. Jill's activities for the year ended December 31, 2018, included the following:

■ Income tax expense for the year was $30,000.
■ Sales for the year were $650,000.
■ Accounts payable decreased $10,000 in 2018.
■ Selling and administration expenses for the year totalled $200,000.
■ Accounts receivable increased $20,000 in 2018.
■ Jill's cost of goods sold in 2018 was $325,000.
■ Jill's inventory decreased $15,000 during the year.
■ Interest expense for the period was $12,000. The interest payable account increased $1,000.
■ Dividends were not declared during the year; however, the dividends payable account decreased $10,000.
■ Sold an at fair value through other comprehensive income investment for $8,000. The cost of the investment and its book value immediately prior to sale was $9,000.
■ Depreciation expense for the year was $13,000.

Required:

a. Prepare the cash flows from operating activities section of the statement of cash flows using the direct method.
b. Identify how the activities listed above that are not operating activities would be reported in the statement of cash flows.

A·S·P·E **PA-12.** Cash flows from operating activities—direct method
(**L.O.** A-3, **L.O.** A-5) (Medium – 10 minutes)

Refer to the information presented in PA-11. Assume that Jill K. Ltd. is a private corporation that elects to report its financial results in accordance with ASPE.

Required:

a. Prepare the cash flows from operating activities section of the cash flow statement using the direct method.

b. Identify how the activities listed above that are not operating activities would be reported in the cash flow statement.

Note: At fair value through other comprehensive income (FVOCI) is IFRS terminology that is not used in Part II of the *CPA Canada Handbook*—Accounting (ASPE). For the purpose of this question, assume that the FVOCI item is an equity instrument that was not acquired for trading purposes.

 PA-13.   Identifying and determining cash flows from operating activities—indirect method   **A·S·P·E**
(**L.O.** A-3, **L.O.** A-5) (Medium – 10 minutes)

Meagan's Psychologist Practice Ltd. is a private corporation that elects to report its financial results in accordance with ASPE. Meagan's activities for the year ended December 31, 2018, included the following:

- Meagan's paid $20,000 in income taxes on its 2018 income before income taxes of $110,000.
- Retained earnings increased $52,000 during the year.
- Accounts receivable decreased $15,000 in 2018.
- Accounts payable increased $16,000 in 2018.
- Prepaid expenses decreased $2,000 in 2018.
- Depreciation expense for the year was $10,000.
- Purchased an investment for trading purposes for $5,000 that is not designated as a cash equivalent.
- Repaid $100,000 in bank indebtedness plus $5,000 in interest.
- Bond interest expense for the period was $14,000. The bonds were previously issued at a discount; $2,000 of the discount was amortized during the year.

Required:

a. Prepare the cash flows from operating activities section of the cash flow statement using the indirect method.

b. Identify how the activities listed above that are not operating activities would be reported in the cash flow statement.

 PA-14.   Identifying and determining cash flows from operating activities—indirect method   **A·S·P·E**
(**L.O.** A-3, **L.O.** A-5) (Medium – 10 minutes)

Gail's Restaurant Ltd. is a private corporation that elects to report its financial results in accordance with ASPE. Gail's activities for the year ended December 31, 2018, included the following:

- Net income after taxes for 2018 totalled $75,000.
- Declared and issued a two-for-one stock split.
- Accounts receivable increased $18,000 in 2018.
- Accounts payable increased $12,000 in 2018.
- Depreciation expense for the year was $15,000.
- Sold an investment acquired for trading purposes for its book value of $9,000.
- Sold an investment not acquired for trading purposes for its book value of $10,000.
- Interest expense for the period was $10,000. The bonds to which this interest expense relates were previously issued at a premium; $2,000 of the premium was amortized during the year. The interest payable account increased $6,000.
- Declared a $20,000 cash dividend payable on January 15, 2019. The dividends payable account increased $15,000 in 2018.
- Gail's recorded a $5,000 impairment loss on a patent it owns.

Required:

a. Prepare the cash flows from operating activities section of the cash flow statement using the indirect method.

b. Identify how the activities listed above that are not operating activities would be reported in the cash flow statement.

PA-15.   Identifying and determining cash flows from investing

L.O. A-3, **L.O.** A-5) (Medium – 10 minutes)

Anne Gapper Crafts Inc.'s policy is to report all cash inflows from interest and dividends in the investing section and cash outflows arising from interest and dividends in the financing section. Anne Gapper Crafts' activities for the year ended December 31, 2021, included the following:

- Purchased an investment for $11,000. The investment, which met the criteria of a cash equivalent, was held for the purpose of meeting short-term cash commitments.
- Purchased an at fair value through other comprehensive income investment for $10,000.
- Paid $85,000 cash for $90,000 in bonds.
- Repaid a $20,000 investment loan plus $1,000 in interest to the bank.
- Sold equipment for $20,000 that originally cost $40,000. The net book value of this item at time of sale was $30,000.
- Received $10,000 in interest and $5,000 in dividends on sundry investments.
- Acquired land and buildings valued at $200,000 by paying $110,000 cash and issuing a $90,000 note payable for the balance.

Required:

a. Prepare the cash flows from investing activities section of the statement of cash flows.
b. Identify how the activities listed above that are not investing activities would be reported in the statement of cash flows assuming that the statement is prepared using the indirect method.

PA-16.   Identifying and determining cash flows from investing

L.O. A-3) (Medium – 10 minutes)

Recon Cile Ltd.'s policy is to report all cash flows arising from interest and dividends in the operating section. Recon Cile's activities for the year ended December 31, 2018, included the following:

- Sold an at fair value through profit or loss investment for $11,000. The book value of this investment, which was held for trading purposes, was $10,000.
- Purchased an at fair value through other comprehensive income investment for $16,000.
- Borrowed $50,000 from the bank for investment purposes.
- Sold equipment for $20,000 that originally cost $30,000. The net book value of this item at time of sale was $25,000.
- Purchased inventory costing $45,000 for cash.
- Received $10,000 in interest and $5,000 in dividends on sundry investments.
- Leased a right-of-use forklift valued at $24,000.
- Acquired land and buildings valued at $300,000 by issuing ordinary shares.
- Bought $100,000 in bonds at a discount, paying $95,000 cash.

Required:

a. Prepare the cash flows from investing activities section of the statement of cash flows.
b. Identify how the activities listed above that are not investing activities would be reported in the statement of cash flows assuming that the statement is prepared using the indirect method.

PA-17.   Identifying and determining cash flows from investing

L.O. A-3, **L.O.** A-5) (Medium – 10 minutes)

Jamie Bleay Law Ltd.'s policy is to report all cash inflows from interest and dividends in the investing section and cash outflows arising from interest and dividends in the financing section. Jamie Bleay Law's activities for the year ended December 31, 2021, included the following:

- Sold an at fair value through profit or loss investment for $11,000. The book value of this investment, which was not held for trading purposes, was $11,000.
- Sold an at fair value through other comprehensive income investment for $12,000. The cost of the investment was $10,000. Its book value immediately prior to sale was $13,000.

- Borrowed $40,000 from the bank for investment purposes.
- Sold equipment for $30,000 that originally cost $50,000. The net book value of this item at time of sale was $20,000.
- Received $8,000 in interest and $9,000 in dividends on sundry investments.
- Paid $2,000 interest on the investment loan.
- Acquired land and buildings valued at $500,000 by paying $300,000 cash and issuing ordinary shares for the balance.
- Bought $100,000 in bonds at a premium, paying $105,000 cash.

Required:

a. Prepare the cash flows from investing activities section of the statement of cash flows.
b. Identify how the activities listed above that are not investing activities would be reported in the statement of cash flows assuming that the statement is prepared using the indirect method.

PA-18.   Identifying and determining cash flows from financing

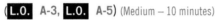 (**L.O.** A-3, **L.O.** A-5) (Medium – 10 minutes)

Angela's Angels Corp.'s policy is to report all cash inflows from interest and dividends in the investing section and cash outflows arising from interest and dividends in the financing section. Angela's activities for the year ended December 31, 2021, included the following:

- Declared and issued a stock dividend valued at $50,000.
- Issued $500,000 in ordinary shares.
- Accounts payable decreased $28,000 during the year.
- Paid $985,000 to repurchase bonds. The book value of the bonds was $1,000,000.
- Made a $10,000 principal payment on a bank loan.
- Interest expense for the period was $18,000. The interest payable account increased $2,000.
- Declared a $10,000 cash dividend payable on January 15, 2022.
- Leased a right-of-use automobile valued at $40,000.

Required:

a. Prepare the cash flows from financing activities section of the statement of cash flows.
b. Identify how the activities listed above that are not financing activities would be reported in the statement of cash flows assuming that the statement is prepared using the indirect method.

 ### PA-19.   Identifying and determining cash flows from financing

(**L.O.** A-3) (Medium – 10 minutes)

Boboto Inc.'s policy is to report all cash flows arising from interest and dividends in the operating section. Boboto's activities for the year ended December 31, 2018, included the following:

- Declared and issued a stock dividend valued at $100,000.
- Paid $40,000 to repurchase ordinary shares and cancelled them. The book value was $30,000.
- Accounts payable increased $32,000 during the year.
- Issued $1,000,000 in bonds. The cash proceeds were $985,000.
- Interest expense for the period was $15,000. The interest payable account decreased $2,000.
- Made a $20,000 principal payment on a bank loan.
- Declared a $20,000 cash dividend payable on January 15, 2019.

Required:

a. Prepare the cash flows from financing activities section of the statement of cash flows.
b. Identify how the activities listed above that are not financing activities would be reported in the statement of cash flows assuming that the statement is prepared using the indirect method.

PA-20.   Identifying and determining cash flows from financing

L.O. A-3, **L.O.** A-5) (Medium – 10 minutes)

Jane's Bookkeeping Services Inc.'s policy is to report all cash inflows from interest and dividends in the investing section and cash outflows arising from interest and dividends in the financing section. Jane's activities for the year ended December 31, 2021, included the following:

- Declared and issued a two-for-one stock split.
- Converted $300,000 of preferred shares into ordinary shares.
- Accounts payable increased $5,000 during the year.
- Paid $505,000 to repurchase bonds. The book value of the bonds was $500,000.
- Interest expense for the period was $10,000. The interest payable account decreased $2,000.
- Paid a $20,000 cash dividend declared in 2020.
- Distributed a stock dividend valued at $25,000.
- Borrowed $40,000 from the bank. $30,000 of the proceeds were used to pay off a lease liability.

Required:

a. Prepare the cash flows from financing activities section of the statement of cash flows.
b. Identify how the activities listed above that are not financing activities would be reported in the statement of cash flows assuming that the statement is prepared using the indirect method.

PA-21.   Statement of cash flows—indirect method—classification of transactions

L.O. A-3) (Difficult – 30 minutes)

Select transactions of Mark Fisher Taxidermy Inc. (MFTI) are listed below. MFTI is a publicly accountable company that uses the indirect method to determine cash flows from operating activities.

1. MFTI purchased a $15,000 bond at a discount, paying $14,500 cash. Management classified the investment as a financial asset at amortized cost.
2. MFTI's comprehensive income for the year totalled $150,000 consisting of $200,000 net income and other comprehensive income of $(50,000).
3. MFTI declared and distributed a stock dividend valued at $20,000.
4. MFTI's retained earnings increased $150,000. The dividends payable account decreased $40,000.
5. MFTI made a payment of $20,000 on a lease liability including interest of $6,000.
6. MFTI exchanged equipment valued at $100,000 for a patent and $40,000 cash.
7. MFTI's income tax expense totalled $10,000. Its income tax payable account decreased $5,000, while its deferred income tax liability account increased $8,000.
8. At year-end, MFTI wrote off $40,000 in bad debts.
9. MFTI amortized $10,000 of the premium on bonds payable.
10. MFTI sold a maturing Treasury bill held to meet short-term cash commitments for $100,000. The book value of the investment equalled the market value.

Required:

Discuss how the activities listed above would be reported in the statement of cash flows. For items with multiple reporting options, identify all available options. For items not reported on the statement of cash flows, indicate the disclosure requirements, if any.

PA-22.   Statement of cash flows—indirect method—classification of transactions

L.O. A-3) (Medium – 30 minutes)

Select transactions of Jack Lin Accounting Inc. (JLAI) are listed below. JLAI is a publicly accountable company that uses the indirect method to determine cash flows from operating activities.

1. JLAI purchased a $100,000, 60-day Treasury bill at fair value through profit or loss investment. The investment was held for trading purposes.
2. JLAI amortized $30,000 of the discount on bonds payable.
3. At year-end, JLAI increased its allowance for bad debts by $50,000.
4. JLAI's income tax expense totalled $40,000. Its income tax payable account increased $7,000, while its deferred income tax liability account decreased $10,000.

5. JLAI leased right-of-use equipment valued at $100,000.
6. JLAI declared and distributed a stock dividend valued at $30,000.
7. JLAI declared a cash dividend of $20,000. The dividends payable account increased $15,000.
8. JLAI's comprehensive income for the year totalled $200,000 consisting of $150,000 net income and $50,000 other comprehensive income.
9. JLAI sold a financial asset at amortized cost investment for $12,000. The investment's amortized cost was $10,000.

Required:

Discuss how the activities listed above would be reported in the statement of cash flows. For items with multiple reporting options, identify all available options. For items not reported on the statement of cash flows, indicate the disclosure requirements, if any.

 PA-23. Analysis of changes in account balances—effects of specific transactions
(**L.O.** A-3, **L.O.** A-4) (Difficult – 30 minutes)

Information pertaining to select activities of Rosamelia Corp. during 2021 is set out below:

1. On January 1, 2021, Rosamelia leased right-of-use equipment. The lease calls for five annual payments of $20,000 due at the beginning of the year. Rosamelia must return the equipment to the lessor at the end of the lease. The payment due on January 1, 2021, was made as agreed. The implicit rate in the lease is 4%; the present value of the lease payments is $92,598.
2. The opening balance in the computer account was $70,000; the closing balance was $80,000. The corresponding balances in the accumulated depreciation accounts were $42,000 and $53,000. During the year, Rosamelia scrapped a computer originally costing $10,000 having a remaining net book value of $2,000 and purchased a replacement machine for cash.
3. The opening balance in the land account was $250,000; the closing balance was $300,000. During the year, land costing $40,000 was given to a creditor in full settlement of a $50,000 loan. The fair value of the land at the time of the exchange was $50,000. The company also purchased a separate parcel of land for cash during the year.

Required:

a. Prepare the underlying journal entries to record the transactions and record events stemming from the transactions (e.g., the accrual of interest at year-end).
b. For each entry, identify the cash flow effects, if any, under both the direct and indirect methods of presentation and classify the cash flow according to its nature.
c. Why does the IASB require that companies classify cash flows as arising from operations, investing, or financing activities?

PA-24. Analysis of changes in account balances—effects of specific transactions
(**L.O.** A-3, **L.O.** A-4) (Medium – 15 minutes)

Information pertaining to select activities of Extravaganza Inc. during 2019 is set out below:

1. Extravaganza converted $2,000,000 in bonds payable into 10,000 ordinary shares. At time of conversion, the book value of the bonds was $1,950,000; the contributed surplus–conversion option was $75,000; and the interest paid was $8,000. The interest had not previously been accrued.
2. During the year, Extravaganza sold production equipment that originally cost $20,000 for $8,000. The net book value at time of sale was $5,000.
3. The opening balance in the land account was $200,000; the closing balance $225,000. During the year, land costing $60,000 was given to a creditor in full settlement of a $70,000 loan. The fair value of the land at the time of the exchange was $70,000. The company also purchased a separate parcel of land for cash during the year.

Required:

a. Prepare the underlying journal entries to record the transactions.
b. For each entry, identify the cash flow effects, if any, under both the direct and indirect methods of presentation and classify the cash flow according to its nature.

🌐 **PA-25.** Contrast the direct and indirect methods of preparing the statement of cash flows

L.O. **A-4**) (Easy – 5 minutes)

a. What are the similarities and differences between the direct and indirect methods of preparing the statement of cash flows?
b. In practice, do more companies use the direct or indirect method of preparation?
c. Does the IASB encourage the use of the direct or indirect method of presenting the statement of cash flows?

PA-26. Presentation and disclosure of cash flows **L.O.** **A-5**) (Easy – 5 minutes)

Summarize the principal presentation, reporting, and disclosure requirements for the statement of cash flows.

PA-27. Preparing a statement of cash flows **L.O.** **A-5**) (Easy – 10 minutes)

a. Briefly discuss how unrealized gains and losses arising from at fair value through profit or loss investments that are held for trading are reported on the statement of cash flows.
b. Briefly discuss how cash flows arising from income taxes are reported on the statement of cash flows.
c. Briefly discuss how stock splits and stock dividends are reported on the statement of cash flows.
d. Briefly discuss how cash flows arising from the purchase and sale of treasury shares are reported on the statement of cash flows.

🌐 **PA-28.** Preparing a statement of cash flows **L.O.** **A-5**) (Medium – 15 minutes)

a. Briefly discuss how the amortization of discounts and premiums on financial instruments are classified in an IFRS-based statement of cash flows.
b. Briefly discuss how other comprehensive income is reported on the statement of cash flows.
c. Briefly discuss how cash flows arising from investments in associates are reported on the statement of cash flows.

A·S·P·E

d. Briefly discuss how the amortization of discounts and premiums on financial instruments are classified in an ASPE-based cash flow statement.

🌐 **PA-29.** Preparing a statement of cash flows **L.O.** **A-4**, **L.O.** **A-5**) (Easy – 10 minutes)

a. List the three primary sources of information required to prepare a statement of cash flows.
b. A company may report its accounts receivable at the gross amount less an allowance for bad debts. Contrast the direct and indirect methods of adjusting for accounts receivable reported at the gross amount.
c. Briefly discuss the alternatives for reporting discontinued operations in the statement of cash flows.

🌐 **PA-30.** Cash flows from operating activities—indirect method

L.O. **A-3**, **L.O.** **A-5**) (Medium – 10 minutes)

Coastal Cares Inc.'s (CCI) policy is to report all cash flows arising from interest and dividends in the operating section. The company's activities for the year ended December 31, 2021, included the following:

■ Comprehensive income totalled $350,000, including $50,000 in other comprehensive income.
■ Paid a cash dividend of $50,000 that was declared in 2020.
■ Interest expense for the year was $30,000; the opening and closing balances in the interest payable account were $25,000 and $10,000, respectively.
■ Accounts receivable increased $24,000 and accounts payable decreased $18,000 during the year.
■ CCI paid $47,000 cash for equipment.
■ CCI sold a financial asset at amortized cost investments for $18,000. The book value of the investment was $20,000.
■ Depreciation expense for the year totalled $37,000.
■ CCI suffered an impairment loss on patents of $12,000.
■ Declared and issued a two-for-one stock split. There were 10,000 ordinary shares outstanding before the split with a collective market value of $2,500,000.

Required:

a. Prepare the cash flows from operating activities section of the statement of cash flows using the indirect method.

b. Identify how the activities detailed above that are not operating activities would be reported in the statement of cash flows.

 PA-31. Cash flows from operating activities—indirect method

(**L.O.** A-5) (Medium – 5 minutes)

Refer to the information presented in PA-30.

Required:

Prepare the cash flows from operating activities section of the statement of cash flows using the indirect method, assuming that Coastal Cares Inc.'s policy is to report interest and dividends received as an investing activity and interest and dividends paid as a financing activity.

PA-32. Cash flows from operating activities—indirect method

(**L.O.** A-3, **L.O.** A-5) (Medium – 15 minutes)

Liz Hicks Accounting Ltd.'s (LHA) policy is to report all cash flows arising from interest and dividends in the operating section. LHA owns a 30% interest in an associated company, LH Bookkeeping Inc. (LHB), and accounts for this investment using the equity method. LHA's activities for the year ended December 31, 2019, included the following:

■ Net income totalled $625,000, including $60,000 in investment income arising from its investment in LHB.

■ Received $20,000 in dividends from LHB that were declared in 2018.

■ Declared a cash dividend of $40,000 that was payable on January 5, 2020.

■ Interest expense for the year was $28,000; the opening and closing balances in the interest payable account were $17,000 and $21,000, respectively.

■ Total income tax expense for the year was $65,000; the current taxes payable account increased $3,000 and the deferred taxes liability increased $5,000.

■ Accounts receivable decreased $16,000 and accounts payable decreased $14,000 during the year.

■ LHA sold equipment for $15,000 cash that had a net book value of $14,000.

■ Depreciation expense for the year totalled $62,000.

■ LHA leased right-of-use equipment valued at $39,000. The company made one payment of $4,500 during the year; $2,900 was allocated to interest expense with the remaining $1,600 reducing the lease liability.

Required:

a. Prepare the cash flows from operating activities section of the statement of cash flows for LHA using the indirect method.

b. Identify how the activities detailed above that are not operating activities would be reported in the statement of cash flows.

PA-33. Cash flows from operating activities—indirect method

(**L.O.** A-3, **L.O.** A-5) (Medium – 10 minutes)

Valley Hospitality Ltd.'s (VHL) policy is to report all cash flows arising from interest and dividends as operating activities. The company's activities for the year ended December 31, 2021, included the following:

■ VHL reported income before income taxes of $400,000. Current income tax expense was $40,000; deferred income tax expense was $10,000.

■ Retained earnings increased $340,000 for the year; the dividends payable account increased $5,000.

■ Current income taxes payable decreased $4,000; deferred income taxes payable increased $6,000.

■ Interest expense for the year was $20,000; the interest payable account increased $12,000.

- Accounts receivable decreased $18,000 and accounts payable increased $40,000 during the year.
- Inventory increased $14,000.
- VHL sold equipment with a net book value of $40,000 for $42,000 cash.
- VHL sold at fair value through other comprehensive income investments for $12,000. The investment cost was $15,000. The book value of the investment immediately preceding the sale was $11,000.
- Depreciation expense for the year totalled $22,000.
- VHL recorded a goodwill impairment loss of $15,000.
- Leased right-of-use equipment valued at $200,000 by way of a $20,000 cash down payment and a $180,000 lease liability.

Required:

a. Prepare the cash flows from operating activities section of the statement of cash flows using the indirect method.
b. Identify how the activities detailed above that are not operating activities would be reported in the statement of cash flows.

PA-34. Cash flows from operating activities—indirect method

(**L.O.** **A-5**) (Medium – 5 minutes)

Refer to the information presented in PA-33.

Required:

Prepare the cash flows from operating activities section of the statement of cash flows using the indirect method, assuming that Valley Hospitality Ltd.'s policy is to report interest and dividends received as an investing activity and interest and dividends paid as a financing activity.

 PA-35. Cash flows from operating activities—indirect method

(**L.O.** **A-5**) (Medium – 5 minutes)

Refer to the information presented in PA-33.

Required:

Prepare the cash flows from operating activities section of the cash flow statement using the indirect method, assuming that Valley Hospitality Ltd. is a private enterprise that elects to report its financial results in accordance with ASPE.

A·S·P·E *Note:* Under ASPE, deferred income taxes are referred to as future income taxes. Also, at fair value through other comprehensive income (FVOCI) is IFRS terminology that is not used in Part II of the *CPA Canada Handbook*—Accounting. For the purposes of this question, assume that the FVOCI is an equity instrument that was not acquired for trading purposes.

 PA-36. Statement of cash flows—indirect method—comprehensive

(**L.O.** **A-3**, **L.O.** **A-5**) (Difficult – 60 minutes)

Brigitte's Bathrooms Ltd.'s balance sheet for the year ended December 31, 2021, follows:

Brigitte's Bathrooms Ltd. Comparative Balance Sheet As at Year Ended December 31		
	2021	2020
Assets		
Cash	$ 17,000	$ 43,000
Accounts receivable	104,000	90,000

(Continued)

Brigitte's Bathrooms Ltd. Comparative Balance Sheet As at Year Ended December 31		
	2021	**2020**
Inventory	80,000	65,000
Prepaid expenses	48,000	45,000
Current assets	249,000	243,000
Land	551,000	310,000
Buildings	860,000	810,000
Accumulated depreciation	(250,000)	(220,000)
Long-term investment (equity)	84,000	90,000
Total assets	$1,494,000	$1,233,000
Liabilities and shareholders' equity		
Accounts payable	$ 50,000	$ 60,000
Accrued interest payable	2,000	5,000
Notes payable	145,000	132,000
Current liabilities	197,000	197,000
Long-term bank loan	600,000	400,000
Deferred income taxes payable	20,000	10,000
Total liabilities	817,000	607,000
Preferred shares	0	100,000
Ordinary shares	285,000	210,000
Retained earnings	392,000	316,000
Total equity	677,000	626,000
Total liabilities and shareholders' equity	$1,494,000	$1,233,000

Additional information:

- During the year, Brigitte declared and paid cash dividends of $50,000. They also declared and distributed stock dividends valued at $20,000.
- Brigitte bought and sold land during the year. The land that was sold for $200,000 originally cost $250,000.
- Brigitte's long-term investment consists of holding ordinary shares in one company (GFF Services Inc.). For most of the year, Brigitte owned 50,000 of the 200,000 ordinary shares outstanding. GFF's net income for the year (which ended December 15) was $40,000. GFF's income from December 16 to December 31 was not material. The company paid dividends of $100,000 on December 15. Brigitte bought additional shares in GFF on December 31.
- A gain of $25,000 was realized on the sale of a building that cost $200,000. Accumulated depreciation at time of sale was $150,000.
- Brigitte borrowed money from a finance company, which accounted for the increase in notes payable.
- The company's expenses for the year included $40,000 for income tax and $30,000 for interest.
- Brigitte's policy is to report investment income and interest paid in the cash flows from operating activities section, while dividends paid are classified as a cash outflow from financing activities.

Required:

a. Prepare a statement of cash flows for Brigitte's Bathrooms Ltd. for 2021 using the indirect method.

b. Identify what supplemental disclosure, if any, is required.

🌐 **PA-37.**　Prepare statement of cash flows from transactions

(L.O. A-3, L.O. A-5) (Difficult – 30 minutes)

Golf Is Great Corp.'s condensed balance sheet for the year ended December 31, 2017, follows:

Golf Is Great Corp. Balance Sheet As at December 31, 2017			
Cash	$ 30,000	Accounts payable	$ 20,000
Inventory	50,000	Other current liabilities	60,000
Other current assets	60,000	Bank loans	50,000
Investments—at fair value through other comprehensive income	40,000	Bonds payable	100,000
Plant and equipment (net)	100,000	Share capital	10,000
Land	80,000	Retained earnings	120,000
	$360,000		$360,000

Golf Is Great's 2018 transactions are as follows:

1. Net income for the year was $27,000 after recording $20,000 in depreciation expense on the plant and equipment.
2. Received cash proceeds of $20,000 from the issuance of preferred shares.
3. Purchased $10,000 inventory on account.
4. Received $19,000 cash from the sale of at fair value through other comprehensive income investments. The investment originally cost $22,000. Its book value immediately preceding the sale was $22,000.
5. Issued $100,000 in bonds to acquire land having a fair value of $100,000.
6. Declared and paid dividends totalling $25,000. Golf Is Great has a policy of including dividends paid in the financing section.
7. Made a $10,000 principal payment on the bank loan.

Required:

a. Prepare a statement of cash flows for 2018 using the indirect method.
b. Discuss how the transaction(s) above that are not reported on the statement of cash flows are reported in the financial statements.
c. Prepare a balance sheet as at December 31, 2018. Assume that other current assets and other current liabilities remain unchanged.
d. Golf's policy is to report dividends paid as a cash outflow from financing activity. What are its alternatives in this respect? How would the statement of cash flows that you prepared in (a) differ if Golf had adopted the alternative presentation method?

🌐 **PA-38.**　Prepare statement of cash flows from transactions

(L.O. A-3, L.O. A-5) (Difficult – 45 minutes)

Squash Forever Corp.'s first year of operations was 2018. Its transactions for the year are as follows:

1. Sold ordinary shares for $50,000 cash and preferred shares for $20,000 cash.
2. Paid $20,000 to acquire at fair value through other comprehensive income securities.
3. Net income for the year was $29,000 after recording $10,000 in depreciation expense on the plant and equipment.
4. Purchased $200,000 inventory on account.
5. Recorded $300,000 in sales on account; cost of goods sold was $140,000.
6. Received $190,000 from customers previously sold to on account.
7. Paid $40,000 cash to a supplier in partial settlement of the inventory purchased in transaction #4.
8. Paid $20,000 cash to redeem ordinary shares redeemed at book value.
9. Received $23,000 cash from the sale of at fair value through other comprehensive income investments purchased in transaction #2.

10. Leased right-of-use equipment valued at $80,000.
11. Declared and paid dividends totalling $20,000. Squash has a policy of reporting dividends as a cash outflow from financing activities.
12. Made a $15,000 payment on the lease liability including $4,000 in interest. Squash has a policy of reporting interest paid as a cash outflow from operating activities.
13. Paid $100,000 cash for various administrative expenses.
14. Paid $20,000 cash in income taxes; cash paid equals income tax expense.

Required:

a. Prepare a statement of cash flows for 2018 using the indirect method.
b. Prepare an income statement for the year ended December 31, 2018.
c. Prepare a balance sheet as at December 31, 2018.
d. Discuss how the transaction(s) above that are not reported on the statement of cash flows are reported in the financial statements.
e. Squash's policy is to report interest paid as a cash outflow from operating activities and dividends paid as a cash outflow from financing activity. What are its alternatives in this respect? How would the statement of cash flows that you prepared in (a) differ if Squash had adopted a policy of reporting the receipt and payment of interest and dividends as operating activities?

 PA-39. Statement of cash flows—operating activities—direct method

(**L.O.** A-3, **L.O.** A-5) (Medium – 15 minutes)

Quitzau's Supplies Inc.'s income statement for the year ended December 31, 2021, follows:

Quitzau's Supplies Inc. Income Statement Year Ended December 31, 2021		
Sales		$1,000,000
Cost of goods sold		
Beginning inventory	$500,000	
Purchases	400,000	
Cost of goods available for sale	900,000	
Ending inventory	300,000	
Cost of goods sold		600,000
Gross profit		400,000
Operating expenses		200,000
Interest expense		10,000
Amortization and depreciation expense		30,000
Income before income taxes		160,000
Income tax expense		40,000
Net income		$ 120,000

Additional information:

- Accounts receivable decreased $20,000 during the year.
- Accounts payable increased $15,000 during the year.
- Prepaid expenses increased $5,000 during the year.
- Income taxes payable decreased $3,000 during the year.
- Accrued interest payable increased $2,000 during the year.
- Quitzau has adopted a policy of reporting the cash flows arising from the receipt and payment of dividends and interest as an operating activity.

Required:

Prepare the operating section of Quitzau's statement of cash flows for the year ended December 31, 2021, using the direct method.

🌐 **PA-40.**   Statement of cash flows—indirect method

(**L.O.** A-3, **L.O.** A-5) (Difficult – 40 minutes)

Financial information for Solnickova Inc. follows:

Solnickova Inc. Balance Sheets As at December 31		
	2021	**2020**
Assets		
Cash	$ 150,000	$ 500,000
Accounts receivable	1,400,000	1,500,000
Inventory	600,000	400,000
Investments—at fair value through profit or loss	100,000	
Investments—financial asset at amortized cost	200,000	—
Property, plant, and equipment	3,250,000	3,250,000
Accumulated depreciation	(1,950,000)	(1,700,000)
Total	$ 3,750,000	$ 3,950,000
Liabilities and shareholders' equity		
Accounts payable	$ 320,000	$ 100,000
Bank loans	1,967,200	2,550,000
Bonds payable	382,800	380,000
Preferred shares	—	10,000
Ordinary shares	600,000	500,000
Retained earnings	480,000	410,000
Total	$ 3,750,000	$ 3,950,000

Additional information:

- Preferred shares were converted to common shares during the year at their book value.
- The face value of the bonds is $400,000; they pay a coupon rate of 5% per annum. The effective rate of interest is 6% per annum.
- Net income was $80,000.
- There was an ordinary stock dividend valued at $4,000 and cash dividends were also paid.
- Interest expense for the year was $125,000. Income tax expense was $20,000.
- Solnickova arranged for a $250,000 bank loan to finance the purchase of the held-to-maturity investments.
- Solnickova has adopted a policy of reporting cash flows arising from the payment of interest and dividends as operating and financing activities, respectively.
- The at fair value through profit or loss investments are held for trading purposes.

Required:

a. Prepare a statement of cash flows for the year ended December 31, 2021, using the indirect method.
b. Discuss how the transaction(s) above that are not reported on the statement of cash flows are reported in the financial statements.
c. Independent of part (a), assume that Solnickova held the $100,000 investment to meet short-term cash commitments. Summarize the impact of this change on the company's statement of cash flows for the year ended December 31, 2021.

PA-41.   Statement of cash flows—operating activities—direct method

(L.O. A-4, L.O. A-5) (Medium – 20 minutes)

Refer to the information presented in PA-40 and the supplemental information below:

Sales	$1,600,000
Cost of goods sold	600,000
Sales and administrative expenses	525,000

Required:

a. Prepare the cash flows from operating activities section of the statement of cash flows using the direct method.
b. Compare and contrast the cash flows from operating activities prepared in this question using the direct method with that prepared in PA-40 part (a) using the indirect method. Which statement do you feel provides investors and other users of the financial statements with more useful information? Why?

 PA-42.   Statement of cash flows—indirect method

(L.O. A-3, L.O. A-5) (Difficult – 40 minutes)

Financial information for Robinson Inc. follows:

Robinson Inc. Balance Sheets As at December 31		
	2021	**2020**
Assets		
Cash	$ 600,000	$ 400,000
Accounts receivable	1,100,000	1,300,000
Inventory	400,000	600,000
Investments—held to meet short-term cash commitments	200,000	—
Investments—financial asset at amortized cost	100,000	—
Property, plant, and equipment	4,200,000	3,400,000
Accumulated depreciation	(2,000,000)	(1,500,000)
Total	$ 4,600,000	$ 4,200,000
Liabilities and shareholders' equity		
Accounts payable	$ 100,000	$ 150,000
Bank loans	2,700,000	2,400,000
Bonds payable	413,860	416,849
Preferred shares	300,000	—
Ordinary shares	300,000	400,000
Retained earnings	786,140	833,151
Total	$ 4,600,000	$ 4,200,000

Additional information:

- Ordinary shares were redeemed during the year at their book value.
- The face value of the bonds is $400,000; they pay a coupon rate of 7% per annum. The effective rate of interest is 6% per annum.
- Net income was $100,000.
- There was an ordinary stock dividend valued at $20,000 and cash dividends were also paid.
- Interest expense for the year was $100,000. Income tax expense was $50,000.
- Robinson arranged for a $500,000 bank loan to finance the purchase of equipment.

- Robinson sold equipment with a net book value of $150,000 (original cost $200,000) for $180,000 cash.
- Robinson leased right-of-use equipment valued at $250,000.
- Robinson has adopted a policy of reporting cash flows arising from the payment of interest and dividends as operating activities.

Required:

a. Prepare a statement of cash flows for the year ended December 31, 2021, using the indirect method.
b. Discuss how the transaction(s) above that are not reported on the statement of cash flows are reported in the financial statements.

PA-43. Statement of cash flows—operating activities—direct method

(**L.O.** A-5) (Medium – 15 minutes)

Refer to the information presented in PA-42 and the supplemental information below:

Sales	$2,000,000
Cost of goods sold	1,200,000
Sales and administrative expenses	30,000

Required:

Prepare the cash flows from operating activities section of the statement of cash flows using the direct method.

 PA-44. Statement of cash flows—indirect method—comprehensive

(**L.O.** A-3, **L.O.** A-5) (Difficult – 60 minutes)

Zippo's financial statements as at December 31, 2021, appear below:

Zippo Ltd. Comparative Balance Sheet As at December 31		
	2021	**2020**
Cash	$ 160,000	$ 100,000
Investments held to meet short-term cash commitments	12,000	10,000
Accounts receivable	300,000	375,000
Less allowance for bad debts and doubtful accounts	(10,000)	(15,000)
Inventory	575,000	498,000
Property, plant, and equipment	1,984,000	1,396,000
Less accumulated depreciation	(650,400)	(487,000)
Intangibles, net	126,000	135,000
Deferred product development costs	564,000	417,000
	3,060,600	2,429,000
Accounts payable	81,000	84,000
Income taxes payable	12,000	2,000
Bonds payable	659,500	674,000
Ordinary shares	1,150,000	700,000
Retained earnings	1,158,100	969,000
	$3,060,600	$2,429,000

Zippo Ltd. Income Statement For the Year Ended December 31, 2021	
Sales	$2,511,100
Cost of goods sold	1,256,000
Gross profit	1,255,100
Depreciation of property, plant, and equipment	334,400
Interest expense	75,000
Other expenses	256,600
Income before income taxes	589,100
Income taxes	300,000
Net income	$ 289,100

Additional information:

- Property, plant, and equipment costing $570,000 was sold for $422,000.
- 100,000 ordinary shares were issued to acquire $450,000 of property, plant, and equipment.
- $212,000 of deferred development costs were capitalized during the year.
- The company nets many items to "Other Expenses," for example, gains and losses on fixed asset sales and some amortization.
- Bad debt expense for the year was $8,000.
- The deferred product development expenditures were all paid in cash.
- The decrease in the bonds payable account was due to the amortization of the premium.
- Zippo has adopted a policy of classifying cash outflows from interest and dividends as financing activities.

Required:

a. Prepare a statement of cash flows for Zippo Ltd. for 2021 using the indirect method.
b. Identify what supplemental disclosure, if any, is required
c. Based on your analysis of Zippo's cash flow activities during the year, do you think that you should consider investing in the company? Why or why not?

 PA-45.   Statement of cash flows—operating activities—direct method

(**L.O.** A-5) (Medium – 15 minutes)

Based on the information set out in PA-44 above, prepare the cash flows from operating activities section of the statement of cash flows using the direct method.

PA-46.   Statement of cash flows—indirect method—comprehensive

(**L.O.** A-3, **L.O.** A-5) (Difficult – 45 minutes)

Tymen's financial statements as at December 31, 2019, appear below (PPE denotes property, plant, and equipment):

Tymen Ltd. Comparative Balance Sheet As at December 31		
	2019	**2018**
Cash	$ 91,000	$ 85,000
Investments at fair value through profit or loss	11,000	13,000
Accounts receivable (net)	406,000	374,000
Inventory	501,000	522,000

(Continued)

Tymen Ltd.
Comparative Balance Sheet
As at December 31

	2019	2018
Property, plant, and equipment (owned and right-of-use)	1,645,000	1,344,000
Less accumulated depreciation	(412,000)	(389,000)
Patent (net)	140,000	162,000
Investment in associate	465,000	312,000
	$2,847,000	$2,423,000
Accounts payable	$ 74,000	$ 77,000
Income taxes payable	12,000	16,000
Lease liability	93,000	0
Bonds payable	608,000	625,000
Deferred tax liability	396,000	442,000
Ordinary shares	329,000	239,000
Preferred shares	400,000	380,000
Retained earnings	935,000	644,000
	$2,847,000	$2,423,000

Tymen Ltd.
Income Statement
For the Year Ended December 31, 2019

Sales	$3,218,575
Cost of goods sold	1,649,125
Gross profit	1,569,450
Depreciation of PPE	318,700
Patent impairment	40,000
Interest expense—bonds	36,000
Interest expense—lease liability	4,500
Other expenses	735,750
Operating income	434,500
Investment income—associate	288,000
Income before income taxes	722,500
Income taxes	293,000
Net income	$ 429,500

Additional information:

- Tymen has adopted a policy of classifying cash inflows and outflows from interest and dividends as operating activities.
- The investments at fair value through profit or loss were purchased for other than trading purposes.
- Tymen accounts for its investment in an associate using the equity method.
- The company nets many items to "Other Expenses"; for example, gains and losses on fixed asset sales.
- During the year, Tymen leased a right-of-use asset valued at $100,000. The payment made on the lease liability was made after the commencement date.
- 90,000 ordinary shares and 10,000 preferred shares were issued to acquire $110,000 of PPE.

- Tymen successfully defended its right to a patent. Related expenditures totalled $18,000.
- The decrease in the bonds payable account was due to the amortization of the premium.
- Property, plant, and equipment costing $420,000 was sold for $75,000.

Required:

a. Prepare a statement of cash flows for Tymen Ltd. for 2019 using the indirect method.
b. Identify what supplemental disclosure, if any, is required.

PA-47. Statement of cash flows—operating activities—direct method

(**L.O.** A-5) (Medium – 15 minutes)

Based on the information set out in problem PA-46 above, prepare the cash flows from operating activities section of the statement of cash flows using the direct method.

PA-48. Statement of cash flows—indirect method—comprehensive income

(**L.O.** A-3, **L.O.** A-5) (Difficult – 60 minutes)

Luke and Angie Inc.'s financial statements as at December 31, 2021, appear below:

Luke and Angie Inc. Comparative Balance Sheet As at December 31		
	2021	**2020**
Cash	$ 85,000	$ 102,000
Investments—held for meeting short-term cash commitments	26,000	26,000
Investments—at fair value through other comprehensive income	33,000	38,000
Accounts receivable	52,000	59,000
Inventory	45,000	39,000
Prepaid expenses	12,000	10,000
Investments—financial asset at amortized cost	90,000	100,000
Plant assets	850,000	490,000
Accumulated depreciation	(160,000)	(110,000)
Goodwill	42,000	82,000
	$1,075,000	$836,000
Accounts payable	$ 48,000	$ 44,000
Accrued liabilities	27,000	30,000
Cash dividends payable	10,000	18,000
Bonds payable	52,000	54,000
Mortgage payable	100,000	—
Lease liability	90,000	
Deferred income tax liability	9,000	4,000
Preferred shares	150,000	—
Ordinary shares	536,000	400,000
Retained earnings	58,000	286,000
Reserves	(5,000)	—
	$1,075,000	$836,000

Luke and Angie Inc. Statement of Comprehensive Income For the Year Ended December 31, 2021	
Sales	$860,000
Cost of sales	(422,000)
Gross profit	438,000
Interest expense	(10,000)
Depreciation expense	(70,000)
Operating expenses	(180,000)
Other gains and losses	(29,000)
Income before income tax	149,000
Income tax expense	(42,000)
Net income	107,000
Other comprehensive income: Holding loss on at fair value through other comprehensive income securities	(5,000)
Comprehensive income	$102,000

Supplemental financial information for the year ended December 31, 2021:

- Luke and Angie exchanged 1,500 preferred shares for plant assets having a fair value of $150,000.
- Luke and Angie declared and issued 1,000 ordinary shares as a stock dividend valued at $10,000.
- Goodwill was determined to be impaired and was written down $40,000.
- Luke and Angie paid $10,000 cash and signed a lease agreement for $90,000 to acquire an ROU asset valued at $100,000.
- Luke and Angie sold equipment (plant assets) with a net book value of $70,000 for $80,000 cash.
- Luke and Angie did not buy or sell any at fair value through other comprehensive income securities during the year.
- Financial asset at amortized cost securities with a book value of $10,000 were called for redemption during the year; $11,000 cash was received.
- The recorded decrease in the bonds payable account was due to the amortization of the premium.
- The deferred income tax liability represents temporary differences relating to the use of capital cost allowance for income tax reporting and straight-line depreciation for financial statement reporting.
- Luke and Angie elects to record interest and dividends paid as an operating activity.

Required:

a. From the information provided, prepare Luke and Angie's statement of cash flows for the year ended December 31, 2021, using the indirect method.
b. Prepare note disclosure(s) for non-cash transactions.

PA-49.   Statement of cash flows—operating activities—direct method
(**L.O.** A-5) (Medium – 15 minutes)

Based on the information presented in PA-48, prepare the cash flows from operating activities section of the statement of cash flows using the direct method.

PA-50.   Statement of cash flows—indirect and direct methods—comprehensive income
(**L.O.** A-3, **L.O.** A-4, **L.O.** A-5) (Difficult – 75 minutes)

Valli Ltd.'s financial statements as at December 31, 2021, appear below:

Valli Ltd. Comparative Balance Sheet As at December 31		
	2021	**2020**
Cash	$ 69,000	$ 21,000
Investments—at fair value through profit or loss held for trading purposes	25,000	22,000
Investments—at fair value through other comprehensive income	30,000	25,000
Accounts receivable	53,000	39,000
Inventory	50,000	60,000
Prepaid expenses	6,000	9,000
Plant assets	540,000	380,000
Accumulated depreciation	(140,000)	(125,000)
Goodwill	51,000	58,000
	$684,000	$489,000
Accounts payable	$ 41,000	$ 46,000
Accrued liabilities	33,000	24,000
Cash dividends payable	8,000	6,000
Bonds payable	50,000	47,000
Mortgage payable	—	136,000
Deferred income tax liability	5,000	8,000
Preferred shares	201,000	—
Ordinary shares	320,000	200,000
Retained earnings	21,000	22,000
Reserves	5,000	—
	$684,000	$489,000

Valli Ltd. Statement of Comprehensive Income For the Year Ended December 31, 2021	
Sales	$660,000
Cost of sales	(359,000)
Gross profit	301,000
Interest expense, long term	(6,000)
Depreciation expense	(25,000)
Operating expenses	(160,000)
Other gains and losses	(4,000)
Income before income tax	106,000
Income tax expense	(39,000)
Net income	67,000
Other comprehensive income: Holding gain on at fair value through other comprehensive income securities	5,000
Comprehensive income	$ 72,000

Supplemental information:

- During the year, Valli exchanged 5,000 ordinary shares for plant assets having a fair value of $100,000.
- During the year, Valli declared and issued a stock dividend of 1,000 ordinary shares. The transaction was valued at $20,000.
- During the year, goodwill was written down $7,000 to reflect a permanent impairment of the asset.
- The deferred income tax liability represents temporary differences relating to the use of capital cost allowance for income tax reporting and straight-line depreciation for financial statement reporting.
- Valli did not buy or sell any at fair value through profit or loss or at fair value through other comprehensive income securities during the year.
- The recorded increase in the bonds payable account was due to the amortization of the discount.
- Valli elects to record interest paid as an operating activity and dividends paid as a financing activity.
- During the year, Valli sold equipment (plant assets) that originally cost $40,000 for $30,000 cash.

Required:

a. From the information above, prepare Valli's statement of cash flows for the year ended December 31, 2021, using the indirect method.
b. Prepare Valli's cash flows from operating activities for the year ended December 31, 2021, using the direct method.
c. Prepare note disclosure(s) for non-cash transactions.

K. MINI-CASES

You have been asked to prepare a statement of cash flows using the balance sheet provided in Exhibit I, the income statement in Exhibit II, and the extracts from the notes provided in Exhibit III. Assume that the term deposits are cash equivalents. Further assume that CompuCo elects to report both the payment and collection of interest as operating activities.

CASE 1
CompuCo Ltd.

(45 minutes)[10]

Required:

1. Use the indirect method to prepare a statement of cash flows for 2021 on a non-comparative basis in good form from the information provided.
2. Use the direct method to prepare the cash flows from operations section of the statement of cash flows for 2021.
3. What are the objectives of a statement of cash flows prepared in accordance with generally accepted accounting principles?

Exhibit I	Extracts from consolidated balance sheet		
CompuCo Ltd.			
Extracts from Consolidated Balance Sheet			
As at December 31			
($000's)			
		2021	**2020**
Assets			
Current			
Cash and term deposits		$ 3,265	$ 3,739
Accounts receivable		23,744	18,399
Inventories		26,083	21,561
Income taxes recoverable		145	0
Prepaid expenses		1,402	1,613
		54,639	45,312
Investments (note 1)		5,960	6,962
Property, plant, and equipment (note 2)		37,332	45,700
Deferred income taxes		4,875	2,245
Goodwill		0	12,737
Intangible assets (note 3)		4,391	1,911
		$107,197	$114,867
Liabilities			
Current			
Bank indebtedness		$ 6,844	$ 6,280
Accounts payable		3,243	4,712
Current portion of long-term debt		1,800	1,200
		11,887	12,192
Long-term debt (note 4)		14,900	14,500
Total liabilities		26,787	26,692

(*Continued*)

[10] Reprinted from Uniform Final Examination 1999, with permission from Chartered Professional Accountants of Canada, Toronto, Canada. Any changes to the original material are the sole responsibility of the author (and/or publisher) and have not been reviewed or endorsed by the Chartered Professional Accountants of Canada.

Exhibit I	Continued

CompuCo Ltd.
Extracts from Consolidated Balance Sheet
As at December 31
($000's)

	2021	2020
Shareholders' equity		
Share capital (Note 5)	79,257	62,965
Retained earnings	1,153	25,210
Total shareholders' equity	80,410	88,175
	$107,197	$114,867

Exhibit II	Extracts from consolidated income statement

CompuCo Ltd.
Extracts from the Consolidated Income Statement
For the Years Ended December 31
(in $000's)

	2021	2020
Revenue		
Operating	$ 89,821	$ 68,820
Interest	1,310	446
	91,131	69,266
Expenses		
Operating	76,766	62,355
General and administrative	13,039	12,482
Depreciation and amortization	10,220	11,709
Goodwill write-off	12,737	0
Interest	1,289	1,521
Loss on sale of property, plant, and equipment	394	0
	114,445	88,067
Income (loss) before income from associates and income taxes	(23,314)	(18,801)
Income (loss) from associates (Note 1)	(2,518)	0
Income (loss) before income taxes	(25,832)	(18,801)
Recovery of income taxes	2,775	5,161
Net loss	$(23,057)	$(13,640)

Exhibit III	Extracts from notes to financial statements

CompuCo Ltd.
Extracts from Notes to Financial Statements
For the Year Ended December 31
(in $000's)

1. Investments

The company's investments at December 31 are as follows:

	2021	2020
XYZ Inc. (investment in associate)		
Shares	$ 5,962	$ 5,962

(*Continued*)

Exhibit III	Continued

CompuCo Ltd.
Extracts from Notes to Financial Statements
For the Year Ended December 31
(in $000's)

Income (loss) from associates	(2,518)	—
	3,444	$ 5,962
Other investments (financial asset at amortized cost)	2,516	1,000
	$ 5,960	$ 6,962

2. Property, plant, and equipment (PPE)

Additions to PPE for the current year amounted to $2.29 million and proceeds from the disposal of PPE amounted to $250,000.

3. Intangible assets

Qualifying development costs of intangible assets are capitalized.

4. Long-term debt

	2021	2020
Debentures	$12,500	$12,500
Bank term loans, due December 31, 2028; principal repayable $150,000 a month (2020, $100,000 a month)	4,200	3,200
	16,700	15,700
Current maturities	(1,800)	(1,200)
	$14,900	$14,500

Debentures bear interest at 12% per annum and are due in 2024. Bank term loans bear interest at 8% and the bank advanced $2.2 million during the year.

5. Share capital

On May 14, 2021, CompuCo Ltd. issued 3.8 million shares with special warrants. Net proceeds from issuing 3.8 million shares amounted to $14.393 million. Net proceeds from issuing 3.8 million warrants amounted to $899,000. On December 31, 2021, a stock dividend of $1 million was distributed.

Big City Gymnastics (BCG or the Club) is a not-for-profit organization that operates a gymnastics club. BCG was incorporated in May 1983 and has operated the Club at the same facility since that time. BCG was started with a generous donation of equipment after a gymnastics competition that was held in April 1983.

BCG is governed by an elected board of directors of 10 members, all of whom are parents of athletes who train at the Club.

BCG trains both male and female athletes, from preschool to young adult. Its programs are preschool gymnastics, recreational gymnastics, and competitive gymnastics. BCG's athletes have qualified for national and international gymnastics meets, with some even going on to full scholarships at Canadian and American universities. BCG's coaches and programs are recognized by the Canadian gymnastics community as being of high quality.

Like most gymnastics clubs, BCG has paid coaching staff. Salaried staff, paid in total $20,000 a month including all required government remittances, include an office

CASE 2
Big City Gymnastics
(60 minutes)[11]

---

[11] Reprinted from Uniform Final Examination 2005, with permission from Chartered Professional Accountants of Canada, Toronto, Canada. Any changes to the original material are the sole responsibility of the author (and/or publisher) and have not been reviewed or endorsed by the Chartered Professional Accountants of Canada.

manager, a program director who coaches and also oversees the program and staffing, and three head coaches who oversee, respectively, the women's competitive, men's competitive, and recreational/preschool programs.

You are the parent of a gymnast. You were appointed to the board of BCG as treasurer three-and-a-half weeks ago. During your short time as treasurer, you have interviewed the office manager (Exhibit I) to become familiar with the workings of BCG, and gathered some historical financial information (Exhibit II).

Today, July 23, 2021, the president of BCG, Jim Taylor, approached you while you were watching your daughter train at BCG's facility. He informed you that the treasurer is responsible for preparing and presenting a financial report to the BCG board of directors at each monthly board meeting. Jim mentioned that, in the past, the report usually consisted of a quick update on the cash balance in the Club's bank account. At the May 2021 board meeting, the report stated a cash balance of $19,823. At the board meeting on June 30, 2021, the cash balance was $4,324. The board was concerned about the deteriorating cash situation and wondered how it would look at the end of the fiscal year.

At previous board meetings, members often asked for more financial information but the previous treasurer was unable to provide it. Jim let you know that the lack of information caused some frustration among the board members and asks you to recommend reporting improvements to the board.

As you think about Jim's comments, you remember that, as a parent of a BCG athlete, you had your own questions about the financial situation of BCG, the success of the various programs and of the fundraisers, and so on. You tell Jim that your report will be different. You will report to the board the findings from your recent discussions and recommendations for improvement, and you will provide some insights into BCG's current financial situation.

Required:

Prepare the report, paying specific attention to (i) BCG's cash flow and (ii) the sufficiency of the financial reports currently being produced.

Exhibit I	Notes from interview with office manager

The office manager is Joan Epp. She was hired three weeks ago to replace the outgoing office manager, Tom Dickens, who quit after only 11 months on the job. Joan's role as office manager:

- Receive payments from athletes' families for their gymnastics fees. These fees are paid monthly in advance. BCG accepts cash, cheques, and credit card payments. Receipts are issued upon request.
- Tally the cash received and credit card slips on a deposit sheet and enter the amounts monthly into the accounting records. Deposits are made on an occasional basis at the nearby bank branch, once sufficient cash has been accumulated to warrant making a deposit.
- Receive and pay suppliers' invoices. One signature is required for all cheques. Signing officers are the office manager, the treasurer, and the president.

Joan reviewed the records on her first day. She had examined the paid invoices, stored in a filing cabinet, to become familiar with BCG's operations. Joan mentioned that there were several small cheques, most of which were posted as debits to the revenue accounts, that did not have corresponding invoices. Most of those cheques were made out to Tom Dickens. Also, one large cheque for $5,617 had a note that it was to reimburse Tom for the purchase of a trampoline, but no supporting invoice was attached. Joan also noted there were several cheques to suppliers, totalling $820, that are still outstanding.

As far as Joan is aware, there is no formal policy established for approval of spending. Joan can order what she needs for her job. Coaches can order the equipment or other gymnastics materials that they believe are needed for BCG's various programs.

(Continued)

Exhibit I	Continued

BCG has a chocolate fundraiser where athletes sell chocolate bars for $3 apiece. An envelope marked Chocolate Fundraiser was in Joan's desk. It had $3,750 cash in it, with various notes on who had paid for chocolate bars. The drawer is locked when Joan is out of the office. Joan will deposit the money as soon as all the chocolate bars are sold, so that she will know the exact amount raised. The chocolate supplier shipped 1,500 chocolate bars. Joan received an invoice for $3,300, dated July 20, from the chocolate supplier. The terms on the invoice are that any unsold chocolate bars cannot be returned and, if payment is made within 30 days, the supplier's discount is 20%.

Exhibit II	CA's notes on BCG's historical financial information

The fiscal year-end of the Club is August 31.

Revenues are seasonal. The fall and winter recreational sessions are busy. The competitive season starts in September and runs through June. The spring recreational session appears to have one-third less revenue than the other two sessions due to the start of competing outdoor sports in the spring (baseball, football, soccer, etc.). The two summer months provide approximately 10% of BCG's annual revenue because of school summer holidays. Some weekly gymnastics camps are run, but attendance is muted due to athletes being away or taking time off. In addition to the chocolate fundraiser, BCG holds two other fundraisers during the year.

BCG receives a grant of $1,200 per month from the citywide gymnastics organization.

General and administrative costs include building rent and utilities, which combined are approximately $2,000 per month.

The net book value of BCG's equipment was $54,563 as of August 31, 2020.

BCG does not have any bank loans or lines of credit because it has never needed credit.

Exhibit III	BCG financial data produced by the system		
		10 months ended June 30, 2021	12 months ended August 31, 2020
Cash Receipts			
Donations/grants		$ 20,549	$ 22,547
Facility rentals		9,094	12,402
Fundraising activities		68,685	73,158
Fees, recreational and competitive		201,864	209,402
		300,192	317,509
Cash Disbursements			
General and administrative		45,301	45,465
Repairs and maintenance		50,281	50,419
Salaries, benefits, and travel		220,603	217,056
Fundraising activities		6,635	9,219
		322,820	322,159
Net change in cash		(22,628)	(4,650)
Beginning cash		26,952	31,602
Ending cash		$ 4,324	$ 26,952

CASE 3
Community Care Services

(60 minutes)[12]

Community Care Services (CCS) is a not-for-profit organization formed in January 2021 and is located in the rural community of Thomas County. CCS is dedicated to serving the needs of seniors. CCS's informational literature and website contain the following statement:

> Our mission is to provide a secure retirement community in a carefully selected location in the heart of our beloved Thomas County. Our organization provides a warm, attractive setting as the surroundings for a vibrant, healthy living space—one that our residents deserve. Our vision is to serve the community, and it encompasses accommodation and leisure as well as the provision of health care.

Background information on CCS is provided in Exhibit I, and some details of CCS's operations are included in Exhibit II. The executive director, Janet Admer, joined the organization in the last month and was recruited from a nearby city. Janet has extensive experience in managing the construction and operations of a major hotel. It was the board of directors' view that, even though Janet's salary of $120,000 seemed high, her hospitality-industry skills would be a good contribution to the operation of CCS.

It is now November 15, 2021. You have known Janet Admer for many years, and she has approached you for advice. Janet has asked your firm, Yelt and Rerdan, Chartered Professional Accountants, to advise her and the board on the issues facing CCS as it moves from the construction phase to the operating phase. Janet has prepared a cash budget, included in Exhibit III, and she is very pleased that her estimate indicates that a surplus will exist in the first year of full operation. Because the board members would like to make sure that CCS will have sufficient cash to meet its obligations as it starts to operate the residences, Janet wants you to look at her budget. The board had approved obtaining a bank loan to complete the construction phase but is still concerned that there is a risk that CCS will run out of cash by the end of the year.

CCS has already appointed KZY, Chartered Professional Accountants, as the auditor, and KZY will be reporting on the first fiscal year-end of December 31, 2021. Janet has deliberately not assigned the engagement to you and your firm so that the functions of auditor and advisor will be independent.

The board is made up of highly respected individuals in the community; however, the members have very little experience in running an operation such as CCS. Janet would like you to help her determine the kind of information, financial and otherwise, that would be useful to them to evaluate the performance of CCS in meeting its goals.

You are pleased at the prospect of bringing in a client to the firm, and you have discussed the engagement with a partner at Yelt and Rerdan. The partner has agreed to accept the engagement and has asked you to prepare a draft report addressing Janet's requests.

Required:

Prepare the draft report addressing Janet's requests, including a comprehensive analysis of CCS's cash flow situation and an analysis of CCS's information needs.

Exhibit I	Background information

In the last decade, foreign investors who believed that land was a bargain as a result of the weak Canadian dollar have purchased many of the farms in Thomas County. The community was concerned that there were no residential alternatives in the county for older farmers who left their farms as a result of a sale or retirement.

Mr. MacDougall, an advocate for the local farmers and seniors, started with the idea of providing residential options to the families. He was instrumental in setting up CCS and was appointed the chairman of the board. He donated 10 acres of land from his farm for the facility.

(Continued)

[12] Reprinted from Uniform Final Examination 2003, with permission from Chartered Professional Accountants of Canada, Toronto, Canada. Any changes to the original material are the sole responsibility of the author (and/ or publisher) and have not been reviewed or endorsed by the Chartered Professional Accountants of Canada.

Exhibit I	Continued

He also donated $1 million for the construction of the residential units. The conditions of the donations were as follows:

1. The land can never be sold.
2. At least one-third of all residential units must be provided to low-income seniors who must meet an annual income test, and the rent charged cannot generate a surplus on the operational costs of these units. (These units have been designated as Building C.)
3. At least one-third of all residential units must provide full health care services. (These units have been designated as Building A, commonly referred to as the "Nursing Home.")
4. One-half of the sales proceeds from the retirement home sales units must be maintained in a separate account to be used for the maintenance and capital repairs of the complex.

If these terms are not met, the land reverts to Mr. MacDougall, or to a special MacDougall trust if the breach occurs after the death of Mr. MacDougall.

The layout of the complex is as follows:

Construction began in February 2021 and is almost complete. The nursing home and both retirement homes are completed. The recreation facility is scheduled to be completed by December 31. All of the units in the nursing home and the rental retirement home have been assigned to residents. Sales contracts have been signed for all of the units in the other retirement home. These sales are expected to close in January 2022. The complex is expected to be fully operational in early January 2022.

The costs of construction and the budget are as follows:

	Original budget	Estimate to December 2021*
Land Improvements	$ 170,000	$ 168,000
Building A – Nursing Home	300,000	421,000
Building B – Retirement Homes for Sale	250,000	250,000
Building C – Retirement Homes for Rent	275,000	270,000
Building D – Recreation Facility	150,000	100,000
Equipment and Furniture	150,000	150,000
	$1,295,000	$1,359,000

* Total actual cost incurred plus revised estimates to complete

(Continued)

Exhibit I	Continued	
Source of funds		
Mr. MacDougall		$1,000,000
Thomas County Grant		200,000
Bank loan—no interest until January 1, 2022, then payments of $20,000 per month, plus annual interest of 5%.		200,000
		$1,400,000

Exhibit II	Additional information

Building A—Nursing Home

This building has 20 beds and its operations will be funded by the provincial government's Ministry of Community and Social Services (the ministry). The funding formula is $130 per day per bed, and any surplus from operations must be returned to the ministry. To determine the surplus, the ministry will allow direct costs plus a reasonable allocation of overheads. The ministry, which provides some funding, has requested the audit of the annual financial statements as part of the funding requirement.

Building B—Retirement Home, Units for Sale

There are 10 unfurnished units and the residents will have a "life-lease" on the land, which means that the residents will have the right to use the portion of the land on which the building is located but they will not own it, and the right will expire at either the death of the resident or sooner if mutually agreed to. In addition to the purchase price, the residents will also pay $550 per month to cover the occupancy costs, and this amount could be adjusted to meet actual costs if necessary. There are two types of "sales" and there are five units of each type:

Type I—The units are "sold" for fair market value. At the end of the lease (i.e., death or resident moves out), CCS must pay back the full price paid.

Type II—The units are "sold" for 120% of fair market value. At the end of the lease (i.e., death or resident moves out), CCS must pay back the fair market value at the date the resident purchased the unit plus 50% of any increase in value.

For both types, CCS has the right to select the next occupant, and the price to be charged for the unit is to be based on fair market value and must be supported by an independent opinion. The fair market value for all the initial sales was determined to be $100,000. The board is confident that the value of these units will increase. These units are designed to appeal to those who want a "premium" unit and can afford to pay for it.

Building C—Retirement Home, Rental Units

There are 15 unfurnished units. The rent will be approximately $400 per month per unit and includes all utilities, cable, etc. To be eligible for these units, the applicants must prove that the combined annual income available to them is not more than $20,000. CCS will receive an annual operating grant of $200,000 from the ministry.

Building D—Recreation Facility

When it is completed, Building D will hold the administration offices and a recreation facility to be used for social activities. The residents of all buildings can use the common area and recreation facility.

Other

Each of the four buildings has a staff member employed as the "Program Director." Each program director has an annual salary of $60,000. The total administrative costs incurred in 2021 are expected to be limited to $115,000.

Exhibit III	Budgeted cash flows

Budgeted operating cash flows
for the Year Ending December 31, 2022
(in $000's)

Cash inflows	
Government funding—Nursing Home (20 beds × $130 × 365 days)	$ 949
Government funding—Retirement Home rental units	200
Sales proceeds—Retirement Home sales units	1,100
Occupancy fees—Retirement Home sales units (10 units × $550 × 12 months)	66
Rent—Retirement Home rental units (15 units × $400 × 12 months)	72
Interest (same amount as earned in 2021)	29
	2,416
Cash outflows	
Salaries and benefits (including medical staff costs of $260)	850
Medical supplies	55
Furniture and equipment (Nursing Home and Administration)	44
Food costs—Nursing Home	160
Staff training (one-time cost)	34
Repairs and maintenance	23
Communications, office, etc.	15
Utilities and property taxes	23
Insurance	10
	1,214
Excess of cash inflows over cash outflows	$1,202

CASE 4
Enviro Ltd.
(60 minutes)[13]

You are employed by McDowell and Partners, Chartered Professional Accountants (M&P). A new client, Community Finance Corporation (CFC), approached M&P for assistance. Enviro Ltd. (Enviro) has asked CFC for a loan of $10 million in the form of long-term debt to fund capital expenditures and other operating requirements. CFC has already conducted a general assessment of Enviro but now needs an accounting firm to look closely at the financial aspects, including the areas of financial risk. In particular, CFC needs to be assured that it will receive the payments of principal and interest over the term of the loan. M&P has accepted the engagement and is responsible for preparing a report to CFC.

It is now August 2021. Enviro's board of directors have provided both CFC and M&P with recent financial statements (Exhibit I) and extracts from the working papers of Enviro's auditors, Y&Z, for the most recent year-end (Exhibit II). The engagement partner wants you to prepare a memo addressing CFC's concerns.

Required:

Prepare the memo requested by the engagement partner.

[13] Reprinted from Uniform Final Examination 2002, with permission from Chartered Professional Accountants of Canada, Toronto, Canada. Any changes to the original material are the sole responsibility of the author (and/or publisher) and have not been reviewed or endorsed by the Chartered Professional Accountants of Canada.

Exhibit I	Extracts from financial statements

Extracts from the Financial Statements of Enviro Ltd.
Consolidated Balance Sheet
As at June 30
(audited, in $000's)

	2021	2020	2019
Assets			
Current assets			
Cash	$ 15	$ 105	$ 655
Marketable securities	0	870	1,495
Accounts receivable	3,870	3,705	3,580
Inventory			
Metals and scrap	7,775	5,260	4,005
Other	610	585	570
Prepaid expenses	130	120	110
	12,400	10,645	10,415
Land	910	1,160	1,160
Building and equipment	8,985	8,720	8,570
Accumulated depreciation	(2,880)	(2,290)	(1,720)
Waste disposal equipment, net of depreciation	2,060	1,435	1,410
Development cost, net of depreciation	330	240	390
Goodwill	640	700	770
Investment in Klens & Breeth	4,990	3,730	3,160
	$27,435	$24,340	$24,155
Liabilities			
Current liabilities			
Bank demand loan, secured	$ 3,000	$ 2,000	$ 2,200
Accounts payable and accrued liabilities	3,815	1,880	1,185
Other liabilities	790	580	315
	7,605	4,460	3,700
Mortgage payable, 12%, due 2022	2,310	2,490	2,670
Notes payable, 13%, due 2022	4,000	4,000	4,000
Bank term loan, 12%, due 2023	2,500	2,200	2,400
	16,415	13,150	12,770
Shareholders' equity			
Ordinary shares	5,000	5,000	5,000
Preferred shares, 11% cumulative dividend	4,000	4,000	4,000
Retained earnings	2,020	2,190	2,385
	11,020	11,190	11,385
	$27,435	$24,340	$24,155

(*Continued*)

Exhibit I	Continued

Enviro Ltd.
Extracts from the Financial Statements
Consolidated Income Statements
For the Year Ended June 30
(audited, in $000's)

	2021	2020	2019
Revenues	$ 9,660	$10,450	$ 8,795
Expenses			
Cost of goods sold	3,180	3,360	2,265
Wages and benefits	3,420	3,210	2,370
Depreciation	950	790	615
Maintenance and insurance	1,440	1,470	1,305
General and administrative	1,335	1,165	865
Gain on disposal of securities	(360)	(910)	0
Gain on sale of land	(1,105)	0	0
	8,860	9,085	7,420
Income before income from associates	800	1,365	1,375
Income from associate—Klens & Breeth	1,260	570	490
Income before interest and income tax expenses	2,060	1,935	1,865
Interest expense	1,670	1,590	1,005
Income tax expense	120	100	320
Net income	$ 270	$ 245	$ 540

Exhibit II	Extracts from working papers

Extracts from Y&Z's Working Papers
For the Year Ended June 30, 2021

Enviro

1. Enviro is a holding company that was incorporated under federal legislation several years ago as an investment company for a small group of investors. Enviro owns the following:
   - 100% of the voting shares of Waste Disposal Corporation (WDC), which collects and disposes of environmentally hazardous chemicals.
   - 50% of a partnership that specializes in designing advertisements for organizations that promote improvements to the environment. The partnership is called Klens & Breeth (KB). KB in turn owns all the voting shares of two corporations involved in advertising design and development.
   - 100% of the voting shares of Scrap Metal Enterprises Ltd. (SMEL), which deals in the collection and sale of non-precious metals (copper, iron, and others).

2. Enviro's existing bank loans are secured by a first charge on receivables. The mortgage payable is secured by a first mortgage on the land and building. The notes payable are secured by inventory and are due in August 2022. The notes payable cannot be renewed because payment in full has been demanded.

3. Enviro is insured for liability and accidents but not for theft and fire.

4. Enviro paid dividends on preferred shares of $440,000 in each of 2019, 2020, and 2021. In addition, the company paid $100,000 of dividends on common shares in 2019.

(Continued)

Exhibit II   Continued

WDC

1. To meet government requirements, WDC's disposal equipment has to be upgraded by October 1, 2022; otherwise, large segments of the operations will have to be suspended and other safe disposal methods will have to be found—an unlikely prospect. Upgrading is really the only alternative if WDC is to avoid having to cancel contracts and incur significant cancellation penalties. Approximately $7 million is needed as soon as possible.

2. Using its own waste disposal technology, WDC builds some of the equipment that it needs to process certain wastes. During fiscal 2021, the following expenditures were capitalized:

Components and parts	$322,100
Wages and benefits	208,220
Overhead costs	208,000
Interest on borrowings	12,680
	$751,000

The overhead costs are allocated based on roughly 100% of wages and benefits.

KB

1. We do not audit KB but have reviewed the audit working papers and have had discussions with KB's auditors. KB's income for the year ended March 31, 2021, was $2,520,000, and Enviro has appropriately accounted for its share using the equity method of accounting. Enviro is a silent partner. However, Enviro provides major assistance in developing new client contracts for KB. The other partner needs the partnership form of ownership for various purposes. Among the more significant transactions during fiscal 2021 were the following:

   a. KB accounts for its investments on an equity basis; its subsidiaries paid cash dividends in fiscal 2021 of $1,200,000. KB retained these funds to develop new technology.

   b. KB earned $1,875,000 from a federal government contract that has expired this month. Most of the fee was recognized in income in 2021 because the ideas had already been generated for another project and few additional costs were necessary.

   c. The other partner of KB operates an advertising firm for non-environmental promotion. KB paid this firm $895,000 for a variety of services.

SMEL

1. SMEL's scrap metal piles are large, and it is difficult to estimate the quantity of metal in the piles. To satisfy ourselves, we photographed the piles, compared them geometrically to photographs of previous years, and discussed important issues with management. We also conducted extra checks of the perpetual inventory system against arrival and departure weights of trucks. The system was operating satisfactorily, but estimates were necessary for wastage.

2. The scrap metal is recorded at cost because resale prices of scrap vary considerably. If prices are low, SMEL stores the metals until selling prices improve. Management believes there is no need to sell at a loss.

3. The government requires a soil test of SMEL's scrap yard every five years. The most recent soil test was conducted four years ago.

You are the assistant controller for StrongBar Ltd., a company that specializes in making energy bars and other high-protein snacks. The company's CFO, Diana Cash, has just stopped by your office. She is meeting with a consortium of banks this afternoon regarding StrongBar's upcoming public debt issue. The bankers have asked her to present the statement of cash flows for 2021 in the meeting. She further states that the controller,

CASE 5
Statement of Cash Flows

(20 minutes)

Exhibit I	**Balance sheets at December 31**		
		2021	**2020**
Cash		$ 69,000	$ 41,000
Trading securities		30,000	26,500
Accounts receivable		86,000	68,000
Inventory		36,000	50,000
Prepaid expenses		6,000	9,000
Plant assets		450,000	380,000
Accumulated depreciation		(150,000)	(125,000)
		$ 527,000	$ 449,500
Accounts payable		$ 60,032	$ 53,000
Accrued liabilities		18,000	19,000
Deferred tax liability		5,000	8,000
Bonds		0	146,500
Convertible bonds		154,968	0
Common shares		230,000	200,000
Retained earnings		31,000	22,000
Reserves—conversion rights		25,000	0
Reserves—accumulated other comprehensive income		3,000	1,000
		$ 527,000	$ 449,500

James Well, was supposed to provide her the statement of cash flows, but this morning he called in sick. She is wondering if you can prepare the report for her. She remembers that yesterday Mr. Well started working on the report and suggests that you check his desk for his notes. You tell Ms. Cash that you will try to help her, and promise to update her in a few hours. Nervously you walk to Mr. Well's office and, searching his desk, you find the following information.
Additional information:

1. In the beginning of 2021, StrongBar had 20,000 shares outstanding.
2. On March 1, the company declared and distributed a 5% stock dividend. At that date StrongBar's shares were trading for $10.
3. A cash dividend of $18,000 was declared and paid in October 2021.
4. On May 1, the company issued common shares for cash.
5. On January 1, 2021, StrongBar extinguished all of its outstanding bonds and replaced them with a new issue of convertible bonds. The old bonds had a face value of 150,000. To induce the retirement of the bonds, it offered bondholders $10,000 above the market value of the bonds. At that date the bonds were trading at $0.99. On the same day, StrongBar issued 150,000, 9%, five-year convertible bonds. The bonds pay interest *annually* on December 31 each year. Similar bonds without conversion options are traded to yield 8%. The company does not remember what the proceeds from the issue were, but the controller's notes say that the fair value of the conversion rights at issuance was $25,000. Because the terms of the old bonds and the new bonds were substantially different, those transactions are not considered a modification of debt.

6. StrongBar has two investments, as follows:

Name	Initial Investment	Fair Value Dec. 31, 2020	Fair Value Dec. 31, 2021	Classification
Prot-In	$13,000	$13,500	$15,000	At fair value through profit or loss
ProBar	12,000	13,000	15,000	At fair value through other comprehensive income

7. In 2021, the company sold plant assets with a gross book value of $30,000 and accumulated depreciation of $25,000. There was no gain or loss on the sale.

One thing that you are unable to locate is the income statement or information about the company's net income. At first you are worried that this will mean you will not be able to prepare the statement of cash flows. However, after carefully examining the information, you feel relief as you realize that this is not going to be a problem, and you start preparing the report.

StrongBar is a public Canadian company located in Vancouver. StrongBar uses the indirect method for reporting the operating activities section of the statement of cash flows. StrongBar's policy is to classify interest expense as an operating activity, dividends paid as a financing activity, and interest and dividends received as investing activities.

Required:

1. Explain how it is possible to prepare the statement of cash flows without having the income statement.
2. Prepare the statement of cash flows. Assume that the bond premium is included in the same category as the underlying interest expense. Ignore the disclosure requirements pertaining to interest and dividends paid and received, income taxes paid, and non-cash transactions.
3. Now assume that the company classified the dividends paid as an operating activity. Without regenerating the entire report again, explain what will change in the statement of cash flows. Be specific.
4. Suppose investors are unaware that companies can choose how to classify interest expense and dividends paid. How can this affect their assessment of StrongBar's statement of cash flows?

APPENDIX B
Time Value of Money and Simple Valuation Techniques

This appendix reviews several aspects of the time value of money, which is covered in introductory finance. The first section looks at the basic relationships and formulas for future and present values. The second section goes through the practical approaches (formulas, calculators, and spreadsheets) to make computations frequently encountered in accounting applications. The third section briefly discusses simple valuation techniques used to estimate the value of assets and enterprises. The end of this appendix includes present and future value tables.

A. FUTURE VALUES AND PRESENT VALUES

The time value of money is a concept that will be useful for many parts of this text. It is simply the idea that people value a dollar received today more than a dollar received tomorrow, next week, or next year. We can ask the question, "In order to be as satisfied as being paid a dollar now, how much would you need to be paid in one year's time?" If the answer is $1.10, then the interest rate you demand is 10% (i.e., 10% more than $1). We usually use "$r$" to denote the interest rate, also called the discount rate. Once we have an interest rate, we can express the value of money at any point in time, at the present time or in the future, giving rise to the concepts of present value and future value.

1. Future value of a single sum received now

In the example just given, $1.10 is the future value in one year's time of $1 today. Changing the example slightly, if you invest $100 now, you expect to obtain $110 in a year's time because you would earn 10% interest. If you invest for two years, you would have $100 \times 1.10 \times 1.10 = \$100 \times 1.10^2 = \$121$. Formally, we can express this relationship by the following equation:

Exhibit B-1	Future value of a single sum

$$FV_t = PV_0 \times (1 + r)^t$$

In this equation, FV_t denotes future value (a dollar amount) at time t, PV_0 denotes present value (a dollar amount) at time 0, and r is the interest rate per period. Time is usually measured in years, but it could be any length of time, as long as the interest rate is defined accordingly.

2. Present value of a single sum to be received in the future

We can rearrange the equation in Exhibit B-1 to isolate PV_0, the present value at time 0, as follows:

Exhibit B-2	Present value of a single sum

$$PV_0 = \frac{FV_t}{(1 + r)^t}$$

Thus, the present value of $121 to be received in two years' time when the interest rate is 10% per year is $PV_0 = \$121 \div 1.10^2 = \$121 \div 1.21 = \$100$. The diagram in Exhibit B-3 summarizes the relationship between the present and future values just calculated.

Exhibit B-3	Timeline illustrating the relationship between present and future values

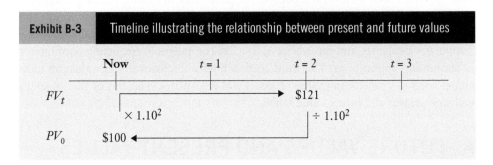

One reason for computing future and present values is to allow us to add together cash flows that occur at different times. For example, if you were to receive $100 next year, $100 in two years, and $100 three years from now, how much are you really receiving? Simply adding together the three cash flows is not appropriate because the cash flows occur at different times and each cash flow has a different time value of money. Instead, all the cash flows need to be expressed in terms of one particular point in time. In most instances, it is most convenient to choose the present time as the point of reference. If the interest rate is 10%, we can compute the present value of each of the three cash flows and then they can be summed up, as follows:

Exhibit B-4	Computation of present value of three cash flows of $100 each

$$PV_0 = \$100/1.1 + \$100/1.1^2 + \$100/1.1^3$$
$$= \$90.91 + \$82.64 + \$75.13$$
$$= \$248.68$$

As you can see, the present value ($248.68) is considerably less than the simple sum of the three cash flows ($300). The diagram in Exhibit B-5 illustrates this computation.

Exhibit B-5	Timeline showing the computation of present value of three cash flows

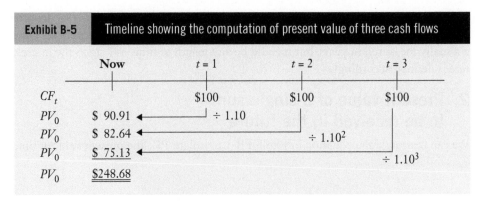

3. Present value of a perpetuity

A **perpetuity** is a series of cash flows in equal amounts occurring at regular intervals for an infinite number of periods. The present value of a perpetuity is not infinite, even though the cash flows occur for an infinite number of periods. In fact, we can compute the value of a perpetuity using the following formula, where each cash flow occurs at the end of period t:

perpetuity A series of cash flows in equal amounts occurring at regular intervals for an infinite number of periods.

Exhibit B-6	Present value of a perpetuity[1]

$$PV_0 = \frac{CF}{r}$$

For example, if each cash flow, denoted CF in the formula, is $100 and received at the end of each year forever into the future, and the discount rate is 10%, then $PV = \$100 \div 0.10 = \$1,000$.

4. Present value of a perpetuity with growth

Instead of the same cash flow every period, a **perpetuity with growth** is one in which the cash flows grow at a constant rate. The present value of a perpetuity with the cash flow CF_1 occurring at the end of one year and growing at rate g, discounted at rate r, is given by the following formula:

perpetuity with growth A series of cash flows occurring at regular intervals for an infinite number of periods with cash flows that grow at a constant rate.

Exhibit B-7	Present value of a perpetuity with growth

$$PV_0 = \frac{CF_1}{r - g}$$

5. Present value of an ordinary annuity

The pattern of cash flows illustrated by the computation in Exhibit B-5 is an example of an **annuity**, which is a series of cash flows in equal amounts occurring at regular intervals (i.e., $CF_1 = CF_2 = \ldots$). In this example, $100 is received at the end of each of three years. In addition, this is an **ordinary annuity** because the cash flows occur at the *end* of each period. In comparison, an **annuity due** is one in which the cash flows occur at the *beginning* of each period.

In cases where there are a small number of cash flows, as in the example illustrated in Exhibit B-5, we can compute the present value by computing the present value of each individual cash flow and then adding them up. However, this approach is laborious even using a spreadsheet if the number of cash flows in the annuity is large. Instead, using the following formula is often more efficient:

annuity A series of cash flows in equal amounts occurring at regular intervals.

ordinary annuity An annuity with cash flows at the *end* of each period.

annuity due An annuity with cash flows at the *beginning* of each period.

[1.] For those curious as to the source of this formula, it is an application of the general formula for the sum of an infinite series from high school algebra: $\sum_{t=1}^{\infty}(1/a^t) = 1/(a - 1)$. For example, if $a = 2$, then $\frac{1}{2} + \frac{1}{4} + \ldots = 1$, which is $1/(a - 1) = 1/(2 - 1)$. If $a = 10$, then $0.1 + 0.01 + 0.001 + \ldots = 0.111 \ldots = 1/9$. If $a = 1 + r$, then $[1/(1 + r)] + [1/(1 + r)^2] + \ldots = 1/(1 + r - 1) = 1/r$.

Exhibit B-8	Present value of an ordinary annuity[2]

$$PV_0 = CF_1 \times \left(\frac{1}{r} - \frac{1}{r(1+r)^t} \right)$$

$$= CF_1 \times \left(\frac{1 - (1+r)^{-t}}{r} \right)$$

$$= CF \times PVFA(r, t)$$

The term in parentheses is known as the *present value factor for an annuity* at discount rate *r* for *t* periods. For convenience of reference, we denote this factor as *PVFA(r, t)*.

For example, if you were to receive $100 at the end of each of the next three years, the present value of those three payments is $248.69, calculated as follows:

Exhibit B-9	Computation of present value of three cash flows of $100 each

$$PV_0 = \$100 \times \left(\frac{1}{0.10} - \frac{1}{0.10(1.10)^3} \right)$$

$$= \$100 \times 2.48685$$

$$= \$248.69$$

Of course, this is the same as the answer obtained using the calculations in Exhibit B-5.

6. Present value of an annuity due

As mentioned above, the cash flows for an annuity due occur at the beginning of the period. The simplest way to deal with such annuities is to recognize that, setting aside the first cash flow, the remainder is just an ordinary annuity with one less period. Thus, we can write the present value factor for an annuity due (*PVFAD*) as follows:

Exhibit B-10	Present value factor for an annuity due *(PVFAD)*

$$PVFAD(r, t) = 1 + PVFA(r, t-1)$$

$$= 1 + \left(\frac{1}{r} - \frac{1}{r(1+r)^{t-1}} \right)$$

For example, if you receive three cash flows of $100 each at the beginning of each of three years, and the discount rate is 10%, then:

Exhibit B-11	Present value of $100 received at the beginning of each of three years

$$PV_0 = CF \times PVFAD(10\%, 3)$$

$$= \$100 \times \left(1 + \frac{1}{0.10} - \frac{1}{0.10(1.10)^2} \right)$$

$$= \$100 \times 2.73554$$

$$= \$273.55$$

---

[2] This formula is derived from the perpetuity formula. A $1 annuity of *t* periods is equivalent to a $1 perpetuity minus a $1 perpetuity that starts at the end of period *t*. The first perpetuity has value $1/r$. The second perpetuity starts after *t* periods, so it has value $(1/r) \times 1/(1+r)^t = 1/r(1+r)^t$. Thus, $PVAF = (1/r) - 1/r(1+r)^t$.

Notice that this present value of $273.55 is 10% more than $248.69, the value of the ordinary annuity ($248.69 $\times$ 1.1 = $273.55). So another way to think of an annuity due is to imagine that it is like an ordinary annuity with every payment shifted by one period closer to the present time. Thus, we can also express the present value annuity factor for an annuity due as follows:

Exhibit B-12	Alternate formula for present value factor for an annuity due

$$PVFAD(r, t) = PVFA(r, t) \times (1 + r)$$

$$= \left(\frac{1}{r} - \frac{1}{r(1 + r)^t} \right) \times (1 + r)$$

B. COMPUTATION TECHNIQUES

The previous section reviewed the fundamentals of present and future values, as well as the formulas for computing these values. Exhibit B-13 summarizes techniques to make these computations using formulas, a financial calculator (Texas Instruments BA II Plus), or a spreadsheet (Microsoft Excel). Notation is as follows:

- FV = future value
- PV = present value
- CF = cash flow
- r = interest rate per period
- t = number of periods
- g = growth rate
- $PVFA$ = present value factor for an annuity

Exhibit B-13	Basic computation techniques for future and present values

Objective	Example	Formula calculation	Texas Instruments BA II Plus	Microsoft Excel
FV of a single sum	A $100 investment earns 5% interest compounded annually. Compute the future value of this investment at the end of 10 years.	$FV_t = PV_0 \times (1 + r)^t$ $FV_{10} = 100 \, (1.05)^{10}$ $= \$162.89$	-100 [PV]; 5 [I/Y]; 10 [N]; [CPT] [FV]; [Output] 162.89	Input: =FV (5%, 10, , −100) Output: 162.89
PV of a single sum	You agree to pay $162.89 at the end of 10 years. If the interest rate is 5%, how much would you need to set aside today to fund that future payment?	$PV_0 = \dfrac{FV_t}{(1 + r)^t}$ $PV_0 = \dfrac{162.89}{(1.05)^{10}}$ $= 100.00$	-162.89 [FV]; 5 [I/Y]; 10 [N]; [CPT] [PV]; [Output] 100.00	Input: =PV (5%, 10, , −162.89) Output: 100.00

(*Continued*)

| Exhibit B-13 | Continued |

PV of a perpetuity	An investment promises to pay $100 at the end of each year indefinitely. If the discount rate is 5%, how much would it cost to buy the investment?	$PV_0 = \dfrac{CF_t}{r}$ $PV_0 = \dfrac{100}{0.05}$ $= 2{,}000$	No special financial functions. Use normal arithmetic functions.	No special financial function. Input according to formula.
PV of a perpetuity with growth	An investment promises to make a stream of payments indefinitely, with payments starting at $100 at the end of the first year and growing at 1% each year. If the interest rate is 5%, how much would it cost to buy the investment?	$PV_0 = \dfrac{CF_1}{r - g}$ $PV_0 = \dfrac{100}{0.05 - 0.01}$ $= 2{,}500$	No special financial functions. Use normal arithmetic functions.	No special financial function. Input according to formula.
PV of an ordinary annuity	You promise to pay $100 at the end of each year for 10 years. If the interest rate is 5%, how much would you need to set aside now to fund these 10 payments?	$PV_0 = CF_1 \times PVFA(r, t)$ $= CF_1 \times \left(\dfrac{1}{r} - \dfrac{1}{r(1 + r)^t}\right)$ $PV_0 = 100 \times PVFA(5\%, 10)$ $= 100 \times \left(\dfrac{1}{0.05} - \dfrac{1}{0.05(1.05)^{10}}\right)$ $= 100 \times 7.7217$ $= 772.17$	−100 PMT 5 I/Y 10 N CPT PV [Output] 772.17	Input: =PV(5%, 10, −100) Output: -772.17
PV of an annuity due	You promise to pay $100 at the beginning of each year for 10 years. If the interest rate is 5%, how much would you need to set aside now to fund these 10 payments?	$PV_0 = CF_1 \times [1 + PVFA(r, t - 1)]$ $= CF_1 \times \left(1 + \dfrac{1}{r} - \dfrac{1}{r(1 + r)^{t-1}}\right)$ $PV_0 = 100 \times [1 + PVFA(5\%, 9)]$ $= 100 \times \left(1 + \dfrac{1}{0.05} - \dfrac{1}{0.05(1.05)^9}\right)$ $= 100 \times 8.1078$ $= 810.78$	2ND BGN 2ND SET 2ND QUIT −100 PMT 5 I/Y 10 N CPT PV [Output] 810.78	Input: =PV (5%, 10, −100, , 1) Output: 810.78

- Subscripts denote the timing of a variable (e.g., 0 is the present, 1 is one period in the future)
- For the calculator entries, keystrokes are either numbers or function keys denoted by ⬭; items in [square brackets] are informational and not for keying

In addition to the above future and present value computations, it is sometimes necessary to determine the interest rate or yield of an annuity or a bond. It is not generally possible to calculate yields using algebraic formulas. Instead, a financial calculator or a spreadsheet is necessary.

Exhibit B-14	Techniques for computing yields on annuities and bonds			
Objective	**Example**	**Formula**	**Texas Instruments BA II Plus**	**Microsoft Excel**
Interest rate or yield of an annuity	An ordinary annuity has annual cash payments of $100 for 10 periods. The present value of the annuity is $772.17. Compute the interest rate of the annuity.	No formula	−100 [PMT] 10 [N] 772.17 [PV] [CPT] [I/Y] [Output] 5.00	Input: = RATE (10, −100, 772.17) Output: 5.00%
Annual yield of a bond	You purchase a bond on Jan. 1, 2013. The bond has an annual coupon rate of 6% and semi-annual coupon payments until maturity on Dec. 31, 2022, at which time it will repay the principal of $1,000. You paid $900 for this bond.	No formula	[Start bond functions] [2ND] [BOND] [Purchase date] 1.0111 [ENTER] [↓] [Coupon rate] 6 [ENTER] [↓] [Maturity date] 12.3120 [ENTER] [↓] [Maturity payment per $100 face value] 100 [ENTER] [↓] [Display shows ACT] [↓] [Display shows 2/Y] [↓] [Display shows YLD] [↓] [Price per $100 face value] 90 [ENTER] [↑] [Display shows YLD] [CPT] [Output] 7.44	Input cell A1: 2013/01/01 Input cell A2: 2022/12/31 Input cell A3: = YIELD(A1, A2, 6%, 90, 100, 2, 0) Output cell A3: 7.44%

The above table shows an example of a bond with standard characteristics, but the number of steps in the calculator is already becoming unwieldy. For more complex bonds, it is advisable to use a spreadsheet that identifies the timing and amount of all cash flows, and then sum the present value of each cash flow.

C. SIMPLE VALUATION METHODS

As noted in Chapter 1, the demand for accounting information arises from uncertainty about the future. Due to this uncertainty, equity investors are only able to make imperfect forecasts about the future prices of shares, which influence whether and in which companies they invest. Given the importance of this topic, it is the subject of many books in finance and investments. The following discussion touches on the basic approaches to equity valuation using accounting information. This will provide a basis for understanding why accounting information is important in equity markets.

In all the methods discussed below, our goal is to estimate a fundamental value (V). If prevailing stock price (P) in the market is below V, then the valuation suggests that the stock is underpriced. In contrast, $P > V$ suggests that the stock is overpriced. However, it is important to recognize that these estimates of V are just that: estimates. Each estimation approach has its limitations because of the assumptions required. Below, we will discuss approaches using book value, dividends, and earnings.

1. Valuation using book value

The simplest method of share valuation is to use a company's book value per share ($BVPS$). "Book value" in this context refers to the amount for common shares, retained earnings, and any other amounts in equity on the balance sheet that pertain to the common shareholders. We divide book value by the number of shares outstanding[3] to obtain a value comparable to the company's stock price, which is naturally expressed on a per share basis.

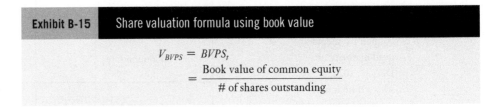

| Exhibit B-15 | Share valuation formula using book value |

$$V_{BVPS} = BVPS_t$$
$$= \frac{\text{Book value of common equity}}{\text{\# of shares outstanding}}$$

While this method is simple, it is useful in very limited circumstances. Specifically, this valuation approach requires the following assumptions to be approximately correct:

- *Completeness:* The company's balance sheet has recorded all significant assets and liabilities. That is, the company cannot have unrecorded assets such as patents, or unrecorded liabilities such as pending lawsuits.
- *Neutrality:* Accounting policies are neutral such that the recorded values of assets and liabilities on the balance sheet approximate their current values. In other words, the accounting can be neither conservative nor aggressive.
- *Stability:* The company's operations are stable rather than growing (or declining). Usually, this also requires that the company's industry be mature and stable.

Using the book value method, the estimate V will usually be substantially below stock price P because (1) the balance sheet does not show all economic assets such as valuable patents and internally generated goodwill; (2) accounting tends to be conservative; and (3) firms tend to grow over time along with growth in the overall economy. Despite these limitations, the book value method often provides a reliable lower bound estimate of fundamental value, and it is a good starting point to gauge the reasonability of the other methods discussed below. For instance, if another valuation method produces a value estimate that is four times book value, is the 300% difference reasonably explained by incomplete accounting of assets, conservative accounting, or future growth?

2. Valuation using dividends

Finance theory suggests that the value of common equity is equal to the present value of expected future dividends. This idea is summarized by the following formula:

[3.] There are some complexities relating to the number of shares that should be used in the denominator. These issues are addressed in Chapter 15 on earnings per share. For simplicity, we use the number of shares outstanding.

Exhibit B-16	Valuation formula using expected dividends

$$V_{Div} = \sum_{t=1}^{\infty} \frac{E(DPS_t)}{(1 + t)^t}$$

$E(DPS_t)$ is the expected dividends per share in period t. This formula is just an application of basic discounted cash flow analysis. However, the difficulty with applying this approach is that dividends are hard to predict: they are at the discretion of companies' boards of directors, and some companies have no history of dividends to help forecast future dividends. One way to overcome these difficulties is to replace expected dividends with another measure of expected cash flow, such as cash flow from operations. Another approach is to use earnings forecasts in place of expected dividends, because earnings eventually result in cash inflows, from which the firm pays dividends.

3. Valuation using earnings and earnings multiples

The earnings forecasting process can be quite elaborate and complex. A good starting point is to use the most recent reported earnings per share. For valuation purposes, it is useful to "normalize" the earnings per share: adjusting the actual earnings for temporary fluctuations so as to obtain a better forecast of permanent earnings. We can then use this normalized earnings per share (EPS_0) as an indicator for future dividend-paying capacity, and apply the perpetuity with growth formula (see Exhibit B-7) to obtain the following formula:

Exhibit B-17	Valuation formula using expected earnings

$$V_{Earn} = \frac{E(EPS_1)}{r - g}$$
$$= \frac{EPS_0 \times (1 + g)}{r - g}$$

In this equation, $E(EPS_1)$ is the expected earnings per share next year. If growth is zero ($g = 0$), then the formula is particularly simple: $V_{Earn} = EPS_0 / r$.

To illustrate this approach and the related computations below, assume the following for Alpha Corporation:

Exhibit B-18	Assumptions about Alpha Corporation	
Item description	Notation	Amount
Current stock price	P_0	$39.00
Most recent year's earnings per share	EPS_0	$1.50
Discount rate	r	9%
Growth rate in earnings per share	g	4%

Applying the equation in Exhibit B-17, we obtain $V_{Earn} = \$1.50 \times 1.04 \div (0.09 - 0.04) = \$1.56 \div 0.05 = \$31.20$ as the estimated value per share for Alpha Corporation.

It is also useful to write the formula for V_{Earn} from Exhibit B-17 in a slightly different way to emphasize what is commonly known as an **earnings multiple**:

Exhibit B-19	Valuation formula using earnings multiples

$$V_{Earn} = EPS_0 \times \frac{1 + g}{r - g}$$
$$= EPS_0 \times \text{Earnings multiple}$$

Using the assumptions for Alpha Corporation shown above in Exhibit B-18, we have the following results:

Exhibit B-20	Valuation of Alpha Corporation using multiples
Earnings multiple	**Value estimate**
Earnings multiple $= \dfrac{1 + g}{r - g} = \dfrac{1.04}{0.09 - 0.04} = 20.8$	$V_{Earn} = EPS_0 \times \text{Earnings multiple}$ $= \$1.50 \times 20.8$ $= \$31.20$

Of course, the estimated value of $31.20 is the same as computing the value using the perpetuity with growth formula in Exhibit B-7.

One of the reasons for isolating the multiple in the earnings valuation method is that it allows for comparisons among different firms. Along the same line, instead of making predictions about r and g directly to calculate the multiple, one can also use the average multiple for a set of firms that is comparable to the firm being analyzed.[4] Thus, if the set of comparable firms has an average earnings multiple of 23, and $EPS_0 = \$1.50$, then $V_{Earn} = 23 \times \$1.50 = \$34.50$.

Another way to use an earnings multiple is to compare it against the price–earnings ratio, or P/E ratio, which is simply the share price divided by earnings per share:

Exhibit B-21	The price–earnings (P/E) ratio

$$P/E \text{ ratio} = \frac{P_0}{EPS_0}$$

If the prevailing stock price (P_0) is $39, then the P/E ratio is $39 \div \$1.50 = 26$. This ratio exceeds the earnings multiple of 20.8, as well as the average multiple of 23 for comparable firms. This analysis suggests that the stock is overpriced. The same inference of overpricing would be drawn by comparing the actual price of $39 with the estimated value of $31.20.

---

[4] This method of using earnings multiples of comparable firms is one application of an approach called the method of comparable multiples. This method involves using multiples of earnings, sales, book value, cash flow, or any other measure that helps to predict share price.

Exhibit B-22	Summary of earnings valuation for Alpha Corporation	
Earnings multiple for the firm (estimated):	$\dfrac{1 + g}{r - g} = 20.8$	The actual P/E ratio of 26 exceeds the earnings multiple corresponding to the discount rate and growth rate estimated for the firm. The P/E ratio also exceeds the earnings multiple for comparable firms.
Earnings multiple for comparable firms (given):	23	
Actual P/E ratio:	$\dfrac{P_0}{EPS_0} = \dfrac{\$39}{\$1.50} = 26$	
Value estimate: Actual price:	$V_{Earn} = \$31.20$ $P_0 = \$39$	The actual market price for the shares at $39 exceeds estimated value of $31.20. Therefore, this analysis suggests that the shares are overvalued.

D. GLOSSARY

annuity: A series of cash flows in equal amounts occurring at regular intervals.

annuity due: An annuity that has cash flows at the *beginning* of each period.

earnings multiple: A number that, when multiplied with earnings, provides an estimate of a share's value. When earnings are expected to grow at rate g and the discount rate is r, the earnings multiple is equal to $(1 + g) / (r - g)$.

ordinary annuity: An annuity that has cash flows at the *end* of each period.

perpetuity: A series of cash flows in equal amounts occurring at regular intervals for an infinite number of periods.

perpetuity with growth: A series of cash flows occurring at regular intervals for an infinite number of periods with cash flows that grow at a constant rate.

E. TABLES OF PRESENT VALUE AND FUTURE VALUE FACTORS

1. Present value factors for a single sum of $1 (PVF)

Periods (t)	Interest rate per period (r)											
	2%	3%	4%	5%	6%	7%	8%	9%	10%	11%	12%	15%
1	0.9804	0.9709	0.9615	0.9524	0.9434	0.9346	0.9259	0.9174	0.9091	0.9009	0.8929	0.8696
2	0.9612	0.9426	0.9246	0.9070	0.8900	0.8734	0.8573	0.8417	0.8264	0.8116	0.7972	0.7561
3	0.9423	0.9151	0.8890	0.8638	0.8396	0.8163	0.7938	0.7722	0.7513	0.7312	0.7118	0.6575
4	0.9238	0.8885	0.8548	0.8227	0.7921	0.7629	0.7350	0.7084	0.6830	0.6587	0.6355	0.5718
5	0.9057	0.8626	0.8219	0.7835	0.7473	0.7130	0.6806	0.6499	0.6209	0.5935	0.5674	0.4972
6	0.8880	0.8375	0.7903	0.7462	0.7050	0.6663	0.6302	0.5963	0.5645	0.5346	0.5066	0.4323
7	0.8706	0.8131	0.7599	0.7107	0.6651	0.6227	0.5835	0.5470	0.5132	0.4817	0.4523	0.3759
8	0.8535	0.7894	0.7307	0.6768	0.6274	0.5820	0.5403	0.5019	0.4665	0.4339	0.4039	0.3269
9	0.8368	0.7664	0.7026	0.6446	0.5919	0.5439	0.5002	0.4604	0.4241	0.3909	0.3606	0.2843
10	0.8203	0.7441	0.6756	0.6139	0.5584	0.5083	0.4632	0.4224	0.3855	0.3522	0.3220	0.2472
11	0.8043	0.7224	0.6496	0.5847	0.5268	0.4751	0.4289	0.3875	0.3505	0.3173	0.2875	0.2149
12	0.7885	0.7014	0.6246	0.5568	0.4970	0.4440	0.3971	0.3555	0.3186	0.2858	0.2567	0.1869
13	0.7730	0.6810	0.6006	0.5303	0.4688	0.4150	0.3677	0.3262	0.2897	0.2575	0.2292	0.1625
14	0.7579	0.6611	0.5775	0.5051	0.4423	0.3878	0.3405	0.2992	0.2633	0.2320	0.2046	0.1413
15	0.7430	0.6419	0.5553	0.4810	0.4173	0.3624	0.3152	0.2745	0.2394	0.2090	0.1827	0.1229
16	0.7284	0.6232	0.5339	0.4581	0.3936	0.3387	0.2919	0.2519	0.2176	0.1883	0.1631	0.1069
17	0.7142	0.6050	0.5134	0.4363	0.3714	0.3166	0.2703	0.2311	0.1978	0.1696	0.1456	0.0929
18	0.7002	0.5874	0.4936	0.4155	0.3503	0.2959	0.2502	0.2120	0.1799	0.1528	0.1300	0.0808
19	0.6864	0.5703	0.4746	0.3957	0.3305	0.2765	0.2317	0.1945	0.1635	0.1377	0.1161	0.0703
20	0.6730	0.5537	0.4564	0.3769	0.3118	0.2584	0.2145	0.1784	0.1486	0.1240	0.1037	0.0611
21	0.6598	0.5375	0.4388	0.3589	0.2942	0.2415	0.1987	0.1637	0.1351	0.1117	0.0926	0.0531
22	0.6468	0.5219	0.4220	0.3418	0.2775	0.2257	0.1839	0.1502	0.1228	0.1007	0.0826	0.0462
23	0.6342	0.5067	0.4057	0.3256	0.2618	0.2109	0.1703	0.1378	0.1117	0.0907	0.0738	0.0402
24	0.6217	0.4919	0.3901	0.3101	0.2470	0.1971	0.1577	0.1264	0.1015	0.0817	0.0659	0.0349
25	0.6095	0.4776	0.3751	0.2953	0.2330	0.1842	0.1460	0.1160	0.0923	0.0736	0.0588	0.0304
26	0.5976	0.4637	0.3607	0.2812	0.2198	0.1722	0.1352	0.1064	0.0839	0.0663	0.0525	0.0264
27	0.5859	0.4502	0.3468	0.2678	0.2074	0.1609	0.1252	0.0976	0.0763	0.0597	0.0469	0.0230
28	0.5744	0.4371	0.3335	0.2551	0.1956	0.1504	0.1159	0.0895	0.0693	0.0538	0.0419	0.0200
29	0.5631	0.4243	0.3207	0.2429	0.1846	0.1406	0.1073	0.0822	0.0630	0.0485	0.0374	0.0174
30	0.5521	0.4120	0.3083	0.2314	0.1741	0.1314	0.0994	0.0754	0.0573	0.0437	0.0334	0.0151
31	0.5412	0.4000	0.2965	0.2204	0.1643	0.1228	0.0920	0.0691	0.0521	0.0394	0.0298	0.0131
32	0.5306	0.3883	0.2851	0.2099	0.1550	0.1147	0.0852	0.0634	0.0474	0.0355	0.0266	0.0114
33	0.5202	0.3770	0.2741	0.1999	0.1462	0.1072	0.0789	0.0582	0.0431	0.0319	0.0238	0.0099
34	0.5100	0.3660	0.2636	0.1904	0.1379	0.1002	0.0730	0.0534	0.0391	0.0288	0.0212	0.0086
35	0.5000	0.3554	0.2534	0.1813	0.1301	0.0937	0.0676	0.0490	0.0356	0.0259	0.0189	0.0075
36	0.4902	0.3450	0.2437	0.1727	0.1227	0.0875	0.0626	0.0449	0.0323	0.0234	0.0169	0.0065
37	0.4806	0.3350	0.2343	0.1644	0.1158	0.0818	0.0580	0.0412	0.0294	0.0210	0.0151	0.0057
38	0.4712	0.3252	0.2253	0.1566	0.1092	0.0765	0.0537	0.0378	0.0267	0.0190	0.0135	0.0049
39	0.4619	0.3158	0.2166	0.1491	0.1031	0.0715	0.0497	0.0347	0.0243	0.0171	0.0120	0.0043
40	0.4529	0.3066	0.2083	0.1420	0.0972	0.0668	0.0460	0.0318	0.0221	0.0154	0.0107	0.0037
45	0.4102	0.2644	0.1712	0.1113	0.0727	0.0476	0.0313	0.0207	0.0137	0.0091	0.0061	0.0019
50	0.3715	0.2281	0.1407	0.0872	0.0543	0.0339	0.0213	0.0134	0.0085	0.0054	0.0035	0.0009

2. Present value factors for an ordinary annuity of $1 (PVFA)

Periods (t)	Interest rate per period (r)											
	2%	3%	4%	5%	6%	7%	8%	9%	10%	11%	12%	15%
1	0.9804	0.9709	0.9615	0.9524	0.9434	0.9346	0.9259	0.9174	0.9091	0.9009	0.8929	0.8696
2	1.9416	1.9135	1.8861	1.8594	1.8334	1.8080	1.7833	1.7591	1.7355	1.7125	1.6901	1.6257
3	2.8839	2.8286	2.7751	2.7232	2.6730	2.6243	2.5771	2.5313	2.4869	2.4437	2.4018	2.2832
4	3.8077	3.7171	3.6299	3.5460	3.4651	3.3872	3.3121	3.2397	3.1699	3.1024	3.0373	2.8550
5	4.7135	4.5797	4.4518	4.3295	4.2124	4.1002	3.9927	3.8897	3.7908	3.6959	3.6048	3.3522
6	5.6014	5.4172	5.2421	5.0757	4.9173	4.7665	4.6229	4.4859	4.3553	4.2305	4.1114	3.7845
7	6.4720	6.2303	6.0021	5.7864	5.5824	5.3893	5.2064	5.0330	4.8684	4.7122	4.5638	4.1604
8	7.3255	7.0197	6.7327	6.4632	6.2098	5.9713	5.7466	5.5348	5.3349	5.1461	4.9676	4.4873
9	8.1622	7.7861	7.4353	7.1078	6.8017	6.5152	6.2469	5.9952	5.7590	5.5370	5.3282	4.7716
10	8.9826	8.5302	8.1109	7.7217	7.3601	7.0236	6.7101	6.4177	6.1446	5.8892	5.6502	5.0188
11	9.7868	9.2526	8.7605	8.3064	7.8869	7.4987	7.1390	6.8052	6.4951	6.2065	5.9377	5.2337
12	10.5753	9.9540	9.3851	8.8633	8.3838	7.9427	7.5361	7.1607	6.8137	6.4924	6.1944	5.4206
13	11.3484	10.6350	9.9856	9.3936	8.8527	8.3577	7.9038	7.4869	7.1034	6.7499	6.4235	5.5831
14	12.1062	11.2961	10.5631	9.8986	9.2950	8.7455	8.2442	7.7862	7.3667	6.9819	6.6282	5.7245
15	12.8493	11.9379	11.1184	10.3797	9.7122	9.1079	8.5595	8.0607	7.6061	7.1909	6.8109	5.8474
16	13.5777	12.5611	11.6523	10.8378	10.1059	9.4466	8.8514	8.3126	7.8237	7.3792	6.9740	5.9542
17	14.2919	13.1661	12.1657	11.2741	10.4773	9.7632	9.1216	8.5436	8.0216	7.5488	7.1196	6.0472
18	14.9920	13.7535	12.6593	11.6896	10.8276	10.0591	9.3719	8.7556	8.2014	7.7016	7.2497	6.1280
19	15.6785	14.3238	13.1339	12.0853	11.1581	10.3356	9.6036	8.9501	8.3649	7.8393	7.3658	6.1982
20	16.3514	14.8775	13.5903	12.4622	11.4699	10.5940	9.8181	9.1285	8.5136	7.9633	7.4694	6.2593
21	17.0112	15.4150	14.0292	12.8212	11.7641	10.8355	10.0168	9.2922	8.6487	8.0751	7.5620	6.3125
22	17.6580	15.9369	14.4511	13.1630	12.0416	11.0612	10.2007	9.4424	8.7715	8.1757	7.6446	6.3587
23	18.2922	16.4436	14.8568	13.4886	12.3034	11.2722	10.3711	9.5802	8.8832	8.2664	7.7184	6.3988
24	18.9139	16.9355	15.2470	13.7986	12.5504	11.4693	10.5288	9.7066	8.9847	8.3481	7.7843	6.4338
25	19.5235	17.4131	15.6221	14.0939	12.7834	11.6536	10.6748	9.8226	9.0770	8.4217	7.8431	6.4641
26	20.1210	17.8768	15.9828	14.3752	13.0032	11.8258	10.8100	9.9290	9.1609	8.4881	7.8957	6.4906
27	20.7069	18.3270	16.3296	14.6430	13.2105	11.9867	10.9352	10.0266	9.2372	8.5478	7.9426	6.5135
28	21.2813	18.7641	16.6631	14.8981	13.4062	12.1371	11.0511	10.1161	9.3066	8.6016	7.9844	6.5335
29	21.8444	19.1885	16.9837	15.1411	13.5907	12.2777	11.1584	10.1983	9.3696	8.6501	8.0218	6.5509
30	22.3965	19.6004	17.2920	15.3725	13.7648	12.4090	11.2578	10.2737	9.4269	8.6938	8.0552	6.5660
31	22.9377	20.0004	17.5885	15.5928	13.9291	12.5318	11.3498	10.3428	9.4790	8.7331	8.0850	6.5791
32	23.4683	20.3888	17.8736	15.8027	14.0840	12.6466	11.4350	10.4062	9.5264	8.7686	8.1116	6.5905
33	23.9886	20.7658	18.1476	16.0025	14.2302	12.7538	11.5139	10.4644	9.5694	8.8005	8.1354	6.6005
34	24.4986	21.1318	18.4112	16.1929	14.3681	12.8540	11.5869	10.5178	9.6086	8.8293	8.1566	6.6091
35	24.9986	21.4872	18.6646	16.3742	14.4982	12.9477	11.6546	10.5668	9.6442	8.8552	8.1755	6.6166
36	25.4888	21.8323	18.9083	16.5469	14.6210	13.0352	11.7172	10.6118	9.6765	8.8786	8.1924	6.6231
37	25.9695	22.1672	19.1426	16.7113	14.7368	13.1170	11.7752	10.6530	9.7059	8.8996	8.2075	6.6288
38	26.4406	22.4925	19.3679	16.8679	14.8460	13.1935	11.8289	10.6908	9.7327	8.9186	8.2210	6.6338
39	26.9026	22.8082	19.5845	17.0170	14.9491	13.2649	11.8786	10.7255	9.7570	8.9357	8.2330	6.6380
40	27.3555	23.1148	19.7928	17.1591	15.0463	13.3317	11.9246	10.7574	9.7791	8.9511	8.2438	6.6418
45	29.4902	24.5187	20.7200	17.7741	15.4558	13.6055	12.1084	10.8812	9.8628	9.0079	8.2825	6.6543
50	31.4236	25.7298	21.4822	18.2559	15.7619	13.8007	12.2335	10.9617	9.9148	9.0417	8.3045	6.6605

3. Present value factors for an annuity due of $1 (PVFAD)

Periods (t)	Interest rate per period (r)											
	2%	3%	4%	5%	6%	7%	8%	9%	10%	11%	12%	15%
1	1.0000	1.0000	1.0000	1.0000	1.0000	1.0000	1.0000	1.0000	1.0000	1.0000	1.0000	1.0000
2	1.9804	1.9709	1.9615	1.9524	1.9434	1.9346	1.9259	1.9174	1.9091	1.9009	1.8929	1.8696
3	2.9416	2.9135	2.8861	2.8594	2.8334	2.8080	2.7833	2.7591	2.7355	2.7125	2.6901	2.6257
4	3.8839	3.8286	3.7751	3.7232	3.6730	3.6243	3.5771	3.5313	3.4869	3.4437	3.4018	3.2832
5	4.8077	4.7171	4.6299	4.5460	4.4651	4.3872	4.3121	4.2397	4.1699	4.1024	4.0373	3.8550
6	5.7135	5.5797	5.4518	5.3295	5.2124	5.1002	4.9927	4.8897	4.7908	4.6959	4.6048	4.3522
7	6.6014	6.4172	6.2421	6.0757	5.9173	5.7665	5.6229	5.4859	5.3553	5.2305	5.1114	4.7845
8	7.4720	7.2303	7.0021	6.7864	6.5824	6.3893	6.2064	6.0330	5.8684	5.7122	5.5638	5.1604
9	8.3255	8.0197	7.7327	7.4632	7.2098	6.9713	6.7466	6.5348	6.3349	6.1461	5.9676	5.4873
10	9.1622	8.7861	8.4353	8.1078	7.8017	7.5152	7.2469	6.9952	6.7590	6.5370	6.3282	5.7716
11	9.9826	9.5302	9.1109	8.7217	8.3601	8.0236	7.7101	7.4177	7.1446	6.8892	6.6502	6.0188
12	10.7868	10.2526	9.7605	9.3064	8.8869	8.4987	8.1390	7.8052	7.4951	7.2065	6.9377	6.2337
13	11.5753	10.9540	10.3851	9.8633	9.3838	8.9427	8.5361	8.1607	7.8137	7.4924	7.1944	6.4206
14	12.3484	11.6350	10.9856	10.3936	9.8527	9.3577	8.9038	8.4869	8.1034	7.7499	7.4235	6.5831
15	13.1062	12.2961	11.5631	10.8986	10.2950	9.7455	9.2442	8.7862	8.3667	7.9819	7.6282	6.7245
16	13.8493	12.9379	12.1184	11.3797	10.7122	10.1079	9.5595	9.0607	8.6061	8.1909	7.8109	6.8474
17	14.5777	13.5611	12.6523	11.8378	11.1059	10.4466	9.8514	9.3126	8.8237	8.3792	7.9740	6.9542
18	15.2919	14.1661	13.1657	12.2741	11.4773	10.7632	10.1216	9.5436	9.0216	8.5488	8.1196	7.0472
19	15.9920	14.7535	13.6593	12.6896	11.8276	11.0591	10.3719	9.7556	9.2014	8.7016	8.2497	7.1280
20	16.6785	15.3238	14.1339	13.0853	12.1581	11.3356	10.6036	9.9501	9.3649	8.8393	8.3658	7.1982
21	17.3514	15.8775	14.5903	13.4622	12.4699	11.5940	10.8181	10.1285	9.5136	8.9633	8.4694	7.2593
22	18.0112	16.4150	15.0292	13.8212	12.7641	11.8355	11.0168	10.2922	9.6487	9.0751	8.5620	7.3125
23	18.6580	16.9369	15.4511	14.1630	13.0416	12.0612	11.2007	10.4424	9.7715	9.1757	8.6446	7.3587
24	19.2922	17.4436	15.8568	14.4886	13.3034	12.2722	11.3711	10.5802	9.8832	9.2664	8.7184	7.3988
25	19.9139	17.9355	16.2470	14.7986	13.5504	12.4693	11.5288	10.7066	9.9847	9.3481	8.7843	7.4338
26	20.5235	18.4131	16.6221	15.0939	13.7834	12.6536	11.6748	10.8226	10.0770	9.4217	8.8431	7.4641
27	21.1210	18.8768	16.9828	15.3752	14.0032	12.8258	11.8100	10.9290	10.1609	9.4881	8.8957	7.4906
28	21.7069	19.3270	17.3296	15.6430	14.2105	12.9867	11.9352	11.0266	10.2372	9.5478	8.9426	7.5135
29	22.2813	19.7641	17.6631	15.8981	14.4062	13.1371	12.0511	11.1161	10.3066	9.6016	8.9844	7.5335
30	22.8444	20.1885	17.9837	16.1411	14.5907	13.2777	12.1584	11.1983	10.3696	9.6501	9.0218	7.5509
31	23.3965	20.6004	18.2920	16.3725	14.7648	13.4090	12.2578	11.2737	10.4269	9.6938	9.0552	7.5660
32	23.9377	21.0004	18.5885	16.5928	14.9291	13.5318	12.3498	11.3428	10.4790	9.7331	9.0850	7.5791
33	24.4683	21.3888	18.8736	16.8027	15.0840	13.6466	12.4350	11.4062	10.5264	9.7686	9.1116	7.5905
34	24.9886	21.7658	19.1476	17.0025	15.2302	13.7538	12.5139	11.4644	10.5694	9.8005	9.1354	7.6005
35	25.4986	22.1318	19.4112	17.1929	15.3681	13.8540	12.5869	11.5178	10.6086	9.8293	9.1566	7.6091
36	25.9986	22.4872	19.6646	17.3742	15.4982	13.9477	12.6546	11.5668	10.6442	9.8552	9.1755	7.6166
37	26.4888	22.8323	19.9083	17.5469	15.6210	14.0352	12.7172	11.6118	10.6765	9.8786	9.1924	7.6231
38	26.9695	23.1672	20.1426	17.7113	15.7368	14.1170	12.7752	11.6530	10.7059	9.8996	9.2075	7.6288
39	27.4406	23.4925	20.3679	17.8679	15.8460	14.1935	12.8289	11.6908	10.7327	9.9186	9.2210	7.6338
40	27.9026	23.8082	20.5845	18.0170	15.9491	14.2649	12.8786	11.7255	10.7570	9.9357	9.2330	7.6380
45	30.0800	25.2543	21.5488	18.6628	16.3832	14.5579	13.0771	11.8605	10.8491	9.9988	9.2764	7.6524
50	32.0521	26.5017	22.3415	19.1687	16.7076	14.7668	13.2122	11.9482	10.9063	10.0362	9.3010	7.6596

4. Future value factors for a single sum of $1 (FVF)

Periods (t)	Interest rate per period (r)											
	2%	3%	4%	5%	6%	7%	8%	9%	10%	11%	12%	15%
1	1.0200	1.0300	1.0400	1.0500	1.0600	1.0700	1.0800	1.0900	1.1000	1.1100	1.1200	1.1500
2	1.0404	1.0609	1.0816	1.1025	1.1236	1.1449	1.1664	1.1881	1.2100	1.2321	1.2544	1.3225
3	1.0612	1.0927	1.1249	1.1576	1.1910	1.2250	1.2597	1.2950	1.3310	1.3676	1.4049	1.5209
4	1.0824	1.1255	1.1699	1.2155	1.2625	1.3108	1.3605	1.4116	1.4641	1.5181	1.5735	1.7490
5	1.1041	1.1593	1.2167	1.2763	1.3382	1.4026	1.4693	1.5386	1.6105	1.6851	1.7623	2.0114
6	1.1262	1.1941	1.2653	1.3401	1.4185	1.5007	1.5869	1.6771	1.7716	1.8704	1.9738	2.3131
7	1.1487	1.2299	1.3159	1.4071	1.5036	1.6058	1.7138	1.8280	1.9487	2.0762	2.2107	2.6600
8	1.1717	1.2668	1.3686	1.4775	1.5938	1.7182	1.8509	1.9926	2.1436	2.3045	2.4760	3.0590
9	1.1951	1.3048	1.4233	1.5513	1.6895	1.8385	1.9990	2.1719	2.3579	2.5580	2.7731	3.5179
10	1.2190	1.3439	1.4802	1.6289	1.7908	1.9672	2.1589	2.3674	2.5937	2.8394	3.1058	4.0456
11	1.2434	1.3842	1.5395	1.7103	1.8983	2.1049	2.3316	2.5804	2.8531	3.1518	3.4785	4.6524
12	1.2682	1.4258	1.6010	1.7959	2.0122	2.2522	2.5182	2.8127	3.1384	3.4985	3.8960	5.3503
13	1.2936	1.4685	1.6651	1.8856	2.1329	2.4098	2.7196	3.0658	3.4523	3.8833	4.3635	6.1528
14	1.3195	1.5126	1.7317	1.9799	2.2609	2.5785	2.9372	3.3417	3.7975	4.3104	4.8871	7.0757
15	1.3459	1.5580	1.8009	2.0789	2.3966	2.7590	3.1722	3.6425	4.1772	4.7846	5.4736	8.1371
16	1.3728	1.6047	1.8730	2.1829	2.5404	2.9522	3.4259	3.9703	4.5950	5.3109	6.1304	9.3576
17	1.4002	1.6528	1.9479	2.2920	2.6928	3.1588	3.7000	4.3276	5.0545	5.8951	6.8660	10.7613
18	1.4282	1.7024	2.0258	2.4066	2.8543	3.3799	3.9960	4.7171	5.5599	6.5436	7.6900	12.3755
19	1.4568	1.7535	2.1068	2.5270	3.0256	3.6165	4.3157	5.1417	6.1159	7.2633	8.6128	14.2318
20	1.4859	1.8061	2.1911	2.6533	3.2071	3.8697	4.6610	5.6044	6.7275	8.0623	9.6463	16.3665
21	1.5157	1.8603	2.2788	2.7860	3.3996	4.1406	5.0338	6.1088	7.4002	8.9492	10.8038	18.8215
22	1.5460	1.9161	2.3699	2.9253	3.6035	4.4304	5.4365	6.6586	8.1403	9.9336	12.1003	21.6447
23	1.5769	1.9736	2.4647	3.0715	3.8197	4.7405	5.8715	7.2579	8.9543	11.0263	13.5523	24.8915
24	1.6084	2.0328	2.5633	3.2251	4.0489	5.0724	6.3412	7.9111	9.8497	12.2392	15.1786	28.6252
25	1.6406	2.0938	2.6658	3.3864	4.2919	5.4274	6.8485	8.6231	10.8347	13.5855	17.0001	32.9190
26	1.6734	2.1566	2.7725	3.5557	4.5494	5.8074	7.3964	9.3992	11.9182	15.0799	19.0401	37.8568
27	1.7069	2.2213	2.8834	3.7335	4.8223	6.2139	7.9881	10.2451	13.1100	16.7386	21.3249	43.5353
28	1.7410	2.2879	2.9987	3.9201	5.1117	6.6488	8.6271	11.1671	14.4210	18.5799	23.8839	50.0656
29	1.7758	2.3566	3.1187	4.1161	5.4184	7.1143	9.3173	12.1722	15.8631	20.6237	26.7499	57.5755
30	1.8114	2.4273	3.2434	4.3219	5.7435	7.6123	10.0627	13.2677	17.4494	22.8923	29.9599	66.2118
31	1.8476	2.5001	3.3731	4.5380	6.0881	8.1451	10.8677	14.4618	19.1943	25.4104	33.5551	76.1435
32	1.8845	2.5751	3.5081	4.7649	6.4534	8.7153	11.7371	15.7633	21.1138	28.2056	37.5817	87.5651
33	1.9222	2.6523	3.6484	5.0032	6.8406	9.3253	12.6760	17.1820	23.2252	31.3082	42.0915	100.6998
34	1.9607	2.7319	3.7943	5.2533	7.2510	9.9781	13.6901	18.7284	25.5477	34.7521	47.1425	115.8048
35	1.9999	2.8139	3.9461	5.5160	7.6861	10.6766	14.7853	20.4140	28.1024	38.5749	52.7996	133.1755
36	2.0399	2.8983	4.1039	5.7918	8.1473	11.4239	15.9682	22.2512	30.9127	42.8181	59.1356	153.1519
37	2.0807	2.9852	4.2681	6.0814	8.6361	12.2236	17.2456	24.2538	34.0039	47.5281	66.2318	176.1246
38	2.1223	3.0748	4.4388	6.3855	9.1543	13.0793	18.6253	26.4367	37.4043	52.7562	74.1797	202.5433
39	2.1647	3.1670	4.6164	6.7048	9.7035	13.9948	20.1153	28.8160	41.1448	58.5593	83.0812	232.9248
40	2.2080	3.2620	4.8010	7.0400	10.2857	14.9745	21.7245	31.4094	45.2593	65.0009	93.0510	267.8635
45	2.4379	3.7816	5.8412	8.9850	13.7646	21.0025	31.9204	48.3273	72.8905	109.5302	163.9876	538.7693
50	2.6916	4.3839	7.1067	11.4674	18.4202	29.4570	46.9016	74.3575	117.3909	184.5648	289.0022	1,083.6574

5. Future value factors for an ordinary annuity of $1 (FVFA)

Periods (t)	Interest rate per period (r)											
	2%	3%	4%	5%	6%	7%	8%	9%	10%	11%	12%	15%
1	1.0000	1.0000	1.0000	1.0000	1.0000	1.0000	1.0000	1.0000	1.0000	1.0000	1.0000	1.0000
2	2.0200	2.0300	2.0400	2.0500	2.0600	2.0700	2.0800	2.0900	2.1000	2.1100	2.1200	2.1500
3	3.0604	3.0909	3.1216	3.1525	3.1836	3.2149	3.2464	3.2781	3.3100	3.3421	3.3744	3.4725
4	4.1216	4.1836	4.2465	4.3101	4.3746	4.4399	4.5061	4.5731	4.6410	4.7097	4.7793	4.9934
5	5.2040	5.3091	5.4163	5.5256	5.6371	5.7507	5.8666	5.9847	6.1051	6.2278	6.3528	6.7424
6	6.3081	6.4684	6.6330	6.8019	6.9753	7.1533	7.3359	7.5233	7.7156	7.9129	8.1152	8.7537
7	7.4343	7.6625	7.8983	8.1420	8.3938	8.6540	8.9228	9.2004	9.4872	9.7833	10.0890	11.0668
8	8.5830	8.8923	9.2142	9.5491	9.8975	10.2598	10.6366	11.0285	11.4359	11.8594	12.2997	13.7268
9	9.7546	10.1591	10.5828	11.0266	11.4913	11.9780	12.4876	13.0210	13.5795	14.1640	14.7757	16.7858
10	10.9497	11.4639	12.0061	12.5779	13.1808	13.8164	14.4866	15.1929	15.9374	16.7220	17.5487	20.3037
11	12.1687	12.8078	13.4864	14.2068	14.9716	15.7836	16.6455	17.5603	18.5312	19.5614	20.6546	24.3493
12	13.4121	14.1920	15.0258	15.9171	16.8699	17.8885	18.9771	20.1407	21.3843	22.7132	24.1331	29.0017
13	14.6803	15.6178	16.6268	17.7130	18.8821	20.1406	21.4953	22.9534	24.5227	26.2116	28.0291	34.3519
14	15.9739	17.0863	18.2919	19.5986	21.0151	22.5505	24.2149	26.0192	27.9750	30.0949	32.3926	40.5047
15	17.2934	18.5989	20.0236	21.5786	23.2760	25.1290	27.1521	29.3609	31.7725	34.4054	37.2797	47.5804
16	18.6393	20.1569	21.8245	23.6575	25.6725	27.8881	30.3243	33.0034	35.9497	39.1899	42.7533	55.7175
17	20.0121	21.7616	23.6975	25.8404	28.2129	30.8402	33.7502	36.9737	40.5447	44.5008	48.8837	65.0751
18	21.4123	23.4144	25.6454	28.1324	30.9057	33.9990	37.4502	41.3013	45.5992	50.3959	55.7497	75.8364
19	22.8406	25.1169	27.6712	30.5390	33.7600	37.3790	41.4463	46.0185	51.1591	56.9395	63.4397	88.2118
20	24.2974	26.8704	29.7781	33.0660	36.7856	40.9955	45.7620	51.1601	57.2750	64.2028	72.0524	102.4436
21	25.7833	28.6765	31.9692	35.7193	39.9927	44.8652	50.4229	56.7645	64.0025	72.2651	81.6987	118.8101
22	27.2990	30.5368	34.2480	38.5052	43.3923	49.0057	55.4568	62.8733	71.4027	81.2143	92.5026	137.6316
23	28.8450	32.4529	36.6179	41.4305	46.9958	53.4361	60.8933	69.5319	79.5430	91.1479	104.6029	159.2764
24	30.4219	34.4265	39.0826	44.5020	50.8156	58.1767	66.7648	76.7898	88.4973	102.1742	118.1552	184.1678
25	32.0303	36.4593	41.6459	47.7271	54.8645	63.2490	73.1059	84.7009	98.3471	114.4133	133.3339	212.7930
26	33.6709	38.5530	44.3117	51.1135	59.1564	68.6765	79.9544	93.3240	109.1818	127.9988	150.3339	245.7120
27	35.3443	40.7096	47.0842	54.6691	63.7058	74.4838	87.3508	102.7231	121.0999	143.0786	169.3740	283.5688
28	37.0512	42.9309	49.9676	58.4026	68.5281	80.6977	95.3388	112.9682	134.2099	159.8173	190.6989	327.1041
29	38.7922	45.2189	52.9663	62.3227	73.6398	87.3465	103.9659	124.1354	148.6309	178.3972	214.5828	377.1697
30	40.5681	47.5754	56.0849	66.4388	79.0582	94.4608	113.2832	136.3075	164.4940	199.0209	241.3327	434.7451
31	42.3794	50.0027	59.3283	70.7608	84.8017	102.0730	123.3459	149.5752	181.9434	221.9132	271.2926	500.9569
32	44.2270	52.5028	62.7015	75.2988	90.8898	110.2182	134.2135	164.0370	201.1378	247.3236	304.8477	577.1005
33	46.1116	55.0778	66.2095	80.0638	97.3432	118.9334	145.9506	179.8003	222.2515	275.5292	342.4294	664.6655
34	48.0338	57.7302	69.8579	85.0670	104.1838	128.2588	158.6267	196.9823	245.4767	306.8374	384.5210	765.3654
35	49.9945	60.4621	73.6522	90.3203	111.4348	138.2369	172.3168	215.7108	271.0244	341.5896	431.6635	881.1702
36	51.9944	63.2759	77.5983	95.8363	119.1209	148.9135	187.1021	236.1247	299.1268	380.1644	484.4631	1,014.3457
37	54.0343	66.1742	81.7022	101.6281	127.2681	160.3374	203.0703	258.3759	330.0395	422.9825	543.5987	1,167.4975
38	56.1149	69.1594	85.9703	107.7095	135.9042	172.5610	220.3159	282.6298	364.0434	470.5106	609.8305	1,343.6222
39	58.2372	72.2342	90.4091	114.0950	145.0585	185.6403	238.9412	309.0665	401.4478	523.2667	684.0102	1,546.1655
40	60.4020	75.4013	95.0255	120.7998	154.7620	199.6351	259.0565	337.8824	442.5926	581.8261	767.0914	1,779.0903
45	71.8927	92.7199	121.0294	159.7002	212.7435	285.7493	386.5056	525.8587	718.9048	986.6386	1,358.2300	3,585.1285
50	84.5794	112.7969	152.6671	209.3480	290.3359	406.5289	573.7702	815.0836	1,163.9085	1,668.7712	2,400.0182	7,217.7163

6. Future value factors for an annuity due of $1 (FVFAD)

Periods (t)	Interest rate per period (r)											
	2%	3%	4%	5%	6%	7%	8%	9%	10%	11%	12%	15%
1	1.0200	1.0300	1.0400	1.0500	1.0600	1.0700	1.0800	1.0900	1.1000	1.1100	1.1200	1.1500
2	2.0604	2.0909	2.1216	2.1525	2.1836	2.2149	2.2464	2.2781	2.3100	2.3421	2.3744	2.4725
3	3.1216	3.1836	3.2465	3.3101	3.3746	3.4399	3.5061	3.5731	3.6410	3.7097	3.7793	3.9934
4	4.2040	4.3091	4.4163	4.5256	4.6371	4.7507	4.8666	4.9847	5.1051	5.2278	5.3528	5.7424
5	5.3081	5.4684	5.6330	5.8019	5.9753	6.1533	6.3359	6.5233	6.7156	6.9129	7.1152	7.7537
6	6.4343	6.6625	6.8983	7.1420	7.3938	7.6540	7.9228	8.2004	8.4872	8.7833	9.0890	10.0668
7	7.5830	7.8923	8.2142	8.5491	8.8975	9.2598	9.6366	10.0285	10.4359	10.8594	11.2997	12.7268
8	8.7546	9.1591	9.5828	10.0266	10.4913	10.9780	11.4876	12.0210	12.5795	13.1640	13.7757	15.7858
9	9.9497	10.4639	11.0061	11.5779	12.1808	12.8164	13.4866	14.1929	14.9374	15.7220	16.5487	19.3037
10	11.1687	11.8078	12.4864	13.2068	13.9716	14.7836	15.6455	16.5603	17.5312	18.5614	19.6546	23.3493
11	12.4121	13.1920	14.0258	14.9171	15.8699	16.8885	17.9771	19.1407	20.3843	21.7132	23.1331	28.0017
12	13.6803	14.6178	15.6268	16.7130	17.8821	19.1406	20.4953	21.9534	23.5227	25.2116	27.0291	33.3519
13	14.9739	16.0863	17.2919	18.5986	20.0151	21.5505	23.2149	25.0192	26.9750	29.0949	31.3926	39.5047
14	16.2934	17.5989	19.0236	20.5786	22.2760	24.1290	26.1521	28.3609	30.7725	33.4054	36.2797	46.5804
15	17.6393	19.1569	20.8245	22.6575	24.6725	26.8881	29.3243	32.0034	34.9497	38.1899	41.7533	54.7175
16	19.0121	20.7616	22.6975	24.8404	27.2129	29.8402	32.7502	35.9737	39.5447	43.5008	47.8837	64.0751
17	20.4123	22.4144	24.6454	27.1324	29.9057	32.9990	36.4502	40.3013	44.5992	49.3959	54.7497	74.8364
18	21.8406	24.1169	26.6712	29.5390	32.7600	36.3790	40.4463	45.0185	50.1591	55.9395	62.4397	87.2118
19	23.2974	25.8704	28.7781	32.0660	35.7856	39.9955	44.7620	50.1601	56.2750	63.2028	71.0524	101.4436
20	24.7833	27.6765	30.9692	34.7193	38.9927	43.8652	49.4229	55.7645	63.0025	71.2651	80.6987	117.8101
21	26.2990	29.5368	33.2480	37.5052	42.3923	48.0057	54.4568	61.8733	70.4027	80.2143	91.5026	136.6316
22	27.8450	31.4529	35.6179	40.4305	45.9958	52.4361	59.8933	68.5319	78.5430	90.1479	103.6029	158.2764
23	29.4219	33.4265	38.0826	43.5020	49.8156	57.1767	65.7648	75.7898	87.4973	101.1742	117.1552	183.1678
24	31.0303	35.4593	40.6459	46.7271	53.8645	62.2490	72.1059	83.7009	97.3471	113.4133	132.3339	211.7930
25	32.6709	37.5530	43.3117	50.1135	58.1564	67.6765	78.9544	92.3240	108.1818	126.9988	149.3339	244.7120
26	34.3443	39.7096	46.0842	53.6691	62.7058	73.4838	86.3508	101.7231	120.0999	142.0786	168.3740	282.5688
27	36.0512	41.9309	48.9676	57.4026	67.5281	79.6977	94.3388	111.9682	133.2099	158.8173	189.6989	326.1041
28	37.7922	44.2189	51.9663	61.3227	72.6398	86.3465	102.9659	123.1354	147.6309	177.3972	213.5828	376.1697
29	39.5681	46.5754	55.0849	65.4388	78.0582	93.4608	112.2832	135.3075	163.4940	198.0209	240.3327	433.7451
30	41.3794	49.0027	58.3283	69.7608	83.8017	101.0730	122.3459	148.5752	180.9434	220.9132	270.2926	499.9569
31	43.2270	51.5028	61.7015	74.2988	89.8898	109.2182	133.2135	163.0370	200.1378	246.3236	303.8477	576.1005
32	45.1116	54.0778	65.2095	79.0638	96.3432	117.9334	144.9506	178.8003	221.2515	274.5292	341.4294	663.6655
33	47.0338	56.7302	68.8579	84.0670	103.1838	127.2588	157.6267	195.9823	244.4767	305.8374	383.5210	764.3654
34	48.9945	59.4621	72.6522	89.3203	110.4348	137.2369	171.3168	214.7108	270.0244	340.5896	430.6635	880.1702
35	50.9944	62.2759	76.5983	94.8363	118.1209	147.9135	186.1021	235.1247	298.1268	379.1644	483.4631	1,013.3457
36	53.0343	65.1742	80.7022	100.6281	126.2681	159.3374	202.0703	257.3759	329.0395	421.9825	542.5987	1,166.4975
37	55.1149	68.1594	84.9703	106.7095	134.9042	171.5610	219.3159	281.6298	363.0434	469.5106	608.8305	1,342.6222
38	57.2372	71.2342	89.4091	113.0950	144.0585	184.6403	237.9412	308.0665	400.4478	522.2667	683.0102	1,545.1655
39	59.4020	74.4013	94.0255	119.7998	153.7620	198.6351	258.0565	336.8824	441.5926	580.8261	766.0914	1,778.0903
40	61.6100	77.6633	98.8265	126.8398	164.0477	213.6096	279.7810	368.2919	486.8518	645.8269	859.1424	2,045.9539
45	73.3306	95.5015	125.8706	167.6852	225.5081	305.7518	417.4261	573.1860	790.7953	1,095.1688	1,521.2176	4,122.8977
50	86.2710	116.1808	158.7738	219.8154	307.7561	434.9860	619.6718	888.4411	1,280.2994	1,852.3360	2,688.0204	8,300.3737

APPENDIX C
Case Solving and Comprehensive Cases

A. INTRODUCTION

If you are like most other business students, you are excited about cases while at the same time intimidated by them. The excitement comes from the realistic context a case provides in which you can apply the skills and knowledge you have learned in the classroom. This realism adds a dimension of difficulty that may be new to you. This difficulty does not arise from the technical nature of the issue—in most instances, cases involve issues that are technically no more demanding than non-case problems—but rather the difficulty results from the complex interplay among issues, facts, alternatives, and decision makers. As a result, case solving is not a linear process (like solving a simple calculation problem).[1]

Given the non-linear, context-specific nature of cases, there can be no universal one-size-fits-all recipe for solving them. However, there are some elements, or ingredients, that are often useful. This appendix lays out a number of these ingredients. Depending on the situation, you will need to use your judgment to use more or less of some ingredients (i.e., to emphasize different elements in different situations) and to omit other ingredients altogether.

B. APPROACHING A CASE

1. Role-playing

Whether explicitly or implicitly, most cases require you to play a role in the scenario rather than act as a passive external observer. To solve a case effectively, you need to take your role seriously. Your role determines the scope of your authority: which decisions can you or can't you make? In some cases, you are an advisor who can only provide suggestions or recommendations, and it is up to the ultimate decision maker to follow or to reject those recommendations. At other times, you are the ultimate decision maker.

The role that you play also determines to what extent different issues are relevant to you. For example, intricate audit issues may be highly relevant to an auditor, but less so to a small business owner. Finally, your role also determines the type of language you need to use (will the reader understand technical terms?) and the form of your communication (should the response be an internal memo or a letter to the client?).

[1.] Some case authors and publications differentiate between a "case" and a "simulation." When there is such a differentiation, a case refers to a real, historically accurate account of facts and circumstances, whereas a simulation refers to an imagined but realistic scenario that mimics real business situations. In this appendix and in the text, a "case" refers to both real case studies and simulated scenarios.

2. Identification of issues

One of the skills required of professional accountants is the ability to identify issues. While some cases clearly lay out issues that you need to address, other cases involve issues that are not readily apparent from a superficial reading of the case. In real life, clients hire professional accountants precisely because the clients do not know all the relevant issues. In some cases, analysis of one issue results in the identification of additional issues that warrant further investigation.

3. Ranking

Related to the identification of issues is the need to rank order them. The rank of an issue affects how much time you devote to addressing the issue and the priority it has in your memo, letter, or report (higher ranking issues should appear earlier in the report). When there are logical or chronological connections between issues, where one issue must be considered before another, the ranking is clear-cut. For example, in a case that involves the recognition and measurement of inventories, the issue of recognition should be addressed before measurement, because recognition is about whether the inventories are recorded on the balance sheet while measurement involves how much should be recorded if the inventories were to be recognized.

When there are no clear logical or chronological connections among issues, ranking should consider two factors: urgency and importance. Your case analysis should address more urgent matters before less urgent ones, and more important matters before less important ones. An issue that is both urgent and important has even more priority. For example, an issue relating to a cash shortage in the short term would be both urgent and important, because not resolving the issue satisfactorily will jeopardize the survival of the enterprise.

Take note that the amount of information relating to an issue is not necessarily indicative of the importance of an issue. Some cases deliberately provide extraneous information that is not relevant to the most urgent or important issue to examine your ability to determine what is actually urgent and important.

4. Analysis (including consideration of alternatives)

Analysis involves applying the facts of the situation and relevant accounting standards. For example, in a particular situation, is it appropriate to record a transaction using a particular accounting policy; or which of several possible accounting policies is more appropriate under the circumstances? Analysis implicitly includes the consideration of alternative courses of action, including the status quo.

The extent of the analysis (i.e., how much time you devote to the issue) depends on the ranking of the issue you made earlier. An issue with high priority will generally require extensive analysis, while some issues with low priority can be dealt with in as little as a sentence or two.

5. Evaluation/conclusion/recommendation

After analyzing the potential alternatives, you must evaluate the overall attractiveness of those alternatives in order to draw a conclusion regarding which is the best alternative under the circumstances. If your role is to provide advice to the decision maker, then these conclusions would be in the form of recommendations.

While most cases require you to draw conclusions, be careful not to jump to conclusions. Conclusions need to logically follow and flow from the analysis with full consideration of the relevant facts. Avoid rushing to a conclusion and then selectively using facts from the case to support that conclusion.

6. Action plan

If the case involves a large number of issues, it would be helpful to lay out an action plan that outlines the sequence in which those issues would be resolved. An action plan explains who does what and when. It chronologically lists the actions required, and it is helpful to identify the person or people responsible for each particular task. Depending on the case, the timing may need to be precise (with specific dates) or general (short, medium, and long term).

C. SUMMARY

The above discussion lays out the ingredients that are useful for solving a variety of styles of cases. You will need to use your judgment to put more or less emphasis on different components. With practice, you will be able to master the art of case solving.

D. COMPREHENSIVE CASES

Your friend is considering investing in Cineplex Inc., a publicly traded company listed on the Toronto Stock Exchange. She believes the failure of DVD retailers has drastically improved prospects for Cineplex. She seeks your advice on accounting matters, and provides you with the following information she obtained on the Internet.

Cineplex is the largest cinema company in Canada, operating over 1,600 screens in theatres across 10 provinces. August is generally its peak season, followed by December and January. The majority of the $1 billion of revenues comes from box office ticket sales, followed by approximately 30% derived from concessions such as soft drinks and popcorn.[2] In 2013, over 73 million patrons watched films at Cineplex theatres, spending an average of $9.15 on a ticket and $4.82 on concessions.[3] Both activities generated healthy profit margins. Film rental costs, which represent the company's largest expenditure, are often difficult to assess. In some cases, the final film cost depends on the ultimate duration of the film's play and, until this is known, management uses its best estimate of the final settlement to match costs with revenues in each reporting period.

Goodwill represents the largest asset on the company's balance sheet at a value of $600 million, and reflects amounts paid on the recent acquisition of two subsidiaries. The property, plant, and equipment balance is the next largest item, reported at a value of $500 million. This amount does not reflect the full economic value of the land and buildings deployed to earn the revenues of a billion dollars. Many of the cinemas and properties are leased, and are therefore not on Cineplex's balance sheet. This may be a concern for Cineplex, since there is a proposal to change the current accounting standards such that most leases would be treated as if Cineplex owned the underlying buildings and property. When setting up these leases as assets, accounting rules assume they were acquired with debt, which creates both an asset and a corresponding liability. While Cineplex management would be pleased with the asset side of this transaction, the additional liability could create issues.

A large and growing item on Cineplex's balance sheet is deferred revenue from gift cards. Unlike typical transactions where payment is received after the good or service is provided, gift cards generate the opposite pattern of cash flows. The bulk of gift cards are sold around Christmas time; therefore, large amounts are typically outstanding when Cineplex closes its books for its December 31 year-end.

Your friend has uncovered additional information from Cineplex's annual general meeting. It appears the CEO's compensation package includes a base salary, share ownership, and a bonus based on multiple performance targets such as:[4]

- Concession revenue target of $3.74 per patron
- Operating expense target of $3.86 per patron
- Adjusted net income of $204.20 million
- Other income target of $144.25 million

Your friend is not sure why these targets exist and why they are made so specific.

Required:
Provide your friend with your view on the qualitative characteristics of the financial statement items. Discuss the proposed change in accounting rules for leases from the perspective of users. Provide some thoughts on the executive compensation package.

CASE 1
Cineplex Inc.
Chapters 1–3
(25 minutes)

[2.] http://irfiles.cineplex.com/investors/investorkit/2013AnnualReport.pdf

[3.] http://irfiles.cineplex.com/investors/presentations/2014/2014Q1InvestorsFINAL.pdf

[4.] http://irfiles.cineplex.com/reportsandfilings/managementinformationcircular/CineplexMIC_FINAL.pdf

CASE 2
Canada Post
Chapters 1–4

(30 minutes)

Canada Post is a Crown corporation with the dual mandate of providing a public service and maximizing profits. With 50,000 employees, Canada Post delivers over 9 billion letters and parcels annually. Approximately half of the $6 billion in revenues is from mail delivered to Canadian addresses, with this service declining rapidly in favour of digital alternatives.[5] Revenues come from the sale of stamps or postage meters. Stamps are sold individually or in booklets, coils, or sheets of up to 100 stamps. A small portion is purchased for stamp collecting or philatelic purpose. A postage meter is a machine that imprints an amount of postage in ink, which functions as a stamp. In the past, postage meters had to be taken to a post office to refill the postage balance, but now this is done remotely through telephone connections or the Internet.

As the new audit senior for this client, you are preparing this year's annual audit plan. While their financial statements are prepared in accordance with IFRS, the operations of Canada Post present a few unique challenges. First, Canada Post is required to provide national postal service for one set price, which means incurring losses on mail delivered to small, rural communities across the country. Second, revenue recognition on stamps is complex. Canada Post receives cash upfront when they sell stamps or refill postage meters, but cannot recognize the revenue until recognition criteria are met. Their legal commitment on postal service is fully discharged once the mail is delivered and the 90-day claim period for damaged items has expired. The stamp income number is significant. Other important items on the financial statements are a rising cost for pension plan obligations and increasingly profitable courier services provided by the Purolator division. As well, the company has recognized gains on the disposal of property, such as the recent sale of their Vancouver mail processing plant.

As you sift through last year's files, you recall having read a news article about a class-action lawsuit, which Canada Post seems likely to lose. They are charged with maintaining inappropriate practices with respect to calculating parcel volume, and dealing with weight calculation discrepancies. The first issue is that volume calculations are based on measuring three sides of a parcel, which overstates the cost of mailing irregular-shaped items such as triangular boxes. The second issue relates to Canada Post's rule of correcting under-calculated weights of parcels, but not over-calculated weights.

Required:

a. Discuss the issues surrounding revenue recognition for Canada Post.
b. Consider whether financial statement users are served by IFRS.
c. How might the lawsuit be reported in the financial statements?

CASE 3
Electronic Arts Inc.
Chapters 1–7

(30 minutes)

Electronic Arts Inc. (EA) is a name that is familiar to most gamers. The company develops and distributes software products such as Battlefield, Mass Effect, Need for Speed, Dragon Age, The Sims, FIFA, and Madden NFL,[6] and provides services that require their hosting support for online games and massively multi-player online (MMO) play. The cornerstones of EA's business strategy are to develop products and services across multiple platforms (such as PlayStation 3 and 4, Xbox, PCs, cellphones, and tablets), while narrowing their product portfolio to reduce production costs.

Some of EA's $4 billion in annual sales comprise both a product element (the software game, delivered physically via a disk or digitally via the Internet) and a service element (online service such as matchmaking players on the Internet). EA reports revenues for product separately from services, where the latter represent about 40% of revenues. Service revenues are growing as a proportion of sales and have a higher profit margin. The largest expenditure on their income statement is research and development, representing about half of the $2 billion in operating expenses.

One of EA's largest assets is cash and cash equivalents, and one of their largest liabilities is deferred revenue from online games, both reported at over $1 billion. The deferred revenue pertains to payments received for online-enabled games that EA

---

[5] http://www.canadapost.ca/cpo/mc/assets/pdf/aboutus/annualreport/2013_ar_financial_en.pdf

[6] http://files.shareholder.com/downloads/ERTS/3699633685x0x762357/F71D53F7-F900-49E2-86D8-093EADA6009B/Electronic_Arts_10K_Proxy_FY14.PDF

expects will need updates. Another smaller, but significant, asset is capitalized software development costs. Notes to the financial statements explain that when a project reaches the development stage and EA can demonstrate its feasibility and investment recoverability, they begin capitalizing costs as an asset rather than expensing them, so as to later match these costs with future revenues from the project. Inventories represent a relatively small portion of assets, and are mostly finished goods. They are measured as the cost of labour, materials, and royalties payments, less any write-down for obsolescence.

EA owns equities as strategic investments. The company has more than 40 subsidiaries, which EA either founded or acquired by purchasing 100% of their outstanding shares.

You are engaged as the consultant for a company poised to launch a competing product for Mass Effect. This company's representatives are aware the auditor did not find material misstatements in the financial statements, but would like to know whether they can take the reported numbers at face value when analyzing EA's performance.

Required:

Prepare a report for your consulting client. Discuss recognition and measurement issues relating to the items mentioned above. Provide some relevant information on reporting for investments.

Canadian Tire Corporation 2016 Consolidated Financial Statements

Index to the Consolidated Financial Statements and Notes

Management's Responsibility for Financial Statements

The Management of Canadian Tire Corporation, Limited (the "Company") is responsible for the integrity and reliability of the accompanying consolidated financial statements. These consolidated financial statements have been prepared by Management in accordance with International Financial Reporting Standards and include amounts based on judgements and estimates. All financial information in our Management's Discussion and Analysis is consistent with these consolidated financial statements.

Management is responsible for establishing and maintaining adequate systems of internal control over financial reporting. These systems are designed to provide reasonable assurance that the financial records are reliable and form a proper basis for the timely and accurate preparation of financial statements. Management has assessed the effectiveness of the Company's internal control over financial reporting based on the framework in Internal Control – Integrated Framework (2013) issued by the Committee of Sponsoring Organizations of the Treadway Commission (COSO) and concluded that the Company's internal controls over financial reporting were effective as at the date of these consolidated financial statements.

The Board of Directors oversees Management's responsibilities for the consolidated financial statements primarily through the activities of its Audit Committee, which is comprised solely of directors who are neither officers nor employees of the Company. This Committee meets with Management and the Company's independent auditors, Deloitte LLP, to review the consolidated financial statements and recommend approval by the Board of Directors. The Audit Committee is responsible for making recommendations to the Board of Directors with respect to the appointment of and, subject to the approval of the shareholders authorizing the Board of Directors to do so, approving the remuneration and terms of engagement of the Company's auditors. The Audit Committee also meets with the auditors, without the presence of Management, to discuss the results of their audit.

The consolidated financial statements have been audited by Deloitte LLP, in accordance with Canadian generally accepted auditing standards. Their report is presented below.

Stephen G. Wetmore
President and Chief Executive Officer

Dean McCann
Executive Vice-President and
Chief Financial Officer

February 15, 2017

Independent Auditor's Report

To the Shareholders of Canadian Tire Corporation, Limited

We have audited the accompanying consolidated financial statements of Canadian Tire Corporation, Limited, which comprise the consolidated balance sheets as at December 31, 2016 and January 2, 2016, and the consolidated statements of income, consolidated statements of comprehensive income, consolidated statements of cash flows and consolidated statements of changes in equity for the years ended December 31, 2016 and January 2, 2016, and a summary of significant accounting policies and other explanatory information.

Management's Responsibility for the Consolidated Financial Statements

Management is responsible for the preparation and fair presentation of these consolidated financial statements in accordance with International Financial Reporting Standards, and for such internal control as management determines is necessary to enable the preparation of consolidated financial statements that are free from material misstatement, whether due to fraud or error.

Auditor's Responsibility

Our responsibility is to express an opinion on these consolidated financial statements based on our audits. We conducted our audits in accordance with Canadian generally accepted auditing standards. Those standards require that we comply with ethical requirements and plan and perform the audit to obtain reasonable assurance about whether the consolidated financial statements are free from material misstatement.

An audit involves performing procedures to obtain audit evidence about the amounts and disclosures in the consolidated financial statements. The procedures selected depend on the auditor's judgment, including the assessment of the risks of material misstatement of the consolidated financial statements, whether due to fraud or error. In making those risk assessments, the auditor considers internal control relevant to the entity's preparation and fair presentation of the consolidated financial statements in order to design audit procedures that are appropriate in the circumstances, but not for the purpose of expressing an opinion on the effectiveness of the entity's internal control. An audit also includes evaluating the appropriateness of accounting policies used and the reasonableness of accounting estimates made by management, as well as evaluating the overall presentation of the consolidated financial statements.

We believe that the audit evidence we have obtained in our audits is sufficient and appropriate to provide a basis for our audit opinion.

Opinion

In our opinion, the consolidated financial statements present fairly, in all material respects, the financial position of Canadian Tire Corporation, Limited as at December 31, 2016 and January 2, 2016, and its financial performance and its cash flows for the years then ended in accordance with International Financial Reporting Standards.

Deloitte LLP

Chartered Professional Accountants
Licensed Public Accountants

February 15, 2017
Toronto, Ontario

Consolidated Balance Sheets

As at (C$ in millions)	December 31, 2016	January 2, 2016
ASSETS		
Cash and cash equivalents (Note 7)	$ 829.7	$ 900.6
Short-term investments	117.2	96.1
Trade and other receivables (Note 8)	690.8	915.0
Loans receivable (Note 9)	5,138.4	4,875.5
Merchandise inventories	1,710.7	1,764.5
Income taxes recoverable	42.5	42.2
Prepaid expenses and deposits	103.8	96.1
Assets classified as held for sale	4.6	2.3
Total current assets	8,637.7	8,692.3
Long-term receivables and other assets (Note 10)	763.7	731.2
Long-term investments	175.2	153.4
Goodwill and intangible assets (Note 11)	1,280.3	1,246.8
Investment property (Note 12)	266.4	137.8
Property and equipment (Note 13)	4,097.2	3,978.2
Deferred income taxes (Note 15)	82.3	48.1
Total assets	$ 15,302.8	$ 14,987.8
LIABILITIES		
Bank indebtedness (Note 7)	$ 5.9	$ —
Deposits (Note 16)	950.7	880.7
Trade and other payables (Note 17)	1,856.9	1,957.1
Provisions (Note 18)	253.2	216.1
Short-term borrowings (Note 20)	199.4	88.6
Loans payable (Note 21)	700.3	655.5
Income taxes payable	61.1	61.5
Current portion of long-term debt (Note 22)	653.4	24.3
Total current liabilities	4,680.9	3,883.8
Long-term provisions (Note 18)	45.9	45.7
Long-term debt (Note 22)	2,667.1	2,971.4
Long-term deposits (Note 16)	1,230.8	1,372.2
Deferred income taxes (Note 15)	104.2	111.1
Other long-term liabilities (Note 23)	836.6	813.9
Total liabilities	9,565.5	9,198.1
EQUITY		
Share capital (Note 25)	648.1	671.2
Contributed surplus	2.9	2.9
Accumulated other comprehensive income	36.7	148.1
Retained earnings	4,250.9	4,172.0
Equity attributable to shareholders of Canadian Tire Corporation	4,938.6	4,994.2
Non-controlling interests (Note 14)	798.7	795.5
Total equity	5,737.3	5,789.7
Total liabilities and equity	$ 15,302.8	$ 14,987.8

The related notes form an integral part of these consolidated financial statements.

Maureen J. Sabia
Director

Diana L. Chant
Director

Consolidated Statements of Income

For the years ended (C$ in millions, except per share amounts)	December 31, 2016		January 2, 2016
Revenue (Note 27)	$	**12,681.0**	$ 12,279.6
Cost of producing revenue (Note 28)		**8,288.5**	8,144.3
Gross margin		**4,392.5**	4,135.3
Other (income)		**(4.3)**	(54.9)
Selling, general and administrative expenses (Note 29)		**3,291.9**	3,096.1
Net finance costs (Note 30)		**93.9**	92.8
Income before income taxes		**1,011.0**	1,001.3
Income taxes (Note 15)		**263.5**	265.4
Net income	$	**747.5**	$ 735.9
Net income attributable to:			
Shareholders of Canadian Tire Corporation	$	**669.1**	$ 659.4
Non-controlling interests (Note 14)		**78.4**	76.5
	$	**747.5**	$ 735.9
Basic EPS	$	**9.25**	$ 8.66
Diluted EPS	$	**9.22**	$ 8.61
Weighted average number of Common and Class A Non-Voting Shares outstanding:			
Basic		**72,360,303**	76,151,321
Diluted		**72,555,732**	76,581,602

The related notes form an integral part of these consolidated financial statements.

Consolidated Statements of Comprehensive Income

For the years ended (C$ in millions)	December 31, 2016	January 2, 2016
Net income	$ 747.5	$ 735.9
Other comprehensive (loss) income, net of taxes		
Items that may be reclassified subsequently to net income:		
Cash flow hedges and available-for-sale financial assets:		
(Losses) gains	(40.5)	275.1
Reclassification of gains to non-financial assets	(67.9)	(207.4)
Reclassification of gains to income	(1.7)	(3.0)
Item that will not be reclassified subsequently to net income:		
Actuarial (losses) gains	(3.0)	0.8
Other comprehensive (loss) income	(113.1)	65.5
Other comprehensive (loss) income attributable to:		
Shareholders of Canadian Tire Corporation	$ (114.3)	$ 68.0
Non-controlling interests	1.2	(2.5)
	$ (113.1)	$ 65.5
Comprehensive income	$ 634.4	$ 801.4
Comprehensive income attributable to:		
Shareholders of Canadian Tire Corporation	$ 554.8	$ 727.4
Non-controlling interests	79.6	74.0
	$ 634.4	$ 801.4

The related notes form an integral part of these consolidated financial statements.

Consolidated Statements of Cash Flows

For the years ended (C$ in millions)	December 31, 2016	January 2, 2016
Cash (used for) generated from:		
Operating activities		
Net income	$ 747.5	$ 735.9
Adjustments for:		
Depreciation of property and equipment and investment property (Notes 28 and 29)	330.8	312.8
Income tax expense	263.5	265.4
Net finance costs (Note 30)	93.9	92.8
Amortization of intangible assets (Note 29)	126.1	111.9
Changes in fair value of derivative instruments	(15.8)	6.9
(Gain) on disposal of property and equipment, investment property, assets held for sale, intangible assets, and lease terminations	(14.9)	(43.9)
Interest paid	(114.0)	(101.4)
Interest received	6.5	8.4
Income taxes paid	(262.8)	(284.0)
Other	5.6	14.6
Total adjustments, except as noted below	1,166.4	1,119.4
Change in operating working capital and other (Note 31)	126.1	(115.3)
Change in loans receivable	(306.1)	(25.2)
Cash generated from operating activities	986.4	978.9
Investing activities		
Additions to property and equipment and investment property	(617.3)	(515.9)
Additions to intangible assets	(163.5)	(94.7)
Total additions	(780.8)	(610.6)
Acquisition of short-term investments	(422.3)	(177.4)
Proceeds from the maturity and disposition of short-term investments	441.4	426.6
Acquisition of long-term investments	(61.4)	(35.0)
Proceeds on disposition of property and equipment, investment property, and assets held for sale	32.8	101.5
Other	7.5	(4.1)
Cash (used for) investing activities	(782.8)	(299.0)
Financing activities		
Dividends paid	(157.5)	(152.2)
Distributions paid to non-controlling interests	(76.4)	(53.8)
Total dividends and distributions paid	(233.9)	(206.0)
Net issuance (repayment) of short-term borrowings	110.7	(111.2)
Issuance of loans payable	288.3	270.1
Repayment of loans payable	(243.5)	(219.0)
Issuance of long-term debt (Note 22)	350.0	856.1
Repayment of long-term debt and finance lease liabilities (Note 22)	(24.5)	(588.5)
Payment of transaction costs related to long-term debt	(3.2)	(6.5)
Repurchase of share capital (Note 25)	(449.4)	(434.6)
Change in deposits	(74.9)	12.5
Cash (used for) financing activities	(280.4)	(427.1)
Cash (used) generated in the period	(76.8)	252.8
Cash and cash equivalents, net of bank indebtedness, beginning of period	900.6	647.8
Cash and cash equivalents, net of bank indebtedness, end of period (Note 7)	$ 823.8	$ 900.6

The related notes form an integral part of these consolidated financial statements.

Consolidated Statements of Changes in Equity

(C$ in millions)	Share capital	Contributed surplus	Total accumulated other comprehensive income	Retained earnings	Equity attributable to shareholders of Canadian Tire Corporation	Equity attributable to non-controlling interests	Total equity
Balance at January 2, 2016	$ 671.2	$ 2.9	$ 148.1	$ 4,172.0	$ 4,994.2	$ 795.5	$ 5,789.7
Net income	–	–	–	669.1	669.1	78.4	747.5
Other comprehensive (loss) income	–	–	(111.4)	(2.9)	(114.3)	1.2	(113.1)
Total comprehensive (loss) income	–	–	(111.4)	666.2	554.8	79.6	634.4
Contributions and distributions to shareholders of Canadian Tire Corporation							
Issuance of Class A Non-Voting Shares (Note 25)	9.3	–	–	–	9.3	–	9.3
Repurchase of Class A Non-Voting Shares (Note 25)	(449.4)	–	–	–	(449.4)	–	(449.4)
Excess of purchase price over average cost (Note 25)	417.0	–	–	(417.0)	–	–	–
Dividends	–	–	–	(170.3)	(170.3)	–	(170.3)
Contributions and distributions to non-controlling interests							
Issuance of trust units to non-controlling interests, net of transaction costs	–	–	–	–	–	2.0	2.0
Distributions and dividends to non-controlling interests	–	–	–	–	–	(78.4)	(78.4)
Total contributions and distributions	(23.1)	–	–	(587.3)	(610.4)	(76.4)	(686.8)
Balance at December 31, 2016	$ 648.1	$ 2.9	$ 36.7	$ 4,250.9	$ 4,938.6	$ 798.7	$ 5,737.3

(C$ in millions)	Share capital	Contributed surplus	Total accumulated other comprehensive income	Retained earnings	Equity attributable to shareholders of Canadian Tire Corporation	Equity attributable to non-controlling interests	Total equity
Balance at January 3, 2015	$ 695.5	$ 2.9	$ 82.0	$ 4,075.1	$ 4,855.5	$ 775.3	$ 5,630.8
Net income	–	–	–	659.4	659.4	76.5	735.9
Other comprehensive income (loss)	–	–	66.1	1.9	68.0	(2.5)	65.5
Total comprehensive income	–	–	66.1	661.3	727.4	74.0	801.4
Contributions and distributions to shareholders of Canadian Tire Corporation							
Issuance of Class A Non-Voting Shares (Note 25)	8.3	–	–	–	8.3	–	8.3
Repurchase of Class A Non-Voting Shares (Note 25)	(434.6)	–	–	–	(434.6)	–	(434.6)
Excess of purchase price over average cost (Note 25)	402.0	–	–	(402.0)	–	–	–
Dividends	–	–	–	(162.4)	(162.4)	–	(162.4)
Contributions and distributions to non-controlling interests							
Issuance of trust units to non-controlling interests, net of transaction costs	–	–	–	–	–	1.8	1.8
Distributions and dividends to non-controlling interests	–	–	–	–	–	(55.6)	(55.6)
Total contributions and distributions	(24.3)	–	–	(564.4)	(588.7)	(53.8)	(642.5)
Balance at January 2, 2016	$ 671.2	$ 2.9	$ 148.1	$ 4,172.0	$ 4,994.2	$ 795.5	$ 5,789.7

The related notes form an integral part of these consolidated financial statements.

1. The Company and its operations

Canadian Tire Corporation, Limited is a Canadian public company primarily domiciled in Canada. Its registered office is located at 2180 Yonge Street, Toronto, Ontario, M4P 2V8, Canada. It is listed on the Toronto Stock Exchange (TSX – CTC, CTC.A). Canadian Tire Corporation, Limited and entities it controls are together referred to in these consolidated financial statements as the "Company" or "Canadian Tire Corporation". Refer to Note 14 for the Company's major subsidiaries.

The Company comprises three main business operations, which offer a range of retail goods and services, including general merchandise, apparel, sporting goods, petroleum, financial services including a bank, and real estate operations. Details of its three reportable operating segments are provided in Note 6.

2. Basis of preparation

Fiscal year

The fiscal year of the Company consists of a 52 or 53-week period ending on the Saturday closest to December 31. The fiscal years for the consolidated financial statements and notes presented for 2016 and 2015 are the 52-week periods ended December 31, 2016 and January 2, 2016, respectively.

Statement of compliance

These consolidated financial statements have been prepared in accordance with International Financial Reporting Standards ("IFRS") using the accounting policies described herein.

These consolidated financial statements were authorized for issuance by the Company's Board of Directors on February 15, 2017.

Basis of presentation

These consolidated financial statements have been prepared on the historical cost basis, except for the following items, which are measured at fair value:
- financial instruments at fair value through profit or loss ("FVTPL");
- derivative financial instruments;
- available-for-sale financial assets;
- liabilities for share-based payment plans; and
- initial recognition of assets acquired and liabilities assumed in a business combination.

In addition, the post-employment defined benefit obligation is recorded at its discounted present value.

Functional and presentation currency

These consolidated financial statements are presented in Canadian dollars ("C$"), the Company's functional currency.

Judgments and estimates

The preparation of these consolidated financial statements in accordance with IFRS requires Management to make judgments and estimates that affect:
- the application of accounting policies;
- the reported amounts of assets and liabilities;
- disclosures of contingent assets and liabilities; and
- the reported amounts of revenue and expenses during the reporting periods.

Actual results may differ from estimates made in these consolidated financial statements.

Judgments are made in the selection and assessment of the Company's accounting policies. Estimates are used mainly in determining the measurement of recognized transactions and balances. Estimates are based on historical experience and other factors, including expectations of future events believed to be reasonable under the circumstances. Judgments and estimates are often interrelated. The Company's judgments and estimates are continually re-evaluated to ensure they remain appropriate. Revisions to accounting estimates are recognized in the period in which the estimates are revised and in future periods affected.

Following are the accounting policies that are subject to judgments and estimates that the Company believes could have the most significant impact on the amounts recognized in these consolidated financial statements.

Impairment of assets

Judgment – The Company uses judgment in determining the grouping of assets to identify its Cash Generating Units ("CGUs") for purposes of testing for impairment of property and equipment and goodwill and intangible assets. The Company has determined that its Retail CGUs comprise individual stores or groups of stores within a geographic market. In testing for impairment, goodwill acquired in a business combination is allocated to the CGUs that are expected to benefit from the synergies of the business combination. In testing for impairment of intangibles with indefinite lives, these assets are allocated to the CGUs to which they relate. Furthermore, on a quarterly basis, judgment has been used in determining whether there has been an indication of impairment, which would require the completion of a quarterly impairment test, in addition to the annual requirement.

Estimation – The Company's estimate of a CGU's or group of CGUs' recoverable amount based on value in use ("VIU") involves estimating future cash flows before taxes. Future cash flows are estimated based on multi-year extrapolation of the most recent historical actual results or budgets and a terminal value calculated by discounting the final year in perpetuity. The growth rate applied to the terminal value is based on the Bank of Canada's target inflation rate or Management's estimate of the growth rate specific to the individual item being tested. The future cash flow estimates are then discounted to their present value using an appropriate pre-tax discount rate that incorporates a risk premium specific to each business. The Company's determination of a CGU's or group of CGUs' recoverable amount based on fair value less cost to sell uses factors such as market rental rates for comparable assets.

Fair value measurement of redeemable financial instrument

Judgment – The Company uses judgment in determining the fair value measurement of the redeemable financial instrument issued in conjunction with the sale of a 20 percent equity interest in the Company's Financial Services business. In calculating the fair value, judgment is used when determining the discount and growth rates applied to the forecast earnings in the discounted cash flow valuation. Refer to Note 32 for further information regarding this financial instrument.

Estimation – The inputs to determine the fair value are taken from observable markets where possible, but where they are unavailable, assumptions are required in establishing fair value. The fair value of the redeemable financial instrument is determined based on the Company's best estimate of forecast normalized earnings attributable to the Financial Services business, adjusted for any undistributed earnings.

Merchandise inventories

Estimation – Merchandise inventories are carried at the lower of cost and net realizable value. The estimation of net realizable value is based on the most reliable evidence available of the amount the merchandise inventories are expected to realize. Additionally, estimation is required for inventory provisions due to shrinkage.

Income and other taxes

Judgment – In calculating current and deferred income and other taxes, the Company uses judgment when interpreting the tax rules in jurisdictions where the Company operates. The Company also uses judgment in classifying transactions and assessing probable outcomes of claimed deductions, which considers expectations of future operating results, the timing and reversal of temporary differences, and possible audits of income tax and other tax filings by tax authorities.

Consolidation

Judgment – The Company uses judgment in determining the entities that it controls and accordingly consolidates. An entity is controlled when the Company has power over an entity, exposure or rights to variable returns from its involvement with the entity, and is able to use its power over the entity to affect its return from the entity. The Company has power over an entity when it has existing rights that give it the current ability to direct the relevant activities, which are the activities that significantly affect the investee's returns. Since power comes from rights, power can result from contractual arrangements. However, certain contractual arrangements contain rights that are designed to protect the Company's interest, without giving it power over the entity.

Loans receivable

Estimation – The Company's estimate of allowances on credit card loans receivable is based on a roll-rate methodology that employs analysis of historical data and experience of delinquency and default, to estimate the amount of loans that will eventually be written off as a result of events occurring before the reporting date, with certain adjustments for other relevant circumstances influencing the recoverability of these loans receivable. Default rates, loss rates, and the expected timing of future recoveries are regularly benchmarked against actual outcomes to ensure that they remain appropriate. Future customer behaviour may be affected by a number of factors, including changes in interest and unemployment rates and program design changes.

Post-employment benefits

Estimation – The accounting for the Company's post-employment benefit plan requires the use of assumptions. The accrued benefit liability is calculated using actuarial determined data and the Company's best estimates of future salary escalations, retirement ages of employees, employee turnover, mortality rates, market discount rates, and expected health and dental care costs.

Other

Other estimates include determining the useful lives of property and equipment, investment property, and intangible assets for the purposes of depreciation and amortization; in accounting for and measuring items such as deferred revenue, customer loyalty and other provisions, and purchase price adjustments on business combinations; and in measuring certain fair values, including those related to the valuation of business combinations, share-based payments, and financial instruments.

Standards, amendments, and interpretations issued and adopted

Disclosure initiative (IAS 1)

In December 2014, the International Accounting Standard Board ("IASB") issued *Disclosure Initiative Amendments to IAS 1* as part of the IASB's Disclosure Initiative. These amendments encourage entities to apply professional judgment regarding disclosure and presentation in their financial statements.

NOTES TO THE CONSOLIDATED FINANCIAL STATEMENTS

These amendments were effective for annual periods beginning on or after January 1, 2016 and were applied prospectively. The implementation of these amendments did not have a significant impact on the Company other than immaterial amendments to current and prior-year note disclosure.

Standards, amendments, and interpretations issued but not yet adopted

The following new standards, amendments, and interpretations have been issued and are expected to impact the Company, but are not effective for the fiscal year ending December 31, 2016 and, accordingly, have not been applied in preparing the consolidated financial statements.

Financial instruments

In July 2014, the IASB issued the final version of IFRS 9 – *Financial Instruments* ("IFRS 9"), which brings together the classification and measurement, impairment, and hedge-accounting phases of the IASB's project to replace IAS 39 – *Financial Instruments: Recognition and Measurement* ("IAS 39").

Classification and measurement – Financial assets are classified and measured based on the business model under which they are managed and the contractual cash flow characteristics of the financial assets. Financial liabilities are classified in a similar manner as under IAS 39, except that financial liabilities measured at fair value will have fair value changes resulting from changes in the entity's own credit risk recognized in Other Comprehensive Income ("OCI") instead of Net Income, unless this would create an accounting mismatch.

Impairment – The measurement of impairment of financial assets is based on an expected credit loss model. It is no longer necessary for a triggering event to have occurred before credit losses are recognized. IFRS 9 also includes new disclosure requirements about expected credit losses and credit risk.

Hedge accounting – The new general hedge accounting model more closely aligns hedge accounting with risk management activities undertaken by entities when hedging their financial and non-financial risk exposures. It will provide more opportunities to apply hedge accounting to reflect actual risk management activities.

IFRS 9 will be applied retrospectively for annual periods beginning on or after January 1, 2018. The impairment requirements of IFRS 9 are expected to have an impact on the Company, particularly with respect to the estimate of allowances on credit card loans receivable. In order to meet the impairment requirements of IFRS 9, a dedicated project team has been established with joint leadership from finance and credit risk. The Company is assessing the potential financial and disclosure impact of this standard.

Revenue from contracts with customers

In May 2014, the IASB issued IFRS 15 – *Revenue from Contracts with Customers* ("IFRS 15"), which replaces IAS 11 – *Construction Contracts*, IAS 18 – *Revenue*, and International Financial Reporting Interpretations Committee 13 – *Customer Loyalty Programmes* ("IFRIC 13"), as well as various other interpretations regarding revenue. IFRS 15 outlines a single comprehensive model for entities to use in accounting for revenue arising from contracts with customers; except for contracts that are within the scope of the standards on leases, insurance contracts, and financial instruments. IFRS 15 also contains enhanced disclosure requirements. IFRS 15 will be applied retrospectively for annual periods beginning on or after January 1, 2018. The Company is assessing the potential impact of this standard.

In April 2016, the IASB published clarifications to IFRS 15 which address three topics (identifying performance obligations, principal versus agent considerations, and licensing) and provide some transition relief for modified contracts and completed contracts. The amendments are effective for annual periods beginning on or after January 1, 2018. Earlier adoption is permitted. The Company is assessing the potential impact of these amendments.

Disclosure initiative (IAS 7)

In January 2016, the IASB issued Disclosure Initiative Amendments to IAS 7 – *Statement of Cash Flows* also as part of the IASB's Disclosure Initiative. These amendments require entities to provide additional disclosures that will enable financial statement users to evaluate changes in liabilities arising from financing activities, including changes from cash flows and non-cash changes.

These amendments are effective for annual periods beginning on or after January 1, 2017. The implementation of these amendments is not expected to have a significant impact on the Company.

Leases

In January 2016, the IASB issued IFRS 16 – *Leases* ("IFRS 16"), which replaced IAS 17 – *Leases* ("IAS 17") and related interpretations. IFRS 16 provides a single lessee accounting model, requiring the recognition of assets and liabilities for all leases, unless the lease term is 12-months or less or the underlying asset has a low value. IFRS 16 substantially carries forward the lessor accounting in IAS 17 with the distinction between operating leases and finance leases being retained.

IFRS 16 is effective for annual periods beginning on or after January 1, 2019. Early adoption is permitted if IFRS 15 has also been applied. The Company is assessing the potential impact of this standard.

Income taxes

In January 2016, the IASB amended IAS 12 – *Income Taxes* by issuing *Recognition of Deferred Tax Assets for Unrealized Losses*. These amendments address the accounting for deferred tax assets for unrealized losses on debt instruments measured at fair value.

These amendments are effective for annual periods beginning on or after January 1, 2017. The implementation of these amendments is not expected to have a significant impact on the Company.

Share-based payment

In June 2016, the IASB issued amendments to IFRS 2 – *Share-based Payment,* clarifying how to account for the effects of vesting and non-vesting conditions on the measurement of cash-settled share-based payments, share-based payment transactions with a net settlement feature, and a modification to the terms and conditions that changes the classification of the transactions.

These amendments are effective for annual periods beginning on or after January 1, 2018. Early adoption is permitted. The Company is assessing the potential impact of these amendments.

Insurance contracts

In September 2016, the IASB issued amendments to IFRS 4 – *Insurance Contracts*, introducing two approaches; an overlay approach and a deferral approach, to address the additional accounting mismatches and volatility that may arise in profit or loss as a result of applying IFRS 9.

The overlay approach can be applied whenever IFRS 9 is applied and the deferral approach permits a company with activities that are predominantly connected with insurance to be exempted from applying IFRS 9 until 2021. The Company is assessing the potential impact of these amendments.

3. Significant accounting policies

The accounting policies set out below have been applied consistently to all periods presented in these consolidated financial statements and have been applied consistently throughout the Company.

Basis of consolidation

These consolidated financial statements include the accounts of Canadian Tire Corporation and entities it controls. An entity is controlled when the Company has the ability to direct the relevant activities of the entity, has exposure or rights to variable returns from its involvement with the entity, and is able to use its power over the entity to affect its returns from the entity.

The results of certain subsidiaries that have different year ends have been included in these consolidated financial statements for the 52-week periods ended December 31, 2016 and January 2, 2016. The year end of CTFS Holdings Limited and its subsidiaries, Franchise Trust, and CT Real Estate Investment Trust ("CT REIT") is December 31.

Income or loss and each component of OCI are attributed to the shareholders of the Company and to the non-controlling interests. Total comprehensive income is attributed to the shareholders of the Company and to the non-controlling interests even if this results in the non-controlling interests having a deficit balance on consolidation.

Business combinations

The Company applies the acquisition method in accounting for business combinations.

The Company measures goodwill as the difference between the fair value of the consideration transferred, including the recognized amount of any non-controlling interests in the acquiree, and the net recognized amount (generally fair value) of the identifiable assets acquired and liabilities assumed, all measured as at the acquisition date.

Consideration transferred includes the fair value of the assets transferred (including cash), liabilities incurred by the Company on behalf of the acquiree, the fair value of any contingent consideration, and equity interests issued by the Company.

Where a business combination is achieved in stages, previously held interests in the acquired entity are remeasured to fair value at the acquisition date, which is the date control is obtained, and the resulting gain or loss, if any, is recognized in net income. Amounts arising from interests in the acquiree prior to the acquisition date that have previously been recognized in OCI are reclassified to net income.

The fair values of property and equipment recognized as a result of a business combination is based on either the cost approach or market approach, as applicable. The market value of property is the estimated amount for which a property could be exchanged on the date of valuation between a willing buyer and a willing seller in an arm's length transaction after proper marketing wherein the parties each act knowledgeably and willingly. For the cost approach, the current replacement cost or reproduction cost for each major asset is calculated.

The fair values of banners and trademarks acquired in a business combination are determined using an income approach. The "relief from royalty" method has been applied to forecast revenue using an appropriate royalty rate. This results in an estimate of the value of the intangible assets acquired by the Company.

The fair values of franchise agreements and other intangibles, such as customer relationships, are determined using an income approach or multi-period excess earnings approach. This method is based on the discounted cash flows expected to be derived from ownership of the assets. The present value of the cash flows represents the value of the intangible asset. The fair value of off-market leases acquired in a business combination is determined based on the present value of the difference between market rates and rates in the existing leases.

The fair values of inventories acquired in a business combination is determined based on the estimated selling price in the ordinary course of business less the estimated costs of sale, and a reasonable profit margin based on the effort required to complete and sell the inventories.

Transaction costs that the Company incurs in connection with a business combination are expensed immediately.

Joint arrangement

A joint arrangement is an arrangement in which two or more parties have joint control. Joint control is the contractually agreed sharing of control whereby decisions about relevant activities require unanimous consent of the parties sharing control. A joint arrangement is classified as a joint operation when the parties that have joint control have rights to the assets and obligations for the liabilities related to the arrangement. The Company records its share of a joint operation's assets, liabilities, revenues, and expenses.

Foreign currency translation

Transactions in foreign currencies are translated into Canadian dollars at rates in effect at the date of the transaction. Monetary assets and liabilities in foreign currencies are translated into Canadian dollars at the closing exchange rate at the balance sheet date. Non-monetary items that are measured in terms of historical cost are translated into Canadian dollars at the exchange rate at the date of the original transaction. Exchange gains or losses arising from translation are recorded in Other income or Cost of producing revenue as applicable in the Consolidated Statements of Income.

Financial instruments

Recognition and measurement

Financial assets and financial liabilities, including derivatives, are recognized in the Consolidated Balance Sheets when the Company becomes a party to the contractual provisions of a financial instrument or non-financial derivative contract. All financial instruments are required to be measured at fair value on initial recognition. Subsequent measurement of these assets and liabilities is based on either fair value or amortized cost using the effective interest method, depending upon their classification.

Transaction costs that are directly attributable to the acquisition or issue of financial assets and financial liabilities (other than financial assets and financial liabilities classified as FVTPL) are added to or deducted from the fair value of the financial assets or financial liabilities, as appropriate, on initial recognition. Transaction costs directly attributable to the acquisition of financial assets or financial liabilities classified as FVTPL are recognized immediately in net income.

The Company classifies financial instruments, at the time of initial recognition, according to their characteristics and Management's choices and intentions related thereto for the purposes of ongoing measurement. Classification choices for financial assets include a) FVTPL, b) held to maturity, c) available for sale, and d) loans and receivables. Classification choices for financial liabilities include a) FVTPL and b) other liabilities.

The Company's financial assets and financial liabilities are generally classified and measured as follows:

Asset/Liability	Category	Measurement
Cash and cash equivalents	Loans and receivables	Amortized cost
Short-term investments[1]	Available for sale	Fair value
Trade and other receivables[2]	Loans and receivables	Amortized cost
Loans receivable	Loans and receivables	Amortized cost
Deposits (recorded in prepaid expenses and deposits)	Loans and receivables	Amortized cost
Long-term receivables and other assets[2]	Loans and receivables	Amortized cost
Long-term investments	Available for sale	Fair value
Bank indebtedness	Other liabilities	Amortized cost
Deposits	Other liabilities	Amortized cost
Trade and other payables[2]	Other liabilities	Amortized cost
Short-term borrowings	Other liabilities	Amortized cost
Loans payable	Other liabilities	Amortized cost
Long-term debt	Other liabilities	Amortized cost
Redeemable financial instrument (recorded in other long-term liabilities)	FVTPL	Fair value

[1] Certain short-term investments are classified as FVTPL and measured at fair value.

[2] Includes derivatives that are classified as FVTPL or are effective hedging instruments, and measured at fair value.

Financial instruments at fair value through profit or loss

Financial instruments are classified as FVTPL when the financial instrument is either held for trading or designated as such upon initial recognition. Financial instruments are classified as held for trading if acquired principally for the purpose of selling in the near future or if part of an identified portfolio of financial instruments that the Company manages together and has a recent actual pattern of short-term profit-making. Derivatives are classified as FVTPL unless they are designated as effective hedging instruments.

Financial instruments classified as FVTPL are measured at fair value, with changes in fair value recorded in net income in the period in which they arise.

Available-for-sale

Financial assets classified as available-for-sale are measured at fair value with changes in fair value recognized in OCI until realized through disposal or other than temporary impairment, at which point the change in fair value is recognized in net income. Dividend income from available-for-sale financial assets is recognized in net income when the Company's right to receive payments is established. Interest income on available-for-sale financial assets, calculated using the effective interest method, is recognized in net income.

Loans and receivables

Loans and receivables are financial assets with fixed or determinable payments that are not quoted in an active market. Subsequent to initial recognition, loans and receivables are measured at amortized cost using the effective interest method, less any impairment, with gains and losses recognized in net income in the period that the asset is derecognized or impaired.

Other liabilities

Subsequent to initial recognition, other financial liabilities are measured at amortized cost using the effective interest method, with gains and losses recognized in net income in the period that the liability is derecognized.

Derecognition of financial instruments

A financial asset is derecognized when the contractual rights to the cash flows from the asset expire or when the Company transfers the financial asset to another party without retaining control or substantially all the risks and rewards of ownership of the asset. Any interest in transferred financial assets created or retained by the Company is recognized as a separate asset or liability.

A financial liability is derecognized when its contractual obligations are discharged, cancelled, or expire.

Derivative financial instruments

The Company enters into various derivative financial instruments as part of the Company's strategy to manage its foreign currency and interest rate exposures. The Company also enters into equity derivative contracts to hedge certain future share-based payment expenses. The Company does not hold or issue derivative financial instruments for trading purposes.

All derivative financial instruments, including derivatives embedded in financial or non-financial contracts not closely related to the host contracts, are measured at fair value. The gain or loss that results from remeasurement at each reporting period is recognized in net income immediately unless the derivative is designated and effective as a hedging instrument, in which case the timing of the recognition in net income depends on the nature of the hedge relationship.

Hedge accounting

Where hedge accounting can be applied, certain criteria are documented at the inception of the hedge and updated at each reporting date.

Cash flow hedges

For cash flow hedges, the effective portion of the changes in the fair value of the hedging derivative, net of taxes, is recognized in OCI, while the ineffective and unhedged portions are recognized immediately in net income. Amounts recorded in Accumulated Other Comprehensive Income ("AOCI") are reclassified to net income in the periods when the hedged item affects net income. However, when a forecast transaction that is hedged results in the recognition of a non-financial asset or liability, the gains and losses previously recognized in AOCI are reclassified from AOCI and included in the initial measurement of the cost of the non-financial asset or liability.

When hedge accounting is discontinued, the amounts previously recognized in AOCI are reclassified to net income during the periods when the variability in the cash flows of the hedged item affects net income. Gains and losses on derivatives are reclassified immediately to net income when the hedged item is sold or terminated early. If hedge accounting is discontinued due to the hedged item no longer being expected to occur, the amount previously recognized in AOCI is reclassified immediately to net income.

The Company enters into foreign currency contracts to hedge the exposure against foreign currency risk on the future payment of foreign-currency-denominated inventory purchases and certain expenses. The changes in fair value of these contracts are included in OCI to the extent the hedges continue to be effective. Once the inventory is received, the Company reclassifies the related AOCI amount to merchandise inventories and subsequent changes in the fair value of the foreign currency contracts are recorded in net income as they occur. When the expenses are incurred, the Company reclassifies the related AOCI amount to the expense.

The Company enters into interest rate-swap contracts to hedge the exposure against interest rate risk on the future interest payments of debt issuances. The changes in fair value of these contracts are included in OCI to the extent that the hedges continue to be effective. When the interest expense is incurred, the Company reclassifies the related AOCI amount to finance costs.

Cash and cash equivalents

Cash and cash equivalents are defined as cash plus highly liquid and rated certificates of deposit or commercial paper with an original term to maturity of three months or less.

Short-term investments

Short-term investments are investments in highly liquid and rated certificates of deposit, commercial paper or other securities, primarily Canadian and United States ("U.S.") government securities, and notes of other creditworthy parties, with an original term to maturity of more than three months and remaining term to maturity of less than one year.

Trade and other receivables

The allowance for impairment of trade and other receivables is established when there is objective evidence that the Company will not be able to collect all amounts due according to the original terms of the receivables. Significant financial difficulties of the debtor, probability that the debtor will enter bankruptcy or financial reorganization, and default or delinquency in payments are considered indicators that the trade receivable is impaired. The amount of the allowance is calculated as the difference between the asset's carrying amount and the present value of estimated future cash flows, discounted at the original effective interest rate. The carrying amount of the asset is reduced through the use of an allowance account, and the amount of the loss is recognized in Selling, general and administrative expenses in the Consolidated Statements of Income. When a trade receivable is deemed uncollectible, it is written off against the allowance account. Subsequent recoveries of amounts previously written off are recognized as a recovery in Selling, general and administrative expenses in the Consolidated Statements of Income.

Loans receivable

Loans receivable consists of credit card and line of credit loans, as well as loans to Associate Dealers ("Dealers"), who are independent third-party operators of Canadian Tire Retail stores. Loans receivable are recognized when cash is advanced to the borrower. They are derecognized when the borrower repays its obligations, the loans are sold or written off, or substantially all of the risks and rewards of ownership are transferred.

Losses for impaired loans are recognized when there is objective evidence that impairment of the loans has occurred. Impairment allowances are calculated on individual loans and on groups of loans assessed collectively. Impairment losses are recorded in Cost of producing revenue in the Consolidated Statements of Income. The carrying amount of impaired loans in the Consolidated Balance Sheets is reduced through the use of impairment allowance accounts. Losses expected from future events are not recognized.

All individually significant loans receivable are assessed for specific impairment. All individually significant loans receivable found not to be specifically impaired are then collectively assessed for any impairment that has been incurred but not yet identified. Loans receivable not individually significant are collectively assessed for impairment by grouping together loans receivable with similar risk characteristics.

The Company uses a roll-rate methodology to calculate allowances for credit card loans. This methodology employs analysis of historical data, economic indicators, and experience of delinquency and default to estimate the amount of loans that will eventually be written off as a result of events occurring before the reporting date, with certain adjustments for other relevant circumstances influencing the recoverability of the loans receivable. Default rates, loss rates, and cash recoveries are regularly benchmarked against actual outcomes to ensure that they remain appropriate.

Merchandise inventories

Merchandise inventories are carried at the lower of cost and net realizable value.

Cash consideration received from vendors is recognized as a reduction to the cost of related inventory, unless the cash consideration received is either a reimbursement of incremental costs incurred by the Company or a payment for assets or services delivered to the vendor.

The cost of merchandise inventories is determined based on weighted average cost and includes costs incurred in bringing the merchandise inventories to their present location and condition. All inventories are finished goods.

Net realizable value is the estimated selling price of inventory during the normal course of business less estimated selling expenses.

Long-term investments

Investments in highly liquid and rated certificates of deposit, commercial paper, or other securities with a remaining term to maturity of greater than one year are classified as long-term investments. The Company's exposure to credit, currency, and interest rate risks related to other investments is disclosed in Note 5.

Intangible assets

Goodwill

Goodwill represents the excess of the cost of an acquisition over the fair value of the Company's share of the identifiable assets acquired and liabilities assumed in a business combination. Goodwill is measured at cost less any accumulated impairment and is not amortized.

Finite life and indefinite life intangible assets

Intangible assets with finite useful lives are measured at cost and are amortized on a straight-line basis over their estimated useful lives, generally for a period of two to ten years. The estimated useful lives and amortization methods are reviewed annually with the effect of any changes in estimate being accounted for on a prospective basis.

Intangible assets with indefinite useful lives are measured at cost, less any accumulated impairment, and are not amortized.

Expenditures on research activities are expensed as incurred.

Investment property

Investment property is property held to earn rental income or for appreciation of capital or both. The Company has determined that properties it provides to its Dealers, franchisees, and agents are not investment property as these relate to the Company's operating activities. This was determined based on certain criteria such as whether the Company provides significant ancillary services to the lessees of the property. The Company includes property that it leases to third parties (other than Dealers, franchisees, or agents) in investment property. Investment property is measured and depreciated in the same manner as property and equipment.

Property and equipment

Property and equipment is measured at cost less accumulated depreciation and any accumulated impairment. Land is measured at cost less any accumulated impairment. Properties in the course of construction are measured at cost less any accumulated impairment. The cost of an item of property or equipment comprises costs that are directly attributed to its acquisition and initial estimates of the cost of dismantling and removing the item and restoring the site on which it is located.

Buildings, fixtures, and equipment are depreciated using a declining balance method to their estimated residual value over their estimated useful lives. The estimated useful lives, amortization method, and residual values are reviewed annually with the effect of any changes in estimate being accounted for on a prospective basis.

Leasehold improvements are amortized on a straight-line basis over the terms of the respective leases or useful life, if shorter.

Assets held under finance leases are depreciated on the same basis as owned assets. If there is no reasonable certainty that the Company will obtain ownership by the end of the lease term, the asset is depreciated over the shorter of lease term and its useful life.

Depreciation and amortization rates are as follows:

Asset Category	Depreciation rate/term
Buildings	4-20%
Fixtures and equipment	5-40%
Leasehold improvements	Shorter of term of lease or useful life
Assets under finance lease	Shorter of term of lease or useful life

Leased assets

Leases are classified as finance leases whenever the terms of the lease transfer substantially all the risks and rewards of ownership to the lessee. All other leases are classified as operating leases.

Lessor

When the Company is the lessor in an operating lease, rental income and licence fees are recognized in net income on a straight-line basis over the term of the lease.

Lessee

When the Company is the lessee in an operating lease, rent payments are charged to net income on a straight-line basis over the term of the lease. Lease incentives are amortized on a straight-line basis over the terms of the respective leases.

Assets under finance leases are recognized as assets of the Company at their fair value or, if lower, at the present value of the minimum lease payments, each determined at the inception of the lease. The corresponding liability is included in the Consolidated Balance Sheets as a finance lease obligation. Lease payments are apportioned between finance costs and reduction of the lease obligations, so as to achieve a constant rate of interest on the remaining balance of the liability.

Sale and leaseback

The accounting treatment of a sale and leaseback transaction is assessed based upon the substance of the transaction and whether the sale is made at the asset's fair value.

For sale and finance leasebacks, any gain or loss from the sale is deferred and amortized over the lease term. For sale and operating leasebacks, the assets are sold at fair value and, accordingly, the gain or loss from the sale is recognized immediately in net income.

Impairment of assets

The carrying amounts of property and equipment, investment property, and intangible assets with finite useful lives are reviewed at the end of each reporting period to determine whether there are any indicators of impairment. Indicators of impairment may include a significant decline in asset market value, material adverse changes in the external operating environment which affect the manner in which the asset is used or is expected to be used, obsolescence, or physical damage of the asset. If any such indicators exist, then the recoverable amount of the asset is estimated. Goodwill and intangible assets with indefinite useful lives and intangible assets not yet available for use are not amortized but are tested for impairment at least annually or whenever there is an indicator that the asset may be impaired.

Cash generating units

When it is not possible to estimate the recoverable amount of an individual asset, the Company estimates the recoverable amount of the CGU to which the asset belongs. The CGUs correspond to the smallest identifiable group of assets whose continuing use generates cash inflows that are largely independent of the cash inflows from other assets or groups of assets.

Goodwill acquired in a business combination is allocated to each of the CGUs (or groups of CGUs) expected to benefit from the synergies of the combination. Intangible assets with indefinite useful lives are allocated to the CGU to which they relate.

Determining the recoverable amount

An impairment loss is recognized when the carrying amount of an asset, or of the CGU to which it belongs, exceeds the recoverable amount. The recoverable amount of an asset or CGU is defined as the higher of its fair value less costs to sell ("FVLCS") and its VIU.

In assessing VIU, the estimated future cash flows are discounted to their present value. Cash flows are discounted using a pre-tax discount rate that includes a risk premium specific to each line of business. The Company estimates cash flows before taxes based on the most recent actual results or budgets. Cash flows are then extrapolated over a period of up to five years, taking into account a terminal value calculated by discounting the final year in perpetuity. The growth rate applied to the terminal values is based on the Bank of Canada's target inflation rate or a growth rate specific to the individual item being tested based on Management's estimate.

Recording impairments and reversals of impairments

Impairments and reversals of impairments are recognized in Other income in the Consolidated Statements of Income. Any impairment loss is allocated first to reduce the carrying amount of any goodwill allocated to the CGU and then to the other assets of the CGU. Impairments of goodwill cannot be reversed. Impairments of other assets recognized in prior periods are assessed at the end of each reporting period to determine if the indicators of impairment have reversed or no longer exist. An impairment loss is reversed if the estimated recoverable amount exceeds the carrying amount. The increased carrying amount of an asset attributable to a reversal of impairment may not exceed the carrying amount that would have been determined had no impairment been recognized in prior periods.

Assets classified as held for sale

Non-current assets and disposal groups are classified as assets held for sale when their carrying amount is to be recovered principally through a sale transaction rather than through continuing use. This condition is regarded as met only when the sale is highly probable and the asset (or disposal group) is available for immediate sale in its present condition. Management must be committed to the sale, and it should be expected to qualify for recognition as a completed sale within one year from the date of classification. Assets (and disposal groups) classified as held for sale are measured at the lower of the carrying amount or FVLCS and are not depreciated. The fair value measurement of assets held for sale is categorized within Level 2 of fair value hierarchy (refer to Note 32.4 for definition of levels).

Borrowing costs

Borrowing costs directly attributable to the acquisition or construction of a qualifying asset are capitalized. Qualifying assets are those that require a minimum of three months to prepare for their intended use. All other borrowing costs are recognized in Cost of producing revenue or in Net finance costs in the Consolidated Statements of Income in the period in which they are incurred.

Employee benefits

Short-term benefits

Short-term employee benefit obligations are measured on an undiscounted basis and are expensed as the related service is provided.

The Company recognizes a liability and an expense for short-term benefits such as bonuses, profit-sharing, and employee stock purchases if the Company has a present legal obligation or constructive obligation to pay this amount as a result of past service provided by the employees and the obligation can be estimated reasonably.

Post-employment benefits

The Company provides certain health care, dental care, life insurance, and other benefits, but not pensions, for certain retired employees pursuant to Company policy. The Company accrues the cost of these employee benefits over the periods in which the employees earn the benefits. The cost of employee benefits earned by employees is actuarially determined using the projected benefit method pro-rated on length of service and Management's best estimate of salary escalation, retirement ages of employees, employee turnover, life expectancy, and expected health and dental care costs. The costs are discounted at a rate that is based on market rates as at the measurement date. Actuarial gains and losses are immediately recorded in OCI.

The Company also provides post-employment benefits with respect to contributions to a Deferred Profit Sharing Plan ("DPSP").

Termination benefits

Termination benefits are payable when employment is terminated by the Company before the normal retirement date or whenever an employee accepts voluntary redundancy in exchange for these benefits. The Company recognizes a provision for termination benefits when it is demonstrably committed to either terminating the employment of current employees according to a detailed formal plan, without possibility of withdrawal, or providing termination benefits as a result of an offer made to encourage voluntary redundancy.

Share-based payments

Stock options with tandem stock appreciation rights ("stock options") are granted with a feature that enables the employee to exercise the stock option or receive a cash payment equal to the difference between the market price of the Company's Class A Non-Voting Shares as at the exercise date and the exercise price of the stock option. These stock options are considered to be compound instruments. The fair value of compound instruments is measured at each reporting date, taking into account the terms and conditions on which the rights to cash or equity instruments are granted. As the fair value of the settlement in cash is the same as the fair value of the settlement as a traditional stock option, the fair value of the stock option is the same as the fair value of the debt component. The corresponding expense and liability are recognized over the respective vesting period.

The fair value of the amount payable to employees with respect to share unit plans and trust unit plans, which are settled in cash, is recorded as the services are provided over the vesting period. The fair value of the liability is remeasured at each reporting date with the change in the liability being recognized in Selling, general and administrative expenses in the Consolidated Statements of Income.

Insurance reserve

Included in trade and other payables is an insurance reserve that consists of an amount determined from loss reports and individual cases and an amount, based on past experience, for losses incurred but not reported. These estimates are continually reviewed and are subject to the impact of future changes in such factors as claim severity and frequency. While Management believes that the amount is adequate, the ultimate liability may be in excess of or less than the amounts provided, and any adjustment will be reflected in net income during the periods in which they become known.

The Company uses actuarial valuations in determining its reserve for outstanding losses and loss-related expenses using an appropriate reserving methodology for each line of business. The Company does not discount its liabilities for unpaid claims.

Provisions

A provision is recognized if, as a result of a past event, the Company has a present legal or constructive obligation that can be estimated reliably and it is probable that an outflow of economic benefits will be required to settle the obligation. The amount recognized as a provision is the best estimate of the consideration required to settle the present obligation at the end of the reporting period, taking into account risks and uncertainty of cash flows. Where the effect of discounting is material, provisions are determined by discounting the expected future cash flows at a pre-tax rate that reflects current market assessments of the time value of money and the risks specific to the liability.

Sales and warranty returns

The provision for sales and warranty returns relates to the Company's obligation for defective goods in current store inventories and defective goods sold to customers that have yet to be returned, after sales service for replacement parts, and future corporate store sales returns. Accruals for sales and warranty returns are estimated on the basis of historical returns and are recorded so as to allocate them to the same period the corresponding revenue is recognized. These accruals are reviewed regularly and updated to reflect Management's best estimate; however, actual returns could vary from these estimates.

Site restoration and decommissioning

Legal or constructive obligations associated with the removal of underground fuel storage tanks and site remediation costs on the retirement of certain property and equipment and with the termination of certain lease agreements, are recognized in the period in which they are incurred, when it is probable that an outflow of resources embodying economic benefits will be required and a reasonable estimate of the amount of the obligation can be made. The obligations are initially measured at the Company's best estimate, using an expected value approach, and are discounted to present value.

Onerous contracts

A provision for onerous contracts is recognized when the expected benefits to be derived by the Company from a contract are lower than the unavoidable costs of meeting its obligations under the contract. The provision is measured at the present value of the lower of the expected cost of terminating the contract or the expected net cost of continuing with the contract.

Customer loyalty

An obligation arises from the "My Canadian Tire 'Money'™" customer loyalty program when the Company issues electronic Canadian Tire 'Money'® and when the Dealers pay the Company to acquire paper-based Canadian Tire 'Money', as the Dealers retain the right to return paper-based Canadian Tire Money to the Company for refund in cash. These obligations are measured at fair value by reference to the fair value of the awards for which they could be redeemed and based on the estimated probability of their redemption. The expense is recorded in Selling, general and administrative expenses in the Consolidated Statements of Income.

Debt

Debt is classified as current when the Company expects to settle the liability in its normal operating cycle, it holds the liability primarily for the purpose of trading, the liability is due to be settled within 12 months after the date of the Consolidated Balance Sheets, or it does not have an unconditional right to defer settlement of the liability for at least 12 months after the date of the Consolidated Balance Sheets.

Share capital

Shares issued by the Company are recorded at the value of proceeds received. Repurchased shares are removed from equity. No gain or loss is recognized in net income on the purchase, sale, issue, or cancellation of the Company's shares.

Share repurchases are charged to share capital at the average cost per share outstanding and the excess between the repurchase price and the average cost is first allocated to contributed surplus, with any remainder allocated to retained earnings.

Dividends

Dividends declared and payable to the Company's shareholders are recognized as a liability in the Consolidated Balance Sheets in the period in which the dividends are approved by the Company's Board of Directors.

Distributions

Distributions to non-controlling interests are recognized as a liability in the Consolidated Balance Sheets in the period in which the distributions are declared.

Revenue

The Company recognizes revenue when the amount can be reliably measured, when it is probable that future economic benefits will flow to the entity, and when specific criteria have been met for each of the Company's activities described below.

Sale of goods

Revenue from the sale of goods includes merchandise sold to Dealers and Mark's Work Wearhouse Ltd. ("Mark's") and FGL Sports Ltd. ("FGL Sports") franchisees, the sale of gasoline through agents, and the sale of goods by Mark's, PartSource, and FGL Sports corporately-owned stores to the general public. This revenue is recognized when the goods are delivered, less an estimate for the sales and warranty returns. Revenue from the sale of goods is measured at the fair value of the consideration received less an appropriate deduction for actual and expected returns, discounts, rebates, and warranty and loyalty program costs, net of sales taxes.

If there is any uncertainty regarding the right of a customer to return goods, no revenue is recognized until the uncertainty is resolved. However, in the case of warranties, if warranty claims can be reasonably estimated, revenue is recorded for the net amount.

Customer loyalty programs

Loyalty award credits issued as part of a sales transaction relating to the Company's Gas Advantage, Cash Advantage, and Sport Chek MasterCard Rewards credit card programs result in revenue being deferred until the loyalty award is redeemed by the customer. The portion of the revenue that is deferred is the fair value of the award. The fair value of the award takes into account the amount for which the award credits could be sold separately, less the proportion of the award credits that are not expected to be redeemed by customers.

Interest income on loans receivable

Interest income includes interest charged on loans receivable and fees that are an integral part of the effective interest rate on financial instruments. Interest income on financial assets that are classified as loans and receivables is determined using the effective interest method.

Services rendered

Service revenue includes Roadside Assistance Club membership revenue; insurance premiums and reinsurance revenue; extended warranty contract fees; merchant, interchange, and processing fees; cash advance fees; foreign exchange fees; and service charges on the loans receivable of the Financial Services operating segment, as well as Mark's clothing alteration revenue. Service revenue is recognized according to the contractual provisions of the arrangement, which is generally when the service is provided or over the contractual period.

Merchant, interchange, and processing fees, cash advance fees, and foreign exchange fees on credit card transactions are recognized as revenue at the time transactions are completed. Revenue from separately priced extended warranty contracts is recorded on a straight-line basis over the term of the contracts.

Reinsurance premiums are recorded on an accrual basis and are included in net income on a pro rata basis over the life of the insurance contract, with the unearned portion deferred in the Consolidated Balance Sheets. Premiums that are subject to adjustment are estimated based on available information. Any variances from the estimates are recorded in the periods in which they become known.

Royalties and licence fees

Royalties and licence fees include licence fees from petroleum agents and Dealers, and royalties from Mark's and FGL Sports franchisees. Royalties and licence fee revenues are recognized as they are earned in accordance with the substance of the relevant agreement and are measured on an accrual basis.

Rental income

Rental income from operating leases where the Company is the lessor is recognized on a straight-line basis over the terms of the respective leases.

Vendor rebates

The Company records cash consideration received from vendors as a reduction in the price of vendors' products and recognizes it as a reduction to the cost of related inventory or, if the related inventory has been sold, to the cost of producing revenue. Certain exceptions apply where the cash consideration received is either a reimbursement of incremental selling costs incurred by the Company or a payment for assets or services delivered to the vendor, in which case the cost is reflected as a reduction in selling, general and administrative expenses.

The Company recognizes rebates that are at the vendor's discretion when the vendor either pays the rebates or agrees to pay them and payment is considered probable and can be reasonably estimated.

Net finance costs

Finance income comprises interest income on funds invested (including available-for-sale financial assets). Interest income is recognized as it accrues using the effective interest method.

Finance costs comprises interest expense on borrowings (including borrowings relating to the Dealer Loan Program), unwinding of the discount on provisions, and is net of borrowing costs that have been capitalized. Interest on deposits is recorded in Cost of producing revenue in the Consolidated Statements of Income.

Income taxes

The income tax expense for the year comprises current and deferred income tax. Income tax expense is recognized in net income except to the extent that it relates to items recognized either in OCI or directly in equity. In this case, the income tax expense is recognized in OCI or in equity, respectively.

The income tax expense is calculated on the basis of the tax laws enacted or substantively enacted at the date of the Consolidated Balance Sheets in the countries where the Company operates and generates taxable income.

Deferred income tax is recognized using the liability method for unused tax losses, unused tax benefits, and temporary differences arising between the tax bases of assets and liabilities and their carrying amounts in these consolidated financial statements. However, deferred income tax is not accounted for if it arises from the initial recognition of goodwill or the initial recognition of an asset or liability in a transaction, other than a business combination, that at the time of the transaction affects neither accounting nor taxable income. Deferred income tax is determined using tax rates (and laws) that have been enacted or substantively enacted at the date of the Consolidated Balance Sheets and are expected to apply when the related deferred income tax asset is realized or the deferred income tax liability is settled.

Deferred income tax assets are recognized only to the extent that it is probable that future taxable income will be available against which the temporary differences can be utilized. Deferred income tax liabilities are provided on temporary differences arising on investments in subsidiaries and associates, except where the timing of the reversal of the temporary difference is controlled by the Company and it is probable that the temporary difference will not reverse in the foreseeable future.

Earnings per share

Basic earnings per share ("Basic EPS") is calculated by dividing the net income attributable to the shareholders of the Company by the weighted average number of Common and Class A Non-Voting shares outstanding during the reporting period. Diluted earnings per share ("Diluted EPS") is calculated by adjusting the net income attributable to the shareholders of the Company and the weighted average number of shares outstanding for the effects of all potentially dilutive equity instruments, which comprise employee stock options. Net income attributable to the shareholders of the Company is the same for both the Basic EPS and Diluted EPS calculations.

Non-controlling interests

When the proportion of the equity held by non-controlling interests changes, the Company adjusts the carrying amounts of the controlling and non-controlling interests to reflect the changes in their relative interest in the subsidiary. The Company recognizes directly in equity any difference between the amount by which the non-controlling interests are adjusted and the fair value of the consideration paid or received, and attribute it to the shareholders of the Company.

4. Capital management

The Company's objectives when managing capital are:

- ensuring sufficient liquidity to support its financial obligations and execute its operating and strategic plans;
- maintaining healthy liquidity reserves and access to capital; and
- minimizing the after-tax cost of capital while taking into consideration current and future industry, market, and economic risks and conditions.

The definition of capital varies from company to company, industry to industry, and for different purposes. In the process of managing the Company's capital, Management includes the following items in its definition of capital, which includes Glacier Credit Card Trust ("GCCT") indebtedness but excludes Franchise Trust indebtedness:

(C$ in millions)		2016	% of total		2015	% of total
Capital components						
Deposits	$	950.7	8.5%	$	880.7	8.2%
Short-term borrowings		199.4	1.8%		88.6	0.8%
Current portion of long-term debt		653.4	5.9%		24.3	0.2%
Long-term debt		2,667.1	24.0%		2,971.4	27.8%
Long-term deposits		1,230.8	11.1%		1,372.2	12.8%
Total debt	$	5,701.4	51.3%	$	5,337.2	49.8%
Redeemable financial instrument		517.0	4.7%		517.0	4.9%
Share capital		648.1	5.8%		671.2	6.3%
Contributed surplus		2.9	0.0%		2.9	0.0%
Retained earnings		4,250.9	38.2%		4,172.0	39.0%
Total capital under management	$	**11,120.3**	**100.0%**	$	10,700.3	100.0%

The Company monitors its capital structure through measuring debt-to-earnings ratios and ensures its ability to service debt and meet other fixed obligations by tracking its interest and other coverage ratios, and forecasting cash flows.

The Company manages its capital structure over the long term to optimize the balance among capital efficiency, financial flexibility, and risk mitigation. Management calculates its ratios to approximate the methodology of debt-rating agencies and other market participants on a current and prospective basis. To assess its effectiveness in managing capital, Management monitors these ratios against targeted ranges.

In order to maintain or adjust the capital structure, the Company has the flexibility to adjust the amount of dividends paid to shareholders, repurchase shares pursuant to a normal course issuer bid ("NCIB") program, repay debt, issue new debt and equity at Canadian Tire Corporation and CT REIT, issue new debt with different characteristics to replace existing debt, engage in additional sale and leaseback transactions of real estate properties, and increase or decrease the amount of sales of co-ownership interests in loans receivable to GCCT.

The Company has a policy in place to manage capital. As part of the overall management of capital, Management and the Audit Committee of the Board of Directors review the Company's compliance with, and performance against, the policy. In addition, periodic review of the policy is performed to ensure consistency with the risk tolerances.

Financial covenants of the existing debt agreements are reviewed by Management on an ongoing basis to monitor compliance with the agreements. The key financial covenant for Canadian Tire Corporation is a requirement for the retail segment to maintain, at all times, a ratio of total indebtedness to total capitalization equal to or lower than a specified maximum ratio (as defined in the applicable bank credit facility agreements, but which excludes consideration of CTFS Holdings, CT REIT, Franchise Trust, and their respective subsidiaries).

The Company was in compliance with this key covenant as at December 31, 2016 and January 2, 2016. Under the covenant, the Company currently has sufficient flexibility to fund business growth.

CT REIT is required to comply with financial covenants established under its Trust Indenture, Bank Credit Agreement, and the Declaration of Trust and was in compliance with the key covenants as at December 31, 2016 and 2015.

In addition, the Company is required to comply with regulatory requirements for capital associated with the operations of Canadian Tire Bank ("CTB" or "the Bank"), a federally chartered bank, and other regulatory requirements that have an impact on its business operations and certain financial covenants established under its unsecured revolving credit facility.

CTB manages its capital under guidelines established by the Office of the Superintendent of Financial Institutions of Canada ("OSFI"). OSFI's regulatory capital guidelines are based on the international Basel Committee on Banking Supervision framework entitled Basel III: A Global Regulatory Framework for More Resilient Banks and Banking Systems ("Basel III"), which came into effect in Canada on January 1, 2013, and measures capital in relation to credit, market, and operational risks. The Bank has various capital policies and procedures and controls, including an Internal Capital Adequacy Assessment Process ("ICAAP"), which it utilizes to achieve its goals and objectives.

The Bank's objectives include:
- providing sufficient capital to maintain the confidence of investors and depositors; and
- being an appropriately capitalized institution, as measured internally, defined by regulatory authorities and compared with the Bank's peers.

OSFI's regulatory capital guidelines under Basel III allow for two tiers of capital. As at December 31, 2016, the Bank's fiscal year end, Common Equity Tier 1 ("CET1") capital includes common shares, retained earnings, and AOCI, less regulatory adjustments including items risk-weighted at 0 percent which are deducted from capital. The Bank currently does not hold any additional Tier 1 or Tier 2 capital instruments. Therefore, the Bank's CET1 is equal to its Tier 1 and total regulatory capital. Risk-weighted assets ("RWA") include a credit risk component for all on-balance-sheet assets weighted for the risk inherent in each type of asset, off-balance sheet financial instruments, an operational risk component based on a percentage of average risk-weighted revenues, and a market-risk component for assets held for trade. For the purposes of calculating RWA, securitization transactions are considered off-balance-sheet transactions and, therefore, securitization assets are not included in the RWA calculation. Assets are classified as held for trade when they are held with trading intent.

The Leverage Ratio prescribed by OSFI's Leverage Requirements Guideline provides an overall measure of the adequacy of an institution's capital and is defined as the all-in Tier 1 capital divided by the leverage ratio exposure. The leverage ratio exposure is the sum of on-balance sheet exposures, derivative exposures, securities financing transaction exposures, and off-balance sheet items.

As at December 31, 2016 and 2015, the Bank complied with all regulatory capital guidelines established by OSFI, its internal targets as determined by its ICAAP, and the financial covenants of its credit facility.

5. Financial risk management

5.1 Overview
The Company has exposure to the following risks from its use of financial instruments:
- credit risk;
- liquidity risk; and
- market risk (including foreign currency and interest rate risk).

This note presents information about the Company's exposure to each of the above risks and the Company's objectives, policy, and processes for measuring and managing risk. Further quantitative disclosures are included throughout these consolidated financial statements and notes thereto.

5.2 Risk management framework
The Company's financial risk management policy serves to identify and analyze the risks faced by the Company, to set acceptable risk tolerance limits and controls, and to monitor risks and adherence to limits. The financial risk management strategies and systems are reviewed regularly to ensure they remain consistent with the objectives and risk tolerance acceptable to the Company and current market trends and conditions. The Company, through its training and management standards and procedures, aims to uphold a disciplined and constructive control environment in which all employees understand their roles and obligations.

5.3 Credit risk
Credit risk is the risk of financial loss to the Company if a customer or counterparty to a financial instrument fails to meet its contractual obligations. Credit risk primarily arises from the Company's credit card customers, Dealer network, and financial instruments held with bank or non-bank counterparties.

NOTES TO THE CONSOLIDATED FINANCIAL STATEMENTS

5.3.1 Financial instrument counterparty credit risk

The Company has a Board-approved financial risk management policy in place to manage the various risks including counterparty credit risk relating to cash balances, investment activity. and the use of financial derivatives. The Company limits its exposure to counterparty credit risk by transacting only with highly-rated financial institutions and other counterparties and by managing within specific limits for credit exposure and term to maturity. The Company's financial instrument portfolio is spread across financial institutions, provincial and federal governments, and, to a lesser extent, corporate issuers that are dual rated and have a credit rating in the "A" category or better.

5.3.2 Consumer and Dealer credit risk

Through the granting of Canadian Tire credit cards to its customers, the Company assumes certain risks with respect to the ability and willingness of its customers to repay debt. In addition, the Company may be required to provide credit enhancement for individual Dealer's borrowings in the form of standby letters of credit (the "LCs") or guarantees of third-party bank debt agreements, with respect to the financing programs available to the Dealers (Note 34).

The Company's maximum exposure to credit risk, over and above amounts recognized in the Consolidated Balance Sheets, include the following:

(C$ in millions)	2016	2015
Undrawn loan commitments	$ 9,517.4	$ 9,514.1
Guarantees	428.5	482.1
Total	$ 9,945.9	$ 9,996.2

Refer to Note 9 for information on the credit quality and performance of loans receivables.

5.4 Liquidity risk

Liquidity risk is the risk that the Company might encounter difficulty in meeting the obligations associated with its financial liabilities that are settled by delivering cash or another financial asset. The Company's approach to managing liquidity is to ensure, as much as possible, that it will always have sufficient liquidity to meet its liabilities when due, under both normal and reasonably stressed conditions. The Company's financial risk management policy serves to manage its exposure to liquidity risk. The Company uses a detailed consolidated cash flow forecast model to regularly monitor its near-term and longer-term cash flow requirements, which assists in optimizing its short-term cash and indebtedness position while evaluating longer-term funding strategies.

In addition, CTB has in place an Asset Liability Management policy. It is CTB's objective to ensure the availability of adequate funds by maintaining a strong liquidity management framework and to satisfy all applicable regulatory and statutory requirements.

As at December 31, 2016, the Company had $4.525 billion in committed bank lines of credit of which $1.975 billion is available to Canadian Tire Corporation under a syndicated credit facility expiring in July 2021, $300.0 million is available to CT REIT under a syndicated credit facility expiring in April 2021, and $2.25 billion is available to CTB expiring October 2019.

In addition to the bank lines of credit, the Company has access to additional funding sources including internal cash generation, access to public and private financial markets, and strategic real estate transactions. Assets of CTB are funded through the securitization of credit card receivables using GCCT, broker guaranteed investment certificate ("GICs") deposits, retail GIC deposits, and high-interest savings ("HIS") account deposits. CTB also holds high quality liquid assets, as required by regulators, which are available to address funding disruptions.

CT REIT filed a base-shelf prospectus on March 5, 2015, under which it may raise up to $1.5 billion of debt and equity capital for the subsequent 25-month period (and under which the Company can sell some of the equity units it owns of CT REIT). On March 31, 2015, GCCT filed a base shelf prospectus permitting it to issue up to $1.5 billion of term notes for the subsequent 25-month period.

Due to the diversification of its funding sources, the Company is not exposed to any concentration risk regarding liquidity.

The following table summarizes the Company's contractual maturity for its financial liabilities, including both principal and interest payments:

(C$ in millions)	2017	2018	2019	2020	2021	Thereafter	Total
Non-derivative financial liabilities							
Deposits[1]	957.8	362.9	413.5	281.9	172.5	–	2,188.6
Trade and other payables	1,626.3	–	–	–	–	–	1,626.3
Short-term borrowings	199.4	–	–	–	–	–	199.4
Loans payable	700.3	–	–	–	–	–	700.3
Long-term debt	636.7	264.6	500.0	500.0	150.0	1,100.0	3,151.3
Finance lease obligations	16.7	14.5	12.7	11.5	11.4	59.0	125.8
Mortgages	1.2	17.1	37.6	–	–	–	55.9
Interest payments[2]	146.0	125.1	103.3	78.7	61.4	437.7	952.2
Total	$ 4,284.4	$ 784.2	$ 1,067.1	$ 872.1	$ 395.3	$ 1,596.7	$ 8,999.8

[1] Deposits exclude the GIC broker fee discount of $7.1 million.
[2] Includes interest payments on deposits, short-term borrowings, loans payable, long-term debt, and finance lease obligations.

It is not expected that the cash flows included in the maturity analysis would occur significantly earlier or at significantly different amounts.

5.5 Market risk

Market risk is the risk that changes in market prices, such as foreign exchange rates, interest rates, and equity prices, will affect the Company's income or the value of its holdings of financial instruments. The objective of market risk management is to manage market risk exposures within acceptable parameters while optimizing the return. The Company's financial risk management policy establishes guidelines on how the Company is to manage the market risk inherent to the business and provides mechanisms to ensure business transactions are executed in accordance with established limits, processes, and procedures.

All such transactions are carried out within the established guidelines and, generally, the Company seeks to apply hedge accounting in order to manage volatility in its net income.

5.5.1 Foreign currency risk

The Company sources its merchandise globally. Approximately 40%, 45%, and 6% of the value of the inventory purchased for the Canadian Tire, Mark's, and FGL Sports banners, respectively, is sourced directly from vendors outside North America, primarily denominated in U.S. dollars. To mitigate the impact of fluctuating foreign exchange rates on the cost of these purchases, the Company has an established foreign exchange risk management program that governs the proportion of forecast U.S. dollar purchases that must be hedged through the purchase of foreign exchange contracts. The purpose of the program is to provide certainty with respect to a portion of the foreign exchange component of future merchandise purchases.

As the Company has hedged a significant portion of the cost of its near-term U.S.-dollar-denominated forecast purchases, a change in foreign currency rates will not impact that portion of the cost of those purchases. Even when a change in rates is sustained, the Company's program to hedge a proportion of forecast U.S. dollar purchases continues. As hedges are placed at current foreign exchange rates, the impact of a sustained change in rate will eventually be reflected in the cost of the Company's U.S. dollar purchases. The hedging program has historically allowed the Company to defer the impact of sudden exchange rate movements on margins and allow it time to develop strategies to mitigate the impact of a sustained change in foreign exchange rates. Some vendors have an underlying exposure to U.S. currency fluctuations which may affect the price they charge the Company for merchandise from time to time; the Company's hedging program does not mitigate that risk. While the Company may be able to pass on changes in foreign currency exchange rates through pricing, any decision to do so will be subject to market conditions.

5.5.2 Interest rate risk

The Company may enter into interest rate swap contracts to manage its current and anticipated exposure to interest rate price risk. The Company's financial risk management policy requires that a minimum of 75 percent of its long-term debt (term greater than one year) and lease obligations must be at fixed interest rates.

A one percent change in interest rates would not materially affect the Company's net income or equity as the Company has minimal floating interest rate exposure given the indebtedness of the Company is predominantly at fixed rates.

The Company's exposure to interest rate changes is predominantly driven by the Financial Services business to the extent that the interest rates on future GIC deposits, HIS account deposits, tax free savings account ("TFSA") deposits, and securitization transactions are market-dependent. Partially offsetting this will be rates charged on credit cards and future liquidity pool investment rates available to the Bank. In addition, the Company has entered into delayed start interest rate swaps to hedge a portion of its planned GCCT term debt issuances in 2017 to 2020.

6. Operating segments

The Company has three reportable operating segments: Retail, CT REIT, and Financial Services. The reportable operating segments are strategic business units offering different products and services. They are separately managed due to their distinct nature. The following summary describes the operations in each of the Company's reportable segments:

- The retail business is conducted under a number of banners including Canadian Tire, Canadian Tire Gas ("Petroleum"), Mark's, PartSource, and various FGL Sports banners. Retail also includes the Dealer Loan Program (the portion [silo] of Franchise Trust that issues loans to Dealers). Non-CT REIT real estate is included in Retail.
- CT REIT is an unincorporated, closed-end real estate investment trust. CT REIT holds a geographically-diversified portfolio of properties comprised largely of Canadian Tire banner stores, Canadian Tire anchored retail developments, mixed-use commercial property, and distribution centres.
- Financial Services markets a range of Canadian Tire branded credit cards including Canadian Tire Options MasterCard, Cash Advantage MasterCard, Gas Advantage MasterCard, and Sport Chek MasterCard and also participates in the Canadian Tire loyalty program. Certain costs associated with these activities were allocated to Financial Services for segment reporting purposes. Financial Services also markets insurance and warranty products and provides settlement services to Canadian Tire affiliates. Financial Services includes CTB, a federally regulated financial institution that manages and finances the Company's consumer MasterCard, Visa, and retail credit card portfolios, as well as an existing block of Canadian Tire-branded line of credit portfolios. CTB also offers high-interest savings deposit accounts, tax free savings accounts, and GIC deposits, both directly and through third-party brokers. Financial Services also includes GCCT, a structured entity established to purchase co-ownership interests in the Company's credit card loans. GCCT issues debt to third-party investors to fund its purchases.

NOTES TO THE CONSOLIDATED FINANCIAL STATEMENTS

Performance is measured based on segment income before income taxes, as included in the internal management reports. Management has determined that this measure is the most relevant in evaluating segment results and allocating resources. Information regarding the results of each reportable operating segment is as follows:

				2016						2015	
(C$ in millions)	Retail	CT REIT	Financial Services	Eliminations and adjustments	Total	Retail	CT REIT	Financial Services	Eliminations and adjustments	Total
External revenue	$ 11,447.6	$ 24.9	$ 1,091.9	$ 116.6	$ 12,681.0	$ 11,069.8	$ 16.3	$ 1,087.6	$ 105.9	$ 12,279.6
Intercompany revenue	5.8	382.3	15.9	(404.0)	–	5.5	361.9	13.6	(381.0)	–
Total revenue	11,453.4	407.2	1,107.8	(287.4)	12,681.0	11,075.3	378.2	1,101.2	(275.1)	12,279.6
Cost of producing revenue	7,890.9	–	449.2	(51.6)	8,288.5	7,747.6	–	452.1	(55.4)	8,144.3
Gross margin	3,562.5	407.2	658.6	(235.8)	4,392.5	3,327.7	378.2	649.1	(219.7)	4,135.3
Other (income) expense	(120.5)	–	0.4	115.8	(4.3)	(160.7)	–	1.9	103.9	(54.9)
Selling, general and administrative expenses	3,099.1	106.7	293.7	(207.6)	3,291.9	2,926.0	96.5	274.7	(201.1)	3,096.1
Net finance (income) costs	(37.9)	85.9	(0.6)	46.5	93.9	(42.5)	87.1	(1.5)	49.7	92.8
Fair value (gain) loss on investment properties	–	(44.5)	–	44.5	–	–	(39.9)	–	39.9	–
Income before income taxes	$ 621.8	$ 259.1	$ 365.1	$ (235.0)	$ 1,011.0	$ 604.9	$ 234.5	$ 374.0	$ (212.1)	$ 1,001.3
Items included in the above:										
Depreciation and amortization	$ 374.9	$ –	$ 9.3	$ 72.7	$ 456.9	$ 350.6	$ –	$ 7.0	$ 67.1	$ 424.7
Interest income	91.4	0.2	871.7	(72.9)	890.4	101.1	0.3	845.4	(80.6)	866.2
Interest expense	39.3	86.1	103.9	(73.2)	156.1	45.5	87.4	109.7	(81.2)	161.4

The eliminations and adjustments include the following items:

- reclassifications of certain revenues and costs in the Financial Services segment to net finance costs;
- reclassifications of revenues and operating expenses to reflect loyalty program accounting in accordance with IFRIC 13 for the Company's Loyalty program;
- conversion from CT REIT's fair value investment property valuation policy to the Company's cost model, including the recording of depreciation; and
- inter-segment eliminations and adjustments including intercompany rent, property management fees, and credit card processing fees.

Capital expenditures by reportable operating segment are as follows:

			2016					2015
(C$ in millions)	Retail	CT REIT[1]	Financial Services	Total	Retail[2]	CT REIT[1]	Financial Services	Total
Capital expenditures[3]	$ 568.7	$ 176.8	$ 9.4	$ 754.9	$ 655.9	$ 42.4	$ 17.8	$ 716.1

[1] CT REIT capital expenditures include the construction of stores under Mark's and FGL Sports banners of $2.0 million (2015 – $17.7 million).
[2] Retail capital expenditures include $17.7 million relating to the acquisition of 12 real estate leases, formerly held by Target Canada which were acquired during 2015, and are recorded in long-term receivables and other assets on the Consolidated Balance Sheets.
[3] Capital expenditures are presented on an accrual basis and include software additions.

Total assets by reporting operating segment are as follows:

(C$ in millions)	2016	2015
Retail	$ 11,024.4	$ 11,128.0
CT REIT	5,014.6	4,350.9
Financial Services	5,773.5	5,520.3
Eliminations and adjustments	(6,509.7)	(6,011.4)
Total assets[1]	$ 15,302.8	$ 14,987.8

[1] The Company employs a shared-services model for several of its back-office functions, including finance, information technology, human resources, and legal. As a result, expenses relating to these functions are allocated on a systematic and rational basis to the reportable operating segments. The associated assets and liabilities are not allocated among segments in the presented measures of segmented assets and liabilities.

Total liabilities by reporting operating segment are as follows:

(C$ in millions)	2016	2015
Retail	$ 3,943.9	$ 3,899.1
CT REIT	2,424.0	2,137.5
Financial Services	4,731.6	4,588.4
Eliminations and adjustments	(1,534.0)	(1,426.9)
Total liabilities[1]	$ 9,565.5	$ 9,198.1

[1] The Company employs a shared-services model for several of its back-office functions, including finance, information technology, human resources, and legal. As a result, expenses relating to these functions are allocated on a systematic and rational basis to the reportable operating segments. The associated assets and liabilities are not allocated among segments in the presented measures of segmented assets and liabilities.

The eliminations and adjustments include the following items:

- conversion from CT REIT's fair value investment property valuation policy to the Company's cost model, including the recording of depreciation; and
- inter-segment eliminations.

7. Cash and cash equivalents

Cash and cash equivalents comprise the following:

(C$ in millions)	2016	2015
Cash	$ 81.0	$ 192.2
Cash equivalents	738.2	698.6
Restricted cash[1]	10.5	9.8
Total cash and cash equivalents[2]	829.7	900.6
Bank indebtedness	(5.9)	–
Cash and cash equivalents, net of bank indebtedness	$ 823.8	$ 900.6

[1] Relates to GCCT and is restricted for the purpose of paying out note holders and additional funding costs.
[2] Included in cash and cash equivalents are amounts held in reserve in support of Financial Services' liquidity and regulatory requirements. Refer to Note 31.1.

8. Trade and other receivables

Trade and other receivables include the following:

(C$ in millions)	2016	2015
Trade and other receivables	$ 614.2	$ 673.6
Derivatives (Note 32)	76.6	241.4
Total financial assets	$ 690.8	$ 915.0

Trade receivables are primarily from Dealers and franchisees, a large and geographically-dispersed group whose receivables, individually, generally comprise less than one percent of the total balance outstanding.

Receivables from Dealers are in the normal course of business, and include cost-sharing and financing arrangements. The net average credit period on sale of goods is between 14 and 120 days.

9. Loans receivable

Quantitative information about the Company's loans receivable portfolio is as follows:

(C$ in millions)	Total principal amount of receivables[1]	
	2016	2015
Credit card loans[2]	$ 5,104.6	$ 4,844.3
Dealer loans[3]	705.4	659.6
Total loans receivable	5,810.0	5,503.9
Less: long-term portion[4]	671.6	628.4
Current portion of loans receivable	$ 5,138.4	$ 4,875.5

[1] Amounts shown are net of allowance for loan impairment.
[2] Includes line of credit loans.
[3] Dealer loans primarily relate to loans issued by Franchise Trust (refer to Note 21).
[4] The long-term portion of loans receivable is included in long-term receivables and other assets and includes Dealer loans of $668.9 million (2015 – $624.9 million).

For the year ended December 31, 2016, cash received from interest earned on credit cards and loans was $820.2 million (2015 – $789.6 million).

The carrying amount of loans includes loans to Dealers that are secured by the assets of the respective Dealer corporations. The Company's exposure to loans receivable credit risk resides at Franchise Trust and at the Bank. Credit risk at the Bank is influenced mainly by the individual characteristics of each credit card customer. The Bank uses sophisticated credit scoring models, monitoring technology, and collection modelling techniques to implement and manage strategies, policies, and limits that are designed to control risk. Loans receivable are generated by a large and geographically-dispersed group of customers. Current credit exposure is limited to the loss that would be incurred if all of the Bank's counterparties were to default at the same time.

A continuity schedule of the Company's allowances for loans receivable[1] is as follows:

(C$ in millions)	2016	2015
Balance, beginning of year	$ 111.5	$ 113.2
Impairments for credit losses, net of recoveries	293.7	301.9
Recoveries	69.4	65.9
Write-offs	(367.7)	(369.5)
Balance, end of year	$ 106.9	$ 111.5

[1] Loans include credit card loans and line of credit loans. No allowances for credit losses have been made with respect to Franchise Trust and FGL Sports loans receivable.

The Company's allowances for credit losses are maintained at levels that are considered adequate to absorb future credit losses.

The Company's aging of the loans receivable that are past due, but not impaired, is as follows:

	2016			2015		
(C$ in millions)	1-90 days	> 90 days	Total	1-90 days	> 90 days	Total
Loans receivable	$ 308.6	$ 58.3	$ 366.9	$ 306.3	$ 62.8	$ 369.1

Credit card loans are considered impaired and written off when a payment is 180 days in arrears. Line of credit loans are considered impaired when a payment is over 90 days in arrears and are written off when a payment is 180 days in arrears. No collateral is held against loans receivable, except for loans to Dealers, as discussed above.

Transfers of financial assets

Glacier Credit Card Trust

GCCT is a structured entity that was created to securitize credit card loans receivable. As at December 31, 2016, the Bank has transferred co-ownership interest in credit card loans receivable to GCCT but has retained substantially all the credit risk associated with the transferred assets. Due to the retention of substantially all of the risks and rewards on these assets, the Bank continues to recognize these assets within loans receivable and the transfers are accounted for as secured financing transactions. The associated liability as at December 31, 2016, secured by these assets, includes the commercial paper and term notes on the Consolidated Balance Sheets and is carried at amortized cost. The Bank is exposed to the majority of ownership risks and rewards of GCCT and, hence, it is consolidated. The carrying amount of the assets approximates their fair value. The difference between the credit card loans receivable transferred and the associated liabilities is shown below:

	2016		2015	
(C$ in millions)	Carrying amount	Fair value	Carrying amount	Fair value
Credit card loans receivable transferred[1]	$ 1,989.0	$ 1,989.0	$ 1,988.0	$ 1,988.0
Associated liabilities	1,985.0	2,017.0	1,982.3	2,021.4
Net position	$ 4.0	$ (28.0)	$ 5.7	$ (33.4)

[1] The fair value measurement of credit card loans receivable is categorized within Level 2 of the fair value hierarchy. For a definitions of the levels refer to Note 32.4.

For legal purposes, the co-ownership interests in the Bank's receivables owned by GCCT have been sold at law to GCCT and are not available to the creditors of the Bank. Furthermore GCCT's liabilities are not legal liabilities of the Company.

The Bank has not identified any factors arising from current market circumstances that could lead to a need for the Bank to extend liquidity and/or credit support to GCCT over and above the existing arrangements or that could otherwise change the substance of the Bank's relationship with GCCT. There have been no relevant changes in the capital structure of GCCT since the Bank's assessment for consolidation.

Franchise Trust

The consolidated financial statements include a portion (silo) of Franchise Trust, a legal entity sponsored by a third-party bank that originates and services loans to Dealers for their purchases of inventory and fixed assets (the "Dealer loans"). The Company has arranged for several major Canadian banks to provide standby LCs to Franchise Trust as credit support for the Dealer loans. Franchise Trust has sold all of its rights in the LCs and outstanding Dealer loans to other independent trusts set up by major Canadian banks (the "Co-owner Trusts") that raise funds in the capital markets to finance their purchase of these undivided co-ownership interests. Due to the retention of substantially all of the risks and rewards relating to these Dealer loans, the transfers are accounted for as secured financing transactions. Accordingly, the Company continues to recognize the current portion of these assets in loans receivable and the long-term portion in long-term receivables and other assets, and records the associated liability secured by these assets as loans payable, being the loans that Franchise Trust has incurred to fund the Dealer loans. The Dealer loans and loans payable are initially recorded at fair value and subsequently carried at amortized cost.

NOTES TO THE CONSOLIDATED FINANCIAL STATEMENTS

(C$ in millions)	2016		2015	
	Carrying amount	Fair value	Carrying amount	Fair value
Dealer loans[1]	$ 700.3	$ 700.3	$ 655.5	$ 655.5
Associated liabilities	700.3	700.3	655.5	655.5
Net position	$ –	$ –	$ –	$ –

[1] The fair value measurement of Dealer loans is categorized within Level 2 of the fair value hierarchy. For a definitions of the levels refer to Note 32.4.

The Dealer loans have been sold at law and are not available to the creditors of the Company. Loans payable are not legal liabilities of the Company.

In the event that a Dealer defaults on a loan, the Company has the right to purchase such loan from the Co-owner Trusts, at which time the Co-owner Trusts will assign such Dealer's debt instrument and related security documentation to the Company. The assignment of this documentation provides the Company with first-priority security rights over all of such Dealer's assets, subject to certain prior ranking statutory claims.

In most cases, the Company would expect to recover any payments made to purchase a defaulted loan, including any associated expenses. In the event the Company does not choose to purchase a defaulted Dealer loan, the Co-owner Trusts may draw against the LCs.

The Co-owner Trusts may also draw against the LCs to cover any shortfalls in certain related fees owing to them. In any case, where a draw is made against the LCs, the Company has agreed to reimburse the bank issuing the LCs for the amount so drawn. Refer to Note 34 for further information.

10. Long-term receivables and other assets

Long-term receivables and other assets include the following:

(C$ in millions)	2016	2015
Loans receivable (Note 9)	$ 671.6	$ 628.4
Derivatives (Note 32)	46.2	50.2
Mortgages receivable	17.1	28.0
Other receivables	3.6	5.1
Total long-term receivables	738.5	711.7
Other	25.2	19.5
	$ 763.7	$ 731.2

11. Goodwill and intangible assets

The following table presents the changes in cost and accumulated amortization and impairment of the Company's intangible assets:

						2016
	Indefinite-life intangible assets and goodwill			Finite-life intangible assets		
(C$ in millions)	Goodwill	Banners and trademarks	Franchise agreements and other intangibles	Software	Other intangibles[1]	Total
Cost						
Balance, beginning of year	$ 438.9	$ 267.4	$ 158.9	$ 1,267.7	$ 23.1	$ 2,156.0
Additions[2]	7.7	–	–	153.8	–	161.5
Disposals/retirements	–	–	–	(10.7)	–	(10.7)
Reclassifications and transfers	–	2.9	(2.9)	–	–	–
Balance, end of year	$ 446.6	$ 270.3	$ 156.0	$ 1,410.8	$ 23.1	$ 2,306.8
Accumulated amortization and impairment						
Balance, beginning of year	$ (1.9)	$ –	$ –	$ (889.6)	$ (17.7)	$ (909.2)
Amortization for the year	–	–	–	(124.6)	(1.5)	(126.1)
Impairment	–	(0.6)	–	–	–	(0.6)
Disposals/retirements	–	–	–	10.7	–	10.7
Reclassifications and transfers	–	–	–	–	(1.3)	(1.3)
Balance, end of year	$ (1.9)	$ (0.6)	$ –	$ (1,003.5)	$ (20.5)	$ (1,026.5)
Net carrying amount, end of year	$ 444.7	$ 269.7	$ 156.0	$ 407.3	$ 2.6	$ 1,280.3

[1] Includes FGL Sports customer relationships, certain private-label brands, and off-market leases.
[2] Additions primarily relate to internally developed intangible assets.

						2015
	Indefinite-life intangible assets and goodwill			Finite-life intangible assets		
(C$ in millions)	Goodwill	Banners and trademarks	Franchise agreements and other intangibles	Software	Other intangibles[1]	Total
Cost						
Balance, beginning of year	$ 438.5	$ 266.6	$ 156.9	$ 1,158.1	$ 23.1	$ 2,043.2
Additions[2]	0.4	0.8	2.0	109.1	–	112.3
Disposals/retirements	–	–	–	0.9	–	0.9
Reclassifications and transfers	–	–	–	(0.4)	–	(0.4)
Balance, end of year	$ 438.9	$ 267.4	$ 158.9	$ 1,267.7	$ 23.1	$ 2,156.0
Accumulated amortization and impairment						
Balance, beginning of year	$ (1.9)	$ –	$ –	$ (775.3)	$ (14.3)	$ (791.5)
Amortization for the year	–	–	–	(109.8)	(2.1)	(111.9)
Disposals/retirements	–	–	–	(4.5)	–	(4.5)
Reclassifications and transfers	–	–	–	–	(1.3)	(1.3)
Balance, end of year	$ (1.9)	$ –	$ –	$ (889.6)	$ (17.7)	$ (909.2)
Net carrying amount, end of year	$ 437.0	$ 267.4	$ 158.9	$ 378.1	$ 5.4	$ 1,246.8

[1] Includes FGL Sports customer relationships, certain private-label brands, and off-market leases.
[2] Additions primarily relate to internally developed intangible assets.

The following table presents the details of the Company's goodwill:

(C$ in millions)	2016	2015
FGL Sports	$ 364.6	$ 356.9
Mark's	56.7	56.7
Canadian Tire	23.4	23.4
Total	$ 444.7	$ 437.0

Banners and trademarks includes FGL Sports and Mark's store banners, which represent legal trademarks of the Company with expiry dates ranging from 2017 to 2030. In addition, banners and trademarks include FGL Sports and Mark's private-label brands that have legal expiry dates. As the Company currently has no approved plans to change its store banners and intends to continue to renew all trademarks and private-label brands at each expiry date for the foreseeable future, there is no foreseeable limit to the period over which the assets are expected to generate net cash inflows. Therefore, these intangible assets are considered to have indefinite useful lives.

Franchise agreements have expiry dates with options to renew, or have indefinite lives. As the Company intends to renew these agreements at each renewal date for the foreseeable future, there is no foreseeable limit to the period over which the franchise agreements and franchise locations will generate net cash inflows. Therefore, these assets are considered to have indefinite useful lives.

Finite-life intangible assets are amortized over a term of two to ten years. Off-market leases are amortized over the term of the lease to which they relate.

The amount of borrowing costs capitalized in 2016 was $5.4 million (2015 – $3.4 million). The capitalization rate used to determine the amount of borrowing costs capitalized during the year was 6.1 percent (2015 – 6.0 percent).

Amortization expense of software and other finite-life intangible assets is included in Selling, general and administrative expenses in the Consolidated Statements of Income.

Impairment of intangible assets and subsequent reversal

The Company performed its annual impairment test on goodwill and indefinite-life intangible assets for all CGUs based on VIU using after-tax discount rates ranging from 7.3 to 10.5 percent and growth rates ranging from 1.1 to 10.7 percent per annum.

The amount of impairment of intangible assets in 2016 was $0.6 million (2015 – $nil). There was no reversal of impairments in 2016 or 2015. The impairment on goodwill in 2016 pertains to the Company's Retail operating segment and is reported in Other Income in the Consolidated Statements of Income.

For all goodwill and intangible assets, the estimated recoverable amount is based on VIU exceeding the carrying amount. There is no reasonably possible change in assumptions that would cause the carrying amount to exceed the estimated recoverable amount.

12. Investment property

The following table presents changes in the cost and the accumulated depreciation and impairment on the Company's investment property:

(C$ in millions)	2016	2015
Cost		
Balance, beginning of year	$ 172.4	$ 178.8
Additions	135.1	11.0
Disposals/retirements	(0.9)	(3.8)
Reclassifications and transfers	(0.3)	(13.6)
Balance, end of year	$ 306.3	$ 172.4
Accumulated depreciation and impairment		
Balance, beginning of year	$ (34.6)	$ (30.2)
Depreciation for the year	(6.1)	(4.0)
Reversal of impairment	0.1	–
Disposal/retirements	0.7	1.1
Reclassifications and transfers	–	(1.5)
Balance, end of year	$ (39.9)	$ (34.6)
Net carrying amount, end of year	$ 266.4	$ 137.8

The investment properties generated rental income of $29.7 million (2015 – $19.2 million).

Direct operating expenses (including repairs and maintenance) arising from investment property recognized in net income were $13.0 million (2015 – $9.7 million).

The estimated fair value of investment property was $357.2 million (2015 – $228.2 million). This recurring fair value measurement is categorized within Level 3 of the fair value hierarchy (refer to Note 32.4 for definition of levels). The Company determines the fair value of investment property by applying a pre-tax capitalization rate to the annual rental income for the current leases. The capitalization rate ranged from 4.9 percent to 11.0 percent (2015 – 5.3 percent to 11.0 percent). The cash flows are for a term of five years, including a terminal value. The Company has real estate management expertise that is used to perform the valuation of investment property and has also completed independent appraisals on certain investment property owned by CT REIT.

Impairment of investment property and subsequent reversal
Any impairment or reversals of impairment are reported in Other income in the Consolidated Statements of Income.

13. Property and equipment

The following table presents changes in the cost and the accumulated depreciation and impairment on the Company's property and equipment:

							2016
(C$ in millions)	Land	Buildings	Fixtures and equipment	Leasehold improvements	Assets under finance lease	Construction in progress	Total
Cost							
Balance, beginning of year	$ 874.4	$ 2,915.9	$ 1,216.6	$ 1,140.7	$ 262.8	$ 359.4	$ 6,769.8
Additions	41.8	44.2	156.4	152.7	0.5	72.7	468.3
Disposals/retirements	(2.5)	(5.3)	(19.0)	(8.2)	(4.0)	(6.2)	(45.2)
Reclassifications and transfers	(2.5)	(10.9)	28.0	21.2	(36.3)	–	(0.5)
Balance, end of year	$ 911.2	$ 2,943.9	$ 1,382.0	$ 1,306.4	$ 223.0	$ 425.9	$ 7,192.4
Accumulated depreciation and impairment							
Balance, beginning of year	$ (6.6)	$ (1,385.8)	$ (794.8)	$ (436.2)	$ (168.2)	$ –	$ (2,791.6)
Depreciation for the year	–	(108.5)	(116.9)	(84.0)	(15.5)	–	(324.9)
Impairment	–	–	(3.3)	(0.2)	–	–	(3.5)
Disposals/retirements	–	3.8	17.8	7.3	4.1	–	33.0
Reclassifications and transfers	–	8.9	(21.9)	(21.9)	26.7	–	(8.2)
Balance, end of year	$ (6.6)	$ (1,481.6)	$ (919.1)	$ (535.0)	$ (152.9)	$ –	$ (3,095.2)
Net carrying amount, end of year	$ 904.6	$ 1,462.3	$ 462.9	$ 771.4	$ 70.1	$ 425.9	$ 4,097.2

							2015
(C$ in millions)	Land	Buildings	Fixtures and equipment	Leasehold improvements	Assets under finance lease	Construction in progress	Total
Cost							
Balance, beginning of year	$ 861.0	$ 2,857.7	$ 1,071.9	$ 1,001.1	$ 256.5	$ 224.3	$ 6,272.5
Additions	9.1	63.3	165.8	155.6	14.0	163.2	571.0
Disposals/retirements	(4.2)	(10.5)	(21.4)	(6.7)	(8.0)	(26.3)	(77.1)
Reclassifications and transfers	8.5	5.4	0.3	(9.3)	0.3	(1.8)	3.4
Balance, end of year	$ 874.4	$ 2,915.9	$ 1,216.6	$ 1,140.7	$ 262.8	$ 359.4	$ 6,769.8
Accumulated depreciation and impairment							
Balance, beginning of year	$ (4.4)	$ (1,289.8)	$ (712.0)	$ (365.7)	$ (157.5)	$ –	$ (2,529.4)
Depreciation for the year	–	(108.4)	(103.8)	(80.0)	(16.5)	–	(308.7)
Impairment	–	(0.2)	(0.2)	–	–	–	(0.4)
Reversal of impairment losses	–	–	0.1	0.1	–	–	0.2
Disposals/retirements	0.1	4.8	18.6	7.1	7.4	–	38.0
Reclassifications and transfers	(2.3)	7.8	2.5	2.3	(1.6)	–	8.7
Balance, end of year	$ (6.6)	$ (1,385.8)	$ (794.8)	$ (436.2)	$ (168.2)	$ –	$ (2,791.6)
Net carrying amount, end of year	$ 867.8	$ 1,530.1	$ 421.8	$ 704.5	$ 94.6	$ 359.4	$ 3,978.2

The Company capitalized borrowing costs of $18.0 million (2015 – $11.8 million) on indebtedness relating to property and equipment under construction. The rate used to determine the amount of borrowing costs capitalized during the year was 6.1 percent (2015 – 6.0 percent).

The carrying amount of assets under finance leases at December 31, 2016, comprises $33.4 million (2015 – $39.3 million) in buildings and $36.7 million (2015 – $55.3 million) in fixtures and equipment.

Impairment of property and equipment and subsequent reversal
The amount of impairment of property and equipment in 2016 was $3.5 million (2015 – $0.4 million). There was no reversal of impairment in 2016 (2015 – $0.2 million). The impairment of property and equipment pertain to the Company's Retail operating segment. Any impairment or reversal of impairment is reported in Other income in the Consolidated Statements of Income.

NOTES TO THE CONSOLIDATED FINANCIAL STATEMENTS

14. Subsidiaries

14.1 Control of subsidiaries and composition of the Company

These consolidated financial statements include entities controlled by Canadian Tire Corporation. Control exists when Canadian Tire Corporation has the ability to direct the relevant activities and the returns of an entity. The financial statements of these entities are included in these consolidated financial statements from the date that control commences until the date that control ceases. Details of the Company's significant entities are as follows:

			Ownership Interest	
Name of subsidiary	Principal activity	Country of incorporation and operation	2016	2015
CTFS Holdings Limited[1]	Marketing of insurance products, processing credit card transactions at Canadian Tire stores, banking, and reinsurance	Canada	80.0%	80.0%
Canadian Tire Real Estate Limited	Real estate	Canada	100.0%	100.0%
CT Real Estate Investment Trust	Real estate	Canada	85.1%	83.8%
FGL Sports Ltd.	Retailer of sporting equipment, apparel and footwear	Canada	100.0%	100.0%
Franchise Trust[2]	Canadian Tire Dealer Loan Program	Canada	0.0%	0.0%
Glacier Credit Card Trust[3]	Financing program to purchase co-ownership interests in Canadian Tire Bank's credit card loans	Canada	0.0%	0.0%
Mark's Work Wearhouse Ltd.	Retailer of clothing and footwear	Canada	100.0%	100.0%

[1] Legal entity CTFS Holdings Limited, incorporated in 2014, is the parent company of CTB and CTFS Bermuda Ltd. CTB's principal activity is banking, marketing of insurance products, and the processing credit card transactions at Canadian Tire stores. CTFS Bermuda Ltd.'s principal activity is reinsurance.

[2] Franchise Trust is a legal entity sponsored by a third-party bank that originates loans to Dealers under the Dealer Loan Program. The Company does not have any share ownership in Franchise Trust. However, the Company has determined that it has the ability to direct the relevant activities and returns on the silo of assets and liabilities of Franchise Trust that relate to the Canadian Tire Dealer Loan Program. As the Company has control over this silo of assets and liabilities, it is consolidated in these financial statements.

[3] GCCT was formed to meet specific business needs of the Company, namely to buy co-ownership interests in the Company's credit card loans. GCCT issues debt to third-party investors to fund its purchases. The Company does not have any share ownership in GCCT. However, the Company has determined that it has the ability to direct the relevant activities and returns of GCCT. As the Company has control over GCCT, it is consolidated in these financial statements.

14.2 Details of non-wholly owned subsidiaries that have non-controlling interests

The portion of net assets and income attributable to third parties is reported as non-controlling interests and net income attributable to non-controlling interests in the Consolidated Balance Sheets and Consolidated Statements of Income, respectively. The non-controlling interests of CT REIT and CTFS Holdings Limited were initially measured at fair value on the date of acquisition.

The following table summarizes the information relating to non-controlling interests:

				2016
(C$ in millions)	CT REIT[1]	CTFS Holdings Limited[2]	Other[3]	Total
Non-controlling interests	14.9%	20.0%	50.0%	
Current assets	$ 11.1	$ 5,539.4	$ 13.6	$ 5,564.1
Non-current assets	5,003.5	234.1	33.0	5,270.6
Current liabilities	219.3	2,201.9	4.3	2,425.5
Non-current liabilities	2,204.8	2,527.2	23.4	4,755.4
Net assets	2,590.5	1,044.4	18.9	3,653.8
Revenue	$ 407.2	$ 1,180.7	$ 184.9	$ 1,772.8
Net income attributable to non-controlling interests	$ 21.4	$ 52.4	$ 4.6	$ 78.4
Equity attributable to non-controlling interests	288.6	504.1	6.0	798.7
Distributions to non-controlling interests	(20.9)	(53.8)	(3.7)	(78.4)

[1] Net income attributable to non-controlling interests is based on net income of CT REIT adjusted to convert to the Company's cost method, including recording of depreciation.

[2] Net income attributable to non-controlling interests is based on the net income of CTFS Holdings Limited adjusted for contractual requirements as stipulated in the Universal Shareholder agreement.

[3] Net income attributable to non-controlling interests is based on net income of the subsidiary adjusted for contractual requirements as stipulated in the ownership agreement.

(C$ in millions)	CT REIT[1]	CTFS Holdings Limited[2]	Other[3]	2015 Total
Non-controlling interests	16.2%	20.0%	50.0%	
Current assets	$ 29.3	$ 5,364.2	$ 13.2	$ 5,406.7
Non-current assets	4,321.6	209.9	32.2	4,563.7
Current liabilities	245.2	1,226.3	4.3	1,475.8
Non-current liabilities	1,892.4	3,305.8	25.6	5,223.8
Net assets	2,213.3	1,042.0	15.5	3,270.8
Revenue	$ 378.2	$ 1,165.2	$ 181.4	$ 1,724.8
Net income attributable to non-controlling interests	$ 20.6	$ 53.0	$ 2.9	$ 76.5
Equity attributable to non-controlling interests	286.5	504.3	4.7	795.5
Distributions to non-controlling interests	(20.3)	(33.6)	(1.7)	(55.6)

[1] Net income attributable to non-controlling interests is based on net income of CT REIT adjusted to convert to the Company's cost method, including recording of depreciation.

[2] Net income attributable to non-controlling interests is based on the net income of CTFS Holdings Limited adjusted for contractual requirements as stipulated in the Universal Shareholder agreement.

[3] Net income attributable to non-controlling interests is based on net income of the subsidiary adjusted for contractual requirements as stipulated in the ownership agreement.

14.3 Continuity of non-controlling interests

(C$ in millions)	2016	2015
Balance at beginning of year	$ 795.5	$ 775.3
Comprehensive income attributable to non-controlling interests for the year[1]	79.6	74.0
Issuance of trust units to non-controlling interests, net of transaction costs	2.0	1.8
Distributions	(78.4)	(55.6)
Balance at end of year	$ 798.7	$ 795.5

[1] Includes $1.2 million [2015 – $(2.5) million] from the Consolidated Statements of Comprehensive Income.

15. Income taxes

15.1 Deferred income tax assets and liabilities

The amount of deferred tax assets or liabilities recognized in the Consolidated Balance Sheets and the corresponding movement recognized in the Consolidated Statements of Income, Consolidated Statements of Changes in Equity, or resulting from a business combination is as follows:

(C$ in millions)	Balance, beginning of year	Recognized in profit or loss	Recognized in other comprehensive income	Other adjustments	2016 Balance, end of year
Provisions, deferred revenue and reserves	$ 143.8	$ 8.8	$ –	$ 0.2	$ 152.8
Property and equipment	(43.8)	5.9	–	–	(37.9)
Intangible assets	(153.5)	(17.1)	–	–	(170.6)
Employee benefits	37.5	1.1	1.1	–	39.7
Cash flow hedges	(53.3)	–	40.1	–	(13.2)
Other	6.3	1.0	–	–	7.3
Net deferred tax asset (liability)[1]	$ (63.0)	$ (0.3)	$ 41.2	$ 0.2	$ (21.9)

[1] Includes the net amount of deferred tax assets of $82.3 million and deferred tax liabilities of $104.2 million.

NOTES TO THE CONSOLIDATED FINANCIAL STATEMENTS

		2015			
(C$ in millions)	Balance, beginning of year	Recognized in profit or loss	Recognized in other comprehensive income	Other adjustments	Balance, end of year
Provisions, deferred revenue and reserves	$ 139.3	$ 4.5	$ –	$ –	$ 143.8
Property and equipment	(56.7)	12.9	–	–	(43.8)
Intangible assets	(147.5)	(5.7)	–	(0.3)	(153.5)
Employee benefits	36.4	1.3	(0.2)	–	37.5
Cash flow hedges	(29.5)	–	(23.8)	–	(53.3)
Other	3.5	2.1	–	0.7	6.3
Net deferred tax asset (liability)[1]	$ (54.5)	$ 15.1	$ (24.0)	$ 0.4	$ (63.0)

[1] Includes the net amount of deferred tax assets of $48.1 million and deferred tax liabilities of $111.1 million.

No deferred tax is recognized on the amount of temporary differences arising from the difference between the carrying amount of the investment in subsidiaries, branches and associates, and interests in joint arrangements accounted for in the financial statements and the cost amount for tax purposes of the investment. The Company is able to control the timing of the reversal of these temporary differences and believes it is probable that they will not reverse in the foreseeable future. The amount of these taxable temporary differences was approximately $2.3 billion at December 31, 2016 (2015 – $2.6 billion).

15.2 Income tax expense

The following are the major components of income tax expense:

(C$ in millions)	2016	2015
Current tax expense		
Current period	$ 261.9	$ 258.9
Adjustments with respect to prior years	1.3	21.6
	$ 263.2	$ 280.5
Deferred tax expense (benefit)		
Deferred income tax expense (benefit) relating to the origination and reversal of temporary differences	$ 2.9	$ (0.3)
Deferred income tax (benefit) adjustments with respect to prior years	(2.6)	(16.6)
Deferred income tax expense resulting from change in tax rate	–	1.8
	0.3	(15.1)
Total income tax expense	$ 263.5	$ 265.4

Income tax (benefit) expense recognized in Other Comprehensive Income was as follows:

(C$ in millions)	2016	2015
(Losses) gains on derivatives designated as cash flow hedges and available-for-sale financial assets	$ (14.7)	$ 99.8
Reclassification of gains to non-financial assets on derivatives designated as cash flow hedges	(24.8)	(74.9)
Reclassification of gains to income on derivatives designated as cash flow hedges and available-for-sale financial assets	(0.6)	(1.1)
Actuarial (losses) gains	(1.1)	0.2
Total income tax (benefit) expense	$ (41.2)	$ 24.0

Reconciliation of income tax expense

Income taxes in the Consolidated Statements of Income vary from amounts that would be computed by applying the statutory income tax rate for the following reasons:

(C$ in millions)	2016	2015
Income before income taxes	$ 1,011.0	$ 1,001.3
Income taxes based on the applicable statutory tax rate of 26.67% (2015 – 26.56%)	$ 269.6	$ 266.0
Adjustment to income taxes resulting from:		
Non-deductibility of stock option expense	5.0	2.5
Non-taxable portion of capital gains	(2.0)	(6.8)
Income attributable to non-controlling interest in flow-through entities	(7.0)	(6.3)
Other	(2.1)	10.0
Income tax expense	$ 263.5	$ 265.4

NOTES TO THE CONSOLIDATED FINANCIAL STATEMENTS

The applicable statutory tax rate is the aggregate of the Canadian federal income tax rate of 15.0 percent (2015 – 15.0 percent) and the Canadian provincial income tax rate of 11.67 percent (2015 – 11.56 percent). The increase in the applicable rate from 2015 is primarily due to changes in the provincial tax rates in the year.

In the ordinary course of business, the Company is subject to ongoing audits by tax authorities. While the Company has determined that its tax filing positions are appropriate and supportable, from time to time certain matters are reviewed and challenged by the tax authorities.

The Company regularly reviews the potential for adverse outcomes with respect to tax matters. The Company believes that the ultimate disposition of these will not have a material adverse effect on its liquidity, consolidated financial position, or net income because the Company has determined that it has adequate provision for these tax matters. Should the ultimate tax liability materially differ from the provision, the Company's effective tax rate and its earnings could be affected positively or negatively in the period in which the matters are resolved.

16. Deposits

Deposits consist of broker deposits and retail deposits.

Cash from broker deposits is raised through sales of GICs through brokers rather than directly to the retail customer. Broker deposits are offered for varying terms ranging from 30 days to five years and issued broker GICs are non-redeemable prior to maturity (except in certain rare circumstances). Total short-term and long-term broker deposits outstanding at December 31, 2016, were $1,515.7 million (2015 – $1,548.5 million).

Retail deposits consist of HIS deposits, retail GICs, and TFSA deposits. Total retail deposits outstanding at December 31, 2016, were $665.8 million (2015 – $704.4 million).

For repayment requirements of deposits refer to Note 5.4. The following are the effective rates of interest:

	2016	2015
GIC deposits	2.78%	2.84%
HIS account deposits	1.39%	1.52%

17. Trade and other payables

Trade and other payables include the following:

(C$ in millions)	2016	2015
Trade payables and accrued liabilities	$ 1,626.3	$ 1,761.2
Derivatives (Note 32)	13.4	0.7
Total financial liabilities	1,639.7	1,761.9
Deferred revenue	39.5	38.4
Insurance reserve	18.4	16.9
Other	159.3	139.9
	$ 1,856.9	$ 1,957.1

Deferred revenue consists mainly of unearned insurance premiums, unearned roadside assistance revenue, and unearned revenue relating to gift cards.

Other consists primarily of the short-term portion of share based payment transactions and sales taxes payable.

The credit range period on trade payables is three to 270 days (2015 – three to 180 days).

18. Provisions

The following table presents the changes to the Company's provisions:

					2016
(C$ in millions)	Sales and warranty returns	Site restoration and decommissioning	Customer loyalty	Other	Total
Balance, beginning of year	$ 120.5	$ 38.3	$ 86.2	$ 16.8	$ 261.8
Charges, net of reversals	301.9	3.9	176.6	6.0	488.4
Utilizations	(279.5)	(1.3)	(161.5)	(8.0)	(450.3)
Discount adjustments	0.6	(1.6)	–	0.2	(0.8)
Balance, end of year	$ 143.5	$ 39.3	$ 101.3	$ 15.0	$ 299.1
Current provisions	137.1	6.5	101.3	8.3	253.2
Long-term provisions	6.4	32.8	–	6.7	45.9

19. Contingencies

Legal and regulatory matters

The Company is party to a number of legal and regulatory proceedings. The Company believes that each such proceeding constitutes a routine matter incidental to the business conducted by the Company. The Company cannot determine with certainty the ultimate outcome of all the outstanding claims but believes that the ultimate disposition of the proceedings will not have a material adverse effect on its consolidated earnings, cash flow, or financial position.

20. Short-term borrowings

Short-term borrowings include commercial paper notes issued by GCCT and bank line of credit borrowings. Short-term borrowings may bear interest payable at maturity or be sold at a discount and mature at face value.

The commercial paper notes are short-term notes issued with varying original maturities of one year or fewer, typically 90 days or fewer, at interest rates fixed at the time of each renewal, and are recorded at amortized cost. As at December 31, 2016, $89.6 million (2015 – $88.6 million) of commercial paper notes were issued.

As at December 31, 2016, $109.8 million (2015 – $nil) of bank line of credit borrowings had been drawn on CT REIT's Bank Credit Facility.

21. Loans payable

Franchise Trust, a special purpose entity, is a legal entity sponsored by a third-party bank that originates loans to Dealers. Loans payable are the loans that Franchise Trust incurs to fund loans to Dealers. These loans are not direct legal liabilities of the Company but have been consolidated in the accounts of the Company as the Company effectively controls the silo of Franchise Trust containing the Dealer Loan Program.

Loans payable, which are initially recognized at fair value and are subsequently measured at amortized cost, are due within one year.

22. Long-term debt

Long-term debt includes the following:

(C$ in millions)	2016 Face value	2016 Carrying amount	2015 Face value	2015 Carrying amount
Senior notes[1]				
Series 2012-1, 2.807%, May 20, 2017	$ 200.0	$ 199.9	$ 200.0	$ 199.7
Series 2012-2, 2.394%, October 20, 2017	400.0	399.6	400.0	399.2
Series 2013-1, 2.755%, November 20, 2018	250.0	249.4	250.0	249.1
Series 2014-1, 2.568%, September 20, 2019	472.5	471.2	472.5	470.7
Series 2015-1, 2.237%, September 20, 2020	465.0	463.3	465.0	462.9
Subordinated notes[1]				
Series 2012-1, 3.827%, May 20, 2017	11.6	11.6	11.6	11.6
Series 2012-2, 3.174%, October 20, 2017	23.3	23.3	23.3	23.3
Series 2013-1, 3.275%, November 20, 2018	14.6	14.6	14.6	14.6
Series 2014-1, 3.068%, September 20, 2019	27.5	27.5	27.5	27.5
Series 2015-1, 3.237%, September 20, 2020	35.0	35.0	35.0	35.0
Medium-term notes and debentures				
2.159% due June 1, 2021	150.0	149.1	–	–
2.85% due June 9, 2022	150.0	149.1	150.0	149.2
3.53% due June 9, 2025	200.0	198.6	200.0	198.8
3.289% due June 1, 2026	200.0	198.6	–	–
6.375% due April 13, 2028	150.0	148.6	150.0	148.5
6.445% due February 24, 2034	200.0	198.1	200.0	198.0
5.61% due September 4, 2035	200.0	199.4	200.0	199.3
Finance lease obligations	125.8	125.8	145.9	145.9
Mortgages	55.9	56.0	60.0	60.1
Promissory note	1.8	1.8	2.3	2.3
Total debt	$ 3,333.0	$ 3,320.5	$ 3,007.7	$ 2,995.7
Current	653.4	653.4	24.3	24.3
Non-current	2,679.6	2,667.1	2,983.4	2,971.4

[1] Senior and subordinated notes are those of GCCT.

The carrying amount of long-term debt is net of debt issuance costs of $12.6 million (2015 – $12.0 million).

Senior and subordinated notes

Asset-backed senior and subordinated notes issued by GCCT are recorded at amortized cost using the effective interest method.

Subject to the payment of certain priority amounts, the senior notes have recourse on a priority basis to the related series ownership interest. The subordinated notes have recourse to the related series ownership interests on a subordinated basis to the senior notes in terms of the priority of payment of principal and, in some circumstances, interest. The asset-backed notes, together with certain other permitted obligations of GCCT, are secured by the assets of GCCT. The entitlement of note holders and other parties to such assets is governed by the priority and payment provisions set forth in the GCCT Indenture and the related series supplements under which these series of notes were issued.

Repayment of the principal of the series 2012-1, 2012-2, 2013-1, 2014-1, and 2015-1 notes is scheduled for the expected repayment dates indicated in the preceding table. Subsequent to the expected repayment date, collections distributed to GCCT with respect to the related ownership interest will be applied to pay any remaining amount owing.

Principal repayments may commence earlier than these scheduled commencement dates if certain events occur including:
- the Bank failing to make required payments to GCCT or failing to meet covenant or other contractual terms;
- the performance of the receivables failing to achieve set criteria; and
- insufficient receivables in the pool.

None of these events occurred in the year ended December 31, 2016.

NOTES TO THE CONSOLIDATED FINANCIAL STATEMENTS

Medium-term notes and debentures

Medium-term notes and debentures are unsecured and are redeemable by the Company, in whole or in part, at any time, at the greater of par or a formula price based upon interest rates at the time of redemption.

Finance lease obligations

Finance leases relate to DCs, fixtures, and equipment. The Company generally has the option to renew such leases or purchase the leased assets at the conclusion of the lease term. During 2016, interest rates on finance leases ranged from 1.09 percent to 11.35 percent. Remaining terms at December 31, 2016, were one to 120 months.

Finance lease obligations are payable as follows:

	2016			2015		
(C$ in millions)	Future minimum lease payments	Interest	Present value of future minimum lease payments	Future minimum lease payments	Interest	Present value of future minimum lease payments
Due in less than one year	$ 24.2	$ 7.5	$ 16.7	$ 27.8	$ 8.2	$ 19.6
Due between one year and two years	21.0	6.5	14.5	24.5	7.2	17.3
Due between two years and three years	18.5	5.8	12.7	21.0	6.5	14.5
Due between three years and four years	16.6	5.1	11.5	18.5	5.8	12.7
Due between four years and five years	15.7	4.3	11.4	16.7	5.1	11.6
Due in more than five years	69.2	10.2	59.0	85.0	14.8	70.2
	$ 165.2	$ 39.4	$ 125.8	$ 193.5	$ 47.6	$ 145.9

Mortgages

Mortgages bear interest rates ranging from 2.93 percent to 3.60 percent and have maturity dates ranging from January 1, 2018 to December 8, 2019.

Promissory notes

Promissory notes were issued as part of franchise acquisitions in 2015. These notes are non-interest bearing.

Debt covenants

The Company has provided covenants to certain of its lenders. The Company was in compliance with all of its covenants as at December 31, 2016. Refer to Note 4 for details on the Company's debt covenants.

23. Other long-term liabilities

Other long-term liabilities include the following:

(C$ in millions)	2016	2015
Redeemable financial instrument[1]	$ 517.0	$ 517.0
Employee benefits (Note 24)	149.3	141.2
Deferred gains	15.2	16.8
Derivatives (Note 32)	8.3	12.9
Deferred revenue	6.1	8.8
Other	140.7	117.2
	$ 836.6	$ 813.9

[1] A financial liability; refer to Note 32 for further information on the redeemable financial instrument.

Deferred gains relate to the sale and leaseback of certain distribution centres. The deferred gains are amortized over the terms of the leases.

Other includes the long-term portion of share-based payment transactions, deferred lease inducements, and straight-line rent liabilities.

24. Employment benefits

Profit-sharing program

The Company has a profit-sharing program for certain employees. The amount awarded to employees is contingent on the Company's profitability but shall be equal to at least one percent of the Company's previous year's net profits after income tax. A portion of the award ("Base Award") is contributed to a DPSP for the benefit of the employees. The maximum amount of the Company's Base Award contribution to the DPSP per employee per year is subject to limits set by the Income Tax Act. Each participating employee is required to invest and maintain 10 percent of the Base Award in a Company share fund of the DPSP. The share fund holds both Common Shares and Class A Non-Voting Shares. The Company's contributions to the DPSP with respect to each employee vest 20 percent after one year of continuous service and 100 percent after two years of continuous service.

In 2016, the Company contributed $22.4 million (2015 – $22.1 million) under the terms of the DPSP.

Defined benefit plan

The Company provides certain health care, dental care, life insurance, and other benefits for certain retired employees pursuant to Company policy. The Company does not have a pension plan. Information about the Company's defined benefit plan is as follows:

(C$ in millions)	2016	2015
Change in the present value of defined benefit obligation		
Defined benefit obligation, beginning of year	$ 141.2	$ 137.5
Current service cost	1.7	2.3
Interest cost	5.7	5.4
Actuarial (gain) arising from changes in demographic assumptions	–	(0.2)
Actuarial loss (gain) arising from changes in financial assumptions	4.8	(4.6)
Actuarial (gain) loss arising from changes in experience assumptions	(1.0)	3.8
Benefits paid	(3.1)	(3.0)
Defined benefit obligation, end of year[1]	$ 149.3	$ 141.2

[1] The accrued benefit obligation is not funded because funding is provided when benefits are paid. Accordingly, there are no plan assets.

Significant actuarial assumptions used:

	2016	2015
Defined benefit obligation, end of year:		
Discount rate	3.90%	4.10%
Net benefit plan expense for the year:		
Discount rate	4.10%	4.00%

For measurement purposes, a 4.80 percent weighted average health care cost trend rate is assumed for 2016 (2015 – 4.91 percent). The rate is assumed to decrease gradually to 2.96 percent for 2032 and remain at that level thereafter.

The most recent actuarial valuation of the obligation was performed as of January 2, 2016. The next required valuation will be as of December 29, 2018.

The cumulative amount of actuarial losses before tax recognized in equity at December 31, 2016, was $47.8 million (2015 – $44.1 million).

Sensitivity analysis:

The Company's defined benefit plan is exposed to actuarial risks such as the health care cost trend rate, the discount rate, and the life expectancy assumptions. The following tables provide the sensitivity of the defined benefit obligation to these assumptions. For each sensitivity test, the impact of a reasonably possible change in a single factor is shown with other assumptions left unchanged.

(C$ in millions)		2016
Sensitivity analysis	Accrued benefit obligation	
	Increase	Decrease
A fifty basis point change in assumed discount rates	$ (11.5)	$ 13.1
A one-percentage-point change in assumed health care cost trend rates	14.2	(11.9)
A one-year change in assumed life expectancy	(3.4)	3.4

The weighted-average duration of the defined benefit plan obligation at December 31, 2016 is 16.4 years (2015 – 16.5 years).

25. Share capital

Share capital consists of the following:

(C$ in millions)	2016	2015
Authorized		
3,423,366 Common Shares		
100,000,000 Class A Non-Voting Shares		
Issued		
3,423,366 Common Shares (2015 – 3,423,366)	$ 0.2	$ 0.2
67,323,781 Class A Non-Voting Shares (2015 – 70,637,987)	647.9	671.0
	$ 648.1	$ 671.2

All issued shares are fully paid. The Company does not hold any of its Common or Class A Non-Voting Shares. Neither the Common nor Class A Non-Voting Shares have a par value.

During 2016 and 2015, the Company issued and repurchased Class A Non-Voting Shares. The Company's share repurchases were made pursuant to its NCIB program.

The following transactions occurred with respect to Class A Non-Voting Shares during 2016 and 2015:

	2016		2015	
(C$ in millions)	Number	$	Number	$
Shares outstanding at beginning of the year	70,637,987	$ 671.0	74,023,208	$ 695.3
Issued under the dividend reinvestment plan	68,069	9.3	65,760	8.3
Repurchased[1]	(3,382,275)	(449.4)	(3,450,981)	(434.6)
Excess of purchase price over average cost	–	417.0	–	402.0
Shares outstanding at end of the period	67,323,781	$ 647.9	70,637,987	$ 671.0

[1] Repurchased shares, pursuant to the Company's NCIB program, have been restored to the status of authorized but unissued shares. The Company records shares repurchased on a transaction date basis.

Conditions of Class A Non-Voting Shares and Common Shares

The holders of Class A Non-Voting Shares are entitled to receive a fixed cumulative preferential dividend at the rate of $0.01 per share per annum. After payment of fixed cumulative preferential dividends at the rate of $0.01 per share per annum on each of the Class A Non-Voting Shares with respect to the current year and each preceding year, and payment of a non-cumulative dividend on each of the Common Shares with respect to the current year at the same rate, the holders of the Class A Non-Voting Shares and the Common Shares are entitled to further dividends declared and paid in equal amounts per share without preference or distinction or priority of one share over another.

In the event of the liquidation, dissolution, or winding up of the Company, all of the property of the Company available for distribution to the holders of the Class A Non-Voting Shares and the Common Shares shall be paid or distributed equally, share for share, to the holders of the Class A Non-Voting Shares, and to the holders of the Common Shares without preference or distinction or priority of one share over another.

The holders of Class A Non-Voting Shares are entitled to receive notice of and to attend all meetings of the shareholders; however, except as provided by the *Business Corporations Act* (Ontario) and as hereinafter noted, they are not entitled to vote at those meetings. Holders of Class A Non-Voting Shares, voting separately as a class, are entitled to elect the greater of (i) three Directors or (ii) one-fifth of the total number of the Company's Directors.

The holders of Common Shares are entitled to receive notice of, to attend, and to have one vote for each Common Share held at all meetings of holders of Common Shares, subject only to the restriction on the right to elect those directors who are elected by the holders of Class A Non-Voting Shares as set out above.

Common Shares can be converted, at any time and at the option of each holder of Common Shares, into Class A Non-Voting Shares on a share-for-share basis. The authorized number of shares of either class cannot be increased without the approval of the holders of at least two-thirds of the shares of each class represented and voted at a meeting of the shareholders called for the purpose of considering such an increase. Neither the Class A Non-Voting Shares nor the Common Shares can be changed in any manner whatsoever whether by way of subdivision, consolidation, reclassification, exchange, or otherwise unless at the same time the other class of shares is also changed in the same manner and in the same proportion.

Should an offer to purchase Common Shares be made to all, or substantially all of the holders of Common Shares, or be required by applicable securities legislation or by the Toronto Stock Exchange to be made to all holders of Common Shares in Ontario and should a majority of the Common Shares then issued and outstanding be tendered and taken up pursuant to such offer, the Class A Non-Voting Shares shall thereupon and thereafter be entitled to one vote per share at all meetings of the shareholders and thereafter the Class A Non-Voting Shares shall be designated as Class A Shares. The foregoing voting entitlement applicable to Class A Non-Voting Shares would not apply in the case where an offer is made to purchase both Class A Non-Voting Shares and Common Shares at the same price per share and on the same terms and conditions.

The foregoing is a summary of certain conditions attached to the Class A Non-Voting Shares of the Company and reference should be made to the Company's articles of amendment dated December 15, 1983 for a full statement of such conditions, which are available on SEDAR at www.sedar.com.

As of December 31, 2016, the Company had dividends declared and payable to holders of Class A Non-Voting Shares and Common Shares of $45.9 million (2015 – $42.6 million) at a rate of $0.650 per share (2015 – $0.575 per share).

On February 15, 2017 the Company's Board of Directors declared a dividend of $0.650 per share payable on June 1, 2017 to shareholders of record as of April 30, 2017.

Dividends per share declared were $2.3750 in 2016 (2015 – $2.1500).

Dilutive effect of employee stock options is 195,429 (2015 – 430,281).

26. Share-based payments

The Company's share-based payment plans are described below.

Stock options

The Company has granted stock options to certain employees that enable such employees to exercise their stock options and subscribe for Class A Non-Voting Shares or surrender their options and receive a cash payment. Such cash payment is calculated as the difference between the fair market value of Class A Non-Voting Shares as at the surrender date and the exercise price of the option. Stock options granted prior to 2012 vested on the third anniversary of their grant. Stock options that were granted in 2012 and later vest over a three-year period. All outstanding stock options have a term of seven years. At December 31, 2016, the aggregate number of Class A Non-Voting Shares that were authorized for issuance under the stock option plan was 3.4 million.

Stock option transactions during 2016 and 2015 were as follows:

	2016		2015	
	Number of options	Weighted average exercise price	Number of options	Weighted average exercise price
Outstanding at beginning of year	1,010,243	$ 97.75	1,526,343	$ 72.21
Granted	404,439	129.92	387,234	129.14
Exercised and surrendered	(337,338)	75.12	(823,888)	65.69
Forfeited	(115,995)	121.13	(79,446)	92.53
Expired	–	–	–	–
Outstanding at end of year	961,349	$ 116.41	1,010,243	$ 97.75
Stock options exercisable at end of year	395,042		243,240	

[1] The weighted average market price of the Company's shares when the options were exercised in 2016 was $131.27 (2015 – $127.12).

The following table summarizes information about stock options outstanding and exercisable at December 31, 2016:

	Options outstanding			Options exercisable	
Range of exercise prices	Number of outstanding options	Weighted average remaining contractual life[1]	Weighted average exercise price	Number of exercisable options	Weighted average exercise price
$ 129.14 to 129.92	658,599	5.72	$ 129.56	166,925	$ 129.34
99.72	192,241	4.19	99.72	117,608	99.72
53.49 to 69.01	110,509	2.78	67.06	110,509	67.06
$ 53.49 to 129.92	961,349	5.08	$ 116.41	395,042	$ 103.10

[1] Weighted average remaining contractual life is expressed in years.

Performance share units and performance units

The Company grants Performance Share Units ("PSUs") to certain of its employees that generally vest after three years. Each PSU entitles the participant to receive a cash payment equal to the fair market value of the Company's Class A Non-Voting Shares on the date set out in the Performance Share Unit Plan, multiplied by a factor determined by specific performance-based criteria and, in the case of PSUs granted in 2016, a relative total shareholder return modifier.

CT REIT grants Performance Units ("PUs") to certain of its employees that generally vest after three years. Each PU entitles the participant to receive a cash payment equal to the fair market value of Units of CT REIT on the date set out in the Performance Unit Plan, multiplied by a factor determined by specific performance-based criteria.

Deferred share units and deferred units

The Company offers Deferred Share Unit ("DSU") Plans to certain of its Executives and to members of its Board of Directors. Under the Executives' DSU Plan, eligible Executives may elect to receive all or a portion of their annual bonus in DSUs. The Executives' DSU Plan also provides for the granting of discretionary DSUs. Under the Directors' DSU Plan, eligible directors may defer all or a portion of their annual director fees into DSUs. DSUs received under both the Executives' and Directors' DSU Plans are settled in cash following termination of service with the Company and/or the Board based on the fair market value of the Company's Class A Non-Voting Shares on the settlement date.

CT REIT also offers a Deferred Unit Plan for members of its Board of Trustees. Under this plan, eligible trustees may elect to receive all or a portion of their annual trustee fees in Deferred Units ("DUs"). DUs are settled through the issuance of an equivalent number of Units of CT REIT or, at the election of the trustee, in cash, following termination of service with the Board.

Restricted Unit Plan

CT REIT offers a Restricted Unit Plan for its Executives. Restricted Units ("RUs") may be issued as discretionary grants or, Executives may elect to receive all or a portion of their annual bonus in RUs. At the end of the vesting period, which is generally three years from the date of grant (in the case of discretionary grants) and five years from the annual bonus payment date (in the case of deferred bonus), an Executive receives an equivalent number of Units issued by CT REIT or, at the Executive's election, the cash equivalent thereof.

The fair value of stock options and PSUs at the end of the year was determined using the Black-Scholes option pricing model with the following inputs:

	2016		2015	
	Stock options	**PSUs**	Stock options	PSUs
Share price at end of year (C$)	**$ 139.27**	**$ 139.27**	$ 118.16	$ 118.16
Weighted average exercise price[1](C$)	**$ 116.23**	**N/A**	$ 97.17	N/A
Expected remaining life (years)	**4.1**	**1.1**	4.0	0.9
Expected dividends	**1.8%**	**2.6%**	1.8%	2.6%
Expected volatility[2]	**20.4%**	**19.2%**	22.3%	21.1%
Risk-free interest rate	**1.4%**	**1.0%**	1.1%	0.9%

[1] Reflects expected forfeitures.
[2] Reflects historical volatility over a period of time similar to the remaining life of the stock options, which may not necessarily be the actual outcome.

Service and non-market performance conditions attached to the transactions are not taken into account in determining fair value.

The Company enters into equity derivative transactions to hedge share-based payments and does not apply hedge accounting. The expense recognized for share-based compensation is summarized as follows:

(C$ in millions)	2016	2015
Expense arising from share-based payment transactions	**$ 64.6**	$ 35.6
Effect of hedging arrangements	**(32.0)**	4.1
Total expense included in net income	**$ 32.6**	$ 39.7

The total carrying amount of liabilities for share-based payment transactions at December 31, 2016, was $101.1 million (2015 – $100.0 million).

The intrinsic value of the liability for vested benefits at December 31, 2016, was $30.7 million (2015 – $23.4 million).

27. Revenue

Revenue consists of the following:

(C$ in millions)	2016	2015
Sale of goods	$ 11,002.7	$ 10,649.9
Interest income on loans receivable	881.0	852.1
Royalties and licence fees	400.0	375.6
Services rendered	329.9	342.6
Rental income	67.4	59.4
	$ 12,681.0	$ 12,279.6

Major customers

The Company does not rely on any one customer.

28. Cost of producing revenue

Cost of producing revenue consists of the following:

(C$ in millions)	2016	2015
Inventory cost of sales[1]	$ 7,898.4	$ 7,747.1
Net impairment loss on loans receivable	287.0	297.1
Finance costs on deposits	52.8	54.5
Other	50.3	45.6
	$ 8,288.5	$ 8,144.3

[1] Inventory cost of sales includes depreciation for the year ended December 31, 2016 of $8.0 million (2015 – $8.9 million).

Inventory writedowns, as a result of net realizable value being lower than cost, recognized in the year ended December 31, 2016 were $61.5 million (2015 – $52.3 million).

Inventory writedowns recognized in prior periods and reversed in the year ended December 31, 2016 were $5.5 million (2015 – $5.7 million). The reversal of writedowns was the result of actual losses being lower than previously estimated.

The writedowns and reversals are included in inventory cost of sales.

29. Selling, general and administrative expenses

Selling, general and administrative expenses consist of the following:

(C$ in millions)	2016	2015
Personnel expenses[1]	$ 1,169.8	$ 1,127.9
Occupancy[1]	659.6	648.6
Marketing and advertising	400.3	365.3
Depreciation of property and equipment and investment property[2]	322.8	303.9
Information systems	153.3	133.4
Amortization of intangible assets	126.1	111.9
Other[1]	460.0	405.1
	$ 3,291.9	$ 3,096.1

[1] As a result of certain changes to business processes, costs previously recorded in "Personnel expenses" and "Occupancy" are presented as "Other" in the current year. $9.9 million of Personnel expenses and $2.0 million of Occupancy recorded in 2015 would have been classified as Other under the current year presentation.

[2] Refer to Note 28 for depreciation included in cost of producing revenue.

30. Net finance costs

Net finance costs consists of the following:

(C$ in millions)	2016	2015
Finance (income)[1]	$ (9.4)	$ (14.1)
Finance costs		
Subordinated and senior notes	$ 48.3	$ 50.2
Medium-term notes	51.3	45.9
Loans payable	12.0	11.1
Finance leases	8.3	9.0
Other[2]	7.2	8.6
	127.1	124.8
Less: Capitalized borrowing costs	23.8	17.9
Total finance costs	**$ 103.3**	$ 106.9
Net finance costs	**$ 93.9**	$ 92.8

[1] Primarily includes short and long-term investments, mortgages, and tax installments.
[2] Includes $1.2 million of amortization of debt issuance costs (2015 – $1.8 million).

31. Notes to the consolidated statements of cash flows

Change in operating working capital and other comprise the following:

(C$ in millions)	2016	2015
Change in operating working capital		
Trade and other receivables	$ 85.0	$ 83.1
Merchandise inventories	70.8	(147.3)
Income taxes	(1.6)	(0.6)
Prepaid expenses and deposits	(7.6)	8.3
Trade and other payables	(82.0)	(80.9)
Total	64.6	(137.4)
Change in other		
Provisions	36.2	12.7
Long-term provisions	2.4	(0.4)
Other long term liabilities	22.9	9.8
Total	61.5	22.1
Change in operating working capital and other	$ 126.1	$ (115.3)

31.1 Cash and marketable investments held in reserve
Cash and marketable investments includes reserves held by the Financial Services segment in support of its liquidity and regulatory requirements. As at December 31, 2016, reserves held by Financial Services totalled $422.1 million (2015 – $275.1 million) and includes restricted cash disclosed in Note 7 as well as short-term investments.

31.2 Supplementary information
During the year ended December 31, 2016, the Company acquired property and equipment and investment property at an aggregate cost of $601.1 million (2015 – $582.0 million). During the year ended December 31, 2016, intangible assets were internally developed or acquired at an aggregate cost of $153.8 million (2015 – $109.9 million).

The amount relating to property and equipment and investment property acquired that is included in trade and other payables at December 31, 2016, is $63.5 million (2015 – $104.1 million). The amount relating to intangible assets that is included in trade and other payables at December 31, 2016, is $28.4 million (2015 – $38.0 million).

During the year ended December 31, 2016, the Company also included in the property and equipment, investment property, and intangible assets acquired non-cash items relating to finance leases, asset retirement obligations, and capitalized interest in the amount of $24.3 million (2015 – $33.7 million).

32. Financial instruments

32.1 Fair value of financial instruments

Fair values have been determined for measurement and/or disclosure purposes based on the following:

The carrying amount of the Company's cash and cash equivalents, trade and other receivables, loans receivable, bank indebtedness, trade and other payables, short-term borrowings, and loans payable approximate their fair value either due to their short-term nature or because they are derivatives, which are carried at fair value.

The carrying amount of the Company's long-term receivables and other assets approximate their fair value either because the interest rates applied to measure their carrying amount approximate current market interest or because they are derivatives, which are carried at fair value.

Fair values of financial instruments reflect the credit risk of the Company and counterparties when appropriate.

Investments in equity and debt securities

The fair values of financial assets at FVTPL, held-to-maturity investments, and available-for-sale financial assets that are traded in active markets are determined by reference to their quoted closing bid price or dealer price quotations at the reporting date. For investments that are not traded in active markets, the Company determines fair values using a combination of discounted cash flow models, comparison to similar instruments for which market-observable prices exist, and other valuation models.

Derivatives

The fair value of a foreign exchange forward contract is estimated by discounting the difference between the contractual forward price and the current forward price for the residual maturity of the contract using a risk-free interest rate (based on government bonds).

The fair value of interest rate swaps is based on counterparty confirmations tested for reasonableness by discounting estimated future cash flows derived from the terms and maturity of each contract, using market interest rates for a similar instrument at the measurement date.

The fair value of equity derivatives is determined by reference to share price movement adjusted for interest using market interest rates specific to the terms of the underlying derivative contracts.

Redeemable financial instrument

On October 1, 2014, The Bank of Nova Scotia ("Scotiabank") acquired a 20.0 percent interest in the Financial Services business from the Company for proceeds of $476.8 million, net of $23.2 million in transaction costs. In conjunction with the transaction, Scotiabank was provided an option to sell and require the Company to purchase all of the interest owned by Scotiabank at any time during the six-month period following the tenth anniversary of the transaction. This obligation gives rise to a liability for the Company (the "redeemable financial instrument") and is recorded on the Company's Consolidated Balance Sheets in Other long-term liabilities. The purchase price will be based on the fair value of the Financial Services business and Scotiabank's proportionate interest in the Financial Services business, at that time.

The redeemable financial instrument was initially recorded at $500.0 million and is subsequently measured at fair value with changes in fair value recorded in net income for the period in which they arise. The subsequent fair value measurements of the redeemable financial instrument are calculated based on a discounted cash flow analysis using normalized earnings attributable to the Financial Services business, adjusted for any undistributed earnings and Scotiabank's proportionate interest in the business. The Company estimates future normalized earnings based on the most recent actual results. The earnings are then forecast over a period of five years, taking into account a terminal value calculated by discounting the final year in perpetuity. The growth rate applied to the terminal value is based on an industry-based estimate of the Financial Services business. The discount rate reflects the cost of equity of the Financial Services business and is based on expected market rates adjusted to reflect the risk profile of the Business. The fair value measurement is performed quarterly using internal estimates and judgment supplemented by periodic input from a third party. This recurring fair value measurement is categorized within Level 3 of the fair value hierarchy (refer to Note 32.4).

32.2 Fair value measurement of debt and deposits

The fair value measurement of debt and deposits is categorized within Level 2 of the fair value hierarchy (refer to Note 32.4). The fair values of the Company's debt and deposits compared to the carrying amounts are as follows:

As at	December 31, 2016		January 2, 2016	
(C$ in millions)	Carrying amount	Fair value	Carrying amount	Fair value
Liabilities carried at amortized cost				
Debt	$ 3,320.5	$ 3,476.9	$ 2,995.7	$ 3,161.1
Deposits	$ 2,181.5	$ 2,197.9	$ 2,252.9	$ 2,276.1

The difference between the fair values and the carrying amounts (excluding transaction costs, which are included in the carrying amount of debt) is due to decreases in market interest rates for similar instruments. The fair values are determined by discounting the associated future cash flows using current market interest rates for items of similar risk.

32.3 Items of income, expense, gains or losses

The following table presents certain amounts of income, expense, gains, or losses, arising from financial instruments that were recognized in net income or equity:

(C$ in millions)	2016	2015
Net gain (loss) on:		
Financial instruments designated and/or classified as FVTPL[1]	$ 29.1	$ (7.5)
Interest income (expense):		
Total interest income calculated using effective interest method for financial instruments that are not at FVTPL	888.6	863.0
Total interest expense calculated using effective interest method for financial instruments that are not at FVTPL	(169.5)	(167.4)
Fee expense arising from financial instruments that are not at FVTPL:		
Other fee expense	(13.9)	(11.6)

[1] Excludes gains (losses) on cash flow hedges, which are effective hedging relationships and gains (losses) on available for sale investments that are both reflected in the Consolidated Statements of Comprehensive Income.

32.4 Fair value of financial assets and financial liabilities classified using the fair value hierarchy

The Company uses a fair value hierarchy to categorize the inputs used to measure the fair value of financial assets and financial liabilities, the levels of which are:

Level 1 – Inputs are unadjusted quoted prices of identical instruments in active markets;

Level 2 – Inputs are other than quoted prices included in Level 1 but are observable for the asset or liability, either directly or indirectly; and

Level 3 – Inputs are not based on observable market data.

The following table presents the financial instruments measured at fair value classified by the fair value hierarchy:

(C$ in million)		2016		2015	
Balance sheet line	**Category**	**Level**		Level	
Short-term investments	FVTPL	2	$ 38.6	2	$ –
Short-term investments	Available for sale	2	78.6	2	96.1
Long-term investments	Available for sale	2	175.2	2	153.4
Trade and other receivables	FVTPL[1]	2	26.7	2	27.3
Trade and other receivables	Effective hedging instruments	2	49.9	2	214.1
Long-term receivables and other assets	FVTPL[1]	2	26.0	2	25.4
Long-term receivables and other assets	Effective hedging instruments	2	20.2	2	24.8
Trade and other payables	FVTPL[1]	2	1.1	2	0.7
Trade and other payables	Effective hedging instruments	2	12.3	2	–
Redeemable financial instrument	FVTPL	3	517.0	3	517.0
Other long-term liabilities	Effective hedging instruments	2	8.3	2	12.9

[1] Includes derivatives that are classified as held for trading.

There were no transfers in either direction between categories in 2016 or 2015.

Changes in fair value measurement for instruments categorized in Level 3

Level 3 financial instruments include a redeemable financial instrument.

As of December 31, 2016, the fair value of the redeemable financial instrument was estimated to be $517.0 million (2015 – $517.0 million). The determination of the fair value of the redeemable financial instrument requires significant judgment on the part of Management. Refer to Note 2 of these consolidated financial statements for further information.

33. Operating leases

The Company as lessee

The Company leases a number of retail stores, distribution centres, petroleum sites, facilities, and office equipment, under operating leases with termination dates extending to March 25, 2060. Generally, the leases have renewal options, primarily at the Company's option.

The annual lease payments for property and equipment under operating leases are as follows:

(C$ in millions)	2016	2015
Less than one year	$ 354.1	$ 343.4
Between one and five years	1,097.7	1,055.5
More than five years	830.2	884.6
	$ 2,282.0	$ 2,283.5

The amounts recognized as an expense are as follows:

(C$ in millions)	2016	2015
Minimum lease payments[1]	$ 369.6	$ 347.0
Sublease payments received	(38.5)	(39.7)
	$ 331.1	$ 307.3

[1] Minimum lease payments includes contingent rent.

Due to the redevelopment or replacement of existing properties, certain leased properties are no longer needed for business operations. Where possible, the Company subleases these properties to third parties, receiving sublease payments to reduce costs. In addition, the Company has certain premises where it is on the head lease and subleases the property to franchisees. The total future minimum sublease payments expected under these non-cancellable subleases were $82.6 million as at December 31, 2016 (2015 – $94.9 million).

The Company as lessor

The Company leases out a number of its investment properties, and has certain sublease arrangements, under operating leases (refer to Note 12), with lease terms between one to 20 years with the majority having an option to renew after the expiry date.

The lessee does not have an option to purchase the property at the expiry of the lease period.

The future annual lease payments receivable from lessees under non-cancellable leases are as follows:

(C$ in millions)	2016	2015
Less than one year	$ 35.9	$ 34.4
Between one and five years	90.0	92.3
More than five years	66.5	55.9
	$ 192.4	$ 182.6

34. Guarantees and commitments

Guarantees

In the normal course of business, the Company enters into numerous agreements that may contain features that meet the definition of a guarantee. A guarantee is defined to be a contract (including an indemnity) that contingently requires the Company to make payments to the guaranteed party based on (i) changes in an underlying interest rate, foreign exchange rate, equity or commodity instrument, index or other variable that is related to an asset, a liability or an equity security of the counterparty; (ii) failure of another party to perform under an obligating agreement; or (iii) failure of a third party to pay its indebtedness when due.

The Company has provided the following significant guarantees and other commitments to third parties:

Standby letters of credit

Franchise Trust, a legal entity sponsored by a third-party bank, originates loans to Dealers for their purchase of inventory and fixed assets. While Franchise Trust is consolidated as part of these financial statements, the Company has arranged for several major Canadian banks to provide standby LCs to Franchise Trust to support the credit quality of the Dealer loan portfolio. The banks may also draw against the LCs to cover any shortfalls in certain related fees owing to it. In any case where a draw is made against the LCs, the Company has agreed to reimburse the banks issuing the standby LCs for the amount so drawn. The Company has not recorded any liability for these amounts due to the credit quality of the Dealer loans and to the nature of the underlying collateral represented by the inventory and fixed assets of the borrowing Dealers. In the unlikely event that all the LCs have been fully drawn simultaneously, the maximum payment by the Company under this reimbursement obligation would have been $141.2 million at December 31, 2016 (2015 – $151.0 million).

The Company has obtained documentary and standby letters of credit aggregating $40.4 million (2015 – $32.3 million) relating to the importation of merchandise inventories and to facilitate various real estate activities.

Business and property dispositions

In connection with agreements for the sale of all or part of a business or property and in addition to indemnifications relating to failure to perform covenants and breach of representations and warranties, the Company has agreed to indemnify the purchasers against claims from its past conduct, including environmental remediation. Typically, the term and amount of such indemnification will be determined by the parties in the agreements. The nature of these indemnification agreements prevents the Company from estimating the maximum potential liability it would be required to pay to counterparties. Historically, the Company has not made any significant indemnification payments under such agreements, and no amount has been accrued in the consolidated financial statements with respect to these indemnification agreements.

Lease agreements guarantees

The Company has guaranteed leases on certain franchise stores in the event the franchisees are unable to meet their remaining lease commitments. These lease agreements have expiration dates through November 2023. The maximum amount that the Company may be required to pay under these agreements was $4.6 million (2015 – $5.3 million). In addition, the Company could be required to make payments for percentage rents, realty taxes, and common area costs. No amount has been accrued in the consolidated financial statements with respect to these lease agreements.

Third-party financial guarantees

The Company has guaranteed the debts of certain Dealers. These third-party financial guarantees require the Company to make payments if the Dealer fails to make scheduled debt payments. The majority of these third-party financial guarantees have expiration dates extending up to and including July 2017. The maximum amount that the Company may be required to pay under these debt agreements was $50.0 million (2015 – $50.0 million), of which $23.4 million (2015 – $32.3 million) was issued at December 31, 2016. No amount has been accrued in the consolidated financial statements with respect to these debt agreements.

The Company has entered into agreements to buy back franchise-owned merchandise inventory should the banks foreclose on any of the franchisees. The terms of the guarantees range from less than a year to the lifetime of the particular underlying franchise agreement. The Company's maximum exposure as at December 31, 2016, was $70.4 million (2015 – $88.0 million).

Indemnification of lenders and agents under credit facilities

In the ordinary course of business, the Company has agreed to indemnify its lenders under various credit facilities against costs or losses resulting from changes in laws and regulations that would increase the lenders' costs and from any legal action brought against the lenders related to the use of the loan proceeds. These indemnifications generally extend for the term of the credit facilities and do not provide any limit on the maximum potential liability. Historically, the Company has not made any significant indemnification payments under such agreements, and no amount has been accrued in the consolidated financial statements with respect to these indemnification agreements.

Other indemnification agreements

In the ordinary course of business, the Company provides other additional indemnification agreements to counterparties in transactions such as leasing transactions, service arrangements, investment banking agreements, securitization agreements, indemnification of trustees under indentures for outstanding public debt, director and officer indemnification agreements, escrow agreements, price escalation clauses, sales of assets (other than dispositions of businesses discussed above), and the arrangements with Franchise Trust discussed above. These additional indemnification agreements require the Company to compensate the counterparties for certain amounts and costs incurred, including costs resulting from changes in laws and regulations (including tax legislation) or as a result of litigation claims or statutory sanctions that may be suffered by a counterparty as a consequence of the transaction.

The terms of these additional indemnification agreements vary based on the contract and do not provide any limit on the maximum potential liability. Historically, the Company has not made any significant payments under such additional indemnifications, and no amount has been accrued in the consolidated financial statements with respect to these additional indemnification commitments.

The Company's exposure to credit risks related to the above-noted guarantees are disclosed in Note 5.

Capital commitments

As at December 31, 2016, the Company had capital commitments for the acquisition of property and equipment, investment property, and intangible assets for an aggregate cost of approximately $54.8 million (2015 – $120.2 million).

35. Related parties

The Company's majority shareholder is Ms. Martha G. Billes, who beneficially owns, or controls or directs approximately 61.4 percent of the Common Shares of the Company through two privately held companies, Tire 'N' Me Pty. Ltd. and Albikin Management Inc.

Transactions with members of the Company's Board of Directors who were also Dealers represented less than one percent of the Company's total revenue and were in accordance with established Company policy applicable to all Dealers. Other transactions with related parties, as defined by IFRS, were not significant during the year.

The following outlines the compensation of the Company's Board of Directors and key Management personnel (the Company's Chief Executive Officer, Chief Financial Officer, and certain other Senior Officers):

(C$ in millions)	2016	2015
Salaries and short-term employee benefits	$ 11.0	$ 12.3
Share-based payments and other	17.9	11.7
	$ 28.9	$ 24.0

36. Comparative figures

Certain of the prior period figures have been restated to align with Management's current view of the Company's operations.

Glossary

accrual An accounting entry that reflects events or transactions in a period different from its corresponding cash flow. *76*

accrual accounting A basis of accounting that records economic events when they happen rather than only when cash exchanges occur; contrast with **cash accounting**. *32, 75*

adverse selection A type of information asymmetry whereby one party to a contract has an information advantage over another party. *7*

agency problem Arises from the inability of the principals to monitor the agents to ensure that the agents make decisions in the best interest of the principals. *8*

aging (of accounts receivable) A process of categorizing accounts receivable according to the length of time that has passed since the invoice date. *216*

agricultural activity The management by an entity of the biological transformation of biological assets for sale or for conversion into agricultural produce or into additional biological assets. *483*

agricultural produce The harvested product of biological assets. *483*

allowance for doubtful accounts (ADA) A contra account relating to accounts receivable; the balance in the allowance for doubtful accounts is management's estimate of the amount that will not be collected from customers. Also called *allowance for bad debts* or *allowance for uncollectible accounts*. *215*

annuity A series of cash flows in equal amounts occurring at regular intervals. *B3*

annuity due An annuity with cash flows at the *beginning* of each period. *B3*

articulation The connection of financial statements with each other. *89*

asset A resource controlled by an entity as a result of past events and from which future economic benefits are expected to flow to the entity. *36*

associate An entity over which the investor has **significant influence** and that is neither a **subsidiary** nor an interest in a **joint venture**. *311*

balance sheet approach An approach to accounting and standard setting that emphasizes the values of the balance sheet over the income statement. *216*

bearer plants Biological assets that are used only to grow agricultural produce over several periods. *485*

biological asset A living animal or plant. *483*

capitalize Recording an **expenditure** as an asset on the balance sheet. *211, 350*

cash Cash on hand and demand deposits. *204*

cash accounting A method of accounting that records only cash exchanges; contrast with **accrual accounting**. *76*

cash cycle: A set of transactions that converts a cash inflow to a cash outflow, or vice versa. A **financing cash cycle** is the receipt of funding from investors, using those funds to generate returns from investments and operations, and returning the funds to investors. An **investing cash cycle** is the purchase of property that has long-term future benefits for the enterprise, using that property to obtain economic benefits that ultimately result in cash inflows, and disposing of the property. An **operating cash cycle** involves the purchase of items such as inventory; production, sales, and delivery of goods or provision of services; and receipts from customers. *73*

cash discount A discount given for immediate or timely payment. *213*

cash equivalents Short-term, highly liquid investments that are readily convertible to known amounts of cash and which are subject to an insignificant risk of changes in value. *98, 204, A3*

cash generating units The smallest identifiable group of assets that generates cash inflows that are largely independent of those from other assets. *465*

change in accounting policy An accounting change made at the discretion of management. *83*

change in estimate An accounting change made necessary by the arrival of new information. *85*

cheap talk Communication of unverifiable information, by means that are virtually costless; contrast with **costly signalling**. *6*

comparability Refers to the ability to compare one set of financial statements with another. The comparison may be with the financial statements of the same enterprise in a different year or with those of a different enterprise. One of four **enhancing qualitative characteristics**. *34*

completed contract method An accounting method that defers revenue and expense recognition until the date when the contractor completes the project. *171*

completeness The inclusion of all material items in the financial statements. One of three attributes of **representational faithfulness**. *34*

component of an entity A portion of an entity that comprises operations and cash flows that can be clearly distinguished, operationally and for financial reporting purposes, from the rest of the entity. *488*

consignment An arrangement where one party (the consignor) provides goods to a second party to sell; however, the second party (the consignee) has the right to return all or a portion of the goods to the first party if the goods are not sold. *160*

contra account A balance sheet account that has the opposite sign of the main balance sheet account to which it is connected. *215*

control The power to govern the financial and operating policies of an entity. *307*

correction of an error An accounting change made necessary by the discovery of an incorrect amount, given information available at the time the amount was reported. *83*

cost allocation The process of apportioning the cost of an asset over its **useful life**. *361*

cost constraint A constraint stating that the cost of reporting financial information should not exceed the benefits that can be obtained from using that information. *38*

cost of goods available for sale (**COGAS**) The total of beginning inventories plus purchases (or goods manufactured). *258*

cost recovery method Recognizes contract costs incurred in the period as expenses and an amount of revenue equal to the costs that are expected to be recoverable as part of the contract. *171*

costly signalling (**or just signalling**) Communication of information that is otherwise unverifiable, by means of an action that is costly to the sender; contrast with **cheap talk**. *6*

costs of disposal The incremental costs directly attributable to the disposal of an asset, excluding finance costs and income tax expense. *468*

current value The value of an asset in an input market or output market on the date of measurement. *360*

cut-off The point in time at which one reporting period ends and the next begins. *81*

debt instrument Any financial instrument that is not an equity instrument or a derivative. *306*

declining-balance method A method of depreciation in which a period's depreciation equals the asset's net carrying amount multiplied by a fixed percentage. *362*

deferral An accounting entry that reflects events or transactions after the related cash flow. *76*

depreciable amount The total amount to be expensed through depreciation: initial cost less residual value. *362*

depreciation The systematic allocation of an asset's depreciable amount over its estimated useful life. Depreciation usually refers to tangible human-made assets, depletion refers to tangible natural resources, and amortization refers to intangible assets. ASPE uses amortization as a generic term that covers all three types of assets. *361*

derivative A financial instrument with all three of the following characteristics: (i) its value changes according to a specified variable, such as an interest rate or stock price; (ii) it requires no initial net investment or a small investment relative to non-derivative contracts with similar exposure to the specified variable; and (iii) it is settled at a future date. *306*

development The application of research findings or other knowledge to a plan or design for the production of new or substantially improved materials, devices, products, processes, systems, or services before the start of commercial production or use. *412*

direct method A method of presenting the statement of cash flows by showing major classes of gross cash receipts and gross cash payments; contrast with **indirect method**. *99, A10*

direct write-off method (**for accounts receivable**) A method that records the expense when an account receivable is deemed to be uncollectible. *214*

discontinued operations A component of an entity that either has been disposed of or is classified as held for sale and (i) represents a separate major line of business or geographical area of operation, (ii) is part of a single coordinated plan to dispose of a separate major line of business or geographical area of operation, or (iii) is a subsidiary acquired exclusively with a view to resale. *488*

disposal group A group of assets and liabilities to be disposed of together in a single transaction. *487*

earnings multiple A number that, when multiplied with earnings, provides an estimate of a share's value. When earnings are expected to grow at rate g and the discount rate is r, the earnings multiple is equal to $(1 + g)/(r - g)$. *B10*

effective interest method Calculates the amortized cost of a financial asset at each reporting date as the present value of the asset's cash flows discounted at the **effective interest rate** or **yield**. *322*

effective interest rate (**or yield**) The discount rate that results in a present value equal to the purchase price of a financial asset. In finance, this is called the internal rate of return (IRR). *322*

efficient securities market (**semi-strong form**) A market in which the prices of securities traded in that market at all times properly reflect all information that is publicly known about those securities. A market that is strong form efficient has prices that reflect all information, whether publicly or privately known. *11*

elimination method (**of accounting for revaluation**) A method that removes the balance in accumulated depreciation and restates the gross carrying amount to fair value. Contrast with **proportional method**. *461*

enhancing qualitative characteristics The characteristics that affect the information's degree of usefulness. Compare with **fundamental qualitative characteristics**. *33*

equity The residual interest in the assets of an entity after deducting all its liabilities. *36*

equity instrument A contract that gives the holder the residual interest in an entity after deducting all of its liabilities; an example is a common share. *306*

equity method A method of accounting whereby the balance sheet value of the investment equals the purchase cost adjusted by the investor's share of the investee's post-acquisition changes in net assets, and the income recognized equals the investor's share of the investee's net income. *310*

expenditure An outflow of cash or other resources; distinguish from **expense**. *211*

expense An amount reported on the income statement that reduces the amount of profit (or increases a loss) for the period. *211*

expenses Decreases in economic benefits during an accounting period in the form of outflows or depletions of assets or incurrence of liabilities that result in decreases in equity, other than those relating to distributions to equity participants. Expenses include **ordinary expenses** and **losses**. *36*

exploration for and evaluation of mineral resources Activities involved in the search for mineral resources, including minerals, oil, natural gas, and similar non-regenerative resources, after the entity has obtained legal rights to explore in a specific area, as well as the determination of the technical feasibility and commercial viability of extracting the mineral resource. *419*

factor (for receivables) A finance company that buys accounts receivable from other companies. *218*

fair value The price that would be received to sell an asset or paid to transfer a liability in an orderly transaction between market participants at the measurement date. *360, 410, 459*

fair value less cost to sell The price that would be received to sell an asset or paid to transfer a liability in an orderly transaction between market participants at the measurement date, less the **costs of disposal**. *467*

fair value model A measurement model that reports assets at fair value on the balance sheet date, with changes in value recognized in profit or loss. *477*

financial asset An asset arising from contractual agreements on future cash flows. *304*

financial capital maintenance The assumption that an entity needs to have as much resource in monetary terms at the end of a period as it did at the beginning of that period to maintain its operating capacity. Amounts in excess of that required to maintain financial capital are profit. *39*

financial instrument Any contract that gives rise to (i) a financial asset for one entity and (ii) a financial liability or equity instrument for another entity. *305*

financing activities Activities that result in changes in the size and composition of the contributed equity and borrowings of the entity. *A5*

first-in, first-out (FIFO) A cost flow assumption that uses the oldest costs in the computation of cost of sales. *259*

franchise A commercial arrangement in which one party (the franchisor) licenses its trademarks, business practices, and so on to another (the franchisee). *157*

free on board (F.O.B.) The point at which the buyer takes legal possession of the goods. *254*

freedom from error The extent to which information is absent of errors or omissions. One of three attributes of **representational faithfulness**. *34*

full cost method (relating to mineral exploration) A method of accounting that capitalizes costs of mineral exploration and evaluation costs without regard to outcome; contrast with the **successful efforts method**. *420*

function (of an expense) The use to which the expense has been put (e.g., cost of sales, distribution, administration, or other activities); contrast with **nature**. *98*

fundamental qualitative characteristics The characteristics that must be present for information to be useful for decision making. Compare with **enhancing qualitative characteristics**. *33*

gains A type of income other than revenue. *36*

generally accepted accounting principles (GAAP) Broad principles and conventions of general application as well as rules and procedures that determine accepted accounting practices. *2*

going concern The assumption that the reporting entity will continue operating into the foreseeable future. *38*

goodwill The difference between the purchase cost of a business and the fair value of identifiable assets, net of liabilities. *410*

gross accounts receivable The face value of accounts receivable before deducting the allowance for doubtful accounts. *215*

gross margin method A method for estimating cost of goods sold by applying an average gross margin to the amount of sales recorded in a period. *265*

gross method (of accounting for cash discounts) Records the gross/face value of receivables and records any discounts taken as a reduction in revenue. *213*

historical cost The actual cost of an asset at the time it was purchased; can also refer to amounts based on historical cost but adjusted by depreciation or impairment. *37, 360, 415*

impairment The process of writing down the value of an asset to recognize declines in its fair value. *350, 415*

income Increases in economic benefits during an accounting period in the form of inflows or enhancements of assets or decreases of liabilities that result in increases in equity, other than those relating to contributions from equity participants. Income encompasses both **revenue** and **gains**. *36*

income statement approach An approach to accounting and standard setting that emphasizes the values of the income statement over the balance sheet. *215*

indirect method A method of presenting the statement of cash flows by adjusting profit or loss for the effects of transactions of a non-cash nature, any deferrals or accruals of past or future operating cash receipts or payments, and items of income or expense associated with investing or financing cash flows. *A10*

indirect method (informal definition) A method of presenting the operating section of the cash flow statement that uses the profit or loss from the income statement as a starting point and then itemizes adjustments to arrive at the net amount of operating cash flows; contrast with **direct method**.   *99*

information Evidence that can potentially affect an individual's decisions.   *4*

information asymmetry A condition in which some people have more information than others.   *4*

installment sale An arrangement whereby the seller allows the buyer to make payments over an extended period of time while the buyer receives the product at the beginning of the installment period.   *161*

intangible asset An identifiable, non-monetary asset without physical substance.   *409*

investing activities The acquisition and disposal of long-term assets and other investments not included in cash equivalents.   *A5*

investment property Land or buildings held to earn rental income or for capital appreciation.   *477*

joint arrangement A contractual arrangement whereby two or more parties undertake an economic activity that is subject to **joint control** by those parties.   *309*

joint control A contractually agreed upon sharing of control over an economic activity; joint control exists only when the strategic decisions relating to the activity require the unanimous consent of the parties sharing control.   *309*

joint operation A joint arrangement in which the investor has rights to the assets and obligations for the liabilities of the arrangement.   *309*

joint venture A joint arrangement in which the investor has rights to the net assets of the arrangement.   *309*

last-in, first-out (LIFO) A cost flow assumption that uses the most recent costs in the computation of cost of sales.   *260*

liability A present obligation of the entity arising from past events, the settlement of which is expected to result in an outflow from the entity of economic resources embodying economic benefits.   *36*

LIFO liquidation The effect on income due to an enterprise using old LIFO cost layers when quantities sold exceed quantities purchased in the year.   *276*

LIFO reserve The difference between the LIFO inventory cost and current replacement cost.   *275*

losses A type of **expense** that is not an **ordinary expense**.   *36*

materiality Whether omitting, misstating, or obscuring a particular piece of information about a reporting entity would influence the primary users' economic decisions.   *33*

measurement The basis for quantifying items reported in the financial statements.   *37*

monetary items Assets and liabilities that have fixed or determinable cash flows.   *370*

moral hazard A type of information asymmetry whereby one party to a contract cannot observe some actions relating to the fulfillment of the contractual terms by the other party.   *7*

nature (of an expense) The source of the expense (depreciation from equipment, costs of employee labour, cost of raw materials, or other means of production); contrast with **function**.   *98*

net accounts receivable The face value of accounts receivable minus the allowance for doubtful accounts.   *215*

net method (of accounting for cash discounts) Records receivables net of cash discounts and records any discounts forfeited as income.   *213*

net realizable value (exit value) The value expected from the sale of an asset, net of any costs of disposal.   *214, 267, 360*

neutrality The extent to which information is free from bias. One of three attributes of **representational faithfulness**.   *34*

non-cash transactions Activities that do not involve cash.   *A7*

onerous contract A contract in which the unavoidable cost of meeting the obligations under the contract exceeds the economic benefits expected to be received under it.   *160*

operating activities The principal revenue-producing activities of the entity and other activities that are not investing or financing activities.   *A5*

ordinary annuity An annuity with cash flows at the *end* of each period.   *B3*

ordinary expense A type of **expense** that arises from the ordinary activities of the entity.   *36*

owner-occupied property Land or buildings for use in the production or supply of goods or services or for administrative purposes.   *477*

parent An entity that controls another entity (the **subsidiary**).   *308*

percentage of completion method An accounting method that recognizes revenues and expenses on a long-term contract in proportion to the degree of progress on the contracted project.   *162*

period costs Costs that should not be capitalized in inventory because they are not closely related to the production process.   *255*

periodic inventory system An inventory control system that relies on periodic inventory counts to infer the amounts withdrawn from inventory.   *252*

perpetual inventory system An inventory control system that directly keeps track of additions to and withdrawals from inventory.   *252*

perpetuity A series of cash flows in equal amounts occurring at regular intervals for an infinite number of periods.   *B3*

perpetuity with growth A series of cash flows occurring at regular intervals for an infinite number of periods with cash flows that grow at a constant rate.   *B3*

positive accounting theory A theory for understanding managers' motivations, accounting choices, and reactions to accounting standards. *10*

principal—agent problem See **agency problem**. *8*

private enterprise In the ASPE standards, any for-profit entity that is not a publicly accountable enterprise. *43*

product costs Costs that should be capitalized in inventory because they are incurred as part of the production process. *255*

promissory note A written promise by one party to repay another party a specified amount at a specified date; sometimes colloquially called an "IOU." *224*

proportional method (of accounting for revaluation) A method that adjusts the gross carrying value and accumulated depreciation (or amortization) by the same percentage such that the net carrying amount equals fair value after revaluation. Contrast with **elimination method**. *460*

prospective adjustment Applying an accounting change only to the current and future reporting periods without any changes to past financial statements. *85*

public companies Firms with equity, debt, or other securities traded in public markets. *11*

publicly accountable enterprise An entity, other than a not-for-profit organization, that has issued debt or equity instruments that are outstanding and traded in a public market (or is in the process of issuing such instruments) or an entity that holds assets in a fiduciary capacity for a broad group of outsiders as one of its primary businesses. *43*

quality of earnings How closely reported earnings correspond to earnings that would be reported in the absence of management bias. *80*

recognition The process of presenting an item in the financial statements, as opposed to merely disclosing that item in the notes. *37, 147*

recoverable amount The higher of an asset's **fair value less cost to sell** and its **value in use**. *467*

recycling (of OCI) The process of recognizing amounts through OCI, accumulating that OCI in reserves, and later recognizing those amounts through net income and retained earnings. *96*

relevance The ability to influence users' economic decisions. Information that is able to provide feedback about past performance or helps make predictions is more relevant. *33*

replacement cost The amount required to be expended to replace an item (of inventory). *267*

replacement cost (entry value) The cost required to replace the productive capacity of an asset. For a used asset, the amount reflects the age and past usage of the asset, not a new asset. *360*

representational faithfulness The extent to which financial information reflects the underlying transactions, resources, and claims of an enterprise. *33*

research Original and planned investigation undertaken with the prospect of gaining new scientific or technical knowledge and understanding. Contrast with **development**. *412*

residual value The estimated amount that an entity would currently obtain from disposal of the asset, after deducting the estimated costs of disposal, if the asset were already of the age and in the condition expected at the end of its useful life. *362*

retail inventory method A method of estimating the cost of ending inventory by applying an average sales margin to the retail price of products. *262*

retrospective adjustment (also retroactive adjustment) Applying an accounting change to all periods affected in the past, present, and future. Retrospective adjustment **with restatement** shows any comparative figures on the same basis as the current period figures. Retrospective adjustment **without restatement** reflects the accounting change's impact on past periods in the current period. *83*

revaluation model Restates the carrying value of an asset to the asset's fair value on the date of revaluation. *459*

revenue A type of income that arises in the course of ordinary activities. *36*

securitization The process of transforming a financial asset into a security. *221*

significant influence The power to participate in the financial and operating policy decisions of the investee (but not to the extent of **control** or **joint control**). *311*

special purpose entity (SPE) An entity that is created for limited purposes; such purposes are specified in the legal documents that create the entity. *221*

specific identification A method of assigning costs to inventories and cost of sales based on actual costs of each item. *258*

stand-alone selling price The price at which an entity would sell a promised good or service separately to a customer. *155*

straight-line method A method of depreciation in which the (remaining) depreciable amount is evenly allocated over the asset's (remaining) estimated useful life. *362*

sub-ledger A listing with details regarding individual accounts receivable including the name of the party who owes money to the firm, the amount they owe, and the dates on which the payments are due. *215*

subsequent-events period The period between the cut-off date and the date when the company authorizes its financial statements for issuance. *82*

subsidiary An entity that is controlled by another entity (known as the **parent**). *308*

successful efforts method (relating to mineral exploration) A method of accounting that capitalizes costs of mineral exploration and evaluation only if the outcome is successful (i.e., production is technically feasible and commercially viable); contrast with the **full cost method**. *420*

timeliness How soon the information becomes available to decision makers. One of four **enhancing qualitative characteristics**. *35*

true and fair An overall evaluation of a set of financial statements as being a fair representation of the enterprise's economic conditions and performance. *79*

unbiased accounting A conceptual accounting outcome that would result from taking an average or consensus from a sample of disinterested accountants. *79*

understandability The ease with which users are able to comprehend financial reports. One of four **enhancing qualitative characteristics**. *34*

units-of-production method A method of depreciation in which the (remaining) depreciable amount is allocated in proportion to the productive capacity used. *362*

useful life The period of time over which an asset is expected to be available for use by an entity, or the number of production units an enterprise expects to obtain from the use of an asset. *362, 415*

value in use The present value of the future cash flows expected to be derived from an asset. *360, 468*

verifiability The degree to which different people would agree with the chosen representation in the financial reports. One of four **enhancing qualitative characteristics**. *35*

weighted-average cost A cost flow assumption that uses the weighted-average cost in the computation of cost of sales; weighted average is computed using cost of goods available for sale divided by the number of units available for sale. *260*

winner's curse The higher likelihood of loss faced by winners of auctions when bidders each have different information. *173*

INDEX

Note: Page numbers followed by *n* denote footnotes.

#	Competency and knowledge items	Level at Entry*	Chapter Coverage 1	2	3	4	5	6	7	8	9	10
Financial reporting												
1.1.1	Evaluates financial reporting needs	B	✓	✓	✓							
	a. Framework of standard setting (IFRS and ASPE)			✓								
	b. Financial statement users and their broad needs, standard setting, and requirement for accountability			✓	✓							
	c. Objectives of financial reporting			✓								
1.1.2	Evaluates the appropriateness of the basis of financial reporting	B	✓	✓	✓	✓	✓	✓	✓	✓	✓	✓
	a. Fundamental accounting concepts and principles (qualitative characteristics of accounting information, basic elements)			✓		✓						
	b. Methods of measurement			✓		✓		✓	✓	✓	✓	✓
	c. Difference between accrual accounting compared to cash accounting				✓	✓	✓			✓		
1.1.3	Evaluates reporting processes to support reliable financial reporting	B	✓					✓				
	a. Accounting information systems							✓				
	b. The role of IT in the reporting of information, including real-time access, remote access to information, dashboard, spreadsheet, report generator, and XBRL											
1.1.4	Explains implications of current trends and emerging issues in financial reporting	C							✓			
1.1.5	Identifies financial reporting needs for the public sector	C										
	a. Unique concepts in the PSAB handbook											
	b. Internal and external users of government accounting information and the uses of that information											
	c. Identifies financial reporting needs for the public sector—objectives of government reporting and major reporting issues											
1.1.6	Identifies specialized financial reporting requirements for specified regulatory and other filing requirements	C										
	a. Legislation that has an impact on accounting (SOX, Bill 198)											
1.2.1	Develops or evaluates appropriate accounting policies and procedures	B	✓	✓	✓	✓	✓	✓	✓	✓	✓	✓
1.2.2	Evaluates treatment for routine transactions	A				✓	✓	✓	✓	✓	✓	✓
	a. Cash and cash equivalents						✓					
	b. Receivables						✓					
	c. Inventories							✓				
	d. Property, plant, and equipment									✓		✓
	e. Goodwill and intangible assets										✓	
	f. Depreciation, amortization, impairment, and disposition/derecognition									✓	✓	✓
	g. Provisions, contingencies, and current liabilities											
	h. Long-term liabilities											
	i. Owners'/shareholders' equity											
	j. Earnings per share (basic, diluted)											
	k. Financial instruments								✓			
	l. Investments in associates/significant influence								◆			
	m. Revenue recognition/revenue from contracts with customers, and accounting for revenue and related expenses						✓					
	n. Leases											
	o. Changes in accounting policies and estimates, and errors					✓	✓	✓	✓	✓	✓	
	p. Foreign currency transactions											
	q. Accounting for income taxes											
	r. Events after the reporting period			✓								
1.2.3	Evaluates treatment for non-routine transactions	B							✓	✓	✓	✓
	a. Uncommon capital assets (e.g., natural resources, exchanges of assets, decommissioning costs)									✓	✓	✓